**Oxford Essential
German Dictionary**

1406

Oxford Essential German Dictionary

GERMAN–ENGLISH

ENGLISH–GERMAN

DEUTSCH–ENGLISCH

ENGLISCH–DEUTSCH

OXFORD
UNIVERSITY PRESS

OXFORD
UNIVERSITY PRESS

Great Clarendon Street, Oxford OX2 6DP

Oxford University Press is a department of the University of Oxford.
It furthers the University's objective of excellence in research, scholarship,
and education by publishing worldwide in

Oxford New York

Auckland Cape Town Dar es Salaam Hong Kong Karachi
Kuala Lumpur Madrid Melbourne Mexico City Nairobi
New Delhi Shanghai Taipei Toronto

With offices in

Argentina Austria Brazil Chile Czech Republic France Greece
Guatemala Hungary Italy Japan Poland Portugal Singapore
South Korea Switzerland Thailand Turkey Ukraine Vietnam

Oxford is a registered trade mark of Oxford University Press
in the UK and in certain other countries

© Oxford University Press 2009

Database right Oxford University Press (maker)

Previously published as the *Oxford German Mini Dictionary*, 2005

First edition 2009

British Library Cataloguing in Publication Data

Data available

ISBN 978-0-19-957639-5

2

Typeset by Interactive Sciences Ltd, Gloucester
Printed in Great Britain by Clays Ltd, St. Ives plc

Contents/Inhalt

List of contributors

Gunhild Prowe, Jill Schneider
Roswitha Morris, Robin Sawers
Nicholas Rollin, Eva Vennebusch

Proprietary terms

This dictionary includes some words which are, or are asserted to be, proprietary names or trade marks. Their inclusion does not imply that they have acquired for legal purposes a non-proprietary or general significance, nor is any other judgement implied concerning their legal status. In cases where the editor has some evidence that a word is used as a proprietary name or trade mark this is indicated by the symbol ®, but no judgement concerning the legal status of such words is made or implied thereby.

Introduction

The *Oxford Essential German Dictionary* has been written for speakers of both
German and English and contains the most useful words and expressions in
use today.

The dictionary provides a handy and comprehensive reference work for
tourists, students, and business people who require quick and reliable answers
to their translation needs.

The text of this dictionary reflects changes to the spelling of German ratified in
July 1996. The symbol * has been introduced to refer from the old spelling to
the new, preferred one:

> **As** * *nt* -ses, -se *s*. Ass
> **dasein** * *vi sep* (*sein*) **da sein**, *s*. **da**
> **Schiffahrt** * *f s*. Schifffahrt

Where both the old and new forms are valid, an equals sign = is used to refer to
the preferred form:

> **aufwändig** *adj* = aufwendig
> **Tunfisch** *m* = Thunfisch

When such forms follow each other alphabetically, they are given with
commas, with the preferred form in first place:

> **Panther, Panter** *m* -s, - panther

In phrases, od (oder) is used:

> ...**deine(r,s)** *poss pron* yours;
> **die D~en** *od* **d~en** *pl* your family *sg*

On the English–German side, only the preferred German form is given.

- A swung dash ~ represents the headword or that part of the headword
  preceding a vertical bar |. The initial letter of a German headword is given to
  show whether or not it is a capital.

- The vertical bar | precedes the part of the headword which is not repeated in
  compounds or derivatives.

- Square brackets [ ] are used for optional material.

- Parentheses are used after a verb translation to indicate the object; before a
  verb translation to indicate the subject; before an adjective to indicate a
  typical noun which it qualifies.

- Parentheses are also used for field or style labels (see the inside covers), and
  for explanatory matter.

Introduction

- A bold bullet indicates a new part of speech within an entry.

- *od* (oder) and *or* denote that words or portions of a phrase are synonymous. An oblique stroke / is used where there is a difference in usage or meaning.

- ≈ is used where no exact equivalent exists in the other language.

- A dagger † indicates that a German verb is irregular and that the parts can be found in the verb table on pages 521–524. Compound verbs are not listed there as they follow the pattern of the basic verb.

- The stressed vowel is marked in a German headword by _ (long) or . (short). A phonetic transcription is only given for words which do not follow the normal rules of pronunciation. A guide to German pronunciation rules can be found on page ix.

- Phonetics are given for all English headwords. In blocks of compounds, if no stress is shown, it falls on the first element.

- A change in pronunciation or stress shown within a block of compounds applies only to that particular word (subsequent entries revert to the pronunciation and stress of the headword).

- German headword nouns are followed by the gender and, with the exception of compound nouns, by the genitive and plural. These are only given at compound nouns if they present some difficulty. Otherwise the user should refer to the final element.

- Nouns that decline like adjectives are entered as follows: **-e(r)** *m/f*, **-e(s)** *nt*.

- Adjectives which have no undeclined form are entered in the feminine form with the masculine and neuter in brackets **-e(r,s)**.

- The reflexive pronoun sich is accusative unless marked (*dat*).

Phonetic symbols used for German words

a	Hand	hant	ŋ	lang	laŋ
aː	Bahn	baːn	o	Moral	moˈraːl
ɐ	Ober	ˈoːbɐ	oː	Boot	boːt
ɐ̯	Uhr	uːɐ̯	o̜	loyal	lo̜aˈjaːl
ã	Conférencier	kõferãˈsi̯e:	õ	Konkurs	kõˈkʊrs
ãː	Abonnement	abɔnəˈmãː	õː	Ballon	baˈlõː
ai̯	weit	vai̯t	ɔ	Post	pɔst
au̯	Haut	hau̯t	ø	Ökonom	økoˈnoːm
b	Ball	bal	øː	Öl	øːl
ç	ich	ɪç	œ	göttlich	ˈɡœtlɪç
d	dann	dan	ɔy̯	heute	ˈhɔy̯tə
dʒ	Gin	dʒɪn	p	Pakt	pakt
e	Metall	meˈtal	r	Rast	rast
eː	Beet	beːt	s	Hast	hast
ɛ	mästen	ˈmɛstən	ʃ	Schal	ʃaːl
ɛː	wählen	ˈvɛːlən	t	Tal	taːl
ɛ̃	Cousin	kuˈzɛ̃	ts	Zahl	tsaːl
ə	Nase	ˈnaːzə	tʃ	Couch	kau̯tʃ
f	Faß	fas	u	Kupon	kuˈpõː
ɡ	Gast	ɡast	uː	Hut	huːt
h	haben	ˈhaːbən	u̯	aktuell	akˈtu̯ɛl
i	Rivale	riˈvaːlə	ʊ	Pult	pʊlt
iː	viel	fiːl	v	was	vas
i̯	Aktion	akˈtsi̯oːn	x	Bach	bax
ɪ	Birke	ˈbɪrkə	y	Physik	fyˈziːk
j	ja	jaː	yː	Rübe	ˈryːbə
k	kalt	kalt	ỹ	Nuance	ˈnỹãːsə
l	Last	last	ʏ	Fülle	ˈfʏlə
m	Mast	mast	z	Nase	ˈnaːzə
n	Naht	naːt	ʒ	Regime	reˈʒiːm

ʔ Glottal stop, e.g. Koordination /koʔɔrdinaˈtsi̯on/.
ː length sign after a vowel, e.g. Chrom /kroːm/.
ˈ Stress mark before stressed syllable, e.g. Balkon/balˈkõː/.

Guide to German pronunciation

Consonants

Pronounced as in English with the following exceptions:

b	as	p	
d	as	t	*at the end of a word or syllable*
g	as	k	

ch	as in Scottish lo<u>ch</u>	*after a, o, u, au*
	like an exaggerated h as in <u>h</u>uge	*after i, e, ä, ö, ü, eu, ei*
-chs	as x	(as in bo<u>x</u>)
-ig	as -ich / ıç /	*when a suffix*
j	as y	(as in <u>y</u>es)
ps		
pn	the p is pronounced	
qu	as k + v	
s	as z	(as in <u>z</u>ero) *at the beginning of a word*
	as s	(as in bu<u>s</u>) *at the end of a word or syllable, before a consonant (except p and t), or when doubled*
sch	as sh	
sp	as shp	*at the beginning of a word or syllable*
st	as sht	*at the beginning of a word or syllable*
v	as f	(as in <u>f</u>or)
	as v	(as in <u>v</u>ery) *within a word*
w	as v	(as in <u>v</u>ery)
z	as ts	

Vowels

Approximately as follows:

a	short	as	u	(as in b<u>u</u>t)
	long	as	a	(as in c<u>a</u>r)
e	short	as	e	(as in p<u>e</u>n)
	long	as	a	(as in p<u>a</u>per)
i	short	as	i	(as in b<u>i</u>t)
	long	as	ee	(as in qu<u>ee</u>n)
o	short	as	o	(as in h<u>o</u>t)
	long	as	o	(as in p<u>o</u>pe)
u	short	as	oo	(as in f<u>oo</u>t)
	long	as	oo	(as in b<u>oo</u>t)

Vowels are always short before a double consonant, and long when followed by an h or when double

ie	is pronounced	ee	(as in k<u>ee</u>p)

Diphthongs

au	as	ow	(as in h<u>ow</u>)
ei ai	as	y	(as in m<u>y</u>)
eu äu	as	oy	(as in b<u>oy</u>)

Die für das Englische verwendeten Zeichen der Lautschrift

ɑː	barn	bɑːn	l	lot	lɒt
ɑ̃	nuance	'njuːɑ̃s	m	mat	mæt
æ	fat	fæt	n	not	nɒt
æ̃	lingerie	'læ̃ʒərɪ	ŋ	sing	sɪŋ
aɪ	fine	faɪn	ɒ	got	gɒt
aʊ	now	naʊ	ɔː	paw	pɔː
b	bat	bæt	ɔɪ	boil	bɔɪl
d	dog	dɒg	p	pet	pet
dʒ	jam	dʒæm	r	rat	ræt
e	met	met	s	sip	sɪp
eɪ	fate	feɪt	ʃ	ship	ʃɪp
eə	fairy	'feərɪ	t	tip	tɪp
əʊ	goat	gəʊt	tʃ	chin	tʃɪn
ə	ago	ə'gəʊ	θ	thin	θɪn
ɜː	fur	fɜː(r)	ð	the	ðə
f	fat	fæt	uː	boot	buːt
g	good	gʊd	ʊ	book	bʊk
h	hat	hæt	ʊə	tourism	'tʊərɪzm
ɪ	bit, happy	bɪt, 'hæpɪ	ʌ	dug	dʌg
ɪə	near	nɪə(r)	v	van	væn
iː	meet	miːt	w	win	wɪn
j	yet	jet	z	zip	zɪp
k	kit	kɪt	ʒ	vision	'vɪʒn

:   bezeichnet Länge des vorhergehenden Vokals, z. B. boot /buːt/.

'   Betonung, steht unmittelbar vor einer betonten Silbe, z. B. ago /ə'gəʊ/.

(r)   Ein „r" in runden Klammern wird nur gesprochen, wenn im Textzusammenhang ein Vokal unmittelbar folgt, z. B. fire /'faɪə(r)/; fire at /'faɪər æt/.

Pronunciation of the alphabet/ Aussprache des Alphabets

English/ Englisch		German/ Deutsch	English/ Englisch		German/ Deutsch
eɪ	**a**	aː	piː	**p**	peː
biː	**b**	beː	kjuː	**q**	kuː
siː	**c**	t͜seː	aː(r)	**r**	ɛr
diː	**d**	deː	es	**s**	ɛs
iː	**e**	eː	tiː	**t**	teː
ef	**f**	ɛf	juː	**u**	uː
dʒiː	**g**	geː	viː	**v**	fau
eɪtʃ	**h**	haː	ˈdʌbljuː	**w**	veː
aɪ	**i**	iː	eks	**x**	ɪks
dʒeɪ	**j**	jɔt	waɪ	**y**	ˈʏpsilɔn
keɪ	**k**	kaː	zed	**z**	t͜sɛt
el	**l**	ɛl	eɪ umlaut	**ä**	ɛː
em	**m**	ɛm	əʊ umlaut	**ö**	øː
en	**n**	ɛn	juː umlaut	**ü**	yː
əʊ	**o**	oː	esˈzed	**ß**	ɛsˈt͜sɛt

Abbreviations/Abkürzungen

adjective	*adj*	Adjektiv
abbreviation	*abbr*	Abkürzung
accusative	*acc*	Akkusativ
Administration	*Admin*	Administration
adverb	*adv*	Adverb
American	*Amer*	amerikanisch
Anatomy	*Anat*	Anatomie
attributive	*attrib*	attributiv
Austrian	*Aust*	österreichisch
Motor vehicles	*Auto*	Automobil
Aviation	*Aviat*	Luftfahrt
Botany	*Bot*	Botanik
collective	*coll*	Kollektivum
Commerce	*Comm*	Handel
conjunction	*conj*	Konjunktion
Cookery	*Culin*	Kochkunst
dative	*dat*	Dativ
definite article	*def art*	bestimmter Artikel
demonstrative	*dem*	Demonstrativ-
Electricity	*Electr*	Elektrizität
something	*etw*	etwas
feminine	*f*	Femininum
figurative	*fig*	figurativ
genitive	*gen*	Genitiv
Geography	*Geog*	Geographie
Grammar	*Gram*	Grammatik
impersonal	*impers*	unpersönlich
inseparable	*insep*	untrennbar
interjection	*int*	Interjektion
invariable	*inv*	unveränderlich
someone	*jd*	jemand
someone (dat)	*jdm*	jemandem
someone (acc)	*jdn*	jemanden
someone's	*jds*	jemandes
Law	*Jur*	Jura
Language	*Lang*	Sprache
masculine	*m*	Maskulinum
Mathematics	*Math*	Mathematik
Medicine	*Med*	Medizin
Military	*Mil*	Militär
Music	*Mus*	Musik
noun	*n*	Substantiv

Nautical	*Naut*	nautisch
nominative	*nom*	Nominativ
neuter	*nt*	Neutrum
or	*od*	oder
pejorative	*pej*	abwertend
Photography	*Phot*	Fotografie
Physics	*Phys*	Physik
plural	*pl*	Plural
Politics	*Pol*	Politik
possessive	*poss*	Possessiv-
past participle	*pp*	zweites Partizip
predicative	*pred*	prädikativ
prefix	*pref*	Präfix, Vorsilbe
preposition	*prep*	Präposition
present	*pres*	Präsens
present participle	*pres p*	erstes Partizip
pronoun	*pron*	Pronomen
past tense	*pt*	Präteritum
Railway	*Rail*	Eisenbahn
regular	*reg*	regelmäßig
relative	*rel*	Relativ-
Religion	*Relig*	Religion
see	*s.*	siehe
School	*Sch*	Schule
separable	*sep*	trennbar
singular	*sg*	Singular
someone	*s.o.*	jemand
Technical	*Techn*	Technik
Telephone	*Teleph*	Telefon
Theatre	*Theat*	Theater
University	*Univ*	Universität
intransitive verb	*vi*	intransitives Verb
reflexive verb	*vr*	reflexives Verb
transitive verb	*vt*	transitives Verb
Zoology	*Zool*	Zoologie

Symbols used in this dictionary

familiar	!	familiär
slang	⊠	Slang
old spelling	*	alte Schreibung
proprietary term	®	Markenzeichen

Aal *m* -[e]s,-e eel

Aas *nt* -es carrion; ⊠ swine

ab *prep* (+ *dat*) from ● *adv* off; (*weg*) away; (*auf Fahrplan*) departs; **ab und zu** now and then; **auf und ab** up and down

abändern *vt sep* alter; (*abwandeln*) modify

Abbau *m* dismantling; (*Kohlen-*) mining. **a~en** *vt sep* dismantle; mine (*Kohle*)

abbeißen† *vt sep* bite off

abbeizen *vt sep* strip

abberufen† *vt sep* recall

abbestellen *vt sep* cancel; **jdn a~** put s.o. off

abbiegen† *vi sep* (*sein*) turn off; **[nach] links a~** turn left

Abbildung *f* -,-en illustration

abblättern *vi sep* (*sein*) flake off

abblend|en *vt/i sep* (*haben*) **[die Scheinwerfer] a~en** dip one's headlights. **A~licht** *nt* dipped headlights *pl*

abbrechen† *v sep* ● *vt* break off; (*abreißen*) demolish; (*Computer*) cancel ● *vi* (*sein/haben*) break off

abbrennen† *v sep* ● *vt* burn off; (*niederbrennen*) burn down ● *vi* (*sein*) burn down

abbringen† *vt sep* dissuade (**von** from)

Abbruch *m* demolition; (*Beenden*) breaking off

abbuchen *vt sep* debit

abbürsten *vt sep* brush down; (*entfernen*) brush off

abdanken *vi sep* (*haben*) resign; (*Herrscher:*) abdicate

abdecken *vt sep* uncover; (*abnehmen*) take off; (*zudecken*) cover; **den Tisch a~** clear the table

abdichten *vt sep* seal

abdrehen *vt sep* turn off

Abdruck *m* (*pl* ⸚e) impression. **a~en** *vt sep* print

abdrücken *vt/i sep* (*haben*) fire; **sich a~** leave an impression

Abend *m* -s,-e evening; **am A~** in the evening; **heute A~** this evening, tonight; **gestern A~** yesterday evening, last night. **A~brot** *nt* supper. **A~essen** *nt* dinner; (*einfacher*) supper. **A~mahl** *nt* (*Relig*) [Holy] Communion. **a~s** *adv* in the evening

Abenteuer *nt* -s,- adventure; (*Liebes-*) affair. **a~lich** *adj* fantastic

aber *conj* but; **oder a~** or else ● *adv* (*wirklich*) really

Aber|glaube *m* superstition. **a~gläubisch** *adj* superstitious

abfahr|en *v sep* ● *vi* (*sein*) leave; (*Auto:*) drive off ● *vt* take away; (*entlangfahren*) drive along; use (*Fahrkarte*); **abgefahrene Reifen** worn tyres. **A~t** *f* departure; (*Talfahrt*) descent; (*Piste*) run; (*Ausfahrt*) exit

Abfall *m* refuse, rubbish; (*auf der Straße*) litter; (*Industrie-*) waste

abfallen† *vi sep* (*sein*) drop, fall; (*übrig bleiben*) be left (**für** for); (*sich neigen*) slope away. **a~d** *adj* sloping

Abfallhaufen *m* rubbish-dump

abfällig *adj* disparaging

abfangen† *vt sep* intercept

abfärben *vi sep* (*haben*) (*Farbe:*) run; (*Stoff:*) not be colour-fast

abfassen *vt sep* draft

abfertigen *vt sep* attend to; (*zollamtlich*) clear; **jdn kurz a~** 🛈 give s.o. short shrift

abfeuern *vt sep* fire

abfind|en† *vt sep* pay off; (*entschädigen*) compensate; **sich a~en mit** come to terms with. **A~ung** *f* -,-en compensation

abfliegen† *vi sep* (*sein*) fly off; (*Aviat*) take off

abfließen† *vi sep* (*sein*) drain *or* run away

Abflug m (Aviat) departure

Abfluss m drainage; (Öffnung) drain. **A~rohr** nt drain-pipe

abfragen vt sep jdn od jdm Vokabeln a~ test s.o. on vocabulary

Abfuhr f - removal; (fig) rebuff

abführ|en vt sep take or lead away. **A~mittel** nt laxative

abfüllen vt sep auf od in Flaschen a~ bottle

Abgase ntpl exhaust fumes

abgeben† vt sep hand in; (abliefern) deliver; (verkaufen) sell; (zur Aufbewahrung) leave; (Fußball) pass; (ausströmen) give off; (abfeuern) fire; (verlauten lassen) give; cast (Stimme); jdm etw a~ give s.o. a share of sth

abgehen† v sep ● vi (sein) leave; (Theat) exit; (sich lösen) come off; (abgezogen werden) be deducted ● vt walk along

abgehetzt adj harassed. **abgelegen** adj remote. **abgeneigt** adj etw (dat) nicht abgeneigt sein not be averse to sth. **abgenutzt** adj worn. **Abgeordnete(r)** m/f deputy; (Pol) Member of Parliament. **abgepackt** adj pre-packed

abgeschieden adj secluded

abgeschlossen adj (fig) complete; (Wohnung) self-contained. **abgesehen** prep apart (from von). **abgespannt** adj exhausted. **abgestanden** adj stale. **abgestorben** adj dead; (Glied) numb. **abgetragen** adj worn. **abgewetzt** adj threadbare

abgewinnen† vt sep win (jdm from s.o.); etw (dat) Geschmack a~ get a taste for sth

abgewöhnen vt sep jdm/sich das Rauchen a~ cure s.o. of/give up smoking

abgießen† vt sep pour off; drain (Gemüse)

Abgott m idol

abgöttisch adv a~ lieben idolize

abgrenz|en vt sep divide off; (fig) define. **A~ung** f - demarcation

Abgrund m abyss; (fig) depths pl

abgucken vt sep ⊡ copy

Abguss m cast

abhacken vt sep chop off

abhaken vt sep tick off

abhalten† vt sep keep off; (hindern) keep, prevent (von from); (veranstalten) hold

abhanden adv a~ kommen get lost

Abhandlung f treatise

Abhang m slope

abhängen[1] vt sep (reg) take down; (abkuppeln) uncouple

abhäng|en[2]† vi sep (haben) depend (von on). **a~ig** adj dependent (von on). **A~igkeit** f - dependence

abhärten vt sep toughen up

abheben† v sep ● vt take off; (vom Konto) withdraw; **sich a~** stand out (gegen against) ● vi (haben) (Cards) cut [the cards]; (Aviat) take off; (Rakete:) lift off

abheften vt sep file

Abhilfe f remedy

abholen vt sep collect

abhör|en vt sep listen to; (überwachen) tap; jdn od jdm Vokabeln a~en test s.o. on vocabulary. **A~gerät** nt bugging device

Abitur nt -s ≈ A levels pl

Abitur The Abitur, or Matura *i*
in Austria, is the final exam
taken by pupils at a ▷**GYMNASIUM**
or comprehensive school. The result is based on continuous assessment during the last two years before the Abitur, plus examinations in four subjects. The Abitur is an obligatory qualification for university entrance.

---

abkaufen vt sep buy (dat from)

abklingen† vi sep (sein) die away; (nachlassen) subside

abkochen vt sep boil

abkommen† vi sep (sein) a~ von stray from; (aufgeben) give up. **A~** nt -s,- agreement

Abkömmling m -s,-e descendant

abkratzen vt sep scrape off

abkühlen *vt/i sep (sein)* cool; **sich a~** cool [down]

Abkunft *f* - origin

abkuppeln *vt sep* uncouple

abkürz|en *vt sep* shorten; abbreviate (*Wort*). **A~ung** *f* short cut; (*Wort*) abbreviation

abladen† *vt sep* unload

Ablage *f* shelf; (*für Akten*) tray

ablager|n *vt sep* deposit. **A~ung** *f* -,-en deposit

ablassen† *vt sep* drain [off]; let off (*Dampf*)

Ablauf *m* drain; (*Verlauf*) course; (*Ende*) end; (*einer Frist*) expiry. **a~en†** *v sep* ● *vi* (*sein*) run or drain off; (*verlaufen*) go off; (*enden*) expire; (*Zeit:*) run out; (*Uhrwerk:*) run down ● *vt* walk along; (*absuchen*) scour (**nach** for)

ableg|en *v sep* ● *vt* put down; discard (*Karte*); (*abheften*) file; (*ausziehen*) take off; sit, take (*Prüfung*); **abgelegte Kleidung** cast-offs *pl* ● *vi* (*haben*) take off one's coat; (*Naut*) cast off. **A~er** *m* -s,- (*Bot*) cutting; (*Schössling*) shoot

ablehn|en *vt sep* refuse; (*missbilligen*) reject. **A~ung** *f* -,-en refusal; rejection

ableit|en *vt sep* divert; **sich a~en** be derived (**von/aus** from). **A~ung** *f* derivation; (*Wort*) derivative

ablenk|en *vt sep* deflect; divert (*Aufmerksamkeit*). **A~ung** *f* -,-en distraction

ablesen† *vt sep* read

ablicht|en *vt sep* photocopy. **A~ung** *f* photocopy

abliefern *vt sep* deliver

ablös|en *vt sep* detach; (*abwechseln*) relieve; **sich a~en** come off; (*sich abwechseln*) take turns. **A~ung** *f* relief

abmach|en *vt sep* remove; (*ausmachen*) arrange; (*vereinbaren*) agree. **A~ung** *f* -,-en agreement

abmager|n *vi sep* (*sein*) lose weight. **A~ungskur** *f* slimming diet

abmelden *vt sep* cancel; **sich a~**

(*im Hotel*) check out; (*Computer*) log off

abmessen† *vt sep* measure

abmühen (sich) *vr sep* struggle

Abnäher *m* -s,- dart

abnehm|en† *v sep* ● *vt* take off, remove; pick up (*Hörer*); **jdm etw a~en** take/(*kaufen*) buy sth from s.o. ● *vi* (*haben*) decrease; (*nachlassen*) decline; (*Person:*) lose weight; (*Mond:*) wane. **A~er** *m* -s,- buyer

Abneigung *f* dislike (**gegen** of)

abnorm *adj* abnormal

abnutz|en *vt sep* wear out. **A~ung** *f* - wear [and tear]

Abon|nement /abɔnə'mã:/ *nt* -s,-s subscription. **A~nent** *m* -en, -en subscriber. **a~nieren** *vt* take out a subscription to

Abordnung *f* -,-en deputation

abpassen *vt sep* wait for; **gut a~** time well

abraten† *vi sep* (*haben*) **jdm von etw a~** advise s.o. against sth

abräumen *vt/i* (*haben*) clear away

abrechn|en *v sep* ● *vt* deduct ● *vi* (*haben*) settle up. **A~ung** *f* settlement; (*Rechnung*) account

Abreise *f* departure. **a~n** *vi sep* (*sein*) leave

abreißen† *v sep* ● *vt* tear off; (*demolieren*) pull down ● *vi* (*sein*) come off

abrichten *vt sep* train

Abriss *m* demolition; (*Übersicht*) summary

abrufen† *vt sep* call away; (*Computer*) retrieve

abrunden *vt sep* round off

abrüst|en *vi sep* (*haben*) disarm. **A~ung** *f* disarmament

abrutschen *vi sep* (*sein*) slip

Absage *f* -,-n cancellation; (*Ablehnung*) refusal. **a~n** *v sep* ● *vt* cancel ● *vi* (*haben*) [**jdm**] **a~n** cancel an appointment [with s.o.]; (*auf Einladung*) refuse [s.o.'s invitation]

Absatz *m* heel; (*Abschnitt*) paragraph; (*Verkauf*) sale

abschaffen | absteigen

4

a

abschaff|en *vt sep* abolish; get rid of (*Auto, Hund*)

abschalten *vt/i sep* (*haben*) switch off

Abscheu *m* - revulsion

abscheulich *adj* revolting

abschicken *vt sep* send off

Abschied *m* -[e]s,-e farewell; (*Trennung*) parting; **A~ nehmen** say goodbye (**von** to)

abschießen† *vt sep* shoot down; (*abfeuern*) fire; launch (*Rakete*)

abschirmen *vt sep* shield

abschlagen† *vt sep* knock off; (*verweigern*) refuse

Abschlepp|dienst *m* breakdown service. **a~en** *vt sep* tow away. **A~seil** *nt* tow-rope

abschließen† *v sep* ● *vt* lock; (*beenden, abmachen*) conclude; make (*Wette*); balance (*Bücher*) ● *vi* (*haben*) lock up; (*enden*) end. **a~d** *adv* in conclusion

Abschluss *m* conclusion. **A~zeugnis** *nt* diploma

abschmecken *vt sep* season

abschmieren *vt sep* lubricate

abschneiden† *v sep* ● *vt* cut off ● *vi* (*haben*) **gut/schlecht a~** do well/badly

Abschnitt *m* section; (*Stadium*) stage; (*Absatz*) paragraph

abschöpfen *vt sep* skim off

abschrauben *vt sep* unscrew

abschreck|en *vt sep* deter; (*Culin*) put in cold water (*Ei*). **a~end** *adj* repulsive. **A~ungsmittel** *nt* deterrent

abschreib|en *v sep* ● *vt* copy; (*Comm & fig*) write off ● *vi* (*haben*) copy. **A~ung** *f* (*Comm*) depreciation

Abschrift *f* copy

Abschuss *m* shooting down; (*Abfeuern*) firing; (*Raketen-*) launch

abschüssig *adj* sloping; (*steil*) steep

abschwellen† *vi sep* (*sein*) go down

abseh|bar *adj* in **a~barer Zeit** in the foreseeable future. **a~en**† *vt/i sep* (*haben*) copy; (*voraussehen*) fore-

see; **a~en von** disregard; (*aufgeben*) refrain from

abseits *adv* apart; (*Sport*) offside ● *prep* (+ *gen*) away from. **A~** *nt* - (*Sport*) offside

absend|en† *vt sep* send off. **A~er** *m* sender

absetzen *v sep* ● *vt* put *or* set down; (*ablagern*) deposit; (*abnehmen*) take off; (*abbrechen*) stop; (*entlassen*) dismiss; (*verkaufen*) sell; (*abziehen*) deduct ● *vi* (*haben*) pause

Absicht *f* -,-en intention; **mit A~** intentionally, on purpose

absichtlich *adj* intentional

absitzen† *v sep* ● *vi* (*sein*) dismount ● *vt* ① serve (*Strafe*)

absolut *adj* absolute

absolvieren *vt* complete; (*bestehen*) pass

absonder|n *vt sep* separate; (*ausscheiden*) secrete. **A~ung** *f* -,-en secretion

absorbieren *vt* absorb

abspeisen *vt sep* fob off (**mit** with)

absperr|en *vt sep* cordon off; (*abstellen*) turn off; (*SGer*) lock. **A~ung** *f* -,-en barrier

abspielen *vt sep* play; (*Fußball*) pass; **sich a~** take place

Absprache *f* agreement

absprechen† *vt sep* arrange; **sich a~** agree

abspringen† *vi sep* (*sein*) jump off; (*mit Fallschirm*) parachute; (*abgehen*) come off

Absprung *m* jump

abspülen *vt sep* rinse

abstamm|en *vi sep* (*haben*) be descended (**von** from). **A~ung** *f* - descent

Abstand *m* distance; (*zeitlich*) interval; **A~ halten** keep one's distance

abstatten *vt sep* **jdm einen Besuch a~** pay s.o. a visit

Abstecher *m* -s,- detour

abstehen† *vi sep* (*haben*) stick out

absteigen† *vi sep* (*sein*) dismount; (*niedersteigen*) descend; (*Fußball*) be relegated

abstell|en vt sep put down; (lagern) store; (parken) park; (abschalten) turn off. **A~gleis** nt siding. **A~raum** m box-room

absterben† vi sep (sein) die; (gefühllos werden) go numb

Abstieg m -[e]s,-e descent; (Fußball) relegation

abstimm|en v sep ● vi (haben) vote (**über** + acc on) ● vt coordinate (**auf** + acc with). **A~ung** f vote

Abstinenzler m -s, - teetotaller

abstoßen† vt sep knock off; (verkaufen) sell; (fig: ekeln) repel. **a~d** adj repulsive

abstreiten† vt sep deny

Abstrich m (Med) smear

abstufen vt sep grade

Absturz m fall; (Aviat) crash

abstürzen vi sep (sein) fall; (Aviat) crash

absuchen vt sep search

absurd adj absurd

Abszess m -es,-e abscess

Abt m -[e]s,ˉe abbot

abtasten vt sep feel; (Techn) scan

abtauen vt/i sep (sein) thaw; (entfrosten) defrost

Abtei f -,-en abbey

Abteil nt compartment

Abteilung f -,-en section; (Admin, Comm) department

abtragen| vt sep clear; (einebnen) level; (abnutzen) wear out

abträglich adj detrimental (dat to)

abtreib|en† vt sep (Naut) drive off course; **ein Kind a~en lassen** have an abortion. **A~ung** f -,-en abortion

abtrennen vt sep detach; (abteilen) divide off

Abtreter m -s,- doormat

abtrocknen vt/i sep (haben) dry; **sich a~** dry oneself

abtropfen vi sep (sein) drain

abtun† vt sep (fig) dismiss

abwägen† vt sep (fig) weigh

abwandeln vt sep modify

abwarten v sep ● vt wait for ● vi (haben) wait [and see]

abwärts adv down[wards]

Abwasch m -[e]s washing-up; (Geschirr) dirty dishes pl. **a~en**† v sep ● vt wash; wash up (Geschirr); (entfernen) wash off ● vi (haben) wash up. **A~lappen** m dishcloth

Abwasser nt -s,ˉ sewage. **A~kanal** m sewer

abwechseln vi/r sep (haben) [**sich**] **a~** alternate; (Personen:) take turns. **a~d** adj alternate

Abwechslung f -,-en change; **zur A~** for a change

abwegig adj absurd

Abwehr f - defence; (Widerstand) resistance; (Pol) counter-espionage. **a~en** vt sep ward off. **A~system** nt immune system

abweich|en† vi sep (sein) deviate/(von Regel) depart (**von** from); (sich unterscheiden) differ (**von** from). **a~end** adj divergent; (verschieden) different. **A~ung** f -,-en deviation

abweis|en† vt sep turn down; turn away (Person). **a~end** adj unfriendly. **A~ung** f rejection

abwenden† vt sep turn away; (verhindern) avert

abwerfen† vt sep throw off; throw (Reiter); (Aviat) drop; (Kartenspiel) discard; shed (Haut, Blätter); yield (Gewinn)

abwert|en vt sep devalue. **A~ung** f -,-en devaluation

Abwesenheit f - absence; absent-mindedness

abwickeln vt sep unwind; (erledigen) settle

abwischen vt sep wipe

abzahlen vt sep pay off

abzählen vt sep count

Abzahlung f instalment

Abzeichen nt badge

abzeichnen vt sep copy

Abzieh|bild nt transfer. **a~en**† v sep ● vt pull off; take off (Laken); strip (Bett); (häuten) skin; (Phot) print; run off (Kopien); (zurückziehen) withdraw; (abrechnen) deduct ● vi (sein) go away, (Rauch:) escape

Abzug m withdrawal; (*Abrechnung*) deduction; (*Phot*) print (*Korrektur-*) proof; (*am Gewehr*) trigger; (*A∼söffnung*) vent; **A∼e** pl deductions

abzüglich prep (+ gen) less

Abzugshaube f [cooker] hood

abzweig|en v sep ● vi (sein) branch off ● vt divert. **A∼ung** f -,-en junction; (*Gabelung*) fork

ach int oh; **a∼ je!** oh dear! **a∼ so I** see

Achse f -,-n axis; (*Rad-*) axle

Achsel f -,-n shoulder. **A∼höhle** f armpit. **A∼zucken** nt -s shrug

acht inv adj, **A∼**¹ f -,-en eight

Acht f **A∼ geben** be careful; **A∼ geben auf** (+ acc) look after; **außer A∼ lassen** disregard; **sich in A∼ nehmen** be careful

acht|e(r,s) adj eighth. **a∼eckig** adj octagonal. **A∼el** nt -s,- eighth

achten vt respect ● vi (haben) **a∼ auf** (+ acc) pay attention to; (*aufpassen*) look after

Achterbahn f roller-coaster

achtlos adj careless

achtsam adj careful

Achtung f - respect (**vor** + dat for); **A∼!** look out!

acht|zehn inv adj eighteen. **a∼zehnte(r,s)** adj eighteenth. **a∼zig** a inv eighty. **a∼zigste(r,s)** adj eightieth

Acker m -s,∺ field. **A∼bau** m agriculture. **A∼land** nt arable land

addieren vt/i (haben) add

Addition /-'tsjo:n/ f -,-en addition

ade int goodbye

Adel m -s nobility

Ader f -,-n vein

Adjektiv nt -s,-e adjective

Adler m -s,- eagle

adlig adj noble. **A∼e(r)** m nobleman

Administration /-'tsjo:n/ f - administration

Admiral m -s,∺e admiral

adop|tieren vt adopt. **A∼tion** f -,-en adoption. **A∼tiveltern** pl adoptive parents. **A∼tivkind** nt adopted child

Adrenalin nt -s adrenalin

Adres|se f -,-n address. **a∼sieren** vt address

Adria f - Adriatic

Adverb nt -s,-ien adverb

Affäre f -,-n affair

Affe m -n,-n monkey; (*Menschen-*) ape

affektiert adj affected

affig adj affected; (*eitel*) vain

Afrika nt -s Africa

Afrikan|er(in) m -s,- (f -,-nen) African. **a∼isch** adj African

After m -s,- anus

Agen|t(in) m -en,-en (f -,-nen) agent. **A∼tur** f -,-en agency

Aggres|sion f -,-en aggression. **a∼siv** adj aggressive

Agnostiker m -s,- agnostic

Ägypt|en /ɛ'gʏptən/ nt -s Egypt. **A∼er(in)** m -s,- (f -,-nen) Egyptian. **ä∼isch** adj Egyptian

ähneln vi (haben) (+ dat) resemble; **sich ä∼** be alike

ahnen vt have a presentiment of; (*vermuten*) suspect

Ahnen mpl ancestors. **A∼forschung** f genealogy

ähnlich adj similar; **jdm ä∼ sehen** resemble s.o. **Ä∼keit** f -,-en similarity; resemblance

Ahnung f -,-en premonition; (*Vermutung*) idea, hunch

Ahorn m -s,-e maple

Ähre f -,-n ear [of corn]

Aids /eːts/ nt - Aids

Airbag /'ɛːɐ̯bɛk/ m -s, -s (*Auto*) air bag

Akademie f -,-n academy

Akadem|iker(in) m -s,- (f -,-nen) university graduate. **a∼isch** adj academic

akklimatisieren (sich) vr become acclimatized

Akkord m -[e]s,-e (*Mus*) chord. **A∼arbeit** f piecework

Akkordeon nt -s,-s accordion

Akkumulator m -s,-en (Electr) accumulator

Akkusativ m -s,-e accusative. A~objekt nt direct object

Akrobat|(in) m -en,-en (f -,-nen) acrobat. a~isch adj acrobatic

Akt m -[e]s,-e act; (Kunst) nude

Akte f -,-n file; A~n documents. A~ntasche f briefcase

Aktie /'aktsiə/ f -,-n (Comm) share. A~ngesellschaft f joint-stock company

Aktion /ak'tsio:n/ f -,-en action. A~är m -s,-e shareholder

aktiv adj active

aktuell adj topical; (gegenwärtig) current

Akupunktur f - acupuncture

Akustik f - acoustics pl.

akut adj acute

Akzent m -[e]s,-e accent

akzept|abel adj acceptable. a~ieren vt accept

Alarm m -s alarm; (Mil) alert. a~ieren vt alert; (beunruhigen) alarm

Albdruck m nightmare

albern adj silly ● vi (haben) play the fool

Albtraum m nightmare

Al|bum nt -s,-ben album

Algebra f - algebra

Algen fpl algae

Algerien /-iən/ nt -s Algeria

Alibi nt -s,-s alibi

Alimente pl maintenance sg

Alkohol m -s alcohol. a~frei adj non-alcoholic

Alkohol|iker(in) m -s,- (f -,-nen) alcoholic. a~isch adj alcoholic

Alkopop nt -(s), -s alcopop

all inv pron all das/mein Geld all the/my money; all dies all this

All nt -s universe

alle pred adj finished

all|e(r,s) pron all; (jeder) every; a~es everything, all; (alle Leute) everyone; a~e pl all; a~es Geld all the money; a~e beide both [of

them/us]; a~e Tage every day; a~e drei Jahre every three years; ohne a~en Grund without any reason; vor a~em above all; a~es in a~em all in all; a~es aussteigen! all change!

Allee f -,-n avenue

allein adv alone; (nur) only; a~ stehend single; a~ der Gedanke the mere thought; von a~[e] of its/(Person) one's own accord; (automatisch) automatically ● conj but. A~erziehende(r) m/f single parent. a~ig adj sole. A~stehende pl single people

allemal adv every time; (gewiss) certainly

allenfalls adv at most; (eventuell) possibly

aller|beste(r,s) adj very best; am a~besten best of all. a~dings adv indeed; (zwar) admittedly. a~erste(r,s) adj very first

Allergie f -,-n allergy

allergisch adj allergic (gegen to)

Aller|heiligen nt -s All Saints Day. a~höchstens adv at the very most. a~lei inv adj all sorts of ● pron all sorts of things. a~letzte(r,s) adj very last. a~liebste(r,s) adj favourite ● adv am a~liebsten for preference; am a~liebsten haben like best of all. a~meiste(r,s) adj most ● adv am a~meisten most of all. A~seelen nt -s All Souls Day. a~wenigste(r,s) adj very least ● adv am a~wenigsten least of all

allgemein adj general; im A~en (a~en) in general. A~heit f - community; (Öffentlichkeit) general public

Allianz f -,-en alliance

Alligator m -s,-en alligator

alliiert adj allied; die A~en pl the Allies

all|jährlich adj annual. a~mählich adj gradual

Alltag m working day; der A~ (fig) everyday life

alltäglich adj daily; (gewöhnlich) everyday; (Mensch) ordinary

alltags adv on weekdays

allzu *adv* [far] too; **a~ oft** all too often; **a~ vorsichtig** over-cautious

Alm *f -,-en* alpine pasture

Almosen *ntpl* alms

Alpdruck* *m* = **Albdruck**

Alpen *pl* Alps

Alphabet *nt -[e]s,-e* alphabet. **a~isch** *adj* alphabetical

Alptraum* *m* = **Albtraum**

als *conj* as; (*zeitlich*) when; (*mit Komparativ*) than; **nichts als** nothing but; **als ob** as if *or* though

also *adv & conj* so; **a~ gut** all right then; **na a~!** there you are!

alt *adj* old; (*gebraucht*) second-hand; (*ehemalig*) former; **alt werden** grow old

Alt *m -s, -e* (*Mus*) contralto

Altar *m -s, ̈e* altar

Alt|e(r) *m/f* old man/woman; **die A~en** old people. **A~eisen** *nt* scrap iron. **A~enheim** *nt* old people's home

Alter *nt -s,-* age; (*Bejahrtheit*) old age; **im A~ von** at the age of

älter *adj* older; **mein ä~er Bruder** my elder brother

altern *vi* (*sein*) age

Alternative *f -,-n* alternative

Alters|grenze *f* age limit. **A~heim** *nt* old people's home. **A~rente** *f* old-age pension. **a~schwach** *adj* old and infirm. **A~vorsorge** *f* provision for old age

Alter|tum *nt -s, ̈er* antiquity. **a~tümlich** *adj* old; (*altmodisch*) old-fashioned

altklug *adj* precocious

alt|modisch *adj* old-fashioned. **A~papier** *nt* waste paper. **A~warenhändler** *m* second-hand dealer

Alufolie *f* [aluminium] foil

Aluminium *nt -s* aluminium, (*Amer*) aluminum

am *prep* = **an dem**; **am Montag** on Monday; **am Morgen** in the morning; **am besten** [the] best

Amateur /-'tøːɐ̯/ *m -s,-e* amateur

Ambition /-'tsi̯oːn/ *f -,-en* ambition

Amboss *m -es,-e* anvil

ambulan|t *adj* out-patient ● *adv* **a~t behandeln** treat as an out-patient. **A~z** *f -,-en* out-patients' department

Ameise *f -,-n* ant

amen *int*, **A~** *nt -s* amen

Amerika *nt -s* America

Amerikan|er(in) *m -s,-* (*f -,-nen*) American. **a~isch** *adj* American

Ammoniak *nt -s* ammonia

Amnestie *f -,-n* amnesty

amoralisch *adj* amoral

Ampel *f -,-n* traffic lights *pl*

Amphitheater *nt* amphitheatre

Amput|ation /-'tsi̯oːn/ *f -,-en* amputation. **a~ieren** *vt* amputate

Amsel *f -,-n* blackbird

Amt *nt -[e]s, ̈er* office; (*Aufgabe*) task; (*Teleph*) exchange. **a~lich** *adj* official. **A~szeichen** *nt* dialling tone

Amulett *nt -[e]s,-e* [lucky] charm

amüs|ant *adj* amusing. **a~ieren** *vt* amuse; **sich a~ieren** be amused (**über** + *acc* at); (*sich vergnügen*) enjoy oneself

an

● *preposition* (+ *dative*)

! Note that **an** plus **dem** can become **am**

⋯➤ (*räumlich*) on; (*Gebäude, Ort*) at. **an der Wand** on the wall. **Frankfurt an der Oder** Frankfurt on [the] Oder. **an der Ecke** at the corner. **am Bahnhof** at the station. **an vorbei** past. **am 24. Mai** on May 24th

⋯➤ (*zeitlich*) on. **am Montag** on Monday. **an jedem Sonntag** every Sunday

⋯➤ (*sonstige Verwendungen*) **arm/reich an Vitaminen** low/rich in vitamins. **jdn an etw erkennen** recognize s.o. by sth. **an etw leiden** suffer from sth. **an einer Krankheit sterben** die of a disease. **an [und für] sich** actually

● *preposition* (+ *accusative*)

> ❗ Note that **an** plus **das** can become **ans**

••••➤ to. **schicke es an deinen Bruder** send it to your brother. **er ging ans Fenster** he went to the window

••••➤ (*auf, gegen*) on. **etw an die Wand hängen** to hang sth on the wall. **lehne es an den Baum** lean it on *or* against the tree

••••➤ (*sonstige Verwendungen*) **an etw/jdn glauben** believe in sth/s.o. **an etw denken** think of sth. **sich an etw erinnern** remember sth

● *adverb*

••••➤ (*auf Fahrplan*) **Köln an: 9.15** arriving Cologne 09.15

••••➤ (*angeschaltet*) on. **die Waschmaschine/der Fernseher/ das Licht/das Gas ist an** the washing machine/television/light/ gas is on

••••➤ (*ungefähr*) around; about. **an [die] 20000 DM** around *or* about 20,000 DM

••••➤ (*in die Zukunft*) **von heute an** from today (onwards)

analog *adj* analogous; (*Computer*) analog. **A~ie** *f* -,-n analogy

Analphabet *m* -en,-en illiterate person. **A~entum** *nt* -s illiteracy

Analy|se *f* -,-n analysis. **a~sieren** *vt* analyse. **A~tiker** *m* -s,- analyst. **a~tisch** *adj* analytical

Anämie *f* - anaemia

Ananas *f* -,-[se] pineapple

Anatomie *f* - anatomy

Anbau *m* cultivation; (*Gebäude*) extension. **a~en** *vt sep* build on; (*anpflanzen*) cultivate, grow

anbei *adv* enclosed

anbeißen† *v sep* ● *vt* take a bite of ● *vi* (*haben*) (*Fisch:*) bite

anbeten *vt sep* worship

Anbetracht *m* in **A~** (+ *gen*) in view of

anbieten† *vt sep* offer; **sich a~** offer (**zu** to)

anbinden† *vt sep* tie up

Anblick *m* sight. **a~en** *vt sep* look at

anbrechen† *v sep* ● *vt* start on; break into (*Vorräte*) ● *vi* (*sein*) begin; (*Tag:*) break; (*Nacht:*) fall

anbrennen† *v sep* ● *vt* light ● *vi* (*sein*) burn

anbringen† *vt sep* bring [along]; (*befestigen*) fix

Anbruch *m* (*fig*) dawn; **bei A~ des Tages/der Nacht** at daybreak/nightfall

Andacht *f* -,-en reverence; (*Gottesdienst*) prayers *pl*

andächtig *adj* reverent; (*fig*) rapt

andauern *vi sep* (*haben*) last; (*anhalten*) continue. **a~d** *adj* persistent; (*ständig*) constant

Andenken *nt* -s,- memory; (*Souvenir*) souvenir

ander|e(r,s) *adj* other; (*verschieden*) different; (*nächste*) next; **ein a~er, eine a~e** another ● *pron* **der a~e/ die a~en** the other/others; **ein a~er** another [one]; (*Person*) someone else; **kein a~er** no one else; **einer nach dem a~en** one after the other; **alles a~e/nichts a~es** everything/nothing else; **unter a~em** among other things. **a~enfalls** *adv* otherwise. **a~erseits** *adv* on the other hand. **a~mal** *adv* **ein a~mal** another time

ändern *vt* alter; (*wechseln*) change; **sich ä~** change

anders *pred adj* different; **a~ werden** change ● *adv* differently; (*riechen, schmecken*) different; (*sonst*) else; **jemand a~** someone else

andersherum *adv* the other way round

anderthalb *inv adj* one and a half; **a~ Stunden** an hour and a half

Änderung *f* -,-en alteration; (*Wechsel*) change

andeut|en *vt sep* indicate; (*anspie-*

a

len) hint at. **A~ung** *f* -,-en indication; hint

Andrang *m* rush (**nach** for); (*Gedränge*) crush

androhen *vt sep* jdm etw a~ threaten s.o. with sth

aneignen *vt sep* sich (*dat*) a~ appropriate; (*lernen*) learn

aneinander *adv & prefix* together; (*denken*) of one another; **a~ vorbei** past one another; **a~ geraten** quarrel

Anekdote *f* -,-n anecdote

anerkannt *adj* acknowledged

anerkenn|en† *vt sep* acknowledge, recognize; (*würdigen*) appreciate. **a~end** *adj* approving. **A~ung** *f* - acknowledgement, recognition; appreciation

anfahren† *v sep* ● *vt* deliver; (*streifen*) hit ● *vi* (*sein*) start

Anfall *m* fit, attack. **a~en†** *v sep* ● *vt* attack ● *vi* (*sein*) arise; (*Zinsen:*) accrue

anfällig *adj* susceptible (**für** to); (*zart*) delicate

Anfang *m* -s,ᵉe beginning, start; **zu** *od* **am A~** at the beginning; (*anfangs*) at first. **a~en†** *vt/i sep* (*haben*) begin, start; (*tun*) do

Anfänger(in) *m* -s,- (*f* -,-nen) beginner

anfangs *adv* at first. **A~buchstabe** *m* initial letter. **A~gehalt** *nt* starting salary

anfassen *vt sep* touch; (*behandeln*) treat; tackle (*Arbeit*); **sich a~** hold hands

anfechten† *vt sep* contest

anfertigen *vt sep* make

anfeuchten *vt sep* moisten

anflehen *vt sep* implore, beg

Anflug *m* (*Avia*) approach

anforder|n *vt sep* demand; (*Comm*) order. **A~ung** *f* demand

Anfrage *f* enquiry. **a~n** *vi sep* (*haben*) enquire, ask

anfreunden (sich) *vr sep* make friends (**mit** with)

anfügen *vt sep* add

anfühlen *vt sep* feel; **sich weich a~** feel soft

anführ|en *vt sep* lead; (*zitieren*) quote; (*angeben*) give. **A~er** *m* leader. **A~ungszeichen** *ntpl* quotation marks

Angabe *f* statement; (*Anweisung*) instruction; (*Tennis*) service; **nähere A~n** particulars

angeb|en† *v sep* ● *vt* state; give (*Namen, Grund*); (*anzeigen*) indicate; set (*Tempo*) ● *vi* (*haben*) (*Tennis*) serve; (🖬: *protzen*) show off. **A~er(in)** *m* -s,- (*f* -,-nen) 🖬 show-off. **A~erei** *f* - 🖬 showing-off

angeblich *adj* alleged

angeboren *adj* innate; (*Med*) congenital

Angebot *nt* offer; (*Auswahl*) range; **A~ und Nachfrage** supply and demand

angebracht *adj* appropriate

angeheiratet *adj* (*Onkel, Tante*) by marriage

angeheitert *adj* 🖬 tipsy

angehen† *v sep* ● *vi* (*sein*) begin, start; (*Licht, Radio:*) come on; (*anwachsen*) take root; **a~ gegen** fight ● *vt* attack; tackle (*Arbeit*); (*bitten*) ask (**um** for); (*betreffen*) concern

angehör|en *vi sep* (*haben*) (+ *dat*) belong to. **A~ige(r)** *m/f* relative

Angeklagte(r) *m/f* accused

Angel *f* -,-n fishing-rod; (*Tür-*) hinge

Angelegenheit *f* matter

Angel|haken *m* fish-hook. **a~n** *vi* (*haben*) fish (**nach** for); **a~n gehen** go fishing ● *vt* (*fangen*) catch. **A~rute** *f* fishing-rod

angelsächsisch *adj* Anglo-Saxon

angemessen *adj* commensurate (*dat* with); (*passend*) appropriate

angenehm *adj* pleasant; (*bei Vorstellung*) **a~!** delighted to meet you!

angeregt *adj* animated

angesehen *adj* respected; (*Firma*) reputable

angesichts *prep* (+ *gen*) in view of

angespannt *adj* intent; (*Lage*) tense

Angestellte(r) m/f employee

angewandt adj applied

angewiesen adj dependent (**auf** + acc on); **auf sich selbst a~** on one's own

angewöhnen vt sep **jdm etw a~** get s.o. used to sth; **sich** (dat) **etw a~** get into the habit of doing sth

Angewohnheit f habit

Angina f - tonsillitis

angleichen† vt sep adjust (**dat** to)

anglikanisch adj Anglican

Anglistik f - English [language and literature]

Angorakatze f Persian cat

angreif|en† vt sep attack; tackle (Arbeit); (schädigen) damage. **A~er** m -s,- attacker; (Pol) aggressor

angrenzen vi sep (haben) adjoin (**an etw** acc sth). **a~d** adj adjoining

Angriff m attack; **in A~ nehmen** tackle. **a~slustig** adj aggressive

Angst f -,-̈e fear; (Psychology) anxiety; (Sorge) worry (**um** about); **A~ haben** be afraid (**vor** + dat of); (sich sorgen) be worried (**um** about); **jdm A~ machen** frighten s.o.

ängstigen vt frighten; (Sorge machen) worry; **sich ä~** be frightened; be worried (**um** about)

ängstlich adj nervous; (scheu) timid; (verängstigt) frightened, scared; (besorgt) anxious

angucken vt sep 🔲 look at

angurten (sich) vr sep fasten one's seat belt

anhaben† vt sep have on; **er/es kann mir nichts a~** (fig) he/it cannot hurt me

anhalt|en† v sep ● vt stop; hold (Atem); **jdn zur Arbeit a~en** urge s.o. to work ● vi (haben) stop; (andauern) continue. **a~end** adj persistent. **A~er(in)** m -s,- (f -,-nen) hitchhiker; **per a~er fahren** hitchhike. **A~spunkt** m clue

anhand prep (+ gen) with the aid of

Anhang m appendix

anhängen¹ vt sep (reg) hang up; (befestigen) attach

anhäng|en²† vi (haben) be a follower of. **A~er** m -s,- follower; (Auto) trailer; (Schild) [tie-on] label; (Schmuck) pendant. **A~erin** f -,-nen follower. **a~lich** adj affectionate

anhäufen vt sep pile up

Anhieb m **auf A~** straight away

Anhöhe f hill

anhören vt sep listen to; **sich gut a~** sound good

animieren vt encourage (**zu** to)

Anis m -es aniseed

Anker m -s,- anchor; **vor A~ gehen** drop anchor. **a~n** vi (haben) anchor; (liegen) be anchored

anketten vt sep chain up

Anklage f accusation; (Jur) charge; (Ankläger) prosecution. **A~bank** f dock. **a~n** vt sep accuse (gen of); (Jur) charge (gen with)

Ankläger m accuser; (Jur) prosecutor

anklammern vt sep clip on; **sich a~** cling (**an** + acc to)

ankleben v sep ● vt stick on ● vi (sein) stick (**an** + dat to)

anklicken vt sep click on

anklopfen vi sep (haben) knock

anknipsen vt sep 🔲 switch on

ankommen† vi sep (sein) arrive; (sich nähern) approach; **gut a~** arrive safely; (fig) go down well (**bei** with); **nicht a~ gegen** (fig) be no match for; **a~ auf** (+ acc) depend on; **das kommt darauf an** it [all] depends

ankreuzen vt sep mark with a cross

ankündig|en vt sep announce. **A~ung** f announcement

Ankunft f - arrival

ankurbeln vt sep (fig) boost

anlächeln vt sep smile at

anlachen vt sep smile at

Anlage f -,-n installation; (Industrie-) plant; (Komplex) complex; (Geld-) investment; (Plan) layout; (Beilage) enclosure; (Veranlagung) aptitude; (Neigung) predisposition; [**öffentliche**] **A~n** [public] gardens; **als A~** enclosed

a

Anlass *m* -es, ⸚e reason; (*Gelegenheit*) occasion; **A~ geben zu** give cause for

anlass|en† *vt sep* (*Auto*) start; ⏚ leave on (*Licht*); keep on (*Mantel*). **A~er** *m* -s,- starter

anlässlich *prep* (+ *gen*) on the occasion of

Anlauf *m* (*Sport*) run-up; (*fig*) attempt. **a~en**† *v sep* ● *vi* (*sein*) start; (*beschlagen*) mist up; (*Metall:*) tarnish; **rot a~en** blush ● *vt* (*Naut*) call at

anlegen *v sep* ● *vt* put on (**an** + *acc* against); put on (*Kleidung, Verband*); lay back (*Ohren*); aim (*Gewehr*); (*investieren*) invest; (*ausgeben*) spend (**für** on); draw up (*Liste*); **es darauf a~** (*fig*) aim (**zu** to) ● *vi* (*haben*) (*Schiff:*) moor; **a~ auf** (+ *acc*) aim at

anlehnen *vt sep* lean (**an** + *acc* against); **sich a~** lean (**an** + *acc* on)

Anleihe *f* -,-n loan

anleit|en *vt sep* instruct. **A~ung** *f* instructions *pl*

anlernen *vt sep* train

Anliegen *nt* -s,- request; (*Wunsch*) desire

anlieg|en† *vi sep* (*haben*) **[eng] a~en** fit closely; **[eng] a~end** close-fitting. **A~er** *mpl* residents; **'A~er frei'** 'access for residents only'

anlügen† *vt sep* lie to

anmachen *vt sep* ⏚ fix; (*anschalten*) turn on; dress (*Salat*)

anmalen *vt sep* paint

Anmarsch *m* (*Mil*) approach

anmeld|en *vt sep* announce; (*Admin*) register; **sich a~en** say that one is coming; (*Admin*) register; (*Sch*) enrol; (*im Hotel*) check in; (*beim Arzt*) make an appointment; (*Computer*) log on. **A~ung** *f* announcement; (*Admin*) registration; (*Sch*) enrolment; (*Termin*) appointment

anmerk|en *vt sep* mark; **sich** (*dat*) **etw a~en lassen** show sth. **A~ung** *f* -,-en note

Anmut *f* - grace; (*Charme*) charm

anmutig *adj* graceful

annähen *vt sep* sew on

annäher|nd *adj* approximate. **A~ungsversuche** *mpl* advances

Annahme *f* -,-n acceptance; (*Adoption*) adoption; (*Vermutung*) assumption

annehm|bar *adj* acceptable. **a~en**† *vt sep* accept; (*adoptieren*) adopt; acquire (*Gewohnheit*); (*sich zulegen, vermuten*) assume; **angenommen, dass** assuming that. **A~lichkeiten** *fpl* comforts

Anno *adv* **A~ 1920** in the year 1920

Annon|ce /aˈnõːsə/ *f* -,-n advertisement. **a~cieren** *vt/i* (*haben*) advertise

annullieren *vt* annul; cancel

Anomalie *f* -,-n anomaly

anonym *adj* anonymous

Anorak *m* -s,-s anorak

anordn|en *vt sep* arrange; (*befehlen*) order. **A~ung** *f* arrangement; order

anorganisch *adj* inorganic

anormal *adj* abnormal

anpass|en *vt sep* try on; (*angleichen*) adapt (*dat* to); **sich a~** adapt (*dat* to). **A~ung** *f* - adaptation. **a~ungsfähig** *adj* adaptable. **A~ungsfähigkeit** *f* adaptability

Anpfiff *m* (*Sport*) kick-off

Anprall *m* -[e]s impact. **a~en** *vi sep* (*sein*) strike (**an etw** *acc* sth)

anpreisen† *vt sep* commend

Anprob|e *f* fitting. **a~ieren** *vt sep* try on

anrechnen *vt sep* count (**als** as); (*berechnen*) charge for; (*verrechnen*) allow (*Summe*)

Anrecht *nt* right (**auf** + *acc* to)

Anrede *f* [form of] address. **a~n** *vt sep* address; speak to

anreg|en *vt sep* stimulate; (*ermuntern*) encourage (**zu** to); (*vorschlagen*) suggest. **a~end** *adj* stimulating. **A~ung** *f* stimulation; (*Vorschlag*) suggestion

Anreise *f* journey; (*Ankunft*) arrival. **a~n** *vi sep* (*sein*) arrive

Anreiz *m* incentive

Anrichte *f* -,-n sideboard. **a~n** *vt sep* (*Culin*) prepare; (*garnieren*) garnish (**mit** with); (*verursachen*) cause

anrüchig *adj* disreputable

Anruf *m* call. **A∼beantworter** *m* **-s,-** answering machine. **a∼en†** *v sep* ● *vt* call to; (*bitten*) call on (**um** for); (*Teleph*) ring ● *vi* (*haben*) ring (**bei jdm** s.o.)

anrühren *vt sep* touch; (*verrühren*) mix

ans *prep* = **an das**

Ansage *f* announcement. **a∼n** *vt sep* announce

ansamm|eln *vt sep* collect; (*anhäufen*) accumulate; **sich a∼eln** collect; (*sich häufen*) accumulate; (*Leute:*) gather. **A∼lung** *f* collection; (*Menschen-*) crowd

ansässig *adj* resident

Ansatz *m* beginning; (*Versuch*) attempt

anschaffen *vt sep* [**sich** *dat*] **etw a∼en** acquire/(*kaufen*) buy sth

anschalten *vt sep* switch on

anschau|en *vt sep* look at. **a∼lich** *adj* vivid. **A∼ung** *f* -,-en (*fig*) view

Anschein *m* appearance. **a∼end** *adv* apparently

anschirren *vt sep* harness

Anschlag *m* notice; (*Vor-*) estimate; (*Überfall*) attack (**auf** + *acc* on); (*Mus*) touch; (*Techn*) stop. **a∼en†** *v sep* ● *vt* put up (*Aushang*); strike (*Note, Taste*); cast on (*Masche*); (*beschädigen*) chip ● *vi* (*haben*) strike/(*stoßen*) knock (**an** + *acc* against); (*wirken*) be effective ● *vi* (*sein*) knock (**an** + *acc* against)

anschließen† *v sep* ● *vt* connect (**an** + *acc* to); (*zufügen*) add; **sich a∼ an** (+ *acc*) (*anstoßen*) adjoin; (*folgen*) follow; (*sich anfreunden*) become friendly with; **sich jdm a∼** join s.o. ● *vi* (*haben*) **a∼ an** (+ *acc*) adjoin; (*folgen*) follow. **a∼d** *adj* adjoining; (*zeitlich*) following ● *adv* afterwards

Anschluss *m* connection; (*Kontakt*) contact; **A∼ finden** make friends; **im A∼ an** (+ *acc*) after

anschmiegsam *adj* affectionate

anschmieren *vt sep* smear

anschnallen *vt sep* strap on; **sich**

a∼ fasten one's seat-belt

anschneiden† *vt sep* cut into; broach (*Thema*)

anschreiben† *vt sep* write (**an** + *acc* on); (*Comm*) put on s.o.'s account; (*sich wenden*) write to

Anschrift *f* address

anschuldig|en *vt sep* accuse. **A∼ung** *f* -,-en accusation

anschwellen† *vi sep* (*sein*) swell

ansehen† *vt sep* look at; (*einschätzen*) regard (**als** as); [**sich** *dat*] **etw a∼** look at sth; (*TV*) watch sth. **A∼** *nt* **-s** respect; (*Ruf*) reputation

ansehnlich *adj* considerable

ansetzen *v sep* ● *vt* join (**an** + *acc* to); (*veranschlagen*) estimate ● *vi* (*haben*) (*anbrennen*) burn; **zum Sprung a∼** get ready to jump

Ansicht *f* view; **meiner A∼ nach** in my view; **zur A∼** (*Comm*) on approval. **A∼s[post]karte** *f* picture postcard. **A∼ssache** *f* matter of opinion

ansiedeln (**sich**) *vr sep* settle

ansonsten *adv* apart from that

anspannen *vt sep* hitch up; (*anstrengen*) strain; tense (*Muskel*)

Anspielung *f* -,-en allusion; hint

Anspitzer *m* **-s,-** pencil-sharpener

Ansprache *f* address

ansprechen† *v sep* ● *vt* speak to; (*fig*) appeal to ● *vi* (*haben*) respond (**auf** + *acc* to)

anspringen† *v sep* ● *vt* jump at ● *vi* (*sein*) (*Auto*) start

Anspruch *m* claim/(*Recht*) right (**auf** + *acc* to); **A∼ haben** be entitled (**auf** + *acc* to); **in A∼ nehmen** make use of; (*erfordern*) demand; take up (*Zeit*); occupy (*Person*); **hohe A∼e stellen** be very demanding. **a∼slos** *adj* undemanding. **a∼svoll** *adj* demanding; (*kritisch*) discriminating; (*vornehm*) up-market

anstacheln *vt sep* (*fig*) spur on

Anstalt *f* -,-en institution

Anstand *m* decency; (*Benehmen*) [good] manners *pl*

anständig *adj* decent; (*ehrbar*) re-

a

spectable; (*richtig*) proper

anstandslos *adv* without any trouble

anstarren *vt sep* stare at

anstatt *conj & prep* (+ *gen*) instead of

ansteck|en *v sep* ● *vt* pin (**an** + *acc* to/on); put on (*Ring*); (*anzünden*) light; (*in Brand stecken*) set fire to; (*Med*) infect; **sich a~en** catch an infection (**bei** from) ● *vi* (*haben*) be infectious. **a~end** *adj* infectious. **A~ung** *f* -,-en infection

anstehen† *vi sep* (*haben*) queue

anstelle *prep* (+ *gen*) instead of

anstell|en *vt sep* put, stand (**an** + *acc* against); (*einstellen*) employ; (*anschalten*) turn on; (*tun*) do; **sich a~en** queue [up]. **A~ung** *f* employment; (*Stelle*) job

Anstieg *m* -[e]s,-e climb; (*fig*) rise

anstifte|n *vt sep* cause; (*anzetteln*) instigate

Anstoß *m* (*Anregung*) impetus; (*Stoß*) knock; (*Fußball*) kick-off; **A~ erregen** give offence. **a~en**† *v sep* ● *vt* knock; (*mit dem Ellbogen*) nudge ● *vi* (*sein*) knock (**an** + *acc* against) ● *vi* (*haben*) adjoin (**an** *etw acc* sth); **a~en auf** (+ *acc*) drink to; **mit der Zunge a~en** lisp

anstößig *adj* offensive

anstrahlen *vt sep* floodlight

anstreichen† *vt sep* paint; (*anmerken*) mark

anstreng|en *vt sep* strain; (*ermüden*) tire; **sich a~en** exert oneself; (*sich bemühen*) make an effort (**zu** to). **a~end** *adj* strenuous; (*ermüdend*) tiring. **A~ung** *f* -,-en strain; (*Mühe*) effort

Anstrich *m* coat [of paint]

Ansturm *m* rush; (*Mil*) assault

Ansuchen *nt* -s,- request

Antarktis *f* - Antarctic

Anteil *m* share; **A~ nehmen** take an interest (**an** + *dat* in). **A~nahme** *f* - interest (**an** + *dat* in); (*Mitgefühl*) sympathy

Antenne *f* -,-n aerial

Anthologie *f* -,-n anthology

Anthrax *m* - anthrax

Anthropologie *f* - anthropology

Anti|alkoholiker *m* teetotaller. **A~biotikum** *nt* -s,-ka antibiotic

antik *adj* antique. **A~e** *f* - [classical] antiquity

Antikörper *m* antibody

Antilope *f* -,-n antelope

Antipathie *f* - antipathy

Antiquariat *nt* -[e]s,-e antiquarian bookshop

Antiquitäten *fpl* antiques. **A~händler** *m* antique dealer

Antrag *m* -[e]s,¨e proposal; (*Pol*) motion; (*Gesuch*) application. **A~steller** *m* -s,- applicant

antreffen† *vt sep* find

antreten† *v sep* ● *vt* start; take up (*Amt*) ● *vi* (*sein*) line up

Antrieb *m* urge; (*Techn*) drive; **aus eigenem A~** of one's own accord

Antritt *m* start; **bei A~ eines Amtes** when taking office

antun† *vt sep* **jdm etw a~** do sth to s.o.; **sich** (*dat*) **etwas a~** take one's own life

Antwort *f* -,-en answer, reply (**auf** + *acc* to). **a~en** *vt/i* (*haben*) answer (**jdm** s.o.)

anvertrauen *vt sep* entrust/(*mitteilen*) confide (**jdm** to s.o.)

Anwalt *m* -[e]s,¨e, **Anwältin** *f* -,-nen lawyer; (*vor Gericht*) counsel

Anwandlung *f* -,-en fit (**von** of)

Anwärter(in) *m(f)* candidate

anweis|en† *vt sep* assign (*dat* to); (*beauftragen*) instruct. **A~ung** *f* instruction; (*Geld-*) money order

anwend|en *vt sep* apply (**auf** + *acc* to); (*gebrauchen*) use. **A~ung** *f* application; use

anwerben† *vt sep* recruit

Anwesen *nt* -s,- property

anwesen|d *adj* present (**bei** at); **die A~den** those present. **A~heit** *f* - presence

anwidern *vt sep* disgust

Anwohner *mpl* residents

Anzahl f number

anzahl|en vt sep pay a deposit on. **A~ung** f deposit

anzapfen vt sep tap

Anzeichen nt sign

Anzeige f -,-n announcement; (*Inserat*) advertisement; **A~ erstatten gegen jdn** report s.o. to the police. **a~n** vt sep announce; (*inserieren*) advertise; (*melden*) report [to the police]; (*angeben*) indicate

anzieh|en† vt sep ● vt attract; (*festziehen*) tighten; put on (*Kleider, Bremse*); (*ankleiden*) dress; **sich a~en** get dressed. **a~end** adj attractive. **A~ungskraft** f attraction; (*Phys*) gravity

Anzug m suit

anzüglich adj suggestive

anzünden vt sep light; (*in Brand stecken*) set fire to

anzweifeln vt sep question

apart adj striking

Apathie f - apathy

apathisch adj apathetic

Aperitif m -s,-s aperitif

Apfel m -s,⁼ apple

Apfelsine f -,-n orange

Apostel m -s,- apostle

Apostroph m -s,-e apostrophe

Apothek|e f -,-n pharmacy. **A~er(in)** m -s,- (f -,-nen) pharmacist, [dispensing] chemist

Apparat m -[e]s,-e device; (*Phot*) camera; (*Radio, TV*) set; (*Teleph*) telephone; **am A~!** speaking!

Appell m -s,-e appeal; (*Mil*) roll-call. **a~ieren** vi (*haben*) appeal (**an** + acc to)

Appetit m -s appetite; **guten A~!** enjoy your meal! **a~lich** adj appetizing

Applaus m -es applause

Aprikose f -,-n apricot

April m -[s] April

Aquarell nt -s,-e water-colour

Aquarium nt -s,-ien aquarium

Äquator m -s equator

Ära f - era

Araber(in) m -s,- (f -,-nen) Arab

arabisch adj Arab; (*Geog*) Arabian; (*Ziffer*) Arabic

Arbeit f -,-en work; (*Anstellung*) employment, job; (*Aufgabe*) task; (*Sch*) [written] test; (*Abhandlung*) treatise; (*Qualität*) workmanship; **sich an die A~ machen** set to work; **sich** (*dat*) **viel A~ machen** go to a lot of trouble. **a~en** v sep ● vi (*haben*) work (**an** + dat on) ● vt make. **A~er(in)** m -s,- (f -,-nen) worker; (*Land-, Hilfs-*) labourer. **A~erklasse** f working class

Arbeit|geber m -s,- employer. **A~nehmer** m -s,- employee

Arbeits|amt nt employment exchange. **A~erlaubnis, A~genehmigung** f work permit. **A~kraft** f worker. **a~los** adj unemployed; **~los sein** be out of work. **A~lose(r)** m/f unemployed person; **die A~losen** the unemployed pl. **A~losenunterstützung** f unemployment benefit. **A~losigkeit** f - unemployment

arbeitsparend adj labour-saving

Arbeitsplatz m job

Archäo|loge m -n,-n archaeologist. **A~logie** f - archaeology

Arche f - **die A~** Noah Noah's Ark

Architek|t(in) m -en,-en (f -,-nen) architect. **a~tonisch** adj architectural. **A~tur** f - architecture

Archiv nt -s,-e archives pl

Arena f -,-nen arena

arg adj bad; (*groß*) terrible

Argentin|ien /-i̯ən/ nt -s Argentina. **a~isch** adj Argentinian

Ärger m -s annoyance; (*Unannehmlichkeit*) trouble. **ä~lich** adj annoyed; (*leidig*) annoying; **ä~lich sein** be annoyed. **ä~n** vt annoy; (*necken*) tease; **sich ä~n** get annoyed (**über jdn/ etw** with s.o./ about sth). **Ä~nis** nt -ses, -se annoyance; **öffentliches Ä~nis** public nuisance

Arglist f - malice

arglos adj unsuspecting

Argument nt -[e]s,-e argument.

a

a~ieren vi (*haben*) argue (**dass** that)

Arie /'a:riə/ f -,-n aria

Aristo|krat m -en,-en aristocrat. **A~kratie** f - aristocracy. **a~kratisch** adj aristocratic

Arkt|is f - Arctic. **a~isch** adj Arctic

arm adj poor

Arm m -[e]s,-e arm; **jdn auf den Arm nehmen** 🔲 pull s.o.'s leg

Armaturenbrett nt instrument panel; (*Auto*) dashboard

Armband nt (*pl* -bänder) bracelet; (*Uhr-*) watch-strap. **A~uhr** f wristwatch

Arm|e(r) m/f poor man/woman; **die A~en** the poor pl

Armee f -,-n army

Ärmel m -s,- sleeve. **Ä~kanal** m [English] Channel. **ä~los** adj sleeveless

Arm|lehne f arm. **A~leuchter** m candelabra

ärmlich adj poor; (*elend*) miserable

armselig adj miserable

Armut f - poverty

Arran|gement /arãʒə'mã:/ nt -s,-s arrangement. **a~gieren** vt arrange

arrogant adj arrogant

Arsch m -[e]s,ᵇe (*vulgar*) arse

Arsen nt -s arsenic

Art f -,-en manner; (*Weise*) way; (*Natur*) nature; (*Sorte*) kind; (*Biology*) species; **auf diese Art** in this way

Arterie /-iə/ f -,-n artery

Arthritis f - arthritis

artig adj well-behaved

Artikel m -s,- article

Artillerie f - artillery

Artischocke f -,-n artichoke

Arznei f -,-en medicine

Arzt m -[e]s,ᵇe doctor

Ärzt|in f -,-nen [woman] doctor. **ä~lich** adj medical

As* nt -ses,-se = Ass

Asbest m -[e]s asbestos

Asche f - ash. **A~nbecher** m ashtray. **A~rmittwoch** m Ash Wednesday

Asiat|(in) m -en,-en (f -,-nen)

Asian. **a~isch** adj Asian

Asien /'a:ziən/ nt -s Asia

asozial adj antisocial

Aspekt m -[e]s,-e aspect

Asphalt m -[e]s asphalt. **a~ieren** vt asphalt

Ass nt -es,-e ace

Assistent(in) m -en,-en (f -,-nen) assistant

Ast m -[e]s,ᵇe branch

ästhetisch adj aesthetic

Asth|ma nt -s asthma. **a~matisch** adj asthmatic

Astro|loge m -n,-n astrologer. **A~logie** f - astrology. **A~naut** m -en,-en astronaut. **A~nomie** f - astronomy

Asyl nt -s,-e home; (*Pol*) asylum. **A~bewerber(in)** m -e, - (f -en, -en) asylum seeker

Atelier /-'lie:/ nt -s,-s studio

Atem m -s breath. **a~los** adj breathless. **A~zug** m breath

Atheist m -en,-en atheist

Äther m -s ether

Äthiopien /-iən/ nt -s Ethiopia

Athlet|(in) m -en,-en (f -,-nen) athlete. **a~isch** adj athletic

Atlant|ik m -s Atlantic. **a~isch** adj Atlantic; **der A~ische Ozean** the Atlantic Ocean

Atlas m -lasses,-lanten atlas

atmen vt/i (*haben*) breathe

Atmosphäre f -,-n atmosphere

Atmung f - breathing

Atom nt -s,-e atom. **A~bombe** f atom bomb. **A~krieg** m nuclear war

Atten|tat nt -[e]s,-e assassination attempt. **A~täter** m assassin

Attest nt -[e]s,-e certificate

Attrak|tion /-'tsio:n/ f -,-en attraction. **a~tiv** adj attractive

Attribut nt -[e]s,-e attribute

ätzen vt corrode; (*Med*) cauterize; (*Kunst*) etch. **ä~d** adj corrosive; (*Spott*) caustic

au int ouch; **au fein!** oh good!

Aubergine /ober'ʒi:nə/ f -,-n aubergine

auch *adv & conj* also, too; (*außerdem*) what's more; (*selbst*) even; **a~ wenn** even if; **sie weiß es a~ nicht** she doesn't know either; **wer/wie/was a~ immer** whoever/however/whatever

Audienz *f* -,-en audience

audiovisuell *adj* audio-visual

Auditorium *nt* -s,-ien (*Univ*) lecture hall

---

auf

● *preposition* (+ *dative*)

••••➤ (*nicht unter*) on. **auf dem Tisch** on the table. **auf Deck** on deck. **auf der Erde** on earth. **auf der Welt** in the world. **auf der Straße** in the street

••••➤ (*bei Institution, Veranstaltung usw.*) at; (*bei Gebäude, Zimmer*) in. **auf der Schule/Uni** at school/university. **auf einer Party/Hochzeit** at a party/wedding. **Geld auf der Bank haben** have money in the bank. **sie ist auf ihrem Zimmer** she's in her room. **auf einem Lehrgang** on a course. **auf Urlaub** on holiday

● *preposition* (+ *accusative*)

••••➤ (*nicht unter*) on[to]. **er legte das Buch auf den Tisch** he laid the book on the table. **auf eine Mauer steigen** climb onto a wall. **auf die Straße gehen** go [out] into the street

••••➤ (*bei Institution, Veranstaltung usw.*) to. **auf eine Party/die Toilette gehen** go to a party/the toilet. **auf die Schule/Uni gehen** go to school/university. **auf einen Lehrgang/auf Urlaub gehen** go on a course/on holiday

••••➤ (*bei Entfernung*) **auf 10 km [Entfernung] zu sehen/hören** visible/audible for [a distance of] 10 km

••••➤ (*zeitlich*) (*wie lange*) for; (*bis*) until; (*wann*) on. **auf Jahre [hinaus]** for years [to come]. **auf ein paar Tage** for a few days. **etw auf nächsten Mittwoch verschieben** postpone sth until next

Wednesday. **das fällt auf einen Montag** it falls on a Monday

••••➤ (*Art und Weise*) in. **auf diese [Art und] Weise** in this way. **auf Deutsch/Englisch** in German/English

••••➤ (*aufgrund*) **auf Wunsch** on request. **auf meine Bitte** on *or* at my request. **auf Befehl** on command

••••➤ (*Proportion*) to. **ein Teelöffel auf einen Liter Wasser** one teaspoon to one litre of water. **auf die Sekunde/den Millimeter [genau]** [precise] to the nearest second/millimetre

••••➤ (*Toast*) to. **auf deine Gesundheit!** your health!

● *adverb*

••••➤ (*aufgerichtet, aufgestanden*) up. **auf!** (*steh auf!*) up you get! **auf und ab** (*hin und her*) up and down

••••➤ (*aufsetzen*) **Helm/Hut/Brille auf!** helmet/hat/glasses on!

••••➤ (*geöffnet, offen*) open. **Fenster/Mund auf!** open the window/your mouth!

---

aufatmen *vi sep* (*haben*) heave a sigh of relief

aufbahren *vt sep* lay out

Aufbau *m* construction; (*Struktur*) structure. **a~en** *v sep* ● *vt* construct, build; (*errichten*) erect; (*schaffen*) build up; (*arrangieren*) arrange; **sich a~en** (*fig*) be based (**auf** + *dat* on) ● *vi* (*haben*) be based (**auf** + *dat* on)

aufbauschen *vt sep* puff out; (*fig*) exaggerate

aufbekommen† *vt sep* get open; (*Sch*) be given [as homework]

aufbessern *vt sep* improve; (*erhöhen*) increase

aufbewahr|en *vt sep* keep; (*lagern*) store. **A~ung** *f* - safe keeping; storage; (*Gepäck-*) left-luggage office

aufblas|bar *adj* inflatable. **a~en**† *vt sep* inflate

aufbleiben† *vi sep* (*sein*) stay open; (*Person:*) stay up

a

aufblenden *vt/i sep* (*haben*) (*Auto*) switch to full beam

aufblühen *vi sep* (*sein*) flower

aufbocken *vt sep* jack up

aufbrauchen *vt sep* use up

aufbrechen† *v sep* ● *vt* break open ● *vi* (*sein*) (*Knospe:*) open; (*sich aufmachen*) set out, start

aufbringen† *vt sep* raise (*Geld*); find (*Kraft*)

Aufbruch *m* start, departure

aufbrühen *vt sep* make (*Tee*)

aufbürden *vt sep* jdm etw a~ (*fig*) burden s.o. with sth

aufdecken *vt sep* (*auflegen*) put on; (*abdecken*) uncover; (*fig*) expose

aufdrehen *vt sep* turn on

aufdringlich *adj* persistent

aufeinander *adv* one on top of the other; (*schießen*) at each other; (*warten*) for each other; a~ **folgend** successive; (*Tage*) consecutive.

Aufenthalt *m* stay; **10 Minuten A~ haben** (*Zug:*) stop for 10 minutes. **A~serlaubnis, A~sgenehmigung** *f* residence permit. **A~sraum** *m* recreation room; (*im Hotel*) lounge

Auferstehung *f* - resurrection

aufessen† *vt sep* eat up

auffahr|en† *vi sep* (*sein*) drive up; (*aufprallen*) crash, run (**auf** + *acc* into). **A~t** *f* drive; (*Autobahn-*) access road, slip road; (*Bergfahrt*) ascent

auffallen† *vi sep* (*sein*) be conspicuous; **unangenehm a~** make a bad impression

auffällig *adj* conspicuous

auffangen† *vt sep* catch; pick up

auffass|en *vt sep* understand; (*deuten*) take. **A~ung** *f* understanding; (*Ansicht*) view

auffordern *vt sep* ask; (*einladen*) invite. **A~ung** *f* request; invitation

auffrischen *v sep* ● *vt* freshen up; revive (*Erinnerung*); **seine Englischkenntnisse a~** brush up one's English

aufführ|en *vt sep* perform; (*angeben*) list; **sich a~en** behave. **A~ung** *f* performance

auffüllen *vt sep* fill up

Aufgabe *f* task; (*Rechen-*) problem; (*Verzicht*) giving up; **A~n** (*Sch*) homework *sg*

Aufgang *m* way up; (*Treppe*) stairs *pl*; (*der Sonne*) rise

aufgeben† *v sep* ● *vt* give up; post (*Brief*); send (*Telegramm*); place (*Bestellung*); register (*Gepäck*); put in the paper (*Annonce*); **jdm eine Aufgabe a~** set s.o. a task; **jdm Suppe a~** serve s.o. with soup ● *vi* (*haben*) give up

Aufgebot *nt* contingent (**an** + *dat* of); (*Relig*) banns *pl*

aufgedunsen *adj* bloated

aufgehen† *vi sep* (*sein*) open; (*sich lösen*) come undone; (*Teig, Sonne:*) rise; (*Saat:*) come up; (*Math*) come out exactly; **in Flammen a~** go up in flames

aufgelegt *adj* **gut/schlecht a~ sein** be in a good/bad mood

aufgeregt *adj* excited; (*erregt*) agitated

aufgeschlossen *adj* (*fig*) open-minded

aufgeweckt *adj* (*fig*) bright

aufgießen† *vt sep* pour on; (*aufbrühen*) make (*Tee*)

aufgreifen† *vt sep* pick up; take up (*Vorschlag, Thema*)

aufgrund *prep* (+ *gen*) on the strength of

Aufguss *m* infusion

aufhaben† *v sep* ● *vt* have on; **den Mund a~** have one's mouth open; **viel a~** (*Sch*) have a lot of homework ● *vi* (*haben*) be open

aufhalten† *vt sep* hold up; (*anhalten*) stop; (*abhalten*) keep; (*offenhalten*) hold open; hold out (*Hand*); **sich a~** stay; (*sich befassen*) spend one's time (**mit** on)

aufhäng|en *vt/i sep* (*haben*) hang up; (*henken*) hang; **sich a~en** hang oneself. **A~er** *m* **-s,-** loop

aufheben† *vt sep* pick up; (*hochheben*) raise; (*aufbewahren*) keep; (*beenden*) end; (*rückgängig machen*) lift;

(*abschaffen*) abolish; (*Jur*) quash (*Urteil*); repeal (*Gesetz*); (*ausgleichen*) cancel out; **gut aufgehoben sein** be well looked after

aufheitern *vt sep* cheer up; **sich a~** (*Wetter:*) brighten up

aufhellen *vt sep* lighten; **sich a~** (*Himmel:*) brighten

aufhetzen *vt sep* incite

aufholen *v sep* ● *vt* make up ● *vi* (*haben*) catch up; (*zeitlich*) make up time

aufhören *vi sep* (*haben*) stop

aufklappen *vt/i sep* (*sein*) open

aufklär|en *vt sep* solve; **jdn a~en** enlighten s.o.; **sich a~en** be solved; (*Wetter:*) clear up. **A~ung** *f* solution; enlightenment; (*Mil*) reconnaissance; **sexuelle A~ung** sex education

aufkleb|en *vt sep* stick on. **A~er** *m* -s,- sticker

aufknöpfen *vt sep* unbutton

aufkochen *v sep* ● *vt* bring to the boil ● *vi* (*sein*) come to the boil

aufkommen† *vi sep* (*sein*) start; (*Wind:*) spring up; (*Mode:*) come in

aufkrempeln *vt sep* roll up

aufladen† *vt sep* load; (*Electr*) charge

Auflage *f* impression; (*Ausgabe*) edition; (*Zeitungs-*) circulation

auflassen† *vt sep* leave open; leave on (*Hut*)

Auflauf *m* crowd; (*Culin*) ≈ soufflé

auflegen *v sep* ● *vt* apply (**auf** + *acc* to); put down (*Hörer*); **neu a~** reprint ● *vi* (*haben*) ring off

auflehn|en (sich) *vr sep* (*fig*) rebel. **A~ung** *f* - rebellion

auflesen† *vt sep* pick up

aufleuchten *vi sep* (*haben*) light up

auflös|en *vt sep* dissolve; close (*Konto*); **sich a~en** dissolve; (*Nebel:*) clear. **A~ung** dissolution; (*Lösung*) solution

aufmach|en *v sep* ● *vt* open; (*lösen*) undo; **sich a~en** set out (**nach** for) ● *vi* (*haben*) open; **jdm a~en** open the door to s.o. **A~ung** *f* -,-en get-up

aufmerksam *adj* attentive; **a~ werden auf** (+ *acc*) notice; **jdn a~ machen auf** (+ *acc*) draw s.o.'s attention to. **A~keit** *f* -,-en attention; (*Höflichkeit*) courtesy

aufmuntern *vt sep* cheer up

Aufnahme *f* -,-n acceptance; (*Empfang*) reception; (*in Klub, Krankenhaus*) admission; (*Einbeziehung*) inclusion; (*Beginn*) start; (*Foto*) photograph; (*Film-*) shot; (*Mus*) recording; (*Band-*) tape recording. **a~fähig** *adj* receptive. **A~prüfung** *f* entrance examination

aufnehmen† *vt sep* pick up; (*absorbieren*) absorb; take (*Nahrung, Foto*); (*fassen*) hold; (*annehmen*) accept; (*leihen*) borrow; (*empfangen*) receive; (*in Klub, Krankenhaus*) admit; (*beherbergen, geistig erfassen*) take in; (*einbeziehen*) include; (*beginnen*) take up; (*niederschreiben*) take down; (*filmen*) film, shoot; (*Mus*) record; **auf Band a~** tape[-record]

aufopfer|n *vt sep* sacrifice; **sich a~n** sacrifice oneself. **A~ung** *f* self-sacrifice

aufpassen *vi sep* (*haben*) pay attention; (*sich vorsehen*) take care; **a~ auf** (+ *acc*) look after

Aufprall *m* -[e]s impact. **a~en** *vi sep* (*sein*) **a~en auf** (+ *acc*) hit

aufpumpen *vt sep* pump up, inflate

aufputsch|en *vt sep* incite. **A~mittel** *nt* stimulant

aufquellen† *vi sep* (*sein*) swell

aufraffen *vt sep* pick up; **sich a~** pick oneself up; (*fig*) pull oneself together

aufragen *vi sep* (*sein*) rise [up]

aufräumen *vt/i sep* (*haben*) tidy up; (*wegräumen*) put away

aufrecht *adj* & *adv* upright. **a~erhalten†** *vt sep* (*fig*) maintain

aufreg|en *vt* excite; (*beunruhigen*) upset; (*ärgern*) annoy; **sich a~en** get excited; (*sich erregen*) get worked up. **a~end** *adj* exciting. **A~ung** *f* excitement

aufreiben† *vt sep* chafe; (*fig*) wear down. **a~d** *adj* trying

a

aufreißen† v sep ● vt tear open; dig up (*Straße*); open wide (*Augen, Mund*) ● vi (*sein*) split open

aufrichtig adj sincere. **A~keit** f -sincerity

aufrollen vt sep roll up; (*entrollen*) unroll

aufrücken vi sep (*sein*) move up; (*fig*) be promoted

Aufruf m appeal (**an** + dat to); **a~en**† vt sep call out (*Namen*); **jdn a~en** call s.o.'s name

Aufruhr m -s,-e turmoil; (*Empörung*) revolt

aufrühr|en vt sep stir up. **A~er** m -s,- rebel. **a~erisch** adj inflammatory; (*rebellisch*) rebellious

aufrunden vt sep round up

aufrüsten vi sep (*haben*) arm

aufsagen vt sep recite

aufsässig adj rebellious

Aufsatz m top; (*Sch*) essay

aufsaugen† vt sep soak up

aufschauen vi sep (*haben*) look up (**zu** at/(*fig*) to)

aufschichten vt sep stack up

aufschieben† vt sep slide open; (*verschieben*) put off, postpone

Aufschlag m impact; (*Tennis*) service; (*Hosen-*) turn-up; (*Ärmel-*) upturned cuff; (*Revers*) lapel; (*Comm*) surcharge. **a~en**† v sep ● vt open; crack (*Ei*); (*hochschlagen*) turn up; (*errichten*) put up; (*erhöhen*) increase; cast on (*Masche*); **sich** (dat) **das Knie a~en** cut [open] one's knee ● vi (*haben*) hit (**auf etw** acc/dat sth); (*Tennis*) serve; (*teurer werden*) go up

aufschließen† v sep ● vt unlock ● vi (*haben*) unlock the door

aufschlussreich adj revealing; (*lehrreich*) informative

aufschneiden† v sep ● vt cut open; (*in Scheiben*) slice ● vi (*haben*) 🗓 exaggerate

Aufschnitt m sliced sausage, cold meat [and cheese]

aufschrauben vt sep screw on; (*abschrauben*) unscrew

Aufschrei m [sudden] cry

aufschreiben† vt sep write down; **jdn a~** (*Polizist:*) book s.o.

Aufschrift f inscription; (*Etikett*) label

Aufschub m delay; (*Frist*) grace

aufschürfen vt sep **sich** (dat) **das Knie a~** graze one's knee

aufschwingen (sich) vr sep find the energy (**zu** for)

Aufschwung m (*fig*) upturn

aufsehen† vi sep (*haben*) look up (**zu** at/(*fig*) to). **A~** nt -s **A~ erregen** cause a sensation; **A~ erregend** sensational

Aufseher(in) m -s,- (f -,-nen) supervisor; (*Gefängnis-*) warder

aufsetzen vt sep put on; (*verfassen*) draw up; (*entwerfen*) draft; **sich a~** sit up

Aufsicht f supervision; (*Person*) supervisor. **A~srat** m board of directors

aufsperren vt sep open wide

aufspielen v sep ● vi (*haben*) play ● vr **sich a~** show off

aufspießen vt sep spear

aufspringen† vi sep (*sein*) jump up; (*aufprallen*) bounce; (*sich öffnen*) burst open

aufspüren vt sep track down

aufstacheln vt sep incite

Aufstand m uprising, rebellion

aufständisch adj rebellious

aufstehen† vi sep (*sein*) get up; (*offen sein*) be open; (*fig*) rise up

aufsteigen† vi sep (*sein*) get on; (*Reiter:*) mount; (*Bergsteiger:*) climb up; (*hochsteigen*) rise [up]; (*fig: befördert werden*) rise (**zu** to); (*Sport*) be promoted

aufstell|en vt sep put up; (*Culin*) put on; (*postieren*) post; (*in einer Reihe*) line up; (*nominieren*) nominate; (*Sport*) select (*Mannschaft*); make out (*Liste*); lay down (*Regel*); make (*Behauptung*); set up (*Rekord*). **A~ung** f nomination; (*Liste*) list

Aufstieg m -[e]s, -e ascent; (*fig*) rise; (*Sport*) promotion

Aufstoßen nt -s burping

aufstrebend *adj* (*fig*) ambitious

Aufstrich *m* [sandwich] spread

aufstützen *vt sep* rest (**auf** + *acc* on); **sich a~** lean (**auf** + *acc* on)

Auftakt *m* (*fig*) start

auftauchen *vi sep* (*sein*) emerge; (*fig*) turn up; (*Frage:*) crop up

auftauen *vt/i sep* (*sein*) thaw

aufteil|en *vt sep* divide [up]. **A~ung** *f* division

auftischen *vt sep* serve [up]

Auftrag *m* -[e]s, ⸚e task; (*Kunst*) commission; (*Comm*) order; **im A~** (+ *gen*) on behalf of. **a~en†** *vt sep* apply; (*servieren*) serve; (*abtragen*) wear out; **jdm a~en** instruct s.o. (**zu** to). **A~geber** *m* -s,- client

auftrennen *vt sep* unpick, undo

auftreten† *vi sep* (*sein*) tread; (*sich benehmen*) behave, act; (*Theat*) appear; (*die Bühne betreten*) enter; (*vorkommen*) occur

Auftrieb *m* buoyancy; (*fig*) boost

Auftritt *m* (*Theat*) appearance; (*auf die Bühne*) entrance; (*Szene*) scene

aufwachen *vi sep* (*sein*) wake up

aufwachsen† *vi sep* (*sein*) grow up

Aufwand *m* -[e]s expenditure; (*Luxus*) extravagance; (*Mühe*) trouble; **A~ treiben** be extravagant

aufwändig *adj* = aufwendig

aufwärmen *vt sep* heat up; (*fig*) rake up; **sich a~** warm oneself; (*Sport*) warm up

Aufwartefrau *f* cleaner

aufwärts *adv* upwards; (*bergauf*) uphill; **es geht a~ mit jdm/etw** someone/something is improving

Aufwartung *f* - cleaner

aufwecken *vt sep* wake up

aufweichen *v sep* ● *vt* soften ● *vi* (*sein*) become soft

aufweisen† *vt sep* have, show

aufwend|en† *vt sep* spend; **Mühe a~en** take pains. **a~ig** *adj* lavish; (*teuer*) expensive

aufwert|en *vt sep* revalue. **A~ung** *f* revaluation

aufwickeln *vt sep* roll up; (*auswickeln*) unwrap

Aufwiegler *m* -s,- agitator

aufwisch|en *vt sep* wipe up; wash (*Fußboden*). **A~lappen** *m* floorcloth

aufwühlen *vt sep* churn up

aufzähl|en *vt sep* enumerate, list. **A~ung** *f* list

aufzeichn|en *vt sep* record; (*zeichnen*) draw. **A~ung** *f* recording; **A~ungen** notes

aufziehen† *v sep* ● *vt* pull up; hoist (*Segel*); (*öffnen*) open; draw (*Vorhang*); (*großziehen*) bring up; rear (*Tier*); mount (*Bild*); thread (*Perlen*); wind up (*Uhr*); (🄸: *necken*) tease ● *vi* (*sein*) approach

Aufzug *m* hoist; (*Fahrstuhl*) lift, (*Amer*) elevator; (*Prozession*) procession; (*Theat*) act

Augapfel *m* eyeball

Auge *nt* -s,-n eye; (*Punkt*) spot; **vier A~n werfen** throw a four; **gute A~n** good eyesight; **unter vier A~n** in private; **im A~ behalten** keep in sight; (*fig*) bear in mind

Augenblick *m* moment; **A~!** just a moment! **a~lich** *adj* immediate; (*derzeitig*) present ● *adv* immediately; (*derzeit*) at present

Augen|braue *f* eyebrow. **A~höhle** *f* eye socket. **A~licht** *nt* sight. **A~lid** *nt* eyelid

August *m* -[s] August

Auktion /'tsio:n/ *f* -,-en auction

Aula *f* -,-len (*Sch*) [assembly] hall

Au-pair-Mädchen /o'pɛːr-/ *nt* aupair

aus *prep* (+ *dat*) out of; (*von*) from; (*bestehend*) [made] of; **aus Angst** from or out of fear; **aus Spaß** for fun ● *adv* out; (*Licht, Radio*) off; **aus sein auf** (+ *acc*) be after; **aus und ein** in and out; **von sich aus** of one's own accord; **von mir aus** as far as I'm concerned

ausarbeiten *vt sep* work out

ausarten *vi sep* (*sein*) degenerate (**in** + *acc* into)

ausatmen vt/i sep (haben) breathe out

ausbauen vt sep remove; (vergrößern) extend; (fig) expand

ausbedingen† vt sep sich (dat) a~ insist on; (zur Bedingung machen) stipulate

ausbesser|n vt sep mend, repair. A~ung f repair

ausbeulen vt sep remove the dents from; (dehnen) make baggy

ausbild|en vt sep train; (formen) form; (entwickeln) develop; sich a~en train (als/zu as); (entstehen) develop. A~ung f training; (Sch) education

ausbitten† vt sep sich (dat) a~ ask for; (verlangen) insist on

ausblasen† vt sep blow out

ausbleiben† vi sep (sein) fail to appear/ (Erfolg:) materialize; (nicht heimkommen) stay out

Ausblick m view

ausbrech|en† vi sep (sein) break out; (Vulkan:) erupt; (fliehen) escape; in Tränen a~en burst into tears. A~er m runaway

ausbreit|en vt sep spread [out]. A~ung f spread

Ausbruch m outbreak; (Vulkan-) eruption; (Wut-) outburst; (Flucht) escape, break-out

ausbrüten vt sep hatch

Ausdauer f perseverance; (körperlich) stamina. a~nd adj persevering; (unermüdlich) untiring

ausdehnen vt sep stretch; (fig) extend; sich a~ stretch; (Phys & fig) expand; (dauern) last

ausdenken† vt sep sich (dat) a~ think up; (sich vorstellen) imagine

Ausdruck m expression; (Fach-) term; (Computer) printout. a~en vt sep print

ausdrücken vt sep squeeze out; squeeze (Zitrone); stub out (Zigarette); (äußern) express

ausdrucks|los adj expressionless. a~voll adj expressive

auseinander adv apart; (entzwei) in pieces; a~ falten unfold; a~ gehen part; (Linien, Meinungen:) diverge; (Ehe:) break up; a~ halten tell apart; a~ nehmen take apart or to pieces; a~ setzen explain (jdm to s.o.); sich a~ setzen sit apart; (sich aussprechen) have it out (mit jdm with s.o.); come to grips (mit einem Problem with a problem). A~setzung f -,-en discussion; (Streit) argument

auserlesen adj select, choice

Ausfahrt f drive; (Autobahn-, Garagen-) exit

Ausfall m failure; (Absage) cancellation; (Comm) loss. a~en† vi sep (sein) fall out; (versagen) fail; (abgesagt werden) be cancelled; gut/schlecht a~en turn out to be good/poor

ausfallend, ausfällig adj abusive

ausfertig|en vt sep make out. A~ung f -,-en in doppelter A~ung in duplicate

ausfindig adj a~ machen find

Ausflug m excursion, outing

Ausflügler m -s,- [day-]tripper

Ausfluss m outlet; (Abfluss) drain; (Med) discharge

ausfragen vt sep question

Ausfuhr f -,-en (Comm) export

ausführ|en vt sep take out; (Comm) export; (erklären) explain. a~lich adj detailed ● adv in detail. A~ung f execution; (Comm) version; (äußere) finish; (Qualität) workmanship; (Erklärung) explanation

Ausgabe f issue; (Buch-) edition; (Comm) version

Ausgang m way out, exit; (Flugsteig) gate; (Ende) end; (Ergebnis) outcome. A~spunkt m starting point. A~sperre f curfew

ausgeben† vt sep hand out; issue (Fahrkarten); spend (Geld); sich a~ als pretend to be

ausgebildet adj trained

ausgebucht adj fully booked; (Vorstellung) sold out

ausgefallen adj unusual

ausgefranst *adj* frayed

ausgeglichen *adj* [well-]balanced

ausgeh|en† *vi sep* (*sein*) go out; (*Haare:*) fall out; (*Vorräte, Geld:*) run out; (*verblassen*) fade; **gut/schlecht a~en** end well/badly; **davon a~en, dass** assume that. **A~verbot** *nt* curfew

ausgelassen *adj* high-spirited

ausgemacht *adj* agreed

ausgenommen *conj* except; **a~ wenn** unless

ausgeprägt *adj* marked

ausgeschlossen *pred adj* out of the question

ausgeschnitten *adj* low-cut

ausgesprochen *adj* marked ● *adv* decidedly

ausgestorben *adj* extinct; [**wie**] **a~** (*Straße:*) deserted

Ausgestoßene(r) *m/f* outcast

ausgezeichnet *adj* excellent

ausgiebig *adj* extensive; (*ausgedehnt*) long; **a~ Gebrauch machen von** make full use of

ausgießen† *vt sep* pour out

Ausgleich *m* -[e]s balance; (*Entschädigung*) compensation. **a~en**† *v sep* ● *vt* balance; even out (*Höhe*); (*wettmachen*) compensate for; **sich a~en** balance out ● *vi* (*haben*) (*Sport*) equalize. **A~streffer** *m* equalizer

ausgrab|en† *vt sep* dig up; (*Archaeology*) excavate. **A~ung** *f* -,-en excavation

Ausguss *m* [kitchen] sink

aushaben† *vt sep* have finished (*Buch*)

aushalten† *vt sep* bear, stand; hold (*Note*); (*Unterhalt zahlen für*) keep; **nicht auszuhalten, nicht zum A~** unbearable

aushändigen *vt sep* hand over

aushängen¹ *vt sep* (*reg*) display; take off its hinges (*Tür*)

aushäng|en²† *vi sep* (*haben*) be displayed. **A~eschild** *nt* sign

ausheben† *vt sep* excavate

aushecken *vt sep* (*fig*) hatch

aushelfen† *vi sep* (*haben*) help out (**jdm** s.o.)

Aushilf|e *f* [temporary] assistant; **zur A~e** to help out. **A~skraft** *f* temporary worker. **a~sweise** *adv* temporarily

aushöhlen *vt sep* hollow out

auskennen† (**sich**) *vr sep* know one's way around; **sich mit/in etw** (*dat*) **a~** know all about sth

auskommen† *vi sep* (*sein*) manage (**mit/ohne** with/without); (*sich vertragen*) get on (**gut** well)

auskugeln *vt sep* **sich** (*dat*) **den Arm a~** dislocate one's shoulder

auskühlen *vt/i sep* (*sein*) cool

auskundschaften *vt sep* spy out

Auskunft *f* -,-̈e information; (*A~sstelle*) information desk/ (*Büro*) bureau; (*Teleph*) enquiries *pl*; **eine A~** a piece of information

auslachen *vt sep* laugh at

Auslage *f* [window] display; **A~n** expenses

Ausland *nt* **im/ins A~** abroad

Ausländ|er(in) *m* -s,- (*f* -,-nen) foreigner. **a~isch** *adj* foreign

Auslandsgespräch *nt* international call

auslass|en† *vt sep* let out; let down (*Saum*); (*weglassen*) leave out; (*versäumen*) miss; (*Culin*) melt; (*fig*) vent (*Ärger*) (**an** ɪ *dat* at on). **A~ungszeichen** *nt* apostrophe

Auslauf *m* run. **a~en**† *vi sep* (*sein*) run out; (*Farbe:*) run; (*Naut*) put to sea; (*Modell:*) be discontinued

ausleeren *vt sep* empty [out]

ausleg|en *vt sep* lay out; display (*Waren*); (*auskleiden*) line (**mit** with); (*bezahlen*) pay; (*deuten*) interpret. **A~ung** *f* -,-en interpretation

ausleihen† *vt sep* lend; **sich** (*dat*) **a~** borrow

Auslese *f* - selection; (*fig*) pick; (*Elite*) elite

ausliefer|n *vt sep* hand over; (*Jur*) extradite. **A~ung** *f* handing over; (*Jur*) extradition; (*Comm*) distribution

ausloggen *vi sep* log off *or* out

a

auslosen *vt sep* draw lots for

auslös|en *vt sep* set off, trigger; (*fig*) cause; arouse (*Begeisterung*); (*einlösen*) redeem; pay a ransom for (*Gefangene*). **A~er** *m* **-s,-** trigger; (*Phot*) shutter release

Auslosung *f* draw

auslüften *vt/i sep* (*haben*) air

ausmachen *vt sep* put out; (*abschalten*) turn off; (*abmachen*) arrange; (*erkennen*) make out; (*betragen*) amount to; (*wichtig sein*) matter

Ausmaß *nt* extent; **A~e** dimensions

Ausnahm|e *f* **-,-n** exception. **A~ezustand** *m* state of emergency. **a~slos** *adv* without exception. **a~sweise** *adv* as an exception

ausnehmen† *vt sep* take out; gut (*Fisch*); **gut a~** look good. **a~d** *adv* exceptionally

ausnutz|en, ausnütz|en *vt sep* exploit. **A~ung** *f* exploitation

auspacken *vt sep* unpack; (*auswickeln*) unwrap

ausplaudern *vt sep* let out, blab

ausprobieren *vt sep* try out

Auspuff *m* **-s** exhaust [system]. **A~gase** *ntpl* exhaust fumes. **A~rohr** *nt* exhaust pipe

auspusten *vt sep* blow out

ausradieren *vt sep* rub out

ausrauben *vt sep* rob

ausräuchern *vt sep* smoke out; fumigate (*Zimmer*)

ausräumen *vt sep* clear out

ausrechnen *vt sep* work out

Ausrede *f* excuse. **a~n** *v sep* ● *vi* (*haben*) finish speaking ● *vt* jdm etw **a~n** talk s.o. out of sth

ausreichen *vi sep* (*haben*) be enough. **a~d** *adj* adequate

Ausreise *f* departure. **a~n** *vi sep* (*sein*) leave the country. **A~visum** *nt* exit visa

ausreißen† *v sep* ● *vt* pull or tear out ● *vi* (*sein*) 🄸 run away

ausrenken *vt sep* dislocate

ausrichten *vt sep* align; (*bestellen*) deliver; (*erreichen*) achieve; jdm **a~** tell s.o. (**dass** that); **ich soll Ihnen**

Grüße von X a~ X sends [you] his regards

ausrotten *vt sep* exterminate; (*fig*) eradicate

Ausruf *m* exclamation. **a~en**† *vt sep* exclaim; call out (*Namen*); (*verkünden*) proclaim; jdn **a~en lassen** put out a call for s.o. **A~ezeichen** *nt* exclamation mark

ausruhen *vt/i sep* (*haben*) rest; **sich a~** have a rest

ausrüst|en *vt sep* equip. **A~ung** *f* equipment; (*Mil*) kit

ausrutschen *vi sep* (*sein*) slip

Aussage *f* **-,-n** statement; (*Jur*) testimony, evidence; (*Gram*) predicate. **a~n** *vt/i sep* (*haben*) state; (*Jur*) give evidence, testify

ausschalten *vt sep* switch off

Ausschank *m* sale of alcoholic drinks; (*Bar*) bar

Ausschau *f* - **A~ halten nach** look out for

ausscheiden† *vi sep* (*sein*) leave; (*Sport*) drop out; (*nicht in Frage kommen*) be excluded

ausschenken *vt sep* pour out

ausscheren *vi sep* (*sein*) (*Auto*) pull out

ausschildern *vt sep* signpost

ausschimpfen *vt sep* tell off

ausschlafen† *vi/r sep* (*haben*) [sich] **a~** get enough sleep; (*morgens*) sleep late

Ausschlag *m* (*Med*) rash; **den A~ geben** (*fig*) tip the balance. **a~gebend** *adj* decisive

ausschließ|en† *vt sep* lock out; (*fig*) exclude; (*entfernen*) expel. **a~lich** *adj* exclusive

ausschlüpfen *vi sep* (*sein*) hatch

Ausschluss *m* exclusion; expulsion; **unter A~ der Öffentlichkeit** in camera

ausschneiden† *vt sep* cut out

Ausschnitt *m* excerpt, extract; (*Zeitungs-*) cutting; (*Hals-*) neckline

ausschöpfen *vt sep* ladle out; (*Naut*) bail out; exhaust (*Möglichkeiten*)

ausschreiben† *vt sep* write out; (*ausstellen*) make out; (*bekanntgeben*) announce; put out to tender (*Auftrag*)

Ausschreitungen *fpl* riots; (*Exzesse*) excesses

Ausschuss *m* committee; (*Comm*) rejects *pl*

ausschütten *vt sep* tip out; (*verschütten*) spill; (*leeren*) empty

aussehen† *vi sep* (*haben*) look; **wie sieht er/es aus?** what does he/it look like? **A∼** *nt* **-s** appearance

außen *adv* [on the] outside; **nach a∼** outwards. **A∼bordmotor** *m* outboard motor. **A∼handel** *m* foreign trade. **A∼minister** *m* Foreign Minister. **A∼politik** *f* foreign policy. **A∼seite** *f* outside. **A∼seiter** *m* -s,- outsider; (*fig*) misfit. **A∼stände** *mpl* outstanding debts

außer *prep* (+ *dat*) except [for], apart from; (*außerhalb*) out of; **a∼ sich** (*fig*) beside oneself ● *conj* except; **a∼ wenn** unless. **a∼dem** *adv* in addition, as well ● *conj* moreover

äußer|e(r,s) *adj* external; (*Teil, Schicht*) outer. **Ä∼e(s)** *nt* exterior; (*Aussehen*) appearance

außer|ehelich *adj* extramarital. **a∼gewöhnlich** *adj* exceptional. **a∼halb** *prep* (+ *gen*) outside ● *adv* **a∼halb wohnen** live outside town

äußer|lich *adj* external; (*fig*) outward. **ä∼n** *vt* express; **sich ä∼n** comment; (*sich zeigen*) manifest itself

außerordentlich *adj* extraordinary

äußerst *adv* extremely

äußerste|(r,s) *adj* outermost; (*weiteste*) furthest; (*höchste*) utmost, extreme; (*letzte*) last; (*schlimmste*) worst. **Ä∼(s)** *nt* **das Ä∼** the limit; (*Schlimmste*) the worst; **sein Ä∼s tun** do one's utmost; **aufs Ä∼** extremely

Äußerung *f* -,-en comment; (*Bemerkung*) remark

aussetzen *v sep* ● *vt* expose (*dat* to); abandon (*Kind*); launch (*Boot*); offer (*Belohnung*); **etwas auszuset-**

zen haben an (+ *dat*) find fault with ● *vi* (*haben*) stop; (*Motor:*) cut out

Aussicht *f* -,-en view/(*fig*) prospect (**auf** + *acc* of); **weitere A∼en** (*Meteorology*) further outlook *sg*. **a∼slos** *adj* hopeless

ausspannen *v sep* ● *vt* spread out; unhitch (*Pferd*) ● *vi* (*haben*) rest

aussperren *vt sep* lock out

ausspielen *v sep* ● *vt* play (*Karte*); (*fig*) play off (**gegen** against) ● *vi* (*haben*) (*Kartenspiel*) lead

Aussprache *f* pronunciation; (*Gespräch*) talk

aussprechen† *vt sep* pronounce; (*äußern*) express; **sich a∼** talk; come out (**für/gegen** in favour of/against)

Ausspruch *m* saying

ausspucken *v sep* ● *vt* spit out ● *vi* (*haben*) spit

ausspülen *vt sep* rinse out

ausstatt|en *vt sep* equip. **A∼ung** *f* -,-en equipment; (*Innen*) furnishings *pl*; (*Theat*) scenery and costumes *pl*

ausstehen† *v sep* ● *vt* suffer; **Angst a∼** be frightened; **ich kann sie nicht a∼** I can't stand her ● *vi* (*haben*) be outstanding

aussteigen† *vi sep* (*sein*) get out; (*aus Bus, Zug*) get off; **alles a∼!** all change!

ausstell|en *vt sep* exhibit; (*Comm*) display; (*ausfertigen*) make out; issue (*Pass*). **A∼ung** *f* exhibition; (*Comm*) display

aussterben† *vi sep* (*sein*) die out; (*Biology*) become extinct

Aussteuer *f* trousseau

Ausstieg *m* -[e]s,-e exit

ausstopfen *vt sep* stuff

ausstoßen† *vt sep* emit; utter (*Fluch*); heave (*Seufzer*); (*ausschließen*) expel

ausstrahl|en *vt/i sep* (*sein*) radiate, emit; (*Radio, TV*) broadcast. **A∼ung** *f* radiation

ausstrecken *vt sep* stretch out; put out (*Hand*)

ausstreichen† *vt sep* cross out

ausströmen *v sep* ● *vi* (*sein*) pour

a

out; (*entweichen*) escape ● *vt* emit;
(*ausstrahlen*) radiate

aussuchen *vt sep* pick, choose

Austausch *m* exchange. **a~bar** *adj*
interchangeable. **a~en** *vt sep* exchange; (*auswechseln*) replace

austeilen *vt sep* distribute

Auster *f* -,-n oyster

austragen† *vt sep* deliver; hold
(*Wettkampf*); play (*Spiel*)

Austral|ien /-i̯ən/ *nt* -s Australia.
A~ier(in) *m* -s,- (*f* -,-nen) Australian. **a~isch** *adj* Australian

austreiben† *vt sep* drive out; (*Relig*)
exorcize

austreten† *v sep* ● *vt* stamp out;
(*abnutzen*) wear down ● *vi* (*sein*)
come out; (*ausscheiden*) leave (**aus
etw** sth); [mal] **a~** 🔟 go to the loo

austrinken† *vt/i sep* (*haben*) drink
up; (*leeren*) drain

Austritt *m* resignation

austrocknen *vt/i sep* (*sein*) dry out

ausüben *vt sep* practise; carry on
(*Handwerk*); exercise (*Recht*); exert
(*Druck, Einfluss*)

Ausverkauf *m* [clearance] sale.
a~t *adj* sold out

Auswahl *f* choice, selection; (*Comm*)
range; (*Sport*) team

auswählen *vt sep* choose, select

Auswander|er *m* emigrant. **a~n**
vi sep (*sein*) emigrate. **A~ung** *f*
emigration

auswärt|ig *adj* non-local; (*auslän-
disch*) foreign. **a~s** *adv* outwards;
(*Sport*) away. **A~sspiel** *nt* away
game

auswaschen† *vt sep* wash out

auswechseln *vt sep* change; (*ersetzen*) replace; (*Sport*) substitute

Ausweg *m* (*fig*) way out

ausweichen† *vi sep* (*sein*) get out
of the way; **jdm/etw a~en** avoid/
(*sich entziehen*) evade someone/
something

Ausweis *m* -es,-e pass; (*Mitglieds-,
Studenten-*) card. **a~en†** *vt sep* deport; **sich a~en** prove one's identity. **A~papiere** *ntpl* identification

papers. **A~ung** *f* deportation

auswendig *adv* by heart

auswerten *vt sep* evaluate

auswickeln *vt sep* unwrap

auswirk|en (sich) *vr sep* have an
effect (**auf** + *acc* on). **A~ung** *f* effect; (*Folge*) consequence

auswringen *vt sep* wring out

auszahlen *vt sep* pay out; (*entlohnen*) pay off; (*abfinden*) buy out; **sich
a~** (*fig*) pay off

auszählen *vt sep* count; (*Boxen*)
count out

Auszahlung *f* payment

auszeichn|en *vt sep* (*Comm*) price;
(*ehren*) honour; (*mit einem Preis*)
award a prize to; (*Mil*) decorate; **sich
a~en** distinguish oneself. **A~ung** *f*
honour; (*Preis*) award; (*Mil*) decoration; (*Sch*) distinction

ausziehen† *v sep* ● *vt* pull out; (*auskleiden*) undress; take off (*Mantel,
Schuhe*) ● *vi* (*sein*) move out; (*sich
aufmachen*) set out

Auszug *m* departure; (*Umzug*) move;
(*Ausschnitt*) extract; (*Bank-*) statement

Auto *nt* -s,-s car; **A~ fahren** drive;
(*mitfahren*) go in the car. **A~bahn** *f*
motorway

Autobiographie *f* autobiography

Auto|bus *m* bus. **A~fahrer(in)**
m(f) driver, motorist. **A~fahrt** *f*
drive

Autogramm *nt* -s,-e autograph

Automat *m* -en,-en automatic device; (*Münz-*) slot-machine; (*Verkaufs-*)
vending-machine; (*Fahrkarten-*) machine; (*Techn*) robot. **A~ik** *f* - automatic mechanism; (*Auto*) automatic
transmission

automatisch *adj* automatic

Autonummer *f* registration number

Autopsie *f* -,-n autopsy

Autor *m* -s,-en author

Auto|reisezug *m* Motorail.
A~rennen *nt* motor race

Autorin *f* -,-nen author[ess]

Autori|sation /-ˈt͡si̯oːn/ *f* - author-

ization. **A~tät** f -,-en authority
Auto|schlosser m motor mech-
anic. **A~skooter** m -s,- dodgem.
A~stopp m -s per A~stopp fahren
hitch-hike. **A~verleih** m car hire
[firm]. **A~waschanlage** f car wash
autsch int ouch
Axt f -,-̈e axe

Bb

B, b /beː/ nt - (Mus) B flat
Baby /'beːbi/ nt -s,-s baby. **B~aus-
stattung** f layette. **B~sitter** m -s,-
babysitter
Bach m -[e]s,-̈e stream
Backbord nt -[e]s port [side]
Backe f -,-n cheek
backen vt/i† (haben) bake; (braten)
fry
Backenzahn m molar
Bäcker m -s,- baker. **B~ei** f -,-en,
B~laden m baker's shop
Back|obst nt dried fruit. **B~ofen** m
oven. **B~pfeife** f 🆃 slap in the face.
B~pflaume f prune. **B~pulver** nt
baking-powder. **B~stein** m brick
Bad nt -[e]s,-̈er bath; (Zimmer) bathroom; (Schwimm-) pool; (Ort) spa
Bade|anstalt f swimming baths pl.
B~anzug m swim-suit. **B~hose** f
swimming trunks pl. **B~kappe** f
bathing-cap. **B~mantel** m bathrobe.
b~n vi (haben) have a bath; (im
Meer) bathe ● vt bath; (waschen)
bathe. **B~ort** m seaside resort.
B~wanne f bath. **B~zimmer** nt
bathroom
Bagger m -s,- excavator; (Nass-)
dredger. **B~see** m flooded gravel-pit
Bahn f -,-en path; (Astronomy) orbit;
(Sport) track; (einzelne) lane; (Rodel-)
run; (Stoff-) width; (Eisen-) railway;
(Zug) train; (Straßen-) tram. **b~bre-
chend** adj (fig) pioneering. **B~hof**
m [railway] station. **B~steig** m

-[e]s,-e platform. **B~übergang** m
level crossing
Bahre f -,-n stretcher
Baiser /bɛˈzeː/ nt -s,-s meringue
Bake f -,-n (Naut, Aviat) beacon
Bakterien /-i̯ən/ fpl bacteria
Balance /baˈlãːsə/ f - balance.
b~ieren vt/i (haben/sein) balance
bald adv soon; (fast) almost
Baldachin /-xiːn/ m -s,-e canopy
bald|ig adj early; (Besserung) speedy.
b~möglichst adv as soon as pos-
sible
Balg nt & m -[e]s,-̈er 🆃 brat
Balkan m -s Balkans pl
Balken m -s,- beam
Balkon /balˈkõː/ m -s,-s balcony;
(Theat) circle
Ball¹ m -[e]s,-̈e ball
Ball² m -[e]s,-̈e (Tanz) ball
Ballade f -,-n ballad
Ballast m -[e]s ballast. **B~stoffe**
mpl roughage sg
Ballen m -s,- bale; (Anat) ball of the
hand/(Fuß-) foot; (Med) bunion
Ballerina f -,-nen ballerina
Ballett nt -s,-e ballet
Ballon /baˈlõː/ m -s,-s balloon
Balsam m -s balm
Balt|ikum nt -s Baltic States pl.
b~isch adj Baltic
Bambus m -ses,-se bamboo
banal adj banal
Banane f -,-n banana
Banause m -n,-n philistine
Band¹ nt -[e]s,-̈er ribbon; (Naht-,
Ton-, Ziel-) tape; **am laufenden B~**
🆃 non-stop
Band² m -[e]s,-̈e volume
Band³ nt -[e]s,-e (fig) bond
Band⁴ /bɛnt/ f -,-s [jazz] band
Bandage /banˈdaːʒə/ f -,-n ban-
dage. **b~ieren** vt bandage
Bande f -,-n gang
bändigen vt control, restrain; (zäh-
men) tame
Bandit m -en,-en bandit
Band|maß nt tape-measure.

B~scheibe f (*Anat*) disc. **B~wurm** m tapeworm

Bang|e f **B~e haben** be afraid; **jdm B~e machen** frighten s.o. **b~en** vi (*haben*) fear (**um** for)

Banjo nt -s,-s banjo

Bank[1] f -,⸚e bench

Bank[2] f -,-en (*Comm*) bank. **B~einzug** m direct debit

Bankett nt -s,-e banquet

Bankier /baŋ'kje:/ m -s,-s banker

Bankkonto nt bank account

Bankrott m -s,-s bankruptcy. **b~** adj bankrupt

Bankwesen nt banking

Bann m -[e]s,-e (*fig*) spell. **b~en** vt exorcize; (*abwenden*) avert; **[wie] gebannt** spellbound

Banner nt -s,- banner

bar adj (*rein*) sheer; (*Gold*) pure; **b~es Geld** cash; **[in] bar bezahlen** pay cash

Bar f -,-s bar

Bär m -en,-en bear

Baracke f -,-n (*Mil*) hut

Barb|ar m -en,-en barbarian. **b~arisch** adj barbaric

bar|fuß adv barefoot. **B~geld** nt cash

barmherzig adj merciful

barock adj baroque. **B~** nt & m -[s] baroque

Barometer nt -s,- barometer

Baron m -s,-e baron. **B~in** f -,-nen baroness

Barren m -s,- (*Gold-*) bar, ingot; (*Sport*) parallel bars pl. **B~gold** nt gold bullion

Barriere f -,-n barrier

Barrikade f -,-n barricade

barsch adj gruff

Barsch m -[e]s,-e (*Zool*) perch

Bart m -[e]s,⸚e beard; (*der Katze*) whiskers pl

bärtig adj bearded

Barzahlung f cash payment

Basar m -s,-e bazaar

Base[1] f -,-n [female] cousin

Base[2] f -,-n (*Chemistry*) alkali, base

Basel nt -s Basle

basieren vi (*haben*) be based (**auf +** dat on)

Basilikum nt -s basil

Basis f -,Basen base; (*fig*) basis

basisch adj (*Chemistry*) alkaline

Bask|enmütze f beret. **b~isch** adj Basque

Bass m -es,⸚e bass

Bassin /ba'sɛ̃:/ nt -s,-s pond; (*Brunnen-*) basin; (*Schwimm-*) pool

Bassist m -en,-en bass player; (*Sänger*) bass

Bast m -[e]s raffia

basteln vt make ● vi (*haben*) do handicrafts

Batterie f -,-n battery

Bau[1] m -[e]s,-e burrow; (*Fuchs-*) earth

Bau[2] m -[e]s,-ten construction; (*Gebäude*) building; (*Auf-*) structure; (*Körper-*) build; (*B~stelle*) building site. **B~arbeiten** fpl building work sg; (*Straßen-*) roadworks

Bauch m -[e]s, Bäuche abdomen, belly; (*Magen*) stomach; (*Bauchung*) bulge. **b~ig** adj bulbous. **B~nabel** m navel. **B~redner** m ventriloquist. **B~schmerzen** mpl stomach-ache sg. **B~speicheldrüse** f pancreas

bauen vt build; (*konstruieren*) construct ● vi (*haben*) build (**an etw** dat sth); **b~ auf** (+ acc) (*fig*) rely on

Bauer[1] m -n,-n farmer; (*Schach*) pawn

Bauer[2] nt -s,- [bird]cage

bäuerlich adj rustic

Bauern|haus nt farmhouse. **B~hof** m farm

bau|fällig adj dilapidated. **B~genehmigung** f planning permission. **B~gerüst** nt scaffolding. **B~jahr** nt year of construction. **B~kunst** f architecture. **b~lich** adj structural

Baum m -[e]s, Bäume tree

baumeln vi (*haben*) dangle

bäumen (sich) vr rear [up]

Baum|schule f [tree] nursery. **B~wolle** f cotton

Bausch *m* -[e]s, Bäusche wad; **in B~ und Bogen** (*fig*) wholesale. **b~en** *vt* puff out

Bau|sparkasse *f* building society. **B~stein** *m* building brick. **B~stelle** *f* building site; (*Straßen-*) roadworks *pl*. **B~unternehmer** *m* building contractor

Bayer|(in) *m* -n,-n (*f* -,-nen) Bavarian. **B~n** *nt* -s Bavaria

bay[e]risch *adj* Bavarian

Bayreuth The Bavarian city of Bayreuth is a magnet for opera fans. The German composer Richard Wagner (1813 83) lived there, and since 1876 the Richard Wagner Festival has been staged annually. The Bayreuth festival theatre was built by Ludwig II, King of Bavaria, who was Wagner's greatest admirer.

Bazillus *m* -,-len bacillus

beabsichtig|en *vt* intend. **b~t** *adj* intended; intentional

beacht|en *vt* take notice of; (*einhalten*) observe; (*folgen*) follow; **nicht b~en** ignore. **b~lich** *adj* considerable. **B~ung** *f* - observance; **etw** (*dat*) **keine B~ung schenken** take no notice of sth

Beamte(r) *m*, **Beamtin** *f* -,-nen official; (*Staats-*) civil servant; (*Schalter-*) clerk

beanspruchen *vt* claim; (*erfordern*) demand

beanstand|en *vt* find fault with; (*Comm*) make a complaint about. **B~ung** *f* -,-en complaint

beantragen *vt* apply for

beantworten *vt* answer

bearbeiten *vt* work; (*weiter-*) process; (*behandeln*) treat (**mit** with); (*Admin*) deal with; (*redigieren*) edit; (*Theat*) adapt; (*Mus*) arrange

Beatmungsgerät *nt* ventilator

beaufsichtig|en *vt* supervise. **B~ung** *f* - supervision

beauftragen *vt* instruct; commission (*Künstler*)

bebauen *vt* build on; (*bestellen*) cultivate

beben *vi* (*haben*) tremble

Becher *m* -s,- beaker; (*Henkel-*) mug; (*Joghurt-, Sahne-*) carton

Becken *nt* -s,- basin; pool; (*Mus*) cymbals *pl*; (*Anat*) pelvis

bedacht *adj* careful; **darauf b~** anxious (**zu** to)

bedächtig *adj* careful; slow

bedanken (sich) *vr* thank (**bei jdm** s.o.)

Bedarf *m* -s need/(*Comm*) demand (**an** + *dat* for); **bei B~** if required. **B~shaltestelle** *f* request stop

bedauer|lich *adj* regrettable. **b~licherweise** *adv* unfortunately. **b~n** *vt* regret; (*bemitleiden*) feel sorry for; **bedaure!** sorry! **b~nswert** *adj* pitiful; (*bedauerlich*) regrettable

bedeckt *adj* covered; (*Himmel*) overcast

bedenken† *vt* consider; (*überlegen*) think over. **B~** *pl* misgivings; **ohne B~** without hesitation

bedenklich *adj* doubtful; (*verdächtig*) dubious; (*ernst*) serious

bedeut|en *vi* (*haben*) mean. **b~end** *adj* important; (*beträchtlich*) considerable. **B~ung** *f* -,-en meaning; (*Wichtigkeit*) importance. **b~ungslos** *adj* meaningless; (*unwichtig*) unimportant. **b~ungsvoll** *adj* significant; (*vielsagend*) meaningful

bedien|en *vt* serve; (*betätigen*) operate; **sich [selbst] b~en** help oneself. **B~ung** *f* -,-en service; (*Betätigung*) operation; (*Kellner*) waiter; (*Kellnerin*) *f* waitress. **B~ungsgeld** *nt* service charge

Bedingung *f* -,-en condition; **B~en** conditions; (*Comm*) terms. **b~slos** *adj* unconditional

bedroh|en *vt* threaten. **b~lich** *adj* threatening. **B~ung** *f* threat

bedrücken *vt* depress

bedruckt *adj* printed

bedürf|en† *vi* (*haben*) (+ *gen*) need. **B~nis** *nt* -ses,-se need

Beefsteak /'bi:fste:k/ *nt* -s,-s steak;

deutsches B~ hamburger

beeilen (sich) *vr* hurry; hasten (**zu** to)

beeindrucken *vt* impress

beeinflussen *vt* influence

beeinträchtigen *vt* mar; (*schädigen*) impair

beengen *vt* restrict

beerdig|en *vt* bury. **B~ung** *f* -,-en funeral

Beere *f* -,-n berry

Beet *nt* -[e]s,-e (*Horticulture*) bed

Beete *f* -,-n Rote B~ beetroot

befähig|en *vt* enable; (*qualifizieren*) qualify. **B~ung** *f* - qualification; (*Fähigkeit*) ability

befahrbar *adj* passable

befallen† *vt* attack; (*Angst:*) seize

befangen *adj* shy; (*gehemmt*) self-conscious; (*Jur*) biased. **B~heit** *f* - shyness; self-consciousness; bias

befassen (sich) *vr* concern oneself/(*behandeln*) deal (**mit** with)

Befehl *m* -[e]s,-e order; (*Leitung*) command (**über** + *acc* of). **b~en** † *vt* **jdm etw b~en** order s.o. to do sth ● *vi* (*haben*) give the orders. **B~sform** *f* (*Gram*) imperative. **B~shaber** *m* -s,- commander

befestigen *vt* fasten (**an** + *dat* to); (*Mil*) fortify

befeuchten *vt* moisten

befinden† (sich) *vr* be. **B~** *nt* -s [state of] health

beflecken *vt* stain

befolgen *vt* follow

beförder|n *vt* transport; (*im Rang*) promote. **B~ung** *f* -,-en transport; promotion

befragen *vt* question

befrei|en *vt* free; (*räumen*) clear (**von** of); (*freistellen*) exempt (**von** from); **sich b~en** free oneself. **B~er** *m* -s,- liberator. **B~ung** *f* - liberation; exemption

befreunden (sich) *vr* make friends; **befreundet sein** be friends

befriedig|en *vt* satisfy. **b~end** *adj*

satisfying; (*zufrieden stellend*) satisfactory. **B~ung** *f* - satisfaction

befrucht|en *vt* fertilize. **B~ung** *f* - fertilization; **künstliche B~ung** artificial insemination

Befugnis *f* -,-se authority

Befund *m* result

befürcht|en *vt* fear. **B~ung** *f* -,-en fear

befürworten *vt* support

begab|t *adj* gifted. **B~ung** *f* -,-en gift, talent

begeben† (sich) *vr* go; **sich in Gefahr b~** expose oneself to danger

begegn|en *vi* (*sein*) **jdm/etw b~en** meet someone/something. **B~ung** *f* -,-en meeting

begehr|en *vt* desire. **b~t** *adj* sought-after

begeister|n *vt* **jdn b~n** arouse someone's enthusiasm. **b~t** *adj* enthusiastic; (*eifrig*) keen. **B~ung** *f* - enthusiasm

Begierde *f* -,-n desire

Beginn *m* -s beginning. **b~en**† *vt/i* (*haben*) start, begin

beglaubigen *vt* authenticate

begleichen† *vt* settle

begleit|en *vt* accompany. **B~er** *m* -s,- companion; (*Mus*) accompanist. **B~ung** *f* -,-en company; (*Mus*) accompaniment

beglück|en *vt* make happy. **b~wünschen** *vt* congratulate (**zu** on)

begnadig|en *vt* (*Jur*) pardon. **B~ung** *f* -,-en (*Jur*) pardon

begraben† *vt* bury

Begräbnis *n* -ses,-se burial; (*Feier*) funeral

begreif|en† *vt* understand; **nicht zu b~en** incomprehensible. **b~lich** *adj* understandable

begrenz|en *vt* form the boundary of; (*beschränken*) restrict. **b~t** *adj* limited. **B~ung** *f* -,-en restriction; (*Grenze*) boundary

Begriff *m* -[e]s,-e concept; (*Aus-*

druck) term; (*Vorstellung*) idea

begründ|en *vt* give one's reason for. **b~et** *adj* justified. **B~ung** *f* -,-en reason

begrüß|en *vt* greet; (*billigen*) welcome. **b~enswert** *adj* welcome. **B~ung** *f* - greeting; welcome

begünstigen *vt* favour

begütert *adj* wealthy

behaart *adj* hairy

behäbig *adj* portly

behag|en *vi* (*haben*) please (**jdm** s.o.). **B~en** *nt* -s contentment; (*Genuss*) enjoyment. **b~lich** *adj* comfortable. **B~lichkeit** *f* - comfort

behalten† *vt* keep; (*sich merken*) remember

Behälter *m* -s,- container

behand|eln *vt* treat; (*sich befassen*) deal with. **B~lung** *f* treatment

beharr|en *vi* (*haben*) persist (**auf** + *dat* in). **b~lich** *adj* persistent

behaupt|en *vt* maintain; (*vorgeben*) claim; (*sagen*) say; (*bewahren*) retain; **sich b~en** hold one's own. **B~ung** *f* -,-en assertion; claim; (*Äußerung*) statement

beheben† *vt* remedy

behelf|en† (**sich**) *vr* make do (**mit** with). **b~smäßig** *adj* makeshift • *adv* provisionally

beherbergen *vt* put up

beherrsch|en *vt* rule over; (*dominieren*) dominate; (*meistern, zügeln*) control; (*können*) know. **b~t** *adj* self-controlled. **B~ung** *f* - control

beherzigen *vt* heed

behilflich *adj* **jdm b~ sein** help s.o.

behinder|n *vt* hinder; (*blockieren*) obstruct. **b~t** *adj* handicapped; (*schwer*) disabled. **B~te(r)** *m/f* handicapped/disabled person. **B~ung** *f* -,-en obstruction; (*Med*) handicap; disability

Behörde *f* -,-n [public] authority

behüte|n *vt* protect. **b~t** *adj* sheltered

behutsam *adj* careful; (*zart*) gentle

---

bei

● *preposition* (+ *dative*)

! Note that **bei** plus **dem** can become **beim**

••••➤ (*nahe*) near; (*dicht an, neben*) by; (*als Begleitung*) with. **wer steht da bei ihm?** who is standing there next to or with him? **etw bei sich haben** have sth with or on one. **bleiben Sie beim Gepäck/bei den Kindern** stay with the luggage/the children. **war heute ein Brief für mich bei der Post?** was there a letter for me in the post today?

••••➤ (*an*) by. **jdn bei der Hand nehmen** take s.o. by the hand

••••➤ (*in der Wohnung von*) at ... 's home or house/flat. **bei mir [zu Hause]** at my home or 🇬🇧 place. **bei seinen Eltern leben** live with one's parents. **wir sind bei Ulrike eingeladen** we have been invited to Ulrike's. **bei Schmidt** at the Schmidts'; (*Geschäft*) at Schmidts'; (*auf Briefen*) c/o Schmidt. **bei jdm/einer Firma arbeiten** work for s.o./a firm. **bei uns tut man das nicht** we don't do that where I come from.

••••➤ (*gegenwärtig*) at; (*verwickelt*) in. **bei einer Hochzeit/einem Empfang** at a wedding/reception. **bei einem Unfall** in an accident

••••➤ (*im Falle von*) in the case of, with; (*bei Wetter*) in. **wie bei den Römern** as with the Romans. **bei Nebel** in fog, if there is fog. **bei dieser Hitze** in this heat

••••➤ (*angesichts*) with; (*trotz*) in spite of. **bei deinen guten Augen** with your good eyesight. **bei all seinen Bemühungen** in spite of or despite all his efforts

••••➤ (*Zeitpunkt*) at, on. **bei diesen Worten errötete er** he blushed at this or on hearing this. **bei seiner Ankunft** on his arrival. **bei Tag/Nacht** by day/night.

b

b

····▶ (*Gleichzeitigkeit, mit Verbalsubstantiv*) **beim ... en** while *or* when ... ing. **beim Spaziergehen im Walde** while walking in the woods. **beim Überqueren der Straße** when crossing the road. **sie war beim Lesen** she was reading. **wir waren beim Frühstück** we were having breakfast

beibehalten† *vt sep* keep

beibringen† *vt sep* **jdm etw b∼** teach s.o. sth; (*mitteilen*) break sth to s.o.; (*zufügen*) inflict sth on s.o.

Beicht|e *f* -,-n confession. **b∼en** *vt/i* (*haben*) confess. **B∼stuhl** *m* confessional

beide *adj & pron* both; **b∼s** both; **dreißig b∼** (*Tennis*) thirty all. **b∼rseitig** *adj* mutual. **b∼rseits** *adv & prep* (+ *gen*) on both sides (of)

beieinander *adv* together

Beifahrer(in) *m(f)* [front-seat] passenger; (*Motorrad*) pillion passenger

Beifall *m* -[e]s applause; (*Billigung*) approval; **B∼ klatschen** applaud

beifügen *vt sep* add; (*beilegen*) enclose

beige /bɛːʒ/ *inv adj* beige

beigeben† *vt sep* add

Beihilfe *f* financial aid; (*Studien-*) grant; (*Jur*) aiding and abetting

Beil *nt* -[e]s,-e hatchet, axe

Beilage *f* supplement; (*Gemüse*) vegetable

beiläufig *adj* casual

beilegen *vt sep* enclose; (*schlichten*) settle

Beileid *nt* condolences *pl*. **B∼sbrief** *m* letter of condolence

beiliegend *adj* enclosed

beim *prep* = bei dem; **b∼ Militär** in the army; **b∼ Frühstück** at breakfast

beimessen† *vt sep* (*fig*) attach (*dat* to)

Bein *nt* -[e]s,-e leg; **jdm ein B∼ stellen** trip s.o. up

beinah[e] *adv* nearly, almost

Beiname *m* epithet

beipflichten *vi sep* (*haben*) agree (*dat* with)

Beirat *m* advisory committee

beisammen *adv* together; **b∼ sein** be together

Beisein *nt* presence

beiseite *adv* aside; (*abseits*) apart; **b∼ legen** put aside; (*sparen*) put by

beisetz|en *vt sep* bury. **B∼ung** *f* -,-en funeral

Beispiel *nt* example; **zum B∼** for example. **b∼sweise** *adv* for example

beißen† *vt/i* (*haben*) bite; (*brennen*) sting; **sich b∼** (*Farben:*) clash

Bei|stand *m* -[e]s help. **b∼stehen**† *vi sep* (*haben*) **jdm b∼stehen** help s.o.

beistimmen *vi sep* (*haben*) agree

Beistrich *m* comma

Beitrag *m* -[e]s,⸚e contribution; (*Mitglieds-*) subscription; (*Versicherungs-*) premium; (*Zeitungs-*) article. **b∼en**† *vt/i sep* (*haben*) contribute

bei|treten† *vi sep* (*sein*) (+ *dat*) join. **B∼tritt** *m* joining

Beize *f* -,-n (*Holz-*) stain

beizeiten *adv* in good time

beizen *vt* stain (*Holz*)

bejahen *vt* answer in the affirmative; (*billigen*) approve of

bejahrt *adj* aged, old

bekämpf|en *vt* fight. **B∼ung** *f* (*gen* against)

bekannt *adj* well-known; (*vertraut*) familiar; **jdn b∼ machen** introduce s.o.; **etw b∼ machen** *od* **geben** announce sth; **b∼ werden** become known. **B∼e(r)** *m/f* acquaintance; (*Freund*) friend. **B∼gabe** *f* announcement. **b∼lich** *adv* as is well known. **B∼machung** *f* -,-en announcement; (*Anschlag*) notice. **B∼schaft** *f* - acquaintance; (*Leute*) acquaintances *pl*; (*Freunde*) friends *pl*

bekehr|en *vt* convert. **B∼ung** *f* -,-en conversion

bekenn|en† *vt* confess, profess (*Glauben*); **sich [für] schuldig b∼en**

admit one's guilt. **B~tnis** nt -ses,-se confession; (Konfession) denomination

beklag|en vt lament; (bedauern) deplore; **sich b~en** complain. **b~enswert** adj unfortunate. **B~te(r)** m/f (Jur) defendant

bekleid|en vt hold (Amt). **B~ung** f clothing

Beklemmung f -,-en feeling of oppression

bekommen† vt get; have (Baby); catch (Erkältung) ● vi (sein) **jdm gut b~** do s.o. good; (Essen:) agree with s.o.

beköstig|en vt feed. **B~ung** f - board; (Essen) food

bekräftigen vt reaffirm

bekreuzigen (sich) vr cross oneself

bekümmert adj troubled; (besorgt) worried

bekunden vt show

Belag m -[e]s, ̈e coating; (Fußboden-) covering; (Brot-) topping; (Zahn-) tartar; (Brems-) lining

belager|n vt besiege. **B~ung** f -,-en siege

Belang m **von B~** of importance; **B~e** pl interests. **b~los** adj irrelevant; (unwichtig) trivial

belassen† vt leave; **es dabei b~** leave it at that

belasten vt load; (fig) burden; (beanspruchen) put a strain on; (Comm) debit; (Jur) incriminate

belästigen vt bother; (bedrängen) pester; (unsittlich) molest

Belastung f -,-en load; (fig) strain; (Comm) debit. **B~smaterial** nt incriminating evidence. **B~szeuge** m prosecution witness

belaufen† (sich) vr amount (auf + acc to)

belauschen vt eavesdrop on

beleb|en vt (fig) revive; (lebhaft machen) enliven. **b~t** adj lively; (Straße) busy

Beleg m -[e]s,-e evidence; (Beispiel) instance (für of); (Quittung) receipt.

b~en vt cover/(garnieren) garnish (mit with); (besetzen) reserve; (Univ) enrol for; (nachweisen) provide evidence for; **den ersten Platz b~en** (Sport) take first place. **B~schaft** f -,-en workforce. **b~t** adj occupied; (Zunge) coated; (Stimme) husky; **b~te Brote** open sandwiches

belehren vt instruct

beleidig|en vt offend; (absichtlich) insult. **B~ung** f -,-en insult

belesen adj well-read

beleucht|en vt light; (anleuchten) illuminate. **B~ung** f -,-en illumination

Belg|ien /-ˈɡi̯ən/ nt -s Belgium. **B~ier(in)** m -s,- (f -,-nen) Belgian. **b~isch** adj Belgian

belicht|en vt (Phot) expose. **B~ung** f - exposure

Belieb|en nt -s **nach B~en** [just] as one likes. **b~ig** adj **eine b~ige Zahl** any number you like ● adv **b~ig oft** as often as one likes. **b~t** adj popular

bellen vi (haben) bark

belohn|en vt reward. **B~ung** f -,-en reward

belustig|en vt amuse. **B~ung** f -,-en amusement

bemalen vt paint

bemängeln vt criticize

bemannt adj manned

bemerk|bar adj **sich b~bar machen** attract attention. **b~en** vt notice; (äußern) remark. **b~enswert** adj remarkable. **B~ung** f -,-en remark

bemitleiden vt pity

bemüh|en vt trouble; **sich b~en** try (zu to; **um etw** to get sth); (sich kümmern) attend (um to); **b~t sein** endeavour (zu to). **B~ung** f -,-en effort

benachbart adj neighbouring

benachrichtig|en vt inform; (amtlich) notify. **B~ung** f -,-en notification

benachteiligen vt discriminate against; (ungerecht sein) treat unfairly

b

benehmen† **(sich)** vr behave. **B~
nt** -s behaviour

beneiden vt envy (**um etw** sth)

Bengel m -s,- boy; (Rüpel) lout

benötigen vt need

benutz|en, (SGer) **benütz|en** vt use;
take (Bahn) **B~ung** f use

Benzin nt -s petrol

beobacht|en vt observe. **B~er** m
-s,- observer. **B~ung** f -,-en obser-
vation

bequem adj comfortable; (mühelos)
easy; (faul) lazy. **b~en (sich)** vr
deign (**zu** to). **B~lichkeit** f -,-en
comfort; (Faulheit) laziness

berat|en† vt advise; (überlegen) dis-
cuss; **sich b~en** confer ● vi (haben)
discuss (**über etw** acc sth); (berat-
schlagen) confer. **B~er(in)** m -s,-, (f
-,-nen) adviser. **B~ung** f -,-en guidance; (Rat) advice; (Besprechung) discussion; (Med, Jur) consultation

berechn|en vt calculate; (anrech-
nen) charge for; (abfordern) charge.
B~ung f calculation

berechtig|en vt entitle; (befugen)
authorize; (fig) justify. **b~t** adj justified, justifiable. **B~ung** f -,-en authorization; (Recht) right; (Recht-
mäßigkeit) justification

bered|en vt talk about; **sich b~en**
talk. **B~samkeit** f - eloquence

beredt adj eloquent

Bereich m -[e]s,-e area; (fig) realm;
(Fach-) field

bereichern vi enrich

bereit adj ready. **b~en** vt prepare;
(verursachen) cause; give (Überra-
schung). **b~halten**† vt sep
have/(ständig) keep ready. **b~legen**
vt sep put out [ready]. **b~machen**
vt sep get ready. **b~s** adv already

Bereitschaft f -,-en readiness; (Einheit) squad. **B~sdienst** m
B~sdienst haben (Mil) be on stand-
by; (Arzt:) be on call. **B~spolizei** f
riot police

bereit|stehen† vi sep (haben) be
ready. **b~stellen** vt sep put out
ready; (verfügbar machen) make avail-

able. **B~ung** f - preparation.
b~willig adj willing

bereuen vt regret

Berg m -[e]s,-e mountain; (Anhöhe)
hill; **in den B~en** in the mountains.
b~ab adv downhill. **B~arbeiter** m
miner. **b~auf** adv uphill. **B~bau** m
-[e]s mining

bergen† vt recover; (Naut) salvage;
(retten) rescue

Berg|führer m mountain guide.
b~ig adj mountainous. **B~kette** f
mountain range. **B~mann** m (pl
-leute) miner. **B~steiger(in)** m -s,-
(f -,-nen) mountaineer, climber

Bergung f - recovery; (Naut) salvage; (Rettung) rescue

Berg|wacht f mountain rescue ser-
vice. **B~werk** nt mine

Bericht m -[e]s,-e report; (Reise-) account. **b~en** vt/i (haben) report; (erzählen) tell (**von** of). **B~erstat-
ter(in)** m -s,- (f -,-nen) reporter

berichtigen vt correct

beriesel|n vt irrigate. **B~ungsan-
lage** f sprinkler system

Berlin nt -s Berlin. **B~er** m -s,- Berliner

Bernhardiner m -s,- St Bernard

Bernstein m amber

berüchtigt adj notorious

berücksichtig|en vt take into
consideration. **B~ung** f - consideration

Beruf m profession; (Tätigkeit) occupation; (Handwerk) trade. **b~en**† vt
appoint; **sich b~en** refer (**auf** + acc
to); (vorgeben) plead (**auf etw** acc
sth); ● adj competent; **b~en sein**
be destined (**zu** to). **b~lich** adj professional; (Ausbildung) vocational
● adv professionally; **b~lich tätig
sein** work, have a job. **B~sberatung**
f vocational guidance. **B~sausbil-
dung** f professional training.
b~smäßig adv professionally.
B~sschule f vocational school.
B~ssoldat m regular soldier.
b~stätig adj working; **b~stätig
sein** work, have a job. **B~stätige(r)**
m/f working man/woman. **B~ung** f

-,-**en** appointment; (*Bestimmung*) vocation; (*Jur*) appeal; **B~ung einlegen** appeal. **B~ungsgericht** *nt* appeal court

beruhen *vi* (*haben*) be based (**auf** + *dat* on)

beruhig|en *vt* calm [down]; (*zuversichtlich machen*) reassure. **b~end** *adj* calming; (*tröstend*) reassuring; (*Med*) sedative. **B~ung** *f* - calming; reassurance; (*Med*) sedation. **B~ungsmittel** *nt* sedative; (*bei Psychosen*) tranquillizer

berühmt *adj* famous. **B~heit** *f* -,-**en** fame; (*Person*) celebrity

berühr|en *vt* touch; (*erwähnen*) touch on. **B~ung** *f* -,-**en** touch; (*Kontakt*) contact

besänftigen *vt* soothe

Besatz *m* -**es**,ˈ**e** trimming

Besatzung *f* -,-**en** crew; (*Mil*) occupying force

beschädig|en *vt* damage. **B~ung** *f* -,-**en** damage

beschaffen *vt* obtain, get ● *adj* so **b~ sein, dass** be such that. **B~heit** *f* - consistency

beschäftig|en *vt* occupy; (*Arbeitgeber:*) employ; **sich b~en** occupy oneself. **b~t** *adj* busy; (*angestellt*) employed (**bei** at). **B~ung** *f* -,-**en** occupation; (*Anstellung*) employment

beschämt *adj* ashamed; (*verlegen*) embarrassed

beschatten *vt* shade; (*überwachen*) shadow

Bescheid *m* -[e]s information; **jdm B~ sagen** *od* **geben** let s.o. know; **B~ wissen** know

bescheiden *adj* modest. **B~heit** *f* - modesty

bescheinen† *vt* shine on; **von der Sonne beschienen** sunlit

bescheinig|en *vt* certify. **B~ung** *f* -,-**en** [written] confirmation; (*Schein*) certificate

beschenken *vt* give a present/presents to

Bescherung *f* -,-**en** distribution of Christmas presents

beschildern *vt* signpost

beschimpf|en *vt* abuse, swear at. **B~ung** *f* -,-**en** abuse

beschirmen *vt* protect

Beschlag *m* **in B~ nehmen** monopolize. **b~en**† *vt* shoe ● *vi* (*sein*) steam *or* mist up ● *adj* steamed *or* misted up. **B~nahme** *f* -,-**n** confiscation; (*Jur*) seizure. **b~nahmen** *vt* confiscate; (*Jur*) seize

beschleunig|en *vt* hasten; (*schneller machen*) speed up (*Schritt*) ● *vi* (*haben*) accelerate. **B~ung** *f* - acceleration

beschließen† *vt* decide; (*beenden*) end ● *vi* (*haben*) decide (**über** + *acc* about)

Beschluss *m* decision

beschmutzen *vt* make dirty

beschneid|en† *vt* trim; (*Horticulture*) prune; (*Relig*) circumcise. **B~ung** *f* - circumcision

beschnüffeln *vt* sniff at

beschönigen *vt* (*fig*) gloss over

beschränken *vt* limit, restrict; **sich b~ auf** (+ *acc*) confine oneself to

beschrankt *adj* (*Bahnübergang*) with barrier[s]

beschränk|t *adj* limited; (*geistig*) dull-witted. **B~ung** *f* -,-**en** limitation, restriction

beschreib|en† *vt* describe. **B~ung** *f* -,-**en** description

beschuldig|en *vt* accuse. **B~ung** *f* -,-**en** accusation

beschummeln *vt* 🄸 cheat

Beschuss *m* (*Mil*) fire; (*Artillerie-*) shelling

beschütz|en *vt* protect. **B~er** *m* -**s**,- protector

Beschwer|de *f* -,-**n** complaint; **B~den** (*Med*) trouble *sg*. **b~en** *vt* weight down; **sich b~en** complain. **b~lich** *adj* difficult

beschwindeln *vt* cheat (**um** out of); (*belügen*) lie to

beschwipst *adj* 🄸 tipsy

beseitig|en *vt* remove. **B~ung** *f* - removal

Besen *m* -**s**,- broom

Besenwirtschaft An inn set up by a local wine-grower for a few weeks after the new wine has been made. An inflated pig's bladder is hung up outside the door to show that the new vintage may be sampled there. This is mainly found in Southern Germany. ▷HEURIGE.

besessen adj obsessed (von by)

besetz|en vt occupy; fill (Posten); (Theat) cast (Rolle); (verzieren) trim (mit with). **b~t** adj occupied; (Toilette, Leitung) engaged; (Zug, Bus) full up; **der Platz ist b~t** this seat is taken. **B~tzeichen** nt engaged tone. **B~ung** f -,-en occupation; (Theat) cast

besichtig|en vt look round (Stadt); (prüfen) inspect; (besuchen) visit. **B~ung** f -,-en visit; (Prüfung) inspection; (Stadt-) sightseeing

besiedelt adj **dünn/dicht b~** sparsely/densely populated

besiegen vt defeat

besinn|en† (sich) vr think, reflect; (sich erinnern) remember (auf jdn/ etw someone/something). **B~ung** f - reflection; (Bewusstsein) consciousness; **bei/ohne B~ung** conscious/ unconscious. **b~ungslos** adj unconscious

Besitz m possession; (Eigentum, Land-) property; (Gut) estate. **b~en†** vt own, possess; (haben) have. **B~er(in)** m -s,- (f -,-nen) owner; (Comm) proprietor

besoffen adj 🗵 drunken; **b~ sein** be drunk

besonder|e(r,s) adj special; (bestimmt) particular; (gesondert) separate. **b~s** adv [e]specially, particularly; (gesondert) separately

besonnen adj calm

besorg|en vt get; (kaufen) buy; (erledigen) attend to; (versorgen) look after. **b~t** adj worried/(bedacht) concerned (um about). **B~ung** f -,-en errand; **B~ungen machen** do shopping

bespitzeln vt spy on

besprech|en† vt discuss; (rezensieren) review. **B~ung** f -,-en discussion; review; (Konferenz) meeting

besser adj & adv better. **b~n** vt improve; **sich b~n** get better. **B~ung** f - improvement; **gute B~ung!** get well soon!

Bestand m -[e]s,⸚e existence; (Vorrat) stock (**an** + dat of)

beständig adj constant; (Wetter) settled; **b~ gegen** resistant to

Bestand|saufnahme f stocktaking. **B~teil** m part

bestätig|en vt confirm; acknowledge (Empfang); **sich b~en** prove to be true. **B~ung** f -,-en confirmation

bestatt|en vt bury. **B~ung** f -,-en funeral

Bestäubung f - pollination

bestaunen vt gaze at in amazement; (bewundern) admire

best|e(r,s) adj best; **b~en Dank!** many thanks! **B~e(r,s)** m/f/nt best; **sein B~es tun** do one's best

bestech|en† vt bribe; (bezaubern) captivate. **b~end** adj captivating. **b~lich** adj corruptible. **B~ung** f - bribery. **B~ungsgeld** nt bribe

Besteck nt -[e]s,-e [set of] knife, fork and spoon; (coll) cutlery

bestehen† vi (haben) exist; (fortdauern) last; (bei Prüfung) pass; **~ aus** consist/(gemacht sein) be made of; **~ auf** (+ dat) insist on ● vt pass (Prüfung)

besteig|en† vt climb; (aufsteigen) mount; ascend (Thron). **B~ung** f ascent

bestell|en vt order; (vor-) book; (ernennen) appoint; (bebauen) cultivate; (ausrichten) tell; **zu sich b~en** send for; **b~t sein** have an appointment; **kann ich etwas b~en?** can I take a message? **B~schein** m order form. **B~ung** f order; (Botschaft) message; (Bebauung) cultivation

besteuer|n vt tax. **B~ung** f - taxation

Bestie /'bɛstiə/ f -,-n beast

bestimm|en vt fix; (entscheiden) de-

cide; (*vorsehen*) intend; (*ernennen*)
appoint; (*ermitteln*) determine; (*definieren*) define; (*Gram*) qualify ● *vi*
(*haben*) be in charge (**über** + *acc* of).
~t *adj* definite; (*gewiss*) certain;
(*fest*) firm. **B~ung** *f* fixing; (*Vorschrift*) regulation; (*Ermittlung*) determination; (*Definition*) definition;
(*Zweck*) purpose; (*Schicksal*) destiny.
B~ungsort *m* destination
Bestleistung *f* (*Sport*) record
bestraf|en *vt* punish. **B~ung** *f*
-,-en punishment
Bestrahlung *f* radiotherapy
Bestreb|en *nt* -s endeavour; (*Absicht*) aim. **B~ung** *f* -,-en effort
bestreiten† *vt* dispute; (*leugnen*)
deny; (*bezahlen*) pay for
bestürz|t *adj* dismayed; (*erschüttert*)
stunned. **B~ung** *f* - dismay, consternation
Bestzeit *f* (*Sport*) record [time]
Besuch *m* -[e]s,-e visit; (*kurz*) call;
(*Schul-*) attendance; (*Gast*) visitor;
(*Gäste*) visitors *pl*; **B~ haben** have a
visitor/visitors; **bei jdm zu** *od* **auf**
B~ sein be staying with s.o. **~en** *vt*
visit; (*kurz*) call on; (*teilnehmen*) attend; go to (*Schule, Ausstellung*).
B~er(in) *m* -s,- (*f* -,-nen) visitor;
caller. **B~szeit** *f* visiting hours *pl*
betagt *adj* aged, old
betätig|en *vt* operate; **sich b~en**
work (**als** as). **B~ung** *f* -,-en operation; (*Tätigkeit*) activity
betäub|en *vt* stun; (*Lärm:*) deafen;
(*Med*) anaesthetize; (*lindern*) ease;
deaden (*Schmerz*); **wie b~t** dazed.
B~ung *f* - daze; (*Med*) anaesthesia.
B~ungsmittel *nt* anaesthetic
Bete *f* -,-n Rote **B~** beetroot
beteilig|en *vt* give a share to; **sich
b~en** take part (**an** + *dat* in); (*beitragen*) contribute (**an** + *dat* to). **b~t**
adj **b~t sein** take part/(*an Unfall*) be
involved/(*Comm*) have a share (**an** +
dat in); **alle B~ten** all those involved. **B~ung** *f* -,-en participation;
involvement; (*Anteil*) share
beten *vi* (*haben*) pray
Beton /be'tɔŋ/ *m* -s concrete

betonen *vt* stressed, emphasize
beton|t *adj* stressed; (*fig*) pointed.
B~ung *f* -,-en stress
Betracht *m* in **B~ ziehen** consider;
außer B~ lassen disregard; **nicht in
B~ kommen** be out of the question. **b~en** *vt* look at; (*fig*) regard
(**als** as)
beträchtlich *adj* considerable
Betrachtung *f* -,-en contemplation; (*Überlegung*) reflection
Betrag *m* -[e]s,ʺe amount. **b~en**†
vt amount to; **sich b~en** behave.
B~en *nt* -s behaviour; (*Sch*) conduct
betreff|en† *vt* affect; (*angehen*) concern. **b~end** *adj* relevant. **b~s** *prep*
(+ *gen*) concerning
betreiben† *vt* (*leiten*) run; (*ausüben*)
carry on
betreten† *vt* step on; (*eintreten*)
enter; '**B~ verboten**' 'no entry'; (*bei
Rasen*) 'keep off [the grass]'
betreu|en *vt* look after. **B~er(in)** *m*
-s,- (*f* -,-nen) helper; (*Kranken-*)
nurse. **B~ung** *f* - care
Betrieb *m* business; (*Firma*) firm;
(*Treiben*) activity; (*Verkehr*) traffic;
außer B~ not in use; (*defekt*) out of
order
Betriebs|anleitung, B~anweisung *f* operating instructions *pl*.
B~ferien *pl* firm's holiday. **B~leitung** *f* management. **B~rat** *m*
works committee. **B~störung** *f*
breakdown
betrinken† (**sich**) *vr* get drunk
betroffen *adj* disconcerted; **b~
sein** be affected (**von** by)
betrüb|en *vt* sadden. **b~t** *adj* sad
Betrug *m* -[e]s deception; (*Jur*)
fraud
betrüg|en† *vt* cheat, swindle; (*Jur*)
defraud; (*in der Ehe*) be unfaithful to.
B~er(in) *m* -s,- (*f* -,-nen) swindler.
B~erei *f* -,-en fraud
betrunken *adj* drunken; **b~ sein**
be drunk. **B~e(r)** *m* drunk
Bett *nt* -[e]s,-en bed. **B~couch** *f*
sofa-bed. **B~decke** *f* blanket;
(*Tages-*) bedspread

Bettel|ei f - begging. **b~n** vi (haben) beg

Bettler(in) m -s,- (f -,-nen) beggar

Bettpfanne f bedpan

Betttuch (**Bettuch**) nt sheet

Bett|wäsche f bed linen. **B~zeug** nt bedding

betupfen vt dab (mit with)

beug|en vt bend; (Gram) decline; conjugate (Verb); **sich b~en** bend; (lehnen) lean; (sich fügen) submit (dat to). **B~ung** f -,-en (Gram) declension; conjugation

Beule f -,-n bump; (Delle) dent

beunruhig|en vt worry; **sich b~en** worry. **B~ung** f - worry

beurlauben vt give leave to

beurteil|en vt judge. **B~ung** f -,-en judgement; (Ansicht) opinion

Beute f - booty, haul; (Jagd-) bag; (eines Raubtiers) prey

Beutel m -s,- bag; (Tabak- & Zool) pouch. **B~tier** nt marsupial

Bevölkerung f -,-en population

bevollmächtigen vt authorize

bevor conj before; **b~ nicht** until

bevormunden vt treat like a child

bevorstehen† vi sep (haben) approach; (unmittelbar) be imminent. **b~d** adj approaching, forthcoming; **unmittelbar b~d** imminent

bevorzug|en vt prefer; (begünstigen) favour. **b~t** adj privileged; (Behandlung) preferential

bewachen vt guard

Bewachung f - guard; **unter B~** under guard

bewaffn|en vt arm. **b~et** adj armed. **B~ung** f - armament; (Waffen) arms pl

bewahren vt protect (vor + dat from); (behalten) keep; **die Ruhe b~** keep calm

bewähren (sich) vr prove one's/(Ding:) its worth; (erfolgreich sein) prove a success

bewähr|t adj reliable; (erprobt) proven. **B~ung** f - (Jur) probation. **B~ungsfrist** f [period of] probation.

B~ungsprobe f (fig) test

bewältigen vt cope with; (überwinden) overcome

bewässer|n vt irrigate. **B~ung** f - irrigation

bewegen[1] vt (reg) move; **sich b~** move; (körperlich) take exercise

bewegen[2]† vt **jdn dazu b~, etw zu tun** induce s.o. to do sth

Beweg|grund m motive. **b~lich** adj movable, mobile; (wendig) agile. **B~lichkeit** f - mobility; agility. **B~ung** f -,-en movement; (Phys) motion; (Rührung) emotion; (Gruppe) movement; **körperliche B~ung** physical exercise. **b~ungslos** adj motionless

Beweis m -es,-e proof; (Zeichen) token; **B~e** evidence sg. **b~en**† vt prove; (zeigen) show; **sich b~en** prove oneself/(Ding:) itself. **B~material** nt evidence

bewerb|en† (**sich**) vr apply (um for; **bei** to). **B~er(in)** m -s,- (f -,-nen) applicant. **B~ung** f -,-en application

bewerten vt value; (einschätzen) rate; (Sch) mark, grade

bewilligen vt grant

bewirken vt cause; (herbeiführen) bring about

bewirt|en vt entertain. **B~ung** f - hospitality

bewohn|bar adj habitable. **b~en** vt inhabit, live in. **B~er(in)** m -s,- (f -,-nen) resident, occupant; (Einwohner) inhabitant

bewölk|en (sich) vr cloud over; **b~t** cloudy. **B~ung** f - clouds pl

bewunder|n vt admire. **b~nswert** adj admirable. **B~ung** f - admiration

bewusst adj conscious (gen of); (absichtlich) deliberate. **b~los** adj unconscious. **B~losigkeit** f - unconsciousness; **B~sein** nt -s consciousness; (Gewissheit) awareness; **bei B~sein** conscious

bezahl|en vt/i (haben) pay; pay for (Ware, Essen). **B~ung** f - payment;

(*Lohn*) pay. **B~fernsehen** *nt* pay television; pay TV

bezaubern *vt* enchant

bezeichn|en *vt* mark; (*bedeuten*) denote; (*beschreiben, nennen*) describe (**als** as). **b~end** *adj* typical. **B~ung** *f* marking; (*Beschreibung*) description (**als** as); (*Ausdruck*) term; (*Name*) name

bezeugen *vt* testify to

bezichtigen *vt* accuse (*gen* of)

bezieh|en† *vt* cover; (*einziehen*) move into; (*beschaffen*) obtain; (*erhalten*) get; (*in Verbindung bringen*) relate (**auf** + *acc* to); **sich b~en** (*bewölken*) cloud over; **sich b~en auf** (+ *acc*) refer to; **das Bett frisch b~en** put clean sheets on the bed. **B~ung** *f* -,-en relation; (*Verhältnis*) relationship; (*Bezug*) respect; **B~ungen haben** have connections. **b~ungsweise** *adv* respectively; (*vielmehr*) or rather

Bezirk *m* -[e]s,-e district

Bezug *m* cover; (*Kissen-*) case; (*Beschaffung*) obtaining; (*Kauf*) purchase; (*Zusammenhang*) reference; **B~̈e** *pl* earnings; **B~ nehmen** refer (**auf** + *acc* to); **in B~ auf** (+ *acc*) regarding

bezüglich *prep* (+ *gen*) regarding ● *adj* relating (**auf** + *acc* to)

bezwecken *vt* (*fig*) aim at

bezweifeln *vt* doubt

BH /beː'haː/ *m* -[s],-[s] bra

Bibel *f* -,-n Bible

Biber *m* -s,- beaver

Biblio|thek *f* -,-en library. **B~thekar(in)** *m* -s,- (*f* -,-nen) librarian

biblisch *adj* biblical

bieg|en† *vt* bend; **sich b~en** bend ● *vi* (*sein*) curve (**nach** to); **um die Ecke b~en** turn the corner. **b~sam** *adj* flexible, supple. **B~ung** *f* -,-en bend

Biene *f* -,-n bee. **B~nstock** *m* beehive. **B~nwabe** *f* honey-comb

Bier *nt* -s,-e beer. **B~deckel** *m* beermat. **B~krug** *m* beer-mug

Bier Germany and Austria rank among the world's top beer consumers. Germans brew more than 5000 varieties, and each beer tastes different. German beer is brewed according to the *Reinheitsgebot* (brewing regulations) of 1516, which stipulate that no ingredients other than hops, malted barley, yeast and water may be used. The standard pale ale or lager is a *Helles*, a dark beer is a *Dunkles*, and a wheat beer is a *Weißbier* (south), *Weizenbier* (northwest) and *Weiße* (Berlin). A *Biergarten* is a rustic open-air pub, or beer garden, which is traditional in Bavaria and Austria. *i*

bieten† *vt* offer; (*bei Auktion*) bid

Bifokalbrille *f* bifocals *pl*

Bigamie *f* - bigamy

bigott *adj* over-pious

Bikini *m* -s,-s bikini

Bilanz *f* -,-en balance sheet; (*fig*) result; **die B~ ziehen** (*fig*) draw conclusions (**aus** from)

Bild *nt* -[e]s,-er picture; (*Theat*) scene

bilden *vt* form; (*sein*) be; (*erziehen*) educate

Bild|erbuch *nt* picture-book. **B~fläche** *f* screen. **B~hauer** *m* -s,- sculptor. **b~lich** *adj* pictorial; (*figurativ*) figurative. **B~nis** *nt* -ses,-se portrait. **B~punkt** *m* pixel. **B~schirm** *m* (*TV*) screen. **B~schirmgerät** *nt* visual display unit, VDU. **b~schön** *adj* very beautiful

Bildung *f* - formation; (*Erziehung*) education; (*Kultur*) culture

Billard /'bɪljart/ *nt* -s billiards *sg*. **B~tisch** *m* billiard table

Billett /bɪl'jɛt/ *nt* -[e]s,-e & -s ticket

Billiarde *f* -,-n thousand million million

billig *adj* cheap; (*dürftig*) poor; **recht und b~** right and proper. **b~en** *vt* approve. **B~flieger** *m* low-cost airline. **B~ung** *f* - approval

Billion /bɪljoːn/ *f* -,-en million million, billion

b

b

Bimsstein *m* pumice stone

Binde *f* -,-n band; (*Verband*) bandage; (*Damen-*) sanitary towel. **B~hautentzündung** *f* conjunctivitis. **b~n†** *vt* tie (**an** + *acc* to); make (*Strauß*); bind (*Buch*); (*fesseln*) tie up; (*Culin*) thicken; **sich b~n** commit oneself. **B~strich** *m* hyphen. **B~wort** *nt* (*pl* -wörter) (*Gram*) conjunction

Bind|faden *m* string. **B~ung** *f* -,-en (*fig*) tie; (*Beziehung*) relationship; (*Verpflichtung*) commitment; (*Ski-*) binding; (*Textiles*) weave

binnen *prep* (+ *dat*) within. **B~handel** *m* home trade

Bio- *prefix* organic

Bio|chemie *f* biochemistry. **b~dynamisch** *m* organic. **B~graphie, B~grafie** *f* -,-n biography

Bio|hof *m* organic farm. **B~laden** *m* health-food store

Biolog|e *m* -n,-n biologist. **B~ie** *f* - biology. **b~isch** *adj* biological; **b~ischer Anbau** organic farming; **b~isch angebaut** organically grown

Bioterrorismus *m* bioterrorism

Birke *f* -,-n birch [tree]

Birm|a *nt* -s Burma. **b~anisch** *adj* Burmese

Birn|baum *m* pear-tree. **B~e** *f* -,-n pear; (*Electr*) bulb

bis *prep* (+ *acc*) as far as, [up] to; (*zeitlich*) until, till; (*spätestens*) by; **bis zu** up to; **bis auf** (+ *acc*) (*einschließlich*) [down] to; (*ausgenommen*) except [for]; **drei bis vier Minuten** three to four minutes; **bis morgen!** see you tomorrow! ● *conj* until

Bischof *m* -s,⸚e bishop

bisher *adv* so far, up to now

Biskuit|rolle /bɪs'kviːt-/ *f* Swiss roll. **B~teig** *m* sponge mixture

Biss *m* -es,-e bite

bisschen *inv pron* **ein b~** a bit, a little; **kein b~** not a bit

Biss|en *m* -s,- bite, mouthful. **b~ig** *adj* vicious; (*fig*) caustic

bisweilen *adv* from time to time

bitt|e *adv* please; (*nach Klopfen*) come in; (*als Antwort auf 'danke'*) don't mention it, you're welcome; **wie b~e?** pardon? **B~e** *f* -,-n request/(*dringend*) plea (**um** for). **b~en†** *vt/i* (*haben*) ask/(*dringend*) beg (**um** for); (*einladen*) invite, ask. **b~end** *adj* pleading

bitter *adj* bitter. **B~keit** *f* - bitterness. **b~lich** *adv* bitterly

Bittschrift *f* petition

bizarr *adj* bizarre

bläh|en *vt* swell; (*Vorhang, Segel:*) billow ● *vi* (*haben*) cause flatulence. **B~ungen** *fpl* flatulence *sg*, Ⓘ wind *sg*

Blamage /bla'maːʒə/ *f* -,-n humiliation; (*Schande*) disgrace

blamieren *vt* disgrace; **sich b~** disgrace oneself; (*sich lächerlich machen*) make a fool of oneself

blanchieren /blã'ʃiːrən/ *vt* (*Culin*) blanch

blank *adj* shiny. **B~oscheck** *m* blank cheque

Blase *f* -,-n bubble; (*Med*) blister; (*Anat*) bladder. **b~n†** *vt/i* (*haben*) blow; play (*Flöte*). **B~nentzündung** *f* cystitis

Blas|instrument *nt* wind instrument. **B~kapelle** *f* brass band

blass *adj* pale; (*schwach*) faint

Blässe *f* - pallor

Blatt *nt* -[e]s,⸚er (*Bot*) leaf; (*Papier*) sheet; (*Zeitung*) paper

Blattlaus *f* greenfly

blau *adj*, **B~** *nt* -s,- blue; **b~er Fleck** bruise; **b~es Auge** black eye; **b~ sein** Ⓘ be tight; **Fahrt ins B~e** mystery tour. **B~beere** *f* bilberry. **B~licht** *nt* blue flashing light

Blech *nt* -[e]s,-e sheet metal; (*Weiß-*) tin; (*Platte*) metal sheet; (*Back-*) baking sheet; (*Mus*) brass; (Ⓘ: *Unsinn*) rubbish. **B~schaden** *m* (*Auto*) damage to the bodywork

Blei *nt* -[e]s lead

Bleibe *f* - place to stay. **b~n†** *vi* (*sein*) remain, stay; (*übrig-*) be left; **ruhig b~n** keep calm; **bei etw b~n** (*fig*) stick to sth; **b~n Sie am Appa-**

rat hold the line; **etw b~n lassen** not do sth. **b~nd** adj permanent; (anhaltend) lasting

bleich adj pale. **b~en†** vi (sein) bleach; (ver-) fade ● vt (reg) bleach. **B~mittel** nt bleach

blei|ern adj leaden. **~frei** adj unleaded. **B~stift** m pencil. **B~stift-absatz** m stiletto heel. **B~stift-spitzer** m -s,- pencil sharpener

Blende f -,-n shade, shield; (Sonnen-) [sun] visor; (Phot) diaphragm; (Öffnung) aperture; (an Kleid) facing. **b~n** vt dazzle, blind

Blick m -[e]s,-e look; (kurz) glance; (Aussicht) view; **auf den ersten B~** at first sight. **b~en** vi (haben) look/(kurz) glance (**auf** + acc at). **B~punkt** m (fig) point of view

blind adj blind; (trübe) dull; **b~er Alarm** false alarm; **b~er Passagier** stowaway. **B~darm** m appendix. **B~darmentzündung** f appendicitis. **B~e(r)** m/f blind man/woman; **die B~en** the blind pl. **B~enhund** m guidedog. **B~enschrift** f braille. **B~gänger** m -s,- (Mil) dud. **B~heit** f - blindness

blink|en vi (haben) flash; (funkeln) gleam; (Auto) indicate. **B~er** m -s,- (Auto) indicator. **B~licht** nt flashing light

blinzeln vi (haben) blink

Blitz m -es,-e [flash of] lightning; (Phot) flash. **B~ableiter** m lightning-conductor. **b~artig** adj lightning ● adv like lightning. **b~en** vi (haben) flash; (funkeln) sparkle; **es hat geblitzt** there was a flash of lightning. **B~eis** nt sheet ice. **B~licht** nt (Phot) flash. **b~sauber** adj spick and span. **b~schnell** adj lightning ● adv like lightning

Block m -[e]s, ̈-e block ● -[e]s,-s & ̈-e pad; (Häuser-) block

Blockade f -,-n blockade

Blockflöte f recorder

blockieren vt block; (Mil) blockade

Blockschrift f block letters pl

blöd[e] adj feeble-minded; (dumm) stupid

Blödsinn m -[e]s idiocy; (Unsinn) nonsense

blöken vi (haben) bleat

blond adj fair-haired; (Haar) fair

bloß adj bare; (alleinig) mere ● adv only, just

bloß|legen vt sep uncover. **b~stellen** vt sep compromise

Bluff m -s,-s bluff. **b~en** vt/i (haben) bluff

blühen vi (haben) flower; (fig) flourish. **b~d** adj flowering; (fig) flourishing, thriving

Blume f -,-n flower; (vom Wein) bouquet. **B~nbeet** nt flower-bed. **B~ngeschäft** nt flower-shop, florist's. **B~nkohl** m cauliflower. **B~nmuster** nt floral design. **B~nstrauß** m bunch of flowers. **B~ntopf** m flowerpot; (Pflanze) pot plant. **B~nzwiebel** f bulb

blumig adj (fig) flowery

Bluse f -,-n blouse

Blut nt -[e]s blood. **b~arm** adj anaemic. **B~bahn** f blood-stream. **B~bild** nt blood count. **B~druck** m blood pressure. **b~dürstig** adj bloodthirsty

Blüte f -,-n flower, bloom; (vom Baum) blossom; (B~zeit) flowering period; (Baum-) blossom time; (Höhepunkt) peak, prime

Blut|egel m -s,- leech. **b~en** vi (haben) bleed

Blüten|blatt nt petal. **B~staub** m pollen

Blut|er m -s,- haemophiliac. **B~erguss** m bruise. **B~gefäß** nt bloodvessel. **B~gruppe** f blood group. **b~ig** adj bloody. **B~körperchen** nt -s,- corpuscle. **B~probe** f blood test. **b~rünstig** adj (fig) bloody, gory. **B~schande** f incest. **B~spender** m blood donor. **B~sturz** m haemorrhage. **B~transfusion, B~übertragung** f blood transfusion. **B~ung** f -,-en bleeding; (Med) haemorrhage; (Regel-) period. **b~unterlaufen** adj bruised; (Auge) bloodshot. **B~vergiftung** f bloodpoisoning. **B~wurst** f black pudding

Bö f -,-en gust; (Regen-) squall

Bob m -s,-s bob[-sleigh]

Bock m -[e]s, ∵e buck; (Ziege) billy goat; (Schaf) ram; (Gestell) support. **b~ig** adj ⊞ stubborn. **B~springen** nt leap-frog

Boden m -s, ∵ ground; (Erde) soil; (Fuß-) floor; (Grundfläche) bottom; (Dach-) loft, attic. **B~satz** m sediment. **B~schätze** mpl mineral deposits. **B~see (der)** Lake Constance

Bogen m -s,- & ∵ curve; (Geometry) arc; (beim Skilauf) turn; (Architecture) arch; (Waffe, Geigen-) bow; (Papier) sheet; **einen großen B~ um jdn/ etw machen** ⊞ give s.o./sth a wide berth. **B~schießen** nt archery

Bohle f -,-n [thick] plank

Böhm|en nt -s Bohemia. **b~isch** adj Bohemian

Bohne f -,-n bean; **grüne B~n** French beans

bohner|n vt polish. **B~wachs** nt floor-polish

bohr|en vt/i (haben) drill (nach for); drive (Tunnel); sink (Brunnen); (Insekt:) bore. **B~er** m -s,- drill. **B~insel** f [offshore] drilling rig. **B~turm** m derrick

Boje f -,-n buoy

Böllerschuss m gun salute

Bolzen m -s,- bolt; (Stift) pin

bombardieren vt bomb; (fig) bombard (mit with)

Bombe f -,-n bomb. **B~nangriff** m bombing raid. **B~nerfolg** m huge success

Bon /bɔŋ/ m -s,-s voucher; (Kassen-) receipt

Bonbon /bɔŋˈbɔŋ/ m & nt -s,-s sweet

Bonus m -[ses],-[se] bonus

Boot nt -[e]s,-e boat. **B~ssteg** m landing-stage

Bord[1] nt -[e]s,-e shelf

Bord[2] m (Naut) **an B~** aboard, on board; **über B~** overboard. **B~buch** nt log[-book]

Bordell nt -s,-e brothel

Bordkarte f boarding-pass

borgen vt borrow; **jdm etw b~** lend s.o. sth

Borke f -,-n bark

Börse f -,-n purse; (Comm) stock exchange. **B~nmakler** m stockbroker

Borst|e f -,-n bristle. **b~ig** adj bristly

Borte f -,-n braid

Böschung f -,-en embankment

böse adj wicked, evil; (unartig) naughty; (schlimm) bad; (zornig) cross; **jdm** od **auf jdn b~ sein** be cross with s.o.

bos|haft adj malicious, spiteful. **B~heit** f -,-en malice; spite; (Handlung) spiteful act/(Bemerkung) remark

böswillig adj malicious

Botani|k f - botany. **B~ker(in)** m -s,- (f -,-nen) botanist

Bot|e m -n,-n messenger. **B~engang** m errand. **B~schaft** f -,-en message; (Pol) embassy. **B~schafter** m -s,- ambassador

Bouillon /bʊlˈjɔŋ/ f -,-s clear soup. **B~würfel** m stock cube

Bowle /ˈboːlə/ f -,-n punch

Box f -,-en box; (Pferde-) loose box; (Lautsprecher-) speaker; (Autorennen) pit

box|en vi (haben) box ● vt punch. **B~en** nt -s boxing. **B~enluder** nt pit babe. **B~er** m -s,- boxer. **B~stopp** m pit stop

brachliegen† vi sep (haben) lie fallow

Branche /ˈbrãːʃə/ f -,-n [line of] business. **B~nverzeichnis** nt (Teleph) classified directory

Brand m -[e]s, ∵e fire; (Med) gangrene; (Bot) blight; **in B~ geraten** catch fire; **in B~ setzen** od **stecken** set on fire. **B~bombe** f incendiary bomb

Brand|stifter m arsonist. **B~stiftung** f arson

Brandung f - surf

Brand|wunde f burn. **B~zeichen** nt brand

Branntwein m spirit; (coll) spirits pl. **B~brennerei** f distillery

b

bras|ilianisch *adj* Brazilian.
B~ilien *nt* -s Brazil

Brat|apfel *m* baked apple. b~en†
vt/i (*haben*) roast; (*in der Pfanne*) fry.
B~en *m* -s,- roast; (*B~stück*) joint.
b~fertig *adj* oven-ready. B~hähn-
chen roasting chicken. B~kartof-
feln *fpl* fried potatoes. B~pfanne *f*
frying-pan

Bratsche *f* -,-n (*Mus*) viola

Bratspieß *m* spit

Brauch *m* -[e]s,Bräuche custom.
b~bar *adj* usable; (*nützlich*) useful.
b~en *vt* need; (*ge-, verbrauchen*)
use; take (*Zeit*); er b~t es nur zu
sagen he only has to say

Braue *f* -,-n eyebrow

brau|en *vt* brew. B~er *m* -s,-
brewer. B~erei *f* -,-en brewery

braun *adj*, B~ *nt* -s,- brown; b~
werden (*Person*:) get a tan; b~ [ge-
brannt] sein be [sun-]tanned

Bräune *f* - [sun-]tan. b~n *vt/i*
(*haben*) brown; (*in der Sonne*) tan

Braunschweig *nt* -s Brunswick

Brause *f* -,-n (*Dusche*) shower; (*an
Gießkanne*) rose; (*B~limonade*) fizzy
drink

Braut *f* -,̈e bride; (*Verlobte*) fiancée

Bräutigam *m* -s,-e bridegroom;
(*Verlobter*) fiancé

Brautkleid *nt* wedding dress

Brautpaar *nt* bridal couple; (*Verlobte*) engaged couple

brav *adj* good; (*redlich*) honest ● *adv*
dutifully; (*redlich*) honestly

bravo *int* bravo!

BRD *abbr* (**Bundesrepublik Deutschland**) FRG

Brech|eisen *nt* jemmy; (*B~stange*)
crowbar. b~en† *vt* break; (*Phys*) re-
fract (*Licht*); (*erbrechen*) vomit; sich
b~en (*Wellen:*) break; (*Licht:*) be re-
fracted; sich (*dat*) den Arm b~en
break one's arm ● *vi* (*sein*) break ● *vi*
(*haben*) vomit, be sick. B~reiz *m*
nausea. B~stange *f* crowbar

Brei *m* -[e]s,-e paste; (*Culin*) purée;
(*Hafer-*) porridge

breit *adj* wide; (*Schultern, Grinsen*)

broad. B~band *nt* broadband. B~e
f -,-n width; breadth; (*Geog*) latitude.
b~en *vt* spread (**über** + *acc* over).
B~engrad *m* [degree of] latitude.
B~enkreis *m* parallel

Bremse¹ *f* -,-n horsefly

Bremse² *f* -,-n brake. b~n *vt* slow
down; (*fig*) restrain ● *vi* (*haben*)
brake

Bremslicht *nt* brake-light

brenn|bar *adj* combustible; leicht
b~bar highly [in]flammable. b~en†
vi (*haben*) burn; (*Licht:*) be on; (*Zigarette:*) be alight; (*weh tun*) smart,
sting ● *vt* burn; (*rösten*) roast; (*im
Brennofen*) fire; (*destillieren*) distil.
b~end *adj* burning; (*angezündet*)
lighted; (*fig*) fervent. B~er *m* -s, -
burner. B~erei *f* -,-en distillery

Brennessel* *f* = Brennnessel

Brenn|holz *nt* firewood. B~ofen *m*
kiln. B~nessel *f* stinging nettle.
B~punkt *m* (*Phys*) focus. B~spiri-
tus *m* methylated spirits. B~stoff *m*
fuel. B~stoffzelle *f* fuel cell

Bretagne /bre'tanjə/ (**die**) - Brittany

Brett *nt* -[e]s,-er board; (*im Regal*)
shelf; schwarzes B~ notice board.
B~spiel *nt* board game

Brezel *f* -,-n pretzel

Bridge /brɪtʃ/ *nt* - (*Spiel*) bridge

Brief *m* -[e]s,-e letter. B~beschwe-
rer *m* -s,- paperweight.
B~freund(in) *m(f)* pen-friend.
B~kasten *m* letter-box. B~kopf *m*
letter-head. b~lich *adj & adv* by letter. B~marke *f* [postage] stamp.
B~öffner *m* paper-knife. B~papier
nt notepaper. B~tasche *f* wallet.
B~träger *m* postman. B~um-
schlag *m* envelope. B~wahl *f*
postal vote. B~wechsel *m* correspondence

Brikett *nt* -s,-s briquette

Brillant *m* -en,-en [cut] diamond

Brille *f* -,-n glasses *pl*, spectacles *pl*;
(*Schutz-*) goggles *pl*; (*Klosett-*) toilet
seat

bringen† *vt* bring; (*fort-*) take; (*ein-*)
yield; (*veröffentlichen*) publish; (*im
Radio*) broadcast; show (*Film*); **ins**

Bett b~ put to bed; **jdn nach Hause b~** take/(*begleiten*) see s.o. home; **um etw b~** deprive of sth; **jdn dazu b~, etw zu tun** get s.o. to do sth; **es weit b~** (*fig*) go far

Brise *f* -,-n breeze

Brit|e *m* -n,-n, **B~in** *f* -,-nen Briton. **b~isch** *adj* British

Bröck|chen *nt* -s,- (*Culin*) crouton. **b~elig** *adj* crumbly; (*Gestein*) friable. **b~eln** *vt/i* (*haben/sein*) crumble

Brocken *m* -s,- chunk; (*Erde, Kohle*) lump

Brokat *m* -[e]s,-e brocade

Brokkoli *pl* broccoli *sg*

Brombeere *f* blackberry

Bronchitis *f* - bronchitis

Bronze /'brõːsə/ *f* -,-n bronze

Brosch|e *f* -,-n brooch. **b~iert** *adj* paperback. **B~üre** *f* -,-n brochure; (*Heft*) booklet

Brösel *mpl* (*Culin*) breadcrumbs

Brot *nt* -[e]s,-e bread; **ein B~** a loaf [of bread]; (*Scheibe*) a slice of bread

Brötchen *nt* -s,- [bread] roll

Brotkrümel *m* breadcrumb

Bruch *m* -[e]s,ᵉe break; (*Brechen*) breaking; (*Rohr-*) burst; (*Med*) fracture; (*Eingeweide-*) rupture, hernia; (*Math*) fraction; (*fig*) breach; (*in Beziehung*) break-up

brüchig *adj* brittle

Bruch|landung *f* crash-landing. **B~rechnung** *f* fractions *pl*. **B~stück** *nt* fragment. **B~teil** *m* fraction

Brücke *f* -,-n bridge; (*Teppich*) rug

Bruder *m* -s,ᵉ brother

brüderlich *adj* brotherly, fraternal

Brügge *nt* -s Bruges

Brüh|e *f* -,-n broth, stock. **B~würfel** *m* stock cube

brüllen *vt/i* (*haben*) roar

brumm|eln *vt/i* (*haben*) mumble. **b~en** *vi* (*haben*) buzz; (*Insekt:*) buzz; (*Bär:*) growl; (*Motor:*) hum; (*murren*) grumble. **B~er** *m* -s,- 🔲 bluebottle. **b~ig** *adj* 🔲 grumpy

brünett *adj* dark-haired

Brunnen *m* -s,- well; (*Spring-*) fountain; (*Heil-*) spa water

brüsk *adj* brusque

Brüssel *nt* -s Brussels

Brust *f* -,ᵉe chest; (*weibliche, Culin: B~stück*) breast. **B~bein** *nt* breastbone

brüsten (sich) *vr* boast

Brust|fellentzündung *f* pleurisy. **B~schwimmen** *nt* breaststroke

Brüstung *f* -,-en parapet

Brustwarze *f* nipple

Brut *f* -,-en incubation

brutal *adj* brutal

brüten *vi* (*haben*) sit (on eggs); (*fig*) ponder (*über* + *dat* over)

Brutkasten *m* (*Med*) incubator

brutto *adv*, **B~-** *prefix* gross

BSE *f* - BSE

Bub *m* -en,-en (*SGer*) boy. **B~e** *m* -n,-n (*Karte*) jack, knave

Buch *nt* -[e]s,ᵉer book; **B~ führen** keep a record (*über* + *acc* of); **die B~er führen** keep the accounts

Buche *f* -,-n beech

buchen *vt* book; (*Comm*) enter

Bücher|ei *f* -,-en library. **B~regal** *nt* bookcase, bookshelves *pl*. **B~schrank** *m* bookcase

Buchfink *m* chaffinch

Buch|führung *f* bookkeeping. **B~halter(in)** *m* -s,- (*f* -,-nen) bookkeeper, accountant. **B~haltung** *f* bookkeeping, accountancy; (*Abteilung*) accounts department. **B~handlung** *f* bookshop

Büchse *f* -,-n box; (*Konserven-*) tin, can

Buch|stabe *m* -n,-n letter. **b~stabieren** *vt* spell [out]. **b~stäblich** *adv* literally

Bucht *f* -,-en (*Geog*) bay

Buchung *f* -,-en booking, reservation; (*Comm*) entry

Buckel *m* -s,- hump; (*Beule*) bump; (*Hügel*) hillock

bücken (sich) *vr* bend down

bucklig *adj* hunchbacked

Bückling *m* -s,-e smoked herring

Buddhis|mus m - Buddhism.
B~t(in) m -en,-en (f -,-nen) Buddhist. **b~tisch** adj Buddhist

Bude f -,-n hut; (*Kiosk*) kiosk; (*Markt-*) stall; (🔲: *Zimmer*) room

Budget /byˈdʒeː/ nt -s,-s budget

Büfett nt -[e]s,-e sideboard; (*Theke*) bar; **kaltes B~** cold buffet

Büffel m -s,- buffalo

Bügel m -s,- frame; (*Kleider-*) coathanger; (*Steig-*) stirrup; (*Brillen-*) sidepiece. **B~brett** nt ironing-board. **B~eisen** nt iron. **B~falte** f crease. **b~frei** adj non-iron. **b~n** vt/i (*haben*) iron

Bühne f -,-n stage. **B~nbild** nt set. **B~neingang** m stage door

Buhrufe mpl boos

Bukett nt -[e]s,-e bouquet

Bulgarien /-jən/ nt -s Bulgaria

Bull|auge nt (*Naut*) porthole. **B~dogge** f bulldog. **B~dozer** m -s,- bulldozer. **B~e** m -n,-n bull; (*sl: Polizist*) cop

Bummel m -s,- 🔲 stroll. **B~lei** f - 🔲 dawdling

bummel|ig adj 🔲 slow; (*nachlässig*) careless. **b~n** vi (*sein*) 🔲 stroll ● vi (*haben*) 🔲 dawdle. **B~streik** m go-slow. **B~zug** m 🔲 slow train

Bums m -es,-e 🔲 bump, thump

Bund¹ nt -[e]s,-e bunch

Bund² m -[e]s,ⁱe association; (*Bündnis*) alliance; (*Pol*) federation; (*Rock-, Hosen-*) waistband; **der B~** the Federal Government

Bündel nt -s,- bundle. **b~n** vt bundle [up]

Bundes|- prefix Federal. **B~genosse** m ally. **B~kanzler** m Federal Chancellor. **B~land** nt [federal] state; (*Aust*) province. **B~liga** f German national league. **B~rat** m Upper House of Parliament. **B~regierung** f Federal Government. **B~republik** f **die B~republik Deutschland** the Federal Republic of Germany. **B~tag** m Lower House of Parliament. **B~wehr** f [Federal German] Army

---

Bundestag The lower house of the German parliament, which is elected every four years. The *Bundestag* is responsible for federal legislation, the federal budget, and electing the *Bundeskanzler*, or Federal Chancellor, (equivalent of prime minister). Half the MPs are elected directly and half by proportional representation. Every citizen has two votes. ⓘ

Bundeswappen ▷WAPPEN ⓘ

---

bünd|ig adj & adv kurz und b~ig short and to the point. **B~nis** nt -ses,-se alliance

Bunker m -s,- bunker; (*Luftschutz-*) shelter

bunt adj coloured; (*farbenfroh*) colourful; (*grell*) gaudy; (*gemischt*) varied; (*wirr*) confused; **b~e Platte** assorted cold meats. **B~stift** m crayon

Bürde f -,-n (*fig*) burden

Burg f -,-en castle

Bürge m -n,-n guarantor. **b~n** vi (*haben*) **b~n für** vouch for; (*fig*) guarantee

Bürger|(in) m -s,- (f -,-nen) citizen. **B~krieg** m civil war. **b~lich** adj civil; (*Pflicht*) civic; (*mittelständisch*) middle-class. **B~liche(r)** m/f commoner. **B~meister** m mayor. **B~rechte** npl civil rights. **B~steig** m -[e]s,-e pavement

Bürgschaft f -,-en surety

Burgunder m -s,- (*Wein*) Burgundy

Büro nt -s,-s office. **B~angestellte(r)** m/f office worker. **B~klammer** f paper clip. **B~kratie** f -,-n bureaucracy. **b~kratisch** adj bureaucratic

Bursche m -n,-n lad, youth

Bürste f -,-n brush. **b~n** vt brush. **B~nschnitt** m crew cut

Bus m -ses,-se bus; (*Reise-*) coach

Busch m -[e]s,ⁱe bush

Büschel nt -s,- tuft

buschig adj bushy

Busen m -s,- bosom

Bussard m -s,-e buzzard

Buße f -,-n penance; (*Jur*) fine

Bußgeld nt (*Jur*) fine

Büste f -,-n bust; (*Schneider-*) dummy. **B~nhalter** m -s,- bra

Butter f - butter. **B~blume** f buttercup. **B~brot** nt slice of bread and butter. **B~milch** f buttermilk. **b~n** vt butter

b.w. abbr (**bitte wenden**) P.T.O.

....

Cc

....

ca. abbr (**circa**) about

Café /ka'fe:/ nt -s,-s café

Camcorder /'kamkɔrdɐ/ m -s, - camcorder

camp|en /'kɛmpən/ vi (*haben*) go camping. **C~ing** nt -s camping. **C~ingplatz** m campsite

Caravan /'ka[:]ravan/ m -s,-s (*Auto*) caravan; (*Kombi*) estate car

CD /tse:'de:/ f -,-s compact disc, CD. **CD-ROM** f -,-(s) CD-ROM

Cell|ist(in) /tʃɛ'lɪst(ɪn)/ m -en,-en (f -,-nen) cellist. **C~o** nt -,-los & -li cello

Celsius /'tsɛlzi̯ʊs/ inv Celsius, centigrade

Cent /tsɛnt/ m -[s], -[s] cent

Champagner /ʃam'panjɐ/ m -s champagne

Champignon /'ʃampɪnjɔŋ/ m -s,-s [field] mushroom

Chance /'ʃã:s[ə]/ f -,-n chance

Chaos /'ka:ɔs/ nt - chaos

Charakter /ka'raktɐ/ m -s,-e character. **c~isieren** vt characterize. **c~istisch** adj characteristic (**für** of)

charm|ant /ʃar'mant/ adj charming. **C~e** m -s charm

Charter|flug /'tʃ-, 'ʃartɐ-/ m charter flight. **c~n** vt charter

Chassis /ʃa'si:/ nt -,- chassis

Chauffeur /ʃɔ'føːɐ/ m -s,-e chauffeur; (*Taxi-*) driver

Chauvinist /ʃovi'nɪst/ m -en,-en chauvinist

Chef /ʃɛf/ m -s,-s head; 🔲 boss

Chemie /çe'mi:/ f - chemistry

Chem|iker(in) /'çe:-/ m -s,- (f -,-nen) chemist. **c~isch** adj chemical; **c~ische Reinigung** dry-cleaning; (*Geschäft*) dry-cleaner's

Chicorée /'ʃikore:/ m -s chicory

Chiffre /'ʃɪfə, 'ʃɪfrə/ f -,-n cipher

Chile /'çi:le/ nt -s Chile

Chin|a /'çi:na/ nt -s China. **C~ese** m -n,-n, **C~esin** f -,-nen Chinese. **c~esisch** adj Chinese. **C~esisch** nt -[s] (*Lang*) Chinese

Chip /tʃɪp/ m -s,-s [micro]chip. **C~s** pl crisps

Chirurg /çi'rʊrk/ m -en,-en surgeon. **C~ie** f - surgery

Chlor /klo:ɐ/ nt -s chlorine

Choke /tʃo:k/ m -s,-s (*Auto*) choke

Cholera /'ko:lera/ f - cholera

cholerisch /ko'le:rɪʃ/ adj irascible

Cholesterin /ço-, kolɛste'ri:n/ nt -s cholesterol

Chor /ko:ɐ/ m -[e]s,-̈e choir

Choreographie, Choreografie /koreografi:/ f -,-n choreography

Christ /krɪst/ m -en,-en Christian. **C~baum** m Christmas tree. **C~entum** nt -s Christianity **c~lich** adj Christian

Christus /'krɪstʊs/ m -ti Christ

Chrom /kro:m/ nt -s chromium

Chromosom /kromo'zo:m/ nt -s,-en chromosome

Chronik /'kro:nɪk/ f -,-en chronicle

chronisch /'kro:nɪʃ/ adj chronic

Chrysantheme /kryzan'te:mə/ f -,-n chrysanthemum

circa /'tsɪrka/ adv about

Clique /'klɪkə/ f -,-n clique

Clou /klu:/ m -s,-s highlight, 🔲 high spot

Clown /klaʊn/ m -s,-s clown

Club /klʊp/ m -s,-s club

Cocktail /'kɔkte:l/ m -s,-s cocktail

Code /'ko:t/ m -s,-s code

Comic-Heft /'kɔmɪk-/ nt comic

Computer /kɔm'pjuːtɐ/ m -s,- computer. **c~isieren** vt computerize. **C~spiel** nt computer game

Conférencier /kõˈferãˈsie:/ m -s,- compère

Cord /kɔrt/ m -s, **C~samt** m corduroy

Couch /kautʃ/ f -,-s settee

Cousin /kuˈzɛ̃:/ m -s,-s [male] cousin. **C~e** f -,-n [female] cousin

Creme /kreːm/ f -s,-s cream; (Speise) cream dessert

Curry /'kari, 'kœri/ nt & m -s curry powder ● nt -s,-s (Gericht) curry

Cursor /'kɔːɐ̯sɐ/ m -s, - cursor

Cyberspace /'saibɐspeːs/ m - cyberspace

Dd

da adv there; (hier) here; (zeitlich) then; (in dem Fall) in that case; **von da an** from then on; **da sein** be there/(hier) here; (existieren) exist; **wieder da sein** be back ● conj as, since

dabei (emphatic: dabei) adv nearby; (daran) with it; (eingeschlossen) included; (hinsichtlich) about it; (währenddem) during this; (gleichzeitig) at the same time; (doch) and yet; **dicht d~** close by; **d~ sein** be present; (mitmachen) be involved; **d~ sein, etw zu tun** be just doing sth

Dach nt -[e]s,ᴗer roof. **D~boden** m loft. **D~luke** f skylight. **D~rinne** f gutter

Dachs m -es,-e badger

Dachsparren m -s,- rafter

Dackel m -s,- dachshund

dadurch (emphatic: dadurch) adv through it/them; (Ursache) by it; (deshalb) because of that; **d~, dass** because

dafür (emphatic: dafür) adv for it/them; (anstatt) instead; (als Aus-gleich) but [on the other hand]; **d~, dass** considering that; **ich kann nichts dafür** it's not my fault

dagegen (emphatic: dagegen) adv against it/them; (Mittel, Tausch) for it; (verglichen damit) by comparison; (jedoch) however; **hast du was d~?** do you mind?

daheim adv at home

daher (emphatic: daher) adv from there; (deshalb) for that reason; **das kommt d~, weil** that's because ● conj that is why

dahin (emphatic: dahin) adv there; **bis d~** up to there; (bis dann) until/(Zukunft) by then; **jdn d~ bringen, dass er etw tut** get s.o. to do sth

dahinten adv back there

dahinter (emphatic: dahinter) adv behind it/them; **d~ kommen** (fig) get to the bottom of it

Dahlie /-lə/ f -,-n dahlia

dalassen† vt sep leave there

daliegen† vi sep (haben) lie there

damalig adj at that time; **der d~e Minister** the then Minister

damals adv at that time

Damast m -es,-e damask

Dame f -,-n lady; (Karte, Schach) queen; (D~spiel) draughts sg. **d~nhaft** adj ladylike

damit (emphatic: damit) adv with it/them; (dadurch) by it; **hör auf d~!** stop it! ● conj so that

Damm m -[e]s,ᴗe dam

dämmer|ig adj dim. **D~licht** nt twilight. **d~n** vi (haben) (Morgen:) dawn; **es d~t** it is getting light/(abends) dark. **D~ung** f dawn; (Abend-) dusk

Dämon m -s,-en demon

Dampf m -es,ᴗe steam; (Chemistry) vapour. **d~en** vi (haben) steam

dämpfen vt (Culin) steam; (fig) muffle (Ton); lower (Stimme)

Dampf|er m -s,- steamer. **D~kochtopf** m pressure-cooker. **D~maschine** f steam engine. **D~walze** f steamroller

dan|ach (*emphatic:* **da**nach) *adv* after it/them; (*suchen*) for it/them; (*riechen*) of it; (*später*) afterwards; (*entsprechend*) accordingly; **es sieht d~ aus** it looks like it

Däne *m* -n,-n Dane

daneben (*emphatic:* **da**neben) *adv* beside it/them; (*außerdem*) in addition; (*verglichen damit*) by comparison

Dän|emark *nt* -s Denmark. **D~in** *f* -,-nen Dane. **d~isch** *adj* Danish

Dank *m* -es thanks *pl*; **vielen D~!** thank you very much! **d~** *prep* (+ *dat or gen*) thanks to. **d~bar** *adj* grateful; (*erleichtert*) thankful; (*lohnend*) rewarding. **D~barkeit** *f* - gratitude. **d~e** *adv* **d~e [schön od sehr]!** thank you [very much]! **d~en** *vi* (*haben*) thank (**jdm** s.o.); (*ablehnen*) decline; **nichts zu d~en!** don't mention it!

dann *adv* then; **selbst d~, wenn** even if

daran (*emphatic:* **da**ran) *adv* on it/them; at it/them; (*denken*) of it; **nahe d~** on the point (**etw zu tun** of doing sth). **d~setzen** *vt sep* **alles d~setzen** do one's utmost (**zu** to)

darauf (*emphatic:* **da**rauf) *adv* on it/them; (*warten*) for it; (*antworten*) to it; (*danach*) after that; (*d~hin*) as a result. **d~hin** *adv* as a result

daraus (*emphatic:* **da**raus) *adv* out of or from it/them; **er macht sich nichts d~** he doesn't care for it

darlegen *vt sep* expound; (*erklären*) explain

Darlehen *nt* -s,- loan

Darm *m* -[e]s,¨e intestine

darstell|en *vt sep* represent; (*bildlich*) portray; (*Theat*) interpret; (*spielen*) play; (*schildern*) describe. **D~er** *m* -s,- actor. **D~erin** *f* -,-nen actress. **D~ung** *f* representation; interpretation; description

darüber (*emphatic:* **da**rüber) *adv* over it/them; (*höher*) above it/them; (*sprechen, lachen, sich freuen*) about it; (*mehr*) more; **d~ hinaus** beyond [it]; (*dazu*) on top of that

darum (*emphatic:* **da**rum) *adv* round it/them; (*bitten, kämpfen*) for it; (*deshalb*) that is why; **d~, weil** because

darunter (*emphatic:* **da**runter) *adv* under it/them; (*tiefer*) below it/them; (*weniger*) less; (*dazwischen*) among them

das *def art & pron* s. **der**

dasein* *vi sep* (*sein*) = **da sein**, s. **da**. **D~** *nt* -s existence

dass *conj* that

dasselbe *pron* s. **derselbe**

Daten|sichtgerät *nt* visual display unit, VDU. **D~verarbeitung** *f* data processing

datieren *vt/i* (*haben*) date

Dativ *m* -s,-e dative. **D~objekt** *nt* indirect object

Dattel *f* -,-n date

Datum *nt* -s,-ten date; **Daten** dates; (*Angaben*) data

Dauer *f* - duration, length; (*Jur*) term; **auf die D~** in the long run. **D~auftrag** *m* standing order. **d~haft** *adj* lasting, enduring; (*fest*) durable. **D~karte** *f* season ticket. **d~n** *vi* (*haben*) last; **lange d~n** take a long time. **d~nd** *adj* lasting; (*ständig*) constant. **D~welle** *f* perm

Daumen *m* -s,- thumb; **jdm den D~ drücken** *od* **halten** keep one's fingers crossed for s.o.

Daunen *fpl* down *sg*. **D~decke** *f* [down-filled] duvet

davon (*emphatic:* **da**von) *adv* from it/them; (*dadurch*) by it; (*damit*) with it/them; (*darüber*) about it; (*Menge*) of it/them; **das kommt d~!** it serves you right! **d~kommen†** *vi sep* (*sein*) escape (**mit dem Leben** with one's life). **d~laufen†** *vi sep* (*sein*) run away. **d~machen** (**sich**) *vr sep* 🔲 make off. **d~tragen†** *vt sep* carry off; (*erleiden*) suffer; (*gewinnen*) win

davor (*emphatic:* **da**vor) *adv* in front of it/them; (*sich fürchten*) of it; (*zeitlich*) before it/them

dazu (*emphatic:* **da**zu) *adv* to it/them; (*damit*) with it/them; (*dafür*) for it; **noch d~** in addition to that; **jdn d~ bringen, etw zu tun** get s.o. to do sth; **ich kam nicht d~** I didn't get round to [doing] it. **d~kommen†** *vi sep* (*sein*) arrive [on the scene]; (*hinzukommen*) be added. **d~rechnen** *vt sep* add to it/them

dazwischen (*emphatic:* **dazwischen**) *adv* between them; in between; (*darunter*) among them. **d~kommen†** *vi sep* (*sein*) (*fig*) crop up; **wenn nichts d~kommt** if all goes well

Debat|te *f* -,-n debate; **zur D~te stehen** be at issue. **d~tieren** *vt/i* (*haben*) debate

Debüt /de'byː/ *nt* -s,-s début

Deck *nt* -[e]s,-s (*Naut*) deck; **an D~** on deck. **D~bett** *nt* duvet

Decke *f* -,-n cover; (*Tisch-*) tablecloth; (*Bett-*) blanket; (*Reise-*) rug; (*Zimmer-*) ceiling; **unter einer D~ stecken** 🛈 be in league

Deckel *m* -s,- lid; (*Flaschen-*) top; (*Buch-*) cover

decken *vt* cover; tile (*Dach*); lay (*Tisch*); (*schützen*) shield; (*Sport*) mark; meet (*Bedarf*); **jdn d~** (*fig*) cover up for s.o.; **sich d~** (*fig*) cover oneself (**gegen** against); (*übereinstimmen*) coincide

Deckname *m* pseudonym

Deckung *f* - (*Mil*) cover; (*Sport*) defence; (*Mann-*) marking; (*Boxen*) guard; (*Sicherheit*) security; **in D~ gehen** take cover

defin|ieren *vt* define. **D~ition** *f* -,-en definition

Defizit *nt* -s,-e deficit

deformiert *adj* deformed

deftig *adj* 🛈 (*Mahlzeit*) hearty; (*Witz*) coarse

Degen *m* -s,- sword; (*Fecht-*) épée

degeneriert *adj* (*fig*) degenerate

degradieren *vt* (*Mil*) demote; (*fig*) degrade

dehn|bar *adj* elastic. **d~en** *vt* stretch; lengthen (*Vokal*); **sich d~en** stretch

Deich *m* -[e]s,-e dike

dein *poss pron* your. **d~e(r,s)** *poss pron* yours; **die D~en** *od* **d~en** *pl*

your family *sg.* **d~erseits** *adv* for your part. **d~etwegen** *adv* for your sake; (*wegen dir*) because of you, on your account. **d~etwillen** *adv* **um d~etwillen** for your sake. **d~ige** *poss pron* **der/die/das d~ige** yours. **d~s** *poss pron* yours

Dekan *m* -s,-e dean

Deklin|ation /-'tsioːn/ *f* -,-en declension. **d~ieren** *vt* decline

Dekolleté, **Dekolletee** /dekɔl'teː/ *nt* -s,-s low neckline

Dekor *m* & *nt* -s decoration. **D~ ateur** *m* -s,-e interior decorator; (*Schaufenster-*) window-dresser. **D~ation** *f* -,-en decoration; (*Schaufenster-*) window-dressing; (*Auslage*) display. **d~ativ** *adj* decorative. **d~ieren** *vt* decorate; dress (*Schaufenster*)

Deleg|ation /-'tsioːn/ *f* -,-en delegation. **D~ierte(r)** *m/f* delegate

delikat *adj* delicate; (*lecker*) delicious; (*taktvoll*) tactful. **D~essengeschäft** *nt* delicatessen

Delikt *nt* -[e]s,-e offence

Delinquent *m* -en,-en offender

Delle *f* -,-n dent

Delphin *m* -s,-e dolphin

Delta *nt* -s,-s delta

dem *def art & pron s.* **der**

dementieren *vt* deny

dem|entsprechend *adj* corresponding; (*passend*) appropriate ● *adv* accordingly; (*passend*) appropriately. **d~nächst** *adv* soon; (*in Kürze*) shortly

Demokrat *m* -en,-en democrat. **D~ie** *f* -,-n democracy. **d~isch** *adj* democratic

demolieren *vt* wreck

Demonstr|ant *m* -en,-en demonstrator. **D~ation** *f* -,-en demonstration. **d~ieren** *vt/i* (*haben*) demonstrate

demontieren *vt* dismantle

Demoskopie *f* - opinion research

Demut *f* - humility

den *def art & pron s.* **der**. **d~en** *pron s.* **der**

denk|bar *adj* conceivable. **d~en†** *vt/i* (*haben*) think (**an** + *acc* of); (*sich erinnern*) remember (**an etw** *acc* sth); **das kann ich mir d~en** I can imagine [that]; **ich d~e nicht daran** I have no intention of doing it. **D~mal** *nt* memorial; (*Monument*) monument. **d~würdig** *adj* memorable

denn *conj* for; **besser/mehr d~ je** better/more than ever ● *adv* **wie/wo d~?** but how/where? **warum d~ nicht?** why ever not? **es sei d~ [, dass]** unless

dennoch *adv* nevertheless

Denunz|iant *m* -en,-en informer. **d~ieren** *vt* denounce

Deodorant *nt* -s,-s deodorant

deplaciert, **deplatziert** /-'tsi:ɐt/ *adj* (*fig*) out of place

Deponie *f* -,-n dump. **d~ren** *vt* deposit

deportieren *vt* deport

Depot /de'po:/ *nt* -s,-s depot; (*Lager*) warehouse; (*Bank-*) safe deposit

Depression *f* -,-en depression

deprimieren *vt* depress

---

der, die, das, *pl* die
● *definite article*

> ! *acc* den, die, das, *pl* die;
> ■ *gen* des, der, des, *pl* der;
> *dat* dem, der, dem, *pl* den

⸱⸱⸱➤ the. **der Mensch** the person; (*als abstrakter Begriff*) man. **die Natur** nature. **das Leben** life. **das Lesen/Tanzen** reading/dancing. **sich** (*dat*) **das Gesicht/die Hände waschen** wash one's face/hands. **3 Euro das Pfund** 3 euros a pound

● *pronoun*

> ! *acc* den, die, das, *pl* die; *gen*
> ■ dessen, deren, dessen, *pl*
> deren; *dat* dem, der, dem, *pl*
> denen

● *demonstrative pronoun*
⸱⸱⸱➤ that; (*pl*) those

⸱⸱⸱➤ (*attributiv*) **der Mann war es** it was 'that man
⸱⸱⸱➤ (*substantivisch*) he, she, it; (*pl*) they. **der war es** it was 'him. **die da** (*person*) that woman/girl; (*thing*) that one
● *relative pronoun*
⸱⸱⸱➤ (*Person*) who. **der Mann, der/ dessen Sohn hier arbeitet** the man who/whose son works here. **die Frau, mit der ich Tennis spiele** the woman with whom I play tennis, the woman I play tennis with. **das Mädchen, das ich gestern sah** the girl I saw yesterday
⸱⸱⸱➤ (*Ding*) which, that. **ich sah ein Buch, das mich interessierte** I saw a book that interested me. **die CD, die ich mir anhöre** the CD I am listening to. **das Auto, mit dem wir nach Deutschland fahren** the car we are going to Germany in *or* in which we are going to Germany

---

derb *adj* tough; (*kräftig*) strong; (*grob*) coarse; (*unsanft*) rough

deren *pron* s. **der**

dergleichen *inv adj* such ● *pron* such a thing/such things

der-/die-/dasselbe, *pl* **dieselben** *pron* the same; **ein- und dasselbe** one and the same thing

derzeit *adv* at present

des *def art* s. **der**

Desert|eur /-'tø:ɐ/ *m* -s,-e deserter. **d~ieren** *vi* (*sein/haben*) desert

desgleichen *adv* likewise ● *pron* the like

deshalb *adv* for this reason; (*also*) therefore

Design *nt* -s, -s design

Designer(in) /di'zainɐ, -nərɪn/ *m* -s,- (*f* -,-nen) designer

Desin|fektion /dɛsʔɪnfɛk'tsio:n/ *f* disinfecting. **D~fektionsmittel** *nt* disinfectant. **d~fizieren** *vt* disinfect

dessen *pron* s. **der**

Destill|ation /-'tsio:n/ *f* - distillation. **d~ieren** *vt* distil

desto *adv* je mehr d~besser the more the better

deswegen *adv* = deshalb

Detektiv *m* -s,-e detective

Deton|ation /-'tsjo:n/ *f* -,-en explosion. **d~ieren** *vi* (*sein*) explode

deut|en *vt* interpret; predict (*Zukunft*) ● *vi* (*haben*) point (**auf** + *acc* at/(*fig*) to). **d~lich** *adj* clear; (*eindeutig*) plain

deutsch *adj* German. **D~** *nt* -[s] (*Lang*) German; **auf D~** in German. **D~e(r)** *m/f* German. **D~land** *nt* -s Germany

Deutung *f* -,-en interpretation

Devise *f* -,-n motto. **D~n** *pl* foreign currency *or* exchange *sg*

Dezember *m* -s,- December

dezent *adj* unobtrusive; (*diskret*) discreet

Dezernat *nt* -[e]s,-e department

Dezimalzahl *f* decimal

d.h. *abbr* (*das heißt*) i.e.

Dia *nt* -s,-s (*Phot*) slide

Diabet|es *m* - diabetes. **D~iker** *m* -s,- diabetic

Diadem *nt* -s,-e tiara

Diagnose *f* -,-n diagnosis

diagonal *adj* diagonal. **D~e** *f* -,-n diagonal

Diagramm *nt* -s,-e diagram; (*Kurven-*) graph

Diakon *m* -s,-e deacon

Dialekt *m* -[e]s,-e dialect

Dialog *m* -[e]s,-e dialogue

Diamant *m* -en,-en diamond

Diapositiv *nt* -s,-e (*Phot*) slide

Diaprojektor *m* slide projector

Diät *f* -,-en (*Med*) diet; **D~ leben** be on a diet

dich *pron* (*acc of* du) you; (*reflexive*) yourself

dicht *adj* dense; (*dick*) thick; (*undurchlässig*) airtight; (*wasser-*) watertight ● *adv* densely; (*nahe*) close (**bei** to). **D~e** density. **d~en¹** *vt* make watertight

dicht|en² *vi* (*haben*) write poetry.

● *vt* write. **D~er(in)** *m* -s,- (*f* -,-nen) poet. **d~erisch** *adj* poetic. **D~ung¹** *f* -,-en poetry; (*Gedicht*) poem

Dichtung² *f* -,-en seal; (*Ring*) washer; (*Auto*) gasket

dick *adj* thick; (*beleibt*) fat; (*geschwollen*) swollen; (*fam: eng*) close; **d~machen** be fattening. **d~flüssig** *adj* thick; (*Phys*) viscous. **D~kopf** *m* Ⅰ stubborn person; **einen D~kopf haben** be stubborn

die *def art & pron s.* der

Dieb|(in) *m* -[e]s,-e (*f* -,-nen) thief. **d~isch** *adj* thieving; (*Freude*) malicious. **D~stahl** *m* -[e]s,∸e theft

Diele *f* -,-n floorboard; (*Flur*) hall

dien|en *vi* (*haben*) serve. **D~er** *m* -s,- servant; (*Verbeugung*) bow. **D~erin** *f* -,-nen maid, servant

Dienst *m* -[e]s,-e service; (*Arbeit*) work; (*Amtsausübung*) duty; **außer D~** off duty; (*pensioniert*) retired; **D~ haben** work; (*Soldat, Arzt:*) be on duty

Dienstag *m* Tuesday. **d~s** *adv* on Tuesdays

Dienst|bote *m* servant. **d~frei** *adj* **d~freier Tag** day off; **d~frei haben** have time off; (*Soldat, Arzt:*) be off duty. **D~grad** *m* rank. **D~leistung** *f* service. **d~lich** *adj* official ● *adv* **d~lich verreist** away on business. **D~mädchen** *nt* maid. **D~reise** *f* business trip. **D~stelle** *f* office. **D~stunden** *fpl* office hours

dies *inv pron* this. **d~bezüglich** *adj* relevant ● *adv* regarding this matter. **d~e(r,s)** *pron* this; (*pl*) these; (*substantivisch*) this [one]; (*pl*) these; **d~e Nacht** tonight; (*letzte*) last night

dieselbe *pron s.* derselbe

Dieselkraftstoff *m* diesel [oil]

diesmal *adv* this time

Dietrich *m* -s,-e skeleton key

Diffamation /-'tsjo:n/ *f* - defamation

Differential* /-'tsja:l/ *nt* -s,-e = Differenzial

Differenz f -,-en difference. **D~ial** nt -s,-e differential. **d~ieren** vt/i (haben) differentiate (**zwischen** + dat between)

digital adj digital

Digital- prefix digital. **D~kamera** f digital camera. **D~uhr** f digital clock/watch

digitalisieren vt digitize

Dikt|at nt -[e]s,-e dictation. **D~ator** m -s,-en dictator. **D~atur** f -,-en dictatorship. **d~ieren** vt/i (haben) dictate

Dill m -s dill

Dimension f -,-en dimension

Ding nt -[e]s,-e & ⊞ -er thing; **guter D~e sein** be cheerful; **vor allen D~en** above all

Dinosaurier /-iɐ/ m -s,- dinosaur

Diözese f -,-n diocese

Diphtherie f - diphtheria

Diplom nt -s,-e diploma; (Univ) degree

Diplomat m -en,-en diplomat

dir pron (dat of du) [to] you; (reflexive) yourself; **ein Freund von dir** a friend of yours

direkt adj direct ● adv directly; (wirklich) really. **D~ion** f - management; (Vorstand) board of directors. **D~or** m -s,-en, **D~orin** f -,-nen director; (Bank-, Theater-) manager; (Sch) head; (Gefängnis) governor. **D~übertragung** f live transmission

Dirig|ent m -en,-en (Mus) conductor. **d~ieren** vt direct; (Mus) conduct

Dirndl nt -s,- dirndl [dress]

Discounter m -s, - discount supermarket

Diskette f -,-n floppy disc

Disko f -,-s ⊞ disco. **D~thek** f -,-en discothèque

diskret adj discreet

Diskus m -,-se & **Disken** discus

Disku|ssion f -,-en discussion. **d~tieren** vt/i (haben) discuss

disponieren vi (haben) make arrangements; **d~ [können] über** (+ acc) have at one's disposal

Disqualifi|kation /-'tsio:n/ f disqualification. **d~zieren** vt disqualify

Dissertation /-'tsio:n/ f -,-en dissertation

Dissident m -en,-en dissident

Distanz f -,-en distance. **d~ieren (sich)** vr dissociate oneself (**von** from). **d~iert** adj aloof

Distel f -,-n thistle

Disziplin f -,-en discipline. **d~arisch** adj disciplinary. **d~iert** adj disciplined

dito adv ditto

diverse attrib a pl various

Divid|ende f -,-en dividend. **d~ieren** vt divide (**durch** by)

Division f -,-en division

DJH abbr (**Deutsche Jugendherberge**) [German] youth hostel

DM abbr (**Deutsche Mark**) DM

doch conj & adv but; (dennoch) yet; (trotzdem) after all; **wenn d~ ...** ! if only ... ! **nicht d~!** don't!

Docht m -[e]s,-e wick

Dock nt -s,-s dock. **d~en** vt/i (haben) dock

documenta This international contemporary arts exhibition takes place in Kassel every four to five years. It includes drama, music and film events. documenta 12 will take place in 2007. The events are subsidized by state and private sponsors.

Dogge f -,-n Great Dane

Dogm|a nt -s,-men dogma. **d~atisch** adj dogmatic

Dohle f -,-n jackdaw

Doktor m -s,-en doctor. **D~arbeit** f [doctoral] thesis

Dokument nt -[e]s,-e document. **D~arbericht** m documentary. **D~arfilm** m documentary film

Dolch m -[e]s,-e dagger

Dollar m -s,- dollar

dolmetsch|en vt/i (haben) interpret. **D~er(in)** m -s,- (f -,-nen) interpreter

Dom m -[e]s,-e cathedral

Domino nt -s,-s dominoes sg.
D~stein m domino

Dompfaff m -en,-en bullfinch

Donau f - Danube

Donner m -s thunder. d~n vi
(haben) thunder

Donnerstag m Thursday. d~s adv
on Thursdays

doof adj ⊞ stupid

Doppel nt -s,- duplicate; (Tennis)
doubles pl. D~bett nt double bed.
D~decker m -s,- doubledecker
[bus]. d~deutig adj ambiguous.
D~gänger m -s,- double. D~kinn
nt double chin. d~klicken vi (haben)
double-click (auf + acc on).
D~name m double-barrelled name.
D~punkt m (Gram) colon.
D~stecker m two-way adaptor.
d~t adj double; (Boden) false; in
d~ter Ausfertigung in duplicate;
die d~te Menge twice the amount
● adv doubly; (zweimal) twice; d~t
so viel twice as much. D~zimmer
nt double room

Dorf nt -[e]s,ˉer village. D~bewoh-
ner m villager

dörflich adj rural

Dorn m -[e]s,-en thorn. d~ig adj
thorny

Dorsch m -[e]s,-e cod

dort adv there. d~ig adj local

Dose f -,-n tin, can

dösen vi (haben) doze

Dosen|milch f evaporated milk.
D~öffner m tin or can opener.
D~pfand nt deposit (on beer cans
etc)

dosieren vt measure out

Dosis f -, Dosen dose

Dotter m & nt -s,- [egg] yolk

Dozent(in) m -en,-en (f -,-nen)
(Univ) lecturer

Dr. abbr (Doktor) Dr

Drache m -n,-n dragon. D~n m -s,-
kite. D~nfliegen nt hang-gliding

Draht m -[e]s,ˉe wire; auf D~ ⊞
on the ball. D~seilbahn f cable railway

Dram|a nt -s,-men drama. D~atik f
- drama. D~atiker m -s,- dramatist.
d~atisch adj dramatic

dran adv ⊞ = daran; gut/schlecht
d~ sein be well off/in a bad way;
ich bin d~ it's my turn

Drang m -[e]s urge; (Druck) pressure

dräng|eln vt/i (haben) push; (be-
drängen) pester. d~en vt push; (bedrängen) urge; sich d~en crowd
(um round) ● vi (haben) push; (eilen)
be urgent; d~en auf (+ acc) press
for

dran|halten† (sich) vr sep hurry.
d~kommen† vi sep (sein) have one's
turn

drauf adv ⊞ = darauf; d~ und dran
sein be on the point (etw zu tun of
doing sth). D~gänger m -s,- dare-
devil

draußen adv outside; (Im Freien) out
of doors

drechseln vt (Techn) turn

Dreck m -s dirt; (Morast) mud

Dreh m -s ⊞ knack; den D~ her-
aushaben have got the hang of it.
D~bank f lathe. D~bleistift m pro-
pelling pencil. D~buch nt screen-
play, script. d~en vt turn; (im Kreis)
rotate; (verschlingen) twist; roll (Zigarette); shoot (Film); lauter/leiser
d~en turn up/down; sich d~en
turn; (im Kreis) rotate; (schnell) spin;
(Wind:) change; sich d~en um revolve around; (sich handeln) be about
● vi (haben) turn; (Wind:) change; an
etw (dat) d~en turn sth. D~stuhl
m swivel chair. D~tür f revolving
door. D~ung f -,-en turn; (im Kreis)
rotation. D~zahl f number of re-
volutions

drei inv adj, D~ f -,-en three; (Sch)
≈ pass. D~eck nt -[e]s,-e triangle.
d~eckig adj triangular. d~erlei inv
adj three kinds of ● pron three
things. d~fach adj triple. d~mal
adv three times. D~rad nt tricycle

dreißig inv adj thirty. d~ste(r,s) adj
thirtieth

dreiviertel* inv adj = drei viertel, s. viertel. D~stunde f three-
quarters of an hour

dreizehn *inv adj* thirteen **d~te(r,s)** *adj* thirteenth

dreschen† *vt* thresh

dress|ieren *vt* train. **D~ur** *f* - training

dribbeln *vi* (*haben*) dribble

Drill *m* -[e]s (*Mil*) drill. **d~en** *vt* drill

Drillinge *mpl* triplets

dringlich *adj* urgent

Drink *m* -[s],-s [alcoholic] drink

drinnen *adv* inside

dritt *adv* zu **d~** in threes; **wir waren zu d~** there were three of us. **d~e(r,s)** *adj* third; **ein D~er** a third person. **d~el** *inv adj* third. **D~el** *nt* -s,- third. **d~ens** *adv* thirdly. **d~rangig** *adj* third-rate

Drog|e *f* -,-n drug. **D~enabhängige(r)** *m/f* drug addict. **D~erie** *f* -,-n chemist's shop. **D~ist** *m* -en,-en chemist

drohen *vi* (*haben*) threaten (**jdm** s.o.)

dröhnen *vi* (*haben*) resound; (*tönen*) boom

Drohung *f* -,-en threat

drollig *adj* funny; (*seltsam*) odd

Drops *m* -,- [fruit] drop

Drossel *f* -,-n thrush

drosseln *vt* (*Techn*) throttle; (*fig*) cut back

drüben *adv* over there

Druck[1] *m* -[e]s,⸚e pressure; **unter D~** **setzen** (*fig*) pressurize

Druck[2] *m* -[e]s,-e printing; (*Schrift, Reproduktion*) print. **D~buchstabe** *m* block letter

drucken *vt* print

drücken *vt/i* (*haben*) press; (*aus-*) squeeze; (*Schuh:*) pinch; (*umarmen*) hug; **Preise d~** force down prices; (*an Tür*) **d~** push; **sich d~** 🔲 make oneself scarce; **sich d~ vor** (+ *dat*) 🔲 shirk. **d~d** *adj* heavy; (*schwül*) oppressive

Drucker *m* -s,- printer

Druckerei *f* -,-en printing works

Druck|fehler *m* misprint. **D~knopf** *m* press-stud. **D~luft** *f* compressed air. **D~sache** *f* printed matter. **D~schrift** *f* type; (*Veröffentlichung*) publication; **in D~schrift** in block letters *pl*

Druckstelle *f* bruise

Drüse *f* -,-n (*Anat*) gland

Dschungel *m* -s,- jungle

du *pron* (*familiar address*) you; **auf Du und Du** on familiar terms

Dübel *m* -s,- plug

Dudelsack *m* bagpipes *pl*

Duell *nt* -s,-e duel

Duett *nt* -s,-e [vocal] duet

Duft *m* -[e]s,⸚e fragrance, scent; (*Aroma*) aroma. **d~en** *vi* (*haben*) smell (**nach** of)

dulden *vt* tolerate; (*erleiden*) suffer ● *vi* (*haben*) suffer

dumm *adj* stupid; (*unklug*) foolish; (🔲: *lästig*) awkward; **wie d~!** how annoying! **d~erweise** *adv* stupidly; (*leider*) unfortunately. **D~heit** *f* -,-en stupidity; (*Torheit*) foolishness; (*Handlung*) folly. **D~kopf** *m* 🔲 fool.

dumpf *adj* dull

Düne *f* -,-n dune

Dung *m* -s manure

Düng|emittel *nt* fertilizer. **d~en** *vt* fertilize. **D~er** *m* -s,- fertilizer

dunk|el *adj* dark; (*vage*) vague; (*fragwürdig*) shady; **d~les Bier** brown ale; **im D~eln** in the dark

Dunkel|heit *f* - darkness. **D~kammer** *f* dark-room. **d~n** *vi* (*haben*) get dark

dünn *adj* thin; (*Buch*) slim; (*spärlich*) sparse; (*schwach*) weak

Dunst *m* -es,⸚e mist, haze; (*Dampf*) vapour

dünsten *vt* steam

dunstig *adj* misty, hazy

Duo *nt* -s,-s [instrumental] duet

Duplikat *nt* -[e]s,-e duplicate

Dur *nt* - (*Mus*) major [key]

durch *prep* (+ *acc*) through; (*mittels*) by; **[geteilt] d~** (*Math*) divided by ● *adv* **die Nacht d~** throughout the night; **d~ und d~ nass** wet through

durch<u>au</u>s *adv* absolutely; **d~nicht** by no means

d<u>u</u>rchblättern *vt sep* leaf through

d<u>u</u>rchblicken *vi sep* (*haben*) look through; **d~ lassen** (*fig*) hint at

D<u>u</u>rchblutung *f* circulation

durchb<u>o</u>hren *vt insep* pierce

durchbr<u>e</u>chen¹† *vt/i sep* (*haben*) break [in two]

durchbr<u>e</u>chen²† *vt insep* break through; break (*Schallmauer*)

durchbr<u>e</u>nnen† *vi sep* (*sein*) burn through; (*Sicherung:*) blow

D<u>u</u>rchbruch *m* breakthrough

d<u>u</u>rchdrehen *v sep* ● *vt* mince ● *vi* (*haben/sein*) 🗊 go crazy

durchdr<u>i</u>ngen† *vi sep* (*sein*) penetrate; (*sich durchsetzen*) get one's way. **d~d** *adj* penetrating; (*Schrei*) piercing

durcheinander *adv* in a muddle; (*Person*) confused; **d~ bringen** muddle [up]; confuse (*Person*); **d~ geraten** get mixed up; **d~ reden** all talk at once. **D~** *nt* **-s** muddle

d<u>u</u>rchfahren *vi sep* (*sein*) drive through; (*Zug:*) go through

D<u>u</u>rchfahrt *f* journey/drive through; **auf der D~** passing through; 'D~ verboten' 'no thoroughfare'

D<u>u</u>rchfall *m* diarrhoea. **d~en/**vi sep (*sein*) fall through; (🗊: *versagen*) flop; (*bei Prüfung*) fail

D<u>u</u>rchfuhr *f* - (*Comm*) transit

d<u>u</u>rchführ|bar *adj* feasible. **d~en** *vt sep* carry out

D<u>u</u>rchgang *m* passage; (*Sport*) round; 'D~ verboten' 'no entry'. **D~sverkehr** *m* through traffic

d<u>u</u>rchgeben† *vt sep* pass through; (*übermitteln*) transmit; (*Radio, TV*) broadcast

d<u>u</u>rchgebraten *adj* gut **d~** well done

d<u>u</u>rchgehen† *vi sep* (*sein*) go through; (*davonlaufen*) run away; (*Pferd:*) bolt; **jdm etw d~ lassen** let s.o. get away with sth. **d~d** *adj* continuous; **d~d geöffnet** open all day; **d~der Zug** through train

d<u>u</u>rchgreifen† *vi sep* (*haben*) reach through; (*vorgehen*) take drastic action. **d~d** *adj* drastic

d<u>u</u>rchhalte|n† *v sep* (*fig*) ● *vi* (*haben*) hold out ● *vt* keep up. **D~vermögen** *nt* stamina

durchk<u>o</u>mmen† *vi sep* (*sein*) come through; (*gelangen, am Telefon*) get through

d<u>u</u>rchlassen† *vt sep* let through

d<u>u</u>rchlässig *adj* permeable; (*undicht*) leaky

D<u>u</u>rchlauferhitzer *m* **-s,-** geyser

d<u>u</u>rchlesen† *vt sep* read through

durchl<u>eu</u>chten *vt insep* X-ray

durchl<u>ö</u>chert *adj* riddled with holes

d<u>u</u>rchmachen *vt sep* go through; (*erleiden*) undergo

D<u>u</u>rchmesser *m* **-s,-** diameter

durchn<u>ä</u>sst *adj* wet through

d<u>u</u>rchnehmen† *vt sep* (*Sch*) do

d<u>u</u>rchnummeriert *adj* numbered consecutively

d<u>u</u>rchpausen *vt sep* trace

durchqu<u>e</u>ren *vt insep* cross

D<u>u</u>rchreiche *f* **-,-n** hatch

D<u>u</u>rchreise *f* journey through; **auf der D~** passing through. **d~n** *vi sep* (*sein*) pass through

durchr<u>ei</u>ßen† *vt/i sep* (*sein*) tear

D<u>u</u>rchsage *f* **-, n** announcement. **d~n** *vt sep* announce

D<u>u</u>rchschlag *m* carbon copy; (*Culin*) colander. **d~en†** *v sep* ● *vt* (*Culin*) rub through a sieve; **sich d~en** (*fig*) struggle through ● *vi* (*sein*) (*Sicherung:*) blow

durchschl<u>a</u>gend *adj* (*fig*) effective; (*Erfolg*) resounding

durchschn<u>ei</u>den† *vt sep* cut

D<u>u</u>rchschnitt *m* average; **im D~** on average. **d~lich** *adj* average ● *adv* on average. **D~s-** *prefix* average

D<u>u</u>rchschrift *f* carbon copy

d<u>u</u>rchsehen† *v sep* ● *vi* (*haben*) see through ● *vt* look through

d<u>u</u>rchseihen *vt sep* strain

d

durchsetzen vt sep force through; **sich d~** assert oneself; (*Mode:*) catch on

Durchsicht f check

durchsichtig adj transparent

durchsickern vi sep (sein) seep through; (*Neuigkeit:*) leak out

durchstehen† vt sep (*fig*) come through

durchstreichen† vt sep cross out

durchsuch|en vt insep search. **D~ung** f -,-en search

durchwachsen adj (*Speck*) streaky; (🔲: *gemischt*) mixed

durchwählen vi sep (haben) (*Teleph*) dial direct

durchweg adv without exception

durchwühlen vt insep rummage through; ransack (*Haus*)

Durchzug m through draught

dürfen†

- *transitive & auxiliary verb*
- ····▶ (*Erlaubnis haben zu*) be allowed; may, can. **etw [tun] dürfen** be allowed to do sth. **darf ich das tun?** may or can I do that? **nein, das darfst du nicht** no you may not or cannot [do that]. **er sagte mir, ich dürfte sofort gehen** he told me I could go at once. **hier darf man nicht rauchen** smoking is prohibited here. **sie darf/durfte es nicht sehen** she must not/was not allowed to see it.
- ····▶ (*in Höflichkeitsformeln*) may. **darf ich rauchen?** may I smoke? **darf/dürfte ich um diesen Tanz bitten?** may/might I have the pleasure of this dance?
- ····▶ **dürfte** (*sollte*) should, ought. **jetzt dürften sie dort angekommen sein** they should or ought to be there by now. **das dürfte nicht allzu schwer sein** that should not be too difficult. **ich hätte es nicht tun/sagen dürfen** I ought not to have done/said it
- *intransitive verb*
- ····▶ (*irgendwohin gehen dürfen*) be allowed to go; may go; can go. **darf ich nach Hause?** may or can I go home? **sie durfte nicht ins Theater** she was not allowed to go the theatre

dürftig adj poor; (*Mahlzeit*) scanty

dürr adj dry; (*Boden*) arid; (*mager*) skinny. **D~e** f -,-n drought

Durst m -[e]s thirst; **D~ haben** be thirsty. **d~ig** adj thirsty

Dusche f -,-n shower. **d~n** vi/r (haben) [sich] **d~n** have a shower

Düse f -,-n nozzle. **D~nflugzeug** nt jet

Dutzend nt -s,-e dozen. **d~weise** adv by the dozen

duzen vt jdn **d~** call s.o. 'du'

DVD f -, -s DVD

Dynam|ik f - dynamics sg; (*fig*) dynamism. **d~isch** adj dynamic; (*Rente*) index-linked

Dynamit nt -es dynamite

Dynamo m -s,-s dynamo

Dynastie f -,-n dynasty

D-Zug /'de:-/ m express [train]

Ee

Ebbe f -,-n low tide

eben adj level; (*glatt*) smooth; **zu e~er Erde** on the ground floor
- adv just; (*genau*) exactly; **e~ noch** only just; (*gerade vorhin*) just now; **das ist es e~!** that's just it! **E~bild** nt image

Ebene f -,-n (*Geog*) plain; (*Geometry*) plane; (*fig: Niveau*) level

eben|falls adv also; **danke, e~falls** thank you, [the] same to you. **E~holz** nt ebony. **e~so** adv just the same; (*ebenso sehr*) just as much; **e~so gut** just as good; adv just as well; **e~so sehr** just as much; **e~so viel** just as much/many; **e~so**

wenig just as little/few; (*noch*) no more

Eber *m* -s,- boar

ebnen *vt* level; (*fig*) smooth

Echo *nt* -s,-s echo

echt *adj* genuine, real; authentic ● *adv* Ⓘ really; typically. **E~heit** *f* - authenticity

Eck|ball *m* (*Sport*) corner. **E~e** *f* -,-n corner; **um die E~e bringen** Ⓘ bump off. **e~ig** *adj* angular; (*Klammern*) square; (*unbeholfen*) awkward. **E~zahn** *m* canine tooth

Ecu, ECU /eˈkyː/ *m* -[s],-[s] ecu

edel *adj* noble; (*wertvoll*) precious; (*fein*) fine. **e~mütig** *adj* magnanimous. **E~stahl** *m* stainless steel. **E~stein** *m* precious stone

Efeu *m* -s ivy

Effekt *m* -[e]s,-e effect. **E~en** *pl* securities. **e~iv** *adj* actual; (*wirksam*) effective

EG *f* - *abbr* (**Europäische Gemeinschaft**) EC

egal *adj* **das ist mir e~** Ⓘ it's all the same to me ● *adv* **e~ wie/wo** no matter how/where

Egge *f* -,-n harrow

Ego|ismus *m* - selfishness. **E~ist(in)** *m* -en,-en (*f* -,-nen) egoist. **e~istisch** *adj* selfish

eh *adv* (*Aust*, Ⓘ) anyway

ehe *conj* before; **ehe nicht** until

Ehe *f* -,-n marriage. **E~bett** *nt* double bed. **E~bruch** *m* adultery. **E~frau** *f* wife. **e~lich** *adj* marital; (*Recht*) conjugal; (*Kind*) legitimate

ehemalig *adj* former. **e~s** *adv* formerly

Ehe|mann *m* (*pl* -männer) husband. **E~paar** *nt* married couple

eher *adv* earlier, sooner; (*lieber, vielmehr*) rather; (*mehr*) more

Ehering *m* wedding ring

Ehr|e *f* -,-n honour. **E~en** *vt* honour. **e~enamtlich** *adj* honorary ● *adv* in an honorary capacity. **E~engast** *m* guest of honour. **e~enhaft** a honourable. **E~ensache** *f* point of honour. **E~enwort** *nt* word of honour.

e~erbietig *adj* deferential. **E~furcht** *f* reverence; (*Scheu*) awe. **e~fürchtig** *adj* reverent. **E~gefühl** *nt* sense of honour. **E~geiz** *m* ambition. **e~geizig** *adj* ambitious. **e~lich** *adj* honest; **e~lich gesagt** to be honest. **E~lichkeit** *f* - honesty. **e~los** *adj* dishonourable. **e~würdig** *adj* venerable; (*als Anrede*) Reverend

Ei *nt* -[e]s,-er egg

Eibe *f* -,-n yew

Eiche *f* -,-n oak. **E~l** *f* -,-n acorn

eichen *vt* standardize

Eichhörnchen *nt* -s,- squirrel

Eid *m* -[e]s,-e oath

Eidechse *f* -,-n lizard

eidlich *adj* sworn ● *adv* on oath

Eidotter *m* & *nt* egg yolk

Eier|becher *m* egg-cup. **E~kuchen** *m* pancake; (*Omelett*) omelette. **E~schale** *f* eggshell. **E~schnee** *m* beaten egg-white. **E~stock** *m* ovary

Eifer *m* -s eagerness. **E~sucht** *f* jealousy. **e~süchtig** *adj* jealous

eifrig *adj* eager

Eigelb *nt* -[e]s,-e [egg] yolk

eigen *adj* own; (*typisch*) characteristic (*dat* of); (*seltsam*) odd; (*genau*) particular. **E~art** *f* peculiarity. **e~artig** *adj* peculiar. **e~händig** *adj* personal; (*Unterschrift*) own. **E~heit** *f* -,-en peculiarity. **E~name** *m* proper name. **e~nützig** *adj* selfish. **e~s** *adv* specially. **E~schaft** *f* -,-en quality; (*Phys*) property; (*Merkmal*) characteristic; (*Funktion*) capacity. **E~schaftswort** *nt* (*pl* -wörter) adjective. **E~sinn** *m* obstinacy. **e~sinnig** *adj* obstinate

eigentlich *adj* actual, real; (*wahr*) true ● *adv* actually, really; (*streng genommen*) strictly speaking

Eigen|tor *nt* own goal. **E~tum** *nt* -s property. **E~tümer(in)** *m* -s,- (*f* -,-nen) owner. **E~tumswohnung** *f* freehold flat. **e~willig** *adj* self-willed; (*Stil*) highly individual

eignen (sich) *vr* be suitable

Eil|brief *m* express letter. **E~e** *f* -

hurry; **E~e haben** be in a hurry;
(*Sache:*) be urgent. **e~en** *vi* (*sein*)
hurry ● (*haben*) (*drängen*) be urgent.
e~ig *adj* hurried; (*dringend*) urgent;
es e~ig haben be in a hurry.
E~zug *m* semi-fast train

Eimer *m* **-s,-** bucket; (*Abfall-*) bin

ein

● *indefinite article*
····➤ a, (*vor Vokal*) an. **ein Kleid/
Apfel/Hotel/Mensch** a dress/an
apple/a[n] hotel/a human being.
so ein such a. **was für ein ...**
(*Frage*) what kind of a ... ? (*Ausruf*) what a ... !
● *adjective*
····➤ (*Ziffer*) one. **eine Minute** one
minute. **wir haben nur eine
Stunde** we only have an/(*betont*)
one hour. **eines Tages/Abends**
one day/evening
····➤ (*derselbe*) the same. **einer
Meinung sein** be of the same
opinion. **mit jdm in einem Zimmer schlafen** sleep in the same
room as s.o.

einander *pron* one another
Einäscherung *f* -,-en cremation
einatmen *vt/i sep* (*haben*) inhale,
breathe in
Einbahnstraße *f* one-way street
einbalsamieren *vt sep* embalm
Einband *m* binding
Einbau *m* installation; (*Montage*) fitting. **e~en** *vt sep* install; (*montieren*)
fit. **E~küche** *f* fitted kitchen
einbegriffen *pred adj* included
Einberufung *f* call-up
Einbettzimmer *nt* single room
einbeulen *vt sep* dent
einbeziehen† *vt sep* **[mit] e~** include; (*berücksichtigen*) take into account
einbiegen† *vi sep* (*sein*) turn
einbild|en *vt sep* **sich** (*dat*) **etw
e~en** imagine sth; **sich** (*dat*) **viel
e~en** be conceited. **E~ung** *f* imagination; (*Dünkel*) conceit. **E~ungskraft** *f* imagination

einblenden *vt sep* fade in
Einblick *m* insight
einbrech|en† *vi sep* (*haben/sein*)
break in; **bei uns ist eingebrochen
worden** we have been burgled.
E~er *m* burglar
einbringen† *vt sep* get in; bring in
(*Geld*)
Einbruch *m* burglary; **bei E~ der
Nacht** at nightfall
einbürger|n *vt sep* naturalize.
E~ung *f* - naturalization
einchecken /-tʃɛkən/ *vt/i sep*
(*haben*) check in
eindecken (sich) *vr sep* stock up
eindeutig *adj* unambiguous; (*deutlich*) clear
eindicken *vt sep* (*Culin*) thicken
eindringen† *vi sep* (*sein*) **e~en in**
(+ *acc*) penetrate into; (*mit Gewalt*)
force one's/(*Wasser:*) its way into;
(*Mil*) invade
Eindruck *m* impression
eindrücken *vt sep* crush
eindrucksvoll *adj* impressive
ein|e(r,s) *pron* one; (*jemand*) someone; (*man*) one, you
einebnen *vt sep* level
eineiig *adj* (*Zwillinge*) identical
eineinhalb *inv adj* one and a half;
e~ Stunden an hour and a half
Einelternfamilie *f* one-parent
family
einengen *vt sep* restrict
Einer *m* **-s,-** (*Math*) unit. **e~** *pron s.*
eine(r,s). e~lei *inv adj* ● *attrib adj*
one kind of; (*eintönig, einheitlich*) the
same ● *pred adj* 🛈 immaterial; **es ist
mir e~lei** it's all the same to me.
e~seits *adv* on the one hand
einfach *adj* simple; (*Essen*) plain;
(*Faden, Fahrt*) single; **e~er Soldat**
private. **E~heit** *f* - simplicity
einfädeln *vt sep* thread; (*fig; arrangieren*) arrange
einfahr|en† *v sep* ● *vi* (*sein*) arrive;
(*Zug:*) pull in ● *vt* (*Auto*) run in. **E~t**
f arrival; (*Eingang*) entrance, way in;
(*Auffahrt*) drive; (*Autobahn-*) access
road; **keine E~t** no entry

Einfall *m* idea; (*Mil*) invasion. **e~en**† *vi sep* (*sein*) collapse; (*eindringen*) invade; **jdm e~en** occur to s.o.; **was fällt ihm ein!** what does he think he is doing!

Einfalt *f* - naïvety

einfarbig *adj* of one colour; (*Stoff, Kleid*) plain

einfass|en *vt sep* edge; set (*Edelstein*). **E~ung** *f* border, edging

einfetten *vt sep* grease

Einfluss *m* influence. **e~reich** *adj* influential

einförmig *adj* monotonous. **E~keit** *f* - monotony

einfrieren† *vt/i sep* (*sein*) freeze

einfügen *vt sep* insert; (*einschieben*) interpolate; **sich e~** fit in

einfühlsam *adj* sensitive

Einfuhr *f* -,-en import

einführ|en *vt sep* introduce; (*einstecken*) insert; (*einweisen*) initiate; (*Comm*) import. **e~end** *adj* introductory. **E~ung** *f* introduction; (*Einweisung*) initiation

Eingabe *f* petition; (*Computer*) input

Eingang *m* entrance, way in; (*Ankunft*) arrival

eingebaut *adj* built-in; (*Schrank*) fitted

eingeben† *vt sep* hand in; (*Computer*) feed in

eingebildet *adj* imaginary; (*überheblich*) conceited

Eingeborene(r) *m/f* native

eingehen† *v sep* ●*vi* (*sein*) come in; (*ankommen*) arrive; (*einlaufen*) shrink; (*sterben*) die; (*Zeitung, Firma:*) fold; **auf etw** (*acc*) **e~** go into sth; (*annehmen*) agree to sth ●*vt* enter into; contract (*Ehe*); make (*Wette*); take (*Risiko*)

eingemacht *adj* (*Culin*) bottled

eingenommen *pred adj* (*fig*) taken (**von** with); prejudiced (**gegen** against)

eingeschneit *adj* snowbound

eingeschrieben *adj* registered

Einge|ständnis *nt* admission. **e~stehen**† *vt sep* admit

eingetragen *adj* registered

Eingeweide *pl* bowels, entrails

eingewöhnen (sich) *vr sep* settle in

eingießen† *vt sep* pour in; (*einschenken*) pour

eingleisig *adj* single-track

einglieder|n *vt sep* integrate. **E~ung** *f* integration

eingravieren *vt sep* engrave

eingreifen† *vi sep* (*haben*) intervene. **E~** *nt* -s intervention

Eingriff *m* intervention; (*Med*) operation

einhaken *vt/r sep* **jdn e~** *od* **sich bei jdm e~** take someone's arm

einhalten† *v sep* ●*vt* keep; (*befolgen*) observe ●*vi* (*haben*) stop

einhändigen *vt sep* hand in

einhängen *vt sep* hang; put down (*Hörer*)

einheimisch *adj* local; (*eines Landes*) native; (*Comm*) homeproduced. **E~e(r)** *m/f* local, native

Einheit *f* -,-en unity; (*Maß-, Mil*) unit. **e~lich** *adj* uniform. **E~spreis** *m* standard price; (*Fahrpreis*) flat fare

einholen *vt sep* catch up with; (*aufholen*) make up for; (*erbitten*) seek; (*einkaufen*) buy

einhüllen *vt sep* wrap

einhundert *inv adj* one hundred

einig *adj* united; [**sich** (*dat*)] **e~ sein** be in agreement

einig|e(r,s) *pron* some; (*ziemlich viel*) quite a lot of; (*substantivisch*) **e~e** *pl* some; (*mehrere*) several; (*ziemlich viele*) quite a lot; **e~es** *sg* some things; **vor e~er Zeit** some time ago

einigen *vt* unite; unify (*Land*); **sich e~** come to an agreement

einigermaßen *adv* to some extent; (*ziemlich*) fairly; (*ziemlich gut*) fairly well

Einigkeit *f* - unity; (*Übereinstimmung*) agreement

einjährig *adj* one-year-old; **e~e Pflanze** annual

einkalkulieren vt sep take into account

einkassieren vt sep collect

Einkauf m purchase; (Einkaufen) shopping; **Einkäufe machen** do some shopping. **e~en** vt sep buy; **e~en gehen** go shopping. **E~swagen** m shopping trolley

einklammern vt sep bracket

Einklang m harmony; **in E~ stehen** be in accord (**mit** with)

einkleben vt sep stick in

einkleiden vt sep fit out

einklemmen vt sep clamp

einkochen v sep ● vi (sein) boil down ● vt preserve, bottle

Einkommen nt -s income. **E~[s]steuer** f income tax

Einkünfte pl income sg; (Einnahmen) revenue sg

einlad|en† vt sep load; (auffordern) invite; (bezahlen für) treat. **E~ung** f invitation

Einlage f enclosure; (Schuh-) arch support; (Programm-) interlude; (Comm) investment; (Bank-) deposit; **Suppe mit E~** soup with noodles/dumplings

Ein|lass m -es admittance. **e~lassen†** vt sep let in; run (Bad, Wasser); **sich auf etw** (acc) **e~lassen** get involved in sth

einleben (sich) vr sep settle in

Einlege|arbeit f inlaid work. **e~n** vt sep put in; lay in (Vorrat); lodge (Protest); (einfügen) insert; (Auto) engage (Gang); (Culin) pickle; (marinieren) marinade; **eine Pause e~n** have a break. **E~sohle** f insole

einleit|en vt sep initiate; (eröffnen) begin. **E~ung** f introduction

einleuchten vi sep (haben) be clear (dat to). **e~d** adj convincing

einliefer|n vt sep take (**ins Krankenhaus** to hospital). **E~ung** f admission

einlösen vt sep cash (Scheck); redeem (Pfand); (fig) keep

einmachen vt sep preserve

einmal adv once; (eines Tages) one or some day; **noch/schon e~** again/before; **noch e~ so teuer** twice as expensive; **auf e~** at the same time; (plötzlich) suddenly; **nicht e~** not even. **E~eins** nt - [multiplication] tables pl. **e~ig** adj (einzigartig) unique; (🄸: großartig) fantastic

einmarschieren vi sep (sein) march in

einmisch|en (sich) vr sep interfere. **E~ung** f interference

Einnahme f -,-n taking; (Mil) capture; **E~n** pl income sg; (Einkünfte) revenue sg; (Comm) receipts; (eines Ladens) takings

einnehmen† vt sep take; have (Mahlzeit); (Mil) capture; take up (Platz)

einordnen vt sep put in its proper place; (klassifizieren) classify; **sich e~** fit in; (Auto) get in lane

einpacken vt sep pack

einparken vt sep park

einpflanzen vt sep plant; implant (Organ)

einplanen vt sep allow for

einprägen vt sep impress (**jdm** [up]on s.o.); **sich** (dat) **etw e~en** memorize sth

einrahmen vt sep frame

einrasten vi sep (sein) engage

einräumen vt sep put away; (zugeben) admit; (zugestehen) grant

einrechnen vt sep include

einreden v sep ● vt **jdm/sich** (dat) **etw e~** persuade s.o./oneself of sth

einreiben† vt sep rub (**mit** with)

einreichen vt sep submit; **die Scheidung e~** file for divorce

Einreih|er m -s,- single-breasted suit. **e~ig** adj single-breasted

Einreise f entry. **e~n** vi sep (sein) enter (**nach Irland** Ireland)

einrenken vt sep (Med) set

einricht|en vt sep fit out; (möblieren) furnish; (anordnen) arrange; (Med) set (Bruch); (eröffnen) set up; **sich e~en** furnish one's home; (sich einschränken) economize; (sich vorbereiten) prepare (**auf** + acc for).

E~ung f furnishing; (*Möbel*) furnishings pl; (*Techn*) equipment; (*Vorrichtung*) device; (*Eröffnung*) setting up; (*Institution*) institution; (*Gewohnheit*) practice

einrosten vi sep (*sein*) rust; (*fig*) get rusty

eins inv adj & pron one; **noch e~** one other thing; **mir ist alles e~** 🔲 it's all the same to me. **E~** f -,-en one; (*Sch*) ≈ A

einsam adj lonely; (*allein*) solitary; (*abgelegen*) isolated. **E~keit** f - loneliness; solitude; isolation

einsammeln vt sep collect

Einsatz m use; (*Mil*) mission; (*Wett-*) stake; (*E~teil*) insert; **im E~** in action

einschalt|en vt sep switch on; (*einschieben*) interpolate; (*fig: beteiligen*) call in; **sich e~en** (*fig*) intervene. **E~quote** f (*TV*) viewing figures pl; ≈ ratings pl

einschätzen vt sep assess; (*bewerten*) rate

einschenken vt sep pour

einscheren vi sep (*sein*) pull in

einschicken vt sep send in

einschieben† vt sep push in; (*einfügen*) insert

einschiff|en (sich) vr sep embark. **E~ung** f - embarkation

einschlafen† vi sep (*sein*) go to sleep; (*aufhören*) peter out

einschläfern vt sep lull to sleep; (*betäuben*) put out; (*töten*) put to sleep. **e~d** adj soporific

Einschlag m impact. **e~en**† v sep ● vt knock in; (*zerschlagen*) smash; (*drehen*) turn; take (*Weg*); take up (*Laufbahn*) ● vi (*haben*) hit/(*Blitz:*) strike (**in etw** acc sth); (*Erfolg haben*) be a hit

einschleusen vt sep infiltrate

einschließ|en† vt sep lock in; (*umgeben*) enclose; (*einkreisen*) surround; (*einbeziehen*) include; **sich e~en** lock oneself in; **Bedienung eingeschlossen** service included. **e~lich** adv inclusive ● prep (+ gen) including

einschneiden† vt/i sep (*haben*) [**in**] **etw** (*acc*) **e~** cut into sth. **e~d** adj (*fig*) drastic

Einschnitt m cut; (*Med*) incision; (*Lücke*) gap; (*fig*) decisive event

einschränk|en vt sep restrict; (*reduzieren*) cut back; **sich e~en** economize. **E~ung** f -,-en restriction; (*Reduzierung*) reduction; (*Vorbehalt*) reservation

Einschreib|[e]brief m registered letter. **e~en**† vt sep enter; register (*Brief*); **sich e~en** put one's name down; (*sich anmelden*) enrol. **E~en** nt registered letter/packet; **als** od **per E~en** by registered post

einschüchtern vt sep intimidate

Einsegnung f -,-en confirmation

einsehen† vt sep inspect; (*lesen*) consult; (*begreifen*) see

einseitig adj one-sided; (*Pol*) unilateral ● adv on one side; (*fig*) one-sidedly; (*Pol*) unilaterally

einsenden† vt sep send in

einsetzen v sep ● vt put in; (*einfügen*) insert; (*verwenden*) use; put on (*Zug*); call out (*Truppen*); (*Mil*) deploy; (*ernennen*) appoint; (*wetten*) stake; (*riskieren*) risk ● vi (*haben*) start; (*Winter, Regen:*) set in

Einsicht f insight; (*Verständnis*) understanding; (*Vernunft*) reason. **e~ig** adj understanding

Einsiedler m hermit

einsinken† vi sep (*sein*) sink in

einspannen vt sep harness; **jdn e~** 🔲 rope s.o. in

einsparen vt sep save

einsperren vt sep shut/(*im Gefängnis*) lock up

einsprachig adj monolingual

einspritzen vt sep inject

Einspruch m objection; **E~ erheben** object; (*Jur*) appeal

einspurig adj single-track; (*Auto*) single-lane

einst adv once; (*Zukunft*) one day

Einstand m (*Tennis*) deuce

einstecken vt sep put in; post (*Brief*); (*Electr*) plug in; (🔲*: behalten*) pocket; (⊞: *hinnehmen*) take; suffer (*Niederlage*); **etw e~** put sth in one's pocket

einsteigen† *vi sep* (*sein*) get in; (*in Bus/Zug*) get on

einstell|en *vt sep* put in; (*anstellen*) employ; (*aufhören*) stop; (*regulieren*) adjust, set; (*Optik*) focus; tune (*Motor, Zündung*); tune to (*Sender*); **sich e~en** turn up; (*Schwierigkeiten:*) arise; **sich e~en auf** (+ *acc*) adjust to; (*sich vorbereiten*) prepare for. **E~ung** *f* employment; (*Regulierung*) adjustment; (*TV, Auto*) tuning; (*Haltung*) attitude

einstig *adj* former

einstimmig *adj* unanimous. **E~keit** *f* - unanimity

einstöckig *adj* single-storey

einstudieren *vt sep* rehearse

einstufen *vt sep* classify

Ein|sturz *m* collapse. **e~stürzen** *vi sep* (*sein*) collapse

einstweilen *adv* for the time being; (*inzwischen*) meanwhile

eintasten *vt sep* key in

eintauchen *vt/i sep* (*sein*) dip in

eintauschen *vt sep* exchange

eintausend *inv adj* one thousand

einteil|en *vt sep* divide (**in** + *acc* into); (*Biology*) classify; **sich** (*dat*) **seine Zeit gut e~en** organize one's time well. **e~ig** *adj* one-piece. **E~ung** *f* division

eintönig *adj* monotonous. **E~keit** *f* - monotony

Eintopf *m*, **E~gericht** *nt* stew

Eintracht *f* - harmony

Eintrag *m* -[e]s,=e entry. **e~en**† *vt sep* enter; (*Admin*) register; **sich e~en** put one's name down

einträglich *adj* profitable

Eintragung *f* -,-en registration

eintreffen† *vi sep* (*sein*) arrive; (*fig*) come true

eintreiben† *vt sep* drive in; (*einziehen*) collect

eintreten† *v sep* ● *vi* (*sein*) enter; (*geschehen*) occur; **in einen Klub e~**

join a club; **e~ für** (*fig*) stand up for ● *vt* kick in

Eintritt *m* entrance; (*zu Veranstaltung*) admission; (*Beitritt*) joining; (*Beginn*) beginning. **E~skarte** *f* [admission] ticket

einüben *vt sep* practise

einundachtzig *inv adj* eighty-one

Einvernehmen *nt* -s understanding; (*Übereinstimmung*) agreement

einverstanden *adj* **e~ sein** agree

Einverständnis *nt* agreement; (*Zustimmung*) consent

Einwand *m* -[e]s,=e objection

Einwander|er *m* immigrant. **e~n** *vi sep* (*sein*) immigrate. **E~ung** *f* immigration

einwandfrei *adj* perfect

einwärts *adv* inwards

einwechseln *vt sep* change

einwecken *vt sep* preserve, bottle

Einweg- *prefix* non-returnable

einweichen *vt sep* soak

einweih|en *vt sep* inaugurate; (*Relig*) consecrate; (*einführen*) initiate; **in ein Geheimnis e~en** let into a secret. **E~ung** *f* -,-en inauguration; consecration; initiation

einweisen† *vt sep* direct; (*einführen*) initiate; **ins Krankenhaus e~** send to hospital

einwerfen† *vt sep* insert; post (*Brief*); (*Sport*) throw in

einwickeln *vt sep* wrap [up]

einwillig|en *vi sep* (*haben*) consent, agree (**in** + *acc* to). **E~ung** *f* - consent

Einwohner|(in) *m* -s,- (*f* -,-nen) inhabitant. **E~zahl** *f* population

Einwurf *m* interjection; (*Einwand*) objection; (*Sport*) throw-in; (*Münz-*) slot

Einzahl *f* (*Gram*) singular

einzahl|en *vt sep* pay in. **E~ung** *f* payment; (*Einlage*) deposit

einzäunen *vt sep* fence in

Einzel *nt* -s,- (*Tennis*) singles *pl*. **E~bett** *nt* single bed. **E~gänger** *m* -s,- loner. **E~haft** *f* solitary confine-

ment. **E~handel** m retail trade.
E~händler m retailer. **E~haus** nt
detached house. **E~heit** f -,-en detail. **E~karte** f single ticket. **E~kind**
nt only child

einzeln adj single; (individuell) individual; (gesondert) separate; odd
(Handschuh, Socken); **e~e Fälle** some
cases. **E~e(r,s)** pron der/die **E~e**
the individual; **E~e** pl some; **im
E~en** in detail

Einzel|teil nt [component] part.
E~zimmer nt single room

einziehen† v sep ● vt pull in; draw
in (Atem, Krallen); (Zool, Techn) retract; indent (Zeile); (aus dem Verkehr
ziehen) withdraw; (beschlagnahmen)
confiscate; (eintreiben) collect; make
(Erkundigungen); (Mil) call up ● vi
(sein) enter; (umziehen) move in; (eindringen) penetrate

einzig adj only; (einmalig) unique;
eine e~e Frage a a single question
● adv only; **e~ und allein** solely.
E~e(r,s) pron der/die/das **E~e** the
only one; **ein/kein E~er** a/not a single one; **das E~e, was mich stört**
the only thing that bothers me

Eis nt -es ice; (Speise-) ice-cream; **Eis
am Stiel** ice lolly; **Eis laufen** skate.
E~bahn f ice rink. **E~bär** m polar
bear. **E~becher** m ice-cream sun-
dae. **E~berg** m iceberg. **E~diele** f
ice-cream parlour

Eisen nt -s,- iron. **E~bahn** f railway

eisern adj iron; (fest) resolute; **e~er
Vorhang** (Theat) safety curtain; (Pol)
Iron Curtain

Eis|fach nt freezer compartment.
e~gekühlt adj chilled. **e~ig** adj icy.
E~kaffee m iced coffee. **E~lauf** m
skating. **E~läufer(in)** m(f) skater.
E~pickel m ice-axe. **E~scholle** f
ice-floe. **E~vogel** m kingfisher.
E~würfel m icecube. **E~zapfen** m
icicle. **E~zeit** f ice age

eitel adj vain; (rein) pure. **E~keit** f -
vanity

Eiter m -s pus. **e~n** vi (haben) discharge pus

Eiweiß nt -es,-e egg-white

Ekel m -s disgust; (Widerwille) revulsion. **e~haft** adj nauseating; (widerlich) repulsive. **e~n** vt/i (haben) **mich
od mir e~t [es] davor** it makes me
feel sick ● vr **sich e~n vor** (+ dat)
find repulsive

eklig adj disgusting, repulsive

Ekzem nt -s,-e eczema

elastisch adj elastic; (federnd)
springy; (fig) flexible

Elch m -[e]s,-e elk

Elefant m -en,-en elephant

elegan|t adj elegant. **E~z** f - ele-
gance

Elektri|ker m -s,- electrician.
e~sch adj electric

Elektrizität f - electricity. **E~s-
werk** nt power station

Elektr|oartikel mpl electrical ap-
pliances. **E~ode** f -,-n electrode.
E~onik f - electronics sg. **e~onisch**
adj electronic

Elend nt -s misery; (Armut) poverty.
e~ adj miserable; (krank) poorly;
(gemein) contemptible. **E~sviertel**
nt slum

elf inv adj eleven, **E~** f -,-en eleven

Elfe f -,-n fairy

Elfenbein nt ivory

Elfmeter m (Fußball) penalty

elfte(r,s) adj eleventh

Ell[en]bogen m elbow

Ellip|se f -,-n ellipse. **e~tisch** adj el-
liptical

Elsass nt - Alsace

elsässisch adj Alsatian

Elster f -,-n magpie

elter|lich adj parental. **E~n** pl par-
ents. **e~nlos** adj orphaned. **E~nteil**
m parent

Email /e'mai/ nt -s,-s, **E~le** f -,-n
enamel

E-Mail /'i:me:l/ f -,-s e-mail; e-mail
message

Emanzi|pation /-'tsio:n/ f - eman-
cipation. **e~piert** adj emancipated

Embargo nt -s,-s embargo

Embryo m -s,-s embryo

Emigr|ant(in) m -en,-en (f -,-nen)

emigrant. **E~ation** f - emigration.
e~ieren vi (sein) emigrate

Empfang m -[e]s, ⸚e reception; (*Erhalt*) receipt; **in E~ nehmen** receive; (*annehmen*) accept. **e~en†** vt receive; (*Biology*) conceive

Empfäng|er m -s,- recipient; (*Post-*) addressee; (*Zahlungs-*) payee; (*Radio, TV*) receiver. **E~nis** f - (*Biology*) conception

Empfängnisverhütung f contraception. **E~smittel** nt contraceptive

Empfangs|bestätigung f receipt. **E~dame** f receptionist. **E~halle** f [hotel] foyer

empfehl|en† vt recommend. **E~ung** f -,-en recommendation; (*Gruß*) regards pl

empfind|en† vt feel. **e~lich** adj sensitive (**gegen** to); (*zart*) delicate. **E~lichkeit** f - sensitivity; delicacy; tenderness; touchiness. **E~ung** f -,-en sensation; (*Regung*) feeling

empor adv (*literarisch*) up[wards]

empören vt incense; **sich e~** be indignant; (*sich auflehnen*) rebel

Emporkömmling m -s,-e upstart

empör|t adj indignant. **E~ung** f - indignation; (*Auflehnung*) rebellion

Ende nt -s,-n end; (*eines Films, Romans*) ending; (🔲: *Stück*) bit; **zu E~ sein** be finished; **etw zu E~ schreiben** finish writing sth; **am E~** at the end; (*schließlich*) in the end; (🔲: *vielleicht*) perhaps; (🔲: *erschöpft*) at the end of one's tether

end|en vi (*haben*) end. **e~gültig** adj final; (*bestimmt*) definite

Endivie /-iə/ f -,-n endive

end|lich adv at last, finally; (*schließlich*) in the end. **e~los** adj endless. **E~station** f terminus. **E~ung** f -,-en (*Gram*) ending

Energie f - energy

energisch adj resolute; (*nachdrücklich*) vigorous

eng adj narrow; (*beengt*) cramped; (*anliegend*) tight; (*nah*) close; **e~ anliegend** tight-fitting

Engagement /ãgaʒə'mã:/ nt -s,-s (*Theat*) engagement; (*fig*) commitment

Engel m -s,- angel

England nt -s England

Engländer m -s,- Englishman; (*Techn*) monkey-wrench; **die E~** the English pl. **E~in** f -,-nen Englishwoman

englisch adj English. **E~** nt -[s] (*Lang*) English; **auf E~** in English

Engpass m (*fig*) bottleneck

en gros /ã'gro:/ adv wholesale

Enkel m -s,- grandson; **E~** pl grandchildren. **E~in** f -,-nen granddaughter. **E~kind** nt grandchild. **E~sohn** m grandson. **E~tochter** f granddaughter

Ensemble /ã'sã:bəl/ nt -s,-s ensemble; (*Theat*) company

entart|en vi (sein) degenerate. **e~et** adj degenerate

entbehren vt do without; (*vermissen*) miss

entbind|en† vt release (**von** from); (*Med*) deliver (**von** of) ● vi (*haben*) give birth. **E~ung** f delivery. **E~ungsstation** f maternity ward

entdeck|en vt discover. **E~er** m -s,- discoverer; (*Forscher*) explorer. **E~ung** f -,-en discovery

Ente f -,-n duck

entehren vt dishonour

enteignen vt dispossess; expropriate (*Eigentum*)

enterben vt disinherit

Enterich m -s,-e drake

entfallen† vi (sein) not apply; **auf jdn e~** be s.o.'s share

entfern|en vt remove; **sich e~en** leave. **e~t** adj distant; (*schwach*) vague; **2 Kilometer e~t** 2 kilometres away; **e~t verwandt** distantly related. **E~ung** f -,-en removal; (*Abstand*) distance; (*Reichweite*) range

entfliehen† vi (sein) escape

entfremden vt alienate

entfrosten vt defrost

entführ|en vt abduct, kidnap; hijack

(*Flugzeug*). **E~er** *m* abductor, kidnapper; hijacker. **E~ung** *f* abduction, kidnapping; hijacking

entgegen *adv* towards ● *prep* (+ *dat*) contrary to. **e~gehen†** *vi sep* (*sein*) (+ *dat*) go to meet; (*fig*) be heading for. **e~gesetzt** *adj* opposite; (*gegensätzlich*) opposing. **e~kommen†** *vi sep* (*sein*) (+ *dat*) come to meet; (*zukommen auf*) come towards; (*fig*) oblige. **E~kommen** *nt* -s helpfulness; (*Zugeständnis*) concession. **e~kommend** *adj* approaching; (*Verkehr*) oncoming; (*fig*) obliging. **e~nehmen†** *vt sep* accept. **e~wirken** *vi sep* (*haben*) (+ *dat*) counteract; (*fig*) oppose

entgegn|en *vt* reply (**auf** + *acc* to). **E~ung** *f* -,-en reply

entgehen† *vi sep* (*sein*) (+ *dat*) escape; **jdm e~** (*unbemerkt bleiben*) escape s.o.'s notice; **sich** (*dat*) **etw e~ lassen** miss sth

Entgelt *nt* -[e]s payment; **gegen E~** for money

entgleis|en *vi* (*sein*) be derailed; (*fig*) make a gaffe. **E~ung** *f* -,-en derailment; (*fig*) gaffe

entgräten *vt* fillet, bone

Enthaarungsmittel *nt* depilatory

enthalt|en† *vt* contain; **in etw** (*dat*) **e~en sein** be contained/ (*eingeschlossen*) included in sth; **sich der Stimme e~en** (*Pol*) abstain. **e~sam** *adj* abstemious. **E~ung** *f* (*Pol*) abstention

enthaupten *vt* behead

entheben† *vt* **jdn seines Amtes e~** relieve s.o. of his post

Enthüllung *f* -,-en revelation

Enthusias|mus *m* - enthusiasm. **E~t** *m* -en,-en enthusiast

entkernen *vt* stone; core (*Apfel*)

entkleiden *vt* undress; **sich e~en** undress

entkommen† *vi* (*sein*) escape

entkorken *vt* uncork

entladen† *vt* unload; (*Electr*) discharge; **sich e~** discharge; (*Gewitter:*) break; (*Zorn:*) explode

entlang *adv & prep* (+ *preceding acc or following dat*) along; **die Straße e~** along the road; **an etw** (*dat*) **e~** along sth. **e~fahren†** *vi sep* (*sein*) drive along. **e~gehen†** *vi sep* (*sein*) walk along

entlarven *vt* unmask

entlass|en† *vt* dismiss; (*aus Krankenhaus*) discharge; (*aus der Haft*) release. **E~ung** *f* -,-en dismissal; discharge; release

entlast|en *vt* relieve the strain on; ease (*Gewissen, Verkehr*); relieve (**von** of); (*Jur*) exonerate. **E~ung** *f* - relief; exoneration

entlaufen† *vi* (*sein*) run away

entleeren *vt* empty

entlegen *adj* remote

entlohnen *vt* pay

entlüft|en *vt* ventilate. **E~er** *m* -s,- extractor fan. **E~ung** *f* ventilation

entmündigen *vt* declare incapable of managing his own affairs

entmutigen *vt* discourage

entnehmen† *vt* take (*dat* from); (*schließen*) gather (*dat* from)

entpuppen (sich) *vr* (*fig*) turn out (**als etw** to be sth)

entrahmt *adj* skimmed

entrichten *vt* pay

entrinnen† *vi* (*sein*) escape

entrüst|en *vt* fill with indignation; **sich e~en** be indignant (**über** + *acc* at). **e~et** *adj* indignant. **E~ung** *f* - indignation

entsaft|en *vt* extract the juice from. **E~er** *m* -s,- juice extractor

entsagen *vi* (*haben*) (+ *dat*) renounce

entschädig|en *vt* compensate. **E~ung** *f* -,-en compensation

entschärfen *vt* defuse

entscheid|en† *vt/i* (*haben*) decide; **sich e~en** decide; (*Sache:*) be decided. **e~end** *adj* decisive; (*kritisch*) crucial. **E~ung** *f* decision

entschließen† (**sich**) *vr* decide, make up one's mind; **sich anders e~** change one's mind

entschlossen *adj* determined;

Entschluss | erbauen

66

(*energisch*) resolute; **kurz e~** without hesitation. **E~heit** f - determination

Entschluss m decision

entschlüsseln vt decode

entschuld|bar adj excusable. **e~igen** vt excuse; **sich e~igen** apologize (**bei** to); **e~igen Sie [bitte]!** sorry! (*bei Frage*) excuse me. **E~igung** f -,-en apology; (*Ausrede*) excuse; **um E~igung bitten** apologize

entsetz|en vt horrify. **E~en** nt -s horror. **e~lich** adj horrible; (*schrecklich*) terrible

Entsorgung f - waste disposal

entspann|en vt relax; **sich e~en** relax; (*Lage:*) ease. **E~ung** f - relaxation; easing; (*Pol*) détente

entsprech|en† vi (*haben*) (+ *dat*) correspond to; (*übereinstimmen*) agree with. **e~end** adj corresponding; (*angemessen*) appropriate; (*zuständig*) relevant ● adv correspondingly; appropriately; (*demgemäß*) accordingly ● prep (+ *dat*) in accordance with

entspringen† vi (*sein*) (*Fluss:*) rise; (*fig*) arise, spring (*dat* from)

entstammen vi (*sein*) come/(*abstammen*) be descended (*dat* from)

entsteh|en† vi (*sein*) come into being; (*sich bilden*) form; (*sich entwickeln*) develop; (*Brand:*) start; (*stammen*) originate. **E~ung** f - origin; formation; development

entstell|en vt disfigure; (*verzerren*) distort. **E~ung** f disfigurement; distortion

entstört adj (*Electr*) suppressed

enttäusch|en vt disappoint. **E~ung** f disappointment

entwaffnen vt disarm

entwässer|n vt drain. **E~ung** f - drainage

entweder conj & adv either

entwerfen† vt design; (*aufsetzen*) draft; (*skizzieren*) sketch

entwert|en vt devalue; (*ungültig machen*) cancel. **E~er** m -s,- ticket-

cancelling machine. **E~ung** f devaluation; cancelling

entwick|eln vt develop; **sich e~eln** develop. **E~lung** f -,-en development; (*Biology*) evolution. **E~lungsland** nt developing country

entwöhnen vt wean (*gen* from); cure (*Süchtige*)

entwürdigend adj degrading

Entwurf m design; (*Konzept*) draft; (*Skizze*) sketch

entwurzeln vt uproot

entzie|hen† vt take away (*dat* from); **jdm den Führerschein e~hen** disqualify s.o. from driving; **sich e~hen** (+ *dat*) withdraw from. **E~hungskur** f treatment for drug/alcohol addiction

entziffern vt decipher

Entzug m withdrawal; (*Vorenthaltung*) deprivation

entzünd|en vt ignite; (*anstecken*) light; (*fig: erregen*) inflame; **sich e~en** ignite; (*Med*) become inflamed. **e~et** adj (*Med*) inflamed. **e~lich** adj inflammable. **E~ung** f (*Med*) inflammation

entzwei adj broken

Enzian m -s,-e gentian

Enzyklo|pädie f -,-en encyclopaedia. **e~pädisch** adj encyclopaedic

Enzym nt -s,-e enzyme

Epidemie f -,-n epidemic

Epi|lepsie f - epilepsy. **E~leptiker(in)** m -s,- (f -,-nen) epileptic. **e~leptisch** adj epileptic

Epilog m -s,-e epilogue

Episode f -,-n episode

Epoche f -,-n epoch

Epos nt -, **Epen** epic

er pron he; (*Ding, Tier*) it

erachten vt consider (**für nötig** necessary). **E~** nt -s **meines E~s** in my opinion

erbarmen (sich) vr have pity/(*Gott:*) mercy (*gen* on). **E~** nt -s pity; mercy

erbärmlich adj wretched

erbauen vt build; (*fig*) edify; **nicht erbaut von** 🛈 not pleased about

Erbe[1] m -n,-n heir

Erbe[2] nt -s inheritance; (*fig*) heritage.
e~n vt inherit

erbeuten vt get; (*Mil*) capture

Erbfolge f (*Jur*) succession

erbieten† (sich) vr offer (**zu** to)

Erbin f -,-nen heiress

erbitten† vt ask for

erbittert adj bitter; (*heftig*) fierce

erblassen vi (*sein*) turn pale

erblich adj hereditary

erblicken vt catch sight of

erblinden vi (*sein*) go blind

erbrechen† vt vomit ● vi/r [sich]
e~ vomit. E~ nt -s vomiting

Erbschaft f -,-en inheritance

Erbse f -,-n pea

Erb|stück nt heirloom. E~teil nt inheritance

Erd|apfel m (*Aust*) potato.
E~beben nt -s,- earthquake.
E~beere f strawberry

Erde f -,-n earth; (*Erdboden*) ground;
(*Fußboden*) floor. e~n vt (*Electr*)
earth

erdenklich adj imaginable

Erd|gas nt natural gas. E~geschoss
nt ground floor. E~kugel f globe.
E~kunde f geography. E~nuss f
peanut. E~öl nt [mineral] oil

erdrosseln vt strangle

erdrücken vt crush to death

Erd|rutsch m landslide. E~teil m
continent

erdulden vt endure

ereignen (sich) vr happen

Ereignis nt -ses,-se event. e~los
adj uneventful. e~reich adj eventful

Eremit m -en,-en hermit

erfahr|en† vt learn, hear; (*erleben*)
experience ● adj experienced.
E~ung f -,-en experience; **in E~ung
bringen** find out

erfassen vt seize; (*begreifen*) grasp;
(*einbeziehen*) include; (*aufzeichnen*)
record

erfind|en† vt invent. E~er m -s,-
inventor. e~erisch adj inventive.
E~ung f -,-en invention

Erfolg m -[e]s,-e success; (*Folge*) result; E~ haben be successful. e~en
vi (*sein*) take place; (*geschehen*) happen. e~los adj unsuccessful.
e~reich adj successful

erforder|lich adj required, necessary. e~n vt require, demand

erforsch|en vt explore; (*untersuchen*) investigate. E~ung f exploration; investigation

erfreu|en vt please. e~lich adj
pleasing. e~licherweise adv happily. e~t adj pleased

erfrier|en† vi (*sein*) freeze to death;
(*Glied:*) become frostbitten; (*Pflanze:*)
be killed by the frost. E~ung f -,-en
frostbite

erfrisch|en vt refresh. E~ung f
-,-en refreshment

erfüll|en vt fill; (*nachkommen*) fulfil;
serve (*Zweck*); discharge (*Pflicht:*) sich
e~en come true. E~ung f fulfilment

erfunden invented

ergänz|en vt complement; (*hinzufügen*) add. E~ung f complement;
supplement; (*Zusatz*) addition

ergeben† vt produce; (*zeigen*) show,
establish; sich e~en result; (*Schwierigkeit:*) arise; (*kapitulieren*) surrender;
(*sich fügen*) submit ● adj devoted;
(*resigniert*) resigned

Ergebnis nt -ses,-se result. e~los
adj fruitless

ergiebig adj productive; (*fig*) rich

ergreifen† vt seize; take (*Maßnahme, Gelegenheit*); take up (*Beruf*);
(*rühren*) move; **die Flucht e~** flee.
e~d adj moving

ergriffen adj deeply moved.
E~heit f - emotion

ergründen vt (*fig*) get to the bottom of

erhaben adj raised; (*fig*) sublime

Erhalt m -[e]s receipt. e~en† vt receive, get; (*gewinnen*) obtain; (*bewahren*) preserve, keep; (*instand halten*) maintain; (*unterhalten*) support;
am Leben e~en keep alive ● adj
gut/schlecht e~en in good/bad
condition; **e~en bleiben** survive

erhältlich *adj* obtainable

Erhaltung *f* - preservation; maintenance

erhängen (sich) *vr* hang oneself

erheb|en† *vt* raise; levy (*Steuer*); charge (*Gebühr*); **Anspruch e~en** lay claim (**auf** + *acc* to); **Protest e~en** protest; **sich e~en** rise; (*Frage:*) arise. **e~lich** *adj* considerable. **E~ung** *f* -,-en elevation; (*Anhöhe*) rise; (*Aufstand*) uprising; (*Ermittlung*) survey

erheiter|n *vt* amuse. **E~ung** *f* - amusement

erhitzen *vt* heat

erhöh|en *vt* raise; (*fig*) increase; **sich e~en** rise, increase. **E~ung** *f* -,-en increase

erhol|en (sich) *vr* recover (**von** from); (*nach Krankheit*) convalesce; (*sich ausruhen*) have a rest. **e~sam** *adj* restful. **E~ung** *f* - recovery; (*Ruhe*) rest

erinner|n *vt* remind (**an** + *acc* of); **sich e~n** remember (**an jdn/etw** s.o./sth). **E~ung** *f* -,-en memory; (*Andenken*) souvenir

erkält|en (sich) *vr* catch a cold; **e~et sein** have a cold. **E~ung** *f* -,-en cold

erkenn|bar *adj* recognizable; (*sichtbar*) visible. **e~en**† *vt* recognize; (*wahrnehmen*) distinguish. **E~tnis** *f* -,-se recognition; realization; (*Wissen*) knowledge; **die neuesten E~tnisse** the latest findings

Erker *m* -s,- bay

erklär|en *vt* declare; (*erläutern*) explain; **sich bereit e~en** agree (**zu** to). **e~end** *adj* explanatory. **e~lich** *adj* explicable; (*verständlich*) understandable. **e~licherweise** *adv* understandably. **E~ung** *f* -,-en declaration; explanation; **öffentliche E~ung** public statement

erkrank|en *vi* (*sein*) fall ill; be taken ill (**an** + *dat* with). **E~ung** *f* -,-en illness

erkundig|en (sich) *vr* enquire (**nach jdm/etw** after s.o./about sth). **E~ung** *f* -,-en enquiry

erlangen *vt* attain, get

Erlass *m* -es,⸚e (*Admin*) decree; (*Befreiung*) exemption; (*Straf-*) remission

erlassen† *vt* (*Admin*) issue; **jdm etw e~** exempt s.o. from sth; let s.o. off (*Strafe*)

erlauben *vt* allow, permit; **ich kann es mir nicht e~** I can't afford it

Erlaubnis *f* - permission. **E~schein** *m* permit

erläutern *vt* explain

Erle *f* -,-n alder

erleb|en *vt* experience; (*mit-*) see; have (*Überraschung*). **E~nis** *nt* -ses, -se experience

erledigen *vt* do; (*sich befassen mit*) deal with; (*beenden*) finish; (*entscheiden*) settle; (*töten*) kill

erleichter|n *vt* lighten; (*vereinfachen*) make easier; (*befreien*) relieve; (*lindern*) ease. **e~t** *adj* relieved. **E~ung** *f* - relief

erleiden† *vt* suffer

erleuchten *vt* illuminate; **hell erleuchtet** brightly lit

erlogen *adj* untrue, false

Erlös *m* -es proceeds *pl*

erlöschen† *vi* (*sein*) go out; (*vergehen*) die; (*aussterben*) die out; (*ungültig werden*) expire; **erloschener Vulkan** extinct volcano

erlös|en *vt* save; (*befreien*) release (**von** from); (*Relig*) redeem. **e~t** *adj* relieved. **E~ung** *f* release; (*Erleichterung*) relief; (*Relig*) redemption

ermächtig|en *vt* authorize. **E~ung** *f* -,-en authorization

Ermahnung *f* exhortation; admonition

ermäßig|en *vt* reduce. **E~ung** *f* -,-en reduction

ermessen† *vt* judge; (*begreifen*) appreciate. **E~** *nt* -s discretion; (*Urteil*) judgement; **nach eigenem E~** at one's own discretion

ermitt|eln *vt* establish; (*herausfinden*) find out ● *vi* (*haben*) investigate (**gegen jdn** s.o.). **E~lungen** *fpl* investigations. **E~lungsverfahren** *nt* (*Jur*) preliminary inquiry

ermöglichen vt make possible

ermord|en vt murder. **E~ung** f -,-en murder

ermüd|en vt tire ● vi (sein) get tired. **E~ung** f - tiredness

ermutigen vt encourage. **e~d** adj encouraging

ernähr|en vt feed; (unterhalten) support, keep; **sich e~en von** live/(Tier:) feed on. **E~er** m -s,- breadwinner. **E~ung** f - nourishment; nutrition; (Kost) diet

ernenn|en† vt appoint. **E~ung** f -,-en appointment

erneu|ern vt renew; (auswechseln) replace; change (Verband); (renovieren) renovate. **E~erung** f renewal; replacement; renovation. **e~t** adj renewed; (neu) new ● adv again

ernst adj serious; **e~ nehmen** take seriously. **E~** m -es seriousness; **im E~** seriously; **mit einer Drohung E~ machen** carry out a threat; **ist das dein E~?** are you serious? **e~haft** adj serious. **e~lich** adj serious

Ernte f -,-n harvest; (Ertrag) crop. **E~dankfest** nt harvest festival. **e~n** vt harvest; (fig) reap, win

ernüchter|n vt sober up; (fig) bring down to earth. **e~nd** adj (fig) sobering

Erober|er m -s,- conqueror. **e~n** vt conquer. **E~ung** f -,-en conquest

eröffn|en vt open; **jdm etw e~en** announce sth to s.o. **E~ung** f opening; (Mitteilung) announcement

erörter|n vt discuss. **E~ung** f -,-en discussion

Erot|ik f - eroticism. **e~isch** adj erotic

Erpel m -s,- drake

erpicht adj **e~ auf** (+ acc) keen on

erpress|en vt extort; blackmail (Person). **E~er** m -s,- blackmailer. **E~ung** f - extortion; blackmail

erprob|en vt test. **e~t** adj proven

erraten† vt guess

erreg|bar adj excitable. **e~en** vt excite; (hervorrufen) arouse; **sich e~en** get worked up. **e~end** adj exciting. **E~er** m -s,- (Med) germ. **e~t** adj agitated; (hitzig) heated. **E~ung** f - excitement

erreich|bar adj within reach; (Ziel) attainable; (Person) available. **e~en** vt reach; catch (Zug); live to (Alter); (durchsetzen) achieve

errichten vt erect

erringen† vt gain, win

erröten vi (sein) blush

Errungenschaft f -,-en achievement; (ⓘ: Anschaffung) acquisition

Ersatz m -es replacement, substitute; (Entschädigung) compensation. **E~reifen** m spare tyre. **E~teil** nt spare part

erschaffen† vt create

erschein|en† vi (sein) appear; (Buch:) be published. **E~ung** f -,-en appearance; (Person) figure; (Phänomen) phenomenon; (Symptom) symptom; (Geist) apparition

erschieß|en† vt shoot [dead]. **E~ungskommando** nt firing squad

erschlaffen vi (sein) go limp

erschlagen† vt beat to death; (tödlich treffen) strike dead; **vom Blitz e~ werden** be killed by lightning

erschließen† vt develop

erschöpf|en vt exhaust. **e~t** adj exhausted. **E~ung** f - exhaustion

erschrecken† vi (sein) get a fright ● vt (reg) startle; (beunruhigen) alarm; **du hast mich e~t** you gave me a fright

erschrocken adj frightened; (erschreckt) startled

erschütter|n vt shake; (ergreifen) upset deeply. **E~ung** f -,-en shock

erschwinglich adj affordable

ersehen† vt (fig) see (aus from)

ersetzen vt replace; make good (Schaden); refund (Kosten); **jdm etw e~** compensate s.o. for sth

ersichtlich adj obvious, apparent

erspar|en vt save. **E~nis** f -,-se saving; **E~nisse** savings

erst adv (zuerst) first; (noch nicht mehr als) only; (nicht vor) not until;

e~ **dann** only then; **eben e~** [only] just

erstarren vi (sein) solidify; (gefrieren) freeze; (steif werden) go stiff; (vor Schreck) be paralysed

erstatten vt (zurück-) refund; **Bericht e~** report (**jdm** to s.o.)

Erstaufführung f first performance, première

erstaun|en vt amaze, astonish. **E~en** nt amazement, astonishment. **e~lich** adj amazing

Erst|ausgabe f first edition. **e~e(r,s)** adj first; (beste) best; **e~e Hilfe** first aid. **E~e(r)** m/f first; (Beste) best; **fürs E~e** for the time being; **als E~es** first of all; **er kam als E~er** he arrived first

erstechen† vt stab to death

ersteigern vt buy at an auction

erst|ens adv firstly, in the first place. **e~ere(r,s)** adj the former; **der/die/das E~ere** the former

ersticken vt suffocate; smother (Flammen) ● vi (sein) suffocate. **E~** nt -s suffocation; **zum E~** stifling

erstklassig adj first-class

ersuchen vt ask, request. **E~** nt -s request

ertappen vt ⬚ catch

erteilen vt give (**jdm** s.o.)

ertönen vi (sein) sound; (erschallen) ring out

Ertrag m -[e]s,=e yield. **e~en†** vt bear

erträglich adj bearable; (leidlich) tolerable

ertränken vt drown

ertrinken† vi (sein) drown

erübrigen (sich) vr be unnecessary

erwachsen adj grown-up. **E~e(r)** m/f adult, grown-up

erwäg|en† vt consider. **E~ung** f -,-en consideration; **in E~ung ziehen** consider

erwähn|en vt mention. **E~ung** f -,-en mention

erwärmen vt warm; **sich e~** warm up; (fig) warm (**für** to)

erwart|en vt expect; (warten auf)

wait for. **E~ung** f -,-en expectation

erweisen† vt prove; (bezeigen) do (Gefallen, Dienst, Ehre); **sich e~ als** prove to be

erweitern vt widen; dilate (Pupille); (fig) extend, expand

Erwerb m -[e]s acquisition; (Kauf) purchase; (Brot-) livelihood; (Verdienst) earnings pl. **e~en†** vt acquire; (kaufen) purchase. **e~slos** adj unemployed. **e~stätig** adj employed

erwider|n vt reply; return (Besuch, Gruß). **E~ung** f -,-en reply

erwirken vt obtain

erwürgen vt strangle

Erz nt -es,-e ore

erzähl|en vt tell (**jdm** s.o.) ● vi (haben) talk (**von** about). **E~er** m -s,- narrator. **E~ung** f -,-en story, tale

Erzbischof m archbishop

erzeug|en vt produce; (Electr) generate. **E~er** m -s,- producer. **E~nis** nt -ses,-se product; **landwirtschaftliche E~nisse** farm produce sg.

erzieh|en† vt bring up; (Sch) educate. **E~er** m -s,- [private] tutor. **E~erin** f -,-nen governess. **E~ung** f - upbringing; education

erzielen vt achieve; score (Tor)

erzogen adj **gut/schlecht e~** well/badly brought up

---

es

● pronoun

····➤ (Sache) it; (weibliche Person) she/her; (männliche Person) he/him. **ich bin es** it's me. **wir sind traurig, ihr seid es auch** we are sad, and so are you. **er ist es, der ...** he is the one who ... **es sind Studenten** they are students

····➤ (impers) it. **es hat geklopft** there was a knock. **es klingelt** someone is ringing. **es wird schöner** the weather is improving. **es geht ihm gut/schlecht** he is well/unwell. **es lässt sich aushalten** it is bearable. **es gibt**

there is or (*pl*) are
····➤ (*als formales Objekt*) **er hat es gut** he has it made; he's well off. **er meinte es gut** he meant well. **ich hoffe/glaube es** I hope/think so

Esche *f* -,-n ash
Esel *m* -s,- donkey; (⚠: *Person*) ass
Eskimo *m* -[s],-[s] Eskimo
Eskort|e *f* -,-n (*Mil*) escort. **e~ieren** *vt* escort
essbar *adj* edible
essen† *vt/i* (*haben*) eat; **zu Mittag/Abend e~** have lunch/supper; **e~ gehen** eat out. **E~** *nt* -s,- food; (*Mahl*) meal; (*festlich*) dinner
Esser(in) *m* -s,- (*f* -,-nen) eater
Essig *m* -s vinegar. **E~gurke** *f* [pickled] gherkin
Esslöffel *m* ≈ dessertspoon. **Essstäbchen** *ntpl* chopsticks. **Esstisch** *m* dining-table. **Esswaren** *fpl* food *sg*; (*Vorräte*) provisions. **Esszimmer** *nt* dining-room
Estland *nt* -s Estonia
Estragon *m* -s tarragon
etablieren (sich) *vr* establish oneself/(*Geschäft:*) itself
Etage /e'ta:ʒə/ *f* -,-n storey. **E~nbett** *nt* bunk-beds *pl*. **E~nwohnung** *f* flat
Etappe *f* -,-n stage
Etat /e'ta:/ *m* -s,-s budget
Eth|ik *f* - ethic; (*Sittenlehre*) ethics *sg*. **e~isch** *adj* ethical
ethnisch *adj* ethnic; **e~e Säuberung** ethnic cleansing
Etikett *nt* -[e]s,-e[n] label; (*Preis-*) tag. **e~ieren** *vt* label
Etui /e'tvi:/ *nt* -s,-s case
etwa *adv* (*ungefähr*) about; (*zum Beispiel*) for instance; (*womöglich*) perhaps; **nicht e~, dass ...** not that ... ; **denkt nicht e~ ...** don't imagine ...
etwas *pron* something; (*fragend/verneint*) anything; (*ein bisschen*) some, a little; **sonst noch e~?** anything else? **so e~ Ärgerliches!** what a nuisance! ● *adv* a bit
Etymologie *f* - etymology

euch *pron* (*acc of* **ihr** *pl*) you; (*dat*) [to] you; (*reflexive*) yourselves; (*einander*) each other
euer *poss pron* *pl* your. **e~e, e~t-** *s.* **eure, euret-**
Eule *f* -,-n owl
Euphorie *f* - euphoria
eur|e *poss pron* *pl* your. **e~e(r,s)** *poss pron* yours. **e~etwegen** *adv* for your sake; (*wegen euch*) because of you, on your account. **e~etwillen** *adv* **um e~etwillen** for your sake. **e~ige** *poss pron* **der/die/das e~ige** yours
Euro *m* -[s],[-s] euro. **E~-** *prefix* Euro-
Europa *nt* -s Europe. **E~-** *prefix* European
Europä|er(in) *m* -s,- (*f* -,-nen) European. **e~isch** *adj* European
Euter *nt* -s,- udder
evakuier|en *vt* evacuate. **E~ung** *f* - evacuation
evan|gelisch *adj* Protestant. **E~gelium** *nt* -s,-ien gospel
eventuell *adj* possible ● *adv* possibly; (*vielleicht*) perhaps
Evolution /-'tsio:n/ *f* - evolution
ewig *adj* eternal; (*endlos*) never-ending; **e~ dauern** ⚠ take ages. **E~keit** *f* - eternity
Examen *nt* -s,- & -mina (*Sch*) examination
Exemplar *nt* -s,-e specimen; (*Buch*) copy. **e~isch** *adj* exemplary
exerzieren *vt/i* (*haben*) (*Mil*) drill; (*üben*) practise
exhumieren *vt* exhume
Exil *nt* -s exile
Existenz *f* -,-en existence; (*Lebensgrundlage*) livelihood
existieren *vi* (*haben*) exist
exklusiv *adj* exclusive. **e~e** *prep* (+ *gen*) excluding
exkommunizieren *vt* excommunicate
Exkremente *npl* excrement *sg*
Expedition /-'tsio:n/ *f* -,-en expedition

Experiment *nt* -[e]s,-e experiment.
e~**ieren** *vi* (*haben*) experiment
Experte *m* -n,-n expert
explo|dieren *vi* (*sein*) explode.
E~**sion** *f* -,-en explosion
Expor|t *m* -[e]s,-e export. E~**teur**
m -s,-e exporter. e~**tieren** *vt* export
extra *adv* separately; (*zusätzlich*)
extra; (*eigens*) specially; (ⅰ: *absichtlich*) on purpose
extravagan|t *adj* flamboyant;
(*übertrieben*) extravagant
extravertiert *adj* extrovert
extrem *adj* extreme. E~**ist** *m* -en,
-en extremist
Exzellenz *f* - (*title*) Excellency
Exzentr|iker *m* -s,- eccentric.
e~**isch** *adj* eccentric

....

Ff

....

Fabel *f* -,-n fable. f~**haft** *adj* ⅰ fantastic
Fabrik *f* -,-en factory. F~**ant** *m*
-en,-en manufacturer. F~**at** *nt*
-[e]s,-e product; (*Marke*) make.
F~**ation** *f* - manufacture
Fach *nt* -[e]s,¨er compartment;
(*Schub-*) drawer; (*Gebiet*) field; (*Sch*)
subject. F~**arbeiter** *m* skilled
worker. F~**arzt** *m*, F~**ärztin** *f* spe-
cialist. F~**ausdruck** *m* technical
term
Fächer *m* -s,- fan
Fach|gebiet *nt* field. f~**kundig** *adj*
expert. f~**lich** *adj* technical; (*beruflich*) professional. F~**mann** *m* (*pl*
-**leute**) expert. f~**männisch** *adj* expert. F~**schule** *f* technical college.
F~**werkhaus** *nt* half-timbered
house. F~**wort** *nt* (*pl* -**wörter**)
technical term
Fackel *f* -,-n torch
fade *adj* insipid; (*langweilig*) dull
Faden *m* -s,¨ thread; (*Bohnen-*)
string; (*Naut*) fathom

Fagott *nt* -[e]s,-e bassoon
fähig *adj* capable (**zu**/*gen* of); (*tüchtig*) able, competent. F~**keit** *f* -,-en
ability; competence
fahl *adj* pale
fahnd|en *vi* (*haben*) search (**nach**
for). F~**ung** *f* -,-en search
Fahne *f* -,-n flag; (*Druck-*) galley
[proof]; **eine F~ haben** ⅰ reek of
alcohol. F~**nflucht** *f* desertion
Fahr|ausweis *m* ticket. F~**bahn** *f*
carriageway; (*Straße*) road. f~**bar** *adj*
mobile
Fähre *f* -,-n ferry
fahr|en† *vi* (*sein*) go, travel; (*Fahrer:*)
drive; (*Radfahrer:*) ride; (*verkehren*)
run, (*ab-*) leave; (*Schiff:*) sail; **mit
dem Auto/Zug f~en** go by car/
train; **was ist in ihn gefahren?** ⅰ
what has got into him? ● *vt* drive;
ride (*Fahrrad*); take (*Kurve*). f~**end**
adj moving; (*f~bar*) mobile; (*nicht
sesshaft*) travelling. F~**er** *m* -s,-
driver. F~**erflucht** *f* failure to stop
after an accident. F~**erhaus** *nt* driver's cab. F~**erin** *f* -,-nen woman
driver. F~**gast** *m* passenger. F~**geld**
nt fare. F~**gestell** *nt* chassis; (*Aviat*)
undercarriage. F~**karte** *f* ticket.
F~**kartenschalter** *m* ticket office.
f~**lässig** *adj* negligent. F~**lässig-
keit** *f* - negligence. F~**lehrer** *m*
driving instructor. F~**plan** *m* timetable. f~**planmäßig** *adj* scheduled
● *adv* according to/(*pünktlich*) on
schedule. F~**preis** *m* fare. F~**prüfung** *f* driving test. F~**rad** *nt* bicycle. F~**schein** *m* ticket. F~**schule**
f driving school. F~**schüler(in)** *m(f)*
learner driver. F~**stuhl** *m* lift
Fahrt *f* -,-en journey; (*Auto*) drive;
(*Ausflug*) trip; (*Tempo*) speed
Fährte *f* -,-n track; (*Witterung*) scent
Fahr|tkosten *pl* travelling ex-
penses. F~**werk** *nt* undercarriage.
F~**zeug** *nt* -[e]s,-e vehicle; (*Wasser-*)
craft, vessel
fair /fɛːɐ̯/ *adj* fair
Fakultät *f* -,-en faculty
Falke *m* -n,-n falcon
Fall *m* -[e]s,¨e fall; (*Jur, Med, Gram*)

case; **im F~[e]** in case (*gen* of); **auf jeden F~** in any case; (*bestimmt*) definitely; **für alle F~e** just in case; **auf keinen F~** on no account

Falle *f -,-n* trap

fallen† *vi* (*sein*) fall; (*sinken*) go down; **[im Krieg] f~** be killed in the war; **f~ lassen** drop (*etw, fig: Plan, jdn*); make (*Bemerkung*)

fällen *vt* fell; (*fig*) pass (*Urteil*)

fällig *adj* due; (*Wechsel*) mature; **längst f~** long overdue. **F~keit** *f -* (*Comm*) maturity

falls *conj* in case; (*wenn*) if

Fallschirm *m* parachute. **F~jäger** *m* paratrooper. **F~springer** *m* parachutist

Falltür *f* trapdoor

falsch *adj* wrong; (*nicht echt, unaufrichtig*) false; (*gefälscht*) forged; (*Geld*) counterfeit; (*Schmuck*) fake ● *adv* wrongly; falsely; (*singen*) out of tune; **f~ gehen** (*Uhr:*) be wrong

fälschen *vt* forge, fake

Falschgeld *nt* counterfeit money

fälschlich *adj* wrong; (*irrtümlich*) mistaken

Falsch|meldung *f* false report; (*absichtlich*) hoax report. **F~münzer** *m -s,-* counterfeiter

Fälschung *f -,-en* forgery, fake

Falte *f -,-n* fold; (*Rock-*) pleat; (*Knitter-*) crease; (*im Gesicht*) line; wrinkle

falten *vt* fold

Falter *m -s,-* butterfly; moth

faltig *adj* creased; (*Gesicht*) lined; wrinkled

familiär *adj* family ; (*vertraut, zudringlich*) familiar; (*zwanglos*) informal

Familie /-iə/ *f -,-n* family. **F~nforschung** *f* genealogy. **F~nname** *m* surname. **F~nplanung** *f* family planning. **F~nstand** *m* marital status

Fan /fɛn/ *m -s,-s* fan

Fana|tiker *m -s,-* fanatic. **f~tisch** *adj* fanatical

Fanfare *f -,-n* trumpet; (*Signal*) fanfare

Fang *m -[e]s,¨e* capture; (*Beute*)

catch; **F~e** (*Krallen*) talons; (*Zähne*) fangs. **F~arm** *m* tentacle. **F~en†** *vt* catch; (*ein-*) capture; **gefangen nehmen** take prisoner. **F~en** *nt -s* **F~en spielen** play tag. **F~frage** *f* catch question

Fantasie *f -,-n* = Phantasie

Farb|aufnahme *f* colour photograph. **F~band** *nt* (*pl* -bänder) typewriter ribbon. **F~e** *f -,-n* colour; (*Maler-*) paint; (*zum Färben*) dye; (*Karten*) suit. **f~echt** *adj* colour-fast

färben *vt* colour; dye (*Textilien, Haare*) ● *vi* (*haben*) not be colour-fast

farb|enblind *adj* colour-blind. **f~enfroh** *adj* colourful. **F~film** *m* colour film. **f~ig** *adj* coloured ● *adv* in colour. **F~ige(r)** *m/f* coloured man/woman. **F~kasten** *m* box of paints. **f~los** *adj* colourless. **F~stift** *m* crayon. **F~stoff** *m* dye; (*Lebensmittel-*) colouring. **F~ton** *m* shade

Färbung *f -,-en* colouring

Farn *m -[e]s,-e* fern

Färse *f -,-n* heifer

Fasan *m -[e]s,-e[n]* pheasant

Faschierte(s) *nt* (*Aust*) mince

Fasching *m -s* (*SGer*) carnival

Fasching, Fastnachtszeit *i*
The carnival season begins at Epiphany and ends on *Aschermittwoch* (Ash Wednesday) for Lent. Depending on the region, it is also called *Karneval* or *Fasnet*, and is celebrated in Germany, Austria and Switzerland. Celebrations reach a climax on *Faschingsdienstag*, or *Rosenmontag* in the Rhineland, when there are street processions.

Faschis|mus *m -* fascism. **F~t** *m -en,-en* fascist. **f~tisch** *adj* fascist

Faser *f -,-n* fibre

Fass *nt -es,¨er* barrel, cask; **Bier vom F~** draught beer

Fassade *f -,-n* façade

fassbar *adj* comprehensible; (*greifbar*) tangible

fassen *vt* take [hold of], grasp; (*ergreifen*) seize; (*fangen*) catch; (*ein-*)

set; (*enthalten*) hold; (*fig: begreifen*) take in, grasp; conceive (*Plan*); make (*Entschluss*); **sich f~** compose oneself; **sich kurz f~** be brief; **nicht zu f~** (*fig*) unbelievable ● *vi* (*haben*) **f~ an** (+ *acc*) touch

Fassung *f* -,-en mount; (*Edelstein-*) setting; (*Electr*) socket; (*Version*) version; (*Beherrschung*) composure; **aus der F~ bringen** disconcert. **f~slos** *adj* shaken; (*erstaunt*) flabbergasted. **F~svermögen** *nt* capacity

fast *adv* almost, nearly; **f~ nie** hardly ever

fast|en *vi* (*haben*) fast. **F~enzeit** *f* Lent. **F~nacht** *f* Shrovetide; (*Karneval*) carnival. **F~nachtsdienstag** *m* Shrove Tuesday

fatal *adj* fatal; (*peinlich*) embarrassing

Fata Morgana *f* - -,- -nen mirage

fauchen *vi* (*haben*) spit, hiss ● *vt* snarl

faul *adj* lazy; (*verdorben*) rotten, bad; (*Ausrede*) lame

faul|en *vi* (*sein*) rot; (*Zahn:*) decay; (*verwesen*) putrefy. **f~enzen** *vi* (*haben*) be lazy. **F~enzer** *m* -s,- lazybones *sg*. **F~heit** *f* - laziness

Fäulnis *f* - decay

Fauna *f* - fauna

Faust *f* -,Fäuste fist; **auf eigene F~** (*fig*) off one's own bat. **F~handschuh** *m* mitten. **F~schlag** *m* punch

Fauxpas /foˈpa/ *m* -,- gaffe

Favorit(in) /favoˈriːt(ɪn)/ *m* -en,-en (*f* -,-nen) (*Sport*) favourite

Fax *nt* -,-[e] fax. **f~en** *vt* fax

Faxen *fpl* 🄵 antics; **F~ machen** fool about

Faxgerät *nt* fax machine

Februar *m* -s,-e February

fecht|en† *vi* (*haben*) fence. **F~er** *m* -s,- fencer

Feder *f* -,-n feather; (*Schreib-*) pen; (*Spitze*) nib; (*Techn*) spring. **F~ball** *m* shuttlecock; (*Spiel*) badminton. **F~busch** *m* plume. **f~leicht** *adj* as light as a feather. **f~n** *vi* (*haben*) be springy; (*nachgeben*) give; (*hoch-*) bounce. **f~nd** *adj* springy; (*elastisch*)

elastic. **F~ung** *f* - (*Techn*) springs *pl*; (*Auto*) suspension

Fee *f* -,-n fairy

Fegefeuer *nt* purgatory

fegen *vt* sweep

Fehde *f* -,-n feud

fehl *adj* **f~ am Platze** out of place. **F~betrag** *m* deficit. **f~en** *vi* (*haben*) be missing/(*Sch*) absent; (*mangeln*) be lacking; **mir f~t die Zeit** I haven't got the time; **was f~t ihm?** what's the matter with him? **das hat uns noch gefehlt!** that's all we need! **f~end** *adj* missing; (*Sch*) absent

Fehler *m* -s,- mistake, error; (*Sport & fig*) fault; (*Makel*) flaw. **f~frei** *adj* faultless. **f~haft** *adj* faulty. **f~los** *adj* flawless

Fehl|geburt *f* miscarriage. **F~griff** *m* mistake. **F~kalkulation** *f* miscalculation. **F~schlag** *m* failure. **f~schlagen†** *vi sep* (*sein*) fail. **F~start** *m* (*Sport*) false start. **F~zündung** *f* (*Auto*) misfire

Feier *f* -,-n celebration; (*Zeremonie*) ceremony; (*Party*) party. **F~abend** *m* end of the working day; **F~abend machen** stop work. **f~lich** *adj* solemn; (*fömlich*) formal. **f~n** *vt* celebrate; hold (*Fest*) ● *vi* (*haben*) celebrate. **F~tag** *m* [public] holiday; (*kirchlicher*) feast-day; **erster/zweiter F~tag** Christmas Day / Boxing Day. **f~tags** *adv* on public holidays

feige *adj* cowardly; **f~ sein** be a coward ● *adv* in a cowardly way

Feige *f* -,-n fig

Feig|heit *f* - cowardice. **F~ling** *m* -s,-e coward

Feile *f* -,-n file. **f~n** *vt/i* (*haben*) file

feilschen *vi* (*haben*) haggle

fein *adj* fine; (*zart*) delicate; (*Strümpfe*) sheer; (*Unterschied*) subtle; (*scharf*) keen; (*vornehm*) refined; (*prima*) great; **sich f~ machen** dress up. **F~arbeit** *f* precision work

Feind(in) *m* -es,-e (*f* -,-nen) enemy. **f~lich** *adj* enemy; (*f~selig*) hostile. **F~schaft** *f* -,-en enmity

fein|fühlig *adj* sensitive. **F~gefühl**

nt sensitivity; (*Takt*) delicacy. **F∼heit** *f* -,-en fineness; delicacy; subtlety; refinement; **F∼heiten** subtleties. **F∼kostgeschäft** *nt* delicatessen [shop]

feist *adj* fat

Feld *nt* -[e]s,-er field; (*Fläche*) ground; (*Sport*) pitch; (*Schach-*) square; (*auf Formular*) box. **F∼bett** *nt* camp-bed. **F∼forschung** *f* fieldwork. **F∼herr** *m* commander. **F∼stecher** *m* -s,- field-glasses *pl*. **F∼webel** *m* -s,- (*Mil*) sergeant. **F∼zug** *m* campaign

Felge *f* -,-n [wheel] rim

Fell *nt* -[e]s,-e (*Zool*) coat; (*Pelz*) fur; (*abgezogen*) skin, pelt

Fels *m* -en,-en rock. **F∼block** *m* boulder. **F∼en** *m* -s,- rock

Femininum *nt* -s,-na (*Gram*) feminine

Feminist|(in) *m* -en,-en (*f* -,-nen) feminist. **f∼isch** *adj* feminist

Fenchel *m* -s fennel

Fenster *nt* -s,- window. **F∼brett** *nt* window sill. **F∼scheibe** *f* [window-]pane

Ferien /ˈfeːriən/ *pl* holidays; (*Univ*) vacation *sg*; **F∼ haben** be on holiday. **F∼ort** *m* holiday resort

Ferkel *nt* -s,- piglet

fern *adj* distant; **der F∼e Osten** the Far East; **sich f∼ halten** keep away ● *adv* far away; **von f∼** from a distance ● *prep* (+ *dat*) far [away] from. **F∼bedienung** *f* remote control. **F∼e** *f* - distance; **in weiter F∼e** far away; (*zeitlich*) in the distant future. **f∼er** *adj* further ● *adv* (*außerdem*) furthermore; (*in Zukunft*) in future. **f∼gelenkt** *adj* remote-controlled; (*Rakete*) guided. **F∼gespräch** *nt* long-distance call. **F∼glas** *nt* binoculars *pl*. **F∼kurs[us]** *m* correspondence course. **F∼licht** *nt* (*Auto*) full beam. **F∼meldewesen** *nt* telecommunications *pl*. **F∼rohr** *nt* telescope. **F∼schreiben** *nt* telex

Fernseh|apparat *m* television set. **f∼en†** *vi sep* (*haben*) watch television. **F∼en** *nt* -s television. **F∼er** *m* -s,- [television] viewer; (*Gerät*) television set

Fernsprech|amt *nt* telephone exchange. **F∼er** *m* telephone

Fern|steuerung *f* remote control. **F∼studium** *nt* distance learning

Ferse *f* -,-n heel

fertig *adj* finished; (*bereit*) ready; (*Comm*) ready-made; (*Gericht*) ready-to-serve; **f∼ werden mit** finish; (*bewältigen*) cope with; **f∼ sein** have finished; (*fig*) be through (**mit jdm** with s.o.); (🗉: *erschöpft*) be all in/(*seelisch*) shattered; **etw f∼ bringen** manage to do sth; (*beenden*) finish sth; **etw/jdn f∼ machen** finish sth; (*bereitmachen*) get sth/s.o. ready; (🗉: *erschöpfen*) wear s.o. out; (*seelisch*) shatter s.o.; **sich f∼ machen** get ready; **etw f∼ stellen** complete sth ● *adv* **f∼ essen/lesen** finish eating/reading. **F∼bau** *m* (*pl* -bauten) prefabricated building. **f∼en** *vt* make. **F∼gericht** *nt* ready-to-serve meal. **F∼haus** *nt* prefabricated house. **F∼keit** *f* -,-en skill. **F∼stellung** *f* completion. **F∼ung** *f* - manufacture

fesch *adj* 🗉 attractive

Fessel *f* -,-n ankle

fesseln *vt* tie up; tie (**an** + *acc* to); (*fig*) fascinate

fest *adj* firm; (*nicht flüssig*) solid; (*erstarrt*) set; (*haltbar*) strong; (*nicht locker*) tight; (*feststehend*) fixed; (*ständig*) steady; (*Anstellung*) permanent; (*Schlaf*) sound; (*Blick, Stimme*) steady; **f∼ werden** harden; (*Gelee:*) set; **f∼e Nahrung** solids *pl* ● *adv* firmly; tightly; steadily; soundly; (*kräftig, tüchtig*) hard; **f∼ schlafen** be fast asleep; **f∼ angestellt** permanent

Fest *nt* -[e]s,-e celebration; (*Party*) party; (*Relig*) festival; **frohes F∼!** happy Christmas!

fest|binden† *vt sep* tie (**an** + *dat* to). **f∼bleiben†** *vi sep* (*sein*) (*fig*) remain firm. **f∼halten†** *v sep* ● *vt* hold on to; (*aufzeichnen*) record; **sich f∼halten** hold on ● *vi* (*haben*)

f

f∼**halten an** (+ *dat*) (*fig*) stick to; cling to (*Tradition*). F∼**igen** *vt* strengthen. F∼**iger** *m* **-s,-** styling lotion/(*Schaum-*) mousse. F∼**igkeit** *f* **-** (*s. fest*) firmness; solidity; strength; steadiness. F∼**land** *nt* mainland; (*Kontinent*) continent. f∼**legen** *vt sep* (*fig*) fix, settle; lay down (*Regeln*); tie up (*Geld*); **sich** f∼**legen** commit oneself

festlich *adj* festive. F∼**keiten** *fpl* festivities

fest|liegen† *vi sep* (*haben*) be fixed, settled. f∼**machen** *v sep* ● *vt* fasten/(*binden*) tie (**an** + *dat* to); (f∼*legen*) fix, settle ● *vi* (*haben*) (*Naut*) moor. F∼**mahl** *nt* feast. F∼**nahme** *f* **-,-n** arrest. f∼**nehmen**† *vt sep* arrest. F∼**netz** *nt* landline network. F∼**platte** *f* hard disk. f∼**setzen** *vt sep* fix, settle; (*inhaftieren*) gaol; **sich** f∼**setzen** collect. f∼**sitzen**† *vi sep* (*haben*) be firm/(*Schraube:*) tight; (*haften*) stick; (*nicht weiterkommen*) be stuck. F∼**spiele** *npl* festival *sg.* f∼**stehen**† *vi sep* (*haben*) be certain. f∼**stellen** *vt sep* fix; (*ermitteln*) establish; (*bemerken*) notice; (*sagen*) state. F∼**tag** *m* special day

Festung *f* **-,-en** fortress

Festzug *m* [grand] procession

Fete /'fe:tə, 'fɛ:tə/ *f* **-,-n** party

fett *adj* fat; fatty; (*fettig*) greasy; (*üppig*) rich; (*Druck*) bold. F∼ *nt* **-[e]s,-e** fat; (*flüssig*) grease. f∼**arm** *adj* low-fat. f∼**en** *vt* grease ● *vi* (*haben*) be greasy. F∼**fleck** *m* grease mark. f∼**ig** *adj* greasy

Fetzen *m* **-s,-** scrap; (*Stoff*) rag

feucht *adj* damp, moist; (*Luft*) humid. F∼**igkeit** *f* **-** dampness; (*Nässe*) moisture; (*Luft-*) humidity. F∼**igkeitscreme** *f* moisturizer

Feuer *nt* **-s,-** fire; (*für Zigarette*) light; (*Begeisterung*) passion; F∼ **machen** light a fire. F∼**alarm** *m* fire alarm. f∼**gefährlich** *adj* [in]flammable. F∼**leiter** *f* fire escape. F∼**löscher** *m* **-s,-** fire extinguisher. F∼**melder** *m* **-s,-** fire alarm. f∼**n** *vi* (*haben*) fire (**auf** + *acc* on). F∼**probe** *f* (*fig*) test.

f∼**rot** *adj* crimson. F∼**stein** *m* flint. F∼**stelle** *f* hearth. F∼**treppe** *f* fire escape. F∼**wache** *f* fire station. F∼**waffe** *f* firearm. F∼**wehr** *f* **-,-en** fire brigade. F∼**wehrauto** *nt* fire engine. F∼**wehrmann** *m* (*pl* **-männer** & **-leute**) fireman. F∼**werk** *nt* firework display, fireworks *pl.* F∼**zeug** *nt* lighter

feurig *adj* fiery; (*fig*) passionate

Fiaker *m* **-s,-** (*Aust*) horse-drawn cab

Fichte *f* **-,-n** spruce

Fieber *nt* **-s** [raised] temperature; F∼ **haben** have a temperature. f∼**n** *vi* (*haben*) be feverish. F∼**thermometer** *nt* thermometer

fiebrig *adj* feverish

Figur *f* **-,-en** figure; (*Roman-, Film-*) character; (*Schach-*) piece

Filet /fi'le:/ *nt* **-s,-s** fillet

Filiale *f* **-,-n** (*Comm*) branch

Filigran *nt* **-s** filigree

Film *m* **-[e]s,-e** film; (*Kino-*) film; (*Schicht*) coating. f∼**en** *vt/i* (*haben*) film. F∼**kamera** *f* cine/(*für Kinofilm*) film camera

Filt|er *m* & (*Techn*) *nt* **-s,-** filter; (*Zigaretten-*) filter-tip. f∼**ern** *vt* filter. F∼**erzigarette** *f* filter-tipped cigarette. f∼**rieren** *vt* filter

Filz *m* **-es** felt. F∼**stift** *m* felt-tipped pen

Fimmel *m* **-s,-** 🛈 obsession

Finale *nt* **-s,-** (*Mus*) finale; (*Sport*) final

Finanz *f* **-,-en** finance. F∼**amt** *nt* tax office. f∼**iell** *adj* financial. f∼**ieren** *vt* finance. F∼**minister** *m* minister of finance

find|en† *vt* find; (*meinen*) think; **den Tod** f∼**en** meet one's death; **wie** f∼**est du das?** what do you think of that? **es wird sich** f∼**en** it'll turn up; (*fig*) it'll be all right ● *vi* (*haben*) find one's way. F∼**er** *m* **-s,-** finder. F∼**erlohn** *m* reward. f∼**ig** *adj* resourceful

Finesse *f* **-,-n** (*Kniff*) trick; F∼**n** (*Techn*) refinements

Finger *m* **-s,-** finger; **die** F∼ **lassen von** 🛈 leave alone. F∼**abdruck** *m*

finger mark; (*Admin*) fingerprint.
F~hut *m* thimble. **F~nagel** *m* fin-
gernail. **F~spitze** *f* fingertip. **F~zeig**
m -[e]s,-e hint

Fink *m* -en,-en finch

Finn|e *m* -n,-n, **F~in** *f* -,-nen Finn.
f~isch *adj* Finnish. **F~land** *nt* -s
Finland

finster *adj* dark; (*düster*) gloomy;
(*unheildrohend*) sinister. **F~nis** *f* -
darkness; (*Astronomy*) eclipse

Firm|a *f* -,-men firm, company

Firmen|wagen *m* company car.
F~zeichen *nt* trade mark, logo

Firmung *f* -,-en (*Relig*) confirmation

Firnis *m* -ses,-se varnish. **f~sen** *vt*
varnish

First *m* -[e]s,-e [roof] ridge

Fisch *m* -[e]s,-e fish; **F~e** (*Astrology*)
Pisces. **F~dampfer** *m* trawler. **f~en**
vt/i (*haben*) fish. **F~er** *m* -s,- fisher-
man. **F~erei** *f* - fishing. **F~händler**
m fishmonger. **F~reiher** *m* heron

Fiskus *m* - der F~ the Treasury

fit *adj* fit. **Fitness** *f* - fitness

fix *adj* 🔲 quick; (*geistig*) bright; **f~e
Idee** obsession; **fix und fertig** all finished; (*bereit*) all ready; (🔲: *erschöpft*) shattered. **F~er** *m* -s,- ✖
junkie

fixieren *vt* stare at; (*Phot*) fix

Fjord *m* -[e]s,-e fiord

flach *adj* flat; (*eben*) level; (*niedrig*)
low; (*nicht tief*) shallow

Flachbildschirm *m* flat screen

Fläche *f* -,-n area; (*Ober-*) surface;
(*Seite*) face. **F~nmaß** *nt* square
measure

Flachs *m* -es flax. **f~blond** *adj*
flaxen-haired; (*Haar*) flaxen

flackern *vi* (*haben*) flicker

Flagge *f* -,-n flag

Flair /flɛːɐ̯/ *nt* -s air, aura

Flak *f* -,-[s] anti-aircraft artillery/
(*Geschütz*) gun

flämisch *adj* Flemish

Flamme *f* -,-n flame; (*Koch-*) burner

Flanell *m* -s (*Textiles*) flannel

Flank|e *f* -,-n flank. **f~ieren** *vt* flank

Flasche *f* -,-n bottle. **F~nbier** *nt*
bottled beer. **F~nöffner** *m* bottle-
opener. **F~npfand** *nt* deposit (*on
bottle*)

flatter|haft *adj* fickle. **f~n** *vi* (*sein/
haben*) flutter; (*Segel:*) flap

flau *adj* (*schwach*) faint; (*Comm*) slack

Flaum *m* -[e]s down. **f~ig** *adj*
downy; **f~ig rühren** (*Aust Culin*)
cream

flauschig *adj* fleecy; (*Spielzeug*)
fluffy

Flausen *fpl* 🔲 silly ideas

Flaute *f* -,-n (*Naut*) calm; (*Comm*)
slack period; (*Schwäche*) low

fläzen (sich) *vr* 🔲 sprawl

Flechte *f* -,-n (*Med*) eczema; (*Bot*) li-
chen; (*Zopf*) plait. **f~n†** *vt* plait;
weave (*Korb*)

Fleck *m* -[e]s,-e[n] spot; (*größer*)
patch; (*Schmutz-*) stain, mark; **blauer
F~** bruise. **f~en** *vi* (*haben*) stain.
f~enlos *adj* spotless. **F~entferner**
m -s,- stain remover. **f~ig** *adj*
stained

Fledermaus *f* bat

Flegel *m* -s,- lout. **f~haft** *adj* loutish

flehen *vi* (*haben*) beg (**um** for)

Fleisch *nt* -[e]s flesh; (*Culin*) meat;
(*Frucht-*) pulp; **F~ fressend** carnivor-
ous. **F~er** *m* -s,- butcher. **F~fresser**
m -s,- carnivore. **f~ig** *adj* fleshy.
f~lich *adj* carnal. **F~wolf** *m* mincer

Fleiß *m* -es diligence; **mit F~** dili-
gently; (*absichtlich*) on purpose. **f~ig**
adj diligent; (*arbeitsam*) industrious

fletschen *vt* **die Zähne f~** (*Tier:*)
bare its teeth

flex|ibel *adj* flexible; (*Einband*) limp.
F~ibilität *f* - flexibility

flicken *vt* mend; (*mit Flicken*) patch.
F~ *m* -s,- patch

Flieder *m* -s lilac

Fliege *f* -,-n fly; (*Schleife*) bow-tie.
f~n† *vi* (*sein*) fly; (*geworfen werden*)
be thrown; (🔲: *fallen*) fall; (🔲: *entlassen werden*) be fired/(*von der Schule*)
expelled; **in die Luft f~n** blow up
● *vt* fly. **f~nd** *adj* flying. **F~r** *m* -s,-
airman; (*Pilot*); pilot; (🔲: *Flugzeug*)

plane. **F~rangriff** m air raid

flieh|en† vi (sein) flee (**vor** + dat from); (entweichen) escape ● vt shun. **f~end** adj fleeing; (Kinn, Stirn) receding

Fliese f -,-n tile

Fließ|band nt assembly line. **f~en**† vi (sein) flow; (aus Wasserhahn) run. **f~end** adj flowing; (Wasser) running; (Verkehr) moving; (geläufig) fluent

flimmern vi (haben) shimmer; (TV) flicker

flink adj nimble; (schnell) quick

Flinte f -,-n shotgun

Flirt /flœgt/ m -s,-s flirtation. **f~en** vi (haben) flirt

Flitter m -s sequins pl. **F~wochen** fpl honeymoon sg

flitzen vi (sein) Ⓘ dash

Flock|e f -,-n flake; (Wolle) tuft. **f~ig** adj fluffy

Floh m -[e]s,⁻e flea. **F~spiel** nt tiddly-winks sg

Flora f - flora

Florett nt -[e]s,-e foil

florieren vi (haben) flourish

Floskel f -,-n [empty] phrase

Floß nt -es,⁻e raft

Flosse f -,-n fin; (Seehund-, Gummi-) flipper; (sl: Hand) paw

Flöt|e f -,-n flute; (Block-) recorder. **f~en** vi (haben) play the flute/recorder; (Ⓘ: pfeifen) whistle ● vt play on the flute/recorder. **F~ist(in)** m -en,-en (f -,-nen) flautist

flott adj quick; (lebhaft) lively; (schick) smart

Flotte f -,-n fleet

flottmachen vt sep wieder f~ (Naut) refloat; get going again (Auto); put back on its feet (Unternehmen)

Flöz nt -es,-e [coal] seam

Fluch m -[e]s,⁻e curse. **f~en** vi (haben) curse, swear

Flucht f - flight; (Entweichen) escape; **die F~ ergreifen** take flight. **f~artig** adj hasty

flücht|en vi (sein) flee (**vor** + dat from); (entweichen) escape ● vr **sich f~en** take refuge. **f~ig** adj fugitive; (kurz) brief; (Blick) fleeting; (Bekanntschaft) passing; (oberflächlich) cursory; (nicht sorgfältig) careless. **f~ig kennen** know slightly. **F~igkeitsfehler** m slip. **F~ling** m -s,-e fugitive; (Pol) refugee

Fluchwort nt (pl -wörter) swear word

Flug m -[e]s,⁻e flight. **F~abwehr** f anti-aircraft defence

Flügel m -s,- wing; (Fenster-) casement; (Mus) grand piano

Fluggast m [air] passenger

flügge adj fully-fledged

Flug|gesellschaft f airline. **F~hafen** m airport. **F~lotse** m air-traffic controller. **F~platz** m airport; (klein) airfield. **F~preis** m air fare. **F~schein** m air ticket. **F~schneise** f flight path. **F~schreiber** m -s,- flight recorder. **F~schrift** f pamphlet. **F~steig** m -[e]s,-e gate. **F~zeug** nt -[e]s,-e aircraft, plane

Flunder f -,-n flounder

flunkern vi (haben) Ⓘ tell fibs

Flur m -[e]s,-e [entrance] hall; (Gang) corridor

Fluss m -es,⁻e river; (Fließen) flow; **im F~** (fig) in a state of flux. **f~abwärts** adv downstream. **f~aufwärts** adv upstream

flüssig adj liquid; (Lava) molten; (fließend) fluent; (Verkehr) freely moving. **F~keit** f -,-en liquid; (Anat) fluid

Flusspferd nt hippopotamus

flüstern vt/i (haben) whisper

Flut f -,-en high tide; (fig) flood

Föderation /-'tsio:n/ f -,-en federation

Fohlen nt -s,- foal

Föhn m -s föhn [wind]; (Haartrockner) hairdrier. **f~en** vt [blow-]dry

Folg|e f -,-n consequence; (Reihe) succession; (Fortsetzung) instalment; (Teil) part. **f~en** vi (sein) follow (**jdm/etw** s.o./sth); (zuhören) listen (dat to); **wie f~t** as follows

● (*haben*) (*gehorchen*) obey (**jdm s.o.**). **f~end** *adj* following; **F~endes** the following

folger|n *vt* conclude (**aus** from). **F~ung** *f* -,-en conclusion

folg|lich *adv* consequently. **f~sam** *adj* obedient

Folie /ˈfoːliə/ *f* -,-n foil; (*Plastik-*) film

Folklore *f* - folklore

Folter *f* -,-n torture. **f~n** *vt* torture

Fön ® *m* -s,-e hairdrier

Fonds /foː/ *m* -,- fund

fönen* *vt* = föhnen

Förder|band *nt* (*pl* -bänder) conveyor belt. **f~lich** *adj* beneficial

fordern *vt* demand; (*beanspruchen*) claim; (*zum Kampf*) challenge

fördern *vt* promote; (*unterstützen*) encourage; (*finanziell*) sponsor; (*gewinnen*) extract

Forderung *f* -,-en demand; (*Anspruch*) claim

Förderung *f* - promotion; encouragement; (*Techn*) production

Forelle *f* -,-n trout

Form *f* -,-en form; (*Gestalt*) shape; (*Culin, Techn*) mould; (*Back-*) tin; [**gut**] **in F~** in good form

Formalität *f* -,-en formality

Format *nt* -[e]s,-e format; (*Größe*) size; (*fig: Bedeutung*) stature

formatieren *vt* format

Formel *f* -,-n formula

formen *vt* shape, mould; (*bilden*) form; **sich f~** take shape

förmlich *adj* formal

form|los *adj* shapeless; (*zwanglos*) informal. **F~sache** *f* formality

Formular *nt* -s,-e [printed] form

formulier|en *vt* formulate, word. **F~ung** *f* -,-en wording

forsch|en *vi* (*haben*) search (**nach** for). **f~end** *adj* searching. **F~er** *m* -s,- research scientist; (*Reisender*) explorer. **F~ung** *f* -,-en research

Forst *m* -[e]s,-e forest

Förster *m* -s,- forester

Forstwirtschaft *f* forestry

Fort *nt* -s,-s (*Mil*) fort

fort *adv* away; **f~ sein** be away; (*gegangen/verschwunden*) have gone; **und so f~** and so on; **in einem f~** continuously. **F~bewegung** *f* locomotion. **F~bildung** *f* further education/training. **f~bleiben†** *vi sep* (*sein*) stay away. **f~bringen†** *vt sep* take away. **f~fahren†** *vi sep* (*sein*) go away ● (*haben/sein*) continue (**zu** to). **f~fallen†** *vi sep* (*sein*) be dropped/ (*ausgelassen*) omitted; (*entfallen*) no longer apply; (*aufhören*) cease. **f~führen** *vt sep* continue. **f~gehen†** *vi sep* (*sein*) leave, go away; (*ausgehen*) go out; (*andauern*) go on. **f~geschritten** *adj* advanced; (*spät*) late. **F~geschrittene(r)** *m/f* advanced student. **f~lassen†** *vt sep* let go; (*auslassen*) omit. **f~laufen†** *vi sep* (*sein*) run away; (*sich f~setzen*) continue. **f~laufend** *adj* consecutive. **f~pflanzen (sich)** *vr sep* reproduce; (*Ton, Licht:*) travel. **F~pflanzung** *f* - reproduction. **F~pflanzungsorgan** *nt* reproductive organ. **f~schicken** *vt sep* send away; (*abschicken*) send off. **f~schreiten†** *vi sep* (*sein*) continue; (*Fortschritte machen*) progress, advance. **f~schreitend** *adj* progressive; (*Alter*) advancing. **f~schritt** *m* progress; **F~schritte machen** make progress. **f~schrittlich** *adj* progressive. **f~setzen** *vt sep* continue; **sich f~setzen** continue. **F~setzung** *f* -,-en continuation; (*Folge*) instalment; **F~setzung folgt** to be continued. **F~setzungsroman** *m* serialized novel, serial. **f~während** *adj* constant. **f~ziehen†** *v sep* ● *vt* pull away ● *vi* (*sein*) move away

Fossil *nt* -s,-ien fossil

Foto *nt* -s,-s photo. **F~apparat** *m* camera. **f~gen** *adj* photogenic

Fotograf|(in) *m* -en,-en (*f* -,-nen) photographer. **F~ie** *f* -,-n photography; (*Bild*) photograph. **f~ieren** *vt* take a photo[graph] of ● *vi* (*haben*) take photographs. **f~isch** *adj* photographic

Fotohandy *nt* camera phone

Fotokopie *f* photocopy. **f~ren** *vt*

photocopy. **F~rgerät** nt photocopier

Föt|us m -,-ten foetus

Foul /faul/ nt -s,-s (Sport) foul. **f~en** vt foul

Fracht f -,-en freight. **F~er** m -s,- freighter. **F~gut** nt freight. **F~schiff** nt cargo boat

Frack m -[e]s,⁼e & -s tailcoat

Frage f -,-n question; **nicht in F~ kommen** s. **infrage**. **F~bogen** m questionnaire. **f~n** vt (haben) ask; **sich f~n** wonder (**ob** whether). **f~nd** adj questioning. **F~zeichen** nt question mark

frag|lich adj doubtful; (Person, Sache) in question. **f~los** adv undoubtedly

Fragment nt -[e]s,-e fragment

fragwürdig adj questionable; (verdächtig) dubious

Fraktion /-'tsio:n/ f -,-en parliamentary party

Franken[1] m -s,- (Swiss) franc

Franken[2] nt -s Franconia

frankieren vt stamp, frank

Frankreich nt -s France

Fransen fpl fringe sg

Franz|ose m -n,-n Frenchman; **die F~osen** the French pl. **F~ösin** f -,-nen Frenchwoman. **f~ösisch** adj French. **F~ösisch** nt -[s] (Lang) French

Fraß m -es feed; (pej: Essen) muck

Fratze f -,-n grotesque face; (Grimasse) grimace

Frau f -,-en woman; (Ehe-) wife; **F~ Thomas** Mrs Thomas; **Unsere Liebe F~** (Relig) Our Lady

Frauen|arzt m, **F~ärztin** f gynaecologist. **F~rechtlerin** f -,-nen feminist

Fräulein nt -s,- single woman; (jung) young lady; (Anrede) Miss

frech adj cheeky; (unverschämt) impudent. **F~heit** f -,-en cheekiness; impudence; (Äußerung) impertinence

frei adj free; (freischaffend) freelance; (Künstler) independent; (nicht besetzt) vacant; (offen) open; (bloß) bare; **f~er Tag** day off; **sich** (dat) **f~ neh-**

men take time off; **f~ machen** (räumen) clear; vacate (Platz); (befreien) liberate; **f~ lassen** leave free; **ist dieser Platz f~?** is this seat taken? **'Zimmer f~'** 'vacancies' ● adv freely; (ohne Notizen) without notes; (umsonst) free

Frei|bad nt open-air swimming pool. **f~beruflich** adj & adv freelance. **F~e** nt **im F~en** in the open air, out of doors. **F~gabe** f release. **f~geben†** v sep ● vt release; (eröffnen) open; **jdm einen Tag f~geben** give s.o. a day off ● vi (haben) **jdm f~geben** give s.o. time off. **f~gebig** adj generous. **F~gebigkeit** f - generosity. **f~haben†** v sep ● vt **eine Stunde f~haben** have an hour off; (Sch) have a free period ● vi (haben) be off work/(Sch) school; (beurlaubt sein) have time off. **f~händig** adv without holding on

Freiheit f -,-en freedom, liberty. **F~sstrafe** f prison sentence

Frei|herr m baron. **F~körperkultur** f naturism. **F~lassung** f - release. **F~lauf** m free-wheel. **f~legen** vt sep expose. **f~lich** adv admittedly; (natürlich) of course. **F~lichttheater** nt open-air theatre. **f~machen** vt sep (frankieren) frank; (entkleiden) bare; **einen Tag f~machen** take a day off. **F~maurer** m Freemason. **f~schaffend** adj freelance. **f~schwimmen†** (sich) v sep pass one's swimming test. **f~sprechen†** vt sep acquit. **F~spruch** m acquittal. **f~stehen†** vi sep (haben) stand empty; **es steht ihm f~** (fig) he is free (**zu** to). **f~stellen** vt sep exempt (**von** from); **jdm etw f~stellen** leave sth up to s.o. **F~stil** m freestyle. **F~stoß** m free kick

Freitag m Friday. **f~s** adv on Fridays

Frei|tod m suicide. **F~umschlag** m stamped envelope. **f~weg** adv freely; (offen) openly. **f~willig** adj voluntary. **F~willige(r)** m/f volunteer. **F~zeichen** nt ringing tone; (Rufzeichen) dialling tone. **F~zeit** f free or spare time; (Muße) leisure. **F~zeit-** prefix leisure; **F~zeitbeklei-**

dung *f* casual wear. **f~zügig** *adj* unrestricted; (*großzügig*) liberal

fremd *adj* foreign; (*unbekannt*) strange; (*nicht das eigene*) other people's; **ein f~er Mann** a stranger; **f~e Leute** strangers; **unter f~em Namen** under an assumed name; **ich bin hier f~** I'm a stranger here. **F~e** *f* - **in der F~e** away from home; (*im Ausland*) in a foreign country. **F~e(r)** *m/f* stranger; (*Ausländer*) foreigner; (*Tourist*) tourist. **F~enführer** *m* [tourist] guide. **F~enverkehr** *m* tourism. **F~enzimmer** *nt* room [to let]; (*Gäste-*) guest room. **f~gehen†** *vi sep* (*sein*) 🅣 be unfaithful. **F~sprache** *f* foreign language. **F~wort** *nt* (*pl* **-wörter**) foreign word

Freske *f* -,-n, **Fresko** *nt* -s,-ken fresco

Fresse *f* -,-n 🗵 (*Mund*) gob; (*Gesicht*) mug. **f~n†** *vt/i* (*haben*) eat. **F~n** *nt* -s feed; (*sl: Essen*) grub

Fressnapf *m* feeding bowl

Freud|e *f* -,-n pleasure; (*innere*) joy; **mit F~en** with pleasure; **jdm eine F~e machen** please s.o. **f~ig** *adj* joyful

freuen *vt* please; **sich f~** be pleased (**über** + *acc* about); **sich f~ auf** (+ *acc*) look forward to; **es freut mich** I'm glad (**dass** that)

Freund *m* -es,-e friend; (*Verehrer*) boyfriend. **F~in** *f* -,-nen friend; (*Liebste*) girlfriend. **f~lich** *adj* kind; (*umgänglich*) friendly; (*angenehm*) pleasant. **f~licherweise** *adv* kindly. **F~lichkeit** *f* -,-en kindness; friendliness; pleasantness

Freundschaft *f* -,-en friendship; **F~ schließen** become friends. **f~lich** *adj* friendly

Frieden *m* -s peace; **F~ schließen** make peace; **im F~** in peacetime; **lass mich in F~!** leave me alone! **F~svertrag** *m* peace treaty

Fried|hof *m* cemetery. **f~lich** *adj* peaceful

frieren† *vi* (*haben*) (*Person:*) be cold; *impers* **es friert/hat gefroren** it is

freezing/there has been a frost; **frierst du?** are you cold? ● (*sein*) (*gefrieren*) freeze

Fries *m* -es,-e frieze

frisch *adj* fresh; (*sauber*) clean; (*leuchtend*) bright; (*munter*) lively; (*rüstig*) fit; **sich f~ machen** freshen up ● *adv* freshly, newly; **ein Bett f~ beziehen** put clean sheets on a bed; **f~ gestrichen!** wet paint! **F~e** *f* - freshness; brightness; liveliness; fitness. **F~haltepackung** *f* vacuum pack

Fri|seur /fri'zøːɐ̯/ *m* -s,-e hairdresser; (*Herren-*) barber. **F~seursalon** *m* hairdressing salon. **F~seuse** *f* -,-n hairdresser

frisier|en *vt* jdn/sich f~en do someone's/one's hair; **die Bilanz/einen Motor f~en** 🅣 fiddle the accounts/soup up an engine

Frisör *m* -s,-e = Friseur

Frist *f* -,-en period; (*Termin*) deadline; (*Aufschub*) time; **drei Tage F~** three days' grace. **f~los** *adj* instant

Frisur *f* -,-en hairstyle

frittieren *vt* deep-fry

frivol /fri'voːl/ *adj* frivolous

froh *adj* happy; (*freudig*) joyful; (*erleichtert*) glad

fröhlich *adj* cheerful; (*vergnügt*) merry. **F~keit** *f* - cheerfulness; merriment

fromm *adj* devout; (*gutartig*) docile

Frömmigkeit *f* - devoutness

Fronleichnam *m* Corpus Christi

Front *f* -,-en front. **f~al** *adj* frontal; (*Zusammenstoß*) head-on ● *adv* from the front; (*zusammenstoßen*) head-on. **F~alzusammenstoß** *m* head-on collision

Frosch *m* -[e]s,⸚e frog. **F~laich** *m* frog-spawn. **F~mann** *m* (*pl* **-männer**) frogman

Frost *m* -[e]s,⸚e frost. **F~beule** *f* chilblain

frösteln *vi* (*haben*) shiver

frost|ig *adj* frosty. **F~schutzmittel** *nt* antifreeze

Frottee *nt* & *m* -s towelling;

F~[hand]tuch nt terry towel

frottieren vt rub down

Frucht f -,-̈e fruit; **F~ tragen** bear fruit. **f~bar** adj fertile; (fig) fruitful. **F~barkeit** f - fertility

früh adj early ● adv early; (morgens) in the morning; **heute f~** this morning; **von f~ an** od **auf** from an early age. **F~aufsteher** m -s,- early riser. **F~e** f - **in aller F~e** bright and early; **in der F~e** (SGer) in the morning. **f~er** adv earlier; (eher) sooner; (ehemals) formerly; (vor langer Zeit) in the old days; **f~er oder später** sooner or later; **ich wohnte f~er in X** I used to live in X. **f~ere(r,s)** adj earlier; (ehemalig) former; (vorige) previous; **in f~eren Zeiten** in former times. **f~estens** adv at the earliest. **F~geburt** f premature birth/(Kind) baby. **F~jahr** nt spring. **F~ling** m -s,-e spring. **f~morgens** adv early in the morning. **f~reif** adj precocious

Frühstück nt breakfast. **f~en** vi (haben) have breakfast

frühzeitig adj & adv early; (vorzeitig) premature

Frustr|ation /-'tsjo:n/ f -,-en frustration. **f~ieren** vt frustrate

Fuchs m -es,-̈e fox; (Pferd) chestnut. **f~en** vt 🔲 annoy

Füchsin f -,-nen vixen

Fuge¹ f -,-n joint

Fuge² f -,-n (Mus) fugue

füg|en vt fit (in + acc into); (an-) join (an + acc on to); (dazu-) add (zu to); **sich f~en** fit (in + acc into); adjoin/(folgen) follow (an etw acc sth); (fig: gehorchen) submit (dat to). **f~sam** adj obedient. **F~ung** f -,-en **eine F~ung des Schicksals** a stroke of fate

fühl|bar adj noticeable. **f~en** vt/i (haben) feel; **sich f~en** feel (krank/einsam ill/lonely); (🔲: stolz sein) fancy oneself. **F~er** m -s,- feeler. **F~ung** f - contact

Fuhre f -,-n load

führ|en vt lead; guide (Tourist); (geleiten) take; (leiten) run; (befehligen) command; (verkaufen) stock; bear (Namen); keep (Liste, Bücher); **bei** od **mit sich f~en** carry ● vi (haben) lead; (verlaufen) go, run; **zu etw f~en** lead to sth. **f~end** adj leading. **F~er** m -s,- leader; (Fremden-) guide; (Buch) guide[book]. **F~erhaus** nt driver's cab. **F~erschein** m driving licence; **den F~erschein machen** take one's driving test. **F~erscheinentzug** m disqualification from driving. **F~ung** f -,-en leadership; (Leitung) management; (Mil) command; (Betragen) conduct; (Besichtigung) guided tour; (Vorsprung) lead; **in F~ung gehen** go into the lead

Fuhr|unternehmer m haulage contractor. **F~werk** nt cart

Fülle f -,-n abundance, wealth (an + dat of); (Körper-) plumpness. **f~n** vt fill; (Culin) stuff

Füllen nt -s,- foal

Füll|er m -s,- 🔲, **F~federhalter** m fountain pen. **F~ung** f -,-en filling; (Braten-) stuffing

fummeln vi (haben) fumble (an + dat with)

Fund m -[e]s,-e find

Fundament nt -[e]s,-e foundations pl. **f~al** adj fundamental

Fundbüro nt lost-property office

fünf inv adj, **F~** f -,-en five; (Sch) ≈ fail mark. **F~linge** mpl quintuplets. **f~te(r,s)** adj fifth. **f~zehn** inv adj fifteen. **f~zehnte(r,s)** adj fifteenth. **f~zig** inv adj fifty. **f~zigste(r,s)** adj fiftieth

fungieren vi (haben) act (als as)

Funk m -s radio. **F~e** m -n,-n spark. **f~eln** vi (haben) sparkle; (Stern:) twinkle. **F~en** m -s,- spark. **f~en** vt radio. **F~sprechgerät** nt walkietalkie. **F~spruch** m radio message. **F~streife** f [police] radio patrol

Funktion /-'tsjo:n/ f -,-en function; (Stellung) position; (Funktionieren) working; **außer F~** out of action. **F~är** m -s,-e official. **f~ieren** vi (haben) work

für prep (+ acc) for; **Schritt für**

Schritt step by step; **was für [ein]** what [a]! (*fragend*) what sort of [a]? **Für** *nt* **das Für und Wider** the pros and cons *pl*

Furche *f* -,-n furrow

Furcht *f* - fear (**vor** + *dat* of); **F~erregend** terrifying. **f~bar** *adj* terrible

fürcht|en *vt/i* (*haben*) fear; **sich f~en** be afraid (**vor** + *dat* of). **f~erlich** *adj* dreadful

füreinander *adv* for each other

Furnier *nt* -s,-e veneer. **f~t** *adj* veneered

Fürsorg|e *f* care; (*Admin*) welfare; (🔲: *Geld*) ≈ social security. **F~er(in)** *m* -s,- (*f* -,-nen) social worker. **f~lich** *adj* solicitous

Fürst *m* -en,-en prince. **F~entum** *nt* -s,⁻er principality. **F~in** *f* -,-nen princess

Furt *f* -,-en ford

Furunkel *m* -s,- (*Med*) boil

Fürwort *nt* (*pl* -wörter) pronoun

Furz *m* -es,-e (*vulgar*) fart

Fusion *f* -,-en fusion; (*Comm*) merger

Fuß *m* -es,⁻e foot; (*Aust: Bein*) leg; (*Lampen-*) base; (*von Weinglas*) stem; **zu Fuß** on foot; **zu Fuß gehen** walk; **auf freiem Fuß** free. **F~abdruck** *m* footprint. **F~abtreter** *m* -s,- doormat. **F~ball** *m* football. **F~ballspieler** *m* footballer. **F~balltoto** *nt* football pools *pl*. **F~bank** *f* footstool. **F~boden** *m* floor

Fussel *f* -,-n & *m* -s,-[n] piece of fluff; **F~n** fluff *sg.* **f~n** *vi* (*haben*) shed fluff

fußen *vi* (*haben*) be based (**auf** + *dat* on)

Fußgänger|(in) *m* -s,- (*f* -,-nen) pedestrian. **F~brücke** *f* footbridge. **F~zone** *f* pedestrian precinct

Fuß|geher *m* -s,- (*Aust*) = **F~gänger. F~gelenk** *nt* ankle. **F~hebel** *m* pedal. **F~nagel** *m* toenail. **F~note** *f* footnote. **F~pflege** *f* chiropody. **F~rücken** *m* instep. **F~sohle** *f* sole of the foot. **F~tritt** *m* kick. **F~weg** *m* footpath; **eine Stunde F~weg** an hour's walk

futsch *pred adj* 🔲 gone

Futter¹ *nt* -s feed; (*Trocken-*) fodder

Futter² *nt* -s,- (*Kleider-*) lining

Futteral *nt* -s,-e case

füttern¹ *vt* feed

füttern² *vt* line

Futur *nt* -s (*Gram*) future

• •

Gg

• •

Gabe *f* -,-n gift; (*Dosis*) dose

Gabel *f* -,-n fork. **g~n (sich)** *vr* fork. **G~stapler** *m* -s,- fork-lift truck. **G~ung** *f* -,-en fork

gackern *vi* (*haben*) cackle

gaffen *vi* (*haben*) gape, stare

Gage /'gaːʒə/ *f* -,-n (*Theat*) fee

gähnen *vi* (*haben*) yawn

Gala *f* - ceremonial dress

Galavorstellung *f* gala performance

Galerie *f* -,-n gallery

Galgen *m* -s,- gallows *sg.* **G~frist** *f* 🔲 reprieve

Galionsfigur *f* figurehead

Galle *f* - bile; (*G~nblase*) gall-bladder. **G~nblase** *f* gall-bladder. **G~nstein** *m* gallstone

Galopp *m* -s gallop; **im G~** at a gallop. **g~ieren** *vi* (*sein*) gallop

gamm|eln *vi* (*haben*) 🔲 loaf around. **G~ler(in)** *m* -s,- (*f* -,-nen) drop-out

Gams *f* -,-en (*Aust*) chamois

Gämse *f* -,-n chamois

Gang *m* -[e]s,⁻e walk; (*G~art*) gait; (*Boten-*) errand; (*Funktionieren*) running; (*Verlauf, Culin*) course; (*Durch-*) passage; (*Korridor*) corridor; (*zwischen Sitzreihen*) aisle, gangway; (*Anat*) duct; (*Auto*) gear; **in G~ bringen** get going; **im G~e sein** be in progress; **Essen mit vier G~en** four-course meal

gängig adj common; (Comm) popular

Gangschaltung f gear change

Gangster /'gɛŋstɐ/ m -s,- gangster

Ganove m -n,-n 🔲 crook

Gans f -,ᴙe goose

Gänse|blümchen nt -s,- daisy. **G~füßchen** ntpl inverted commas. **G~haut** f goose-pimples pl. **G~rich** m -s,-e gander

ganz adj whole, entire; (vollständig) complete; (🔲: heil) undamaged, intact; **die g~e Zeit** all the time, the whole time; **eine g~e Weile/Menge** quite a while/lot; inv **g~ Deutschland** the whole of Germany; **wieder g~ machen** 🔲 mend; **im Großen und G~en** on the whole ● adv quite; (völlig) completely, entirely; (sehr) very; **nicht g~** not quite; **g~ allein** all on one's own; **g~ und gar** completely, totally; **g~ und gar nicht** not at all. **G~e(s)** nt whole. **g~jährig** adv all the year round. **g~tägig** adj & adv full-time; (geöffnet) all day. **g~tags** adv all day; (arbeiten) full-time

gar¹ adj done, cooked

gar² adv **gar nicht/nichts/niemand** not/nothing/no one at all

Garage /ga'ra:ʒə/ f -,-n garage

Garantie f -,-n guarantee. **g~ren** vt/i (haben) [für] etw **g~ren** guarantee sth. **G~schein** m guarantee

Garderobe f -,-n (Kleider) wardrobe; (Ablage) cloakroom; (Künstler-) dressing-room. **G~nfrau** f cloakroom attendant

Gardine f -,-n curtain

garen vt/i (haben) cook

gären† vi (haben) ferment; (fig) seethe

Garn nt -[e]s,-e yarn; (Näh-) cotton

Garnele f -,-n shrimp; prawn

garnieren vt decorate; (Culin) garnish

Garnison f -,-en garrison

Garnitur f -,-en set; (Möbel-) suite

Garten m -s,ᴙ garden. **G~arbeit** f gardening. **G~bau** m horticulture.

G~haus nt, **G~laube** f summerhouse. **G~schere** f secateurs pl

Gärtner|(in) m -s,- (f -,-nen) gardener. **G~ei** f -,-en nursery

Gärung f - fermentation

Gas nt -es,-e gas; **Gas geben** 🔲 accelerate. **G~maske** f gas mask. **G~pedal** nt (Auto) accelerator

Gasse f -,-n alley; (Aust) street

Gast m -[e]s,ᴙe guest; (Hotel-) visitor; (im Lokal) patron; **zum Mittag G~e haben** have people to lunch; **bei jdm zu G~ sein** be staying with s.o. **G~arbeiter** m foreign worker. **G~bett** nt spare bed

Gäste|bett nt spare bed. **G~buch** nt visitors' book. **G~zimmer** nt [hotel] room; (privat) spare room

gast|freundlich adj hospitable. **G~freundschaft** f hospitality. **G~geber** m -s,- host. **G~geberin** f -,-nen hostess. **G~haus** nt, **G~hof** m inn, hotel

gastlich adj hospitable

Gastronomie f - gastronomy

Gast|spiel nt guest performance. **G~spielreise** f (Theat) tour. **G~stätte** f restaurant. **G~wirt** m landlord. **G~wirtin** f landlady. **G~wirtschaft** f restaurant

Gas|werk nt gasworks sg. **G~zähler** m gas meter

Gatte m -n,-n husband

Gattin f -,-nen wife

Gattung f -,-en kind; (Biology) genus; (Kunst) genre

Gaudi f - (Aust, 🔲) fun

Gaumen m -s,- palate

Gauner m -s,- crook, swindler. **G~ei** f -,-en swindle

Gaze /'ga:zə/ f - gauze

Gazelle f -,-n gazelle

Gebäck nt -s [cakes and] pastries pl; (Kekse) biscuits pl

Gebälk nt -s timbers pl

geballt adj (Faust) clenched

Gebärde f -,-n gesture

gebär|en† vt give birth to, bear; **ge-**

boren werden be born. **G~mutter**
f womb, uterus

Gebäude nt -s,- building

Gebeine ntpl [mortal] remains

Gebell nt -s barking

geben† vt give; (tun, bringen) put;
(Karten) deal; (aufführen) perform;
(unterrichten) teach; **etw verloren
g~** give sth up as lost; **viel/wenig
g~ auf** (+ acc) set great/little store
by; **sich g~** (nachlassen) wear off;
(besser werden) get better; (sich verhalten) behave ● impers **es gibt** there
is/are; **was gibt es Neues/zum
Mittag/im Kino?** what's the news/
for lunch/on the cinema? **es wird
Regen g~** it's going to rain ● vi
(haben) (Karten) deal

Gebet nt -[e]s,-e prayer

Gebiet nt -[e]s,-e area; (Hoheits-) territory; (Sach-) field

gebieten† vt command; (erfordern)
demand ● vi (haben) rule

Gebilde nt -s,- structure

gebildet adj educated; (kultiviert)
cultured

Gebirg|e nt -s,- mountains pl. **g~ig**
adj mountainous

Gebiss nt -es,-e teeth pl; (künstliches)
false teeth pl; dentures pl, (des Zau-
mes) bit

geblümt adj floral, flowered

gebogen adj curved

geboren adj born; **g~er Deutscher**
German by birth; **Frau X, g~e Y** Mrs
X, née Y

Gebot nt -[e]s,-e rule

gebraten adj fried

Gebrauch m use; (Sprach-) usage;
Gebräuche customs; **in G~** in use;
G~ machen von make use of.
g~en vt use; **zu nichts zu g~en**
useless

gebräuchlich adj common; (Wort)
in common use

**Gebrauch|sanleitung, G~san-
weisung** f directions pl for use. **g~t**
adj used; (Comm) secondhand.
G~twagen m used car

gebrechlich adj frail, infirm

gebrochen adj broken ● adv
g~Englisch sprechen speak broken
English

Gebrüll nt -s roaring

Gebühr f -,-en charge, fee; **über G~**
excessively. **g~end** adj due; (gezie-
mend) proper. **g~enfrei** adj free
● adv free of charge. **g~enpflichtig**
adj & adv subject to a charge; **g~en-
pflichtige Straße** toll road

Geburt f -,-en birth; **von G~** by
birth. **G~enkontrolle, G~enrege-
lung** f birth control. **G~enziffer** f
birth rate

gebürtig adj native (**aus** of); **g~er
Deutscher** German by birth

Geburts|datum nt date of birth.
G~helfer m obstetrician. **G~hilfe** f
obstetrics sg. **G~ort** m place of
birth. **G~tag** m birthday. **G~ur-
kunde** f birth certificate

Gebüsch nt -[e]s,-e bushes pl

Gedächtnis nt -ses memory; **aus
dem G~** from memory

Gedanke m -ns,-n thought (**an** +
acc of); (Idee) idea; **sich** (dat) **G~n
machen** worry (**über** + acc about).
g~nlos adj thoughtless; (zerstreut)
absent-minded. **G~nstrich** m dash

Gedärme ntpl intestines; (Tier-) entrails

Gedeck nt -[e]s,-e place setting; (auf
Speisekarte) set meal

gedeihen† vi (sein) thrive, flourish

gedenken† vi (haben) propose (**etw
zu tun** to do sth); **jds g~** remember
s.o. **G~** nt -s memory

Gedenk|feier f commemoration.
G~gottesdienst m memorial service

Gedicht nt -[e]s,-e poem

Gedräng|e nt -s crush, crowd. **g~t**
adj (knapp) concise ● adv **g~t voll**
packed

Geduld f - patience; **G~ haben** be
patient. **g~en** (sich) vr be patient.
g~ig adj patient. **G~[s]spiel** nt
puzzle

gedunsen adj bloated

g

geehrt *adj* honoured; **Sehr g~er Herr X** Dear Mr X

geeignet *adj* suitable; **im g~en Moment** at the right moment

Gefahr *f* -,-en danger; **in G~** in danger; **auf eigene G~** at one's own risk; **G~ laufen** run the risk (**etw zu tun** of doing sth)

gefähr|den *vt* endanger; (*fig*) jeopardize. **g~lich** *adj* dangerous

gefahrlos *adj* safe

Gefährt *nt* -[e]s,-e vehicle

Gefährte *m* -n,-n, **Gefährtin** *f* -,-nen companion

gefahrvoll *adj* dangerous, perilous

Gefälle *nt* -s,- slope; (Straßen-) gradient

gefallen† *vi* (haben) **jdm g~** please s.o.; **er/es gefällt mir** I like him/it; **sich** (*dat*) **etw g~ lassen** put up with sth

Gefallen¹ *m* -s,- favour

Gefallen² *nt* -s pleasure (**an** + *dat* in); **dir zu G~** to please you

Gefallene(r) *m* soldier killed in the war

gefällig *adj* pleasing; (hübsch) attractive; (hilfsbereit) obliging; **noch etwas g~?** will there be anything else? **G~keit** *f* -,-en favour; (Freundlichkeit) kindness

Gefangen|e(r) *m/f* prisoner. **G~nahme** *f* - capture. **g~nehmen*** *vt sep* = **g~ nehmen**, s. **fangen**. **G~schaft** *f* - captivity

Gefängnis *nt* -ses,-se prison; (Strafe) imprisonment. **G~strafe** *f* imprisonment; (Urteil) prison sentence. **G~wärter** *m* [prison] warder

Gefäß *nt* -es,-e container; (Blut-) vessel

gefasst *adj* composed; (ruhig) calm; **g~ sein auf** (+ *acc*) be prepared for

gefedert *adj* sprung

gefeiert *adj* celebrated

Gefieder *nt* -s plumage

gefleckt *adj* spotted

Geflügel *nt* -s poultry. **G~klein** *nt* -s giblets *pl*. **g~t** *adj* winged

Geflüster *nt* -s whispering

Gefolge *nt* -s retinue, entourage

gefragt *adj* popular

Gefreite(r) *m* lance corporal

gefrier|en† *vi* (sein) freeze. **G~fach** *nt* freezer compartment. **G~punkt** *m* freezing point. **G~schrank** *m* upright freezer. **G~truhe** *f* chest freezer

gefroren *adj* frozen

gefügig *adj* compliant; (gehorsam) obedient

Gefühl *nt* -[e]s,-e feeling; (Empfindung) sensation; (G~sregung) emotion; **im G~ haben** know instinctively. **g~los** *adj* insensitive; (herzlos) unfeeling; (taub) numb. **g~smäßig** *adj* emotional; (instinktiv) instinctive. **G~sregung** *f* emotion. **g~voll** *adj* sensitive; (sentimental) sentimental

gefüllt *adj* filled; (voll) full

gefürchtet *adj* feared, dreaded

gefüttert *adj* lined

gegeben *adj* given; (bestehend) present; (passend) appropriate. **g~enfalls** *adv* if need be

gegen *prep* (+ *acc*) against; (Sport) versus; (g~über) to[-wards]; (Vergleich) compared with; (Richtung, Zeit) towards; (ungefähr) around; **ein Mittel g~** a remedy for ● *adv* **g~ 100 Leute** about 100 people. **G~angriff** *m* counter-attack

Gegend *f* -,-en area, region; (Umgebung) neighbourhood

gegeneinander *adv* against/(gegenüber) towards one another

Gegen|fahrbahn *f* opposite carriageway. **G~gift** *nt* antidote. **G~maßnahme** *f* countermeasure. **G~satz** *m* contrast; (Widerspruch) contradiction; (G~teil) opposite; **im G~satz zu** unlike. **g~seitig** *adj* mutual; **sich g~seitig hassen** hate one another. **G~stand** *m* object; (Gram, Gesprächs-) subject. **G~stück** *nt* counterpart; (G~teil) opposite. **G~teil** *nt* opposite, contrary; **im G~teil** on the contrary. **g~teilig** *adj* opposite

gegenüber *prep* (+ *dat*) opposite;

(*Vergleich*) compared with; **jdm g~ höflich sein** be polite to s.o. ● *adv* opposite. **G~** *nt* **-s** person opposite. **g~liegend** *adj* opposite. **g~stehen†** *vi sep* (*haben*) (+ *dat*) face; **feindlich g~stehen** (+ *dat*) be hostile to s.o. **g~stellen** *vt sep* confront; (*vergleichen*) compare

Gegen|verkehr *m* oncoming traffic. **G~vorschlag** *m* counterproposal. **G~wart** *f* - present; (*Anwesenheit*) presence. **g~wärtig** *adj* present ● *adv* at present. **G~wehr** *f* - resistance. **G~wert** *m* equivalent. **G~wind** *m* head wind. **g~zeichnen** *vt sep* countersign

geglückt *adj* successful

Gegner|(in) *m* **-s,-** (*f* **-,-nen**) opponent. **g~isch** *adj* opposing

Gehabe *nt* **-s** affected behaviour

Gehackte(s) *nt* mince

Gehalt *nt* **-[e]s,ᵚer** salary. **G~serhöhung** *f* rise

gehässig *adj* spiteful

gehäuft *adj* heaped

Gehäuse *nt* **-s,-** case; (*TV, Radio*) cabinet; (*Schnecken-*) shell

Gehege *nt* **-s,-** enclosure

geheim *adj* secret; **g~ halten** keep secret; **im g~en** secretly. **G~dienst** *m* Secret Service. **G~nis** *nt* **-ses,-se** secret. **g~nisvoll** *adj* mysterious

gehemmt *adj* (*fig*) inhibited

---

gehen†

● *intransitive verb* (*sein*)

⋯▸ (*sich irgendwohin begeben*) go; (*zu Fuß*) walk. **tanzen/ schwimmen/einkaufen gehen** go dancing/swimming/shopping. **schlafen gehen** go to bed. **zum Arzt gehen** go to the doctor's. **in die Schule gehen** go to school. **auf und ab gehen** walk up and down. **über die Straße gehen** cross the street

⋯▸ (*weggehen; fam: abfahren*) go; leave. **ich muss bald gehen** I must go soon. **Sie können gehen** you may go. **der Zug geht um zehn Uhr** 🛈 the train leaves *or* goes at ten o'clock

⋯▸ (*funktionieren*) work. **der Computer geht wieder/nicht mehr** the computer is working again/has stopped working. **meine Uhr geht falsch/richtig** my watch is wrong/right

⋯▸ (*möglich sein*) be possible. **ja, das geht** yes, I *or* we can manage that. **das geht nicht** that can't be done; (🛈: *ist nicht akzeptabel*) it's not good enough, it's not on 🛈. **es geht einfach nicht, dass du so spät nach Hause kommst** it simply won't do for you to come home so late

⋯▸ (🛈: *gerade noch angehen*) **es geht [so]** it is all right. **Wie war die Party? — Es ging so** How was the party? — Not bad *or* So-so

⋯▸ (*sich entwickeln*) do; go. **der Laden geht gut** the shop is doing well. **es geht alles nach Wunsch** everything is going to plan

⋯▸ (*impers*) **wie geht es Ihnen?** how are you? **jdm geht es gut/ schlecht** (*gesundheitlich*) s.o. is doing well/badly

⋯▸ (*impers; sich um etw handeln*) **es geht um** it concerns. **worum geht es hier?** what is this all about? **es geht ihr nur ums Geld** she is only interested in money

---

Geheul *nt* **-s** howling

Gehilfe *m* **-n,-n**, **Gehilfin** *f* **-,-nen** trainee; (*Helfer*) assistant

Gehirn *nt* **-s** brain; (*Verstand*) brains *pl* **G~erschütterung** *f* concussion. **G~hautentzündung** *f* meningitis. **G~wäsche** *f* brainwashing

gehoben *adj* (*fig*) superior

Gehöft *nt* **-[e]s,-e** farm

Gehör *nt* **-s** hearing

gehorchen *vi* (*haben*) (+ *dat*) obey

gehören *vi* (*haben*) belong (*dat* to); **dazu gehört Mut** that takes courage; **es gehört sich nicht** it isn't done

gehörlos adj deaf

Gehörn nt -s,-e horns pl; (Geweih) antlers pl

gehorsam adj obedient. **G~** m -s obedience

Geh|steig m -[e]s,-e pavement. **G~weg** m = Gehsteig; (Fußweg) footpath

Geier m -s,- vulture

Geig|e f -,-n violin. **g~en** vi (haben) play the violin ● vt play on the violin. **G~er(in)** m -s,- (f -,-nen) violinist

geil adj lecherous; randy; (🔲: toll) great

Geisel f -,-n hostage

Geiß f -,-en (SGer) [nanny-]goat. **G~blatt** nt honeysuckle

Geist m -[e]s,-er mind; (Witz) wit; (Gesinnung) spirit; (Gespenst) ghost; **der Heilige G~** the Holy Ghost or Spirit

geistes|abwesend adj absent-minded. **G~blitz** m brainwave. **g~gegenwärtig** adv with great presence of mind. **g~gestört** adj [mentally] deranged. **g~krank** adj mentally ill. **G~krankheit** f mental illness. **G~wissenschaften** fpl arts. **G~zustand** m mental state

geist|ig adj mental; (intellektuell) intellectual. **g~lich** adj spiritual; (religiös) religious; (Musik) sacred; (Tracht) clerical. **G~liche(r)** m clergyman. **G~lichkeit** f - clergy. **g~reich** adj clever; (witzig) witty

Geiz m -es meanness. **g~en** vi (haben) be mean (mit with). **G~hals** m 🔲 miser. **g~ig** adj mean, miserly. **G~kragen** m 🔲 miser

Gekicher nt -s giggling

geknickt adj 🔲 dejected

gekonnt adj accomplished ● adv expertly

gekränkt adj offended, hurt

Gekritzel nt -s scribble

Gelächter nt -s laughter

geladen adj loaded

gelähmt adj paralysed

Geländer nt -s,- railings pl; (Treppen-) banisters

gelangen vi (sein) reach/(fig) attain (zu etw/an etw acc sth)

gelassen adj composed; (ruhig) calm. **G~heit** f - equanimity; (Fassung) composure

Gelatine /ʒela-/ f - gelatine

geläufig adj common, current; (fließend) fluent; **jdm g~ sein** be familiar to s.o.

gelaunt adj **gut/schlecht g~ sein** be in a good/bad mood

gelb adj yellow; (bei Ampel) amber; **das G~e vom Ei** the yolk of the egg. **G~** nt -s,- yellow. **g~lich** adj yellowish. **G~sucht** f jaundice

Geld nt -es,-er money; **öffentliche G~er** public funds. **G~automat** m cashpoint machine. **G~beutel** m, **G~börse** f purse. **G~geber** m -s,- backer. **g~lich** adj financial. **G~mittel** ntpl funds. **G~schein** m banknote. **G~schrank** m safe. **G~strafe** f fine. **G~stück** nt coin

Gelee /ʒe'le:/ nt -s,-s jelly

gelegen adj situated; (passend) convenient

Gelegenheit f -,-en opportunity, chance; (Anlass) occasion; (Comm) bargain; **bei G~** some time. **G~sarbeit** f casual work. **G~skauf** m bargain

gelegentlich adj occasional ● adv occasionally; (bei Gelegenheit) some time

Gelehrte(r) m/f scholar

Geleit nt -[e]s escort; **freies G~** safe conduct. **g~en** vt escort

Gelenk nt -[e]s,-e joint. **g~ig** adj supple; (Techn) flexible

gelernt adj skilled

Geliebte(r) m/f lover

gelingen† vi (sein) succeed, be successful. **G~** nt -s success

gellend adj shrill

geloben vt promise [solemnly]; **das Gelobte Land** the Promised Land

Gelöbnis nt -ses,-se vow

gelöst adj (fig) relaxed

gelten† vi (haben) be valid; (Regel:) apply; **g~ als** be regarded as; **etw nicht g~ lassen** not accept sth; **wenig/viel g~** be worth/(fig) count for little/a lot; **jdm g~** be meant for s.o.; **das gilt nicht** that doesn't count. **g~d** adj valid; (Preise) current; (Meinung) prevailing; **g~d machen** assert (Recht, Forderung); bring to bear (Einfluss)

Geltung f - validity; (Ansehen) prestige; **zur G~ bringen** set off

Gelübde nt -s,- vow

gelungen adj successful

Gelüst nt -[e]s,-e desire

gemächlich adj leisurely ● adv in a leisurely manner

Gemahl m -s,-e husband. **G~in** f -,-nen wife

Gemälde nt -s,- painting. **G~galerie** f picture gallery

gemäß prep (+ dat) in accordance with

gemäßigt adj moderate; (Klima) temperate

gemein adj common; (unanständig) vulgar; (niederträchtig) mean; **g~er Soldat** private

Gemeinde f -,-n [local] community; (Admin) borough; (Pfarr-) parish; (bei Gottesdienst) congregation. **G~rat** m local council-/(Person) councillor. **G~wahlen** fpl local elections

gemein|gefährlich adj dangerous. **G~heit** f -,-en commonness; vulgarity; meanness; (Bemerkung, Handlung) mean thing [to say/do]; **so eine G~heit!** how mean! **G~kosten** pl overheads. **g~nützig** adj charitable. **g~sam** adj common ● adv together

Gemeinschaft f -,-en community. **g~lich** adj joint; (Besitz) communal ● adv jointly; (zusammen) together. **G~sarbeit** f team work

Gemenge nt -s,- mixture

Gemisch nt -[e]s,-e mixture. **g~t** adj mixed

Gemme f -,-n engraved gem

Gemse* f -,-n = **Gämse**

Gemurmel nt -s murmuring

Gemüse nt -s,- vegetable; (coll) vegetables pl. **G~händler** m greengrocer

gemustert adj patterned

Gemüt nt -[e]s,-er nature, disposition; (Gefühl) feelings pl

gemütlich adj cosy; (gemächlich) leisurely; (zwanglos) informal; (Person) genial; **es sich** (dat) **g~ machen** make oneself comfortable. **G~keit** f - cosiness

Gen nt -s,-e gene

genau adj exact, precise; (Waage, Messung) accurate; (sorgfältig) meticulous; (ausführlich) detailed; **nichts G~es wissen** not know any details; **g~ genommen** strictly speaking; **g~!** exactly! **G~igkeit** f - exactitude; precision; accuracy; meticulousness

genauso adv just the same; (g~sehr) just as much; **g~ teuer** just as expensive; **g~ gut** just as good; adv just as well; **g~ sehr** just as much; **g~ viel** just as much/many; **g~ wenig** just as little/few; (noch) no more

Gendarm /ʒã'darm/ m -en,-en (Aust) policeman

Genealogie f - genealogy

genehmig|en vt grant; approve (Plan). **G~ung** f -,-en permission; (Schein) permit

geneigt adj sloping, inclined; (fig) well-disposed (dat towards)

General m -s, ̈e general. **G~direktor** m managing director. **G~probe** f dress rehearsal. **G~streik** m general strike

Generation /-'tsioːn/ f -,-en generation

Generator m -s,-en generator

generell adj general

genes|en† vi (sein) recover. **G~ung** f - recovery; (Erholung) convalescence

Genetik f - genetics sg

genetisch adj genetic

Genf nt -s Geneva. **G~er** adj Geneva; **G~er See** Lake Geneva

g

genial *adj* brilliant. **G~ität** *f* genius

Genick *nt* **-s,-e** [back of the] neck; **sich** (*dat*) **das G~ brechen** break one's neck

Genie /ʒeˈniː/ *nt* **-s,-s** genius

genieren /ʒeˈniːrən/ *vt* embarrass; **sich g~** feel *or* be embarrassed

genieß|bar *adj* fit to eat/drink. **g~en†** *vt* enjoy; (*verzehren*) eat/drink

Genitiv *m* **-s,-e** genitive

genmanipuliert *adj* genetically modified

Genom *nt* **-s, -e** genome

Genosse *m* **-n,-n** (*Pol*) comrade. **G~nschaft** *f* **-,-en** cooperative

Gentechnologie *f* genetic engineering

genug *inv adj & adv* enough

Genüge *f* **zur G~** sufficiently. **g~n** *vi* (*haben*) be enough. **g~nd** *inv adj* sufficient, enough; (*Sch*) fair ● *adv* sufficiently, enough

Genuss *m* **-es,¨e** enjoyment; (*Vergnügen*) pleasure; (*Verzehr*) consumption

geöffnet *adj* open

Geo|graphie, **G~grafie** *f* - geography. **g~graphisch**, **g~grafisch** *adj* geographical. **G~logie** *f* - geology. **g~logisch** *adj* geological. **G~meter** *m* **-s,-** surveyor. **G~metrie** *f* - geometry. **g~metrisch** *adj* geometric[al]

geordnet *adj* well-ordered; (*stabil*) stable; **alphabetisch g~** in alphabetical order

Gepäck *nt* **-s** luggage, baggage. **G~ablage** *f* luggage-rack. **G~aufbewahrung** *f* left-luggage office. **G~schein** *m* left-luggage ticket; (*Aviat*) baggage check. **G~träger** *m* porter; (*Fahrrad-*) luggage carrier; (*Dach-*) roof-rack

Gepard *m* **-s,-e** cheetah

gepflegt *adj* well-kept; (*Person*) well-groomed; (*Hotel*) first-class

gepunktet *adj* spotted

gerade *adj* straight; (*direkt*) direct; (*aufrecht*) upright; (*aufrichtig*) straightforward; (*Zahl*) even ● *adv* straight; directly; (*eben*) just; (*genau*) exactly; (*besonders*) especially; **g~ sitzen/stehen** sit/stand [up] straight; **g~ erst** only just. **G~** *f* **-,-n** straight line. **g~aus** *adv* straight ahead/on. **g~heraus** *adv* (*fig*) straight out. **g~so** *adv* just the same; **g~so gut** just as good; *adv* just as well. **g~stehen†** *vi sep* (*haben*) (*fig*) accept responsibility (**für** for). **g~zu** *adv* virtually; (*wirklich*) absolutely

Geranie /-iə/ *f* **-,-n** geranium

Gerät *nt* **-[e]s,-e** tool; (*Acker-*) implement; (*Küchen-*) utensil; (*Elektro-*) appliance; (*Radio-, Fernseh-*) set; (*Turn-*) piece of apparatus; (*coll*) equipment

geraten† *vi* (*sein*) get; **in Brand g~** catch fire; **in Wut g~** get angry; **gut g~** turn out well

Geratewohl *nt* **aufs G~** at random

geräuchert *adj* smoked

geräumig *adj* spacious, roomy

Geräusch *nt* **-[e]s,-e** noise. **g~los** *adj* noiseless

gerben *vt* tan

gerecht *adj* just; (*fair*) fair. **g~fertigt** *adj* justified. **G~igkeit** *f* - justice; fairness

Gerede *nt* **-s** talk

geregelt *adj* regular

gereizt *adj* irritable

Geriatrie *f* - geriatrics *sg*

Gericht¹ *nt* **-[e]s,-e** (*Culin*) dish

Gericht² *nt* **-[e]s,-e** court [of law]; **vor G~** in court; **das jüngste G~** the Last Judgement. **g~lich** *adj* judicial; (*Verfahren*) legal ● *adv* **g~lich vorgehen** take legal action. **G~shof** *m* court of justice. **G~smedizin** *f* forensic medicine. **G~ssaal** *m* court room. **G~svollzieher** *m* **-s,-** bailiff

gerieben *adj* grated; (⬛: *schlau*) crafty

gering *adj* small; (*niedrig*) low; (*g~fügig*) slight. **g~fügig** *adj* slight. **g~schätzig** *adj* contemptuous; (*Bemerkung*) disparaging. **g~ste(r,s)** *adj* least; **nicht im G~sten** not in the least

gerinnen† vi (sein) curdle; (Blut:) clot

Gerippe nt -s,- skeleton; (fig) framework

gerissen adj 🔲 crafty

Germ m -[e]s & (Aust) f - yeast

German|e m -n,-n [ancient] German. **g~isch** adj Germanic. **G~istik** f - German [language and literature]

gern[e] adv gladly; **g~ haben** like; (lieben) be fond of; **ich tanze g~** I like dancing; **willst du mit?—g~!** do you want to come?—I'd love to!

Gerste f - barley. **G~nkorn** nt (Med) stye

Geruch m -[e]s,ᵉe smell (**von/nach** of). **g~los** adj odourless. **G~ssinn** m sense of smell

Gerücht nt -[e]s,-e rumour

gerührt adj (fig) moved, touched

Gerümpel nt -s lumber, junk

Gerüst nt -[e]s,-e scaffolding; (fig) framework

gesammelt adj collected; (gefasst) composed

gesamt adj entire, whole. **G~ausgabe** f complete edition. **G~eindruck** m overall impression. **G~heit** f - whole. **G~schule** f comprehensive school. **G~summe** f total

Gesandte(r) m/f envoy

Gesang m -[e]s,ᵉe singing; (Lied) song; (Kirchen-) hymn. **G~verein** m choral society

Gesäß nt -es buttocks pl

Geschäft nt -[e]s,-e business; (Laden) shop, store; (Transaktion) deal; **schmutzige G~e** shady dealings; **ein gutes G~ machen** do very well (**mit** out of). **g~ig** adj busy; (Treiben) bustling. **G~igkeit** f - activity. **g~lich** adj business ● adv on business

Geschäfts|brief m business letter. **G~führer** m manager; (Vereins-) secretary. **G~mann** m (pl -leute) businessman. **G~stelle** f office; (Zweigstelle) branch. **g~tüchtig** adj **g~tüchtig sein** be a good

businessman/-woman. **G~zeiten** fpl hours of business

geschehen† vi (sein) happen (dat to); **das geschieht dir recht!** it serves you right! **gern g~!** you're welcome! **G~** nt -s events pl

gescheit adj clever

Geschenk nt -[e]s,-e present, gift

Geschicht|e f -,-n history; (Erzählung) story; (🔲: Sache) business. **g~lich** adj historical

Geschick nt -[e]s fate; (Talent) skill. **G~lichkeit** f - skilfulness, skill. **g~t** adj skilful; (klug) clever

geschieden adj divorced

Geschirr nt -s,-e (coll) crockery; (Porzellan) china; (Service) service; (Pferde-) harness; **schmutziges G~** dirty dishes pl. **G~spülmaschine** f dishwasher. **G~tuch** nt tea towel

Geschlecht nt -[e]s,-er sex; (Gram) gender; (Generation) generation. **g~lich** adj sexual. **G~skrankheit** f venereal disease. **G~steile** ntpl genitals. **G~sverkehr** m sexual intercourse. **G~swort** nt (pl -wörter) article

geschliffen adj (fig) polished

Geschmack m -[e]s,ᵉe taste; (Aroma) flavour; (G~ssinn) sense of taste; **einen guten G~ haben** (fig) have good taste. **g~los** adj tasteless; **g~los sein** (fig) be in bad taste. **g~voll** adj (fig) tasteful

Geschoss nt -es,-e missile; (Stockwerk) storey, floor

Geschrei nt -s screaming; (fig) fuss

Geschütz nt -es,-e gun, cannon

geschützt adj protected; (Stelle) sheltered

Geschwader nt -s,- squadron

Geschwätz nt -es talk

geschweige conj **g~ denn** let alone

Geschwindigkeit f -,-en speed; (Phys) velocity. **G~sbegrenzung, G~sbeschränkung** f speed limit

Geschwister pl brother[s] and sister[s]; siblings

g

geschwollen adj swollen; (fig) pompous

Geschworene|(r) m/f juror; **die G~n** the jury sg

Geschwulst f -,-̈e swelling; (Tumor) tumour

geschwungen adj curved

Geschwür nt -s,-e ulcer

gesellig adj sociable; (Zool) gregarious; (unterhaltsam) convivial; **g~er Abend** social evening

Gesellschaft f -,-en company; (Veranstaltung) party; **die G~** society; **jdm G~ leisten** keep s.o. company. **g~lich** adj social. **G~sspiel** nt party game

Gesetz nt -es,-e law. **G~entwurf** m bill. **g~gebend** adj legislative. **G~gebung** f - legislation. **g~lich** adj legal. **g~mäßig** adj lawful; (gesetzlich) legal. **g~widrig** adj illegal

gesichert adj secure

Gesicht nt -[e]s,-er face; (Aussehen) appearance. **G~sfarbe** f complexion. **G~spunkt** m point of view. **G~szüge** mpl features

Gesindel nt -s riff-raff

Gesinnung f -,-en mind; (Finstellung) attitude

gesondert adj separate

Gespann nt -[e]s,-e team; (Wagen) horse and cart/carriage

gespannt adj taut; (fig) tense; (Beziehungen) strained; (neugierig) eager; (erwartungsvoll) expectant; **g~ sein, ob** wonder whether; **auf etw g~ sein** look forward eagerly to sth

Gespenst nt -[e]s,-er ghost. **g~isch** adj ghostly; (unheimlich) eerie

Gespött nt -[e]s mockery; **zum G~ werden** become a laughing stock

Gespräch nt -[e]s-e conversation; (Telefon-) call; **ins G~ kommen** get talking; **im G~ sein** be under discussion. **g~ig** adj talkative. **G~sthema** nt topic of conversation

Gestalt f -,-en figure; (Form) shape, form; **G~ annehmen** (fig) take shape. **g~en** vt shape; (organisieren) arrange; (schaffen) create; (entwerfen) design; **sich g~en** turn out

Geständnis nt -ses,-se confession

Gestank m -s stench, [bad] smell

gestatten vt allow, permit; **nicht gestattet** prohibited; **g~ Sie?** may I?

Geste /'gɛ-, 'ge:stə/ f -,-n gesture

Gesteck nt -[e]s,-e flower arrangement

gestehen† vt/i (haben) confess; confess to (Verbrechen)

Gestein nt -[e]s,-e rock

Gestell nt -[e]s,-e stand; (Flaschen-) rack; (Rahmen) frame

gesteppt adj quilted

gestern adv yesterday; **g~ Nacht** last night

gestrandet adj stranded

gestreift adj striped

gestrichelt adj (Linie) dotted

gestrichen adj **g~er Teelöffel** level teaspoon[ful]

gestrig /'gɛstrɪç/ adj yesterday's; **am g~en Tag** yesterday

Gestrüpp nt -s,-e undergrowth

Gestüt nt -[e]s,-e stud [farm]

Gesuch nt -[e]s,-e request; (Admin) application. **g~t** adj sought-after

gesund adj healthy; **g~ sein** be in good health; (Sport, Getränk:) be good for one; **wieder g~ werden** get well again

Gesundheit f - health; **G~!** (bei Niesen) bless you! **g~lich** adj health; **g~licher Zustand** state of health ● adv **es geht ihm g~lich gut/ schlecht** he is in good/poor health. **g~sschädlich** adj harmful

getäfelt adj panelled

Getöse nt -s racket, din

Getränk nt -[e]s,-e drink. **G~e-karte** f wine-list

getrauen vt sich (dat) etw g~ dare [to] do sth; **sich g~** dare

Getreide nt -s (coll) grain

getrennt adj separate; **g~ leben** live apart; **g~ schreiben** write as two words

getreu *adj* faithful ● *prep* (+ *dat*) true to. **g~lich** *adv* faithfully

Getriebe *nt* -s,- bustle; (*Techn*) gear; (*Auto*) transmission; (*Gehäuse*) gearbox

getrost *adv* with confidence

Getto *nt* -s,-s ghetto

Getue *nt* -s 🛈 fuss

Getümmel *nt* -s tumult

geübt *adj* skilled

Gewächs *nt* -es,-e plant

gewachsen *adj* jdm g~ sein be a match for s.o.

Gewächshaus *nt* greenhouse

gewagt *adj* daring

gewählt *adj* refined

gewahr *adj* g~ werden become aware (*acc/gen* of)

Gewähr *f* - guarantee

gewähr|en *vt* grant; (*geben*) offer. **g~leisten** *vt* guarantee

Gewahrsam *m* -s safekeeping; (*Haft*) custody

Gewalt *f* -,-en power; (*Kraft*) force; (*Brutalität*) violence; **mit G~** by force. **G~herrschaft** *f* tyranny. **g~ig** *adj* powerful; (🛈: *groß*) enormous; (*stark*) tremendous. **g~sam** *adj* forcible; (*Tod*) violent. **g~tätig** *adj* violent. **G~tätigkeit** *f* -,-en violence; (*Handlung*) act of violence

Gewand *nt* -[e]s,-̈er robe

gewandt *adj* skilful. **G~heit** *f* - skill

Gewebe *nt* -s,- fabric; (*Anat*) tissue

Gewehr *nt* -s,-e rifle, gun

Geweih *nt* -[e]s,-e antlers *pl*

Gewerb|e *nt* -s,- trade. **g~lich** *adj* commercial. **g~smäßig** *adj* professional

Gewerkschaft *f* -,-en trade union. **G~ler(in)** *m* -s,- (*f* -,-nen) trade unionist

Gewicht *nt* -[e]s,-e weight; (*Bedeutung*) importance. **G~heben** *nt* -s weight lifting

Gewinde *nt* -s,- [screw] thread

Gewinn *m* -[e]s,-e profit; (*fig*) gain, benefit; (*beim Spiel*) winnings *pl*; (*Preis*) prize; (*Los*) winning ticket.

G~beteiligung *f* profit-sharing. **g~en†** *vt* win; (*erlangen*) gain; (*fördern*) extract ● *vi* (*haben*) win; **g~en an** (+ *dat*) gain in. **g~end** *adj* engaging. **G~er(in)** *m* -s,- (*f* -,-nen) winner

Gewirr *nt* -s,-e tangle; (*Straßen-*) maze

gewiss *adj* certain

Gewissen *nt* -s,- conscience. **g~haft** *adj* conscientious. **g~los** *adj* unscrupulous. **G~sbisse** *mpl* pangs of conscience

gewissermaßen *adv* to a certain extent; (*sozusagen*) as it were

Gewissheit *f* - certainty

Gewitt|er *nt* -s,- thunderstorm. **g~rig** *adj* thundery

gewogen *adj* (*fig*) well-disposed (*dat* towards)

gewöhnen *vt* jdn/sich g~ an (+ *acc*) get s.o. used to/get used to; [an] jdn/etw gewöhnt sein be used to s.o./sth

Gewohnheit *f* -,-en habit. **G~srecht** *nt* common law

gewöhnlich *adj* ordinary; (*üblich*) usual; (*ordinär*) common

gewohnt *adj* customary; (*vertraut*) familiar; (*üblich*) usual; **etw** (*acc*) **g~ sein** be used to sth

Gewölbe *nt* -s,- vault

Gewühl *nt* -[e]s crush

gewunden *adj* winding

Gewürz *nt* -es,-e spice. **G~nelke** *f* clove

gezackt *adj* serrated

gezähnt *adj* serrated; (*Säge*) toothed

Gezeiten *fpl* tides

gezielt *adj* specific; (*Frage*) pointed

geziert *adj* affected

gezwungen *adj* forced. **g~ermaßen** *adv* of necessity

Gicht *f* - gout

Giebel *m* -s,- gable

Gier *f* - greed (**nach** for). **g~ig** *adj* greedy

gieß|en† *vt* pour; water (*Blumen, Garten*); (*Techn*) cast ● *v impers* es

g~t it is pouring [with rain].
G~kanne f watering can

Gift nt -[e]s,-e poison; (Schlangen-)
venom; (Med) toxin. **g~ig** adj poi-
sonous; (Schlange) venomous; (Med,
Chemistry) toxic; (fig) spiteful.
G~müll m toxic waste. **G~pilz** m
toadstool

Gilde f -,-n guild

Gin /dʒɪn/ m -s gin

Ginster m -s (Bot) broom

Gipfel m -s,- summit, top; (fig) peak.
G~konferenz f summit conference.
g~n vi (haben) culminate (in + dat
in)

Gips m -es plaster. **G~verband** m
(Med) plaster cast

Giraffe f -,-n giraffe

Girlande f -,-n garland

Girokonto /ˈʒiːro-/ nt current account

Gischt m -[e]s & f - spray

Gitar|re f -,-n guitar. **G~rist(in)** m
-en,-en (f -,-nen) guitarist

Gitter nt -s,- bars pl; (Rost) grating,
grid; (Geländer, Zaun) railings pl;
(Fenster-) grille; (Draht-) wire screen

Glanz m -es shine; (von Farbe, Papier)
gloss; (Seiden-) sheen; (Politur) polish;
(fig) brilliance; (Pracht) splendour

glänzen vi (haben) shine. **g~d** adj
shining, bright; (Papier) glossy; (fig)
brilliant

glanz|los adj dull. **G~stück** nt mas-
terpiece

Glas nt -es,∵er glass; (Brillen-) lens;
(Fern-) binoculars pl; (Marmeladen-)
[glass] jar. **G~er** m -s,- glazier

glasieren vt glaze; ice (Kuchen)

glas|ig adj glassy; (durchsichtig)
transparent. **G~scheibe** f pane

Glasur f -,-en glaze; (Culin) icing

glatt adj smooth; (eben) even; (Haar)
straight; (rutschig) slippery; (einfach)
straightforward; (Absage) flat; **g~
streichen** smooth out; **g~ rasiert**
clean-shaven; **g~ gehen** go off
smoothly; **das ist g~ gelogen** it's a
downright lie

Glätte f - smoothness; (Rutschigkeit)
slipperiness

Glatt|eis nt [black] ice. **g~weg** adv
🄸 outright

Glatz|e f -,-n bald patch; (Voll-) bald
head; **eine G~e bekommen** go
bald. **g~köpfig** adj bald

Glaube m -ns belief (an + acc in);
(Relig) faith; **G~n schenken** (+ dat)
believe. **g~n** vt/i (haben) believe (an
+ acc in); (vermuten) think; **jdm g~n**
believe s.o.; **nicht zu g~n** unbelievable, incredible. **G~nsbekenntnis** nt
creed

gläubig adj religious; (vertrauend)
trusting. **G~e(r)** m/f (Relig) believer;
die G~en the faithful. **G~er** m -s,-
(Comm) creditor

glaub|lich adj kaum g~lich
scarcely believable. **g~würdig** adj
credible; (Person) reliable

gleich adj same; (identisch) identical;
(g~wertig) equal; **g~ bleibend**
constant; **2 mal 5 [ist] g~ 10** two
times 5 equals 10; **das ist mir g~**
it's all the same to me; **ganz g~,
wo/wer** no matter where/who ● adv
equally; (übereinstimmend) identi-
cally, the same; (sofort) immediately;
(in Kürze) in a minute; (fast) nearly;
(direkt) right. **g~altrig** adj [of] the
same age. **g~bedeutend** adj synonymous. **g~berechtigt** adj equal.
G~berechtigung f equality

gleichen† vi (haben) jdm/etw g~
be like or resemble s.o./something

gleich|ermaßen adv equally.
g~falls adv also, likewise; **danke
g~falls** thank you, the same to you.
G~gewicht nt balance; (Phys & fig)
equilibrium. **g~gültig** adj indifferent; (unwichtig) unimportant.
G~gültigkeit f indifference. **g~ma-
chen** vt sep make equal; **dem Erdboden g~machen** raze to the ground.
g~mäßig adj even, regular; (beständig) constant. **G~mäßigkeit** f - re-
gularity

Gleichnis nt -ses,-se parable

Gleich|schritt m im G~schritt in
step. **g~setzen** vt sep equate/

(g~stellen) place on a par (dat/mit with). **g~stellen** vt sep place on a par (dat with). **G~strom** m direct current

Gleichung f -,-en equation

gleichwertig adv adj of equal value. **g~zeitig** adj simultaneous

Gleis nt -es,-e track; (Bahnsteig) platform; **G~** 5 platform 5

gleiten† vi (sein) glide; (rutschen) slide. **g~d** adj sliding. **g~de Arbeitszeit** flexitime

Gleitzeit f flexitime

Gletscher m -s,- glacier

Glied nt -[e]s,-er limb; (Teil) part; (Ketten-) link; (Mitglied) member; (Mil) rank. **g~ern** vt arrange; (einteilen) divide. **G~maßen** fpl limbs

glitschig adj slippery

glitzern vi (haben) glitter

global adj global

globalisier|en vt globalize. **G~ung** f -,-en globalization

Globus m - & -busses,-ben & -busse globe

Glocke f -,-n bell. **G~nturm** m bell tower, belfry

glorreich adj glorious

Glossar nt -s,-e glossary

Glosse f -,-n comment

glotzen vi (haben) stare

Glück nt -[e]s [good] luck; (Zufriedenheit) happiness; **G~ bringend** lucky; **G~/kein G~ haben** be lucky/unlucky; **zum G~** luckily, fortunately; **auf gut G~** on the off chance; (wahllos) at random. **g~en** vi (sein) succeed

glücklich adj lucky, fortunate; (zufrieden) happy; (sicher) safe ● adv happily; safely. **g~erweise** adv luckily, fortunately

Glücksspiel nt game of chance; (Spielen) gambling

Glückwunsch m good wishes pl; (Gratulation) congratulations pl; **herzlichen G~!** congratulations! (zum Geburtstag) happy birthday! **G~karte** f greetings card

Glüh|birne f light bulb. **g~en** vi

(haben) glow. **g~end** adj glowing; (rot-) red-hot; (Hitze) scorching; (leidenschaftlich) fervent. **G~faden** m filament. **G~wein** m mulled wine. **G~würmchen** nt -s,- glow-worm

Glukose f - glucose

Glut f - embers pl; (Röte) glow; (Hitze) heat; (fig) ardour

Glyzinie /-iə/ f -,-n wisteria

GmbH abbr (Gesellschaft mit beschränkter Haftung) ≈ plc

Gnade f - mercy; (Gunst) favour; (Relig) grace. **G~nfrist** f reprieve

gnädig adj gracious; (mild) lenient; **g~e Frau** Madam

Gnom m -en,-en gnome

Gobelin /gobə'lɛ̃:/ m -s,-s tapestry

Gold nt -[e]s gold. **g~en** adj gold; (g~farben) golden. **G~fisch** m goldfish. **g~ig** adj sweet, lovely. **G~lack** m wallflower. **G~regen** m laburnum. **G~schmied** m goldsmith

Golf¹ m -[e]s,-e (Geog) gulf

Golf² nt -s golf. **G~platz** m golf course. **G~schläger** m golf club. **G~spieler(in)** m(f) golfer

Gondel f -,-n gondola; (Kabine) cabin

gönnen vt jdm etw g~ not begrudge s.o. sth; **jdm etw nicht g~** begrudge s.o. sth

googeln vt/i ® google

Gör nt -s,-en, **Göre** f -,-n 🄸 kid

Gorilla m -s,-s gorilla

Gosse f -,-n gutter

Got|ik f - Gothic. **g~isch** adj Gothic

Gott m -[e]s,⸚er God; (Myth) god

Götterspeise f jelly

Gottes|dienst m service. **G~lästerung** f blasphemy

Gottheit f -,-en deity

Göttin f -,-nen goddess

göttlich adj divine

gottlos adj ungodly; (atheistisch) godless

Grab nt -[e]s,⸚er grave

graben† vi (haben) dig

Graben m -s,⸚ ditch; (Mil) trench

Grab|mal nt tomb. **G~stein** m gravestone, tombstone

Grad m -[e]s,-e degree

Graf m -en,-en count

Grafik f -,-en graphics sg; (Kunst) graphic arts pl; (Druck) print

Gräfin f -,-nen countess

grafisch adj graphic; g~e Darstellung diagram

Grafschaft f -,-en county

Gram m -s grief

grämen (sich) vr grieve

Gramm nt -s,-e gram

Gram|matik f -,-en grammar. g~matikalisch adj grammatical

Granat m -[e]s,-e garnet. G~e f -,-n shell; (Hand-) grenade

Granit m -s,-e granite

Gras nt -es,ᵉer grass. g~en vi (haben) graze. G~hüpfer m -s,- grasshopper

grässlich adj dreadful

Grat m -[e]s,-e [mountain] ridge

Gräte f -,-n fishbone

Gratifikation /-'tsio:n/ f -,-en bonus

gratis adv free [of charge]. G~probe f free sample

Gratu|lant(in) m -en,-en (f -,-nen) well-wisher. G~lation f -,-en congratulations pl; (Glückwünsche) best wishes pl. g~lieren vi (haben) jdm g~lieren congratulate s.o. (zu on); (zum Geburtstag) wish s.o. happy birthday

grau adj, G~ nt -s,- grey

Gräuel m -s,- horror

grauen v impers mir graut [es] davor I dread it. G~ nt -s dread. g~haft adj gruesome; (grässlich) horrible

gräulich adj horrible

grausam adj cruel. G~keit f -,-en cruelty

graus|en v impers mir graust davor I dread it. G~en nt -s horror, dread. g~ig adj gruesome

gravieren vt engrave. g~d adj (fig) serious

graziös adj graceful

greifen† vt take hold of; (fangen) catch ● vi (haben) reach (nach for); um sich g~ (fig) spread

Greis m -es,-e old man. G~in f -,-nen old woman

grell adj glaring; (Farbe) garish; (schrill) shrill

Gremium nt -s,-ien committee

Grenz|e f -,-n border; (Staats-) frontier; (Grundstücks-) boundary; (fig) limit. g~en vi (haben) border (an + acc on). g~enlos adj boundless; (maßlos) infinite

Griech|e m -n,-n Greek. G~enland nt -s Greece. G~in f -,-nen Greek woman. g~isch adj Greek. G~isch nt -[s] (Lang) Greek

Grieß m -es semolina

Griff m -[e]s,-e grasp, hold; (Hand-) movement of the hand; (Tür-, Messer-) handle; (Schwert-) hilt. g~bereit adj handy

Grill m -s,-s grill; (Garten-) barbecue

Grille f -,-n (Zool) cricket

grill|en vt grill; (im Freien) barbecue ● vi (haben) have a barbecue. G~fest nt barbecue

Grimasse f -,-n grimace; G~n schneiden pull faces

grimmig adj furious; (Kälte) bitter

grinsen vi (haben) grin

Grippe f -,-n influenza, 🄸 flu

grob adj coarse; (unsanft, ungefähr) rough; (unhöflich) rude; (schwer) gross; (Fehler) bad; g~ geschätzt roughly. G~ian m -s,-e brute

Groll m -[e]s resentment. g~en vi (haben) be angry (dat with); (Donner:) rumble

Grönland nt -s Greenland

Gros nt -es,- (Maß) gross

Groschen m -s,- (Aust) groschen; 🄸 ten-pfennig piece

groß adj big; (Anzahl, Summe) large; (bedeutend, stark) great; (g~artig) grand; (Buchstabe) capital; g~e Ferien summer holidays; der größte Teil the majority or bulk; g~ werden (Person:) grow up; g~ in etw (dat) sein be good at sth; G~ und Klein young and old; im G~en und

Ganzen on the whole ● *adv* (*feiern*) in style; (🔢: *viel*) much

groß|artig *adj* magnificent. **G~auf-nahme** *f* close-up. **G~britannien** *nt* -s Great Britain. **G~buchstabe** *m* capital letter. **G~e(r)** *m/f* unser G~er our eldest; **die G~en** the grown-ups; (*fig*) the great *pl*

Größe *f* -,-n size; (*Ausmaß*) extent; (*Körper-*) height; (*Bedeutsamkeit*) greatness; (*Math*) quantity; (*Person*) great figure

Großeltern *pl* grandparents

Groß|handel *m* wholesale trade. **G~händler** *m* wholesaler. **G~macht** *f* superpower. **g~mütig** *adj* magnanimous. **G~mutter** *f* grandmother. **G~schreibung** *f* capitalization. **g~spurig** *adj* pompous; (*überheblich*) arrogant. **G~stadt** *f* [large] city. **g~städtisch** *adj* city; **G~teil** *m* large proportion; (*Haupt-teil*) bulk

größtenteils *adv* for the most part

groß|tun† (**sich**) *vr sep* brag. **G~vater** *m* grandfather. **g~ziehen†** *vt sep* bring up; rear (*Tier*). **g~zügig** *adj* generous. **G~zügigkeit** *f* - generosity

Grotte *f* -,-n grotto

Grübchen *nt* -s,- dimple

Grube *f* -,-n pit

grübeln *vi* (*haben*) brood

Gruft *f* -,⁺e [burial] vault

grün *adj* green; **im G~en** out in the country; **die G~en** the Greens

Grund *m* -[e]s,⁺e ground; (*Boden*) bottom; (*Hinter-*) background; (*Ursache*) reason; **aus diesem G~e** for this reason; **im G~e [genommen]** basically; **auf G~ laufen** (*Naut*) run aground; **zu G~e richten/gehen** s. **zugrunde**. **G~begriffe** *mpl* basics. **G~besitzer** *m* landowner

gründ|en *vt* found, set up; start (*Familie*); (*fig*) base (**auf** + *acc* on); **sich g~en** be based (**auf** + *acc* on). **G~er(in)** *m* -s,- (*f* -,-nen) founder

Grund|farbe *f* primary colour. **G~form** *f* (*Gram*) infinitive. **G~ge-**

setz *nt* (*Pol*) constitution. **G~lage** *f* basis, foundation

---

Grundgesetz The written German constitution, or "basic law", which came into force in May 1949. It lays down the basic rights of German citizens and the legal framework of the German state. *i*

---

gründlich *adj* thorough. **G~keit** *f* - thoroughness

Gründonnerstag *m* Maundy Thursday

Grund|regel *f* basic rule. **G~riss** *m* ground plan; (*fig*) outline. **G~satz** *m* principle. **g~sätzlich** *adj* fundamental; (*im Allgemeinen*) in principle; (*prinzipiell*) on principle. **G~schule** *f* primary school. **G~stück** *nt* plot [of land]

Gründung *f* -,-en foundation

Grün|span *m* verdigris. **G~streifen** *m* grass verge; (*Mittel-*) central reservation

grunzen *vi* (*haben*) grunt

Gruppe *f* -,-n group; (*Reise-*) party

gruppieren *vt* group

Grusel|geschichte *f* horror story. **g~ig** *adj* creepy

Gruß *m* -es,⁺e greeting; (*Mil*) salute; **einen schönen G~ an X** give my regards to X; **viele/herzliche G~e** regards; **Mit freundlichen G~en** Yours sincerely/faithfully

grüßen *vt/i* (*haben*) say hallo (**jdn** to s.o.); (*Mil*) salute; **g~ Sie X von mir** give my regards to X; **grüß Gott!** (*SGer, Aust*) good morning/afternoon/ evening!

gucken *vi* (*haben*) 🔢 look

Guerilla /ge'rɪlja/ *f* - guerrilla warfare. **G~kämpfer** *m* guerrilla

Gulasch *nt* & *m* -[e]s goulash

gültig *adj* valid

Gummi *m* & *nt* -s,-[s] rubber; (*Harz*) gum. **G~band** *nt* (*pl* -bänder) elastic *or* rubber band

gummiert *adj* gummed

Gummi|knüppel *m* truncheon.

g

G~stiefel *m* gumboot, wellington. **G~zug** *m* elastic

Gunst *f* - favour

günstig *adj* favourable; (*passend*) convenient

Gurgel *f* -,-n throat. **g~n** *vi* (*haben*) gargle

Gurke *f* -,-n cucumber; (*Essig-*) gherkin

Gurt *m* -[e]s,-e strap; (*Gürtel*) belt; (*Auto*) safety belt. **G~band** *nt* (*pl* -bänder) waistband

Gürtel *m* -s,- belt. **G~linie** *f* waistline. **G~rose** *f* shingles *sg*

Guss *m* -es,⸚e (*Techn*) casting; (*Strom*) stream; (*Regen-*) downpour; (*Torten-*) icing. **G~eisen** *nt* cast iron

gut *adj* good; (*Gewissen*) clear; (*gütig*) kind (**zu** to); **jdm gut sein** be fond of s.o.; **im G~en** amicably; **schon gut** that's all right ● *adv* well; (*schmecken, riechen*) good; (*leicht*) easily; **gut zu sehen** clearly visible; **gut drei Stunden** a good three hours

Gut *nt* -[e]s,⸚er possession, property; (*Land-*) estate; **Gut und Böse** good and evil; **Güter** (*Comm*) goods

Gutacht|en *nt* -s,- expert's report. **G~er** *m* -s,- expert

gutartig *adj* good-natured; (*Med*) benign

Gute|(s) *nt* etwas/nichts G~s something/nothing good; **G~s tun** do good; **alles G~!** all the best!

Güte *f* -,-n goodness, kindness; (*Qualität*) quality

Güterzug *m* goods train

gut|gehen* *vi sep* (*sein*) gut gehen, s. gehen. **g~gehend*** *adj* gut gehend, s. gehen. **g~gläubig** *adj* trusting. **g~haben†** *vt sep* fünfzig Euro g~haben have fifty euros credit (**bei** with). **G~haben** *nt* -s,- [credit] balance; (*Kredit*) credit

gut|machen *vt sep* make up for; make good (*Schaden*). **g~mütig** *adj* good-natured. **G~mütigkeit** *f* - good nature. **G~schein** *m* credit note; (*Bon*) voucher; (*Geschenk-*) gift

token. **g~schreiben†** *vt sep* credit. **G~schrift** *f* credit

Guts|haus *nt* manor house

gut|tun* *vi sep* (*haben*) gut tun, s. tun. **g~willig** *adj* willing

Gymnasium *nt* -s,-ien ≈ grammar school

Gymnasium The secondary i school that prepares pupils for the Abitur. After primary school the most academically gifted pupils go to a *Gymnasium*, or grammar school, for eight or nine years. In their last three years they have some choice as to which subjects they study.

Gymnastik *f* - [keep-fit] exercises *pl*; (*Turnen*) gymnastics *sg*

Gynäko|loge *m* -n,-n gynaecologist. **G~logie** *f* - gynaecology

Hh

H, h /ha:/ *nt* -,- (*Mus*) B, b

Haar *nt* -[e]s,-e hair; **sich** (*dat*) **die Haare** *od* **das H~ waschen** wash one's hair; **um ein H~** ⊡ very nearly. **H~bürste** *f* hairbrush. **h~en** *vi* (*haben*) shed hairs; (*Tier:*) moult ● *vr* **sich h~en** moult. **h~ig** *adj* hairy; ⊡ tricky. **H~klemme** *f* hair grip. **H~nadelkurve** *f* hairpin bend. **H~schnitt** *m* haircut. **H~spange** *f* slide. **H~waschmittel** *nt* shampoo

Habe *f* - possessions *pl*

---

haben†

● *transitive verb*

····▸ have; (*im Präsens*) have got ⊡. **er hat kein Geld** he has no money *or* ⊡ he hasn't got any money. **ich habe/hatte die Grippe** I've got flu/had flu. **was haben Sie da?** what have you got there? **wenn ich die Zeit**

(margin tabs) **g** **h**

hätte if I had the time

····▸ (*empfinden*) **Angst**/**Hunger**/ **Durst haben** be frightened/hungry/thirsty. **was hat er?** what's wrong with him?

····▸ (+ *Adj., es*) **es gut**/**schlecht haben** be well/badly off. **es schwer haben** be having a difficult time

····▸ (+ *zu*) (*müssen*) **du hast zu gehorchen** you must obey

● *auxiliary verb*

····▸ have. **ich habe**/**hatte ihn eben gesehen** I have *or* I've/I had *or* I'd just seen him. **er hat es gewusst** he knew it. **er hätte ihr geholfen** he would have helped her

● *reflexive verb*

····▸ (⊡: *sich aufregen*) make a fuss. **hab dich nicht so!** don't make such a fuss!

Habgier *f* greed. **h~ig** *adj* greedy

Habicht *m* -[e]s,-e hawk

Hachse *f* -,-n (*Culin*) knuckle

Hackbraten *m* meat loaf

Hacke[1] *f* -,-n hoe; (*Spitz-*) pick

Hacke[2] *f* -,-n, **Hacken** *m* -s,- heel

hack|en *vt* hoe; (*schlagen, zerkleinern*) chop; (*Vogel:*) peck. **H~fleisch** *nt* mince

Hafen *m* -s,∺ harbour; (*See-*) port. **H~arbeiter** *m* docker. **H~stadt** *f* port

Hafer *m* -s oats *pl*. **H~flocken** *fpl* [rolled] oats

Haft *f* - (*Jur*) custody; (*H~strafe*) imprisonment. **h~bar** *adj* (*Jur*) liable. **H~befehl** *m* warrant

haften *vi* (*haben*) cling; (*kleben*) stick; (*bürgen*) vouch/(*Jur*) be liable (**für** for)

Häftling *m* -s,-e detainee

Haftpflicht *f* (*Jur*) liability. **H~versicherung** *f* (*Auto*) third-party insurance

Haftung *f* - (*Jur*) liability

Hagebutte *f* -,-n rose hip

Hagel *m* -s hail. **h~n** *vi* (*haben*) hail

hager *adj* gaunt

Hahn *m* -[e]s,∺e cock; (*Techn*) tap

Hähnchen *nt* -s,- (*Culin*) chicken

Hai[fisch] *m* -[e]s,-e shark

Häkchen *nt* -s,- tick

häkel|n *vt*/*i* (*haben*) crochet. **H~nadel** *f* crochet hook

Haken *m* -s,- hook; (*Häkchen*) tick; (⊡: *Schwierigkeit*) snag. **h~** *vt* hook (**an** + *acc* to). **H~kreuz** *nt* swastika

halb *adj* half; **auf h~em Weg** halfway ● *adv* half; **h~ drei** half past two; **fünf [Minuten] vor**/**nach h~ vier** twenty-five [minutes] past three/to four. **H~e(r,s)** *f*/*m*/*nt* half [a litre]

halber *prep* (+ *gen*) for the sake of; **Geschäfte h~** on business

Halbfinale *nt* semifinal

halbieren *vt* halve, divide in half; (*Geometry*) bisect

Halb|insel *f* peninsula. **H~kreis** *m* semicircle. **H~kugel** *f* hemisphere. **h~laut** *adj* low ● *adv* in an undertone. **h~mast** *adv* at half-mast. **H~mond** *m* half moon. **H~pension** *f* half board. **h~rund** *adj* semicircular. **H~schuh** *m* [flat] shoe. **h~tags** *adv* [for] half a day; **h~tags arbeiten** ≈ work part-time. **H~ton** *m* semitone. **h~wegs** *adv* half-way; (*ziemlich*) more or less. **h~wüchsig** *adj* adolescent. **H~zeit** *f* (*Sport*) half-time; (*Spielzeit*) half

Halde *f* -,-n dump, tip

Hälfte *f* -,-n half; **zur H~** half

Halfter *f* -,-n & *nt* -s,- holster

Halle *f* -,-n hall; (*Hotel-*) lobby; (*Bahnhofs-*) station concourse

hallen *vi* (*haben*) resound; (*wider-*) echo

Hallen- *prefix* indoor

hallo *int* hallo

Halluzination /-'tsio:n/ *f* -,-en hallucination

Halm *m* -[e]s,-e stalk; (*Gras-*) blade

Hals *m* -es,∺e neck; (*Kehle*) throat; **aus vollem H~e** at the top of one's voice; (*lachen*) out loud. **H~band** *nt*

h

(*pl* -bänder) collar. **H~schmerzen**
mpl sore throat *sg*

halt *int* stop! (*Mil*) halt!; ⚠ wait a
minute!

Halt *m* -[e]s,-e hold; (*Stütze*) support;
(*innerer*) stability; (*Anhalten*) stop;
H~ machen stop. **h~bar** *adj* durable; (*Textiles*) hard-wearing; (*fig*)
tenable; **h~bar bis** (*Comm*) use by

halten† *vt* hold; make (*Rede*); give
(*Vortrag*); (*einhalten, bewahren*) keep;
[**sich** (*dat*)] **etw h~** keep (*Hund*);
take (*Zeitung*); **h~ für** regard as; **viel
h~ von** think highly of; **sich links
h~** keep left; **sich h~ an** (+ *acc*)
(*fig*) keep to ● *vi* (*haben*) hold; (*haltbar sein, bestehen bleiben*) keep;
(*Freundschaft, Blumen:*) last; (*Halt machen*) stop; **auf sich** (*acc*) **h~** take
pride in oneself; **zu jdm h~** be loyal
to s.o.

Halte|stelle *f* stop. **H~verbot** *nt*
waiting restriction; **'H~verbot**' 'no
waiting'

Haltung *f* -,-en (*Körper-*) posture;
(*Verhalten*) manner; (*Einstellung*) attitude; (*Fassung*) composure; (*Halten*)
keeping

Hammel *m* -s,- ram; (*Culin*) mutton.
H~fleisch *nt* mutton

Hammer *m* -s,: hammer

hämmern *vt/i* (*haben*) hammer

Hamster *m* -s,- hamster. **h~n** *vt/i*
⚠ hoard

Hand *f* -,:e hand; **jdm die H~
geben** shake hands with s.o.;
rechter/linker H~ on the right/left;
zweiter H~ second-hand; **unter der
H~** unofficially; (*geheim*) secretly;
H~ und Fuß haben (*fig*) be sound.
H~arbeit *f* manual work; (*handwerk-
lich*) handicraft; (*Nadelarbeit*) needlework; (*Gegenstand*) hand-made article. **H~ball** *m* [German] handball.
H~bewegung *f* gesture.
H~bremse *f* handbrake. **H~buch**
nt handbook, manual

Händedruck *m* handshake

Handel *m* -s trade, commerce; (*Unternehmen*) business; (*Geschäft*) deal;
H~ treiben trade. **h~n** *vi* (*haben*)

act; (*Handel treiben*) trade (**mit** in);
von etw *od* **über etw** (*acc*) **h~n**
deal with sth; **sich h~n um** be
about, concern. **H~smarine** *f* merchant navy. **H~sschiff** *nt* merchant
vessel. **H~sschule** *f* commercial college. **H~sware** *f* merchandise

Hand|feger *m* -s,- brush. **H~flä-
che** *f* palm. **H~gelenk** *nt* wrist.
H~gemenge *nt* -s,- scuffle. **H~ge-
päck** *nt* hand luggage. **h~geschrie-
ben** *adj* hand-written. **h~greiflich**
adj tangible; **h~greiflich werden**
become violent. **H~griff** *m* handle

handhaben *vt insep* (*reg*) handle

Handikap /'hɛndikɛp/ *nt* -s,-s
handicap

Handkuss *m* kiss on the hand

Händler *m* -s,- dealer, trader

handlich *adj* handy

Handlung *f* -,-en act; (*Handeln*) action; (*Roman-*) plot; (*Geschäft*) shop.
H~sweise *f* conduct

Hand|schellen *fpl* handcuffs.
H~schlag *m* handshake. **H~schrift**
f handwriting; (*Text*) manuscript.
H~schuh *m* glove. **H~stand** *m*
handstand. **H~tasche** *f* handbag.
H~tuch *nt* towel

Handwerk *nt* craft, trade. **H~er** *m*
-s,- craftsman; (*Arbeiter*) workman

Handy /'hɛndi/ *nt* -s,-s mobile
phone, cell phone *Amer*

Hanf *m* -[e]s hemp

Hang *m* -[e]s,:e slope; (*fig*) inclination

Hänge|brücke *f* suspension
bridge. **H~matte** *f* hammock

hängen¹ *vt* (*reg*) hang

hängen²† *vi* (*haben*) hang; **h~ an** (+
dat) (*fig*) be attached to; **h~ lassen**
leave

Hannover *nt* -s Hanover

hänseln *vt* tease

hantieren *vi* (*haben*) busy oneself

Happen *m* -s,- mouthful; **einen H~
essen** have a bite to eat

Harfe *f* -,-n harp

Harke *f* -,-n rake. **h~n** *vt/i* (*haben*)
rake

h

harmlos *adj* harmless; (*arglos*) innocent

Harmonie *f* -,-n harmony

Harmonika *f* -,-s accordion; (*Mund-*) mouth organ

harmonisch *adj* harmonious

Harn *m* -[e]s urine. **H∼blase** *f* bladder

Harpune *f* -,-n harpoon

hart *adj* hard; (*heftig*) violent; (*streng*) harsh

Härte *f* -,-n hardness; (*Strenge*) harshness; (*Not*) hardship. **h∼n** *vt* harden

Hart|faserplatte *f* hardboard. **h∼näckig** *adj* stubborn; (*ausdauernd*) persistent. **H∼näckigkeit** *f* - stubbornness; persistence

Harz *nt* -es,-e resin

Haschee *nt* -s,-s (*Culin*) hash

Haschisch *nt* & *m* -[s] hashish

Hase *m* -n,-n hare

Hasel *f* -,-n hazel. **H∼maus** *f* dormouse. **H∼nuss** *f* hazel nut

Hass *m* -es hatred

hassen *vt* hate

hässlich *adj* ugly; (*unfreundlich*) nasty. **H∼keit** *f* - ugliness; nastiness

Hast *f* - haste. **h∼ig** *adj* hasty, *adv* -ily, hurried

hast, hat, hatte, hätte *s.* haben

Haube *f* -,-n cap; (*Trocken-*) drier; (*Kühler-*) bonnet

Hauch *m* -[e]s breath; (*Luft-*) breeze; (*Duft*) whiff; (*Spur*) tinge. **h∼dünn** *adj* very thin

Haue *f* -,-n pick; (🄁: *Prügel*) beating. **h∼n†** *vt* beat; (*hämmern*) knock; (*meißeln*) hew; **sich h∼n** fight; **übers Ohr h∼n** 🄁 cheat ● *vi* (*haben*) bang (**auf** + *acc* on); **jdm ins Gesicht h∼n** hit s.o. in the face

Haufen *m* -s,- heap, pile; (*Leute*) crowd

häufen *vt* heap *or* pile [up]; **sich h∼** pile up; (*zunehmen*) increase

häufig *adj* frequent

Haupt *nt* -[e]s, Häupter head. **H∼bahnhof** *m* main station.

H∼fach *nt* main subject. **H∼gericht** *nt* main course

Häuptling *m* -s,-e chief

Haupt|mahlzeit *f* main meal **H∼mann** *m* (*pl* -leute) captain. **H∼post** *f* main post office. **H∼quartier** *nt* headquarters *pl*. **H∼rolle** *f* lead; (*fig*) leading role. **H∼sache** *f* main thing; **in der H∼sache** in the main. **h∼sächlich** *adj* main. **H∼satz** *m* main clause. **H∼stadt** *f* capital. **H∼verkehrsstraße** *f* main road. **H∼verkehrszeit** *f* rush hour. **H∼wort** *nt* (*pl* -wörter) noun

Haus *nt* -es, Häuser house; (*Gebäude*) building; (*Schnecken-*) shell; **zu H∼e** at home; **nach H∼e** home. **H∼arbeit** *f* housework; (*Sch*) homework. **H∼arzt** *m* family doctor. **H∼aufgaben** *fpl* homework *sg*. **H∼besetzer** *m* -s,- squatter

hausen *vi* (*haben*) live; (*wüten*) wreak havoc

Haus|frau *f* housewife. **h∼gemacht** *adj* home-made. **H∼halt** *m* -[e]s,-e household; (*Pol*) budget. **h∼halten†** *vi sep* (*haben*) **h∼halten mit** manage carefully; conserve (*Kraft*). **H∼hälterin** *f* -,-nen housekeeper. **H∼haltsgeld** *nt* housekeeping [money]. **H∼haltsplan** *m* budget. **H∼herr** *m* head of the household; (*Gastgeber*) host

Hausierer *m* -s,- hawker

Hauslehrer *m* [private] tutor. **H∼in** *f* governess

häuslich *adj* domestic, (*Person*) domesticated

Haus|meister *m* caretaker. **H∼ordnung** *f* house rules *pl*. **H∼putz** *m* cleaning. **H∼rat** *m* -[e]s household effects *pl*. **H∼schlüssel** *m* front-door key. **H∼schuh** *m* slipper. **H∼suchung** *f* [police] search. **H∼suchungsbefehl** *m* search warrant. **H∼tier** *nt* domestic animal; (*Hund, Katze*) pet. **H∼tür** *f* front door. **H∼wirt** *m* landlord. **H∼wirtin** *f* landlady

Haut *f* -,Häute skin; (*Tier-*) hide.

H~arzt m dermatologist

häuten vt skin; **sich h~** moult

haut|eng adj skin-tight. **H~farbe** f colour; (Teint) complexion

Hebamme f -,-n midwife

Hebel m -s,- lever

heben† vt lift; (hoch-, steigern) raise; **sich h~** rise; (Nebel:) lift; (sich verbessern) improve

hebräisch adj Hebrew

hecheln vi (haben) pant

Hecht m -[e]s,-e pike

Heck nt -s,-s (Naut) stern; (Aviat) tail; (Auto) rear

Hecke f -,-n hedge

Heck|fenster nt rear window. **H~tür** f hatchback

Heer nt -[e]s,-e army

Hefe f - yeast

Heft nt -[e]s,-e booklet; (Sch) exercise book; (Zeitschrift) issue. **h~en** vt (nähen) tack; (stecken) pin/(klammern) clip/(mit Heftmaschine) staple (**an** + acc to). **H~er** m -s,- file

heftig adj fierce, violent; (Regen) heavy; (Schmerz, Gefühl) intense

Heft|klammer f staple; (Büro-) paper clip. **H~maschine** f stapler. **H~zwecke** f -,-n drawing pin

Heide[1] m -n,-n heathen

Heide[2] f -,-n heath; (Bot) heather. **H~kraut** nt heather

Heidelbeere f bilberry

Heidin f -,-nen heathen

heikel adj difficult, tricky

heil adj undamaged, intact; (Person) unhurt; **mit h~er Haut** ① unscathed

Heil nt -s salvation

Heiland m -s (Relig) Saviour

Heil|anstalt f sanatorium; (Nerven-) mental hospital. **H~bad** nt spa. **h~bar** adj curable

Heilbutt m -[e]s,-e halibut

heilen vt cure; heal (Wunde) • vi (sein) heal

Heilgymnastik f physiotherapy

heilig adj holy; (geweiht) sacred; **der**

H~e Abend Christmas Eve; **die h~e Anna** Saint Anne; (Feiertag); **h~ sprechen** canonize. **H~abend** m Christmas Eve. **H~e(r)** m/f saint. **H~enschein** m halo. **H~keit** f - sanctity, holiness. **H~tum** nt -s,-̈er shrine

heil|kräftig adj medicinal. **H~kräuter** ntpl medicinal herbs. **H~mittel** nt remedy. **H~praktiker** m -s,- practitioner of alternative medicine. **H~sarmee** f Salvation Army. **H~ung** f - cure

Heim nt -[e]s,-e home; (Studenten-) hostel. **h~** adv home

Heimat f -,-en home; (Land) native land. **H~stadt** f home town

heim|begleiten vt sep see home. **H~computer** m home computer. **h~fahren**† v sep • vi (sein) go/drive home • vt take/drive home. **H~fahrt** f way home. **h~gehen**† vi sep (sein) go home

heimisch adj native, indigenous; (Pol) domestic

Heim|kehr f - return [home]. **h~kehren** vi sep (sein) return home. **h~kommen**† vi sep (sein) come home

heimlich adj secret; **etw h~ tun** do sth secretly. **H~keit** f -,-en secrecy; **H~keiten** secrets

Heim|reise f journey home. **H~spiel** nt home game. **h~suchen** vt sep afflict. **h~tückisch** adj treacherous; (Krankheit) insidious. **h~wärts** adv home. **H~weg** m way home. **H~weh** nt -s homesickness; **H~weh haben** be homesick. **H~werker** m -s,- [home] handyman. **h~zahlen** vt sep jdm etw h~zahlen (fig) pay s.o. back for sth

Heirat f -,-en marriage. **h~en** vt/i (haben) marry. **H~santrag** m proposal; **jdm einen H~santrag machen** propose to s.o.

heiser adj hoarse. **H~keit** f - hoarseness

heiß adj hot; (hitzig) heated; (leidenschaftlich) fervent

heißen† vi (haben) be called; (bedeu-

ten) mean; **ich heiße ...** my name is
...; **wie h∼Sie?** what is your name?
wie heißt ... auf Englisch? what's
the English for ...? ● *vt* call; **jdn etw
tun h∼** tell s.o. to do sth

heiter *adj* cheerful; *(Wetter)* bright;
(amüsant) amusing; **aus h∼em Himmel** *(fig)* out of the blue

Heiz|anlage *f* heating; *(Auto)*
heater. **H∼decke** *f* electric blanket.
h∼en *vt* heat; light *(Ofen)* ● *vi*
(haben) put the heating on; *(Ofen:)*
give out heat. **H∼gerät** *nt* heater.
H∼kessel *m* boiler. **H∼körper** *m*
radiator. **H∼lüfter** *m* **-s,-** fan heater.
H∼material *nt* fuel. **H∼ung** *f* **-,-en**
heating; *(Heizkörper)* radiator

Hektar *nt* & *m* **-s,-** hectare

Held *m* **-en,-en** hero. **h∼enhaft** *adj*
heroic. **H∼entum** *nt* **-s** heroism.
H∼in *f* **-,-nen** heroine

helf|en† *vi (haben)* help *(jdm* s.o.)*;
(nützen) be effective; **sich** *(dat)* **nicht
zu h∼en wissen** not know what to
do; **es hilft nichts** it's no use.
H∼er(in) *m* **-s,-** *(f* **-,-nen)** helper,
assistant

hell *adj* light; *(Licht ausstrahlend, klug)*
bright; *(Stimme)* clear; (🆈: *völlig)*
utter; **h∼es Bier** ≈ lager ● *adv*
brightly

Hell|igkeit *f* - brightness. **H∼se-
her(in)** *m* **-s,-** *(f* **-,-nen)** clairvoyant

Helm *m* **-[e]s,-e** helmet

Hemd *nt* **-[e]s,-en** vest; *(Ober-)* shirt

Hemisphäre *f* **-,-n** hemisphere

hemm|en *vt* check; *(verzögern)* im-
pede; *(fig)* inhibit. **H∼ung** *f* **-,-en**
(fig) inhibition; *(Skrupel)* scruple;
H∼ungen haben be inhibited.
h∼ungslos *adj* unrestrained

Hendl *nt* **-s,-[n]** *(Aust)* chicken

Hengst *m* **-[e]s,-e** stallion

Henkel *m* **-s,-** handle

Henne *f* **-,-n** hen

her *adv* here; *(zeitlich)* ago; **her
mit ...! give me ...! von Norden/
weit her** from the north/far away;
vom Thema her as far as the subject is concerned; **her sein** come
(von from); **es ist schon lange her** it

was a long time ago

herab *adv* down [here]; **von oben
h∼** from above; *(fig)* condescending

herablassen† *vt sep* let down; **sich
h∼** condescend **(zu** to)

herab|sehen† *vi sep (haben)* look
down *(auf + acc* on). **h∼setzen** *vt
sep* reduce, cut; *(fig)* belittle

Heraldik *f* - heraldry

heran *adv* near; **[bis] h∼ an** (+ *acc)*
up to. **h∼kommen**† *vi sep (sein)* approach; **h∼kommen an** (+ *acc)*
come up to; *(erreichen)* get at; *(fig)*
measure up to. **h∼machen (sich)** *vr
sep* **sich h∼machen an** (+ *acc)* approach; get down to *(Arbeit)*.
h∼wachsen† *vi sep (sein)* grow up.
h∼ziehen† *v sep* ● *vt* pull up **(an** +
acc to); *(züchten)* raise; *(h∼bilden)*
train; *(hinzuziehen)* call in ● *vi (sein)*
approach

herauf *adv* up [here]; **die Treppe
h∼** up the stairs. **h∼setzen** *vt sep*
raise, increase

heraus *adv* out (aus of); **h∼ damit
od mit der Sprache!** out with it!
h∼bekommen† *vt sep* get out; *(ausfindig machen)* find out; *(lösen)* solve;
Geld h∼bekommen get change.
h∼finden† *v sep* ● *vt* find out ● *vi
(haben)* find one's way out. **h∼for-
dern** *vt sep* provoke; challenge *(Person)*. **H∼forderung** *f* provocation;
challenge. **H∼gabe** *f* handing over;
(Admin) issue; *(Veröffentlichung)* publication. **h∼geben**† *vt sep* hand over;
(Admin) issue; *(veröffentlichen)* publish; edit *(Zeitschrift)*; **jdm Geld
h∼geben** give s.o. change ● *vi
(haben)* give change **(auf** + *acc* for).
H∼geber *m* **-s,-** publisher; editor.
h∼halten† **(sich)** *vr sep (fig)* keep
out (aus of). **h∼kommen**† *vi sep
(sein)* come out; *(aus Schwierigkeit,
Takt)* get out; **auf eins** *od* **dasselbe
h∼kommen** 🆈 come to the same
thing. **h∼lassen**† *vt sep* let out.
h∼nehmen† *vt sep* take out; **sich zu
viel h∼nehmen** *(fig)* take liberties.
h∼reden (sich) *vr sep* make ex-
cuses. **h∼rücken** *v sep* ● *vt* move

h (in right margin tab)

out; (*hergeben*) hand over ● *vi* (*sein*) h∼**rücken mit** hand over; (*fig: sagen*) come out with. **h∼schlagen**† *vt sep* knock out; (*fig*) gain. **h∼stellen** *vt sep* put out; **sich h∼stellen** turn out (**als** to be; **dass** that). **h∼ziehen**† *vt sep* pull out

herb *adj* sharp; (*Wein*) dry; (*fig*) harsh

herbei *adv* here. **h∼führen** *vt sep* (*fig*) bring about. **h∼schaffen** *vt sep* get. **h∼sehnen** *vt sep* long for

Herberg|e *f* -,-n [youth] hostel; (*Unterkunft*) lodging. **H∼svater** *m* warden

herbestellen *vt sep* summon

herbitten† *vt sep* ask to come

herbringen† *vt sep* bring [here]

Herbst *m* -[e]s,-e autumn. **h∼lich** *adj* autumnal

Herd *m* -[e]s,-e stove, cooker

Herde *f* -,-n herd; (*Schaf-*) flock

herein *adv* in [here]; **h∼!** come in! **h∼bitten**† *vt sep* ask in. **h∼fallen**† *vi sep* (*sein*) 🛈 be taken in (**auf** + *acc* by). **h∼kommen**† *vi sep* (*sein*) come in. **h∼lassen**† *vt sep* let in. **h∼legen** *vt sep* 🛈 take for a ride

Herfahrt *f* journey/drive here

herfallen† *vi sep* (*sein*) ∼ **über** (+ *acc*) attack; fall upon (*Essen*)

hergeben† *vt sep* hand over; (*fig*) give up

hergehen† *vi sep* (*sein*) **h∼ vor** (+ *dat*) walk along in front of; **es ging lustig her** 🛈 there was a lot of merriment

herholen *vt sep* fetch; **weit hergeholt** (*fig*) far-fetched

Hering *m* -s,-e herring; (*Zeltpflock*) tent peg

her|kommen† *vi sep* (*sein*) come here; **wo kommt das her?** where does it come from? **h∼kömmlich** *adj* traditional. **H∼kunft** *f* - origin

herleiten *vt sep* derive

hermachen *vt sep* **viel/wenig h∼** be impressive/unimpressive; (*wichtig nehmen*) make a lot of/little fuss (**von** of); **sich h∼ über** (+ *acc*) fall

upon; tackle (*Arbeit*)

Hermelin[1] *nt* -s,-e (*Zool*) stoat

Hermelin[2] *m* -s,-e (*Pelz*) ermine

Hernie /ˈhɛrniə/ *f* -,-n hernia

Heroin *nt* -s heroin

heroisch *adj* heroic

Herr *m* -n,-en gentleman; (*Gebieter*) master (**über** + *acc* of); **[Gott,] der H∼** the Lord [God]; **H∼ Meier** Mr Meier; **Sehr geehrte H∼en** Dear Sirs. **H∼enhaus** *nt* manor [house]. **h∼enlos** *adj* ownerless; (*Tier*) stray

Herrgott *m* **der H∼** the Lord

herrichten *vt sep* prepare; **wieder h∼** renovate

Herrin *f* -,-nen mistress

herrlich *adj* marvellous; (*großartig*) magnificent

Herrschaft *f* -,-en rule; (*Macht*) power; (*Kontrolle*) control; **meine H∼en!** ladies and gentlemen!

herrsch|en *vi* (*haben*) rule; (*verbreitet sein*) prevail; **es h∼te Stille** there was silence. **H∼er(in)** *m* -s,- (*f* -,-nen) ruler

herrühren *vi sep* (*haben*) stem (**von** from)

herstammen *vi sep* (*haben*) come (**aus/von** from)

herstell|en *vt sep* establish; (*Comm*) manufacture, make. **H∼er** *m* -s,- manufacturer, maker. **H∼ung** *f* - establishment; manufacture

herüber *adv* over [here]

herum *adv* **im Kreis h∼** [round] in a circle; **falsch h∼** the wrong way round; **um ... h∼** round ... ; (*ungefähr*) [round] about ; **h∼ sein** be over. **h∼drehen** *vt sep* turn round/ (*wenden*) over; turn (*Schlüssel*). **h∼gehen**† *vi sep* (*sein*) walk around; (*Zeit:*) pass; **h∼gehen um** go round. **h∼kommen**† *vi sep* (*sein*) get about; **h∼kommen um** get round; come round (*Ecke*); **um etw [nicht] h∼kommen** (*fig*) [not] get out of sth. **h∼sitzen**† *vi sep* (*haben*) sit around; **h∼sitzen um** sit round. **h∼sprechen**† (**sich**) *vr sep* (*Gerücht:*) get about. **h∼treiben**† (**sich**) *vr sep*

hang around. **h~ziehen†** *vi sep* (*sein*)
move around; (*ziellos*) wander about

herunter *adv* down [here]; **die
Treppe h~** down the stairs. **h~fal-
len†** *vi* fall off. **h~gekommen** *adj*
(*fig*) run-down; (*Gebäude*) dilapidated; (*Person*) down-at-heel.
h~kommen† *vi sep* (*sein*) come
down; (*fig*) go to rack and ruin;
(*Firma, Person:*) go downhill; (*gesundheitlich*) get run down. **h~laden** *sep*
vt † download. **h~lassen†** *vt sep* let
down, lower. **h~machen** *vt sep* 🛈
reprimand; (*herabsetzen*) run down.
h~spielen *vt sep* (*fig*) play down

hervor *adv* out (**aus** of). **h~brin-
gen†** *vt sep* produce; utter (*Wort*).
h~gehen† *vi sep* (*sein*) come/(*sich
ergeben*) emerge/(*folgen*) follow (**aus**
from). **h~heben†** *vt sep* (*fig*) stress,
emphasize. **h~ragen** *vi sep* (*haben*)
jut out; (*fig*) stand out. **h~ragend**
adj (*fig*) outstanding. **h~rufen†** *vt
sep* (*fig*) cause. **h~stehen†** *vi sep*
(*haben*) protrude. **h~treten†** *vi sep*
(*sein*) protrude, bulge; (*fig*) stand
out. **h~tun† (sich)** *vr sep* (*fig*) distinguish oneself; (*angeben*) show off

Herweg *m* way here

Herz *nt* **-ens,-en** heart; (*Kartenspiel*)
hearts *pl*; **sich** (*dat*) **ein H~ fassen**
pluck up courage. **H~anfall** *m* heart
attack

herzhaft *adj* hearty; (*würzig*) savoury

herziehen† *v sep* ● *vt* **hinter sich**
(*dat*) **h~** pull along [behind one] ● *vi*
(*sein*) **hinter jdm h~** follow along
behind s.o.; **über jdn h~** 🛈 run s.o.
down

herz|ig *adj* sweet, adorable.
H~infarkt *m* heart attack.
H~klopfen *nt* **-s** palpitations *pl*

herzlich *adj* cordial; (*warm*) warm;
(*aufrichtig*) sincere; **h~en Dank!**
many thanks! **h~e Grüße** kind regards

herzlos *adj* heartless

Herzog *m* **-s,** ̈e duke. **H~in** *f* **-,-nen**
duchess. **H~tum** *nt* **-s,** ̈er duchy

Herzschlag *m* heartbeat; (*Med*)
heart failure

Hessen *nt* **-s** Hesse

heterosexuell *adj* heterosexual

Hetze *f* **-** rush; (*Kampagne*) virulent
campaign (**gegen** against). **h~n** *vt*
chase; **sich h~n** hurry

Heu *nt* **-s** hay

Heuchelei *f* **-** hypocrisy

heuch|eln *vt* feign ● *vi* (*haben*) pre-
tend. **H~ler(in)** *m* **-s,-** (*f* -,-nen)
hypocrite. **h~lerisch** *adj* hypocritical

heuer *adv* (*Aust*) this year

heulen *vi* (*haben*) howl; (🛈: *weinen*)
cry

Heurige This is an Austrian *i*
term for both a new wine
and an inn with new wine on tap,
especially an inn with its own vineyard in the Vienna region. A garland of pine twigs outside the
gates of the *Heurige* shows that the
new barrel has been tapped.

Heu|schnupfen *m* hay fever.
H~schober *m* **-s,-** haystack.
H~schrecke *f* **-,-n** grasshopper

heut|e *adv* today; (*heutzutage*) now-
adays; **h~e früh** *od* **Morgen** this
morning; **von h~e auf morgen**
from one day to the next. **h~ig** *adj*
today's; (*gegenwärtig*) present; **der
h~ige Tag** today. **h~zutage** *adv*
nowadays

Hexe *f* **-,-n** witch. **h~n** *vi* (*haben*)
work magic. **H~nschuss** *m* lumbago

Hieb *m* **-[e]s,-e** blow; (*Peitschen-*)
lash; **H~e** hiding *sg*

hier *adv* here; **h~ sein/bleiben/
lassen/behalten** be/stay/leave/keep
here; **h~ und da** here and there;
(*zeitlich*) now and again

hier|auf *adv* on this/these; (*antwor-
ten*) to this; (*zeitlich*) after this.
h~aus *adv* out of or from this/
these. **h~durch** *adv* through this/
these; (*Ursache*) as a result of this.
h~her *adv* here. **h~hin** *adv* here.
h~in *adv* in this/these. **h~mit** *adv*
with this/these; (*Comm*) herewith;
(*Admin*) hereby. **h~nach** *adv* after

h

this/these; (*demgemäß*) according to this/these. **h~über** *adv* over/(*höher*) above this/these; (*sprechen, streiten*) about this/these. **h~von** *adv* from this/these; (*h~über*) about this/these; (*Menge*) of this/these. **h~zu** *adv* to this/these; (*h~für*) for this/these. **h~zulande** *adv* here

hiesig *adj* local. **H~e(r)** *m/f* local

Hilf|e *f* -,-**n** help, aid; **um H~e rufen** call for help. **h~los** *adj* helpless. **H~losigkeit** *f* - helplessness. **h~reich** *adj* helpful

Hilfs|arbeiter *m* unskilled labourer. **h~bedürftig** *adj* needy; **h~bedürftig sein** be in need of help. **h~bereit** *adj* helpful. **H~kraft** *f* helper. **H~mittel** *nt* aid. **H~verb** *nt* auxiliary verb

Himbeere *f* raspberry

Himmel *m* -s,- sky; (*Relig & fig*) heaven; (*Bett-*) canopy; **unter freiem H~** in the open air. **H~bett** *nt* four-poster [bed]. **H~fahrt** *f* Ascension

himmlisch *adj* heavenly

hin *adv* there; **hin und her** to and fro; **hin und zurück** there and back; (*Rail*) return; **hin und wieder** now and again; **an** (+ *dat*) ... **hin** along; **auf** (+ *acc*) ... **hin** in reply to (*Brief, Anzeige*); on (*jds Rat*); **zu** *od* **nach** ... **hin** towards; **hin sein** 🄸 be gone; **es ist noch lange hin** it's a long time yet

hinauf *adv* up [there]. **h~gehen†** *vi sep* (*sein*) go up. **h~setzen** *vt sep* raise

hinaus *adv* out [there]; (*nach draußen*) outside; **zur Tür h~** out of the door; **auf Jahre h~** for years to come; **über etw** (*acc*) **h~** beyond sth; (*Menge*) [over and] above sth; **über etw** (*acc*) **h~ sein** (*fig*) be past sth. **h~gehen†** *vi sep* (*sein*) go out; (*Zimmer:*) face (**nach Norden** north); **h~gehen über** (+ *acc*) go beyond, exceed. **h~laufen†** *vi sep* (*sein*) run out; **h~laufen auf** (+ *acc*) (*fig*) amount to. **h~lehnen (sich)** *vr sep* lean out. **h~schieben†** *vt sep* push out; (*fig*) put off. **h~werfen†** *vt sep*

throw out; (🄸: *entlassen*) fire. **h~wollen†** *vi sep* (*haben*) want to go out; **h~wollen auf** (+ *acc*) (*fig*) aim at. **h~ziehen†** *v sep* ● *vt* pull out; (*in die Länge ziehen*) drag out; (*verzögern*) delay; **sich h~ziehen** drag on; be delayed ● *vi* (*sein*) move out. **h~zögern** *vt* delay; **sich h~zögern** be delayed

Hinblick *m* **im H~ auf** (+ *acc*) in view of; (*hinsichtlich*) regarding

hinder|lich *adj* awkward; **jdm h~lich sein** hamper s.o. **h~n** *vt* hamper; (*verhindern*) prevent. **H~nis** *nt* -ses,-se obstacle. **H~nisrennen** *nt* steeplechase

Hindu *m* -s,-s Hindu.

hindurch *adv* through it/them

hinein *adv* in [there]; (*nach drinnen*) inside; **h~ in** (+ *acc*) into. **h~fallen†** *vi sep* (*sein*) fall in. **h~gehen†** *vi sep* (*sein*) go in; **h~gehen in** (+ *acc*) go into. **h~reden** *vi sep* (*haben*) **jdm h~reden** interrupt s.o.; (*sich einmischen*) interfere in s.o.'s affairs. **h~versetzen (sich)** *vr sep* **sich in jds Lage h~versetzen** put oneself in s.o.'s position. **h~ziehen†** *vt sep* pull in; **h~ziehen in** (+ *acc*) pull into; **in etw** (*acc*) **h~gezogen werden** (*fig*) become involved in sth

hin|fahren† *v sep* ● *vi* (*sein*) go/drive there ● *vt* take/drive there. **H~fahrt** *f* journey/drive there; (*Rail*) outward journey. **h~fallen†** *vi sep* (*sein*) fall. **h~fliegen†** *v sep* ● *vi* (*sein*) fly there; 🄸 fall ● *vt* fly there. **H~flug** *m* flight there; (*Aviat*) outward flight

Hingeb|ung *f* - devotion. **h~ungsvoll** *adj* devoted

hingehen† *vi sep* (*sein*) go/(*zu Fuß*) walk there; (*vergehen*) pass; **h~ zu** go up to; **wo gehst du hin?** where are you going?

hingerissen *adj* rapt; **h~ sein** be carried away (**von** by)

hinhalten† *vt sep* hold out; (*warten lassen*) keep waiting

hinken *vi* (*haben/sein*) limp

hin|knien (sich) *vr sep* kneel down.

h~kommen† *vi sep* (*sein*) get there; (*h~gehören*) belong, go; (⊡: *auskommen*) manage (**mit** with); (⊡: *stimmen*) be right. **h~laufen**† *vi sep* (*sein*) run/(*gehen*) walk there. **h~legen** *vt sep* lay *or* put down; **sich h~legen** lie down. **h~nehmen**† *vt sep* (*fig*) accept

hinreichen *v sep* ● *vt* hand (*dat* to) ● *vi* (*haben*) extend (**bis** to); (*ausreichen*) be adequate. **h~d** *adj* adequate

Hinreise *f* journey there; (*Rail*) outward journey

hinreißen† *vt sep* (*fig*) carry away; **sich h~ lassen** get carried away. **h~d** *adj* ravishing

hinricht|en *vt sep* execute. **H~ung** *f* execution

hinschreiben† *vt sep* write there; (*aufschreiben*) write down

hinsehen† *vi sep* (*haben*) look

hinsetzen *vt sep* put down; **sich h~** sit down

Hinsicht *f* - **in dieser H~** in this respect; **in finanzieller H~** financially. **h~lich** *prep* (+ *gen*) regarding

hinstellen *vt sep* put *or* set down; park (*Auto*)

hinstrecken *vt sep* hold out; **sich h~** extend

hinten *adv* at the back; **dort h~** back there; **nach/von h~** to the back/from behind. **h~herum** *adv* round the back; ⊡ by devious means

hinter *prep* (+ *dat/acc*) behind; (*nach*) after; **h~ jdm/etw herlaufen** run after s.o./something; **h~ etw** (*dat*) **stecken** (*fig*) be behind sth; **h~ etw** (*acc*) **kommen** (*fig*) get to the bottom of sth; **etw h~ sich** (*acc*) **bringen** get sth over [and done] with

Hinterbliebene *pl* (*Admin*) surviving dependants; **die H~n** the bereaved family *sg*

hintere|(r,s) *adj* back, rear; **h~s Ende** far end

hintereinander *adv* one behind/(*zeitlich*) after the other; **dreimal h~** three times in succession

Hintergedanke *m* ulterior motive

hintergehen† *vt* deceive

Hinter|grund *m* background. **H~halt** *m* -[e]s,-e ambush. **h~hältig** *adj* underhand

hinterher *adv* behind, after; (*zeitlich*) afterwards

Hinter|hof *m* back yard. **H~kopf** *m* back of the head

hinterlassen† *vt* leave [behind]; (*Jur*) leave, bequeath (*dat* to). **H~schaft** *f* -,-en (*Jur*) estate

hinterlegen *vt* deposit

Hinter|leib *m* (*Zool*) abdomen. **H~list** *f* deceit. **h~listig** *adj* deceitful. **H~n** *m* -s,- ⊡ bottom, backside. **H~rad** *nt* rear *or* back wheel. **h~rücks** *adv* from behind. **h~ste(r,s)** *adj* last; **h~ste Reihe** back row. **H~teil** *nt* ⊡ behind. **H~treppe** *f* back stairs *pl*

hinterziehen† *vt* (*Admin*) evade

hinüber *adv* over *or* across [there]; **h~ sein** (⊡: *unbrauchbar, tot*) have had it. **h~gehen**† *vi sep* (*sein*) go over *or* across; **h~gehen über** (+ *acc*) cross

hinunter *adv* down [there]. **h~gehen**† *vi sep* (*sein*) go down. **h~schlucken** *vt sep* swallow

Hinweg *m* way there

hinweg *adv* away, off; **h~ über** (+ *acc*) over; **über eine Zeit h~** over a period. **h~kommen**† *vt sep* (*sein*) **h~kommen über** (+ *acc*) (*fig*) get over. **h~sehen**† *vi sep* (*haben*) **h~sehen über** (+ *acc*) see over; (*fig*) overlook. **h~setzen** (**sich**) *vr sep* **sich h~setzen über** (+ *acc*) ignore

Hinweis *m* -es,-e reference; (*Andeutung*) hint; (*Anzeichen*) indication; **unter H~ auf** (+ *acc*) with reference to. **h~en**† *v sep* ● *vi* (*haben*) point (**auf** + *acc* to) ● *vt* **jdn auf etw** (*acc*) **h~en** point sth out to s.o.

hinwieder *adv* on the other hand

hin|zeigen *vi sep* (*haben*) point (**auf** + *acc* to). **h~ziehen**† *vt sep* pull; (*fig: in die Länge ziehen*) drag out; (*verzögern*) delay; **sich h~ziehen** drag on

hinzu *adv* in addition. **h~fügen** *vt*

sep add. **h~kommen†** vt sep (sein) be added; (ankommen) arrive [on the scene]; join (zu jdm s.o.). **h~ziehen†** vt sep call in

Hiobsbotschaft f bad news sg

Hirn nt -s brain; (Culin) brains pl. **H~hautentzündung** f meningitis

Hirsch m -[e]s,-e deer; (männlich) stag; (Culin) venison

Hirse f - millet

Hirt m -en,-en, **Hirte** m -n,-n shepherd

hissen vt hoist

Histor|iker m -s,- historian. **h~isch** adj historical; (bedeutend) historic

Hitz|e f - heat. **h~ig** adj (fig) heated; (Person) hot-headed; (jähzornig) hot-tempered. **H~schlag** m heat-stroke

H-Milch /'ha:-/ f long-life milk

Hobby nt -s,-s hobby

Hobel m -s,- (Techn) plane; (Culin) slicer. **h~n** vt/i (haben) plane. **H~späne** mpl shavings

hoch adj (attrib hohe(r,s)) high; (Baum, Mast) tall; (Offizier) high-ranking; (Alter) great; (Summe) large; (Strafe) heavy; **hohe Schuhe** ankle boots ● adv high; (sehr) highly; **h~gewachsen** tall; **h~ begabt** highly gifted; **h~ gestellte Persönlichkeit** important person; **die Treppe h~** up the stairs; **sechs Mann h~** six of us/them. **H~** nt -s,-s cheer; (Meteorology) high

Hoch|achtung f high esteem. **H~achtungsvoll** adv Yours faithfully. **H~betrieb** m great activity; **in den Geschäften herrscht H~betrieb** the shops are terribly busy. **H~deutsch** nt High German. **H~druck** m high pressure. **H~ebene** f plateau. **h~fahren†** vi sep (sein) go up; (auffahren) start up; (aufbrausen) flare up. **h~gehen†** vi sep (sein) go up; (explodieren) blow up; (aufbrausen) flare up. **h~gestellt** attrib adj (Zahl) superior; (fig) *h~gestellt, s. hoch. **H~glanz** m high

gloss. **h~gradig** adj extreme. **h~hackig** adj high-heeled. **h~halten†** vt sep hold up; (fig) uphold. **H~haus** nt high-rise building. **h~heben†** vt sep lift up; raise (Hand). **h~kant** adv on end. **h~kommen†** vi sep (sein) come up; (aufstehen) get up; (fig) get on [in the world]. **H~konjunktur** f boom. **h~krempeln** vt sep roll up. **h~leben** vi sep (haben) **h~leben lassen** give three cheers for; **H~mut** m pride, arrogance. **h~näsig** adj 🗉 snooty. **H~ofen** m blast-furnace. **h~ragen** vi sep rise [up]; (Turm:) soar. **H~ruf** m cheer. **H~saison** f high season. **h~schlagen†** vt sep turn up (Kragen). **H~schule** f university; (Musik-, Kunst-) academy. **H~sommer** m midsummer. **H~spannung** f high/(fig) great tension. **h~spielen** vt sep (fig) magnify. **H~sprung** m high jump

---

Hochdeutsch There are many regional dialects in Germany, Austria and Switzerland. *Hochdeutsch* (High German) is the standard language that can be understood by all German speakers. Newspapers and books are generally printed in *Hochdeutsch*. ℹ️

---

höchst adv extremely, most

Hochstapler m -s,- confidence trickster

höchst|e(r,s) adj highest; (Baum, Turm) tallest; (oberste, größte) top; **es ist h~e Zeit** it is high time. **h~ens** adv at most; (es sei denn) except perhaps. **H~geschwindigkeit** f top or maximum speed. **H~maß** nt maximum. **h~persönlich** adv in person. **H~preis** m top price. **H~temperatur** f maximum temperature

Hoch|verrat m high treason. **H~wasser** nt high tide; (Überschwemmung) floods pl. **H~würden** m -s Reverend; (Anrede) Father

Hochzeit f -,-en wedding. **H~skleid** nt wedding dress. **H~sreise** f honeymoon [trip].

H~stag m wedding day/(*Jahrestag*) anniversary

Hocke f - in der H~ sitzen squat. **h~n** vi (*haben*) squat ● vr sich h~n squat down

Hocker m -s,- stool

Höcker m -s,- bump; (*Kamel-*) hump

Hockey /hɔki/ nt -s hockey

Hode f -,-n, **Hoden** m -s,- testicle

Hof m -[e]s, ⁼e [court]yard; (*Bauern-*) farm; (*Königs-*) court; (*Schul-*) playground; (*Astronomy*) halo

hoffen vt/i (*haben*) hope (**auf** + acc for). **h~tlich** adv I hope so, hopefully

Hoffnung f -,-en hope. **h~slos** adj hopeless. **h~svoll** adj hopeful

höflich adj polite. **H~keit** f -,-en politeness, courtesy

hohe(r,s) adj s. hoch

Höhe f -,-n height; (*Aviat, Geog*) altitude; (*Niveau*) level; (*einer Summe*) size; (*An-*) hill

Hoheit f -,-en (*Staats-*) sovereignty; (*Titel*) Highness. **H~sgebiet** nt [sovereign] territory. **H~szeichen** nt national emblem

Höhe|nlinie f contour line. **H~nsonne** f sun lamp. **H~punkt** m (*fig*) climax, peak. **h~r** adj & adv higher; **h~re Schule** secondary school

hohl adj hollow; (*leer*) empty

Höhle f -,-n cave; (*Tier-*) den; (*Hohlraum*) cavity; (*Augen-*) socket

Hohl|maß nt measure of capacity. **H~raum** m cavity

Hohn m -s scorn, derision

höhnen vt deride

holen vt fetch, get; (*kaufen*) buy; (*nehmen*) take (**aus** from)

Holland nt -s Holland

Holländ|er m -s,- Dutchman; die H~er the Dutch pl. **H~erin** f -,-nen Dutchwoman. **h~isch** adj Dutch

Höll|e f - hell. **h~isch** adj infernal; (*schrecklich*) terrible

Holunder m -s (*Bot*) elder

Holz nt -es, ⁼er wood; (*Nutz-*) timber.

H~blasinstrument nt woodwind instrument

hölzern adj wooden

Holz|hammer m mallet. **~ig** adj woody. **H~kohle** f charcoal. **H~schnitt** m woodcut. **H~wolle** f wood shavings pl

Homöopathie f - homoeopathy

homöopathisch adj homoeopathic

homosexuell adj homosexual. **H~e(r)** m/f homosexual

Honig m -s honey. **H~wabe** f honeycomb

Hono|rar nt -s,-e fee. **h~rieren** vt remunerate; (*fig*) reward

Hopfen m -s hops pl; (*Bot*) hop

hopsen vi (*sein*) jump

horchen vi (*haben*) listen (**auf** + acc to); (*heimlich*) eavesdrop

hören vt hear; (*an-*) listen to ● vi (*haben*) hear; (*horchen*) listen; (*gehorchen*) obey; **h~ auf** (+ acc) listen to

Hör|er m -s,- listener; (*Teleph*) receiver. **H~funk** m radio. **H~gerät** nt hearing aid

Horizon|t m -[e]s horizon. **h~tal** adj horizontal

Hormon nt -s,-e hormone

Horn nt -s, ⁼er horn. **H~haut** f hard skin; (*Augen-*) cornea

Hornisse f -,-n hornet

Horoskop nt -[e]s,-e horoscope

Horrorfilm m horror film

Hör|saal m (*Univ*) lecture hall. **H~spiel** nt radio play

Hort m -[e]s,-e (*Schatz*) hoard; (*fig*) refuge. **h~en** vt hoard

Hortensie /-iə/ f -,-n hydrangea

Hose f -,-n, **Hosen** pl trousers pl. **H~nrock** m culottes pl. **H~nschlitz** m fly, flies pl. **H~nträger** mpl braces

Hostess f -,-tessen hostess; (*Aviat*) air hostess

Hostie /ˈhɔstiə/ f -,-n (*Relig*) host

Hotel nt -s,-s hotel

hübsch adj pretty; (*nett*) nice

Hubschrauber m -s,- helicopter

Huf *m* -[e]s,-e hoof. **H~eisen** *nt* horseshoe

Hüft|e *f* -,-n hip. **H~gürtel** *m* -s,- girdle

Hügel *m* -s,- hill. **h~ig** *adj* hilly

Huhn *nt* -s,⁼er chicken; (*Henne*) hen

Hühn|chen *nt* -s,- chicken. **H~erauge** *nt* corn **H~erstall** *m* henhouse

Hülle *f* -,-n cover; (*Verpackung*) wrapping; (*Platten-*) sleeve. **h~n** *vt* wrap

Hülse *f* -,-n (*Bot*) pod; (*Etui*) case. **H~nfrüchte** *fpl* pulses

human *adj* humane. **H~ität** *f* - humanity

Hummel *f* -,-n bumble bee

Hummer *m* -s,- lobster

Hum|or *m* -s humour; **H~or haben** have a sense of humour. **h~orvoll** *adj* humorous

humpeln *vi* (*sein/haben*) hobble

Humpen *m* -s,- tankard

Hund *m* -[e]s,-e dog; (*Jagd-*) hound. **H~ehütte** *f* kennel

hundert *inv adj* one/a hundred. **H~** *nt* -s,-e hundred; **H~e** *od* **h~e von** hundreds of. **H~jahrfeier** *f* centenary. **h~prozentig** *adj & adv* one hundred per cent. **h~ste(r,s)** *adj* hundredth. **H~stel** *nt* -s,- hundredth

Hündin *f* -,-nen bitch

Hüne *m* -n,-n giant

Hunger *m* -s hunger; **H~ haben** be hungry. **h~n** *vi* (*haben*) starve. **H~snot** *f* famine

hungrig *adj* hungry

Hupe *f* -,-n (*Auto*) horn. **h~n** *vi* (*haben*) sound one's horn

hüpfen *vi* (*sein*) skip; (*Frosch:*) hop; (*Grashüpfer:*) jump

Hürde *f* -,-n (*Sport & fig*) hurdle; (*Schaf-*) pen, fold

Hure *f* -,-n whore

hurra *int* hurray

husten *vi* (*haben*) cough. **H~** *m* -s cough. **H~saft** *m* cough mixture

Hut¹ *m* -[e]s,⁼e hat; (*Pilz-*) cap

Hut² *f* - **auf der H~ sein** be on one's guard (**vor** + *dat* against)

hüten *vt* watch over; tend (*Tiere*); (*aufpassen*) look after; **das Bett h~ müssen** be confined to bed; **sich h~** be on one's guard (**vor** + *dat* against); **sich h~, etw zu tun** take care not to do sth

Hütte *f* -,-n hut; (*Hunde-*) kennel; (*Techn*) iron and steel works. **H~nkäse** *m* cottage cheese. **H~nkunde** *f* metallurgy

Hyäne *f* -,-n hyena

hydraulisch *adj* hydraulic

Hygien|e /hyˈgiːnə/ *f* - hygiene. **h~isch** *adj* hygienic

Hypno|se *f* - hypnosis. **h~tisch** *adj* hypnotic. **H~tiseur** *m* -s,-e hypnotist. **h~tisieren** *vt* hypnotize

Hypochonder /hypoˈxɔndɐ/ *m* -s,- hypochondriac

Hypothek *f* -,-en mortgage

Hypothese *f* -,-n hypothesis

Hys|terie *f* - hysteria. **h~terisch** *adj* hysterical

I i

ich *pron* I; **ich bins** it's me. **Ich** *nt* -[s],-[s] self; (*Psychology*) ego

IC-Zug /iˈtseː-/ *m* inter-city train

ideal *adj* ideal. **I~** *nt* -s,-e ideal. **I~ismus** *m* - idealism. **I~ist(in)** *m* -en,-en (*f* -,-nen) idealist. **i~istisch** *adj* idealistic

Idee *f* -,-n idea; **fixe I~** obsession

identifizieren *vt* identify

identisch *adj* identical

Identität *f* -, -en identity

Ideo|logie *f* -,-n ideology. **i~logisch** *adj* ideological

idiomatisch *adj* idiomatic

Idiot *m* -en,-en idiot. **i~isch** *adj* idiotic

idyllisch /iˈdʏlɪʃ/ *adj* idyllic

Igel *m* -s,- hedgehog

ihm pron (dat of **er, es**) [to] him;
(Ding, Tier) [to] it
ihn pron (acc of **er**) him; (Ding, Tier)
it. **i∼en** pron (dat of **sie** pl) [to]
them. **I∼en** pron (dat of **Sie**) [to]
you

ihr pron (2nd pers pl) you ● (dat of **sie**
sg) [to] her; (Ding, Tier) [to] it ● poss
pron her; (Ding, Tier) its; (pl) their.
Ihr poss pron your. **i∼e(r,s)** poss
pron hers; (pl) theirs. **I∼e(r,s)** poss
pron yours. **i∼erseits** adv for
her/(pl) their part. **I∼erseits** adv on
your part. **i∼etwegen** adv for
her/(Ding, Tier) its/(pl) their sake;
(wegen) because of her/it/them, on
her/its/their account. **I∼etwegen**
adv for your sake; (wegen) because of
you, on your account. **i∼ige** poss
pron der/die/das **i∼ige** hers; (pl)
theirs. **I∼ige** poss pron der/die/das
I∼ige poss pron hers; (pl)
theirs. **i∼s** poss pron hers; (pl)
theirs. **I∼s** poss pron yours

Ikone f -,-n Icon
illegal adj illegal
Illus|ion f -,-en illusion. **i∼orisch**
adj illusory
Illustr|ation /-ˈtsi̯oːn/ f -,-en illus-
tration. **i∼ieren** vt illustrate.
I∼ierte f -n,-[n] [illustrated] magazine
Iltis m -ses,-se polecat
im prep = in dem
Imbiss m snack. **I∼stube** f snack
bar
Imit|ation /-ˈtsi̯oːn/ f -,-en imita-
tion. **i∼ieren** vt imitate
Imker m -s,- bee-keeper
Immatrikul|ation /-ˈtsi̯oːn/ f -
(Univ) enrolment. **i∼ieren** vt (Univ)
enrol; **sich i∼ieren** enrol
immer adv always; **für i∼** for ever;
(endgültig) for good; **i∼ noch** still;
i∼ mehr more and more; **was i∼**
whatever. **i∼hin** adv (wenigstens) at
least; (trotzdem) all the same;
(schließlich) after all. **i∼zu** adv all the
time
Immobilien /-i̯ən/ pl real estate sg.
I∼makler m estate agent
immun adj immune (**gegen** to)

Imperialismus m - imperialism
impf|en vt vaccinate, inoculate.
I∼stoff m vaccine. **I∼ung** f -,-en
vaccination, inoculation
imponieren vi (haben) impress
(jdm s.o.)
Impor|t m -[e]s,-e import. **I∼teur**
m -s,-e importer. **i∼tieren** vt import
impoten|t adj (Med) impotent. **I∼z**
f - (Med) impotence
imprägnieren vt waterproof
Impressionismus m - impression-
ism
improvisieren vt/i (haben) improvise
imstande pred adj able (**zu** to); capable (**etw zu tun** of doing sth)
in prep (+ dat) in; (+ acc) into, in; (bei
Bus, Zug) on; **in der Schule** at
school; **in die Schule** to school ● adj
in sein be in
Inbegriff m embodiment
indem conj (während) while; (dadurch) by (+ -ing)
Inder(in) m -s,- (f -,-nen) Indian
indessen conj while ● adv (unterdessen) meanwhile
Indian|er(in) m -s,- (f -,-nen)
(American) Indian. **i∼isch** adj Indian
Indien /ˈɪndi̯ən/ nt -s India
indirekt adj indirect
indisch adj Indian
indiskret adj indiscreet
indiskutabel adj out of the question
Individu|alist m -en,-en individual-
ist. **I∼alität** f - individuality. **i∼ell**
adj individual
Indizienbeweis /ɪnˈdiːtsi̯ən-/ m
circumstantial evidence
industr|ialisiert adj industrialized.
I∼ie f -,-n industry. **i∼iell** adj industrial
ineinander adv in/into one another
Infanterie f - infantry
Infektion /-ˈtsi̯oːn/ f -,-en infection.
I∼skrankheit f infectious disease
infizieren vt infect; **sich i∼** be-

come/ (*Person:*) be infected

Inflation /-'tsi̯oːn/ *f* - inflation. **i~är** *adj* inflationary

infolge *prep* (+ *gen*) as a result of. **i~dessen** *adv* consequently

Inform|atik *f* - information science. **I~ation** *f* -,-en information; **I~ationen** information *sg*. **i~ieren** *vt* inform; **sich i~ieren** find out (**über** + *acc* about)

infrage *adv* **etw i~ stellen** question sth; (*ungewiss machen*) make sth doubtful; **nicht i~ kommen** be out of the question

infrarot *adj* infra-red

Ingenieur /ɪnʒe'ni̯øːɐ̯/ *m* -s,-e engineer

Ingwer *m* -s ginger

Inhaber(in) *m* -s,- (*f* -,-nen) holder; (*Besitzer*) proprietor; (*Scheck-*) bearer

inhaftieren *vt* take into custody

inhalieren *vt/i* (*haben*) inhale

Inhalt *m* -[e]s,-e contents *pl*; (*Bedeutung, Gehalt*) content; (*Geschichte*) story. **I~sangabe** *f* summary. **I~sverzeichnis** *nt* list/(*in Buch*) table of contents

Initiative /initsi̯a'tiːvə/ *f* -,-n initiative

inklusive *prep* (+ *gen*) including ● *adv* inclusive

inkonsequent *adj* inconsistent

inkorrekt *adj* incorrect

Inkubationszeit /-'tsi̯oːns-/ *f* (*Med*) incubation period

Inland *nt* -[e]s home country; (*Binnenland*) interior. **I~sgespräch** *nt* inland call

inmitten *prep* (+ *gen*) in the middle of; (*unter*) amongst

innen *adv* inside; **nach i~** inwards. **I~architekt(in)** *m*(*f*) interior designer. **I~minister** *m* Minister of the Interior; (*in UK*) Home Secretary. **I~politik** *f* domestic policy. **I~stadt** *f* town centre

inner|e(r,s) *adj* inner; (*Med, Pol*) internal. **I~e(s)** *nt* interior; (*Mitte*) cen-

tre; (*fig: Seele*) inner being. **I~eien** *fpl* (*Culin*) offal *sg*. **i~halb** *prep* (+ *gen*) inside; (*zeitlich & fig*) within; (*während*) during ● *adv* **i~halb von** within. **i~lich** *adj* internal

innig *adj* sincere

innovativ *adj* innovative

Innung *f* -,-en guild

ins *prep* = **in das**

Insasse *m* -n,-n inmate; (*im Auto*) occupant; (*Passagier*) passenger

insbesondere *adv* especially

Inschrift *f* inscription

Insekt *nt* -[e]s,-en insect. **I~envertilgungsmittel** *nt* insecticide

Insel *f* -,-n island

Inser|at *nt* -[e]s,-e [newspaper] advertisement. **i~ieren** *vt/i* (*haben*) advertise

insge|heim *adv* secretly. **i~samt** *adv* [all] in all

insofern, **insoweit** *adv* in this respect; **i~ als** in as much as

Insp|ektion /ɪnspɛk'tsi̯oːn/ *f* -,-en inspection. **I~ektor** *m* -en,-en inspector

Install|ateur /ɪnstala'tøːɐ̯/ *m* -s,-e fitter; (*Klempner*) plumber. **i~ieren** *vt* install

instand *adv* **i~ halten** maintain; (*pflegen*) look after. **I~haltung** *f* - maintenance, upkeep

Instandsetzung *f* - repair

Instanz /-st-/ *f* -,-en authority

Instinkt /-st-/ *m* -[e]s,-e instinct. **i~iv** *adj* instinctive

Institut /-st-/ *nt* -[e]s,-e institute

Instrument /-st-/ *nt* -[e]s,-e instrument. **I~almusik** *f* instrumental music

Insulin *nt* -s insulin

inszenier|en *vt* (*Theat*) produce. **I~ung** *f* -,-en production

Integr|ation /-'tsi̯oːn/ *f* - integration. **i~ieren** *vt* integrate; **sich i~ieren** integrate

Intellekt *m* -[e]s intellect. **i~uell** *adj* intellectual

intelligen|t *adj* intelligent. **I~z** *f* - intelligence

Intendant *m* **-en,-en** director

Intensivstation *f* intensive-care unit

interaktiv *adj* interactive

inter|essant *adj* interesting. **I~esse** *nt* **-s,-n** interest; **I~esse haben** be interested (**an** + *dat* in). **I~essengruppe** *f* pressure group. **I~essent** *m* **-en,-en** interested party; (*Käufer*) prospective buyer. **i~essieren** *vt* interest; **sich i~essieren** be interested (**für** in)

Inter|nat *nt* **-[e]s,-e** boarding school. **i~national** *adj* international. **I~nist** *m* **-en,-en** specialist in internal diseases. **I~pretation** /-'tsi:ʃo:n/ *f* **-,-en** interpretation. **i~pretieren** *vt* interpret. **I~vall** *nt* **-s,-e** interval. **I~vention** /-'tsi:ʃo:n/ *f* **-,-en** intervention

Internet *nt* **-s,-s** Internet; **im I~** on the Internet

Interview /'mtɐvju:/ *nt* **-s,-s** interview. **i~en** *vt* interview

intim *adj* intimate

intoleran|t *adj* intolerant. **I~z** *f* - intolerance

intravenös *adj* intravenous

Intrige *f* **-,-n** intrigue

introvertiert *adj* introverted

Invalidenrente *f* disability pension

Invasion *f* **-,-en** invasion

Inven|tar *nt* **-s,-e** furnishings and fittings *pl*; (*Techn*) equipment; (*Bestand*) stock; (*Liste*) inventory. **I~tur** *f* **-,-en** stock-taking

investieren *vt* invest

inwie|fern *adv* in what way. **i~weit** *adv* how far, to what extent

Inzest *m* **-[e]s** incest

inzwischen *adv* in the meantime

Irak (der) -[s] Iraq. **i~isch** *adj* Iraqi

Iran (der) -[s] Iran. **i~isch** *adj* Iranian

irdisch *adj* earthly

Ire *m* **-n,-n** Irishman; **die I~n** the Irish *pl*

irgend *adv* **wenn i~ möglich** if at all possible. **i~ein** *indefinite article* some/any; **i~ein anderer** someone/anyone else. **i~eine(r,s)** *pron* any one; (*jemand*) someone/anyone. **i~etwas** *pron* something; anything. **i~jemand** *pron* someone; anyone. **i~wann** *pron* at some time [or other]/at any time. **i~was** *pron* 🔲 something [or other]/anything. **i~welche(r,s)** *pron* any. **i~wer** *pron* someone/anyone. **i~wie** *adv* somehow [or other]. **i~wo** *adv* somewhere

Irin *f* **-,-nen** Irishwoman

irisch *adj* Irish

Irland *nt* **-s** Ireland

Ironie *f* **-** irony

ironisch *adj* ironic

irre *adj* mad, crazy; (🔲: *gewaltig*) incredible. **I~(r)** *m/f* lunatic. **i~führen** *vt sep* (*fig*) mislead

irre|machen *vt sep* confuse. **i~n** *vi/r* (*haben*) [**sich**] **i~n** be mistaken ● *vi* (*sein*) wander. **I~nanstalt** *f*, **I~nhaus** *nt* lunatic asylum. **i~werden†** *vi sep* (*sein*) get confused

Irrgarten *m* maze

irritieren *vt* irritate

Irr|sinn *m* madness, lunacy. **i~sinnig** *adj* mad; (🔲: *gewaltig*) incredible. **I~tum** *m* **-s,⁼er** mistake

Ischias *m & nt* **-** sciatica

Islam (der) -[s] Islam. **islamisch** *adj* Islamic

Island *nt* **-s** Iceland

Isolier|band *nt* insulating tape. **i~en** *vt* isolate; (*Phys, Electr*) insulate; (*gegen Schall*) soundproof. **I~ung** *f* **-** isolation; insulation; soundproofing

Isra|el /'ɪsrae:l/ *nt* **-s** Israel. **I~eli** *m* **-[s],-s** & *f* **-,-[s]** Israeli. **i~elisch** *adj* Israeli

ist *s.* sein; **er ist** he is

Ital|ien /-jən/ *nt* **-s** Italy. **I~iener(in)** *m* **-s,-** (*f* **-,-nen**) Italian. **i~ienisch** *adj* Italian. **I~ienisch** *nt* **-[s]** (*Lang*) Italian

Jj

ja adv, **Ja** nt -[s] yes; **ich glaube ja** I think so; **ja nicht!** not on any account! **da seid ihr ja!** there you are!

Jacht f -,-en yacht

Jacke f -,-n jacket; (Strick-) cardigan

Jackett /ʒa'kɛt/ nt -s,-s jacket

Jade m -[s] & f - jade

Jagd f -,-en hunt; (Schießen) shoot; (Jagen) hunting; shooting; (fig) pursuit (nach of); **auf die J∼ gehen** go hunting/shooting. **J∼gewehr** nt sporting gun. **J∼hund** m gun-dog: (Hetzhund) hound

jagen vt hunt; (schießen) shoot; (verfolgen, wegjagen) chase; (treiben) drive; **sich j∼** chase each other; **in die Luft j∼** blow up ● vi (haben) hunt, go hunting/shooting; (fig) chase (nach after) ● vi (sein) race, dash

Jäger m -s,- hunter

Jahr nt -[e]s,-e year. **j∼elang** adv for years. **J∼eszahl** f year. **J∼eszeit** f season. **J∼gang** m year; (Wein) vintage. **J∼hundert** nt century

jährlich adj annual, yearly

Jahr|markt m fair. **J∼tausend** nt millennium. **J∼zehnt** nt -[e]s,-e decade

Jähzorn m violent temper. **j∼ig** adj hot-tempered

Jalousie /ʒalu'ziː/ f -,-n venetian blind

Jammer m -s misery

jämmerlich adj miserable; (Mitleid erregend) pitiful

jammern vi (haben) lament ● vt jdn j∼n arouse s.o.'s pity

Jänner m -s,- (Aust) January

Januar m -s,-e January

Jap|an nt -s Japan. **J∼aner(in)** m -s,- (f -,-nen) Japanese. **j∼anisch** adj Japanese. **J∼anisch** nt -[s] (Lang) Japanese

jäten vt/i (haben) **weed**

jaulen vi (haben) yelp

Jause f -,-n (Aust) snack

jawohl adv yes

Jazz /jats, dʒɛs/ m - jazz

je adv (jemals) ever; (jeweils) each; (pro) per; **je nach** according to; **seit eh und je** always ● conj **je mehr, desto besser** the more the better ● prep (+ acc) per

Jeans /dʒiːns/ pl jeans

jed|e(r,s) pron every; (j∼er Einzelne) each; (j∼er Beliebige) any; (substantivisch) everyone; each one; anyone; **ohne j∼en Grund** without any reason. **j∼enfalls** adv in any case; (wenigstens) at least. **j∼ermann** pron everyone. **j∼erzeit** adv at any time. **j∼esmal** adv every time

jedoch adv & conj however

jemals adv ever

jemand pron someone, somebody; (fragend, verneint) anyone, anybody

jen|e(r,s) pron that; (pl) those; (substantivisch) that one; (pl) those. **j∼seits** prep (+ gen) [on] the other side of

jetzt adv now

jiddisch adj. **J∼** nt -[s] Yiddish

Job /dʒɔp/ m -s,-s job. **j∼ben** vi (haben) Ⓘ work

Joch nt -[e]s,-e yoke

Jockei, Jockey /'dʒɔki/ m -s,-s jockey

Jod nt -[e]s iodine

jodeln vi (haben) yodel

Joga m & nt -[s] yoga

joggen /'dʒɔgən/ vi (haben/sein) jog

Joghurt, Jogurt m & nt -[s] yoghurt

Johannisbeere f redcurrant

Joker m -s,- (Karte) joker

Jolle f -,-n dinghy

Jongleur /ʒõ'gløː*ɐ*/ m -s,-e juggler

Jordanien /-iən/ nt -s Jordan

Journalis|mus /ʒʊrna'lɪsmʊs/ m - journalism. **J∼t(in)** m -en,-en (f -,-nen) journalist

Jubel m -s rejoicing, jubilation. **j∼n** vi (haben) rejoice

Jubiläum nt -s,-äen jubilee; (Jahrestag) anniversary

jucken vi (haben) itch; **sich j∼en** scratch; **es j∼t mich** I have an itch

Jude m -n,-n Jew. **J∼ntum** nt -s Judaism; (Juden) Jewry

Jüd|in f -,-nen Jewess. **j∼isch** adj Jewish

Judo nt -[s] judo

Jugend f - youth; (junge Leute) young people pl. **J∼herberge** f youth hostel. **J∼kriminalität** f juvenile delinquency. **j∼lich** adj youthful. **J∼liche(r)** m/f young man/woman. **J∼liche** pl young people. **J∼stil** m art nouveau

Jugoslaw|ien /-i̯ən/ nt -s Yugoslavia. **j∼isch** adj Yugoslav

Juli m -[s],-s July

jung adj young; (Wein) new ● pron **J∼ und Alt** young and old. **J∼e** m -n,-n boy. **J∼e(s)** nt young animal/bird; (Katzen-) kitten; (Bären-) cub; (Hunde-) pup; **die J∼en** the young pl

Jünger m -s,- disciple

Jung|frau f virgin; (Astrology) Virgo. **J∼geselle** m bachelor

Jüngling m -s,-e youth

jüngst|e(r,s) adj youngest; (neueste) latest; **in j∼er Zeit** recently

Juni m -[s],-s June

Jura pl law sg

Jurist|(in) m -en,-en (f -,-nen) lawyer. **j∼isch** adj legal

Jury /ʒyˈriː/ f -,-s jury; (Sport) judges pl

Justiz f - **die J∼** justice

Juwel nt -s,-en & (fig) -e jewel. **J∼ier** m -s,-e jeweller

Jux m -es,-e 🔟 joke; **aus Jux** for fun

Kk

Kabarett nt -s,-s & -e cabaret

Kabel nt -s,- cable. **K∼fernsehen** nt cable television

Kabeljau m -s,-e & -s cod

Kabine f -,-n cabin; (Umkleide-) cu-

bicle; (Telefon-) booth; (einer K∼nbahn) car. **K∼nbahn** f cable-car

Kabinett nt -s,-e (Pol) Cabinet

Kabriolett nt -s,-s convertible

Kachel f -,-n tile. **k∼n** vt tile

Kadenz f -,-en (Mus) cadence

Käfer m -s,- beetle

Kaffee /ˈkafeː, kaˈfeː/ m -s,-s coffee. **K∼kanne** f coffee pot. **K∼maschine** f coffee maker. **K∼mühle** f coffee grinder

Käfig m -s,-e cage

kahl adj bare; (haarlos) bald; **k∼ geschoren** shaven

Kahn m -s,⸚e boat; (Last-) barge

Kai m -s,-s quay

Kaiser m -s,- emperor. **K∼in** f -,-nen empress. **k∼lich** adj imperial. **K∼reich** nt empire. **K∼schnitt** m Caesarean [section]

Kajüte f -,-n (Naut) cabin

Kakao /kaˈkaʊ/ m -s cocoa

Kakerlak m -s & -en,-en cockroach

Kaktus m -,-teen cactus

Kalb nt -[e]s,⸚er calf. **K∼fleisch** nt veal

Kalender m -s,- calendar; (Termin-) diary

Kaliber nt -s,- calibre; (Gewehr-) bore

Kalium nt -s potassium

Kalk m -[e]s,-e lime; (Kalzium) calcium. **k∼en** vt whitewash. **K∼stein** m limestone

Kalkul|ation /-ˈtsi̯oːn/ f -,-en calculation. **k∼ieren** vt/i (haben) calculate

Kalorie f -,-n calorie

kalt adj cold; **mir ist k∼** I am cold

Kälte f - cold; (Gefühls-) coldness; **10 Grad K∼** 10 degrees below zero

Kalzium nt -s calcium

Kamel nt -s,-e camel

Kamera f -,-s camera

Kamerad(in) m -en,-en (f -,-nen) companion; (Freund) mate; (Mil, Pol) comrade

Kameramann m (pl -männer & -leute) cameraman

Kamille f - chamomile

j

k

Kamin m -s,-e fireplace; (SGer: Schornstein) chimney

Kamm m -[e]s,¨e comb; (Berg-) ridge; (Zool, Wellen-) crest

kämmen vt comb; **jdn/sich k∼** comb someone's/one's hair

Kammer f -,-n small room; (Techn, Biology, Pol) chamber. **K∼musik** f chamber music

Kammgarn nt (Textiles) worsted

Kampagne /kam'panjə/ f -,-n (Pol, Comm) campaign

Kampf m -es,¨e fight; (Schlacht) battle; (Wett-) contest; (fig) struggle

kämpf|en vi (haben) fight; **k∼en durch** fight one's way through. **K∼er(in)** m -s,- (f -,-nen) fighter

Kampfrichter m (Sport) judge

Kanada nt -s Canada

Kanad|ier(in) /-iɐ, -iɐrn/ m -s,- (f -,-nen) Canadian. **k∼isch** adj Canadian

Kanal m -s,¨e canal; (Abfluss-) drain, sewer; (Radio, TV) channel; **der K∼** the [English] Channel

Kanalisation /-'tsio:n/ f - sewerage system, drains pl

Kanarienvogel /-iən-/ m canary

Kanarisch adj K∼e Inseln Canaries

Kandidat(in) m -en,-en (f -,-nen) candidate

kandiert adj candied

Känguru nt -s,-s kangaroo

Kaninchen nt -s,- rabbit

Kanister m -s,- canister; (Benzin-) can

Kännchen nt -s,- [small] jug; (Kaffee-) pot

Kanne f -,-n jug; (Tee-) pot; (Öl-) can; (große Milch-) churn

Kannibal|e m -n,-n cannibal. **K∼ismus** m - cannibalism

Kanon m -s,-s canon; (Lied) round

Kanone f -,-n cannon, gun

kanonisieren vt canonize

Kantate f -,-n cantata

Kante f -,-n edge

Kanten m -s,- crust [of bread]

Kanter m -s,- canter

kantig adj angular

Kantine f -,-n canteen

Kanton m -s,-e (Swiss) canton

> **Kanton** The name for the individual autonomous states that make up Switzerland. There are 26 cantons, each with its own government and constitution. *i*

Kanu nt -s,-s canoe

Kanzel f -,-n pulpit; (Aviat) cockpit

Kanzler m -s,- chancellor

Kap nt -s,-s (Geog) cape

Kapazität f -,-en capacity

Kapelle f -,-n chapel; (Mus) band

kapern vt (Naut) seize

kapieren vt ⊡ understand

Kapital nt -s capital. **K∼ismus** m - capitalism. **K∼ist** m -en,-en capitalist. **k∼istisch** adj capitalist

Kapitän m -s,-e captain

Kapitel nt -s,- chapter

Kaplan m -s,¨e curate

Kappe f -,-n cap

Kapsel f -,-n capsule; (Flaschen-) top

kaputt adj ⊡ broken; (zerrissen) torn; (defekt) out of order; (ruiniert) ruined; (erschöpft) worn out. **k∼gehen†** vi sep (sein) ⊡ break; (zerreißen) tear; (defekt werden) pack up; (Ehe, Freundschaft:) break up. **k∼lachen (sich)** vr sep ⊡ be in stitches. **k∼machen** vt sep ⊡ break; (zerreißen) tear; (defekt machen) put out of order; (erschöpfen) wear out; **sich k∼machen** wear oneself out

Kapuze f -,-n hood

Kapuzinerkresse f nasturtium

Karaffe f -,-n carafe; (mit Stöpsel) decanter

Karamell m -s caramel. **K∼bonbon** m & nt ≈ toffee

Karat nt -[e]s,-e carat

Karawane f -,-n caravan

Kardinal m -s,¨e cardinal. **K∼zahl** f cardinal number

Karfreitag m Good Friday

karg adj meagre; (frugal) frugal;

(*spärlich*) sparse; (*unfruchtbar*) barren; (*gering*) scant

Karibik f - Caribbean

kariert adj check[ed]; (*Papier*) squared; **schottisch k~** tartan

Karik|atur f -,-en caricature; (*Journalism*) cartoon. **k~ieren** vt caricature

Karneval m -s,-e & -s carnival

Kärnten nt -s Carinthia

Karo nt -s,-s (*Raute*) diamond; (*Viereck*) square; (*Muster*) check (*Kartenspiel*) diamonds pl

Karosserie f -,-n bodywork

Karotte f -,-n carrot

Karpfen m -s,- carp

Karren m -s,- cart; (*Hand-*) barrow. **k~** vt cart

Karriere /ka'rjɛːrə/ f -,-n career; **K~ machen** get to the top

Karte f -,-n card; (*Eintritts-, Fahr-*) ticket; (*Speise-*) menu; (*Land-*) map

Kartei f -,-en card index

Karten|spiel nt card game; (*Spielkarten*) pack of cards. **K~vorverkauf** m advance booking

Kartoffel f -,-n potato. **K~brei** m mashed potatoes

Karton /kar'tɔŋ/ m -s,-s cardboard; (*Schachtel*) carton

Karussell nt -s,-s & -e roundabout

Käse m -s, cheese

Kaserne f -,-n barracks pl

Kasino nt -s,-s casino

Kasperle nt & m -s,- Punch. **K~theater** nt Punch and Judy show

Kasse f -,-n till; (*Registrier-*) cash register; (*Zahlstelle*) cash desk; (*im Supermarkt*) check out; (*Theater-*) box office; (*Geld*) pool [of money], 🅣 kitty; (*Kranken-*) health insurance scheme; **knapp bei K~ sein** 🅣 be short of cash. **K~nwart** m -[e]s,-e treasurer. **K~nzettel** m receipt

Kasserolle f -,-n saucepan

Kassette f -,-n cassette; (*Film-, Farbband-*) cartridge. **K~nrekorder** m -s,- cassette recorder

kassier|en vi (*haben*) collect the money/(*im Bus*) the fares ● vt collect. **K~er(in)** m -s,- (f -,-nen) cashier

Kastanie /kas'taːnjə/ f -,-n [horse] chestnut, 🅣 conker

Kasten m -s,= box; (*Brot-*) bin; (*Flaschen-*) crate; (*Brief-*) letter box; (*Aust: Schrank*) cupboard

kastrieren vt castrate; neuter

Katalog m -[e]s,-e catalogue

Katalysator m -s,-en catalyst; (*Auto*) catalytic converter

Katapult nt -[e]s,-e catapult

Katarrh, **Katarr** m -s,-e catarrh

Katastrophe f -,-n catastrophe

Katechismus m - catechism

Kategorie f -,-n category

Kater m -s,- tom cat; (🅣: *Katzenjammer*) hangover

Kathedrale f -,-n cathedral

Kath|olik(in) m -en,-en (f -,-nen) Catholic. **k~olisch** adj Catholic. **K~olizismus** m - Catholicism

Kätzchen nt -s,- kitten; (*Bot*) catkin

Katze f -,-n cat. **K~njammer** m 🅣 hangover. **K~nsprung** m **ein K~nsprung** 🅣 a stone's throw

Kauderwelsch nt -[s] gibberish

kauen vt/i (*haben*) chew; bite (*Nägel*)

Kauf m -[e]s, Käufe purchase; **guter K~** bargain; **in K~ nehmen** (fig) put up with. **k~en** vt/i (*haben*) buy; **k~en bei** shop at

Käufer(in) m -s,- (f -,-nen) buyer; (*im Geschäft*) shopper

Kauf|haus nt department store. **K~laden** m shop

käuflich adj saleable; (*bestechlich*) corruptible; **k~ erwerben** buy

Kauf|mann m (pl -leute) businessman; (*Händler*) dealer; (*Dialekt*) grocer. **K~preis** m purchase price

Kaugummi m chewing gum

Kaulquappe f -,-n tadpole

kaum adv hardly

Kaution /-'tsjoːn/ f -,-en surety; (*Jur*) bail; (*Miet-*) deposit

Kautschuk m -s rubber

Kauz m -es, Käuze owl

Kavalier m -s,-e gentleman

Kavallerie | Kinderarzt

Kavallerie *f* - cavalry

Kaviar *m* -s caviare

keck *adj* bold; cheeky

Kegel *m* -s,- skittle, (*Geometry*) cone. **K~bahn** *f* skittle-alley. **k~n** *vi* (*haben*) play skittles

Kehl|e *f* -,-n throat; **aus voller K~e** at the top of one's voice. **K~kopf** *m* larynx. **K~kopfentzündung** *f* laryngitis

Kehr|e *f* -,-n [hairpin] bend. **k~en** *vi* (*haben*) (*fegen*) sweep ● *vt* sweep; (*wenden*) turn; **sich nicht k~en an** (+ *acc*) not care about. **K~icht** *m* -[e]s sweepings *pl*. **K~reim** *m* refrain. **K~seite** *f* (*fig*) drawback. **k~tmachen** *vi sep* (*haben*) turn back; (*sich umdrehen*) turn round

Keil *m* -[e]s,-e wedge

Keilriemen *m* fan belt

Keim *m* -[e]s,-e (*Bot*) sprout; (*Med*) germ. **k~en** *vi* (*haben*) germinate; (*austreiben*) sprout. **k~frei** *adj* sterile

kein *pron* no; not a; **k~e fünf Minuten** less than five minutes. **k~e(r,s)** *pron* no one, nobody; (*Ding*) none, not one. **k~esfalls** *adv* on no account. **k~eswegs** *adv* by no means. **k~mal** *adv* not once. **k~s** *pron* none, not one

Keks *m* -[es],-[e] biscuit

Kelch *m* -[e]s,-e goblet, cup; (*Relig*) chalice; (*Bot*) calyx

Kelle *f* -,-n ladle; (*Maurer*) trowel

Keller *m* -s,- cellar. **K~ei** *f* -,-en winery. **K~wohnung** *f* basement flat

Kellner *m* -s,- waiter. **K~in** *f* -,-nen waitress

keltern *vt* press

keltisch *adj* Celtic

Kenia *nt* -s Kenya

kenn|en† *vt* know; **k~en lernen** get to know; (*treffen*) meet; **sich k~en lernen** meet; (*näher*) get to know one another. **K~er** *m* -s,-, **K~erin** *f* -,-nen connoisseur; (*Experte*) expert. **k~tlich** *adj* recognizable; **k~tlich machen** mark. **K~tnis** *f* -,-se knowledge; **zur K~tnis nehmen** take note of; **in K~tnis setzen** inform

(**von** of). **K~wort** *nt* (*pl* -wörter) reference; (*geheimes*) password. **K~zeichen** *nt* distinguishing mark or feature; (*Merkmal*) characteristic, (*Markierung*) marking; (*Auto*) registration. **k~zeichnen** *vt* distinguish; (*markieren*) mark

kentern *vi* (*sein*) capsize

Keramik *f* -,-en pottery

Kerbe *f* -,-n notch

Kerker *m* -s,- dungeon; (*Gefängnis*) prison

Kerl *m* -s,-e & -s 🔲 fellow, bloke

Kern *m* -s,-e pip; (*Kirsch-*) stone; (*Nuss-*) kernel; (*Techn*) core; (*Atom-, Zell-* & *fig*) nucleus; (*Stadt-*) centre; (*einer Sache*) heart. **K~energie** *f* nuclear energy. **K~gehäuse** *nt* core. **k~los** *adj* seedless. **K~physik** *f* nuclear physics *sg*

Kerze *f* -,-n candle. **K~nhalter** *m* -s,- candlestick

kess *adj* pert

Kessel *m* -s,- kettle

Kette *f* -,-n chain; (*Hals-*) necklace. **k~n** *vt* chain (**an** + *acc* to). **K~nladen** *m* chain store

Ketze|r(in) *m* -s,- (*f* -,-nen) heretic. **K~rei** *f* - heresy

keuch|en *vi* (*haben*) pant. **K~husten** *m* whooping cough

Keule *f* -,-n club; (*Culin*) leg; (*Hühner-*) drumstick

keusch *adj* chaste

Khaki *nt* - khaki

kichern *vi* (*haben*) giggle

Kiefer[1] *f* -,-n pine[-tree]

Kiefer[2] *m* -s,- jaw

Kiel *m* -s,-e (*Naut*) keel

Kiemen *fpl* gills

Kies *m* -es gravel. **K~el** *m* -s,-, **K~elstein** *m* pebble

Kilo *nt* -s,-[s] kilo. **K~gramm** *nt* kilogram. **K~hertz** *nt* kilohertz. **K~meter** *m* kilometre. **K~meterstand** *m* ≈ mileage. **K~watt** *nt* kilowatt

Kind *nt* -es,-er child; **von K~ auf** from childhood

Kinder|arzt *m*, **K~ärztin** *f* paediat-

rician. **K~bett** nt child's cot.
K~garten m nursery school.
K~geld nt child benefit. **K~läh-mung** f polio. **k~leicht** adj very
easy. **k~los** adj childless. **K~mäd-chen** nt nanny. **K~reim** m nursery
rhyme. **K~spiel** nt children's game.
K~tagesstätte f day nursery.
K~teller m children's menu.
K~wagen m pram. **K~zimmer** nt
child's/children's room; (für Baby)
nursery

Kind|heit f - childhood. **k~isch** adj
childish. **k~lich** adj childlike

kinetisch adj kinetic

Kinn nt -[e]s,-e chin. **K~lade** f jaw

Kino nt -s,-s cinema

Kiosk m -[e]s,-e kiosk

Kippe f -,-n (Müll-) dump; (🄵:
Zigaretten-) fag end. **k~n** vt tilt;
(schütten) tip (in + acc into) ● vi
(sein) topple

Kirch|e f -,-n church. **K~enbank** f
pew. **K~endiener** m verger. **K~en-lied** nt hymn. **K~enschiff** nt nave.
K~hof m churchyard. **k~lich** adj
church ● adv **k~lich getraut wer-den** be married in church. **K~turm**
m church tower, steeple. **K~weih** f
-,-en [village] fair

Kirmes f -,-sen = Kirchweih

Kirsche f -,-n cherry

Kissen nt -s,- cushion; (Kopf-) pillow

Kiste f -,-n crate; (Zigarren-) box

Kitsch m -es sentimental rubbish;
(Kunst) kitsch

Kitt m -s [adhesive] cement; (Fenster-)
putty

Kittel m -s,- overall, smock

Kitz nt -es,-e (Zool) kid

Kitz|el m -s,- tickle; (Nerven-) thrill.
k~eln vt/i (haben) tickle. **k~lig** adj
ticklish

kläffen vi (haben) yap

Klage f -,-n lament; (Beschwerde)
complaint; (Jur) action. **k~n** vi
(haben) lament; (sich beklagen) com-plaint; (Jur) sue

Kläger(in) m -s,- (f -,-nen) (Jur)
plaintiff

klamm adj cold and damp; (steif)
stiff. **K~** f -,-en (Geog) gorge

Klammer f -,-n (Wäsche-) peg;
(Büro-) paper clip; (Heft-) staple;
(Haar-) grip; (für Zähne) brace;
(Techn) clamp; (Typography) bracket.
k~n (sich) vr cling (**an** + acc to)

Klang m -[e]s,⸚e sound; (K~farbe)
tone

Klapp|e f -,-n flap; (🄵: Mund) trap.
k~en vt fold; (hoch-) tip up ● vi
(haben) 🄵 work out. **K~handy** nt
folding mobile phone

Klapper f -,-n rattle. **k~n** vi (haben)
rattle. **K~schlange** rattlesnake

klapp|rig adj rickety; (schwach) de-crepit. **K~stuhl** m folding chair

Klaps m -es,-e pat, smack

klar adj clear; **sich** (dat) **k~ werden**
make up one's mind; (erkennen) real-ize (**dass** that); **sich** (dat) **k~** od **im
K~en sein** realize (**dass** that) ● adv
clearly; (🄵: natürlich) of course

klären vt clarify; **sich k~** clear; (fig:
sich lösen) resolve itself

Klarheit f -,- clarity

Klarinette f -,-n clarinet

klar|machen vt sep make clear (dat
to); **sich** (dat) **etw k~machen**
understand sth. **k~stellen** vt sep
clarify

Klärung f - clarification

Klasse f -,-n class; (Sch) class, form;
(Zimmer) classroom. **k~** inv adj 🄵
super. **K~narbeit** f [written] test.
K~nzimmer nt classroom

Klass|ik f - classicism; (Epoche) clas-sical period. **K~iker** m -s,- classical
author/(Mus) composer. **k~isch** adj
classical; (typisch) classic

Klatsch m -[e]s gossip. **K~base** f 🄵
gossip. **k~en** vt slap; **Beifall k~en**
applaud ● vi (haben) make a slapping
sound; (im Wasser) splash; (tratschen)
gossip; (applaudieren) clap. **k~nass**
adj 🄵 soaking wet

klauen vt/i (haben) 🄵 steal

Klausel f -,-n clause

Klaustrophobie f - claustrophobia

Klausur f -,-en (Univ) paper

Klavier nt -s,-e piano.
K~spieler(in) m(f) pianist

kleb|en vt stick/(mit Klebstoff) glue
(an + acc to). ● vi (haben) stick (an +
dat to). **k~rig** adj sticky. **K~stoff** m
adhesive, glue. **K~streifen** m adhesive tape

Klecks m -es,-e stain; (Tinten-) blot;
(kleine Menge) dab. **k~en** vi (haben)
make a mess

Klee m -s clover

Kleid nt -[e]s,-er dress; **K~er**
dresses; (Kleidung) clothes. **k~en** vt
dress; (gut stehen) suit. **K~erbügel**
m coat hanger. **K~erbürste** f
clothes brush. **K~erhaken** m coat-
hook. **K~erschrank** m wardrobe.
k~sam adj becoming. **K~ung** f -
clothes pl, clothing. **K~ungsstück**
nt garment

Kleie f - bran

klein adj small, little; (von kleinem
Wuchs) short; **k~ schneiden** cut up
small. **von k~ auf** from childhood.
K~arbeit f painstaking work.
K~e(r,s) m/f/nt little one. **K~geld**
nt [small] change. **K~handel** m retail trade. **K~heit** f - smallness;
(Wuchs) short stature. **K~holz** nt
firewood. **K~igkeit** f -,-en trifle;
(Mahl) snack. **K~kind** nt infant.
k~laut adj subdued. **k~lich** adj
petty

klein|schreiben† vt sep write with
a small [initial] letter. **K~stadt** f
small town. **k~städtisch** adj provin-
cial

Kleister m -s paste. **k~n** vt paste

Klemme f -,-n [hair-]grip. **k~n** vt
jam; **sich** (dat) **den Finger k~n** get
one's finger caught ● vi (haben) jam,
stick

Klempner m -s,- plumber

Klerus (der) - the clergy

Klette f -,-n burr

kletter|n vi (sein) climb. **K~pflanze**
f climber

Klettverschluss m Velcro ® fas-
tening

klicken vi (haben) click

Klient(in) /kli'ɛnt(m)/ m -en,-en (f
-,-nen) (Jur) client

Kliff nt -[e]s,-e cliff

Klima nt -s climate. **K~anlage** f air
conditioning

klimat|isch adj climatic. **k~isiert**
adj air-conditioned

klimpern vi (haben) jingle; **k~ auf**
(+ dat) tinkle on (Klavier); strum (Gitarre)

Klinge f -,-n blade

Klingel f -,-n bell. **k~n** vi (haben)
ring; **es k~t** there's a ring at the
door

klingen† vi (haben) sound

Klinik f -,-en clinic

Klinke f -,-n [door] handle

Klippe f -,-n [submerged] rock

Klips m -es,-e clip; (Ohr-) clip-on ear
ring

klirren vi (haben) rattle; (Glas:) chink

Klo nt -s,-s 🆉 loo

Klon m -s, -e clone. **k~en** vt clone

klopfen vi (haben) knock; (leicht)
tap; (Herz:) pound; **es k~te** there
was a knock at the door

Klops m -es,-e meatball

Klosett nt -s,-e lavatory

Kloß m -es,¨e dumpling

Kloster nt -s,¨ monastery; (Nonnen-)
convent

klösterlich adj monastic

Klotz m -es,¨e block

Klub m -s,-s club

Kluft f -,¨e cleft; (fig: Gegensatz) gulf

klug adj intelligent; (schlau) clever.
K~heit f - cleverness

Klump|en m -s,- lump

knabbern vt/i (haben) nibble

Knabe m -n,-n boy. **k~nhaft** adj
boyish

Knäckebrot nt crispbread

knack|en vt/i (haben) crack. **K~s** m
-es,-e crack

Knall m -[e]s,-e bang. **K~bonbon**
m cracker. **k~en** vi (haben) go bang;
(Peitsche:) crack ● vt (🆉: werfen)
chuck; **jdm eine k~en** 🆉 clout s.o.
k~ig adj 🆉 gaudy

knapp *adj* (*gering*) scant; (*kurz*) short; (*mangelnd*) scarce; (*gerade ausreichend*) bare; (*eng*) tight. **K~heit** *f* - scarcity

knarren *vi* (*haben*) creak

Knast *m* -[e]s 🔲 prison

knattern *vi* (*haben*) crackle; (*Gewehr:*) stutter

Knäuel *m* & *nt* -s,- ball

Knauf *m* -[e]s, Knäufe knob

knauserig *adj* 🔲 stingy

knautschen *vt* 🔲 crumple ● *vi* (*haben*) crease

Knebel *m* -s,- gag. **k~n** *vt* gag

Knecht *m* -[e]s,-e farm-hand; (*fig*) slave

kneif|en† *vt* pinch ● *vi* (*haben*) pinch; (🔲: *sich drücken*) chicken out. **K~zange** *f* pincers *pl*

Kneipe *f* -,-n 🔲 pub

knet|en *vt* knead; (*formen*) mould. **K~masse** *f* Plasticine®

Knick *m* -[e]s,-e bend; (*Kniff*) crease. **k~en** *vt* bend; (*kniffen*) fold; **geknickt sein** 🔲 be dejected

Knicks *m* -es,-e curtsy. **k~en** *vi* (*haben*) curtsy

Knie *nt* -s,- knee

knien /'kni:ən/ *vi* (*haben*) kneel ● *vr* **sich k~** kneel [down]

Kniescheibe *f* kneecap

Kniff *m* -[e]s,-e pinch; (*Falte*) crease; (🔲: *Trick*) trick. **k~en** *vt* fold

knipsen *vt* (*lochen*) punch; (*Phot*) photograph ● *vi* (*haben*) take a photograph/photographs

Knirps *m* -es,-e 🔲 little chap; ® (*Schirm*) telescopic umbrella

knirschen *vi* (*haben*) grate; (*Schnee, Kies:*) crunch

knistern *vi* (*haben*) crackle; (*Papier:*) rustle

Knitter|falte *f* crease. **k~frei** *adj* crease-resistant. **k~n** *vi* (*haben*) crease

knobeln *vi* (*haben*) toss (**um** for)

Knoblauch *m* -s garlic

Knöchel *m* -s,- ankle; (*Finger-*) knuckle

Knochen *m* -s,- bone. **K~mark** *nt* bone marrow

knochig *adj* bony

Knödel *m* -s,- (*SGer*) dumpling

Knoll|e *f* -,-n tuber

Knopf *m* -[e]s,¨e button; (*Griff*) knob

knöpfen *vt* button

Knopfloch *nt* buttonhole

Knorpel *m* -s gristle; (*Anat*) cartilage

Knospe *f* bud

Knoten *m* -s,- knot; (*Med*) lump; (*Haar-*) bun, chignon. **k~** *vt* knot. **K~punkt** *m* junction

knüll|en *vt* crumple ● *vi* (*haben*) crease. **K~er** *m* -s,- 🔲 sensation

knüpfen *vt* knot; (*verbinden*) attach (**an** + *acc* to)

Knüppel *m* -s,- club; (*Gummi-*) truncheon

knurren *vi* (*haben*) growl; (*Magen:*) rumble

knusprig *adj* crunchy, crisp

knutschen *vi* (*haben*) 🔲 smooch

k.o. /ka'?o:/ *adj* **k.o. schlagen** knock out; **k.o. sein** 🔲 be worn out

Koalition /koali'tsio:n/ *f* -,-en coalition

Kobold *m* -[e]s,-e goblin, imp

Koch *m* -[e]s,¨e cook; (*im Restaurant*) chef. **K~buch** *nt* cookery book. **k~en** *vt* cook; (*sieden*) boil; make (*Kaffee, Tee*); **hart gekochtes Ei** hard-boiled egg ● *vi* (*haben*) cook; (*sieden*) boil; 🔲 seethe (**vor** + *dat* with). **K~en** *nt* -s cooking; (*Sieden*) boiling. **k~end** *adj* boiling. **K~herd** *m* cooker, stove

Köchin *f* -,-nen [woman] cook

Koch|löffel *m* wooden spoon. **K~nische** *f* kitchenette. **K~platte** *f* hotplate. **K~topf** *m* saucepan

Köder *m* -s,- bait

Koffein /kɔfe'i:n/ *nt* -s caffeine. **k~frei** *adj* decaffeinated

Koffer *m* -s,- suitcase. **K~kuli** *m* luggage trolley. **K~raum** *m* (*Auto*) boot

Kognak /'kɔnjak/ *m* -s,-s brandy

Kohl m -[e]s cabbage

Kohle f -,-n coal. **K~[n]hydrat** nt -[e]s,-e carbohydrate. **K~nbergwerk** nt coal mine, colliery. **K~ndioxid** nt carbon dioxide. **K~nsäure** f carbon dioxide. **K~nstoff** m carbon

Koje f -,-n (Naut) bunk

Kokain /koka'i:n/ nt -s cocaine

kokett adj flirtatious. **k~ieren** vi (haben) flirt

Kokon /ko'kõ:/ m -s,-s cocoon

Kokosnuss f coconut

Koks m -es coke

Kolben m -s,- (Gewehr-) butt; (Mais-) cob; (Techn) piston; (Chemistry) flask

Kolibri m -s,-s humming bird

Kolik f -,-en colic

Kollaborateur /-'tø:ɐ̯/ m -s,-e collaborator

Kolleg nt -s,-s & -ien (Univ) course of lectures

Kolleg|e m -n,-n, **K~in** f -,-nen colleague. **K~ium** nt -s,-ien staff

Kollek|te f -,-n (Relig) collection. **K~tion** /-'tsi̯o:n/ f -,-en collection

Köln nt -s Cologne. **K~ischwasser**, **K~isch Wasser** nt eau-de-Cologne

Kolonie f -,-n colony

Kolonne f -,-n column; (Mil) convoy

Koloss m -es,-e giant

Koma nt -s,-s coma

Kombi m -s,-s = **K~wagen**. **K~nation** /-'tsi̯o:n/ f -,-en combination; (Folgerung) deduction; (Kleidung) co-ordinating outfit. **k~nieren** vt combine; (fig) reason; (folgern) deduce. **K~wagen** m estate car

Kombüse f -,-n (Naut) galley

Komet m -en,-en comet

Komfort /kɔm'fo:ɐ̯/ m -s comfort; (Luxus) luxury

Komik f - humour. **K~er** m -s,- comic, comedian

komisch adj funny; (Oper) comic; (sonderbar) odd, funny. **k~erweise** adv funnily enough

Komitee nt -s,-s committee

Komma nt -s,-s & -ta comma;

(Dezimal-) decimal point; **drei K~ fünf** three point five

Kommando nt -s,-s order; (Befehlsgewalt) command; (Einheit) detachment. **K~brücke** f bridge

kommen† vi (sein) come; (eintreffen) arrive; (gelangen) get (nach to); **k~ lassen** send for; **auf/hinter etw** (acc) **k~** think of/find out about sth; **um/zu etw k~** lose/acquire sth; **wieder zu sich k~** come round; **wie kommt das?** why is that? **k~d** adj coming; **k~den Montag** next Monday

Kommen|tar m -s,-e commentary; (Bemerkung) comment. **k~tieren** vt comment on

kommerziell adj commercial

Kommissar m -s,-e commissioner; (Polizei-) superintendent

Kommission f -,-en commission; (Gremium) committee

Kommode f -,-n chest of drawers

Kommunalwahlen fpl local elections

Kommunion f -,-en [Holy] Communion

Kommun|ismus m - Communism. **K~ist(in)** m -en,-en (f -,-nen) Communist. **k~istisch** adj Communist

kommunizieren vi (haben) receive [Holy] Communion

Komödie /ko'mø:di̯ə/ f -,-n comedy

Kompagnon /'kɔmpanjõ:/ m -s,-s (Comm) partner

Kompanie f -,-n (Mil) company

Komparse m -n,-n (Theat) extra

Kompass m -es,-e compass

komplett adj complete

Komplex m -es,-e complex

Komplikation /-'tsi̯o:n/ f -,-en complication

Kompliment nt -[e]s,-e compliment

Komplize m -n,-n accomplice

komplizier|en vt complicate. **k~t** adj complicated

Komplott nt -[e]s,-e plot

kompo|nieren vt/i (haben) compose. **K~nist** m -en,-en composer

Kompost m -[e]s compost

Kompott nt -[e]s,-e stewed fruit

Kompromiss m -es,-e compromise; **einen K~ schließen** compromise. **k~los** adj uncompromising

Konden|sation /-'tsio:n/ f - condensation. **k~sieren** vt condense

Kondensmilch f evaporated/(gesüßt) condensed milk

Kondition /-'tsio:n/ f - (Sport) fitness; **in K~** in form

Konditor m -s,-en confectioner. **K~ei** f -,-en patisserie

Kondo|lenzbrief m letter of condolence. **k~lieren** vi (haben) express one's condolences

Kondom nt & m -s,-e condom

Konfekt nt -[e]s confectionery; (Pralinen) chocolates pl

Konfektion /-'tsio:n/ f - ready-to-wear clothes pl

Konferenz f -,-en conference; (Besprechung) meeting

Konfession f -,-en [religious] denomination. **k~ell** adj denominational

Konfetti nt -s confetti

Konfirm|and(in) m -en,-en (f -,-nen) candidate for confirmation. **K~ation** f -,-en (Relig) confirmation. **k~ieren** vt (Relig) confirm

Konfitüre f -,-n jam

Konflikt m -[e]s,-e conflict

Konföderation /-'tsio:n/ f confederation

konfus adj confused

Kongress m -es,-e congress

König m -s,-e king. **K~in** f -,-nen queen. **k~lich** adj royal; (hoheitsvoll) regal; (großzügig) handsome. **K~reich** nt kingdom

Konjunktiv m -s,-e subjunctive

Konjunktur f - economic situation; (Hoch-) boom

konkret adj concrete

Konkurren|t(in) m -en,-en (f -,-nen) competitor, rival. **K~z** f - competition; **jdm K~z machen** compete with s.o. **K~zkampf** m competition, rivalry

konkurrieren vi (haben) compete

Konkurs m -es,-e bankruptcy

---

können†

● auxiliary verb

····➤ (vermögen) be able to; (Präsens) can; (Vergangenheit, Konditional) could. **ich kann nicht schlafen** I cannot or can't sleep. **kann ich Ihnen helfen?** can I help you? **kann/könnte das explodieren?** can/could it explode? **es kann sein, dass er kommt** he may come

❗ Distinguish **konnte** and **könnte** (both can be 'could'): **er konnte sie nicht retten** he couldn't or was unable to rescue them. **er konnte sie noch retten** he was able to rescue them. **er könnte sie noch retten, wenn ...** he could still rescue them if ...

····➤ (dürfen) can, may. **kann ich gehen?** can or may I go? **können wir mit[kommen]?** can or may we come too?

● transitive verb

····➤ (beherrschen) know (language); be able to play (game). **können Sie Deutsch?** do you know any German? **sie kann das [gut]** she can do that [well]. **ich kann nichts dafür** I can't help that, I'm not to blame

● intransitive verb

····➤ (fähig sein) **ich kann [heute] nicht** I can't [today]. **er kann nicht anders** there's nothing else he can do; (es ist seine Art) he can't help it. **er kann nicht mehr** 🔃 he can't go on; (nicht mehr essen) he can't eat any more

····➤ (irgendwohin gehen können) be able to go; can go. **ich kann nicht ins Kino** I can't go to the cinema. **er konnte endlich nach Florenz** at last he was able to go to Florence

konsequen|t *adj* consistent; (*logisch*) logical. **K~z** *f* -,-en consequence

konservativ *adj* conservative

Konserv|en *fpl* tinned or canned food *sg*. **K~endose** *f* tin, can. **K~ierungsmittel** *nt* preservative

Konsonant *m* -en,-en consonant

Konstitution /-'tsio:n/ *f* -,-en constitution. **k~ell** *adj* constitutional

konstruieren *vt* construct; (*entwerfen*) design

Konstruk|tion /-'tsio:n/ *f* -,-en construction; (*Entwurf*) design. **k~tiv** *adj* constructive

Konsul *m* -s,-n consul. **K~at** *nt* -[e]s,-e consulate

Konsum *m* -s consumption. **K~güter** *npl* consumer goods

Kontakt *m* -[e]s,-e contact. **K~linsen** *fpl* contact lenses. **K~person** *f* contact

kontern *vt/i* (*haben*) counter

Kontinent /'kɔn-, kɔnti'nɛnt/ *m* -[e]s,-e continent

Konto *nt* -s,-s account. **K~auszug** *m* [bank] statement. **K~nummer** *f* account number. **K~stand** *m* [bank] balance

Kontrabass *m* double bass

Kontroll|abschnitt *m* counterfoil. **K~e** *f* -,-n control; (*Prüfung*) check. **K~eur** *m* -s,-e [ticket] inspector. **k~ieren** *vt* check; inspect (*Fahrkarten*); (*beherrschen*) control

Kontroverse *f* -,-n controversy

Kontur *f* -,-en contour

konventionell *adj* conventional

Konversationslexikon *nt* encyclopaedia

konvert|ieren *vi* (*haben*) (*Relig*) convert. **K~it** *m* -en,-en convert

Konzentration /-'tsio:n/ *f* -,-en concentration. **K~slager** *nt* concentration camp

konzentrieren *vt* concentrate; **sich k~** concentrate (**auf** + *acc* on)

Konzept *nt* -[e]s,-e [rough] draft; **jdn aus dem K~bringen** put s.o. off his stroke

Konzern *m* -s,-e (*Comm*) group [of companies]

Konzert *nt* -[e]s,-e concert; (*Klavier-*) concerto

Konzession *f* -,-en licence; (*Zugeständnis*) concession

Konzil *nt* -s,-e (*Relig*) council

Kooperation /koʔopera'tsio:n/ *f* co-operation

Koordin|ation /koʔɔrdina'tsio:n/ *f* - co-ordination. **k~ieren** *vt* co-ordinate

Kopf *m* -[e]s,ˉe head; **ein K~ Kohl/Salat** a cabbage/lettuce; **aus dem K~** from memory; (*auswendig*) by heart; **auf dem K~** (*verkehrt*) upside down; **K~ stehen** stand on one's head; **sich** (*dat*) **den K~ waschen** wash one's hair; **sich** (*dat*) **den K~ zerbrechen** rack one's brains. **K~ball** *m* header

köpfen *vt* behead; (*Fußball*) head

Kopf|ende *nt* head. **K~haut** *f* scalp. **K~hörer** *m* headphones *pl*. **K~kissen** *nt* pillow. **k~los** *adj* panic-stricken. **K~rechnen** *nt* mental arithmetic. **K~salat** *m* lettuce. **K~schmerzen** *mpl* headache *sg*. **K~sprung** *m* header, dive. **K~stand** *m* headstand. **K~steinpflaster** *nt* cobblestones *pl*. **K~tuch** *nt* headscarf. **k~über** *adv* head first; (*fig*) headlong. **K~wäsche** *f* shampoo. **K~weh** *nt* headache

Kopie *f* -,-n copy. **k~ren** *vt* copy. **K~rschutz** *m* copy protection

Koppel[1] *f* -,-n enclosure; (*Pferde-*) paddock

Koppel[2] *nt* -s,- (*Mil*) belt. **k~n** *vt* couple

Koralle *f* -,-n coral

Korb *m* -[e]s,ˉe basket; **jdm einen K~ geben** (*fig*) turn s.o. down. **K~ball** *m* [kind of] netball

Kord *m* -s (*Textiles*) corduroy

Kordel *f* -,-n cord

Korinthe *f* -,-n currant

Kork *m* -s,-e cork. **K~en** *m* -s,- cork. **K~enzieher** *m* -s,- corkscrew

Korn *nt* -[e]s,ˉer grain, (*Samen-*)

seed; (*am Visier*) front sight

Körn|chen *nt* -s,- granule. **k~ig** *adj* granular

Körper *m* -s,- body; (*Geometry*) solid. **K~bau** *m* build, physique. **k~behindert** *adj* physically disabled. **k~lich** *adj* physical; (*Strafe*) corporal. **K~pflege** *f* personal hygiene. **K~schaft** *f* -,-en corporation, body

korrekt *adj* correct. **K~or** *m* -s,-en proof reader. **K~ur** *f* -,-en correction. **K~urabzug** *m* proof

Korrespon|dent(in) *m* -en,-en (*f* -,-nen) correspondent. **K~denz** *f* -,-en correspondence

Korridor *m* -s,-e corridor

korrigieren *vt* correct

Korrosion *f* - corrosion

korrup|t *adj* corrupt. **K~tion** *f* - corruption

Korsett *nt* -[e]s,-e corset

koscher *adj* kosher

Kosename *m* pet name

Kosmet|ik *f* - beauty culture. **K~ika** *ntpl* cosmetics. **K~ikerin** *f* -,-nen beautician. **k~isch** *adj* cosmetic; (*Chirurgie*) plastic

kosm|isch *adj* cosmic. **K~onaut(in)** *m* -en,-en (*f* -,-nen) cosmonaut

Kosmos *m* - cosmos

Kost *f* - food; (*Ernährung*) diet; (*Verpflegung*) board

kostbar *adj* precious. **K~keit** *f* -,-en treasure

kosten¹ *vt/i* (*haben*) [von] etw k~ taste sth

kosten² *vt* cost; (*brauchen*) take; **wie viel kostet es?** how much is it? **K~** *pl* expense *sg*, cost *sg*; (*Jur*) costs; **auf meine K~** at my expense. **K~[vor]anschlag** *m* estimate. **k~los** *adj* free ● *adv* free [of charge]

köstlich *adj* delicious; (*entzückend*) delightful

Kostprobe *f* taste; (*fig*) sample

Kostüm *nt* -s,-e (*Theat*) costume; (*Verkleidung*) fancy dress; (*Schneider-*)

suit. **k~iert** *adj* **k~iert sein** be in fancy dress

Kot *m* -[e]s excrement

Kotelett /kɔt'lɛt/ *nt* -s,-s chop, cutlet. **K~en** *pl* sideburns

Köter *m* -s,- (*pej*) dog

Kotflügel *m* (*Auto*) wing

kotzen *vi* (*haben*) 🗙 throw up

Krabbe *f* -,-n crab, shrimp

krabbeln *vi* (*sein*) crawl

Krach *m* -[e]s,⁺e din, racket; (*Knall*) crash; (🗓: *Streit*) row; (🗓: *Ruin*) crash. **k~en** *vi* (*haben*) crash; **es hat gekracht** there was a bang/(🗓: *Unfall*) a crash ● (*sein*) break, crack; (*auftreffen*) crash (**gegen** into)

krächzen *vi* (*haben*) croak

Kraft *f* -,⁺e strength; (*Gewalt*) force; (*Arbeits-*) worker; **in/außer K~** in/no longer in force. **K~fahrer** *m* driver. **K~fahrzeug** *nt* motor vehicle. **K~fahrzeugbrief** *m* [vehicle] registration document

kräftig *adj* strong; (*gut entwickelt*) sturdy; (*nahrhaft*) nutritious; (*heftig*) hard

kraft|los *adj* weak. **K~probe** *f* trial of strength. **K~stoff** *m* (*Auto*) fuel. **K~wagen** *m* motor car. **K~werk** *nt* power station

Kragen *m* -s,- collar

Krähe *f* -,-n crow

krähen *vi* (*haben*) crow

Kralle *f* -,-n claw

Kram *m* -s 🗓 things *pl*, 🗓 stuff; (*Angelegenheiten*) business. **k~en** *vi* (*haben*) rummage about (**in** + *dat* in; **nach** for)

Krampf *m* -[e]s,⁺e cramp. **K~adern** *fpl* varicose veins. **k~haft** *adj* convulsive; (*verbissen*) desperate

Kran *m* -[e]s,⁺e (*Techn*) crane

Kranich *m* -s,-e (*Zool*) crane

krank *adj* sick; (*Knie, Herz*) bad; **k~ sein/werden** be/fall ill. **K~e(r)** *m/f* sick man/woman, invalid; **die K~en** the sick *pl*

kränken *vt* offend, hurt

Kranken|bett *nt* sick bed. **K~geld** *nt* sickness benefit. **K~gymnast(in)**

m -en,-en (*f* -,-nen) physiotherapist. **K~gymnastik** *f* physiotherapy. **K~haus** *nt* hospital. **K~kasse** *f* health insurance scheme/(*Amt*) office. **K~pflege** *f* nursing. **K~saal** *m* [hospital] ward. **K~schein** *m* certificate of entitlement to medical treatment. **K~schwester** *f* nurse. **K~versicherung** *f* health insurance. **K~wagen** *m* ambulance

Krankheit *f* -,-en illness, disease

kränklich *adj* sickly

krank|melden *vt sep* jdn k~melden report s.o. sick; **sich k~melden** report sick

Kranz *m* -es,-e wreath

Krapfen *m* -s,- doughnut

Krater *m* -s,- crater

kratzen *vt/i* (*haben*) scratch. **K~er** *m* -s,- scratch

Kraul *nt* -s (*Sport*) crawl. **k~en¹** *vi* (*haben/sein*) (*Sport*) do the crawl

kraulen² *vt* tickle; **sich am Kopf k~** scratch one's head

kraus *adj* wrinkled; (*Haar*) frizzy; (*verworren*) muddled. **K~e** *f* -,-n frill

kräuseln *vt* wrinkle; frizz (*Haar-*); gather (*Stoff*); **sich k~** wrinkle; (*sich kringeln*) curl; (*Haar:*) go frizzy

Kraut *nt* -[e]s, Kräuter herb; (*SGer*) cabbage; (*Sauer-*) sauerkraut

Krawall *m* -s,-e riot; (*Lärm*) row

Krawatte *f* -,-n [neck]tie

krea|tiv /krea'ti:f/ *adj* creative. **K~tur** *f* -,-en creature

Krebs *m* -es,-e crayfish; (*Med*) cancer; (*Astrology*) Cancer

Kredit *m* -s,-e credit; (*Darlehen*) loan; **auf K~** on credit. **K~karte** *f* credit card

Kreid|e *f* - chalk. **k~ig** *adj* chalky

kreieren /kre'i:rən/ *vt* create

Kreis *m* -es,-e circle; (*Admin*) district

kreischen *vt/i* (*haben*) screech; (*schreien*) shriek

Kreisel *m* -s,- [spinning] top

kreis|en *vi* (*haben*) circle; revolve (**um** around). **k~förmig** *adj* circular. **K~lauf** *m* cycle; (*Med*) circulation. **K~säge** *f* circular saw. **K~verkehr**

m [traffic] roundabout

Krem *f* -,-s & *m* -s,-e cream

Krematorium *nt* -s,-ien crematorium

Krempe *f* -,-n [hat] brim

krempeln *vt* turn (**nach oben** up)

Krepp *m* -s,-s & -e crêpe

Krepppapier *nt* crêpe paper

Kresse *f* -,-n cress; (*Kapuziner-*) nasturtium

Kreta *nt* -s Crete

Kreuz *nt* -es,-e cross; (*Kreuzung*) intersection; (*Mus*) sharp; (*Kartenspiel*) clubs *pl*; (*Anat*) small of the back; **über K~** crosswise; **das K~ schlagen** cross oneself. **k~en** *vt* cross; **sich k~en** cross; (*Straßen:*) intersect; (*Meinungen:*) clash ● *vi* (*haben/sein*) cruise. **K~fahrt** *f* (*Naut*) cruise. **K~gang** *m* cloister

kreuzig|en *vt* crucify. **K~ung** *f* -,-en crucifixion

Kreuz|otter *f* adder, common viper. **K~ung** *f* -,-en intersection; (*Straßen-*) crossroads *sg*. **K~verhör** *nt* cross-examination. **k~weise** *adv* crosswise. **K~worträtsel** *nt* crossword [puzzle]. **K~zug** *m* crusade

kribbel|ig *adj* 🄐 edgy. **k~n** *vi* (*haben*) tingle; (*kitzeln*) tickle

kriech|en† *vi* (*sein*) crawl; (*fig*) grovel (**vor** + *dat* to). **K~spur** *f* (*Auto*) crawler lane. **K~tier** *nt* reptile

Krieg *m* -[e]s,-e war

kriegen *vt* 🄐 get; **ein Kind k~** have a baby

kriegs|beschädigt *adj* war-disabled. **K~dienstverweigerer** *m* -s,- conscientious objector. **K~gefangene(r)** *m* prisoner of war. **K~gefangenschaft** *f* captivity. **K~gericht** *nt* court martial. **K~list** *f* stratagem. **K~rat** *m* council of war. **K~recht** *nt* martial law

Krimi *m* -s,-s 🄐 crime story/film. **K~nalität** *f* - crime; (*Vorkommen*) crime rate. **K~nalpolizei** *f* criminal investigation department. **K~nalroman** *m* crime novel. **k~nell** *adj* criminal

Krippe f -,-n manger; (Weihnachts-) crib; (Kinder-) crèche. **K~nspiel** nt Nativity play

Krise f -,-n crisis

Kristall nt -s crystal; (geschliffen) cut glass

Kritik f -,-en criticism; (Rezension) review; **unter aller K~** 🖭 abysmal

Kriti|ker m -s,- critic; (Rezensent) reviewer. **k~sch** adj critical. **k~sieren** vt criticize; review

kritzeln vt/i (haben) scribble

Krokodil nt -s,-e crocodile

Krokus m -,-n [se] crocus

Krone f -,-n crown; (Baum-) top

krönen vt crown

Kronleuchter m chandelier

Krönung f -,-en coronation; (fig: Höhepunkt) crowning event

Kropf m -[e]s,ᵉe (Zool) crop; (Med) goitre

Kröte f -,-n toad

Krücke f -,-n crutch

Krug m -[e]s,ᵉe jug; (Bier-) tankard

Krümel m -s,- crumb. **k~ig** adj crumbly. **k~n** vt crumble ● vi (haben) be crumbly

krumm adj crooked; (gebogen) curved; (verbogen) bent

krümmen vt bend; crook (Finger); **sich k~** bend; (sich winden) writhe; (vor Lachen) double up

Krümmung f -,-en bend, curve

Krüppel m -s,- cripple

Kruste f -,-n crust; (Schorf) scab

Kruzifix nt -es,-e crucifix

Kub|a nt -s Cuba. **k~anisch** adj Cuban

Kübel m -s,- tub; (Eimer) bucket; (Techn) skip

Küche f -,-n kitchen; (Kochkunst) cooking; **kalte/warme K~** cold/hot food

Kuchen m -s,- cake

Küchen|herd m cooker, stove. **K~maschine** f food processor, mixer. **K~schabe** f -,-n cockroach

Kuckuck m -s,-e cuckoo

Kufe f -,-n [sledge] runner

Kugel f -,-n ball; (Geometry) sphere; (Gewehr-) bullet; (Sport) shot. **k~förmig** adj spherical. **K~lager** nt ball-bearing. **k~n** vt/i (haben) roll; **sich k~n** (vor Lachen) fall about. **K~schreiber** m -s,- ballpoint [pen]. **k~sicher** adj bulletproof. **K~stoßen** nt -s shot-putting

Kuh f -,ᵉe cow

kühl adj cool; (kalt) chilly. **K~box** f -,-en cool box. **K~e** f - coolness; chilliness. **k~en** vt cool; refrigerate (Lebensmittel); chill (Wein). **K~er** m -s,- (Auto) radiator. **K~erhaube** f bonnet. **K~fach** nt frozen-food compartment. **K~raum** m cold store. **K~schrank** m refrigerator. **K~truhe** f freezer. **K~wasser** nt [radiator] water

kühn adj bold

Kuhstall m cowshed

Küken nt -s,- chick; (Enten-) duckling

Kulissen fpl (Theat) scenery sg; (seitlich) wings; **hinter den K~** (fig) behind the scenes

Kult m -[e]s,-e cult

kultivier|en vt cultivate. **k~t** adj cultured

Kultur f -,-en culture. **K~beutel** m toilet bag. **k~ell** adj cultural. **K~film** m documentary film. **K~tourismus** m cultural tourism

Kultusminister m Minister of Education and Arts

Kümmel m -s caraway; (Getränk) kümmel

Kummer m -s sorrow, grief; (Sorge) worry; (Ärger) trouble

kümmer|lich adj puny; (dürftig) meagre; (armselig) wretched. **k~n** vt concern; **sich k~n um** look after; (sich befassen) concern oneself with; (beachten) take notice of

kummervoll adj sorrowful

Kumpel m -s,- 🖭 mate

Kunde m -n,-n customer. **K~ndienst** m [after-sales] service

Kundgebung f -,-en (Pol) rally

kündig|en vt cancel (Vertrag); give notice of withdrawal for (Geld); give notice to quit (*Wohnung*); **seine Stellung k~en** give [in one's] notice ● *vi* (*haben*) give [in one's] notice; **jdm k~en** give s.o. notice. **K~ung** *f* -,-en cancellation; notice [of withdrawal/dismissal/to quit]; (*Entlassung*) dismissal. **K~ungsfrist** *f* period of notice

Kund|in *f* -,-nen [woman] customer. **K~schaft** *f* - clientele, customers *pl*

künftig *adj* future ● *adv* in future

Kunst *f* -,ᵈe art; (*Können*) skill. **K~faser** *f* synthetic fibre. **K~galerie** *f* art gallery. **K~geschichte** *f* history of art. **K~gewerbe** *nt* arts and crafts *pl*. **K~griff** *m* trick

Künstler *m* -s,- artist; (*Könner*) master. **K~in** *f* -,-nen [woman] artist. **k~isch** *adj* artistic

künstlich *adj* artificial

Kunst|stoff *m* plastic. **K~stück** *nt* trick; (*große Leistung*) feat. **k~voll** *adj* artistic; (*geschickt*) skilful

kunterbunt *adj* multicoloured; (*gemischt*) mixed

Kupfer *nt* -s copper

Kupon /kuˈpõː/ *m* -s,-s voucher; (*Zins-*) coupon; (*Stoff-*) length

Kuppe *f* -,-n [rounded] top

Kuppel *f* -,-n dome

kupp|eln *vt* couple (**an** + *acc* to) ● *vi* (*haben*) (*Auto*) operate the clutch. **K~lung** *f* -,-en coupling; (*Auto*) clutch

Kur *f* -,-en course of treatment, cure

> **Kur** A health cure in a spa town may last up to 6 weeks and usually involves a special diet, exercise programmes, physiotherapy and massage. The cure is intended for people with minor complaints or who are recovering from illness, and it plays an important role in preventative medicine in Germany. *i*

Kür *f* -,-en (*Sport*) free exercise; (*Eislauf*) free programme

Kurbel *f* -,-n crank. **K~welle** *f* crankshaft

Kürbis *m* -ses,-se pumpkin

Kurier *m* -s,-e courier

kurieren *vt* cure

kurios *adj* curious, odd. **K~ität** *f* -,-en oddness; (*Objekt*) curiosity

Kurort *m* health resort; (*Badeort*) spa

Kurs *m* -es,-e course; (*Aktien-*) price. **K~buch** *nt* timetable

kursieren *vi* (*haben*) circulate

kursiv *adj* italic ● *adv* in italics. **K~schrift** *f* italics *pl*

Kursus *m* -,Kurse course

Kurswagen *m* through carriage

Kurtaxe *f* visitors' tax

Kurve *f* -,-n curve; (*Straßen-*) bend

kurz *adj* short; (*knapp*) brief; (*rasch*) quick; (*schroff*) curt; **k~e Hosen** shorts; **vor k~em** a short time ago; **seit k~em** lately; **den Kürzeren ziehen** get the worst of it; **k~ vor** shortly before; **sich k~ fassen** be brief; **k~ und gut** in short; **zu k~ kommen** get less than one's fair share. **k~ärmelig** *adj* short-sleeved. **k~atmig** *adj* **k~atmig sein** be short of breath

Kürze *f* - shortness; (*Knappheit*) brevity; **in K~** shortly. **k~n** *vt* shorten; (*verringern*) cut

kurzfristig *adj* short-term ● *adv* at short notice

kürzlich *adv* recently

Kurz|meldung *f* newsflash. **K~schluss** *m* short circuit. **K~schrift** *f* shorthand. **k~sichtig** *adj* short-sighted. **K~sichtigkeit** *f* - short-sightedness. **K~streckenrakete** *f* short-range missile

Kürzung *f* -,-en shortening; (*Verringerung*) cut (*gen* in)

Kurz|waren *fpl* haberdashery *sg*. **K~welle** *f* short wave

kuscheln (sich) *vr* snuggle (**an** + *acc* up to)

Kusine *f* -,-n [female] cousin

Kuss *m* -es,ᵈe kiss

küssen *vt/i* (*haben*) kiss; **sich k~** kiss

Küste *f* -,-n coast

Küster *m* -s,- verger

Kutsch|e *f* -,-n [horse-drawn] carriage/(*geschlossen*) coach. **K~er** *m*

-s,- coachman, driver
Kutte f -,-n (Relig) habit
Kutter m -s,- (Naut) cutter
Kuvert /ku've:ɐ̯/ nt -s,-s envelope

• •

L

• •

Labor nt -s,-s & -e laboratory.
L∼ant(in) m -en,-en (f -,-nen) laboratory assistant
Labyrinth nt -[e]s,-e maze, labyrinth
Lache f -,-n puddle; (Blut-) pool
lächeln vi (haben) smile. L∼ nt -s
smile. l∼d adj smiling
lachen vi (haben) laugh. L∼ nt -s
laugh; (Gelächter) laughter
lächerlich adj ridiculous; sich l∼
machen make a fool of oneself.
L∼keit f -,-en ridiculousness; (Klei-
nigkeit) triviality
Lachs m -es,-e salmon
Lack m -[e]s,-e varnish; (Japan-) lacquer; (Auto) paint. l∼en vt varnish.
l∼ieren vt varnish; (spritzen) spray.
L∼schuhe mpl patent-leather shoes
laden† vt load; (Electr) charge; (Jur:
vor-) summon
Laden m -s,ⁿ shop; (Fenster-) shutter.
L∼dieb m shoplifter. L∼schluss m
[shop] closing time. L∼tisch m
counter
Laderaum m (Naut) hold
lädieren vt damage
Ladung f -,-en load; (Naut, Aviat)
cargo; (elektrische) charge
Lage f -,-n position, situation;
(Schicht) layer; nicht in der L∼ sein
not be in a position (zu to)
Lager nt -s,- camp; (L∼haus) warehouse; (Vorrat) stock; (Techn) bearing; (Erz-, Ruhe-) bed; (eines Tieres)
lair; [nicht] auf L∼ [not] in stock.
L∼haus nt warehouse. l∼n vt store;
(legen) lay; sich l∼n settle. L∼raum
m store-room. L∼ung f - storage

Lagune f -,-n lagoon
lahm adj lame. l∼en vi (haben) be
lame
lähmen vt paralyse
Lähmung f -,-en paralysis
Laib m -[e]s,-e loaf
Laich m -[e]s (Zool) spawn
Laie m -n,-n layman; (Theat) amateur.
l∼nhaft adj amateurish
Laken nt -s,- sheet
Lakritze f - liquorice
lallen vt/i (haben) mumble; (Baby:)
babble
Lametta nt -s tinsel
Lamm nt -[e]s,ⁿer lamb
Lampe f -,-n lamp; (Decken-, Wand-)
light; (Glüh-) bulb. L∼nfieber nt
stage fright
Lampion /lam'piɔŋ/ m -s,-s Chinese
lantern
Land nt -[e]s,ⁿer country; (Fest-)
land; (Bundes-) state, Land; (Ausl)
province; auf dem L∼e in the coun-
try; an L∼ gehen (Naut) go ashore.
L∼arbeiter m agricultural worker.
L∼ebahn f runway. l∼en vt/i (sein)
land; (🆒: gelangen) end up

Land Germany is a federal
republic consisting of 16
member states called Länder or
Bundesländer. Each Land is responsible for local government, educa-
tional and cultural affairs, police
and the environment. Austria has 9
Länder, while the Swiss equivalent
is the ▸KANTON.

Ländereien pl estates
Länderspiel nt international
Landesverrat m treason
Landkarte f map
ländlich adj rural
Land|schaft f -,-en scenery; (Geog,
Kunst) landscape; (Gegend) country-
[side]. l∼schaftlich adj scenic; (regional) regional. L∼streicher m -s,-
tramp. L∼tag m state/(Aust) provin-
cial parliament
Landung f -,-en landing
Land|vermesser m -s,- surveyor.

k

l

L~weg m country lane; **auf dem L~weg** overland. **L~wirt** m farmer. **L~wirtschaft** f agriculture; (*Hof*) farm. **l~wirtschaftlich** adj agricultural

lang¹ adv & prep (+ preceding acc or preceding **an** + dat) along; **den** od **am Fluss l~** along the river

lang² adj long; (*groß*) tall; **seit l~em** for a long time ● adv **eine Stunde l~** for an hour; **mein Leben l~** all my life. **l~ärmelig** adj long-sleeved. **l~atmig** adj long-winded. **l~e** adv a long time; (*schlafen*) late; **schon l~e** [for] a long time; (*zurückliegend*) a long time ago; **l~e nicht** not for a long time; (*bei weitem nicht*) nowhere near

Länge f -,-n length; (*Geog*) longitude; **der L~ nach** lengthways

Läng|engrad m degree of longitude. **l~er** adj & adv longer; (*längere Zeit*) [for] some time

Langeweile f - boredom; **L~ haben** be bored

lang|fristig adj long-term; (*Vorhersage*) long-range. **l~jährig** adj long-standing; (*Erfahrung*) long

länglich adj oblong; **l~ rund** oval

längs adv & prep (+ gen/dat) along; (*der Länge nach*) lengthways

lang|sam adj slow. **L~samkeit** f - slowness

längst adv [**schon**] **l~** for a long time; (*zurückliegend*) a long time ago; **l~ nicht** nowhere near

Lang|strecken- prefix long-distance; (*Mil, Aviat*) long-range. **l~weilen** vt bore; **sich l~weilen** be bored. **l~weilig** adj boring

Lanze f -,-n lance

Lappalie /la'pa:liə/ f -,-n trifle

Lappen m -s,- cloth; (*Anat*) lobe

Laptop m -s,-s laptop

Lärche f -,-n larch

Lärm m -s noise. **l~end** adj noisy

Larve /'larfə/ f -,-n larva; (*Maske*) mask

lasch adj listless; (*schlaff*) limp

Lasche f -,-n tab, flap

Laser /'le:-, 'la:zɐ/ m -s,- laser

lassen†

● *transitive verb*

····▸ (+ *infinitive; veranlassen*) **etw tun lassen** have or get sth done. **jdn etw tun lassen** make s.o. do sth; get s.o. to do sth **sich** dat **die Haare schneiden lassen** have or get one's hair cut. **jdn warten lassen** make or let s.o. wait; keep s.o. waiting. **jdn grüßen lassen** send one's regards to s.o. **jdn kommen/rufen lassen** send for s.o.

····▸ (+ *infinitive; erlauben*) let; allow; (*hineinlassen/herauslassen*) let or allow (**in** + acc into, **aus** + dat out of). **jdn etw tun lassen** let s.o. do sth; allow s.o. to do sth. **er ließ mich nicht ausreden** he didn't let me finish [what I was saying]

····▸ (*belassen, bleiben lassen*) leave. **jdn in Frieden lassen** leave s.o. in peace. **etw ungesagt lassen** leave sth unsaid

····▸ (*unterlassen*) stop. **das Rauchen lassen** stop smoking. **er kann es nicht lassen, sie zu quälen** he can't stop or he is forever tormenting her

····▸ (*überlassen*) **jdm etw lassen** let s.o. have sth

····▸ (*als Aufforderung*) **lass/lasst uns gehen/fahren!** let's go!

● *reflexive verb*

····▸ **das lässt sich machen** that can be done. **das lässt sich nicht beweisen** it can't be proved. **die Tür lässt sich leicht öffnen** the door opens easily

● *intransitive verb*

····▸ 🛈 **Lass mal. Ich mache das schon** Leave it. I'll do it

lässig adj casual. **L~keit** f - casualness

Lasso nt -s,-s lasso

Last f -,-en load; (*Gewicht*) weight; (*fig*) burden; **L~en** charges; (*Steuern*) taxes. **L~auto** nt lorry. **l~en** vi (*haben*) weigh heavily/(*liegen*) rest (**auf** + *dat* on)

Laster[1] *m* -s,- 🔲 lorry

Laster[2] *nt* -s,- vice

läster|n *vt* blaspheme ● *vi* (*haben*) make disparaging remarks (**über** + *acc* about). **L~ung** *f* -,-en blasphemy

lästig *adj* troublesome; **l~ sein/ werden** be/become a nuisance

Last|kahn *m* barge. **L~[kraft]wagen** *m* lorry

Latein *nt* -[s] Latin. **L~amerika** *nt* Latin America. **l~isch** *adj* Latin

Laterne *f* -,-n lantern; (*Straßen-*) street lamp. **L~npfahl** *m* lamp-post

latschen *vi* (*sein*) 🔲 traipse

Latte *f* -,-n slat; (*Tor-, Hochsprung-*) bar

Latz *m* -es,⁓e bib

Lätzchen *nt* -s,- [baby's] bib

Latzhose *f* dungarees *pl*

Laub *nt* -[e]s leaves *pl*; (*L~werk*) foliage. **L~baum** *m* deciduous tree

Laube *f* -,-n summer-house

Laub|säge *f* fretsaw. **L~wald** *m* deciduous forest

Lauch *m* -[e]s leeks *pl*

Lauer *f* **auf der L~ liegen** lie in wait. **l~n** *vi* (*haben*) lurk; **l~n auf** (+ *acc*) lie in wait for

Lauf *m* -[e]s, Läufe run; (*Laufen*) running; (*Verlauf*) course; (*Wett-*) race; (*Sport: Durchgang*) heat; (*Gewehr-*) barrel; **im L~[e]** (+ *gen*) in the course of. **L~bahn** *f* career. **l~en** *vi* (*sein*) run; (*zu Fuß gehen*) walk; (*gelten*) be valid; **Ski/Schlittschuh l~en** ski/skate. **l~end** *adj* running; (*gegenwärtig*) current; (*regelmäßig*) regular; **auf dem L~enden sein** be up to date ● *adv* continually

Läufer *m* -s,- (*Person, Teppich*) runner; (*Schach*) bishop

Lauf|gitter *nt* play-pen. **L~masche** *f* ladder. **L~text** *m* marquee text. **L~zettel** *m* circular

Lauge *f* -,-n soapy water

Laun|e *f* -,-n mood; (*Einfall*) whim; **guter L~e sein, gute L~e haben**

be in a good mood. **l~isch** *adj* moody

Laus *f* -,Läuse louse; (*Blatt-*) greenfly

lauschen *vi* (*haben*) listen

laut *adj* loud; (*geräuschvoll*) noisy; **l~ lesen** read aloud; **l~er stellen** turn up ● *prep* (+ *gen/dat*) according to. **L~** *m* -es,-e sound

Laute *f* -,-n (*Mus*) lute

lauten *vi* (*haben*) (*Text:*) run, read

läuten *vt/i* (*haben*) ring

lauter *adj* pure; (*ehrlich*) honest; (*Wahrheit*) plain ● *adj inv* sheer; (*nichts als*) nothing but

laut|hals *adv* at the top of one's voice, (*lachen*) out loud. **l~los** *adj* silent, (*Stille*) hushed. **L~schrift** *f* phonetics *pl*. **L~sprecher** *m* loudspeaker. **L~stärke** *f* volume

lauwarm *adj* lukewarm

Lava *f* -,-ven lava

Lavendel *m* -s lavender

lavieren *vi* (*haben*) manœuvre

Lawine *f* -,-n avalanche

Lazarett *nt* -[e]s,-e military hospital

leasen /'li:sən/ *vt* rent

Lebehoch *nt* cheer

leben *vt/i* (*haben*) live (**von** on); **leb wohl!** farewell! **L~** *nt* -s,- life, (*Treiben*) bustle; **am L~** alive. **l~d** *adj* living

lebendig *adj* live; (*lebhaft*) lively; (*anschaulich*) vivid; **l~ sein** be alive. **L~keit** *f* - liveliness; vividness

Lebens|abend *m* old age. **L~alter** *nt* age. **l~fähig** *adj* viable. **L~gefahr** *f* mortal danger; **in L~gefahr** in mortal danger; (*Patient*) critically ill. **l~gefährlich** *adj* extremely dangerous; (*Verletzung*) critical. **L~haltungskosten** *pl* cost of living *sg*. **l~länglich** *adj* life-long ● *adv* for life. **L~lauf** *m* curriculum vitae. **L~mittel** *ntpl* food *sg*. **L~mittelgeschäft** *nt* food shop. **L~mittelhändler** *m* grocer. **L~retter** *m* rescuer; (*beim Schwimmen*) life-guard. **L~unterhalt** *m* livelihood; **seinen L~unterhalt verdienen** earn one's living. **L~versicherung** *f* life assurance.

L~wandel m conduct. **l~wichtig** adj vital. **L~zeit** f **auf l~zeit** for life

Leber f -,-n liver. **L~fleck** m mole

Lebe|wesen nt living being. **L~wohl** nt -s,-s & -e farewell

leb|haft adj lively; (Farbe) vivid. **L~kuchen** m gingerbread. **l~los** adj lifeless. **L~zeiten** fpl **zu jds L~zeiten** in s.o.'s lifetime

leck adj leaking. **L~** nt -s,-s leak. **l~en**[1] vi (haben) leak

lecken[2] vi (haben) lick

lecker adj tasty. **L~bissen** m delicacy

Leder nt -s,- leather

ledig adj single, unmarried

leer adj empty; (unbesetzt) vacant; **l~ laufen** (Auto) idle. **l~en** vt empty; **sich l~en** empty. **L~lauf** m (Auto) neutral. **L~ung** f -,-en (Post) collection

legal adj legal. **l~isieren** vt legalize. **L~ität** f - legality

Legas|thenie f - dyslexia **L~theniker** m -s,- dyslexic

legen vt put; (hin-, ver-) lay; set (Haare); **sich l~** lie down; (nachlassen) subside

Legende f -,-n legend

leger /leˈʒeːɐ̯/ adj casual

Legierung f -,-en alloy

Legion f -,-en legion

Legislative f - legislature

legitim adj legitimate. **L~ität** f - legitimacy

Lehm m -s clay

Lehn|e f -,-n (Rücken-) back; (Arm-) arm. **l~en** vt lean (an + acc against); **sich l~en** lean (an + acc against) ● vi (haben) be leaning (an + acc against)

Lehr|buch nt textbook. **L~e** f -,-n apprenticeship; (Anschauung) doctrine; (Theorie) theory; (Wissenschaft) science; (Erfahrung) lesson. **l~en** vt/i (haben) teach. **L~er** m -s,- teacher; (Fahr-) instructor. **L~erin** f -,-nen teacher. **L~erzimmer** nt staff-room. **L~fach** nt (Sch) subject. **L~gang** m course. **L~kraft** f teacher. **L~ling** m

-s,-e apprentice; (Auszubildender) trainee. **L~plan** m syllabus. **l~reich** adj instructive. **L~stelle** f apprenticeship. **L~stuhl** m (Univ) chair. **L~zeit** f apprenticeship

Leib m -es,-er body; (Bauch) belly. **L~eserziehung** f (Sch) physical education. **L~gericht** nt favourite dish. **l~lich** adj physical; (blutsverwandt) real, natural. **L~wächter** m bodyguard

Leiche f -,-n [dead] body; corpse. **L~nbestatter** m -s,- undertaker. **L~nhalle** f mortuary. **L~nwagen** m hearse. **L~nzug** m funeral procession, cortège

Leichnam m -s,-e [dead] body

leicht adj light; (Stoff) lightweight; (gering) slight; (mühelos) easy; **jdm l~ fallen** be easy for s.o.; **etw l~ machen** make sth easy (dat for); **es sich** (dat) **l~ machen** take the easy way out; **etw l~ nehmen** (fig) take sth lightly. **L~athletik** f [track and field] athletics sg. **L~gewicht** nt (Boxen) lightweight. **l~gläubig** adj gullible. **l~hin** adv casually. **L~igkeit** f - lightness; (Mühelosigkeit) ease; (L~sein) easiness; **mit L~igkeit** with ease. **L~sinn** m carelessness; recklessness; (Frivolität) frivolity. **l~sinnig** adj careless; (unvorsichtig) reckless

Leid nt -[e]s sorrow, grief; (Böses) harm; **es tut mir L~** I am sorry; **er tut mir L~** I feel sorry for him. **l~** adj **jdn/etw l~ sein/werden** be/get tired of s.o./something

Leide|form f passive. **l~n†** vt/i (haben) suffer (an + dat from); **jdn/etw nicht l~n können** dislike s.o./something. **L~n** nt -s,- suffering; (Med) complaint; (Krankheit) disease. **l~nd** adj suffering. **L~nschaft** f -,-en passion. **l~nschaftlich** adj passionate

leider adv unfortunately; **l~er ja/nicht** I'm afraid so/not

Leier|kasten m barrel-organ. **l~n** vt/i (haben) wind; (herunter-) drone out

Leih|e f -,-n loan. **l∼en†** vt lend; **sich** (dat) etw **l∼en** borrow sth. **L∼gabe** f loan. **L∼gebühr** f rental; lending charge. **L∼haus** nt pawnshop. **L∼wagen** m hire-car. **l∼weise** adv on loan

Leim m -s glue. **l∼en** vt glue

Leine f -,-n rope; (Wäsche-) line; (Hunde-) lead, leash

Lein|en nt -s linen. **L∼wand** f linen; (Kunst) canvas; (Film-) screen

leise adj quiet; (Stimme, Berührung) soft; (schwach) faint; (leicht) light; **l∼r stellen** turn down

Leiste f -,-n strip; (Holz-) batten; (Anat) groin

leist|en vt achieve, accomplish; **sich** (dat) etw **l∼en** treat oneself to sth; (🏛: anstellen) get up to sth; **ich kann es mir nicht l∼en** I can't afford it. **L∼ung** f -,-en achievement; (Sport, Techn) performance; (Produktion) output; (Zahlung) payment

Leit|artikel m leader, editorial. **l∼en** vt run, manage; (an-/hinführen) lead; (Mus, Techn, Phys) conduct; (lenken, schicken) direct. **l∼end** adj leading; (Posten) executive

Leiter¹ f -,-n ladder

Leit|er² m -s,- director; (Comm) manager; (Führer) leader; (Mus, Phys) conductor. **L∼erin** f -,-nen director; manageress; leader. **L∼planke** f crash barrier. **L∼spruch** m motto. **L∼ung** f -,-en (Führung) direction; (Comm) management; (Aufsicht) control; (Electr: Schnur) lead, flex; (Kabel) cable; (Telefon-) line; (Rohr-) pipe; (Haupt-) main. **L∼ungswasser** nt tap water

Lektion /-'tsio:n/ f -,-en lesson

Lekt|or m -s,-en, **L∼orin** f -,-nen (Univ) assistant lecturer; (Verlags-) editor. **L∼üre** f -,-n reading matter

Lende f -,-n loin

lenk|en vt guide; (steuern) steer; (regeln) control; **jds Aufmerksamkeit auf sich** (acc) **l∼en** attract s.o.'s attention. **L∼rad** nt steering-wheel. **L∼stange** f handlebars pl. **L∼ung** f - steering

Leopard m -en,-en leopard

Lepra f - leprosy

Lerche f -,-n lark

lernen vt/i (haben) learn; (für die Schule) study

Lernkurve f learning curve

Lesb|ierin /'lɛsbjərm/ f -,-nen lesbian. **l∼isch** adj lesbian

les|en† vt/i (haben) read; (Univ) lecture • vt pick, gather. **L∼en** nt -s reading. **L∼er(in)** m -s,- (f -,-nen) reader. **l∼erlich** adj legible. **L∼ezeichen** nt bookmark

lethargisch adj lethargic

Lettland nt -s Latvia

letzt|e(r,s) adj last; (neueste) latest; **in l∼er Zeit** recently; **l∼en Endes** in the end. **l∼ens** adv recently; (zuletzt) lastly. **l∼ere(r,s)** adj the latter; **der/die/das L∼ere** (**l∼ere**) the latter

Leucht|e f -,-n light. **l∼en** vi (haben) shine. **l∼end** adj shining. **L∼er** m -s,- candlestick. **L∼feuer** nt beacon. **L∼rakete** f flare. **L∼reklame** f neon sign. **L∼röhre** f fluorescent tube. **L∼turm** m lighthouse

leugnen vt deny

Leukämie f - leukaemia

Leumund m -s reputation

Leute pl people; (Mil) men; (Arbeiter) workers

Leutnant m -s,-s second lieutenant

Lexikon nt -s,-ka encyclopaedia; (Wörterbuch) dictionary

Libanon (der) -s Lebanon

Libelle f -,-n dragonfly

liberal adj (Pol) liberal

Libyen nt -s Libya

Licht nt -[e]s,-er light; (Kerze) candle; **l∼ machen** turn on the light. **l∼** adj bright; (Med) lucid; (spärlich) sparse. **L∼bild** nt [passport] photograph; (Dia) slide. **L∼blick** m (fig) ray of hope. **l∼en** vt thin out; **den Anker l∼en** (Naut) weigh anchor; **sich l∼en** become less dense; thin. **L∼hupe** f headlight flasher; **die L∼hupe betätigen** flash one's headlights. **L∼maschine** f dynamo.

L∼ung f -,-en clearing

Lid nt -[e]s,-er [eye]lid. **L∼schatten** m eye-shadow

lieb adj dear; (nett) nice; (artig) good; jdn l∼ haben be fond of s.o.; (lieben) love s.o.; es wäre mir l∼er I should prefer it (wenn if)

Liebe f -,-n love. l∼n vt love; (mögen) like; sich l∼n love each other; (körperlich) make love. l∼nd adj loving. l∼nswert a lovable. l∼nswürdig adj kind. l∼nswürdigerweise adv very kindly

lieber adv rather; (besser) better; l∼ mögen like better; ich trinke l∼ Tee I prefer tea

Liebes|brief m love letter. L∼dienst m favour. L∼kummer m heartache. L∼paar nt [pair of] lovers pl

lieb|evoll adj loving, affectionate. L∼haber m -s,- lover; (Sammler) collector. L∼haberei f -,-en hobby. L∼kosung f -,-en caress. l∼lich adj lovely; (sanft) gentle; (süß) sweet. L∼ling m -s,-e darling; (Bevorzugte) favourite. L∼lings- prefix favourite. l∼los adj loveless; (Eltern) uncaring; (unfreundlich) unkind. L∼schaft f -,-en [love] affair. l∼ste(r,s) adj dearest; (bevorzugt) favourite ● adv am l∼sten best [of all]; jdn/etw am l∼sten mögen like s.o./something best [of all]. L∼ste(r) m/f beloved; (Schatz) sweetheart

Lied nt -[e]s,-er song

liederlich adj slovenly; (unordentlich) untidy. L∼keit f - slovenliness; untidiness

Lieferant m -en,-en supplier

liefer|bar adj (Comm) available. l∼n vt supply; (zustellen) deliver; (hervorbringen) yield. L∼ung f -,-en delivery; (Sendung) consignment

Liege f -,-n couch. l∼n† vi (haben) lie; (gelegen sein) be situated; l∼n bleiben remain lying [there]; (im Bett) stay in bed; (Ding:) be left; (Schnee:) settle; (Arbeit:) remain undone; (zurückgelassen werden) be left

behind; l∼n lassen leave; (zurücklassen) leave behind; (nicht fortführen) leave undone; l∼n an (+ dat) (fig) be due to; (abhängen) depend on; jdm [nicht] l∼n [not] suit s.o.; mir liegt viel daran it is very important to me. L∼stuhl m deck-chair. L∼stütz m -es,-e press-up, (Amer) push-up. L∼wagen m couchette car

Lift m -[e]s,-e & -s lift

Liga f -,-gen league

Likör m -s,-e liqueur

lila inv adj mauve; (dunkel) purple

Lilie /'li:li̯ə/ f -,-n lily

Liliputaner(in) m -s,- (f -,-nen) dwarf

Limo f -,-[s] 1, L∼nade f -,-n fizzy drink; lemonade

Limousine /limu'zi:nə/ f -,-n saloon

lind adj mild

Linde f -,-n lime tree

linder|n vt relieve, ease. L∼ung f - relief

Lineal nt -s,-e ruler

Linie /-i̯ə/ f -,-n line; (Zweig) branch; (Bus-) route; l∼ 4 number 4 [bus/tram]; in erster L∼ primarily. L∼nflug m scheduled flight. L∼nrichter m linesman

lin[i]iert adj lined, ruled

Link|e f -n,-n left side; (Hand) left hand; (Boxen) left; die L∼e (Pol) the left. l∼e(r,s) adj left; (Pol) leftwing; l∼e Masche purl

links adv on the left; (bei Stoff) on the wrong side; (verkehrt) inside out; l∼stricken purl. L∼händer(in) m -s,- (f -,-nen) lefthander. l∼händig adj & adv lefthanded

Linoleum /-leʊm/ nt -s lino, linoleum

Linse f -,-n lens; (Bot) lentil

Lippe f -,-n lip. L∼nstift m lipstick

Liquid|ation /-'tsi̯o:n/ f -,-en liquidation. l∼ieren vt liquidate

lispeln vt/i (haben) lisp

List f -,-en trick, ruse

Liste f -,-n list

listig *adj* cunning, crafty

Litanei *f* -,-en litany

Litauen *nt* -s Lithuania

Liter *m* & *nt* -s,- litre

Literatur *f* - literature

Liturgie *f* -,-n liturgy

Litze *f* -,-n braid

Lizenz *f* -,-en licence

Lob *nt* -[e]s praise

Lobby /'lɔbi/ *f* - (*Pol*) lobby

loben *vt* praise

löblich *adj* praiseworthy

Lobrede *f* eulogy

Loch *nt* -[e]s, ̈er hole. **l⁓en** *vt* punch a hole/holes in; punch (*Fahrkarte*). **L⁓er** *m* -s,- punch

löcherig *adj* full of holes

Locke *f* -,-n curl. **l⁓n¹** *vt* curl; **sich l⁓n** curl

locken² *vt* lure, entice; (*reizen*) tempt. **l⁓d** *adj* tempting

Lockenwickler *m* -s,- curler; (*Rolle*) roller

locker *adj* loose; (*Seil*) slack; (*Erde*) light; (*zwanglos*) casual; (*zu frei*) lax. **l⁓n** *vt* loosen; slacken (*Seil*); break up (*Boden*); relax (*Griff*); **sich l⁓n** become loose; (*Seil:*) slacken; (*sich entspannen*) relax

lockig *adj* curly

Lockmittel *nt* bait

Loden *m* -s (*Textiles*) loden

Löffel *m* -s,- spoon; (*L⁓ voll*) spoonful. **l⁓n** *vt* spoon up

Logarithmus *m* -,-men logarithm

Logbuch *nt* (*Naut*) log-book

Loge /'lo:ʒə/ *f* -,-n lodge; (*Theat*) box

Log|ik *f* - logic. **l⁓isch** *adj* logical

Logo *nt* -s,-s logo

Lohn *m* -[e]s, ̈e wages *pl*, pay; (*fig*) reward. **L⁓empfänger** *m* wage-earner. **l⁓en** *vi|r* (*haben*) [sich] **l⁓en** be worth it *or* worth while ● *vt* be worth. **l⁓end** *adj* worthwhile; (*befriedigend*) rewarding. **L⁓erhöhung** *f* [pay] rise. **L⁓steuer** *f* income tax

Lok *f* -,-s ⊞ = Lokomotive

Lokal *nt* -s,-e restaurant; (*Trink-*) bar

Lokomotiv|e *f* -,-n engine, locomotive. **L⁓führer** *m* engine driver

London *nt* -s London. **L⁓er** *adj* London ● *m* -s,- Londoner

Lorbeer *m* -s,-en laurel. **L⁓blatt** *nt* (*Culin*) bay-leaf

Lore *f* -,-n (*Rail*) truck

Los *nt* -es,-e lot; (*Lotterie-*) ticket; (*Schicksal*) fate

los *pred adj* **los sein** be loose; **jdn/ etw los sein** be rid of s.o./something; **was ist [mit ihm] los?** what's the matter [with him]? ● *adv* **los!** go on! **Achtung, fertig, los!** ready, steady, go!

lösbar *adj* soluble

losbinden† *vt sep* untie

Lösch|blatt *nt* sheet of blotting-paper. **l⁓en** *vt* put out, extinguish; quench (*Durst*); blot (*Tinte*); (*tilgen*) cancel; (*streichen*) delete

Löschfahrzeug *nt* fire-engine

lose *adj* loose

Lösegeld *nt* ransom

losen *vt* (*haben*) draw lots (**um** for)

lösen *vt* undo; (*lockern*) loosen; (*entfernen*) detach; (*klären*) solve; (*auflösen*) dissolve; cancel (*Vertrag*); break off (*Beziehung*); (*kaufen*) buy; **sich l⁓** come off; (*sich trennen*) detach oneself/itself; (*lose werden*) come undone; (*sich klären*) resolve itself; (*sich auflösen*) dissolve

los|fahren† *vi sep* (*sein*) start; (*Auto:*) drive off; **l⁓fahren nach** (+ *dat*) head for. **l⁓gehen**† *vi sep* (*sein*) set off; (⊞: *anfangen*) start; (*Bombe:*) go off; **l⁓gehen nach** (+ *dat*) head for; (*fig: angreifen*) go for. **l⁓kommen**† *vi sep* (*sein*) get away (**von** from). **l⁓lassen**† *vt sep* let go of; (*freilassen*) release

löslich *adj* soluble

los|lösen *vt sep* detach; **sich l⁓lösen** become detached; (*fig*) break away (**von** from). **l⁓machen** *vt sep* detach; untie. **l⁓reißen**† *vt sep* tear off; **sich l⁓reißen** break free; (*fig*)

tear oneself away. **l~schicken** vt sep
send off. **l~sprechen†** vt sep absolve
(**von** from)

Losung f -,-en (Pol) slogan; (Mil)
password

Lösung f -,-en solution. **L~smittel**
nt solvent

loswerden† vt sep get rid of

Lot nt -[e]s,-e perpendicular; (Blei-)
plumb[-bob]. **l~en** vt plumb

löt|en vt solder. **L~lampe** f blow-
lamp

lotrecht adj perpendicular

Lotse m -n,-n (Naut) pilot. **l~n** vt
(Naut) pilot; (fig) guide

Lotterie f -,-n lottery

Lotto nt -s,-s lotto; (Lotterie) lottery

Love Parade A techno
music and dance festival,
which takes place in Berlin every
summer. Originally a celebration of
youth culture and very popular
with young people, this festival has
become a major tourist attraction.

Löw|e m -n,-n lion; (Astrology) Leo.
L~enzahn m (Bot) dandelion. **L~in**
f -,-nen lioness

loyal /loaˈjaːl/ adj loyal. **L~ität** f -
loyalty

Luchs m -es,-e lynx

Lücke f -,-n gap. **l~nhaft** adj incomplete; (Wissen) patchy. **l~nlos** adj
complete; (Folge) unbroken

Luder nt -s,- ⊠ (Frau) bitch

Luft f -,ːe air; **tief L~ holen** take a
deep breath; **in die L~ gehen** explode. **L~angriff** m air raid. **L~auf-
nahme** f aerial photograph. **L~bal-
lon** m balloon. **L~blase** f air bubble.
L~druck m atmospheric pressure

lüften vt air; raise (Hut); reveal (Geheimnis)

Luft|fahrt f aviation. **L~fahrtge-
sellschaft** f airline. **L~gewehr** nt
airgun. **l~ig** adj airy; (Kleid) light.
L~kissenfahrzeug nt hovercraft.
L~krieg m aerial warfare. **l~leer**
adj **l~leerer Raum** vacuum. **L~linie**

f **100 km L~linie** 100 km as the
crow flies. **L~matratze** f air-bed, inflatable mattress. **L~pirat** m hijacker. **L~post** f airmail. **L~röhre** f
windpipe. **L~schiff** nt airship.
L~schlange f [paper] streamer.
L~schutzbunker m air-raid shelter

Lüftung f - ventilation

Luft|veränderung f change of
air. **L~waffe** f air force. **L~zug** m
draught

Lüg|e f -,-n lie. **l~en†** vt/i (haben) lie.
L~ner(in) m -s,- (f -,-nen) liar.
l~nerisch adj untrue; (Person) un-
truthful

Luke f -,-n hatch; (Dach-) skylight

Lümmel m -s,- lout

Lump m -en,-en scoundrel. **L~en** m
-s,- rag; **in L~en** in rags. **L~enpack**
nt riff-raff. **L~ensammler** m rag-
and-bone man. **l~ig** adj mean,
shabby

Lunge f -,-n lungs pl; (L~nflügel)
lung. **L~nentzündung** f pneumonia

Lupe f -,-n magnifying glass

Lurch m -[e]s,-e amphibian

Lust f -,ːe pleasure; (Verlangen) desire; (sinnliche Begierde) lust; **L~
haben** feel like (**auf etw** acc sth); **ich
habe keine L~** I don't feel like it;
(will nicht) I don't want to

lustig adj jolly; (komisch) funny; **sich
l~ machen über** (+ acc) make
fun of

Lüstling m -s,-e lecher

lust|los adj listless. **L~mörder** m
sex killer. **L~spiel** nt comedy

lutsch|en vt/i (haben) suck. **L~er** m
-s,- lollipop

Lüttich nt -s Liège

Luv f & nt - **nach Luv** (Naut) to wind-
ward

luxuriös adj luxurious

Luxus m - luxury

Lymph|drüse /ˈlʏmf-/ f, **L~knoten**
m lymph gland

lynchen /ˈlʏnçən/ vt lynch

Lyr|ik f - lyric poetry. **L~iker** m -s,-
lyric poet. **l~isch** adj lyrical

Mm

Machart f style

machen

● *transitive verb*

····▸ (*herstellen, zubereiten*) make (*money, beds, music, exception, etc*). **aus Plastik/Holz gemacht** made of plastic/wood. **sich** (*dat*) **etw machen lassen** have sth made. **etw aus jdm machen** make s.o. into sth. **jdn zum Präsidenten machen** make s.o. president. **er machte sich** (*dat*) **viele Freunde/Feinde** he made a lot of friends/enemies. **jdm/sich** (*dat*) **[einen] Kaffee machen** make [some] coffee for s.o./oneself. **ein Foto machen** take a photo

····▸ (*verursachen*) make, cause (*difficulties*); cause (*pain, anxiety*). **jdm Arbeit machen** make [extra] work for s.o., cause s.o. extra work. **jdm Mut/Hoffnung machen** give s.o. courage/hope. **das macht Hunger/Durst** this makes you hungry/thirsty. **das macht das Wetter** that's [because of] the weather

····▸ (*ausführen, ordnen*) do (*job, repair, fam: room, washing, etc.*).; take (*walk, trip, exam, course*). **sie machte mir die Haare** 🛈 she did my hair for me. **einen Besuch [bei jdm] machen** pay [s.o.] a visit

····▸ (*tun*) do (*nothing, everything*). **was machst du [da]?** what are you doing? **so etwas macht man nicht** that [just] isn't done

····▸ **was macht ... ?** (*wie ist es um bestellt?*) how is ...? **was macht die Gesundheit/Arbeit?** how are you keeping/how is the job [getting on]?

····▸ (*Math: ergeben*) be. **zwei mal** **zwei macht vier** two times two is four. **das macht 6 Euro [zusammen]** that's *or* that comes to six euros [altogether]

····▸ (*schaden*) **was macht das schon?** what does it matter? **[das] macht nichts!** 🛈 it doesn't matter

····▸ **mach's gut!** 🛈 look after yourself!; (*auf Wiedersehen*) so long!

● *reflexive verb*

····▸ **sich machen** 🛈 do well

····▸ **sich an etw** (*acc*) **machen** get down to sth. **sie machte sich an die Arbeit** she got down to work

● *intransitive verb*

····▸ **das macht hungrig/durstig** it makes you hungry/thirsty. **das macht dick** it's fattening

Macht f -,⸚e power. **M∼haber** m -s,- ruler

mächtig adj powerful ● adv 🛈 terribly

machtlos adj powerless

Mädchen nt -s,- girl; (*Dienst-*) maid. **m∼haft** adj girlish. **M∼name** m girl's name; (*vor der Ehe*) maiden name

Made f -,-n maggot

madig adj maggoty

Madonna f -,-nen madonna

Magazin nt -s,-e magazine; (*Lager*) warehouse; store-room

Magd f -,⸚e maid

Magen m -s,⸚ stomach. **M∼verstimmung** f stomach upset

mager adj thin; (*Fleisch*) lean; (*Boden*) poor; (*dürftig*) meagre. **M∼keit** f - thinness; leanness. **M∼sucht** f anorexia

Magie f - magic

Mag|ier /'ma:giɐ/ m -s,- magician. **m∼isch** adj magic

Magistrat m -s,-e city council

Magnet m -en & -[e]s,-e magnet. **m∼isch** adj magnetic

Mahagoni nt -s mahogany

Mäh|drescher m -s,- combine harvester. **m~en** vt/i (haben) mow

Mahl nt -[e]s, ˸er & -e meal

mahlen† vt grind

Mahlzeit f meal; **M~!** enjoy your meal!

Mähne f -,-n mane

mahn|en vt/i (haben) remind (**wegen** about); (ermahnen) admonish; (auffordern) urge (**zu** to). **M~ung** f -,-en reminder; admonition

Mai m -[e]s,-e May; **der Erste Mai** May Day. **M~glöckchen** nt -s,- lily of the valley

Mailand nt -s Milan

Mais m -es maize; (Culin) sweet corn

Majestät f -,-en majesty. **m~isch** adj majestic

Major m -s,-e major

Majoran m -s marjoram

makaber adj macabre

Makel m -s,- blemish; (Defekt) flaw

Makkaroni pl macaroni sg

Makler m -s,- (Comm) broker

Makrele f -,-n mackerel

Makrone f -,-n macaroon

mal adv (Math) times; (bei Maßen) by; (🔲: einmal) once; (eines Tages) one day; **nicht mal** not even

Mal nt -[e]s,-e time; **zum ersten/letzten Mal** for the first/last time; **ein für alle Mal** once and for all; **jedes Mal** every time; **jedes Mal, wenn** whenever

Mal|buch nt colouring book. **m~en** vt/i (haben) paint. **M~er** m -s,- painter. **M~erei** f -,-en painting. **M~erin** f -,-nen painter. **m~erisch** adj picturesque

Mallorca /ma'lɔrka, -'jɔrka/ nt -s Majorca

malnehmen† vt sep multiply (**mit** by)

Malz nt -es malt

Mama /'mama, ma'ma:/ f -s mummy

Mammut nt -s,-e & -s mammoth

mampfen vt 🔲 munch

man pron one, you; (die Leute)

people, they; **man sagt** they say, it is said

manch|e(r,s) pron many a; [so] **m~es Mal** many a time; **m~e Leute** some people ● (substantivisch) **m~er/m~e** many a man/woman; **m~e** pl some; (Leute) some people; (viele) many [people]; **m~es** some things; (vieles) many things. **m~erlei** inv adj various ● pron various things

manchmal adv sometimes

Mandant(in) m -en,-en (f -,-nen) (Jur) client

Mandarine f -,-n mandarin

Mandat nt -[e]s,-e mandate; (Jur) brief; (Pol) seat

Mandel f -,-n almond; (Anat) tonsil. **M~entzündung** f tonsillitis

Manege /ma'ne:ʒə/ f -,-n ring; (Reit-) arena

Mangel[1] m -s,˸ lack; (Knappheit) shortage; (Med) deficiency; (Fehler) defect

Mangel[2] f -,-n mangle

mangel|haft adj faulty, defective; (Sch) unsatisfactory. **m~n**[1] vi (haben) **es m~t an** (+ dat) there is a lack/(Knappheit) shortage of

mangeln[2] vt put through the mangle

Manie f -,-n mania

Manier f -,-en manner; **M~en** manners. **m~lich** adj well-mannered ● adv properly

Manifest nt -[e]s,-e manifesto

Maniküre f -,-n manicure; (Person) manicurist. **m~n** vt manicure

Manko nt -s,-s disadvantage; (Fehlbetrag) deficit

Mann m -[e]s,˸er man; (Ehe-) husband

Männchen nt -s,- little man; (Zool) male

Mannequin /'manəkɛ̃/ nt -s,-s model

männlich adj male; (Gram & fig) masculine; (mannhaft) manly; (Frau) mannish. **M~keit** f - masculinity; (fig) manhood

Mannschaft *f* -,-en team; (*Naut*) crew

Manöv|er *nt* -s,- manœuvre; (*Winkelzug*) trick. **m~rieren** *vt/i* (*haben*) manœuvre

Mansarde *f* -,-n attic room; (*Wohnung*) attic flat

Manschette *f* -,-n cuff. **M~nknopf** *m* cuff-link

Mantel *m* -s,: coat; overcoat

Manuskript *nt* -[e]s,-e manuscript

Mappe *f* -,-n folder; (*Akten-*) briefcase; (*Schul-*) bag

Märchen *nt* -s,- fairy-tales

Margarine *f* - margarine

Marienkäfer /ma'riːən-/ *m* ladybird

Marihuana *nt* -s marijuana

Marine *f* marine; (*Kriegs-*) navy. **m~blau** *adj* navy [blue]

marinieren *vt* marinade

Marionette *f* -,-n puppet, marionette

Mark[1] *f* -,- (*alte Währung*) mark; **drei M~** three marks

Mark[2] *nt* -[e]s (*Knochen-*) marrow (*Bot*)pith; (*Frucht-*) pulp

markant *adj* striking

Marke *f* -,-n token; (*rund*) disc; (*Erkennungs-*) tag; (*Brief-*) stamp; (*Lebensmittel-*) coupon; (*Spiel-*) counter; (*Markierung*) mark; (*Fabrikat*) make, (*Tabak-*) brand. **M~nartikel** *m* branded article

markieren *vt* mark; (🛈: *vortäuschen*) fake

Markise *f* -,-n awning

Markstück *nt* one-mark piece

Markt *m* -[e]s,:e market; (*M~-platz*) market-place. **M~forschung** *f* market research

Marmelade *f* -,-n jam; (*Orangen-*) marmalade

Marmor *m* -s marble

Marokko *nt* -s Morocco

Marone *f* -,-n [sweet] chestnut

Marsch *m* -[e]s,:e march. **m~** *int* (*Mil*) march!

Marschall *m* -s,:e marshal

marschieren *vi* (*sein*) march

Marter *f* -,-n torture. **m~n** *vt* torture

Märtyrer(in) *m* -s,- (*f* -,-nen) martyr

Marxismus *m* - Marxism

März *m* -,-e March

Marzipan *nt* -s marzipan

Masche *f* -,-n stitch; (*im Netz*) mesh; (🛈: *Trick*) dodge. **M~ndraht** *m* wire netting

Maschin|e *f* -,-n machine; (*Flugzeug*) plane; (*Schreib-*) typewriter; **M~e schreiben** type. **m~egeschrieben** *adj* typewritten, typed. **m~ell** *adj* machine ● *adv* by machine. **M~enbau** *m* mechanical engineering. **M~engewehr** *nt* machine-gun. **M~ist** *m* -en,-en machinist; (*Naut*) engineer

Masern *pl* measles *sg*

Maserung *f* -,-en [wood] grain

Maske *f* -,-n mask; (*Theat*) make-up

maskieren *vt* mask; **sich m~** dress up (**als** as)

maskulin *adj* masculine

Masochist *m* -en,-en masochist

Maß[1] *nt* -es,-e measure; (*Abmessung*) measurement; (*Grad*) degree; (*Mäßigung*) moderation; **in hohem Maße** to a high degree

Maß[2] *f* -,- (*SGer*) litre [of beer]

Massage /ma'saːʒə/ *f* -,-n massage

Massaker *nt* -s,- massacre

Maßband *nt* (*pl* -bänder) tapemeasure

Masse *f* -,-n mass; (*Culin*) mixture; (*Menschen-*) crowd; **eine M~ Arbeit** 🛈 masses of work. **m~nhaft** *adv* in huge quantities. **M~nproduktion** *f* mass production. **M~nvernichtungswaffen** *fpl* weapons of mass destruction. **m~nweise** *adv* in huge numbers

Masseu|r /ma'søːɐ̯/ *m* -s,-e masseur. **M~se** *f* -,-n masseuse

maß|gebend *adj* authoritative; (*einflussreich*) influential. **m~geblich** *adj* decisive. **m~geschneidert** *adj* made-to-measure

massieren vt massage

massig adj massive

mäßig adj moderate; (mittelmäßig) indifferent. **m~en** vt moderate; **sich m~en** moderate; (sich beherrschen) restrain oneself. **M~ung** f - moderation

massiv adj solid; (stark) heavy

Maß|krug m beer mug. **m~los** adj excessive; (grenzenlos) boundless; (äußerst) extreme. **M~nahme** f -,-n measure

Maßstab m scale; (Norm & fig) standard. **m~sgerecht, m~sgetreu** adj scale ● adv to scale

Mast[1] m -[e]s,-en pole; (Überland-) pylon; (Naut) mast

Mast[2] f - fattening

mästen vt fatten

masturbieren vi (haben) masturbate

Material nt -s,-ien material; (coll) materials pl. **M~ismus** m - materialism. **m~istisch** adj materialistic

Mathe f - 🔲 maths sg

Mathe|matik f - mathematics sg. **M~matiker** m -s,- mathematician. **m~matisch** adj mathematical

Matinee f -,-n (Theat) morning performance

Matratze f -,-n mattress

Matrose m -n,-n sailor

Matsch m -[e]s mud; (Schnee-) slush

matt adj weak; (gedämpft) dim; (glanzlos) dull; (Politur, Farbe) matt. **M~** nt -s (Schach) mate

Matte f -,-n mat

Mattglas nt frosted glass

Matura f - (Aust) ≈ A levels pl

Matura ▷ **Abitur**

Mauer f -,-n wall. **M~werk** nt masonry

Maul nt -[e]s, Mäuler (Zool) mouth; halts M~! 🔲 shut up! **M~- und Klauenseuche** f foot-and-mouth disease. **M~korb** m muzzle. **M~tier** nt mule. **M~wurf** m mole

Maurer m -s,- bricklayer

Maus f -,Mäuse mouse

Maut f -,-en (Aust) toll. **M~straße** f toll road

maximal adj maximum

Maximum nt -s,-ma maximum

Mayonnaise /majo'nɛːzə/ f -,-n mayonnaise

Mechan|ik /me'çaːnɪk/ f - mechanics sg; (Mechanismus) mechanism. **M~iker** m -s,- mechanic. **m~isch** adj mechanical. **m~isieren** vt mechanize. **M~ismus** m -,-men mechanism

meckern vi (haben) bleat; (🔲: nörgeln) grumble

Medaill|e /me'daljə/ f -,-n medal. **M~on** nt -s,-s medallion (Schmuck) locket

Medikament nt -[e]s,-e medicine

Medit|ation /-'tsjoːn/ f -,-en meditation. **m~ieren** vi (haben) meditate

Medium nt -s,-ien medium; **die Medien** the media

Medizin f -,-en medicine. **M~er** m -s,- doctor; (Student) medical student; **m~isch** adj medical; (heilkräftig) medicinal

Meer nt -[e]s,-e sea. **M~busen** m gulf. **M~enge** f strait. **M~esspiegel** m sea-level. **M~jungfrau** f mermaid. **M~rettich** m horseradish. **M~schweinchen** nt -s,- guinea-pig

Mehl nt -[e]s flour. **M~schwitze** f (Culin) roux

mehr pron & adv more; **nicht m~** no more; (zeitlich) no longer; **nichts m~** no more; (nichtsweiter) nothing else; **nie m~** never again. **m~eres** pron several things pl. **m~fach** adj multiple; (mehrmalig) repeated ● adv several times. **M~fahrtenkarte** f book of tickets. **M~heit** f -,-en majority. **m~malig** adj repeated. **m~mals** adv several times. **m~sprachig** adj multilingual. **M~wertsteuer** f value-added tax, VAT. **M~zahl** f majority; (Gram) plural. **M~zweck-** prefix multipurpose

meiden† vt avoid, shun

Meile *f* -,-n mile. **m～nweit** *adv* [for] miles

mein *poss pron* my. **m～e(r,s)** *poss pron* mine; **die M～en** *od* **m～en** *pl* my family *sg*

Meineid *m* perjury

meinen *vt* mean; (*glauben*) think; (*sagen*) say

mein|erseits *adv* for my part. **m～etwegen** *adv* for my sake; (*wegen mir*) because of me; (Ⅱ: *von mir aus*) as far as I'm concerned

Meinung *f* -,-en opinion; **jdm die M～ sagen** give s.o. a piece of one's mind. **M～sumfrage** *f* opinion poll

Meise *f* -,-n (*Zool*) tit

Meißel *m* -s,- chisel. **m～n** *vt/i* (*haben*) chisel

meist *adv* mostly; (*gewöhnlich*) usually. **m～e** *adj* **der/die/das m～e** most; **die m～en Leute** most people; **am m～en** [the] most ● *pron* **das m～e** most [of it]; **die m～en** most. **m～ens** *adv* mostly; (*gewöhnlich*) usually

Meister *m* -s,- master craftsman; (*Könner*) master; (*Sport*) champion. **m～n** *vt* master. **M～schaft** *f* -,-en mastery; (*Sport*) championship

meld|en *vt* report; (*anmelden*) register; (*ankündigen*) announce; **sich m～en** report (**bei** to); (*zum Militär*) enlist; (*freiwillig*) volunteer; (*Teleph*) answer; (*Sch*) put up one's hand; (*von sich hören lassen*) get in touch (**bei** with). **M～ung** *f* -,-en report; (*Anmeldung*) registration

melken† *vt* milk

Melodie *f* -,-n tune, melody

melodisch *adj* melodic; melodious

Melone *f* -,-n melon

Memoiren /me'mǫa:rən/ *pl* memoirs

Menge *f* -,-n amount, quantity; (*Menschen-*) crowd; (*Math*) set; **eine M～ Geld** a lot of money. **m～n** *vt* mix

Mensa *f* -,-sen (*Univ*) refectory

Mensch *m* -en,-en human being; **der M～** man; **die M～en** people;

jeder/kein **M～** everybody/nobody. **M～enaffe** *m* ape. **m～enfeindlich** *adj* antisocial. **M～enfresser** *m* -s,- cannibal; (*Zool*) man-eater. **m～enfreundlich** *adj* philanthropic. **M～enleben** *nt* human life; (*Lebenszeit*) lifetime. **m～enleer** *adj* deserted. **M～enmenge** *f* crowd. **M～enraub** *m* kidnapping. **M～enrechte** *ntpl* human rights. **m～enscheu** *adj* unsociable. **m～enwürdig** *adj* humane. **M～heit** *f* - **die M～heit** mankind, humanity. **m～lich** *adj* human; (*human*) humane. **M～lichkeit** *f* - humanity

Menstru|ation /-'tsio:n/ *f* - menstruation. **m～ieren** *vi* (*haben*) menstruate

Mentalität *f* -,-en mentality

Menü *nt* -s,-s menu; (*festes M～*) set meal

Meridian *m* -s,-e meridian

merk|bar *adj* noticeable. **M～blatt** *nt* [explanatory] leaflet. **m～en** *vt* notice; **sich** (*dat*) **etw m～en** remember sth. **M～mal** *nt* feature

merkwürdig *adj* odd, strange

Messe[1] *f* -,-n (*Relig*) mass; (*Comm*) [trade] fair

Messe[2] *f* -,-n (*Mil*) mess

messen† *vt/i* (*haben*) measure; (*ansehen*) look at; **[bei jdm] Fieber m～** take s.o.'s temperature; **sich mit jdm m～ können** be a match for s.o.

Messer *nt* -s,- knife

Messias *m* - Messiah

Messing *nt* -s brass

Messung *f* -,-en measurement

Metabolismus *m* - metabolism

Metall *nt* -s,-e metal. **m～isch** *adj* metallic

Metamorphose *f* -,-n metamorphosis

metaphorisch *adj* metaphorical

Meteor *m* -s,-e meteor. **M～ologie** *f* - meteorology

Meter *m & nt* -s,- metre. **M～maß** *nt* tape-measure

Method|e *f* -,-n method. **m～isch** *adj* methodical

m

Metropole f -,-n metropolis

Metzger m -s,- butcher. **M~ei** f -,-en butcher's shop

Meuterei f -,-en mutiny

meutern vi (haben) mutiny; (🔲: schimpfen) grumble

Mexikan|er(in) m -s,- (f -,-nen) Mexican. **m~isch** adj Mexican

Mexiko nt -s Mexico

miauen vi (haben) mew, miaow

mich pron (acc of ich) me; (reflexive) myself

Mieder nt -s,- bodice

Miene f -,-n expression

mies adj 🔲 lousy

Miet|e f -,-n rent; (Mietgebühr) hire charge; **zur M~e wohnen** live in rented accommodation. **m~en** vt rent (Haus, Zimmer); hire (Auto, Boot). **M~er(in)** m -s,- (f -,-nen) tenant. **m~frei** adj & adv rent-free. **M~shaus** nt block of rented flats. **M~vertrag** m lease. **M~wagen** m hire-car. **M~wohnung** f rented flat; (zu vermieten) flat to let

Migräne f -,-n migraine

Mikro|chip m microchip. **M~computer** m microcomputer. **M~film** m microfilm

Mikro|fon, M~phon nt -s,-e microphone. **M~skop** nt -s,-e microscope. **m~skopisch** adj microscopic

Mikrowelle f microwave. **M~nherd** m microwave oven

Milbe f -,-n mite

Milch f - milk. **M~glas** nt opal glass. **m~ig** adj milky. **M~mann** m (pl -männer) milkman. **M~straße** f Milky Way

mild adj mild; (nachsichtig) lenient. **M~e** f - mildness; leniency. **m~ern** vt make milder; (mäßigen) moderate; (lindern) ease; **sich m~ern** become milder; (sich mäßigen) moderate; (Schmerz:) ease; **m~ernde Umstände** mitigating circumstances

Milieu /mi'liø:/ nt -s,-s [social] environment

Militär nt -s army; (Soldaten) troops pl; **beim M~** in the army. **m~isch** adj military

Miliz f -,-en militia

Milliarde /mɪl'liardə/ f -,-n thousand million, billion

Milli|gramm nt milligram. **M~meter** m & nt millimetre. **M~meterpapier** nt graph paper

Million /mɪl'lio:n/ f -,-en million. **M~är** m -s,-e millionaire

Milz f - (Anat) spleen. **~brand** m anthrax

mimen vt (🔲: vortäuschen) act

Mimose f -,-n mimosa

Minderheit f -,-en minority

minderjährig adj (Jur) under-age. **M~e(r)** m/f (Jur) minor

mindern vt diminish; decrease

minderwertig adj inferior. **M~keit** f - inferiority. **M~keitskomplex** m inferiority complex

Mindest- prefix minimum. **m~e** adj & pron **der/die/das M~e** od **m~e** the least; **nicht im M~en** not in the least. **m~ens** adv at least. **M~lohn** m minimum wage. **M~maß** nt minimum

Mine f -,-n mine; (Bleistift-) lead; (Kugelschreiber-) refill. **M~nräumboot** nt minesweeper

Mineral nt -s,-e & -ien mineral. **m~isch** adj mineral. **M~wasser** nt mineral water

Miniatur f -,-en miniature

Minigolf nt miniature golf

minimal adj minimal

Minimum nt -s,-ma minimum

Mini|ster m, -s,- minister. **m~steriell** adj ministerial. **M~sterium** nt -s,-ien ministry

minus conj, adv & prep (+ gen) minus. **M~** nt - deficit; (Nachteil) disadvantage. **M~zeichen** nt minus [sign]

Minute f -,-n minute

mir pron (dat of ich) [to] me; (reflexive) myself

Misch|ehe f mixed marriage. **m~en** vt mix; blend (Tee, Kaffee); toss (Salat); shuffle (Karten); **sich**

m~en mix; (*Person;*) mingle (**unter**
+ *acc* with); **sich m~en in** (+ *acc*)
join in (*Gespräch*); meddle in (*Angelegenheit*) ● *vi* (*haben*) shuffle the
cards. **M~ling** *m* -s,-e half-caste.
M~ung *f* -,-en mixture; blend

miserabel *adj* abominable

missachten *vt* disregard

Miss|achtung *f* disregard.
M~bildung *f* deformity

missbilligen *vt* disapprove of

Miss|billigung *f* disapproval.
M~brauch *m* abuse

missbrauchen *vt* abuse; (*vergewaltigen*) rape

Misserfolg *m* failure

Misse|tat *f* misdeed. **M~täter** *m*
⊞ culprit

missfallen† *vi* (*haben*) displease
(*jdm s.o.*)

Miss|fallen *nt* -s displeasure; (*Miss-
billigung*) disapproval. **M~geburt** *f*
freak; (*fig*) monstrosity. **M~ge-
schick** *nt* mishap; (*Unglück*) misfortune

miss|glücken *vi* (*sein*) fail.
m~gönnen *vt* begrudge

misshandeln *vt* ill-treat

Misshandlung *f* ill-treatment

Mission *f* -,-en mission

Missionar(in) *m* -s,-e (*f* -,-nen)
missionary

Missklang *m* discord

misslingen† *vi* (*sein*) fail; **es miss-
lang ihr** she failed. **M~** *nt* -s failure

Missmut *m* ill humour. **m~ig** *adj*
morose

missraten† *vi* (*sein*) turn out badly

Miss|stand *m* abuse; (*Zustand*) un-
desirable state of affairs. **M~stim-
mung** *f* discord; (*Laune*) bad mood

misstrauen *vi* (*haben*) **jdm/etw
m~** mistrust s.o./sth; (*Argwohn
hegen*) distrust s.o./sth

Misstrau|en *nt* -s mistrust; (*Arg-
wohn*) distrust. **M~ensvotum** *nt*
vote of no confidence. **m~isch** *adj*
distrustful; (*argwöhnisch*) suspicious

Miss|verständnis *nt* misunder-
standing. **m~verstehen**† *vt* misun-

derstand. **M~wirtschaft** *f* misman-
agement

Mist *m* -[e]s manure; ⊞ rubbish

Mistel *f* -,-n mistletoe

Misthaufen *m* dungheap

mit *prep* (+ *dat*) with; (*sprechen*) to;
(*mittels*) by; (*inklusive*) including; (*bei*)
at; **mit Bleistift** in pencil; **mit lauter
Stimme** in a loud voice; **mit drei
Jahren** at the age of three ● *adv*
(*auch*) as well; **mit anfassen** (*fig*)
lend a hand

Mitarbeit *f* collaboration. **m~en** *vi
sep* collaborate (**an** + *dat* on).
M~er(in) *m*(*f*) collaborator; (*Kollege*) colleague; employee

Mitbestimmung *f*
co-determination

mitbringen† *vt sep* bring [along]

miteinander *adv* with each other

Mitesser *m* (*Med*) blackhead

mitfahren† *vi sep* (*sein*) go/come
along; **mit jdm m~** go with s.o.;
(*mitgenommen werden*) be given a lift
by s.o.

mitfühlen *vi sep* (*haben*) sympathize

mitgeben† *vt sep* **jdm etw m~**
give s.o. sth to take with him

Mitgefühl *nt* sympathy

mitgehen† *vi sep* (*sein*) **mit jdm
m~** go with s.o.

Mitgift *f* -,-en dowry

Mitglied *nt* member. **M~schaft** *f* -
membership

mithilfe *prep* (+ *gen*) with the aid of

Mithilfe *f* assistance

mitkommen† *vi sep* (*sein*) come
[along] too; (*fig: folgen können*) keep
up; (*verstehen*) follow

Mitlaut *m* consonant

Mitleid *nt* pity, compassion; **M~ erregend** pitiful. **m~ig** *adj* pitying;
(*mitfühlend*) compassionate. **m~slos**
adj pitiless

mitmachen *v sep* ● *vt* take part in;
(*erleben*) go through ● *vi* (*haben*)
join in

Mitmensch *m* fellow man

mitnehmen† *vt sep* take along;
(*mitfahren lassen*) give a lift to; (*fig:*

schädigen) affect badly; (erschöpfen) exhaust; **'zum M~'** 'to take away'

mitreden vi sep (haben) join in [the conversation]; (mit entscheiden) have a say (**bei** in)

mitreißen† vt sep sweep along; (fig: begeistern) carry away; **m~d** rousing

mitsamt prep (+ dat) together with

mitschreiben† vt sep (haben) take down

Mitschuld f partial blame. **m~ig** adj **m~ig sein** be partly to blame

Mitschüler(in) m(f) fellow pupil

mitspielen vi sep (haben) join in; (Theat) be in the cast; (beitragen) play a part

Mittag m midday, noon; (Mahlzeit) lunch; (Pause) lunch-break; **heute/ gestern M~** at lunch-time today/ yesterday; **[zu] M~ essen** have lunch. **M~essen** nt lunch. **m~s** adv at noon; (als Mahlzeit) for lunch; **um 12 Uhr m~s** at noon. **M~spause** f lunch-hour; (Pause) lunch-break. **M~sschlaf** m after-lunch nap

Mittäter|(in) m(f) accomplice. **M~schaft** f - complicity

Mitte f -,-n middle; (Zentrum) centre; **die goldene M~** the golden mean; **M~ Mai** in mid-May; **in unserer M~** in our midst

mitteil|en vt sep **jdm etw m~en** tell s.o. sth; (amtlich) inform s.o. of sth. **M~ung** f -,-en communication; (Nachricht) piece of news

Mittel nt -s,- means sg; (Heil-) remedy; (Medikament) medicine; (M~wert) mean; (Durchschnitt) average; **M~** pl (Geld-) funds, resources. **m~** pred adj medium; (m~mäßig) middling. **M~alter** nt Middle Ages pl. **m~alterlich** adj medieval. **M~ding** nt (fig) cross. **m~europäisch** adj Central European. **M~finger** m middle finger. **m~los** adj destitute. **m~mäßig** adj middling; [**nur**] **m~mäßig** mediocre. **M~meer** nt Mediterranean. **M~punkt** m centre; (fig) centre of attention

mittels prep (+ gen) by means of

Mittel|schule f = Realschule. **M~smann** m (pl -männer) intermediary, go-between. **M~stand** m middle class. **m~ste(r,s)** adj middle. **M~streifen** m (Auto) central reservation. **M~stürmer** m centreforward. **M~welle** f medium wave. **M~wort** nt (pl -wörter) participle

mitten adv **m~ in/auf** (dat/acc) in the middle of. **m~durch** adv [right] through the middle

Mitternacht f midnight

mittler|e(r,s) adj middle; (Größe, Qualität) medium; (durchschnittlich) mean, average. **m~weile** adv meanwhile; (seitdem) by now

Mittwoch m -s,-e Wednesday. **m~s** adv on Wednesdays

mitunter adv now and again

mitwirk|en vi sep (haben) take part; (helfen) contribute. **M~ung** f participation

mix|en vt mix. **M~er** m -s,- (Culin) liquidizer, blender

mobb|en vt bully, harass. **M~ing** nt -s bullying, harassment

Möbel pl furniture sg. **M~stück** nt piece of furniture. **M~wagen** m removal van

Mobiliar nt -s furniture

mobilisier|en vt mobilize. **M~ung** f - mobilization

Mobil|machung f - mobilization. **M~telefon** nt mobile phone

möblier|en vt furnish; **m~tes Zimmer** furnished room

mochte, möchte s. **mögen**

Mode f -,-n fashion; **M~ sein** be fashionable

Modell nt -s,-e model. **m~ieren** vt model

Modenschau f fashion show

Modera|tor m -s,-en, **M~torin** f -,-nen (TV) presenter

modern adj modern; (modisch) fashionable. **m~isieren** vt modernize

Mode|schmuck m costume jewellery. **M~schöpfer** m fashion designer

modisch adj fashionable
Modistin f -,-nen milliner
modrig adj musty
modulieren vt modulate
Mofa nt -s,-s moped
mogeln vi (haben) ▯ cheat

---

mögen†

● transitive verb

····➤ like. **sie mag ihn sehr [gern]** she likes him very much. **möchten Sie ein Glas Wein?** would you like a glass of wine? **lieber mögen** prefer. **ich möchte lieber Tee** I would prefer tea

● auxiliary verb

····➤ (wollen) want to. **sie mochte nicht länger bleiben** she didn't want to stay any longer. **ich möchte ihn [gerne] sprechen** I'd like to speak to him. **möchtest du nach Hause?** do you want to go home? or would you like to go home?

····➤ (Vermutung, Möglichkeit) may. **ich mag mich irren** I may be wrong. **wer/was mag das sein?** whoever/whatever can it be? **[das] mag sein** that may well be. **mag kommen, was da will** come what may

---

möglich adj possible; **alle m∼en** all sorts of; **über alles M∼e sprechen** talk about all sorts of things. **m∼erweise** adv possibly. **M∼keit** f -,-en possibility. **M∼keitsform** f subjunctive. **m∼st** adv if possible; **m∼st viel** as much as possible
Mohn m -s poppy
Möhre, **Mohrrübe** f -,-n carrot
Mokka m -s mocha; (Geschmack) coffee
Molch m -[e]s,-e newt
Mole f -,-n (Naut) mole
Molekül nt -s,-e molecule
Molkerei f -,-en dairy
Moll nt - (Mus) minor
mollig adj cosy; (warm) warm; (rundlich) plump
Moment m -s,-e moment;

M∼[mal]! just a moment! **m∼an** adj momentary; (gegenwärtig) at the moment
Monarch m -en,-en monarch. **M∼ie** f -,-n monarchy
Monat m -s,-e month. **m∼elang** adv for months. **m∼lich** adj & adv monthly
Mönch m -[e]s,-e monk
Mond m -[e]s,-e moon
mondän adj fashionable
Mond|finsternis f lunar eclipse. **m∼hell** adj moonlit. **M∼sichel** f crescent moon. **M∼schein** m moonlight
monieren vt criticize
Monitor m -s,-en (Techn) monitor
Monogramm nt -s,-e monogram
Mono|log m -s,-e monologue. **M∼pol** nt -s,-e monopoly. **m∼ton** adj monotonous
Monster nt -s,- monster
Monstrum nt -s,-stren monster
Monsun m -s,-e monsoon
Montag m Monday
Montage /mɔnˈtaːʒə/ f -,-n fitting; (Zusammenbau) assembly; (Film-) editing; (Kunst) montage
montags adv on Mondays
Montanindustrie f coal and steel industry
Monteur /mɔnˈtøːɐ̯/ m -s,-e fitter. **M∼anzug** m overalls pl
montieren vt fit; (zusammenbauen) assemble
Monument nt -[e]s,-e monument. **m∼al** a monumental
Moor nt -[e]s,-e bog; (Heide-) moor
Moos nt es,-e moss **m∼ig** adj mossy
Moped nt -s,-s moped
Mopp m -s,-s mop
Moral f - morals pl, (Selbstvertrauen) morale; (Lehre) moral. **m∼isch** adj moral
Mord m -[e]s,-e murder, (Pol) assassination. **M∼anschlag** m murder/assassination attempt. **m∼en** vt/i (haben) murder, kill

Mörder m -s,- murderer, (Pol) assassin. **M~in** f -,-nen murderess. **m~isch** adj murderous; (🗵: schlimm) dreadful

morgen adv tomorrow; **m~ Abend** tomorrow evening

Morgen m -s,- morning; (Maß) ≈ acre; **am M~** in the morning; **heute/Montag M~** this/Monday morning. **M~dämmerung** f dawn. **M~rock** m dressing-gown. **M~rot** nt red sky in the morning. **m~s** adj in the morning

morgig adj tomorrow's; **der m~e Tag** tomorrow

Morphium nt -s morphine

morsch adj rotten

Morsealphabet nt Morse code

Mörtel m -s mortar

Mosaik /moza'i:k/ nt -s,-e[n] mosaic

Moschee f -,-n mosque

Mosel f - Moselle

Moskau nt -s Moscow

Moskito m -s,-s mosquito

Moslem m -s,-s Muslim

Motiv nt -s,-e motive; (Kunst) motif

Motor /'mo:tor, mo'to:ɐ̯/ m -s,-en engine; (Elektro-) motor. **M~boot** nt motor boat

motorisieren vt motorize

Motor|rad nt motor cycle. **M~roller** m motor scooter

Motte f -,-n moth. **M~nkugel** f mothball

Motto nt -s,-s motto

Möwe f -,-n gull

Mücke f -,-n gnat; (kleine) midge; (Stech-) mosquito

müd|e adj tired; **es m~e sein** be tired (etw zu tun of doing sth). **M~igkeit** f - tiredness

muffig adj musty; (🗵: mürrisch) grumpy

Mühe f -,-n effort; (Aufwand) trouble; **sich** (dat) **M~ geben** make an effort; (sich bemühen) try; nicht der **M~ wert** not worth while; mit **M~ und Not** with great difficulty; (gerade noch) only just. **m~los** adj effortless

muhen vi (haben) moo

Mühl|e f -,-n mill; (Kaffee-) grinder. **M~stein** m millstone

Müh|sal f -,-e (literarisch) toil; (Mühe) trouble. **m~sam** adj laborious; (beschwerlich) difficult

Mulde f -,-n hollow

Müll m -s refuse. **M~abfuhr** f refuse collection

Mullbinde f gauze bandage

Mülleimer m waste bin; (Mülltonne) dustbin

Müller m -s,- miller

Müll|halde f [rubbish] dump. **M~schlucker** m refuse chute. **M~tonne** f dustbin

multi|national adj multinational. **M~plikation** f -,-en multiplication. **m~plizieren** vt multiply

Mumie /'mu:miə/ f -,-n mummy

Mumm m -s 🗵 energy

Mumps m - mumps

Mund m -[e]s,ːer mouth; **ein M~ voll Suppe** a mouthful of soup; **halt den M~!** 🗵 shut up! **M~art** f dialect. **m~artlich** adj dialect

Mündel nt & m -s,- (Jur) ward. **m~sicher** adj gilt-edged

münden vi (sein) flow/(Straße:) lead (in + acc into)

Mundharmonika f mouth-organ

mündig adj **m~ sein/werden** (Jur) be/come of age. **M~keit** f - (Jur) majority

mündlich adj verbal; **m~e Prüfung** oral

Mündung f -,-en (Fluss-) mouth; (Gewehr-) muzzle

Mundwinkel m corner of the mouth

Munition /-'tsio:n/ f - ammunition

munkeln vt/i (haben) talk (von of); **es wird gemunkelt** rumour has it (dass that)

Münster nt -s,- cathedral

munter adj lively; (heiter) merry; **m~ sein** (wach) be wide awake ; **gesund und m~** fit and well

Münz|e *f* -,-n coin; (*M~stätte*) mint. **M~fernsprecher** *m* payphone

mürbe *adj* crumbly; (*Obst*) mellow; (*Fleisch*) tender. **M~teig** *m* short pastry

Murmel *f* -,-n marble

murmeln *vt/i* (*haben*) murmur; (*undeutlich*) mumble

Murmeltier *nt* marmot

murren *vt/i* (*haben*) grumble

mürrisch *adj* surly

Mus *nt* -es purée

Muschel *f* -,-n mussel; [sea] shell

Museum /mu'ze:ʊm/ *nt* -s,-seen museum

Musik *f* - music. **m~alisch** *adj* musical

Musiker(in) *m* -s,- (*f* -,-nen) musician

Musik|instrument *nt* musical instrument. **M~kapelle** *f* band. **M~pavillon** *m* bandstand

musisch *adj* artistic

musizieren *vi* (*haben*) make music

Muskat *m* -[e]s nutmeg

Muskel *m* -s,-n muscle. **M~kater** *m* stiff and aching muscles *pl*

muskulös *adj* muscular

Muslim(in) *m* -s,-e (*f* -,-nen) Muslim. **m~isch** *adj* Muslim

muss *s.* müssen

Muße *f* - leisure

---

müssen†

● *auxiliary verb*

····▸ (*gezwungen/verpflichtet/notwendig sein*) have to; must. **er muss es tun** he must *or* has to do it; Ⓘ he's got to do it. **ich musste schnell fahren** I had to drive fast. **das muss 1968 gewesen sein** it must have been in 1968. **er muss gleich hier sein** he must be here at any moment

····▸ (*in negativen Sätzen; ungezwungen*) **sie muss es nicht tun** she does not have to *or* Ⓘ she hasn't got to do it. **es musste nicht so sein** it didn't have to be like that

---

····▸ **es müsste** (*sollte*) **doch möglich sein** it ought to *or* should be possible. **du müsstest es mal versuchen** you ought to *or* should try it

● *intransitive verb*

····▸ (*irgendwohin gehen müssen*) have to *or* must go. **ich muss nach Hause/zum Arzt** I have to *or* must go home/to the doctor. **ich musste mal [aufs Klo]** I had to go [to the loo]

---

müßig *adj* idle

musste, müsste *s.* müssen

Muster *nt* -s,- pattern; (*Probe*) sample; (*Vorbild*) model. **M~beispiel** *nt* typical example; (*Vorbild*) perfect example. **m~gültig, m~haft** *adj* exemplary. **m~n** *vt* eye; (*inspizieren*) inspect. **M~ung** *f* -,-en inspection; (*Mil*) medical; (*Muster*) pattern

Mut *m* -[e]s courage; **jdm Mut machen** encourage s.o.; **zu M~e sein** feel like it; *s.* zumute

mut|ig *adj* courageous. **m~los** *adj* despondent

mutmaßen *vt* presume; (*Vermutungen anstellen*) speculate

Mutprobe *f* test of courage

Mutter[1] *f* -,⸚ mother

Mutter[2] *f* -,-n (*Techn*) nut

Muttergottes *f* - madonna

Mutterland *nt* motherland

mütterlich *adj* maternal; (*fürsorglich*) motherly. **m~erseits** *adv* on one's/the mother's side

Mutter|mal *nt* birthmark; (*dunkel*) mole. **M~schaft** *f* - motherhood. **m~seelenallein** *adj & adv* all alone. **M~sprache** *f* mother tongue. **M~tag** *m* Mother's Day

Mütze *f* -,-n cap; **wollene M~** woolly hat

MwSt. *abbr* (**Mehrwertsteuer**) VAT

mysteriös *adj* mysterious

Mystik /'mʏstɪk/ *f* - mysticism

myth|isch *adj* mythical. **M~ologie** *f* - mythology

Nn

na *int* well; **na gut** all right then

Nabel *m* **-s,-** navel. **N~schnur** *f* umbilical cord

---

nach

● **preposition** (+ *dative*)

····➤ (*räumlich*) to. **nach London fahren** go to London. **der Zug nach München** the train to Munich; (*noch nicht abgefahren*) the train for Munich; the Munich train. **nach Hause gehen** go home. **nach Osten [zu]** eastwards; towards the east

····➤ (*zeitlich*) after; (*Uhrzeit*) past. **nach fünf Minuten/dem Frühstück** after five minutes/breakfast. **zehn [Minuten] nach zwei** ten [minutes] past two

····➤ ([*räumliche und zeitliche*] *Reihenfolge*) after. **nach Ihnen/dir!** after you!

····➤ (*mit bestimmten Verben*) for. **greifen/streben/schicken nach** grasp/strive/send for

····➤ (*gemäß*) according to. **nach der neuesten Mode gekleidet** dressed in [accordance with] the latest fashion. **dem Gesetz nach** in accordance with the law; by law. **nach meiner Ansicht** *od* **Meinung, meiner Ansicht** *od* **Meinung nach** in my view or opinion. **nach etwas schmecken/riechen** taste/smell of sth

● **adverb**

····➤ (*zeitlich*) **nach und nach** little by little; gradually. **nach wie vor** still

---

nachahm|en *vt sep* imitate. **N~ung** *f* **-,-en** imitation

Nachbar|(in) *m* **-n,-n** (*f* **-,-nen**) neighbour. **N~haus** *nt* house next door. **n~lich** *adj* neighbourly;

(*Nachbar-*) neighbouring. **N~schaft** *f* - neighbourhood

nachbestell|en *vt sep* reorder. **N~ung** *f* repeat order

nachbild|en *vt sep* copy, reproduce. **N~ung** *f* copy, reproduction

nachdatieren *vt sep* backdate

nachdem *conj* after; **je n~** it depends

nachdenk|en† *vi sep* (*haben*) think (**über** + *acc* about). **n~lich** *adj* thoughtful

nachdrücklich *adj* emphatic

nacheinander *adv* one after the other

Nachfahre *m* **-n,-n** descendant

Nachfolg|e *f* succession. **N~er(in)** *m* **-s,-** (*f* **-,-nen**) successor

nachforsch|en *vi sep* (*haben*) make enquiries. **N~ung** *f* enquiry

Nachfrage *f* (*Comm*) demand. **n~n** *vi sep* (*haben*) enquire

nachfüllen *vt sep* refill

nachgeben† *v sep* ● *vi* (*haben*) give way; (*sich fügen*) give in, yield ● *vt* **jdm Suppe n~** give s.o. more soup

Nachgebühr *f* surcharge

nachgehen† *vi sep* (*sein*) (*Uhr:*) be slow; **jdm/etw n~** follow s.o./something; follow up (*Spur, Angelegenheit*); pursue (*Angelegenheit*)

Nachgeschmack *m* after-taste

nachgiebig *adj* indulgent; (*gefällig*) compliant. **N~keit** *f* - indulgence; compliance

nachgrübeln *vi sep* (*haben*) ponder (**über** + *acc* on)

nachhaltig *adj* lasting

nachhelfen† *vi sep* (*haben*) help

nachher *adv* later; (*danach*) afterwards; **bis n~!** see you later!

Nachhilfeunterricht *m* coaching

Nachhinein *adv* **im N~** afterwards

nachhinken *vi sep* (*sein*) (*fig*) lag behind

nachholen *vt sep* (*später holen*) fetch later; (*mehr holen*) get more; (*später machen*) do later; (*aufholen*) catch up on

Nachkomme *m* -n,-n descendant.
n~n† *vi sep* (*sein*) follow [later],
come later; **etw** (*dat*) **n~n** (*fig*)
comply with (*Bitte*); carry out
(*Pflicht*). **N~nschaft** *f* - descendants
pl, progeny

Nachkriegszeit *f* post-war period

Nachlass *m* -es,:̈e discount; (*Jur*)
[deceased's] estate

nachlassen† *v sep* ● *vi* (*haben*) decrease; (*Regen, Hitze*:) let up;
(*Schmerz*:) ease; (*Sturm*:) abate;
(*Augen, Leistungen*:) deteriorate ● *vt*
etw vom Preis n~ take sth off the
price

nachlässig *adj* careless; (*leger*) casual; (*unordentlich*) sloppy. **N~keit** *f* -
carelessness; sloppiness

nachlesen† *vt sep* look up

nachlöse|n *vi sep* (*haben*) pay one's
fare on the train/on arrival.
N~schalter *m* excess-fare office

nachmachen *vt sep* (*später machen*) do later; (*imitieren*) imitate,
copy; (*fälschen*) forge

Nachmittag *m* afternoon; **heute/
gestern N~** this/yesterday afternoon. **n~s** *adv* in the afternoon

Nachnahme *f* **etw per N~** schi-
cken send sth cash on delivery *or*
COD

Nachname *m* surname

Nachporto *nt* excess postage

nachprüfen *vt sep* check, verify

Nachricht *f* -,-en [piece of] news
sg; **N~en** news *sg*; **eine N~** hinter-
lassen leave a message; **jdm N~
geben** inform s.o. **N~endienst** *m*
(*Mil*) intelligence service

nachrücken *vi sep* (*sein*) move up

Nachruf *m* obituary

nachsagen *vt sep* repeat (**jdm** after
s.o.); **jdm Schlechtes/Gutes n~**
speak ill/well of s.o.

Nachsaison *f* late season

nachschicken *vt sep* (*später schicken*) send later; (*hinterher-*) send
after (**jdm** s.o.); send on (*Post*) (**jdm**
to s.o.)

nachschlagen† *v sep* ● *vt* look up

● *vi* (*haben*) **in einem Wörterbuch
n~en** consult a dictionary; **jdm
n~en** take after s.o.

Nachschrift *f* transcript; (*Nachsatz*)
postscript

Nachschub *m* (*Mil*) supplies *pl*

nachsehen† *v sep* ● *vt* (*prüfen*)
check; (*nachschlagen*) look up; (*hin-
wegsehen über*) overlook ● *vi* (*haben*)
have a look; (*prüfen*) check; **im Wörterbuch n~** consult a dictionary

nachsenden† *vt sep* forward (*Post*)
(**jdm** to s.o.); '**bitte n~**' 'please forward'

nachsichtig *adj* forbearing; lenient;
indulgent

Nachsilbe *f* suffix

nachsitzen† *vi sep* (*haben*) **n~
müssen** be kept in [after school];
jdn n~ lassen give s.o. detention.
N~ *nt* -s (*Sch*) detention

Nachspeise *f* dessert, sweet

nachsprechen† *vt sep* repeat (**jdm**
after s.o.)

nachspülen *vt sep* rinse

nächst /-çst/ *prep* (+ *dat*) next to.
n~beste(r,s) *adj* first [available];
(*zweitbeste*) next best. **n~e(r,s)** *adj*
next; (*nächstgelegene*) nearest; (*Ver-
wandte*) closest; **in n~er Nähe** close
by; **am n~en sein** be nearest *or*
closest ● *pron* **der/die/das N~e**
(**n~e**) the next; **der N~c** (**n~e**)
bitte next please; **als N~es** (**n~es**)
next; **fürs N~e** (**n~e**) for the time
being. **N~e(r)** *m* fellow man

nachstehend *adj* following ● *adv*
below

Nächst|enliebe *f* charity. **n~ens**
adv shortly. **n~gelegen** *adj* nearest

nachsuchen *vi sep* (*haben*) search;
n~ um request

Nacht *f* -,:̈e night; **über/bei N~**
overnight/at night; **morgen N~** tomorrow night; **heute N~** tonight;
(*letzte Nacht*) last night; **gestern N~**
last night; (*vorletzte Nacht*) the night
before last. **N~dienst** *m* night duty

Nachteil *m* disadvantage; **zum N~**
to the detriment (*gen* of)

n

nachschlagen† *v sep* ● *vt* look up

Nacht|falter m moth. **N~hemd** nt
night-dress; (*Männer-*) night-shirt
Nachtigall f -,-en nightingale
Nachtisch m dessert
Nachtklub m night-club
nächtlich adj nocturnal, night
Nacht|lokal nt night-club. **N~mahl**
nt (*Aust*) supper
Nachtrag m postscript; (*Ergänzung*)
supplement. **n~en†** vt sep add; **jdm
etw n~en** (*fig*) bear a grudge
against s.o. for sth. **n~end** adj vindictive; **n~end sein** bear grudges
nachträglich adj subsequent, later;
(*verspätet*) belated ● adv later; (*nachher*) afterwards; (*verspätet*) belatedly
Nacht|ruhe f night's rest; **ange-
nehme N~ruhe!** sleep well! **n~s**
adv at night; **2 Uhr n~s** 2 o'clock in
the morning. **N~schicht** f night-
shift. **N~tisch** m bedside table.
N~tischlampe f bedside lamp.
N~topf m chamber-pot. **N~wäch-
ter** m night-watchman. **N~zeit** f
night-time
Nachuntersuchung f check-up
Nachwahl f by-election
Nachweis m -es,-e proof. **n~bar**
adj demonstrable. **n~en†** vt sep
prove; (*aufzeigen*) show; (*vermitteln*)
give details of; **jdm nichts n~en
können** have no proof against s.o.
Nachwelt f posterity
Nachwirkung f after-effect
Nachwuchs m new generation; (▣:
Kinder) offspring. **N~spieler** m
young player
nachzahlen vt/i sep (*haben*) pay
extra; (*später zahlen*) pay later; **Steuern n~** pay tax arrears
nachzählen vt/i sep (*haben*) count
again; (*prüfen*) check
Nachzahlung f extra/later payment; (*Gehalts-*) back-payment
nachzeichnen vt sep copy
Nachzügler m -s,- late-comer; (*Zu-
rückgebliebener*) straggler
Nacken m -s,- nape or back of the
neck
nackt adj naked; (*bloß, kahl*) bare;

(*Wahrheit*) plain. **N~heit** f - naked-
ness, nudity. **N~kultur** f nudism.
N~schnecke f slug
Nadel f -,-n needle; (*Häkel-*) hook;
(*Schmuck-, Hut-*) pin. **N~arbeit** f
needlework. **N~baum** m conifer.
N~stich m stitch; (*fig*) pinprick.
N~wald m coniferous forest
Nagel m -s,̈ nail. **N~haut** f cuticle.
N~lack m nail varnish. **n~n** vt nail.
n~neu adj brand-new
nagen vt/i (*haben*) gnaw (**an** + *dat*
at); **n~d** (*fig*) nagging
Nagetier nt rodent
nah adj, adv & prep = nahe
Näharbeit f sewing
Nahaufnahme f close-up
nahe adj nearby; (*zeitlich*) imminent;
(*eng*) close; **der N~ Osten** the Middle East; **in n~r Zukunft** in the near
future; **von n~m** [from] close to;
n~ sein be close (*dat* to) ● adv near,
close; (*verwandt*) closely; **n~ an** (+
acc/dat) near [to], close to; **n~
daran sein, etw zu tun** nearly do
sth; **n~ liegen** be close; (*fig*) be
highly likely; **n~ legen** (*fig*) recommend (**dat** to); **jdm n~ legen, etw
zu tun** urge s.o. to do sth; **jdm n~
gehen** (*fig*) affect s.o. deeply; **jdm
zu n~ treten** (*fig*) offend s.o. ● prep
(+ *dat*) near [to], close to
Nähe f - nearness, proximity; **aus der
N~** [from] close to; **in der N~** near
or close by
nahe|gehen* vi sep (*sein*) **n~
gehen**, s. **nahe. n~legen*** vt sep
n~ legen, s. **nahe. n~liegen*** vi sep
(*haben*) **n~ liegen**, s. **nahe**
nähen vt/i (*haben*) sew; (*anfertigen*)
make; (*Med*) stitch [up]
näher adj closer; (*Weg*) shorter; (*Einzelheiten*) further ● adv closer; (*ge-
nauer*) more closely; **n~ kommen**
come closer; (*fig*) get closer (**dat** to);
sich n~ erkundigen make further
enquiries; **n~an** (+ *acc/dat*) nearer
[to], closer to ● prep (+ *dat*) nearer
[to], closer to. **N~e[s]** nt [further]
details pl. **n~n (sich)** vr approach
nahezu adv almost

Nähgarn *nt* [sewing] cotton

Nahkampf *m* close combat

Näh|maschine *f* sewing machine. **N~nadel** *f* sewing-needle

nähren *vt* feed; (*fig*) nurture

nahrhaft *adj* nutritious

Nährstoff *m* nutrient

Nahrung *f* - food, nourishment. **N~smittel** *nt* food

Nährwert *m* nutritional value

Naht *f* -,⸚e seam; (*Med*) suture. **n~los** *adj* seamless

Nahverkehr *m* local service

Nähzeug *nt* sewing; (*Zubehör*) sewing kit

naiv /naˈiːf/ *adj* naïve. **N~ität** *f* - naïvety

Name *m* -ns,-n name; **im N~n** (+ *gen*) in the name of; (*handeln*) on behalf of. **n~nlos** *adj* nameless; (*unbekannt*) unknown, anonymous. **N~nstag** *m* name-day. **N~nsvetter** *m* namesake. **N~nszug** *m* signature. **n~ntlich** *adv* by name; (*besonders*) especially

namhaft *adj* noted; (*ansehnlich*) considerable; **n~ machen** name

nämlich *adv* (*und zwar*) namely; (*denn*) because

Nanotechnologie *f* nanotechnology

nanu *int* hallo

Napf *m* -[e]s,⸚e bowl

Narbe *f* -,-n scar

Narkose *f* -,-n general anaesthetic. **N~arzt** *m* anaesthetist. **N~mittel** *nt* anaesthetic

Narr *m* -en,-en fool; **zum N~en halten** make a fool of. **n~en** *vt* fool

Närr|in *f* -,-nen fool. **n~isch** *adj* foolish; (**🛈**: *verrückt*) crazy (**auf** + *acc* about)

Narzisse *f* -,-n narcissus

naschen *vt/i* (*haben*) nibble (**an** + *dat* at)

Nase *f* -,-n nose

näseln *vi* (*haben*) speak through one's nose; **n~d** nasal

Nasen|bluten *nt* -s nosebleed. **N~loch** *nt* nostril

Nashorn *nt* rhinoceros

nass *adj* wet

Nässe *f* - wet; wetness. **n~n** *vt* wet

Nation /naˈtsi̯oːn/ *f* -,-en nation. **n~al** *adj* national. **N~alhymne** *f* national anthem. **N~alismus** *m* - nationalism. **N~alität** *f* -,-en nationality. **N~alspieler** *m* international

---

Nationalrat In Austria the *Nationalrat* is the Federal Assembly's lower house, whose 183 members are elected for four years under a system of proportional representation. In Switzerland, the *Nationalrat* is made up of 200 representatives. *i*

Natrium *nt* -s sodium

Natron *nt* -s **doppeltkohlensaures N~** bicarbonate of soda

Natter *f* -,-n snake; (*Gift-*) viper

Natur *f* -,-en nature; **von N~ aus** by nature. **n~alisieren** *vt* naturalize. **N~alisierung** *f* -,-en naturalization

Naturell *nt* -s,-e disposition

Natur|erscheinung *f* natural phenomenon. **N~forscher** *m* naturalist. **N~heilkunde** *f* natural medicine. **N~kunde** *f* natural history

natürlich *adj* natural ● *adv* naturally; (*selbstverständlich*) of course. **N~keit** *f* - naturalness

natur|rein *adj* pure. **N~schutz** *m* nature conservation; **unter N~schutz stehen** be protected. **N~schutzgebiet** *nt* nature reserve. **N~wissenschaft** *f* [natural] science. **N~wissenschaftler** *m* scientist

nautisch *adj* nautical

Navigation /-ˈtsi̯oːn/ *f* - navigation

Nazi *m* -s,-s Nazi

n.Chr. *abbr* (**nach Christus**) AD

Nebel *m* -s,- fog; (*leicht*) mist

neben *prep* (+ *dat/acc*) next to, beside; (+ *dat*) (*außer*) apart from. **n~an** *adv* next door

Neben|anschluss *m* (*Teleph*) ex-

n

tension. **N~ausgaben** *fpl* incidental expenses

nebenb<u>ei</u> *adv* in addition; (*beiläufig*) casually

N<u>e</u>ben|bemerkung *f* passing remark. **N~beruf** *m* second job

nebeneinander *adv* next to each other, side by side

N<u>e</u>ben|eingang *m* side entrance. **N~fach** *nt* (*Univ*) subsidiary subject. **N~fluss** *m* tributary

nebenh<u>e</u>r *adv* in addition

nebenh<u>i</u>n *adv* casually

N<u>e</u>ben|höhle *f* sinus. **N~kosten** *pl* additional costs. **N~produkt** *nt* by-product. **N~rolle** *f* supporting role; (*Kleine*) minor role. **N~sache** *f* unimportant matter. **n~sächlich** *adj* unimportant. **N~satz** *m* subordinate clause. **N~straße** *f* minor road; (*Seiten-*) side street. **N~wirkung** *f* side-effect. **N~zimmer** *nt* room next door

neblig *adj* foggy; (*leicht*) misty

neck|en *vt* tease. **N~erei** *f* - teasing. **n~isch** *adj* teasing

Neffe *m* -n,-n nephew

negativ *adj* negative. **N~** *nt* -s,-e (*Phot*) negative

Neger *m* -s,- Negro

nehmen† *vt* take (*dat* from); **sich** (*dat*) **etw n~** take sth; help oneself to (*Essen*)

Neid *m* -[e]s envy, jealousy. **n~isch** *adj* envious, jealous (**auf** + *acc* of); **auf jdn n~isch sein** envy s.o.

neig|en *vt* incline; (*zur Seite*) tilt; (*beugen*) bend; **sich n~en** incline; (*Boden:*) slope; (*Person:*) bend (**über** + *acc* over) ● *vi* (*haben*) **n~en zu** (*fig*) have a tendency towards; be prone to (*Krankheit*); incline towards (*Ansicht*); **dazu n~en, etw zu tun** tend to do sth. **N~ung** *f* -,-en inclination; (*Gefälle*) slope; (*fig*) tendency

nein *adv*, **N~** *nt* -s no

Nektar *m* -s nectar

Nelke *f* -,-n carnation; (*Culin*) clove

nenn|en† *vt* call; (*taufen*) name; (*angeben*) give; (*erwähnen*) mention;

sich n~en call oneself. **n~enswert** *adj* significant

Neon *nt* -s neon. **N~beleuchtung** *f* fluorescent lighting

Nerv *m* -s,-en nerve; **die N~en verlieren** lose control of oneself. **n~en** *vt* **jdn n~en** ✕ get on s.o.'s nerves. **N~enarzt** *m* neurologist. **n~enaufreibend** *adj* nerve-racking. **N~enkitzel** *m* 🔁 thrill. **N~ensystem** *nt* nervous system. **N~enzusammenbruch** *m* nervous breakdown

nervös *adj* nervy, edgy; (*Med*) nervous; **n~ sein** be on edge

Nervosität *f* - nerviness, edginess

Nerz *m* -es,-e mink

Nessel *f* -,-n nettle

Nest *nt* -[e]s,-er nest; (🔁: *Ort*) small place

nett *adj* nice; (*freundlich*) kind

netto *adv* net

Netz *nt* -es,-e net; (*Einkaufs-*) string bag; (*Spinnen-*) web; (*auf Landkarte*) grid; (*System*) network; (*Electr*) mains *pl*. **N~haut** *f* retina. **N~karte** *f* area season ticket. **N~werk** *nt* network

neu *adj* new; (*modern*) modern; **wie neu** as good as new; **das ist mir neu** it's news to me; **von n~em** all over again ● *adv* newly; (*gerade erst*) only just; (*erneut*) again; **etw neu schreiben** rewrite sth; **neu vermähltes Paar** newly-weds *pl*. **N~auflage** *f* new edition; (*unverändert*) reprint. **N~bau** *m* (*pl* -ten) new house/building

Neu|e(r) *m/f* new person, newcomer; (*Schüler*) new boy/girl. **N~e(s)** *nt* **das N~e** the new; **etwas N~es** something new; (*Neuigkeit*) a piece of news; **was gibt's N~es?** what's the news?

neuerdings *adv* [just] recently

neuest|e(r,s) *adj* newest; (*letzte*) latest; **seit n~em** just recently. **N~e** *nt* **das N~e** the latest thing; (*Neuigkeit*) the latest news *sg*

neugeboren *adj* newborn

Neugier, Neugierde *f* - curiosity; (*Wissbegierde*) inquisitiveness

neugierig adj curious (**auf** + acc about); (wissbegierig) inquisitive

Neuheit f -,-en novelty; newness

Neuigkeit f -,-en piece of news; **N~en** news sg

Neujahr nt New Year's Day; **über N~** over the New Year

neulich adv the other day

Neumond m new moon

neun inv adj. **N~** f -,-en nine. **n~te(r,s)** adj ninth. **n~zehn** inv adj nineteen. **n~zehnte(r,s)** adj nineteenth. **n~zig** inv adj ninety. **n~zigste(r,s)** adj ninetieth

Neuralgie f -,-n neuralgia

neureich adj nouveau riche

Neurologe m -n,-n neurologist

Neurose f -,-n neurosis

Neuschnee m fresh snow

Neuseeland nt -s New Zealand

neuste(r,s) adj = neueste(r,s)

neutral adj neutral. **N~ität** f - neutrality

Neutrum nt -s,-tra neuter noun

neu|vermählt* adj n~ vermählt, s. neu. **N~zeit** f modern times pl

nicht adv not; **ich kann n~** I cannot or can't; **er ist n~ gekommen** he hasn't come; **bitte n~!** please don't! **n~ berühren!** do not touch! **du kennst ihn doch, n~?** you do know him, don't you?

Nichte f -,-n niece

Nichtraucher m non-smoker

nichts pron & a nothing; **n~ mehr** no more; **n~ ahnend** unsuspecting; **n~ sagend** meaningless; (uninteressant) nondescript. **N~** nt - nothingness; (fig: Leere) void

Nichtschwimmer m nonswimmer

nichts|nutzig adj good-for-nothing; (**I**: unartig) naughty. **n~sagend*** adj n~ sagend, s. nichts. **N~tun** nt -s idleness

Nickel nt -s nickel

nicken vi (haben) nod

Nickerchen nt -s,-, **I** nap

nie adv never

nieder adj low ● adv down. **n~brennen†** vt/i sep (sein) burn down. **N~deutsch** nt Low German. **N~gang** m (fig) decline. **n~gedrückt** adj (fig) depressed. **n~geschlagen** adj dejected, despondent. **N~kunft** f -,ᵉe confinement. **N~lage** f defeat

Niederlande (die) pl the Netherlands

Niederländ|er m -s,- Dutchman; **die N~er** the Dutch pl. **N~erin** f -,-nen Dutchwoman. **n~isch** adj Dutch

nieder|lassen† vt sep let down; **sich n~lassen** settle; (sich setzen) sit down. **N~lassung** f -,-en settlement; (Zweigstelle) branch. **n~legen** vt sep put or lay down; resign (Amt); **die Arbeit n~legen** go on strike. **n~metzeln** vt sep massacre. **N~sachsen** nt Lower Saxony. **N~schlag** m precipitation; (Regen) rainfall; (radioaktiver) fallout. **n~schlagen†** vt sep knock down; lower (Augen); (unterdrücken) crush. **n~schmettern** vt sep (fig) shatter. **n~setzen** vt sep put or set down; **sich n~setzen** sit down. **n~strecken** vt sep fell; (durch Schuss) gun down. **n~trächtig** adj base, vile. **n~walzen** vt sep flatten

niedlich adj pretty; sweet

niedrig adj low; (fig: gemein) base ● adv low

niemals adv never

niemand pron nobody, no one

Niere f -,-n kidney; **künstliche N~** kidney machine

niesel|n vi (haben) drizzle. **N~regen** m drizzle

niesen vi (haben) sneeze. **N~** nt -s sneezing; (Nieser) sneeze

Niete¹ f -,-n rivet; (an Jeans) stud

Niete² f -,-n blank; **I** failure

nieten vt rivet

Nikotin nt -s nicotine

Nil m -[s] Nile. **N~pferd** nt hippopotamus

nimmer adv (SGer) not any more; **nie und n~** never

nirgend|s, n~wo adv nowhere

Nische f -,-n recess, niche

nisten vi (haben) nest

Nitrat nt -[e]s,-e nitrate

Niveau /ni'vo:/ nt -s,-s level; (geistig, künstlerisch) standard

nix adv 🔲 nothing

Nixe f -,-n mermaid

nobel adj noble; (🔲: luxuriös) luxurious; (🔲: großzügig) generous

noch adv still; (zusätzlich) as well; (mit Komparativ) even; **n~ nicht** not yet; **gerade n~** only just; **n~ immer** od **immer n~** still; **n~ letzte Woche** only last week; **wer n~?** who else? **n~ etwas** something else; (Frage) anything else? **n~ einmal** again; **n~ ein Bier** another beer; **n~ größer** even bigger; **n~ so sehr** however much ● conj **weder n~ ...** neither nor ...

nochmals adv again

Nomad|e m -n,-n nomad. **n~isch** adj nomadic

nominier|en vt nominate. **N~ung** f -,-en nomination

Nonne f -,-n nun. **N~nkloster** nt convent

Nonstopflug m direct flight

Nord m -[e]s north. **N~amerika** nt North America

Norden m -s north

nordisch adj Nordic

nördlich adj northern; (Richtung) northerly ● adv & prep (+ gen) **n~ [von] der Stadt** [to the] north of the town

Nordosten m north-east

Nord|pol m North Pole. **N~see** f - North Sea. **N~westen** m north-west

Nörgelei f -,-en grumbling

nörgeln vi (haben) grumble

Norm f -,-en norm; (Techn) standard; (Soll) quota

normal adj normal. **n~erweise** adv normally

normen vt standardize

Norwe|gen nt -s Norway. **N~ger(in)** m -s,- (f -,-nen) Norwe-

gian. **n~gisch** adj Norwegian

Nost|algie f - nostalgia. **n~algisch** adj nostalgic

Not f -,⸚e need; (Notwendigkeit) necessity; (Entbehrung) hardship; (seelisch) trouble; **Not leiden** be in need, suffer hardship; **Not leidende Menschen** needy people; **zur Not** if need be; (äußerstenfalls) at a pinch

Notar m -s,-e notary public

Not|arzt m emergency doctor. **N~ausgang** m emergency exit. **N~behelf** m -[e]s,-e makeshift. **N~bremse** f emergency brake. **N~dienst** m **N~dienst haben** be on call

Note f -,-n note; (Zensur) mark; **ganze/halbe N~** (Mus) semi-breve/minim; **N~n lesen** read music; **persönliche N~** personal touch. **N~nblatt** nt sheet of music. **N~nschlüssel** m clef

Notfall m emergency; **für den N~** just in case. **n~s** adv if need be

notieren vt note down; (Comm) quote; **sich** (dat) **etw n~** make a note of sth

nötig adj necessary; **n~ haben** need; **das N~ste** the essentials pl ● adv urgently. **n~enfalls** adv if need be. **N~ung** f - coercion

Notiz f -,-en note; (Zeitungs-) item; **[keine] N~ nehmen von** take [no] notice of. **N~buch** nt notebook. **N~kalender** m diary

Not|lage f plight. **n~landen** vi (sein) make a forced landing. **N~landung** f forced landing. **n~leidend*** adj **Not leidend**, s. **Not**. **N~lösung** f stopgap

Not|ruf m emergency call; (Naut, Aviat) distress call; (Nummer) emergency services number. **N~signal** nt distress signal. **N~stand** m state of emergency. **N~unterkunft** f emergency accommodation. **N~wehr** f - (Jur) self-defence

notwendig adj necessary; essential ● adv urgently. **N~keit** f -,-en necessity

Notzucht f - (Jur) rape

Nougat /'nu:gat/ *m & nt* **-s** nougat

Novelle *f -,-n* novella; (*Pol*) amendment

November *m -s,-* November

Novize *m -n,-n,* **Novizin** *f -,-nen* (*Relig*) novice

Nu *m* **im Nu** 🛈 in a flash

nüchtern *adj* sober; (*sachlich*) matter-of-fact; (*schmucklos*) bare; (*ohne Würze*) bland; **auf n~en Magen** on an empty stomach

Nudel *f -,-n* piece of pasta; **N~n** pasta *sg*; (*Band-*) noodles. **N~holz** *nt* rolling-pin

Nudist *m -en,-en* nudist

nuklear *adj* nuclear

null *inv adj* zero, nought; (*Teleph*) O; (*Sport*) nil; (*Tennis*) love; **n~ Fehler** no mistakes; **n~ und nichtig** (*Jur*) null and void. **N~** *f -,-en* nought, zero; (*fig: Person*) nonentity. **N~punkt** *m* zero

numerieren[+] *vt =* **nummerieren**

Nummer *f -,-n* number; (*Ausgabe*) issue; (*Darbietung*) item; (*Zirkus-*) act; (*Größe*) size. **n~ieren** *vt* number. **N~nschild** *nt* number-plate

nun *adv* now; (*na*) well; (*halt*) just; **nun gut!** very well then!

nur *adv* only, just; **wo kann sie nur sein?** wherever can she be? **er soll es nur versuchen!** just let him try!

Nürnberg *nt -s* Nuremberg

nuscheln *vt/i* (*haben*) mumble

Nuss *f -,⸗e* nut. **N~knacker** *m -s,-* nutcrackers *pl*

Nüstern *fpl* nostrils

Nut *f -,-en,* **Nute** *f -,-n* groove

Nutte *f -,-n* 🗙 tart 🗙

nutz|bar *adj* usable; **n~bar machen** utilize; cultivate (*Boden*). **n~bringend** *adj* profitable

nutzen *vt* use, utilize; (*aus-*) take advantage of ● *vi* (*haben*) = **nützen.** **N~** *m* **-s** benefit; (*Comm*) profit; **N~ziehen aus** benefit from; **von N~ sein** be useful

nützen *vi* (*haben*) be useful *or* of use (*dat* to); (*Mittel:*) be effective; **nichts n~** be useless *or* no use; **was nützt**

mir das? what good is that to me? ● *vt =* **nutzen**

nützlich *adj* useful. **N~keit** *f -* usefulness

nutz|los *adj* useless; (*vergeblich*) vain. **N~losigkeit** *f -* uselessness. **N~ung** *f -* use, utilization

Nylon /'nailɔn/ *nt* **-s** nylon

Nymphe /'nymfə/ *f -,-n* nymph

Oo

o *int* **o ja/nein!** oh yes/no!

Oase *f -,-n* oasis

ob *conj* whether; **ob reich, ob arm** rich or poor; **und ob!** 🛈 you bet!

Obacht *f* **O~ geben** pay attention; **O~!** look out!

Obdach *nt* **-[e]s** shelter. **o~los** *adj* homeless. **O~lose(r)** *m/f* homeless person; **die O~losen** the homeless *pl*

Obduktion /-'tsio:n/ *f -,-en* post-mortem

O-Beine *ntpl* 🛈 bow-legs, bandy legs

oben *adv* at the top; (*auf der Oberseite*) on top; (*eine Treppe hoch*) upstairs; (*im Text*) above; **da o~** up there; **o~ im Norden** up in the north; **siehe o~** see above; **o~ auf** (+ *acc/dat*) on top of; **nach o~** up-[wards]; (*die Treppe hinauf*) upstairs; **von o~** from above/upstairs; **von o~ bis unten** from top to bottom/(*Person*) to toe; **jdn von o~ bis unten mustern** look s.o. up and down; **o~ erwähnt** *od* **genannt** above-mentioned. **o~drein** *adv* on top of that

Ober *m -s,-* waiter

Ober|arm *m* upper arm. **O~arzt** *m* ≈ senior registrar. **O~deck** *nt* upper deck. **o~e(r,s)** *adj* upper; (*höhere*) higher. **O~fläche** *f* surface. **o~flächlich** *adj* superficial. **O~ge-**

n

o

schoss *nt* upper storey. **o~halb** *adv* & *prep* (+ *gen*) above. **O~haupt** *nt* (*fig*) head. **O~haus** *nt* (*Pol*) upper house; (*in UK*) House of Lords. **O~hemd** *nt* [man's] shirt. **o~irdisch** *adj* surface ● *adv* above ground. **O~kiefer** *m* upper jaw. **O~körper** *m* upper part of the body. **O~leutnant** *m* lieutenant. **O~lippe** *f* upper lip

Obers *nt* - (*Aust*) cream

Ober|schenkel *m* thigh. **O~schule** *f* grammar school. **O~seite** *f* upper/(*rechte Seite*) right side

Oberst *m* -en & -s,-en colonel

oberste(r,s) *adj* top; (*höchste*) highest; (*Befehlshaber, Gerichtshof*) supreme; (*wichtigste*) first

Ober|stimme *f* treble. **O~teil** *nt* top. **O~weite** *f* chest/(*der Frau*) bust size

obgleich *conj* although

Obhut *f* - care

obig *adj* above

Objekt *nt* -[e]s,-e object; (*Haus, Grundstück*) property

Objektiv *nt* -s,-e lens. **o~** *adj* objective. **O~ität** *f* - objectivity

Oblate *f* -,-n (*Relig*) wafer

Obmann *m* (*pl* -männer) [jury] foreman; (*Sport*) referee

Oboe /o'bo:ə/ *f* -,-n oboe

Obrigkeit *f* - authorities *pl*

obschon *conj* although

Observatorium *nt* -s,-ien observatory

obskur *adj* obscure; dubious

Obst *nt* -es (*coll*) fruit. **O~baum** *m* fruit-tree. **O~garten** *m* orchard. **O~händler** *m* fruiterer

obszön *adj* obscene

O-Bus *m* trolley bus

obwohl *conj* although

Ochse *m* -n,-n ox

öde *adj* desolate; (*unfruchtbar*) barren; (*langweilig*) dull. **Öde** *f* - desolation; barrenness; dullness

oder *conj* or; **du kennst ihn doch, o~?** you know him, don't you?

Ofen *m* -s, stove; (*Heiz-*) heater; (*Back-*) oven; (*Techn*) furnace

offen *adj* open; (*Haar*) loose; (*Flamme*) naked; (*o~herzig*) frank; (*o~ gezeigt*) overt; (*unentschieden*) unsettled; **o~e Stelle** vacancy; **Wein o~ verkaufen** sell wine by the glass; **o~ bleiben** remain open; **o~ halten** hold open (*Tür*); keep open (*Mund, Augen*); **o~ lassen** leave open; leave vacant (*Stelle*); **o~ stehen** be open; (*Rechnung:*) be outstanding; **jdm o~ stehen** (*fig*) be open to s.o.; *adv* **o~ gesagt** *od* **gestanden** to be honest. **o~bar** *adj* obvious ● *adv* apparently. **o~baren** *vt* reveal. **O~barung** *f* -,-en revelation. **O~heit** *f* - frankness, openness. **o~sichtlich** *adj* obvious

offenstehen* *vi sep* (*haben*) **offen stehen**, *s.* **offen**

öffentlich *adj* public. **Ö~keit** *f* - public; **in aller Ö~keit** in public, publicly

Offerte *f* -,-n (*Comm*) offer

offiziell *adj* official

Offizier *m* -s,-e (*Mil*) officer

öffn|en *vt/i* (*haben*) open; **sich ö~en** open. **Ö~er** *m* -s,- opener. **Ö~ung** *f* -,-en opening. **Ö~ungszeiten** *fpl* opening hours

oft *adv* often

öfter *adv* quite often. **ö~e(r,s)** *adj* frequent; **des Ö~en (ö~en)** frequently. **ö~s** *adv* [!] quite often

oh *int* oh!

ohne *prep* (+ *acc*) without; **o~ mich!** count me out! **oben o~** topless ● *conj* **o~ zu überlegen** without thinking; **o~ dass ich es merkte** without my noticing it. **o~dies** *adv* anyway. **o~gleichen** *pred adj* unparalleled. **o~hin** *adv* anyway

Ohn|macht *f* -,-en faint; (*fig*) powerlessness; **in O~macht fallen** faint. **o~mächtig** *adj* unconscious; (*fig*) powerless; **o~mächtig werden** faint

Ohr *nt* -[e]s,-en ear

Öhr *nt* -[e]s,-e eye (*of needle*)

Ohrenschmalz *nt* ear-wax.

O∼schmerzen *mpl* earache *sg*

Ohrfeige *f* slap in the face. **o∼n** *vt* **jdn o∼n** slap s.o.'s face

Ohr|läppchen *nt* -s,- ear-lobe. **O∼ring** *m* ear-ring. **O∼wurm** *m* earwig

oje *int* oh dear!

okay /o'ke:/ *adj & adv* 🇬🇧 OK

Öko|logie *f* - ecology. **ö∼logisch** *adj* ecological. **Ö∼nomie** *f* - economy; (*Wissenschaft*) economics *sg*. **ö∼nomisch** *adj* economic; (*sparsam*) economical

Oktave *f* -,-n octave

Oktober *m* -s,- October

> *i*
> **Oktoberfest** Germany's biggest beer festival and funfair, which takes place every year in Munich. Over 16 days more than 5 million litres of beer are drunk in marquees erected by the major breweries. The festival goes back to 1810, when a horse race was held to celebrate the wedding of Ludwig, Crown Prince of Bavaria.

ökumenisch *adj* ecumenical

Öl *nt* -[e]s,-e oil; **in Öl malen** paint in oils. **Ölbaum** *m* olivetree. **ölen** *vt* oil. **Ölfarbe** *f* oil-paint. **Ölfeld** *nt* oilfield. **Ölgemälde** *nt* oil-painting. **ölig** *adj* oily

Oliv|e *f* -,-n olive. **O∼enöl** *nt* olive oil

Ölmessstab *m* dip-stick. **Ölsardinen** *fpl* sardines in oil. **Ölstand** *m* oil-level. **Öltanker** *m* oil-tanker. **Ölteppich** *m* oil-slick

Olympiade *f* -,-n Olympic Games *pl*, Olympics *pl*

Olymp|iasieger(in) /o'lʏmpɪa-/ *m*(*f*) Olympic champion. **o∼isch** *adj* Olympic; **O∼ische Spiele** Olympic Games

Ölzeug *nt* oilskins *pl*

Oma *f* -,-s 🇬🇧 granny

Omnibus *m* bus; (*Reise-*) coach

onanieren *vi* (*haben*) masturbate

Onkel *m* -s,- uncle

Opa *m* -s,-s 🇬🇧 grandad

Opal *m* -s,-e opal

Oper *f* -,-n opera

Operation /-'tsio:n/ *f* -,-en operation. **O∼ssaal** *m* operating theatre

Operette *f* -,-n operetta

operieren *vt* operate on (*Patient, Herz*); **sich o∼ lassen** have an operation ● *vi* (*haben*) operate

Opernglas *nt* opera-glasses *pl*

Opfer *nt* -s,- sacrifice; (*eines Unglücks*) victim; **ein O∼ bringen** make a sacrifice; **jdm/etw zum O∼ fallen** fall victim to s.o./something. **o∼n** *vt* sacrifice

Opium *nt* -s opium

Opposition /-'tsio:n/ *f* - opposition. **O∼spartei** *f* opposition party

Optik *f* - optics *sg*, (🇬🇧: *Objektiv*) lens. **O∼er** *m* -s,- optician

optimal *adj* optimum

Optimis|mus *m* - optimism. **O∼t** *m* -en,-en optimist. **o∼tisch** *adj* optimistic

optisch *adj* optical; (*Eindruck*) visual

Orakel *nt* -s,- oracle

Orange /o'rã:ʒə/ *f* -,-n orange. **o∼** *inv adj* orange. **O∼ade** *f* -,-n orangeade. **O∼nmarmelade** *f* [orange] marmalade

Oratorium *nt* -s,-ien oratorio

Orchester /or'kɛstɐ/ *nt* -s,- orchestra

Orchidee /orçi'de:ə/ *f* -,-n orchid

Orden *m* -s,- (*Ritter-, Kloster-*) order; (*Auszeichnung*) medal, decoration

ordentlich *adj* neat. tidy; (*anständig*) respectable; (*ordnungsgemäß, fam: richtig*) proper; (*Mitglied, Versammlung*) ordinary; (🇬🇧: *gut*) decent; (🇬🇧: *gehörig*) good

Order *f* -,-s & -n order

ordinär *adj* common

Ordination /-'tsio:n/ *f* -,-en (*Relig*) ordination; (*Aust*) surgery

ordn|en *vt* put in order; tidy; (*an-*) arrange. **O∼er** *m* -s,- steward; (*Akten-*) file

Ordnung *f* - order; **O∼ machen** tidy up; **in O∼ bringen** put in order; (*aufräumen*) tidy; (*reparieren*) mend;

O

(*fig*) put right; **in O~ sein** be in order; (*ordentlich sein*) be tidy; (*fig*) be all right; **[geht] in O~!** OK! **o~s-gemäß** *adj* proper. **O~sstrafe** *f* (*Jur*) fine. **o~swidrig** *adj* improper

Ordonnanz, Ordonanz *f -,-en* (*Mil*) orderly

Organ *nt -s,-e* organ; voice

Organisation /-'tsio:n/ *f -,-en* organization

organisch *adj* organic

organisieren *vt* organize; (🔲: *be-schaffen*) get [hold of]

Organismus *m -,-men* organism; (*System*) system

Organspenderkarte *f* donor card

Orgasmus *m -,-men* orgasm

Orgel *f -,-n* (*Mus*) organ. **O~pfeife** *f* organ-pipe

Orgie /'ɔrgiə/ *f -,-n* orgy

Orien|t /'o:riɛnt/ *m -s* Orient. **o~talisch** *adj* Oriental

orientier|en /oriɛn'ti:rən/ *vt* inform (**über** + *acc* about); **sich o~en** get one's bearings, orientate oneself; (*unterrichten*) inform oneself (**über** + *acc* about). **O~ung** *f -* orientation; **die O~ung verlieren** lose one's bearings

original *adj* original. **O~** *nt -s,-e* original. **O~übertragung** *f* live transmission

originell *adj* original; (*eigenartig*) un-usual

Orkan *m -s,-e* hurricane

Ornament *nt -[e]s,-e* ornament

Ort *m -[e]s,-e* place; (*Ortschaft*) [small] town; **am Ort** locally; **am Ort des Verbrechens** at the scene of the crime

ortho|dox *adj* orthodox. **O~gra-phie, O~grafie** *f -* spelling. **O~päde** *m -n,-n* orthopaedic spe-cialist

örtlich *adj* local

Ortschaft *f -,-en* [small] town; (*Dorf*) village; **geschlossene O~** (*Auto*) built-up area

Orts|gespräch *nt* (*Teleph*) local

call. **O~verkehr** *m* local traffic. **O~zeit** *f* local time

Öse *f -,-n* eyelet; (*Schlinge*) loop; **Haken und Öse** hook and eye

Ost *m -[e]s* east

Osten *m -s* east; **nach O~** east

ostentativ *adj* pointed

Osteopath *m -en,-en* osteopath

Oster|ei /'o:stɐʔai/ *nt* Easter egg. **O~fest** *nt* Easter. **O~glocke** *f* daffo-dil. **O~n** *nt -,-* Easter; **frohe O~n!** happy Easter!

Österreich *nt -s* Austria. **Ö~er** *m, -s,-,* **Ö~erin** *f -,-nen* Austrian. **ö~isch** *adj* Austrian

östlich *adj* eastern; (*Richtung*) east-erly ● *adv* & *prep* (+ *gen*) **ö~ [von] der Stadt** [to the] east of the town

Ostsee *f* Baltic [Sea]

Otter¹ *m -s,-* otter

Otter² *f -,-n* adder

Ouverture /uvɛr'ty:rə/ *f -,-n* over-ture

oval *adj* oval. **O~** *nt -s,-e* oval

Oxid, Oxyd *nt -[e]s,-e* oxide

Ozean *m -s,-e* ocean

Ozon *nt -s* ozone. **O~loch** *nt* hole in the ozone layer. **O~schicht** *f* ozone layer

Pp

paar *pron inv* **ein p~** a few; **ein p~ Mal** a few times; **alle p~ Tage** every few days. **P~** *nt -[e]s,-e* pair; (*Ehe-, Liebes-*) couple. **p~en** *vt* mate; (*ver-binden*) combine; **sich p~en** mate. **P~ung** *f -,-en* mating. **p~weise** *adv* in pairs, in twos

Pacht *f -,-en* lease; (*P~summe*) rent. **p~en** *vt* lease

Pächter *m -s,-* lessee; (*eines Hofes*) tenant

Pachtvertrag *m* lease

Päckchen nt -s,- package, small packet

pack|en vt/i (haben) pack; (ergreifen) seize; (fig: fesseln) grip. **P~en** m -s,- bundle. **p~end** adj (fig) gripping. **P~papier** nt [strong] wrapping paper. **P~ung** f -,-en packet; (Med) pack

Pädagog|e m -n,-n educationalist; (Lehrer) teacher. **P~ik** f - educational science

Paddel nt -s,- paddle. **P~boot** nt canoe. **p~n** vt/i (haben/sein) paddle. **P~sport** m canoeing

Page /'pa:ʒə/ m -n,-n page

Paillette /pai'jɛtə/ f -,-n sequin

Paket nt -[e]s,-e packet; (Post-) parcel

Pakist|an nt -s Pakistan. **P~aner(in)** m -s,- (f -,-nen) Pakistani. **p~anisch** adj Pakistani

Palast m -[e]s,ˣe palace

Paläst|ina nt -s Palestine. **P~inenser(in)** m -s,- (f -,-nen) Palestinian. **p~inensisch** adj Palestinian

Palette f -,-n palette

Palme f -,-n palm[-tree]

Pampelmuse f -,-n grapefruit

Panier|mehl nt (Culin) breadcrumbs pl. **p~t** adj (Culin) breaded

Panik f - panic

Panne f -,-n breakdown; (Reifen-) flat tyre; (Missgeschick) mishap

Panter, Panther m -s,- panther

Pantine f -,-n [wooden] clog

Pantoffel m -s,-n slipper; mule

Pantomime¹ f -,-n mime

Pantomime² m -n,-n mime artist

Panzer m -s,- armour; (Mil) tank; (Zool) shell. **p~n** vt armourplate. **P~schrank** m safe

Papa /'papa, pa'pa:/ m -s,-s daddy

Papagei m -s & -en,-en parrot

Papier nt -[e]s,-e paper. **P~korb** m waste-paper basket. **P~schlange** f streamer. **P~waren** fpl stationery sg

Pappe f - cardboard

Pappel f -,-n poplar

pappig adj Ⓣ sticky

Papp|karton m, **P~schachtel** f cardboard box

Paprika m -s,-[s] [sweet] pepper; (Gewürz) paprika

Papst m -[e]s,ˣe pope

päpstlich adj papal

Parade f -,-n parade

Paradies nt -es,-e paradise

Paraffin nt -s paraffin

Paragraf, Paragraph m -en,-en section

parallel adj & adv parallel. **P~e** f -,-n parallel

Paranuss f Brazil nut

Parasit m -en,-en parasite

parat adj ready

Parcours /par'kuːɐ̯/ m -,- /-[s],-s/ (Sport) course

Pardon /par'dõː/ int sorry!

Parfüm nt -s,-e & -s perfume, scent. **p~iert** adj perfumed, scented

parieren vi (haben) Ⓣ obey

Park m -s,-s park. **p~en** vt/i (haben) park. **P~en** nt -s parking; 'P~en verboten' 'no parking'

Parkett nt -[e]s, -e parquet floor; (Theat) stalls pl

Park|haus nt multi-storey car park. **P~kralle** f wheel clamp. **P~lücke** f parking space. **P~platz** m car park; parking space. **P~scheibe** f parking-disc. **P~schein** m car-park ticket. **P~uhr** f parking-meter. **P~verbot** nt parking ban; 'P~verbot' 'no parking'

Parlament nt -[e]s,-e parliament. **p~arisch** adj parliamentary

Parodie f -,-n parody

Parole f -,-n slogan; (Mil) password

Partei f -,-en (Pol, Jur) party; (Miet-) tenant; **für jdn P~ ergreifen** take s.o.'s part. **p~isch** adj biased

Parterre /par'tɛr/ nt -s,-s ground floor; (Theat) rear stalls pl

Partie f -,-n part; (Tennis, Schach) game; (Golf) round; (Comm) batch; **eine gute P~ machen** marry well

Partikel nt -s,- particle

Partitur f -,-en (Mus) full score

Partizip nt -s,-ien participle
Partner|(in) m -s,- (f -,-nen) partner. **P~schaft** f -,-en partnership. **P~stadt** f twin town
Party /'pa:ɐti/ f -,-s party
Parzelle f -,-n plot [of ground]
Pass m -es,-̈e passport; (Geog, Sport) pass
Passage /pa'sa:ʒə/ f -,-n passage; (Einkaufs-) shopping arcade
Passagier /pasa'ʒi:ɐ/ m -s,-e passenger
Passant(in) m -en,-en (f -,-nen) passer-by
Passe f -,-n yoke
passen vi (haben) fit; (geeignet sein) be right (für for); (Sport) pass the ball; (aufgeben) pass; **p~ zu** go [well] with; (übereinstimmen) match; **jdm p~** fit s.o.; (gelegen sein) suit s.o.; **[ich] passe** pass. **p~d** adj suitable; (angemessen) appropriate; (günstig) convenient; (übereinstimmend) matching
passier|en vt pass; cross (Grenze); (Culin) rub through a sieve ● vi (sein) happen (jdm to s.o.); **es ist ein Unglück p~t** there has been an accident. **P~schein** m pass
Passiv nt -s,-e (Gram) passive
Passstraße f pass
Paste f -,-n paste
Pastell nt -[e]s,-e pastel
Pastete f -,-n pie; (Gänseleber-) pâté
pasteurisieren /pastøri'zi:rən/ vt pasteurize
Pastor m -s,-en pastor
Pate m -n,-n godfather; (fig) sponsor; **P~n** godparents. **P~nkind** nt godchild
Patent nt -[e]s,-e patent; (Offiziers-) commission. **p~** adj 🆃 clever; (Person) resourceful. **p~ieren** vt patent
Pater m -s,- (Relig) Father
Patholog|e m -n,-n pathologist. **p~isch** adj pathological
Patience /pa'sjã:s/ f -,-n patience
Patient(in) /pa'tsjɛnt(ɪn)/ m -en,-en (f -,-nen) patient
Patin f -,-nen godmother

Patriot|(in) m -en,-en (f -,-nen) patriot. **p~isch** adj patriotic. **P~ismus** m - patriotism
Patrone f -,-n cartridge
Patrouille /pa'trʊljə/ f -,-n patrol
Patsch|e f in der **P~e sitzen** 🆃 be in a jam. **p~nass** adj 🆃 soaking wet
Patt nt -s stalemate
Patz|er m -s,- 🆃 slip. **p~ig** adj 🆃 insolent
Pauk|e f -,-n kettledrum; **auf die P~e hauen** 🆃 have a good time; (prahlen) boast. **p~en** vt/i (haben) 🆃 swot
pauschal adj all-inclusive; (einheitlich) flat-rate; (fig) sweeping (Urteil); **p~e Summe** lump sum. **P~e** f -,-n lump sum. **P~reise** f package tour. **P~summe** f lump sum
Pause[1] f -,-n break; (beim Sprechen) pause; (Theat) interval; (im Kino) intermission; (Mus) rest; **P~ machen** have a break
Pause[2] f -,-n tracing. **p~n** vt trace
pausenlos adj incessant
pausieren vi (haben) have a break; (ausruhen) rest
Pauspapier nt tracing-paper
Pavian m -s,-e baboon
Pavillon /'paviljõ/ m -s,-s pavilion
Pazifi|k m -s Pacific [Ocean]. **p~sch** adj Pacific
Pazifist m -en,-en pacifist
Pech nt -s pitch; (Unglück) bad luck; **P~ haben** be unlucky
Pedal nt -s,-e pedal
Pedant m -en,-en pedant
Pediküre f -,-n pedicure
Pegel m -s,- level; (Gerät) water-level indicator. **P~stand** m [water] level
peilen vt take a bearing on
peinigen vt torment
peinlich adj embarrassing, awkward; (genau) scrupulous; **es war mir sehr p~** I was very embarrassed
Peitsche f -,-n whip. **p~n** vt whip; (fig) lash ● vi (sein) lash (**an** + acc against). **P~nhieb** m lash
Pelikan m -s,-e pelican

Pell|e f -,-n skin. p∼en vt peel; shell (Ei); **sich p∼en** peel

Pelz m -es,-e fur

Pendel nt -s,- pendulum. **p∼n** vi (haben) swing ● vi (sein) commute. **P∼verkehr** m shuttle-service; (für Pendler) commuter traffic

Pendler m -s,- commuter

penetrant adj penetrating; (fig) obtrusive

Penis m -,-se penis

Penne f -,-n 🔢 school

Pension /pā'zio:n/ f -,-en pension; (Hotel) guest-house; **bei voller/ halber P∼** with full/half board. **P∼är(in)** m -s,-e (f -,-nen) pensioner. **P∼at** nt -[e]s,-e boardingschool. **p∼ieren** vt retire. **P∼ierung** f - retirement

Pensum nt -s [allotted] work

Peperoni f -,- chilli

per prep (+ acc) by

Perfekt nt -s (Gram) perfect

Perfektion /-'tsio:n/ f - perfection

perforiert adj perforated

Pergament nt -[e]s,-e parchment. **P∼papier** nt grease-proof paper

Period|e f -,-n period. **p∼isch** adj periodic

Perl|e f -,-n pearl; (Glas-, Holz-) bead; (Sekt-) bubble. **P∼mutt** nt -s mother-of-pearl

Pers|ien /-iən/ nt -s Persia. **p∼isch** adj Persian

Person f -,-en person; (Theat) character; **für vier P∼en** for four people

Personal nt -s personnel, staff. **P∼ausweis** m identity card. **P∼chef** m personnel manager. **P∼ien** pl personal particulars. **P∼mangel** m staff shortage

persönlich adj personal ● adv personally, in person. **P∼keit** f -,-en personality

Perücke f -,-n wig

pervers adj [sexually] perverted. **P∼ion** f -,-en perversion

Pessimis|mus m - pessimism. **P∼t** m -en,-en pessimist. **p∼tisch** adj pessimistic

Pest f - plague

Petersilie /-iə/ f - parsley

Petroleum /-leʊm/ nt -s paraffin

Petze f -,-n 🔢 sneak. **p∼n** vi (haben) 🔢 sneak

Pfad m -[e]s,-e path. **P∼finder** m -s,- [Boy] Scout. **P∼finderin** f -,-nen [Girl] Guide

Pfahl m -[e]s,-̈e stake, post

Pfalz (die) - the Palatinate

Pfand nt -[e]s,-̈er pledge; (beim Spiel) forfeit; (Flaschen-) deposit

pfänd|en vt (Jur) seize. **P∼erspiel** nt game of forfeits

Pfandleiher m -s,- pawnbroker

Pfändung f -,-en (Jur) seizure

Pfann|e f -,-n [frying-]pan. **P∼kuchen** m pancake

Pfarr|er m -s,- vicar, parson; (katholischer) priest. **P∼haus** nt vicarage

Pfau m -s,-en peacock

Pfeffer m -s pepper. **P∼kuchen** m gingerbread. **P∼minze** f - (Bot) peppermint. **p∼n** vt pepper; (🔢: schmeißen) chuck. **P∼streuer** m -s,- pepperpot

Pfeif|e f -,-n whistle; (Tabak-, Orgel-) pipe. **p∼en†** vt/i (haben) whistle; (als Signal) blow the whistle

Pfeil m -[e]s,-e arrow

Pfeiler m -s,- pillar; (Brücken-) pier

Pfennig m -s,-e pfennig

Pferch m -[e]s,-e [sheep] pen

Pferd nt -es,-e horse; **zu P∼e** on horseback. **P∼erennen** nt horserace; (als Sport) [horse-]racing. **P∼eschwanz** m horse's tail; (Frisur) pony-tail. **P∼estall** m stable. **P∼estärke** f horsepower

Pfiff m -[e]s,-e whistle

Pfifferling m -s,-e chanterelle

pfiffig adj 🔢 smart

Pfingst|en nt -s Whitsun. **P∼rose** f peony

Pfirsich m -s,-e peach

Pflanz|e f -,-n plant. **p∼en** vt plant. **P∼enfett** nt vegetable fat. **p∼lich** adj vegetable

Pflaster nt -s,- pavement; (Heft-)

p

plaster. **p~n** vt pave
Pflaume f -,-n plum
Pflege f - care; (*Kranken-*) nursing; **in P~ nehmen** look after; (*Admin*) foster (*Kind*). **p~bedürftig** adj in need of care. **P~eltern** pl foster-parents. **P~kind** nt foster-child. **p~leicht** adj easy-care. **p~n** vt look after, care for; nurse (*Kranke*); cultivate (*Künste, Freundschaft*). **P~r(in)** m -s,- (f -,-nen) nurse; (*Tier-*) keeper
Pflicht f -,-en duty; (*Sport*) compulsory exercise/routine. **p~bewusst** adj conscientious. **P~gefühl** nt sense of duty
pflücken vt pick
Pflug m -[e]s,-̈e plough
pflügen vt/i (*haben*) plough
Pforte f -,-n gate
Pförtner m -s,- porter
Pfosten m -s,- post
Pfote f -,-n paw
Pfropfen m -s,- stopper; (*Korken*) cork. **p~** vt graft (**auf** + acc on [to]); (🔲: *pressen*) cram (**in** + acc into)
pfui int ugh
Pfund nt -[e]s,-e & - pound
Pfusch|arbeit f 🔲 shoddy work. **p~en** vi (*haben*) 🔲 botch one's work. **P~erei** f -,-en 🔲 botch-up
Pfütze f -,-n puddle
Phantasie f -,-n imagination; **P~n** fantasies; (*Fieber-*) hallucinations. **p~los** adj unimaginative. **p~ren** vi (*haben*) fantasize; (*im Fieber*) be delirious. **p~voll** adj imaginative
phantastisch adj fantastic
pharma|zeutisch adj pharmaceutical. **P~zie** f - pharmacy
Phase f -,-n phase
Philologie f - [study of] language and literature
Philosoph m -en,-en philosopher. **P~ie** f -,-n philosophy
philosophisch adj philosophical
Phobie f -,-n phobia
Phonet|ik f - phonetics sg. **p~isch** adj phonetic
Phosphor m -s phosphorus

Photo nt, **Photo-** = Foto, Foto-
Phrase f -,-n empty phrase
Physik f - physics sg. **p~alisch** adj physical
Physiker(in) m -s,- (f -,-nen) physicist
Physiologie f - physiology
physisch adj physical
Pianist(in) m -en,-en (f -,-nen) pianist
Pickel m -s,- pimple, spot; (*Spitzhacke*) pick. **p~ig** adj spotty
Picknick nt -s,-s picnic
piep[s]|en vi (*haben*) (*Vogel:*) cheep; (*Maus:*) squeak; (*Techn*) bleep. **P~er** m -s,- bleeper
Pier m -s,-e [harbour] pier
Pietät /pie'tɛ:t/ f - reverence. **p~los** adj irreverent
Pigment nt -[e]s,-e pigment. **P~ierung** f - pigmentation
Pik nt -s,-s (*Karten*) spades pl
pikant adj piquant; (*gewagt*) racy
piken vt 🔲 prick
pikiert adj offended, hurt
Pilger|(in) m -s,- (f -,-nen) pilgrim. **P~fahrt** f pilgrimage. **p~n** vi (*sein*) make a pilgrimage
Pille f -,-n pill
Pilot m -en,-en pilot
Pilz m -es,-e fungus; (*essbarer*) mushroom
pingelig adj 🔲 fussy
Pinguin m -s,-e penguin
Pinie /-jə/ f -,-n stone-pine
pinkeln vi (*haben*) 🔲 pee
Pinsel m -s,- [paint]brush
Pinzette f -,-n tweezers pl
Pionier m -s,-e (*Mil*) sapper; (*fig*) pioneer
Pirat m -en,-en pirate
Piste f -,-n (*Ski-*) run, piste; (*Renn-*) track; (*Aviat*) runway
Pistole f -,-n pistol
pitschnass adj 🔲 soaking wet
pittoresk adj picturesque
Pizza f -,-s pizza
Pkw /'pe:kave:/ m -s,-s car

plädieren vi (haben) plead (**für** for);
auf Freispruch p~ (Jur) ask for an
acquittal

Plädoyer /plɛdoa'je:/ nt -s,-s (Jur)
closing speech; (fig) plea

Plage f -,-n [hard] labour; (Mühe)
trouble; (Belästigung) nuisance. **p~n**
vt torment, plague; (bedrängen) pester; **sich p~n** struggle

Plakat nt -[e]s,-e poster

Plakette f -,-n badge

Plan m -[e]s,ːe plan

Plane f -,-n tarpaulin; (Boden-)
groundsheet

planen vt/i (haben) plan

Planet m -en,-en planet

planier|en vt level. **P~raupe** f bull-
dozer

Planke f -,-n plank

plan|los adj unsystematic.
p~mäßig adj systematic; (Ankunft)
scheduled

Plansch|becken nt paddling pool.
p~en vi (haben) splash about

Plantage /plan'ta:ʒə/ f -,-n plantation

Planung f - planning

plappern vi (haben) chatter ● vt talk
(Unsinn)

plärren vi (haben) bawl

Plasma nt -s plasma

Plastik[1] f -,-en sculpture

Plast|ik[2] nt -s plastic. **p~isch** adj
three-dimensional; (formbar) plastic;
(anschaulich) graphic

Plateau /pla'to:/ nt -s,-s plateau

Platin nt -s platinum

platonisch adj platonic

plätschern vi (haben) splash; (Bach:)
babble ● vi (sein) (Bach:) babble
along

platt adj & adv flat. **P~** nt -[s] (Lang)
Low German

Plättbrett nt ironing-board

Platte f -,-n slab; (Druck-) plate;
(Metall-, Glas-) sheet; (Fliese) tile;
(Koch-) hotplate; (Tisch-) top; (Schall-)
record, disc; (zum Servieren) [flat]
dish, platter; **kalte P~** assorted cold

meats and cheeses pl

Plätt|eisen nt iron. **p~en** vt/i
(haben) iron

Plattenspieler m record-player

Platt|form f -,-en platform.
P~füße mpl flat feet

Platz m -es,ːe place; (von Häusern
umgeben) square; (Sitz-) seat; (Sport-)
ground; (Fußball-) pitch; (Tennis-)
court; (Golf-) course; (freier Raum)
room, space; **P~ nehmen** take a
seat; **P~ machen** make room; **vom
P~ stellen** (Sport) send off. **P~an-
weiserin** f -,-nen usherette

Plätzchen nt -s,- spot; (Culin) biscuit

platzen vi (sein) burst; (auf-) split;
([I]: scheitern) fall through; (Verlobung:) be off

Platz|karte f seat reservation ticket.
P~mangel m lack of space. **P~pa-
trone** f blank. **P~verweis** m (Sport)
sending off. **P~wunde** f laceration

Plauderei f -,-en chat

plaudern vi (haben) chat

plausibel adj plausible

pleite adj [I] **p~ sein** be broke;
(Firma:) be bankrupt. **P~** f -,-n [I]
bankruptcy; (Misserfolg) flop; **P~
gehen** od **machen** go bankrupt

plissiert adj [finely] pleated

Plomb|e f -,-n seal; (Zahn-) filling.
p~ieren vt seal; fill (Zahn)

plötzlich adj sudden

plump adj plump; clumsy

plumpsen vi (sein) [I] fall

plündern vt/i (haben) loot

Plunderstück nt Danish pastry

Plural m -s,-e plural

plus adv, conj & prep (+ dat) plus. **P~**
nt - surplus; (Gewinn) profit (Vorteil)
advantage, plus. **P~punkt** m (Sport)
point; (fig) plus

Po m -s,-s [I] bottom

Pöbel m -s mob, rabble. **p~haft** adj
loutish

pochen vi (haben) knock, (Herz:)
pound; **p~ auf** (+ acc) (fig) insist on

pochieren /pɔ'ʃiːrən/ vt poach

Pocken pl smallpox sg
Podest nt -[e]s,-e rostrum
Podium nt -s,-ien platform; (Podest) rostrum
Poesie /poe'zi:/ f - poetry
poetisch adj poetic
Pointe /'poɛ̃:tə/ f -,-n punchline (of a joke)
Pokal m -s,-e goblet; (Sport) cup
pökeln vt (Culin) salt
Poker nt -s poker
Pol m -s,-e pole. **p~ar** adj polar
Polarstern m pole-star
Pole m, -n,-n Pole. **P~n** nt -s Poland
Police /po'li:sə/ f -,-n policy
Polier m -s,-e foreman
polieren vt polish
Polin f -,-nen Pole
Politesse f -,-n [woman] traffic warden
Politik f - politics sg; (Vorgehen, Maßnahme) policy
Polit|iker(in) m -s,- (f, -,-nen) politician. **p~isch** adj political
Politur f -,-en polish
Polizei f - police pl. **p~lich** adj police ● adv by the police; (sich anmelden) with the police. **P~streife** f police patrol. **P~stunde** f closing time. **P~wache** f police station
Polizist m -en,-en policeman. **P~in** f -,-nen policewoman
Pollen m -s pollen
polnisch adj Polish
Polster nt -s,- pad; (Kissen) cushion; (Möbel-) upholstery. **p~n** vt pad; upholster (Möbel). **P~ung** f - padding; upholstery
Polter|abend m eve-of-wedding party. **p~n** vi (haben) thump bang

Polyäthylen nt -s polythene
Polyester m -s polyester
Polyp m -en,-en polyp. **P~en** adenoids pl
Pommes frites /pɔm'fri:t/ pl chips; (dünner) French fries
Pomp m -s pomp
Pompon /põ'põ:/ m -s,-s pompon
pompös adj ostentatious
Pony[1] nt -s,-s pony
Pony[2] m -s,-s fringe
Pop m -[s] pop
Popo m -s,-s Ⓣ bottom
populär adj popular
Pore f -,-n pore
Porno|grafie, Pornographie f - pornography. **p~grafisch, p~graphisch** adj pornographic
Porree m -s leeks pl
Portal nt -s,-e portal
Portemonnaie /pɔrtmɔ'ne:/ nt -s,-s purse
Portier /pɔr'tje:/ m -s,-s doorman, porter
Portion /-'tsjo:n/ f -,-en helping, portion
Portmonee nt -s,-s = Portemonnaie
Porto nt -s postage. **p~frei** adv post free, post paid
Porträ|t /pɔr'trɛ:/ nt -s,-s portrait. **p~tieren** vt paint a portrait of
Portugal nt -s Portugal
Portugies|e m -n,-n, **P~in** f -,-nen Portuguese. **p~isch** adj Portuguese
Portwein m port
Porzellan nt -s china, porcelain
Posaune f -,-n trombone
Position /-'tsjo:n/ f -,-en position
positiv adj positive. **P~** nt -s,-e (Phot) positive
Post f - post office; (Briefe) mail, post; mit der **P~** by post
postalisch adj postal
Post|amt nt post office. **P~anweisung** f postal money order. **P~bote** m postman
Posten m -s,- post; (Wache) sentry;

p

(*Waren-*) batch; (*Rechnungs-*) item, entry

Poster *nt & m* **-s,-** poster

Postfach *nt* post-office *or* PO box

Post|karte *f* postcard. **p~lagernd** *adv* poste restante. **P~leitzahl** *f* postcode. **P~scheckkonto** *nt* ≈ National Girobank account. **P~stempel** *m* postmark

postum *adj* posthumous

post|wendend *adv* by return of post. **P~wertzeichen** *nt* [postage] stamp

Potenz *f* **-,-en** potency; (*Math & fig*) power

Pracht *f* **-** magnificence, splendour

prächtig *adj* magnificent; splendid

prachtvoll *adj* magnificent

Prädikat *nt* **-[e]s,-e** rating; (*Comm*) grade; (*Gram*) predicate

prägen *vt* stamp (**auf** + *acc* on); emboss (*Leder*); mint (*Münze*); coin (*Wort*); (*fig*) shape

prägnant *adj* succinct

prähistorisch *adj* prehistoric

prahl|en *vi* (*haben*) boast, brag (**mit** about)

Prakti|k *f* **-,-en** practice. **P~kant(in)** *m* **-en,-en** (*f* **-,-nen**) trainee

Prakti|kum *nt* **-s,-ka** practical training. **p~sch** *adj* practical; (*nützlich*) handy; (*tatsächlich*) virtual; **p~scher Arzt** general practitioner ● *adv* practically; virtually; (*in der Praxis*) in practice. **p~zieren** *vt/i* (*haben*) practise; (*anwenden*) put into practice; (**⬚**: *bekommen*) get

Praline *f* **-,-n** chocolate

prall *adj* bulging; (*dick*) plump; (*Sonne*) blazing ● *adv* **p~ gefüllt** full to bursting. **p~en** *vi* (*sein*) **p~ auf** (+ *acc*)/**gegen** collide with, hit; (*Sonne:*) blaze down on

Prämie /-iə/ *f* **-,-n** premium; (*Preis*) award

präm[i]ieren *vt* award a prize to

Pranger *m* **-s,-** pillory

Pranke *f* **-,-n** paw

Präparat *nt* **-[e]s,-e** preparation

Präsens *nt* **-** (*Gram*) present

präsentieren *vt* present

Präsenz *f* **-** presence

Präservativ *nt* **-s,-e** condom

Präsident|(in) *m* **-en,-en** (*f* **-,-nen**) president. **P~schaft** *f* **-** presidency

Präsidium *nt* **-s** presidency; (*Gremium*) executive committee; (*Polizei-*) headquarters *pl*

prasseln *vi* (*haben*) (*Regen:*) beat down; (*Feuer:*) crackle

> *i*
> **Prater** Vienna's largest amusement park was a private game reserve for the Austrian royal family until 1766. The *Prater* is famous for its old-fashioned carousels. A *Riesenrad*, big wheel or Ferris wheel, with a diameter of 67 metres was built there for the World Exhibition of 1897.

Präteritum *nt* **-s** imperfect

Praxis *f* **-,-xen** practice; (*Erfahrung*) practical experience; (*Arzt-*) surgery; **in der P~** in practice

Präzedenzfall *m* precedent

präzis[e] *adj* precise

predig|en *vt/i* (*haben*) preach. **P~t** *f* **-,-en** sermon

Preis *m* **-es,-e** price; (*Belohnung*) prize. **P~ausschreiben** *nt* competition

Preiselbeere *f* (*Bot*) cowberry; (*Culin*) ≈ cranberry

preisen† *vt* praise

preisgeben† *vt sep* abandon (*dat* to); reveal (*Geheimnis*)

preis|gekrönt *adj* award-winning. **p~günstig** *adj* reasonably priced ● *adv* at a reasonable price. **P~lage** *f* price range. **p~lich** *adj* price ● *adv* in price. **P~richter** *m* judge. **P~schild** *nt* price-tag. **P~träger(in)** *m*(*f*) prize-winner. **p~wert** *adj* reasonable

Prell|bock *m* buffers *pl*. **p~en** *vt* bounce; (*verletzen*) bruise; (**⬚**: *betrügen*) cheat. **P~ung** *f* **-,-en** bruise

Premiere /prə'mie:rə/ *f* **-,-n** première

p

Premierminister(in) /prə'mjeː-/ m(f) Prime Minister

Presse f -,-n press. **p~n** vt press

Pressluftbohrer m pneumatic drill

Preuß|en nt -s Prussia. **p~isch** adj Prussian

prickeln vi (haben) tingle

Priester m -s,- priest

prima inv adj 🔢 first-class, first-rate; (toll) fantastic

primär adj primary

Primel f -,-n primula

primitiv adj primitive

Prinz m -en,-en prince. **P~essin** f -,-nen princess

Prinzip nt -s,-ien principle. **p~iell** adj (Frage) of principle ● adv on principle

Prise f -,-n P~ Salz pinch of salt

Prisma nt -s,-men prism

privat adj private, personal. **P~adresse** f home address. **p~isieren** vt privatize

Privileg nt -[e]s,-ien privilege. **p~iert** adj privileged

pro prep (+ dat) per. **Pro** nt - das Pro und Kontra the pros and cons pl

Probe f -,-n test, trial; (Menge, Muster) sample; (Theat) rehearsal; **auf die P~ stellen** put to the test; **ein Auto P~ fahren** test-drive a car. **p~n** vt/i (haben) (Theat) rehearse. **p~weise** adv on a trial basis. **P~zeit** f probationary period

probieren vt/i (haben) try; (kosten) taste; (proben) rehearse

Problem nt -s,-e problem. **p~atisch** adj problematic

problemlos adj problem-free ● adv without any problems

Produkt nt -[e]s,-e product

Produk|tion /-'tsjoːn/ f -,-en production. **p~tiv** adj productive

Produ|zent m -en,-en producer. **p~zieren** vt produce

Professor m -s,-en professor

Profi m -s,-s (Sport) professional

Profil nt -s,-e profile; (Reifen-) tread; (fig) image

Profit m -[e]s,-e profit. **p~ieren** vi (haben) profit (**von** from)

Prognose f -,-n forecast; (Med) prognosis

Programm nt -s,-e programme; (Computer-) program; (TV) channel; (Comm: Sortiment) range. **p~ieren** vt/i (haben) (Computer) program. **P~ierer(in)** m -s,- (f -,-nen) [computer] programmer

Projekt nt -[e]s,-e project

Projektor m -s,-en projector

Prolet m -en,-en boor. **P~ariat** nt -[e]s proletariat

Prolog m -s,-e prologue

Promenade f -,-n promenade

Promille pl 🔢 alcohol level sg in the blood; **zu viel P~ haben** 🔢 be over the limit

Prominenz f - prominent figures pl

Promiskuität f - promiscuity

promovieren vi (haben) obtain one's doctorate

prompt adj prompt

Pronomen nt -s,- pronoun

Propaganda f - propaganda; (Reklame) publicity

Propeller m -s,- propeller

Prophet m -en,-en prophet

prophezei|en vt prophesy. **P~ung** f -,-en prophecy

Proportion /-'tsjoːn/ f -,-en proportion

Prosa f - prose

prosit int cheers!

Prospekt m -[e]s,-e brochure; (Comm) prospectus

prost int cheers!

Prostitu|ierte f -n,-n prostitute. **P~tion** f - prostitution

Protest m -[e]s,-e protest

Protestant|(in) m -en,-en (f -,-nen) (Relig) Protestant. **p~isch** adj (Relig) Protestant

protestieren vi (haben) protest

Prothese f -,-n artificial limb; (Zahn-) denture

Protokoll nt -s,-e record; (Sitzungs-) minutes pl; (diplomatisches) protocol

protz|en vi (haben) show off (**mit etw** sth). **p~ig** adj ostentatious

Proviant m -s provisions pl

Provinz f -,-en province

Provision f -,-en (Comm) commission

provisorisch adj provisional, temporary

Provokation /-'tsjo:n/ f -,-en provocation

provozieren vt provoke

Prozedur f -,-en [lengthy] business

Prozent nt -[e]s,-e & - per cent; 5 **P~** 5 per cent. **P~satz** m percentage. **p~ual** adj percentage

Prozess m -es,-e process; (Jur) lawsuit; (Kriminal-) trial

Prozession f -,-en procession

Prozessor m -s,-en processor

prüde adj prudish

prüf|en vt test/(über-) check (**auf** + acc for); audit (Bücher); (Sch) examine; **p~ender Blick** searching look. **P~er** m -s,- inspector; (Buch-) auditor; (Sch) examiner. **P~ling** m -s,-e examination candidate. **P~ung** f -,-en examination; (Test) test; (Bücher-) audit; (fig) trial

Prügel m -s,- cudgel; **P~** pl hiding sg, beating sg. **P~ei** f -,-en brawl, fight. **p~n** vt beat, thrash

Prunk m -[e]s magnificence, splendour

Psalm m -s,-en psalm

Pseudonym nt -s,-e pseudonym

pst int shush!

Psychi|ater m -s,- psychiatrist. **P~atrie** f - psychiatry. **p~atrisch** adj psychiatric

psychisch adj psychological

Psycho|analyse f psychoanalysis. **P~loge** m -n,-n psychologist. **P~logie** f - psychology. **p~logisch** adj psychological

Pubertät f - puberty

Publi|kum nt -s public; (Zuhörer) audience; (Zuschauer) spectators pl. **p~zieren** vt publish

Pudding m -s,-s blancmange; (im Wasserbad gekocht) pudding

Pudel m -s,- poodle

Puder m & nt -s,- powder. **P~dose** f [powder] compact. **p~n** vt powder. **P~zucker** m icing sugar

Puff m & nt -s,-s ⊠ brothel

Puffer m -s,- (Rail) buffer; (Culin) pancake. **P~zone** f buffer zone

Pull|i m -s,-s jumper. **P~over** m -s,- jumper; (Herren-) pullover

Puls m -es pulse. **P~ader** f artery

Pult nt -[e]s,-e desk

Pulver nt -s,- powder. **p~ig** adj powdery

Pulverkaffee m instant coffee

pummelig adj ⊡ chubby

Pumpe f -,-n pump vt/i (haben) pump; (⊡: leihen) lend; [sich (dat)] etw p~n (⊡: borgen) borrow sth

Pumps /pœmps/ pl court shoes

Punkt m -[e]s,-e dot; (Textiles) spot; (Geometry, Sport & fig) point; (Gram) full stop, period; **P~ sechs Uhr** at six o'clock sharp

pünktlich adj punctual. **P~keit** f - punctuality

Pupille f -,-n (Anat) pupil

Puppe f -,-n doll; (Marionette) puppet; (Schaufenster-, Schneider-) dummy; (Zool) chrysalis

pur adj pure; (⊡: bloß) sheer

Püree nt -s,-s purée; (Kartoffel-) mashed potatoes pl

purpurrot adj crimson

Purzel|baum m ⊡ somersault. **p~n** vi (sein) ⊡ tumble

Puste f - ⊡ breath. **p~n** vt/i (haben) ⊡ blow

Pute f -,-n turkey

Putsch m -[e]s,-e coup

Putz m -es plaster; (Staat) finery. **p~en** vt clean; (Aust) dry-clean; (zieren) adorn; **sich p~en** dress up; **sich (dat) die Zähne/Nase p~en** clean one's teeth/blow one's nose. **P~frau** f cleaner, charwoman. **p~ig** adj ⊡ amusing, cute; (seltsam) odd

p

Puzzlespiel /'pazl-/ nt jigsaw
Pyramide f -,-n pyramid

Qq

Quacksalber m -s,- quack
Quadrat nt -[e]s,-e square. **q~isch** adj square
quaken vi (haben) quack; (Frosch:) croak
Quäker(in) m -s,- (f -,-nen) Quaker
Qual f -,-en torment; (Schmerz) agony
quälen vt torment; (foltern) torture; (bedrängen) pester; **sich q~** torment oneself; (leiden) suffer; (sich mühen) struggle
Quälerei f -,-en torture
Qualifi|kation /-'tsio:n/ f -,-en qualification. **q~zieren** vt qualify. **q~ziert** adj qualified; (fähig) competent; (Arbeit) skilled
Qualität f -,-en quality
Qualle f -,-n jellyfish
Qualm m -s [thick] smoke
qualvoll adj agonizing
Quantum nt -s,-ten quantity; (Anteil) share, quota
Quarantäne f - quarantine
Quark m -s quark, ≈ curd cheese
Quartal nt -s,-e quarter
Quartett nt -[e]s,-e quartet
Quartier nt -s,-e accommodation; (Mil) quarters pl
Quarz m -es quartz
quasseln vi (haben) ⚏ jabber
Quaste f -,-n tassel
Quatsch m -[e]s ⚏ nonsense, rubbish; **Q~ machen** (Unfug machen) fool around; (etw falsch machen) do a silly thing. **q~en** ⚏ vi (haben) talk; (Wasser, Schlamm:) squelch ● vt talk
Quecksilber nt mercury
Quelle f -,-n spring; (Fluss- & fig) source

quengeln vi ⚏ whine
quer adv across, crosswise; (schräg) diagonally; **q~ gestreift** horizontally striped
Quere f - der **Q~ nach** across, crosswise; **jdm in die Q~ kommen** get in s.o.'s way
Quer|latte f crossbar. **Q~schiff** nt transept. **Q~schnitt** m cross-section. **q~schnittsgelähmt** adj paraplegic. **Q~straße** f side-street. **Q~verweis** m cross-reference
quetschen vt squash; (drücken) squeeze; (zerdrücken) crush; (Culin) mash; **sich q~ in** (+ acc) squeeze into
Queue /kø:/ nt -s,-s cue
quieken vi (haben) squeal; (Maus:) squeak
quietschen vi (haben) squeal; (Tür, Dielen:) creak
Quintett nt -[e]s,-e quintet
quirlen vt mix
Quitte f -,-n quince
quittieren vt receipt (Rechnung); sign for (Geldsumme, Sendung); **den Dienst q~** resign
Quittung f -,-en receipt
Quiz /kvɪs/ nt -,- quiz
Quote f -,-n proportion

Rr

Rabatt m -[e]s,-e discount
Rabatte f -,-n (Horticulture) border
Rabattmarke f trading stamp
Rabbiner m -s,- rabbi
Rabe m -n,-n raven
Rache f - revenge, vengeance
Rachen m -s,- pharynx
rächen vt avenge; **sich r~** take revenge (**an** + dat on); (Fehler:) cost s.o. dear
Rad nt -[e]s, ̈er wheel; (Fahr-) bicycle, ⚏ bike; **Rad fahren** cycle

Radar m & nt **-s** radar
Radau m **-s** 🔊 din, racket
radeln vi (sein) 🔊 cycle
Rädelsführer m ringleader
radfahr|en* vi sep (sein) Rad fahren, s. Rad. **R~er(in)** m(f) **-s,-** (f -,-nen) cyclist
radier|en vt/i (haben) rub out; (Kunst) etch. **R~gummi** m eraser, rubber. **R~ung** f **-,-en** etching
Radieschen /-'diːsçən/ nt **-s,-** radish
radikal adj radical, drastic
Radio nt **-s,-s** radio
radioaktiv adj radioactive. **R~ität** f **-** radioactivity
Radius m **-,-ien** radius
Rad|kappe f hub-cap. **R~ler** m **-s,-** cyclist; (Getränk) shandy
raffen vt grab; (kräuseln) gather; (kürzen) condense
Raffin|ade f **-** refined sugar. **R~erie** f **-,-n** refinery. **R~esse** f **-,-n** refinement; (Schlauheit) cunning. **r~iert** adj ingenious; (durchtrieben) crafty
ragen vi (haben) rise [up]
Rahm m **-s** (SGer) cream
rahmen vt frame. **R~** m **-s,-** frame; (fig) framework; (Grenze) limits pl; (einer Feier) setting
Rakete f **-,-n** rocket; (Mil) missile
Rallye /'rɛli/ nt **-s,-s** rally
rammen vt ram
Rampe f **-,-n** ramp; (Theat) front of the stage
Ramsch m **-[e]s** junk
ran adv = heran
Rand m **-[e]s,ᴇe** edge; (Teller-, Gläser-, Brillen-) rim; (Zier-) border, edging; (Brief-) margin; (Stadt-) outskirts pl; (Ring) ring
randalieren vi (haben) rampage
Randstreifen m (Auto) hard shoulder
Rang m **-[e]s,ᴇe** rank; (Theat) tier; **erster/zweiter R~** (Theat) dress/upper circle; **ersten R~es** first-class
rangieren / raŋ'ʒiːrən/ vt shunt ● vi (haben) rank (**vor** + dat before)
Rangordnung f order of import-

ance; (Hierarchie) hierarchy
Ranke f **-,-n** tendril; (Trieb) shoot
ranken (sich) vr (Bot) trail; (in die Höhe) climb
Ranzen m **-s,-** (Sch) satchel
ranzig adj rancid
Rappe m **-n,-n** black horse
Raps m **-es** (Bot) rape
rar adj rare; **er macht sich rar** 🔊 we don't see much of him. **R~ität** f **-,-en** rarity
rasant adj fast; (schnittig, schick) stylish
rasch adj quick
rascheln vi (haben) rustle
Rasen m **-s,-** lawn
rasen vi (sein) tear [along]; (Puls:) race; (Zeit:) fly; **gegen eine Mauer r~** career Into a wall ● vi (haben) rave; (Sturm:) rage. **r~d** adj furious; (tobend) raving; (Sturm, Durst) raqinq; (Schmerz) excruciating; (Beifall) tumultuous
Rasenmäher m lawn-mower
Rasier|apparat m razor. **r~en** vt shave; **sich r~en** shave. **R~klinge** f razor blade. **R~wasser** nt aftershave [lotion]
Raspel f **-,-n** rasp; (Culin) grater. **r~n** vt grate
Rasse f **-,-n** race. **R~hund** m pedigree dog
Rassel f **-,-n** rattle. **r~n** vi (haben) rattle; (Schlüssel:) jangle; (Kette:) clank
Rassendiskriminierung f racial discrimination
Rassepferd nt thoroughbred.
rasisch adj racial
Rassis|mus m **-** racism. **r~tisch** adj racist
Rast f **-,-en** rest. **R~platz** m picnic area. **R~stätte** f motorway restaurant [and services]
Rasur f **-,-en** shave
Rat m **-[e]s** [piece of] advice; **sich** (dat) **keinen Rat wissen** not know what to do; **zu Rat[e] ziehen** = zurate ziehen, s. zurate
Rate f **-,-n** instalment

r

raten† vt guess; (empfehlen) advise
  ● vi (haben) guess; **jdm r~** advise
  s.o.

Ratenzahlung f payment by instalments

Rat|geber m -s,- adviser; (Buch)
  guide. **R~haus** nt town hall

ratifizier|en vt ratify. **R~ung** f
  -,-en ratification

Ration /raˈtsi̯oːn/ f -,-en ration.
  r~ell adj efficient. **r~ieren** vt ration

rat|los adj helpless; **r~los sein** not
  know what to do. **r~sam** pred adj
  advisable; prudent. **R~schlag** m
  piece of advice; **R~schläge** advice sg

Rätsel nt -s,- riddle; (Kreuzwort-) puzzle; (Geheimnis) mystery. **r~haft** adj
  puzzling, mysterious. **r~n** vi (haben)
  puzzle

Ratte f -,-n rat

rau adj rough; (unfreundlich) gruff;
  (Klima) harsh, raw; (heiser) husky;
  (Hals) sore

Raub m -[e]s robbery; (Menschen-)
  abduction; (Beute) loot, booty. **r~en**
  vt steal; abduct (Menschen)

Räuber m -s,- robber

Raub|mord m robbery with murder. **R~tier** nt predator. **R~vogel** m
  bird of prey

Rauch m -[e]s smoke. **r~en** vt/i
  (haben) smoke. **R~en** nt -s smoking;
  'R~en verboten' 'no smoking'.
  R~er m -s,-smoker

Räucher|lachs m smoked salmon.
  r~n vt (Culin) smoke

rauf adv = herauf, hinauf

rauf|en vt pull ● vr/i (haben) [sich]
  r~en fight. **R~erei** f -,-en fight

rauh* adj = rau

Raum m -[e]s, Räume room; (Gebiet)
  area; (Welt-) space

räumen vt clear; vacate (Wohnung);
  evacuate (Gebäude, Gebiet, (Mil) Stellung); (bringen) put (**in/auf** + acc
  into/on); (holen) get (**aus** out of)

Raum|fahrer m astronaut.
  R~fahrt f space travel. **R~inhalt** m
  volume

räumlich adj spatial

Raum|pflegerin f cleaner.
  R~schiff nt spaceship

Räumung f - clearing; vacating;
  evacuation. **R~sverkauf** m clearance/closing-down sale

Raupe f -,-n caterpillar

raus adv = heraus, hinaus

Rausch m -[e]s, Räusche intoxication; (fig) exhilaration; **einen R~
  haben** be drunk

rauschen vi (haben) (Wasser, Wind:)
  rush; (Bäume Blätter:) rustle ● vi ⊞
  (sein) rush [along]

Rauschgift nt [narcotic] drug; (coll)
  drugs pl. **R~süchtige(r)** m/f drug
  addict

räuspern (sich) vr clear one's
  throat

rausschmeißen† vt sep ⊞ throw
  out; (entlassen) sack

Raute f -,-n diamond

Razzia f -,-ien [police] raid

Reagenzglas nt test-tube

reagieren vi (haben) react (**auf** +
  acc to)

Reaktion /-ˈtsi̯oːn/ f -,-en reaction.
  r~är adj reactionary

Reaktor m -s,-en reactor

realisieren vt realize

Realis|mus m - realism. **R~t** m
  -en,-en realist. **r~tisch** adj realistic

Realität f -,-en reality

Realschule f ≈ secondary modern
  school

Rebe f -,-n vine

Rebell m -en,-en rebel. **r~ieren** vi
  (haben) rebel. **R~ion** f -,-en rebellion

rebellisch adj rebellious

Rebhuhn nt partridge

Rebstock m vine

Rechen m -s,- rake

Rechen|aufgabe f arithmetical
  problem; (Sch) sum. **R~maschine** f
  calculator

recherchieren /reʃɛrˈʃiːrən/ vt/i
  (haben) investigate; (Journalism) research

rechnen vi (haben) do arithmetic;

(*schätzen*) reckon; (*zählen*) count (**zu** among; **auf** + *acc* on); **r~ mit** reckon with; (*erwarten*) expect ● *vt* calculate, work out; (*fig*) count (**zu** among). **R~** *nt* **-s** arithmetic

Rechner *m* **-s,-** calculator; (*Computer*) computer

Rechnung *f* **-,-en** bill; (*Comm*) invoice; (*Berechnung*) calculation; **R~ führen über** (+ *acc*) keep account of. **R~sjahr** *nt* financial year. **R~sprüfer** *m* auditor

Recht *nt* **-[e]s,-e** law; (*Berechtigung*) right (**auf** + *acc* to); **im R~ sein** be in the right; **R~ haben/behalten** be right; **R~ bekommen** be proved right; **jdm R~ geben** agree with s.o.; **mit** *od* **zu R~** rightly

recht *adj* right; (*wirklich*) real; **ich habe keine r~e Lust** I don't really feel like it; **es jdm r~ machen** please s.o.; **jdm r~ sein** be all right with s.o. **r~ vielen Dank** many thanks

Recht|e *f* **-n,-[n]** right side; (*Hand*) right hand; (*Boxen*) right; **die R~e** (*Pol*) the right; **zu meiner R~en** on my right. **r~e(r,s)** *adj* right; (*Pol*) right-wing; **r~e Masche** plain stitch. **R~e(r)** *m/f* **der/die R~e** the right man/woman; **R~e(s)** *nt* **das R~e** the right thing; **etwas R~es lernen** learn something useful; **nach dem R~en sehen** see that everything is all right

Rechteck *nt* **-[e]s,-e** rectangle. **r~ig** *adj* rectangular

rechtfertigen *vt* justify; **sich r~en** justify oneself

recht|haberisch *adj* opinionated. **r~lich** *adj* legal. **r~mäßig** *adj* legitimate

rechts *adv* on the right; (*bei Stoff*) on the right side; **von/nach r~** from/to the right; **zwei r~, zwei links stricken** knit two, purl two. **R~anwalt** *m*, **R~anwältin** *f* lawyer

Rechtschreib|programm *nt* spell checker. **R~ung** *f* **-** spelling

Rechts|händer(in) *m* **-s,-** (*f* **-,-nen**) right-hander. **r~händig** *adj*

& *adv* right-handed. **r~kräftig** *adj* legal. **R~streit** *m* law suit. **R~verkehr** *m* driving on the right. **r~widrig** *adj* illegal. **R~wissenschaft** *f* jurisprudence

rechtzeitig *adj & adv* in time

Reck *nt* **-[e]s,-e** horizontal bar

recken *vt* stretch

Redakteur /redakˈtøːɐ̯/ *m* **-s,-e** editor; (*Radio, TV*) producer

Redaktion /-ˈtsi̯oːn/ *f* **-,-en** editing; (*Radio, TV*) production; (*Abteilung*) editorial/production department

Rede *f* **-,-n** speech; **zur R~stellen** demand an explanation from; **nicht der R~ wert** not worth mentioning

reden *vi* (*haben*) talk (**von** about; **mit** to); (*eine Rede halten*) speak ● *vt* talk; speak (*Wahrheit*). **R~sart** *f* saying

Redewendung *f* idiom

redigieren *vt* edit

Redner *m* **-s,-** speaker

reduzieren *vt* reduce

Reeder *m* **-s,-** shipowner. **R~ei** *f* **-,-en** shipping company

Refer|at *nt* **-[e]s,-e** report; (*Abhandlung*) paper; (*Abteilung*) section. **R~ent(in)** *m* **-en,-en** (*f* **-,-nen**) speaker; (*Sachbearbeiter*) expert. **R~enz** *f* **-,-en** reference

Reflex *m* **-es,-e** reflex; (*Widerschein*) reflection. **R~ion** *f* **-,-en** reflection. **r~iv** *adj* reflexive

Reform *f* **-,-en** reform. **R~ation** *f* **-** (*Relig*) Reformation

Reform|haus *nt* health-food shop. **r~ieren** *vt* reform

Refrain /rəˈfrɛ̃ː/ *m* **-s,-s** refrain

Regal *nt* **-s,-e** [set of] shelves *pl*

Regatta *f* **-,-ten** regatta

rege *adj* active; (*lebhaft*) lively; (*geistig*) alert; (*Handel*) brisk

Regel *f* **-,-n** rule; (*Monats-*) period. **r~mäßig** *adj* regular. **r~n** *vt* regulate; direct (*Verkehr*); (*erledigen*) settle. **r~recht** *adj* real, proper ● *adv* really. **R~ung** *f* **-,-en** regulation; settlement

r

regen vt move; **sich r~** move; (wach werden) stir

Regen m -s,- rain. **R~bogen** m rainbow. **R~bogenhaut** f iris

Regener|ation /-'tsio:n/ f - regeneration. **r~ieren** vt regenerate

Regen|mantel m raincoat. **R~schirm** m umbrella. **R~tag** m rainy day. **R~wetter** nt wet weather. **R~wurm** m earthworm

Regie /re'ʒiː/ f - direction; **R~ führen** direct

regier|en vt/i (haben) govern, rule; (Monarch:) reign [over]; (Gram) take. **R~ung** f -,-en government; (Herrschaft) rule; (eines Monarchen) reign

Regiment nt -[e]s,-er regiment

Region f -,-en region. **r~al** adj regional

Regisseur /reʒɪ'søːɐ̯/ m -s,-e director

Register nt -s,- register; (Inhaltsverzeichnis) index; (Orgel-) stop

Regler m -s,- regulator

reglos adj & adv motionless

regn|en vi (haben) rain; **es r~et** it is raining. **r~erisch** adj rainy

regul|är adj normal; (rechtmäßig) legitimate. **r~ieren** vt regulate

Regung f -,-en movement; (Gefühls-) emotion. **r~slos** adj & adv motionless

Reh nt -[e]s,-e roe-deer; (Culin) venison

Rehbock m roebuck

reib|en vt rub; (Culin) grate ● vi (haben) rub. **R~ung** f - friction. **r~ungslos** adj (fig) smooth

reich adj rich (an + dat in)

Reich nt -[e]s,-e empire; (König-) kingdom; (Bereich) realm

Reiche(r) m/f rich man/woman; **die R~en** the rich pl

reichen vt hand; (anbieten) offer ● vi (haben) be enough; (in der Länge) be long enough; **r~ bis zu** reach [up to]; (sich erstrecken) extend to; **mit dem Geld r~** have enough money

reich|haltig adj extensive, large (Mahlzeit) substantial. **r~lich** adj

ample; (Vorrat) abundant. **R~tum** m -s,-tümer wealth (**an** + dat of); **R~tümer** riches. **R~weite** f reach; (Techn, Mil) range

Reif m -[e]s [hoar-]frost

reif adj ripe; (fig) mature; **r~ für** ready for. **r~en** vi (sein) ripen; (Wein, Käse & fig) mature

Reifen m -s,- hoop; (Arm-) bangle; (Auto-) tyre. **R~druck** m tyre pressure. **R~panne** f puncture, flat tyre

reiflich adj careful

Reihe f -,-n row; (Anzahl & Math) series; **der R~ nach** in turn; **wer ist an der R~?** whose turn is it? **r~n** (sich) vr **sich r~n an** (+ acc) follow. **R~nfolge** f order. **R~nhaus** nt terraced house

Reiher m -s,- heron

Reim m -[e]s,-e rhyme. **r~en** vt rhyme; **sich r~en** rhyme

rein¹ adj pure; (sauber) clean; (Unsinn, Dummheit) sheer; **ins R~e (r~e) schreiben** make a fair copy of

rein² adv = herein, hinein

Reineclaude /rɛːnə'kloːdə/ f -,-n greengage

Reinfall m Ⓘ let-down; (Misserfolg) flop

Rein|gewinn m net profit. **R~heit** f - purity

reinig|en vt clean; (chemisch) dry-clean. **R~ung** f -,-en cleaning; (chemische) dry-cleaning; (Geschäft) dry cleaner's

reinlegen vt sep put in; Ⓘ dupe; (betrügen) take for a ride

reinlich adj clean. **R~keit** f - cleanliness

Reis m -es rice

Reise f -,-n journey; (See-) voyage; (Urlaubs-, Geschäfts-) trip. **R~andenken** nt souvenir. **R~büro** nt travel agency. **R~bus** m coach. **R~führer** m tourist guide; (Buch) guide. **R~gesellschaft** f tourist group. **R~leiter(in)** m(f) courier. **r~n** vi (sein) travel. **R~nde(r)** m/f traveller. **R~pass** m passport. **R~scheck** m traveller's cheque. **R~veranstalter** m -s,- tour operator. **R~ziel** nt destination

Reisig nt -s brushwood

Reißaus m R~ nehmen Ⅱ run away

Reißbrett nt drawing-board

reißen† vt tear; (weg-) snatch; (töten) kill; **Witze r~** crack jokes; **an sich** (acc) r~snatch; seize (Macht); **sich r~ um** Ⅱ fight for ●vi (sein) tear; (Seil, Faden:) break ●vi (haben) r~ an (+ dat) pull at

Reißer m -s,- thriller; (Erfolg) big hit

Reiß|nagel m – R~zwecke. **R~verschluss** m zip [fastener]. **R~wolf** m shredder. **R~zwecke** f -,-n drawing-pin

reit|en† vt/i (sein) ride. **R~er(in)** m -s,- (f -,-nen) rider. **R~hose** f riding breeches pl. **R~pferd** nt saddlehorse. **R~weg** m bridle path

Reiz m -es,-e stimulus; (Anziehungskraft) attraction, appeal; (Charme) charm. **r~bar** adj irritable. **R~barkeit** f - irritability. **r~en** vt provoke; (Med) irritate; (interessieren, locken) appeal to, attract; arouse (Neugier); (beim Kartenspiel) bid. **R~ung** f -,-en (Med) irritation. **r~voll** adj attractive

rekeln (sich) vr Ⅱ stretch

Reklamation /-'tsi̯o:n/ f -,-en (Comm) complaint

Reklam|e f -,-n advertising, publicity; (Anzeige) advertisement; (TV, Radio) commercial; **R~e machen** advertise (für etw sth). **r~ieren** vt complain about; (fordern) claim ●vi (haben) complain

Rekord m -[e]s,-e record

Rekrut m -en,-en recruit

Rek|tor m -s,-en (Sch) head[master]; (Univ) vice-chancellor. **R~torin** f -,-nen head, headmistress; vicechancellor

Relais /rə'lɛː/ nt -,- /-s,-s/ (Electr) relay

relativ adj relative

Religi|on f -,-en religion; (Sch) religious education. **r~ös** adj religious

Reling f -,-s (Naut) rail

Reliquie /re'liːkvi̯ə/ f -,-n relic

rempeln vt jostle; (stoßen) push

Reneklode f -,-n greengage

Rennbahn f race-track; (Pferde-) racecourse. **R~boot** nt speed-boat. **r~en**† vi (sein) run; **um die Wette r~en** have a race. **R~en** nt -s,- race. **R~pferd** nt racehorse. **R~sport** m racing. **R~wagen** m racing car

renommiert adj renowned; (Hotel, Firma) of repute

renovier|en vt renovate; redecorate (Zimmer). **R~ung** f - renovation; redecoration

rentabel adj profitable

Rente f -,-n pension; **in R~ gehen** Ⅱ retire. **R~nversicherung** f pension scheme

Rentier nt reindeer

rentieren (sich) vr be profitable; (sich lohnen) be worth while

Rentner(in) m -s,- (f -,-nen) [oldage] pensioner

Reparatur f -,-en repair. **R~werkstatt** f repair workshop; (Auto) garage

reparieren vt repair, mend

Reportage /-'taːʒə/ f -,-n report

Reporter(in) m -s,- (f -,-nen) reporter

repräsentativ adj representative (für of); (eindrucksvoll) imposing

Reprodu|ktion /-'tsi̯o:n/ f -,-en reproduction. **r~zieren** vt reproduce

Reptil nt -s,-ien reptile

r

Republik f -,-en republic. **r~anisch** adj republican

Requisiten pl (Theat) properties, 🖭 props

Reservat nt -[e]s,-e reservation

Reserve f -,-n reserve; (Mil, Sport) reserves pl. **R~rad** nt spare wheel

reservier|en vt reserve; **r~en lassen** book. **r~t** adj reserved. **R~ung** f -,-en reservation

Reservoir /rezɛr'voaːɐ̯/ nt -s,-s reservoir

Residenz f -,-en residence

Resign|ation /-'tsi̯oːn/ f - resignation. **r~ieren** vi (haben) (fig) give up. **r~iert** adj resigned

resolut adj resolute

Resonanz f -,-en resonanance

Respekt /-sp-, -ʃp-/ m -[e]s respect (**vor** + dat for). **r~ieren** vt respect

respektlos adj disrespectful

Ressort /rɛ'soːɐ̯/ nt -s,-s department

Rest m -[e]s,-e remainder, rest; **R~e** remains; (Essens-) leftovers

Restaurant /rɛsto'rãː/ nt -s,-s restaurant

Restaur|ation /rɛstaura'tsi̯oːn/ f - restoration. **r~ieren** vt restore

Rest|betrag m balance. **r~lich** adj remaining

Resultat nt -[e]s,-e result

rett|en vt save (**vor** + dat from); (aus Gefahr befreien) rescue; **sich r~en** save oneself; (flüchten) escape. **R~er** m -s,- rescuer; (fig) saviour

Rettich m -s,-e white radish

Rettung f -,-en rescue; (fig) salvation; **jds letzte R~** s.o.'s last hope. **R~sboot** nt lifeboat. **R~sdienst** m rescue service. **R~sgürtel** m lifebelt. **r~slos** adv hopelessly. **R~sring** m lifebelt. **R~ssanitäter(in)** m(f) paramedic. **R~swagen** m ambulance

retuschieren vt (Phot) retouch

Reue f - remorse; (Relig) repentance

Revanch|e /re'vãːʃə/ f -,-n revenge; **R~e fordern** (Sport) ask for a return match. **r~ieren (sich)** vr take revenge; (sich erkenntlich zeigen) reciprocate (**mit** with)

Revers /re've:ɐ̯/ nt -,- /-[s],-s/ lapel

Revier nt -s,-e district; (Zool & fig) territory; (Polizei-) [police] station

Revision f -,-en revision; (Prüfung) check; (Jur) appeal

Revolution /-'tsi̯oːn/ f -,-en revolution. **r~är** adj revolutionary. **r~ieren** vt revolutionize

Revolver m -s,- revolver

rezen|sieren vt review. **R~sion** f -,-en review

Rezept nt -[e]s,-e prescription; (Culin) recipe

Rezession f -,-en recession

R-Gespräch nt reverse-charge call

Rhabarber m -s rhubarb

Rhein m -s Rhine. **R~land** nt -s Rhineland. **R~wein** m hock

Rhetorik f - rhetoric

Rheum|a nt -s rheumatism. **r~atisch** adj rheumatic. **R~atismus** m - rheumatism

Rhinozeros nt -[ses],-se rhinoceros

rhyth|misch /'rʏt-/ adj rhythmic[al]. **R~mus** m -,-men rhythm

richten vt direct (**auf** + acc at); address (Frage) (**an** + acc to); aim (Waffe) (**auf** + acc at); (einstellen) set; (vorbereiten) prepare; (reparieren) mend; **in die Höhe r~** raise [up]; **sich r~** be directed (**auf** + acc at; **gegen** against); (Blick:) turn (**auf** + acc on); **sich r~nach** comply with (Vorschrift); fit in with (jds Plänen); (abhängen) depend on ● vi (haben) **r~ über** (+ acc) judge

Richter m -s,- judge

richtig adj right, correct; (wirklich, echt) real; **das R~e** the right thing ● adv correctly; really; **r~ stellen** put right (Uhr); (fig) correct (Irrtum); **die Uhr geht r~** the clock is right

Richtlinien fpl guidelines

Richtung f -,-en direction

riechen† vt/i (haben) smell (**nach** of; **an etw** dat sth)

Riegel m -s,- bolt; (Seife) bar

Riemen m -s,- strap; (*Ruder*) oar

Riese m -n,-n giant

rieseln vi (*sein*) trickle; (*Schnee:*) fall lightly

riesengroß adj huge, enormous

riesig adj huge; (*gewaltig*) enormous ● adv 🅸 terribly

Riff nt -[e]s,-e reef

Rille f -,-n groove

Rind nt -es,-er ox; (*Kuh*) cow; (*Stier*) bull; (*R~fleisch*) beef; **R~er** cattle pl

Rinde f -,-n bark; (*Käse-*) rind; (*Brot-*) crust

Rinder|braten m roast beef. **R~wahnsinn** m 🅸 mad cow disease

Rindfleisch nt beef

Ring m -[e]s,-e ring

ringeln (sich) vr curl

ring|en† vi (*haben*) wrestle; (*fig*) struggle (**um/nach** for) ● vt wring (*Hände*). **R~er** m -s,- wrestler. **R~kampf** m wrestling match; (*als Sport*) wrestling

rings|herum, **r~um** adv all around

Rinn|e f -,-n channel; (*Dach-*) gutter. **r~en†** vi (*sein*) run; (*Sand:*) trickle. **R~stein** m gutter

Rippe f -,-n rib. **R~nfellentzündung** f pleurisy

Risiko nt -s,-s & -ken risk

risk|ant adj risky. **r~ieren** vt risk

Riss m -es,-e tear; (*Mauer-*) crack; (*fig*) rift

rissig adj cracked; (*Haut*) chapped

Rist m -[e]s,-e instep

Ritt m -[e]s,-e ride

Ritter m -s,- knight

Ritual nt -s,-e ritual

Ritz m -es,-e scratch. **R~e** f -,-n crack; (*Fels-*) cleft; (*zwischen Betten, Vorhängen*) gap. **r~en** vt scratch

Rival|e m -n,-n, **R~in** f -,-nen rival. **R~ität** f -,-en rivalry

Robbe f -,-n seal

Robe f -,-n gown; (*Talar*) robe

Roboter m -s,- robot

robust adj robust

röcheln vi (*haben*) breathe noisily

Rochen m -s,- (*Zool*) ray

Rock¹ m -[e]s,ᵉe skirt; (*Jacke*) jacket

Rock² m -[s] (*Mus*) rock

rodel|n vi (*sein/haben*) toboggan. **R~schlitten** m toboggan

roden vt clear (*Land*); grub up (*Stumpf*)

Rogen m -s,- [hard] roe

Roggen m -s rye

roh adj rough; (*ungekocht*) raw; (*Holz*) bare; (*brutal*) brutal. **R~bau** m -[e]s,-ten shell. **R~kost** f raw [vegetarian] food. **R~ling** m -s,-e brute. **R~öl** nt crude oil

Rohr nt -[e]s,-e pipe; (*Geschütz-*) barrel; (*Bot*) reed; (*Zucker-, Bambus-*) cane

Röhre f -,-n tube; (*Radio-*) valve; (*Back-*) oven

Rohstoff m raw material

Rokoko nt -s rococo

Roll|bahn f taxiway; (*Start-/Landebahn*) runway. **R~balken** m scroll bar

Rolle f -,-n roll; (*Garn-*) reel; (*Draht-*) coil; (*Techn*) roller; (*Seil-*) pulley; (*Lauf-*) castor; (*Theat*) part, role; **das spielt keine R~** (*fig*) that doesn't matter. **r~n** vt roll; (*auf-*) roll up; (*Computer*) scroll; **sich r~n** roll ● vi (*sein*) roll; (*Flugzeug.*) Laxi. **R~r** m -s,- scooter. **R~rblades®** /-ble:ds/ mpl Rollerblades®

Roll|feld nt airfield. **R~kragen** m polo-neck. **R~mops** m rollmop[s] sg

Rollo nt -s,-s [roller] blind

Roll|schuh m roller-skate; **R~schuh laufen** roller-skate. **R~stuhl** m wheelchair. **R~treppe** f escalator

Rom nt -s Rome

Roman m -s,-e novel. **r~isch** adj Romanesque; (*Sprache*) Romance

Romant|ik f - romanticism. **r~isch** adj romantic

Röm|er(in) m -s,- (f -,-nen) Roman. **r~isch** adj Roman

r

Rommé, Rommee /'rɔmeː/ nt -s rummy

röntgen vt X-ray. **R~aufnahme** f, **R~bild** nt X-ray. **R~strahlen** mpl X-rays

rosa inv adj, **R~** nt -[s],- pink

Rose f -,-n rose. **R~nkohl** m [Brussels] sprouts pl. **R~nkranz** m (Relig) rosary

Rosine f -,-n raisin

Rosmarin m -s rosemary

Ross nt -es, ̈er horse

Rost¹ m -[e]s,-e grating; (Kamin-) grate; (Brat-) grill

Rost² m -[e]s rust. **r~en** vi (haben) rust

rösten vt roast; toast (Brot)

rostfrei adj stainless

rostig adj rusty

rot adj, **Rot** nt -s,- red; **rot werden** turn red; (erröten) go red, blush

Röte f - redness; (Scham-) blush

Röteln pl German measles sg

röten vt redden; **sich r~** turn red

rothaarig adj red-haired

rotieren vi (haben) rotate

Rot|kehlchen nt -s,- robin. **R~kohl** m red cabbage

rötlich adj reddish

Rotwein m red wine

Rou|lade /ru'laːdə/ f -,-n beef olive. **R~leau** nt -s,-s [roller] blind

Routin|e /ru'tiːnə/ f -,-n routine; (Erfahrung) experience. **r~emäßig** adj routine ● adv routinely. **r~iert** adj experienced

Rowdy /'raʊdi/ m -s,-s hooligan

Rübe f -,-n beet; **rote R~** beetroot

Rubin m -s,-e ruby

Rubrik f -,-en column

Ruck m -[e]s,-e jerk

ruckartig adj jerky

rück|bezüglich adj (Gram) reflexive. **R~blende** f flashback. **R~blick** m (fig) review (auf + acc of). **r~blickend** adv in retrospect. **r~datieren** vt (infinitive & pp only) backdate

Rücken m -s,- back; (Buch-) spine; (Berg-) ridge. **R~lehne** f back. **R~mark** nt spinal cord. **R~schwimmen** nt backstroke. **R~wind** m following wind; (Aviat) tail wind

rückerstatten vt (infinitive & pp only) refund

Rückfahr|karte f return ticket. **R~t** f return journey

Rück|fall m relapse. **R~flug** m return flight. **R~frage** f [further] query. **r~fragen** vi (haben) (infinitive & pp only) check (bei with). **R~gabe** f return. **r~gängig** adj **r~gängig machen** cancel; break off (Verlobung). **R~grat** nt -[e]s,-e spine, backbone. **R~hand** f backhand. **R~kehr** return. **R~lagen** fpl reserves. **R~licht** nt rear-light. **R~reise** f return journey

Rucksack m rucksack

Rück|schau f review. **R~schlag** m (Sport) return; (fig) set-back. **r~schrittlich** adj retrograde. **R~seite** f back; (einer Münze) reverse

Rücksicht f -,-en consideration. **R~nahme** f - consideration. **r~slos** adj inconsiderate; (schonungslos) ruthless. **r~svoll** adj considerate

Rück|sitz m back seat; (Sozius) pillion. **R~spiegel** m rear-view mirror. **R~spiel** nt return match. **R~stand** m (Chemistry) residue; (Arbeits-) backlog; **im R~stand sein** be behind. **r~ständig** adj (fig) backward. **R~stau** m (Auto) tailback. **R~strahler** m -s,- reflector. **R~tritt** m resignation; (Fahrrad) back pedalling

rückwärt|ig adj back, rear. **r~s** adv backwards. **R~sgang** m reverse [gear]

Rückweg m way back

rück|wirkend adj retrospective. **R~wirkung** f retrospective force; **mit R~wirkung vom** backdated to. **R~zahlung** f repayment

Rüde m -n,-n [male] dog

Rudel nt -s,- herd; (Wolfs-) pack; (Löwen-) pride

Ruder *nt* **-s,-** oar; (*Steuer-*) rudder; **am R~** (*Naut & fig*) at the helm. **R~boot** *nt* rowing boat. **r~n** *vt/i* (*haben/sein*) row

Ruf *m* **-[e]s,-e** call; (*laut*) shout; (*Telefon*) telephone number; (*Ansehen*) reputation. **r~en†** *vt/i* (*haben*) call (**nach** for); **r~en lassen** send for

Ruf|name *m* forename by which one is known. **R~nummer** *f* telephone number. **R~zeichen** *nt* dialling tone

Rüge *f* **-,-n** reprimand. **r~n** *vt* reprimand; (*kritisieren*) criticize

Ruhe *f* **-** rest; (*Stille*) quiet; (*Frieden*) peace; (*innere*) calm; (*Gelassenheit*) composure; **R~ [da]!** quiet! **r~los** *adj* restless. **r~n** *vi* (*haben*) rest (**auf** + *dat* on); (*Arbeit, Verkehr:*) have stopped. **R~pause** *f* rest, break. **R~stand** *m* retirement; **im R~stand** retired. **R~störung** *f* disturbance of the peace. **R~tag** *m* day of rest; '**Montag R~tag**' 'closed on Mondays'

ruhig *adj* quiet; (*erholsam*) restful; (*friedlich*) peaceful; (*unbewegt, gelassen*) calm; **man kann r~ darüber sprechen** there's no harm in talking about it

Ruhm *m* **-[e]s** fame; (*Ehre*) glory

rühmen *vt* praise

ruhmreich *adj* glorious

Ruhr *f* **-** (*Med*) dysentery

Rühr|ei *nt* scrambled eggs *pl.* **r~en** *vt* move; (*Culin*) stir; **sich r~en** move ● *vi* (*haben*) stir; **r~en an** (+ *acc*) touch; (*fig*) touch on. **r~end** *adj* touching

Rührung *f* **-** emotion

Ruin *m* **-s** ruin. **R~e** *f* **-,-n** ruin; ruins *pl* (*gen* of). **r~ieren** *vt* ruin

rülpsen *vi* (*haben*) 🔲 belch

Rum *m* **-s** rum

Rumän|ien /-iən/ *nt* **-s** Romania. **r~isch** *adj* Romanian

Rummel *m* **-s** 🔲 hustle and bustle; (*Jahrmarkt*) funfair

Rumpelkammer *f* junk-room

Rumpf *m* **-[e]s,-̈e** body, trunk; (*Schiffs-*) hull; (*Aviat*) fuselage

rund *adj* round ● *adv* approximately; **r~ um** [a]round. **R~blick** *m* panoramic view. **R~brief** *m* circular [letter]

Runde *f* **-,-n** round; (*Kreis*) circle; (*eines Polizisten*) beat; (*beim Rennen*) lap; **eine R~ Bier** a round of beer

Rund|fahrt *f* tour. **R~frage** *f* poll

Rundfunk *m* radio; **im R~** on the radio. **R~gerät** *nt* radio [set]

Rund|gang *m* round; (*Spaziergang*) walk (**durch** round). **r~heraus** *adv* straight out. **r~herum** *adv* all around. **r~lich** *adj* rounded; (*mollig*) plump. **R~reise** *f* [circular] tour. **R~schreiben** *nt* circular. **r~um** *adv* all round. **R~ung** *f* **-,-en** curve

Runzel *f* **-,-n** wrinkle

runzlig *adj* wrinkled

Rüpel *m* **-s,-** 🔲 lout

rupfen *vt* pull out; pluck (*Geflügel*)

Rüsche *f* **-,-n** frill

Ruß *m* **-es** soot

Russe *m* **-n,-n** Russian

Rüssel *m* **-s,-** (*Zool*) trunk

Russ|in *f* **-,-nen** Russian. **r~isch** *adj* Russian. **R~isch** *nt* **-[s]** (*Lang*) Russian

Russland *nt* **-s** Russia

rüsten *vi* (*haben*) prepare (**zu/für** for) ● *vr* **sich r~** get ready

rüstig *adj* sprightly

rustikal *adj* rustic

Rüstung *f* **-,-en** armament; (*Harnisch*) armour. **R~skontrolle** *f* arms control

Rute *f* **-,-n** twig; (*Angel-, Wünschel-*) rod; (*zur Züchtigung*) birch; (*Schwanz*) tail

Rutsch *m* **-[e]s,-e** slide. **R~bahn** *f* slide. **R~e** *f* **-,-n** chute. **r~en** *vt* slide; (*rücken*) move ● *vi* (*sein*) slide; (*aus-, ab-*) slip; (*Auto*) skid. **r~ig** *adj* slippery

rütteln *vt* shake ● *vi* (*haben*) **r~ an** (+ *dat*) rattle

r

Ss

Saal m -[e]s,Säle hall; (*Theat*) auditorium; (*Kranken-*) ward

Saat f -,-en seed; (*Säen*) sowing; (*Gesätes*) crop

sabbern vi (*haben*) ⚀ slobber; (*Baby:*) dribble; (*reden*) jabber

Säbel m -s,- sabre

Sabo|tage /zabo'ta:ʒə/ f - sabotage. **S~teur** m -s,-e saboteur. **s~tieren** vt sabotage

Sach|bearbeiter m expert. **S~buch** nt non-fiction book

Sache f -,-n matter, business; (*Ding*) thing; (*fig*) cause

Sach|gebiet nt (*fig*) area, field. **s~kundig** adj expert. **s~lich** adj factual; (*nüchtern*) matter-of-fact

sächlich adj (*Gram*) neuter

Sachse m -n,-n Saxon. **S~n** nt -s Saxony

sächsisch adj Saxon

Sach|verhalt m -[e]s facts pl. **S~verständige(r)** m/f expert

Sack m -[e]s,ᴬe sack

Sack|gasse f cul-de-sac; (*fig*) impasse. **S~leinen** nt sacking

Sadis|mus m - sadism. **S~t** m -en,-en sadist

säen vt/i (*haben*) sow

Safe /ze:f/ m -s,-s safe

Saft m -[e]s,ᴬe juice; (*Bot*) sap. **s~ig** adj juicy

Sage f -,-n legend

Säge f -,-n saw. **S~mehl** nt sawdust

sagen vt say; (*mitteilen*) tell; (*bedeuten*) mean

sägen vt/i (*haben*) saw

sagenhaft adj legendary

Säge|späne mpl wood shavings. **S~werk** nt sawmill

Sahn|e f - cream. **S~ebonbon** m & nt ≈ toffee. **s~ig** adj creamy

Saison /zɛ'zõ:/ f -,-s season

Saite f -,-n (*Mus, Sport*) string. **S~ninstrument** nt stringed instrument

Sakko m & nt -s,-s sports jacket

Sakrament nt -[e]s,-e sacrament

Sakristei f -,-en vestry

Salat m -[e]s,-e salad. **S~soße** f salad-dressing

Salbe f -,-n ointment

Salbei m -s & f - sage

salben vt anoint

Saldo m -s,-dos & -den balance

Salon /za'lõ:/ m -s,-s salon

salopp adj casual; (*Benehmen*) informal

Salto m -s,-s somersault

Salut m -[e]s,-e salute. **s~ieren** vi (*haben*) salute

Salve f -,-n volley; (*Geschütz-*) salvo, (*von Gelächter*) burst

Salz nt -es,-e salt. **s~en†** vt salt. **S~fass** nt salt-cellar. **s~ig** adj salty. **S~kartoffeln** fpl boiled potatoes. **S~säure** f hydrochloric acid

> **Salzburger Festspiele** The Austrian city of Salzburg, the home of Wolfgang Amadeus Mozart (1756-91), hosts this annual festival as a tribute to the great composer. Every summer since 1920, Mozart-lovers have enjoyed his music at the Salzburg Festival. ℹ️

Samen m -s,- seed; (*Anat*) semen, sperm

Sammel|becken nt reservoir. **s~n** vt/i (*haben*) collect; (*suchen, versammeln*) gather; **sich s~n** collect; (*sich versammeln*) gather; (*sich fassen*) collect oneself. **S~name** m collective noun

Samm|ler(in) m -s,- (f -,-nen) collector. **S~lung** f -,-en collection; (*innere*) composure

Samstag m -s Saturday. **s~s** adv on Saturdays

samt prep (+ dat) together with

Samt m -[e]s velvet

sämtlich indefinite pronoun inv all. **s~e(r,s)** indefinite pronoun all the;

s~e **Werke** complete works

Sanatorium nt -s,-ien sanatorium

Sand m -[e]s sand

Sandale f -,-n sandal

Sand|bank f sandbank. **S~kasten** m sand-pit. **S~papier** nt sandpaper

sanft adj gentle

Sänger(in) m -s,-(f -,-nen) singer

sanieren vt clean up; redevelop (Gebiet); (modernisieren) modernize; make profitable (Industrie, Firma); **sich s~** become profitable

sanitär adj sanitary

Sanität|er m -s,- first-aid man; (Fahrer) ambulance man; (Mil) medical orderly. **S~swagen** m ambulance

Sanktion /zaŋk'tsjoːn/ f -,-en sanction. **s~ieren** vt sanction

Saphir m -s,-e sapphire

Sardelle f -,-n anchovy

Sardine f -,-n sardine

Sarg m -[e]s,ᵈe coffin

Sarkasmus m - sarcasm

Satan m -s Satan; (🖾: Teufel) devil

Satellit m -en,-en satellite. **S~enfernsehen** nt satellite television. **S~enschüssel** f satellite dish. **S~entelefon** nt satphone

Satin /za'tɛn/ m -s satin

Satire f -,-n satire

satt adj full; (Farbe) rich; **s~ sein** have had enough [to eat]; **etw s~ haben** 🖾 be fed up with sth

Sattel m -s,ᵈ saddle. **s~n** vt saddle. **S~zug** m articulated lorry

sättigen vt satisfy; (Chemistry & fig) saturate ● vi (haben) be filling

Satz m -es,ᵈe sentence; (Teil-) clause; (These) proposition; (Math) theorem; (Mus) movement; (Tennis, Zusammengehöriges) set; (Boden-) sediment; (Kaffee-) grounds pl; (Steuer-, Zins-) rate; (Druck-) setting; (Schrift-) type; (Sprung) leap, bound. **S~aussage** f predicate. **S~gegenstand** m subject. **S~zeichen** nt punctuation mark

Sau f -,Säue sow

sauber adj clean; (ordentlich) neat;

(anständig) decent; **s~ machen** clean. **S~keit** f - cleanliness; neatness

säuberlich adj neat

Sauce /'zoːsə/ f -,-n sauce; (Braten-) gravy

Saudi-Arabien /-iən/ nt -s Saudi Arabia

sauer adj sour; (Chemistry) acid; (eingelegt) pickled; (schwer) hard; **saurer Regen** acid rain

Sauerkraut nt sauerkraut

säuerlich adj slightly sour

Sauerstoff m oxygen

saufen† vt/i (haben) drink; 🖾 booze

Säufer m -s,- 🖾 boozer

saugen† vt/i (haben) suck; (staub-) vacuum, hoover; **sich voll Wasser s~** soak up water

säugen vt suckle

Säugetier nt mammal

saugfähig adj absorbent

Säugling m -s,-e infant

Säule f -,-n column

Saum m -[e]s,Säume hem; (Rand) edge

säumen vt hem; (fig) line

Sauna f -,-nas & -nen sauna

Säure f -,-n acidity; (Chemistry) acid

sausen vi (haben) rush; (Ohren:) buzz ● vi (sein) rush [along]

Saxophon, Saxofon nt -s,-e saxophone

S-Bahn f city and suburban railway

Scanner m -s,- scanner

sch int shush! (fort) shoo!

Schabe f -,-n cockroach

schaben vt/i (haben) scrape

schäbig adj shabby

Schablone f -,-n stencil; (Muster) pattern; (fig) stereotype

Schach nt -s chess; **S~!** check! **S~brett** nt chessboard

Schachfigur f chess-man

schachmatt adj **s~ setzen** checkmate; **s~!** checkmate!

Schachspiel nt game of chess

Schacht m -[e]s,ᵈe shaft

S

Schachtel f -,-n box; (*Zigaretten-*) packet

Schachzug m move

schade adj s~ sein be a pity or shame: **zu s~ für** too good for

Schädel m -s, skull. **S~bruch** m fractured skull

schaden vi (*haben*) (+ *dat*) damage; (*nachteilig sein*) hurt. **S~** m -s,: damage; (*Defekt*) defect; (*Nachteil*) disadvantage. **S~ersatz** m damages pl. **S~freude** f malicious glee. **s~froh** adj gloating

schädig|en vt damage, harm. **S~ung** f -,-en damage

schädlich adj harmful

Schädling m -s,-e pest. **S~sbekämpfungsmittel** nt pesticide

Schaf nt -[e]s,-e sheep. **S~bock** m ram

Schäfer m -s,- shepherd. **S~hund** m sheepdog; **Deutscher S~hund** alsatian

schaffen[1]† vt create; (*herstellen*) establish; make (*Platz*)

schaffen[2] v (*reg*) ● vt manage [to do]; pass (*Prüfung*); catch (*Zug*); (*bringen*) take

Schaffner m -s,- conductor; (*Zug-*) ticket-inspector

Schaffung f - creation

Schaft m -[e]s,:e shaft; (*Gewehr-*) stock; (*Stiefel-*) leg

Schal m -s,-s scarf

Schale f -,-n skin; (*abgeschält*) peel; (*Eier-, Nuss-, Muschel-*) shell; (*Schüssel*) dish

schälen vt peel; **sich s~** peel

Schall m -[e]s sound. **S~dämpfer** m silencer. **s~dicht** adj soundproof. **s~en** vi (*haben*) ring out; (*nachhallen*) resound. **S~mauer** f sound barrier. **S~platte** f record, disc

schalt|en vt switch ● vi (*haben*) switch/(*Ampel:*) turn (**auf** + *acc* to); (*Auto*) change gear; (II: *begreifen*) catch on. **S~er** m -s,- switch; (*Post-, Bank-*) counter; (*Fahrkarten-*) ticket window. **S~hebel** m switch; (*Auto*) gear lever. **S~jahr** nt leap year.

S~ung f -,-en circuit: (*Auto*) gear change

Scham f - shame; (*Anat*) private parts pl

schämen (sich) vr be ashamed

scham|haft adj modest. **s~los** adj shameless

Schampon nt -s shampoo. **s~ieren** vt shampoo

Schande f - disgrace, shame

schändlich adj disgraceful

Schanktisch m bar

Schanze f, -,-n [ski-]jump

Schar f -,-en crowd; (*Vogel-*) flock

Scharade f -,-n charade

scharen vt um sich s~ gather round one; **sich s~ um** flock round. **s~weise** adv in droves

scharf adj sharp; (*stark*) strong; (*stark gewürzt*) hot; (*Geruch*) pungent; (*Wind, Augen, Verstand*) keen; (*streng*) harsh; (*Galopp*) hard; (*Munition*) live; (*Hund*) fierce; **s~ einstellen** (*Phot*) focus; **s~ sein** (*Phot*) be in focus; **s~ sein auf** (+ *acc*) II be keen on

Schärfe f sharpness; strength; hotness; pungency; keenness; harshness. **s~n** vt sharpen

Scharf|richter m executioner. **S~schütze** m marksman. **S~sinn** m astuteness

Scharlach m -s scarlet fever

Scharlatan m -s,-e charlatan

Scharnier nt -s,-e hinge

Schärpe f -,-n sash

scharren vi (*haben*) scrape; (*Huhn*) scratch ● vt scrape

Schaschlik m & nt -s,-s kebab

Schatten m -s,- shadow; (*schattige Stelle*) shade. **S~riss** m silhouette. **S~seite** f shady side; (*fig*) disadvantage

schattier|en vt shade. **S~ung** f -,-en shading

schattig adj shady

Schatz m -es,:e treasure; (*Freund, Freundin*) sweetheart

schätzen vt estimate; (*taxieren*)

value; (*achten*) esteem; (*würdigen*) appreciate

Schätzung *f* -,-en estimate; (*Taxierung*) valuation

Schau *f* -,-en show. **S~ bild** *nt* diagram

Schauder *m* -s shiver; (*vor Abscheu*) shudder. **s~ haft** *adj* dreadful. **s~n** *vi* (*haben*) shiver; (*vor Abscheu*) shudder

schauen *vi* (*haben*) (*SGer, Aust*) look; **s~, dass** make sure that

Schauer *m* -s,- shower; (*Schauder*) shiver. **S~geschichte** *f* horror story. **s~lich** *adj* ghastly

Schaufel *f* -,-n shovel; (*Kehr-*) dustpan. **s~n** *vt* shovel; (*graben*) dig

Schaufenster *nt* shop-window. **S~puppe** *f* dummy

Schaukel *f* -,-n swing. **s~n** *vt* rock ● *vi* (*haben*) rock; (*auf einer Schaukel*) swing; (*schwanken*) sway. **S~pferd** *nt* rocking-horse. **S~stuhl** *m* rocking-chair

Schaum *m* -[e]s foam; (*Seifen-*) lather; (*auf Bier*) froth; (*als Frisier-, Rasiermittel*) mousse

schäumen *vi* (*haben*) foam, froth; (*Seife:*) lather

Schaum|gummi *m* foam rubber. **s~ig** *a* frothy; **s~ig rühren** (*Culin*) cream. **S~stoff** *m* [synthetic] foam. **S~wein** *m* sparkling wine

Schauplatz *m* scene

schaurig *adj* dreadful; (*unheimlich*) eerie

Schauspiel *nt* play; (*Anblick*) spectacle. **S~er** *m* actor. **S~erin** *f* actress

Scheck *m* -s,-s cheque. **S~buch, S~heft** *nt* cheque-book. **S~karte** *f* cheque card

Scheibe *f* -,-n disc; (*Schieß-*) target; (*Glas-*) pane; (*Brot-, Wurst-*) slice. **S~nwischer** *m* -s,- windscreen-wiper

Scheich *m* -s,-e & -s sheikh

Scheide *f* -,-n sheath; (*Anat*) vagina

scheid|en† *vt* separate; (*unterscheiden*) distinguish; dissolve (*Ehe*); **sich**

s~en lassen get divorced ● *vi* (*sein*) leave; (*voneinander*) part. **S~ung** *f* -,-en divorce

Schein *m* -[e]s,-e light; (*Anschein*) appearance; (*Bescheinigung*) certificate; (*Geld-*) note. **s~bar** *adj* apparent. **s~en†** *vi* (*haben*) shine; (*den Anschein haben*) seem, appear

scheinheilig *adj* hypocritical

Scheinwerfer *m* -s,- floodlight; (*Such-*) searchlight; (*Auto*) headlight; (*Theat*) spotlight

Scheiße *f* - (*vulgar*) shit. **s~n†** *vi* (*haben*) (*vulgar*) shit

Scheit *nt* -[e]s,-e log

Scheitel *m* -s,- parting

scheitern *vi* (*sein*) fail

Schelle *f* -,-n bell. **s~n** *vi* (*haben*) ring

Schellfisch *m* haddock

Schelm *m* -s,-e rogue

Schelte *f* - scolding

Schema² *nt* -s,-mata model, pattern; (*Skizze*) diagram

Schemel *m* -s,- stool

Schenke *f* -,-n tavern

Schenkel *m* -s,- thigh

schenken *vt* give [as a present]; **jdm Vertrauen s~** trust s.o.

Scherbe *f* -,-n [broken] piece

Schere *f* -,-n scissors *pl*; (*Techn*) shears *pl*; (*Hummer-*) claw. **s~n¹†** *vt* shear; crop (*Haar*)

scheren² *vt* (*reg*) ⊞ bother; **sich nicht s~ um** not care about

Scherenschnitt *m* silhouette

Scherereien *fpl* ⊞ trouble *sg*

Scherz *m* -es,-e joke; **im/zum S~** as a joke. **s~en** *vi* (*haben*) joke

scheu *adj* shy; (*Tier*) timid; **s~ werden** (*Pferd:*) shy

scheuchen *vt* shoo

scheuen *vt* be afraid of; (*meiden*) shun; **keine Mühe/Kosten s~** spare no effort/expense; **sich s~** be afraid (**vor** + *dat* of); shrink (**etw zu tun** from doing sth)

scheuern *vt* scrub; (*reiben*) rub;

[wund] s~n chafe ● vi (haben) rub, chafe

Scheuklappen fpl blinkers

Scheune f -, n barn

Scheusal nt -s,-e monster

scheußlich adj horrible

Schi m -s,-v ski; **S~ fahren** od **laufen** ski

Schicht f -,-en layer; (Geology) stratum; (Gesellschafts-) class; (Arbeits-) shift. **S~arbeit** f shift work. **s~en** vt stack [up]

schick adj stylish; (Frau) chic. **S~** m -[e]s style

schicken vt/i (haben) send; **s~ nach** send for

Schicksal nt -s,-e fate. **S~sschlag** m misfortune

Schieb|edach nt (Auto) sun-roof. **s~en†** vt push; (gleitend) slide; (🔲: handeln mit) traffic in; **etw s~en auf** (+ acc) (fig) put sth down to; shift (Schuld) on to ● vi (haben) push. **S~etür** f sliding door. **S~ung** f -,-en 🔲 illicit deal; (Betrug) rigging, fixing

Schieds|gericht nt panel of judges; (Jur) arbitration tribunal. **S~richter** m referee; (Tennis) umpire; (Jur) arbitrator

schief adj crooked; (unsymmetrisch) lopsided; (geneigt) slanting, sloping; (nicht senkrecht) leaning; (Winkel) oblique; (fig) false; suspicious ● adv not straight; **s~ gehen** 🔲 go wrong

Schiefer m -s slate

schielen vi (haben) squint

Schienbein nt shin

Schiene f -,-n rail; (Gleit-) runner; (Med) splint. **s~n** vt (Med) put in a splint

Schieß|bude f shooting-gallery. **s~en†** vt shoot; fire (Kugel); score (Tor) ● vi (haben) shoot, fire (auf + acc at). **S~scheibe** f target. **S~stand** m shooting-range

Schifahr|en nt skiing. **S~er(in)** m(f) skier

Schiff nt -[e]s,-e ship; (Kirchen-) nave; (Seiten-) aisle

Schiffahrt f = Schifffahrt

schiff|bar adj navigable. **S~bruch** m shipwreck. **s~brüchig** adj shipwrecked. **S~fahrt** f shipping

Schikan|e f -,-n harassment; **mit allen S~en** 🔲 with every refinement. **s~ieren** vt harass

Schi|laufen nt -s skiing. **S~läufer(in)** m(f) -s,- (f -,-nen) skier

Schild¹ m -[e]s,-e shield

Schild² nt -[e]s,-er sign; (Nummern-) plate; (Mützen-) badge; (Etikett) label

Schilddrüse f thyroid [gland]

schilder|n vt describe. **S~ung** f -,-en description

Schild|kröte f tortoise; (See-) turtle. **S~patt** nt -[e]s tortoiseshell

Schilf nt -[e]s reeds pl

schillern vi (haben) shimmer

Schimmel m -s,- mould; (Pferd) white horse. **s~n** vi (haben/sein) go mouldy

schimmern vi (haben) gleam

Schimpanse m -n,-n chimpanzee

schimpf|en vi (haben) grumble (mit at; über + acc about); scold (mit jdm s.o.) ● vt call. **S~wort** nt (pl -wörter) swear-word

Schinken m -s,- ham. **S~speck** m bacon

Schippe f -,-n shovel. **s~n** vt shovel

Schirm m -[e]s,-e umbrella; (Sonnen-) sunshade; (Lampen-) shade; (Augen-) visor; (Mützen-) peak; (Ofen-, Bild-) screen; (fig: Schutz) shield. **S~herrschaft** f patronage. **S~mütze** f peaked cap

schizophren adj schizophrenic. **S~ie** f - schizophrenia

Schlacht f -,-en battle

schlachten vt slaughter, kill

Schlacht|feld nt battlefield. **S~hof** m abattoir

Schlacke f -,-n slag

Schlaf m -[e]s sleep; **im S~** in one's sleep. **S~anzug** m pyjamas pl

Schläfe f -,-n (Anat) temple

schlafen† vi (haben) sleep; **s~**

gehen go to bed; **er schläft noch** he is still asleep

schlaff *adj* limp; (*Seil*) slack; (*Muskel*) flabby

Schlaf|lied *nt* lullaby. **s~los** *adj* sleepless. **S~losigkeit** *f* - insomnia. **S~mittel** *nt* sleeping drug

schläfrig *adj* sleepy

Schlaf|saal *m* dormitory. **S~sack** *m* sleeping-bag. **S~tablette** *f* sleeping-pill. **S~wagen** *m* sleeping-car, sleeper. **s~wandeln** *vi* (*haben/sein*) sleep-walk. **S~zimmer** *nt* bed-room

Schlag *m* -[e]s,⸚e blow; (*Faust-*) punch; (*Herz-, Puls-, Trommel-*) beat; (*einer Uhr*) chime; (*Glocken-, Gong- & Med*) stroke; (*elektrischer*) shock; (*Art*) type; **S~e bekommen** get a beating; **S~ auf S~** in rapid succession. **S~ader** *f* artery. **S~anfall** *m* stroke. **S~baum** *m* barrier

schlagen† *vt* hit, strike; (*fällen*) fell; knock (*Loch, Nagel*) (**in** + *acc* into); (*prügeln, besiegen*) beat; (*Culin*) whisk (*Eiweiß*); whip (*Sahne*); (*legen*) throw; (*wickeln*) wrap; **sich s~** fight ● *vi* (*haben*) beat; (*Tür:*) bang; (*Uhr:*) strike; (*melodisch*) chime; **mit den Flügeln s~** flap its wings ● *vi* (*sein*) **in etw** (*acc*) **s~** (*Blitz, Kugel:*) strike sth; **nach jdm s~** (*fig*) take after s.o.

Schlager *m* -s,- popular song; (*Erfolg*) hit

Schläger *m* -s,- racket; (*Tischtennis-*) bat; (*Golf-*) club; (*Hockey-*) stick. **S~ei** *f* -,-en fight, brawl

schlag|fertig *adj* quick-witted. **S~loch** *nt* pot-hole. **S~sahne** *f* whipped cream; (*ungeschlagen*) whipping cream. **S~seite** *f* (*Naut*) list. **S~stock** *m* truncheon. **S~wort** *nt* (*pl* -worte) slogan. **S~zeile** *f* headline. **S~zeug** *nt* (*Mus*) percussion. **S~zeuger** *m* -s,- percussionist; (*in Band*) drummer

Schlamm *m* -[e]s mud. **s~ig** *adj* muddy

Schlamp|e *f* -,-n ☒ slut. **s~en** *vi* (*haben*) ☒ be sloppy (**bei** in). **s~ig**

adj slovenly; (*Arbeit*) sloppy

Schlange *f* -,-n snake; (*Menschen-, Auto-*) queue; **S~ stehen** queue

schlängeln (sich) *vr* wind; (*Person:*) weave (**durch** through)

schlank *adj* slim. **S~heitskur** *f* slimming diet

schlapp *adj* tired; (*schlaff*) limp

schlau *adj* clever; (*gerissen*) crafty; **ich werde nicht s~ daraus** I can't make head or tail of it

Schlauch *m* -[e]s,Schläuche tube; (*Wasser-*) hose[pipe]. **S~boot** *nt* rubber dinghy

Schlaufe *f* -,-n loop

schlecht *adj* bad; (*böse*) wicked; (*unzulänglich*) poor; **s~ werden** go bad; (*Wetter:*) turn bad; **mir ist s~** I feel sick; **s~ machen** ☒ run down. **s~gehen*** *vi sep* (*sein*) **s~ gehen,** *s.* **gehen**

schlecken *vt/i* (*haben*) lick (**an etw** *dat* sth); (*auf-*) lap up

Schlegel *m* -s,- (*SGer: Keule*) leg; (*Hühner-*) drumstick

schleichen† *vi* (*sein*) creep; (*langsam gehen/fahren*) crawl ● *vr* **sich s~** creep. **s~d** *adj* creeping

Schleier *m* -s,- veil; (*fig*) haze

Schleife *f* -,-n bow; (*Fliege*) bowtie; (*Biegung*) loop

schleifen[1] *v* (*reg*) ● *vt* drag ● *vi* (*haben*) trail, drag

schleifen[2]† *vt* grind; (*schärfen*) sharpen; cut (*Edelstein, Glas*)

Schleim *m* -[e]s slime; (*Anat*) mucus; (*Med*) phlegm. **s~ig** *adj* slimy

schlendern *vi* (*sein*) stroll

schlenkern *vt/i* (*haben*) swing; **s~ mit** swing; dangle (*Beine*)

Schlepp|dampfer *m* tug. **S~e** *f* -,-n train. **s~en** *vt* drag; (*tragen*) carry; (*ziehen*) tow; **sich s~en** drag oneself; (*sich hinziehen*) drag on; **sich s~en mit** carry. **S~er** *m* -s,- tug; (*Traktor*) tractor. **S~kahn** *m* barge. **S~lift** *m* T-bar lift. **S~tau** *nt* towrope; **ins S~tau nehmen** take in tow

S

Schleuder f -,-n catapult; (*Wäsche-*) spin-drier. **s~n** vt hurl; spin (*Wäsche*) ● vi (*sein*) skid; **ins S~n geraten** skid. **S~sitz** m ejector seat

Schleuse f -,-n lock; (*Sperre*) sluice[-gate]. **s~n** vt steer

Schliche pl tricks

schlicht adj plain; simple

Schlichtung f - settlement; (*Jur*) arbitration

Schließe f -,-n clasp; buckle

schließen† vt close (*ab-*) lock; fasten (*Kleid, Verschluss*); (*stilllegen*) close down; (*beenden, folgern*) conclude; enter into (*Vertrag*); **sich s~** close; **etw s~ an** (+ *acc*) connect sth to; **sich s~ an** (+ *acc*) follow ● vi (*haben*) close, (*den Betrieb einstellen*) close down; (*den Schlüssel drehen*) turn the key; (*enden, folgern*) conclude

Schließ|fach nt locker. **s~lich** adv finally, in the end; (*immerhin*) after all. **S~ung** f -,-en closure

Schliff m -[e]s cut; (*Schleifen*) cutting; (*fig*) polish

schlimm adj bad

Schlinge f -,-n loop; (*Henkers-*) noose; (*Med*) sling; (*Falle*) snare

Schlingel m -s,- ☐ rascal

schlingen† vt wind, wrap; tie (*Knoten*) ● vt/i (*haben*) bolt one's food

Schlips m -es,-e tie

Schlitten m -s,- sledge; (*Rodel-*) toboggan; (*Pferde-*) sleigh; **S~ fahren** toboggan

schlittern vi (*haben/ sein*) slide

Schlittschuh m skate; **S~ laufen** skate. **S~läufer(in)** m(f) -s,- (f -,-nen) skater

Schlitz m -es,-e slit; (*für Münze*) slot; (*Jacken-*) vent; (*Hosen-*) flies pl. **s~en** vt slit

Schloss nt -es,-er lock; (*Vorhänge-*) padlock; (*Verschluss*) clasp; (*Gebäude*) castle; palace

Schlosser m -s,- locksmith; (*Auto-*) mechanic

Schlucht f -,-en ravine, gorge

schluchzen vi (*haben*) sob

Schluck m -[e]s,-e mouthful; (*klein*) sip

Schluckauf m -s hiccups pl

schlucken vt/i (*haben*) swallow

Schlummer m -s slumber

Schlund m -[e]s [back of the] throat; (*fig*) mouth

schlüpf|en vi (*sein*) slip; [aus dem Ei] **s~en** hatch. **S~er** m -s,- knickers pl. **s~rig** adj slippery

schlürfen vt/i (*haben*) slurp

Schluss m -es,-e end; (*S~folgerung*) conclusion; **zum S~** finally; **S~ machen** stop (**mit etw** sth); finish (**mit jdm** with s.o.)

Schlüssel m -s,- key; (*Schrauben-*) spanner; (*Geheim-*) code; (*Mus*) clef. **S~bein** nt collar-bone. **S~bund** m & nt bunch of keys. **S~loch** nt keyhole

Schlussfolgerung f conclusion

schlüssig adj conclusive

Schluss|licht nt rear-light. **S~verkauf** m sale

schmächtig adj slight

schmackhaft adj tasty

schmal adj narrow; (*dünn*) thin; (*schlank*) slender; (*karg*) meagre

schmälern vt diminish; (*herabsetzen*) belittle

Schmalz[1] nt -es lard; (*Ohren-*) wax

Schmalz[2] m -es ☐ schmaltz

Schmarotzer m -s,- parasite; (*Person*) sponger

schmatzen vi (*haben*) eat noisily

schmausen vi (*haben*) feast

schmecken vi (*haben*) taste (**nach** of); [gut] **s~** taste good ● vt taste

Schmeichelei f -,-en flattery; (*Kompliment*) compliment

schmeichel|haft adj complimentary, flattering. **s~n** vi (*haben*) (+ *dat*) flatter

schmeißen† vt/i (*haben*) **s~** [mit] ☐ chuck

Schmeißfliege f bluebottle

schmelz|en† vt/i (*sein*) melt; smelt (*Erze*). **S~wasser** nt melted snow and ice

Schmerbauch m 🔟 paunch

Schmerz m -es,-en pain; (Kummer) grief; S~en haben be in pain. s~en vt hurt; (fig) grieve ● vi (haben) hurt, be painful. S~ensgeld nt compensation for pain and suffering. s~haft adj painful. S~los adj painless s~stillend adj pain-killing; s~stillendes Mittel analgesic, pain-killer. S~tablette f pain-killer

Schmetterball m (Tennis) smash

Schmetterling m -s,-e butterfly

schmettern vt hurl; (Tennis) smash; (singen) sing ● vi (haben) sound

Schmied m -[e]s,-e blacksmith

Schmiede f -,-n forge. S~eisen nt wrought iron. s~n vt forge

Schmier|e f -,-n grease; (Schmutz) mess. s~en vt lubricate; (streichen) spread; (schlecht schreiben) scrawl ● vi (haben) smudge; (schreiben) scrawl. S~geld nt 🔟 bribe. s~ig adj greasy; (schmutzig) grubby. S~mittel nt lubricant

Schminke f -,-n make-up. s~n vt make up; sich s~n put on make-up; sich (dat) die Lippen s~n put on lipstick

schmirgel|n vt sand down. S~papier nt emery-paper

schmollen vi (haben) sulk

schmor|en vt/i (haben) braise. S~topf m casserole

Schmuck m -[e]s jewellery; (Verzierung) ornament, decoration

schmücken vt decorate, adorn

schmuck|los adj plain. S~stück nt piece of jewellery

Schmuggel m -s smuggling. s~n vt smuggle. S~ware f contraband

Schmuggler m -s,- smuggler

schmunzeln vi (haben) smile

schmusen vi (haben) cuddle

Schmutz m -es dirt. s~en vi (haben) get dirty. s~ig adj dirty

Schnabel m -s,⁼ beak, bill; (eines Kruges) lip; (Tülle) spout

Schnalle f -,-n buckle. s~n vt strap; (zu-) buckle

schnalzen vi (haben) mit der

Zunge s~ click one's tongue

schnapp|en vi (haben) s~en nach snap at; gasp for (Luft) ● vt snatch, grab; (🔟: festnehmen) nab. S~schloss nt spring lock. S~schuss m snapshot

Schnaps m -es,⁼e schnapps

schnarchen vi (haben) snore

schnaufen vi (haben) puff, pant

Schnauze f -,-n muzzle; (eines Kruges) lip; (Tülle) spout

schnäuzen (sich) vr blow one's nose

Schnecke f -,-n snail; (Nackt-) slug; (Spirale) scroll. S~nhaus nt snail-shell

Schnee m -s snow; (Eier-) beaten egg-white. S~besen m whisk. S~brille f snow-goggles pl. S~fall m snow-fall. S~flocke f snowflake. S~glöckchen nt -s,- snowdrop. S~kette f snow chain. S~mann m (pl -männer) snowman. S~pflug m snowplough. S~schläger m whisk. S~sturm m snowstorm, blizzard. S~wehe f -,-n snowdrift

Schneide f -,-n [cutting] edge; (Klinge) blade

schneiden† vt cut; (in Scheiben) slice; (kreuzen) cross; (nicht beachten) cut dead; Gesichter s~ pull faces; sich s~ cut oneself; (über-) intersect

Schneider m -s,- tailor. S~in f -,-nen dressmaker. s~n vt make (Anzug, Kostüm)

Schneidezahn m incisor

schneien vi (haben) snow; es schneit it is snowing

Schneise f -,-n path

schnell adj quick; (Auto, Tempo) fast ● adv quickly; (in s~em Tempo) fast; (bald) soon; mach s~! hurry up! S~igkeit f - rapidity; (Tempo) speed. S~kochtopf m pressure-cooker. s~stens adv as quickly as possible. S~zug m express [train]

schnetzeln vt cut into thin strips

Schnipsel m & nt -s,- scrap

Schnitt m -[e]s,-e cut; (Film-) cutting; (S~muster) [paper] pattern; im

S

S∼ (*durchschnittlich*) on average

Schnitte *f* -,-n slice [of bread]

schnittig *adj* stylish; (*stromlinienförmig*) streamlined

Schnitt|lauch *m* chives *pl*. **S∼muster** *nt* [paper] pattern. **S∼punkt** *m* [point of] intersection. **S∼stelle** *f* interface. **S∼wunde** *f* cut

Schnitzel *nt* -s,- scrap; (*Culin*) escalope. **s∼n** *vt* shred

schnitzen *vt/i* (*haben*) carve

schnodderig *adj* 🔲 brash

Schnorchel *m* -s,- snorkel

Schnörkel *m* -s,- flourish; (*Kunst*) scroll. **s∼ig** *adj* ornate

schnüffeln *vi* (*haben*) sniff (**an** etw *dat* sth); (🔲: *spionieren*) snoop [around]

Schnuller *m* -s,- [baby's] dummy

Schnupf|en *m* -s,- [head] cold. **S∼tabak** *m* snuff

schnuppern *vt/i* (*haben*) sniff (**an** etw *dat* sth)

Schnur *f* -,¨e string; (*Kordel*) cord; (*Electr*) flex

schnüren *vt* tie; lace [up] (*Schuhe*)

Schnurr|bart *m* moustache. **s∼en** *vi* (*haben*) hum; (*Katze:*) purr

Schnürsenkel *m* [shoe-]lace

Schock *m* -[e]s,-s shock. **s∼en** *vt* 🔲 shock. **s∼ieren** *vt* shock

Schöffe *m* -n,-n lay judge

Schokolade *f* - chocolate

Scholle *f* -,-n clod [of earth]; (*Eis-*) [ice-]floe; (*Fisch*) plaice

schon *adv* already; (*allein*) just; (*sogar*) even; (*ohnehin*) anyway; **s∼ einmal** before; (*jemals*) ever; **s∼ immer/oft/wieder** always/often/ again; **s∼ deshalb** for that reason alone; **das ist s∼ möglich** that's quite possible; **ja s∼, aber** well yes, but

schön *adj* beautiful; (*Wetter*) fine; (*angenehm, nett*) nice; (*gut*) good; (🔲: *beträchtlich*) pretty; **s∼en Dank!** thank you very much!

schonen *vt* spare; (*gut behandeln*) look after. **s∼d** *adj* gentle

Schönheit *f* -,-en beauty. **S∼sfehler** *m* blemish. **S∼skonkurrenz** *f* beauty contest

Schonung *f* -,-en gentle care; (*nach Krankheit*) rest; (*Baum-*) plantation. **s∼slos** *adj* ruthless

Schonzeit *f* close season

schöpf|en *vt* scoop [up]; ladle (*Suppe*); **Mut s∼en** take heart. **s∼erisch** *adj* creative. **S∼kelle** *f*. **S∼löffel** *m* ladle. **S∼ung** *f* -,-en creation

Schoppen *m* -s,- (*SGer*) ≈ pint

Schorf *m* -[e]s scab

Schornstein *m* chimney. **S∼feger** *m* -s,- chimney sweep

Schoß *m* -es,¨e lap; (*Frack-*) tail

Schössling *m* -s,-e (*Bot*) shoot

Schote *f* -,-n pod; (*Erbse*) pea

Schotte *m* -n,-n Scot, Scotsman

Schottin *f* -nen Scot, Scotswoman

Schotter *m* -s gravel

schott|isch *adj* Scottish, Scots. **S∼land** *nt* -s Scotland

schraffieren *vt* hatch

schräg *adj* diagonal; (*geneigt*) sloping; **s∼ halten** tilt. **S∼strich** *m* oblique stroke

Schramme *f* -,-n scratch

Schrank *m* -[e]s,¨e cupboard; (*Kleider-*) wardrobe; (*Akten-, Glas-*) cabinet

Schranke *f* -,-n barrier

Schraube *f* -,-n screw; (*Schiffs-*) propeller. **s∼n** *vt* screw; (*ab-*) unscrew; (*drehen*) turn. **S∼nschlüssel** *m* spanner. **S∼nzieher** *m* -s,- screwdriver

Schraubstock *m* vice

Schreck *m* -[e]s,-e fright. **S∼en** *m* -s,- fright; (*Entsetzen*) horror

Schreck|gespenst *nt* spectre. **s∼haft** *adj* easily frightened; (*nervös*) jumpy. **s∼lich** *adj* terrible.

Schrei *m* -[e]s,-e cry, shout; (*gellend*) scream; **der letzte S∼** 🔲 the latest thing

schreib|en† *vt/i* (*haben*) write; (*auf der Maschine*) type; **richtig/falsch s∼en** spell right/wrong; **sich s∼en** (*Wort:*) be spelt; (*korrespondieren*) correspond. **S∼en** *nt* -s,- writing;

(*Brief*) letter. **S~fehler** *m* spelling mistake. **S~heft** *nt* exercise book. **S~kraft** *f* clerical assistant; (*für Maschineschreiben*) typist. **S~maschine** *f* typewriter. **S~tisch** *m* desk. **S~ung** *f* -,-en spelling. **S~waren** *fpl* stationery *sg*.

schreien† *vt/i* (*haben*) cry; (*gellend*) scream; (*rufen, laut sprechen*) shout

Schreiner *m* -s,- joiner

schreiten† *vi* (*sein*) walk

Schrift *f* -,-en writing; (*Druck-*) type; (*Abhandlung*) paper; **die Heilige S~** the Scriptures *pl*. **S~führer** *m* secretary. **s~lich** *adj* written ● *adv* in writing. **S~sprache** *f* written language. **S~steller(in)** *m* -s,- (*f* -,-nen) writer. **S~stück** *nt* document. **S~zeichen** *nt* character

schrill *adj* shrill

Schritt *m* -[e]s,-e step; (*Entfernung*) pace; (*Gangart*) walk; (*der Hose*) crotch. **S~macher** *m* -s,- pacemaker. **s~weise** *adv* step by step

schroff *adj* precipitous; (*abweisend*) brusque; (*unvermittelt*) abrupt; (*Gegensatz*) stark

Schrot *m & nt* -[e]s coarse meal; (*Blei-*) small shot. **S~flinte** *f* shotgun

Schrott *m* -[e]s scrap[-metal]; **zu S~ fahren** Ⓣ write off. **S~platz** *m* scrap-yard

schrubben *vt/i* (*haben*) scrub

Schrull|e *f* -,-n whim; **alte S~e** Ⓣ old crone. **s~ig** *adj* cranky

schrumpfen *vi* (*sein*) shrink

schrump[e]lig *adj* wrinkled

Schub *m* -[e]s,ⸯe (*Phys*) thrust; (*S~fach*) drawer; (*Menge*) batch. **S~fach** *nt* drawer. **S~karre** *f*, **S~karren** *m* wheelbarrow. **S~lade** *f* drawer

Schubs *m* -es,-e push, shove. **s~en** *vt* push, shove

schüchtern *adj* shy. **S~heit** *f* - shyness

Schuft *m* -[e]s,-e (*pej*) swine

Schuh *m* -[e]s,-e shoe. **S~anzieher** *m* -s,- shoehorn. **S~band** *nt* (*pl* -bänder) shoe-lace. **S~creme** *f* shoe-polish. **S~löffel** *m* shoehorn.

S~macher *m* -s,- shoemaker

Schul|abgänger *m* -s,- schoolleaver. **S~arbeiten, S~aufgaben** *fpl* homework *sg*.

Schuld *f* -,-en guilt; (*Verantwortung*) blame; (*Geld-*) debt; **S~en machen** get into debt; **S~ haben** be to blame (**an** + *dat* for); **jdm S~ geben** blame s.o. ● **s~ sein** be to blame (**an** + *dat* for). **s~en** *vt* owe

schuldig *adj* guilty (*gen* of); (*gebührend*) due; **jdm etw s~sein** owe s.o. sth. **S~keit** *f* - duty

schuld|los *adj* innocent. **S~ner** *m* -s,- debtor. **S~spruch** *m* guilty verdict

Schule *f* -,-n school; **in der/die S~** at/to school. **s~n** *vt* train

Schüler(in) *m* -s,- (*f* -,-nen) pupil

schul|frei *adj* **s~freier Tag** day without school; **wir haben morgen s~frei** there's no school tomorrow. **S~hof** *m* [school] playground. **S~jahr** *nt* school year; (*Klasse*) form. **S~kind** *nt* schoolchild. **S~stunde** *f* lesson

Schulter *f* -,-n shoulder. **S~blatt** *nt* shoulder-blade

Schulung *f* - training

schummeln *vi* (*haben*) Ⓣ cheat

Schund *m* -[e]s trash

Schuppe *f* -,-n scale; **S~n** *pl* dandruff *sg*. **s~n (sich)** *vr* flake [off]

Schuppen *m* -s,- shed

schürf|en *vt* mine; **sich** (*dat*) **das Knie s~en** graze one's knee ● *vi* (*haben*) **s~en nach** prospect for. **S~wunde** *f* abrasion, graze

Schürhaken *m* poker

Schurke *m* -n,-n villain

Schürze *f* -,-n apron

Schuss *m* -es,ⸯe shot; (*kleine Menge*) dash

Schüssel *f* -,-n bowl; (*TV*) dish

Schuss|fahrt *f* (*Ski*) schuss. **S~waffe** *f* firearm

Schuster *m* -s,- = Schuhmacher

Schutt *m* -[e]s rubble. **S~abladeplatz** *m* rubbish dump

Schüttel|frost *m* shivering fit. **s~n**

schütten | Schwein

188

vt shake; **sich s∼n** shake oneself/itself; (*vor Ekel*) shudder; **jdm die Hand s∼n** shake s.o.'s hand

schütten *vt* pour; (*kippen*) tip; (*ver-*) spill ● *vi* (*haben*) **es schüttet** it is pouring [with rain]

Schutz *m* **-es** protection; (*Zuflucht*) shelter; (*Techn*) guard; **S∼ suchen** take refuge. **S∼anzug** *m* protective suit. **S∼blech** *nt* mudguard. **S∼brille** goggles *pl*

Schütze *m* **-n,-n** marksman; (*Tor-*) scorer; (*Astrology*) Sagittarius

schützen *vt* protect; (*Zuflucht gewähren*) shelter (**vor** + *dat* from) ● *vi* (*haben*) give protection/shelter (**vor** + *dat* from)

Schutz|engel *m* guardian angel. **S∼heilige(r)** *m/f* patron saint

Schützling *m* **-s,-e** charge

schutz|los *adj* defenceless, helpless. **S∼mann** *m* (*pl* **-männer** & **-leute**) policeman. **S∼umschlag** *m* dustjacket

Schwaben *nt* **-s** Swabia

schwäbisch *adj* Swabian

schwach *adj* weak; (*nicht gut; gering*) poor; (*leicht*) faint

Schwäche *f* **-,-n** weakness. **s∼n** *vt* weaken

schwäch|lich *adj* delicate. **S∼ling** *m* **-s,-e** weakling

Schwachsinn *m* mental deficiency. **s∼ig** *adj* mentally deficient; 🔲 idiotic

Schwager *m* **-s,⁑** brother-in-law

Schwägerin *f* **-,-nen** sister-in-law

Schwalbe *f* **-,-n** swallow

Schwall *m* **-[e]s** torrent

Schwamm *m* **-[e]s,⁑e** sponge; (*SGer: Pilz*) fungus; (*essbar*) mushroom. **s∼ig** *adj* spongy

Schwan *m* **-[e]s,⁑e** swan

schwanger *adj* pregnant

Schwangerschaft *f* **-,-en** pregnancy

Schwank *m* **-[e]s,⁑e** (*Theat*) farce

schwank|en *vi* (*haben*) sway; (*Boot:*) rock; (*sich ändern*) fluctuate; (*unentschieden sein*) be undecided

● (*sein*) stagger. **S∼ung** *f* **-,-en** fluctuation

Schwanz *m* **-es,⁑e** tail

schwänzen *vt* 🔲 skip; **die Schule s∼** play truant

Schwarm *m* **-[e]s,⁑e** swarm; (*Fisch-*) shoal; (🔲: *Liebe*) idol

schwärmen *vi* (*haben*) swarm; **s∼ für** 🔲 adore; (*verliebt sein*) have a crush on

Schwarte *f* **-,-n** (*Speck-*) rind

schwarz *adj* black; (🔲: *illegal*) illegal; **s∼er Markt** black market; **s∼ gekleidet** dressed in black; **s∼ auf weiß** in black and white; **s∼ sehen** (*fig*) be pessimistic; **ins S∼e treffen** score a bull's-eye. **S∼** *nt* **-[e]s,-** black. **S∼arbeit** *f* moonlighting. **s∼arbeiten** *vi sep* (*haben*) moonlight. **S∼e(r)** *m/f* black

Schwärze *f* **-** blackness. **s∼n** *vt* blacken

Schwarz|fahrer *m* fare-dodger. **S∼handel** *m* black market (**mit** in). **S∼händler** *m* black marketeer. **S∼markt** *m* black market. **S∼wald** *m* Black Forest. **s∼weiß** *adj* black and white

schwatzen, (*SGer*) **schwätzen** *vi* (*haben*) chat; (*klatschen*) gossip; (*Sch*) talk [in class] ● *vt* talk

Schwebe *f* **-** **in der S∼** (*fig*) undecided. **S∼bahn** *f* cable railway. **s∼n** *vi* (*haben*) float; (*fig*) be undecided; (*Verfahren:*) be pending; **in Gefahr s∼n** be in danger ● (*sein*) float

Schwed|e *m* **-n,-n** Swede. **S∼en** *nt* **-s** Sweden. **S∼in** *f* **-,-nen** Swede. **s∼isch** *adj* Swedish

Schwefel *m* **-s** sulphur

schweigen† *vi* (*haben*) be silent; **ganz zu s∼ von** let alone. **S∼** *nt* **-s** silence; **zum S∼ bringen** silence

schweigsam *adj* silent; (*wortkarg*) taciturn

Schwein *nt* **-[e]s,-e** pig; (*Culin*) pork; 🔲 *Schuft*) swine; **S∼haben** 🔲 be lucky. **S∼ebraten** *m* roast pork. **S∼efleisch** *nt* pork. **S∼erei** *f* **-,-en** 🔲 [dirty] mess; (*Gemeinheit*) dirty trick. **S~estall** *m* pigsty. **S~sleder** *nt* pigskin

Schweiß *m* **-es** sweat

schweißen *vt* weld

Schweiz (die) - Switzerland. **S~er** *adj & m* **-s,-**, **S~erin** *f* **-,-nen** Swiss. **s~erisch** *adj* Swiss

> **Schweizerische** **Eidgenossenschaft** The Swiss Confederation is the official name for Switzerland. The confederation was established in 1291 when the cantons (▷**KANTON**) of Uri, Schwyz and Unterwalden swore to defend their traditional rights against the Habsburg Empire. The unified federal state as it is known today was formed in 1848.

Schwelle *f* **-,-n** threshold; (*Eisenbahn-*) sleeper

schwell|en† *vi* (*sein*) swell. **S~ung** *f* **-,-en** swelling

schwer *adj* heavy; (*schwierig*) difficult; (*mühsam*) hard; (*ernst*) serious; (*schlimm*) bad; **3 Pfund s~ sein** weigh 3 pounds ● *adv* heavily; with difficulty; (*mühsam*) hard; (*schlimm, sehr*) badly, seriously; **s~ krank/ verletzt** seriously ill/injured; **s~ hören** be hard of hearing; **etw s~ nehmen** take sth seriously; **jdm s~ fallen** be hard for s.o.; **es jdm s~ machen** make it *or* things difficult for s.o.; **sich s~ tun** have difficulty (**mit** with); **s~ zu sagen** difficult *or* hard to say

Schwere *f* **-** heaviness; (*Gewicht*) weight; (*Schwierigkeit*) difficulty; (*Ernst*) gravity. **S~losigkeit** *f* **-** weightlessness

schwer|fällig *adj* ponderous, clumsy. **S~gewicht** *nt* heavyweight. **s~hörig** *adj* **s~hörig sein** be hard of hearing. **S~kraft** *f* (*Phys*) gravity. **s~mütig** *adj* melancholic. **S~punkt** *m* centre of gravity; (*fig*) emphasis

Schwert *nt* **-[e]s,-er** sword. **S~lilie** *f* iris

Schwer|verbrecher *m* serious of-

fender. **s~wiegend** *adj* weighty

Schwester *f* **-,-n** sister; (*Kranken-*) nurse. **s~lich** *adj* sisterly

Schwieger|eltern *pl* parents-in-law. **S~mutter** *f* mother-in-law. **S~sohn** *m* son-in-law. **S~tochter** *f* daughter-in-law. **S~vater** *m* father-in-law

schwierig *adj* difficult. **S~keit** *f* **-,-en** difficulty

Schwimm|bad *nt* swimming-baths *pl*. **S~becken** *nt* swimming-pool. **s~en†** *vt/i* (*sein/haben*) swim; (*auf dem Wasser treiben*) float. **S~weste** *f* life-jacket

Schwindel *m* **-s** dizziness, vertigo; (🛈: *Betrug*) fraud; (*Lüge*) lie. **S~anfall** *m* dizzy spell. **s~frei** *adj* **s~frei sein** have a good head for heights. **s~n** *vi* (*haben*) lie

Schwindl|er *m* **-s,-** liar; (*Betrüger*) fraud, con-man. **s~ig** *adj* dizzy; **mir ist** *od* **wird s~ig** I feel dizzy

schwing|en† *vi* (*haben*) swing; (*Phys*) oscillate; (*vibrieren*) vibrate ● *vt* swing; wave (*Fahne*); (*drohend*) brandish. **S~ung** *f* **-,-en** oscillation; vibration

Schwips *m* **-es,-e einen S~ haben** 🛈 be tipsy

schwitzen *vi* (*haben*) sweat; **ich s~e** I am hot

schwören† *vt/i* (*haben*) swear (**auf** + *acc* by)

schwul *adj* (🛈: *homosexuell*) gay

schwül *adj* close. **S~e** *f* **-** closeness

Schwung *m* **-[e]s,-̈e** swing; (*Bogen*) sweep; (*Schnelligkeit*) momentum; (*Kraft*) vigour. **s~los** *adj* dull. **s~voll** *adj* vigorous; (*Bogen, Linie*) sweeping; (*mitreißend*) spirited

Schwur *m* **-[e]s,-̈e** vow; (*Eid*) oath. **S~gericht** *nt* jury [court]

sechs *inv adj*, **S~** *f* **-,-en** six; (*Sch*) ≈ fail mark. **s~eckig** *adj* hexagonal. **s~te(r,s)** *adj* sixth

sech|zehn *inv adj* sixteen. **s~zehnte(r,s)** *adj* sixteenth. **s~zig** *inv adj* sixty. **s~zigste(r,s)** *adj* sixtieth

See¹ *m* **-s,-n** lake

S

See² f - sea; **an die/der See** to/at the seaside; **auf See** at sea. **S~fahrt** f [sea] voyage; (*Schifffahrt*) navigation. **S~gang** m **schwerer S~gang** rough sea. **S~hund** m seal. **s~krank** adj seasick

Seele f -,-n soul

seelisch adj psychological; (*geistig*) mental

See|macht f maritime power. **S~mann** m (pl -leute) seaman, sailor. **S~not** f **in S~not** in distress. **S~räuber** m pirate. **S~reise** f [sea] voyage. **S~rose** f water-lily. **S~sack** m kitbag. **S~stern** m starfish. **S~tang** m seaweed. **s~tüchtig** adj seaworthy. **S~zunge** f sole

Segel nt -s,- sail. **S~boot** nt sailing-boat. **S~flugzeug** nt glider. **s~n** vt/i (*sein/haben*) sail. **S~schiff** nt sailing-ship. **S~sport** m sailing. **S~tuch** nt canvas

Segen m -s blessing

Segler m -s,- yachtsman

segnen vt bless

sehen† vt see; watch (*Fernsehsendung*); **jdn/etw wieder s~** see s.o./sth again; **sich s~ lassen** show oneself ● vi (*haben*) see; (*blicken*) look (**auf** + acc at); (*ragen*) show (**aus** above); **gut/schlecht s~** have good/bad eyesight; **vom S~ kennen** know by sight; **s~ nach** keep an eye on; (*betreuen*) look after; (*suchen*) look for. **s~swert, s~swürdig** adj worth seeing. **S~swürdigkeit** f -,-en sight

Sehne f -,-n tendon; (*eines Bogens*) string

sehnen (sich) vr long (**nach** for)

Sehn|sucht f - longing (**nach** for). **s~süchtig** adj longing; (*Wunsch*) dearest

sehr adv very; (*mit Verb*) very much; **so s~, dass** so much that

seicht adj shallow

seid s. sein¹

Seide f -,-n silk

Seidel nt -s,- beer-mug

seiden adj silk **S~papier** nt tissue paper. **S~raupe** f silk-worm

seidig adj silky

Seife f -,-n soap. **S~npulver** nt soap powder. **S~nschaum** m lather

Seil nt -[e]s,-e rope; (*Draht-*) cable. **S~bahn** f cable railway. **s~springen†** vi (*sein*) (*infinitive & pp only*) skip. **S~tänzer(in)** m(f) tightrope walker

sein†¹

● *intransitive verb* (*sein*)

····▶ be. **ich bin glücklich** I am happy. **er ist Lehrer/Schwede** he is a teacher/Swedish. **bist du es?** is that you? **sei still!** be quiet! **sie waren in Paris** they were in Paris. **morgen bin ich zu Hause** I shall be at home tomorrow. **er ist aus Berlin** he is or comes from Berlin

····▶ (*impers + dat*) **mir ist kalt/besser** I am cold/better. **ihr ist schlecht** she feels sick

····▶ (*existieren*) be. **es ist/sind ...** there is/are .... **es ist keine Hoffnung mehr** there is no more hope. **es sind vier davon** there are four of them. **es war einmal ein Prinz** once upon a time there was a prince

● *auxiliary verb*

····▶ (*zur Perfektumschreibung*) have. **er ist gestorben** he has died. **sie sind angekommen** they have arrived. **sie war dort gewesen** she had been there. **ich wäre gefallen** I would have fallen

····▶ (*zur Bildung des Passivs*) be. **wir sind gerettet worden/wir waren gerettet** we were saved

····▶ (+ *zu + Infinitiv*) be to be. **es war niemand zu sehen** there was no one to be seen. **das war zu erwarten** that was to be expected. **er ist zu bemitleiden** he is to be pitied. **die Richtlinien sind strengstens zu beachten** the guidelines are to be strictly followed

sein² poss pron his; (*Ding, Tier*) its;

(*nach man*) one's; **sein Glück versuchen** try one's luck. **s~e(r,s)** *poss
pron* his; (*nach man*) one's own; **das
S~e tun** do one's share. **s~erseits**
adv for his part. **s~erzeit** *adv* in
those days. **s~etwegen** *adv* for his
sake; (*wegen ihm*) because of him,
on his account. **s~ige** *poss pron*
der/die/das s~ige his

seins *poss pron* his; (*nach man*) one's
own

seit *conj & prep* (+ *dat*) since; **s~ eini-
ger** Zeit for some time [past]; **ich
wohne s~ zehn Jahren hier** I've
lived here for ten years. **s~dem** *conj*
since ● *adv* since then

Seite *f* **-,-n** side; (*Buch-*) page; **zur
S~ treten** step aside; **auf der
einen/anderen S~** (*fig*) on the one/
other hand

seitens *prep* (+ *gen*) on the part of

Seiten|schiff *nt* [side] aisle.
S~sprung *m* infidelity. **S~stechen**
nt **-s** (*Med*) stitch. **S~straße** *f* side-
street. **S~streifen** *m* verge;
(*Autobahn-*) hard shoulder

seither *adv* since then

seit|lich *adj* side ● *adv* at/on the
side; **s~lich von** to one side of
● *prep* (+ *gen*) to one side of.
s~wärts *adv* on/to one side; (*zur
Seite*) sideways

Sekret|är *m* **-s,-e** secretary;
(*Schrank*) bureau. **S~ariat** *nt* **-[e]s,-e**
secretary's office. **S~ärin** *f* **-,-nen**
secretary

Sekt *m* **-[e]s** [German] sparkling wine

Sekte *f* **-,-n** sect

Sektor *m* **-s,-en** sector

Sekunde *f* **-,-n** second

Sekundenschlaf *m* microsleep

selber *pron* ① = **selbst**

selbst *pron* oneself; **ich/du/er/sie s~**
I myself /you yourself/ he himself/she
herself; **wir/ihr/sie s~** we ourselves/
you yourselves/they themselves; **ich
schneide mein Haar s~** I cut my
own hair; **von s~** of one's own accord; (*automatisch*) automatically; **s~
gemacht** home-made ● *adv* even

selbständig *adj* = **selbstständig**.

S~keit *f* - = Selbstständigkeit

Selbst|bedienung *f* self-service.
S~befriedigung *f* masturbation.
s~bewusst *adj* self-confident.
S~bewusstsein *nt* self-confidence.
S~bildnis *nt* self-portrait. **S~erhal-
tung** *f* self-preservation. **s~ge-
macht*** *adj* = **s~ gemacht**, *s.*
selbst. **s~haftend** *adj* self-adhesive.
S~hilfe *f* self-help. **s~klebend** *adj*
self-adhesive. **S~kostenpreis** *m* cost
price. **S~laut** *m* vowel. **s~los** *adj*
selfless. **S~mord** *m* suicide.
S~mordattentat *nt* suicide attack.
S~mörder(in) *m(f)* suicide.
s~mörderisch *adj* suicidal.
S~porträt *nt* self-portrait. **s~sicher**
adj self-assured. **s~ständig** *adj* independent; self-employed (*Handwerker*);
sich s~ständig machen set up on
one's own. **S~ständigkeit** *f* - independence. **s~süchtig** *adj* selfish.
S~tanken *nt* self-service (*for petrol*). **s~tätig** *adj* automatic. **S~ver-
sorgung** *f* self-catering. **s~ver-
ständlich** *adj* natural; **etw für
s~verständlich halten** take sth for
granted; **das ist s~verständlich** that
goes without saying; **s~verständ-
lich!** of course! **S~verteidigung** *f*
self-defence. **S~vertrauen** *nt* self-
confidence. **S~verwaltung** *f* self-
government

selig *adj* blissfully happy; (*Relig*)
blessed; (*verstorben*) late. **S~keit** *f* -
bliss

Sellerie *m* **-s,-s** & *f* **-,-** celeriac;
(*Stangen-*) celery

selten *adj* rare ● *adv* rarely, seldom;
(*besonders*) exceptionally. **S~heit** *f*
-,-en rarity

seltsam *adj* odd, strange. **s~er-
weise** *adv* oddly

Semester *nt* **-s,-** (*Univ*) semester

Semikolon *nt* **-s,-s** semicolon

Seminar *nt* **-s,-e** seminar; (*Institut*)
department; (*Priester-*) seminary

Semmel *f* **-,-n** (*Aust, SGer*) [bread]
roll. **S~brösel** *pl* breadcrumbs

Senat *m* **-[e]s,-e** senate. **S~or** *m*
-s,-en senator

senden¹† *vt* send

sende|n² vt (reg) broadcast; (über Funk) transmit, send. **S~r** m **-s,-** [broadcasting] station; (Anlage) transmitter. **S~reihe** f series

Sendung f -,-en consignment, shipment; (TV) programme

Senf m **-s** mustard

senil adj senile. **S~ität** f - senility

Senior m **-s,-en** senior; **S~en** senior citizens. **S~enheim** nt old people's home

senken vt lower; bring down (Fieber, Preise); bow (Kopf); **sich s~** come down, fall; (absinken) subside

senkrecht adj vertical. **S~e** f **-n,-n** perpendicular

Sensation /-'tsjo:n/ f -,-en sensation. **s~ell** adj sensational

Sense f -,-n scythe

sensibel adj sensitive

sentimental adj sentimental

September m **-s,-** September

Serie /'ze:rjə/ f -,-n series; (Briefmarken) set; (Comm) range. **S~nnummer** f serial number

seriös adj respectable; (zuverlässig) reliable

Serpentine f -,-n winding road; (Kehre) hairpin bend

Serum nt **-s,Sera** serum

Server m **-s,-** server

Service¹ /zɛr'vi:s/ nt **-[s],-** service, set

Service² /'zø:ɐ̯vɪs/ m & nt **-s** (Comm, Tennis) service

servier|en vt/i (haben) serve. **S~erin** f -,-nen waitress

Serviette f -,-n napkin, serviette

Servus int (Aust) cheerio; (Begrüßung) hallo

Sessel m **-s,-** armchair. **S~bahn** f, **S~lift** m chairlift

sesshaft adj settled

Set /zɛt/ nt & m **-[s],-s** set; (Deckchen) place-mat

setz|en vt put; (abstellen) set down; (hin-) sit down (Kind); move (Spielstein); (pflanzen) plant; (schreiben, wetten) put; **sich s~en** sit down;

(sinken) settle ● vi (sein) leap ● vi (haben) **s~en auf** (+ acc) back

Seuche f -,-n epidemic

seufz|en vi (haben) sigh. **S~er** m **-s,-** sigh

Sex /zɛks/ m **-[es]** sex

Sexu|alität f - sexuality. **s~ell** adj sexual

sezieren vt dissect

Shampoo /ʃam'pu:/, **Shampoon** /ʃam'po:n/ nt **-s** shampoo

siamesisch adj Siamese

sich reflexive pron oneself; (mit er/sie/ es) himself/herself/itself; (mit sie pl) themselves; (mit Sie) yourself; (pl) yourselves; (einander) each other; **s~ kennen** know oneself/(einander) each other; **s~ waschen** have a wash; **s~** (dat) **die Haare kämmen** comb one's hair; **s~ wundern** be surprised; **s~ gut verkaufen** sell well; **von s~ aus** of one's own accord

Sichel f -,-n sickle

sicher adj safe; (gesichert) secure; (gewiss) certain; (zuverlässig) reliable; sure (Urteil); steady (Hand); (selbstbewusst) self-confident; **bist du s~?** are you sure? ● adv safely; securely; certainly; reliably; self-confidently; (wahrscheinlich) most probably; **s~!** certainly! **s~gehen†** vi sep (sein) (fig) be sure

Sicherheit f - safety; (Pol, Psych, Comm) security; (Gewissheit) certainty; (Zuverlässigkeit) reliability; (des Urteils) surety; (Selbstbewusstsein) self-confidence. **S~sgurt** m safety belt; (Auto) seat belt. **S~snadel** f safety pin

sicherlich adv certainly; (wahrscheinlich) most probably

sicher|n vt secure; (garantieren) safeguard; (schützen) protect; put the safety catch on (Pistole). **S~ung** f -,-en safeguard, protection; (Gewehr-) safety catch; (Electr) fuse

Sicht f - view; (S~weite) visibility; **auf lange S~** in the long term. **s~bar** adj visible. **S~vermerk** m visa. **S~weite** f visibility; **außer S~weite** out of sight

sie *pron* (*nom*) (*sg*) she; (*Ding, Tier*) it; (*pl*) they; (*acc*) (*sg*) her; (*Ding, Tier*) it; (*pl*) them

Sie *pron* you; **gehen/warten Sie!** go/wait!

Sieb *nt* -[e]s,-e sieve; (*Tee-*) strainer. **s~en¹** *vt* sieve, sift

sieben² *inv adj*, **S~** *f* -,-en seven. **S~sachen** *fpl* 🔲 belongings. **s~te(r,s)** *adj* seventh

sieb|te(r,s) *adj* seventh. **s~zehn** *inv adj* seventeen. **s~zehnte(r,s)** *adj* seventeenth. **s~zig** *inv adj* seventy. **s~zigste(r,s)** *adj* seventieth

siede|n *vt/i* (*haben*) boil. **S~punkt** *m* boiling point

Siedlung *f* -,-en [housing] estate; (*Niederlassung*) settlement

Sieg *m* -[e]s,-e victory

Siegel *nt* -s,- seal. **S~ring** *m* signet-ring

sieg|en *vi* (*haben*) win. **S~er(in)** *m* -s,- (*f* -,-nen) winner. **s~reich** *adj* victorious

siezen *vt* jdn s~ call s.o. 'Sie'

Signal *nt* -s,-e signal

Silbe *f* -,-n syllable

Silber *nt* -s silver. **s~n** *adj* silver

Silhouette /zɪ'lʊɛtə/ *f* -,-n silhouette

Silizium *nt* -s silicon

Silo *m & nt* -s,-s silo

Silvester *nt* -s New Year's Eve

Sims *m & nt* -es,-e ledge

simsen *vt/i* text, send a text message

simultan *adj* simultaneous

sind *s.* sein¹

Sinfonie *f* -,-n symphony

singen† *vt/i* (*haben*) sing

Singvogel *m* songbird

sinken† *vi* (*sein*) sink; (*nieder-*) drop; (*niedriger werden*) go down, fall; **den Mut s~ lassen** lose courage

Sinn *m* -[e]s,-e sense; (*Denken*) mind; (*Zweck*) point; **in gewissem S~e** in a sense; **es hat keinen S~** it is pointless. **S~bild** *nt* symbol

sinnlich *adj* sensory; (*sexuell*) sens-

ual; (*Genüsse*) sensuous. **S~keit** *f* - sensuality; sensuousness

sinn|los *adj* senseless; (*zwecklos*) pointless. **s~voll** *adj* meaningful; (*vernünftig*) sensible

Sintflut *f* flood

Siphon /'zi:fõ/ *m* -s,-s siphon

Sippe *f* -,-n clan

Sirene *f* -,-n siren

Sirup *m* -s,-e syrup; treacle

Sitte *f* -,-n custom; S~n manners

sittlich *adj* moral. **S~keit** *f* - morality. **S~keitsverbrecher** *m* sex offender

sittsam *adj* well-behaved; (*züchtig*) demure

Situ|ation /-'tsi̯o:n/ *f* -,-en situation. **s~iert** *adj* **gut/schlecht s~iert** well/badly off

Sitz *m* -es,-e seat; (*Passform*) fit

sitzen† *vi* (*haben*) sit; (*sich befinden*) be; (*passen*) fit; (🔲: *treffen*) hit home; **[im Gefängnis] s~** 🔲 be in jail; **s~ bleiben** remain seated; 🔲 (*Sch*) stay *or* be kept down; (*nicht heiraten*) be left on the shelf; **s~ bleiben auf** (+ *dat*) be left with

Sitz|gelegenheit *f* seat. **S~platz** *m* seat. **S~ung** *f* -,-en session

Sizilien /-i̯ən/ *nt* -s Sicily

Skala *f* -,-len scale; (*Reihe*) range

Skalpell *nt* -s,-e scalpel

skalpieren *vt* scalp

Skandal *m* -s,-e scandal. **s~ös** *adj* scandalous

Skandinav|ien /-i̯ən/ *nt* -s Scandinavia. **s~isch** *adj* Scandinavian

Skat *m* -s skat

Skateboard /'ske:tbɔɐ̯t/ *nt* -s, -s skateboard

Skelett *nt* -[e]s,-e skeleton

Skep|sis *f* - scepticism. **s~tisch** *adj* sceptical

Ski /ʃiː/ *m* -s,-er ski; **Ski fahren** *od* **laufen** ski. **S~fahrer(in), S~läufer(in)** *m(f)* -s,- (*f* -,-nen) skier. **S~sport** *m* skiing

Skizz|e *f* -,-n sketch. **s~ieren** *vt* sketch

s

Sklav|e *m* -n,-n slave. **S~erei** *f* - slavery. **S~in** *f* -,-nen slave

Skorpion *m* -s,-e scorpion; (*Astrology*) Scorpio

Skrupel *m* -s,- scruple. **s~los** *adj* unscrupulous

Skulptur *f* -,-en sculpture

Slalom *m* -s,-s slalom

Slaw|e *m* -n,-n, **S~in** *f* -,-nen Slav. **s~isch** *adj* Slav; (*Lang*) Slavonic

Slip *m* -s,-s briefs *pl*

Smaragd *m* -[e]s,-e emerald

Smoking *m* -s,-s dinner jacket

SMS-Nachricht *f* text message

Snob *m* -s,-s snob. **S~ismus** *m* - snobbery **s~istisch** *adj* snobbish

so *adv* so; (*so sehr*) so much; (*auf diese Weise*) like this/that; (*solch*) such; (🄸: *sowieso*) anyway; (🄸: *umsonst*) free; (🄸: *ungefähr*) about; **so viel** so much; **so gut/bald wie** as good/ soon as; **so ein Zufall!** what a coincidence! **mir ist so, als ob** I feel as if; **so oder so** in any case; **so um zehn Euro** 🄸 about ten euros; **so?** really? ● *conj* (*also*) so; (*dann*) then; **so dass** = sodass

sobald *conj* as soon as

Söckchen *nt* -s,- [ankle] sock

Socke *f* -,-n sock

Sockel *m* -s,- plinth, pedestal

Socken *m* -s,- sock

sodass *conj* so that

Sodawasser *nt* soda water

Sodbrennen *nt* -s heartburn

soeben *adv* just [now]

Sofa *nt* -s,-s settee, sofa

sofern *adv* provided [that]

sofort *adv* at once, immediately; (*auf der Stelle*) instantly

Software /'zɔftvɛːɐ̯/ *f* - software

sogar *adv* even

sogenannt *adj* so-called

sogleich *adv* at once

Sohle *f* -,-n sole; (*Tal-*) bottom

Sohn *m* -[e]s,⸚e son

Sojabohne *f* soya bean

solange *conj* as long as

solch *inv pron* such; **s~ ein(e)** such

a; **s~ einer/eine/eins** one/(*Person*) someone like that. **s~e(r,s)** *pron* such ● (*substantivisch*) **ein s~er/eine s~e/ein s~es** one/(*Person*) someone like that; **s~e** *pl* those; (*Leute*) people like that

Soldat *m* -en,-en soldier

Söldner *m* -s,- mercenary

Solidarität *f* - solidarity

solide *adj* solid; (*haltbar*) sturdy; (*sicher*) sound; (*anständig*) respectable

Solist(in) *m* -en,-en (*f* -,-nen) soloist

Soll *nt* -s (*Comm*) debit; (*Produktions-*) quota

---

sollen†

● *auxiliary verb*

····▸ (*Verpflichtung*) be [supposed or meant] to. **er soll morgen zum Arzt gehen** he is [supposed] to go to the doctor tomorrow. **die beiden Flächen sollen fluchten** the two surfaces are meant to be *or* should be in alignment. **du solltest ihn anrufen** you were meant to phone him *or* should have phoned him

····▸ (*Befehl*) **du sollst sofort damit aufhören** you're to stop that at once. **er soll hereinkommen** he is to come in; (*sagen Sie es ihm*) tell him to come in

····▸ **sollte** (*subjunctive*) should; ought to. **wir sollten früher aufstehen** we ought to *or* should get up earlier. **das hätte er nicht tun/sagen sollen** he shouldn't have done/said that

····▸ (*Zukunft, Geplantes*) be to. **ich soll die Abteilung übernehmen** I am to take over the department. **du sollst dein Geld zurückbekommen** you are to *or* shall get your money back. **es soll nicht wieder vorkommen** it won't happen again. **sie sollten ihr Reiseziel nie erreichen** they were never to reach their destination

····➤ (*Ratlosigkeit*) be to; shall. **was soll man nur machen?** what is one to do?; what shall I/we do? **ich weiß nicht, was ich machen soll** I don't know what I should do *or* what to do

····➤ (*nach Bericht*) be supposed to. **er soll sehr reich sein** he is supposed *or* is said to be very rich. **sie soll geheiratet haben** they say *or* I gather she has got married

····➤ (*Absicht*) be meant *or* supposed to. **was soll dieses Bild darstellen?** what is this picture supposed to represent? **das sollte ein Witz sein** that was meant *or* supposed to be a joke

····➤ (*in Bedingungssätzen*) should. **sollte er anrufen, falls** *od* **wenn er anrufen sollte** should he *or* if he should telephone

● *intransitive verb*

····➤ (*irgendwohin gehen sollen*) be [supposed] to go. **er soll morgen zum Arzt/nach Berlin** he is [supposed] to go to the doctor/ to Berlin tomorrow. **ich sollte ins Theater** I was supposed to go to the theatre

····➤ (*sonstige Wendungen*) **soll er doch!** let him! **was soll das?** what's that in aid of? ⓣ

Solo *nt* **-s,-los** & **-li** solo
somit *adv* therefore, so
Sommer *m* **-s,-** summer. **s~lich** *adj* summery; (*Sommer-*) summer ● *adv* **s~lich warm** as warm as summer. **S~sprossen** *fpl* freckles
Sonate *f* **-,-n** sonata
Sonde *f* **-,-n** probe
Sonder|angebot *nt* special offer. **s~bar** *adj* odd. **S~fahrt** *f* special excursion. **S~fall** *m* special case. **s~gleichen** *adv* eine Gemeinheit **s~gleichen** unparalleled meanness. **S~ling** *m* **-s,-e** crank. **S~marke** *f* special stamp
sondern *conj* but; **nicht nur ... s~ auch** not only ... but also

Sonder|preis *m* special price. **S~schule** *f* special school
Sonett *nt* **-[e]s,-e** sonnet
Sonnabend *m* **-s,-e** Saturday. **s~s** *adv* on Saturdays
Sonne *f* **-,-n** sun. **s~n (sich)** *vr* sun oneself
Sonnen|aufgang *m* sunrise. **s~baden** *vi* (*haben*) sunbathe. **S~bank** *f* sun-bed. **S~blume** *f* sunflower. **S~brand** *m* sunburn. **S~brille** *f* sunglasses *pl*. **S~energie** *f* solar energy. **S~finsternis** *f* solar eclipse. **S~milch** *f* sun-tan lotion. **S~öl** *nt* sun-tan oil. **S~schein** *m* sunshine. **S~schirm** *m* sunshade. **S~stich** *m* sunstroke. **S~uhr** *f* sundial. **S~untergang** *m* sunset. **S~wende** *f* solstice
sonnig *adj* sunny
Sonntag *m* **-s,-e** Sunday. **s~s** *adv* on Sundays
sonst *adv* (*gewöhnlich*) usually; (*im Übrigen*) apart from that; (*andernfalls*) otherwise, or [else]; **wer/was/wie/wo s~?** who/what/how/where else? **s~ niemand** no one else; **s~ noch etwas?** anything else? **s~ noch Fragen?** any more questions? **s~ jemand** *od* **wer** someone/(*fragend, verneint*) anyone else; (*irgendjemand*) [just] anyone; **s~ wo** somewhere/(*fragend, verneint*) anywhere else; (*irgendwo*) [just] anywhere. **s~ig** *adj* other
sooft *conj* whenever
Sopran *m* **-s,-e** soprano
Sorge *f* **-,-n** worry (**um** about); (*Fürsorge*) care; **sich** (*dat*) **S~n machen** worry. **s~n** *vi* (*haben*) **s~n für** look after, care for; (*vorsorgen*) provide for; (*sich kümmern*) see to; **dafür s~n, dass** see *or* make sure that ● *vr* **sich s~n** worry. **s~nfrei** *adj* carefree. **s~nvoll** *adj* worried. **S~recht** *nt* (*Jur*) custody
Sorg|falt *f* **-** care. **s~fältig** *adj* careful
Sorte *f* **-,-n** kind, sort; (*Comm*) brand
sort|ieren *vt* sort [out]; (*Comm*) grade. **S~iment** *nt* **-[e]s,-e** range

s

sosehr *conj* however much

Soße *f* -,-n sauce; (*Braten-*) gravy; (*Salat-*) dressing

Souvenir /zuvə'niːɐ̯/ *nt* -s,-s souvenir

souverän /zuvə'rɛːn/ *adj* sovereign

soviel *conj* however much; **s∼ ich weiß** as far as I know ● *adv* *so viel, s. viel

soweit *conj* as far as; (*insoweit*) [in] so far as ● *adv** so weit, s. weit

sowenig *conj* however little ● *adv* *so wenig, s. wenig

sowie *conj* as well as; (*sobald*) as soon as

sowieso *adv* anyway, in any case

sowjet|isch *adj* Soviet. **S∼union** *f* - Soviet Union

sowohl *adv* **s∼ ... als** *od* **wie auch** as well as ...

sozial *adj* social; (*Einstellung, Beruf*) caring. **S∼arbeit** *f* social work. **S∼demokrat** *m* social democrat. **S∼hilfe** *f* social security

Sozialis|mus *m* - socialism. **S∼t** *m* -en,-en socialist

Sozial|versicherung *f* National Insurance. **S∼wohnung** *f* ≈ council flat

Soziologie *f* - sociology

Sozius *m* -,-se (*Comm*) partner; (*Beifahrersitz*) pillion

Spachtel *m* -s,- & *f* -,-n spatula

Spagat *m* -[e]s,-e (*Aust*) string; **S∼ machen** do the splits *pl*

Spaghetti, Spagetti *pl* spaghetti *sg*

Spalier *nt* -s,-e trellis

Spalt|e *f* -,-n crack; (*Gletscher-*) crevasse; (*Druck-*) column; (*Orangen-*) segment. **s∼en†** *vt* split. **S∼ung** *f* -,-en splitting; (*Kluft*) split; (*Phys*) fission

Span *m* -[e]s,ːe [wood] chip

Spange *f* -,-n clasp; (*Haar-*) slide; (*Zahn-*) brace

Span|ien /-i̯ən/ *nt* -s Spain. **S∼ier** *m* -s,-, **S∼ierin** *f* -,-nen Spaniard. **s∼isch** *adj* Spanish. **S∼isch** *nt* -[s] (*Lang*) Spanish

Spann *m* -[e]s instep

Spanne *f* -,-n span; (*Zeit-*) space; (*Comm*) margin

spann|en *vt* stretch; put up (*Leine*); (*straffen*) tighten; (*an-*) harness (**an** + *acc* to); **sich s∼en** tighten ● *vi* (*haben*) be too tight. **s∼end** *adj* exciting. **S∼ung** *f* -,-en tension; (*Erwartung*) suspense; (*Electr*) voltage

Spar|buch *nt* savings book. **S∼büchse** *f* money-box. **s∼en** *vt/i* (*haben*) save; (*sparsam sein*) economize (**mit/an** + *dat* on). **S∼er** *m* -s,- saver

Spargel *m* -s,- asparagus

Spar|kasse *f* savings bank. **S∼konto** *nt* deposit account

sparsam *adj* economical; (*Person*) thrifty. **S∼keit** *f* - economy; thrift

Sparschwein *nt* piggy bank

Sparte *f* -,-n branch; (*Zeitungs-*) section; (*Rubrik*) column

Spaß *m* -es,ːe fun; (*Scherz*) joke; **im/aus/zum S∼** for fun; **S∼ machen** be fun; (*Person:*) be joking; **viel S∼!** have a good time! **s∼en** *vi* (*haben*) joke. **S∼vogel** *m* joker

Spastiker *m* -s,- spastic

spät *adj & adv* late; **wie s∼ ist es?** what time Is It? **zu s∼ kommen** be late

Spaten *m* -s,- spade

später *adj* later; (*zukünftig*) future ● *adv* later

spätestens *adv* at the latest

Spatz *m* -en,-en sparrow

Spätzle *pl* (*Culin*) noodles

spazieren *vi* (*sein*) stroll; **s∼ gehen** go for a walk

Spazier|gang *m* walk; **einen S∼gang machen** go for a walk. **S∼gänger(in)** *m* -s,- (*f* -,-nen) walker. **S∼stock** *m* walking-stick

Specht *m* -[e]s,-e woodpecker

Speck *m* -s bacon. **s∼ig** *adj* greasy

Spedi|teur /ʃpedi'tøːɐ̯/ *m* -s,-e haulage/(*für Umzüge*) removals contractor. **S∼tion** *f* -,-en carriage; haulage; (*Firma*) haulage/(*für Umzüge*) removals firm

Speer *m* -[e]s,-e spear; (*Sport*) javelin

Speiche f -,-n spoke
Speichel m -s saliva
Speicher m -s,- warehouse; (*Dialekt:* *Dachboden*) attic; (*Computer*) memory. **s~n** vt store
Speise f -,-n food; (*Gericht*) dish; (*Pudding*) blancmange. **S~eis** nt ice-cream. **S~kammer** f larder. **S~karte** f menu. **s~n** vi (*haben*) eat ● vt feed. **S~röhre** f oesophagus. **S~saal** m dining room. **S~wagen** m dining car
Spektrum nt -s,-tra spectrum
Spekul|ant m -en,-en speculator. **s~ieren** vi (*haben*) speculate; **s~ieren auf** (+ acc) ⊡ hope to get
Spelze f -,-n husk
spendabel adj generous
Spende f -,-n donation. **s~n** vt donate; give (*Blut, Schatten*); **Beifall s~n** applaud. **S~r** m -s,- donor; (*Behälter*) dispenser
spendieren vt pay for
Sperling m -s,-e sparrow
Sperre f -,-n barrier; (*Verbot*) ban; (*Comm*) embargo. **s~n** vt close; (*ver-*) block; (*verbieten*) ban; cut off (*Strom, Telefon*); stop (*Scheck, Kredit*); **s~n in** (+ acc) put in (*Gefängnis, Käfig*)
Sperr|holz nt plywood. **S~müll** m bulky refuse. **S~stunde** f closing time
Spesen pl expenses
spezial|isieren (sich) vr specialize (**auf** + acc in). **S~ist** m -en,-en specialist. **S~ität** f -,-en speciality
spicken vt (*Culin*) lard; **gespickt mit** (*fig*) full of ● vi (*haben*) ⊡ crib (**bei** from)
Spiegel m -s,- mirror; (*Wasser-, Alkohol-*) level. **S~bild** nt reflection. **S~ei** nt fried egg. **s~n** vt reflect; **sich s~n** be reflected ● vi (*haben*) reflect [the light]; (*glänzen*) gleam. **S~ung** f -,-en reflection
Spiel nt -[e]s,-e game; (*Spielen*) playing; (*Glücks-*) gambling; (*Schau-*) play; (*Satz*) set; **auf dem S~ stehen** be at stake; **aufs S~ setzen** risk. **S~auto-**

mat m fruit machine. **S~bank** f casino. **S~dose** f musical box. **s~en** vt/i (*haben*) play; (*im Glücksspiel*) gamble; (*vortäuschen*) act; (*Roman:*) be set (**in** + dat in); **s~en mit** (*fig*) toy with
Spieler(in) m -s,- (f -,-nen) player; (*Glücks-*) gambler
Spiel|feld nt field, pitch. **S~marke** f chip. **S~plan** m programme. **S~platz** m playground. **S~raum** m (*fig*) scope; (*Techn*) clearance. **S~regeln** fpl rules [of the game]. **S~sachen** fpl toys. **S~verderber** m -s,- spoilsport. **S~waren** fpl toys. **S~warengeschäft** nt toyshop. **S~zeug** nt toy; (*S~sachen*) toys pl
Spieß m -es,-e spear; (*Brat-*) spit; skewer; (*Fleisch-*) kebab. **S~er** m -s,- [petit] bourgeois. **s~ig** adj bourgeois
Spike[s]reifen /'ʃpaik[s]-/ m studded tyre
Spinat m -s spinach
Spindel f -,-n spindle
Spinne f -,-n spider
spinn|en† vt/i (*haben*) spin; **er spinnt** ⊡ he's crazy. **S~[en]gewebe** nt, **S~webe** f -,-n cobweb
Spion m -s,-e spy
Spionage /ʃpio'naːʒə/ f - espionage, spying. **S~abwehr** f counter-espionage
spionieren vi (*haben*) spy
Spionin f -,-nen [woman] spy
Spiral|e f -,-n spiral. **s~ig** adj spiral
Spirituosen pl spirits
Spiritus m - alcohol; (*Brenn-*) methylated spirits pl. **S~kocher** m spirit stove
spitz adj pointed; (*scharf*) sharp; (*schrill*) shrill; (*Winkel*) acute. **S~bube** m scoundrel
Spitze f -,-n point; (*oberer Teil*) top; (*vorderer Teil*) front; (*Pfeil-, Finger-, Nasen-*) tip; (*Schuh-, Strumpf-*) toe; (*Zigarren-, Zigaretten-*) holder; (*Höchstleistung*) maximum; (*Textiles*) lace; (⊡: *Anspielung*) dig; **an der S~ liegen** be in the lead

S

Spitzel *m* -s,- informer

spitzen *vt* sharpen; purse (*Lippen*); prick up (*Ohren*). **S~geschwindigkeit** *f* top speed

Spitzname *m* nickname

Spleen /ʃpliːn/ *m* -s,-e obsession

Splitter *m* -s,- splinter. **s~n** *vi* (*sein*) shatter

sponsern *vt* sponsor

Spore *f* -,-n (*Biology*) spore

Sporn *m* -[e]s, **Sporen** spur

Sport *m* -[e]s sport; (*Hobby*) hobby. **S~art** *f* sport. **S~ler** *m* -s,- sportsman. **S~lerin** *f* -,-nen sportswoman. **s~lich** *adj* sports; (*fair*) sporting; (*schlank*) sporty. **S~platz** *m* sports ground. **S~verein** *m* sports club. **S~wagen** *m* sports car; (*Kinder-*) push-chair, (*Amer*) stroller

Spott *m* -[e]s mockery

spotten *vi* (*haben*) mock; **s~ über** (+ *acc*) make fun of; (*höhnend*) ridicule

spöttisch *adj* mocking

Sprach|e *f* -,-n language; (*Sprechfähigkeit*) speech; **zur S~e bringen** bring up. **S~fehler** *m* speech defect. **S~labor** *nt* language laboratory. **s~lich** *adj* linguistic. **s~los** *adj* speechless

Spray /ʃpreː/ *nt & m* -s,-s spray. **S~dose** *f* aerosol [can]

Sprechanlage *f* intercom

sprechen† *vi* (*haben*) speak/(*sich unterhalten*) talk (**über** + *acc*/**von** about/of); **Deutsch s~** speak German ● *vt* speak; (*sagen*) say; (*pronounce* (*Urteil*); **schuldig s~** find guilty; **Herr X ist nicht zu s~** Mr X is not available

Sprecher(in) *m* -s,- (*f* -,-nen) speaker; (*Radio, TV*) announcer; (*Wortführer*) spokesman, *f* spokeswoman

Sprechstunde *f* consulting hours *pl*; (*Med*) surgery. **S~nhilfe** *f* (*Med*) receptionist

Sprechzimmer *nt* consulting room

spreizen *vt* spread

spreng|en *vt* blow up; blast (*Felsen*); (*fig*) burst; (*begießen*) water; (*mit Sprenger*) sprinkle; dampen (*Wäsche*). **S~er** *m* -s,- sprinkler. **S~kopf** *m* warhead. **S~körper** *m* explosive device. **S~stoff** *m* explosive

Spreu *f* - chaff

Sprich|wort *nt* (*pl* -wörter) proverb. **s~wörtlich** *adj* proverbial

Springbrunnen *m* fountain

spring|en† *vi* (*sein*) jump; (*Schwimmsport*) dive; (*Ball:*) bounce; (*spritzen*) spurt; (*zer-*) break; (*rissig werden*) crack; (*SGer: laufen*) run. **S~er** *m* -s,- jumper; (*Kunst-*) diver; (*Schach*) knight. **S~reiten** *nt* show-jumping

Sprint *m* -s,-s sprint

Spritz|e *f* -,-n syringe; (*Injektion*) injection; (*Feuer-*) hose. **S~en** *vt* spray; (*be-, ver-*) splash; (*Culin*) pipe; (*Med*) inject ● *vi* (*haben*) splash; (*Fett:*) spit ● *vi* (*sein*) splash; (*hervor-*) spurt. **S~er** *m* -s,- splash; (*Schuss*) dash

spröde *adj* brittle; (*trocken*) dry

Sprosse *f* -,-n rung

Sprotte *f* -,-n sprat

Spruch *m* -[e]s,-̈e saying; (*Denk-*) motto; (*Zitat*) quotation. **S~band** *nt* (*pl* -bänder) banner

Sprudel *m* -s,- sparkling mineral water. **s~n** *vi* (*haben/sein*) bubble

Sprüh|dose *f* aerosol [can]. **s~en** *vt* spray ● *vi* (*sein*) (*Funken:*) fly; (*fig*) sparkle

Sprung *m* -[e]s,-̈e jump, leap; (*Schwimmsport*) dive; (⬜: *Katzen-*) stone's throw; (*Riss*) crack. **S~brett** *nt* springboard. **S~schanze** *f* skijump. **S~seil** *nt* skipping rope

Spucke *f* - spit. **s~n** *vt/i* (*haben*) spit; (*sich übergeben*) be sick

Spuk *m* -[e]s,-e [ghostly] apparition. **s~en** *vi* (*haben*) (*Geist:*) walk; **in diesem Haus s~t es** this house is haunted

Spülbecken *nt* sink

Spule *f* -,-n spool

Spüle *f* -,-n sink

spulen *vt* spool

spül|en *vt* rinse; (*schwemmen*) wash;

Geschirr s~**en** wash up ● *vi* (*haben*) flush [the toilet]. **S~kasten** *m* cistern. **S~mittel** *nt* washing-up liquid

Spur *f* -,-**en** track; (*Fahr*-) lane; (*Fährte*) trail; (*Anzeichen*) trace; (*Hinweis*) lead

spürbar *adj* noticeable

spür|en *vt* feel; (*seelisch*) sense. **S~hund** *m* tracker dog

spurlos *adv* without trace

spurten *vi* (*sein*) put on a spurt

sputen (sich) *vr* hurry

Staat *m* -[e]s,-en state; (*Land*) country; (*Putz*) finery. **s~lich** *adj* state ● *adv* by the state

Staatsangehörig|e(r) *m/f* national. **S~keit** *f* - nationality

Staats|anwalt *m* state prosecutor. **S~beamte(r)** *m* civil servant. **S~besuch** *m* state visit. **S~bürger(in)** *m*(*f*) national. **S~mann** *m* (*pl* -**männer**) statesman. **S~streich** *m* coup

Stab *m* -[e]s,ⁿe rod; (*Gitter*-) bar (*Sport*) baton; (*Mil*) staff

Stäbchen *ntpl* chopsticks

Stabhochsprung *m* pole-vault

stabil *adj* stable; (*gesund*) robust; (*solide*) sturdy

Stachel *m* -s,- spine; (*Gift*-) sting; (*Spitze*) spike. **S~beere** *f* gooseberry. **S~draht** *m* barbed wire. **S~schwein** *nt* porcupine

Stadion *nt* -s,-ien stadium

Stadium *nt* -s,-ien stage

Stadt *f* -,ⁿe town; (*Groß*-) city

städtisch *adj* urban; (*kommunal*) municipal

Stadt|mitte *f* town centre. **S~plan** *m* street map. **S~teil** *m* district

Staffel *f* -,-n team; (*S~lauf*) relay; (*Mil*) squadron

Staffelei *f* -,-en easel

Staffel|lauf *m* relay race. **s~n** *vt* stagger; (*abstufen*) grade

Stahl *m* -s steel. **S~beton** *m* reinforced concrete

Stall *m* -[e]s,ⁿe stable; (*Kuh*-) shed; (*Schweine*-) sty; (*Hühner*-) coop; (*Kaninchen*-) hutch

Stamm *m* -[e]s,ⁿe trunk; (*Sippe*) tribe; (*Wort*-) stem. **S~baum** *m* family tree; (*eines Tieres*) pedigree

stammeln *vt/i* (*haben*) stammer

stammen *vi* (*haben*) come/(*zeitlich*) date (**von**/**aus** from)

stämmig *adj* sturdy

Stamm|kundschaft *f* regulars *pl*. **S~lokal** *nt* favourite pub

> [!info] 𝒊
> **Stammtisch** A large table reserved for regulars in most German *Kneipen* (pubs). The word is also used to refer to the group of people who meet around this table for a drink and lively discussion.

stampfen *vi* (*haben*) stamp; (*Maschine:*) pound ● *vi* (*sein*) tramp ● *vt* pound; mash (*Kartoffeln*)

Stand *m* -[e]s,ⁿe standing position; (*Zustand*) state; (*Spiel*-) score; (*Höhe*) level; (*gesellschaftlich*) class; (*Verkaufs*-) stall; (*Messe*-) stand; (*Taxi*-) rank; **auf den neuesten S~ bringen** up-date

Standard *m* -s,-s standard

Standbild *nt* statue

Ständer *m* -s,- stand; (*Geschirr*-) rack; (*Kerzen*-) holder

Standes|amt *nt* registry office. **S~beamte(r)** *m* registrar

standhaft *adj* steadfast

ständig *adj* constant; (*fest*) permanent

Stand|licht *nt* sidelights *pl*. **S~ort** *m* position; (*Firmen*-) location; (*Mil*) garrison. **S~punkt** *m* point of view. **S~uhr** *f* grandfather clock

Stange *f* -,-n bar; (*Holz*-) pole; (*Gardinen*-) rail; (*Hühner*-) perch; (*Zimt*-) stick; **von der S~** 🔢 off the peg

Stängel *m* -s,- stalk, stem

Stangenbohne *f* runner bean

Stanniol *nt* -s tin foil. **S~papier** *nt* silver paper

stanzen *vt* stamp; punch (*Loch*)

Stapel *m* -s,- stack, pile. **S~lauf** *m* launch[ing]. **s~n** *vt* stack *or* pile up

S

Star¹ m -[e]s,-e starling

Star² m -[e]s (Med) [grauer] S~ cataract; grüner S~ glaucoma

Star³ m -s,-s (Theat, Sport) star

stark adj strong; (Motor) powerful; (Verkehr, Regen) heavy; (Hitze, Kälte) severe; (groß) big; (schlimm) bad; (dick) thick; (korpulent) stout ● adv (sehr) very much

Stärk|e f -,-n strength; power; thickness; stoutness; (Größe) size; (Mais-, Wäsche-) starch. **S~emehl** nt cornflour. **s~en** vt strengthen; starch (Wäsche); **sich s~en** fortify oneself. **S~ung** f -,-en strengthening; (Erfrischung) refreshment

starr adj rigid; (steif) stiff

starren vi (haben) stare

Starr|sinn m obstinacy. **s~sinnig** adj obstinate

Start m -s,-s start; (Aviat) take-off. **S~bahn** f runway. **s~en** vi (sein) start; (Aviat) take off ● vt start; (fig) launch

Station /-'tsjo:n/ f -,-en station; (Haltestelle) stop; (Abschnitt) stage; (Med) ward; **S~ machen** break one's journey. **s~är** adv as an inpatient. **s~ieren** vt station

statisch adj static

Statist(in) m -en,-en (f -,-nen) (Theat) extra

Statisti|k f -,-en statistics sg; (Aufstellung) statistics pl. **s~sch** adj statistical

Stativ nt -s,-e (Phot) tripod

statt prep (+ gen) instead of; **an seiner s~** in his place; **an Kindes s~ annehmen** adopt ● conj **s~ etw zu tun** instead of doing sth. **s~dessen** adv instead

statt|finden† vi sep (haben) take place. **s~haft** adj permitted

Statue /'ʃta:tuə/ f -,-n statue

Statur f - build, stature

Status m - status. **S~symbol** nt status symbol

Statut nt -[e]s,-en statute

Stau m -[e]s,-s congestion; (Auto) [traffic] jam; (Rück-) tailback

Staub m -[e]s dust; **S~ wischen** dust; **S~ saugen** vacuum, hoover

Staubecken nt reservoir

staub|ig adj dusty. **s~saugen** vt/i (haben) vacuum, hoover. **S~sauger** m vacuum cleaner, Hoover®

Staudamm m dam

stauen vt dam up; **sich s~** accumulate; (Autos:) form a tailback

staunen vi (haben) be amazed or astonished

Stau|see m reservoir. **S~ung** f -,-en congestion; (Auto) [traffic] jam

Steak /ʃte:k, ste:k/ nt -s,-s steak

stechen† vt stick (in + acc in); (verletzen) prick; (mit Messer) stab; (Insekt:) sting; (Mücke:) bite ● vi (haben) prick; (Insekt:) sting; (Mücke:) bite; (mit Stechuhr) clock in/out; **in See s~** put to sea

Stech|ginster m gorse. **S~kahn** m punt. **S~palme** f holly. **S~uhr** f time clock

Steck|brief m 'wanted' poster. **S~dose** f socket. **s~en** vt put; (mit Nadel, Reißzwecke) pin; (pflanzen) plant ● vi (haben) be; (fest-) be stuck; **s~ bleiben** get stuck; **den Schlüssel s~ lassen** leave the key in the lock

Steckenpferd nt hobby-horse

Steck|er m -s,- (Electr) plug. **S~nadel** f pin

Steg m -[e]s,-e foot-bridge; (Boots-) landing-stage; (Brillen-) bridge

stehen† vi (haben) stand; (sich befinden) be; (still-) be stationary; (Maschine, Uhr:) have stopped; **s~ bleiben** remain standing; (gebäude:) be left standing; (anhalten) stop; (Motor:) stall; (Zeit:) stand still; **vor dem Ruin s~** face ruin; **zu jdm/etw s~** (fig) stand by s.o./sth **jdm [gut] s~** suit s.o.; **sich gut s~** be on good terms; **es steht 3 zu 1** the score is 3–1. **s~d** adj standing; (sich nicht bewegend) stationary; (Gewässer) stagnant

Stehlampe f standard lamp

stehlen† vt/i (haben) steal; **sich s~** steal, creep

Steh|platz m standing place.
S~vermögen nt stamina, staying-power

steif adj stiff

Steig|bügel m stirrup. **S~eisen** nt crampon

steigen† vi (sein) climb; (hochgehen) rise, go up; (Schulden, Spannung:) mount; **s~ auf** (+ acc) climb on [to] (Stuhl); climb (Berg, Leiter); get on (Pferd, Fahrrad); **s~ in** (+ acc) climb into; get in (Auto); get on (Bus, Zug); **s~ aus** climb out of; get out of (Bett, Auto); get off (Bus, Zug); **s~de Preise** rising prices

steiger|n vt increase; **sich s~n** increase; (sich verbessern) improve. **S~ung** f -,-en increase; improvement; (Gram) comparison

steil adj steep. **S~küste** f cliffs pl

Stein m -[e]s,-e stone; (Ziegel-) brick; (Spiel-) piece. **S~bock** m ibex; (Astrology) Capricorn. **S~bruch** m quarry. **S~garten** m rockery. **S~gut** nt earthenware. **s~ig** adj stony. **s~igen** vt stone. **S~kohle** f [hard] coal. **S~schlag** m rock fall

Stelle f -,-n place; (Fleck) spot; (Abschnitt) passage; (Stellung) job, post; (Behörde) authority; **auf der S~** immediately

stellen vt put; (aufrecht) stand; set (Wecker, Aufgabe); ask (Frage); make (Antrag, Forderung, Diagnose); **zur Verfügung s~** provide; **lauter/leiser s~** turn up/down; **kalt/warm s~** chill/keep hot; **sich s~** [go and] stand; give oneself up (**der Polizei** to the police); **sich tot s~** pretend to be dead; **gut gestellt sein** be well off

Stellen|anzeige f job advertisement. **S~vermittlung** f employment agency. **S~weise** adv in places

Stellung f -,-en position; (Arbeit) job; **S~nehmen** make a statement (**zu** on). **S~suche** f job-hunting

Stellvertreter m deputy

Stelzen fpl stilts. **s~** vi (sein) stalk

stemmen vt press; lift (Gewicht)

Stempel m -s,- stamp; (Post-) post-mark; (Präge-) die; (Feingehalts-) hallmark. **s~n** vt stamp; hallmark (Silber); cancel (Marke)

Stengel m -s,- * **Stängel**

Steno f - ⊞ shorthand

Steno|gramm nt -[e]s,-e shorthand text. **S~grafie** f - shorthand. **s~grafieren** vt take down in shorthand ● vi (haben) do shorthand

Steppdecke f quilt

Steppe f -,-n steppe

Stepptanz m tap-dance

sterben† vi (sein) die (**an** + dat of); **im S~ liegen** be dying

sterblich adj mortal. **S~keit** f - mortality

stereo adv in stereo. **S~anlage** f stereo [system]

steril adj sterile. **s~isieren** vt sterilize. **S~ität** f - sterility

Stern m -[e]s,-e star. **S~bild** nt constellation. **S~chen** nt -s,- asterisk. **S~kunde** f astronomy. **S~schnuppe** f -,-n shooting star. **S~warte** f -,-n observatory

stets adv always

Steuer[1] nt -s,- steering-wheel; (Naut) helm; **am S~** at the wheel

Steuer[2] f -,-n tax

Steuer|bord nt -[e]s starboard [side]. **S~erklärung** f tax return. **s~frei** adj & adv tax-free. **S~mann** m (pl -leute) helmsman; (beim Rudern) cox. **s~n** vt steer; (Aviat) pilot; (Techn) control ● vi (haben) be at the wheel/(Naut) helm. **s~pflichtig** adj taxable. **S~rad** nt steering-wheel. **S~ruder** nt helm. **S~ung** f - steering; (Techn) controls pl. **S~zahler** m -s,- taxpayer

Stewardess /'stju:ɐdɛs/ f -,-en air hostess, stewardess

Stich m -[e]s,-e prick; (Messer-) stab; (S~wunde) stab wound; (Bienen-) sting; (Mücken-) bite; (Schmerz) stabbing pain; (Näh-) stitch; (Kupfer-) engraving; (Kartenspiel) trick

stick|en vt/i (haben) embroider. **S~erei** f - embroidery

Stickstoff m nitrogen

S

Stiefel *m* -s,- boot

Stief|kind *nt* stepchild. **S~mutter** *f* stepmother. **S~mütterchen** *nt* -s,- pansy. **S~sohn** *m* stepson. **S~tochter** *f* stepdaughter. **S~vater** *m* stepfather

Stiege *f* -,-n stairs *pl*

Stiel *m* -[e]s,-e handle; (*Blumen-, Gläser-*) stem; (*Blatt-*) stalk

Stier *m* -[e]s,-e bull; (*Astrology*) Taurus

Stierkampf *m* bullfight

Stift¹ *m* -[e]s,-e pin; (*Nagel*) tack; (*Blei-*) pencil; (*Farb-*) crayon

Stift² *nt* -[e]s,-e [endowed] foundation. **s~en** *vt* endow; (*spenden*) donate; create (*Unheil, Verwirrung*); bring about (*Frieden*). **S~ung** *f* -,-en foundation; (*Spende*) donation

Stil *m* -[e]s,-e style

still *adj* quiet; (*reglos, ohne Kohlensäure*) still; (*heimlich*) secret; **der S~e Ozean** the Pacific; **im S~en** secretly. **S~e** *f* - quiet; (*Schweigen*) silence

Stilleben* *nt* = Stillleben

stillen *vt* satisfy; quench (*Durst*); stop (*Schmerzen, Blutung*); breastfeed (*Kind*)

still|halten† *vi sep* (*haben*) keep still. **S~leben** *nt* still life. **s~legen** *vt sep* close down. **S~schweigen** *nt* silence. **S~stand** *m* standstill; **zum S~stand bringen/kommen** stop. **s~stehen†** *vi sep* (*haben*) stand still; (*anhalten*) stop; (*Verkehr:*) be at a standstill

Stimm|bänder *ntpl* vocal cords. **s~berechtigt** *adj* entitled to vote. **S~bruch** *m* **er ist im S~bruch** his voice is breaking

Stimme *f* -,-n voice; (*Wahl-*) vote

stimmen *vi* (*haben*) be right; (*wählen*) vote ● *vt* tune

Stimmung *f* -,-en mood; (*Atmosphäre*) atmosphere

Stimmzettel *m* ballot-paper

stink|en† *vi* (*haben*) smell/(*stark*) stink (*nach* of). **S~tier** *nt* skunk

Stipendium *nt* -s,-ien scholarship; (*Beihilfe*) grant

Stirn *f* -,-en forehead

stochern *vi* (*haben*) **s~ in** (+ *dat*) poke (*Feuer*); pick at (*Essen*)

Stock¹ *m* -[e]s,¨e stick; (*Ski-*) pole; (*Bienen-*) hive; (*Rosen-*) bush; (*Reb-*) vine

Stock² *m* -[e]s,- storey, floor. **S~bett** *nt* bunk-beds *pl.*

stock|en *vi* (*haben*) stop; (*Verkehr:*) come to a standstill; (*Person:*) falter. **S~ung** *f* -,-en hold-up

Stockwerk *nt* storey, floor

Stoff *m* -[e]s,-e substance; (*Textiles*) fabric, material; (*Thema*) subject [matter]; (*Gesprächs-*) topic. **S~wechsel** *m* metabolism

stöhnen *vi* (*haben*) groan, moan

Stola *f* -,-len stole

Stollen *m* -s,- gallery; (*Kuchen*) stollen

stolpern *vi* (*sein*) stumble; **s~ über** (+ *acc*) trip over

stolz *adj* proud (*auf* + *acc* of). **S~** *m* -es pride

stopfen *vt* stuff; (*stecken*) put; (*ausbessern*) darn ● *vi* (*haben*) be constipating

Stopp *m* -s,-s stop. **s~** *int* stop!

stoppelig *adj* stubbly

stopp|en *vt* stop; (*Sport*) time ● *vi* (*haben*) stop. **S~uhr** *f* stop-watch

Stöpsel *m* -s,- plug; (*Flaschen-*) stopper

Storch *m* -[e]s,¨e stork

Store /ʃtoːɐ/ *m* -s,-s net curtain

stören *vt* disturb; disrupt (*Rede*); jam (*Sender*); (*missfallen*) bother ● *vi* (*haben*) be a nuisance

stornieren *vt* cancel

störrisch *adj* stubborn

Störung *f* -,-en disturbance; disruption; (*Med*) trouble; (*Radio*) interference; **technische S~** technical fault

Stoß *m* -es,¨e push, knock; (*mit Ellbogen*) dig; (*Hörner-*) butt; (*mit Waffe*) thrust; (*Schwimm-*) stroke; (*Ruck*) jolt; (*Erd-*) shock; (*Stapel*) stack, pile. **S~dämpfer** *m* -s,- shock absorber

stoßen† vt push, knock; (*mit Füßen*) kick; (*mit Kopf*) butt; (*an-*) poke, nudge; (*treiben*) thrust; **sich s~** knock oneself; **sich** (*dat*) **den Kopf s~** hit one's head ● vi (*haben*) push; **s~ an** (+ *acc*) knock against; (*angrenzen*) adjoin ● vi (*sein*) **s~ gegen** knock against; bump into (*Tür*); **s~ auf** (+ *acc*) bump into; (*entdecken*) come across; strike (*Öl*)

Stoß|stange f bumper. **S~verkehr** m rush-hour traffic. **S~zahn** m tusk. **S~zeit** f rush-hour

stottern vt/i (*haben*) stutter, stammer

Str. abbr (**Straße**) St

Strafanstalt f prison

Strafe f -,-n punishment; (*Jur & fig*) penalty; (*Geld-*) fine; (*Freiheits-*) sentence. **s~n** vt punish

straff adj tight, taut. **s~en** vt tighten

Strafgesetz nt criminal law

sträf|lich adj criminal. **S~ling** m -s,-e prisoner

Straf|mandat nt (*Auto*) [parking/speeding] ticket. **S~porto** nt excess postage. **S~raum** m penalty area. **S~stoß** m penalty. **S~tat** f crime

Strahl m -[e]s,-en ray; (*einer Taschenlampe*) beam; (*Wasser-*) jet. **s~en** vi (*haben*) shine; (*funkeln*) sparkle; (*lächeln*) beam. **S~enbehandlung** f radiotherapy. **S~ung** f - radiation

Strähne f -,-n strand

stramm adj tight

Strampel|höschen /-sç-/ nt -s,- rompers pl. **s~n** vi (*haben*) (*Baby:*) kick

Strand m -[e]s,¨e beach. **s~en** vi (*sein*) run aground

Strang m -[e]s,¨e rope

Strapaz|e f -,-n strain. **s~ieren** vt be hard on; tax (*Nerven*)

Strass m - & -es paste

Straße f -,-n road; (*in der Stadt auch*) street; (*Meeres-*) strait. **S~nbahn** f tram. **S~nkarte** f road-map. **S~nsperre** f road-block

Strat|egie f -,-n strategy. **s~egisch** adj strategic

Strauch m -[e]s, Sträucher bush

Strauß[1] m -es, Sträuße bunch [of flowers]; (*Bukett*) bouquet

Strauß[2] m -es,-e ostrich

streben vi (*haben*) strive (**nach** for) ● vi (*sein*) head (**nach/zu** for)

Streber m -s,- pushy person

Strecke f -,-n stretch, section; (*Entfernung*) distance; (*Rail*) line; (*Route*) route

strecken vt stretch; (*aus-*) stretch out; (*gerade machen*) straighten; (*Culin*) thin down; **den Kopf aus dem Fenster s~** put one's head out of the window

Streich m -[e]s,-e prank, trick

streicheln vt stroke

streichen† vt spread; (*weg-*) smooth; (*an-*) paint; (*aus-*) delete; (*kürzen*) cut ● vi (*haben*) **s~ über** (+ *acc*) stroke

Streichholz nt match

Streich|instrument nt stringed instrument. **S~käse** m cheese spread. **S~orchester** nt string orchestra. **S~ung** f -,-en deletion; (*Kürzung*) cut

Streife f -,-n patrol

streifen vt brush against; (*berühren*) touch; (*verletzen*) graze; (*fig*) touch on (*Thema*)

Streifen m -s,- stripe; (*Licht-*) streak; (*auf der Fahrbahn*) line; (*schmales Stück*) strip

Streifenwagen m patrol car

Streik m -s,-s strike; **in den S~ treten** go on strike. **S~brecher** m strike-breaker, (*pej*) scab. **s~en** vi (*haben*) strike; (🔲) refuse; (*versagen*) pack up

Streit m -[e]s,-e quarrel; (*Auseinandersetzung*) dispute. **s~en**† vr/i (*haben*) [**sich**] **s~en** quarrel. **S~igkeiten** fpl quarrels. **S~kräfte** fpl armed forces

streng adj strict; (*Blick, Ton*) stern; (*rau, nüchtern*) severe; (*Geschmack*) sharp; **s~ genommen** strictly speaking. **S~e** f - strictness; sternness; severity

Stress m -es,-e stress

stressig adj stressful

streuen vt spread; (ver-) scatter; sprinkle (Zucker, Salz); **die Straßen s~** grit the roads

streunen vi (sein) roam

Strich m -[e]s,-e line; (Feder-, Pinsel-) stroke; (Morse-, Gedanken-) dash. **S~kode** m bar code. **S~punkt** m semicolon

Strick m -[e]s,-e cord; (Seil) rope

strick|en vt/i (haben) knit. **S~jacke** f cardigan. **S~leiter** f rope ladder. **S~nadel** f knitting-needle. **S~waren** fpl knitwear sg. **S~zeug** nt knitting

striegeln vt groom

strittig adj contentious

Stroh nt -[e]s straw. **S~blumen** fpl everlasting flowers. **S~dach** nt thatched roof. **S~halm** m straw

Strolch m -[e]s,-e 🔲 rascal

Strom m -[e]s, ̈e river; (Menschen-, Auto-, Blut-) stream; (Tränen-) flood; (Schwall) torrent; (Electr) current, power; **gegen den S~** (fig) against the tide. **s~abwärts** adv downstream. **s~aufwärts** adv upstream

strömen vi (sein) flow; (Menschen, Blut:) stream, pour

Strom|kreis m circuit. **s~linienförmig** adj streamlined. **S~sperre** f power cut

Strömung f -,-en current

Strophe f -,-n verse

Strudel m -s,- whirlpool; (SGer Culin) strudel

Strumpf m -[e]s, ̈e stocking; (Knie-) sock. **S~band** nt (pl -bänder) suspender. **S~hose** f tights pl

Strunk m -[e]s, ̈e stalk

struppig adj shaggy

Stube f -,-n room. **s~nrein** adj house-trained

Stuck m -s stucco

Stück nt -[e]s,-e piece; (Zucker-) lump; (Seife) tablet; (Theater-) play; (Gegenstand) item; (Exemplar) speci-

men; **ein S~** (Entfernung) some way. **S~chen** nt -s,- [little] bit. **s~weise** adv bit by bit; (einzeln) singly

Student|(in) m -en,-en (f -,-nen) student. **s~isch** adj student

Studie /-iə/ f -,-n study

studieren vt/i (haben) study

Studio nt -s,-s studio

Studium nt -s,-ien studies pl

Stufe f -,-n step; (Treppen-) stair; (Raketen-) stage; (Niveau-) level. **s~n** vt terrace; (staffeln) grade

Stuhl m -[e]s, ̈e chair; (Med) stools pl. **S~gang** m bowel movement

stülpen vt put (über + acc over)

stumm adj dumb; (schweigsam) silent

Stummel m -s,- stump; (Zigaretten-) butt; (Bleistift-) stub

Stümper m -s,- bungler

stumpf adj blunt; (Winkel) obtuse; (glanzlos) dull; (fig) apathetic. **S~** m -[e]s, ̈e stump

Stumpfsinn m apathy; tedium

Stunde f -,-n hour; (Sch) lesson

stunden vt **jdm eine Schuld s~** give s.o. time to pay a debt

Stunden|kilometer mpl kilometres per hour. **s~lang** adv for hours. **S~lohn** m hourly rate. **S~plan** m timetable. **s~weise** adv by the hour

stündlich adj & adv hourly

stur adj pigheaded

Sturm m -[e]s, ̈e gale; storm; (Mil) assault

stürm|en vi (haben) (Wind:) blow hard ● vi (sein) rush ● vt storm; (bedrängen) besiege. **S~er** m -s,- forward. **s~isch** adj stormy; (Überfahrt) rough

Sturz m -es, ̈e [heavy] fall; (Preis-) sharp drop; (Pol) overthrow

stürzen vi (sein) fall [heavily]; (in die Tiefe) plunge; (Preise:) drop sharply; (Regierung:) fall; (eilen) rush ● vt throw; (umkippen) turn upside down; turn out (Speise, Kuchen); (Pol) overthrow, topple; **sich s~** throw oneself (aus/in + acc out of/into)

Sturzhelm *m* crash-helmet
Stute *f* -,-n mare
Stütze *f* -,-n support
stützen *vt* support; (*auf-*) rest; **sich s~ auf** (+ *acc*) lean on
stutzig *adj* puzzled; (*misstrauisch*) suspicious
Stützpunkt *m* (*Mil*) base
Substantiv *nt* -s,-e noun
Substanz *f* -,-en substance
Subvention /-'tsjo:n/ *f* -,-en subsidy. **s~ieren** *vt* subsidize
Such|e *f* - search; **auf der S~e nach** looking for. **s~en** *vt* look for; (*intensiv*) search for; seek (*Hilfe, Rat*); 'Zimmer gesucht' 'room wanted' ● *vi* (*haben*) look, search (**nach** for). **S~er** *m* -s,- (*Phot*) viewfinder. **S~maschine** *f* search engine
Sucht *f* -,ᵉe addiction; (*fig*) mania
süchtig *adj* addicted. **S~e(r)** *m/f* addict
Süd *m* -[e]s south. **S~afrika** *nt* South Africa. **S~amerika** *nt* South America. **s~deutsch** *adj* South German
Süden *m* -s south; **nach S~** south
Süd|frucht *f* tropical fruit. **s~lich** *adj* southern; (*Richtung*) southerly ● *adv & prep* (+ *gen*) **s~lich der Stadt** south of the town. **S~pol** *m* South Pole. **s~wärts** *adv* southwards
Sühne *f* -,-n atonement; (*Strafe*) penalty. **s~n** *vt* atone for
Sultanine *f* -,-n sultana
Sülze *f* -,-n [meat] jelly
Summe *f* -,-n sum
summen *vi* (*haben*) hum; (*Biene:*) buzz ● *vt* hum
summieren (sich) *vr* add up
Sumpf *m* -[e]s,ᵉe marsh, swamp
Sünd|e *f* -,-n sin. **S~enbock** *m* scapegoat. **S~er(in)** *m* -s,- (*f* -,-nen) sinner. **s~igen** *vi* (*haben*) sin
super *inv adj* 🅸 great. **S~markt** *m* supermarket
Suppe *f* -,-n soup. **S~nlöffel** *m* soup-spoon. **S~nteller** *m* soup plate. **S~nwürfel** *m* stock cube

Surf|brett /'sø:ɐ̯f-/ *nt* surfboard. **s~en** *vi* (*haben*) surf. **S~en** *nt* -s surfing
surren *vi* (*haben*) whirr
süß *adj* sweet. **S~e** *f* - sweetness. **s~en** *vt* sweeten. **S~igkeit** *f* -,-en sweet. **s~lich** *adj* sweetish; (*fig*) sugary. **S~speise** *f* sweet. **S~stoff** *m* sweetener. **S~waren** *fpl* confectionery *sg*, sweets *pl*. **S~wasser-** *prefix* freshwater
Sylvester *nt* -s = Silvester
Symbol *nt* -s,-e symbol. **S~ik** *f* - symbolism. **s~isch** *adj* symbolic
Sym|metrie *f* - symmetry. **s~metrisch** *adj* symmetrical
Sympathie *f* -,-n sympathy
sympathisch *adj* agreeable; (*Person*) likeable
Symptom *nt* -s,-e symptom. **s~atisch** *adj* symptomatic
Synagoge *f* -,-n synagogue
synchronisieren /zynkroni'zi:rən/ *vt* synchronize; dub (*Film*)
Syndikat *nt* -[e]s,-e syndicate
Syndrom *nt* -s,-e syndrome
synonym *adj* synonymous
Synthese *f* -,-n synthesis
Syrien /-jən/ *nt* -s Syria
System *nt* -s,-e system. **s~atisch** *adj* systematic
Szene *f* -,-n scene

Tt

Tabak *m* -s,-e tobacco
Tabelle *f* -,-n table; (*Sport*) league table
Tablett *nt* -[e]s,-s tray
Tablette *f* -,-n tablet
tabu *adj* taboo. **T~** *nt* -s,-s taboo
Tacho *m* -s,-s, **Tachometer** *m & nt* speedometer
Tadel *m* -s,- reprimand; (*Kritik*) cen-

sure; (Sch) black mark. **t~los** adj impeccable. **t~n** vt reprimand; censure

Tafel f -,-n (Tisch, Tabelle) table; (Platte) slab; (Anschlag-, Hinweis-) board; (Gedenk-) plaque; (Schiefer-) slate; (Wand-) blackboard; (Bild-) plate; (Schokolade) bar

Täfelung f - panelling

Tag m -[e]s,-e day; **unter T~e** underground; **es wird Tag** it is getting light; **guten Tag!** good morning/afternoon!

Tage|buch nt diary. **t~lang** adv for days

Tages|anbruch m daybreak. **T~ausflug** m day trip. **T~decke** f bedspread. **T~karte** f day ticket; (Speise-) menu of the day. **T~licht** nt daylight. **T~mutter** f child-minder. **T~ordnung** f agenda. **T~rückfahrkarte** f day return [ticket]. **T~zeit** f time of the day. **T~zeitung** f daily [news]paper

täglich adj & adv daily; **zweimal t~** twice a day

tags adv by day; **t~ zuvor/darauf** the day before/after

tagsüber adv during the day

tag|täglich adj daily ● adv every single day. **T~ung** f -,-en meeting; conference

Taill|e /'taljə/ f -,-n waist. **t~iert** adj fitted

Takt m -[e]s,-e tact; (Mus) bar; (Tempo) time; (Rhythmus) rhythm; **im T~** in time

Taktik f - tactics pl.

takt|los adj tactless. **T~losigkeit** f - tactlessness. **T~stock** m baton. **t~voll** adj tactful

Tal nt -[e]s,-er valley

Talar m -s,-e robe; (Univ) gown

Talent nt -[e]s,-e talent. **t~iert** adj talented

Talg m -s tallow; (Culin) suet

Talsperre f dam

Tampon /tam'põ:/ m -s,-s tampon

Tank m -s,-s tank. **t~en** vt fill up with (Benzin) ● vi (haben) fill up with petrol; (Aviat) refuel. **T~er** m -s,-

tanker. **T~stelle** f petrol station. **T~wart** m -[e]s,-e petrol-pump attendant

Tanne f -,-n fir [tree]. **T~nbaum** m fir tree; (Weihnachtsbaum) Christmas tree. **T~nzapfen** m fir cone

Tante f -,-n aunt

Tantiemen /tan'tje:mən/ pl royalties

Tanz m -es,-e dance. **t~en** vt/i (haben) dance

Tänzer(in) m -s,- (f -,-nen) dancer

Tapete f -,-n wallpaper

tapezieren vt paper

tapfer adj brave. **T~keit** f - bravery

Tarif m -s,-e rate; (Verzeichnis) tariff

tarn|en vt disguise; (Mil) camouflage. **T~ung** f - disguise; camouflage

Tasche f -,-n bag; (Hosen-, Mantel-) pocket. **T~nbuch** nt paperback. **T~ndieb** m pickpocket. **T~ngeld** nt pocket-money. **T~nlampe** f torch. **T~nmesser** nt penknife. **T~ntuch** nt handkerchief

Tasse f -,-n cup

Tastatur f -,-en keyboard

Tast|e f -,-n key; (Druck-) push button. **t~en** vi (haben) feel, grope (nach for) ● vt key in (Daten); **sich t~en** feel one's way (zu to)

Tat f -,-en action; (Helden-) deed; (Straf-) crime; **auf frischer Tat ertappt** caught in the act

Täter(in) m -s,- (f -,-nen) culprit; (Jur) offender

tätig adj active; **t~ sein** work. **T~keit** f -,-en activity; (Arbeit) work, job

Tatkraft f energy

Tatort m scene of the crime

tätowier|en vt tattoo. **T~ung** f -,-en tattooing; (Bild) tattoo

Tatsache f fact. **T~nbericht** m documentary

tatsächlich adj actual

Tatze f -,-n paw

Tau[1] m -[e]s dew

Tau[2] nt -[e]s,-e rope

taub *adj* deaf; (*gefühllos*) numb

Taube *f* -,-n pigeon; dove. T~schlag *m* pigeon loft

Taub|heit *f* - deafness. **t~stumm** *adj* deaf and dumb

tauch|en *vt* dip, plunge; (*unter-*) duck ● *vi* (*haben/sein*) dive/(*ein-*) plunge (**in** + *acc* into); (*auf-*) appear (**aus** out of). **T~er** *m* -s,- diver. **T~eranzug** *m* diving-suit

tauen *vi* (*sein*) melt, thaw ● *impers* **es taut** it is thawing

Tauf|becken *nt* font. **T~e** *f* -,-n christening, baptism. **t~en** *vt* christen, baptize. **T~pate** *m* godfather

taugen *vi* (*haben*) **etwas/nichts t~n** be good/no good

tauglich *adj* suitable; (*Mil*) fit

Tausch *m* -[e]s,-e exchange, ⊞ swap. **t~en** *vt* exchange/(*handeln*) barter (*gegen* for) ● *vi* (*haben*) swap (**mit etw** sth; **mit jdm** with s.o.)

täuschen *vt* deceive, fool; betray (*Vertrauen*); **sich t~** delude oneself; (*sich irren*) be mistaken ● *vi* (*haben*) be deceptive. **t~d** *adj* deceptive; (*Ähnlichkeit*) striking

Täuschung *f* -,-en deception; (*Irrtum*) mistake; (*Illusion*) delusion

tausend *inv adj* one/a thousand. **T~** *nt* -s,-e thousand. **T~füßler** *m* -s,- centipede. **t~ste(r, s)** *adj* thousandth. **T~stel** *nt* -s,- thousandth

Tau|tropfen *m* dewdrop. **T~wetter** *nt* thaw

Taxe *f* -,-n charge; (*Kur-*) tax; (*Taxi*) taxi

Taxi *nt* -s,-s taxi, cab

Taxi|fahrer *m* taxi driver. **T~stand** *m* taxi rank

Teakholz /'ti:k-/ *nt* teak

Team /ti:m/ *nt* -s,-s team

Techni|k *f* -,-en technology; (*Methode*) technique. **T~ker** *m* -s,- technician. **t~sch** *adj* technical; (*technologisch*) technological; **T~sche Hochschule** Technical University

Techno|logie *f* -,-n technology. **t~logisch** *adj* technological

Teddybär *m* teddy bear

Tee *m* -s,-s tea. **T~beutel** *m* tea-bag. **T~kanne** *f* teapot. **T~löffel** *m* teaspoon

Teer *m* -s tar. **t~en** *vt* tar

Tee|sieb *nt* tea strainer. **T~wagen** *m* [tea] trolley

Teich *m* -[e]s,-e pond

Teig *m* -[e]s,-e pastry; (*Knet-*) dough; (*Rühr-*) mixture; (*Pfannkuchen-*) batter. **T~rolle** *f* rolling-pin. **T~waren** *fpl* pasta *sg*

Teil *m* -[e]s,-e part; (*Bestand-*) component; (*Jur*) party; **zum T~** partly; **zum großen/größten T~** for the most part ● *m & nt* -[e]s (*Anteil*) share; **ich für mein[en] T~** for my part ● *nt* -[e]s,-e part; (*Ersatz-*) spare part; (*Anbau-*) unit

teil|bar *adj* divisible. **T~chen** *nt* -s,- particle. **t~en** *vt* divide; (*auf-*) share out; (*gemeinsam haben*) share; (*Pol*) partition (*Land*); **sich** (*dat*) **etw t~en** share sth; **sich t~en** divide; (*sich gabeln*) fork; (*Meinungen:*) differ ● *vi* (*haben*) share

Teilhaber *m* -s,- (*Comm*) partner

Teilnahme *f* - participation; (*innere*) interest; (*Mitgefühl*) sympathy

teilnehm|en† *vi sep* (*haben*) **t~en an** (+ *dat*) take part in; (*mitfühlen*) share [in]. **T~er(in)** *m* -s,- (*f* -,-nen) participant; (*an Wettbewerb*) competitor

teil|s *adv* partly. **T~ung** *f* -,-en division; (*Pol*) partition. **t~weise** *adj* partial ● *adv* partially, partly. **T~zahlung** *f* part payment; (*Rate*) instalment. **T~zeitbeschäftigung** *f* part-time job

Teint /tɛ̃:/ *m* -s,-s complexion

Telearbeit *f* teleworking

Telefax *nt* fax

Telefon *nt* -s,-e [tele]phone. **T~anruf** *m*, **T~at** *nt* -[e]s,-e [tele]phone call. **T~buch** *nt* [tele]phone book. **t~ieren** *vi* (*haben*) [tele]phone

telefon|isch *adj* [tele]phone ● *adv* by [tele]phone. **T~ist(in)** *m* -en,-en (*f* -,-nen) telephonist. **T~karte** *f* phone card. **T~nummer** *f* [tele]-

t

phone number. **T~zelle** f [tele]-
phone box
Telegraf m -en,-en telegraph.
  T~enmast m telegraph pole.
  t~ieren vi (haben) send a telegram.
  t~isch adj telegraphic ● adv by tele-
  gram
Telegramm nt -s,-e telegram
Teleobjektiv nt telephoto lens
Telepathie f - telepathy
Teleskop nt -s,-e telescope
Telex nt -,-[e] telex. **t~en** vt telex
Teller m -s,- plate
Tempel m -s,- temple
Temperament nt -s,-e tempera-
  ment; (Lebhaftigkeit) vivacity
Temperatur f -,-en temperature
Tempo nt -s,-s speed; **T~ [T~]!**
  hurry up!
Tendenz f -,-en trend; (Neigung) ten-
  dency
Tennis nt - tennis. **T~platz** m
  tennis-court. **T~schläger** m tennis-
  racket
Teppich m -s,-e carpet. **T~boden**
  m fitted carpet
Termin m -s,-e date; (Arzt-) appoint-
  ment. **T~kalender** m [appoint-
  ments] diary
Terpentin nt -s turpentine
Terrasse f -,-n terrace
Terrier /'tɛriɐ/ m -s,- terrier
Terrine f -,-n tureen
Territorium nt -s,-ien territory
Terror m -s terror. **t~isieren** vt ter-
  rorize. **T~ismus** m - terrorism.
  T~ist m -en,-en terrorist
Tesafilm® m ≈ Sellotape®
Test m -[e]s,-s & -e test
Testament nt -[e]s,-e will; Altes/
  Neues **T~** Old/New Testament.
  T~svollstrecker m -s,- executor
testen vt test
Tetanus m - tetanus
teuer adj expensive; (lieb) dear; **wie
  t~?** how much?
Teufel m -s,- devil. **T~skreis** m vi-
  cious circle
teuflisch adj fiendish

Text m -[e]s,-e text; (Passage) pas-
  sage; (Bild-) caption; (Lied-) lyrics pl.
  T~er m -s,- copywriter; (Schlager-)
  lyricist
Textilien /-iən/ pl textiles; (Textilwa-
  ren) textile goods
Text|nachricht f text message.
  T~verarbeitungssystem nt word
  processor
Theater nt -s,- theatre; (🔲: Getue)
  fuss. **T~kasse** f box-office. **T~stück**
  nt play
Theke f -,-n bar; (Ladentisch) counter
Thema nt -s,-men subject
Themse f - Thames
Theolo|ge m -n,-n theologian.
  T~gie f - theology
theor|etisch adj theoretical. **T~ie** f
  -,-n theory
Therapeut(in) m -en,-en (f
  -,-nen) therapist
Therapie f -,-n therapy
Thermalbad nt thermal bath
Thermometer nt -s,- thermometer
Thermosflasche® f Thermos
  flask®
Thermostat m -[e]s,-e thermostat
These f -,-n thesis
Thrombose f -,-n thrombosis
Thron m -[e]s,-e throne. **t~en** vi
  (haben) sit [in state]. **T~folge** f succession. **T~folger** m -s,- heir to the
  throne
Thunfisch m tuna
Thymian m -s thyme
ticken vi (haben) tick
tief adj deep; (t~ liegend, niedrig)
  low; (t~gründig) profound; **t~er Teller** soup-plate ● adv deep; low; (sehr)
  deeply, profoundly; (schlafen)
  soundly. **T~** nt -s,-s (Meteorology)
  depression. **T~bau** m civil engineering. **T~e** f -,-n depth. **T~garage** f
  underground car park. **t~gekühlt**
  adj [deep-]frozen
Tiefkühl|fach nt freezer compart-
  ment. **T~kost** f frozen food.
  T~truhe f deep-freeze
Tiefsttemperatur f minimum
  temperature

Tier *nt* -[e]s,-e animal. **T~arzt** *m*, **T~ärztin** *f* vet, veterinary surgeon. **T~garten** *m* zoo. **T~kreis** *m* zodiac. **T~kunde** *f* zoology. **T~quälerei** *f* cruelty to animals

Tiger *m* -s,- tiger

tilgen *vt* pay off (*Schuld*); (*streichen*) delete; (*fig: auslöschen*) wipe out

Tinte *f* -,-n ink. **T~nfisch** *m* squid

Tipp (**Tip**) *m* -s,-s ⊞ tip

tipp|en *vt* ⊞ type ● *vi* (*haben*) (*berühren*) touch (**auf/an etw** *acc* sth); (⊞: *Maschine schreiben*) type; **t~en auf** (+ *acc*) (⊞: *wetten*) bet on. **T~schein** *m* pools/lottery coupon

tipptopp *adj* ⊞ immaculate

Tirol *nt* -s [the] Tyrol

Tisch *m* -[e]s,-e table; (*Schreib-*) desk; **nach T~** after the meal. **T~decke** *f* table-cloth. **T~gebet** *nt* grace. **T~ler** *m* -s,- joiner; (*Möbel-*) cabinet-maker. **T~rede** *f* after-dinner speech. **T~tennis** *nt* table tennis

Titel *m* -s,- title

Toast /to:st/ *m* -[e]s,-e toast; (*Scheibe*) piece of toast. **T~er** *m* -s,- toaster

toben *vi* (*haben*) rave; (*Sturm:*) rage; (*Kinder:*) play boisterously

Tochter *f* -,- daughter. **T~gesellschaft** *f* subsidiary

Tod *m* -es death

Todes|angst *f* mortal fear. **T~anzeige** *f* death announcement; (*Zeitungs-*) obituary. **T~fall** *m* death. **T~opfer** *nt* fatality, casualty. **T~strafe** *f* death penalty. **T~urteil** *nt* death sentence

todkrank *adj* dangerously ill

tödlich *adj* fatal; (*Gefahr*) mortal

Toilette /tɔa'lɛtə/ *f* -,-n toilet. **T~npapier** *nt* toilet paper

toler|ant *adj* tolerant. **T~anz** *f* - tolerance. **t~ieren** *vt* tolerate

toll *adj* crazy, mad; (⊞: *prima*) fantastic; (*schlimm*) awful ● *adv* (*sehr*) very; (*schlimm*) badly. **t~kühn** *adj* foolhardy. **T~wut** *f* rabies. **t~wütig** *adj* rabid

Tölpel *m* -s,- fool

Tomate *f* -,-n tomato. **T~nmark** *nt* tomato purée

Tombola *f* -,-s raffle

Ton¹ *m* -[e]s clay

Ton² *m* -[e]s,-e tone; (*Klang*) sound; (*Note*) note; (*Betonung*) stress; (*Farb-*) shade; **der gute Ton** (*fig*) good form. **T~abnehmer** *m* -s,- pick-up. **t~angebend** *adj* (*fig*) leading. **T~art** *f* tone [of voice]; (*Mus*) key. **T~band** *nt* (*pl* -bänder) tape. **T~bandgerät** *nt* tape recorder

tönen *vi* (*haben*) sound ● *vt* tint

Tonleiter *f* scale

Tonne *f* -,-n barrel, cask; (*Müll-*) bin; (*Maß*) tonne, metric ton

Topf *m* -[e]s,-e pot; (*Koch-*) pan

Topfen *m* -s (Aust) ≈ curd cheese

Töpferei *f* -,-en pottery

Topf|lappen *m* oven-cloth. **T~pflanze** *f* potted plant

Tor *nt* -[e]s,-e gate; (*Einfahrt*) gateway; (*Sport*) goal

Torf *m* -s peat

torkeln *vi* (*sein/habe*) stagger

Tornister *m* -s,- knapsack; (*Sch*) satchel

Torpedo *m* -s,-s torpedo

Torpfosten *m* goal-post

Torte *f* -,-n gateau; (*Obst-*) flan

Tortur *f* -,-en torture

Torwart *m* -s,-e goalkeeper

tot *adj* dead; **tot geboren** stillborn; **sich tot stellen** pretend to be dead

total *adj* total. **T~schaden** *m* ≈ write-off

Tote|(r) *m/f* dead man/woman; (*Todesopfer*) fatality; **die T~n** the dead *pl*

töten *vt* kill

Toten|gräber *m* -s,- grave-digger. **T~kopf** *m* skull. **T~schein** *m* death certificate

totfahren† *vt sep* run over and kill

Toto *nt* & *m* -s football pools *pl*. **T~schein** *m* pools coupon

tot|schießen† *vt sep* shoot dead. **T~schlag** *m* (*Jur*) manslaughter. **t~schlagen**† *vt sep* kill

t

Tötung f -,-en killing; **fahrlässige T~** (Jur) manslaughter

Toup|et /tu'pe:/ nt -s,-s toupee. **t~ieren** vt back-comb

Tour /tu:ɐ/ f -,-en tour; (Ausflug) trip; (Auto-) drive; (Rad-) ride; (Strecke) distance; (Techn) revolution; ([I]: Weise) way

Touris|mus /tu'rɪsmʊs/ m - tourism. **T~t m** -en,-en tourist

Tournee /tʊr'ne:/ f -,-n tour

Trab m -[e]s trot

Trabant m -en,-en satellite

traben vi (haben/sein) trot

Tracht f -,-en [national] costume

Tradition /-'tsio:n/ f -,-en tradition. **t~ell** adj traditional

Trag|bahre f stretcher. **t~bar** adj portable; (Kleidung) wearable

tragen† vt carry; (an-/ aufhaben) wear; (fig) bear ● vi (haben) carry; **gut t~** (Baum:) produce a good crop

Träger m -s,- porter; (Inhaber) bearer; (eines Ordens) holder; (Bau-) beam; (Stahl-) girder; (Achsel-) [shoulder] strap. **T~kleid** nt pinafore dress

Trag|etasche f carrier bag. **T~flächenboot, T~flügelboot** nt hydrofoil

Trägheit f - sluggishness; (Faulheit) laziness; (Phys) inertia

Trag|ik f - tragedy. **t~isch** adj tragic

Tragödie /- iə/ f -,-n tragedy

Train|er /'trɛ:nɐ/ m -s,- trainer; (Tennis-) coach. **t~ieren** vt/i (haben) train

Training /'trɛ:nɪŋ/ nt -s training. **T~sanzug** m tracksuit. **T~s-schuhe** mpl trainers

Traktor m -s,-en tractor

trampeln vi (haben) stamp one's feet ● vi (sein) trample (**auf** + acc on) ● vt trample

trampen /'trɛmpən/ vi (sein) [I] hitch-hike

Tranchiermesser /trã'ʃiːɐ-/ nt carving knife

Träne f -,-n tear. **t~n** vi (haben) water. **T~ngas** nt tear-gas

Tränke f -,-n watering place; (Trog)

drinking trough. **t~n** vt water (Pferd); (nässen) soak (mit with)

Trans|formator m -s,-en transformer. **T~fusion** f -,-en [blood] transfusion

Transit /tran'zi:t/ m -s transit

Transparent nt -[e]s,-e banner; (Bild) transparency

transpirieren vi (haben) perspire

Transport m -[e]s,-e transport; (Güter-) consignment. **t~ieren** vt transport

Trapez nt -es,-e trapeze

Tratte f -,-n (Comm) draft

Traube f -,-n bunch of grapes; (Beere) grape; (fig) cluster. **T~nzucker** m glucose

trauen vi (haben) (+ dat) trust ● vt marry; **sich t~** dare (**etw zu tun** [to] do sth); venture (**in** + acc/**aus** into/out of)

Trauer f - mourning; (Schmerz) grief (um for); **T~ tragen** be [dressed] in mourning. **T~fall** m bereavement. **T~feier** f funeral service. **t~n** vi (haben) grieve; **t~n um** mourn [for]. **T~spiel** nt tragedy. **T~weide** f weeping willow

Traum m -[e]s, Träume dream

Trauma nt -s,-men trauma

träumen vt/i (haben) dream

traumhaft adj dreamlike; (schön) fabulous

traurig adj sad; (erbärmlich) sorry. **T~keit** f - sadness

Trau|ring m wedding-ring. **T~schein** m marriage certificate. **T~ung** f -,-en wedding [ceremony]

Treff nt -s,-s (Karten) spades pl

treff|en† vt hit; (Blitz:) strike; (fig: verletzen) hurt; (zusammenkommen mit) meet; take (Maßnahme); **sich t~en** meet (**mit jdm** s.o.); **sich gut t~en** be convenient; **es gut/ schlecht t~en** be lucky/unlucky ● vi (haben) hit the target; **t~en auf** (+ acc) meet; (fig) meet with. **T~en** nt -s,- meeting. **T~er** m -s,- hit; (Los) winner. **T~punkt** m meeting-place

treiben† vt drive; (sich befassen mit)

do; carry on (*Gewerbe*); indulge in (*Luxus*); get up to (*Unfug*); **Handel t~** trade ● *vi* (*sein*) drift; (*schwimmen*) float ● *vi* (*haben*) (*Bot*) sprout. **T~** *nt* **-s** activity

Treib|haus *nt* hothouse. **T~hauseffekt** *m* greenhouse effect. **T~holz** *nt* driftwood. **T~riemen** *m* transmission belt. **T~sand** *m* quicksand. **T~stoff** *m* fuel

trenn|bar *adj* separable. **t~en** *vt* separate/(*abmachen*) detach (**von** from); divide, split (*Wort*); **sich t~en** separate; (*auseinander gehen*) part; **sich t~en von** leave; (*fortgeben*) part with. **T~ung** *f* -,-en separation; (*Silben-*) division. **T~ungsstrich** *m* hyphen. **T~wand** *f* partition

trepp|ab *adv* downstairs. **t~auf** *adv* upstairs

Treppe *f* -,-n stairs *pl*; (*Außen-*) steps *pl*. **T~ngeländer** *nt* banisters *pl*

Tresor *m* -s,-e safe

Tresse *f* -,-n braid

Treteimer *m* pedal bin

treten† *vi* (*sein/haben*) step; (*versehentlich*) tread; (*ausschlagen*) kick (**nach** at); **in Verbindung t~** get in touch ● *vt* tread; (*mit Füßen*) kick

treu *adj* faithful; (*fest*) loyal. **T~e** *f* - faithfulness; loyalty; (*eheliche*) fidelity. **T~ekarte** *f* loyalty card. **T~händer** *m* -s,- trustee. **t~los** *adj* disloyal; (*untreu*) unfaithful

Tribüne *f* -,-n platform; (*Zuschauer-*) stand

Trichter *m* -s,- funnel; (*Bomben-*) crater

Trick *m* -s,-s trick. **T~film** *m* cartoon. **t~reich** *adj* clever

Trieb *m* -[e]s,-e drive, urge; (*Instinkt*) instinct; (*Bot*) shoot. **T~verbrecher** *m* sex offender. **T~werk** *nt* (*Aviat*) engine; (*Uhr-*) mechanism

triefen† *vi* (*haben*) drip; (*nass sein*) be dripping (**von/vor** + *dat* with)

Trigonometrie *f* - trigonometry

Trikot¹ /triˈkoː/ *m* -s (*Textiles*) jersey

Trikot² *nt* -s,-s (*Sport*) jersey; (*Fußball-*) shirt

Trimester *nt* -s,- term

Trimm-dich *nt* -s keep-fit

trimmen *vt* trim; tune (*Motor*); **sich t~** keep fit

trink|en† *vt/i* (*haben*) drink. **T~er(in)** *m* -s,- (*f* -,-nen) alcoholic. **T~geld** *nt* tip. **T~spruch** *m* toast

trist *adj* dreary

Tritt *m* -[e]s,-e step; (*Fuß-*) kick. **T~brett** *nt* step

Triumph *m* -s,-e triumph. **t~ieren** *vi* (*haben*) rejoice

trocken *adj* dry. **T~haube** *f* drier. **T~heit** *f* -,-en dryness; (*Dürre*) drought. **t~legen** *vt sep* change (*Baby*); drain (*Sumpf*). **T~milch** *f* powdered milk

trockn|en *vt/i* (*sein*) dry. **T~er** *m* -s,- drier

Trödel *m* -s 🔲 junk. **t~n** *vi* (*haben*) dawdle

Trödler *m* -s,- 🔲 slowcoach; (*Händler*) junk-dealer

Trog *m* -[e]s,ˉe trough

Trommel *f* -,-n drum. **T~fell** *nt* eardrum. **t~n** *vi* (*haben*) drum

Trommler *m* -s,- drummer

Trompete *f* -,-n trumpet. **T~r** *m* -s,- trumpeter

Tropen *pl* tropics

Tropf *m* -[e]s,-e (*Med*) drip

tröpfeln *vt/i* (*sein/haben*) drip

tropfen *vt/i* (*sein/haben*) drip. **T~** *m* -s,- drop; (*fallend*) drip. **t~weise** *adv* drop by drop

Trophäe /troˈfɛːə/ *f* -,-n trophy

tropisch *adj* tropical

Trost *m* -[e]s consolation, comfort

tröst|en *vt* console, comfort; **sich t~en** console oneself. **t~lich** *adj* comforting

trost|los *adj* desolate; (*elend*) wretched; (*reizlos*) dreary. **T~preis** *m* consolation prize

Trott *m* -s amble; (*fig*) routine

Trottel *m* -s,- 🔲 idiot

Trottoir /trɔˈto̯aːɐ̯/ *nt* -s,-s pavement

trotz *prep* (+ *gen*) despite, in spite of. **T~** *m* -es defiance. **t~dem** *adv*

t

nevertheless. **t~ig** adj defiant; stubborn

trübe adj dull; (Licht) dim; (Flüssigkeit) cloudy; (fig) gloomy

Trubel m -s bustle

trüben vt dull; make cloudy (Flüssigkeit); (fig) spoil; strain (Verhältnis); **sich t~** (Flüssigkeit:) become cloudy; (Himmel:) cloud over; (Augen:) dim

Trüb|sal f - misery. **T~sinn** m melancholy. **t~sinnig** adj melancholy

trügen† vt deceive ● vi (haben) be deceptive

Trugschluss m fallacy

Truhe f -,-n chest

Trümmer pl rubble sg; (T~teile) wreckage sg, (fig) ruins

Trumpf m -[e]s,=e trump [card]. **t~en** vi (haben) play trumps

Trunk m -[e]s drink. **T~enheit** f - drunkenness; **T~enheit am Steuer** drink-driving

Trupp m -s,-s group; (Mil) squad. **T~e** f -,-n (Mil) unit; (Theat) troupe; **T~en** troops

Truthahn m turkey

Tschech|e m -n,-n, **T~in** f -,-nen Czech. **t~isch** adj Czech. **T~oslowakei (die)** - Czechoslovakia

tschüs, tschüss int bye, cheerio

Tuba f -,-ben (Mus) tuba

Tube f -,-n tube

Tuberkulose f - tuberculosis

Tuch nt -[e]s,=er cloth; (Hals-, Kopf-) scarf; (Schulter-) shawl

tüchtig adj competent; (reichlich, beträchtlich) good; (groß) big ● adv competently; (ausreichend) well

Tück|e f -,-n malice. **t~isch** adj malicious; (gefährlich) treacherous

Tugend f -,en virtue. **t~haft** adj virtuous

Tülle f -,-n spout

Tulpe f -,-n tulip

Tümmler m -s,- porpoise

Tumor m -s,-en tumour

Tümpel m -[e]s,- pond

Tumult m -[e]s,-e commotion; (Aufruhr) riot

tun† vt do; take (Schritt, Blick); work (Wunder); (bringen) put (in + acc into); **sich tun** happen; **jdm etwas tun** hurt s.o.; **das tut nichts** it doesn't matter ● vi (haben) act (**als ob** as if); **er tut nur so** he's just pretending; **jdm/etw gut tun** do s.o./ sth good; **zu tun haben** have things/ work to do; **[es] zu tun haben mit** have to deal with. **Tun** nt -s actions pl

Tünche f -,-n whitewash; (fig) veneer. **t~n** vt whitewash

Tunesien /-ịạn/ nt -s Tunisia

Tunfisch m **Thunfisch**

Tunnel m -s,- tunnel

tupf|en vt dab ● vi (haben) **t~en an/auf** (+ acc) touch. **T~en** m -s,- spot. **T~er** m -s,- spot; (Med) swab

Tür f -,-en door

Turban m -s,-e turban

Turbine f -,-n turbine

Türk|e m -n,-n Turk. **T~ei (die)** - Turkey. **T~in** f -,-nen Turk

türkis inv adj turquoise

türkisch adj Turkish

Turm m -[e]s,=e tower; (Schach) rook, castle

Türm|chen nt -s,- turret. **t~en** vt pile [up]; **sich t~en** pile up

Turmspitze f spire

turn|en vi (haben) do gymnastics. **T~en** nt -s gymnastics sg; (Sch) physical education, 🔲 gym. **T~er(in)** m -s,- (f -,-nen) gymnast. **T~halle** f gymnasium

Turnier nt -s,-e tournament; (Reit-) show

Turnschuhe mpl gym shoes; trainers

Türschwelle f doorstep, threshold

Tusche f -,-n [drawing] ink

tuscheln vt/i (haben) whisper

Tüte f -,-n bag; (Comm) packet; (Eis-) cornet; **in die T~ blasen** 🔲 be breathalysed

TÜV m - ≈ MOT [test]

Typ m -s,-en type; (🔲: Kerl) bloke. **T~e** f -,-n type

Typhus m - typhoid

typisch adj typical (**für** of)

Typus m -, **Typen** type

Tyrann m -en,-en tyrant. **T~ei** f - tyranny. **t~isch** adj tyrannical. **t~i-sieren** vt tyrannize

....

Uu

....

U-Bahn f underground

übel adj bad; (*hässlich*) nasty; **mir ist ü~** I feel sick; **jdm etw ü~ nehmen** hold sth against s.o. **Ü~keit** f - nausea

üben vt/i (*haben*) practise

über prep (+ dat/acc) over; (*höher als*) above; (*betreffend*) about; (*Buch, Vortrag*) on; (*Scheck, Rechnung*) for; (*quer ü~*) across; **ü~ Köln fahren** go via Cologne; **ü~ Ostern** over Easter; **die Woche ü~** during the week; **Fehler ü~ Fehler** mistake after mistake • adv **ü~ und ü~** all over; **jdm ü~ sein** be better/(*stärker*) stronger than s.o. • adj ① **ü~ sein** be left over; **etw ü~ sein** be fed up with sth

überall adv everywhere

überanstrengen vt insep overtax; strain (*Augen*)

überarbeiten vt insep revise; **sich ü~en** overwork

überbieten† vt insep outbid; (*übertreffen*) surpass

Überblick m overall view; (*Abriss*) summary

überblicken vt insep overlook; (*abschätzen*) assess

überbringen† vt insep deliver

überbrücken vt insep (*fig*) bridge

überbuchen vt insep overbook

überdies adv moreover

überdimensional adj oversized

Überdosis f overdose

überdrüssig adj **ü~ sein/werden** be/grow tired (*gen* of)

übereignen vt insep transfer

übereilt adj over-hasty

übereinander adv one on top of/above the other; (*sprechen*) about each other

überein|kommen† vi sep (*sein*) agree. **Ü~kunft** f - agreement. **ü~stimmen** vi sep (*haben*) agree; (*Zahlen:*) tally; (*Ansichten:*) coincide; (*Farben:*) match. **Ü~stimmung** f agreement

überfahren† vt insep run over

Überfahrt f crossing

Überfall m attack; (*Bank-*) raid

überfallen† vt insep attack; raid (*Bank*); (*bestürmen*) bombard (**mit** with)

Überfluss m abundance; (*Wohlstand*) affluence

überflüssig adj superfluous

überfordern vt insep overtax

überführ|en vt insep transfer; (*Jur*) convict (*gen* of). **Ü~ung** f transfer; (*Straße*) flyover; (*Fußgänger-*) footbridge

überfüllt adj overcrowded

Übergabe f handing over; transfer

Übergang m crossing; (*Wechsel*) transition

übergeben† vt insep hand over; (*übereignen*) transfer; **sich ü~** be sick

übergehen† vt insep (*fig*) pass over; (*nicht beachten*) ignore; (*auslassen*) leave out

Übergewicht nt excess weight; (*fig*) predominance. **Ü~ haben** be overweight

über|greifen† vi sep (*haben*) spread (**auf** + acc to). **Ü~griff** m infringement

über|groß adj outsize; (*übertrieben*) exaggerated. **Ü~größe** f outsize

überhand adv **ü~ nehmen** increase alarmingly

überhäufen vt insep inundate (**mit** with)

überhaupt adv (*im Allgemeinen*) altogether; (*eigentlich*) anyway; (*überdies*) besides; **ü~ nicht/nichts** not/nothing at all

t

u

überheblich *adj* arrogant. **Ü~keit** *f* - arrogance

überhol|en *vt insep* overtake; *(reparieren)* overhaul. **ü~t** *adj* out-dated. **Ü~ung** *f* -,-en overhaul. **Ü~verbot** *nt* 'Ü~verbot' 'no overtaking'

überhören *vt insep* fail to hear; *(nicht beachten)* ignore

überirdisch *adj* supernatural

überkochen *vi sep (sein)* boil over

überlassen† *vt insep* **jdm etw ü~** leave sth to s.o.; *(geben)* let s.o. have sth; **sich** *(dat)* **selbst ü~ sein** be left to one's own devices

Überlauf *m* overflow

überlaufen† *vi sep (sein)* overflow; *(Mil, Pol)* defect

Überläufer *m* defector

überleben *vt/i insep (haben)* survive. **Ü~de(r)** *m/f* survivor

überlegen¹ *vt sep* put over

überlegen² *v insep* ● *vt* [**sich** *dat*] **ü~** think over, consider; **es sich** *(dat)* **anders ü~** change one's mind ● *vi (haben)* think, reflect

überlegen³ *adj* superior. **Ü~heit** *f* - superiority

Überlegung *f* -,-en reflection

überliefer|n *vt insep* hand down. **Ü~ung** *f* tradition

überlisten *vt insep* outwit

Übermacht *f* superiority

übermäßig *adj* excessive

Übermensch *m* superman. **ü~lich** *adj* superhuman

übermitteln *vt insep* convey; *(senden)* transmit

übermorgen *adv* the day after tomorrow

übermüdet *adj* overtired

Über|mut *m* high spirits *pl.* **ü~mütig** *adj* high-spirited

übernächst|e(r,s) *adj* next but one; **ü~es Jahr** the year after next

übernacht|en *vi insep (haben)* stay overnight. **Ü~ung** *f* -,-en overnight stay; **Ü~ung und Frühstück** bed and breakfast

Übernahme *f* - taking over; *(Comm)* take-over

übernatürlich *adj* supernatural

übernehmen† *vt insep* take over; *(annehmen)* take on; **sich ü~** overdo things; *(finanziell)* over-reach oneself

überqueren *vt insep* cross

überrasch|en *vt insep* surprise. **ü~end** *adj* surprising; *(unerwartet)* unexpected. **Ü~ung** *f* -,-en surprise

überreden *vt insep* persuade

Überreste *mpl* remains

Überschall- *prefix* supersonic

überschätzen *vt insep* overestimate

Überschlag *m* rough estimate; *(Sport)* somersault

überschlagen¹† *vt sep* cross *(Beine)*

überschlagen²† *vt insep* estimate roughly; *(auslassen)* skip; **sich ü~** somersault; *(Ereignisse:)* happen fast ● *adj* tepid

überschneiden† (sich) *vr insep* intersect, cross; *(zusammenfallen)* overlap

überschreiten† *vt insep* cross; *(fig)* exceed

Überschrift *f* heading; *(Zeitungs-)* headline

Über|schuss *m* surplus. **ü~schüssig** *adj* surplus

überschwemm|en *vt insep* flood; *(fig)* inundate. **Ü~ung** *f* -,-en flood

Übersee **in/nach Ü~** overseas; **aus/von Ü~** from overseas. **Ü~dampfer** *m* ocean liner. **ü~isch** *adj* overseas

übersehen† *vt insep* look out over; *(abschätzen)* assess; *(nicht sehen)* overlook, miss; *(ignorieren)* ignore

übersenden† *vt insep* send

übersetzen¹ *vi sep (haben/sein)* cross [over]

übersetz|en² *vt insep* translate. **Ü~er(in)** *m* -s,- *(f* -,-nen*)* translator. **Ü~ung** *f* -,-en translation

Übersicht *f* overall view; *(Abriss)* summary; *(Tabelle)* table. **ü~lich** *adj* clear

Übersiedlung *f* move

überspielen *vt insep* (*fig*) cover up; **auf Band ü~** tape

überstehen† *vt insep* come through; get over (*Krankheit*); (*überleben*) survive

übersteigen† *vt insep* climb [over]; (*fig*) exceed

überstimmen *vt insep* outvote

Überstunden *fpl* overtime *sg*; **Ü~ machen** work overtime

überstürz|en *vt insep* rush; **sich ü~en** (*Ereignisse:*) happen fast. **ü~t** *adj* hasty

übertrag|bar *adj* transferable; (*Med*) infectious. **ü~en†** *vt insep* transfer; (*übergeben*) assign (*dat* to); (*Techn, Med*) transmit; (*Radio, TV*) broadcast; (*übersetzen*) translate; (*anwenden*) apply (**auf** + *acc* to) ● *adj* transferred, figurative. **Ü~ung** *f* -,-en transfer; transmission; broadcast; translation, application

übertreffen† *vt insep* surpass; (*übersteigen*) exceed; **sich selbst ü~** excel oneself

übertreib|en† *vt insep* exaggerate; (*zu weit treiben*) overdo. **Ü~ung** *f* -,-en exaggeration

übertreten¹† *vi sep* (*sein*) step over the line; (*Pol*) go over/(*Relig*) convert (**zu** to)

übertret|en²† *vt insep* infringe; break (*Gesetz*). **Ü~ung** *f* -,-en infringement; breach

übertrieben *adj* exaggerated

übervölkert *adj* overpopulated

überwachen *vt insep* supervise; (*kontrollieren*) monitor; (*bespitzeln*) keep under surveillance

überwältigen *vt insep* overpower; (*fig*) overwhelm

überweis|en† *vt insep* transfer; refer (*Patienten*). **Ü~ung** *f* transfer; (*ärztliche*) referral

überwiegen† *v insep* ● *vi* (*haben*) predominate, ● *vt* outweigh

überwind|en† *vt insep* overcome; **sich ü~en** force oneself. **Ü~ung** *f* effort

Über|zahl *f* majority. **ü~zählig** *adj* spare

überzeug|en *vt insep* convince; **sich [selbst] ü~en** satisfy oneself. **ü~end** *adj* convincing. **Ü~ung** *f* -,-en conviction

überziehen¹† *vt sep* put on

überziehen²† *vt insep* cover; overdraw (*Konto*)

Überzug *m* cover; (*Schicht*) coating

üblich *adj* usual; (*gebräuchlich*) customary

U-Boot *nt* submarine

übrig *adj* remaining; (*andere*) other; **alles Ü~e** [all] the rest; **im Ü~en** besides; (*ansonsten*) apart from that; **ü~ sein** *od* **bleiben** be left [over]; **etw ü~ lassen** leave sth [over]; **uns blieb nichts anderes ü~** we had no choice

Übung *f* -,-en exercise; (*Üben*) practice; (*Üben*) prac- tice; **außer** *od* **aus der Ü~** out of practice

Ufer *nt* -s,- shore; (*Fluss-*) bank

Uhr *f* -,-en clock; (*Armband-*) watch; (*Zähler*) meter; **um ein U~** at one o'clock; **wie viel U~ ist es?** what's the time? **U~macher** *m* -s,- watch and clockmaker. **U~werk** *nt* clock/ watch mechanism. **U~zeiger** *m* [clock-/watch-]hand. **U~zeit** *f* time

Uhu *m* -s,-s eagle owl

UKW *abbr* (*Ultrakurzwelle*) VHF

ulkig *adj* funny; (*seltsam*) odd

Ulme *f* -,-n elm

Ultimatum *nt* -s,-ten ultimatum

Ultra|kurzwelle *f* very high fre- quency. **U~leichtflugzeug** *nt* micro- light [aircraft]

Ultraschall *m* ultrasound

ultraviolett *adj* ultraviolet

um *prep* (+ *acc*) [a]round; (*Uhrzeit*) at; (*bitten*) for; (*streiten*) over; (*sich sor- gen*) about; (*betrügen*) out of; (*bei Angabe einer Differenz*) by; **um [... herum]** around, [round] about; **Tag um Tag** day after day; **um seinetwil- len** for his sake ● *adv* (*ungefähr*) around, about; **um sein** 🅸 be over; (*Zeit*) be up ● *conj* **um zu** to; (*Ab-*

u

sicht) [in order] to; **zu müde, um zu ...** too tired to ...

umarm|en *vt insep* embrace, hug. **U~ung** *f -,-en* embrace, hug

Umbau *m* rebuilding; conversion (**zu** into). **u~en** *vt sep* rebuild; convert (**zu** into)

Umbildung *f* reorganization; (*Pol*) reshuffle

umbinden† *vt sep* put on

umblättern *v sep* ● *vt* turn [over] ● *vi* (*haben*) turn the page

umbringen† *vt sep* kill; **sich u~** kill oneself

umbuchen *v sep* ● *vt* change; (*Comm*) transfer ● *vi* (*haben*) change one's booking

umdrehen *v sep* ● *vt* turn round/(*wenden*) over; turn (*Schlüssel*); (*umkrempeln*) turn inside out; **sich u~** turn round; (*im Liegen*) turn over ● *vi* (*haben/sein*) turn back

Umdrehung *f* turn; (*Motor-*) revolution

umeinander *adv* around each other; **sich u~ sorgen** worry about each other

umfahren¹† *vt sep* run over

umfahren²† *vt insep* go round; bypass (*Ort*)

umfallen† *vi sep* (*sein*) fall over; (*Person:*) fall down

Umfang *m* girth; (*Geometry*) circumference; (*Größe*) size

umfangreich *adj* extensive; (*dick*) big

umfassen *vt insep* consist of, comprise; (*umgeben*) surround. **u~d** *adj* comprehensive

Umfrage *f* survey, poll

umfüllen *vt sep* transfer

umfunktionieren *vt sep* convert

Umgang *m* [social] contact; (*Umgehen*) dealing (**mit** with)

Umgangssprache *f* colloquial language

umgeb|en† *vt/i insep* (*haben*) surround ● *adj* **u~en von** surrounded by. **U~ung** *f -,-en* surroundings *pl*

umgehen† *vt insep* avoid; (*nicht be-*

achten) evade; (*Straße:*) bypass

umgehend *adj* immediate

Umgehungsstraße *f* bypass

umgekehrt *adj* inverse; (*Reihenfolge*) reverse; **es war u~** it was the other way round

umgraben† *vt sep* dig [over]

Umhang *m* cloak

umhauen† *vt sep* knock down; (*fällen*) chop down

umhören (sich) *vr sep* ask around

Umkehr *f -* turning back. **u~en** *v sep* ● *vi* (*sein*) turn back ● *vt* turn round; turn inside out (*Tasche*); (*fig*) reverse

umkippen *v sep* ● *vt* tip over; (*versehentlich*) knock over ● *vi* (*sein*) fall over; (*Boot:*) capsize

Umkleide|kabine *f* changing-cubicle. **u~n (sich)** *vr sep* change. **U~raum** *m* changing-room

umknicken *v sep* ● *vt* bend; (*falten*) fold ● *vi* (*sein*) bend; (*mit dem Fuß*) go over on one's ankle

umkommen† *vi sep* (*sein*) perish

Umkreis *m* surroundings *pl*; **im U~ von** within a radius of

umkreisen *vt insep* circle; (*Astronomy*) revolve around; (*Satellit:*) orbit

umkrempeln *vt sep* turn up; (*von innen nach außen*) turn inside out; (*ändern*) change radically

Umlauf *m* circulation; (*Astronomy*) revolution. **U~bahn** *f* orbit

Umlaut *m* umlaut

umlegen *vt sep* lay *or* put down; flatten (*Getreide*); turn down (*Kragen*); put on (*Schal*); throw (*Hebel*); (*verlegen*) transfer; (**1**: *töten*) kill

umleit|en *vt sep* divert. **U~ung** *f* diversion

umliegend *adj* surrounding

umpflanzen *vt sep* transplant

umranden *vt insep* edge

umräumen *vt sep* rearrange

umrechn|en *vt sep* convert. **U~ung** *f* conversion

umreißen† *vt insep* outline

Umriss *m* outline

u

umrühren vt/i sep (haben) stir

ums pron = um das

Umsatz m (Comm) turnover

umschalten vt/i sep (haben) switch over; **auf Rot u~** (Ampel:) change to red

Umschau f U~ **halten nach** look out for

Umschlag m cover; (Schutz-) jacket; (Brief-) envelope; (Med) compress; (Hosen-) turn-up. **u~en†** v sep ● vt turn up; turn over (Seite); (fällen) chop down ● vi (sein) topple over; (Wetter:) change; (Wind:) veer

umschließen† vt insep enclose

umschreib|en vt insep define; (anders ausdrücken) paraphrase

umschulen vt sep retrain; (Sch) transfer to another school

Umschwung m (fig) change; (Pol) U-turn

umsehen† (sich) vr sep look round; (zurück) look back; **sich u~ nach** look for

umseln* vi sep (sein) um sein, s. um

umseitig adj & adv overleaf

umsetzen vt sep move; (umpflanzen) transplant; (Comm) sell

umsied|eln v sep ● vt resettle ● vi (sein) move. **U~lung** f resettlement

umso conj ~ **besser/mehr** all the better/more; **je mehr, ~ besser** the more the better

umsonst adv in vain; (grundlos) without reason; (gratis) free

Umstand m circumstance; (Tatsache) fact; (Aufwand) fuss; (Mühe) trouble; **unter U~en** possibly; **jdm U~e machen** put s.o. to trouble; **in andern U~en** pregnant

umständlich adj laborious; (kompliziert) involved

Umstands|kleid nt maternity dress. **U~wort** nt (pl -wörter) adverb

Umstehende pl bystanders

umsteigen† vi sep (sein) change

umstellen¹ vt insep surround

umstell|en² vt sep rearrange; transpose (Wörter); (anders einstellen) reset; (Techn) convert; (ändern) change; **sich u~en** adjust. **U~ung** f rearrangement; transposition; resetting; conversion; change; adjustment

umstritten adj controversial; (ungeklärt) disputed

umstülpen vt sep turn upside down; (von innen nach außen) turn inside out

Um|sturz m coup. **u~stürzen** v sep ● vt overturn; (Pol) overthrow ● vi (sein) fall over

umtaufen vt sep rename

Umtausch m exchange. **u~en** vt sep change; exchange (**gegen** for)

umwechseln vt sep change

Umweg m detour; **auf U~en** (fig) in a roundabout way

Umwelt f environment. **u~freundlich** adj environmentally friendly. **U~schutz** m protection of the environment

umwerfen† vt sep knock over; (fig) upset (Plan)

umziehen† v sep ● vi (sein) move ● vt change; **sich u~** change

umzingeln vt insep surround

Umzug m move; (Prozession) procession

unabänderlich adj irrevocable; (Tatsache) unalterable

unabhängig adj independent; **u~ davon, ob** irrespective of whether. **U~keit** f - independence

unablässig adj incessant

unabsehbar adj incalculable

unabsichtlich adj unintentional

unachtsam adj careless

unangebracht adj inappropriate

unangenehm adj unpleasant; (peinlich) embarrassing

Unannehmlichkeiten fpl trouble sg

unansehnlich adj shabby

unanständig adj indecent

unappetitlich adj unappetizing

Unart f -,-en bad habit. **u~ig** adj naughty

u

unauffällig *adj* inconspicuous; unobtrusive

unaufgefordert *adv* without being asked

unauf|haltsam *adj* inexorable. **u~hörlich** *adj* incessant

unaufmerksam *adj* inattentive

unaufrichtig *adj* insincere

unausbleiblich *adj* inevitable

unausstehlich *adj* insufferable

unbarmherzig *adj* merciless

unbeabsichtigt *adj* unintentional

unbedenklich *adj* harmless ● *adv* without hesitation

unbedeutend *adj* insignificant; (*geringfügig*) slight

unbedingt *adj* absolute; **nicht u~** not necessarily

unbefriedig|end *adj* unsatisfactory. **u~t** *adj* dissatisfied

unbefugt *adj* unauthorized ● *adv* without authorization

unbegreiflich *adj* incomprehensible

unbegrenzt *adj* unlimited ● *adv* indefinitely

unbegründet *adj* unfounded

Unbehagen *nt* unease; (*körperlich*) discomfort

unbekannt *adj* unknown; (*nicht vertraut*) unfamiliar. **U~e(r)** *m/f* stranger

unbekümmert *adj* unconcerned; (*unbeschwert*) carefree

unbeliebt *adj* unpopular. **U~heit** *f* unpopularity

unbemannt *adj* unmanned

unbemerkt *adj & adv* unnoticed

unbenutzt *adj* unused

unbequem *adj* uncomfortable; (*lästig*) awkward

unberechenbar *adj* unpredictable

unberechtigt *adj* unjustified; (*unbefugt*) unauthorized

unberührt *adj* untouched; (*fig*) virgin; (*Landschaft*) unspoilt

unbescheiden *adj* presumptuous

unbeschrankt *adj* unguarded

unbeschränkt *adj* unlimited ● *adv* without limit

unbeschwert *adj* carefree

unbesiegt *adj* undefeated

unbespielt *adj* blank

unbeständig *adj* inconsistent; (*Wetter*) unsettled

unbestechlich *adj* incorruptible

unbestimmt *adj* indefinite; (*Alter*) indeterminate; (*ungewiss*) uncertain; (*unklar*) vague

unbestritten *adj* undisputed ● *adv* indisputably

unbeteiligt *adj* indifferent; **u~ an** (+ *dat*) not involved in

unbetont *adj* unstressed

unbewacht *adj* unguarded

unbewaffnet *adj* unarmed

unbeweglich *adj & adv* motionless, still

unbewohnt *adj* uninhabited

unbewusst *adj* unconscious

unbezahlbar *adj* priceless

unbrauchbar *adj* useless

und *conj* and; **und so weiter** and so on; **nach und nach** bit by bit

Undank *m* ingratitude. **u~bar** *adj* ungrateful; (*nicht lohnend*) thankless. **U~barkeit** *f* ingratitude

undeutlich *adj* indistinct; vague

undicht *adj* leaking; **u~e Stelle** leak

Unding *nt* absurdity

undiplomatisch *adj* undiplomatic

unduldsam *adj* intolerant

undurch|dringlich *adj* impenetrable; (*Miene*) inscrutable. **u~führbar** *adj* impracticable

undurch|lässig *adj* impermeable. **u~sichtig** *adj* opaque; (*fig*) doubtful

uneben *adj* uneven. **U~heit** *f* -,-en unevenness; (*Buckel*) bump

unecht *adj* false; **u~er Schmuck** imitation jewellery

unehelich *adj* illegitimate

uneinig *adj* (*fig*) divided; [**sich** (*dat*)] **u~ sein** disagree

uneins *adj* ~ **sein** be at odds

unempfindlich *adj* insensitive

(**gegen** to); (*widerstandsfähig*) tough; (*Med*) immune

unendlich *adj* infinite; (*endlos*) endless. **U~keit** *f* - infinity

unentbehrlich *adj* indispensable

unentgeltlich *adj* free, (*Arbeit*) unpaid ● *adv* free of charge

unentschieden *adj* undecided; (*Sport*) drawn; **u~ spielen** draw. **U~** *nt* -s,- draw

unentschlossen *adj* indecisive; (*unentschieden*) undecided

unentwegt *adj* persistent; (*unaufhörlich*) incessant

unerfahren *adj* inexperienced. **U~heit** *f* - inexperience

unerfreulich *adj* unpleasant

unerhört *adj* enormous; (*empörend*) outrageous

unerklärlich *adj* inexplicable

unerlässlich *adj* essential

unerlaubt *adj* unauthorized ● *adv* without permission

unerschwinglich *adj* prohibitive

unersetzlich *adj* irreplaceable; (*Verlust*) irreparable

unerträglich *adj* unbearable

unerwartet *adj* unexpected

unerwünscht *adj* unwanted; (*Besuch*) unwelcome

unfähig *adj* incompetent; **u~, etw zu tun** incapable of doing sth; (*nicht in der Lage*) unable to do sth. **U~keit** *f* incompetence; inability (**zu** to)

unfair *adj* unfair

Unfall *m* accident. **U~flucht** *f* failure to stop after an accident. **U~station** *f* casualty department

unfassbar *adj* incomprehensible

Unfehlbarkeit *f* - infallibility

unfolgsam *adj* disobedient

unförmig *adj* shapeless

unfreiwillig *adj* involuntary; (*unbeabsichtigt*) unintentional

unfreundlich *adj* unfriendly; (*unangenehm*) unpleasant. **U~keit** *f* unfriendliness; unpleasantness

Unfriede[n] *m* discord

unfruchtbar *adj* infertile; (*fig*) unproductive. **U~keit** *f* infertility

Unfug *m* -s mischief; (*Unsinn*) nonsense

Ungar|(in) *m* -n,-n (*f* -,-nen) Hungarian. **u~isch** *adj* Hungarian. **U~n** *nt* -s Hungary

ungeachtet *prep* (+ *gen*) in spite of; **dessen u~** notwithstanding [this]. **ungebraucht** *adj* unused. **ungedeckt** *adj* uncovered; (*Sport*) unmarked; (*Tisch*) unlaid

Ungeduld *f* impatience. **u~ig** *adj* impatient

ungeeignet *adj* unsuitable

ungefähr *adj* approximate, rough

ungefährlich *adj* harmless

ungeheuer *adj* enormous. **U~** *nt* -s,- monster

ungehorsam *adj* disobedient. **U~** *m* disobedience

ungeklärt *adj* unsolved; (*Frage*) unsettled; (*Ursache*) unknown

ungelegen *adj* inconvenient

ungelernt *adj* unskilled

ungemütlich *adj* uncomfortable; (*unangenehm*) unpleasant

ungenau *adj* inaccurate; vague. **U~igkeit** *f* -,-en inaccuracy

ungeniert /'ʊnʒeniːɐ̯t/ *adj* uninhibited ● *adv* openly

ungenießbar *adj* inedible; (*Getränk*) undrinkable. **ungenügend** *adj* inadequate; (*Sch*) unsatisfactory. **ungepflegt** *adj* neglected; (*Person*) unkempt. **ungerade** *adj* (*Zahl*) odd

ungerecht *adj* unjust. **U~igkeit** *f* -,-en injustice

ungern *adv* reluctantly

ungesalzen *adj* unsalted

Ungeschick|lichkeit *f* clumsiness. **u~t** *adj* clumsy

ungeschminkt *adj* without make-up; (*Wahrheit*) unvarnished. **ungesetzlich** *adj* illegal. **ungestört** *adj* undisturbed. **ungesund** *adj* unhealthy. **ungesüßt** *adj* unsweetened. **ungetrübt** *adj* perfect

Ungetüm *nt* -s,-e monster

ungewiss *adj* uncertain; **im Unge-**

wissen sein/lassen be/leave in the dark. **U~heit** f uncertainty

ungewöhnlich adj unusual. **ungewohnt** adj unaccustomed; (nicht vertraut) unfamiliar

Ungeziefer nt -s vermin

ungezogen adj naughty

ungezwungen adj informal; (natürlich) natural

ungläubig adj incredulous

unglaublich adj incredible, unbelievable

ungleich adj unequal; (verschieden) different. **U~heit** f - inequality. **u~mäßig** adj uneven

Unglück nt -s,-e misfortune; (Pech) bad luck; (Missgeschick) mishap; (Unfall) accident. **u~lich** adj unhappy; (ungünstig) unfortunate. **u~licherweise** adv unfortunately

ungültig adj invalid; (Jur) void

ungünstig adj unfavourable; (unpassend) inconvenient

Unheil nt -s disaster; **U~ anrichten** cause havoc

unheilbar adj incurable

unheimlich adj eerie; (gruselig) creepy; (🔲: groß) terrific ● adv eerily; (🔲: sehr) terribly

unhöflich adj rude. **U~keit** f rudeness

unhygienisch adj unhygienic

Uni f -,-s 🔲 university

uni /yˈniː/ inv adj plain

Uniform f -,-en uniform

uninteressant adj uninteresting

Union f -,-en union

universell adj universal

Universität f -,-en university

Universum nt -s universe

unkenntlich adj unrecognizable

unklar adj unclear; (ungewiss) uncertain; (vage) vague; **im U~en (u~en) sein** be in the dark

unkompliziert adj uncomplicated

Unkosten pl expenses

Unkraut nt weed; (coll) weeds pl; **U~ jäten** weed. **U~vertilgungsmittel** nt weed-killer

unlängst adv recently

unlauter adj dishonest; (unfair) unfair

unleserlich adj illegible

unleugbar adj undeniable

unlogisch adj illogical

Unmenge f enormous amount/(Anzahl) number

Unmensch m 🔲 brute. **u~lich** adj inhuman

unmerklich adj imperceptible

unmittelbar adj immediate; (direkt) direct

unmöbliert adj unfurnished

unmodern adj old-fashioned

unmöglich adj impossible. **U~keit** f - impossibility

Unmoral f immorality. **u~isch** adj immoral

unmündig adj under-age

Unmut m displeasure

unnatürlich adj unnatural

unnormal adj abnormal

unnötig adj unnecessary

unord|entlich adj untidy; (nachlässig) sloppy. **U~nung** f disorder; (Durcheinander) muddle

unorthodox adj unorthodox ● adv in an unorthodox manner

unparteiisch adj impartial

unpassend adj inappropriate; (Moment) inopportune

unpersönlich adj impersonal

unpraktisch adj impractical

unpünktlich adj unpunctual ● adv late

unrealistisch adj unrealistic

unrecht adj wrong ● n **jdm u~ tun** do s.o. an injustice. **U~** nt wrong; **zu U~** wrongly; **U~ haben** be wrong; **jdm U~ geben** disagree with s.o. **u~mäßig** adj unlawful

unregelmäßig adj irregular

unreif adj unripe; (fig) immature

unrein adj impure; (Luft) polluted; (Haut) bad; **ins U~e schreiben** make a rough draft of

unrentabel adj unprofitable

Unruh|e f -,-n restlessness; (Erre-

gung) agitation; (*Besorgnis*) anxiety; **U~en** (*Pol*) unrest *sg.* **u~ig** *adj* restless; (*laut*) noisy; (*besorgt*) anxious

uns *pron* (*acc/dat of* **wir**) us; (*reflexive*) ourselves; (*einander*) each other

unsauber *adj* dirty; (*nachlässig*) sloppy

unschädlich *adj* harmless

unscharf *adj* blurred

unschätzbar *adj* inestimable

unscheinbar *adj* inconspicuous

unschlagbar *adj* unbeatable

unschlüssig *adj* undecided

Unschuld *f* - innocence; (*Jungfräulichkeit*) virginity. **u~ig** *adj* innocent

unselbstständig, unselbständig *adj* dependent ● *adv* **u~ denken** not think for oneself

unser *poss pron* our. **u~e(r,s)** *poss pron* ours. **u~erseits** *adv* for our part. **u~twegen** *adv* for our sake; (*wegen uns*) because of us, on our account

unsicher *adj* unsafe; (*ungewiss*) uncertain; (*nicht zuverlässig*) unreliable; (*Schritte, Hand*) unsteady; (*Person*) insecure ● *adv* unsteadily. **U~heit** *f* uncertainty; unreliability; insecurity

unsichtbar *adj* invisible

Unsinn *m* nonsense. **u~ig** *adj* nonsensical, absurd

Unsitt|e *f* bad habit. **u~lich** *adj* indecent

unsportlich *adj* not sporty; (*unfair*) unsporting

uns|re(r,s) *poss pron* = **unsere(r,s)**. **u~rige** *poss pron* **der/die/das u~rige** ours

unsterblich *adj* immortal. **U~keit** *f* immortality

Unsumme *f* vast sum

unsympathisch *adj* unpleasant; **er ist mir u~** I don't like him

untätig *adj* idle

untauglich *adj* unsuitable; (*Mil*) unfit

unten *adv* at the bottom; (*auf der Unterseite*) underneath; (*eine Treppe tiefer*) downstairs; (*im Text*) below; **hier/da u~** down here/there; **nach**

u~ down[wards]; (*die Treppe hinunter*) downstairs; **siehe u~** see below

unter *prep* (+ *dat/acc*) under; (*niedriger als*) below; (*inmitten, zwischen*) among; **u~ anderem** among other things; **u~ der Woche** during the week; **u~ sich** by themselves

Unter|arm *m* forearm. **U~bewusstsein** *nt* subconscious

unterbieten† *vt insep* undercut; beat (*Rekord*)

unterbinden† *vt insep* stop

unterbrech|en† *vt insep* interrupt; break (*Reise*). **U~ung** *f* -,-en interruption, break

unterbringen† *vt sep* put; (*beherbergen*) put up

unterdessen *adv* in the meantime

Unterdrückung *f* - suppression; oppression

untere(r,s) *adj* lower

untereinander *adv* one below the other; (*miteinander*) among ourselves/yourselves/themselves

unterernähr|t *adj* undernourished. **U~ung** *f* malnutrition

Unterführung *f* underpass; (*Fußgänger-*) subway

Untergang *m* (*der Sonne*) setting; (*Naut*) sinking; (*Zugrundegehen*) disappearance; (*der Welt*) end

Untergebene(r) *m/f* subordinate

untergehen† *vi sep* (*sein*) (*Astronomy*) set; (*versinken*) go under; (*Schiff:*) go down, sink; (*zugrunde gehen*) disappear; (*Welt:*) come to an end

Untergeschoss *nt* basement

Untergrund *m* foundation; (*Hintergrund*) background. **U~bahn** *f* underground [railway]

unterhaken *vt sep* **jdn u~** take s.o.'s arm; **untergehakt** arm in arm

unterhalb *adv & prep* (+ *gen*) below

Unterhalt *m* maintenance

unterhalt|en† *vt insep* maintain; (*ernähren*) support; (*betreiben*) run; (*erheitern*) entertain; **sich u~en** talk; (*sich vergnügen*) enjoy oneself. **U~ung** *f* -,-en maintenance; (*Ge-*

u

spräch) conversation; (*Zeitvertreib*) entertainment

Unter|haus nt (*Pol*) lower house; (*in UK*) House of Commons. **U~hemd** nt vest. **U~hose** f underpants pl. **u~irdisch** adj & adv underground

Unterkiefer m lower jaw

unterkommen† vi sep (*sein*) find accommodation; (*eine Stellung finden*) get a job

Unterkunft f -,-künfte accommodation

Unterlage f pad; **U~n** papers

Unterlass m ohne **U~** incessantly

Unterlassung f -,-en omission

unterlegen adj inferior; (*Sport*) losing; **zahlenmäßig u~** out-numbered (*dat* by). **U~e(r)** m/f loser

Unterleib m abdomen

unterliegen† vi insep (*sein*) lose (*dat* to); (*unterworfen sein*) be subject (*dat* to)

Unterlippe f lower lip

Untermiete f **zur U~ wohnen** be a lodger. **U~r(in)** m(f) lodger

unternehm|en† vt insep undertake; take (*Schritte*); **etw/nichts u~en** do sth/nothing. **U~en** nt -s,- undertaking, enterprise (*Betrieb*) concern. **U~er** m -s,- employer; (*Bau-*) contractor; (*Industrieller*) industrialist. **u~ungslustig** adj enterprising

Unteroffizier m non-commissioned officer

unterordnen vt sep subordinate

Unterredung f -,-en talk

Unterricht m -[e]s teaching; (*Privat-*) tuition; (*U~sstunden*) lessons pl

unterrichten vt/i insep (*haben*) teach; (*informieren*) inform; **sich u~** inform oneself

Unterrock m slip

untersagen vt insep forbid

Untersatz m mat; (*mit Füßen*) stand; (*Gläser-*) coaster

unterscheid|en† vt/i insep (*haben*) distinguish; (*auseinander halten*) tell

apart; **sich u~en** differ. **U~ung** f -,-en distinction

Unterschied m -[e]s,-e difference; (*Unterscheidung*) distinction; **im U~ zu ihm** unlike him. **u~lich** adj different; (*wechselnd*) varying

unterschlag|en† vt insep embezzle; (*verheimlichen*) suppress. **U~ung** f -,-en embezzlement; suppression

Unterschlupf m -[e]s shelter; (*Versteck*) hiding-place

unterschreiben† vt/i insep (*haben*) sign

Unter|schrift f signature; (*Bild-*) caption. **U~seeboot** nt submarine

Unterstand m shelter

unterste(r,s) adj lowest, bottom

unterstehen† v insep ● vi (*haben*) be answerable (*dat* to); (*unterliegen*) be subject (*dat* to)

unterstellen¹ vt sep put underneath; (*abstellen*) store; **sich u~** shelter

unterstellen² vt insep place under the control (*dat* of); (*annehmen*) assume; (*fälschlich zuschreiben*) impute (*dat* to)

unterstreichen† vt insep underline

unterstütz|en vt insep support; (*helfen*) aid. **U~ung** f -,-en support; (*finanziell*) aid; (*regelmäßiger Betrag*) allowance; (*Arbeitslosen-*) benefit

untersuch|en vt insep examine; (*Jur*) investigate; (*prüfen*) test; (*überprüfen*) check; (*durchsuchen*) search. **U~ung** f -,-en examination; investigation; test; check; search. **U~ungshaft** f detention on remand

Untertan m -s & -en,-en subject

Untertasse f saucer

Unterteil nt bottom (part)

Untertitel m subtitle

untervermieten vt/i insep (*haben*) sublet

Unterwäsche f underwear

unterwegs adv on the way; (*außer Haus*) out; (*verreist*) away

Unterwelt f underworld

unterzeichnen vt insep sign

u

unterziehen† *vt insep* **etw einer Untersuchung/Überprüfung u~** examine/ check sth; **sich einer Operation/Prüfung u~** have an operation/take a test

Untier *nt* monster

untragbar *adj* intolerable

untrennbar *adj* inseparable

untreu *adj* disloyal; (*in der Ehe*) unfaithful. **U~e** *f* disloyalty; infidelity

untröstlich *adj* inconsolable

unübersehbar *adj* obvious; (*groß*) immense

ununterbrochen *adj* incessant

unveränderlich *adj* invariable; (*gleichbleibend*) unchanging

unverändert *adj* unchanged

unverantwortlich *adj* irresponsible

unverbesserlich *adj* incorrigible

unverbindlich *adj* non-committal; (*Comm*) not binding ● *adv* without obligation

unverdaulich *adj* indigestible

unver|gesslich *adj* unforgettable. **u~gleichlich** *adj* incomparable. **u~heiratet** *adj* unmarried. **u~käuflich** *adj* not for sale; (*Muster*) free

unverkennbar *adj* unmistakable

unverletzt *adj* unhurt

unvermeidlich *adj* inevitable

unver|mindert *adj & adv* undiminished. **u~mutet** *adj* unexpected

Unver|nunft *f* folly. **u~nünftig** *adj* foolish

unverschämt *adj* insolent; (🔢: *ungeheuer*) outrageous. **U~heit** *f* -,-en insolence

unver|sehens *adv* suddenly. **u~sehrt** *adj* unhurt; (*unbeschädigt*) intact

unverständlich *adj* incomprehensible; (*undeutlich*) indistinct

unverträglich *adj* incompatible; (*Person*) quarrelsome; (*unbekömmlich*) indigestible

unver|wundbar *adj* invulnerable. **u~wüstlich** *adj* indestructible; (*Person, Humor*) irrepressible; (*Gesundheit*) robust. **u~zeihlich** *adj* unforgivable

unverzüglich *adj* immediate

unvollendet *adj* unfinished

unvollkommen *adj* imperfect; (*unvollständig*) incomplete

unvollständig *adj* incomplete

unvor|bereitet *adj* unprepared. **u~hergesehen** *adj* unforeseen

unvorsichtig *adj* careless

unvorstellbar *adj* unimaginable

unvorteilhaft *adj* unfavourable; (*nicht hübsch*) unattractive

unwahr *adj* untrue. **U~heit** *f* -,-en untruth. **u~scheinlich** *adj* unlikely; (*unglaublich*) improbable; (🔢: *groß*) incredible

unweit *adv & prep* (+ *gen*) not far

unwesentlich *adj* unimportant

Unwetter *nt* -s,- storm

unwichtig *adj* unimportant

unwider|legbar *adj* irrefutable. **u~stehlich** *adj* irresistible

Unwill|e *m* displeasure. **u~ig** *adj* angry; (*widerwillig*) reluctant

unwirklich *adj* unreal

unwirksam *adj* ineffective

unwirtschaftlich *adj* uneconomic

unwissen|d *adj* ignorant. **U~heit** *f* - ignorance

unwohl *adj* unwell; (*unbehaglich*) uneasy

unwürdig *adj* unworthy (*gen* of)

Unzahl *f* vast number. **unzählig** *adj* innumerable, countless

unzerbrechlich *adj* unbreakable

unzerstörbar *adj* indestructible

unzertrennlich *adj* inseparable

Unzucht *f* sexual offence; **gewerbsmäßige U~** prostitution

unzüchtig *adj* indecent; (*Schriften*) obscene

unzufrieden *adj* dissatisfied; (*innerlich*) discontented. **U~heit** *f* dissatisfaction

unzulässig *adj* inadmissible

unzurechnungsfähig *adj* insane. **U~keit** *f* insanity

unzusammenhängend *adj* incoherent

unzutreffend *adj* inapplicable; (*falsch*) incorrect

u

unzuverlässig *adj* unreliable

unzweifelhaft *adj* undoubted

üppig *adj* luxuriant; (*überreichlich*) lavish

uralt *adj* ancient

Uran *nt* -s uranium

Uraufführung *f* first performance

Urenkel *m* great-grandson; (*pl*) great-grandchildren

Urgroß|mutter *f* great-grandmother. **U~vater** *m* great-grandfather

Urheber *m* -s,- originator; (*Verfasser*) author. **U~recht** *nt* copyright

Urin *m* -s,-e urine

Urkunde *f* -,-n certificate; (*Dokument*) document

Urlaub *m* -s holiday; (*Mil, Admin*) leave; **auf U~** on holiday/leave; **U~ haben** be on holiday/leave. **U~er(in)** *m* -s,- (*f* -,-nen) holidaymaker. **U~sort** *m* holiday resort

Urne *f* -,-n urn; (*Wahl-*) ballot-box

Ursache *f* cause; (*Grund*) reason; **keine U~!** don't mention it!

Ursprung *m* origin

ursprünglich *adj* original; (*anfänglich*) initial; (*natürlich*) natural

Urteil *nt* -s,-e judgement; (*Meinung*) opinion; (*U~sspruch*) verdict; (*Strafe*) sentence. **u~en** *vi* (*haben*) judge

Urwald *m* primeval forest; (*tropischer*) jungle

Urzeit *f* primeval times *pl*

USA *pl* USA *sg*

usw. *abbr* (**und so weiter**) etc.

utopisch *adj* Utopian

Vv

Vakuum /ˈvaːkuʊm/ *nt* -s vacuum. **v~verpackt** *adj* vacuum-packed

Vanille /vaˈnɪljə/ *f* - vanilla

variieren *vt/i* (*haben*) vary

Vase /ˈvaːzə/ *f* -,-n vase

Vater *m* -s,- father. **V~land** *nt* fatherland

väterlich *adj* paternal; (*fürsorglich*) fatherly. **v~erseits** *adv* on one's/the father's side

Vater|schaft *f* - fatherhood; (*Jur*) paternity. **V~unser** *nt* -s,- Lord's Prayer

v. Chr. *abbr* (**vor Christus**) BC

Vegetar|ier(in) /vegeˈtaːriɐ, -jərın/ *m*(*f*) -s,- (*f* -,-nen) vegetarian. **v~isch** *adj* vegetarian

Veilchen *nt* -s,-n violet

Vene /ˈveːnə/ *f* -,-n vein

Venedig /veˈneːdɪç/ *nt* -s Venice

Ventil /vɛnˈtiːl/ *nt* -s,-e valve. **V~ator** *m* -s,-en fan

verabred|en *vt* arrange; **sich [mit jdm] v~en** arrange to meet [s.o.]. **V~ung** *f* -,-en arrangement; (*Treffen*) appointment

verabschieden *vt* say goodbye to; (*aus dem Dienst*) retire; pass (*Gesetz*); **sich v~** say goodbye

verachten *vt* despise

Verachtung *f* - contempt

verallgemeinern *vt/i* (*haben*) generalize

veränder|lich *adj* changeable; (*Math*) variable. **v~n** *vt* change; **sich v~n** change; (*beruflich*) change one's job. **V~ung** *f* change

verängstigt *adj* frightened, scared

verankern *vt* anchor

veranlag|t *adj* künstlerisch/ musikalisch **v~t sein** have an artistic/a musical bent; **praktisch v~t** practically minded. **V~ung** *f* -,-en disposition; (*Neigung*) tendency; (*künstlerisch*) bent

veranlassen *vt* (*reg*) arrange for; (*einleiten*) institute; **jdn v~** prompt s.o. (**zu** to)

veranschlagen *vt* (*reg*) estimate

veranstalt|en *vt* organize; hold, give (*Party*); make (*Lärm*). **V~er** *m* -s,- organizer. **V~ung** *f* -,-en event

verantwort|lich *adj* responsible; **v~lich machen** hold responsible. **V~ung** *f* - responsibility. **v~ungs-**

bewusst *adj* responsible. **v~ungslos** *adj* irresponsible. **v~ungsvoll** *adj* responsible

verarbeiten *vt* use; (*Techn*) process; (*verdauen & fig*) digest

verärgern *vt* annoy

verausgaben (sich) *vr* spend all one's money (*or*) strength

veräußern *vt* sell

Verb /vɛrp/ *nt* -s,-en verb

Verband *m* -[e]s,-̈e association; (*Mil*) unit; (*Med*) bandage; (*Wund-*) dressing. **V~szeug** *nt* first-aid kit

verbann|en *vt* exile; (*fig*) banish. **V~ung** *f* - exile

verbergen† *vt* hide; **sich v~** hide

verbesser|n *vt* improve; (*berichtigen*) correct. **V~ung** *f* -,-en improvement; correction

verbeug|en (sich) *vr* bow. **V~ung** *f* bow

verbeulen *vt* dent

verbiegen| *vt* bend

verbieten† *vt* forbid; (*Admin*) prohibit, ban

verbillig|en *vt* reduce [in price]. **v~t** *adj* reduced

verbinden| *vt* connect (**mit** to); (*zusammenfügen*) join; (*verknüpfen*) combine; (*in Verbindung bringen*) associate; (*Med*) bandage; dress (*Wunde*); **jdm verbunden sein** (*fig*) be obliged to s.o.

verbindlich *adj* friendly; (*bindend*) binding

Verbindung *f* connection; (*Verknüpfung*) combination; (*Kontakt*) contact; (*Vereinigung*) association; **chemiche V~** chemical compound; **in V~ stehen/sich in V~ setzen** be/get in touch

verbissen *adj* grim

verbitter|n *vt* make bitter. **v~t** *adj* bitter. **V~ung** *f* - bitterness

verblassen *vi* (*sein*) fade

Verbleib *m* -s whereabouts *pl*

verbleit *adj* (*Benzin*) leaded

verblüff|en *vt* amaze, astound. **V~ung** *f* - amazement

verblühen *vi* (*sein*) wither, fade

verbluten *vi* (*sein*) bleed to death

verborgen *vt* lend

Verbot *nt* -[e]s,-e ban. **v~en** *adj* forbidden; (*Admin*) prohibited

Verbrauch *m* -[e]s consumption. **v~en** *vt* use; consume (*Lebensmittel*); (*erschöpfen*) use up. **V~er** *m* -s,- consumer

Verbrechen† *nt* -s,- crime

Verbrecher *m* -s,- criminal

verbreit|en *vt* spread. **v~et** *adj* widespread. **V~ung** *f* - spread; (*Verbreiten*) spreading

verbrenn|en† *vt/i* (*sein*) burn; cremate (*Leiche*). **V~ung** *f* -,-en burning; cremation; (*Wunde*) burn

verbringen† *vt* spend

verbrühen *vt* scald

verbuchen *vt* enter

verbünd|en (sich) *vr* form an alliance. **V~ete(r)** *m/f* ally

verbürgen *vt* guarantee; **sich v~ für** vouch for

Verdacht *m* -[e]s suspicion; **in** *or* **im V~ haben** suspect

verdächtig *adj* suspicious. **v~en** *vt* suspect (*gen* of). **V~te(r)** *m/f* suspect

verdamm|en *vt* condemn; (*Relig*) damn. **v~t** *adj & adv* 🖾 damned; **v~t!** damn!

verdampfen *vt/i* (*sein*) evaporate

verdanken *vt* owe (*dat* to)

verdau|en *vt* digest. **v~lich** *adj* digestible. **V~ung** *f* - digestion

Verdeck *nt* -[e]s,-e hood; (*Oberdeck*) top deck

verderb|en† *vi* (*sein*) spoil; (*Lebensmittel:*) go bad ● *vt* spoil; **ich habe mir den Magen verdorben** I have an upset stomach. **V~en** *nt* -s ruin. **v~lich** *adj* perishable; (*schädlich*) pernicious

verdien|en *vt/i* (*haben*) earn; (*fig*) deserve. **V~er** *m* -s,- wage-earner

Verdienst¹ *m* -[e]s earnings *pl*

Verdienst² *nt* -[e]s,-e merit

verdient *adj* well-deserved

verdoppeln *vt* double

verdorben *adj* spoilt, ruined; (*Magen*) upset; (*moralisch*) corrupt; (*verkommen*) depraved

verdreh|en *vt* twist; roll (*Augen*); (*fig*) distort. **v~t** *adj* 🔲 crazy

verdreifachen *vt* treble, triple

verdrücken *vt* crumple; (🔲: *essen*) polish off; **sich v~** 🔲 slip away

Verdruss *m* -es annoyance

verdünnen *vt* dilute; **sich v~** taper off

verdunst|en *vi* (*sein*) evaporate. **V~ung** *f* - evaporation

verdursten *vi* (*sein*) die of thirst

veredeln *vt* refine; (*Horticulture*) graft

verehr|en *vt* revere; (*Relig*) worship; (*bewundern*) admire; (*schenken*) give. **V~er(in)** *m* -s,- (*f* -,-nen) admirer. **V~ung** *f* - veneration; worship; admiration

vereidigen *vt* swear in

Verein *m* -s,-e society; (*Sport-*) club

vereinbar *adj* compatible. **v~en** *vt* arrange. **V~ung** *f* -,-en agreement

vereinfachen *vt* simplify

vereinheitlichen *vt* standardize

vereinig|en *vt* unite; merge (*Firmen*); **wieder v~en** reunite; reunify (*Land*); **sich v~en** unite; **V~te Staaten [von Amerika]** United States *sg* [of America]. **V~ung** *f* -,-en union; (*Organisation*) organization

vereinzelt *adj* isolated ● *adv* occasionally

vereist *adj* frozen; (*Straße*) icy

vereitert *adj* septic

verenden *vi* (*sein*) die

verengen *vt* restrict; **sich v~** narrow; (*Pupille:*) contract

vererb|en *vt* leave (*dat* to); (*Biology & fig*) pass on (*dat* to). **V~ung** *f* - heredity

verfahren† *vi* (*sein*) proceed; **v~ mit** deal with ● *vr* **sich v~** lose one's way ● *adj* muddled. **V~** *nt* -s,- procedure; (*Techn*) process; (*Jur*) proceedings *pl*

Verfall *m* decay; (*eines Gebäudes*) dilapidation; (*körperlich & fig*) decline;

(*Ablauf*) expiry. **v~en**† *vi* (*sein*) decay; (*Person, Sitten:*) decline; (*ablaufen*) expire; **v~en in** (+ *acc*) lapse into; **v~en auf** (+ *acc*) hit on (*Idee*)

verfärben (sich) *vr* change colour; (*Stoff:*) discolour

verfass|en *vt* write; (*Jur*) draw up; (*entwerfen*) draft. **V~er** *m* -s,- author. **V~ung** *f* (*Pol*) constitution; (*Zustand*) state

verfaulen *vi* (*sein*) rot, decay

verfechten† *vt* advocate

verfehlen *vt* miss

verfeinde|n (sich) *vr* become enemies; **v~t sein** be enemies

verfeinern *vt* refine; (*verbessern*) improve

verfilmen *vt* film

verfluch|en *vt* curse. **v~t** *adj* & *adv* 🔲 damned; **v~t!** damn!

verfolg|en *vt* pursue; (*folgen*) follow; (*bedrängen*) pester; (*Pol*) persecute; **strafrechtlich v~en** prosecute. **V~er** *m* -s,- pursuer. **V~ung** *f* - pursuit; persecution

verfrüht *adj* premature

verfügbar *adj* available

verfüg|en *vt* order; (*Jur*) decree ● *vi* (*haben*) **v~en über** (+ *acc*) have at one's disposal. **V~ung** *f* -,-en order; (*Jur*) decree; **jdm zur V~ung stehen** be at s.o.'s disposal

verführ|en *vt* seduce; tempt. **V~ung** *f* seduction; temptation

vergangen *adj* past; (*letzte*) last. **V~heit** *f* - past; (*Gram*) past tense

vergänglich *adj* transitory

vergas|en *vt* gas. **V~er** *m* -s,- carburettor

vergeb|en† *vt* award (**an** + *dat* to); (*weggeben*) give away; (*verzeihen*) forgive. **v~lich** *adj* futile, vain ● *adv* in vain. **V~ung** *f* - forgiveness

vergehen† *vi* (*sein*) pass; **sich v~** violate (**gegen etw** sth). **V~** *nt* -s,- offence

vergelt|en† *vt* repay. **V~ung** *f* - retaliation; (*Rache*) revenge

vergessen† *vt* forget; (*liegen lassen*) leave behind

vergesslich *adj* forgetful. **V~keit** *f* - forgetfulness

vergeuden *vt* waste, squander

vergewaltig|en *vt* rape. **V~ung** *f* -,-en rape

vergießen† *vt* spill; shed (*Tränen, Blut*)

vergift|en *vt* poison. **V~ung** *f* -,-en poisoning

Vergissmeinnicht *nt* -[e]s,-[e] forget-me-not

vergittert *adj* barred

verglasen *vt* glaze

Vergleich *m* -[e]s,-e comparison; (*Jur*) settlement. **v~bar** *adj* comparable. **v~en**† *vt* compare (**mit** with/to)

vergnüg|en (sich) *vr* enjoy oneself. **V~en** *nt* -s,- pleasure; (*Spaß*) fun; **viel V~en!** have a good time! **v~t** *adj* cheerful; (*zufrieden*) happy. **V~ungen** *fpl* entertainments

vergolden *vt* gild; (*plattieren*) goldplate

vergraben† *vt* bury

vergriffen *adj* out of print

vergrößer|n *vt* enlarge; (*Linse:*) magnify; (*vermehren*) increase; (*erweitern*) extend; expand (*Geschäft*); **sich v~n** grow bigger; (*Firma:*) expand; (*zunehmen*) increase. **V~ung** *f* -,-en magnification; increase; expansion; (*Phot*) enlargement. **V~ungsglas** *nt* magnifying glass

vergüt|en *vt* pay for; **jdm etw v~en** reimburse s.o. for sth. **V~ung** *f* -,-en remuneration; (*Erstattung*) reimbursement

verhaft|en *vt* arrest. **V~ung** *f* -,-en arrest

verhalten† **(sich)** *vr* behave; (*handeln*) act; (*beschaffen sein*) be. **V~** *nt* -s behaviour, conduct

Verhältnis *nt* -ses,-se relationship; (*Liebes-*) affair; (*Math*) ratio; **V~se** circumstances; conditions. **v~mäßig** *adv* comparatively, relatively

verhand|eln *vt* discuss; (*Jur*) try ● *vi* (*haben*) negotiate. **V~lung** *f* (*Jur*) trial; **V~lungen** negotiations

Verhängnis *nt* -ses fate, doom

verhärten *vt/i* (*sein*) harden

verhasst *adj* hated

verhätscheln *vt* spoil

verhauen† *vt* 🗉 beat; make a mess of (*Prüfung*)

verheilen *vi* (*sein*) heal

verheimlichen *vt* keep secret

verheirat|en (sich) *vr* get married (**mit** to); **sich wieder v~en** remarry. **v~et** *adj* married

verhelfen† *vi* (*haben*) **jdm zu etw v~** help s.o. get sth

verherrlichen *vt* glorify

verhexen *vt* bewitch

verhindern *vt* prevent; **v~t sein** be unable to come

Verhör *nt* -s,-e interrogation; **ins V~ nehmen** interrogate. **v~en** *vt* interrogate; **sich v~en** mishear

verhungern *vi* (*sein*) starve

verhüt|en *vt* prevent. **V~ung** *f* - prevention. **V~ungsmittel** *nt* contraceptive

verirren (sich) *vr* get lost

verjagen *vt* chase away

verjüngen *vt* rejuvenate

verkalkt *adj* 🗉 senile

verkalkulieren (sich) *vr* miscalculate

Verkauf *m* sale; **zum V~** for sale. **v~en** *vt* sell; **zu v~en** for sale

Verkäufer(in) *m(f)* seller; (*im Geschäft*) shop assistant

Verkehr *m* -s traffic; (*Kontakt*) contact; (*Geschlechts-*) intercourse; **aus dem V~ ziehen** take out of circulation. **v~en** *vi* (*haben*) operate; (*Bus, Zug:*) run; (*Umgang haben*) associate, mix (**mit** with); (*Gast sein*) visit (**bei jdm** s.o.)

Verkehrs|ampel *f* traffic lights *pl*. **V~unfall** *m* road accident. **V~verein** *m* tourist office. **V~zeichen** *nt* traffic sign

verkehrt *adj* wrong; **v~ herum** *adv* the wrong way round; (*links*) inside out

verklagen *vt* sue (**auf** + *acc* for)

v

verkleid|en vt disguise; (Techn) line;
sich v~en disguise oneself; (für Kostümfest) dress up. **V~ung** f -,-en
disguise; (Kostüm) fancy dress;
(Techn) lining

verkleiner|n vt reduce [in size].
V~ung f - reduction

verknittern vt/i (sein) crumple

verknüpfen vt knot together

verkommen† vi (sein) be neglected; (sittlich) go to the bad; (verfallen) decay; (Haus:) fall into disrepair; (Gegend:) become run-down;
(Lebensmittel:) go bad ● adj neglected; (sittlich) depraved; (Haus) dilapidated; (Gegend) run-down

verkörpern vt embody, personify

verkraften vt cope with

verkrampft adj (fig) tense

verkriechen† (sich) vr hide

verkrümmt adj crooked, bent

verkrüppelt adj crippled; (Glied)
deformed

verkühl|en (sich) vr catch a chill.
V~ung f -,-en chill

verkümmern vi (sein)
waste/(Pflanze:) wither away

verkünden vt announce; pronounce (Urteil)

verkürzen vt shorten; (verringern)
reduce; (abbrechen) cut short; while
away (Zeit)

Verlag m -[e]s,-e publishing firm

verlangen vt ask for; (fordern) demand; (berechnen) charge. **V~** nt -s
desire; (Bitte) request

verlänger|n vt extend; lengthen
(Kleid); (zeitlich) prolong; renew (Pass,
Vertrag); (Culin) thin down. **V~ung** f
-,-en extension; renewal. **V~ungsschnur** f extension cable

verlassen† vt leave; (im Stich lassen)
desert; sich v~ auf (+ acc) rely or
depend on ● adj deserted. **V~heit** f
- desolation

verlässlich adj reliable

Verlauf m course; im V~ (+ gen) in
the course of. v~en† vi (sein) run;
(ablaufen) go; gut v~en go [off] well
● vr sich v~en lose one's way

verlegen vt move; (verschieben)
postpone; (vor-) bring forward; (verlieren) mislay; (versperren) block;
(legen) lay (Teppich, Rohre); (veröffentlichen) publish; sich v~ auf (+ acc)
take up (Beruf); resort to (Bitten)
● adj embarrassed. **V~heit** f - embarrassment

Verleger m -s,- publisher

verleihen† vt lend; (gegen Gebühr)
hire out; (überreichen) award, confer;
(fig) give

verlernen vt forget

verletz|en vt injure; (kränken) hurt;
(verstoßen gegen) infringe; violate
(Grenze). v~end adj hurtful, wounding. **V~te(r)** m/f injured person; (bei
Unfall) casualty. **V~ung** f -,-en (Verstoß) infringement; violation

verleugnen vt deny; disown
(Freund)

verleumd|en vt slander; (schriftlich)
libel. v~erisch adj slanderous; libellous. **V~ung** f -,-en slander; (schriftlich) libel

verlieben (sich) vr fall in love (in +
acc with); verliebt sein be in love (in
+ acc with)

verlier|en† vt lose; shed (Laub) ● vi
(haben) lose (an etw dat sth). **V~er**
m -s,- loser

verlob|en (sich) vr get engaged
(mit to); v~t sein be engaged.
V~te f fiancée. **V~te(r)** m fiancé.
V~ung f -,-en engagement

verlock|en vt tempt. **V~ung** f
-,-en temptation

verloren adj lost; v~ gehen get
lost

verlos|en vt raffle. **V~ung** f -,-en
raffle; (Ziehung) draw

Verlust m -[e]s,-e loss

vermachen vt leave, bequeath

Vermächtnis nt -ses,-se legacy

vermähl|en (sich) vr marry.
V~ung f -,-en marriage

vermehren vt increase; propagate
(Pflanzen); sich v~ increase; (sich
fortpflanzen) breed

vermeiden† vt avoid

Vermerk *m* -[e]s,-e note. **v~en** note [down]

vermessen† *vt* measure; survey (*Gelände*) ● *adj* presumptuous

vermiet|en *vt* let, rent [out]; hire out (*Boot, Auto*); **zu v~en** to let; (*Boot:*) for hire. **V~er** *m* landlord. **V~erin** *f* landlady

vermindern *vt* reduce

vermischen *vt* mix

vermissen *vt* miss

vermisst *adj* missing

vermitteln *vi* (*haben*) mediate ● *vt* arrange; (*beschaffen*) find; place (*Arbeitskräfte*)

Vermittl|er *m* -s,- agent; (*Schlichter*) mediator. **V~ung** *f* -,-en arrangement; (*Agentur*) agency; (*Teleph*) exchange; (*Schlichtung*) mediation

Vermögen *nt* -s,- fortune. **v~d** *adj* wealthy

vermut|en *vt* suspect; (*glauben*) presume. **v~lich** *adj* probable ● *adv* presumably. **V~ung** *f* -,-en supposition; (*Verdacht*) suspicion

vernachlässigen *vt* neglect

vernehm|en† *vt* hear; (*verhören*) question; (*Jur*) examine. **V~ung** *f* -,-en questioning

verneigen (sich) *vr* bow

vernein|en *vt* answer in the negative; (*ablehnen*) reject. **v~end** *adj* negative. **V~ung** *f* -,-en negative answer

vernicht|en *vt* destroy; (*ausrotten*) exterminate. **V~ung** *f* - destruction; extermination

Vernunft *f* - reason

vernünftig *adj* reasonable, sensible

veröffentlich|en *vt* publish. **V~ung** *f* -,-en publication

verordn|en *vt* prescribe (*dat* for). **V~ung** *f* -,-en prescription; (*Verfügung*) decree

verpachten *vt* lease [out]

verpack|en *vt* pack; (*einwickeln*) wrap. **V~ung** *f* packaging; wrapping

verpassen *vt* miss; (🔲: *geben*) give

verpfänden *vt* pawn

verpflanzen *vt* transplant

verpfleg|en *vt* feed: **sich selbst v~en** cater for oneself. **V~ung** *f* -board; (*Essen*) food; **Unterkunft und V~ung** board and lodging

verpflicht|en *vt* oblige; (*einstellen*) engage; (*Sport*) sign; **sich v~en** undertake/(*versprechen*) promise (**zu** to); (*vertraglich*) sign a contract. **V~ung** *f* -,-en obligation, commitment

verprügeln *vt* beat up, thrash

Verputz *m* -es plaster. **v~en** *vt* plaster

Verrat *m* -[e]s betrayal, treachery. **v~en**† *vt* betray; give away (*Geheimnis*)

Verräter *m* -s,- traitor

verrech|nen *vt* settle; clear (*Scheck*); **sich v~nen** make a mistake; (*fig*) miscalculate. **V~nungsscheck** *m* crossed cheque

verreisen *vi* (*sein*) go away; **verreist sein** be away

verrenken *vt* dislocate

verrichten *vt* perform, do

verriegeln *vt* bolt

verringer|n *vt* reduce; **sich v~n** decrease. **V~ung** *f* - reduction; decrease

verrost|en *vi* (*sein*) rust. **v~et** *adj* rusty

verrückt *adj* crazy, mad. **V~e(r)** *m/f* lunatic, **V~heit** *f* -,-en madness; (*Torheit*) folly

verrühren *vt* mix

verrunzelt *adj* wrinkled

verrutschen *vt* (*sein*) slip

Vers /fɛrs/ *m* -es,-e verse

versag|en *vi* (*haben*) fail ● *vt* **sich etw v~en** deny oneself sth. **V~en** *nt* -s,- failure. **V~er** *m* -s,- failure

versalzen† *vt* put too much salt in/on; (*fig*) spoil

versamm|eln *vt* assemble. **V~lung** *f* assembly, meeting

Versand *m* -[e]s dispatch. **V~haus** *nt* mail-order firm

versäumen *vt* miss; lose (*Zeit*); (*unterlassen*) neglect; **[es] v~en, etw**

V

zu tun fail to do sth

verschärfen *vt* intensify; tighten (*Kontrolle*); increase (*Tempo*); aggravate (*Lage*); **sich v~** intensify; increase; (*Lage:*) worsen

verschätzen (sich) *vr* sich v~ in (+ *dat*) misjudge

verschenken *vt* give away

verscheuchen *vt* shoo/(*jagen*) chase away

verschicken *vt* send; (*Comm*) dispatch

verschieb|en† *vt* move; (*aufschieben*) put off, postpone; **sich v~en** move, shift; (*verrutschen*) slip; (*zeitlich*) be postponed. **V~ung** *f* shift; postponement

verschieden *adj* different; **v~e** *pl* different; (*mehrere*) various; **V~es** some things; (*dieses und jenes*) various things; **das ist v~** it varies ● *adv* differently; **v~ groß** of different sizes. **v~artig** *adj* diverse

verschimmel|n *vi* (*sein*) go mouldy. **v~t** *adj* mouldy

verschlafen† *vi* (*haben*) oversleep ● *vt* sleep through (*Tag*); **sich v~** oversleep ● *adj* sleepy

verschlagen† *vt* lose (*Seite*); jdm die Sprache/den Atem v~ leave s.o. speechless/take s.o.'s breath away ● *adj* sly

verschlechter|n *vt* make worse; **sich v~n** get worse, deteriorate. **V~ung** *f* -,-en deterioration

Verschleiß *m* -es wear and tear

verschleppen *vt* carry off; (*entführen*) abduct; spread (*Seuche*); neglect (*Krankheit*); (*hinausziehen*) delay

verschleudern *vt* sell at a loss

verschließen† *vt* close; (*abschließen*) lock; (*einschließen*) lock up

verschlimmer|n *vt* make worse; aggravate (*Lage*); **sich v~n** get worse, deteriorate. **V~ung** *f* -,-en deterioration

verschlossen *adj* reserved. **V~heit** *f* - reserve

verschlucken *vt* swallow; **sich v~**

choke (**an** + *dat* on)

Verschluss *m* -es,-̈e fastener, clasp; (*Koffer-*) catch; (*Flaschen-*) top; (*luftdicht*) seal; (*Phot*) shutter

verschlüsselt *adj* coded

verschmelzen† *vt/i* (*sein*) fuse

verschmerzen *vt* get over

verschmutz|en *vt* soil; pollute (*Luft*) ● *vi* (*sein*) get dirty. **V~ung** *f* - pollution

verschneit *adj* snow-covered

verschnörkelt *adj* ornate

verschnüren *vt* tie up

verschollen *adj* missing

verschonen *vt* spare

verschossen *adj* faded

verschränken *vt* cross

verschreiben† *vt* prescribe; **sich v~** make a slip of the pen

verschulden *vt* be to blame for. **V~** *nt* -s fault

verschuldet *adj* **v~ sein** be in debt

verschütten *vt* spill; (*begraben*) bury

verschweigen† *vt* conceal, hide

verschwend|en *vt* waste. **V~ung** *f* - extravagance; (*Vergeudung*) waste

verschwiegen *adj* discreet

verschwinden† *vi* (*sein*) disappear; [mal] **v~** Ⅰ spend a penny

verschwommen *adj* blurred

verschwör|en (**sich**) *vr* conspire. **V~ung** *f* -,-en conspiracy

versehen† *vt* perform; hold (*Posten*); keep (*Haushalt*); **v~ mit** provide with; **sich v~** make a mistake. **V~** *nt* -s,- oversight; (*Fehler*) slip; **aus V~** by mistake. **v~tlich** *adv* by mistake

Versehrte(r) *m* disabled person

versengen *vt* singe; (*stärker*) scorch

versenken *vt* sink

versessen *adj* keen (**auf** + *acc* on)

versetz|en *vt* move; transfer (*Person*); (*Sch*) move up; (*verpfänden*) pawn; (*verkaufen*) sell; (*vermischen*) blend; jdn **v~en** (Ⅰ: *warten lassen*) stand s.o. up; **jdm in Angst/ Erstaunen v~en** frighten/astonish s.o.; **sich in jds Lage v~en** put oneself in s.o.'s place. **V~ung** f -,-en move; transfer; (Sch) move to a higher class

verseuchen vt contaminate

versicher|n vt insure; (bekräftigen) affirm; **jdm v~n** assure s.o. (**dass** that). **V~ung** f -,-en insurance; assurance

versiegeln vt seal

versiert /vɛrˈʒiːɐt/ adj experienced

versilbert adj silver-plated

Versmaß /ˈfɛrs-/ nt metre

versöhn|en vt reconcile; **sich v~en** become reconciled. **V~ung** f -,-en reconciliation

versorg|en vt provide, supply (**mit** with); provide for (Familie); (betreuen) look after. **V~ung** f - provision, supply; (Betreuung) care

verspät|en (sich) vr be late. **v~et** adj late; (Zug) delayed; (Dank) belated. **V~ung** f - lateness; **V~ung haben** be late

versperren vt block; bar (Weg)

verspiel|en vt gamble away. **v~t** adj playful

verspotten vt mock, ridicule

versprech|en† vt promise; **sich v~en** make a slip of the tongue; **sich** (dat) **viel v~en von** have high hopes of; **ein viel v~ender Anfang** a promising start. **V~en** nt -s,- promise. **V~ungen** fpl promises

verstaatlich|en vt nationalize. **V~ung** f - nationalization

Verstand m -[e]s mind; (Vernunft) reason; **den V~ verlieren** go out of one's mind

verständig adj sensible; (klug) intelligent. **v~en** vt notify, inform; **sich v~en** communicate; (sich verständlich machen) make oneself understood. **V~ung** f - notification; communication; (Einigung) agreement

verständlich adj comprehensible; (deutlich) clear; (begreiflich) under-

standable; **sich v~ machen** make oneself understood. **v~erweise** adv understandably

Verständnis nt -ses understanding

verstärk|en vt strengthen, reinforce; (steigern) intensify, increase; amplify (Ton). **V~er** m -s,- amplifier. **V~ung** f reinforcement; increase; amplification; (Truppen) reinforcements pl

verstaubt adj dusty

verstauchen vt sprain

Versteck nt -[e]s,-e hiding-place; **V~ spielen** play hide-and-seek. **v~en** vt hide; **sich v~en** hide

verstehen† vt understand; (können) know; **falsch v~** misunderstand; **sich v~** understand one another; (auskommen) get on

versteiger|n vt auction. **V~ung** f auction

versteinert adj fossilized

verstell|en vt adjust; (versperren) block; (verändern) disguise; **sich v~en** pretend. **V~ung** f - pretence

versteuern vt pay tax on

verstimm|t adj disgruntled; (Magen) upset; (Mus) out of tune. **V~ung** f - ill humour; (Magen-) upset

verstockt adj stubborn

verstopf|en vt plug; (versperren) block; **v~t** blocked; (Person) constipated. **V~ung** f -,-en blockage; (Med) constipation

verstorben adj late, deceased. **V~e(r)** m/f deceased

verstört adj bewildered

Verstoß m infringement. **v~en†** vt disown ● vi (haben) **v~en gegen** contravene, infringe

verstreuen vt scatter

verstümmeln vt mutilate; garble (Text)

Versuch m -[e]s,-e attempt; (Experiment) experiment. **v~en** vt (haben) try; **v~t sein** be tempted (**zu** to). **V~ung** f -,-en temptation

vertagen vt adjourn; (aufschieben)

postpone; **sich v~** adjourn

vertauschen vt exchange; (verwechseln) mix up

verteidig|en vt defend. **V~er** m -s,- defender; (Jur) defence counsel. **V~ung** f -,-en defence

verteil|en vt distribute; (zuteilen) allocate; (ausgeben) hand out; (verstreichen) spread. **V~ung** f - distribution; allocation

vertief|en vt deepen; **v~t sein in** (+ acc) be engrossed in. **V~ung** f -,-en hollow, depression

vertikal /vɛrti'ka:l/ adj vertical

vertilgen vt exterminate; kill [off] (Unkraut)

vertippen (sich) vr make a typing mistake

vertonen vt set to music

Vertrag m -[e]s,⸚e contract; (Pol) treaty

vertragen† vt tolerate, stand; take (Kritik, Spaß); **sich v~** get on

vertraglich adj contractual

verträglich adj good-natured; (bekömmlich) digestible

vertrauen vi (haben) trust (**jdm/ etw** s.o./sth); **auf** + acc in). **V~** nt -s trust, confidence (**zu** in); **im V~** in confidence. **v~swürdig** adj trustworthy

vertraulich adj confidential; (intim) familiar

vertraut adj intimate; (bekannt) familiar. **V~heit** f - intimacy; familiarity

vertreib|en† vt drive away; drive out (Feind); (Comm) sell; **sich (dat) die Zeit v~en** pass the time. **V~ung** f -,-en expulsion

vertret|en† vt represent; (einspringen für) stand in or deputize for; (verfechten) support; hold (Meinung); **sich (dat) den Fuß v~en** twist one's ankle. **V~er** m -s,- representative; deputy; (Arzt-) locum; (Verfechter) supporter. **V~ung** f -,-en representation; (Person) deputy; (eines Arztes) locum; (Handels-) agency

Vertrieb m -[e]s (Comm) sale

vertrocknen vi (sein) dry up

verüben vt commit

verunglücken vi (sein) be involved in an accident; (▯: missglücken) go wrong; **tödlich v~** be killed in an accident

verunreinigen vt pollute; (verseuchen) contaminate

verursachen vt cause

verurteil|en vt condemn; (Jur) convict (**wegen** of); sentence (**zum Tode** to death). **V~ung** f - condemnation; (Jur) conviction

vervielfachen vt multiply

vervielfältigen vt duplicate

vervollständigen vt complete

verwählen (sich) vr misdial

verwahren vt keep; (verstauen) put away

Verwahrung f - keeping; **in V~ nehmen** take into safe keeping

verwaist adj orphaned

verwalt|en vt administer; (leiten) manage; govern (Land). **V~er** m -s,- administrator; manager. **V~ung** f -,-en administration; management; government

verwand|eln vt transform, change (**in** + acc into); **sich v~eln** change, turn (**in** + acc into). **V~lung** f transformation

verwandt adj related (**mit** to). **V~e(r)** m/f relative. **V~schaft** f - relationship; (Menschen) relatives pl

verwarn|en vt warn, caution. **V~ung** f warning, caution

verwechs|eln vt mix up, confuse; (halten für) mistake (**mit** for). **V~lung** f -,-en mix-up

verweiger|n vt/i (haben) refuse (**jdm etw** s.o. sth). **V~ung** f refusal

Verweis m -es,-e reference (**auf** + acc to); (Tadel) reprimand; **v~en†** vt refer (**auf/an** + acc to); (tadeln) reprimand; **von der Schule v~en** expel

verwelken vi (sein) wilt

verwend|en† vt use; spend (Zeit, Mühe). **V~ung** f use

verwerten vt utilize, use

verwesen vi (sein) decompose

verwick|eln vt involve (**in** + acc in); **sich v~eln** get tangled up. **v~elt** adj complicated

verwildert adj wild; (Garten) overgrown; (Aussehen) unkempt

verwinden† vt (fig) get over

verwirklichen vt realize

verwirr|en vt tangle up; (fig) confuse; **sich v~en** get tangled; (fig) become confused. **v~t** adj confused. **V~ung** f - confusion

verwischen vt smudge

verwittert adj weathered

verwitwet adj widowed

verwöhn|en vt spoil. **v~t** adj spoilt

verworren adj confused

verwund|bar adj vulnerable. **v~en** vt wound

verwunder|lich adj surprising. **v~n** vt surprise; **sich v~n** be surprised. **V~ung** f - surprise

Verwund|ete(r) m wounded soldier; **die V~eten** the wounded pl. **V~ung** f -,-en wound

verwüst|en vt devastate, ravage. **V~ung** f -,-en devastation

verzählen (sich) vr miscount

verzaubern vt bewitch; (fig) enchant; **v~ in** (+ acc) turn into

Verzehr m -s consumption. **v~en** vt eat

verzeih|en† vt forgive; **v~en Sie!** excuse me! **V~ung** f - forgiveness; **um V~ung bitten** apologize; **V~ung!** sorry! (bei Frage) excuse me!

Verzicht m -[e]s renunciation (**auf** + acc of). **v~en** vi (haben) do without; **v~en auf** (+ acc) give up; renounce (Recht, Erbe)

verziehen† vt pull out of shape; (verwöhnen) spoil; **sich v~** lose shape; (Holz:) warp; (Gesicht:) twist; (verschwinden) disappear; (Nebel:) dis-

perse; (Gewitter:) pass ● vi (sein) move [away]

verzier|en vt decorate. **V~ung** f -,-en decoration

verzinsen vt pay interest on

verzöger|n vt delay; (verlangsamen) slow down. **V~ung** f -,-en delay

verzollen vt pay duty on; **haben Sie etwas zu v~?** have you anything to declare?

verzweif|eln vi (sein) despair. **v~elt** adj desperate. **V~lung** f - despair; (Ratlosigkeit) desperation

verzweigen (sich) vr branch [out]

Veto /'ve:to/ nt -s,-s veto

Vetter m -s,-n cousin

vgl. abbr (vergleiche) cf.

Viadukt /via'dʊkt/ nt -[e]s,-e viaduct

Video /'vi:deo/ nt -s,-s video. **V~handy** nt vision phone. **V~kassette** f video cassette. **V~recorder** m -s,- video recorder

Vieh nt -[e]s livestock; (Rinder) cattle pl; (🆃: Tier) creature

viel pron a great deal/🆃 a lot of; (pl) many, 🆃 a lot of; (substantivisch) **v~[es]** much, 🆃 a lot; **nicht/so/wie/zu v~** not/so/how/too much/ (pl) many; **v~e** pl many; **das v~e Geld** all that money ● adv much, 🆃 a lot; **v~ mehr/weniger** much more/less; **v~zu groß/klein** much or far too big/small; **so v~ wie möglich** as much as possible; **so/zu v~ arbeiten** work so/too much

viel|deutig adj ambiguous. **v~fach** adj multiple ● adv many times; (🆃: oft) frequently. **V~falt** f - diversity, [great] variety

vielleicht adv perhaps, maybe; (🆃: wirklich) really

vielmals adv very much

vielmehr adv rather; (im Gegenteil) on the contrary

vielseitig adj varied; (Person) versatile. **V~keit** f - versatility

vielversprechend* adj viel versprechend, *s.* **versprechen**

vier *inv adj,* **V~** *f* **-,-en** four; (*Sch*) ≈ fair. **V~eck** *nt* **-[e]s,-e** oblong, rectangle; (*Quadrat*) square. **v~eckig** *adj* oblong, rectangular; square. **V~linge** *mpl* quadruplets

viertel /'fɪrtəl/ *inv adj* quarter; **um v~ neun** at [a] quarter past eight; **um drei v~ neun** at [a] quarter to nine. **V~** *nt* **-s,-** quarter; (*Wein*) quarter litre; **V~ vor/nach sechs** [a] quarter to/past six. **V~finale** *nt* quarter-final. **V~jahr** *nt* three months *pl*; (*Comm*) quarter. **v~jährlich** *adj & adv* quarterly. **V~stunde** *f* quarter of an hour

vier|zehn /'fɪr-/ *inv adj* fourteen. **v~zehnte(r,s)** *adj* fourteenth. **v~zig** *inv adj* forty. **v~zigste(r,s)** *adj* fortieth

Villa /'vɪla/ *f* **-,-len** villa

violett /vi̯o'lɛt/ *adj* violet

Vio|line /vi̯o'liːnə/ *f* **-,-n** violin. **V~linschlüssel** *m* treble clef

Virus /'viːrʊs/ *nt* **-,-ren** virus

Visier /vi'ziːɐ̯/ *nt* **-s,-e** visor

Visite /vi'ziːtə/ *f* **-,-n** round; **V~ machen** do one's round

Visum /'viːzʊm/ *nt* **-s,-sa** visa

Vitamin /vita'miːn/ *nt* **-s,-e** vitamin

Vitrine /vi'triːnə/ *f* **-,-n** display cabinet/(*im Museum*) case

Vizepräsident /'fiːtsə-/ *m* vice president

Vogel *m* **-s,** ⸚ bird; **einen V~ haben** ⊞ have a screw loose. **V~scheuche** *f* **-,-n** scarecrow

Vokabeln /vo'kaːbəln/ *fpl* vocabulary *sg*

Vokal /vo'kaːl/ *m* **-s,-e** vowel

Volant /vo'lãː/ *m* **-s,-s** flounce

Volk *nt* **-[e]s,** ⸚er people *sg*; (*Bevölkerung*) people *pl*

Völker|kunde *f* ethnology. **V~mord** *m* genocide. **V~recht** *nt* international law

Volks|abstimmung *f* plebiscite. **V~fest** *nt* public festival. **V~hochschule** *f* adult education classes

pl/(*Gebäude*) centre. **V~lied** *nt* folksong. **V~tanz** *m* folk-dance. **v~tümlich** *adj* popular. **V~wirt** *m* economist. **V~wirtschaft** *f* economics *sg*. **V~zählung** *f* [national] census

voll *adj* full (**von** *od* **mit** of); (*Haar*) thick; (*Erfolg, Ernst*) complete; (*Wahrheit*) whole; **v~ machen** fill up; **v~ tanken** fill up with petrol ● *adv* (*ganz*) completely; (*arbeiten*) full-time; (*auszahlen*) in full; **v~ und ganz** completely

Vollblut *nt* thoroughbred

vollende|n *vt insep* complete. **v~t** *adj* perfect

Vollendung *f* completion; (*Vollkommenheit*) perfection

voller *inv adj* full of

Volleyball /'vɔli-/ *m* volleyball

vollführen *vt insep* perform

vollfüllen *vt sep* fill up

Vollgas *nt* **V~ geben** put one's foot down; **mit V~** flat out

völlig *adj* complete

volljährig *adj* **v~ sein** (*Jur*) be of age. **V~keit** *f* **-** (*Jur*) majority

Vollkaskoversicherung *f* fully comprehensive insurance

vollkommen *adj* perfect; (*völlig*) complete

Voll|kornbrot *nt* wholemeal bread. **V~macht** *f* **-,-en** authority; (*Jur*) power of attorney. **V~mond** *m* full moon. **V~pension** *f* full board

vollständig *adj* complete

vollstrecken *vt insep* execute; carry out (*Urteil*)

volltanken* *vi sep* (*haben*) **voll tanken**, *s.* **voll**

Volltreffer *m* direct hit

vollzählig *adj* complete

vollziehen† *vt insep* carry out; perform (*Handlung*); consummate (*Ehe*); **sich v~** take place

Volt /vɔlt/ *nt* **-[s],-** volt

Volumen /vo'luːmən/ *nt* **-s,-** volume

vom *prep* = **von dem**

von

● *preposition* (+ *dative*)

> ❗ Note that **von dem** can become **vom**

····▸ (*räumlich*) from; (*nach Richtungen*) of. **von hier an** from here on[ward]. **von Wien aus** [starting] from Vienna. **nördlich/südlich von Mannheim** [to the] north/south of Mannheim. **rechts/links von mir** to the right/left of me; on my right/left

····▸ (*zeitlich*) from. **von jetzt an** from now on. **von heute/morgen an** [as] from today/tomorrow; starting today/tomorrow

····▸ (*zur Angabe des Urhebers, der Ursache; nach Passiv*) by. **der Roman ist von Fontane** the novel is by Fontane. **sie hat ein Kind von ihm**. she has a child by him. **er ist vom Blitz erschlagen worden** he was killed by lightning

····▸ (*anstelle eines Genitivs; Hingehören, Beschaffenheit, Menge etc.*) of. **ein Stück von dem Kuchen** a piece of the cake. **einer von euch** one of you. **eine Fahrt von drei Stunden** a drive of three hours; a three-hour drive. **das Brot von gestern** yesterday's bread. **ein Tal von erstaunlicher Schönheit** a valley of extraordinary beauty

····▸ (*betreffend*) about. **handeln/wissen/erzählen** *od* **reden von** ... be/know/talk about .... **eine Geschichte von zwei Elefanten** a story about *or* of two elephants

voneinander *adv* from each other; (*abhängig*) on each other

vonseiten *prep* (+ *gen*) on the part of

vonstatten *adv* **v~ gehen** take place

vor *prep* (+ *dat/acc*) in front of; (*zeit-lich, Reihenfolge*) before; (+ *dat*) (*bei Uhrzeit*) to; (*warnen, sich fürchten*) of; (*schützen, davonlaufen*) from; (*Respekt haben*) for; **vor Angst zittern** tremble with fear; **vor drei Tagen** three days ago; **vor allen Dingen** above all ● *adv* forward; **vor und zurück** backwards and forwards

Vorabend *m* eve

voran *adv* at the front; (*voraus*) ahead; (*vorwärts*) forward. **v~gehen†** *vi sep* (*sein*) lead the way; (*Fortschritte machen*) make progress. **v~kommen†** *vi sep* (*sein*) make progress; (*fig*) get on

Vor|anschlag *m* estimate. **V~anzeige** *f* advance notice. **V~arbeiter** *m* foreman

voraus *adv* ahead (*dat* of); (*vorn*) at the front; (*vorwärts*) forward ● **im Voraus** in advance. **v~bezahlen** *vt sep* pay in advance. **v~gehen†** *vi sep* (*sein*) go on ahead; **jdm/etw v~gehen** precede s.o./sth. **V~sage** *f* **-,-n** prediction. **v~sagen** *vt sep* predict

voraussetz|en *vt sep* take for granted; (*erfordern*) require; **vorausgesetzt, dass** provided that. **V~ung** *f* **-,-en** assumption; (*Erfordernis*) prerequisite

voraussichtlich *adj* anticipated, expected ● *adv* probably

Vorbehalt *m* **-[e]s,-e** reservation

vorbei *adv* past (**an** *jdm/etw* s.o./sth); (*zu Ende*) over. **v~fahren†** *vi sep* (*sein*) drive/go past. **v~gehen†** *vi sep* (*sein*) go past; (*verfehlen*) miss; (*vergehen*) pass; (🄸: *besuchen*) drop in (**bei** on)

vorbereit|en *vt sep* prepare; prepare for (*Reise*); **sich v~en** prepare [oneself] (**auf** + *acc* for). **V~ung** *f* **-,-en** preparation

vorbestellen *vt sep* order/(*im Theater, Hotel*) book in advance

vorbestraft *adj* **v~ sein** have a [criminal] record

Vorbeugung *f* **-** prevention

Vorbild *nt* model. **v~lich** *adj* exemplary, model ● *adv* in an exemplary manner

V

vorbringen† *vt sep* put forward; offer (*Entschuldigung*)

vordatieren *vt sep* post-date

Vorder|bein *nt* foreleg. **v~e(r,s)** *adj* front. **V~grund** *m* foreground. **V~rad** *nt* front wheel. **V~seite** *f* front; (*einer Münze*) obverse. **v~ste(r,s)** *adj* front, first. **V~teil** *nt* front

vor|drängeln (sich) *vr sep* 🔲 jump the queue. **v~drängen (sich)** *vr sep* push forward. **v~dringen**† *vi sep* (*sein*) advance

voreilig *adj* rash

voreingenommen *adj* biased, prejudiced. **V~heit** *f* - bias

vorenthalten† *vt sep* withhold

vorerst *adv* for the time being

Vorfahr *m* -en,-en ancestor

Vorfahrt *f* right of way; **'V~ beachten'** 'give way'. **V~sstraße** *f* ≈ major road

Vorfall *m* incident. **v~en**† *vi sep* (*sein*) happen

vorfinden† *vt sep* find

Vorfreude *f* [happy] anticipation

vorführ|en *vt sep* present, show; (*demonstrieren*) demonstrate; (*aufführen*) perform. **V~ung** *f* presentation; demonstration; performance

Vor|gabe *f* (*Sport*) handicap. **V~gang** *m* occurrence; (*Techn*) process. **V~gänger(in)** *m* -s,- (*f* -,-nen*) predecessor

vorgehen† *vi sep* (*sein*) go forward; (*voraus-*) go on ahead; (*Uhr:*) be fast; (*wichtig sein*) take precedence; (*verfahren*) act, proceed; (*geschehen*) happen, go on. **V~** *nt* -s action

vor|geschichtlich *adj* prehistoric. **V~geschmack** *m* foretaste. **V~gesetzte(r)** *m/f* superior. **v~gestern** *adv* the day before yesterday; **v~gestern Abend** the evening before last

vorhaben† *vt sep* propose, intend (**zu** to); **etw v~** have sth planned. **V~** *nt* -s,- plan

Vorhand *f* (*Sport*) forehand

vorhanden *adj* existing; **v~ sein** exist; be available

Vorhang *m* curtain

Vorhängeschloss *nt* padlock

vorher *adv* before[hand]

vorhergehend *adj* previous

vorherrschend *adj* predominant

Vorher|sage *f* -,-n prediction; (*Wetter-*) forecast. **v~sagen** *vt sep* predict; forecast (*Wetter*). **v~sehen**† *vt sep* foresee

vorhin *adv* just now

vorige(r,s) *adj* last, previous

Vor|kehrungen *fpl* precautions. **V~kenntnisse** *fpl* previous knowledge *sg*

vorkommen† *vi sep* (*sein*) happen; (*vorhanden sein*) occur; (*nach vorn kommen*) come forward; (*hervorkommen*) come out; (*zu sehen sein*) show; **jdm bekannt v~** seem familiar to s.o.

Vorkriegszeit *f* pre-war period

vorlad|en† *vt sep* (*Jur*) summons. **V~ung** *f* summons

Vorlage *f* model; (*Muster*) pattern; (*Gesetzes-*) bill

vorlassen† *vt sep* admit; **jdn v~** 🔲 let s.o. pass; (*den Vortritt lassen*) let s.o. go first

Vor|lauf *m* (*Sport*) heat. **V~läufer** *m* forerunner. **v~läufig** *adj* provisional; (*zunächst*) for the time being. **v~laut** *adj* forward. **V~leben** *nt* past

vorleg|en *vt sep* put on (*Kette*); (*unterbreiten*) present; (*vorzeigen*) show. **V~er** *m* -s,- mat; (*Bett-*) rug

vorles|en† *vt sep* read [out]; **jdm v~en** read to s.o. **V~ung** *f* lecture

vorletzt|e(r,s) *adj* last ... but one; **v~es Jahr** the year before last

Vorliebe *f* preference

vorliegen† *vt sep* (*haben*) be present/(*verfügbar*) available; (*bestehen*) exist, be

vorlügen† *vt sep* lie (*dat* to)

vormachen *vt sep* put up; put on (*Kette*); push (*Riegel*); (*zeigen*) demonstrate; **jdm etwas v~** (🔲: *täuschen*) kid s.o.

Vormacht *f* supremacy

vormals *adv* formerly

vormerken *vt sep* make a note of; (*reservieren*) reserve

Vormittag *m* morning; **gestern/ heute V~** yesterday/this morning. **v~s** *adv* in the morning

Vormund *m* -[e]s,-munde & -münder guardian

vorn *adv* at the front; **nach v~** to the front; **von v~** from the front/(*vom Anfang*) beginning; **von v~ anfangen** start afresh

Vorname *m* first name

vorne *adv* = vorn

vornehm *adj* distinguished; smart

vornehmen† *vt sep* carry out; **sich** (*dat*) **v~, etw zu tun** plan to do sth

vornherein *adv* **von v~herein** from the start

Vor|ort *m* suburb. **V~rang** *m* priority, precedence (**vor** + *dat* over). **V~rat** *m* -[e]s,-räte supply, stock (**an** + *dat* of). **v~rätig** *adj* available; **v~rätig haben** have in stock. **V~ratskammer** *f* larder. **V~recht** *nt* privilege. **V~richtung** *f* device

Vorrunde *f* qualifying round

vorsagen *vt/i sep* (*haben*) recite; **jdm v~** tell s.o. the answer

Vor|satz *m* resolution. **v~sätzlich** *adj* deliberate; (*Jur*) premeditated

Vorschau *f* preview; (*Film-*) trailer

Vorschein *m* **zum V~kommen** appear

Vorschlag *m* suggestion, proposal. **v~en**† *vt sep* suggest, propose

vorschnell *adj* rash

vorschreiben† *vt sep* lay down; dictate (*dat* to); **vorgeschriebene Dosis** prescribed dose

Vorschrift *f* regulation; (*Anweisung*) instruction; **jdm V~en machen** tell s.o. what to do. **v~smäßig** *adj* correct

Vorschule *f* nursery school

Vorschuss *m* advance

vorseh|en† *v sep* ● *vt* intend (**für/ als** for/as); (*planen*) plan; **sich v~en** be careful (**vor** + *dat* of) ● *vi* (*haben*) peep out. **V~ung** *f* - providence

Vorsicht *f* - care; (*bei Gefahr*) caution; **V~!** careful! (*auf Schild*) 'caution'. **v~ig** *adj* careful; cautious. **V~smaßnahme** *f* precaution

Vorsilbe *f* prefix

Vorsitz *m* chairmanship; **den V~ führen** be in the chair. **V~ende(r)** *m/f* chairman

Vorsorge *f* **V~ treffen** take precautions; make provisions (**für** for). **v~n** *vi sep* (*haben*) provide (**für** for)

Vorspeise *f* starter

Vorspiel *nt* prelude. **v~en** *v sep* ● *vt* perform/ (*Mus*) play (*dat* for) ● *vi* (*haben*) audition

vorsprechen† *v sep* ● *vt* recite; (*zum Nachsagen*) say (*dat* to) ● *vi* (*haben*) (*Theat*) audition; **bei jdm v~** call on s.o.

Vor|sprung *m* projection; (*Fels-*) ledge; (*Vorteil*) lead (**vor** + *dat* over). **V~stadt** *f* suburb. **V~stand** *m* board [of directors]; (*Vereins-*) committee; (*Partei-*) executive

vorsteh|en† *vi sep* (*haben*) project, protrude; **einer Abteilung v~en** be in charge of a department. **V~er** *m* -s,- head

vorstell|en *vt sep* put forward (*Bein, Uhr*); (*darstellen*) represent; (*bekannt-machen*) introduce; **sich v~en** introduce oneself; (*als Bewerber*) go for an interview; **sich** (*dat*) **etw v~en** imagine sth. **V~ung** *f* introduction; (*bei Bewerbung*) interview; (*Aufführung*) performance; (*Idee*) idea; (*Phantasie*) imagination. **V~ungsgespräch** *nt* interview

Vorstoß *m* advance

Vorstrafe *f* previous conviction

Vortag *m* day before

vortäuschen *vt sep* feign, fake

Vorteil *m* advantage. **v~haft** *adj* advantageous; flattering

Vortrag *m* -[e]s,-̈e talk; (*wissenschaftlich*) lecture. **v~en**† *vt sep* perform; (*aufsagen*) recite; (*singen*) sing; (*darlegen*) present (*dat* to)

vortrefflich *adj* excellent

Vortritt *m* precedence; **jdm den**

V

V∼ **lassen** let s.o. go first

vorüber adv v∼ **sein** be over; **an etw** (dat) v∼ past sth. **v∼gehend** adj temporary

Vor|urteil nt prejudice. **V∼verkauf** m advance booking

vorverlegen vt sep bring forward

Vor|wahl[nummer] f dialling code. **V∼wand** m -[e]s,⁀e pretext; (Ausrede) excuse

vorwärts adv forward[s]; v∼ **kommen** make progress; (fig) get on or ahead

vorwegnehmen† vt sep anticipate

vorweisen† vt sep show

vorwiegend adv predominantly

Vorwort nt (pl -worte) preface

Vorwurf m reproach; **jdm Vorwürfe machen** reproach s.o. **v∼svoll** adj reproachful

Vorzeichen nt sign; (fig) omen

vorzeigen vt sep show

vorzeitig adj premature

vorziehen† vt sep pull forward; draw (Vorhang); (lieber mögen) prefer; favour

Vor|zimmer nt anteroom; (Büro) outer office. **V∼zug** m preference; (gute Eigenschaft) merit, virtue; (Vorteil) advantage

vorzüglich adj excellent

vulgär /vʊlˈgɛːɐ̯/ adj vulgar ● adv in a vulgar way

Vulkan /vʊlˈkaːn/ m -s,-e volcano

••••••••••••••••••••••••••••••

Ww

••••••••••••••••••••••••••••••

Waage f -,-n scales pl; (Astrology) Libra. **w∼recht** adj horizontal

Wabe f -,-n honeycomb

wach adj awake; (aufgeweckt) alert; w∼ **werden** wake up

Wach|e f -,-n guard; (Posten) sentry; (Dienst) guard duty; (Naut) watch; (Polizei-) station; **W∼e halten** keep watch. **W∼hund** m guard-dog

Wacholder m -s juniper

Wachposten m sentry

Wachs nt -es wax

wach|sam adj vigilant. **W∼keit** f - vigilance

wachsen†¹ vi (sein) grow

wachs|en² vt (reg) wax. **W∼figur** f waxwork

Wachstum nt -s growth

Wächter m -s,- guard; (Park-) keeper; (Parkplatz-) attendant

Wacht|meister m [police] constable. **W∼posten** m sentry

wackel|ig adj wobbly; (Stuhl) rickety; (Person) shaky. **W∼kontakt** m loose connection. **w∼n** vi (haben) wobble; (zittern) shake

Wade f -,-n (Anat) calf

Waffe f -,-n weapon; **W∼n** arms

Waffel f -,-n waffle; (Eis-) wafer

Waffen|ruhe f cease-fire. **W∼schein** m firearms licence. **W∼stillstand** m armistice

Wagemut m daring

wagen vt risk; **es w∼, etw zu tun** dare [to] do sth; **sich w∼** (gehen) venture

Wagen m -s,- cart; (Eisenbahn-) carriage, coach; (Güter-) wagon; (Kinder-) pram; (Auto) car. **W∼heber** m -s,- jack

Waggon /vaˈgõː/ m -s,-s wagon

Wahl f -,-en choice; (Pol, Admin) election; (geheime) ballot; **zweite W∼** (Comm) seconds pl

wähl|en vt/i (haben) choose; (Pol, Admin) elect; (stimmen) vote; (Teleph) dial. **W∼er(in)** m -s,- (f -,-nen) voter. **w∼erisch** adj choosy, fussy

Wahl|fach nt optional subject. **w∼frei** adj optional. **W∼kampf** m election campaign. **W∼kreis** m constituency. **W∼lokal** nt polling-station. **w∼los** adj indiscriminate

Wahl|spruch m motto. **W∼urne** f ballot-box

Wahn m -[e]s delusion; (Manie) mania

Wahnsinn m madness. **w∼ig** adj

mad, insane; (🄵: *unsinnig*) crazy; (🄵: *groß*) terrible; **w∼ig werden** go mad ● *adv* 🄵 terribly. **W∼ige(r)** *m/f* maniac

wahr *adj* true; (*echt*) real; **du kommst doch, nicht w∼?** you are coming, aren't you?

während *prep* (+ *gen*) during ● *conj* while; (*wohingegen*) whereas

Wahrheit *f* -,-en truth. **w∼sgemäß** *adj* truthful

wahrnehm|en† *vt sep* notice; (*nutzen*) take advantage of; exploit (*Vorteil*); look after (*Interessen*). **W∼ung** *f* -,-en perception

Wahrsagerin *f* -,-nen fortune teller

wahrscheinlich *adj* probable. **W∼keit** *f* - probability

Währung *f* -,-en currency

Wahrzeichen *nt* symbol

Waise *f* -,-n orphan. **W∼nhaus** *nt* orphanage. **W∼nkind** *nt* orphan

Wal *m* -[e]s,-e whale

Wald *m* -[e]s,⸚er wood; (*groß*) forest. **w∼ig** *adj* wooded

---

Waldorfschule An increasingly popular type of private school originally inspired by the Austrian educationist Rudolf Steiner (1861-1925) in the 1920s. The main aim of Waldorf schools is to develop pupils' creative and cognitive abilities through music, art and crafts.   *i*

Waliser *m* -s,- Welshman

Waliserin *f* -,-nen Welshwoman

walisisch *adj* Welsh

Wall *m* -[e]s,⸚e mound

Wallfahr|er(in) *m(f)* pilgrim. **W∼t** *f* pilgrimage

Walnuss *f* walnut

Walze *f* -,-n roller. **w∼n** *vt* roll

Walzer *m* -s,- waltz

Wand *f* -,⸚e wall; (*Trenn-*) partition; (*Seite*) side; (*Fels-*) face

Wandel *m* -s change

Wander|er *m* -s,-, **W∼in** *f* -,-nen hiker, rambler. **w∼n** *vi* (*sein*) hike,

ramble; (*ziehen*) travel; (*gemächlich gehen*) wander; (*ziellos*) roam. **W∼schaft** *f* - travels *pl*. **W∼ung** *f* -,-en hike, ramble. **W∼weg** *m* footpath

Wandlung *f* -,-en change, transformation

Wand|malerei *f* mural. **W∼tafel** *f* blackboard. **W∼teppich** *m* tapestry

Wange *f* -,-n cheek

wann *adv* when

Wanne *f* -,-n tub

Wanze *f* -,-n bug

Wappen *nt* -s,- coat of arms. **W∼kunde** *f* heraldry

Bundeswappen The federal coat of arms features a heraldic eagle, which was originally the emblem of Roman emperors. It was incorporated into the coat of arms of the German Empire when it was founded in 1871. In 1950 it was revived as the official coat of arms of the Federal Republic of Germany.   *i*

---

war, **wäre** *s.* **sein**[1]

Ware *f* -,-n article; (*Comm*) commodity; (*coll*) merchandise; **W∼n** goods. **W∼nhaus** *nt* department store. **W∼nprobe** *f* sample. **W∼nzeichen** *nt* trademark

warm *adj* warm; (*Mahlzeit*) hot; **w∼ machen** heat ● *adv* warmly; **w∼ essen** have a hot meal

Wärm|e *f* - warmth; (*Phys*) heat; **10 Grad W∼e** 10 degrees above zero. **w∼en** *vt* warm; heat (*Essen, Wasser*). **W∼flasche** *f* hot-water bottle

Warn|blinkanlage *f* hazard [warning] lights *pl*. **w∼en** *vt/i* (*haben*) warn (**vor** + *dat* of). **W∼ung** *f* -,-en warning

Warteliste *f* waiting list

warten *vi* (*haben*) wait (**auf** + *acc* for) ● *vt* service

Wärter(in) *m* -s,- (*f* -,-nen) keeper; (*Museums-*) attendant; (*Gefängnis-*) warder; (*Kranken-*) orderly

W

Warte|raum, W~saal *m*
waiting-room. **W~zimmer** *nt* (*Med*)
waiting-room

Wartung *f* - (*Techn*) service

warum *adv* why

Warze *f* -,-n wart

was *pron* what ● *rel pron* that; **alles,
was ich brauche** all [that] I need
● *indefinite pronoun* (①: *etwas*)
something; (*fragend, verneint*) anything; **so was Ärgerliches!** what a
nuisance! ● *adv* ① (*warum*) why;
(*wie*) how

wasch|bar *adj* washable.
W~becken *nt* wash-basin

Wäsche *f* - washing; (*Unter-*) underwear

waschecht *adj* colour-fast

Wäscheklammer *f* clothes-peg

waschen† *vt* wash; **sich w~** have a
wash; **W~ und Legen** shampoo and
set ● *vi* (*haben*) do the washing

Wäscherei *f* -,-en laundry

Wäsche|schleuder *f* spin-drier.
W~trockner *m* tumble-drier

Wasch|küche *f* laundry-room.
W~lappen *m* face-flannel. **W~ma-
schine** *f* washing machine. **W~mit-
tel** *nt* detergent. **W~pulver** *nt*
washing-powder. **W~salon** *m* laun-
derette. **W~zettel** *m* blurb

Wasser *nt* -s water. **W~ball** *m*
beach-ball; (*Spiel*) water polo.
w~dicht *adj* watertight; (*Kleidung*)
waterproof. **W~fall** *m* waterfall.
W~farbe *f* water-colour. **W~hahn**
m tap. **W~kraft** *f* water-power.
W~kraftwerk *nt* hydroelectric
power-station. **W~leitung** *f* water-
main; **aus der W~leitung** from the
tap. **W~mann** *m* (*Astrology*) Aquar-
ius

wässern *vt* soak; (*begießen*) water
● *vi* (*haben*) water

Wasser|ski *nt* -s water-skiing.
W~stoff *m* hydrogen. **W~straße** *f*
waterway. **W~waage** *f* spirit-level

wässrig *adj* watery

watscheln *vi* (*sein*) waddle

Watt *nt* -s,- (*Phys*) watt

Watt|e *f* - cotton wool. **w~iert** *adj*
padded; (*gesteppt*) quilted

WC /ve:'tse:/ *nt* -s,-s WC

Web|cam *f* -,-s web camera.
W~design *nt* web design

web|en *vt/i* (*haben*) weave. **W~er**
m -s,- weaver

Web|seite /'vep-/ *f* web page.
W~site *f* -, -s website

Wechsel *m* -s,- change; (*Tausch*) exchange; (*Comm*) bill of exchange.
W~geld *nt* change. **w~haft** *adj*
changeable. **W~jahre** *npl* menopause *sg.* **W~kurs** *m* exchange rate.
w~n *vt* change; (*tauschen*) exchange
● *vi* (*haben*) change; vary. **w~nd** *adj*
changing; varying. **W~strom** *m* al-
ternating current. **W~stube** *f* bureau de change

weck|en *vt* wake [up]; (*fig*) awaken
● *vi* (*haben*) (*Wecker:*) go off. **W~er**
m -s,- alarm [clock]

wedeln *vi* (*haben*) wave; **mit dem
Schwanz w~** wag its tail

weder *conj* **w~ ... noch** neither ...
nor

Weg *m* -[e]s,-e way; (*Fuß-*) path;
(*Fahr-*) track; (*Gang*) errand; **sich auf
den Weg machen** set off

weg *adv* away, off; (*verschwunden*)
gone; **weg sein** be away; (*gegangen/
verschwunden*) have gone; **Hände
weg!** hands off!

wegen *prep* (+ *gen*) because of; (*um
... willen*) for the sake of; (*bezüglich*)
about

weg|fahren† *vi sep* (*sein*) go away;
(*abfahren*) leave. **W~fahrsperre** *f*
immobilizer. **w~fallen†** *vi sep* (*sein*)
be dropped/(*ausgelassen*) omitted;
(*entfallen*) no longer apply. **w~ge-
ben†** *vt sep* give away. **w~gehen†** *vi
sep* (*sein*) leave, go away; (*ausgehen*)
go out. **w~kommen†** *vi sep* (*sein*)
get away; (*verloren gehen*) disappear;
schlecht w~kommen ① get a raw
deal. **w~lassen†** *vt sep* let go; (*auslassen*) omit. **w~laufen†** *vi sep* (*sein*)
run away. **w~räumen** *vt sep* put
away; (*entfernen*) clear away.
w~schicken *vt sep* send away; (*ab-*

schicken) send off. **w~tun†** *vt sep*
put away; (*wegwerfen*) throw away

Wegweiser *m* **-s,-** signpost

weg|werfen† *vt sep* throw away.
w~ziehen† *v sep* ● *vt* pull away ● *vi*
(*sein*) move away

weh *adj* sore; **weh tun** hurt; (*Kopf,
Rücken:*) ache; **jdm weh tun** hurt s.o.

wehe *int* alas; **w~** **[dir/euch]!** (*drohend*) don't you dare!

wehen *vi* (*haben*) blow; (*flattern*)
flutter ● *vt* blow

Wehen *fpl* contractions

Wehr[1] *nt* **-[e]s,-e** weir

Wehr[2] *f* **sich zur W~** **setzen** resist.
W~dienst *m* military service.
W~dienstverweigerer *m* **-s,-** con-
scientious objector

wehren (sich) *vr* resist; (*gegen An-
schuldigung*) protest; (*sich sträuben*)
refuse

wehr|los *adj* defenceless.
W~macht *f* armed forces *pl*.
W~pflicht *f* conscription

Weib *nt* **-[e]s,-er** woman; (*Ehe-*) wife.
W~chen *nt* **-s,-** (*Zool*) female.
w~lich *adj* feminine; (*Biology*) female

weich *adj* soft; (*gar*) done

Weiche *f* **-,-n** (*Rail*) points *pl*

Weich|heit *f* **-** softness. **w~lich**
adj soft; (*Charakter*) weak. **W~spü-
ler** *m* **-s,-** (*Textiles*) conditioner.
W~tier *nt* mollusc

Weide[1] *f* **-,-n** (*Bot*) willow

Weide[2] *f* **-,-n** pasture. **w~n** *vt/i*
(*haben*) graze

weiger|n (sich) *vr* refuse. **W~ung**
f **-,-en** refusal

Weihe *f* **-,-n** consecration; (*Priester-*)
ordination. **w~n** *vt* consecrate; (*zum
Priester*) ordain

Weiher *m* **-s,-** pond

Weihnacht|en *nt* **-s** & *pl* Christ-
mas. **w~lich** *adj* Christmassy.
W~sbaum *m* Christmas tree.
W~slied *nt* Christmas carol.
W~smann *m* (*pl* **-männer**) Father
Christmas. **W~stag** *m* **erster/**

zweiter **W~stag** Christmas Day/
Boxing Day

Weihnachtsmarkt During
the weeks of Advent, Christmas markets are held in most German towns. Visitors can buy Christmas decorations, handmade toys
and crib figures, traditional Christmas biscuits, and mulled wine to
sustain them while they shop.

Weih|rauch *m* incense. **W~was-
ser** *nt* holy water

weil *conj* because; (*da*) since

Weile *f* **-** while

Wein *m* **-[e]s,-e** wine; (*Bot*) vines *pl*;
(*Trauben*) grapes *pl*. **W~bau** *m*
winegrowing. **W~berg** *m* vineyard.
W~brand *m* **-[e]s** brandy

weinen *vt/i* (*haben*) cry, weep

Wein|glas *nt* wine glass. **W~karte**
f wine list. **W~lese** *f* grape harvest.
W~liste *f* wine list. **W~probe** *f*
wine tasting. **W~rebe** *f*, **W~stock**
m vine. **W~stube** *f* wine bar.
W~traube *f* bunch of grapes;
(*W~beere*) grape

weise *adj* wise

Weise *f* **-,-n** way; (*Melodie*) tune

Weisheit *f* **-,-en** wisdom.
W~szahn *m* wisdom tooth

weiß *adj*, **W~** *nt* **-,-** white

weissag|en *vt/i insep* (*haben*)
prophesy. **W~ung** *f* **-,-en** prophecy

Weiß|brot *nt* white bread.
W~e(r) *m/f* white man/woman.
w~en *vt* whitewash. **W~wein** *m*
white wine

Weisung *f* **-,-en** instruction; (*Befehl*)
order

weit *adj* wide; (*ausgedehnt*) extensive;
(*lang*) long ● *adv* widely; (*offen, öffnen*) wide; (*lang*) far; **von w~em**
from a distance; **bei w~em** by far;
w~ und breit far and wide; **ist es
noch w~?** is it much further? **so
w~ wie möglich** as far as possible;
ich bin so w~ I'm ready; **w~ verbreitet** widespread; **w~ reichende
Folgen** far-reaching consequences

Weite *f* **-,-n** expanse; (*Entfernung*)

W

distance; (*Größe*) width. **w~n** *vt*
widen; stretch (*Schuhe*)

weiter *adj* further ● *adv* further; (*außerdem*) in addition; (*anschließend*)
then; **etw w~ tun** go on doing sth;
w~ nichts/niemand nothing/no one
else; **und so w~** and so on

weiter|e(r,s) *adj* further; **ohne
w~es** just like that; (*leicht*) easily

weiter|erzählen *vt sep* go on
with; (*w~sagen*) repeat. **w~fahren†**
vi sep (*sein*) go on. **w~geben†** *vt sep*
pass on. **w~hin** *adv* (*immer noch*)
still; (*in Zukunft*) in future; (*außerdem*) furthermore; **etw w~hin tun**
go on doing sth. **w~machen** *vi sep*
(*haben*) carry on

weit|gehend *adj* extensive ● *adv*
to a large extent. **w~sichtig** *adj*
long-sighted; (*fig*) far-sighted.
W~sprung *m* long jump. **w~ver-
breitet** *adj* = **w~ verbreitet**, *s*. **weit**

Weizen *m* **-s** wheat

welch *inv pron* what; **w~ ein(e)**
what a. **w~e(r,s)** *pron* which; **um
w~e Zeit?** at what time? ● *rel pron*
which; (*Person*) who ● *indefinite pronoun* some; (*fragend*) any; **was für
w~e?** what sort of?

Wellblech *nt* corrugated iron

Well|e *f* **-,-n** wave; (*Techn*) shaft.
W~enlänge *f* wavelength. **W~en-
linie** *f* wavy line. **W~enreiten** *nt*
surfing. **W~ensittich** *m* **-s,-e** budg-
erigar. **w~ig** *adj* wavy.

Wellness *f* **-** mental and physical
wellbeing

Welt *f* **-,-en** world; **auf der W~** in
the world; **auf die** *od* **zur W~ kommen** be born. **W~all** *nt* universe.
w~berühmt *adj* world-famous.
w~fremd *adj* unworldly. **W~kugel**
f globe. **w~lich** *adj* worldly; (*nicht
geistlich*) secular

Weltmeister|(in) *m(f)* world
champion. **W~schaft** *f* world championship

Weltraum *m* space. **W~fahrer** *m*
astronaut

Weltrekord *m* world record

wem *pron* (*dat of* **wer**) to whom

wen *pron* (*acc of* **wer**) whom

Wende *f* **-,-n** change. **W~kreis** *m*
(*Geog*) tropic

Wendeltreppe *f* spiral staircase

wenden¹ *vt* (*reg*) turn ● *vi* (*haben*)
turn [round]

wenden²† (& *reg*) *vt* turn; **sich w~**
turn; **sich an jdn w~**
turn/(*schriftlich*) write to s.o.

Wend|epunkt *m* (*fig*) turning-
point. **W~ung** *f* **-,-en** turn; (*Biegung*) bend; (*Veränderung*) change

wenig *pron* little; (*pl*) few; **so/zu
w~** so/too little/(*pl*) few; **w~e** *pl*
few ● *adv* little; (*kaum*) not much; **so
w~ wie möglich** as little as possible. **w~er** *pron* less; (*pl*) fewer;
immer w~er less and less ● *adv* &
conj less. **w~ste(r,s)** least; **am
w~sten** least [of all]. **w~stens** *adv*
at least

wenn *conj* if; (*sobald*) when; **immer
w~** whenever; **w~ nicht** *od* **außer
w~** unless; **w~ auch** even though

wer *pron* who; (🄸: *jemand*) someone; (*fragend*) anyone

Werbe|agentur *f* advertising
agency. **w~n†** *vt* recruit; attract
(*Kunden, Besucher*) ● *vi* (*haben*) **w~n
für** advertise; canvass for (*Partei*).
W~spot *m* **-s,-s** commercial

Werbung *f* **-** advertising

---

werden†

● *intransitive verb* (*sein*)

····➤ (+ *adjective*) become; get; (*allmählich*) grow. **müde/alt/länger
werden** become *or* get/grow
tired/old/longer. **taub/blind/
wahnsinnig werden** go deaf/
blind/mad. **blass werden** become *or* turn pale. **krank
werden** become *or* fall ill. **es
wird warm/dunkel** it is getting
warm/dark. **mir wurde schlecht/
schwindlig** I began to feel sick/
dizzy

····➤ (+ *noun*) become. **Arzt/
Lehrer/Mutter werden** become
a doctor/teacher/mother. **er will**

Lehrer werden he wants to be a teacher. **was ist aus ihm geworden?** what has become of him?

····▶ **werden zu** become; turn into. **das Erlebnis wurde zu einem Albtraum** the experience became or turned into a nightmare. **zu Eis werden** turn into ice

● *auxiliary verb*

····▶ (*Zukunft*) will; shall. **er wird bald hier sein** he will or he'll soon be here. **wir werden sehen** we shall see. **es wird bald regnen** it's going to rain soon

····▶ (*Konjunktiv*) **würde(n)** would. **ich würde es kaufen, wenn ...** I would buy it if .... **würden Sie so nett sein?** would you be so kind?

····▶ (*beim Passiv; pp* **worden**) be. **geliebt/geboren werden** be loved/born. **du wirst gerufen** you are being called. **er wurde gebeten** he was asked. **es wurde gemunkelt** it was rumoured. **mir wurde gesagt, dass ...** I was told that .... **das Haus ist soeben/1995 renoviert worden** the house has just been renovated/was renovated in 1995

werfen† *vt* throw; cast (*Blick, Schatten*); **sich w~** (*Holz:*) warp

Werft *f -,-en* shipyard

Werk *nt -[e]s,-e* work; (*Fabrik*) works *sg*, factory; (*Trieb-*) mechanism. **W~en** *nt -s* (*Sch*) handicraft. **W~statt** *f -,-̈en* workshop; (*Auto-*) garage. **W~tag** *m* weekday. **w~tags** *adv* on weekdays. **w~tätig** *adj* working

Werkzeug *nt* tool; (*coll*) tools *pl*. **W~leiste** *f* toolbar

Wermut *m -s* vermouth

wert *adj* **viel w~** worth a lot; **nichts w~ sein** be worthless; **jds w~ sein** be worthy of s.o. **W~** *m -[e]s,-e* value; (*Nenn-*) denomination; **im W~ von** worth. **w~en** *vt* rate

Wert|gegenstand *m* object of value. **w~los** *adj* worthless.

W~minderung *f* depreciation. **W~papier** *nt* (*Comm*) security. **W~sachen** *fpl* valuables. **w~voll** *adj* valuable

Wesen *nt -s,-* nature; (*Lebe-*) being; (*Mensch*) creature

wesentlich *adj* essential; (*grundlegend*) fundamental ● *adv* considerably, much

weshalb *adv* why

Wespe *f -,-n* wasp

wessen *pron* (*gen of* **wer**) whose

westdeutsch *adj* West German

Weste *f -,-n* waistcoat

Westen *m -s* west

Western *m -[s],-* western

Westfalen *nt -s* Westphalia

Westindien *nt* West Indies *pl*

west|lich *adj* western; (*Richtung*) westerly ● *adv & prep* (+ *gen*) **w~lich [von] der Stadt** [to the] west of the town. **w~wärts** *adv* westwards

weswegen *adv* why

Wettbewerb *m -s,-e* competition

Wette *f -,-n* bet; **um die W~ laufen** race (**mit jdm** s.o.)

wetten *vt/i* (*haben*) bet (**auf** + *acc* on); **mit jdm w~** have a bet with s.o.

Wetter *nt -s,-* weather; (*Un-*) storm. **W~bericht** *m* weather report. **W~vorhersage** *f* weather forecast. **W~warte** *f -,-n* meteorological station

Wett|kampf *m* contest. **W~kämpfer(in)** *m(f)* competitor. **W~lauf** *m* race. **W~rennen** *nt* race. **W~streit** *m* contest

Whisky *m -s* whisky

wichtig *adj* important; **w~ nehmen** take seriously. **W~keit** *f -* importance

Wicke *f -,-n* sweet pea

Wickel *m -s,-* compress

wickeln *vt* wind; (*ein-*) wrap; (*bandagieren*) bandage; **ein Kind frisch w~** change a baby

Widder *m -s,-* ram; (*Astrology*) Aries

wider *prep* (+ *acc*) against; (*entge-*

w

gen) contrary to; **w~ Willen** against one's will

widerlegen *vt insep* refute

wider|lich *adj* repulsive. **W~rede** *f* contradiction; **keine W~rede!** don't argue!

widerrufen† *vt/i insep (haben)* retract; revoke *(Befehl)*

Widersacher *m* -s,- adversary

widersetzen (sich) *vr insep* resist **(jdm/etw** s.o./sth)

widerspiegeln *vt sep* reflect

widersprechen† *vi insep (haben)* contradict **(jdm/etw** s.o./something)

Wider|spruch *m* contradiction; *(Protest)* protest. **w~sprüchlich** *adj* contradictory. **w~spruchslos** *adv* without protest

Widerstand *m* resistance; **W~ leisten** resist. **w~sfähig** *adj* resistant; *(Bot)* hardy

widerstehen† *vi insep (haben)* resist **(jdm/etw** s.o./sth); *(anwidern)* be repugnant **(jdm** to s.o.)

Widerstreben *nt* -s reluctance

widerwärtig *adj* disagreeable

Widerwill|e *m* aversion, repugnance. **w~ig** *adj* reluctant

widm|en *vt* dedicate *(dat* to); *(verwenden)* devote *(dat* to); **sich w~en** *(+ dat)* devote oneself to. **W~ung** *f* -,-en dedication

wie *adv* how; **wie viel** how much/*(pl)* many; **um wie viel Uhr?** at what time? **wie viele?** how many? **wie ist Ihr Name?** what is your name? **wie ist das Wetter?** what is the weather like? ● *conj* as; *(gleich wie)* like; *(sowie)* as well as; *(als)* when, as; **so gut wie** as good as; **nichts wie** nothing but

wieder *adv* again; **jdn/etw w~ erkennen** recognize s.o./something; **etw w~ verwenden/verwerten** reuse/recycle sth; **etw w~ gutmachen** make up for *(Schaden)*; redress *(Unrecht)*; *(bezahlen)* pay for sth

Wiederaufbau *m* reconstruction

wieder|bekommen† *vt sep* get back. **W~belebung** *f* - resuscita-

tion. **w~bringen**† *vt sep* bring back. **w~erkennen**† *vt sep* * **w~ erkennen,** *s.* wieder. **w~geben**† *vt sep* give back, return; *(darstellen)* portray; *(ausdrücken, übersetzen)* render; *(zitieren)* quote. **W~geburt** *f* reincarnation

Wiedergutmachung *f* - reparation; *(Entschädigung)* compensation

wiederherstellen *vt sep* re-establish; restore *(Gebäude)*; restore to health *(Kranke)*

wiederhol|en *vt insep* repeat; *(Sch)* revise; **sich w~en** recur; *(Person:)* repeat oneself. **w~t** *adj* repeated. **W~ung** *f* -,-en repetition; *(Sch)* revision

Wieder|hören *nt* **auf W~hören!** goodbye! **W~käuer** *m* -s,- ruminant. **W~kehr** *f* - return; *(W~holung)* recurrence. **w~kommen**† *vi sep (sein)* come back

wiedersehen * *vt sep* **wieder sehen,** *s.* sehen. **W~** *nt* -s,- reunion; **auf W~!** goodbye!

wiedervereinig|en * *vt sep* **wieder vereinigen,** *s.* vereinigen. **W~ung** *f* reunification

---

Wiedervereinigung The re-unification of Germany officially took place on 3 October 1990, when the former German Democratic Republic (East Germany) was incorporated into the Federal Republic. It followed the collapse of Communism in 1989 and the fall of *die Mauer* (the Berlin Wall).

---

wieder|verwenden† *vt sep* * **w~ verwenden,** *s.* wieder. **w~verwerten** * *vt sep* **w~ verwerten,** *s.* wieder

Wiege *f* -,-n cradle

wiegen¹† *vt/i (haben)* weigh

wiegen² *vt (reg)* rock. **W~lied** *nt* lullaby

wiehern *vi (haben)* neigh

Wien *nt* -s Vienna. **W~er** *adj* Viennese ● *m* -s,- Viennese ● *f* -,- ≈ frankfurter. **w~erisch** *adj* Viennese

Wiese f -,-n meadow
Wiesel nt -s,- weasel
wieso adv why
wieviel* pron wie viel, s. wie.
  w~te(r,s) adj which; **der W~te ist
  heute?** what is the date today?
wieweit adv how far
wild adj wild; (Stamm) savage; **w~er
  Streik** wildcat strike; **w~ wachsen**
  grow wild. **W~** nt -[e]s game; (Rot-)
  deer; (Culin) venison. **W~e(r)** m/f
  savage
Wilder|er m -s,- poacher. **w~n** vt/i
  (haben) poach
Wild|heger, W~hüter m -s,-
  gamekeeper. **W~leder** nt suede.
  W~nis f - wilderness. **W~schwein**
  nt wild boar. **W~westfilm** m western
Wille m -ns will
Willenskraft f will-power
willig adj willing
willkommen adj welcome; **w~
  heißen** welcome. **W~** nt -s welcome
wimmeln vi (haben) swarm
wimmern vi (haben) whimper
Wimpel m -s,- pennant
Wimper f -,-n [eye]lash;
  W~ntusche f mascara
Wind m -[e]s,-e wind
Winde f -,-n (Techn) winch
Windel f -,-n nappy
winden† vt wind; make (Kranz); **in
  die Höhe w~** winch up; **sich w~**
  wind (**um** round); (sich krümmen)
  writhe
Wind|hund m greyhound. **w~ig**
  adj windy. **W~mühle** f windmill.
  W~park m wind farm. **W~pocken**
  fpl chickenpox sg. **W~schutz-
  scheibe** f windscreen. **W~stille** f
  calm. **W~stoß** m gust of wind.
  W~surfen nt windsurfing
Windung f -,-en bend; (Spirale)
  spiral
Winkel m -s,- angle; (Ecke) corner.
  W~messer m -s,- protractor
winken vi (haben) wave
Winter m -s,- winter. **w~lich** adj

wintry; (Winter-) winter **W~schlaf** m
hibernation; **W~sport** m winter
sports pl
Winzer m -s,- winegrower
winzig adj tiny, minute
Wipfel m -s,- [tree-]top
Wippe f -,-n see-saw
wir pron we; **wir sind es** it's us
Wirbel m -s,- eddy; (Drehung) whirl;
  (Trommel-) roll; (Anat) vertebra;
  (Haar-) crown; (Aufsehen) fuss. **w~n**
  vt/i (sein/haben) whirl. **W~säule** f
  spine. **W~sturm** m cyclone.
  W~tier nt vertebrate. **W~wind** m
  whirlwind
wird s. werden
wirken vi (haben) have an effect
  (**auf** + acc on); (zur Geltung kommen)
  be effective; (tätig sein) work; (scheinen) seem ● vt (Textiles) knit
wirklich adj real. **W~keit** f -,-en
  reality
wirksam adj effective
Wirkung f -,-en effect. **w~slos** adj
  ineffective. **w~svoll** adj effective
wirr adj tangled; (Haar) tousled; (ver-
  wirrt, verworren) confused
Wirt m -[e]s,-e landlord. **W~in** f
  -,-nen landlady
Wirtschaft f -,-en economy; (Gast-)
  restaurant; (Kneipe) pub. **w~en** vi
  (haben) manage one's finances.
  w~lich adj economic; (sparsam)
  economical. **W~sflüchtling** m economic refugee. **W~sgeld** nt house-
  keeping [money]. **W~sprüfer** m
  auditor
Wirtshaus nt inn; (Kneipe) pub
wischen vt/i (haben) wipe; wash
  (Fußboden)
wissen† vt/i (haben) know; **weißt du
  noch?** do you remember? **nichts
  w~ wollen von** not want anything
  to do with. **W~** nt -s knowledge;
  meines W~s to my knowledge
Wissenschaft f -,-en science.
  W~ler m -s,- academic; (Natur-) scientist. **w~lich** adj academic; scien-
  tific
wissenswert adj worth knowing

w

witter|n *vt* scent; (*ahnen*) sense.
W~ung *f* - scent; (*Wetter*) weather

Witwe *f* -,-n widow. **W~r** *m* -s,-
widower

Witz *m* -es,-e joke; (*Geist*) wit.
W~bold *m* -[e]s,-e joker. **w~ig** *adj*
funny; witty

wo *adv* where; (*als*) when; (*irgendwo*)
somewhere; **wo immer** wherever
● *conj* seeing that; (*obwohl*) although; (*wenn*) if

woanders *adv* somewhere else

wobei *adv* how; (*relativ*) during the
course of which

Woche *f* -,-n week. **W~nende** *nt*
weekend. **W~nkarte** *f* weekly
ticket. **w~nlang** *adv* for weeks.
W~ntag *m* day of the week; (*Werk-
tag*) weekday. **w~tags** *adv* on weekdays

wöchentlich *adj* & *adv* weekly

Wodka *m* -s vodka

wofür *adv* what ... for; (*relativ*) for
which

Woge *f* -,-n wave

woher *adv* where from; **woher
weißt du das?** how do you know
that? **wohin** *adv* where [to]; **wohin
gehst du?** where are you going?

wohl *adv* well; (*vermutlich*) probably;
(*etwa*) about; (*zwar*) perhaps; **w~
kaum** hardly; **sich w~ fühlen** feel
well/(*behaglich*) comfortable; **jdm
w~ tun** do s.o. good. **W~** *nt* -[e]s
welfare, well-being; **zum W~** (+ *gen*)
for the good of; **zum W~!** cheers!

Wohl|befinden *nt* well-being.
W~behagen *nt* feeling of well-
being. **W~ergehen** *nt* -s welfare.
w~erzogen *adj* well brought-up

Wohlfahrt *f* - welfare. **W~sstaat**
m Welfare State

wohl|habend *adj* prosperous, well-
to-do. **w~ig** *adj* comfortable.
w~schmeckend *adj* tasty

Wohlstand *m* prosperity.
W~sgesellschaft *f* affluent society

Wohltat *f* [act of] kindness; (*An-
nehmlichkeit*) treat; (*Genuss*) bliss

Wohltät|er *m* benefactor. **w~ig**
adj charitable

wohl|tuend *adj* agreeable.
w~tun* *vi sep* (*haben*) **w~ tun**, *s.*
wohl

Wohlwollen *nt* -s goodwill;
(*Gunst*) favour. **w~d** *adj* benevolent

Wohn|block *m* block of flats.
w~en *vi* (*haben*) live; (*vorübergehend*) stay. **W~gegend** *f* residential
area. **w~haft** *adj* resident.
W~haus *nt* house. **W~heim** *nt*
hostel; (*Alten-*) home. **w~lich** *adj*
comfortable. **W~mobil** *nt* -s,-e
camper. **W~ort** *m* place of residence. **W~sitz** *m* place of residence

Wohnung *f* -,-en flat; (*Unterkunft*)
accommodation. **W~snot** *f* housing
shortage

Wohn|wagen *m* caravan.
W~zimmer *nt* living-room

wölb|en *vt* curve; arch (*Rücken*).
W~ung *f* -,-en curve; (*Architecture*)
vault

Wolf *m* -[e]s, ̈e wolf; (*Fleisch-*) mincer; (*Reiß-*) shredder

Wolk|e *f* -,-n cloud. **W~enbruch** *m*
cloudburst. **W~enkratzer** *m* sky-
scraper. **w~enlos** *adj* cloudless.
w~ig *adj* cloudy

Woll|decke *f* blanket. **W~e** *f* -,-n
wool

wollen†1

● *auxiliary verb*
····▸ (*den Wunsch haben*) want to.
ich will nach Hause gehen I
want to go home. **ich wollte Sie
fragen, ob ...** I wanted to ask
you if ...
····▸ (*im Begriff sein*) be about to.
wir wollten gerade gehen we
were just about to go
····▸ (*sich in der gewünschten Weise
verhalten*) **will nicht** refuses to.
**der Motor will nicht ansprin-
gen** the engine won't start
● *intransitive verb*
····▸ want to. **ob du willst oder
nicht** whether you want to or
not. **ganz wie du willst** just as

you like

····➤ (🔲: *irgendwohin zu gehen wünschen*) **ich will nach Hause** I want to go home. **zu wem wollen Sie?** who[m] do you want to see?

····➤ (🔲: *funktionieren*) **will nicht** won't go. **meine Beine wollen nicht mehr** my legs are giving up 🔲

● *transitive verb*

····➤ want; (*beabsichtigen*) intend. **er will nicht, dass du ihm hilfst** he does not want you to help him. **das habe ich nicht gewollt** I never intended *or* meant that to happen

Wollsachen *fpl* woollens

womit *adv* what ... with; (*relativ*) with which. **wonach** *adv* what ... after/(*suchen*) for/(*riechen*) of; (*relativ*) after/for/of which

woran *adv* what ... on/(*denken, sterben*) of; (*relativ*) on/of which; **woran hast du ihn erkannt?** how did you recognize him? **worauf** *adv* what on .../(*warten*) for; (*relativ*) on/for which; (*woraufhin*) whereupon. **woraus** *adv* what ... from; (*relativ*) from which

Wort *nt* -[e]s,¨er & -e word; **jdm ins W~ fallen** interrupt s.o.

Wörterbuch *nt* dictionary

Wort|führer *m* spokesman. **w~getreu** *adj & adv* word-for-word. **w~karg** *adj* taciturn. **W~laut** *m* wording

wörtlich *adj* literal; (*wortgetreu*) word-for-word

wort|los *adj* silent ● *adv* without a word. **W~schatz** *m* vocabulary. **W~spiel** *nt* pun, play on words

worüber *adv* what ... over/(*lachen, sprechen*) about; (*relativ*) over/about which. **worum** *adv* what ... round/(*bitten, kämpfen*) for; (*relativ*) round/for which; **worum geht es?** what is it about? **wovon** *adv* what ... from/(*sprechen*) about; (*relativ*) from/about which. **wovor** *adv* what ... in front of; (*sich fürchten*) what of; (*rela-*

tiv) in front of which; of which.

wozu *adv* what ... to/(*brauchen, benutzen*) for; (*relativ*) to/for which; **wozu?** what for?

Wrack *nt* -s,-s wreck

wringen† *vt* wring

Wucher|preis *m* extortionate price. **W~ung** *f* -,-en growth

Wuchs *m* -es growth; (*Gestalt*) stature

Wucht *f* - force

wühlen *vi* (*haben*) rummage; (*in der Erde*) burrow ● *vt* dig

Wulst *m* -[e]s,¨e bulge; (*Fett-*) roll

wund *adj* sore; **w~ reiben** chafe; **sich w~ liegen** get bedsores. **W~brand** *m* gangrene

Wunde *f* -,-n wound

Wunder *nt* -s,- wonder, marvel; (*übernatürliches*) miracle; **kein W~!** no wonder! **w~bar** *adj* miraculous; (*herrlich*) wonderful. **W~kind** *nt* infant prodigy. **w~n** *vt* surprise; **sich w~n** be surprised (**über** + *acc* at). **w~schön** *adj* beautiful

Wundstarrkrampf *m* tetanus

Wunsch *m* -[e]s,¨e wish; (*Verlangen*) desire; (*Bitte*) request

wünschen *vt* want; **sich** (*dat*) **etw w~** want sth; (*bitten um*) ask for sth; **jdm Glück/gute Nacht w~** wish s.o. luck/good night; **Sie w~?** can I help you? **w~swert** *adj* desirable

Wunschkonzert *nt* musical request programme

wurde, würde *s.* werden

Würde *f* -,-n dignity; (*Ehrenrang*) honour. **w~los** *adj* undignified. **W~nträger** *m* dignitary. **w~voll** *adj* dignified ● *adv* with dignity

würdig *adj* dignified; (*wert*) worthy

Wurf *m* -[e]s,¨e throw; (*Junge*) litter

Würfel *m* -s,- cube; (*Spiel-*) dice; (*Zucker-*) lump. **w~n** *vi* (*haben*) throw the dice; **w~n um** play dice for ● *vt* throw; (*in Würfel schneiden*) dice. **W~zucker** *m* cube sugar

würgen *vt* choke ● *vi* (*haben*) retch; choke (**an** + *dat* on)

Wurm *m* -[e]s,¨er worm; (*Made*)

W

maggot. **w~en** vi (haben) **jdn
w~en** 🔲 rankle [with s.o.]

Wurst f -,⸚e sausage; **das ist mir
W~** 🔲 I couldn't care less

Würze f -,-n spice; (Aroma) aroma

Wurzel f -,-n root; **W~n schlagen**
take root. **w~n** vi (haben) root

würz|en vt season. **w~ig** adj tasty;
(aromatisch) aromatic; (pikant) spicy

wüst adj chaotic; (wirr) tangled; (öde)
desolate; (wild) wild; (schlimm) terrible

Wüste f -,-n desert

Wut f - rage, fury. **W~anfall** m fit
of rage

wüten vi (haben) rage. **w~d** adj
furious; **w~d machen** infuriate

Xx

x /ɪks/ inv adj (Math) x; 🔲 umpteen.
X-Beine ntpl knock-knees. **x-beinig,
X-beinig** adj knock-kneed.
x-beliebig adj 🔲 any. **x-mal** adv 🔲
umpteen times

Yy

Yoga /ˈjoːɡa/ m & nt -[s] yoga

Zz

Zack|e f -,-n point; (Berg-) peak;
(Gabel-) prong. **z~ig** adj jagged; (gezackt) serrated

zaghaft adj timid; (zögernd) tentative

zäh adj tough; (hartnäckig) tenacious.
z~flüssig adj viscous; (Verkehr) slow-
moving. **Z~igkeit** f - toughness;
tenacity

Zahl f -,-en number; (Ziffer, Betrag)
figure

zahlen vt/i (haben) pay; (bezahlen)
pay for; **bitte z~!** the bill please!

zählen vi (haben) count; **z~ zu** (fig)
be one/(pl) some of ● vt count; **z~
zu** add to; (fig) count among

zahlenmäßig adj numerical

Zähler m -s,- meter

Zahl|grenze f fare-stage. **Z~karte**
f paying-in slip. **z~los** adj countless.
z~reich adj numerous; (Anzahl,
Gruppe) large ● adv in large numbers. **Z~ung** f -,-en payment; **in
Z~ung nehmen** take in part-
exchange

Zählung f -,-en count

Zahlwort nt (pl -wörter) numeral

zahm adj tame

zähmen vt tame; (fig) restrain

Zahn m -[e]s,⸚e tooth; (am Zahnrad)
cog. **Z~arzt** m, **Z~ärztin** f dentist.
Z~belag m plaque. **Z~bürste** f
toothbrush. **Z~fleisch** nt gums pl.
z~los adj toothless. **Z~pasta** f
-,-en toothpaste. **Z~rad** nt cog-
wheel. **Z~schmelz** m enamel.
Z~schmerzen mpl toothache sg.
Z~spange f brace. **Z~stein** m tartar. **Z~stocher** m -s,- toothpick

Zange f -,-n pliers pl; (Kneif-) pincers
pl; (Kohlen-, Zucker-) tongs pl;
(Geburts-) forceps pl

Zank m -[e]s squabble. **z~en** vr sich
z~en squabble

Zäpfchen nt -s,- (Anat) uvula; (Med)
suppository

zapfen vt tap, draw. **Z~streich** m
(Mil) tattoo

Zapf|hahn m tap. **Z~säule** f
petrol-pump

zappeln vi (haben) wriggle; (Kind:)
fidget

zart adj delicate; (weich, zärtlich) tender; (sanft) gentle. **Z~gefühl** nt tact

zärtlich adj tender; (liebevoll) loving.

w
x
y
z

Z~keit f -,-en tenderness; (*Liebko-sung*) caress

Zauber m -s magic; (*Bann*) spell. **Z~er** m -s,- magician. **z~haft** adj enchanting. **Z~künstler** m conjuror. **z~n** vi (*haben*) do magic; (*Zauber-tricks ausführen*) do conjuring tricks ● vt produce as if by magic. **Z~stab** m magic wand. **Z~trick** m conjuring trick

Zaum m -[e]s,Zäume bridle

Zaun m -[e]s,Zäune fence

z.B. abbr (**zum Beispiel**) e.g.

Zebra nt -s,-s zebra. **Z~streifen** m zebra crossing

Zeche f -,-n bill; (*Bergwerk*) pit

zechen vi (*haben*) 🗉 drink

Zeder f -,-n cedar

Zeh m -[e]s,-en toe. **Z~e** f -,-n toe; (*Knoblauch-*) clove

zehn inv adj, **Z~** f -,-en ten. **z~te(r,s)** adj tenth. **Z~tel** nt -s,- tenth

Zeichen nt -s,- sign; (*Signal*) signal. **Z~setzung** f - punctuation. **Z~trickfilm** m cartoon

zeichn|en vt/i (*haben*) draw; (*kenn-*) mark; (*unter-*) sign. **Z~ung** f -,-en drawing

Zeige|finger m index finger. **z~n** vt show; **sich z~n** appear; (*sich her-ausstellen*) become clear ● vi (*haben*) point (**auf** + acc to). **Z~r** m -s,- pointer; (*Uhr-*) hand

Zeile f -,-n line; (*Reihe*) row

Zeit f -,-en time; **sich** (*dat*) **Z~ las-sen** take one's time; **es hat Z~** theres's no hurry; **mit der Z~** in time; **in nächster Z~** in the near fu-ture; **zur Z~** (*rechtzeitig*) in time; *(derzeit*) s. **zurzeit**; **eine Z~ lang** for a time or while

Zeit|alter nt age, era. **z~gemäß** adj modern, up-to-date. **Z~genosse** m, **Z~genossin** f contemporary. **z~genössisch** adj contemporary. **z~ig** adj & adv early

zeitlich adj (*Dauer*) in time; (*Folge*) chronological. ● adv **z~ begrenzt** for a limited time

zeit|los adj timeless. **Z~lupe** f slow motion. **Z~punkt** m time. **z~rau-bend** adj time-consuming. **Z~raum** m period. **Z~schrift** f magazine, periodical

Zeitung f -,-en newspaper. **Z~spapier** nt newspaper

Zeit|verschwendung f waste of time. **Z~vertreib** m pastime. **z~weise** adv at times. **Z~wort** nt (pl -wörter) verb. **Z~zünder** m time fuse

Zelle f -,-n cell; (*Telefon-*) box

Zelt nt -[e]s,-e tent; (*Fest-*) marquee. **z~en** vi (*haben*) camp. **Z~en** nt -s camping. **Z~plane** f tarpaulin. **Z~platz** m campsite

Zement m -[e]s cement

zen|sieren vt (*Sch*) mark; censor (*Presse, Film*). **Z~sur** f -,-en (*Sch*) mark; (*Presse-*) censorship

Zentimeter m & nt centimetre. **Z~maß** nt tape-measure

Zentner m -s,- [metric] hundred-weight (*50 kg*)

zentral adj central. **Z~e** f -,-n cen-tral office; (*Partei-*) headquarters pl; (*Teleph*) exchange. **Z~heizung** f cen-tral heating

Zentrum nt -s,-tren centre

zerbrech|en† vt/i (*sein*) break. **z~lich** adj fragile

zerdrücken vt crush

Zeremonie f -,-n ceremony

Zerfall m disintegration; (*Verfall*) decay. **z~en†** vi (*sein*) disintegrate; (*verfallen*) decay

zergehen† vi (*sein*) melt; (*sich auflö-sen*) dissolve

zerkleinern vt chop/(*schneiden*) cut up; (*mahlen*) grind

zerknüllen vt crumple [up]

zerkratzen vt scratch

zerlassen† vt melt

zerlegen vt take to pieces, disman-tle; (*zerschneiden*) cut up; (*tranchie-ren*) carve

zerlumpt adj ragged

zermalmen vt crush

zermürben vt (*fig*) wear down

z

zerplatzen vi (sein) burst

zerquetschen vt squash; crush

Zerrbild nt caricature

zerreißen† vt tear; (in Stücke) tear up; break (Faden, Seil) ● vi (sein) tear; break

zerren vt drag; pull (Muskel) ● vi (haben) pull (an + dat at)

zerrissen adj torn

zerrütten vt ruin, wreck; shatter (Nerven)

zerschlagen† vt smash; smash up (Möbel); **sich z~** (fig) fall through; (Hoffnung:) be dashed

zerschmettern vt/i (sein) smash

zerschneiden† vt cut; (in Stücke) cut up

zersplittern vi (sein) splinter; (Glas:) shatter ● vt shatter

zerspringen† vi (sein) shatter; (bersten) burst

Zerstäuber m -s,- atomizer

zerstör|en vt destroy; (zunichte machen) wreck. **Z~er** m -s,- destroyer. **Z~ung** f destruction

zerstreu|en vt scatter; disperse (Menge); dispel (Zweifel); **sich z~en** disperse; (sich unterhalten) amuse oneself. **z~t** adj absent-minded

Zertifikat nt -[e]s,-e certificate

zertrümmern vt smash [up]; wreck (Gebäude, Stadt)

Zettel m -s,- piece of paper; (Notiz) note; (Bekanntmachung) notice

Zeug nt -s 🗊 stuff; (Sachen) things pl; (Ausrüstung) gear; **dummes Z~** nonsense

Zeuge m -n,-n witness. **z~n** vi (haben) testify; **z~n von** (fig) show ● vt father. **Z~naussage** f testimony. **Z~nstand** m witness box

Zeugin f -,-nen witness

Zeugnis nt -ses,-se certificate; (Sch) report; (Referenz) reference; (fig: Beweis) evidence

Zickzack m -[e]s,-e zigzag

Ziege f -,-n goat

Ziegel m -s,- brick; (Dach-) tile. **Z~stein** m brick

ziehen† vt pull; (sanfter; zücken; zeichnen) draw; (heraus-) pull out; extract (Zahn); raise (Hut); put on (Bremse); move (Schachfigur); (dehnen) stretch; make (Grimasse, Scheitel); (züchten) breed; grow (Rosen); **nach sich z~** (fig) entail ● vr **sich z~** (sich erstrecken) run; (sich verziehen) warp ● vi (haben) pull (an + dat on/at); (Tee, Ofen:) draw; (Culin) simmer; **es zieht** there is a draught; **solche Filme z~ nicht mehr** films like that are no longer popular ● vi (sein) (um-) move (nach to); (Menge:) march; (Vögel:) migrate; (Wolken, Nebel:) drift

Ziehharmonika f accordion

Ziehung f -,-en draw

Ziel nt -[e]s,-e destination; (Sport) finish; (Z~scheibe & Mil) target; (Zweck) aim, goal. **z~bewusst** adj purposeful. **z~en** vi (haben) aim (auf + acc at). **z~los** adj aimless. **Z~scheibe** f target

ziemlich adj 🗊 fair ● adv rather, fairly

Zier|de f -,-n ornament. **z~en** vt adorn

zierlich adj dainty

Ziffer f -,-n figure, digit; (Zahlzeichen) numeral. **Z~blatt** nt dial

Zigarette f -,-n cigarette

Zigarre f -,-n cigar

Zigeuner(in) m -s,- (f -,-nen) gypsy

Zimmer nt -s,- room. **Z~mädchen** nt chambermaid. **Z~mann** m (pl -leute) carpenter. **Z~nachweis** m accommodation bureau. **Z~pflanze** f house plant

Zimt m -[e]s cinnamon

Zink nt -s zinc

Zinn m -s tin; (Gefäße) pewter

Zins|en mpl interest sg; **Z~en tragen** earn interest. **Z~eszins** m -es,-en compound interest. **Z~fuß, Z~satz** m interest rate

Zipfel m -s,- corner; (Spitze) point

zirka adv about

z

Zirkel m -s,- [pair of] compasses pl;
(Gruppe) circle

Zirkul|ation /-'tsi̯o:n/ f - circulation.
z~ieren vi (sein) circulate

Zirkus m -,-se circus

zirpen vi (haben) chirp

zischen vi (haben) hiss; (Fett:) sizzle
● vt hiss

Zit|at nt -[e]s,-e quotation. z~ieren
vt/i (haben) quote

Zitr|onat nt -[e]s candied lemon-
peel. Z~one f -,-n lemon

zittern vi (haben) tremble; (vor Kälte)
shiver; (beben) shake

zittrig adj shaky

Zitze f -,-n teat

zivil adj civilian; (Ehe, Recht) civil. Z~
nt -s civilian clothes pl. Z~dienst m
community service

Zivili|sation /-'tsi̯o:n/ f -,-en civil-
ization. z~sieren vt civilize. z~siert
adj civilized ● adv in a civilized manner

Zivilist m -en,-en civilian

zögern vi (haben) hesitate. Z~ nt -s
hesitation. z~d adj hesitant

Zoll¹ m -[e]s,- inch

Zoll² m -[e]s,ˇe [customs] duty; (Behörde) customs pl. Z~abfertigung f
customs clearance. Z~beamte(r) m
customs officer. z~frei adj & adv
duty-free. Z~kontrolle f customs
check

Zone f -,-n zone

Zoo m -s,-s zoo

zoologisch adj zoological

Zopf m -[e]s,ˇe plait

Zorn m -[e]s anger. z~ig adj angry

---

zu

● preposition (+ dative)

> **!** Note that **zu dem** can be-
> come **zum** and **zu der, zur**

····▸ (Richtung) to; (bei Beruf) into.
wir gehen zur Schule we are
going to school. **ich muss zum
Arzt** I must go to the doctor's.
zu ... hin towards. **er geht zum**

Theater/Militär he is going into
the theatre/army

····▸ (zusammen mit) with. **zu dem
Käse gab es Wein** there was
wine with the cheese. **zu etw
passen** go with sth

····▸ (räumlich; zeitlich) at. **zu
Hause** at home. **zu ihren Füßen**
at her feet. **zu Ostern** at Easter.
zur Zeit (+ gen) at the time of

····▸ (preislich) at; for. **zum halben
Preis** at half price. **das Stück zu
zwei Euro** at or for two euros
each. **eine Marke zu 60 Cent** a
60-cent stamp

····▸ (Zweck, Anlass) for. **zu diesem
Zweck** for this purpose. **zum
Spaß** for fun. **zum Lesen** for
reading. **zum Geburtstag bekam
ich** ... for my birthday I got ... .
zum ersten Mal for the first
time

····▸ (Art und Weise) **zu meinem
Erstaunen/Entsetzen** to my sur-
prise/horror. **zu Fuß/Pferde** on
foot/horseback. **zu Dutzenden**
by the dozen. **wir waren zu
dritt/viert** there were three/four
of us

····▸ (Zahlenverhältnis) to. **es steht
5 zu 3** the score is 5–3

····▸ (Ziel, Ergebnis) into. **zu etw
werden** turn into sth

····▸ (gegenüber) to; towards.
freundlich/hässlich zu jdm sein
be friendly/nasty to s.o.

····▸ (über) on; about. **sich zu etw
äußern** to comment on sth

● adverb

····▸ (allzu) too. **zu groß/viel/weit**
too big/much/far

····▸ (Richtung) towards. **nach dem
Fluss zu** towards the river

····▸ (geschlossen) closed; (an Schalter, Hahn) off. **Augen zu!** close
your eyes! **Tür zu!** shut the door!

● conjunction

····▸ to. **etwas zu essen** something to eat. **nicht zu glauben**
unbelievable. **zu erörternde Probleme** problems to be discussed

zualler|erst *adv* first of all. **z~letzt**
adv last of all

Zubehör *nt* -s accessories *pl*

zubereit|en *vt sep* prepare. **Z~ung**
f - preparation; (*in Rezept*) method

zubinden† *vt sep* tie [up]

zubring|en† *vt sep* spend. **Z~er** *m*
-s,- access road; (*Bus*) shuttle

Zucchini /tsuˈkiːni/ *pl* courgettes

Zucht *f* -,-en breeding; (*Pflanzen-*)
cultivation; (*Art, Rasse*) breed; (*von
Pflanzen*) strain; (*Z~farm*) farm;
(*Pferde-*) stud

zücht|en *vt* breed; cultivate, grow
(*Rosen*). **Z~er** *m* -s,- breeder; grower

Zuchthaus *nt* prison

Züchtung *f* -,-en breeding;
(*Pflanzen-*) cultivation; (*Art, Rasse*)
breed; (*von Pflanzen*) strain

zucken *vi* (*haben*) twitch; (*sich z~d
bewegen*) jerk; (*Blitz:*) flash; (*Flamme:*)
flicker ● *vt* **die Achseln z~** shrug
one's shoulders

Zucker *m* -s sugar. **Z~dose** *f* sugar
basin. **Z~guss** *m* icing. **z~krank** *adj*
diabetic. **Z~krankheit** *f* diabetes.
z~n *vt* sugar. **Z~rohr** *nt* sugar
cane. **Z~rübe** *f* sugar beet.
Z~watte *f* candyfloss

zudecken *vt sep* cover up; (*im Bett*)
tuck up; cover (*Topf*)

zudem *adv* moreover

zudrehen *vt sep* turn off

zueinander *adv* to one another;
z~ passen go together; **z~ halten**
(*fig*) stick together

zuerkennen† *vt sep* award (*dat* to)

zuerst *adv* first; (*anfangs*) at first

zufahr|en† *vi sep* (*sein*) **z~en auf** (+
acc) drive towards. **Z~t** *f* access;
(*Einfahrt*) drive

Zufall *m* chance; (*Zusammentreffen*)
coincidence; **durch Z~** by chance/
coincidence. **z~en**† *vi sep* (*sein*)
close, shut; **jdm z~en** (*Aufgabe:*)
fall/(*Erbe:*) go to s.o.

zufällig *adj* chance, accidental ● *adv*
by chance

Zuflucht *f* refuge; (*Schutz*) shelter

zufolge *prep* (+ *dat*) according to

zufrieden *adj* contented; (*befriedigt*)
satisfied; **sich z~ geben** be satisfied;
jdn z~ lassen leave s.o. in peace;
jdn z~ stellen satisfy s.o.; **z~ stellend** satisfactory. **Z~helt** *f* - contentment; satisfaction

zufrieren† *vi sep* (*sein*) freeze over

zufügen *vt sep* inflict (*dat* on); do
(*Unrecht*) (*dat* to)

Zufuhr *f* - supply

Zug *m* -[e]s,⁻e train; (*Kolonne*) column; (*Um-*) procession; (*Mil*) platoon;
(*Vogelschar*) flock; (*Ziehen, Zugkraft*)
pull; (*Wandern, Ziehen*) migration;
(*Schluck, Luft-*) draught; (*Atem-*)
breath; (*beim Rauchen*) puff; (*Schach-*)
move; (*beim Schwimmen, Rudern*)
stroke; (*Gesichts-*) feature; (*Wesens-*)
trait

Zugabe *f* (*Geschenk*) [free] gift;
(*Mus*) encore

Zugang *m* access

zugänglich *adj* accessible; (*Mensch:*)
approachable

Zugbrücke *f* drawbridge

zugeben† *vt sep* add; (*gestehen*)
admit; (*erlauben*) allow

zugehen† *vi sep* (*sein*) close; **jdm
z~** be sent to s.o.; **z~ auf** (+ *acc*)
go towards; **dem Ende z~** draw to a
close; (*Vorräte:*) run low; **auf der
Party ging es lebhaft zu** the party
was pretty lively

Zugehörigkeit *f* - membership

Zügel *m* -s,- rein

zugelassen *adj* registered

zügel|los *adj* unrestrained. **z~n** *vt*
rein in; (*fig*) curb

Zuge|ständnis *nt* concession.
z~stehen† *vt sep* grant

zügig *adj* quick

Zugkraft *f* pull; (*fig*) attraction

zugleich *adv* at the same time

Zugluft *f* draught

zugreifen† *vi sep* (*haben*) grab
it/them; (*bei Tisch*) help oneself; (*bei
Angebot*) jump at it; (*helfen*) lend a
hand

zugrunde *adv* **z~ richten** destroy;
z~ gehen be destroyed; (*sterben*)

die; z~ **liegen** form the basis (*dat* of)

zugunsten *prep* (+ *gen*) in favour of; (*Sammlung*) in aid of

zugute *adv* jdm/etw z~ **kommen** benefit s.o./something

Zugvogel *m* migratory bird

zuhalten† *v sep* ● *vt* keep closed; (*bedecken*) cover; **sich** (*dat*) **die Nase** z~ hold one's nose

Zuhälter *m* -s,- pimp

zuhause *adv* = **zu Hause**, *s*. **Haus**. **Z~** *nt* -s,- home

zuhör|en *vi sep* (*haben*) listen (*dat* to). **Z~er(in)** *m(f)* listener

zujubeln *vi sep* (*haben*) jdm z~ cheer s.o.

zukleben *vt sep* seal

zuknöpfen *vt sep* button up

zukommen† *vi sep* (*sein*) z~ **auf** (+ *acc*) come towards; (*sich nähern*) approach; z~ **lassen** send (jdm s.o.); devote (*Pflege*) (*dat* to); **jdm** z~ be s.o.'s right

Zukunft *f* - future. **zukünftig** *adj* future ● *adv* in future

zulächeln *vi sep* (*haben*) smile (*dat* at)

zulangen *vi sep* (*haben*) help oneself

zulassen† *vt sep* allow, permit; (*teilnehmen lassen*) admit; (*Admin*) license, register; (*geschlossen lassen*) leave closed; leave unopened (*Brief*)

zulässig *adj* permissible

Zulassung *f* -,-en admission; registration; (*Lizenz*) licence

zuleide *adv* jdm etwas z~ **tun** hurt s.o.

zuletzt *adv* last; (*schließlich*) in the end

zuliebe *adv* jdm/etw z~ for the sake of someone/something

zum *prep* = **zu dem**; **zum Spaß** for fun; **etw zum Lesen** sth to read

zumachen *v sep* ● *vt* close, shut; do up (*Jacke*); seal (*Umschlag*); turn off (*Hahn*); (*stilllegen*) close down ● *vi* (*haben*) close, shut; (*stillgelegt werden*) close down

zumal *adv* especially ● *conj* especially since

zumindest *adv* at least

zumutbar *adj* reasonable

zumute *adv* mir ist nicht danach z~ I don't feel like it

zumut|en *vt sep* jdm etw z~en ask or expect sth of s.o.; **sich** (*dat*) **zu viel** z~en overdo things. **Z~ung** *f* - imposition

zunächst *adv* first [of all]; (*anfangs*) at first; (*vorläufig*) for the moment ● *prep* (+ *dat*) nearest to

Zunahme *f* -,-n increase

Zuname *m* surname

zünd|en *vt/i* (*haben*) ignite. **Z~er** *m* -s,- detonator, fuse. **Z~holz** *nt* match. **Z~kerze** *f* sparking-plug. **Z~schlüssel** *m* ignition key. **Z~schnur** *f* fuse. **Z~ung** *f* -,-en ignition

zunehmen† *vi sep* (*haben*) increase (**an** + *dat* in); (*Mond:*) wax; (*an Gewicht*) put on weight. **z~d** *adj* increasing

Zuneigung *f* - affection

Zunft *f* -,⸗e guild

Zunge *f* -,-n tongue. **Z~nbrecher** *m* tongue-twister

zunutze *adj* sich (*dat*) etw z~ **machen** make use of sth; (*ausnutzen*) take advantage of sth

zuoberst *adv* right at the top

zuordnen *vt sep* assign (*dat* to)

zupfen *vt/i* (*haben*) pluck (**an** + *dat* at); pull out (*Unkraut*)

zur *prep* = **zu der**; **zur Schule** to school; **zur Zeit** at present

zurate *adv* z~ **ziehen** consult

> **Zürcher Festspiele** The Zurich festival in Switzerland is an annual celebration of classical music, opera, dance and art, with special performances held throughout the city. The festival concludes with a brilliant Midsummer Night's Ball in central Zurich. *i*

zurechnungsfähig *adj* of sound mind

z

zurecht|finden† **(sich)** vr sep find one's way. **z~kommen**† vi sep (sein) cope (**mit** with); (rechtzeitig kommen) be in time. **z~legen** vt sep put out ready; **sich** (dat) **eine Ausrede z~legen** have an excuse all ready. **z~machen** vt sep get ready. **Z~weisung** f reprimand

zureden vi sep (haben) **jdm z~** try to persuade s.o.

zurichten vt sep prepare; (beschädigen) damage; (verletzen) injure

zuriegeln vt sep bolt

zurück adv back; **Berlin, hin und z~** return to Berlin. **z~bekommen**† vt sep get back. **z~bleiben**† vi sep (sein) stay behind; (nicht mithalten) lag behind. **z~bringen**† vt sep bring back; (wieder hinbringen) take back. **z~erstatten** vt sep refund. **z~fahren**† v sep ● vt drive back ● vi (sein) return, go back; (im Auto) drive back; (z~weichen) recoil. **z~finden**† vi sep (haben) find one's way back. **z~führen** v sep ● vt take back; (fig) attribute (**auf** + acc to) ● vi (haben) lead back. **z~geben**† vt sep give back, return. **z~geblieben** adj retarded. **z~gehen**† vi sep (sein) go back, return; (abnehmen) go down; **z~gehen auf** (+ acc) (fig) go back to

zurückgezogen adj secluded. **Z~heit** f - seclusion

zurückhalt|en† vt sep hold back; (abhalten) stop; **sich z~en** restrain oneself. **z~end** adj reserved. **Z~ung** f - reserve

zurück|kehren vi sep (sein) return. **z~kommen**† vi sep (sein) come back, return; (ankommen) get back. **z~lassen**† vt sep leave behind; (z~kehren lassen) allow back. **z~legen** vt sep put back; (reservieren) keep; (sparen) put by; (Strecke) cover. **z~liegen**† vi sep (haben) be in the past; (Sport) be behind; **das liegt lange zurück** that was long ago. **z~melden (sich)** vr sep report back. **z~schicken** vt sep send back. **z~schlagen**† v sep ● vi (haben) hit back ● vt hit back; (umschlagen) turn back. **z~schrecken**† vi sep (sein)

shrink back, recoil; (fig) shrink (**vor** + dat from). **z~stellen** vt sep put back; (reservieren) keep; (fig) put aside; (aufschieben) postpone. **z~stoßen**† v sep ● vt push back ● vi (sein) reverse, back. **z~treten**† vi sep (sein) step back; (vom Amt) resign; (verzichten) withdraw. **z~weisen**† vt sep turn away; (fig) reject. **z~zahlen** vt sep pay back. **z~ziehen**† vt sep draw back; (fig) withdraw; **sich z~ziehen** withdraw; (vom Beruf) retire

Zuruf m shout. **z~en**† vt sep shout (dat to)

zurzeit adv at present

Zusage f -,-n acceptance; (Versprechen) promise. **z~n** v sep ● vt promise ● vi (haben) accept

zusammen adv together; (insgesamt) altogether; **z~ sein** be together. **Z~arbeit** f co-operation. **z~arbeiten** vi sep (haben) co-operate. **z~bauen** vt sep assemble. **z~bleiben**† vi sep (sein) stay together. **z~brechen**† vi sep (sein) collapse. **Z~bruch** m collapse; (Nerven- & fig) breakdown. **z~fallen**† vi sep (sein) collapse; (zeitlich) coincide. **z~fassen** vt sep summarize, sum up. **Z~fassung** f summary. **z~fügen** vt sep fit together. **z~gehören** vi sep (haben) belong together; (z~passen) go together. **z~gesetzt** adj (Gram) compound. **z~halten** v sep ● vt hold together; (beisammenhalten) keep together ● vi (haben) (fig) stick together. **Z~hang** m connection; (Kontext) context. **z~hanglos** adj incoherent. **z~klappen** v sep ● vt fold up ● vi (sein) collapse. **z~kommen**† vi sep (sein) meet; (sich sammeln) accumulate. **Z~kunft** f -,⸚e meeting. **z~laufen**† vi sep (sein) gather; (Flüssigkeit:) collect; (Linien:) converge. **z~leben** vi sep (haben) live together. **z~legen** v sep ● vt put together; (z~falten) fold up; (vereinigen) amalgamate; pool (Geld) ● vi (haben) club together. **z~nehmen**† vt sep gather up; summon up (Mut); collect (Gedanken);

sich z~nehmen pull oneself together. **z~passen** vi sep (haben) go together, match. **Z~prall** m collision. **z~rechnen** vt sep add up. **z~schlagen†** vt sep smash up; (prügeln) beat up. **z~schließen† (sich)** vr sep join together; (Firmen:) merge. **Z~schluss** m union; (Comm) merger

Zusammensein nt -s get-together

zusammensetz|en vt sep put together; (Techn) assemble; **sich z~en** sit [down] together; (bestehen) be made up (aus from). **Z~ung** f -,-en composition; (Techn) assembly; (Wort) compound

zusammen|stellen vt sep put together; (gestalten) compile. **Z~stoß** m collision; (fig) clash. **z~treffen†** vi sep (sein) meet; (zeitlich) coincide. **z~zählen** vt sep add up. **z~ziehen** v sep ● vt draw together; (addieren) add up; (konzentrieren) mass; **sich z~ziehen** contract; (Gewitter:) gather ● vi (sein) move in together; move in (mit with)

Zusatz m addition; (Jur) rider; (Lebensmittel-) additive. **zusätzlich** adj additional ● adv in addition

zuschau|en vi sep (haben) watch. **Z~er(in)** m -s,- (f -,-nen) spectator; (TV) viewer

Zuschlag m surcharge; (Zug) supplement. **z~pflichtig** adj (Zug) for which a supplement is payable

zuschließen† v sep ● vt lock ● vi (haben) lock up

zuschneiden† vt sep cut out; cut to size (Holz)

zuschreiben† vt sep attribute (dat to); **jdm die Schuld z~** blame s.o.

Zuschrift f letter; (auf Annonce) reply

zuschulden adv **sich** (dat) **etwas z~ kommen lassen** do wrong

Zuschuss m contribution; (staatlich) subsidy

zusehends adv visibly

zusein* vi sep (sein) **zu sein**, s. zu

zusenden† vt sep send (dat to)

zusetzen v sep ● vt add; (einbüßen) lose

zusicher|n vt sep promise. **Z~ung** f promise.

zuspielen vt sep (Sport) pass

zuspitzen (sich) vr sep (fig) become critical

Zustand m condition, state

zustande adv **z~ bringen/kommen** bring/come about

zuständig adj competent; (verantwortlich) responsible

zustehen† vi sep (haben) **jdm z~** be s.o.'s right; (Urlaub:) be due to s.o.

zusteigen† vi sep (sein) get on; **noch jemand zugestiegen?** ≈ tickets please; (im Bus) ≈ any more fares please?

zustell|en vt sep block; (bringen) deliver. **Z~ung** f delivery

zusteuern v sep ● vi (sein) head (auf + acc for) ● vt contribute

zustimm|en vi sep (haben) agree; (billigen) approve (dat of). **Z~ung** f consent; approval

zustoßen† vi sep (sein) happen (dat to)

Zustrom m influx

Zutat f (Culin) ingredient

zuteil|en vt sep allocate; assign (Aufgabe). **Z~ung** f allocation

zutiefst adv deeply

zutragen† vt sep carry/(fig) report (dat to); **sich z~** happen

zutrau|en vt sep **jdm etw z~** believe s.o. capable of sth. **Z~en** nt -s confidence

zutreffen† vi sep (haben) be correct; **z~ auf** (+ acc) apply to

Zutritt m admittance

zuunterst adv right at the bottom

zuverlässig adj reliable. **Z~keit** f - reliability

Zuversicht f - confidence. **z~lich** adj confident

zuviel* pron & adv **zu viel**, s. viel

zuvor adv before; (erst) first

zuvorkommen† vi sep (sein) (+

z

dat) anticipate. **z~d** *adj* obliging

Zuwachs *m* **-es** increase

Zuwanderung *f* immigration

zuwege *adv* **z~ bringen** achieve

zuweilen *adv* now and then

zuweisen† *vt sep* assign

Zuwendung *f* donation; (*Fürsorge*) care

zuwenig* *pron & adv* **zu wenig**, *s.* **wenig**

zuwerfen† *vt sep* slam (*Tür*); **jdm etw z~** throw s.o. sth

zuwider *adv* **jdm z~ sein** be repugnant to s.o. ● *prep* (+ *dat*) contrary to

zuzahlen *vt sep* pay extra

zuziehen† *v sep* ● *vt* pull tight; draw (*Vorhänge*); (*hinzu-*) call in; **sich** (*dat*) **etw z~** contract (*Krankheit*); sustain (*Verletzung*); incur (*Zorn*) ● *vi* (*sein*) move into the area

zuzüglich *prep* (+ *gen*) plus

Zwang *m* **-[e]s,⁼e** compulsion; (*Gewalt*) force; (*Verpflichtung*) obligation

zwängen *vt* squeeze

zwanglos *adj* informal. **Z~igkeit** *f* - informality

Zwangsjacke *f* straitjacket

zwanzig *inv adj* twenty. **z~ste(r,s)** *adj* twentieth

zwar *adv* admittedly

Zweck *m* **-[e]s,-e** purpose; (*Sinn*) point. **z~los** *adj* pointless. **z~mäßig** *adj* suitable; (*praktisch*) functional

zwei *inv adj*, **Z~** *f* **-,-en** two; (*Sch*) ≈ B. **Z~bettzimmer** *nt* twin-bedded room

zweideutig *adj* ambiguous

zweierlei *inv adj* two kinds of ● *pron* two things. **z~fach** *adj* double

Zweifel *m* **-s,-** doubt. **z~haft** *adj* doubtful; (*fragwürdig*) dubious. **z~los** *adv* undoubtedly. **z~n** *vi* (*haben*) doubt (**an etw** *dat* sth)

Zweig *m* **-[e]s,-e** branch. **Z~stelle** *f* branch [office]

Zwei|kampf *m* duel. **z~mal** *adv* twice. **z~reihig** *adj* (*Anzug*) double-breasted. **z~sprachig** *adj* bilingual

zwoit *adv* **zu z~** in twos; **wir waren zu z~** there were two of us. **z~beste(r,s)** *adj* second-best. **z~e(r,s)** *adj* second

zweitens *adv* secondly

Zwerchfell *nt* diaphragm

Zwerg *m* **-[e]s,-e** dwarf

Zwickel *m* **-s,-** gusset

zwicken *vt/i* (*haben*) pinch

Zwieback *m* **-[e]s,⁼e** rusk

Zwiebel *f* **-,-n** onion; (*Blumen-*)bulb

Zwielicht *nt* half-light; (*Dämmerlicht*) twilight. **z~ig** *adj* shady

Zwiespalt *m* conflict

Zwilling *m* **-s,-e** twin; **Z~e** (*Astrology*) Gemini

zwingen† *vt* force; **sich z~** force oneself. **z~d** *adj* compelling

Zwinger *m* **-s,-** run; (*Zucht-*) kennels *pl*

zwinkern *vi* (*haben*) blink; (*als Zeichen*) wink

Zwirn *m* **-[e]s** button thread

zwischen *prep* (+ *dat/acc*) between; (*unter*) among[st]. **Z~bemerkung** *f* interjection. **z~durch** *adv* in between; (*in der Z~zeit*) in the meantime. **Z~fall** *m* incident. **Z~landung** *f* stopover. **Z~raum** *m* gap, space. **Z~wand** *f* partition. **Z~zeit** *f* **in der Z~zeit** in the meantime

Zwist *m* **-[e]s,-e** discord; (*Streit*) feud

zwitschern *vi* (*haben*) chirp

zwo *inv adj* two

zwölf *inv adj* twelve. **z~te(r,s)** *adj* twelfth

Zylind|er *m* **-s,-** cylinder; (*Hut*) top hat. **z~risch** *adj* cylindrical

Zyn|iker *m* **-s,-** cynic. **z~isch** *adj* cynical. **Z~ismus** *m* **-** cynicism

Zypern *nt* **-s** Cyprus

Zypresse *f* **-,-n** cypress

Zyste /ˈtsʏstə/ *f* **-,-n** cyst

z

a /ə/, *betont* /eɪ/

! vor einem Vokal **an**

● *indefinite article*

····➤ ein (*m*), eine (*f*), ein (*nt*). **a problem** ein Problem. **an apple** ein Apfel. **a cat** eine Katze. **have you got a pencil?** hast du einen Bleistift? **I gave it to a beggar** ich gab es einem Bettler

! There are some cases where **a** is not translated, such as when talking about people's professions or nationalities: **she is a lawyer** sie ist Rechtsanwältin. **he's an Italian** er ist Italiener

····➤ (*with 'not'*) kein (*m*), keine (*f*), kein (*nt*), keine (*pl*). **that's not a problem/not a good idea** das ist kein Problem/keine gute Idee. **there was not a chance that ...** es bestand keine Möglichkeit, dass .... **she did not say a word** sie sagte kein Wort. **I didn't tell a soul** ich habe es keinem Menschen gesagt

····➤ (*per; each*) pro. **£300 a week** 300 Pfund pro Woche. **30 miles an hour** 30 Meilen pro Stunde. (*in prices*) **it costs 90p a pound** es kostet 90 Pence das Pfund.

aback /əˈbæk/ *adv* **be taken ~** verblüfft sein

abandon /əˈbændən/ *vt* verlassen; (*give up*) aufgeben

abate /əˈbeɪt/ *vi* nachlassen

abattoir /ˈæbətwɑː(r)/ *n* Schlachthof *m*

abb|ey /ˈæbɪ/ *n* Abtei *f*. **~ot** *n* Abt *m*

abbreviat|e /əˈbriːvɪeɪt/ *vt* abkürzen. **~ion** *n* Abkürzung *f*

abdicat|e /ˈæbdɪkeɪt/ *vi* abdanken.

~ion *n* Abdankung *f*

abdom|en /ˈæbdəmən/ *n* Unterleib *m*. **~inal** *adj* Unterleibs-

abduct /əbˈdʌkt/ *vt* entführen. **~ion** *n* Entführung *f*

aberration /æbəˈreɪʃn/ *n* Abweichung *f*; (*mental*) Verwirrung *f*

abeyance /əˈbeɪəns/ *n* **in ~** [zeitweilig] außer Kraft

abhor /əbˈhɔː(r)/ *vt* (*pt/pp* **abhorred**) verabscheuen. **~rent** *adj* abscheulich

abide /əˈbaɪd/ *vt* (*pt/pp* **abided**) (*tolerate*) aushalten; ausstehen (*person*)

ability /əˈbɪlətɪ/ *n* Fähigkeit *f*; (*talent*) Begabung *f*

abject /ˈæbdʒekt/ *adj* erbärmlich; (*humble*) demütig

ablaze /əˈbleɪz/ *adj* in Flammen

able /ˈeɪbl/ *adj* (-r, -st) fähig; **be ~ to do sth** etw tun können. **~-'bodied** *adj* körperlich gesund

ably /ˈeɪblɪ/ *adv* gekonnt

abnormal /æbˈnɔːml/ *adj* anormal; (*Med*) abnorm. **~ity** *n* Abnormität *f*. **~ly** *adv* ungewöhnlich

aboard /əˈbɔːd/ *adv & prep* an Bord (+ *gen*)

abol|ish /əˈbɒlɪʃ/ *vt* abschaffen. **~ition** *n* Abschaffung *f*

abominable /əˈbɒmɪnəbl/ *adj*, **-bly** *adv* abscheulich

aborigines /æbəˈrɪdʒəniːz/ *npl* Ureinwohner *pl*

abort /əˈbɔːt/ *vt* abtreiben. **~ion** *n* Abtreibung *f*. **~ive** *adj* (*attempt*) vergeblich

about /əˈbaʊt/ *adv* umher, herum; (*approximately*) ungefähr; **be ~** (*in circulation*) umgehen; (*in existence*) vorhanden sein; **be ~ to do sth** im Begriff sein, etw zu tun; **there was no one ~** es war kein Mensch da; **run/play ~** herumlaufen/-spielen ● *prep* um (+ *acc*) [... herum]; (*concerning*) über (+ *acc*); **what is it ~?**

a

worum geht es? (*book:*) wovon handelt es? **I know nothing ~ it** ich weiß nichts davon; **talk/know ~** reden/wissen von

about: ~**-ʹface** n, -ʹ**turn** n Kehrtwendung f

above /əˈbʌv/ adv oben ● *prep* über (+ *dat/acc*); ~ **all** vor allem.

above: ~-ʹ**board** adj legal. ~**-mentioned** adj oben erwähnt

abrasive /əˈbreɪsɪv/ adj Scheuer-; (*remark*) verletzend ● n Scheuermittel nt; (*Techn*) Schleifmittel nt

abreast /əˈbrest/ adv nebeneinander; **keep ~ of** Schritt halten mit

abridge /əˈbrɪdʒ/ vt kürzen

abroad /əˈbrɔːd/ adv im Ausland; **go ~** ins Ausland fahren

abrupt /əˈbrʌpt/ adj abrupt; (*sudden*) plötzlich; (*curt*) schroff

abscess /ˈæbsɪs/ n Abszess m

absence /ˈæbsəns/ n Abwesenheit f

absent /ˈæbsənt/ adj abwesend; **be ~** fehlen

absentee /æbsənˈtiː/ n Abwesende(r) m/f

absent-minded /æbsəntˈmaɪndɪd/ adj geistesabwesend; (*forgetful*) zerstreut

absolute /ˈæbsəluːt/ adj absolut

absorb /əbˈsɔːb/ vt absorbieren, aufsaugen; ~**ed in** vertieft in (+ *acc*). ~**ent** adj saugfähig

absorption /əbˈsɔːpʃn/ n Absorption f

abstain /əbˈsteɪn/ vi sich enthalten (**from** gen)

abstemious /əbˈstiːmɪəs/ adj enthaltsam

abstention /əbˈstenʃn/ n (*Pol*) [Stimm]enthaltung f

abstract /ˈæbstrækt/ adj abstrakt ● n (*summary*) Abriss m

absurd /əbˈsɜːd/ adj absurd. ~**ity** n Absurdität f

abundan|ce /əˈbʌndəns/ n Fülle f (**of** an + *dat*). ~**t** adj reichlich

abuse[1] /əˈbjuːz/ vt missbrauchen; (*insult*) beschimpfen

abus|e[2] /əˈbjuːs/ n Missbrauch m;

(*insults*) Beschimpfungen pl. ~**ive** ausfallend

abysmal /əˈbɪzml/ adj 🄵 katastrophal

abyss /əˈbɪs/ n Abgrund m

academic /ækəˈdemɪk/ adj, -**ally** adv akademisch

academy /əˈkædəmɪ/ n Akademie f

accelerat|e /əkˈseləreɪt/ vt/i beschleunigen. ~**ion** n Beschleunigung f. ~**or** n (*Auto*) Gaspedal nt

accent /ˈæksənt/ n Akzent m

accept /əkˈsept/ vt annehmen; (*fig*) akzeptieren ● vi zusagen. ~**able** adj annehmbar. ~**ance** n Annahme f; (*of invitation*) Zusage f

access /ˈækses/ n Zugang m. ~**ible** adj zugänglich

accessor|y /əkˈsesərɪ/ n (*Jur*) Mitschuldige(r) m/f; ~**ies** pl (*fashion*) Accessoires pl; (*Techn*) Zubehör nt

accident /ˈæksɪdənt/ n Unfall m; (*chance*) Zufall m; **by ~** zufällig; (*unintentionally*) versehentlich. ~**al** adj zufällig; (*unintentional*) versehentlich

acclaim /əˈkleɪm/ vt feiern (**as** als)

acclimatize /əˈklaɪmətaɪz/ vt **become ~d** sich akklimatisieren

accommodat|e /əˈkɒmədeɪt/ vt unterbringen. ~**ing** adj entgegenkommend. ~**ion** n (*rooms*) Unterkunft f

accompan|iment /əˈkʌmpənɪmənt/ n Begleitung f. ~**ist** n (*Mus*) Begleiter(in) m(f)

accompany /əˈkʌmpənɪ/ vt (*pt/pp* -**ied**) begleiten

accomplice /əˈkʌmplɪs/ n Komplize/-zin m/f

accomplish /əˈkʌmplɪʃ/ vt erfüllen (*task*); (*achieve*) erreichen. ~**ed** adj fähig. ~**ment** n Fertigkeit f; (*achievement*) Leistung f

accord /əˈkɔːd/ n of one's own ~ aus eigenem Antrieb. ~**ance** n in ~**ance with** entsprechend (+ *dat*)

according /əˈkɔːdɪŋ/ adv ~ **to** nach (+ *dat*). ~**ly** adv entsprechend

accordion /əˈkɔːdɪən/ n Akkordeon nt

account /ə'kaʊnt/ n Konto nt; (bill) Rechnung f; (description) Darstellung f; (report) Bericht m; ~s pl (Comm) Bücher pl; on ~ of wegen (+ gen); on no ~ auf keinen Fall; take into ~ in Betracht ziehen, berücksichtigen ● vi ~ for Rechenschaft ablegen für; (explain) erklären

accountant /ə'kaʊntənt/ n Buchhalter(in) m(f); (chartered) Wirtschaftsprüfer m

accumulat|e /ə'kju:mjʊleɪt/ vt ansammeln, anhäufen ● vi sich ansammeln, sich anhäufen. ~ion n Ansammlung f, Anhäufung f

accura|cy /'ækʊrəsɪ/ n Genauigkeit f. ~te adj genau

accusation /ækju:'zeɪʃn/ n Anklage f

accusative /ə'kju:zətɪv/ adj & n ~ [case] (Gram) Akkusativ m

accuse /ə'kju:z/ vt (Jur) anklagen (of gen); ~ s.o. of doing sth jdn beschuldigen, etw getan zu haben

accustom /ə'kʌstəm/ vt gewöhnen (to an + dat); grow or get ~ed to sich gewöhnen an (+ acc). ~ed adj gewohnt

ace /eɪs/ n (Cards, Sport) Ass nt

ache /eɪk/ n Schmerzen pl ● vi weh tun, schmerzen

achieve /ə'tʃi:v/ vt leisten; (gain) erzielen; (reach) erreichen. ~ment n (feat) Leistung f

acid /'æsɪd/ adj sauer; (fig) beißend ● n Säure f. ~ity n Säure f. ~'rain n saurer Regen m

acknowledge /ək'nɒlɪdʒ/ vt anerkennen; (admit) zugeben; erwidern (greeting); ~ receipt of den Empfang bestätigen (+ gen). ~ment n Anerkennung f; (of letter) Empfangsbestätigung f

acne /'æknɪ/ n Akne f

acorn /'eɪkɔ:n/ n Eichel f

acoustic /ə'ku:stɪk/ adj, -ally adv akustisch. ~s npl Akustik f

acquaint /ə'kweɪnt/ vt be ~ed with kennen; vertraut sein mit (fact). ~ance n (person) Bekannte(r)

m/f; make s.o.'s ~ance jdn kennen lernen

acquire /ə'kwaɪə(r)/ vt erwerben

acquisit|ion /ækwɪ'zɪʃn/ n Erwerb m; (thing) Erwerbung f. ~ive adj habgierig

acquit /ə'kwɪt/ vt (pt/pp acquitted) freisprechen

acre /'eɪkə(r)/ n ≈ Morgen m

acrimon|ious /'ækrɪ'məʊnɪəs/ adj bitter

acrobat /'ækrəbæt/ n Akrobat(in) m(f). ~ic adj akrobatisch

across /ə'krɒs/ adv hinüber/herüber; (wide) breit; (not lengthwise) quer; (in crossword) waagerecht; come ~ sth auf etw (acc) stoßen; go ~ hinübergehen; bring ~ herüberbringen ● prep über (+ acc); (on the other side of) auf der anderen Seite (+ gen)

act /ækt/ n Tat f; (action) Handlung f; (law) Gesetz nt; (Theat) Akt m; (item) Nummer f ● vi handeln; (behave) sich verhalten; (Theat) spielen; (pretend) sich verstellen; ~ as fungieren als ● vt spielen (role). ~ing adj (deputy) stellvertretend ● n (Theat) Schauspielerei f

action /'ækʃn/ n Handlung f; (deed) Tat f; (Mil) Einsatz m; (Jur) Klage f; (effect) Wirkung f; (Techn) Mechanismus m; out of ~ (machine:) außer Betrieb; take ~ handeln; killed in ~ gefallen

activate /'æktɪveɪt/ vt betätigen

activ|e /'æktɪv/ adj aktiv; on ~e service im Einsatz. ~ity n Aktivität f

act|or /'æktə(r)/ n Schauspieler m. ~ress n Schauspielerin f

actual /'æktʃʊəl/ adj eigentlich; (real) tatsächlich

acupuncture /'ækjʊ-/ n Akupunktur f

acute /ə'kju:t/ adj scharf; (angle) spitz; (illness) akut. ~ly adv sehr

ad /æd/ n Ⅰ = advertisement

AD abbr (Anno Domini) n.Chr.

adamant /'ædəmənt/ adj be ~ that darauf bestehen, dass

adapt /ə'dæpt/ vt anpassen; bearbeiten (*play*) ● *vi* sich anpassen. ~**able** *adj* anpassungsfähig

adaptation /ædæp'teɪʃn/ *n* (*Theat*) Bearbeitung *f*

add /æd/ *vt* hinzufügen; (*Math*) addieren ● *vi* zusammenzählen, addieren; ~ **to** hinzufügen zu; (*fig: increase*) steigern; (*compound*) verschlimmern. ~ **up** *vt* zusammenzählen (*figures*) ● *vi* zusammenzählen, addieren

adder /'ædə(r)/ *n* Kreuzotter *f*

addict /'ædɪkt/ *n* Süchtige(r) *m/f*

addict|ed /ə'dɪktɪd/ *adj* süchtig; ~**ed to drugs** drogensüchtig. ~**ion** *n* Sucht *f*

addition /ə'dɪʃn/ *n* Hinzufügung *f*; (*Math*) Addition *f*; (*thing added*) Ergänzung *f*; **in** ~ zusätzlich. ~**al** *adj* zusätzlich

additive /'ædɪtɪv/ *n* Zusatz *m*

address /ə'dres/ *n* Adresse *f*, Anschrift *f*; (*speech*) Ansprache *f* ● *vt* adressieren (**to** an + *acc*); (*speak to*) anreden (*person*); sprechen vor (+ *dat*) (*meeting*). ~**ee** *n* Empfänger *m*

adequate /'ædɪkwət/ *adj* ausreichend

adhere /əd'hɪə(r)/ *vi* kleben/(*fig*) festhalten (**to** an + *dat*)

adhesive /əd'hi:sɪv/ *adj* klebend ● *n* Klebstoff *m*

adjacent /ə'dʒeɪsnt/ *adj* angrenzend

adjective /'ædʒɪktɪv/ *n* Adjektiv *nt*

adjoin /ə'dʒɔɪn/ *vt* angrenzen an (+ *acc*). ~**ing** *adj* angrenzend

adjourn /ə'dʒɜ:n/ *vt* vertagen (**until** auf + *acc*) ● *vi* sich vertagen. ~**ment** *n* Vertagung *f*

adjudicate /ə'dʒu:dɪkeɪt/ *vi* (*in competition*) Preisrichter sein

adjust /ə'dʒʌst/ *vt* einstellen; (*alter*) verstellen ● *vi* sich anpassen (**to** *dat*). ~**able** *adj* verstellbar. ~**ment** *n* Einstellung *f*; Anpassung *f*

ad lib /æd'lɪb/ *adv* aus dem Stegreif ● *vi* (*pt/pp* **ad libbed**) 🆒 improvisieren

administer /əd'mɪnɪstə(r)/ *vt* verwalten; verabreichen (*medicine*)

administration /ədmɪnɪ'streɪʃn/ *n* Verwaltung *f*; (*Pol*) Regierung *f*

admirable /'ædmərəbl/ *adj* bewundernswert

admiral /'ædmərəl/ *n* Admiral *m*

admiration /ædmə'reɪʃn/ *n* Bewunderung *f*

admire /əd'maɪə(r)/ *vt* bewundern. ~**r** *n* Verehrer(in) *m(f)*

admission /əd'mɪʃn/ *n* Eingeständnis *nt*; (*entry*) Eintritt *m*

admit /əd'mɪt/ *vt* (*pt/pp* **admitted**) (*let in*) hereinlassen; (*acknowledge*) zugeben; ~ **to sth** etw zugeben. ~**tance** *n* Eintritt *m*. ~**tedly** *adv* zugegebenermaßen

admonish /əd'mɒnɪʃ/ *vt* ermahnen

adolescen|ce /ædə'lesns/ *n* Jugend *f*, Pubertät *f*. ~**t** *adj* Jugend-; (*boy, girl*) halbwüchsig ● *n* Jugendliche(r) *m/f*

adopt /ə'dɒpt/ *vt* adoptieren; ergreifen (*measure*); (*Pol*) annehmen (*candidate*). ~**ion** *n* Adoption *f*

ador|able /ə'dɔ:rəbl/ *adj* bezaubernd. ~**ation** *n* Anbetung *f*

adore /ə'dɔ:(r)/ *vt* (*worship*) anbeten; (🆒: *like*) lieben

adorn /ə'dɔ:n/ *vt* schmücken. ~**ment** *n* Schmuck *m*

Adriatic /eɪdrɪ'ætɪk/ *adj & n* ~ [**Sea**] Adria *f*

adrift /ə'drɪft/ *adj* **be** ~ treiben

adroit /ə'drɔɪt/ *adj* gewandt, geschickt

adulation /ædjʊ'leɪʃn/ *n* Schwärmerei *f*

adult /'ædʌlt/ *n* Erwachsene(r) *m/f*

adulterate /ə'dʌltəreɪt/ *vt* verfälschen; panschen (*wine*)

adultery /ə'dʌltərɪ/ *n* Ehebruch *m*

advance /əd'vɑ:ns/ *n* Fortschritt *m*; (*Mil*) Vorrücken *nt*; (*payment*) Vorschuss *m*; **in** ~ im Voraus ● *vi* vorankommen; (*Mil*) vorrücken; (*make progress*) Fortschritte machen ● *vt* fördern (*cause*); vorbringen (*idea*); vorschießen (*money*). ~**d** *adj* fortgeschritten; (*progressive*) fortschrittlich. ~**ment** *n* Förderung *f*; (*promotion*) Beförderung *f*

advantage /əd'vɑːntɪdʒ/ n Vorteil m; **take ~ of** ausnutzen. **~ous** adj vorteilhaft

adventur|e /əd'ventʃə(r)/ n Abenteuer nt. **~er** n Abenteurer m. **~ous** adj abenteuerlich; (person) abenteuerlustig

adverb /'ædvɜːb/ n Adverb nt

adverse /'ædvɜːs/ adj ungünstig

advert /'ædvɜːt/ n 🔲 = advertisement

advertise /'ædvətaɪz/ vt Reklame machen für; (by small ad) inserieren ● vi Reklame machen; inserieren

advertisement /əd'vɜːtɪsmənt/ n Anzeige f; (publicity) Reklame f; (small ad) Inserat nt

advertis|er /'ædvətaɪzə(r)/ n Inserent m. **~ing** n Werbung f

advice /əd'vaɪs/ n Rat m

advisable /əd'vaɪzəbl/ adj ratsam

advis|e /əd'vaɪz/ vt raten (s.o. jdm); (counsel) beraten; (inform) benachrichtigen; **~e s.o. against sth** jdm von etw abraten ● vi raten. **~er** n Berater(in) m(f). **~ory** adj beratend

advocate[1] /'ædvəkət/ n (supporter) Befürworter m

advocate[2] /'ædvəkeɪt/ vt befürworten

aerial /'eərɪəl/ adj Luft- ● n Antenne f

aerobics /eə'rəʊbɪks/ n Aerobic nt

aero|drome /'eərədrəʊm/ n Flugplatz m. **~plane** n Flugzeug nt

aerosol /'eərəsɒl/ n Spraydose f

aesthetic /iːs'θetɪk/ adj ästhetisch

affair /ə'feə(r)/ n Angelegenheit f, Sache f; (scandal) Affäre f; **[love-]~** [Liebes]verhältnis nt

affect /ə'fekt/ vt sich auswirken auf (+ acc); (concern) betreffen; (move) rühren; (pretend) vortäuschen. **~ation** n Affektiertheit f. **~ed** adj affektiert

affection /ə'fekʃn/ n Liebe f. **~ate** adj liebevoll

affirm /ə'fɜːm/ vt behaupten

affirmative /ə'fɜːmətɪv/ adj bejahend ● n Bejahung f

afflict /ə'flɪkt/ vt be **~ed with** behaftet sein mit. **~ion** n Leiden nt

affluen|ce /'æfluəns/ n Reichtum m. **~t** adj wohlhabend. **~t society** n Wohlstandsgesellschaft f

afford /ə'fɔːd/ vt be able to **~ sth** sich (dat) etw leisten können. **~able** adj erschwinglich

affront /ə'frʌnt/ n Beleidigung f ● vt beleidigen

afloat /ə'fləʊt/ adj be **~** (ship:) flott sein; **keep ~** (person:) sich über Wasser halten

afraid /ə'freɪd/ adj be **~** Angst haben (of vor + dat); **I'm ~ not** leider nicht; **I'm ~ so** [ja] leider

Africa /'æfrɪkə/ n Afrika nt. **~n** adj afrikanisch ● n Afrikaner(in) m(f)

after /'ɑːftə(r)/ adv danach ● prep nach (+ dat); **~ that** danach; **~ all** schließlich; **the day ~ tomorrow** übermorgen; **be ~** aus sein auf (+ acc) ● conj nachdem

after: ~-effect n Nachwirkung f. **~math** /-mɑːθ/ n Auswirkungen pl. **~'noon** n Nachmittag m; **good ~noon!** guten Tag! **~-sales service** n Kundendienst m. **~shave** n Rasierwasser nt. **~thought** n nachträglicher Einfall m. **~wards** adv nachher

again /ə'gen/ adv wieder; (once more) noch einmal; **~ and ~** immer wieder

against /ə'genst/ prep gegen (+ acc)

age /eɪdʒ/ n Alter nt; (era) Zeitalter nt; **~s** 🔲 ewig; **under ~** minderjährig; **of ~** volljährig; **two years of ~** zwei Jahre alt ● v (pres p ageing) ● vt älter machen ● vi altern; (mature) reifen

aged[1] /eɪdʒd/ adj **~ two** zwei Jahre alt

aged[2] /'eɪdʒɪd/ adj betagt ● n **the ~** pl die Alten

ageless /'eɪdʒlɪs/ adj ewig jung

agency /'eɪdʒənsɪ/ n Agentur f; (office) Büro nt

agenda /ə'dʒendə/ n Tagesordnung f

agent /'eɪdʒənt/ n Agent(in) m(f);

a

(*Comm*) Vertreter(in) *m(f)*; (*substance*) Mittel *nt*

aggravat|e /ˈægrəveɪt/ *vt* verschlimmern; (🔲: *annoy*) ärgern. **∼ion** *n* 🔲 Ärger *m*

aggregate /ˈægrɪgət/ *adj* gesamt ● *n* Gesamtzahl *f*; (*sum*) Gesamtsumme *f*

aggress|ion /əˈgreʃn/ *n* Aggression *f*. **∼ive** *adj* aggressiv. **∼or** *n* Angreifer(in) *m(f)*

aggro /ˈægrəʊ/ *n* 🔲 Ärger *m*

aghast /əˈgɑːst/ *adj* entsetzt

agil|e /ˈædʒaɪl/ *adj* flink, behände; (*mind*) wendig. **∼ity** *n* Flinkheit *f*, Behändigkeit *f*

agitat|e /ˈædʒɪteɪt/ *vt* bewegen; (*shake*) schütteln ● *vi* (*fig*) **∼ for** agitieren für. **∼ed** *adj* erregt. **∼ion** *n* Erregung *f*; (*Pol*) Agitation *f*

ago /əˈgəʊ/ *adv* vor (+ *dat*); **a long time ∼** vor langer Zeit; **how long ∼ is it?** wie lange ist es her?

agony /ˈægənɪ/ *n* Qual *f*; **be in ∼** furchtbare Schmerzen haben

agree /əˈgriː/ *vt* vereinbaren; (*admit*) zugeben; **∼ to do sth** sich bereit erklären, etw zu tun ● *vi* (*people, figures:*) übereinstimmen; (*reach agreement*) sich einigen; (*get on*) gut miteinander auskommen; (*consent*) einwilligen (**to** in + *acc*); **∼ with s.o.** jdm zustimmen; (*food:*) jdm bekommen; **∼ with sth** (*approve of*) mit etw einverstanden sein

agreeable /əˈgriːəbl/ *adj* angenehm

agreed /əˈgriːd/ *adj* vereinbart

agreement /əˈgriːmənt/ *n* Übereinstimmung *f*; (*consent*) Einwilligung *f*; (*contract*) Abkommen *nt*; **reach ∼** sich einigen

agricultur|al /ægrɪˈkʌltʃərəl/ *adj* landwirtschaftlich. **∼e** *n* Landwirtschaft *f*

aground /əˈgraʊnd/ *adj* gestrandet; **run ∼** (*ship:*) stranden

ahead /əˈhed/ *adv* **straight ∼** geradeaus; **be ∼ of s.o./sth** vor jdm/etw sein; (*fig*) voraus sein; **go on ∼** vorgehen; **get ∼** vorankommen; **go ∼!**

🔲 bitte! **look/plan ∼** vorausblicken/-planen

aid /eɪd/ *n* Hilfe *f*; (*financial*) Unterstützung *f*; **in ∼ of** zugunsten (+ *gen*) ● *vt* helfen (+ *dat*)

Aids /eɪdz/ *n* Aids *nt*

aim /eɪm/ *n* Ziel *nt*; **take ∼** zielen ● *vt* richten (**at** auf + *acc*); ● *vi* zielen (**at** auf + *acc*); **∼ to do sth** beabsichtigen, etw zu tun. **∼less** *adj* ziellos

air /eə(r)/ *n* Luft *f*; (*expression*) Miene *f*; (*appearance*) Anschein *m*; **be on the ∼** (*programme:*) gesendet werden; (*person:*) auf Sendung sein; **by ∼** auf dem Luftweg; (*airmail*) mit Luftpost ● *vt* lüften; vorbringen (*views*)

air: **∼ bag** *n* (*Auto*) Airbag *m*. **∼-conditioned** *adj* klimatisiert. **∼-conditioning** *n* Klimaanlage *f*. **∼craft** *n* Flugzeug *nt*. **∼field** *n* Flugplatz *m*. **∼ force** *n* Luftwaffe *f*. **∼ freshener** *n* Raumspray *nt*. **∼gun** *n* Luftgewehr *nt*. **∼ hostess** *n* Stewardess *f*. **∼ letter** *n* Aerogramm *nt*. **∼line** *n* Fluggesellschaft *f*. **∼mail** *n* Luftpost *f*. **∼man** *n* Flieger *m*. **∼plane** *n* (*Amer*) Flugzeug *nt*. **∼port** *n* Flughafen *m*. **∼-raid** *n* Luftangriff *m*. **∼-raid shelter** *n* Luftschutzbunker *m*. **∼ship** *n* Luftschiff *nt*. **∼ ticket** *n* Flugschein *m*. **∼tight** *adj* luftdicht. **∼-traffic controller** *n* Fluglotse *m*

airy /ˈeərɪ/ *adj* luftig; (*manner*) nonchalant

aisle /aɪl/ *n* Gang *m*

ajar /əˈdʒɑː(r)/ *adj* angelehnt

alarm /əlɑːm/ *n* Alarm *m*; (*device*) Alarmanlage *f*; (*clock*) Wecker *m*; (*fear*) Unruhe *f* ● *vt* erschrecken

alas /əˈlæs/ *int* ach!

album /ˈælbəm/ *n* Album *nt*

alcohol /ˈælkəhɒl/ *n* Alkohol *m*. **∼ic** *adj* alkoholisch ● *n* Alkoholiker(in) *m(f)*. **∼ism** *n* Alkoholismus *m*

alert /əˈlɜːt/ *adj* aufmerksam ● *n* Alarm *m*

algebra /ˈældʒɪbrə/ *n* Algebra *f*

Algeria /ælˈdʒɪərɪə/ *n* Algerien *nt*

alias /'eɪlɪəs/ n Deckname m ● adv alias

alibi /'ælɪbaɪ/ n Alibi nt

alien /'eɪlɪən/ adj fremd ● n Ausländer(in) m(f)

alienate /'eɪlɪəneɪt/ vt entfremden

alight¹ /ə'laɪt/ vi aussteigen (**from** aus)

alight² adj be ∼ brennen; **set** ∼ anzünden

align /ə'laɪn/ vt ausrichten. ∼**ment** n Ausrichtung f

alike /ə'laɪk/ adj & adv ähnlich; (same) gleich; **look** ∼ sich (dat) ähnlich sehen

alive /ə'laɪv/ adj lebendig; **be** ∼ leben; **be** ∼ **with** wimmeln von

---

all /ɔːl/

● adjective

····➤ (plural) alle. **all [the] children** alle Kinder. **all our children** alle unsere Kinder. **all the books** alle Bücher. **all the others** alle anderen

····➤ (singular = whole) ganz. **all the wine** der ganze Wein. **all the town** die ganze Stadt. **all my money** mein ganzes Geld; all mein Geld. **all day** den ganzen Tag. **all Germany** ganz Deutschland

● pronoun

····➤ (plural = all persons/things) alle. **all are welcome** alle sind willkommen. **they all came** sie sind alle gekommen. **are we all here?** sind wir alle da? **the best pupils of all** die besten Schüler (von allen). **the most beautiful of all** der/die/das schönste von allen

····➤ (singular = everything) alles. **that is all** das ist alles. **all that I possess** alles, was ich besitze

····➤ **all of** ganz; (with plural) alle. **all of the money** das ganze Geld. **all of the paintings** alle Gemälde. **all of you/them** Sie/sie alle

····➤ (in phrases) **all in all** alles in

---

allem. **in all** insgesamt. **most of all** am meisten. **once and for all** ein für alle Mal. **not at all** gar nicht

● adverb

····➤ (completely) ganz. **she was all alone** sie war ganz allein. **I was all dirty** ich war ganz schmutzig

····➤ (in scores) **four all** vier zu vier

····➤ **all right** (things) in Ordnung. **is everything all right?** ist alles in Ordnung? **is that all right for you?** passt das Ihnen? **I'm all right** mir geht es gut. **did you get home all right?** sind Sie gut nach Hause gekommen? **is it all right to go in?** kann ich reingehen? **yes, all right** ja, gut. **work out all right** gut gehen; klappen ⚠

····➤ (in phrases) **all but** (almost) fast. **all at once** auf einmal. **all the better** umso besser. **all the same** (nevertheless) trotzdem

---

allege /ə'ledʒ/ vt behaupten. ∼**d** adj angeblich

allegiance /ə'liːdʒəns/ n Treue f

allerg|ic /ə'lɔːdʒɪk/ adj allergisch (**to** gegen). ∼**y** n Allergie f

alleviate /ə'liːvɪeɪt/ vt lindern

alley /'ælɪ/ n Gasse f; (for bowling) Bahn f

alliance /ə'laɪəns/ n Verbindung f, (Pol) Bündnis nt

allied /'ælaɪd/ adj alliiert

alligator /'ælɪgeɪtə(r)/ n Alligator m

allocat|e /'æləkeɪt/ vt zuteilen; (share out) verteilen. ∼**ion** n Zuteilung f

allot /ə'lɒt/ vt (pt/pp **allotted**) zuteilen (**s.o.** jdm)

allow /ə'laʊ/ vt erlauben; (give) geben; (grant) gewähren; (reckon) rechnen; (agree, admit) zugeben; ∼ **for** berücksichtigen; ∼ **s.o. to do sth** jdm erlauben, etw zu tun; **be** ∼**ed to do sth** etw tun dürfen

allowance /ə'laʊəns/ n [finanzielle] Unterstützung f; **make** ∼**s for** berücksichtigen

alloy /'ælɔɪ/ n Legierung f

allude /ə'luːd/ vi anspielen (**to** auf + *acc*)

allusion /ə'luːʒn/ n Anspielung f

ally[1] /'ælaɪ/ n Verbündete(r) m/f; **the Allies** pl die Alliierten

ally[2] /ə'laɪ/ vt (pt/pp -ied) verbinden; **~ oneself with** sich verbünden mit

almighty /ɔːl'maɪtɪ/ adj allmächtig; (🔢: big) Riesen- ● n **the A~** der Allmächtige

almond /'ɑːmənd/ n (Bot) Mandel f

almost /'ɔːlməʊst/ adv fast, beinahe

alone /ə'ləʊn/ adj & adv allein; **leave me ~** lass mich in Ruhe; **leave that ~!** lass die Finger davon! **let ~** ganz zu schweigen von

along /ə'lɒŋ/ prep entlang (+ acc); **~ the river** den Fluss entlang ● adv **~ with** zusammen mit; **all ~** die ganze Zeit; **come ~** komm doch; **I'll bring it ~** ich bringe es mit

along'side adv daneben ● prep neben (+ dat)

aloud /ə'laʊd/ adv laut

alphabet /'ælfəbet/ n Alphabet nt. **~ical** adj alphabetisch

alpine /'ælpaɪn/ adj alpin; **A~** Alpen-

Alps /ælps/ npl Alpen pl

already /ɔːl'redɪ/ adv schon

Alsace /æl'sæs/ n Elsass nt

Alsatian /æl'seɪʃn/ n (dog) [deutscher] Schäferhund m

also /'ɔːlsəʊ/ adv auch

altar /'ɔːltə(r)/ n Altar m

alter /'ɔːltə(r)/ vt ändern ● vi sich verändern. **~ation** n Änderung f

alternate[1] /'ɔːltəneɪt/ vi [sich] abwechseln ● vt abwechseln

alternate[2] /ɔːl'tɜːnət/ adj abwechselnd; **on ~ days** jeden zweiten Tag

alternative /ɔːl'tɜːnətɪv/ adj andere(r,s); **~ medicine** Alternativmedizin f ● n Alternative f. **~ly** adv oder aber

although /ɔːl'ðəʊ/ conj obgleich, obwohl

altitude /'æltɪtjuːd/ n Höhe f

altogether /ɔːltə'geðə(r)/ adv insge-

samt; (on the whole) alles in allem

aluminium /æljʊ'mɪnɪəm/ n, (Amer) **aluminum** n Aluminium nt

always /'ɔːlweɪz/ adv immer

am /æm/ see be

a.m. abbr (ante meridiem) vormittags

amass /ə'mæs/ vt anhäufen

amateur /'æmətə(r)/ n Amateur m ● attrib Amateur-; (Theat) Laien-. **~ish** adj laienhaft

amaze /ə'meɪz/ vt erstaunen. **~d** adj erstaunt. **~ment** n Erstaunen nt

amazing /ə'meɪzɪŋ/ adj erstaunlich

ambassador /æm'bæsədə(r)/ n Botschafter m

amber /'æmbə(r)/ n Bernstein m ● adj (colour) gelb

ambigu|ity /æmbɪ'gjuːətɪ/ n Zweideutigkeit f. **~ous** adj -ly adv zweideutig

ambiti|on /æm'bɪʃn/ n Ehrgeiz m; (aim) Ambition f. **~ous** adj ehrgeizig

amble /'æmbl/ vi schlendern

ambulance /'æmbjʊləns/ n Krankenwagen m. **~ man** n Sanitäter m

ambush /'æmbʊʃ/ n Hinterhalt m ● vt aus dem Hinterhalt überfallen

amen /ɑː'men/ int amen

amend /ə'mend/ vt ändern. **~ment** n Änderung f

amenities /ə'miːnətɪz/ npl Einrichtungen pl

America /ə'merɪkə/ n Amerika nt. **~n** adj amerikanisch ● n Amerikaner(in) m(f). **~nism** n Amerikanismus m

---

American dream Der 𝒊 Glaube, dass Amerika das Land unbegrenzter Möglichkeiten ist, in dem jeder sein Leben erfolgreich gestalten kann. Für Minderheiten und Einwanderer bedeutet der Traum weitgehende Toleranz und Anspruch auf eigene freie Lebensgestaltung. Der American dream verkörpert eine optimistische allgemeine Grundhaltung mit auf Erfolg gerichtetem Denken und Handeln.

amiable /'eɪmɪəbl/ *adj* nett

amicable /'æmɪkəbl/ *adj*, **-bly** *adv* freundschaftlich; (*agreement*) gütlich

amid[st] /ə'mɪd[st]/ *prep* inmitten (+ *gen*)

ammonia /ə'məʊnɪə/ *n* Ammoniak *nt*

ammunition /æmjʊ'nɪʃn/ *n* Munition *f*

amnesty /'æmnəstɪ/ *n* Amnestie *f*

among[st] /ə'mʌŋ[st]/ *prep* unter (+ *dat/acc*); ~ **yourselves** untereinander

amoral /eɪ'mɒrəl/ *adj* amoralisch

amorous /'æmərəs/ *adj* zärtlich

amount /ə'maʊnt/ *n* Menge *f*; (*sum of money*) Betrag *m*; (*total*) Gesamtsumme *f* ● *vi* ~ **to** sich belaufen auf (+ *acc*); (*fig*) hinauslaufen auf (+ *acc*)

amphibi|an /æm'fɪbɪən/ *n* Amphibie *f*. ~**ous** *adj* amphibisch

amphitheatre /'æmfɪ-/ *n* Amphitheater *nt*

ample /'æmpl/ *adj* (**-r,-st**) reichlich; (*large*) füllig

amplif|ier /'æmplɪfaɪə(r)/ *n* Verstärker *m*. ~**y** *vt* (*pt/pp* **-ied**) weiter ausführen; verstärken (*sound*)

amputat|e /'æmpjʊteɪt/ *vt* amputieren. ~**ion** *n* Amputation *f*

amuse /ə'mjuːz/ *vt* amüsieren, belustigen; (*entertain*) unterhalten. ~**ment** *n* Belustigung *f*; Unterhaltung *f*

amusing /ə'mjuːzɪŋ/ *adj* amüsant

an /ən/, *betont* /æn/ *see* **a**

anaem|ia /ə'niːmɪə/ *n* Blutarmut *f*, Anämie *f*. ~**ic** *adj* blutarm

anaesthetic /ænəs'θetɪk/ *n* Narkosemittel *nt*, Betäubungsmittel *nt*; **under [an]** ~ in Narkose

anaesthetist /ə'niːsθətɪst/ *n* Narkosearzt *m*

analogy /ə'nælədʒɪ/ *n* Analogie *f*

analyse /'ænəlaɪz/ *vt* analysieren

analysis /ə'næləsɪs/ *n* Analyse *f*

analyst /'ænəlɪst/ *n* Chemiker(in) *m(f)*; (*psychologist*) Analytiker *m*

analytical /ænə'lɪtɪkl/ *adj* analytisch

anarch|ist /'ænəkɪst/ *n* Anarchist *m*. ~**y** *n* Anarchie *f*

anatom|ical /ænə'tɒmɪkl/ *adj* anatomisch. ~**y** *n* Anatomie *f*

ancest|or /'ænsestə(r)/ *n* Vorfahr *m*. ~**ry** *n* Abstammung *f*

anchor /'æŋkə(r)/ *n* Anker *m* ● *vi* ankern ● *vt* verankern

ancient /'eɪnʃənt/ *adj* alt

and /ənd/, *betont* /ænd/ *conj* und; ~ **so on** und so weiter; **six hundred** ~ **two** sechshundertzwei; **more** ~ **more** immer mehr; **nice** ~ **warm** schön warm

anecdote /'ænɪkdəʊt/ *n* Anekdote *f*

angel /'eɪndʒl/ *n* Engel *m*. ~**ic** *adj* engelhaft

anger /'æŋgə(r)/ *n* Zorn *m* ● *vt* zornig machen

angle /'æŋgl/ *n* Winkel *m*; (*fig*) Standpunkt *m*; **at an** ~ schräg

angler /'æŋglə(r)/ *n* Angler *m*

Anglican /'æŋglɪkən/ *adj* anglikanisch ● *n* Anglikaner(in) *m(f)*

Anglo-Saxon /æŋgləʊ'sæksn/ *adj* angelsächsisch ● *n* (*Lang*) Angelsächsisch *nt*

angry /'æŋgrɪ/ *adj*, **-ily** *adv* zornig; **be** ~ **with** böse sein auf (+ *acc*)

anguish /'æŋgwɪʃ/ *n* Qual *f*

angular /'æŋgjʊlə(r)/ *adj* eckig; (*features*) kantig

animal /'ænɪml/ *n* Tier *nt* ● *adj* tierisch

animat|e /'ænɪmeɪt/ *vt* beleben. ~**ed** *adj* lebhaft

animosity /ænɪ'mɒsətɪ/ *n* Feindseligkeit *f*

ankle /'æŋkl/ *n* [Fuß]knöchel *m*

annex[e] /'æneks/ *n* Nebengebäude *nt*; (*extension*) Anbau *m*

annihilate /ə'naɪəleɪt/ *vt* vernichten

anniversary /ænɪ'vɜːsərɪ/ *n* Jahrestag *m*

annotate /'ænəteɪt/ *vt* kommentieren

announce /ə'naʊns/ *vt* bekannt geben; (*over loudspeaker*) durchsagen; (*at reception*) ankündigen; (*Radio, TV*) ansagen; (*in newspaper*) anzeigen.

a

~ment n Bekanntgabe f, Bekanntmachung f; Durchsage f; Ansage f;
Anzeige f. ~r n Ansager(in) m(f)

annoy /əˈnɔɪ/ vt ärgern; (pester) belästigen; **get ~ed** sich ärgern.
~ance n Ärger m. ~ing adj ärgerlich

annual /ˈænjʊəl/ adj jährlich ● n
(book) Jahresalbum nt

anonymous /əˈnɒnɪməs/ adj anonym

anorak /ˈænəræk/ n Anorak m

anorexi|a /ænəˈreksɪə/ n Mager-
sucht f; **be ~c** an Magersucht leiden

another /əˈnʌðə(r)/ adj & pron ein
anderer/eine andere/ein anderes;
(additional) noch ein(e); ~ [one]
noch einer/eine/eins; ~ time ein an-
dermal; **one ~** einander

answer /ˈɑːnsə(r)/ n Antwort f; (solution) Lösung f ● vt antworten (**s.o.**
jdm); beantworten (question, letter);
~ the door/telephone an die Tür/
ans Telefon gehen ● vi antworten;
(Teleph) sich melden; ~ **back** eine
freche Antwort geben. ~ing **machine** n (Teleph) Anrufbeantworter m

ant /ænt/ n Ameise f

antagonis|m /ænˈtægənɪzm/ n
Antagonismus m. ~tic adj feindselig

Antarctic /ænˈtɑːktɪk/ n Antarktis f

antelope /ˈæntɪləʊp/ n Antilope f

antenatal /æntɪˈneɪtl/ adj ~ **care**
Schwangerschaftsfürsorge f

antenna /ænˈtenə/ n Fühler m;
(Amer: aerial) Antenne f

anthem /ˈænθəm/ n Hymne f

anthology /ænˈθɒlədʒɪ/ n Anthologie f

anthrax /ˈænθræks/ n Milzbrand m,
Anthrax m

anthropology /ænθrəˈpɒlədʒɪ/ n
Anthropologie f

antibiotic /æntɪbaɪˈɒtɪk/ n Antibio-
tikum nt

anticipat|e /ænˈtɪsɪpeɪt/ vt vorher-
sehen; (forestall) zuvorkommen (+
dat); (expect) erwarten. ~ion n Erwartung f

anti'climax n Enttäuschung f

anti'clockwise adj & adv gegen
den Uhrzeigersinn

antics /ˈæntɪks/ npl Mätzchen pl

antidote /ˈæntɪdəʊt/ n Gegengift nt

'antifreeze n Frostschutzmittel nt

antipathy /ænˈtɪpəθɪ/ n Abneigung
f, Antipathie f

antiquated /ˈæntɪkweɪtɪd/ adj veraltet

antique /ænˈtiːk/ adj antik ● n Anti-
quität f. ~ **dealer** n Antiquitäten-
händler m

antiquity /ænˈtɪkwətɪ/ n Alter-
tum nt

anti'septic adj antiseptisch ● n An-
tiseptikum nt

anti'social adj asozial; 🔢 ungesellig

antlers /ˈæntləz/ npl Geweih nt

anus /ˈeɪnəs/ n After m

anvil /ˈænvɪl/ n Amboss m

anxiety /æŋˈzaɪətɪ/ n Sorge f

anxious /ˈæŋkʃəs/ adj ängstlich;
(worried) besorgt; **be ~ to do sth**
etw gerne machen wollen

any /ˈenɪ/ adj irgendein(e); (every)
jede(r,s); pl alle; (after
negative) kein(e); pl keine; ~ **colour/
number you like** eine beliebige
Farbe/Zahl; **have you ~ wine/ap-
ples?** haben Sie Wein/Äpfel? ● pron
[irgend]einer/eine/eins; pl [irgend]-
welche; (some) welche(r,s); pl welche;
(all) alle pl; (negative) keiner/keine/
keins; pl keine; **I don't want ~ of it**
ich will nichts davon; **there aren't ~**
es gibt keine ● adv noch; ~ **quicker/
slower** noch schneller/langsamer; **is
it ~ better?** geht es etwas besser?
would you like ~ more? möchten
Sie noch [etwas]? **I can't eat ~**
more ich kann nichts mehr essen

'anybody pron [irgend]jemand;
(after negative) niemand; ~ **can do
that** das kann jeder

'anyhow adv jedenfalls; (nevertheless) trotzdem; (badly) irgendwie

'anyone pron = anybody

'anything pron [irgend]etwas; (after
negative) nichts; (everything) alles

'**anyway** adv jedenfalls; (in any case) sowieso

'**anywhere** adv irgendwo; (after negative) nirgendwo; (be, live) überall; (go) überallhin

apart /ə'pɑːt/ adv auseinander; **live** ~ getrennt leben; ~ **from** abgesehen von

apartment /ə'pɑːtmənt/ n Zimmer nt; (flat) Wohnung f

ape /eɪp/ n [Menschen]affe m ● vt nachäffen

aperitif /ə'perətiːf/ n Aperitif m

apologetic /əpɒlə'dʒetɪk/ adj, -**ally** adv entschuldigend; **be** ~ sich entschuldigen

apologize /ə'pɒlədʒaɪz/ vi sich entschuldigen (**to** bei)

apology /ə'pɒlədʒɪ/ n Entschuldigung f

apostle /ə'pɒsl/ n Apostel m

apostrophe /ə'pɒstrəfɪ/ n Apostroph m

appal /ə'pɔːl/ vt (pt/pp **appalled**) entsetzen. ~**ling** adj entsetzlich

apparatus /æpə'reɪtəs/ n Apparatur f; (Sport) Geräte pl; (single piece) Gerät nt

apparent /ə'pærənt/ adj offenbar; (seeming) scheinbar. ~**ly** adv offenbar, anscheinend

appeal /ə'piːl/ n Appell m, Aufruf m; (request) Bitte f; (attraction) Reiz m; (Jur) Berufung f ● vi appellieren (**to** an + acc); (ask) bitten (**for** um); (be attractive) zusagen (**to** dat); (Jur) Berufung einlegen. ~**ing** adj ansprechend

appear /ə'pɪə(r)/ vi erscheinen; (seem) scheinen; (Theat) auftreten. ~**ance** n Erscheinen nt; (look) Aussehen nt; **to all** ~**ances** allem Anschein nach

appendicitis /əpendɪ'saɪtɪs/ n Blinddarmentzündung f

appendix /ə'pendɪks/ n (pl **-ices** /-ɪsiːz/) (of book) Anhang m ● (pl **-es**) (Anat) Blinddarm m

appetite /'æpɪtaɪt/ n Appetit m

appetizing /'æpɪtaɪzɪŋ/ adj appetitlich

applau|d /ə'plɔːd/ vt/i Beifall klatschen (+ dat). ~**se** n Beifall m

apple /'æpl/ n Apfel m

appliance /ə'plaɪəns/ n Gerät nt

applicable /'æplɪkəbl/ adj anwendbar (**to** auf + acc); (on form) **not** ~ nicht zutreffend

applicant /'æplɪkənt/ n Bewerber(in) m(f)

application /æplɪ'keɪʃn/ n Anwendung f; (request) Antrag m; (for job) Bewerbung f; (diligence) Fleiß m

applied /ə'plaɪd/ adj angewandt

apply /ə'plaɪ/ vt (pt/pp **-ied**) auftragen (paint); anwenden (force, rule) ● vi zutreffen (**to** auf + acc); ~ **for** beantragen; sich bewerben um (job)

appoint /ə'pɔɪnt/ vt ernennen; (fix) festlegen. ~**ment** n Ernennung f; (meeting) Verabredung f; (at doctor's, hairdresser's) Termin m; (job) Posten m; **make an** ~**ment** sich anmelden

appreciable /ə'priːʃəbl/ adj merklich; (considerable) beträchtlich

appreciat|e /ə'priːʃɪeɪt/ vt zu schätzen wissen; (be grateful for) dankbar sein für; (enjoy) schätzen; (understand) verstehen ● vi (increase in value) im Wert steigen. ~**ion** n (gratitude) Dankbarkeit f. ~**ive** adj dankbar

apprehens|ion /æprɪ'henʃn/ n Festnahme f; (fear) Angst f. ~**ive** adj ängstlich

apprentice /ə'prentɪs/ n Lehrling m. ~**ship** n Lehre f

approach /ə'prəʊtʃ/ n Näherkommen nt; (of time) Nahen nt; (access) Zugang m; (road) Zufahrt f ● vi sich nähern; (time:) nahen ● vt sich nähern (+ dat); (with request) herantreten an (+ acc); (set about) sich heranmachen an (+ acc). ~**able** adj zugänglich

appropriate /ə'prəʊprɪət/ adj angebracht, angemessen

approval /ə'pruːvl/ n Billigung f; **on** ~ zur Ansicht

approv|e /əˈpruːv/ vt billigen ● vi ~**e of sth/s.o.** mit etw/jdm einverstanden sein. ~**ing** adj anerkennend

approximate /əˈprɒksɪmət/ adj. -**ly** adv ungefähr

approximation /əprɒksɪˈmeɪʃn/ n Schätzung f

apricot /ˈeɪprɪkɒt/ n Aprikose f

April /ˈeɪprəl/ n April m; **make an ~ fool of** in den April schicken

apron /ˈeɪprən/ n Schürze f

apt /æpt/ adj passend; **be ~ to do sth** dazu neigen, etw zu tun

aqualung /ˈækwəlʌŋ/ n Tauchgerät nt

aquarium /əˈkweərɪəm/ n Aquarium nt

aquatic /əˈkwætɪk/ adj Wasser-

Arab /ˈærəb/ adj arabisch ● n Araber(in) m(f). ~**ian** adj arabisch

Arabic /ˈærəbɪk/ adj arabisch

arbitrary /ˈɑːbɪtrəri/ adj, -**ily** adv willkürlich

arbitrat|e /ˈɑːbɪtreɪt/ vi schlichten. ~**ion** n Schlichtung f

arc /ɑːk/ n Bogen m

arcade /ɑːˈkeɪd/ n Laubengang m; (shops) Einkaufspassage f

arch /ɑːtʃ/ n Bogen m; (of foot) Gewölbe nt ● vt ~ **its back** (cat:) einen Buckel machen

archaeological /ɑːkɪəˈlɒdʒɪkl/ adj archäologisch

archaeolog|ist /ɑːkɪˈɒlədʒɪst/ n Archäologe m/-login f. ~**y** n Archäologie f

archaic /ɑːˈkeɪɪk/ adj veraltet

arch'bishop /ɑːtʃ-/ n Erzbischof m

archer /ˈɑːtʃə(r)/ n Bogenschütze m. ~**y** n Bogenschießen nt

architect /ˈɑːkɪtekt/ n Architekt(in) m(f). ~**ural** adj architektonisch

architecture /ˈɑːkɪtektʃə(r)/ n Architektur f

archives /ˈɑːkaɪvz/ npl Archiv nt

archway /ˈɑːtʃweɪ/ n Torbogen m

Arctic /ˈɑːktɪk/ adj arktisch ● n **the ~** die Arktis

ardent /ˈɑːdənt/ adj leidenschaftlich

ardour /ˈɑːdə(r)/ n Leidenschaft f

arduous /ˈɑːdjʊəs/ adj mühsam

are /ɑː(r)/ see **be**

area /ˈeərɪə/ n (surface) Fläche f; (Geometry) Flächeninhalt m; (region) Gegend f; (fig) Gebiet nt

arena /əˈriːnə/ n Arena f

Argentina /ɑːdʒənˈtiːnə/ n Argentinien nt

Argentin|e /ˈɑːdʒəntaɪn/, ~**ian** /-ˈtɪnɪən/ adj argentinisch

argue /ˈɑːgjuː/ vi streiten (**about** über + acc); (two people:) sich streiten; (debate) diskutieren; **don't ~!** keine Widerrede! ● vt (debate) diskutieren; (reason) ~ **that** argumentieren, dass

argument /ˈɑːgjʊmənt/ n Streit m, Auseinandersetzung f; (reasoning) Argument nt; **have an ~** sich streiten. ~**ative** adj streitlustig

aria /ˈɑːrɪə/ n Arie f

arise /əˈraɪz/ vi (pt **arose**, pp **arisen**) sich ergeben (**from** aus)

aristocracy /ærɪˈstɒkrəsi/ n Aristokratie f

aristocrat /ˈærɪstəkræt/ n Aristokrat(in) m(f). ~**ic** adj aristokratisch

arithmetic /əˈrɪθmətɪk/ n Rechnen nt

arm /ɑːm/ n Arm m; (of chair) Armlehne f; ~**s** pl (weapons) Waffen pl; (Heraldry) Wappen nt ● vt bewaffnen

armament /ˈɑːməmənt/ n Bewaffnung f; ~**s** pl Waffen pl

'armchair n Sessel m

armed /ɑːmd/ adj bewaffnet; ~ **forces** Streitkräfte pl

armour /ˈɑːmə(r)/ n Rüstung f. ~**ed** adj Panzer-

'armpit n Achselhöhle f

army /ˈɑːmi/ n Heer nt; (specific) Armee f; **join the ~** zum Militär gehen

aroma /əˈrəʊmə/ n Aroma nt, Duft m. ~**tic** adj aromatisch

arose /əˈrəʊz/ see **arise**

around /əˈraʊnd/ adv [**all**] ~ rings herum; **he's not ~** er ist nicht da; **travel ~** herumreisen ● prep um (+

acc) ... herum; (*approximately, nearly*) gegen

arouse /əˈraʊz/ *vt* aufwecken; (*excite*) erregen

arrange /əˈreɪndʒ/ *vt* arrangieren; anordnen (*furniture, books*); (*settle*) abmachen. **∼ment** *n* Anordnung *f*; (*agreement*) Vereinbarung *f*; (*of flowers*) Gesteck *nt*; **make ∼ments** Vorkehrungen treffen

arrest /əˈrest/ *n* Verhaftung *f*; **under ∼** verhaftet ● *vt* verhaften

arrival /əˈraɪvl/ *n* Ankunft *f*; **new ∼s** *pl* Neuankömmlinge *pl*

arrive /əˈraɪv/ *vi* ankommen; **∼ at** (*fig*) gelangen zu

arrogan|ce /ˈærəgəns/ *n* Arroganz *f*. **∼t** *adj* arrogant

arrow /ˈærəʊ/ *n* Pfeil *m*

arse /ɑːs/ *n* (*vulgar*) Arsch *m*

arson /ˈɑːsn/ *n* Brandstiftung *f*. **∼ist** *n* Brandstifter *m*

art /ɑːt/ *n* Kunst *f*; **work of ∼** Kunstwerk *nt*; **∼s and crafts** *pl* Kunstgewerbe *nt*; **A∼s** *pl* (*Univ*) Geisteswissenschaften *pl*

artery /ˈɑːtəri/ *n* Schlagader *f*, Arterie *f*

'art gallery *n* Kunstgalerie *f*

arthritis /ɑːˈθraɪtɪs/ *n* Arthritis *f*

artichoke /ˈɑːtɪtʃəʊk/ *n* Artischocke *f*

article /ˈɑːtɪkl/ *n* Artikel *m*; (*object*) Gegenstand *m*; **∼ of clothing** Kleidungsstück *nt*

artificial /ɑːtɪˈfɪʃl/ *adj* künstlich

artillery /ɑːˈtɪləri/ *n* Artillerie *f*

artist /ˈɑːtɪst/ *n* Künstler(in) *m(f)*

artiste /ɑːˈtiːst/ *n* (*Theat*) Artist(in) *m(f)*

artistic /ɑːˈtɪstɪk/ *adj*, **-ally** *adv* künstlerisch

as /æz/ *conj* (*because*) da; (*when*) als; (*while*) während ● *prep* als; **as a child/foreigner** als Kind/Ausländer ● *adv* **as well** auch; **as soon as** sobald; **as much as** so viel wie; **as quick as you** so schnell wie du; **as you know** wie Sie wissen; **as far as I'm concerned** was mich betrifft

asbestos /æzˈbestɒs/ *n* Asbest *m*

ascend /əˈsend/ *vi* [auf]steigen ● *vt* besteigen (*throne*)

ascent /əˈsent/ *n* Aufstieg *m*

ascertain /æsəˈteɪn/ *vt* ermitteln

ash¹ /æʃ/ *n* (*tree*) Esche *f*

ash² *n* Asche *f*

ashamed /əˈʃeɪmd/ *adj* beschämt; **be ∼** sich schämen (**of** über + *acc*)

ashore /əˈʃɔː(r)/ *adv* an Land

'ashtray *n* Aschenbecher *m*

Asia /ˈeɪʃə/ *n* Asien *nt*. **∼n** *adj* asiatisch ● *n* Asiat(in) *m(f)*. **∼tic** *adj* asiatisch

aside /əˈsaɪd/ *adv* beiseite

ask /ɑːsk/ *vt/i* fragen; stellen (*question*); (*invite*) einladen; **∼ for** bitten um; verlangen (*s.o.*); **∼ after** sich erkundigen nach; **∼ s.o. in** jdn hereinbitten; **∼ s.o. to do sth** jdn bitten, etw zu tun

asleep /əˈsliːp/ *adj* **be ∼** schlafen; **fall ∼** einschlafen

asparagus /əˈspærəgəs/ *n* Spargel *m*

aspect /ˈæspekt/ *n* Aspekt *m*

asphalt /ˈæsfælt/ *n* Asphalt *m*

aspire /əˈspaɪə(r)/ *vi* **∼ to** streben nach

ass /æs/ *n* Esel *m*

assail /əˈseɪl/ *vt* bestürmen. **∼ant** *n* Angreifer(in) *m(f)*

assassin /əˈsæsɪn/ *n* Mörder(in) *m(f)*. **∼ate** *vt* ermorden. **∼ation** *n* [politischer] Mord *m*

assault /əˈsɔːlt/ *n* (*Mil*) Angriff *m*; (*Jur*) Körperverletzung *f* ● *vt* [tätlich] angreifen

assemble /əˈsembl/ *vi* sich versammeln ● *vt* versammeln; (*Techn*) montieren

assembly /əˈsemblɪ/ *n* Versammlung *f*; (*Sch*) Andacht *f*; (*Techn*) Montage *f*. **∼ line** *n* Fließband *nt*

assent /əˈsent/ *n* Zustimmung *f*

assert /əˈsɜːt/ *vt* behaupten; **∼ oneself** sich durchsetzen. **∼ion** *n* Behauptung *f*

assess /əˈses/ *vt* bewerten; (*fig & for*

a

tax purposes) einschätzen: schätzen (*value*). ∼**ment** *n* Einschätzung *f*; (*of tax*) Steuerbescheid *m*

asset /'æset/ *n* Vorteil *m*; ∼**s** *pl* (*money*) Vermögen *nt*; (*Comm*) Aktiva *pl*

assign /ə'saɪn/ *vt* zuweisen (**to** *dat*). ∼**ment** *n* (*task*) Aufgabe *f*

assist /ə'sɪst/ *vt/i* helfen (+ *dat*). ∼**ance** *n* Hilfe *f*. ∼**ant** *adj* Hilfs- ● *n* Assistent(in) *m*(*f*); (*in shop*) Verkäufer(in) *m*(*f*)

associat|e[1] /ə'səʊʃɪeɪt/ *vt* verbinden; (*Psychology*) assoziieren ● *vi* ∼ **with** verkehren mit. ∼**ion** *n* Verband *m*

associate[2] /ə'səʊʃɪət/ *adj* assoziiert ● *n* Kollege *m*/-gin *f*

assort|ed /ə'sɔ:tɪd/ *adj* gemischt. ∼**ment** *n* Mischung *f*

assum|e /ə'sju:m/ *vt* annehmen; übernehmen (*office*); ∼**ing that** angenommen, dass

assumption /ə'sʌmpʃn/ *n* Annahme *f*; **on the** ∼ in der Annahme (**that** dass)

assurance /ə'ʃʊərəns/ *n* Versicherung *f*; (*confidence*) Selbstsicherheit *f*

assure /ə'ʃʊə(r)/ *vt* versichern (**s.o.** jdm); **I** ∼ **you [of that]** das versichere ich Ihnen. ∼**d** *adj* sicher

asterisk /'æstərɪsk/ *n* Sternchen *nt*

asthma /'æsmə/ *n* Asthma *nt*

astonish /ə'stɒnɪʃ/ *vt* erstaunen. ∼**ing** *adj* erstaunlich. ∼**ment** *n* Erstaunen *nt*

astray /ə'streɪ/ *adv* **go** ∼ verloren gehen; (*person:*) sich verlaufen

astride /ə'straɪd/ *adv* rittlings ● *prep* rittlings auf (+ *dat/acc*)

astrolog|er /ə'strɒlədʒə(r)/ *n* Astrologe *m*/-gin *f*. ∼**y** *n* Astrologie *f*

astronaut /'æstrənɔ:t/ *n* Astronaut(in) *m*(*f*)

astronom|er /ə'strɒnəmə(r)/ *n* Astronom *m*. ∼**ical** *adj* astronomisch. ∼**y** *n* Astronomie *f*

astute /ə'stju:t/ *adj* scharfsinnig

asylum /ə'saɪləm/ *n* Asyl *nt*; **[lunatic]** ∼ Irrenanstalt *f*. ∼**-seeker** *n*

Asylbewerber(in) *m*(*f*)

---

at /æt/, *unbetont* /ət/

● *preposition*

····▸ (*expressing place*) an (+ *dat*). **at the station** am Bahnhof. **at the end** am Ende. **at the corner** an der Ecke. **at the same place** an der gleichen Stelle

····▸ (*at s.o.'s house or shop*) bei (+ *dat*). **at Lisa's** bei Lisa. **at my uncle's** bei meinem Onkel. **at the baker's/butcher's** beim Bäcker/Fleischer

····▸ (*inside a building*) in (+ *dat*). **at the theatre/supermarket** im Theater/Supermarkt. **we spent the night at a hotel** wir übernachteten in einem Hotel. **he is still at the office** er ist noch im Büro

····▸ (*expressing time*) (*with clock time*) um; (*with main festivals*) zu. **at six o'clock** um sechs Uhr. **at midnight** um Mitternacht. **at midday** um zwölf Uhr mittags. **at Christmas/Easter** zu Weihnachten/Ostern

····▸ (*expressing age*) mit. **at [the age of] forty** mit vierzig; im Alter von vierzig

····▸ (*expressing price*) zu. **at £2.50 [each]** zu od für [je] 2,50 Pfund

····▸ (*expressing speed*) mit. **at 30 m.p.h.** mit dreißig Meilen pro Stunde

····▸ (*in phrases*) **good/bad at languages** gut/schlecht in Sprachen. **two at a time** zwei auf einmal. **at that** (*at that point*) dabei; (*at that provocation*) daraufhin; (*moreover*) noch dazu

---

ate /et/ *see* **eat**

atheist /'eɪθɪɪst/ *n* Atheist(in) *m*(*f*)

athlet|e /'æθli:t/ *n* Athlet(in) *m*(*f*). ∼**ic** *adj* sportlich. ∼**ics** *n* Leichtathletik *f*

Atlantic /ət'læntɪk/ *adj & n* **the** ∼ **[Ocean]** der Atlantik

atlas /'ætləs/ *n* Atlas *m*

atmosphere /ˈætməsfɪə(r)/ n Atmosphäre f

atom /ˈætəm/ n Atom nt. ~ **bomb** n Atombombe f

atomic /əˈtɒmɪk/ adj Atom-

atrocious /əˈtrəʊʃəs/ adj abscheulich

atrocity /əˈtrɒsəti/ n Gräueltat f

attach /əˈtætʃ/ vt befestigen (**to** an + dat); beimessen (importance) (**to** dat); **be ~ed to** (fig) hängen an (+ dat)

attack /əˈtæk/ n Angriff m; (Med) Anfall m ● vt/i angreifen. ~**er** n Angreifer m

attain /əˈteɪn/ vt erreichen. ~**able** adj erreichbar

attempt /əˈtempt/ n Versuch m ● vt versuchen

attend /əˈtend/ vt anwesend sein bei; (go regularly to) besuchen; (take part in) teilnehmen an (+ dat); (accompany) begleiten; (doctor:) behandeln ● vi anwesend sein; (pay attention) aufpassen; ~ **to** sich kümmern um; (in shop) bedienen. ~**ance** n Anwesenheit f; (number) Besucherzahl f. ~**ant** n Wärter(in) m(f); (in car park) Wächter m

attention /əˈtenʃn/ n Aufmerksamkeit f; ~! (Mil) stillgestanden! **pay** ~ aufpassen; **pay** ~ **to** beachten, achten auf (+ acc)

attentive /əˈtentɪv/ adj aufmerksam

attic /ˈætɪk/ n Dachboden m

attitude /ˈætɪtjuːd/ n Haltung f

attorney /əˈtɜːnɪ/ n (Amer: lawyer) Rechtsanwalt m; **power of** ~ Vollmacht f

attract /əˈtrækt/ vt anziehen; erregen (attention); ~ **s.o.'s attention** jds Aufmerksamkeit auf sich (acc) lenken. ~**ion** n Anziehungskraft f; (charm) Reiz m; (thing) Attraktion f. ~**ive** adj, -ly adv attraktiv

attribute /əˈtrɪbjuːt/ vt zuschreiben (**to** dat)

aubergine /ˈəʊbəʒiːn/ n Aubergine f

auburn /ˈɔːbən/ adj kastanienbraun

auction /ˈɔːkʃn/ n Auktion f Versteigerung f ● vt versteigern. ~**eer** n Auktionator m

audaci|ous /ɔːˈdeɪʃəs/ adj verwegen. ~**ty** n Verwegenheit f; (impudence) Dreistigkeit f

audible /ˈɔːdəbl/ adj, -**bly** adv hörbar

audience /ˈɔːdɪəns/ n Publikum nt; (Theat, TV) Zuschauer pl; (Radio) Zuhörer pl; (meeting) Audienz f

audit /ˈɔːdɪt/ n Bücherrevision f ● vt (Comm) prüfen

audition /ɔːˈdɪʃn/ n (Theat) Vorsprechen nt; (Mus) Vorspielen nt (for singer) Vorsingen nt ● vi vorsprechen; vorspielen; vorsingen

auditor /ˈɔːdɪtə(r)/ n Buchprüfer m

auditorium /ɔːdɪˈtɔːrɪəm/ n Zuschauerraum m

August /ˈɔːgəst/ n August m

aunt /ɑːnt/ n Tante f

au pair /əʊˈpeə(r)/ n ~ [**girl**] Au-pair-Mädchen nt

aura /ˈɔːrə/ n Fluidum nt

auspicious /ɔːˈspɪʃəs/ adj günstig; (occasion) freudig

auster|e /ɒˈstɪə(r)/ adj streng; (simple) nüchtern. ~**ity** n Strenge f; (hardship) Entbehrung f

Australia /ɒˈstreɪlɪə/ n Australien nt. ~**n** adj australisch ● n Australier(in) m(f)

Austria /ˈɒstrɪə/ n Österreich nt ~**n** adj österreichisch ● n Österreicher(in) m(f)

authentic /ɔːˈθentɪk/ adj echt, authentisch. ~**ate** vt beglaubigen. ~**ity** n Echtheit f

author /ˈɔːθə(r)/ n Schriftsteller m, Autor m; (of document) Verfasser m

authoritarian /ɔːθɒrɪˈteərɪən/ adj autoritär

authoritative /ɔːˈθɒrɪtətɪv/ adj maßgebend

authority /ɔːˈθɒrətɪ/ n Autorität f; (public) Behörde f; **in** ~ verantwortlich

authorization /ɔːθəraɪˈzeɪʃn/ n Ermächtigung f

authorize /ˈɔːθəraɪz/ vt ermächtigen (s.o.); genehmigen (sth) a **autobi'ography** /ɔːtə-/ n Autobiographie f

b **autograph** /'ɔːtə-/ n Autogramm nt

automatic /ɔːtə'mætɪk/ adj, **-ally** adv automatisch

automation /ɔːtə'meɪʃn/ n Automation f

automobile /'ɔːtəməbiːl/ n Auto nt

autonom|ous /ɔː'tɒnəməs/ adj autonom. ~**y** n Autonomie f

autumn /'ɔːtəm/ n Herbst m. ~**al** adj herbstlich

auxiliary /əːg'zɪlɪərɪ/ adj Hilfs- • n Helfer(in) m(f), Hilfskraft f

avail /ə'veɪl/ n **to no** ~ vergeblich

available /ə'veɪləbl/ adj verfügbar; (obtainable) erhältlich

avalanche /'ævəlɑːnʃ/ n Lawine f

avenge /ə'vendʒ/ vt rächen

avenue /'ævənjuː/ n Allee f

average /'ævərɪdʒ/ adj Durchschnitts-, durchschnittlich • n Durchschnitt m; **on** ~ im Durchschnitt, durchschnittlich • vt durchschnittlich schaffen

averse /ə'vɜːs/ adj **not be** ~**e to sth** etw (dat) nicht abgeneigt sein

avert /ə'vɜːt/ vt abwenden

aviary /'eɪvɪərɪ/ n Vogelhaus nt

aviation /eɪvɪ'eɪʃn/ n Luftfahrt f

avocado /ævə'kɑːdəʊ/ n Avocado f

avoid /ə'vɔɪd/ vt vermeiden; ~ **s.o.** jdm aus dem Weg gehen. ~**able** adj vermeidbar. ~**ance** n Vermeidung f

await /ə'weɪt/ vt warten auf (+ acc)

awake /ə'weɪk/ adj wach; **wide** ~ hellwach • vi (pt **awoke**, pp **awoken**) erwachen

awaken /ə'weɪkn/ vt wecken • vi erwachen. ~**ing** n Erwachen nt

award /ə'wɔːd/ n Auszeichnung f; (prize) Preis m • vt zuerkennen (**to s.o.** dat); verleihen (prize)

aware /ə'weə(r)/ adj **become** ~ gewahr werden (of gen); **be** ~ **that** wissen, dass. ~**ness** n Bewusstsein nt

away /ə'weɪ/ adv weg, fort; (absent) abwesend; **four kilometres** ~ vier

Kilometer entfernt; **play** ~ (Sport) auswärts spielen. ~ **game** n Auswärtsspiel nt

awful /'ɔːfl/ adj furchtbar

awkward /'ɔːkwəd/ adj schwierig; (clumsy) ungeschickt; (embarrassing) peinlich; (inconvenient) ungünstig. ~**ly** adv ungeschickt; (embarrassedly) verlegen

awning /'ɔːnɪŋ/ n Markise f

awoke(n) /ə'wəʊk(n)/ see **awake**

axe /æks/ n Axt f • vt (pres p **axing**) streichen

axle /'æksl/ n (Techn) Achse f

Bb

B /biː/ n (Mus) H nt

baboon /bə'buːn/ n Pavian m

baby /'beɪbɪ/ n Baby nt; (Amer, 🆃) Schätzchen nt

baby: ~**ish** adj kindisch. ~**-sit** vi babysitten. ~**-sitter** n Babysitter m

bachelor /'bætʃələ(r)/ n Junggeselle m

back /bæk/ n Rücken m; (reverse) Rückseite f; (of chair) Rückenlehne f; (Sport) Verteidiger m; **at**/(Auto) **in the** ~ hinten; **on the** ~ auf der Rückseite; ~ **to front** verkehrt • adj Hinter- • adv zurück; ~ **here/there** hier/da hinten; ~ **at home** zu Hause. **go/pay** ~ zurückgehen/-zahlen • vt (support) unterstützen; (with money) finanzieren; (Auto) zurücksetzen; (Betting) [Geld] setzen auf (+ acc); (cover the back of) mit einer Verstärkung versehen • vi (Auto) zurücksetzen. ~ **down** vi klein beigeben. ~ **in** vi rückwärts hineinfahren. ~ **out** vi rückwärts hinaus-/herausfahren; (fig) aussteigen (of aus). ~ **up** vt unterstützen; (confirm) bestätigen • vi (Auto) zurücksetzen

back: ~**ache** n Rückenschmerzen pl. ~**biting** n gehässiges Gerede nt.

~**bone** n Rückgrat nt. ~**date** vt rückdatieren; ~**dated to** rückwirkend von. ~ **'door** n Hintertür f

backer /ˈbækə(r)/ n Geldgeber m

back: ~**'fire** vi (Auto) fehlzünden; (fig) fehlschlagen. ~**ground** n Hintergrund m; **family** ~**ground** Familienverhältnisse pl. ~**hand** n (Sport) Rückhand f. ~**'handed** adj (compliment) zweifelhaft

backing /ˈbækɪŋ/ n (support) Unterstützung f; (material) Verstärkung f

back: ~**lash** n (fig) Gegenschlag m. ~**log** n Rückstand m (of an + dat). ~**pack** n Rucksack m. ~ **'seat** n Rücksitz m. ~**side** n ▣ Hintern m. ~**stroke** n Rückenschwimmen nt. ~**-up** n Unterstützung f; (Amer: traffic jam) Stau m

backward /ˈbækwəd/ adj zurückgeblieben; (country) rückständig ● adv rückwärts. ~**s** rückwärts; ~**s and forwards** hin und her

back'yard n Hinterhof m; **not in my** ~**yard** ▣ nicht vor meiner Haustür

bacon /ˈbeɪkn/ n [Schinken]speck m

bacteria /bækˈtɪərɪə/ npl Bakterien pl

bad /bæd/ adj (**worse, worst**) schlecht; (serious) schwer, schlimm; (naughty) unartig; ~ **language** gemeine Ausdrucksweise f; **feel** ~ sich schlecht fühlen; (feel guilty) ein schlechtes Gewissen haben

badge /bædʒ/ n Abzeichen nt

badger /ˈbædʒə(r)/ n Dachs m ● vt plagen

badly /ˈbædlɪ/ adv schlecht; (seriously) schwer; ~ **off** schlecht gestellt; ~ **behaved** unerzogen; **want** ~ sich (dat) sehnsüchtig wünschen; **need** ~ dringend brauchen

bad-'mannered adj mit schlechten Manieren

badminton /ˈbædmɪntən/ n Federball m

bad-'tempered adj schlecht gelaunt

baffle /ˈbæfl/ vt verblüffen

bag /bæg/ n Tasche f; (of paper) Tüte

f; (pouch) Beutel m; ~**s of** ▣ jede Menge ● vt (▣: reserve) in Beschlag nehmen

baggage /ˈbægɪdʒ/ n [Reise]gepäck nt

baggy /ˈbægɪ/ adj (clothes) ausgebeult

'bagpipes npl Dudelsack m

bail /beɪl/ n Kaution f; **on** ~ gegen Kaution ● vt ~ **s.o. out** jdn gegen Kaution freibekommen; (fig) jdm aus der Patsche helfen

bait /beɪt/ n Köder m ● vt mit einem Köder versehen; (fig: torment) reizen

bake /beɪk/ vt/i backen

baker /ˈbeɪkə(r)/ n Bäcker m; ~**'s [shop]** Bäckerei f. ~**y** n Bäckerei f

baking /ˈbeɪkɪŋ/ n Backen nt. ~**-powder** n Backpulver nt

balance /ˈbæləns/ n (equilibrium) Gleichgewicht nt, Balance f; (scales) Waage f; (Comm) Saldo m; (outstanding sum) Restbetrag m; **[bank]** ~ Kontostand m; **in the** ~ (fig) in der Schwebe ● vt balancieren; (equalize) ausgleichen; (Comm) abschließen (books) ● vi balancieren; (fig & Comm) sich ausgleichen. ~**d** adj ausgewogen

balcony /ˈbælkənɪ/ n Balkon m

bald /bɔːld/ adj (**-er, -est**) kahl; (person) kahlköpfig

bald|ly adv unverblümt. ~**ness** n Kahlköpfigkeit f

ball¹ /bɔːl/ n Ball m; (Billiards, Croquet) Kugel f; (of yarn) Knäuel m & nt; **on the** ~ ▣ auf Draht

ball² n (dance) Ball m

ball-'bearing n Kugellager nt

ballerina /bæləˈriːnə/ n Ballerina f

ballet /ˈbæleɪ/ m Ballett nt. ~ **dancer** n Balletttänzer(in) m(f)

balloon /bəˈluːn/ n Luftballon m; (Aviat) Ballon m

ballot /ˈbælət/ n [geheime] Wahl f; (on issue) [geheime] Abstimmung f. ~**-box** n Wahlurne f. ~**-paper** n Stimmzettel m

ball: ~**point** [ˈpen] n Kugelschreiber m. ~**room** n Ballsaal m

balm /bɑːm/ n Balsam m

balmy /'bɑːmɪ/ adj sanft

Baltic /'bɔːltɪk/ adj & n the ~ [Sea] die Ostsee

bamboo /bæm'buː/ n Bambus m

ban /bæn/ n Verbot nt ● vt (pt/pp banned) verbieten

banal /bə'nɑːl/ adj banal. ~ity n Banalität f

banana /bə'nɑːnə/ n Banane f

band /bænd/ n Band nt; (stripe) Streifen m; (group) Schar f; (Mus) Kapelle f

bandage /'bændɪdʒ/ n Verband m; (for support) Bandage f ● vt verbinden; bandagieren (limb)

b. & b. abbr bed and breakfast

bandit /'bændɪt/ n Bandit m

band: ~stand n Musikpavillon m. ~wagon n jump on the ~wagon (fig) sich einer erfolgreichen Sache anschließen

bang /bæŋ/ n (noise) Knall m; (blow) Schlag m ● adv go ~ knallen ● int bums! peng! ● vt knallen; (shut noisily) zuknallen; (strike) schlagen auf (+ acc); ~ one's head sich (dat) den Kopf stoßen (on an + acc) ● vi schlagen; (door:) zuknallen

banger /'bæŋə(r)/ n (firework) Knallfrosch m; (⬚: sausage) Wurst f; old ~ (⬚: car) Klapperkiste f

bangle /'bæŋgl/ n Armreifen m

banish /'bænɪʃ/ vt verbannen

banisters /'bænɪstəz/ npl [Treppen]geländer nt

banjo /'bændʒəʊ/ n Banjo nt

bank¹ /bæŋk/ n (of river) Ufer nt; (slope) Hang m ● vi (Aviat) in die Kurve gehen

bank² n Bank f ● ~ on vt sich verlassen auf (+ acc)

'bank account n Bankkonto nt

banker /'bæŋkə(r)/ n Bankier m

bank: ~ 'holiday n gesetzlicher Feiertag m. ~ing n Bankwesen nt. ~note n Banknote f

bankrupt /'bæŋkrʌpt/ adj bankrott; go ~ Bankrott machen ● n Bankrot-

teur m ● vt Bankrott machen. ~cy n Bankrott m

banner /'bænə(r)/ n Banner nt; (carried by demonstrators) Transparent nt, Spruchband nt

banquet /'bæŋkwɪt/ n Bankett nt

baptism /'bæptɪzm/ n Taufe f

baptize /bæp'taɪz/ vt taufen

bar /bɑː(r)/ n Stange f; (of cage) [Gitter]stab m; (of gold) Barren m; (of chocolate) Tafel f; (of soap) Stück nt; (long) Riegel m; (café) Bar f; (counter) Theke f; (Mus) Takt m; (fig: obstacle) Hindernis nt; **parallel** ~s (Sport) Barren m; **behind** ~s ⬚ hinter Gittern ● vt (pt/pp **barred**) versperren (way, door); ausschließen (person)

barbar|ic /bɑː'bærɪk/ adj barbarisch. ~ity n Barbarei f. ~ous adj barbarisch

barbecue /'bɑːbɪkjuː/ n Grill m; (party) Grillfest nt ● vt [im Freien] grillen

barbed /'bɑːbd/ adj ~ wire Stacheldraht m

barber /'bɑːbə(r)/ n [Herren]friseur m

'bar code n Strichkode m

bare /beə(r)/ adj (-r, -st) nackt, bloß; (tree) kahl; (empty) leer; (mere) bloß

bare: ~back adv ohne Sattel. ~faced adj schamlos. ~foot adv barfuß. ~'headed adj mit unbedecktem Kopf

barely /'beəlɪ/ adv kaum

bargain /'bɑːgɪn/ n (agreement) Geschäft nt; (good buy) Gelegenheitskauf m; **into the** ~ noch dazu; **make a** ~ sich einigen ● vi handeln; (haggle) feilschen; ~ **for** (expect) rechnen mit

barge /bɑːdʒ/ n Lastkahn m; (towed) Schleppkahn m ● vi ~ **in** ⬚ hereinplatzen

baritone /'bærɪtəʊn/ n Bariton m

bark¹ /bɑːk/ n (of tree) Rinde f

bark² n Bellen nt ● vi bellen

barley /'bɑːlɪ/ n Gerste f

bar: ~maid n Schankmädchen nt. ~man n Barmann m

barmy /'bɑːmɪ/ adj 🆔 verrückt

barn /bɑːn/ n Scheune f

barometer /bə'rɒmɪtə(r)/ n Barometer nt

baron /'bærn/ n Baron m. **~ess** n Baronin f

barracks /'bærəks/ npl Kaserne f

barrage /'bærɑːʒ/ n (in river) Wehr nt; (Mil) Sperrfeuer nt; (fig) Hagel m

barrel /'bærl/ n Fass nt; (of gun) Lauf m; (of cannon) Rohr nt. **~-organ** n Drehorgel f

barren /'bærn/ adj unfruchtbar; (landscape) öde

barricade /bærɪ'keɪd/ n Barrikade f ● vt verbarrikadieren

barrier /'bærɪə(r)/ n Barriere f; (across road) Schranke f; (Rail) Sperre f; (fig) Hindernis nt

barrow /'bærəʊ/ n Karre f, Karren m

base /beɪs/ n Fuß m; (fig) Basis f; (Mil) Stützpunkt m ● vt stützen (**on** auf + acc); **be ~d on** basieren auf (+ dat)

base: ~ball n Baseball m. **~less** adj unbegründet. **~ment** n Kellergeschoss nt

bash /bæʃ/ n Schlag m; **have a ~!** 🆔 probier es mal! ● vt hauen

basic /'beɪsɪk/ adj Grund-; (fundamental) grundlegend; (essential) wesentlich; (unadorned) einfach; **the ~s** das Wesentliche. **~ally** adv grundsätzlich

basin /'beɪsn/ n Becken nt; (for washing) Waschbecken nt; (for food) Schüssel f

basis /'beɪsɪs/ n (pl **-ses** /-siːz/) Basis f

bask /bɑːsk/ vi sich sonnen

basket /'bɑːskɪt/ n Korb m. **~ball** n Basketball m

Basle /bɑːl/ n Basel nt

bass /beɪs/ adj Bass-; **~ voice** Bassstimme f ● n Bass m; (person) Bassist m

bassoon /bə'suːn/ n Fagott nt

bastard /'bɑːstəd/ n 🆇 Schuft m

bat¹ /bæt/ n Schläger m; **off one's own ~** 🆔 auf eigene Faust ● vt (pt/

pp **batted**) schlagen; **not ~ an eyelid** (fig) nicht mit der Wimper zucken

bat² n (Zool) Fledermaus f

batch /bætʃ/ n (of people) Gruppe f; (of papers) Stoß m; (of goods) Sendung f; (of bread) Schub m

bath /bɑːθ/ n (pl **~s** /bɑːðz/) Bad nt; (tub) Badewanne f; **~s** pl Badeanstalt f; **have a ~** baden

bathe /beɪð/ n Bad nt ● vt/i baden. **~r** n Badende(r) m/f

bathing /'beɪðɪŋ/ n Baden nt. **~cap** n Bademütze f. **~costume** n Badeanzug m

bath: ~mat n Bademattte f. **~room** n Badezimmer nt. **~towel** n Badetuch nt

battalion /bə'tælɪən/ n Bataillon nt

batter /'bætə(r)/ n (Culin) flüssiger Teig m ● vt schlagen. **~ed** adj (car) verbeult; (wife) misshandelt

battery /'bætərɪ/ n Batterie f

battle /'bætl/ n Schlacht f; (fig) Kampf m ● vi (fig) kämpfen (**for** um)

battle: ~field n Schlachtfeld nt. **~ship** n Schlachtschiff nt

batty /'bætɪ/ adj 🆔 verrückt

Bavaria /bə'veərɪə/ n Bayern nt. **~n** adj bayrisch ● n Bayer(in) m(f)

bawl /bɔːl/ vt/i brüllen

bay¹ /beɪ/ n (Geog) Bucht f; (in room) Erker m

bay² n (Bot) [echter] Lorbeer m. **~-leaf** n Lorbeerblatt nt

bayonet /'beɪənet/ n Bajonett nt

bay 'window n Erkerfenster nt

bazaar /bə'zɑː(r)/ n Basar m

BC abbr (**before Christ**) v.Chr.

be /biː/

❗ (pres **am, are, is**, pl **are**; pt **was**, pl **were**; pp **been**)

● intransitive verb

⋯► (expressing identity, nature, state, age etc.) sein. **he is a teacher** er ist Lehrer. **she is French** sie ist Französin. **he is**

b

very nice er ist sehr nett. **I am tall** ich bin groß. **you are thirty** du bist dreißig. **it was very cold** es war sehr kalt

••••➤ (expressing general position) sein; (lie) liegen; (stand) stehen. **where is the bank?** wo ist die Bank? **the book is on the table** das Buch liegt auf dem Tisch. **the vase is on the shelf** die Vase steht auf dem Brett

••••➤ (feel) **I am cold/hot** mir ist kalt/heiß. **I am ill** ich bin krank. **I am well** mir geht es gut. **how are you?** wie geht es Ihnen?

••••➤ (date) **it is the 5th today** heute haben wir den Fünften

••••➤ (go, come, stay) sein. **I have been to Vienna** ich bin in Wien gewesen. **have you ever been to London?** bist du schon einmal in London gewesen? **has the postman been?** war der Briefträger schon da? **I've been here for an hour** ich bin seit einer Stunde hier

••••➤ (origin) **where are you from?** woher stammen od kommen Sie? **she is from Australia** sie stammt od ist aus Australien

••••➤ (cost) kosten. **how much are the eggs?** was kosten die Eier?

••••➤ (in calculations) **two threes are six** zweimal drei ist od sind sechs

••••➤ (exist) **there is/are** es gibt (+ acc). **there's no fish left** es gibt keinen Fisch mehr

● auxiliary verb

••••➤ (forming continuous tenses: not translated) **I'm working** ich arbeite. **I'm leaving tomorrow** ich reise morgen [ab]. **they were singing** sie sangen. **they will be coming on Tuesday** sie kommen am Dienstag

••••➤ (forming passive) werden. **the child was found** das Kind wurde gefunden. **German is spoken here** hier wird Deutsch gesprochen; hier spricht man Deutsch

••••➤ (expressing arrangement, obligation, destiny) sollen. **I am to go/inform you** ich soll gehen/Sie unterrichten. **they were to fly today** sie sollten heute fliegen. **you are to do that immediately** das sollst du sofort machen. **you are not to ...** (prohibition) du darfst nicht .... **they were never to meet again** (destiny) sie sollten sich nie wieder treffen

••••➤ (in short answers) **Are you disappointed? — Yes I am** Bist du enttäuscht? — Ja. (negating previous statement) **Aren't you coming? — Yes I am!** Kommst du nicht? — Doch!

••••➤ (in tag questions) **isn't it? wasn't she? aren't they?** etc. nicht wahr. **it's a beautiful house, isn't it?** das Haus ist sehr schön, nicht wahr?

beach /biːtʃ/ n Strand m

bead /biːd/ n Perle f

beak /biːk/ n Schnabel m

beam /biːm/ n Balken m; (of light) Strahl m ● vi strahlen. **~ing** adj [freude]strahlend

bean /biːn/ n Bohne f

bear¹ /beə(r)/ n Bär m

bear² vt/i (pt bore, pp borne) tragen; (endure) ertragen; gebären (child); **~ right** sich rechts halten. **~able** adj erträglich

beard /bɪəd/ n Bart m. **~ed** adj bärtig

bearer /ˈbeərə(r)/ n Träger m; (of news, cheque) Überbringer m; (of passport) Inhaber(in) m(f)

bearing /ˈbeərɪŋ/ n Haltung f; (Techn) Lager nt; **get one's ~s** sich orientieren

beast /biːst/ n Tier nt; (🛈: person) Biest nt

beastly /ˈbiːstlɪ/ adj 🛈 scheußlich; (person) gemein

beat /biːt/ n Schlag m; (of policeman) Runde f; (rhythm) Takt m ● vt/i (pt beat, pp beaten) schlagen; (thrash) verprügeln; klopfen (carpet); (ham-

mer) hämmern (**on** an + *acc*); ~ **it!** 🔲 hau ab! **it** ~**s me** 🔲 das begreife ich nicht. ~ **up** *vt* zusammenschlagen

beat|en /'biːtn/ *adj* **off the** ~**en track** abseits. ~**ing** *n* Prügel *pl*

beauti|ful /'bjuːtɪfl/ *adj* schön. ~**fy** *vt* (*pt/pp* -**ied**) verschönern

beauty /'bjuːtɪ/ *n* Schönheit *f*. ~ **parlour** *n* Kosmetiksalon *m*. ~ **spot** *n* Schönheitsfleck *m*; (*place*) landschaftlich besonders reizvolles Fleckchen *nt*.

beaver /'biːvə(r)/ *n* Biber *m*

became /bɪ'keɪm/ *see* **become**

because /bɪ'kɒz/ *conj* weil ● *adv* ~ **of** wegen (+ *gen*)

becom|e /bɪ'kʌm/ *vt/i* (*pt* **became**, *pp* **become**) werden. ~**ing** *adj* (*clothes*) kleidsam

bed /bed/ *n* Bett *nt*; (*layer*) Schicht *f*; (*of flowers*) Beet *nt*; **in** ~ im Bett; **go to** ~ ins *od* zu Bett gehen; ~ **and breakfast** Zimmer mit Frühstück. ~**clothes** *npl*, ~**ding** *n* Bettzeug *nt*. ~**room** *n* Schlafzimmer *nt*

---

bed and breakfast Überall in Großbritannien sieht man Schilder mit der Aufschrift *Bed & Breakfast* oder *B & B*. Sie weisen auf Privathäuser hin, die preisgünstige Unterkunft anbieten, wobei im Zimmerpreis das Frühstück mit eingeschlossen ist. Zum traditionellen Frühstück gehört vor allem, Cornflakes, *bacon and eggs* (Spiegelei mit Speck), Toast und Orangenmarmelade und Tee.

'**bedside** *n* **at his** ~ an seinem Bett. ~ '**lamp** *n* Nachttischlampe *f*. ~ '**table** *n* Nachttisch *m*

bed: ~'**sitter** *n*, ~-'**sitting-room** *n* Wohnschlafzimmer *nt*. ~'**spread** *n* Tagesdecke *f*. ~**time** *n* **at** ~**time** vor dem Schlafengehen

bee /biː/ *n* Biene *f*

beech /biːtʃ/ *n* Buche *f*

beef /biːf/ *n* Rindfleisch *nt*. ~**burger** *n* Hamburger *m*

bee: ~**hive** *n* Bienenstock *m*. ~-**line**

n **make a** ~-**line for** 🔲 zusteuern auf (+ *acc*)

been /biːn/ *see* **be**

beer /bɪə(r)/ *n* Bier *nt*

beet /biːt/ *n* (*Amer: beetroot*) rote Bete *f*; [**sugar**] ~ Zuckerrübe *f*

beetle /'biːtl/ *n* Käfer *m*

'**beetroot** *n* rote Bete *f*

before /bɪ'fɔː(r)/ *prep* vor (+ *dat/acc*); **the day** ~ **yesterday** vorgestern; ~ **long** bald ● *adv* vorher; (*already*) schon; **never** ~ noch nie; ~ **that** davor ● *conj* (*time*) ehe, bevor. ~**hand** *adv* vorher, im Voraus

beg /beg/ *v* (*pt/pp* **begged**) ● *vi* betteln ● *vt* (*entreat*) anflehen; (*ask*) bitten (**for** um)

began /bɪ'gæn/ *see* **begin**

beggar /'begə(r)/ *n* Bettler(in) *m(f)*; 🔲 Kerl *m*

begin /bɪ'gɪn/ *vt/i* (*pt* **began**, *pp* **begun**, *pres p* **beginning**) anfangen, beginnen; **to** ~ **with** anfangs. ~**ner** *n* Anfänger(in) *m(f)*. ~**ning** *n* Anfang *m*, Beginn *m*

begun /bɪ'gʌn/ *see* **begin**

behalf /bɪ'hɑːf/ *n* **on** ~ **of** im Namen von; **on my** ~ meinetwegen

behave /bɪ'heɪv/ *vi* sich verhalten; ~ **oneself** sich benehmen

behaviour /bɪ'heɪvjə(r)/ *n* Verhalten *nt*; **good/bad** ~ gutes/ schlechtes Benehmen *nt*

behind /bɪ'haɪnd/ *prep* hinter (+ *dat/ acc*); **be** ~ **sth** hinter etw (*dat*) stecken ● *adv* hinten; (*late*) im Rückstand; **a long way** ~ weit zurück ● *n* 🔲 Hintern *m*. ~**hand** *adv* im Rückstand

beige /beɪʒ/ *adj* beige

being /'biːɪŋ/ *n* Dasein *nt*; **living** ~ Lebewesen *nt*; **come into** ~ entstehen

belated /bɪ'leɪtɪd/ *adj* verspätet

belfry /'belfrɪ/ *n* Glockenstube *f*; (*tower*) Glockenturm *m*

Belgian /'beldʒən/ *adj* belgisch ● *n* Belgier(in) *m(f)*

Belgium /'beldʒəm/ *n* Belgien *nt*

belief /bɪ'liːf/ *n* Glaube *m*

believable /bɪˈliːvəbl/ adj glaubhaft

believe /bɪˈliːv/ vt/i glauben (s.o. jdm; **in** an + acc). **~r** n (Relig) Gläubige(r) m/f

belittle /bɪˈlɪtl/ vt herabsetzen

bell /bel/ n Glocke f; (on door) Klingel f

bellow /ˈbeləʊ/ vt/i brüllen

belly /ˈbelɪ/ n Bauch m

belong /bɪˈlɒŋ/ vi gehören (**to** dat); (be member) angehören (**to** dat). **~ings** npl Sachen pl

beloved /bɪˈlʌvɪd/ adj geliebt ● n Geliebte(r) m/f

below /bɪˈləʊ/ prep unter (+ dat/acc) ● adv unten; (Naut) unter Deck

belt /belt/ n Gürtel m; (area) Zone f; (Techn) [Treib]riemen m ● vi (⊞: rush) rasen ● vt (⊞: hit) hauen

bench /bentʃ/ n Bank f; (work-) Werkbank f

bend /bend/ n Biegung f; (in road) Kurve f; **round the ~** ⊞ verrückt ● v (pt/pp bent) ● vt biegen; beugen (arm, leg) ● vi sich bücken; (thing:) sich biegen; (road:) eine Biegung machen. **~ down** vi sich bücken. **~ over** vi sich vornüberbeugen

beneath /bɪˈniːθ/ prep unter (+ dat/acc); **~ him** (fig) unter seiner Würde ● adv darunter

benefactor /ˈbenɪfæktə(r)/ n Wohltäter(in) m(f)

beneficial /benɪˈfɪʃl/ adj nützlich

benefit /ˈbenɪfɪt/ n Vorteil m; (allowance) Unterstützung f; (insurance) Leistung f; **sickness ~** Krankengeld nt ● v (pt/pp -fited, pres p -fiting) ● vt nützen (+ dat) ● vi profitieren (**from** von)

benevolen|ce /bɪˈnevələns/ n Wohlwollen nt. **~t** adj wohlwollend

bent /bent/ see **bend** ● adj (person) gebeugt; (distorted) verbogen; (⊞: dishonest) korrupt; **be ~ on doing sth** darauf erpicht sein, etw zu tun ● n Hang m, Neigung f (**for** zu); **artistic ~** künstlerische Ader f

bequeath /bɪˈkwiːð/ vt vermachen (**to** dat)

bereave|d /bɪˈriːvd/ n **the ~d** pl die Hinterbliebenen

beret /ˈbereɪ/ n Baskenmütze f

Berne /bɜːn/ n Bern nt

berry /ˈberɪ/ n Beere f

berth /bɜːθ/ n (on ship) [Schlaf]koje f; (ship's anchorage) Liegeplatz m; **give a wide ~ to** ⊞ einen großen Bogen machen um

beside /bɪˈsaɪd/ prep neben (+ dat/acc); **~ oneself** außer sich (dat)

besides /bɪˈsaɪdz/ prep außer (+ dat) ● adv außerdem

besiege /bɪˈsiːdʒ/ vt belagern

best /best/ adj & n beste(r,s); **the ~** der/die/das Beste; **at ~** bestenfalls; **all the ~!** alles Gute! **do one's ~** sein Bestes tun; **the ~ part of a year** fast ein Jahr; **to the ~ of my knowledge** so viel ich weiß; **make the ~ of it** das Beste daraus machen ● adv am besten; **as ~ I could** so gut ich konnte. **~ 'man** n ≈ Trauzeuge m. **~'seller** n Bestseller m

bet /bet/ n Wette f ● v (pt/pp bet or betted) ● vt **~ s.o. £5** mit jdm um £5 wetten ● vi wetten; **~ on** [Geld] setzen auf (+ acc)

betray /bɪˈtreɪ/ vt verraten. **~al** n Verrat m

better /ˈbetə(r)/ adj besser; **get ~** sich bessern; (after illness) sich erholen ● adv besser; **~ off** besser dran; **~ not** lieber nicht; **all the ~** umso besser; **the sooner the ~** je eher, desto besser; **think ~ of sth** sich eines Besseren besinnen; **you'd ~ stay** du bleibst am besten hier ● vt verbessern; (do better than) übertreffen; **~ oneself** sich verbessern

between /bɪˈtwiːn/ prep zwischen (+ dat/acc); **~ you and me** unter uns; **~ us** (together) zusammen ● adv [in] **~** dazwischen

beware /bɪˈweə(r)/ vi sich in Acht nehmen (**of** vor + dat); **~ of the dog!** Vorsicht, bissiger Hund!

bewilder /bɪˈwɪldə(r)/ vt verwirren. **~ment** n Verwirrung f

bewitch /bɪˈwɪtʃ/ vt verzaubern; (fig) bezaubern

beyond /bɪ'jɒnd/ prep über (+ acc) ... hinaus; (further) weiter als; ~ **reach** außer Reichweite; ~ **doubt** ohne jeden Zweifel; **it's ~ me** 🔲 das geht über meinen Horizont ● adv darüber hinaus

bias /'baɪəs/ n Voreingenommenheit f; (preference) Vorliebe f; (Jur) Befangenheit f ● vt (pt/pp **biased**) (influence) beeinflussen. ~**ed** adj voreingenommen; (Jur) befangen

bib /bɪb/ n Lätzchen nt

Bible /'baɪbl/ n Bibel f

biblical /'bɪblɪkl/ adj biblisch

bibliography /bɪblɪ'ɒgrəfɪ/ n Bibliographie f

bicycle /'baɪsɪkl/ n Fahrrad nt ● vi mit dem Rad fahren

bid /bɪd/ n Gebot nt; (attempt) Versuch m ● vt/i (pt/pp **bid**, pres p **bidding**) bieten (**for** auf + acc); (Cards) reizen

bidder /'bɪdə(r)/ n Bieter(in) m(f)

bide /baɪd/ vt ~ **one's time** den richtigen Moment abwarten

big /bɪg/ adj (**bigger, biggest**) groß ● adv **talk ~** 🔲 angeben

bigam|ist /'bɪgəmɪst/ n Bigamist m. ~**y** n Bigamie f

big-'headed adj 🔲 eingebildet

bigot /'bɪgət/ n Eiferer m. ~**ed** adj engstirnig

'bigwig n 🔲 hohes Tier nt

bike /baɪk/ n 🔲 [Fahr]rad nt

bikini /bɪ'kiːnɪ/ n Bikini m

bile /baɪl/ n Galle f

bilingual /baɪ'lɪŋgwəl/ adj zweisprachig

bilious /'bɪljəs/ adj (Med) ~ **attack** verdorbener Magen m

bill¹ /bɪl/ n Rechnung f; (poster) Plakat nt; (Pol) Gesetzentwurf m; (Amer: note) Banknote f; ~ **of exchange** Wechsel m ● vt eine Rechnung schicken (+ dat)

bill² n (beak) Schnabel m

'billfold n (Amer) Brieftasche f

billiards /'bɪljədz/ n Billard nt

billion /'bɪljən/ n (thousand million) Milliarde f; (million million) Billion f

bin /bɪn/ n Mülleimer m; (for bread) Kasten m

bind /baɪnd/ vt (pt/pp **bound**) binden (**to** an + acc); (bandage) verbinden; (Jur) verpflichten; (cover the edge of) einfassen. ~**ing** adj verbindlich ● n Einband m; (braid) Borte f; (on ski) Bindung f

binge /bɪndʒ/ n 🔲 **go on the ~** eine Sauftour machen

binoculars /bɪ'nɒkjʊləz/ npl [**pair of**] ~ Fernglas nt

bio|'chemistry /baɪəʊ-/ n Biochemie f. ~**degradable** adj biologisch abbaubar

biograph|er /baɪ'ɒgrəfə(r)/ n Biograph(in) m(f). ~**y** n Biographie f

biological /baɪə'lɒdʒɪkl/ adj biologisch

biolog|ist /baɪ'ɒlədʒɪst/ n Biologe m. ~**y** n Biologie f

bio'terrorism /baɪəʊ-/ n Bioterrorismus m

birch /bɜːtʃ/ n Birke f; (whip) Rute f

bird /bɜːd/ n Vogel m; (🔲: girl) Mädchen nt; **kill two ~s with one stone** zwei Fliegen mit einer Klappe schlagen

Biro ® /'baɪrəʊ/ n Kugelschreiber m

birth /bɜːθ/ n Geburt f

birth: ~ **certificate** n Geburtsurkunde f. ~-**control** n Geburtenregelung f. ~**day** n Geburtstag m. ~-**rate** n Geburtenziffer f

biscuit /'bɪskɪt/ n Keks m

bishop /'bɪʃəp/ n Bischof m

bit¹ /bɪt/ n Stückchen nt; (for horse) Gebiss nt; (Techn) Bohreinsatz m; **a ~** ein bisschen; ~ **by** ~ nach und nach; **a ~ of bread** ein bisschen Brot; **do one's ~** sein Teil tun

bit² see **bite**

bitch /bɪtʃ/ n Hündin f; 🔲 Luder nt. ~**y** adj gehässig

bit|e /baɪt/ n Biss m; [**insect**] ~ Stich m; (mouthful) Bissen m ● vt/i (pt **bit**, pp **bitten**) beißen; (insect:) stechen; kauen (one's nails). ~**ing** adj beißend

bitten /'bɪtn/ see **bite**

bitter /'bɪtə(r)/ adj bitter; ~ly cold bitterkalt ● n bitteres Bier nt. ~ness n Bitterkeit f

b

bitty /'bɪtɪ/ adj zusammengestoppelt

bizarre /bɪ'zɑː(r)/ adj bizarr

black /blæk/ adj (-er, -est) schwarz; be ~and blue grün und blau sein ● n Schwarz nt; (person) Schwarze(r) m/f ● vt schwärzen; boykottieren (goods)

black: ~berry n Brombeere f. ~bird n Amsel f. ~board n (Sch) [Wand]tafel f. ~'currant n schwarze Johannisbeere f

blacken vt/i schwärzen

black: ~ 'eye n blaues Auge nt. B ~ 'Forest n Schwarzwald m. ~ 'ice n Glatteis nt. ~list vt auf die schwarze Liste setzen. ~mail n Erpressung f ● vt erpressen. ~mailer n Erpresser(in) m(f). ~ 'market n schwarzer Markt m. ~-out n have a ~-out (Med) das Bewusstsein verlieren. ~ 'pudding n Blutwurst f

bladder /'blædə(r)/ n (Anat) Blase f

blade /bleɪd/ n Klinge f; (of grass) Halm m

blame /bleɪm/ n Schuld f ● vt die Schuld geben (+ dat); no one is to ~ keiner ist schuld daran. ~less adj schuldlos

bland /blænd/ adj (-er, -est) mild

blank /blæŋk/ adj leer; (look) ausdruckslos ● n Lücke f; (cartridge) Platzpatrone f. ~ 'cheque n Blankoscheck m

blanket /'blæŋkɪt/ n Decke f; wet ~ 🅴 Spielverderber(in) m(f)

blare /bleə(r)/ vt/i schmettern

blasé /'blɑːzeɪ/ adj blasiert

blast /blɑːst/ n (gust) Luftstoß m; (sound) Schmettern nt; (of horn) Tuten nt ● vt sprengen ● int 🅴 verdammt. ~ed adj 🅴 verdammt

'blast-off n (of missile) Start m

blatant /'bleɪtənt/ adj offensichtlich

blaze /bleɪz/ n Feuer nt ● vi brennen

blazer /'bleɪzə(r)/ n Blazer m

bleach /bliːtʃ/ n Bleichmittel nt ● vt/i bleichen

bleak /bliːk/ adj (-er, -est) öde; (fig) trostlos

bleary-eyed /'blɪərɪ-/ adj mit trüben/(on waking up) verschlafenen Augen

bleat /bliːt/ vi blöken

bleed /bliːd/ v (pt/pp bled) ● vi bluten ● vt entlüften (radiator)

bleep /bliːp/ n Piepton m ● vi piepsen ● vt mit dem Piepser rufen. ~er n Piepser m

blemish /'blemɪʃ/ n Makel m

blend /blend/ n Mischung f ● vt mischen ● vi sich vermischen

bless /bles/ vt segnen. ~ed adj heilig; 🅴 verflixt. ~ing n Segen m

blew /bluː/ see blow²

blight /blaɪt/ n (Bot) Brand m

blind /blaɪnd/ adj blind; (corner) unübersichtlich; ~ man/woman Blinde(r) m/f ● n [roller] ~ Rouleau nt ● vt blenden

blind: ~ 'alley n Sackgasse f. ~fold adj & adv mit verbundenen Augen ● n Augenbinde f ● vt die Augen verbinden (+ dat). ~ly adv blindlings. ~ness n Blindheit f

blink /blɪŋk/ vi blinzeln; (light:) blinken

bliss /blɪs/ n Glückseligkeit f. ~ful adj glücklich

blister /'blɪstə(r)/ n (Med) Blase f

blitz /blɪts/ n 🅴 Großaktion f

blizzard /'blɪzəd/ n Schneesturm m

bloated /'bləʊtɪd/ adj aufgedunsen

blob /blɒb/ n Klecks m

block /blɒk/ n Block m; (of wood) Klotz m; (of flats) [Wohn]block m ● vt blockieren. ~ up vt zustopfen

blockade /blɒ'keɪd/ n Blockade f ● vt blockieren

blockage /'blɒkɪdʒ/ n Verstopfung f

block: ~head n 🅴 Dummkopf m. ~ 'letters npl Blockschrift f

bloke /bləʊk/ n 🅴 Kerl m

blonde /blɒnd/ adj blond ● n Blondine f

blood /blʌd/ n Blut nt

blood: ~-curdling adj markerschütternd. ~ **donor** n Blutspender m. ~ **group** n Blutgruppe f. **~hound** n Bluthund m. **~-poisoning** n Blutvergiftung f. ~ **pressure** n Blutdruck m. **~shed** n Blutvergießen nt. **~shot** adj blutunterlaufen. ~ **sports** npl Jagdsport m. **~-stained** adj blutbefleckt. ~ **test** n Blutprobe f. **~thirsty** adj blutdürstig. **~-vessel** n Blutgefäß nt

bloody /'blʌdɪ/ adj blutig; ☒ verdammt. **~-'minded** adj ☒ stur

bloom /bluːm/ n Blüte f ● vi blühen

blossom /'blɒsəm/ n Blüte f ● vi blühen

blot /blɒt/ n [Tinten]klecks m; (fig) Fleck m ● ~ **out** vt (fig) auslöschen

blotch /blɒtʃ/ n Fleck m. **~y** adj fleckig

'blotting-paper n Löschpapier nt

blouse /blaʊz/ n Bluse f

blow[1] /bləʊ/ n Schlag m

blow[2] v (pt **blew**, pp **blown**) ● vt blasen; (fam; squander) verpulvern; ~ **one's nose** sich (dat) die Nase putzen ● vi blasen; (fuse:) durchbrennen. ~ **away** vt wegblasen ● vi wegfliegen. ~ **down** vt umwehen ● vi umfallen. ~ **out** vt (extinguish) ausblasen. ~ **over** vi umfallen; (fig: die down) vorübergehen. ~ **up** vt (inflate) aufblasen; (enlarge) vergrößern; (shatter by explosion) sprengen ● vi explodieren

'blowlamp n Lötlampe f

blown /bləʊn/ see **blow**[2]

'blowtorch n (Amer) Lötlampe f

blowy /'bləʊɪ/ adj windig

blue /bluː/ adj (-r, -st) blau; **feel** ~ deprimiert sein ● n Blau nt; **have the ~s** deprimiert sein; **out of the** ~ aus heiterem Himmel

blue: **~bell** n Sternhyazinthe f. **~berry** n Heidelbeere f. **~bottle** n Schmeißfliege f. ~ **film** n Pornofilm m. **~print** n (fig) Entwurf m

bluff /blʌf/ n Bluff m ● vi bluffen

blunder /'blʌndə(r)/ n Schnitzer m ● vi einen Schnitzer machen

blunt /blʌnt/ adj stumpf; (person)

geradeheraus. **~ly** adv unverblümt, geradeheraus

blur /blɜː(r)/ n **it's all a** ~ alles ist verschwommen ● vt (pt/pp **blurred**) verschwommen machen; **~red** verschwommen

blush /blʌʃ/ n Erröten nt ● vi erröten

bluster /'blʌstə(r)/ n Großtuerei f. **~y** adj windig

boar /bɔː(r)/ n Eber m

board /bɔːd/ n Brett nt; (for notices) schwarzes Brett nt; (committee) Ausschuss m; (of directors) Vorstand m; **on** ~ an Bord; **full** ~ Vollpension f; ~ **and lodging** Unterkunft und Verpflegung pl ● vt einsteigen in (+ acc); (Naut, Aviat) besteigen ● vi an Bord gehen. ~ **up** vt mit Brettern verschlagen

boarder /'bɔːdə(r)/ n Pensionsgast m; (Sch) Internatsschüler(in) m(f)

board: **~-game** n Brettspiel nt. **~ing-house** n Pension f. **~ing-school** n Internat nt

boast /bəʊst/ vt sich rühmen (+ gen) ● vi prahlen (**about** mit). **~ful** adj prahlerisch

boat /bəʊt/ n Boot nt; (ship) Schiff nt

Boat Race Seit 1829 findet jährlich (meist am Samstag vor Ostern) ein Ruderrennen auf der Themse in London statt. Das Achterrennen wird von den Rudermannschaften der Universitäten Oxford und Cambridge ausgetragen. Im Gegensatz zu anderen sportlichen Universitätswettbewerben wird dieses Ruderrennen landesweit im Fernsehen übertragen.

---

bob /bɒb/ vi (pt/pp **bobbed**) ~ **up and down** sich auf und ab bewegen

'bob-sleigh n Bob m

bodily /'bɒdɪlɪ/ adj körperlich ● adv (forcibly) mit Gewalt

body /'bɒdɪ/ n Körper m; (corpse) Leiche f; (corporation) Körperschaft f. **~guard** n Leibwächter m. ~ **part** n Leichenteil nt. **~work** n (Auto) Karosserie f

bog /bɒg/ n Sumpf m

b

bogus | bother

b

bogus /'bəʊgəs/ adj falsch

boil¹ /bɔɪl/ n Furunkel m

boil² n bring/come to the ~ zum Kochen bringen/kommen ● vt/i kochen; ~ed potatoes Salzkartoffeln pl. ~ down vi (fig) hinauslaufen (to auf + acc). ~ over vi überkochen

boiler /'bɔɪlə(r)/ n Heizkessel m

'boiling point n Siedepunkt m

boisterous /'bɔɪstərəs/ adj übermütig

bold /bəʊld/ adj (-er, -est) kühn; (Printing) fett. ~ness n Kühnheit f

bolster /'bəʊlstə(r)/ n Nackenrolle f ● vt ~ up Mut machen (+ dat)

bolt /bəʊlt/ n Riegel m; (Techn) Bolzen m ● vt schrauben (to an + acc); verriegeln (door); hinunterschlingen (food) ● vi abhauen; (horse:) durchgehen

bomb /bɒm/ n Bombe f ● vt bombardieren

bombard /bɒm'bɑːd/ vt beschießen; (fig) bombardieren

bombastic /bɒm'bæstɪk/ adj bombastisch

bomber /'bɒmə(r)/ n (Aviat) Bomber m; (person) Bombenleger(in) m(f)

bond /bɒnd/ n (fig) Band nt; (Comm) Obligation f

bone /bəʊn/ n Knochen m; (of fish) Gräte f ● vt von den Knochen lösen (meat); entgräten (fish). ~-'dry adj knochentrocken

bonfire /'bɒn-/ n Gartenfeuer nt; (celebratory) Freudenfeuer nt

bonus /'bəʊnəs/ n Prämie f; (gratuity) Gratifikation f; (fig) Plus nt

bony /'bəʊnɪ/ adj knochig; (fish) grätig

boo /buː/ int buh! ● vt ausbuhen ● vi buhen

boob /buːb/ n (🄵 mistake) Schnitzer m

book /bʊk/ n Buch nt; (of tickets) Heft nt; keep the ~s (Comm) die Bücher führen ● vt/i buchen; (reserve) [vor]bestellen; (for offence) aufschreiben

book: ~case n Bücherregal nt.

~-ends npl Buchstützen pl. ~ing-office n Fahrkartenschalter m. ~keeping n Buchführung f. ~let n Broschüre f. ~maker n Buchmacher m. ~mark n Lesezeichen nt. ~seller n Buchhändler(in) m(f). ~shop n Buchhandlung f. ~stall n Bücherstand m

boom /buːm/ n (Comm) Hochkonjunktur f; (upturn) Aufschwung m ● vi dröhnen; (fig) blühen

boon /buːn/ n Segen m

boost /buːst/ n Auftrieb m ● vt Auftrieb geben (+ dat)

boot /buːt/ n Stiefel m; (Auto) Kofferraum m

booth /buːð/ n Bude f; (cubicle) Kabine f

booty /'buːtɪ/ n Beute f

booze /buːz/ n 🄵 Alkohol m ● vi 🄵 saufen

border /'bɔːdə(r)/ n Rand m; (frontier) Grenze f; (in garden) Rabatte f ● vi ~ on grenzen an (+ acc). ~line case n Grenzfall m

bore¹ /bɔː(r)/ see bear²

bor|e² n (of gun) Kaliber nt; (person) langweiliger Mensch m; (thing) langweilige Sache f ● vt langweilen; be ~ed sich langweilen. ~edom n Langeweile f. ~ing adj langweilig

born /bɔːn/ pp be ~ geboren werden ● adj geboren

borne /bɔːn/ see bear²

borrow /'bɒrəʊ/ vt [sich (dat)] borgen od leihen (from von)

bosom /'bʊzm/ n Busen m

boss /bɒs/ n 🄵 Chef m ● vt herumkommandieren. ~y adj herrschsüchtig

botanical /bə'tænɪkl/ adj botanisch

botan|ist /'bɒtənɪst/ n Botaniker(in) m(f). ~y n Botanik f

both /bəʊθ/ adj & pron beide; ~[of] the children beide Kinder; ~ of them beide [von ihnen] ● adv ~ men and women sowohl Männer als auch Frauen

bother /'bɒðə(r)/ n Mühe f; (minor trouble) Ärger m ● int 🄵 verflixt! ● vt belästigen; (*disturb*) stören ● *vi* sich kümmern (**about** um)

bottle /'bɒtl/ *n* Flasche *f* ● *vt* auf Flaschen abfüllen; (*preserve*) einmachen

bottle: ~-**neck** *n* (*fig*) Engpass *m*. ~-**opener** *n* Flaschenöffner *m*

bottom /'bɒtəm/ *adj* unterste(i,s) ● *n* (*of container*) Boden *m*; (*of river*) Grund *m*; (*of page, hill*) Fuß *m*; (*buttocks*) Hintern *m*; **at the** ~ unten; **get to the** ~ **of sth** (*fig*) hinter etw (*acc*) kommen

bought /bɔːt/ *see* buy

bounce /baʊns/ *vi* [auf]springen; (*cheque:*) ⊞ nicht gedeckt sein ● *vt* aufspringen lassen (*ball*)

bouncer /'baʊnsə(r)/ *n* ⊞ Rausschmeißer *m*

bound[1] /baʊnd/ *n* Sprung *m* ● *vi* springen

bound[2] *see* bind ● *adj* ~ **for** (*ship*) mit Kurs auf (+ *acc*); **be** ~ **to do sth** etw bestimmt machen; (*obliged*) verpflichtet sein, etw zu machen

boundary /'baʊndəri/ *n* Grenze *f*

bounds /baʊndz/ *npl* (*fig*) Grenzen *pl*; **out of** ~ verboten

bouquet /bʊ'keɪ/ *n* [Blumen]strauß *m*; (*of wine*) Bukett *nt*

bourgeois /'bʊəʒwɑː/ *adj* (*pej*) spießbürgerlich

bout /baʊt/ *n* (*Med*) Anfall *m*; (*Sport*) Kampf *m*

bow[1] /bəʊ/ *n* (*weapon & Mus*) Bogen *m*; (*knot*) Schleife *f*

bow[2] /baʊ/ *n* Verbeugung *f* ● *vi* sich verbeugen ● *vt* neigen (*head*)

bow[3] /baʊ/ *n* (*Naut*) Bug *m*

bowel /'baʊəl/ *n* Darm *m*. ~**s** *pl* Eingeweide *pl*

bowl[1] /bəʊl/ *n* Schüssel *f*; (*shallow*) Schale *f*

bowl[2] *n* (*ball*) Kugel *f* ● *vt/i* werfen. ~ **over** *vt* umwerfen

bowler /'bəʊlə(r)/ *n* (*Sport*) Werfer *m*

bowling /'bəʊlɪŋ/ *n* Kegeln *nt*. ~-**alley** *n* Kegelbahn *f*

bowls /bəʊlz/ *n* Bowlsspiel *nt*

bow-'tie /bəʊ-/ *n* Fliege *f*

box[1] /bɒks/ *n* Schachtel *f*; (*wooden*) Kiste *f*; (*cardboard*) Karton *m*; (*Theat*) Loge *f*

box[2] *vt/i* (*Sport*) boxen

box|er /'bɒksə(r)/ *n* Boxer *m*. ~**ing** *n* Boxen *nt*. **B**~**ing Day** *n* zweiter Weihnachtstag *m*

box: ~-**office** *n* (*Theat*) Kasse *f*. ~-**room** *n* Abstellraum *m*

boy /bɔɪ/ *n* Junge *m*. ~ **band** *n* Jungenband *f*

boycott /'bɔɪkɒt/ *n* Boykott *m* ● *vt* boykottieren

boy: ~**friend** *n* Freund *m*. ~**ish** *adj* jungenhaft

bra /brɑː/ *n* BH *m*

brace /breɪs/ *n* Strebe *f*, Stütze *f*; (*dental*) Zahnspange *f*; ~**s** *npl* Hosenträger *mpl*

bracelet /'breɪslɪt/ *n* Armband *nt*

bracing /'breɪsɪŋ/ *adj* stärkend

bracket /'brækɪt/ *n* Konsole *f*; (*group*) Gruppe *f*; (*Printing*) **round**/**square** ~**s** runde/eckige Klammern ● *vt* einklammern

brag /bræg/ *vi* (*pt/pp* **bragged**) prahlen (**about** mit)

braille /breɪl/ *n* Blindenschrift *f*

brain /breɪn/ *n* Gehirn *nt*; ~**s** (*fig*) Intelligenz *f*

brain: ~**less** *adj* dumm. ~**wash** *vt* einer Gehirnwäsche unterziehen. ~**wave** *n* Geistesblitz *m*

brainy /'breɪnɪ/ *adj* klug

brake /breɪk/ *n* Bremse *f* ● *vt/i* bremsen. ~-**light** *n* Bremslicht *nt*

bramble /'bræmbl/ *n* Brombeerstrauch *m*

branch /brɑːntʃ/ *n* Ast *m*; (*fig*) Zweig *m*; (*Comm*) Zweigstelle *f*; (*shop*) Filiale *f* ● *vi* sich gabeln

brand /brænd/ *n* Marke *f* ● *vt* (*fig*) brandmarken als

brandish /'brændɪʃ/ *vt* schwingen

brand-'new *adj* nagelneu

brandy /'brændɪ/ *n* Weinbrand *m*

brash /bræʃ/ *adj* nassforsch

brass /brɑːs/ *n* Messing *nt*; (*Mus*) Blech *nt*; **top** ~ ⊞ hohe Tiere *pl*. ~

band n Blaskapelle f

brassy /'brɑːsɪ/ adj ⒤ ordinär

brat /bræt/ n (pej) Balg nt

bravado /brə'vɑːdəʊ/ n Forschheit f

brave /breɪv/ adj (-r, -st) tapfer • vt die Stirn bieten (+ dat). ~ry n Tapferkeit f

bravo /brɑː'vəʊ/ int bravo!

brawl /brɔːl/ n Schlägerei f

brawn /brɔːn/ n (Culin) Sülze f

brawny /'brɔːnɪ/ adj muskulös

bray /breɪ/ vi iahen

brazen /'breɪzn/ adj unverschämt

Brazil /brə'zɪl/ n Brasilien nt. ~ian adj brasilianisch. ~ nut n Paranuss f

breach /briːtʃ/ n Bruch m; (Mil & fig) Bresche f; ~ of contract Vertragsbruch m

bread /bred/ n Brot nt; slice of ~ and butter Butterbrot nt. ~crumbs npl Brotkrümel pl; (Culin) Paniermehl nt

breadth /bredθ/ n Breite f

break /breɪk/ n Bruch m; (interval) Pause f; (interruption) Unterbrechung f; (⒤: chance) Chance f • v (pt broke, pp broken) • vt brechen; (smash) zerbrechen; (damage) kaputtmachen ⒤; (interrupt) unterbrechen; ~ one's arm sich (dat) den Arm brechen • vi brechen; (day:) anbrechen; (storm:) losbrechen; (thing:) kaputtgehen ⒤; (rope, thread:) reißen; (news:) bekannt werden; his voice is ~ing er ist im Stimmbruch. ~ away vi sich losreißen/(fig) sich absetzen (from von). ~ down vi zusammenbrechen; (Techn) eine Panne haben; (negotiations:) scheitern • vt aufgliedern (door); aufgliedern (figures). ~ in vi einbrechen. ~ off vt/i abbrechen; lösen (engagement). ~ out vi ausbrechen. ~ up vt zerbrechen • vi (crowd:) sich zerstreuen; (marriage, couple:) auseinander gehen; (Sch) Ferien bekommen

break|able /'breɪkəbl/ adj zerbrechlich. ~age n Bruch m. ~down n (Techn) Panne f; (Med) Zusammenbruch m; (of figures) Aufgliederung f. ~er n (wave) Brecher m

breakfast /'brekfəst/ n Frühstück nt

break: ~through n Durchbruch m. ~water n Buhne f

breast /brest/ n Brust f. ~bone n Brustbein nt. ~-feed vt stillen. ~-stroke n Brustschwimmen nt

breath /breθ/ n Atem m; out of ~ außer Atem; under one's ~ vor sich (acc) hin

breathe /briːð/ vt/i atmen. ~ in vt/i einatmen. ~ out vt/i ausatmen

breathing n Atmen nt

breath: ~less adj atemlos. ~-taking adj atemberaubend

bred /bred/ see breed

breed /briːd/ n Rasse f • v (pt/pp bred) • vt züchten; (give rise to) erzeugen • vi sich vermehren. ~er n Züchter m. ~ing n Zucht f; (fig) [gute] Lebensart f

breez|e /briːz/ n Lüftchen nt; (Naut) Brise f. ~y adj windig

brevity /'brevətɪ/ n Kürze f

brew /bruː/ n Gebräu nt • vt brauen; kochen (tea). ~er n Brauer m. ~ery n Brauerei f

bribe /braɪb/ n (money) Bestechungsgeld nt • vt bestechen. ~ry n Bestechung f

brick /brɪk/ n Ziegelstein m, Backstein m

'bricklayer n Maurer m

bridal /'braɪdl/ adj Braut-

bride /braɪd/ n Braut f. ~groom n Bräutigam m. ~smaid n Brautjungfer f

bridge¹ /brɪdʒ/ n Brücke f; (of nose) Nasenrücken m; (of spectacles) Steg m

bridge² n (Cards) Bridge nt

bridle /'braɪdl/ n Zaum m

brief¹ /briːf/ adj (-er, -est) kurz; be ~ (person:) sich kurz fassen

brief² n Instruktionen pl; (Jur: case) Mandat nt. ~case n Aktentasche f

brief|ing /'briːfɪŋ/ n Informationsgespräch nt. ~ly adv kurz. ~ness n Kürze f

briefs /briːfs/ npl Slip m

brigade /brɪ'geɪd/ n Brigade f

bright /braɪt/ adj (-er, -est) hell; (day) heiter; ~ **red** hellrot

bright|en /ˈbraɪtn/ v ~**en [up]** • vt aufheitern. • vi sich aufheitern. ~**ness** n Helligkeit f

brilliance /ˈbrɪljəns/ n Glanz m; (of person) Genialität f

brilliant /ˈbrɪljənt/ adj glänzend; (person) genial

brim /brɪm/ n Rand m; (of hat) Krempe f

bring /brɪŋ/ vt (pt/pp brought) bringen; ~ **them with you** bring sie mit; **I can't b~ myself to do it** ich bringe es nicht fertig. ~ **about** vt verursachen. ~ **along** vt mitbringen. ~ **back** vt zurückbringen. ~ **down** vt herunterbringen; senken (price). ~ **off** vt vollbringen. ~ **on** vt (cause) verursachen. ~ **out** vt herausbringen. ~ **round** vt vorbeibringen; (persuade) überreden; wieder zum Bewusstsein bringen (unconscious person). ~ **up** vt heraufbringen; (vomit) erbrechen; aufziehen (children); erwähnen (question)

brink /brɪŋk/ n Rand m

brisk /brɪsk/ adj (-er, -est,) -ly adv lebhaft; (quick) schnell

bristle /ˈbrɪsl/ n Borste f

Brit|ain /ˈbrɪtn/ n Großbritannien nt. ~**ish** adj britisch; **the** ~**ish** die Briten pl. ~**on** n Brite m/Britin f

Brittany /ˈbrɪtəni/ n die Bretagne

brittle /ˈbrɪtl/ adj brüchig, spröde

broad /brɔːd/ adj (-er, -est) breit; (hint) deutlich; **in** ~ **daylight** am helllichten Tag. ~ **beans** npl dicke Bohnen pl

broadband /ˈbrɔːdbænd/ n Breitband nt

'broadcast n Sendung f • vt/i (pt/pp -cast) senden. ~**er** n Rundfunk- und Fernsehpersönlichkeit f. ~**ing** n Funk und Fernsehen pl

broaden /ˈbrɔːdn/ vt verbreitern; (fig) erweitern • vi sich verbreitern

broadly /ˈbrɔːdlɪ/ adv breit; ~ **speaking** allgemein gesagt

broad'minded adj tolerant

broccoli /ˈbrɒkəlɪ/ n inv Brokkoli pl

brochure /ˈbrəʊʃə(r)/ n Broschüre f

broke /brəʊk/ see break • adj 🔲 pleite

broken /ˈbrəʊkn/ see break • adj zerbrochen, 🔲 kaputt. ~-**hearted** adj untröstlich

broker /ˈbrəʊkə(r)/ n Makler m

brolly /ˈbrɒlɪ/ n 🔲 Schirm m

bronchitis /brɒŋˈkaɪtɪs/ n Bronchitis f

bronze /brɒnz/ n Bronze f

brooch /brəʊtʃ/ n Brosche f

brood /bruːd/ vi (fig) grübeln

broom /bruːm/ n Besen m; (Bot) Ginster m

broth /brɒθ/ n Brühe f

brothel /ˈbrɒθl/ n Bordell nt

brother /ˈbrʌðə(r)/ n Bruder m

brother: ~-**in-law** n (pl -s-in-law) Schwager m. ~**ly** adj brüderlich

brought /brɔːt/ see bring

brow /braʊ/ n Augenbraue f; (forehead) Stirn f; (of hill) [Berg]kuppe f

brown /braʊn/ adj (-er, -est) braun; ~ '**paper** Packpapier nt • n Braun nt • vt bräunen • vi braun werden

browse /braʊz/ vi (read) schmökern; (in shop) sich umsehen. ~**r** n (Computing) Browser m

bruise /bruːz/ n blauer Fleck m • vt beschädigen (fruit); ~ **one's arm** sich (dat) den Arm quetschen

brunette /bruːˈnet/ n Brünette f

brush /brʌʃ/ n Bürste f; (with handle) Handfeger m; (for paint, pastry) Pinsel m; (bushes) Unterholz nt; (fig: conflict) Zusammenstoß m • vt bürsten; putzen (teeth); ~ **against** streifen [gegen]; ~ **aside** (fig) abtun. ~ **off** vt abbürsten. ~ **up** vt/i (fig) ~ **up [on]** auffrischen

brusque /brʊsk/ adj brüsk

Brussels /ˈbrʌslz/ n Brüssel nt. ~ **sprouts** npl Rosenkohl m

brutal /ˈbruːtl/ adj brutal. ~**ity** n Brutalität f

brute /bruːt/ n Unmensch m. ~ **force** n rohe Gewalt f

BSE *abbr* (bovine spongiform en-cephalopathy) BSE *f*

bubble /ˈbʌbl/ *n* [Luft]blase *f* ● *vi* sprudeln

buck[1] /bʌk/ *n* (*deer & Gym*) Bock *m*; (*rabbit*) Rammler *m* ● *vi* (*horse:*) bocken

buck[2] *n* (*Amer* 🔲) Dollar *m*

buck[3] *n* pass the ~ die Verantwortung abschieben

bucket /ˈbʌkɪt/ *n* Eimer *m*

buckle /ˈbʌkl/ *n* Schnalle *f* ● *vt* zuschnallen ● *vi* sich verbiegen

bud /bʌd/ *n* Knospe *f*

buddy /ˈbʌdɪ/ *n* 🔲 Freund *m*

budge /bʌdʒ/ *vt* bewegen ● *vi* sich [von der Stelle] rühren

budget /ˈbʌdʒɪt/ *n* Budget *nt*; (*Pol*) Haushaltsplan *m*; (*money available*) Etat *m* ● *vi* (*pt/pp* budgeted) ~ for sth etw einkalkulieren

buff /bʌf/ *adj* (*colour*) sandfarben ● *n* Sandfarbe *f*; 🔲 Fan *m* ● *vt* polieren

buffalo /ˈbʌfələʊ/ *n* (*inv or pl* -es) Büffel *m*

buffer /ˈbʌfə(r)/ *n* (*Rail*) Puffer *m*

buffet[1] /ˈbʊfeɪ/ *n* Büfett *nt*; (*on station*) Imbissstube *f*

buffet[2] /ˈbʌfɪt/ *vt* (*pt/pp* buffeted) hin und her werfen

bug /bʌg/ *n* Wanze *f*; (🔲: *virus*) Bazillus *m*; (🔲: *device*) Abhörgerät *nt*, 🔲 Wanze *f* ● *vt* (*pt/pp* bugged) 🔲 verwanzen (*room*); abhören (*telephone*); (*Amer: annoy*) ärgern

bugle /ˈbjuːgl/ *n* Signalhorn *nt*

build /bɪld/ *n* (*of person*) Körperbau *m* ● *vt/i* (*pt/pp* built) bauen. ~ on *vt* anbauen (to an + *acc*). ~ up *vt* aufbauen ● *vi* zunehmen

builder /ˈbɪldə(r)/ *n* Bauunternehmer *m*

building /ˈbɪldɪŋ/ *n* Gebäude *nt*. ~ site *n* Baustelle *f*. ~ society *n* Bausparkasse *f*

built /bɪlt/ *see* build. ~-in *adj* eingebaut. ~-in 'cupboard *n* Einbauschrank *m*. ~-up area *n* bebautes Gebiet *nt*; (*Auto*) geschlossene Ortschaft *f*

bulb /bʌlb/ *n* [Blumen]zwiebel *f*; (*Electr*) [Glüh]birne *f*

bulbous /ˈbʌlbəs/ *adj* bauchig

Bulgaria /bʌlˈgeərɪə/ *n* Bulgarien *nt*

bulg|e /bʌldʒ/ *n* Ausbauchung *f* ● *vi* sich ausbauchen. ~ing *adj* prall; (*eyes*) hervorquellend

bulk /bʌlk/ *n* Masse *f*; (*greater part*) Hauptteil *m*. ~y *adj* sperrig; (*large*) massig

bull /bʊl/ *n* Bulle *m*, Stier *m*

'bulldog *n* Bulldogge *f*

bulldozer /ˈbʊldəʊzə(r)/ *n* Planierraupe *f*

bullet /ˈbʊlɪt/ *n* Kugel *f*

bulletin /ˈbʊlɪtɪn/ *n* Bulletin *nt*

'bullet-proof *adj* kugelsicher

'bullfight *n* Stierkampf *m*. ~er *n* Stierkämpfer *m*

'bullfinch *n* Dompfaff *m*

bullock /ˈbʊlək/ *n* Ochse *m*

bull: ~ring *n* Stierkampfarena *f*. ~'s-eye *n* score a ~'s-eye ins Schwarze treffen

bully /ˈbʊlɪ/ *n* Tyrann *m* ● *vt* tyrannisieren

bum /bʌm/ *n* 🔲 Hintern *m*

bumble-bee /ˈbʌmbl-/ *n* Hummel *f*

bump /bʌmp/ *n* Bums *m*; (*swelling*) Beule *f*; (*in road*) holperige Stelle *f* ● *vt* stoßen; ~ into stoßen gegen; (*meet*) zufällig treffen. ~ off *vt* 🔲 um die Ecke bringen

bumper /ˈbʌmpə(r)/ *adj* Rekord- ● *n* (*Auto*) Stoßstange *f*

bumpy /ˈbʌmpɪ/ *adj* holperig

bun /bʌn/ *n* Milchbrötchen *nt*; (*hair*) [Haar]knoten *m*

bunch /bʌntʃ/ *n* (*of flowers*) Strauß *m*; (*of radishes, keys*) Bund *m*; (*of people*) Gruppe *f*; ~ of grapes [ganze] Weintraube *f*

bundle /ˈbʌndl/ *n* Bündel *nt* ● *vt* ~ [up] bündeln

bungalow /ˈbʌŋgələʊ/ *n* Bungalow *m*

bungle /ˈbʌŋgl/ *vt* verpfuschen

bunk /bʌŋk/ *n* [Schlaf]koje *f*. ~-beds *npl* Etagenbett *nt*

bunker /ˈbʌŋkə(r)/ n Bunker m

bunny /ˈbʌnɪ/ n 🄸 Kaninchen nt

buoy /bɔɪ/ n Boje f

buoyan|cy /ˈbɔɪənsɪ/ n Auftrieb m. ～t adj be ～t schwimmen

burden /ˈbɜːdn/ n Last f

bureau /ˈbjʊərəʊ/ n (pl -x or ～s) (desk) Sekretär m; (office) Büro nt

bureaucracy /bjʊəˈrɒkrəsɪ/ n Bürokratie f

bureaucratic /ˌbjʊərəkrætɪk/ adj bürokratisch

burger /ˈbɜːɡə(r)/ n Hamburger m

burglar /ˈbɜːɡlə(r)/ n Einbrecher m. ～ **alarm** n Alarmanlage f

burglary n Einbruch m

burgle /ˈbɜːɡl/ vt einbrechen in (+ acc); **they have been** ～**d** bei ihnen ist eingebrochen worden

burial /ˈberɪəl/ n Begräbnis nt

burly /ˈbɜːlɪ/ adj stämmig

Burm|a /ˈbɜːmə/ n Birma nt. ～**ese** adj birmanisch

burn /bɜːn/ n Verbrennung f; (on skin) Brandwunde f; (on material) Brandstelle f ● v (pt/pp burnt or burned) ● vt verbrennen ● vi brennen; (food:) anbrennen. ～ **down** vt/i niederbrennen

burner /ˈbɜːnə(r)/ n Brenner m

burnt /bɜːnt/ see burn

burp /bɜːp/ vi 🄸 aufstoßen

burrow /ˈbʌrəʊ/ n Bau m ● vi wühlen

burst /bɜːst/ n Bruch m; (surge) Ausbruch m ● v (pt/pp burst) ● vt platzen machen ● vi platzen; (bud:) aufgehen; ～ **into tears** in Tränen ausbrechen

bury /ˈberɪ/ vt (pt/pp -ied) begraben; (hide) vergraben

bus /bʌs/ n [Auto]bus m

bush /bʊʃ/ n Strauch m; (land) Busch m. ～**y** adj buschig

busily /ˈbɪzɪlɪ/ adv eifrig

business /ˈbɪznɪs/ n Angelegenheit f; (Comm) Geschäft nt; **on** ～ geschäftlich; **he has no** ～ er hat kein Recht (**to** zu); **mind one's own** ～

sich um seine eigenen Angelegenheiten kümmern; **that's none of your** ～ das geht Sie nichts an. ～**-like** adj geschäftsmäßig. ～**man** n Geschäftsmann m

'bus-stop n Bushaltestelle f

bust¹ /bʌst/ n Büste f

bust² adj 🄸 kaputt; **go** ～ Pleite gehen ● v (pt/pp busted or bust) 🄸 ● vt kaputtmachen ● vi kaputtgehen

busy /ˈbɪzɪ/ adj beschäftigt; (day) voll; (street) belebt; (with traffic) stark befahren; (Amer Teleph) besetzt; **be** ～ zu tun haben ● vt ～ **oneself** sich beschäftigen (**with** mit)

but /bʌt/, unbetont /bət/ conj aber; (after negative) sondern ● prep außer (+ dat); ～ **for** (without) ohne (+ acc); **the last** ～ **one** der/die/das vorletzte; **the next** ～ **one** der/die/das übernächste ● adv nur

butcher /ˈbʊtʃə(r)/ n Fleischer m, Metzger m; ～**'s [shop]** Fleischerei f, Metzgerei f ● vt [ab]schlachten

butler /ˈbʌtlə(r)/ n Butler m

butt /bʌt/ n (of gun) [Gewehr]kolben m; (fig: target) Zielscheibe f; (of cigarette) Stummel m; (for water) Regentonne f ● vi ～ **in** unterbrechen

butter /ˈbʌtə(r)/ n Butter f ● vt mit Butter bestreichen. ～ **up** vt 🄸 schmeicheln (+ dat)

butter: ～**cup** adj Butterblume f, Hahnenfuß m. ～**fly** n Schmetterling m

buttocks /ˈbʌtəks/ npl Gesäß nt

button /ˈbʌtn/ n Knopf m ● vt ～ **[up]** zuknöpfen. ～**hole** n Knopfloch nt

buy /baɪ/ n Kauf m ● vt (pt/pp bought) kaufen. ～**er** n Käufer(in) m(f)

buzz /bʌz/ n Summen nt ● vi summen

buzzer /ˈbʌzə(r)/ n Summer m

by /baɪ/ prep (close to) bei (+ dat); (next to) neben (+ dat/acc); (past) an (+ dat) ... vorbei; (to the extent of) um (+ acc); (at the latest) bis; (by means of) durch; **by Mozart/Dickens** von Mozart/Dickens; ～ **oneself** allein; ~ **the sea** am Meer; ~ **car/bus** mit dem Auto/Bus; ~ **sea** mit dem Schiff; ~ **day/night** bei Tag/Nacht; ~ **the hour** pro Stunde; ~ **the metre** meterweise; **six metres** ~ **four** sechs mal vier Meter; **win** ~ **a length** mit einer Länge Vorsprung gewinnen; **miss the train** ~ **a minute** den Zug um eine Minute verpassen ● *adv* ~ **and large** im Großen und Ganzen; **put** ~ beiseite legen; **go/pass** ~ vorbeigehen

bye /baɪ/ *int* 🔲 tschüs

by: ~**-election** *n* Nachwahl *f*. ~**pass** *n* Umgehungsstraße *f*; (*Med*) Bypass *m* ● *vt* umfahren. ~**-product** *n* Nebenprodukt *m*. ~**stander** *n* Zuschauer(in) *m(f)*

....

Cc

....

cab /kæb/ *n* Taxi *nt*; (*of lorry, train*) Führerhaus *nt*

cabaret /ˈkæbəreɪ/ *n* Kabarett *nt*

cabbage /ˈkæbɪdʒ/ *n* Kohl *m*

cabin /ˈkæbɪn/ *n* Kabine *f*; (*hut*) Hütte *f*

cabinet /ˈkæbɪnɪt/ *n* Schrank *m*; **[display]** ~ Vitrine *f*; **C**~ (*Pol*) Kabinett *nt*

cable /ˈkeɪbl/ *n* Kabel *nt*; (*rope*) Tau *nt*. ~ ˈ**railway** *n* Seilbahn *f*. ~ ˈ**television** *n* Kabelfernsehen *nt*

cackle /ˈkækl/ *vi* gackern

cactus /ˈkæktəs/ *n* (*pl* **-ti** *or* **-tuses**) Kaktus *m*

cadet /kəˈdet/ *n* Kadett *m*

cadge /kædʒ/ *vt/i* 🔲 schnorren

Caesarean /sɪˈzeərɪən/ *adj & n* ~ **[section]** Kaiserschnitt *m*

café /ˈkæfeɪ/ *n* Café *nt*

cafeteria /kæfəˈtɪərɪə/ *n* Selbstbedienungsrestaurant *nt*

cage /keɪdʒ/ *n* Käfig *m*

cagey /ˈkeɪdʒɪ/ *adj* 🔲 **be** ~ mit der Sprache nicht herauswollen

cake /keɪk/ *n* Kuchen *m*; (*of soap*) Stück *nt*. ~**d** *adj* verkrustet (**with** mit)

calamity /kəˈlæmətɪ/ *n* Katastrophe *f*

calculat|e /ˈkælkjʊleɪt/ *vt* berechnen; (*estimate*) kalkulieren. ~**ing** *adj* (*fig*) berechnend. ~**ion** *n* Rechnung *f*, Kalkulation *f*. ~**or** *n* Rechner *m*

calendar /ˈkælɪndə(r)/ *n* Kalender *m*

calf[1] /kɑːf/ *n* (*pl* **calves**) Kalb *nt*

calf[2] *n* (*pl* **calves**) (*Anat*) Wade *f*

calibre /ˈkælɪbə(r)/ *n* Kaliber *nt*

call /kɔːl/ *n* Ruf *m*; (*Teleph*) Anruf *m*; (*visit*) Besuch *m* ● *vt* rufen; (*Teleph*) anrufen; (*wake*) wecken; ausrufen (*strike*) (*name*) nennen; **be** ~**ed** heißen ● *vi* rufen; ~ **[in** *or* **round]** vorbeikommen. ~ **back** *vt* zurückrufen ● *vi* noch einmal vorbeikommen. ~ **for** *vt* rufen nach; (*demand*) verlangen; (*fetch*) abholen. ~ **off** *vt* zurückrufen (*dog*); (*cancel*) absagen. ~ **on** *vt* bitten (**for** um); (*appeal to*) appellieren an (+ *acc*); (*visit*) besuchen. ~ **out** *vt* rufen; aufrufen (*names*) ● *vi* rufen. ~ **up** *vt* (*Mil*) einberufen; (*Teleph*) anrufen

call: ~**-box** *n* Telefonzelle *f*. ~ **centre** *n* Callcenter *nt*. ~**er** *n* Besucher *m*; (*Teleph*) Anrufer *m*. ~**ing** *n* Berufung *f*. ~**-up** *n* (*Mil*) Einberufung *f*

calm /kɑːm/ *adj* (**-er, -est**) ruhig ● *n* Ruhe *f* ● *vt* ~ **[down]** beruhigen ● *vi* ~ **down** sich beruhigen. ~**ness** *n* Ruhe *f*; (*of sea*) Stille *f*

calorie /ˈkælərɪ/ *n* Kalorie *f*

calves /kɑːvz/ *npl see* **calf**[1] & [2]

camcorder /ˈkæmkɔːdə(r)/ *n* Camcorder *m*

came /keɪm/ *see* **come**

camel /ˈkæml/ *n* Kamel *nt*

camera /ˈkæmərə/ *n* Kamera *f*

camouflage /ˈkæmɒflɑːʒ/ *n* Tarnung *f* ● *vt* tarnen

camp /kæmp/ *n* Lager *nt* ● *vi* campen; (*Mil*) kampieren

campaign /kæmˈpeɪn/ *n* Feldzug *m*; (*Comm, Pol*) Kampagne *f* ● *vi* (*Pol*) im Wahlkampf arbeiten

camp: ~**-bed** n Feldbett nt. ~**er** n Camper m; (Auto) Wohnmobil nt. ~**ing** n Camping nt. ~**site** n Campingplatz m

can¹ /kæn/ n (for petrol) Kanister m; (tin) Dose f, Büchse f; **a** ~ **of beer** eine Dose Bier

---

can² /kæn/, unbetont /kən/

❗ pres **can**, pt **could**

● modal verb

····➤ (be able to) können. **I can't** or **cannot go** ich kann nicht gehen. **she couldn't** or **could not go** (was unable to) sie konnte nicht gehen; (would not be able to) sie könnte nicht gehen. **he could go if he had time** er könnte gehen, wenn er Zeit hätte. **if I could go** wenn ich gehen könnte. **that cannot be true** das kann nicht stimmen

····➤ (know how to) können. **can you swim?** können Sie schwimmen? **she can drive** sie kann Auto fahren

····➤ (be allowed to) dürfen. **you can't smoke here** hier dürfen Sie nicht rauchen. **can I go?** kann ich gehen?

····➤ (in requests) können. **can I have a glass of water, please?** kann ich ein Glas Wasser haben, bitte? **could you ring me tomorrow?** könnten Sie mich morgen anrufen?

····➤ **could** (expressing possibility) könnte. **that could be so** das könnte od kann sein. **I could have killed him** ich hätte ihn umbringen können

---

Canad|a /'kænədə/ n Kanada nt. ~**ian** adj kanadisch ● n Kanadier(in) m(f)

canal /kə'næl/ n Kanal m

canary /kə'neərɪ/ n Kanarienvogel m

cancel /'kænsl/ vt/i (pt/pp **cancelled**) absagen; abbestellen (newspaper);

(Computing) abbrechen; **be** ~**led** ausfallen. ~**lation** n Absage f

cancer /'kænsə(r)/ n (also Astrology) C~ Krebs m. ~**ous** adj krebsig

candid /'kændɪd/ adj offen

candidate /'kændɪdət/ n Kandidat(in) m(f)

candle /'kændl/ n Kerze f. ~**stick** n Kerzenständer m, Leuchter m

candy /'kændɪ/ n (Amer) Süßigkeiten pl; **[piece of]** ~ Bonbon m

cane /keɪn/ n Rohr nt; (stick) Stock m ● vt mit dem Stock züchtigen

canine /'keɪnaɪn/ adj Hunde-. ~ **tooth** n Eckzahn m

cannabis /'kænəbɪs/ n Haschisch nt

canned /kænd/ adj Dosen-, Büchsen-

cannibal /'kænɪbl/ n Kannibale m. ~**ism** n Kannibalismus m

cannon /'kænən/ n inv Kanone f

cannot /'kænɒt/ see can²

canoe /kə'nuː/ n Paddelboot nt; (Sport) Kanu nt

'can-opener n Dosenöffner m

can't /kɑːnt/ = cannot. See can²

canteen /kæn'tiːn/ n Kantine f; ~ **of cutlery** Besteckkasten m

canter /'kæntə(r)/ n Kanter m ● vi kantern

canvas /'kænvəs/ n Segeltuch nt; (Art) Leinwand f; (painting) Gemälde nt

canvass /'kænvəs/ vi um Stimmen werben

canyon /'kænjən/ n Cañon m

cap /kæp/ n Kappe f, Mütze f; (nurse's) Haube f; (top, lid) Verschluss m

capability /keɪpə'bɪlətɪ/ n Fähigkeit f

capable /'keɪpəbl/ adj, **-bly** adv fähig; **be** ~ **of doing sth** fähig sein, etw zu tun

capacity /kə'pæsətɪ/ n Fassungsvermögen nt; (ability) Fähigkeit f; **in my** ~ **as** in meiner Eigenschaft als

cape¹ /keɪp/ n (cloak) Cape nt

cape² n (Geog) Kap nt

capital /'kæpɪtl/ adj (letter) groß ● n

(*town*) Hauptstadt *f*; (*money*) Kapital *nt*; (*letter*) Großbuchstabe *m*

capital|ism /'kæpɪtəlɪzm/ *n* Kapitalismus *m*. **~ist** *adj* kapitalistisch ● *n* Kapitalist *m*. **~ 'letter** *n* Großbuchstabe *m*. **~ 'punishment** *n* Todesstrafe *f*

> **Capitol** Der Sitz des amerikanischen ▷**CONGRESS** auf dem Capitol Hill in Washington D.C.   *i*

capsize /kæp'saɪz/ *vi* kentern ● *vt* zum Kentern bringen

captain /'kæptɪn/ *n* Kapitän *m*; (*Mil*) Hauptmann *m* ● *vt* anführen (*team*)

caption /'kæpʃn/ *n* Überschrift *f*; (*of illustration*) Bildtext *m*

captivate /'kæptɪveɪt/ *vt* bezaubern

captiv|e /'kæptɪv/ *adj* **hold/take ~e** gefangen halten/nehmen ● *n* Gefangene(r) *m/f*. **~ity** *n* Gefangenschaft *f*

capture /'kæptʃə(r)/ *n* Gefangennahme *f* ● *vt* gefangen nehmen; [ein]fangen (*animal*); (*Mil*) einnehmen (*town*)

car /kɑ:(r)/ *n* Auto *nt*, Wagen *m*; **by ~** mit dem Auto *od* Wagen

caramel /'kærəmel/ *n* Karamell *m*

carat /'kærət/ *n* Karat *nt*

caravan /'kærəvæn/ *n* Wohnwagen *m*; (*procession*) Karawane *f*

carbon /'kɑ:bən/ *n* Kohlenstoff *m*; (*paper*) Kohlepapier *nt*; (*copy*) Durchschlag *m*

carbon: ~ copy *n* Durchschlag *m*. **~ paper** *n* Kohlepapier *nt*

carburettor /kɑ:bjʊ'retə(r)/ *n* Vergaser *m*

carcass /'kɑ:kəs/ *n* Kadaver *m*

card /kɑ:d/ *n* Karte *f*

'cardboard *n* Pappe *f*, Karton *m*. **~ 'box** *n* Pappschachtel *f*; (*large*) [Papp]karton *m*

'card-game *n* Kartenspiel *nt*

cardigan /'kɑ:dɪgən/ *n* Strickjacke *f*

cardinal /'kɑ:dɪnl/ *adj* Kardinal- ● *n* (*Relig*) Kardinal *m*

card 'index *n* Kartei *f*

care /keə(r)/ *n* Sorgfalt *f*; (*caution*)

Vorsicht *f*; (*protection*) Obhut *f*; (*looking after*) Pflege *f*; (*worry*) Sorge *f*; **~ of** (*on letter abbr* c/o) bei; **take ~** vorsichtig sein; **take into ~** in Pflege nehmen; **take ~ of** sich kümmern um ● *vi* **~ for** (*like*) mögen; (*look after*) betreuen; **I don't ~** das ist mir gleich

career /kə'rɪə(r)/ *n* Laufbahn *f*; (*profession*) Beruf *m* ● *vi* rasen

care: ~free *adj* sorglos. **~ful** *adj* sorgfältig; (*cautious*) vorsichtig. **~less** *adj* nachlässig. **~lessness** *n* Nachlässigkeit *f*. **~r** *n* Pflegende(r) *m/f*

'caretaker *n* Hausmeister *m*

'car ferry *n* Autofähre *f*

cargo /'kɑ:gəʊ/ *n* (*pl* -es) Ladung *f*

Caribbean /kærɪ'bi:ən/ *n* **the ~** die Karibik

caricature /'kærɪkətjʊə(r)/ *n* Karikatur *f* ● *vt* karikieren

caring /'keərɪŋ/ *adj* (*parent*) liebevoll; (*profession, attitude*) sozial

carnation /kɑ:'neɪʃn/ *n* Nelke *f*

carnival /'kɑ:nɪvl/ *n* Karneval *m*

carol /'kærl/ *n* **[Christmas] ~** Weihnachtslied *nt*

carp¹ /kɑ:p/ *n inv* Karpfen *m*

carp² *vi* nörgeln

'car park *n* Parkplatz *m*; (*multistorey*) Parkhaus *nt*; (*underground*) Tiefgarage *f*

carpent|er /'kɑ:pɪntə(r)/ *n* Zimmermann *m*; (*joiner*) Tischler *m*. **~ry** *n* Tischlerei *f*

carpet /'kɑ:pɪt/ *n* Teppich *m*

carriage /'kærɪdʒ/ *n* Kutsche *f*; (*Rail*) Wagen *m*; (*of goods*) Beförderung *f*; (*cost*) Frachtkosten *pl*; (*bearing*) Haltung *f*

carrier /'kærɪə(r)/ *n* Träger(in) *m(f)*; (*Comm*) Spediteur *m*; **~[-bag]** Tragetasche *f*

carrot /'kærət/ *n* Möhre *f*, Karotte *f*

carry /'kærɪ/ *vt/i* (*pt/pp* -ied) tragen; **be carried away** 🔢 hingerissen sein. **~ off** *vt* wegtragen; gewinnen (*prize*). **~ on** *vi* weitermachen; **~ on with** 🔢 eine Affäre haben mit ● *vt*

führen; (*continue*) fortführen. ~ **out**
vt hinaus-/heraustragen; (*perform*)
ausführen

cart /kɑːt/ *n* Karren *m*; **put the ~**
before the horse das Pferd beim
Schwanz aufzäumen ● *vt* karren; (🗊:
carry) schleppen

carton /'kɑːtn/ *n* [Papp]karton *m*;
(*for drink*) Tüte *f*; (*of cream, yoghurt*)
Becher *m*

cartoon /kɑːˈtuːn/ *n* Karikatur *f*;
(*joke*) Witzzeichnung *f*; (*strip*) Comic
Strips *pl*; (*film*) Zeichentrickfilm *m*.
~**ist** *n* Karikaturist *m*

cartridge /'kɑːtrɪdʒ/ *n* Patrone *f*;
(*for film*) Kassette *f*

carve /kɑːv/ *vt* schnitzen; (*in stone*)
hauen; (*Culin*) aufschneiden

carving /'kɑːvɪŋ/ *n* Schnitzerei *f*.
~-**knife** *n* Tranchiermesser *nt*

'car wash *n* Autowäsche *f*; (*place*)
Autowaschanlage *f*

case¹ /keɪs/ *n* Fall *m*; **in any ~** auf
jeden Fall; **just in ~** für alle Fälle; **in**
~ **he comes** falls er kommt

case² *n* Kasten *m*; (*crate*) Kiste *f*; (*for
spectacles*) Etui *nt*; (*suitcase*) Koffer *m*;
(*for display*) Vitrine *f*

cash /kæʃ/ *n* Bargeld *nt*; **pay [in] ~**
[in] bar bezahlen; ~ **on delivery** per
Nachnahme ● *vt* einlösen (*cheque*).
~ **desk** *n* Kasse *f*

cashier /kæˈʃɪə(r)/ *n* Kassierer(in)
m(f)

cash: ~**point [machine]** *n* Geldau-
tomat *m*. ~ **register** *n* Registrier-
kasse *f*

cassette /kəˈset/ *n* Kassette *f*. ~ **recorder** *n* Kassettenrecorder *m*

cast /kɑːst/ *n* (*mould*) Form *f*; (*model*)
Abguss *m*; (*Theat*) Besetzung *f*; [**plaster**] ~ (*Med*) Gipsverband *m* ● *vt*
(*pt/pp* **cast**) (*throw*) werfen; (*shed*)
abwerfen; abgeben (*vote*); gießen
(*metal*); (*Theat*) besetzen (*role*). ~
off *vi* (*Naut*) ablegen

castle /'kɑːsl/ *n* Schloss *nt*; (*fortified*)
Burg *f*; (*Chess*) Turm *m*

'cast-offs *npl* abgelegte Kleidung *f*

castor /'kɑːstə(r)/ *n* (*wheel*)
[Lauf]rolle *f*

'castor sugar *n* Streuzucker *m*

casual /'kæʒʊəl/ *adj* (*chance*) zufällig;
(*offhand*) lässig; (*informal*) zwanglos;
(*not permanent*) Gelegenheits-; ~
wear Freizeitbekleidung *f*

casualty /'kæʒʊəltɪ/ *n* [Todes]opfer
nt; (*injured person*) Verletzte(r) *m/f*;
~ [**department**] Unfallstation *f*

cat /kæt/ *n* Katze *f*

catalogue /'kætəlɒg/ *n* Katalog *m*
● *vt* katalogisieren

catapult /'kætəpʌlt/ *n* Katapult *nt*
● *vt* katapultieren

cataract /'kætərækt/ *n* (*Med*) grauer
Star *m*

catarrh /kəˈtɑː(r)/ *n* Katarrh *m*

catastroph|e /kəˈtæstrəfɪ/ *n* Kata-
strophe *f*. ~**ic** *adj* katastrophal

catch /kætʃ/ *n* (*of fish*) Fang *m*; (*fastener*) Verschluss *m*; (*on door*) Klinke
f; (🗊: *snag*) Haken *m* 🗊 ● *v* (*pt/pp*
caught) ● *vt* fangen; (*be in time for*)
erreichen; (*travel by*) fahren mit; bekommen (*illness*); ~ **a cold** sich er-
kälten; ~ **sight of** erblicken; ~ **s.o.**
stealing jdn beim Stehlen erwischen;
~ **one's finger in the door** sich
(*dat*) den Finger in der Tür [ein]klem-
men ● *vi* (*burn*) anbrennen; (*get
stuck*) klemmen. ~ **on** *vi* 🗊 (*understand*) kapieren; (*become popular*)
sich durchsetzen. ~ **up** *vt* einholen
● *vi* aufholen; ~ **up with** einholen
(*s.o.*); nachholen (*work*)

catching /'kætʃɪŋ/ *adj* ansteckend

catch: ~-**phrase** *n*, ~**word** *n*
Schlagwort *nt*

catchy /'kætʃɪ/ *adj* einprägsam

categor|ical /kætɪˈgɒrɪkl/ *adj* kate-
gorisch. ~**y** *n* Kategorie *f*

cater /'keɪtə(r)/ *vi* ~ **for** beköstigen;
(*firm:*) das Essen liefern für (*party*);
(*fig*) eingestellt sein auf (+ *acc*).
~**ing** *n* (*trade*) Gaststättenge-
werbe *nt*

caterpillar /'kætəpɪlə(r)/ *n* Raupe *f*

cathedral /kəˈθiːdrl/ *n* Dom *m*, Kathedrale *f*

Catholic /'kæθəlɪk/ adj katholisch
● n Katholik(in) m(f). **C ~ism** n Katholizismus m

cattle /'kætl/ npl Vieh nt

catty /'kætɪ/ adj boshaft

caught /kɔːt/ see **catch**

cauliflower /'kɒlɪ-/ n Blumenkohl m

cause /kɔːz/ n Ursache f; (reason) Grund m; **good ~** gute Sache f ● vt verursachen; **~ s.o. to do sth** jdn veranlassen, etw zu tun

caution /'kɔːʃn/ n Vorsicht f; (warning) Verwarnung f ● vt (Jur) verwarnen

cautious /'kɔːʃəs/ adj vorsichtig

cavalry /'kævəlrɪ/ n Kavallerie f

cave /keɪv/ n Höhle f ● vi **~ in** einstürzen

cavern /'kævən/ n Höhle f

caviare /'kævɪɑː(r)/ n Kaviar m

cavity /'kævɪtɪ/ n Hohlraum m; (in tooth) Loch nt

CCTV abbr (closed-circuit television) CCTV nt; (surveillance) Videoüberwachung f

CD abbr (compact disc) CD f; **~-ROM** CD-ROM f

cease /siːs/ vt/i aufhören. **~-fire** n Waffenruhe f. **~less** adj unaufhörlich

cedar /'siːdə(r)/ n Zeder f

ceiling /'siːlɪŋ/ n [Zimmer]decke f; (fig) oberste Grenze f

celebrat|e /'selɪbreɪt/ vt/i feiern. **~ed** adj berühmt (**for** wegen). **~ion** n Feier f

celebrity /sɪ'lebrətɪ/ n Berühmtheit f

celery /'selərɪ/ n [Stangen]sellerie m & f

cell /sel/ n Zelle f

cellar /'selə(r)/ n Keller m

cellist /'tʃelɪst/ n Cellist(in) m(f)

cello /'tʃeləʊ/ n Cello nt

cellphone /'selfəʊn/ n Handy nt

Celsius /'selsɪəs/ adj Celsius

Celt /kelt/ n Kelte m/ Keltin f. **~ic** adj keltisch

cement /sɪ'ment/ n Zement m; (adhesive) Kitt m

cemetery /'semətrɪ/ n Friedhof m

censor /'sensə(r)/ n Zensor m ● vt zensieren. **~ship** n Zensur f

census /'sensəs/ n Volkszählung f

cent /sent/ n Cent m

centenary /sen'tiːnərɪ/ n, (Amer) **centennial** n Hundertjahrfeier f

center /'sentə(r)/ n (Amer) = **centre**

centi|grade /'sentɪ-/ adj Celsius. **~metre** n Zentimeter m & nt

central /'sentrəl/ adj zentral. **~ 'heating** n Zentralheizung f. **~ize** vt zentralisieren

centre /'sentə(r)/ n Zentrum nt; (middle) Mitte f ● v (pt/pp **centred**) ● vt zentrieren. **~-'forward** n Mittelstürmer m

century /'sentʃərɪ/ n Jahrhundert nt

ceramic /sɪ'ræmɪk/ adj Keramik-

cereal /'sɪərɪəl/ n Getreide nt; (breakfast food) Frühstücksflocken pl

ceremon|ial /serɪ'məʊnɪəl/ adj zeremoniell, feierlich ● n Zeremoniell nt. **~ious** adj formell

ceremony /'serɪmənɪ/ n Zeremonie f, Feier f

certain /'sɜːtn/ adj sicher; (not named) gewiss; **for ~** mit Bestimmtheit; **make ~** (check) sich vergewissern (**that** dass); (ensure) dafür sorgen (**that** dass); **he is ~ to win** er wird ganz bestimmt siegen. **~ly** adv bestimmt, sicher; **~ly not!** auf keinen Fall! **~ty** n Sicherheit f, Gewissheit f; **it's a ~ty** es ist sicher

certificate /sə'tɪfɪkət/ n Bescheinigung f; (Jur) Urkunde f; (Sch) Zeugnis nt

certify /'sɜːtɪfaɪ/ vt (pt/pp **-ied**) bescheinigen; (declare insane) für geisteskrank erklären

cf. abbr (compare) vgl.

chafe /tʃeɪf/ vt wund reiben

chaffinch /'tʃæfɪntʃ/ n Buchfink m

chain /tʃeɪn/ n Kette f ● vt ketten (**to** an + acc). **~ up** vt anketten

chain: ~ re'action n Kettenreaktion f. **~-smoker** n Kettenraucher m. **~**

store n Kettenladen m

chair /tʃeə(r)/ n Stuhl m; (Univ) Lehrstuhl m; (Adm) Vorsitzende(r) m/f. ~**-lift** n Sessellift m. ~**man** n Vorsitzende(r) m/f

chalet /'ʃæleɪ/ n Chalet nt

chalk /tʃɔːk/ n Kreide f

challeng|e /'tʃælɪndʒ/ n Herausforderung f; (Mil) Anruf m • vt herausfordern; (Mil) anrufen; (fig) anfechten (statement). ~**er** n Herausforderer m. ~**ing** adj herausfordernd; (demanding) anspruchsvoll

chamber /'tʃeɪmbə(r)/ n Kammer f. C~ **of Commerce** Handelskammer f. ~ **music** n Kammermusik f

chamois /'ʃæmɪ/ n ~**[-leather]** Ledertuch nt

champagne /ʃæm'peɪn/ n Champagner m

champion /'tʃæmpɪən/ n (Sport) Meister(in) m(f); (of cause) Verfechter m • vt sich einsetzen für. ~**ship** n (Sport) Meisterschaft f

chance /tʃɑːns/ n Zufall m; (prospect) Chancen pl; (likelihood) Aussicht f; (opportunity) Gelegenheit f; **by** ~ zufällig; **take a** ~ ein Risiko eingehen; **give s.o. a** ~ jdm eine Chance geben • attrib zufällig • vt ~ **it** es riskieren

chancellor /'tʃɑːnsələ(r)/ n Kanzler m; (Univ) Rektor m

chancy /'tʃɑːnsɪ/ adj riskant

change /tʃeɪndʒ/ n Veränderung f; (alteration) Änderung f; (money) Wechselgeld nt; **for a** ~ zur Abwechslung • vt wechseln; (alter) ändern; (exchange) umtauschen (**for** gegen); (transform) verwandeln; trocken legen (baby); ~ **one's clothes** sich umziehen; ~ **trains** umsteigen • vi sich verändern; (~ clothes) sich umziehen; (~ trains) umsteigen; **all** ~! alles aussteigen!

changeable /'tʃeɪndʒəbl/ adj wechselhaft

'**changing-room** n Umkleideraum m

channel /'tʃænl/ n Rinne f; (Radio, TV) Kanal m; (fig) Weg m; **the [English] C~** der Ärmelkanal; **the C~ Islands** die Kanalinseln

chant /tʃɑːnt/ vt singen; (demonstrators:) skandieren

chao|s /'keɪɒs/ n Chaos nt. ~**tic** adj chaotisch

chap /tʃæp/ n 🆙 Kerl m

chapel /'tʃæpl/ n Kapelle f

chaplain /'tʃæplɪn/ n Geistliche(r) m

chapped /tʃæpt/ adj (skin) aufgesprungen

chapter /'tʃæptə(r)/ n Kapitel nt

character /'kærɪktə(r)/ n Charakter m; (in novel, play) Gestalt f; (Printing) Schriftzeichen nt; **out of** ~ uncharakteristisch; **quite a** ~ 🆙 ein Original

characteristic /kærɪktə'rɪstɪk/ adj, **-ally** adv charakteristisch (**of** für) • n Merkmal nt

characterize /'kærɪktəraɪz/ vt charakterisieren

charge /tʃɑːdʒ/ n (price) Gebühr f; (Electr) Ladung f; (attack) Angriff m; (Jur) Anklage f; **free of** ~ kostenlos; **be in** ~ verantwortlich sein (**of** für); **take** ~ die Aufsicht übernehmen (**of** über + acc) • vt berechnen (fee); (Electr) laden; (attack) angreifen; (Jur) anklagen (**with** gen); ~ **s.o. for sth** jdm etw berechnen

charitable /'tʃærɪtəbl/ adj wohltätig; (kind) wohlwollend

charity /'tʃærətɪ/ n Nächstenliebe f; (organization) wohltätige Einrichtung f; **for** ~ für Wohltätigkeitszwecke

charm /tʃɑːm/ n Reiz m; (of person) Charme f; (object) Amulett nt • vt bezaubern. ~**ing** adj reizend; (person, smile) charmant

chart /tʃɑːt/ n Karte f; (table) Tabelle f

charter /'tʃɑːtə(r)/ n ~ **[flight]** Charterflug m • vt chartern; ~**ed accountant** Wirtschaftsprüfer, Wirtschaftsprüferin m(f)

chase /tʃeɪs/ n Verfolgungsjagd f • vt jagen, verfolgen. ~ **away** or **off** vt wegjagen

chassis /ˈʃæsɪ/ n (pl **chassis**) Chassis nt

chaste /tʃeɪst/ adj keusch

chat /tʃæt/ n Plauderei f; **have a ~ with** plaudern mit ● vi (pt/pp **chatted**) plaudern. **~ show** n Talkshow f

chatter /ˈtʃætə(r)/ n Geschwätz nt ● vi schwatzen; (child:) plappern; (teeth:) klappern. **~box** n ⧉ Plappermaul nt

chatty /ˈtʃætɪ/ adj geschwätzig

chauffeur /ˈʃəʊfə(r)/ n Chauffeur m

cheap /tʃiːp/ adj & adv (**-er, -est**) billig. **~en** vt entwürdigen

cheat /tʃiːt/ n Betrüger(in) m(f); (at games) Mogler m ● vt betrügen ● vi (at games) mogeln ⧉

check¹ /tʃek/ adj (squared) kariert ● n Karo nt

check² n Überprüfung f; (inspection) Kontrolle f; (Chess) Schach nt; (Amer: bill) Rechnung f; (Amer: cheque) Scheck m; (Amer: tick) Haken m; **keep a ~ on** kontrollieren ● vt [über]prüfen; (inspect) kontrollieren; (restrain) hemmen; (stop) aufhalten ● vi [**go and**] **~** nachsehen. **~ in** vi sich anmelden; (Aviat) einchecken ● vt abfertigen; einchecken. **~ out** vi sich abmelden. **~ up** vi prüfen, kontrollieren; **~ up on** überprüfen

checked /tʃekt/ adj kariert

check: ~-out n Kasse f. **~room** n (Amer) Garderobe f. **~-up** n (Med) [Kontroll]untersuchung f

cheek /tʃiːk/ n Backe f; (impudence) Frechheit f. **~y** adj, **-ily** adv frech

cheer /tʃɪə(r)/ n Beifallsruf m; **three ~s** ein dreifaches Hoch (**for** auf + acc); **~s!** prost! (goodbye) tschüs! ● vt zujubeln (+ dat) ● vi jubeln. **~ up** vt aufmuntern; aufheitern ● vi munterer werden. **~ful** adj fröhlich. **~fulness** n Fröhlichkeit f

cheerio /tʃɪərɪˈəʊ/ int ⧉ tschüs!

cheese /tʃiːz/ n Käse m. **~cake** n Käsekuchen m

chef /ʃef/ n Koch m

chemical /ˈkemɪkl/ adj chemisch ● n Chemikalie f

chemist /ˈkemɪst/ n (pharmacist) Apotheker(in) m(f); (scientist) Chemiker(in) m(f); **~'s [shop]** Drogerie f; (dispensing) Apotheke f. **~ry** n Chemie f

cheque /tʃek/ n Scheck m. **~-book** n Scheckbuch nt. **~ card** n Scheckkarte f

cherish /ˈtʃerɪʃ/ vt lieben; (fig) hegen

cherry /ˈtʃerɪ/ n Kirsche f ● attrib Kirsch-

chess /tʃes/ n Schach nt

chess: ~board n Schachbrett nt. **~-man** n Schachfigur f

chest /tʃest/ n Brust f; (box) Truhe f

chestnut /ˈtʃesnʌt/ n Esskastanie f, Marone f; (horse-) [Ross]kastanie f

chest of 'drawers n Kommode f

chew /tʃuː/ vt kauen. **~ing-gum** n Kaugummi m

chick /tʃɪk/ n Küken nt

chicken /ˈtʃɪkɪn/ n Huhn nt ● attrib Hühner- ● adj ⧉ feige

chief /tʃiːf/ adj Haupt- ● n Chef m; (of tribe) Häuptling m. **~ly** adv hauptsächlich

child /tʃaɪld/ n (pl **~ren**) Kind nt

child: ~birth n Geburt f. **~hood** n Kindheit f. **~ish** adj kindisch. **~less** adj kinderlos. **~like** adj kindlich. **~-minder** n Tagesmutter f

children /ˈtʃɪldrən/ npl see **child**

Chile /ˈtʃɪlɪ/ n Chile nt

chill /tʃɪl/ n Kälte f; (illness) Erkältung f ● vt kühlen

chilly /ˈtʃɪlɪ/ adj kühl; **I felt ~** mich fröstelte [es]

chime /tʃaɪm/ vi läuten; (clock:) schlagen

chimney /ˈtʃɪmnɪ/ n Schornstein m. **~-pot** n Schornsteinaufsatz m. **~-sweep** n Schornsteinfeger m

chin /tʃɪn/ n Kinn nt

china /ˈtʃaɪnə/ n Porzellan nt

Chin|a n China nt. **~ese** adj chinesisch ● n (Lang) Chinesisch nt; **the ~ese** pl die Chinesen

chink¹ /tʃɪŋk/ n (slit) Ritze f

chink² *n* Geklirr *nt* ● *vi* klirren; (*coins:*) klimpern

chip /tʃɪp/ *n* (*fragment*) Span *m*; (*in china, paintwork*) angeschlagene Stelle *f*; (*Computing, Gambling*) Chip *m*; ~**s** *pl* (*Culin*) Pommes frites *pl*; (*Amer: crisps*) Chips *pl* ● *vt* (*pt/pp* **chipped**) (*damage*) anschlagen. ~**ped** *adj* angeschlagen

chirp /tʃɜːp/ *vi* zwitschern; (*cricket:*) zirpen. ~**y** *adj* 🔲 munter

chit /tʃɪt/ *n* Zettel *m*

chocolate /'tʃɒkələt/ *n* Schokolade *f*; (*sweet*) Praline *f*

choice /tʃɔɪs/ *n* Wahl *f*; (*variety*) Auswahl *f* ● *adj* auserlesen

choir /'kwaɪə(r)/ *n* Chor *m*. ~**boy** *n* Chorknabe *m*

choke /tʃəʊk/ *n* (*Auto*) Choke *m* ● *vt* würgen; (*to death*) erwürgen ● *vi* sich verschlucken; ~ **on** [fast] ersticken an (+ *dat*)

choose /tʃuːz/ *vt/i* (*pt* **chose**, *pp* **chosen**) wählen; (*select*) sich (*dat*) aussuchen; ~ **to do/go** [freiwillig] tun/gehen; **as you** ~ wie Sie wollen

choos[e]y /'tʃuːzɪ/ *adj* 🔲 wählerisch

chop /tʃɒp/ *n* (*blow*) Hieb *m*; (*Culin*) Kotelett *nt* ● *vt* (*pt/pp* **chopped**) hacken. ~ **down** *vt* abhacken; fällen (*tree*). ~ **off** *vt* abhacken

chop|per /'tʃɒpə(r)/ *n* Beil *nt*; 🔲 Hubschrauber *m*. ~**py** *adj* kabbelig

'chopsticks *npl* Essstäbchen *pl*

choral /'kɔːrəl/ *adj* Chor-

chord /kɔːd/ *n* (*Mus*) Akkord *m*

chore /tʃɔː(r)/ *n* lästige Pflicht *f*; [**household**] ~**s** Hausarbeit *f*

chorus /'kɔːrəs/ *n* Chor *m*; (*of song*) Refrain *m*

chose, chosen *see* **choose**

Christ /kraɪst/ *n* Christus *m*

christen /'krɪsn/ *vt* taufen

Christian /'krɪstʃən/ *adj* christlich ● *n* Christ(in) *m*(*f*). ~**ity** *n* Christentum *nt*. ~ **name** *n* Vorname *m*

Christmas /'krɪsməs/ *n* Weihnachten *nt*. ~ **card** *n* Weihnachtskarte *f*. ~ '**Day** *n* erster Weihnachtstag *m*. ~ '**Eve** *n* Heiligabend *m*. ~ **tree** *n* Weihnachtsbaum *m*

chrome /krəʊm/ *n*, **chromium** *n* Chrom *nt*

chronic /'krɒnɪk/ *adj* chronisch

chronicle /'krɒnɪkl/ *n* Chronik *f*

chrysanthemum /krɪ'sænθəməm/ *n* Chrysantheme *f*

chubby /'tʃʌbɪ/ *adj* mollig

chuck /tʃʌk/ *vt* 🔲 schmeißen. ~ **out** *vt* 🔲 rausschmeißen

chuckle /'tʃʌkl/ *vi* in sich (*acc*) hineinlachen

chum /tʃʌm/ *n* Freund(in) *m*(*f*)

chunk /tʃʌŋk/ *n* Stück *nt*

church /tʃɜːtʃ/ *n* Kirche *f*. ~**yard** *n* Friedhof *m*

churn /tʃɜːn/ *vt* ~ **out** am laufenden Band produzieren

cider /'saɪdə(r)/ *n* ≈ Apfelwein *m*

cigar /sɪ'gɑː(r)/ *n* Zigarre *f*

cigarette /sɪgə'ret/ *n* Zigarette *f*

cine-camera /'sɪnɪ-/ *n* Filmkamera *f*

cinema /'sɪnɪmə/ *n* Kino *nt*

cinnamon /'sɪnəmən/ *n* Zimt *m*

circle /'sɜːkl/ *n* Kreis *m*; (*Theat*) Rang *m* ● *vt* umkreisen ● *vi* kreisen

circuit /'sɜːkɪt/ *n* Runde *f*; (*racetrack*) Rennbahn *f*; (*Electr*) Stromkreis *m*. ~**ous** *adj* ~ **route** Umweg *m*

circular /'sɜːkjʊlə(r)/ *adj* kreisförmig ● *n* Rundschreiben *nt*. ~ '**saw** *n* Kreissäge *f*. ~ '**tour** *n* Rundfahrt *f*

circulat|e /'sɜːkjʊleɪt/ *vt* in Umlauf setzen ● *vi* zirkulieren. ~**ion** *n* Kreislauf *m*; (*of newspaper*) Auflage *f*

circumference /sə'kʌmfərəns/ *n* Umfang *m*

circumstance /'sɜːkəmstəns/ *n* Umstand *m*; ~**s** *pl* Umstände *pl*; (*financial*) Verhältnisse *pl*

circus /'sɜːkəs/ *n* Zirkus *m*

cistern /'sɪstən/ *n* (*tank*) Wasserbehälter *m*; (*of WC*) Spülkasten *m*

cite /saɪt/ *vt* zitieren

citizen /'sɪtɪzn/ *n* Bürger(in) *m*(*f*). ~**ship** *n* Staatsangehörigkeit *f*

citrus /'sɪtrəs/ *n* ~ [**fruit**] Zitrusfrucht *f*

city /'sɪtɪ/ n [Groß]stadt f

> ℹ️ **City** The City of London ist das Gebiet innerhalb der alten Stadtgrenzen von London. Heute ist es das Geschäfts- und Finanzzentrum Londons und viele Banken und andere Geldinstitute haben dort ihre Hauptstellen. Wenn Leute über die City sprechen, beziehen sie sich oft auf diese Institutionen und nicht auf den Ort.

civic /'sɪvɪk/ adj Bürger-

civil /'ʃɪvl/ adj bürgerlich; (aviation, defence) zivil; (polite) höflich. ~ **engi'neering** n Hoch- und Tiefbau m

civilian /sɪ'vɪljən/ adj Zivil-; **in ~ clothes** in Zivil ● n Zivilist m

civiliz|ation /sɪvəlar'zeɪʃn/ n Zivilisation f. ~**e** vt zivilisieren

civil: ~'**servant** n Beamte(r) m/Beamtin f. **C~** '**Service** n Staatsdienst m

claim /kleɪm/ n Anspruch m; (application) Antrag m; (demand) Forderung f; (assertion) Behauptung f ● vt beanspruchen; (apply for) beantragen; (demand) fordern; (assert) behaupten; (collect) abholen

clam /klæm/ n Klaffmuschel f

clamber /'klæmbə(r)/ vi klettern

clammy /'klæmɪ/ adj feucht

clamour /'klæmə(r)/ n Geschrei nt ● vi ~ **for** schreien nach

clamp /klæmp/ n Klammer f; **[wheel]** ~ Parkkralle f ● vt [ein] spannen ● vi 🔲 ~ **down on** vorgehen gegen

clan /klæn/ n Clan m

clang /klæŋ/ n Schmettern nt. ~**er** n 🔲 Schnitzer m

clank /klæŋk/ vi klirren

clap /klæp/ n **give s.o. a** ~ jdm Beifall klatschen; ~ **of thunder** Donnerschlag m ● vt/i (pt/pp **clapped**) Beifall klatschen (+ dat); ~ **one's hands** [in die Hände] klatschen

clari|fication /klærɪfɪ'keɪʃn/ n Klärung f. ~**fy** vt/i (pt/pp -**ied**) klären

clarinet /klærɪ'net/ n Klarinette f

clarity /'klærətɪ/ n Klarheit f

clash /klæʃ/ n Geklirr nt; (fig) Konflikt m ● vi klirren; (colours:) sich beißen; (events:) ungünstig zusammenfallen

clasp /klɑːsp/ n Verschluss m ● vt ergreifen; (hold) halten

class /klɑːs/ n Klasse f; **travel first/ second** ~ erster/zweiter Klasse reisen ● vt einordnen

classic /'klæsɪk/ adj klassisch ● n Klassiker m. ~**al** adj klassisch

classi|fication /klæsɪfɪ'keɪʃn/ n Klassifikation f. ~**fy** vt (pt/pp -**ied**) klassifizieren

'**classroom** n Klassenzimmer nt

classy /'klɑːsɪ/ adj 🔲 schick

clatter /'klætə(r)/ n Geklapper nt ● vi klappern

clause /klɔːz/ n Klausel f; (Gram) Satzteil m

claw /klɔː/ n Kralle f; (of bird of prey & Techn) Klaue f; (of crab, lobster) Schere f ● vt kratzen

clay /kleɪ/ n Lehm m; (pottery) Ton m

clean /kliːn/ adj (-er, -est) sauber ● adv glatt ● vt sauber machen; putzen (shoes, windows); ~ **one's teeth** sich (dat) die Zähne putzen; **have sth ~ed** etw reinigen lassen. ~ **up** vt sauber machen

cleaner /'kliːnə(r)/ n Putzfrau f; (substance) Reinigungsmittel nt; **[dry]** ~'**s** chemische Reinigung f

cleanliness /'klenlɪnɪs/ n Sauberkeit f

cleanse /klenz/ vt reinigen

clear /klɪə(r)/ adj (-er, -est) klar; (obvious) eindeutig; (distinct) deutlich; (conscience) rein; (without obstacles) frei; **make sth ~** etw klarmachen (**to** dat) ● adv **stand ~** zurücktreten; **keep ~ of** aus dem Wege gehen (+ dat) ● vt räumen; abräumen (table); (acquit) freisprechen; (authorize) genehmigen; (jump over) überspringen; ~ **one's throat** sich räuspern ● vi (fog:) sich auflösen. ~ **away** vt wegräumen. ~ **off** vi 🔲 abhauen. ~ **out** vt ausräumen ● vi 🔲 abhauen. ~ **up** vt (tidy) aufräumen; (solve) aufklären

● *vi* (*weather*): sich aufklären

clearance /ˈklɪərəns/ *n* Räumung *f*; (*authorization*) Genehmigung *f*; (*customs*) [Zoll]abfertigung *f*; (*Techn*) Spielraum *m*. ~ **sale** *n* Räumungsverkauf *m*

clench /klentʃ/ *vt* ~ **one's fist** die Faust ballen; ~ **one's teeth** die Zähne zusammenbeißen

clergy /ˈklɜːdʒɪ/ *npl* Geistlichkeit *f*. ~**man** *n* Geistliche(r) *m*

clerk /klɑːk, *Amer*: /klɜːk/ *n* Büroangestellte(r) *m/f*; (*Amer: shop assistant*) Verkäufer(in) *m*(*f*)

clever /ˈklevə(r)/ *adj* (**-er, -est**), **-ly** *adv* klug; (*skilful*) geschickt

cliché /ˈkliːʃeɪ/ *n* Klischee *nt*

click /klɪk/ *vi* klicken

client /ˈklaɪənt/ *n* Kunde *m*/ Kundin *f*; (*Jur*) Klient(in) *m*(*f*)

cliff /klɪf/ *n* Kliff *nt*

climat|e /ˈklaɪmət/ *n* Klima *nt*

climax /ˈklaɪmæks/ *n* Höhepunkt *m*

climb /klaɪm/ *n* Aufstieg *m* ● *vt* besteigen (*mountain*); steigen auf (+ *acc*) (*ladder, tree*) ● *vi* klettern; (*rise*) steigen; (*road*:) ansteigen. ~ **down** *vi* hinunter-/herunterklettern; (*from ladder, tree*) heruntersteigen; 🛈 nachgeben

climber /ˈklaɪmə(r)/ *n* Bergsteiger *m*; (*plant*) Kletterpflanze *f*

cling /klɪŋ/ *vi* (*pt/pp* **clung**) sich klammern (**to** an + *acc*); (*stick*) haften (**to** an + *dat*). ~ **film** *n* Sichtfolie *f* mit Hafteffekt

clinic /ˈklɪnɪk/ *n* Klinik *f*. ~**al** *adj* klinisch

clink /klɪŋk/ *vi* klirren

clip¹ /klɪp/ *n* Klammer *f*; (*jewellery*) Klipp *m* ● *vt* (*pt/pp* **clipped**) anklammern (**to** an + *acc*)

clip² *n* (*extract*) Ausschnitt *m* ● *vt* schneiden; knipsen (*ticket*). ~**ping** *n* (*extract*) Ausschnitt *m*

cloak /kləʊk/ *n* Umhang *m*. ~**room** *n* Garderobe *f*; (*toilet*) Toilette *f*

clobber /ˈklɒbə(r)/ *n* 🛈 Zeug *nt* ● *vt* (🛈: *hit, defeat*) schlagen

clock /klɒk/ *n* Uhr *f*; (🛈: *speedom-*

eter) Tacho *m* ● *vi* ~ **in/out** stechen

clock: ~**wise** *adj & adv* im Uhrzeigersinn. ~**work** *n* Uhrwerk *nt*; (*of toy*) Aufziehmechanismus *m*; **like** ~**work** 🛈 wie am Schnürchen

clod /klɒd/ *n* Klumpen *m*

clog /klɒg/ *vt/i* (*pt/pp* **clogged**) ~ **[up]** verstopfen

cloister /ˈklɔɪstə(r)/ *n* Kreuzgang *m*

clone /kləʊn/ *n* Klon *m* ● *vt* klonen

close¹ /kləʊs/ *adj* (**-r, -st**) nah[e] (**to** *dat*); (*friend*) eng; (*weather*) schwül; **have a** ~ **shave** 🛈 mit knapper Not davonkommen ● *adv* nahe ● *n* (*street*) Sackgasse *f*

close² /kləʊz/ *n* Ende *nt*; **draw to a** ~ sich dem Ende nähern ● *vt* zumachen, schließen; (*bring to an end*) beenden; sperren (*road*) ● *vi* sich schließen; (*shop*:) schließen, zumachen; (*end*) enden. ~ **down** *vt* schließen; stilllegen (*factory*) ● *vi* schließen; (*factory*:) stillgelegt werden

closely /ˈkləʊslɪ/ *adv* eng, nah[e]; (*with attention*) genau

closet /ˈklɒzɪt/ *n* (*Amer*) Schrank *m*

close-up /ˈkləʊs-/ *n* Nahaufnahme *f*

closure /ˈkləʊʒə(r)/ *n* Schließung *f*; (*of factory*) Stilllegung *f*; (*of road*) Sperrung *f*

clot /klɒt/ *n* [Blut]gerinnsel *nt*; (🛈: *idiot*) Trottel *m*

cloth /klɒθ/ *n* Tuch *nt*

clothe /kləʊð/ *vt* kleiden

clothes /kləʊðz/ *npl* Kleider *pl*. ~**-line** *n* Wäscheleine *f*

clothing /ˈkləʊðɪŋ/ *n* Kleidung *f*

cloud /klaʊd/ *n* Wolke *f* ● *vi* ~ **over** sich bewölken

cloudy /ˈklaʊdɪ/ *adj* wolkig, bewölkt; (*liquid*) trübe

clout /klaʊt/ *n* 🛈 Schlag *m*; (*influence*) Einfluss *m*

clove /kləʊv/ *n* [Gewürz]nelke *f*; ~ **of garlic** Knoblauchzehe *f*

clover /ˈkləʊvə(r)/ *n* Klee *m*. ~ **leaf** *n* Kleeblatt *nt*

clown /klaʊn/ *n* Clown *m* ● *vi* ~ **[about]** herumalbern

club /klʌb/ n Klub m; (*weapon*) Keule f; (*Sport*) Schläger m; ~s pl (*Cards*) Kreuz nt, Treff nt

clue /klu:/ n Anhaltspunkt m; (*in crossword*) Frage f; **I haven't a** ~ 🖪 ich habe keine Ahnung

clump /klʌmp/ n Gruppe f

clumsiness /'klʌmzɪnɪs/ n Unge-schicklichkeit f

clumsy /'klʌmzɪ/ adj , **-ily** adv unge-schickt; (*unwieldy*) unförmig

clung /klʌŋ/ see **cling**

clutch /klʌtʃ/ n Griff m; (*Auto*) Kupp-lung f; **be in s.o.'s** ~**es** 🖪 in jds Klauen sein ● vt festhalten; (*grab*) er-greifen ● vi ~ **at** greifen nach

clutter /'klʌtə(r)/ n Kram m ● vt ~ [**up**] vollstopfen

c/o abbr (**care of**) bei

coach /kəʊtʃ/ n [Reise]bus m; (*Rail*) Wagen m; (*horse-drawn*) Kutsche f; (*Sport*) Trainer m ● vt Nachhilfestun-den geben (+ *dat*); (*Sport*) trainieren

coal /kəʊl/ n Kohle f

coalition /kəʊə'lɪʃn/ n Koalition f

'coal-mine n Kohlenbergwerk nt

coarse /kɔ:s/ adj (**-r, -st**) grob

coast /kəʊst/ n Küste f ● vi (*free-wheel*) im Freilauf fahren. (*Auto*) im Leerlauf fahren. ~**er** n (*mat*) Unter-satz m

coast: ~**guard** n Küstenwache f. ~**line** n Küste f

coat /kəʊt/ n Mantel m; (*of animal*) Fell nt; (*of paint*) Anstrich m; ~ **of arms** Wappen nt ● vt überziehen; (*with paint*) streichen. ~**-hanger** n Kleiderbügel m. ~**-hook** n Kleiderha-ken m

coating /'kəʊtɪŋ/ n Überzug m, Schicht f; (*of paint*) Anstrich m

coax /kəʊks/ vt gut zureden (+ *dat*)

cobble[1] /'kɒbl/ n Kopfstein m; ~**s** pl Kopfsteinpflaster nt

cobble[2] vt flicken. ~**r** n Schuster m

cobweb /'kɒb-/ n Spinnengewebe nt

cock /kɒk/ n Hahn m; (*any male bird*) Männchen nt ● vt (*animal:*) ~ **its ears** die Ohren spitzen; ~ **the gun** den Hahn spannen

cockerel /'kɒkərəl/ n [junger] Hahn m

cockney /'kɒknɪ/ n (*dialect*) Cockney nt; (*person*) Cockney m

cock: ~**pit** n (*Aviat*) Cockpit nt. ~**roach** /-rəʊtʃ/ n Küchenschabe f. ~**tail** n Cocktail m. ~**-up** n 🖾 **make a** ~**-up** Mist bauen (**of** bei)

cocky /'kɒkɪ/ adj 🖪 eingebildet

cocoa /'kəʊkəʊ/ n Kakao m

coconut /'kəʊkənʌt/ n Kokosnuss f

cod /kɒd/ n inv Kabeljau m

COD abbr (**cash on delivery**) per Nachnahme

coddle /'kɒdl/ vt verhätscheln

code /kəʊd/ n Kode m; (*Computing*) Code m; (*set of rules*) Kodex m. ~**d** adj verschlüsselt

coerc|e /kəʊ'ɜ:s/ vt zwingen. ~**ion** n Zwang m

coffee /'kɒfɪ/ n Kaffee m

coffee: ~**-grinder** n Kaffeemühle f. ~**-pot** n Kaffeekanne f. ~**-table** n Couchtisch m

coffin /'kɒfɪn/ n Sarg m

cogent /'kəʊdʒənt/ adj überzeugend

coherent /kəʊ'hɪərənt/ adj zusam-menhängend; (*comprehensible*) ver-ständlich

coil /kɔɪl/ n Rolle f; (*Electr*) Spule f; (*one ring*) Windung f ● vt ~[**up**] zu-sammenrollen

coin /kɔɪn/ n Münze f ● vt prägen

coincide /kəʊɪn'saɪd/ vi zusammen-fallen; (*agree*) übereinstimmen

coinciden|ce /kəʊ'ɪnsɪdəns/ n Zu-fall m. ~**tal** adj zufällig

coke /kəʊk/ n Koks m

Coke (R) n (*drink*) Cola f

cold /kəʊld/ adj (**-er, -est**) kalt; **I am** or **feel** ~ mir ist kalt ● n Kälte f; (*Med*) Erkältung f

cold: ~**-'blooded** adj kaltblütig. ~**-'hearted** adj kaltherzig. ~**ly** adv (*fig*) kalt, kühl. ~**ness** n Kälte f

collaborat|e /kə'læbəreɪt/ vi zu-sammenarbeiten (**with** mit); ~**e on sth** mitarbeiten bei etw. ~**ion** n Zu-sammenarbeit f, Mitarbeit f; (*with enemy*) Kollaboration f. ~**or** n Mitar-

299

collapse | comfy

beiter(in) *m*(*f*); Kollaborateur *m*

collaps|e /kə'læps/ *n* Zusammenbruch *m*; Einsturz *m* ● *vi* zusammenbrechen; (*roof, building*) einstürzen. ∼**ible** *adj* zusammenklappbar

collar /'kɒlə(r)/ *n* Kragen *m*; (*for animal*) Halsband *nt*. ∼**-bone** *n* Schlüsselbein *nt*

colleague /'kɒliːg/ *n* Kollege *m*/Kollegin *f*

collect /kə'lekt/ *vt* sammeln; (*fetch*) abholen; einsammeln (*tickets*); einziehen (*taxes*) ● *vi* sich [an]sammeln ● *adv* **call** ∼ (*Amer*) ein R-Gespräch führen

collection /kə'lekʃn/ *n* Sammlung *f*; (*in church*) Kollekte *f*; (*of post*) Leerung *f*; (*designer's*) Kollektion *f*

collector /kə'lektə(r)/ *n* Sammler(in) *m*(*f*)

college /'kɒlɪdʒ/ *n* College *nt*

collide /kə'laɪd/ *vi* zusammenstoßen

colliery /'kɒlɪərɪ/ *n* Kohlengrube *f*

collision /kə'lɪʒn/ *n* Zusammenstoß *m*

colloquial /kə'ləʊkwɪəl/ *adj* umgangssprachlich

Cologne /kə'ləʊn/ *n* Köln *nt*

colon /'kəʊlən/ *n* Doppelpunkt *m*

colonel /'kɜːnl/ *n* Oberst *m*

colonial /kə'ləʊnɪəl/ *adj* Kolonial-

colony /'kɒlənɪ/ *n* Kolonie *f*

colossal /kə'lɒsl/ *adj* riesig

colour /'kʌlə(r)/ *n* Farbe *f*; (*complexion*) Gesichtsfarbe *f*; (*race*) Hautfarbe *f*; **off** ∼ 🔲 nicht ganz auf der Höhe ● *vt* färben; ∼ **[in]** ausmalen

colour: ∼**-blind** *adj* farbenblind. ∼**ed** *adj* farbig ● *n* (*person*) Farbige(r) *m/f*. ∼**-fast** *adj* farbecht. ∼**film** *n* Farbfilm *m*. ∼**ful** *adj* farbenfroh. ∼**less** *adj* farblos. ∼ **photo [graph]** *n* Farbaufnahme *f*. ∼ **television** *n* Farbfernsehen *nt*

column /'kɒləm/ *n* Säule *f*; (*of soldiers, figures*) Kolonne *f*; (*Printing*) Spalte *f*; (*newspaper*) Kolumne *f*

comb /kəʊm/ *n* Kamm *m* ● *vt* kämmen; (*search*) absuchen; ∼ **one's hair** sich (*dat*) [die Haare] kämmen

combat /'kɒmbæt/ *n* Kampf *m*

combination /kɒmbɪ'neɪʃn/ *n* Kombination *f*

combine[1] /kəm'baɪn/ *vt* verbinden ● *vi* sich verbinden; (*people:*) sich zusammenschließen

combine[2] /'kɒmbaɪn/ *n* (*Comm*) Konzern *m*

combustion /kəm'bʌstʃn/ *n* Verbrennung *f*

come /kʌm/ *vi* (*pt* **came**, *pp* **come**) kommen; (*reach*) reichen (**to** an + *acc*); **that** ∼ **s to £10** das macht £10; ∼ **into money** zu Geld kommen; ∼ **true** wahr werden; ∼ **in two sizes** in zwei Größen erhältlich sein; **the years to** ∼ die kommenden Jahre; **how** ∼**?** 🔲 wie das? ∼ **about** *vi* geschehen. ∼ **across** *vi* herüberkommen; 🔲 klar werden ● *vt* stoßen auf (+ *acc*). ∼ **apart** *vi* sich auseinander nehmen lassen; (*accidentally*) auseinander gehen. ∼ **away** *vi* weggehen; (*thing:*) abgehen. ∼ **back** *vi* zurückkommen. ∼ **by** *vi* vorbeikommen ● *vt* (*obtain*) bekommen. ∼ **in** *vi* hereinkommen. ∼ **off** *vi* abgehen; (*take place*) stattfinden; (*succeed*) klappen 🔲. ∼ **out** *vi* herauskommen; (*book:*) erscheinen; (*stain:*) herausgehen. ∼ **round** *vi* vorbeikommen; (*after fainting*) [wieder] zu sich kommen; (*change one's mind*) sich umstimmen lassen. ∼ **to** *vi* [wieder] zu sich kommen. ∼ **up** *vi* heraufkommen; (*plant:*) aufgehen; (*reach*) reichen (**to** bis); ∼ **up with** sich (*dat*) einfallen lassen

'come-back *n* Comeback *nt*

comedian /kə'miːdɪən/ *n* Komiker *m*

'come-down *n* Rückschritt *m*

comedy /'kɒmədɪ/ *n* Komödie *f*

comet /'kɒmɪt/ *n* Komet *m*

comfort /'kʌmfət/ *n* Bequemlichkeit *f*; (*consolation*) Trost *m* ● *vt* trösten

comfortable /'kʌmfətəbl/ *adj*, **-bly** *adv* bequem

'comfort station *n* (*Amer*) öffentliche Toilette *f*

comfy /'kʌmfɪ/ *adj* 🔲 bequem

comic /'kɒmɪk/ adj komisch ● n Komiker m; (periodical) Comic-Heft nt

coming /'kʌmɪŋ/ adj kommend ● n Kommen nt

comma /'kɒmə/ n Komma nt

command /kə'mɑːnd/ n Befehl m; (Mil) Kommando nt; (mastery) Beherrschung f ● vt befehlen (+ dat); kommandieren (army)

command|er /kə'mɑːndə(r)/ n Befehlshaber m. **~ing officer** n Befehlshaber m

commemorat|e /kə'meməreɪt/ vt gedenken (+ gen). **~ion** n Gedenken nt

commence /kə'mens/ vt/i anfangen, beginnen

commend /kə'mend/ vt loben; (recommend) empfehlen (to dat)

comment /'kɒment/ n Bemerkung f; **no ~!** kein Kommentar! ● vi sich äußern (on zu); **~ on** (an event) kommentieren

commentary /'kɒməntrɪ/ n Kommentar m; **[running] ~** (Radio, TV) Reportage f

commentator /'kɒmənteɪtə(r)/ n Kommentator m; (Sport) Reporter m

commerce /'kɒmɜːs/ n Handel m

commercial /kə'mɜːʃl/ adj kommerziell ● n (Radio, TV) Werbespot m

commission /kə'mɪʃn/ n (order for work) Auftrag m; (body of people) Kommission f; (payment) Provision f; (Mil) [Offiziers]patent nt; **out of ~** außer Betrieb ● vt beauftragen (s.o.); in Auftrag geben (thing); (Mil) zum Offizier ernennen

commit /kə'mɪt/ vt (pt/pp committed) begehen; (entrust) anvertrauen (to dat); (consign) einweisen (to in + acc); **~ oneself** sich festlegen; (involve oneself) sich engagieren. **~ment** n Verpflichtung f; (involvement) Engagement nt. **~ted** adj engagiert

committee /kə'mɪtɪ/ n Ausschuss m, Komitee nt

common /'kɒmən/ adj (-er, -est) gemeinsam; (frequent) häufig; (ordinary) gewöhnlich; (vulgar) ordinär ● n Gemeindeland nt; **have in ~** gemeinsam haben; **House of C~s** Unterhaus nt

common: ~ly adv allgemein. **C~ 'Market** n Gemeinsamer Markt m. **~place** adj häufig. **~-room** n Aufenthaltsraum m. **~ 'sense** n gesunder Menschenverstand m

> **Commonwealth** Seit 1931 ist das Commonwealth die Gemeinschaft der 53 unabhängigen Staaten des ehemaligen britischen Weltreichs. Die Mitgliedsländer, die jetzt bildungs- und kulturpolitisch miteinander verbunden sind, nehmen alle zwei Jahre an den Commonwealth-Konferenzen teil. Alle vier Jahre finden die Commonwealth-Spiele statt. In den USA ist Commonwealth die offizielle Bezeichnung der vier US-Staaten: Kentucky, Massachusetts, Pennsylvania und Virginia.

commotion /kə'məʊʃn/ n Tumult m

communal /'kɒmjʊnl/ adj gemeinschaftlich

communicate /kə'mjuːnɪkeɪt/ vt mitteilen (to dat); übertragen (disease) ● vi sich verständigen

communication /kəmjuːnɪ'keɪʃn/ n Verständigung f; (contact) Verbindung f; (message) Mitteilung f; **~s** pl (technology) Nachrichtenwesen nt

communicative /kə'mjuːnɪkətɪv/ adj mitteilsam

Communion /kə'mjuːnɪən/ n **[Holy] ~** das [heilige] Abendmahl; (Roman Catholic) die [heilige] Kommunion

communis|m /'kɒmjʊnɪzm/ n Kommunismus m. **~t** adj kommunistisch ● n Kommunist(in) m(f)

community /kə'mjuːnətɪ/ n Gemeinschaft f; **local ~** Gemeinde f

commute /kə'mjuːt/ vi pendeln. **~r** n Pendler(in) m(f)

compact /kəm'pækt/ adj kompakt

companion /kəm'pænjən/ n Begleiter(in) m(f). **~ship** n Gesellschaft f

company /ˈkʌmpənɪ/ n Gesellschaft f; (firm) Firma f; (Mil) Kompanie f; (🚹: guests) Besuch m. **~ car** n Firmenwagen m

comparable /ˈkɒmpərəbl/ adj vergleichbar

comparative /kəmˈpærətɪv/ adj vergleichend; (relative) relativ ● n (Gram) Komparativ m. **~ly** adv verhältnismäßig

compare /kəmˈpeə(r)/ vt vergleichen (**with/to** mit) ● vi sich vergleichen lassen

comparison /kəmˈpærɪsn/ n Vergleich m

compartment /kəmˈpɑːtmənt/ n Fach nt; (Rail) Abteil nt

compass /ˈkʌmpəs/ n Kompass m

compassion /kəmˈpæʃn/ n Mitleid nt. **~ate** adj mitfühlend

compatible /kəmˈpætəbl/ adj vereinbar; (drugs) verträglich; (Techn) kompatibel; **be ~** (people:) |gut| zueinander passen

compatriot /kəmˈpætrɪət/ n Landsmann m /-männin f

compel /kəmˈpel/ vt (pt/pp **compelled**) zwingen

compensat|e /ˈkɒmpənseɪt/ vt entschädigen. **~ion** n Entschädigung f; (fig) Ausgleich m

compete /kəmˈpiːt/ vi konkurrieren; (take part) teilnehmen (**in** an + dat)

competen|ce /ˈkɒmpɪtəns/ n Fähigkeit f. **~t** adj fähig

competition /kɒmpəˈtɪʃn/ n Konkurrenz f; (contest) Wettbewerb m; (in newspaper) Preisausschreiben nt

competitive /kəmˈpetətɪv/ adj (Comm) konkurrenzfähig

competitor /kəmˈpetɪtə(r)/ n Teilnehmer m; (Comm) Konkurrent m

compile /kəmˈpaɪl/ vt zusammenstellen

complacen|cy /kəmˈpleɪsənsɪ/ n Selbstzufriedenheit f. **~t** adj selbstzufrieden

complain /kəmˈpleɪn/ vi klagen (**about/of** über + acc); (formally) sich beschweren. **~t** n Klage f; (formal) Beschwerde f; (Med) Leiden nt

complement¹ /ˈkɒmplɪmənt/ n Ergänzung f; **full ~** volle Anzahl f

complement² /ˈkɒmplɪment/ vt ergänzen

complete /kəmˈpliːt/ adj vollständig; (finished) fertig; (utter) völlig ● vt vervollständigen; (finish) abschließen; (fill in) ausfüllen. **~ly** adv völlig

completion /kəmˈpliːʃn/ n Vervollständigung f; (end) Abschluss m

complex /ˈkɒmpleks/ adj komplex ● n Komplex m

complexion /kəmˈplekʃn/ n Teint m; (colour) Gesichtsfarbe f

complexity /kəmˈpleksətɪ/ n Komplexität f

complicat|e /ˈkɒmplɪkeɪt/ vt komplizieren. **~ed** adj kompliziert. **~ion** n Komplikation f

compliment /ˈkɒmplɪmənt/ n Kompliment nt; **~s** pl Grüße pl ● vt ein Kompliment machen (+ dat). **~ary** adj schmeichelhaft; (given free) Frei-

comply /kəmˈplaɪ/ vi (pt/pp -ied) **~ with** nachkommen (+ dat)

compose /kəmˈpəʊz/ vt verfassen; (Mus) komponieren; **be ~d of** sich zusammensetzen aus. **~r** n Komponist m

composition /kɒmpəˈzɪʃn/ n Komposition f; (essay) Aufsatz m

compost /ˈkɒmpɒst/ n Kompost m

composure /kəmˈpəʊzə(r)/ n Fassung f

compound /ˈkɒmpaʊnd/ adj zusammengesetzt; (fracture) kompliziert ● n (Chemistry) Verbindung f; (Gram) Kompositum nt

comprehen|d /kɒmprɪˈhend/ vt begreifen, verstehen. **~sible** adj, **-bly** adv verständlich. **~sion** n Verständnis nt

comprehensive /kɒmprɪˈhensɪv/ adj & n umfassend; **~ [school]** Gesamtschule f. **~ insurance** n (Auto) Vollkaskoversicherung f

compress /kəm'pres/ vt zusammen-pressen; **~ed air** Druckluft f

comprise /kəm'praɪz/ vt umfassen, bestehen aus

compromise /'kɒmprəmaɪz/ n Kompromiss m ● vt kompromittieren (person) ● vi einen Kompromiss schließen

compuls|ion /kəm'pʌlʃn/ n Zwang m. **~ive** adj zwanghaft. **~ory** adj obligatorisch

comput|e /kəm'pju:t/ vb berechnen. **~er** Computer m. **~er game** n Computerspiel. **~erize** vt computeri-sieren (data); auf Computer umstel-len (firm). **~-'literate** adj mit Com-putern vertraut. **~ing** n Computer-technik f

comrade /'kɒmreɪd/ n Kamerad m; (Pol) Genosse m/Genossin f

con[1] /kɒn/ see **pro**

con[2] n 🄸 Schwindel m ● vt (pt/pp conned) 🄸 beschwindeln

concave /'kɒnkeɪv/ adj konkav

conceal /kən'si:l/ vt verstecken; (keep secret) verheimlichen

concede /kən'si:d/ vt zugeben; (give up) aufgeben

conceit /kən'si:t/ n Einbildung f. **~ed** adj eingebildet

conceivable /kən'si:vəbl/ adj denk-bar

conceive /kən'si:v/ vt (child) emp-fangen; (fig) sich (dat) ausdenken ● vi schwanger werden

concentrat|e /'kɒnsəntreɪt/ vt kon-zentrieren ● vi sich konzentrieren. **~ion** n Konzentration f

concern /kən'sɜ:n/ n Angelegenheit f; (worry) Sorge f; (Comm) Unterneh-men nt ● vt (be about, affect) betref-fen; (worry) kümmern; **be ~ed about** besorgt sein um; **~ oneself with** sich beschäftigen mit; **as far as I am ~ed** was mich angeht od be-trifft. **~ing** prep bezüglich (+ gen)

concert /'kɒnsət/ n Konzert nt

concerto /kən'tʃeətəʊ/ n Konzert nt

concession /kən'seʃn/ n Zuge-ständnis nt; (Comm) Konzession f;

(reduction) Ermäßigung f

concise /kən'saɪs/ adj kurz

conclude /kən'klu:d/ vt/i schließen

conclusion /kən'klu:ʒn/ n Schluss m; **in ~** abschließend, zum Schluss

conclusive /kən'klu:sɪv/ adj schlüs-sig

concoct /kən'kɒkt/ vt zusammen-stellen; (fig) fabrizieren. **~ion** n Zu-sammenstellung f; (drink) Gebräu nt

concrete /'kɒnkri:t/ adj konkret ● n Beton m ● vt betonieren

concurrently /kən'kʌrəntlɪ/ adv gleichzeitig

concussion /kən'kʌʃn/ n Gehirner-schütterung f

condemn /kən'dem/ vt verurteilen; (declare unfit) für untauglich erklären. **~ation** n Verurteilung f

condensation /kɒnden'seɪʃn/ n Kondensation f

condense /kən'dens/ vt zusammen-fassen

condescend /kɒndɪ'send/ vi sich herablassen (**to** zu). **~ing** adj herab-lassend

condition /kən'dɪʃn/ n Bedingung f; (state) Zustand m; **~s** pl Verhältnisse pl; **on ~ that** unter der Bedingung, dass ● vt (mentally) konditionieren. **~al** adj bedingt ● n (Gram) Konditio-nal m. **~er** n Pflegespülung f; (for fabrics) Weichspüler m

condolences /kən'dəʊlənsɪz/ npl Beileid nt

condom /'kɒndəm/ n Kondom nt

condominium /kɒndə'mɪnɪəm/ n (Amer) ≈ Eigentumswohnung f

conduct[1] /'kɒndʌkt/ n Verhalten nt; (Sch) Betragen nt

conduct[2] /kən'dʌkt/ vt führen; (Phys) leiten; (Mus) dirigieren. **~or** n Dirigent m; (of bus) Schaffner m; (Phys) Leiter m

cone /kəʊn/ Kegel m; (Bot) Zapfen m; (for ice-cream) [Eis]tüte f; (Auto) Leit-kegel m

confectioner /kən'fekʃənə(r)/ n Konditor m. **~y** n Süßwaren pl

conference /ˈkɒnfərəns/ n Konferenz f

confess /kənˈfes/ vt/i gestehen; (*Relig*) beichten. **∼ion** n Geständnis nt; (*Relig*) Beichte f

confetti /kənˈfeti/ n Konfetti nt

confide /kənˈfaɪd/ vt anvertrauen ● vi ∼ **in s.o.** sich jdm anvertrauen

confidence /ˈkɒnfɪdəns/ n (*trust*) Vertrauen nt; (*self-assurance*) Selbstvertrauen nt; (*secret*) Geheimnis nt; **in** ∼ im Vertrauen. ∼ **trick** n Schwindel m

confident /ˈkɒnfɪdənt/ adj zuversichtlich; (*self-assured*) selbstsicher

confidential /kɒnfɪˈdenʃl/ adj vertraulich

configuration /kənfɪɡəˈreɪʃn/ n Anordnung f, Konfiguration f

confine /kənˈfaɪn/ vt beschränken (**to** auf + *acc*). ∼**d** adj (*narrow*) eng

confirm /kənˈfɜːm/ vt bestätigen; (*Relig*) konfirmieren; (*Roman Catholic*) firmen. ∼**ation** n Bestätigung f; Konfirmation f; Firmung f

confiscat|e /ˈkɒnfɪskeɪt/ vt beschlagnahmen. ∼**ion** n Beschlagnahme f

conflict[1] /ˈkɒnflɪkt/ n Konflikt m

conflict[2] /kənˈflɪkt/ vi im Widerspruch stehen (**with** zu). ∼**ing** adj widersprüchlich

conform /kənˈfɔːm/ vi (*person:*) sich anpassen; (*thing:*) entsprechen (**to** *dat*). ∼**ist** n Konformist m

confounded /kənˈfaʊndɪd/ adj 🔲 verflixt

confront /kənˈfrʌnt/ vt konfrontieren. ∼**ation** n Konfrontation f

confus|e /kənˈfjuːz/ vt verwirren; (*mistake for*) verwechseln (**with** mit). ∼**ing** adj verwirrend. ∼**ion** n Verwirrung f; (*muddle*) Durcheinander nt

congenial /kənˈdʒiːnɪəl/ adj angenehm

congest|ed /kənˈdʒestɪd/ adj verstopft; (*with people*) überfüllt. ∼**ion** n Verstopfung f; Überfüllung f

congratulat|e /kənˈɡrætjʊleɪt/ vt gratulieren (+ *dat*) (**on** zu). ∼**ions** npl Glückwünsche pl; ∼**ions!** [ich] gratuliere!

congregation /kɒŋɡrɪˈɡeɪʃn/ n (*Relig*) Gemeinde f

congress /ˈkɒŋɡres/ n Kongress m. ∼**man** n Kongressabgeordnete(r) m

C

Congress Die nationale gesetzgebende Versammlung in den Vereinigten Staaten. Der Kongress tritt im ▷CAPITOL zusammen und besteht aus zwei Kammern, dem Senat und dem Repräsentantenhaus. Der Kongress erlässt Gesetze, die von beiden Kammern angenommen und anschließend vom Präsidenten verabschiedet werden.

conical /ˈkɒnɪkl/ adj kegelförmig

conifer /ˈkɒnɪfə(r)/ n Nadelbaum m

conjecture /kənˈdʒektʃə(r)/ n Mutmaßung f

conjunction /kənˈdʒʌŋkʃn/ n Konjunktion f; **in** ∼ **with** zusammen mit

conjur|e /ˈkʌndʒə(r)/ vi zaubern ● vt ∼**e up** heraufbeschwören. ∼**or** n Zauberkünstler m

conk /kɒŋk/ vi ∼ **out** 🔲 (*machine:*) kaputtgehen

conker /ˈkɒŋkə(r)/ n 🔲 Kastanie f

'con-man n 🔲 Schwindler m

connect /kəˈnekt/ vt verbinden (**to** mit); (*Electr*) anschließen (**to** ən + *acc*) ● vi verbunden sein; (*train:*) Anschluss haben (**with** an + *acc*); **be** ∼**ed with** zu tun haben mit; (*be related to*) verwandt sein mit

connection /kəˈnekʃn/ n Verbindung f; (*Rail, Electr*) Anschluss m; **in** ∼ **with** in Zusammenhang mit. ∼**s** npl Beziehungen pl

connoisseur /kɒnəˈsɜː(r)/ n Kenner m

conquer /ˈkɒŋkə(r)/ vt erobern; (*fig*) besiegen. ∼**or** n Eroberer m

conquest /ˈkɒŋkwest/ n Eroberung f

conscience /ˈkɒnʃəns/ n Gewissen nt

conscientious /kɒnʃɪˈenʃəs/ adj gewissenhaft

conscious /'kɒnʃəs/ *adj* bewusst; [fully] ~ bei [vollem] Bewusstsein; **be/become** ~ **of sth** sich (*dat*) etw (*gen*) bewusst sein/werden. ~**ness** *n* Bewusstsein *nt*

conscript /'kɒnskrɪpt/ *n* Einberufene(r) *m*

consecrat|e /'kɒnsɪkreɪt/ *vt* weihen; einweihen (*church*). ~**ion** *n* Weihe *f*; Einweihung *f*

consecutive /kən'sekjʊtɪv/ *adj* aufeinanderfolgend. **-ly** *adv* fortlaufend

consent /kən'sent/ *n* Einwilligung *f*, Zustimmung *f* ● *vi* einwilligen (**to** in + *acc*), zustimmen (**to** *dat*)

consequen|ce /'kɒnsɪkwəns/ *n* Folge *f*. ~**t** *adj* daraus folgend. ~**tly** *adv* folglich

conservation /kɒnsə'veɪʃn/ *n* Erhaltung *f*, Bewahrung *f*. ~**ist** *n* Umweltschützer *m*

conservative /kən'sɜːvətɪv/ *adj* konservativ; (*estimate*) vorsichtig. **C~** (*Pol*) *adj* konservativ ● *n* Konservative(r) *m/f*

conservatory /kən'sɜːvətrɪ/ *n* Wintergarten *m*

conserve /kən'sɜːv/ *vt* erhalten, bewahren; sparen (*energy*)

consider /kən'sɪdə(r)/ *vt* erwägen; (*think over*) sich (*dat*) überlegen; (*take into account*) berücksichtigen; (*regard as*) betrachten als; ~ **doing sth** erwägen, etw zu tun. ~**able** *adj*, **-ably** *adv* erheblich

consider|ate /kən'sɪdərət/ *adj* rücksichtsvoll. ~**ation** *n* Erwägung *f*; (*thoughtfulness*) Rücksicht *f*; (*payment*) Entgelt *nt*; **take into** ~**ation** berücksichtigen. ~**ing** *prep* wenn man bedenkt (**that** dass)

consist /kən'sɪst/ *vi* ~ **of** bestehen aus

consisten|cy /kən'sɪstənsɪ/ *n* Konsequenz *f*; (*density*) Konsistenz *f*. ~**t** *adj* konsequent; (*unchanging*) gleichbleibend. ~**tly** *adv* konsequent; (*constantly*) ständig

consolation /kɒnsə'leɪʃn/ *n* Trost *m*. ~ **prize** *n* Trostpreis *m*

console /kən'səʊl/ *vt* trösten

consonant /'kɒnsənənt/ *n* Konsonant *m*

conspicuous /kən'spɪkjʊəs/ *adj* auffällig

conspiracy /kən'spɪrəsɪ/ *n* Verschwörung *f*

constable /'kʌnstəbl/ *n* Polizist *m*

constant /'kɒnstənt/ *adj* beständig; (*continuous*) ständig

constipat|ed /'kɒnstɪpeɪtɪd/ *adj* verstopft. ~**ion** *n* Verstopfung *f*

constituency /kən'stɪtjʊənsɪ/ *n* Wahlkreis *m*

constitut|e /'kɒnstɪtjuːt/ *vt* bilden. ~**ion** *n* (*Pol*) Verfassung *f*; (*of person*) Konstitution *f*

constraint /kən'streɪnt/ *n* Zwang *m*; (*restriction*) Beschränkung *f*; (*strained manner*) Gezwungenheit *f*

construct /kən'strʌkt/ *vt* bauen. ~**ion** *n* Bau *m*; (*Gram*) Konstruktion *f*; (*interpretation*) Deutung *f*; **under** ~**ion** im Bau

consul /'kɒnsl/ *n* Konsul *m*. ~**ate** *n* Konsulat *nt*

consult /kən'sʌlt/ *vt* [um Rat] fragen; konsultieren (*doctor*); nachschlagen in (+ *dat*) (*book*). ~**ant** *n* Berater *m*; (*Med*) Chefarzt *m*. ~**ation** *n* Beratung *f*; (*Med*) Konsultation *f*

consume /kɒn'sjuːm/ *vt* verzehren; (*use*) verbrauchen. ~**r** *n* Verbraucher *m*

consumption /kən'sʌmpʃn/ *n* Konsum *m*; (*use*) Verbrauch *m*

contact /'kɒntækt/ *n* Kontakt *m*; (*person*) Kontaktperson *f* ● *vt* sich in Verbindung setzen mit. ~ **'lenses** *npl* Kontaktlinsen *pl*

contagious /kən'teɪdʒəs/ *adj* direkt übertragbar

contain /kən'teɪn/ *vt* enthalten; (*control*) beherrschen. ~**er** *n* Behälter *m*; (*Comm*) Container *m*

contaminat|e /kən'tæmɪneɪt/ *vt* verseuchen. ~**ion** *n* Verseuchung *f*

contemplat|e /'kɒntəmpleɪt/ *vt* betrachten; (*meditate*) nachdenken über (+ *acc*). ~**ion** *n* Betrachtung *f*; Nachdenken *nt*

305

contemporary | converge

contemporary /kən'tempərərɪ/ *adj* zeitgenössisch ● *n* Zeitgenosse *m*/ -genossin *f*

contempt /kən'tempt/ *n* Verachtung *f*; **beneath** ~ verabscheuungswürdig. **~ible** *adj* verachtenswert. **~uous** *adj* verächtlich

content[1] /'kɒntent/ *n* (*also* **contents**) *pl* Inhalt *m*

content[2] /kən'tent/ *adj* zufrieden ● *n* **to one's heart's** ~ nach Herzenslust ● *vt* ~ **oneself** sich begnügen (**with** mit). **~ed** *adj* zufrieden

contentment /kən'tentmənt/ *n* Zufriedenheit *f*

contest /'kɒntest/ *n* Kampf *m*; (*competition*) Wettbewerb *m*. **~ant** *n* Teilnehmer *m*

context /'kɒntekst/ *n* Zusammenhang *m*

continent /'kɒntɪnənt/ *n* Kontinent *m*

continental /kɒntɪ'nentl/ *adj* Kontinental-. ~ **breakfast** *n* kleines Frühstück *nt*. ~ **quilt** *n* Daunendecke *f*

continual /kən'tɪnjʊəl/ *adj* dauernd

continuation /kən'tɪnjʊ'eɪʃn/ *n* Fortsetzung *f*

continue /kən'tɪnju:/ *vt* fortsetzen; ~ **doing** *or* **to do sth** fortfahren, etw zu tun; **to be ~d** Fortsetzung folgt ● *vi* weitergehen; (*doing sth*) weitermachen; (*speaking*) fortfahren; (*weather:*) anhalten

continuity /kɒntɪ'nju:ətɪ/ *n* Kontinuität *f*

continuous /kən'tɪnjʊəs/ *adj* anhaltend, ununterbrochen

contort /kən'tɔ:t/ *vt* verzerren. **~ion** *n* Verzerrung *f*

contour /'kɒntʊə(r)/ *n* Kontur *f*; (*line*) Höhenlinie *f*

contracep|tion /kɒntrə'sepʃn/ *n* Empfängnisverhütung *f*. **~tive** *n* Empfängnisverhütungsmittel *nt*

contract[1] /'kɒntrækt/ *n* Vertrag *m*

contract[2] /kən'trækt/ *vi* sich zusammenziehen. **~or** *n* Unternehmer *m*

contradict /kɒntrə'dɪkt/ *vt* widersprechen (+ *dat*). **~ion** *n* Widerspruch *m*. **~ory** *adj* widersprüchlich

contralto /kən'træltəʊ/ *n* Alt *m*; (*singer*) Altistin *f*

contraption /kən'træpʃn/ *n* Apparat *m*

contrary /'kɒntrərɪ/ *adj & adv* entgegengesetzt; ~ **to** entgegen (+ *dat*) ● *n* Gegenteil *nt*; **on the** ~ im Gegenteil

contrast[1] /'kɒntrɑ:st/ *n* Kontrast *m*

contrast[2] /kən'trɑ:st/ *vt* gegenüberstellen (**with** *dat*) ● *vi* einen Kontrast bilden (**with** zu). **~ing** *adj* gegensätzlich; (*colour*) Kontrast-

contribut|e /kən'trɪbju:t/ *vt/i* beitragen; beisteuern (*money*); (*donate*) spenden. **~ion** *n* Beitrag *m*; (*donation*) Spende *f*. **~or** *n* Beitragende(r) *m/f*

contrivance /kən'traɪvəns/ *n* Vorrichtung *f*

control /kən'trəʊl/ *n* Kontrolle *f*; (*mastery*) Beherrschung *f*; (*Techn*) Regler *m*; ~**s** *pl* (*of car, plane*) Steuerung *f*; **get out of** ~ außer Kontrolle geraten ● *vt* (*pt/pp* **controlled**) kontrollieren; (*restrain*) unter Kontrolle halten; ~ **oneself** sich beherrschen

controvers|ial /kɒntrə'vɜ:ʃl/ *adj* umstritten. **~y** *n* Kontroverse *f*

convalesce /kɒnvə'les/ *vi* sich erholen. **~nce** *n* Erholung *f*

convalescent /kɒnvə'lesnt/ *adj* ~ **home** *n* Erholungsheim *nt*

convenience /kən'vi:nɪəns/ *n* Bequemlichkeit *f*; **[public]** ~ öffentliche Toilette *f*; **with all modern** ~**s** mit allem Komfort

convenient /kən'vi:nɪənt/ *adj* günstig; **be** ~ **for s.o.** jdm gelegen sein *od* jdm passen; **if it is** ~ **[for you]** wenn es Ihnen passt

convent /'kɒnvənt/ *n* [Nonnen-] kloster *nt*

convention /kən'venʃn/ *n* (*custom*) Brauch *m*, Sitte *f*. **~al** *adj* konventionell

converge /kən'vɜ:dʒ/ *vi* zusammenlaufen

conversation /kɒnvə'seɪʃn/ n Gespräch nt; (Sch) Konversation f

conversion /kən'vɜːʃn/ n Umbau m; (Relig) Bekehrung f; (calculation) Umrechnung f

convert¹ /'kɒnvɜːt/ n Bekehrte(r) m/f, Konvertit m

convert² /kən'vɜːt/ vt bekehren (person); (change) umwandeln (**into** in + acc); umbauen (building); (calculate) umrechnen; (Techn) umstellen. **~ible** a verwandelbar ● n (Auto) Kabrio[lett] nt

convex /'kɒnveks/ adj konvex

convey /kən'veɪ/ vt befördern; vermitteln (idea, message). **~or belt** n Förderband nt

convict¹ /'kɒnvɪkt/ n Sträfling m

convict² /kən'vɪkt/ vt verurteilen (of wegen). **~ion** n Verurteilung f; (belief) Überzeugung f; **previous ~ion** Vorstrafe f

convinc|e /kən'vɪns/ vt überzeugen. **~ing** adj überzeugend

convoy /'kɒnvɔɪ/ n Konvoi m

convulse /kən'vʌls/ vt **be ~ed** sich krümmen (**with** vor + dat)

coo /kuː/ vi gurren

cook /kʊk/ n Koch m/ Köchin f ● vt/i kochen; **is it ~ed?** ist es gar? **~ the books** ⓣ die Bilanz frisieren. **~book** n Kochbuch nt

cooker /'kʊkə(r)/ n [Koch]herd m; (apple) Kochapfel m. **~y** n Kochen nt. **~y book** n Kochbuch nt

cookie /'kʊkɪ/ n (Amer) Keks m

cool /kuːl/ adj (-er, -est) kühl ● n Kühle f ● vt kühlen ● vi abkühlen. **~-box** n Kühlbox f. **~ness** n Kühle f

coop /kuːp/ vt **~ up** einsperren

co-operat|e /kəʊ'ɒpəreɪt/ vi zusammenarbeiten. **~ion** n Kooperation f

co-operative /kəʊ'ɒpərətɪv/ adj hilfsbereit ● n Genossenschaft f

cop /kɒp/ n ⓣ Polizist m

cope /kəʊp/ vi ⓣ zurechtkommen; **~ with** fertig werden mit

copious /'kəʊpɪəs/ adj reichlich

copper¹ /'kɒpə(r)/ n Kupfer nt ● adj kupfern

copper² n ⓣ Polizist m

copper 'beech n Blutbuche f

coppice /'kɒpɪs/ n, **copse** n Gehölz nt

copy /'kɒpɪ/ n Kopie f; (book) Exemplar nt ● vt (pt/pp **-ied**) kopieren; (imitate) nachahmen; (Sch) abschreiben

copy: ~right n Copyright nt. **~-writer** n Texter m

coral /'kɒrl/ n Koralle f

cord /kɔːd/ n Schnur f; (fabric) Cordsamt m; **~s** pl Cordhose f

cordial /'kɔːdɪəl/ adj herzlich ● n Fruchtsirup m

cordon /'kɔːdn/ n Kordon m ● vt **~ off** absperren

corduroy /'kɔːdərɔɪ/ n Cordsamt m

core /kɔː(r)/ n Kern m; (of apple, pear) Kerngehäuse nt

cork /kɔːk/ n Kork m; (for bottle) Korken m. **~screw** n Korkenzieher m

corn¹ /kɔːn/ n Korn nt; (Amer: maize) Mais m

corn² n (Med) Hühnerauge nt

corned beef /kɔːnd'biːf/ n Cornedbeef nt

corner /'kɔːnə(r)/ n Ecke f; (bend) Kurve f; (football) Eckball m ● vt (fig) in die Enge treiben; (Comm) monopolisieren (market). **~stone** n Eckstein m

cornet /'kɔːnɪt/ n (Mus) Kornett nt; (for ice-cream) [Eis]tüte f

corn: ~flour n, (Amer) **~starch** n Stärkemehl nt

corny /'kɔːnɪ/ adj ⓣ abgedroschen

coronation /kɒrə'neɪʃn/ n Krönung f

coroner /'kɒrənə(r)/ n Beamte(r) m, der verdächtige Todesfälle untersucht

corporal /'kɔːpərəl/ n (Mil) Stabsunteroffizier m

corps /kɔː(r)/ n (pl **corps** /kɔːz/) Korps nt

corpse /kɔːps/ n Leiche f

correct /kə'rekt/ adj richtig; (proper) korrekt ● vt verbessern; (text, school work) korrigieren. **~ion** n Verbesserung f; (Typ) Korrektur f

correspond /kɒrɪ'spɒnd/ vi entsprechen (**to** dat); (two things:) sich entsprechen; (write) korrespondieren. ~**ence** n Briefwechsel m; (Comm) Korrespondenz f. ~**ent** n Korrespondent(in) m(f). ~**ing** adj entsprechend

corridor /'kɒrɪdɔː(r)/ n Gang m; (Pol, Aviat) Korridor m

corro|de /kə'rəʊd/ vt zerfressen ● vi rosten. ~**sion** n Korrosion f

corrugated /'kɒrəgeɪtɪd/ adj gewellt. ~ **iron** n Wellblech nt

corrupt /kə'rʌpt/ adj korrupt ● vt korrumpieren; (spoil) verderben. ~**ion** n Korruption f

corset /'kɔːsɪt/ n Korsett nt

Corsica /'kɔːsɪkə/ n Korsika nt

cosh /kɒʃ/ n Totschläger m

cosmetic /kɒz'metɪk/ adj kosmetisch ● n ~**s** pl Kosmetika pl

cosset /'kɒsɪt/ vt verhätscheln

cost /kɒst/ n Kosten pl; ~**s** pl (Jur) Kosten; **at all** ~**s** um jeden Preis ● vt (pt/pp **cost**) kosten; **it** ~ **me £20** es hat mich £20 gekostet ● vt (pt/pp **costed**) ~ **[out]** die Kosten kalkulieren für

costly /'kɒstlɪ/ adj teuer

cost: ~ **of 'living** n Lebenshaltungskosten pl. ~ **price** n Selbstkostenpreis m

costume /'kɒstjuːm/ n Kostüm nt; (national) Tracht f. ~ **jewellery** n Modeschmuck m

cosy /'kəʊzɪ/ adj gemütlich ● n (tea-, egg-) Wärmer m

cot /kɒt/ n Kinderbett nt; (Amer: camp bed) Feldbett nt

cottage /'kɒtɪdʒ/ n Häuschen nt. ~ **'cheese** n Hüttenkäse m

cotton /'kɒtn/ n Baumwolle f; (thread) Nähgarn nt ● adj baumwollen ● vi ~ **on** 🅸 kapieren

cotton 'wool n Watte f

couch /kaʊtʃ/ n Liege f

couchette /kuː'ʃet/ n (Rail) Liegeplatz m

cough /kɒf/ n Husten m ● vi husten. ~ **up** vt/i husten; (🅸: pay) blechen

'cough mixture n Hustensaft m

could /kʊd/, unbetont /kəd/ see can²

council /'kaʊnsl/ n Rat m; (Admin) Stadtverwaltung f; (rural) Gemeindeverwaltung f. ~ **house** n ≈ Sozialwohnung f

councillor /'kaʊnsələ(r)/ n Ratsmitglied nt

'council tax n Gemeindesteuer f

count¹ /kaʊnt/ n Graf m

count² n Zählung f; **keep** ~ zählen ● vt/i zählen. ~ **on** vt rechnen auf (+ acc)

counter¹ /'kaʊntə(r)/ n (in shop) Ladentisch m; (in bank) Schalter m; (in café) Theke f; (Games) Spielmarke f

counter² adj Gegen- ● vt/i kontern

counter'act vt entgegenwirken (+ dat)

'counterfeit /-fɪt/ adj gefälscht

'counterfoil n Kontrollabschnitt m

'counterpart n Gegenstück nt

counter-pro'ductive adj be ~ das Gegenteil bewirken

'countersign vt gegenzeichnen

countess /'kaʊntɪs/ n Gräfin f

countless /'kaʊntlɪs/ adj unzählig

country /'kʌntrɪ/ n Land nt; (native land) Heimat f; (countryside) Landschaft f; **in the** ~ auf dem Lande. ~**man** n [**fellow**] ~**man** Landsmann m. ~**side** n Landschaft f

county /'kaʊntɪ/ n Grafschaft f

coup /kuː/ n (Pol) Staatsstreich m

couple /'kʌpl/ n Paar nt; **a** ~ **of** (two) zwei ● vt verbinden

coupon /'kuːpɒn/ n Kupon m; (voucher) Gutschein m; (entry form) Schein m

courage /'kʌrɪdʒ/ n Mut m. ~**ous** adj mutig

courgettes /kʊə'ʒets/ npl Zucchini pl

courier /'kʊrɪə(r)/ n Bote m; (diplomatic) Kurier m; (for tourists) Reiseleiter(in) m(f)

course /kɔːs/ n (Naut, Sch) Kurs m; (Culin) Gang m; (for golf) Platz m; ~ **of treatment** (Med) Kur f; **of** ~ na-

court | crease

308

türlich, selbstverständlich; **in the ~ of** im Lauf[e] (+ gen)

court /kɔːt/ n Hof m; (Sport) Platz m; (Jur) Gericht nt

courteous /ˈkɜːtɪəs/ adj höflich

courtesy /ˈkɜːtəsɪ/ n Höflichkeit f

court: ~ 'martial n (pl ~s martial) Militärgericht nt. **~yard** n Hof m

cousin /ˈkʌzn/ n Vetter m, Cousin m; (female) Kusine f

cove /kəʊv/ n kleine Bucht f

cover /ˈkʌvə(r)/ n Decke f; (of cushion) Bezug m; (of umbrella) Hülle f; (of typewriter) Haube f; (of book, lid) Deckel m; (of magazine) Umschlag m; (protection) Deckung f, Schutz m; **take ~** Deckung nehmen; **under separate ~** mit getrennter Post ● vt bedecken; beziehen (cushion); decken (costs, needs); zurücklegen (distance); berichten über (+ acc) event; (insure) versichern. **~ up** vt zudecken; (fig) vertuschen

coverage /ˈkʌvərɪdʒ/ n (Journalism) Berichterstattung f (**of** über + acc)

cover: ~ing n Decke f; (for floor) Belag m. **~-up** n Vertuschung f

cow /kaʊ/ n Kuh f

coward /ˈkaʊəd/ n Feigling m. **~ice** n Feigheit f. **~ly** adj feige

'cowboy n Cowboy m; (I) unsolider Handwerker m

cower /ˈkaʊə(r)/ vi sich [ängstlich] ducken

'cowshed n Kuhstall m

cox /kɒks/ n, **coxswain** n Steuermann m

coy /kɔɪ/ adj (-er, -est) gespielt schüchtern

crab /kræb/ n Krabbe f

crack /kræk/ n Riss m; (in china, glass) Sprung m; (noise) Knall m; (I: joke) Witz m; (I: attempt) Versuch m ● adj I erstklassig ● vt knacken (nut, code); einen Sprung machen in (+ acc) (china, glass); I reißen (joke); I lösen (problem) ● vi (china, glass:) springen; (whip:) knallen. **~ down** vi I durchgreifen

cracked /krækt/ adj gesprungen;

(rib) angebrochen; (I: crazy) verrückt

cracker /ˈkrækə(r)/ n (biscuit) Kräcker m; (firework) Knallkörper m; **[Christmas] ~** Knallbonbon m. **~s** adj **be ~s** I einen Knacks haben

crackle /ˈkrækl/ vi knistern

cradle /ˈkreɪdl/ n Wiege f

craft n Handwerk nt; (technique) Fertigkeit f. **~sman** n Handwerker m

crafty /ˈkrɑːftɪ/ adj , **-ily** adv gerissen

crag /kræg/ n Felszacken m

cram /kræm/ v (pt/pp crammed) ● vt hineinstopfen (**into** in + acc); vollstopfen (**with** mit) ● vi (for exams) pauken

cramp /kræmp/ n Krampf m. **~ed** adj eng

cranberry /ˈkrænbərɪ/ n (Culin) Preiselbeere f

crane /kreɪn/ n Kran m; (bird) Kranich m

crank /kræŋk/ n I Exzentriker m

'crankshaft n Kurbelwelle f

crash /kræʃ/ n (noise) Krach m; (Auto) Zusammenstoß m; (Aviat) Absturz m ● vi krachen (**into** gegen); (cars:) zusammenstoßen; (plane:) abstürzen ● vt einen Unfall haben mit (car)

crash: ~-helmet n Sturzhelm m. **~-landing** n Bruchlandung f

crate /kreɪt/ n Kiste f

crater /ˈkreɪtə(r)/ n Krater m

crawl /krɔːl/ n (Swimming) Kraul nt; **do the ~** kraulen; **at a ~** im Kriechtempo ● vi kriechen; (baby:) krabbeln; **~ with** wimmeln von

crayon /ˈkreɪən/ n Wachsstift m; (pencil) Buntstift m

craze /kreɪz/ n Mode f

crazy /ˈkreɪzɪ/ adj verrückt; **be ~ about** verrückt sein nach

creak /kriːk/ vi knarren

cream /kriːm/ n Sahne f; (Cosmetic, Med, Culin) Creme f ● adj (colour) cremefarben ● vt (Culin) cremig rühren. **~y** adj sahnig; (smooth) cremig

crease /kriːs/ n Falte f; (unwanted) Knitterfalte f ● vt falten; (accidentally) zerknittern ● *vi* knittern

creat|e /kriːˈeɪt/ *vt* schaffen. **~ion** *n* Schöpfung *f*. **~ive** *adj* schöpferisch. **~or** *n* Schöpfer *m*

creature /ˈkriːtʃə(r)/ *n* Geschöpf *nt*

crèche /kreʃ/ *n* Kinderkrippe *f*

credibility /kredəˈbɪlətɪ/ *n* Glaubwürdigkeit *f*

credible /ˈkredəbl/ *adj* glaubwürdig

credit /ˈkredɪt/ *n* Kredit *m*; (*honour*) Ehre *f* ● *vt* glauben; **~ s.o. with sth** (*Comm*) jdm etw gutschreiben; (*fig*) jdm etw zuschreiben. **~able** *adj* lobenswert

credit: ~ card *n* Kreditkarte *f*. **~or** *n* Gläubiger *m*

creep /kriːp/ *vi* (*pt/pp* **crept**) schleichen ● *n* 🅸 fieser Kerl *m*; **it gives me the ~s** es ist mir unheimlich. **~er** *n* Kletterpflanze *f*. **~y** *adj* gruselig

cremat|e /krɪˈmeɪt/ *vt* einäschern. **~ion** *n* Einäscherung *f*

crêpe /kreɪp/ *n* Krepp *m*. **~ paper** *n* Krepppapier *nt*

crept /krept/ *see* **creep**

crescent /ˈkresənt/ *n* Halbmond *m*

cress /kres/ *n* Kresse *f*

crest /krest/ *n* Kamm *m*; (*coat of arms*) Wappen *nt*

crew /kruː/ *n* Besatzung *f*; (*gang*) Bande *f*. **~ cut** *n* Bürstenschnitt *m*

crib[1] /krɪb/ *n* Krippe *f*

crib[2] *vt/i* (*pt/pp* **cribbed**) 🅸 abschreiben

cricket /ˈkrɪkɪt/ *n* Kricket *nt*. **~er** *n* Kricketspieler *m*

crime /kraɪm/ *n* Verbrechen *nt*; (*rate*) Kriminalität *f*

criminal /ˈkrɪmɪnl/ *adj* kriminell, verbrecherisch; (*law, court*) Straf- ● *n* Verbrecher *m*

crimson /ˈkrɪmzn/ *adj* purpurrot

crinkle /ˈkrɪŋkl/ *vt/i* knittern

cripple /ˈkrɪpl/ *n* Krüppel *m* ● *vt* zum Krüppel machen; (*fig*) lahmlegen. **~d** *adj* verkrüppelt

crisis /ˈkraɪsɪs/ *n* (*pl* **-ses** /-siːz/) Krise *f*

crisp /krɪsp/ *adj* (**-er, -est**) knusprig. **~bread** *n* Knäckebrot *nt*. **~s** *npl* Chips *pl*

criss-cross /ˈkrɪs-/ *adj* schräg gekreuzt

criterion /kraɪˈtɪərɪən/ *n* (*pl* **-ria** /-rɪə/) Kriterium *nt*

critic /ˈkrɪtɪk/ *n* Kritiker *m*. **~al** *adj* kritisch. **~ally** *adv* kritisch; **~ally ill** schwer krank

criticism /ˈkrɪtɪsɪzm/ *n* Kritik *f*

criticize /ˈkrɪtɪsaɪz/ *vt* kritisieren

croak /krəʊk/ *vi* krächzen; (*frog:*) quaken

crockery /ˈkrɒkərɪ/ *n* Geschirr *nt*

crocodile /ˈkrɒkədaɪl/ *n* Krokodil *nt*

crocus /ˈkrəʊkəs/ *n* (*pl* **-es**) Krokus *m*

crony /ˈkrəʊnɪ/ *n* Kumpel *m*

crook /krʊk/ *n* (*stick*) Stab *m*; (🅸: *criminal*) Schwindler *m*, Gauner *m*

crooked /ˈkrʊkɪd/ *adj* schief; (*bent*) krumm; (🅸: *dishonest*) unehrlich

crop /krɒp/ *n* Feldfrucht *f*; (*harvest*) Ernte *f* ● *v* (*pt/pp* **cropped**) ● *vt* stutzen ● *vi* **~ up** 🅸 zur Sprache kommen; (*occur*) dazwischenkommen

croquet /ˈkrəʊkeɪ/ *n* Krocket *nt*

cross /krɒs/ *adj* (*annoyed*) böse (**with** auf + *acc*); **talk at ~ purposes** aneinander vorbeireden ● *n* Kreuz *nt*; (*Bot, Zool*) Kreuzung *f* ● *vt* kreuzen (*cheque, animals*); überqueren (*road*); **~ oneself** sich bekreuzigen; **~ one's arms** die Arme verschränken; **~ one's legs** die Beine übereinander schlagen; **keep one's fingers ~ed for s.o.** jdm die Daumen drücken; **it ~ed my mind** es fiel mir ein ● *vi* (*go across*) hinübergehen/-fahren; (*lines:*) sich kreuzen. **~ out** *vt* durchstreichen

cross: ~-'country *n* (*Sport*) Crosslauf *m*. **~-'eyed** *adj* schielend; **be ~-eyed** schielen. **~fire** *n* Kreuzfeuer *nt*. **~ing** *n* Übergang *m*; (*sea journey*) Überfahrt *f*. **~roads** *n* [Straßen]kreuzung *f*. **~-'section** *n* Querschnitt *m*. **~wise** *adv* quer. **~word** *n* **~word [puzzle]** Kreuzworträtsel *nt*

crotchety /ˈkrɒtʃɪtɪ/ adj griesgrämig

crouch /krautʃ/ vi kauern

crow /krəʊ/ n Krähe f; **as the ~ flies** Luftlinie

crowd /kraʊd/ n [Menschen]menge f ● vi sich drängen. **~ed** adj [gedrängt] voll

crown /kraʊn/ n Krone f ● vt krönen; überkronen (tooth)

crucial /ˈkru:ʃl/ adj höchst wichtig; (decisive) entscheidend (to für)

crude /ˈkru:d/ adj (-r, -st) primitiv; (raw) roh

cruel /ˈkru:əl/ adj (crueller, cruellest) grausam (to gegen). **~ty** n Grausamkeit f

cruis|e /kru:z/ n Kreuzfahrt f ● vi kreuzen; (car:) fahren. **~er** n (Mil) Kreuzer m; (motor boat) Kajütboot nt

crumb /krʌm/ n Krümel m

crumb|le /ˈkrʌmbl/ vt/i krümeln; (collapse) einstürzen

crumple /ˈkrʌmpl/ vt zerknittern ● vi knittern

crunch /krʌntʃ/ n 🄃 **when it comes to the ~** wenn es [wirklich] drauf ankommt ● vt mampfen ● vi knirschen

crusade /kru:ˈseɪd/ n Kreuzzug m; (fig) Kampagne f. **~r** n Kreuzfahrer m; (fig) Kämpfer m

crush /krʌʃ/ n (crowd) Gedränge nt ● vt zerquetschen; zerknittern (clothes); (fig: subdue) niederschlagen

crust /krʌst/ n Kruste f

crutch /krʌtʃ/ n Krücke f

cry /kraɪ/ n Ruf m; (shout) Schrei m; **a far ~ from** (fig) weit entfernt von ● vi (pt/pp cried) (weep) weinen; (baby:) schreien; (call) rufen

crypt /krɪpt/ n Krypta f. **~ic** adj rätselhaft

crystal /ˈkrɪstl/ n Kristall m; (glass) Kristall nt

cub /kʌb/ n (Zool) Junge(s) nt

Cuba /ˈkju:bə/ n Kuba nt

cubby-hole /ˈkʌbɪ-/ n Fach nt

cub|e /kju:b/ n Würfel m. **~ic** adj Kubik-

cubicle /ˈkju:bɪkl/ n Kabine f

cuckoo /ˈkʊku:/ n Kuckuck m. **~ clock** n Kuckucksuhr f

cucumber /ˈkju:kʌmbə(r)/ n Gurke f

cuddl|e /ˈkʌdl/ vt herzen ● vi **~e up to** sich kuscheln an (+ acc). **~y** adj kuschelig

cue¹ /kju:/ n Stichwort nt

cue² n (Billiards) Queue nt

cuff /kʌf/ n Manschette f; (Amer: turn-up) [Hosen]aufschlag m; (blow) Klaps m; **off the ~** 🄃 aus dem Stegreif. **~-link** n Manschettenknopf m

cul-de-sac /ˈkʌldəsæk/ n Sackgasse f

culinary /ˈkʌlɪnərɪ/ adj kulinarisch

culprit /ˈkʌlprɪt/ n Täter m

cult /kʌlt/ n Kult m

cultivate /ˈkʌltɪveɪt/ vt anbauen (crop); bebauen (land)

cultural /ˈkʌltʃərəl/ adj kulturell

culture /ˈkʌltʃə(r)/ n Kultur f. **~d** adj kultiviert

cumbersome /ˈkʌmbəsəm/ adj hinderlich; (unwieldy) unhandlich

cunning /ˈkʌnɪŋ/ adj listig ● n List f

cup /kʌp/ n Tasse f; (prize) Pokal m

cupboard /ˈkʌbəd/ n Schrank m

Cup 'Final n Pokalendspiel nt

curable /ˈkjʊərəbl/ adj heilbar

curate /ˈkjʊərət/ n Vikar m; (Roman Catholic) Kaplan m

curb /kɜ:b/ vt zügeln

curdle /ˈkɜ:dl/ vi gerinnen

cure /kjʊə(r)/ n [Heil]mittel nt ● vt heilen; (salt) pökeln; (smoke) räuchern; gerben (skin)

curiosity /kjʊərɪˈɒsətɪ/ n Neugier f; (object) Kuriosität f

curious /ˈkjʊərɪəs/ adj neugierig; (strange) merkwürdig, seltsam

curl /kɜ:l/ n Locke f ● vt locken ● vi sich locken

curly /ˈkɜ:lɪ/ adj lockig

currant /ˈkʌrənt/ n (dried) Korinthe f

currency /ˈkʌrənsɪ/ n Geläufigkeit f;

(*money*) Währung *f*; **foreign** ~ Devisen *pl*

current /ˈkʌrənt/ *adj* augenblicklich, gegenwärtig; (*in general use*) geläufig, gebräuchlich ● *n* Strömung *f*; (*Electr*) Strom *m*. ~ **affairs** *or* **events** *npl* Aktuelle(s) *nt*. ~**ly** *adv* zurzeit

curriculum /kəˈrɪkjʊləm/ *n* Lehrplan *m*. ~ **vitae** *n* Lebenslauf *m*

curry /ˈkʌrɪ/ *n* Curry *nt* & *m*; (*meal*) Currygericht *nt*

curse /kɜːs/ *n* Fluch *m* ● *vt* verfluchen ● *vi* fluchen

cursor /ˈkɜːsə(r)/ *n* Cursor *m*

cursory /ˈkɜːsərɪ/ *adj* flüchtig

curt /kɜːt/ *adj* barsch

curtain /ˈkɜːtn/ *n* Vorhang *m*

curtsy /ˈkɜːtsɪ/ *n* Knicks *m* ● *vi* (*pt/pp* -**led**) knicksen

curve /kɜːv/ *n* Kurve *f* ● *vi* einen Bogen machen; ~ **to the right**/**left** nach rechts/links biegen. ~**d** *adj* gebogen

cushion /ˈkʊʃn/ *n* Kissen *nt* ● *vt* dämpfen; (*protect*) beschützen

cushy /ˈkʊʃɪ/ *adj* **I** bequem

custard /ˈkʌstəd/ *n* Vanillesoße *f*

custom /ˈkʌstəm/ *n* Brauch *m*; (*habit*) Gewohnheit *f*; (*Comm*) Kundschaft *f*. ~**ary** *adj* üblich; (*habitual*) gewohnt. ~**er** *n* Kunde *m*/Kundin *f*

customs /ˈkʌstəmz/ *npl* Zoll *m*. ~ **officer** *n* Zollbeamte(r) *m*

cut /kʌt/ *n* Schnitt *m*; (*Med*) Schnittwunde *f*; (*reduction*) Kürzung *f*; (*in price*) Senkung *f*; ~ **[of meat]** [Fleisch]stück *nt* ● *vt/i* (*pt/pp* **cut**, *pres p* **cutting**) schneiden; (*mow*) mähen; abheben (*cards*); (*reduce*) kürzen; senken (*price*); ~ **one's finger** sich in den Finger schneiden; ~ **s.o.'s hair** jdm die Haare schneiden; ~ **short** abkürzen. ~ **back** *vt* zurückschneiden; (*fig*) einschränken, kürzen. ~ **down** *vt* fällen; (*fig*) einschränken. ~ **off** *vt* abschneiden; (*disconnect*) abstellen; **be** ~ **off** (*Teleph*) unterbrochen werden. ~ **out** *vt* ausschneiden; (*delete*) strei-

chen; **be** ~ **out for** **I** geeignet sein zu. ~ **up** *vt* zerschneiden; (*slice*) aufschneiden

'cut-back *n* Kürzung *f*

cute /kjuːt/ *adj* (-**r**, -**st**) **I** niedlich

cut 'glass *n* Kristall *nt*

cutlery /ˈkʌtlərɪ/ *n* Besteck *nt*

cutlet /ˈkʌtlɪt/ *n* Kotelett *nt*

'cut-price *adj* verbilligt

cutting /ˈkʌtɪŋ/ *adj* (*remark*) bissig ● *n* (*from newspaper*) Ausschnitt *m*; (*of plant*) Ableger *m*

CV *abbr* **curriculum vitae**

cyberspace /ˈsaɪbəspeɪs/ *n* Cyberspace *m*

cycl|e /ˈsaɪkl/ *n* Zyklus *m*; (*bicycle*) [Fahr]rad *nt* ● *vi* mit dem Rad fahren. ~**ing** *n* Radfahren *nt*. ~**ist** *n* Radfahrer(in) *m*(*f*)

cylind|er /ˈsɪlɪndə(r)/ *n* Zylinder *m*. ~**rical** *adj* zylindrisch

cynic /ˈsɪnɪk/ *n* Zyniker *m*. ~**al** *adj* zynisch. ~**ism** *n* Zynismus *m*

Cyprus /ˈsaɪprəs/ *n* Zypern *nt*

Czech /tʃek/ *adj* tschechisch; ~ **Republic** Tschechische Republik *f* ● *n* Tscheche *m*/ Tschechin *f*

Dd

dab /dæb/ *n* Tupfer *m*; (*of butter*) Klecks *m*

dabble /ˈdæbl/ *vi* ~ **in sth** (*fig*) sich nebenbei mit etw befassen

dachshund /ˈdækshʊnd/ *n* Dackel *m*

dad[dy] /ˈdæd[ɪ]/ *n* **I** Vati *m*

daddy-'long-legs *n* [Kohl]schnake *f*; (*Amer: spider*) Weberknecht *m*

daffodil /ˈdæfədɪl/ *n* Osterglocke *f*, gelbe Narzisse *f*

daft /dɑːft/ *adj* (-**er**, -**est**) dumm

dagger /ˈdægə(r)/ *n* Dolch *m*

dahlia /ˈdeɪlɪə/ *n* Dahlie *f*

Dáil Éireann Das Repräsentantenhaus, der *Dáil Éireann* (ausgesprochen daːlˈɛrn) ist das Unterhaus und gesetzgebende Organ des irischen Parlaments in der Republik Irland. Es setzt sich aus 166 Abgeordneten zusammen, die für fünf Jahre durch allgemeine Wahlen (Verhältniswahlsystem) bestimmt werden. Die Verfassung sorgt dafür, dass ein Abgeordneter je 20- bis 30 000 Einwohner vertritt.

daily /ˈdeɪlɪ/ adj & adv täglich

dainty /ˈdeɪntɪ/ adj zierlich

dairy /ˈdeərɪ/ n Molkerei f; *(shop)* Milchgeschäft nt. ~ **products** pl Milchprodukte pl

daisy /ˈdeɪzɪ/ n Gänseblümchen nt

dam /dæm/ n [Stau]damm m ● vt *(pt/pp* **dammed***)* eindämmen

damag|e /ˈdæmɪdʒ/ n Schaden m **(to** an + *dat)*; ~**es** pl *(Jur)* Schadenersatz m ● vt beschädigen; *(fig)* beeinträchtigen

damn /dæm/ adj, int & adv 🆔 verdammt ● n **I don't care** or **give a** ~ 🆔 ich schere mich einen Dreck darum ● vt verdammen. ~**ation** n Verdammnis f

damp /dæmp/ adj (-er, -est) feucht ● n Feuchtigkeit f

damp|en vt anfeuchten; *(fig)* dämpfen. ~**ness** n Feuchtigkeit f

dance /dɑːns/ n Tanz m; *(function)* Tanzveranstaltung f ● vt/i tanzen. ~ **music** n Tanzmusik f

dancer /ˈdɑːnsə(r)/ n Tänzer(in) m(f)

dandelion /ˈdændɪlaɪən/ n Löwenzahn m

dandruff /ˈdændrʌf/ n Schuppen pl

Dane /deɪn/ n Däne m/Dänin f

danger /ˈdeɪndʒə(r)/ n Gefahr f; **in/out of** ~ in/außer Gefahr. ~**ous** adj gefährlich; ~**ously ill** schwer erkrankt

dangle /ˈdæŋgl/ vi baumeln ● vt baumeln lassen

Danish /ˈdeɪnɪʃ/ adj dänisch. ~ **'pas-**

try n Hefeteilchen nt

Danube /ˈdænjuːb/ n Donau f

dare /deə(r)/ vt/i *(challenge)* herausfordern **(to** zu); ~ **[to] do sth** [es] wagen, etw zu tun. ~**devil** n Draufgänger m

daring /ˈdeərɪŋ/ adj verwegen ● n Verwegenheit f

dark /dɑːk/ adj (-er, -est) dunkel; ~ **blue/brown** dunkelblau/ -braun; ~ **horse** *(fig)* stilles Wasser nt ● n Dunkelheit f; **after** ~ nach Einbruch der Dunkelheit; **in the** ~ im Dunkeln

dark|en /ˈdɑːkn/ vt verdunkeln ● vi dunkler werden. ~**ness** n Dunkelheit f

'dark-room n Dunkelkammer f

darling /ˈdɑːlɪŋ/ adj allerliebst ● n Liebling m

darn /dɑːn/ vt stopfen

dart /dɑːt/ n Pfeil m; ~**s** sg *(game)* [Wurf]pfeil m ● vi flitzen

dash /dæʃ/ n *(Printing)* Gedankenstrich m; **a** ~ **of milk** ein Schuss Milch ● vi rennen ● vt schleudern. ~ **off** vi losstürzen ● vt *(write quickly)* hinwerfen

'dashboard n Armaturenbrett nt

data /ˈdeɪtə/ npl & sg Daten pl. ~ **processing** n Datenverarbeitung f

date¹ /deɪt/ n *(fruit)* Dattel f

date² n Datum nt; 🆔 Verabredung f; **to** ~ bis heute; **out of** ~ überholt; *(expired)* ungültig; **be up to** ~ auf dem Laufenden sein ● vt/i datieren; *(Amer, fam: go out with)* ausgehen mit

dated /ˈdeɪtɪd/ adj altmodisch

dative /ˈdeɪtɪv/ adj & n *(Gram)* ~ **[case]** Dativ m

daub /dɔːb/ vt beschmieren **(with** mit); schmieren *(paint)*

daughter /ˈdɔːtə(r)/ n Tochter f. ~-**in-law** n *(pl* ~**s-in-law***)* Schwiegertochter f

dawdle /ˈdɔːdl/ vi trödeln

dawn /dɔːn/ n Morgendämmerung f; **at** ~ bei Tagesanbruch ● vi anbrechen; **it** ~**ed on me** *(fig)* es ging mir auf

day /deɪ/ n Tag m; ~ **by** ~ Tag für Tag; ~ **after** ~ Tag um Tag; **these** ~s heutzutage; **in those** ~s zu der Zeit

day: ~-**dream** n Tagtraum m • vi [mit offenen Augen] träumen. ~**light** n Tageslicht nt. ~**time** n in the ~**time** am Tage

daze /deɪz/ n in a ~ wie benommen. ~d adj benommen

dazzle /'dæzl/ vt blenden

dead /ded/ adj tot; (flower) verwelkt; (numb) taub; ~ **body** Leiche f; ~ **centre** genau in der Mitte • adv ~ **tired** todmüde; ~ **slow** sehr langsam • n the ~ pl die Toten; **in the** ~ **of night** mitten in der Nacht

deaden /'dedn/ vt dämpfen (sound); betäuben (pain)

dead: ~ '**end** n Sackgasse f. ~ '**heat** n totes Rennen nt. ~**line** n [letzter] Termin m

deadly /'dedlɪ/ adj tödlich; (🔲: dreary) sterbenslangweilig

deaf /def/ adj (-er, -est) taub; ~ **and dumb** taubstumm

deaf|en /'defn/ vt betäuben; (permanently) taub machen. ~**ening** adj ohrenbetäubend. ~**ness** n Taubheit f

deal /diːl/ n (transaction) Geschäft nt; **whose** ~? (Cards) wer gibt? **a good** or **great** ~ eine Menge; **get a raw** ~ 🔲 schlecht wegkommen • v (pt/pp **dealt** /delt/) • vt (Cards) geben; ~ **out** austeilen • vi ~ **in** handeln mit; ~ **with** zu tun haben mit; (handle) sich befassen mit; (cope with) fertig werden mit; (be about) handeln von; **that's been dealt with** das ist schon erledigt

deal|er /'diːlə(r)/ n Händler m

dean /diːn/ n Dekan m

dear /dɪə(r)/ adj (-er, -est) lieb; (expensive) teuer; (in letter) liebe(r,s)/ (formal) sehr geehrte(r,s) • n Liebe(r) m/f • int oh ~! oje! ~**ly** adv (love) sehr; (pay) teuer

death /deθ/ n Tod m; **three** ~s drei Todesfälle. ~ **certificate** n Sterbeurkunde f

deathly adj ~ **silence** Totenstille f

• adv ~ **pale** totenblass

death: ~ **penalty** n Todesstrafe f. ~-**trap** n Todesfalle f

debatable /dɪ'beɪtəbl/ adj strittig

debate /dɪ'beɪt/ n Debatte f • vt/i debattieren

debauchery /dɪ'bɔːtʃərɪ/ n Ausschweifung f

debit /'debɪt/ n [side] Soll nt • vt (pt/pp **debited**) belasten; abbuchen (sum)

debris /'debriː/ n Trümmer pl

debt /det/ n Schuld f; **in** ~ verschuldet. ~ **or** n Schuldner m

début /'deɪbuː/ n Debüt nt

decade /'dekeɪd/ n Jahrzehnt nt

decaden|ce /'dekədəns/ n Dekadenz f. ~**t** adj dekadent

decaffeinated /dɪ'kæfɪneɪtɪd/ adj koffeinfrei

decay /dɪ'keɪ/ n Verfall m; (rot) Verwesung f; (of tooth) Zahnfäule f • vi verfallen; (rot) verwesen; (tooth:) schlecht werden

deceased /dɪ'siːsd/ adj verstorben • n the ~d der/die Verstorbene

deceit /dɪ'siːt/ n Täuschung f. ~**ful** adj unaufrichtig

deceive /dɪ'siːv/ vt täuschen; (be unfaithful to) betrügen

December /dɪ'sembə(r)/ n Dezember m

decency /'diːsənsɪ/ n Anstand m

decent /'diːsənt/ adj anständig

decept|ion /dɪ'sepʃn/ n Täuschung f; (fraud) Betrug m. ~**ive** adj täuschend

decide /dɪ'saɪd/ vt entscheiden • vi sich entscheiden (**on** für)

decided /dɪ'saɪdɪd/ adj entschieden

decimal /'desɪml/ adj Dezimal- • n Dezimalzahl f. ~ '**point** n Komma nt

decipher /dɪ'saɪfə(r)/ vt entziffern

decision /dɪ'sɪʒn/ n Entscheidung f; (firmness) Entschlossenheit f

decisive /dɪ'saɪsɪv/ adj ausschlaggebend; (firm) entschlossen

deck[1] /dek/ vt schmücken

deck[2] n (Naut) Deck nt; **on** ~ an

d

Deck; ~ **of cards** (*Amer*) [Karten]-
spiel *nt*. ~**-chair** *n* Liegestuhl *m*

declaration /deklə'reɪʃn/ *n* Erklärung *f*

declare /dɪ'kleə(r)/ *vt* erklären; angeben (*goods*); **anything to ~?**
etwas zu verzollen?

decline /dɪ'klaɪn/ *n* Rückgang *m*; (*in
health*) Verfall *m* ● *vt* ablehnen;
(*Gram*) deklinieren ● *vi* ablehnen;
(*fall*) sinken; (*decrease*) nachlassen

decommission /di:kə'mɪʃn/ *vt*
stilllegen; außer Dienst stellen
(*Schiff*)

décor /'deɪkɔ:(r)/ *n* Ausstattung *f*

decorat|e /'dekəreɪt/ *vt* (*adorn*)
schmücken; verzieren (*cake*); (*paint*)
streichen; (*wallpaper*) tapezieren;
(*award medal to*) einen Orden verleihen (+ *dat*). ~**ion** *n* Verzierung *f*;
(*medal*) Orden *m*; ~**ions** *pl* Schmuck
m. ~**ive** *adj* dekorativ. ~**or** *n*
painter and ~or Maler und Tapezie-
rer *m*

decoy /'di:kɔɪ/ *n* Lockvogel *m*

decrease[1] /'di:kri:s/ *n* Verringerung
f; (*in number*) Rückgang *m*

decrease[2] /dɪ'kri:s/ *vt* verringern;
herabsetzen (*price*) ● *vi* sich verringern; (*price:*) sinken

decrepit /dɪ'krepɪt/ *adj* alters-
schwach

dedicat|e /'dedɪkeɪt/ *vt* widmen;
(*Relig*) weihen. ~**ed** *adj* hingebungs-
voll; (*person*) aufopfernd. ~**ion** *n*
Hingabe *f*; (*in book*) Widmung *f*

deduce /dɪ'dju:s/ *vt* folgern (**from**
aus)

deduct /dɪ'dʌkt/ *vt* abziehen

deduction /dɪ'dʌkʃn/ *n* Abzug *m*;
(*conclusion*) Folgerung *f*

deed /di:d/ *n* Tat *f*; (*Jur*) Urkunde *f*

deep /di:p/ *adj* (**-er, -est**) tief; **go off
the ~ end** [I] auf die Palme gehen
● *adv* tief

deepen /'di:pn/ *vt* vertiefen

deep-'freeze *n* Gefriertruhe *f*; (*upright*) Gefrierschrank *m*

deer /dɪə(r)/ *n inv* Hirsch *m*; (*roe*)
Reh *nt*

deface /dɪ'feɪs/ *vt* beschädigen

default /dɪ'fɔ:lt/ *n* **win by ~** (*Sport*)
kampflos gewinnen

defeat /dɪ'fi:t/ *n* Niederlage *f*; (*de-
feating*) Besiegung *f*; (*rejection*) Ablehnung *f* ● *vt* besiegen; ablehnen;
(*frustrate*) vereiteln

defect /'di:fekt/ *n* Fehler *m*; (*Techn*)
Defekt *m*. ~**ive** *adj* fehlerhaft;
(*Techn*) defekt

defence /dɪ'fens/ *n* Verteidigung *f*.
~**less** *adj* wehrlos

defend /dɪ'fend/ *vt* verteidigen; (*justify*) rechtfertigen. ~**ant** *n* (*Jur*) Be-
klagte(r) *m/f*; (*in criminal court*) An-
geklagte(r) *m/f*

defensive /dɪ'fensɪv/ *adj* defensiv

defer /dɪ'fɜ:(r)/ *vt* (*pt/pp* **deferred**)
(*postpone*) aufschieben

deferen|ce /'defərəns/ *n* Ehrerbie-
tung *f*. ~**tial** *adj* ehrerbietig

defian|ce /dɪ'faɪəns/ *n* Trotz *m*; **in
~ce of** zum Trotz (+ *dat*). ~**t** *adj*
aufsässig

deficien|cy /dɪ'fɪʃənsɪ/ *n* Mangel *m*.
~**t** *adj* mangelhaft

deficit /'defɪsɪt/ *n* Defizit *nt*

define /dɪ'faɪn/ *vt* bestimmen; definieren (*word*)

definite /'defɪnɪt/ *adj* bestimmt;
(*certain*) sicher

definition /defɪ'nɪʃn/ *n* Definition *f*;
(*Phot, TV*) Schärfe *f*

definitive /dɪ'fɪnətɪv/ *adj* endgültig;
(*authoritative*) maßgeblich

deflat|e /dɪ'fleɪt/ *vt* die Luft auslas-
sen aus. ~**ion** *n* (*Comm*) Deflation *f*

deflect /dɪ'flekt/ *vt* ablenken

deform|ed /dɪ'fɔ:md/ *adj* missgebil-
det. ~**ity** *n* Missbildung *f*

defraud /dɪ'frɔ:d/ *vt* betrügen (**of**
um)

defray /dɪ'freɪ/ *vt* bestreiten

defrost /di:'frɒst/ *vt* entfrosten; abtauen (*fridge*); auftauen (*food*)

deft /deft/ *adj* (**-er, -est**) geschickt.
~**ness** *n* Geschicklichkeit *f*

defuse /di:'fju:z/ *vt* entschärfen

defy /dɪ'faɪ/ *vt* (*pt/pp* **-ied**) trotzen (+
dat); widerstehen (+ *dat*) (*attempt*)

degrading /dɪˈɡreɪdɪŋ/ *adj* entwürdigend

degree /dɪˈɡriː/ *n* Grad *m*; (*Univ*) akademischer Grad *m*; **20 ~s** 20 Grad

de-ice /diːˈaɪs/ *vt* enteisen

deity /ˈdiːɪtɪ/ *n* Gottheit *f*

dejected /dɪˈdʒektɪd/ *adj* niedergeschlagen

delay /dɪˈleɪ/ *n* Verzögerung *f*; (*of train, aircraft*) Verspätung *f*; **without ~** unverzüglich ● *vt* aufhalten; (*postpone*) aufschieben ● *vi* zögern

delegate[1] /ˈdelɪɡət/ *n* Delegierte(r) *m/f*

delegat|e[2] /ˈdelɪɡeɪt/ *vt* delegieren. **~ion** *n* Delegation *f*

delet|e /dɪˈliːt/ *vt* streichen. **~ion** *n* Streichung *f*

deliberate /dɪˈlɪbərət/ *adj* absichtlich; (*slow*) bedächtig

delicacy /ˈdelɪkəsɪ/ *n* Feinheit *f*; Zartheit *f*; (*food*) Delikatesse *f*

delicate /ˈdelɪkət/ *adj* fein; (*fabric, health*) zart; (*situation*) heikel; (*mechanism*) empfindlich

delicatessen /delɪkəˈtesn/ *n* Delikatessengeschäft *nt*

delicious /dɪˈlɪʃəs/ *adj* köstlich

delight /dɪˈlaɪt/ *n* Freude *f* ● *vt* entzücken ● *vi* **~ in** sich erfreuen an (+ *dat*). **~ed** *adj* hocherfreut; **be ~ed** sich sehr freuen. **~ful** *adj* reizend

delinquent /dɪˈlɪŋkwənt/ *adj* straffällig ● *n* Straffällige(r) *m/f*

deli|rious /dɪˈlɪrɪəs/ *adj* **be ~rious** im Delirium sein. **~rium** *n* Delirium *nt*

deliver /dɪˈlɪvə(r)/ *vt* liefern; zustellen (*post, newspaper*); halten (*speech*); überbringen (*message*); versetzen (*blow*); (*set free*) befreien; **~ a baby** ein Kind zur Welt bringen. **~y** *n* Lieferung *f*; (*of post*) Zustellung *f*; (*Med*) Entbindung *f*; **cash on ~y** per Nachnahme

delta /ˈdeltə/ *n* Delta *nt*

deluge /ˈdeljuːdʒ/ *n* Flut *f*; (*heavy rain*) schwerer Guss *m*

delusion /dɪˈluːʒn/ *n* Täuschung *f*

de luxe /dəˈlʌks/ *adj* Luxus-

demand /dɪˈmɑːnd/ *n* Forderung *f*; (*Comm*) Nachfrage *f*; **in ~** gefragt; **on ~** auf Verlangen ● *vt* verlangen, fordern (**of**/**from** von). **~ing** *adj* anspruchsvoll

demented /dɪˈmentɪd/ *adj* verrückt

demister /diːˈmɪstə(r)/ *n* (*Auto*) Defroster *m*

demo /ˈdeməʊ/ *n* (*pl* **~s**) 🔲 Demonstration *f*

democracy /dɪˈmɒkrəsɪ/ *n* Demokratie *f*

democrat /ˈdeməkræt/ *n* Demokrat *m*. **~ic** *adj*, **-ally** *adv* demokratisch

demo|lish /dɪˈmɒlɪʃ/ *vt* abbrechen; (*destroy*) zerstören. **~lition** *n* Abbruch *m*

demon /ˈdiːmən/ *n* Dämon *m*

demonstrat|e /ˈdemənstreɪt/ *vt* beweisen; vorführen (*appliance*) ● *vi* (*Pol*) demonstrieren. **~ion** *n* Vorführung *f*; (*Pol*) Demonstration *f*

demonstrator /ˈdemənstreɪtə(r)/ *n* Vorführer *m*; (*Pol*) Demonstrant *m*

demoralize /dɪˈmɒrəlaɪz/ *vt* demoralisieren

demote /dɪˈməʊt/ *vt* degradieren

demure /dɪˈmjʊə(r)/ *adj* sittsam

den /den/ *n* Höhle *f*; (*room*) Bude *f*

denial /dɪˈnaɪəl/ *n* Leugnen *nt*; **official ~** Dementi *nt*

denim /ˈdenɪm/ *n* Jeansstoff *m*; **~s** *pl* Jeans *pl*

Denmark /ˈdenmɑːk/ *n* Dänemark *nt*

denounce /dɪˈnaʊns/ *vt* denunzieren; (*condemn*) verurteilen

dens|e /dens/ *adj* (**-r, -st**) dicht; (🔲: *stupid*) blöd[e]. **~ity** *n* Dichte *f*

dent /dent/ *n* Delle *f*, Beule *f* ● *vt* einbeulen. **~ed** verbeult

dental /ˈdentl/ *adj* Zahn-; (*treatment*) zahnärztlich. **~ floss** *n* Zahnseide *f*. **~ surgeon** *n* Zahnarzt *m*

dentist /ˈdentɪst/ *n* Zahnarzt *m*/-ärztin *f*. **~ry** *n* Zahnmedizin *f*

denture /ˈdentʃə(r)/ *n* Zahnprothese *f*; **~s** *pl* künstliches Gebiss *nt*

deny /dɪˈnaɪ/ *vt* (*pt/pp* **-ied**) leugnen;

d

(*officially*) dementieren; ~ **s.o. sth** jdm etw verweigern

deodorant /diːˈəʊdərənt/ n Deodorant nt

depart /dɪˈpɑːt/ vi abfahren; (*Aviat*) abfliegen; (*go away*) weggehen/- fahren; (*deviate*) abweichen (**from** von)

department /dɪˈpɑːtmənt/ n Abteilung f; (*Pol*) Ministerium nt. ~ **store** n Kaufhaus nt

departure /dɪˈpɑːtʃə(r)/ n Abfahrt f; (*Aviat*) Abflug m; (*from rule*) Abweichung f

depend /dɪˈpend/ vi abhängen (**on** von); (*rely*) sich verlassen (**on** auf + *acc*); **it all** ~**s** das kommt darauf an. ~**able** adj zuverlässig. ~**ant** n Abhängige(r) m/f. ~**ence** n Abhängigkeit f. ~**ent** adj abhängig (**on** von)

depict /dɪˈpɪkt/ vt darstellen

deplor|able /dɪˈplɔːrəbl/ adj bedauerlich. ~**e** vt bedauern

deploy /dɪˈplɔɪ/ vt (*Mil*) einsetzen

depopulate /diːˈpɒpjʊleɪt/ vt entvölkern

deport /dɪˈpɔːt/ vt deportieren, ausweisen. ~**ation** n Ausweisung f

depose /dɪˈpəʊz/ vt absetzen

deposit /dɪˈpɒzɪt/ n Anzahlung f; (*against damage*) Kaution f; (*on bottle*) Pfand nt; (*sediment*) Bodensatz m; (*Geology*) Ablagerung f ● vt (*pt/pp* **deposited**) legen; (*for safety*) deponieren; (*Geology*) ablagern. ~ **account** n Sparkonto nt

depot /ˈdepəʊ/ n Depot nt; (*Amer: railway station*) Bahnhof m

deprav|e /dɪˈpreɪv/ vt verderben. ~**ed** adj verkommen

depreciat|e /dɪˈpriːʃɪeɪt/ vi an Wert verlieren. ~**ion** n Wertminderung f; (*Comm*) Abschreibung f

depress /dɪˈpres/ vt deprimieren; (*press down*) herunterdrücken. ~**ed** adj deprimiert. ~**ing** adj deprimierend. ~**ion** n Vertiefung f; (*Med*) Depression f; (*weather*) Tiefdruckgebiet nt

deprivation /deprɪˈveɪʃn/ n Entbehrung f

deprive /dɪˈpraɪv/ vt ~ **s.o. of sth** jdm etw entziehen. ~**d** adj benachteiligt

depth /depθ/ n Tiefe f; **in** ~ gründlich; **in the** ~**s of winter** im tiefsten Winter

deputize /ˈdepjʊtaɪz/ vi ~ **for** vertreten

deputy /ˈdepjʊtɪ/ n Stellvertreter m ● attrib stellvertretend

derail /dɪˈreɪl/ vt be ~**ed** entgleisen. ~**ment** n Entgleisung f

derelict /ˈderəlɪkt/ adj verfallen; (*abandoned*) verlassen

derisory /dɪˈraɪsərɪ/ adj höhnisch; (*offer*) lächerlich

derivation /derɪˈveɪʃn/ n Ableitung f

derivative /dɪˈrɪvətɪv/ adj abgeleitet ● n Ableitung f

derive /dɪˈraɪv/ vt/i (*obtain*) gewinnen (**from** aus); **be** ~**d from** (*word:*) hergeleitet sein aus

derogatory /dɪˈrɒɡətrɪ/ adj abfällig

derv /dɜːv/ n Diesel[kraftstoff] m

descend /dɪˈsend/ vt/i hinunter-/ heruntergehen; (*vehicle, lift:*) hinunter-/herunterfahren; **be** ~**ed from** abstammen von. ~**ant** n Nachkomme m

descent /dɪˈsent/ n Abstieg m; (*lineage*) Abstammung f

describe /dɪˈskraɪb/ vt beschreiben

descrip|tion /dɪˈskrɪpʃn/ n Beschreibung f; (*sort*) Art f. ~**tive** adj beschreibend; (*vivid*) anschaulich

desecrate /ˈdesɪkreɪt/ vt entweihen

desert[1] /ˈdezət/ n Wüste f. ~ **island** verlassene Insel f

desert[2] /dɪˈzɜːt/ vt verlassen ● vt desertieren. ~**ed** adj verlassen. ~**er** n (*Mil*) Deserteur m. ~**ion** n Fahnenflucht f

deserv|e /dɪˈzɜːv/ vt verdienen. ~**edly** adv verdientermaßen. ~**ing** adj verdienstvoll

design /dɪˈzaɪn/ n Entwurf m; (*pattern*) Muster nt; (*construction*) Konstruktion f; (aim) Absicht f ● vt entwerfen; (construct) konstruieren; **be ~ed for** bestimmt sein für

designer /dɪ'zaɪnə(r)/ n Designer m; (Techn) Konstrukteur m; (Theat) Bühnenbildner m

desirable /dɪ'zaɪrəbl/ adj wünschenswert; (sexually) begehrenswert

desire /dɪ'zaɪə(r)/ n Wunsch m; (longing) Verlangen nt (**for** nach); (sexual) Begierde f ● vt [sich (dat)] wünschen; (sexually) begehren

desk /desk/ n Schreibtisch m; (Sch) Pult m

desolat|e /'desələt/ adj trostlos. **~ion** n Trostlosigkeit f

despair /dɪ'speə(r)/ n Verzweiflung f; **in ~** verzweifelt ● vi verzweifeln

desperat|e /'despərət/ adj verzweifelt; (urgent) dringend; **be ~e for** dringend brauchen. **~ion** n Verzweiflung f

despicable /dɪ'spɪkəbl/ adj verachtenswert

despise /dɪ'spaɪz/ vt verachten

despite /dɪ'spaɪt/ prep trotz (+ gen)

despondent /dɪ'spɒndənt/ adj niedergeschlagen

dessert /dɪ'zɜːt/ n Dessert nt, Nachtisch m. **~ spoon** n Dessertlöffel m

destination /destɪ'neɪʃn/ n [Reise]ziel nt; (of goods) Bestimmungsort m

destiny /'destɪnɪ/ n Schicksal nt

destitute /'destɪtjuːt/ adj völlig mittellos

destroy /dɪ'strɔɪ/ vt zerstören; (totally) vernichten. **~er** n (Naut) Zerstörer m

destruc|tion /dɪ'strʌkʃn/ n Zerstörung f; Vernichtung f. **-tive** adj zerstörerisch; (fig) destruktiv

detach /dɪ'tætʃ/ vt abnehmen; (tear off) abtrennen. **~able** adj abnehmbar. **~ed** adj **~ed house** Einzelhaus nt

detail /'diːteɪl/ n Einzelheit f, Detail nt; **in ~** ausführlich ● vt einzeln aufführen. **~ed** adj ausführlich

detain /dɪ'teɪn/ vt aufhalten; (police:)

in Haft behalten; (take into custody) in Haft nehmen

detect /dɪ'tekt/ vt entdecken; (perceive) wahrnehmen. **~ion** n Entdeckung f

detective /dɪ'tektɪv/ n Detektiv m. **~ story** n Detektivroman m

detention /dɪ'tenʃn/ n Haft f; (Sch) Nachsitzen nt

deter /dɪ'tɜː(r)/ vt (pt/pp deterred) abschrecken; (prevent) abhalten

detergent /dɪ'tɜːdʒənt/ n Waschmittel nt

deteriorat|e /dɪ'tɪərɪəreɪt/ vi sich verschlechtern. **~ion** n Verschlechterung f

determination /dɪtɜːmɪ'neɪʃn/ n Entschlossenheit f

determine /dɪ'tɜːmɪn/ vt bestimmen. **~d** adj entschlossen

deterrent /dɪ'terənt/ n Abschreckungsmittel nt

detest /dɪ'test/ vt verabscheuen. **~able** adj abscheulich

detonate /'detəneɪt/ vt zünden

detour /'diːtʊə(r)/ n Umweg m

detract /dɪ'trækt/ vi **~ from** beeinträchtigen

detriment /'detrɪmənt/ n **to the ~ (of)** zum Schaden (+ gen). **~al** adj schädlich (**to** dat)

deuce /djuːs/ n (Tennis) Einstand m

devaluation /diːvæljʊ'eɪʃn/ n Abwertung f

de'value vt abwerten (currency)

devastat|e /'devəsteɪt/ vt verwüsten. **~ing** adj verheerend. **~ion** n Verwüstung f

develop /dɪ'veləp/ vt entwickeln; bekommen (illness); erschließen (area) ● vi sich entwickeln (**into** zu). **~er** n **[property] ~er** Bodenspekulant m

development /dɪ'veləpmənt/ n Entwicklung f

deviat|e /'diːvɪeɪt/ vi abweichen. **~ion** n Abweichung f

device /dɪ'vaɪs/ n Gerät nt; (fig) Mittel nt

devil /'devl/ n Teufel m. **~ish** adj teuflisch

d

devious /'di:vɪəs/ adj verschlagen

devise /dɪ'vaɪz/ vt sich (dat) ausdenken

devot|e /dɪ'vəʊt/ vt widmen (**to** dat). **~ed** adj ergeben; (care) liebevoll; **be ~ed to s.o.** sehr an jdm hängen

devotion /dɪ'vəʊʃn/ n Hingabe f

devour /dɪ'vaʊə(r)/ vt verschlingen

devout /dɪ'vaʊt/ adj fromm

dew /dju:/ n Tau m

dexterity /dek'sterətɪ/ n Geschicklichkeit f

diabet|es /daɪə'bi:ti:z/ n Zuckerkrankheit f. **~ic** n Diabetiker(in) m(f)

diabolical /daɪə'bɒlɪkl/ adj teuflisch

diagnose /daɪəg'nəʊz/ vt diagnostizieren

diagnosis /daɪəg'nəʊsɪs/ n (pl **-oses** /-si:z/) Diagnose f

diagonal /daɪ'ægənl/ adj diagonal ● n Diagonale f

diagram /'daɪəgræm/ n Diagramm nt

dial /'daɪəl/ n (of clock) Zifferblatt nt; (Techn) Skala f; (Teleph) Wählscheibe f ● vt/i (pt/pp **dialled**) (Teleph) wählen; **~ direct** durchwählen

dialect /'daɪəlekt/ n Dialekt m

dialling: ~ code n Vorwahlnummer f. **~ tone** n Amtszeichen nt

dialogue /'daɪəlɒg/ n Dialog m

diameter /daɪ'æmɪtə(r)/ n Durchmesser m

diamond /'daɪəmənd/ n Diamant m; (cut) Brillant m; (shape) Raute f; **~s** pl (Cards) Karo nt

diaper /'daɪəpə(r)/ n (Amer) Windel f

diarrhoea /daɪə'ri:ə/ n Durchfall m

diary /'daɪərɪ/ n Tagebuch nt; (for appointments) [Termin]kalender m

dice /daɪs/ n inv Würfel m

dictat|e /dɪk'teɪt/ vt/i diktieren. **~ion** n Diktat nt

dictator /dɪk'teɪtə(r)/ n Diktator m. **~ial** adj diktatorisch. **~ship** n Diktatur f

dictionary /'dɪkʃənrɪ/ n Wörterbuch nt

did /dɪd/ see **do**

didn't /'dɪdnt/ = **did not**

die[1] /daɪ/ n (Techn) Prägestempel m; (metal mould) Gussform f

die[2] vi (pres p **dying**) sterben (**of** an + dat); (plant, animal:) eingehen; (flower:) verwelken; **be dying to do sth** 🄸 darauf brennen, etw zu tun; **be dying for sth** 🄸 sich nach etw sehnen. **~ down** vi nachlassen; (fire:) herunterbrennen. **~ out** vi aussterben

diesel /'di:zl/ n Diesel m. **~ engine** n Dieselmotor m

diet /'daɪət/ n Kost f; (restricted) Diät f; (for slimming) Schlankheitskur f; **be on a ~** Diät leben; eine Schlankheitskur machen ● vi Diät leben; eine Schlankheitskur machen

differ /'dɪfə(r)/ vi sich unterscheiden; (disagree) verschiedener Meinung sein

differen|ce /'dɪfrəns/ n Unterschied m; (disagreement) Meinungsverschiedenheit f. **~t** adj andere(r,s); (various) verschiedene; **be ~t** anders sein (**from** als)

differential /dɪfə'renʃl/ adj Differenzial- ● n Unterschied m; (Techn) Differenzial nt

differentiate /dɪfə'renʃɪeɪt/ vt/i unterscheiden (**between** zwischen + dat)

differently /'dɪfrəntlɪ/ adv anders

difficult /'dɪfɪkəlt/ adj schwierig, schwer. **~y** n Schwierigkeit f

diffiden|ce /'dɪfɪdəns/ n Zaghaftigkeit f. **~t** adj zaghaft

dig /dɪg/ n (poke) Stoß m; (remark) spitze Bemerkung f; (archaeological) Ausgrabung f ● vt/i (pt/pp **dug**, pres p **digging**) graben; umgraben (garden). **~ out** vt ausgraben. **~ up** vt ausgraben; umgraben (garden); aufreißen (street)

digest /dɪ'dʒest/ vt verdauen. **~ible** adj verdaulich. **~ion** n Verdauung f

digit /'dɪdʒɪt/ n Ziffer f; (finger) Finger m; (toe) Zehe f. **~ize** vt digitalisieren

digital /'dɪdʒɪtl/ adj Digital-; **~ cam-**

era Digitalkamera f; **~ television** Digitalfernsehen nt

dignified /'dɪɡnɪfaɪd/ adj würdevoll

dignity /'dɪɡnɪtɪ/ n Würde f

dilapidated /dɪ'læpɪdeɪtɪd/ adj baufällig

dilatory /'dɪlətərɪ/ adj langsam

dilemma /dɪ'lemə/ n Dilemma nt

dilettante /dɪlɪ'tæntɪ/ n Dilettant(in) m(f)

diligen|ce /'dɪlɪdʒəns/ n Fleiß m. **~t** adj fleißig

dilute /daɪ'luːt/ vt verdünnen

dim /dɪm/ adj (**dimmer, dimmest**). **-ly** adv (weak) schwach; (dark) trüb[e]; (indistinct) undeutlich; (🖪: stupid) dumm, 🖪 doof ● v (pt/pp **dimmed**) ● vt dämpfen

dime /daɪm/ n (Amer) Zehncentstück nt

dimension /daɪ'menʃn/ n Dimension f; **~s** pl Maße pl

diminutive /dɪ'mɪnjʊtɪv/ adj winzig ● n Verkleinerungsform f

dimple /'dɪmpl/ n Grübchen nt

din /dɪn/ n Krach m, Getöse nt

dine /daɪn/ vi speisen. **~r** n Speisende(r) m/f; (Amer: restaurant) Esslokal nt

dinghy /'dɪŋɡɪ/ n Dinghi nt; (inflatable) Schlauchboot nt

dingy /'dɪndʒɪ/ adj trübe

dining /'daɪnɪŋ/: **~-car** n Speisewagen m. **~-room** n Esszimmer nt. **~-table** n Esstisch m

dinner /'dɪnə(r)/ n Abendessen nt; (at midday) Mittagessen nt; (formal) Essen nt. **~-jacket** n Smoking m

dinosaur /'daɪnəsɔː(r)/ n Dinosaurier m

diocese /'daɪəsɪs/ n Diözese f

dip /dɪp/ n (in ground) Senke f; (Culin) Dip m ● v (pt/pp **dipped**) vt [ein]tauchen; **~ one's headlights** (Auto) [die Scheinwerfer] abblenden ● vi sich senken

diploma /dɪ'pləʊmə/ n Diplom nt

diplomacy /dɪ'pləʊməsɪ/ n Diplomatie f

diplomat /'dɪpləmæt/ n Diplomat m. **~ic** adj, **-ally** adv diplomatisch

'dip-stick n (Auto) Ölmessstab m

dire /'daɪə(r)/ adj (**-r, -st**) bitter; (consequences) furchtbar

direct /dɪ'rekt/ adj & adv direkt ● vt (aim) richten (**at** auf / (fig) an + acc); (control) leiten; (order) anweisen; **~ a film/play** bei einem Film/Theaterstück Regie führen

direction /dɪ'rekʃn/ n Richtung f; (control) Leitung f; (of play, film) Regie f; **~s** pl Anweisungen pl; **~s for use** Gebrauchsanweisung f

directly /dɪ'rektlɪ/ adv direkt; (at once) sofort

director /dɪ'rektə(r)/ n (Comm) Direktor m; (of play, film) Regisseur m, Regisseurin f

directory /dɪ'rektərɪ/ n Verzeichnis nt; (Teleph) Telefonbuch nt

dirt /dɜːt/ n Schmutz m; (soil) Erde f; **~ cheap** 🖪 spottbillig

dirty /'dɜːtɪ/ adj schmutzig

dis|a'bility /dɪs-/ n Behinderung f. **~abled** adj [körper]behindert

disad'vantage n Nachteil m; **at a ~** im Nachteil. **~d** adj benachteiligt

disa'gree vi nicht übereinstimmen (**with** mit); **I ~** ich bin anderer Meinung; **oysters ~ with me** Austern bekommen mir nicht

disa'greeable adj unangenehm

disa'greement n Meinungsverschiedenheit f

disap'pear vi verschwinden. **~ance** n Verschwinden nt

disap'point vt enttäuschen. **~ment** n Enttäuschung f

disap'proval n Missbilligung f

disap'prove vi dagegen sein; **~ of** missbilligen

dis'arm vt entwaffnen ● vi (Mil) abrüsten. **~ament** n Abrüstung f. **~ing** adj entwaffnend

disast|er /dɪ'zɑːstə(r)/ n Katastrophe f; (accident) Unglück nt. **~rous** adj katastrophal

disbe'lief n Ungläubigkeit f; **in ~** ungläubig

disc /dɪsk/ n Scheibe f; (record) [Schall]platte f; (CD) CD f

discard /dɪˈskɑːd/ vt ablegen; (throw away) wegwerfen

discerning /dɪˈsɜːnɪŋ/ adj anspruchsvoll

'**discharge**¹ n Ausstoßen nt; (Naut, Electr) Entladung f; (dismissal) Entlassung f; (Jur) Freispruch m; (Med) Ausfluss m

dis'charge² vt ausstoßen; (Naut, Electr) entladen; (dismiss) entlassen; (Jur) freisprechen (accused)

disciplinary /ˈdɪsɪplɪnəri/ adj disziplinarisch

discipline /ˈdɪsɪplɪn/ n Disziplin f ● vt Disziplin beibringen (+ dat); (punish) bestrafen

'**disc jockey** n Diskjockey m

dis'claim vt abstreiten. ~er n Verzichterklärung f

dis'clos|e vt enthüllen. ~ure n Enthüllung f

disco /ˈdɪskəʊ/ n ⓘ Disko f

dis'colour vt verfärben ● vi sich verfärben

dis'comfort n Beschwerden pl; (fig) Unbehagen nt

discon'nect vt trennen; (Electr) ausschalten; (cut supply) abstellen

discon'tent n Unzufriedenheit f. ~ed adj unzufrieden

discon'tinue vt einstellen; (Comm) nicht mehr herstellen

'**discord** n Zwietracht f; (Mus & fig) Missklang m

discothèque /ˈdɪskətek/ n Diskothek f

'**discount** n Rabatt m

dis'courage vt entmutigen; (dissuade) abraten (+ dat)

dis'courteous adj unhöflich

discover /dɪˈskʌvə(r)/ vt entdecken. ~y n Entdeckung f

discreet /dɪˈskriːt/ adj diskret

discretion /dɪˈskreʃn/ n Diskretion f; (judgement) Ermessen nt

discriminat|e /dɪˈskrɪmɪneɪt/ vi unterscheiden (**between** zwischen + dat); ~e **against** diskriminieren. ~ing adj anspruchsvoll. ~ion n Diskriminierung f

discus /ˈdɪskəs/ n Diskus m

discuss /dɪˈskʌs/ vt besprechen; (examine critically) diskutieren. ~ion n Besprechung f; Diskussion f

disdain /dɪsˈdeɪn/ n Verachtung f

disease /dɪˈziːz/ n Krankheit f

disem'bark vi an Land gehen

disen'chant vt ernüchtern

disen'gage vt losmachen

disen'tangle vt entwirren

dis'figure vt entstellen

dis'grace n Schande f; **in** ~ in Ungnade ● vt Schande machen (+ dat). ~ful adj schändlich

disgruntled /dɪsˈgrʌntld/ adj verstimmt

disguise /dɪsˈgaɪz/ n Verkleidung f; **in** ~ verkleidet ● vt verkleiden; verstellen (voice)

disgust /dɪsˈgʌst/ n Ekel m; **in** ~ empört ● vt anekeln; (appal) empören. ~ing adj eklig; (appalling) abscheulich

dish /dɪʃ/ n Schüssel f; (shallow) Schale f; (small) Schälchen nt; (food) Gericht nt. ~ **out** vt austeilen. ~ **up** vt auftragen

'**dishcloth** n Spültuch nt

dis'hearten vt entmutigen

dis'honest adj -ly adv unehrlich. ~y n Unehrlichkeit f

dis'honour n Schande f. ~able adj, -bly adv unehrenhaft

'**dishwasher** n Geschirrspülmaschine f

disil'lusion vt ernüchtern. ~ment n Ernüchterung f

disin'fect vt desinfizieren. ~ant n Desinfektionsmittel nt

disin'herit vt enterben

dis'integrate vi zerfallen

dis'jointed adj unzusammenhängend

disk /dɪsk/ n = disc

dis'like n Abneigung f ● vt nicht mögen

dislocate /ˈdɪsləkeɪt/ vt ausrenken

dis'lodge vt entfernen

dis'loyal adj illoyal. **~ty** n Illoyalität f

dismal /'dɪzməl/ adj trüb[e]; (person) trübselig

dismantle /dɪs'mæntl/ vt auseinander nehmen; (take down) abbauen

dis'may n Bestürzung f. **~ed** adj bestürzt

dis'miss vt entlassen; (reject) zurückweisen. **~al** n Entlassung f; Zurückweisung f

diso'bedien|ce n Ungehorsam m. **~t** adj ungehorsam

diso'bey vt/i nicht gehorchen (+ dat); nicht befolgen (rule)

dis'order n Unordnung f; (Med) Störung f. **~ly** adj unordentlich

dis'organized adj unorganisiert

dis'own vt verleugnen

disparaging /dɪ'spærɪdʒɪŋ/ adj abschätzig

dispassionate /dɪ'spæʃənət/ adj gelassen; (impartial) unparteiisch

dispatch /dɪ'spætʃ/ n (Comm) Versand m; (Mil) Nachricht f; (report) Bericht m ● vt [ab]senden; (kill) töten

dispel /dɪ'spel/ vt (pt/pp dispelled) vertreiben

dispensary /dɪ'spensərɪ/ n Apotheke f

dispense /dɪ'spens/ vt austeilen; **~ with** verzichten auf (+ acc). **~r** n (device) Automat m

disperse /dɪ'spɜːs/ vt zerstreuen ● vi sich zerstreuen

dispirited /dɪ'spɪrɪtɪd/ adj entmutigt

display /dɪ'spleɪ/ n Ausstellung f; (Comm) Auslage f; (performance) Vorführung f ● vt zeigen; ausstellen (goods)

dis'please vt missfallen (+ dat)

dis'pleasure n Missfallen nt

disposable /dɪ'spəʊzəbl/ adj Wegwerf-; (income) verfügbar

disposal /dɪ'spəʊzl/ n Beseitigung f; **be at s.o.'s ~** jdm zur Verfügung stehen

dispose /dɪ'spəʊz/ vi **~ of** beseiti-

gen; (deal with) erledigen

disposition /dɪspə'zɪʃn/ n Veranlagung f; (nature) Wesensart f

disproportionate /dɪsprə'pɔːʃənət/ adj unverhältnismäßig

dis'prove vt widerlegen

dispute /dɪ'spjuːt/ n Disput m; (quarrel) Streit m ● vt bestreiten

disqualifi'cation n Disqualifikation f

dis'qualify vt disqualifizieren; **~ s.o. from driving** jdm den Führerschein entziehen

disre'gard vt nicht beachten

disre'pair n **fall into ~** verfallen

disre'putable adj verrufen

disre'pute n Verruf m

disre'spect n Respektlosigkeit f. **~ful** adj respektlos

disrupt /dɪs'rʌpt/ vt stören. **~ion** n Störung f

dissatis'faction n Unzufriedenheit f

dis'satisfied adj unzufrieden

dissect /dɪ'sekt/ vt zergliedern; (Med) sezieren. **~ion** n Zergliederung f; (Med) Sektion f

dissent /dɪ'sent/ n Nichtübereinstimmung f ● vi nicht übereinstimmen

dissident /'dɪsɪdənt/ n Dissident m

dis'similar adj unähnlich (to dat)

dissociate /dɪ'səʊʃɪeɪt/ vt **~ one-self** sich distanzieren (from von)

dissolute /'dɪsəluːt/ adj zügellos; (life) ausschweifend

dissolve /dɪ'zɒlv/ vt auflösen ● vi sich auflösen

dissuade /dɪ'sweɪd/ vt abbringen (from von)

distance /'dɪstəns/ n Entfernung f; **long/short ~** lange/kurze Strecke f; **in the/from a ~** in/aus der Ferne

distant /'dɪstənt/ adj fern; (aloof) kühl; (relative) entfernt

dis'tasteful adj unangenehm

distil /dɪ'stɪl/ vt (pt/pp distilled) brennen; (Chemistry) destillieren. **~lery** n Brennerei f

distinct /dɪˈstɪŋkt/ adj deutlich; (different) verschieden. ∼ion n Unterschied m; (Sch) Auszeichnung f. ∼ive adj kennzeichnend; (unmistakable) unverwechselbar. ∼ly adv deutlich

distinguish /dɪˈstɪŋgwɪʃ/ vt/i unterscheiden; (make out) erkennen; ∼ oneself sich auszeichnen. ∼ed adj angesehen; (appearance) distinguiert

distort /dɪˈstɔːt/ vt verzerren; (fig) verdrehen. ∼ion n Verzerrung f; (fig) Verdrehung f

distract /dɪˈstrækt/ vt ablenken. ∼ion n Ablenkung f; (despair) Verzweiflung f

distraught /dɪˈstrɔːt/ adj [völlig] aufgelöst

distress /dɪˈstres/ n Kummer m; (pain) Schmerz m; (poverty, danger) Not f ● vt Kummer/Schmerz bereiten (+ dat); (sadden) bekümmern; (shock) erschüttern. ∼ing adj schmerzlich; (shocking) erschütternd

distribut|e /dɪˈstrɪbjuːt/ vt verteilen; (Comm) vertreiben. ∼ion n Verteilung f; Vertrieb m. ∼or n Verteiler m

district /ˈdɪstrɪkt/ n Gegend f; (Admin) Bezirk m

disˈtrust n Misstrauen nt ● vt misstrauen (+ dat). ∼ful adj misstrauisch

disturb /dɪˈstɜːb/ vt stören; (perturb) beunruhigen; (touch) anrühren. ∼ance n Unruhe f; (interruption) Störung f. ∼ed adj beunruhigt; [mentally] ∼ed geistig gestört. ∼ing adj beunruhigend

disˈused adj stillgelegt; (empty) leer

ditch /dɪtʃ/ n Graben m ● vt (🔲: abandon) fallen lassen (plan)

dither /ˈdɪðə(r)/ vi zaudern

ditto /ˈdɪtəʊ/ n dito; 🔲 ebenfalls

dive /daɪv/ n [Kopf]sprung m; (Aviat) Sturzflug m; (🔲: place) Spelunke f ● vi einen Kopfsprung machen; (when in water) tauchen; (Aviat) einen Sturzflug machen; (🔲: rush) stürzen

diver /ˈdaɪvə(r)/ n Taucher m; (Sport) [Kunst]springer m

diverse /daɪˈvɜːs/ adj verschieden

diversify /daɪˈvɜːsɪfaɪ/ vt/i (pt/pp -ied) variieren; (Comm) diversifizieren

diversion /daɪˈvɜːʃn/ n Umleitung f; (distraction) Ablenkung f

diversity /daɪˈvɜːsətɪ/ n Vielfalt f

divert /daɪˈvɜːt/ vt umleiten; ablenken (attention); (entertain) unterhalten

divide /dɪˈvaɪd/ vt teilen; (separate) trennen; (Math) dividieren (by durch) ● vi sich teilen

dividend /ˈdɪvɪdend/ n Dividende f

divine /dɪˈvaɪn/ adj göttlich

diving /ˈdaɪvɪŋ/ n (Sport) Kunstspringen nt. ∼-board n Sprungbrett nt

divinity /dɪˈvɪnətɪ/ n Göttlichkeit f; (subject) Theologie f

division /dɪˈvɪʒn/ n Teilung f; (separation) Trennung f; (Math, Mil) Division f; (Parl) Hammelsprung m; (line) Trennlinie f; (group) Abteilung f

divorce /dɪˈvɔːs/ n Scheidung f ● vt sich scheiden lassen von. ∼d adj geschieden; **get** ∼d sich scheiden lassen

DIY abbr do-it-yourself

dizziness /ˈdɪzɪnɪs/ n Schwindel m

dizzy /ˈdɪzɪ/ adj schwindlig; **I feel** ∼ mir ist schwindlig

---

do /duː/, unbetont /də/

❗ 3 sg pres tense **does**; pt **did**;
❗ pp **done**

● transitive verb

••••➤ (perform) machen (homework, housework, exam, handstand etc); tun (duty, favour, something, nothing); vorführen (trick, dance); durchführen (test). **what are you doing?** was tust od machst du? **what can I do for you?** was kann ich für Sie tun? **do something!** tu doch etwas! **have you nothing better to do?** hast du nichts Besseres zu tun? **do the washing-up/cleaning** abwaschen/sauber machen

••••➤ (as job) **what does your father do?** was macht dein Vater?; was ist dein Vater von Beruf?

····➤ (*clean*) putzen; (*arrange*) [zurecht]machen (*hair*)

····➤ (*cook*) kochen; (*roast, fry*) braten. **well done** (*meat*) durch[gebraten]. **the potatoes aren't done yet** die Kartoffeln sind noch nicht richtig durch

····➤ (*solve*) lösen (*problem, riddle*); machen (*puzzle*)

····➤ (🔲: *swindle*) reinlegen. **do s.o. out of sth** jdn um etw bringen

● *intransitive verb*

····➤ (*with as or adverb*) es tun; es machen. **do as they do** mach es wie sie. **he can do as he likes** er kann tun *od* machen, was er will. **you did well** du hast es gut gemacht

····➤ (*get on*) vorankommen; (*in exams*) abschneiden. **do well/ badly at school** gut/schlecht in der Schule sein. **how are you doing?** wie geht's dir? **how do you do?** (*formal*) guten Tag!

····➤ **will do** (*serve purpose*) es tun; (*suffice*) [aus]reichen; (*be suitable*) gehen. **that won't do** das geht nicht. **that will do!** jetzt aber genug!

● *auxiliary verb*

····➤ (*in questions*) **do you know him?** kennst du ihn? **what does he want?** was will er?

····➤ (*in negation*) **I don't** or **do not wish to take part** ich will nicht teilnehmen. **don't be so noisy!** seid [doch] nicht so laut!

····➤ (*as verb substitute*) **you mustn't act as he does** du darfst nicht so wie er handeln. **come in, do!** komm doch herein!

····➤ (*in tag questions*) **don't you, doesn't he** *etc.* nicht wahr. **you went to Paris, didn't you?** du warst in Paris, nicht wahr?

····➤ (*in short questions*) **Does he live in London? — Yes, he does** Wohnt er in London? — Ja, stimmt

····➤ (*for special emphasis*) **I do love Greece** Griechenland gefällt mir wirklich gut

····➤ (*for inversion*) **little did he know that ...** er hatte keine Ahnung, dass ...

● *noun*

❗ *pl* **do's** or **dos** /duːz/

····➤ (🔲: *celebration*) Feier *f*

● *phrasal verbs*

● **do away with** *vt* abschaffen.

● **do for** *vt* 🔲: **do for s.o.** jdn fertig machen 🔲; **be done for** erledigt sein. ● **do in** *vt* (*sl: kill*) kaltmachen 🔲. ● **do up** *vt* (*fasten*) zumachen; binden (*shoe-lace, bow-tie*); (*wrap*) einpacken; (*renovate*) renovieren. ● **do with** *vt*: **I could do with ...** ich brauche .... ● **do without** *vt*: **do without sth** auf etw (*acc*) verzichten; *vi* darauf verzichten

docile /ˈdəʊsaɪl/ *adj* fügsam

dock¹ /dɒk/ *n* (*Jur*) Anklagebank *f*

dock² *n* Dock *nt* ● *vi* anlegen. ~**er** *n* Hafenarbeiter *m*. ~**yard** *n* Werft *f*

doctor /ˈdɒktə(r)/ *n* Arzt *m*/ Ärztin *f*; (*Univ*) Doktor *m* ● *vt* kastrieren; (*spay*) sterilisieren

doctrine /ˈdɒktrɪn/ *n* Lehre *f*

document /ˈdɒkjʊmənt/ *n* Dokument *nt*. ~**ary** *adj* Dokumentar- ● *n* Dokumentarbericht *m*; (*film*) Dokumentarfilm *m*

dodge /dɒdʒ/ *n* 🔲 Trick *m*, Kniff *m* ● *vt/i* ausweichen (+ *dat*)

dodgy /ˈdɒdʒɪ/ *adj* 🔲 (*awkward*) knifflig; (*dubious*) zweifelhaft

doe /dəʊ/ *n* Ricke *f*; (*rabbit*) [Kaninchen]weibchen *nt*

does /dʌz/ *see* **do**

doesn't /ˈdʌznt/ = **does not**

dog /dɒg/ *n* Hund *m*

dog: ~**-biscuit** *n* Hundekuchen *m*. ~**-collar** *n* Hundehalsband *nt*; (*Relig*, 🔲) Kragen *m* eines Geistlichen. ~**-eared** *adj* **be** ~**-eared** Eselsohren haben

dogged /ˈdɒgɪd/ *adj* beharrlich

d

dogma /'dɒgmə/ n Dogma nt. **~tic** adj dogmatisch

do-it-yourself /duːɪtjə'self/ n Heimwerken nt. **~ shop** n Heimwerkerladen m

doldrums /'dɒldrəmz/ npl be in the ~ niedergeschlagen sein; (business:) danniederliegen

dole /dəʊl/ n 🔲 Stempelgeld nt; be on the ~ arbeitslos sein ● vt ~ out austeilen

doll /dɒl/ n Puppe f ● vt 🔲 ~ oneself up sich herausputzen

dollar /'dɒlə(r)/ n Dollar m

dolphin /'dɒlfɪn/ n Delphin m

domain /də'meɪn/ n Gebiet nt

dome /dəʊm/ n Kuppel m

domestic /də'mestɪk/ adj häuslich; (Pol) Innen-; (Comm) Binnen-. **~ animal** n Haustier nt. **~ flight** n Inlandflug m

domestic flight n Inlandflug m

dominant /'dɒmɪnənt/ adj vorherrschend

dominat|e /'dɒmɪneɪt/ vt beherrschen ● vi dominieren. **~ion** n Vorherrschaft f

domineering /dɒmɪ'nɪə(r)ɪŋ/ adj herrschsüchtig

domino /'dɒmɪnəʊ/ n (pl -es) Dominostein m; **~es** sg (game) Domino nt

donat|e /dəʊ'neɪt/ vt spenden. **~ion** n Spende f

done /dʌn/ see do

donkey /'dɒŋkɪ/ n Esel m; **~'s years** 🔲 eine Ewigkeit. **~-work** n Routinearbeit f

donor /'dəʊnə(r)/ n Spender m, Spenderin f

don't /dəʊnt/ = do not

doom /duːm/ n Schicksal nt; (ruin) Verhängnis nt

door /dɔː(r)/ n Tür f; out of ~s im Freien

door: **~man** n Portier m. **~mat** n [Fuß]abtreter m. **~step** n Türschwelle f; on the **~step** vor der Tür. **~way** n Türöffnung f

dope /dəʊp/ n 🔲 Drogen pl; (🔲:

information) Informationen pl; (🔲: idiot) Trottel m ● vt betäuben; (Sport) dopen

dormant /'dɔːmənt/ adj ruhend

dormitory /'dɔːmɪtərɪ/ n Schlafsaal m

dormouse /'dɔː-/ n Haselmaus f

dosage /'dəʊsɪdʒ/ n Dosierung f

dose /dəʊs/ n Dosis f

dot /dɒt/ n Punkt m; on the ~ pünktlich

dote /dəʊt/ vi ~ on vernarrt sein in (+ acc)

dotted /'dɒtɪd/ adj ~ line punktierte Linie f; be ~ with bestreut sein mit

dotty /'dɒtɪ/ adj 🔲 verdreht

double /'dʌbl/ adj & adv doppelt; (bed, chin) Doppel-; (flower) gefüllt ● n das Doppelte; (person) Doppelgänger m; **~s** pl (Tennis) Doppel nt; ● vt verdoppeln; (fold) falten ● vi sich verdoppeln. ~ up vi sich krümmen (with vor + dat)

double: **~-'bass** n Kontrabass m. **~-breasted** adj zweireihig. **~-click** vt/i doppelklicken (on auf + acc). **~-'cross** vt ein Doppelspiel treiben mit. **~-'decker** n Doppeldecker m. **~ 'glazing** n Doppelverglasung f. **~ 'room** n Doppelzimmer nt

doubly /'dʌblɪ/ adv doppelt

doubt /daʊt/ n Zweifel m ● vt bezweifeln. **~ful** adj zweifelhaft; (disbelieving) skeptisch. **~less** adv zweifellos

dough /dəʊ/ n [fester] Teig m; (🔲: money) Pinke f. **~nut** n Berliner [Pfannkuchen] m

dove /dʌv/ n Taube f

dowdy /'daʊdɪ/ adj unschick

down¹ /daʊn/ n (feathers) Daunen pl

down² adv unten; (with movement) nach unten; go ~ hinuntergehen; come ~ herunterkommen; ~ there da unten; £50 ~ £50 Anzahlung; ~! (to dog) Platz! ~ with ...! nieder mit ...! ● prep ~ the road/stairs die Straße/Treppe hinunter; ~ the river den Fluss abwärts ● vt 🔲 (drink) runterkippen; ~ **tools** die Arbeit niederlegen

down: ~**cast** adj niedergeschlagen. ~**fall** n Sturz m; (ruin) Ruin m. ~**'hearted** adj entmutigt. ~**hill** adv bergab. ~**load** vt herunterladen. ~ **payment** n Anzahlung f. ~**pour** n Platzregen m. ~**right** adj & adv ausgesprochen. ~**size** vt verschlanken ● vi abspecken. ~**'stairs** adv unten; (go) nach unten ● adj im Erdgeschoss. ~**'stream** adv stromabwärts. ~**-to-'earth** adj sachlich. ~**town** adv (Amer) im Stadtzentrum. ~**ward** adj nach unten; (slope) abfallend ● adv ~**[s]** abwärts, nach unten

> ***i*** **Downing Street** Der Name einer Straße im Zentrum von London. Das Haus mit der Nummer 10 in der *Downing Street* ist der offizielle Sitz des Premierministers und das mit der Nummer 11 der des Finanzministers. Unter Journalisten bezieht sich der Ausdruck *Downing Street* oder *Number 10* auf den Amtssitz des Premierministers.

doze /dəʊz/ n Nickerchen nt ● vi dösen. ~ **off** vi einnicken

dozen /'dʌzn/ n Dutzend nt

Dr abbr **doctor**

draft[1] /drɑːft/ n Entwurf m; (Comm) Tratte f; (Amer Mil) Einberufung f ● vt entwerfen; (Amer Mil) einberufen

draft[2] n (Amer) = **draught**

drag /dræg/ n **in** ~ 🔲 (man) als Frau gekleidet ● vt (pt/pp **dragged**) schleppen; absuchen (river). ~ **on** vi sich in die Länge ziehen

dragon /'drægən/ n Drache m. ~**fly** n Libelle f

drain /dreɪn/ n Abfluss m; (underground) Kanal m; **the** ~**s** die Kanalisation ● vt entwässern (land); ablassen (liquid); das Wasser ablassen aus (tank); abgießen (vegetables); austrinken (glass) ● vi ~ **[away]** ablaufen

drain|age /'dreɪnɪdʒ/ n Kanalisation f; (of land) Dränage f. ~**ing board** n Abtropfbrett nt. ~**pipe** n Abflussrohr nt

drake /dreɪk/ n Enterich m

drama /'drɑːmə/ n Drama nt

dramatic /drə'mætɪk/ adj, **-ally** adv dramatisch

dramat|ist /'dræmətɪst/ n Dramatiker m. ~**ize** vt für die Bühne bearbeiten; (fig) dramatisieren

drank /dræŋk/ see **drink**

drape /dreɪp/ n (Amer) Vorhang m ● vt drapieren

drastic /'dræstɪk/ adj, **-ally** adv drastisch

draught /drɑːft/ n [Luft]zug m; ~**s** sg (game) Damespiel nt; **there is a** ~ es zieht

draught beer n Bier nt vom Fass

draughty /'drɑːftɪ/ adj zugig

draw /drɔː/ n Attraktion f; (Sport) Unentschieden nt; (in lottery) Ziehung f ● v (pt **drew**, pp **drawn**) ● vt ziehen; (attract) anziehen; zeichnen (picture); abheben (money); ~ **the curtains** die Vorhänge zuziehen/ (back) aufziehen ● vi (Sport) unentschieden spielen. ~ **back** vt zurückziehen ● vi (recoil) zurückweichen. ~ **in** vt einziehen ● vi einfahren. ~ **out** vt herausziehen; abheben (money) ● vi ausfahren. ~ **up** vt aufsetzen (document); herrücken (chair) ● vi [an]halten

draw: ~**back** n Nachteil m. ~**bridge** n Zugbrücke f

drawer /drɔː(r)/ n Schublade f

drawing /'drɔːɪŋ/ n Zeichnung f

drawing: ~**board** n Reißbrett nt. ~**-pin** n Reißzwecke f. ~**-room** n Wohnzimmer nt

drawl /drɔːl/ n schleppende Aussprache f

drawn /drɔːn/ see **draw**

dread /dred/ n Furcht f (of vor + dat) ● vt fürchten. ~**ful** adj, **-fully** adv fürchterlich

dream /driːm/ n Traum m ● vt/i (pt/ pp **dreamt** or **dreamed**) träumen (about/of von)

dreary /'drɪərɪ/ adj trüb[e]; (boring) langweilig

dregs /dregz/ npl Bodensatz m

drench /drentʃ/ vt durchnässen

dress /dres/ n Kleid nt; (clothing) Kleidung f ● vt anziehen; (Med) verbinden; ~ **oneself, get** ~ed sich anziehen ● vi sich anziehen. ~ **up** vi sich schön anziehen; (in disguise) sich verkleiden (**as** als)

dress: ~ **circle** n (Theat) erster Rang m. ~**er** n (furniture) Anrichte f; (Amer: dressing-table) Frisiertisch m

dressing n (Culin) Soße f; (Med) Verband m

dressing: ~-**gown** n Morgenmantel m. ~-**room** n Ankleidezimmer nt; (Theat) [Künstler]garderobe f. ~-**table** n Frisiertisch m

dress: ~**maker** n Schneiderin f. ~ **rehearsal** n Generalprobe f

drew /druː/ see **draw**

dried /draɪd/ adj getrocknet; ~ **fruit** Dörrobst nt

drier /'draɪə(r)/ n Trockner m

drift /drɪft/ n Abtrift f; (of snow) Schneewehe f; (meaning) Sinn m ● vi treiben; (off course) abtreiben; (snow:) Wehen bilden; (fig) (person:) sich treiben lassen

drill /drɪl/ n Bohrer m; (Mil) Drill m ● vt/i bohren (**for** nach); (Mil) drillen

drily /'draɪlɪ/ adv trocken

drink /drɪŋk/ n Getränk nt; (alcoholic) Drink m; (alcohol) Alkohol m ● vt/i (pt **drank**, pp **drunk**) trinken. ~ **up** vt/i austrinken

drink|able /'drɪŋkəbl/ adj trinkbar. ~**er** n Trinker m

'drinking-water n Trinkwasser nt

drip /drɪp/ n Tropfen nt; (drop) Tropfen m; (Med) Tropf m; (⊞: person) Niete f ● vi (pt/pp **dripped**) tropfen

drive /draɪv/ n [Auto]fahrt f; (entrance) Einfahrt f; (energy) Elan m; (Psychology) Trieb m; (Pol) Aktion f; (Sport) Treibschlag m; (Techn) Antrieb m ● v (pt **drove**, pp **driven**) ● vt treiben; fahren (car); (Sport: hit) schlagen; (Techn) antreiben; ~ **s.o. mad** ⊞ jdn verrückt machen; **what are you driving at?** ⊞ worauf willst du hinaus? ● vi fahren. ~ **away** vt vertreiben ● vi abfahren. ~ **off** vt ver-

treiben ● vi abfahren. ~ **on** vi weiterfahren. ~ **up** vi vorfahren

drivel /'drɪvl/ n ⊞ Quatsch m

driven /'drɪvn/ see **drive**

driver /'draɪvə(r)/ n Fahrer(in) m(f); (of train) Lokführer m

driving: ~ **lesson** n Fahrstunde f. ~ **licence** n Führerschein m. ~ **school** n Fahrschule f. ~ **test** Fahrprüfung f

drizzle /'drɪzl/ n Nieselregen m ● vi nieseln

drone /drəʊn/ n (sound) Brummen m

droop /druːp/ vi herabhängen

drop /drɒp/ n Tropfen m; (fall) Fall m; (in price, temperature) Rückgang m ● v (pt/pp **dropped**) ● vt fallen lassen; abwerfen (bomb); (omit) auslassen; (give up) aufgeben ● vi fallen; (fall lower) sinken; (wind:) nachlassen. ~ **in** vi vorbeikommen. ~ **off** vt absetzen (person) ● vi abfallen; (fall asleep) einschlafen. ~ **out** vi herausfallen; (give up) aufgeben

drought /draʊt/ n Dürre f

drove /drəʊv/ see **drive**

drown /draʊn/ vi ertrinken ● vt ertränken; übertönen (noise); **be** ~**ed** ertrinken

drowsy /'draʊzɪ/ adj schläfrig

drudgery /'drʌdʒərɪ/ n Plackerei f

drug /drʌɡ/ n Droge f ● vt (pt/pp **drugged**) betäuben

drug: ~ **addict** n Drogenabhängige(r) m/f. ~**store** n (Amer) Drogerie f; (dispensing) Apotheke f

drum /drʌm/ n Trommel f; (for oil) Tonne f ● v (pt/pp **drummed**) ● vi trommeln ● vt ~**sth into s.o.** ⊞ jdm etw einbläuen. ~**mer** n Trommler m; (in pop-group) Schlagzeuger m. ~**stick** n Trommelschlegel m; (Culin) Keule f

drunk /drʌŋk/ see **drink** ● adj betrunken; **get** ~ sich betrinken ● n Betrunkene(r) m

drunk|ard /'drʌŋkəd/ n Trinker m. ~**en** adj betrunken

dry /draɪ/ adj (**drier, driest**) trocken

● *vt/i* trocknen. ~ **up** *vt/i* austrocknen

dry: ~-'**clean** *vt* chemisch reinigen. ~-'**cleaner's** *n* (*shop*) chemische Reinigung *f*. ~**ness** *n* Trockenheit *f*

dual /'dju:əl/ *adj* doppelt

dual 'carriageway *n* ≈ Schnellstraße *f*

dubious /'dju:bɪəs/ *adj* zweifelhaft

duchess /'dʌtʃɪs/ *n* Herzogin *f*

duck /dʌk/ *n* Ente *f* ● *vt* (*in water*) untertauchen ● *vi* sich ducken

duct /dʌkt/ *n* Rohr *nt*; (*Anat*) Gang *m*

dud /dʌd/ *adj* 🔲 nutzlos; (*coin*) falsch; (*cheque*) ungedeckt; (*forged*) gefälscht

due /dju:/ *adj* angemessen; **be** ~ fällig sein; (*baby:*) erwartet werden; (*train:*) planmäßig ankommen; ~ **to** (*owing to*) wegen (+ *gen*); **be** ~ **to** zurückzuführen sein auf (+ *acc*) ● *adv* ~ **west** genau westlich

duel /'dju:əl/ *n* Duell *nt*

duet /dju:'et/ *n* Duo *nt*; (*vocal*) Duett *nt*

dug /dʌg/ *see* **dig**

duke /dju:k/ *n* Herzog *m*

dull /dʌl/ *adj* (-er, -est) (*overcast, not bright*) trüb[e]; (*not shiny*) matt; (*sound*) dumpf; (*boring*) langweilig; (*stupid*) schwerfällig

duly /'dju:lɪ/ *adv* ordnungsgemäß

dumb /dʌm/ *adj* (-er, -est) stumm. ~ **down** *vt/i* verflachen

dummy /'dʌmɪ/ *n* (*tailor's*) [Schneider]puppe *f*; (*for baby*) Schnuller *m*; (*Comm*) Attrappe *f*

dump /dʌmp/ *n* Abfallhaufen *m*; (*for refuse*) Müllhalde *f*, Deponie *f*; (🔲: *town*) Kaff *nt*; **be down in the** ~**s** 🔲 deprimiert sein ● *vt* abladen

dumpling /'dʌmplɪŋ/ *n* Kloß *m*

dunce /dʌns/ *n* Dummkopf *m*

dune /dju:n/ *n* Düne *f*

dung /dʌŋ/ *n* Mist *m*

dungarees /dʌŋgə'ri:z/ *npl* Latzhose *f*

dungeon /'dʌndʒən/ *n* Verlies *nt*

dunk /dʌŋk/ *vt* eintunken

duo /'dju:əʊ/ *n* Paar *nt*; (*Mus*) Duo *nt*

dupe /dju:p/ *n* Betrogene(r) *m/f* ● *vt* betrügen

duplicate[1] /'dju:plɪkət/ *n* Doppel *nt*; **in** ~ in doppelter Ausfertigung *f*

duplicat|e[2] /'dju:plɪkeɪt/ *vt* kopieren; (*do twice*) zweimal machen

durable /'djʊərəbl/ *adj* haltbar

duration /djʊə'reɪʃn/ *n* Dauer *f*

during /'djʊərɪŋ/ *prep* während (+ *gen*)

dusk /dʌsk/ *n* [Abend]dämmerung *f*

dust /dʌst/ *n* Staub *m* ● *vt* abstauben; (*sprinkle*) bestäuben (**with** mit) ● *vi* Staub wischen

dust: ~**bin** *n* Mülltonne *f*. ~-**cart** *n* Müllwagen *m*. ~**er** *n* Staubtuch *nt*. ~-**jacket** *n* Schutzumschlag *m*. ~**man** *n* Müllmann *m*. ~**pan** *n* Kehrschaufel *f*

dusty /'dʌstɪ/ *adj* staubig

Dutch /dʌtʃ/ *adj* holländisch ● *n* (*Lang*) Holländisch *nt*; **the** ~ *pl* die Holländer. ~**man** *n* Holländer *m*

dutiful /'dju:tɪfl/ *adj* pflichtbewusst

duty /'dju:tɪ/ *n* Pflicht *f*; (*task*) Aufgabe *f*; (*tax*) Zoll *m*; **be on** ~ Dienst haben. ~-**free** *adj* zollfrei

duvet /'du:veɪ/ *n* Steppdecke *f*

DVD *abbr* (**digital versatile disc**) DVD *f*

dwarf /dwɔ:f/ *n* (*pl* -**s** or **dwarves**) Zwerg *m*

dwell /dwel/ *vi* (*pt/pp* **dwelt**); ~ **on** (*fig*) verweilen bei. ~**ing** *n* Wohnung *f*

dwindle /'dwɪndl/ *vi* abnehmen, schwinden

dye /daɪ/ *n* Farbstoff *m* ● *vt* (*pres p* **dyeing**) färben

dying /'daɪɪŋ/ *see* **die**[2]

dynamic /daɪ'næmɪk/ *adj* dynamisch

dynamite /'daɪnəmaɪt/ *n* Dynamit *nt*

dyslex|ia /dɪs'leksɪə/ *n* Legasthenie *f*. ~**ic** *adj* legasthenisch; **be** ~**ic** Legastheniker sein

d

Ee

each /iːtʃ/ *adj & pron* jede(r,s); (*per*) je; ~ **other** einander; **£1** ~ £1 pro Person; (*for thing*) pro Stück

eager /ˈiːɡə(r)/ *adj* eifrig; **be** ~ **to do sth** etw gerne machen wollen. ~**ness** *n* Eifer *m*

eagle /ˈiːɡl/ *n* Adler *m*

ear *n* Ohr *nt*. ~**ache** *n* Ohrenschmerzen *pl*. ~**drum** *n* Trommelfell *nt*

earl /ɜːl/ *n* Graf *m*

early /ˈɜːlɪ/ *adj & adv* (-ier, -iest) früh; (*reply*) baldig; **be** ~ früh dran sein

earn /ɜːn/ *vt* verdienen

earnest /ˈɜːnɪst/ *adj* ernsthaft ● *n* **in** ~ im Ernst

earnings /ˈɜːnɪŋz/ *npl* Verdienst *m*

ear: ~**phones** *npl* Kopfhörer *pl*. ~**-ring** *n* Ohrring *m*; (*clip-on*) Ohrklips *m*. ~**shot** *n* **within/out of** ~**shot** in/außer Hörweite

earth /ɜːθ/ *n* Erde *f*; (*of fox*) Bau *m* ● *vt* (*Electr*) erden

earthenware /ˈɜːθn-/ *n* Tonwaren *pl*

earthly /ˈɜːθlɪ/ *adj* irdisch; **be no** ~ **use** 🄸 völlig nutzlos sein

'earthquake *n* Erdbeben *nt*

earthy /ˈɜːθɪ/ *adj* erdig; (*coarse*) derb

ease /iːz/ *n* Leichtigkeit *f* ● *vt* erleichtern; lindern (*pain*) ● *vi* (*pain:*) nachlassen; (*situation:*) sich entspannen

easily /ˈiːzɪlɪ/ *adv* leicht, mit Leichtigkeit

east /iːst/ *n* Osten *m*; **to the** ~ **of** östlich von ● *adj* Ost-, ost- ● *adv* nach Osten

Easter /ˈiːstə(r)/ *n* Ostern *nt* ● *attrib* Oster-. ~ **egg** *n* Osterei *nt*

east|erly /ˈiːstəlɪ/ *adj* östlich. ~**ern** *adj* östlich. ~**ward[s]** *adv* nach Osten

easy /ˈiːzɪ/ *adj* leicht; **take it** ~ 🄸 sich schonen; **go** ~ **with** 🄸 sparsam umgehen mit

easy: ~ **chair** *n* Sessel *m*. ~**'going** *adj* gelassen

eat /iːt/ *vt/i* (*pt* ate, *pp* eaten) essen; (*animal:*) fressen. ~ **up** *vt* aufessen

eatable /ˈiːtəbl/ *adj* genießbar

eau-de-Cologne /əʊdəkəˈləʊn/ *n* Kölnisch Wasser *nt*

eaves /iːvz/ *npl* Dachüberhang *m*. ~**drop** *vi* (*pt/pp* ~ dropped) [heimlich] lauschen

ebb /eb/ *n* (*tide*) Ebbe *f* ● *vi* zurückgehen; (*fig*) verebben

ebony /ˈebənɪ/ *n* Ebenholz *nt*

EC *abbr* (**European Community**) EG *f*

eccentric /ɪkˈsentrɪk/ *adj* exzentrisch ● *n* Exzentriker *m*

ecclesiastical /ɪkliːzɪˈæstɪkl/ *adj* kirchlich

echo /ˈekəʊ/ *n* (*pl* -es) Echo *nt*, Widerhall *m* ● *v* (*pt/pp* echoed, *pres p* echoing) ● *vi* widerhallen (**with** von)

eclipse /ɪˈklɪps/ *n* (*Astronomy*) Finsternis *f*

ecolog|ical /iːkəˈlɒdʒɪkl/ *adj* ökologisch. ~**y** *n* Ökologie *f*

e-commerce /ˈiːkɒmɜːs/ *n* E-Commerce *m*

economic /iːkəˈnɒmɪk/ *adj* wirtschaftlich. ~**al** *adj* sparsam. ~**ally** *adv* wirtschaftlich; (*thriftily*) sparsam. ~ **refugee** *n* Wirtschaftsflüchtling *m*. ~**s** *n* Volkswirtschaft *f*

economist /ɪˈkɒnəmɪst/ *n* Volkswirt *m*; (*Univ*) Wirtschaftswissenschaftler *m*

economize /ɪˈkɒnəmaɪz/ *vi* sparen (**on** an + *dat*)

economy /ɪˈkɒnəmɪ/ *n* Wirtschaft *f*; (*thrift*) Sparsamkeit *f*

ecstasy /ˈekstəsɪ/ *n* Ekstase *f*

ecstatic /ɪkˈstætɪk/ *adj*, -**ally** *adv* ekstatisch

eczema /ˈeksɪmə/ *n* Ekzem *nt*

eddy /ˈedɪ/ *n* Wirbel *m*

edge /edʒ/ *n* Rand *m*; (*of table, lawn*) Kante *f*; (*of knife*) Schneide *f*; **on** ~ 🄸 nervös ● *vt* einfassen. ~ **forward** *vi* sich nach vorn schieben

edgy /ˈedʒɪ/ *adj* 🄸 nervös

edible /ˈedɪbl/ *adj* essbar

edifice /'edɪfɪs/ n [großes] Gebäude nt

Edinburgh Festival Großbritanniens berühmtestes Kunst- und Theaterfestival findet seit 1947 jedes Jahr im August in der schottischen Hauptstadt statt. Die Festspiele ziehen Besucher aus aller Welt an. Ergänzt wird das Programm durch das gleichzeitig stattfindende *Edinburgh Festival Fringe*, das ein Forum für unbekannte Künstler, experimentelle Kunst und alternative Veranstaltungen ist.

edit /'edɪt/ vt (pt/pp **edited**) redigieren; herausgeben (*anthology, dictionary*); schneiden (*film, tape*)

edition /ɪ'dɪʃn/ n Ausgabe f; (*impression*) Auflage f

editor /'edɪtə(r)/ n Redakteur m; (*of anthology, dictionary*) Herausgeber m; (*of newspaper*) Chefredakteur m; (*of film*) Cutter(in) m(f)

editorial /edɪ'tɔːrɪəl/ adj redaktionell, Redaktions- ● n (*in newspaper*) Leitartikel m

educate /'edjʊkeɪt/ vt erziehen. ~**d** adj gebildet

education /edjʊ'keɪʃn/ n Erziehung f; (*culture*) Bildung f. ~**al** adj pädagogisch; (*visit*) kulturell

eel /iːl/ n Aal m

eerie /'ɪərɪ/ adj unheimlich

effect /ɪ'fekt/ n Wirkung f, Effekt m; **take** ~ in Kraft treten

effective /ɪ'fektɪv/ adj wirksam, effektiv; (*striking*) wirkungsvoll, effektvoll; (*actual*) tatsächlich. ~**ness** n Wirksamkeit f

effeminate /ɪ'femɪnət/ adj unmännlich

effervescent /efə'vesnt/ adj sprudelnd

efficiency /ɪ'fɪʃənsɪ/ n Tüchtigkeit f; (*of machine, organization*) Leistungsfähigkeit f

efficient /ɪ'fɪʃənt/ adj tüchtig; (*machine, organization*) leistungsfähig; (*method*) rationell. ~**ly** adv gut; (*function*) rationell

effort /'efət/ n Anstrengung f; **make an** ~ sich (dat) Mühe geben. ~**less** adj mühelos

e.g. abbr (**exempli gratia**) z.B.

egalitarian /ɪgælɪ'teərɪən/ adj egalitär

egg n Ei nt. ~**-cup** n Eierbecher m. ~**shell** n Eierschale f

ego /'iːgəʊ/ n Ich nt. ~**ism** n Egoismus m. ~**ist** n Egoist m. ~**tism** n Ichbezogenheit f. ~**tist** n ichbezogener Mensch m

Egypt /'iːdʒɪpt/ n Ägypten nt. ~**ian** adj ägyptisch ● n Ägypter(in) m(f)

eiderdown /'aɪdə-/ n (*quilt*) Daunendecke f

eigh|t /eɪt/ adj acht ● n Acht f; (*boat*) Achter m. ~'**teen** adj achtzehn. ~'**teenth** adj achtzehnte(r,s)

eighth /eɪtθ/ adj achte(r,s) ● n Achtel nt

eightieth /'eɪtɪɪθ/ adj achtzigste(r,s)

eighty /'eɪtɪ/ adj achtzig

either /'aɪðə(r)/ adj & pron ~ [**of them**] einer von [den] beiden; (*both*) beide; **on** ~ **side** auf beiden Seiten ● adv **I don't** ~ ich auch nicht ● conj ~ ... **or** entweder ... oder

eject /ɪ'dʒekt/ vt hinauswerfen

elaborate /ɪ'læbərət/ adj kunstvoll; (*fig*) kompliziert

elapse /ɪ'læps/ vi vergehen

elastic /ɪ'læstɪk/ adj elastisch. ~'**band** n Gummiband nt

elasticity /ɪlæs'tɪsətɪ/ n Elastizität f

elated /ɪ'leɪtɪd/ adj überglücklich

elbow /'elbəʊ/ n Ellbogen m

elder[1] /'eldə(r)/ n Holunder m

eld|er[2] adj ältere(r,s) ● n **the** ~**er** der/die Ältere. ~**erly** adj alt. ~**est** adj älteste(r,s) ● n **the** ~**est** der/die Älteste

elect /ɪ'lekt/ vt wählen. ~**ion** n Wahl f

elector /ɪ'lektə(r)/ n Wähler(in) m(f). ~**ate** n Wählerschaft f

electric /ɪ'lektrɪk/ adj, -**ally** adv elektrisch

electrical /ɪ'lektrɪkl/ adj elektrisch; ~ **engineering** Elektrotechnik f

e

electric: ~ **'blanket** n Heizdecke f.
~ **'fire** n elektrischer Heizofen m
electrician /ɪlek'trɪʃn/ n Elektri-
ker m
electricity /ɪlek'trɪsəti/ n Elektrizität f; (supply) Strom m
electrify /ɪ'lektrɪfaɪ/ vt (pt/pp -ied)
elektrifizieren. ~**ing** adj (fig) elektri-
sierend
electrocute /ɪ'lektrəkju:t/ vt durch
einen elektrischen Schlag töten
electrode /ɪ'lektrəʊd/ n Elektrode f
electronic /ɪlek'trɒnɪk/ adj elektro-
nisch. ~**s** n Elektronik f
elegance /'elɪgəns/ n Eleganz f
elegant /'elɪgənt/ adj elegant
elegy /'elɪdʒɪ/ n Elegie f
element /'elɪmənt/ n Element nt.
~**ary** adj elementar
elephant /'elɪfənt/ n Elefant m
elevat|e /'elɪveɪt/ vt heben; (fig) er-
heben. ~**ion** n Erhebung f
elevator /'elɪveɪtə(r)/ n (Amer) Aufzug m, Fahrstuhl m
eleven /ɪ'levn/ adj elf ● n Elf f. ~**th**
adj elfte(r,s); **at the** ~**th hour** 🔲 in
letzter Minute
eligible /'elɪdʒəbl/ adj berechtigt
eliminate /ɪ'lɪmɪneɪt/ vt ausschalten
élite /er'li:t/ n Elite f
elm /elm/ n Ulme f
elocution /elə'kju:ʃn/ n Sprecher-
ziehung f
elope /ɪ'əʊp/ vi durchbrennen 🔲
eloquen|ce /'eləkwəns/ n Bered-
samkeit f. ~**t** adj, ~**ly** adv beredt
else /els/ adv sonst; **nothing** ~ sonst
nichts; **or** ~ oder; (otherwise) sonst;
someone/somewhere ~ jemand/
irgendwo anders; **anyone** ~ jeder
andere; (as question) sonst noch jemand? **anything** ~ alles andere; (as
question) sonst noch etwas?
~**where** adv woanders
elucidate /ɪ'lu:sɪdeɪt/ vt erläutern
elusive /ɪ'lu:sɪv/ adj **be** ~ schwer zu
fassen sein
emaciated /ɪ'meɪsɪeɪtɪd/ adj abge-
zehrt

e-mail /'i:meɪl/ n E-Mail f ● vt per
E-Mail übermitteln (Ergebnisse, Datei
usw.); ~ **s.o.** jdm eine E-Mail schicken. ~ **address** n E-Mail-Adresse f.
~ **message** n E-Mail f
emancipat|ed /ɪ'mænsɪpeɪtɪd/ adj
emanzipiert. ~**ion** n Emanzipation f;
(of slaves) Freilassung f
embankment /ɪm'bæŋkmənt/ n
Böschung f; (of railway) Bahn-
damm m
embark /ɪm'bɑ:k/ vi sich einschiffen.
~**ation** n Einschiffung f
embarrass /ɪm'bærəs/ vt in Verle-
genheit bringen. ~**ed** adj verlegen.
~**ing** adj peinlich. ~**ment** n Verle-
genheit f
embassy /'embəsɪ/ n Botschaft f
embellish /ɪm'belɪʃ/ vt verzieren;
(fig) ausschmücken
embezzle /ɪm'bezl/ vt unterschla-
gen. ~**ment** n Unterschlagung f
emblem /'embləm/ n Emblem nt
embodiment /ɪm'bɒdɪmənt/ n Ver-
körperung f
embody /ɪm'bɒdɪ/ vt (pt/pp -ied)
verkörpern; (include) enthalten
embrace /ɪm'breɪs/ n Umarmung f
● vt umarmen; (fig) umfassen ● vi
sich umarmen
embroider /ɪm'brɔɪdə(r)/ vt besti-
cken; sticken (design) ● vi sticken.
~**y** n Stickerei f
embryo /'embrɪəʊ/ n Embryo m
emerald /'emərəld/ n Smaragd m
emer|ge /ɪ'mɜ:dʒ/ vi auftauchen
(**from** aus); (become known) sich herausstellen; (come into being) entstehen. ~**gence** n Auftauchen nt; Ent-
stehung f
emergency /ɪ'mɜ:dʒənsɪ/ n Notfall
m. ~ **exit** n Notausgang m
emigrant /'emɪgrənt/ n Auswande-
rer m
emigrat|e /'emɪgreɪt/ vi auswan-
dern. ~**ion** n Auswanderung f
eminent /'emɪnənt/ adj eminent
emission /ɪ'mɪʃn/ n Ausstrahlung f;
(of pollutant) Emission f
emit /ɪ'mɪt/ vt (pt/pp **emitted**) aus-

strahlen (*light, heat*); ausstoßen
(*smoke, fumes, cry*)

emotion /ɪˈməʊʃn/ n Gefühl nt. ∼**al**
adj emotional; **become** ∼**al** sich erregen

empathy /ˈempəθɪ/ n Einfühlungs-
vermögen nt

emperor /ˈempərə(r)/ n Kaiser m

emphasis /ˈemfəsɪs/ n Betonung f

emphasize /ˈemfəsaɪz/ vt betonen

emphatic /ɪmˈfætɪk/ adj, **-ally** adv
nachdrücklich

empire /ˈempaɪə(r)/ n Reich nt

employ /ɪmˈplɔɪ/ vt beschäftigen;
(*appoint*) einstellen; (*fig*) anwenden.
∼**ee** n Beschäftigte(r) m/f; (*in contrast to employer*) Arbeitnehmer m.
∼**er** n Arbeitgeber m. ∼**ment** n Beschäftigung f; (*work*) Arbeit f.
∼**ment agency** n Stellenvermitt-
lung f

empress /ˈemprɪs/ n Kaiserin f

emptiness /ˈemptɪnɪs/ n Leere f

empty /ˈemptɪ/ adj leer ● vt leeren;
ausleeren (*container*) ● vi sich leeren

emulsion /ɪˈmʌlʃn/ n Emulsion f

enable /ɪˈneɪbl/ vt ∼ s.o. to es jdm
möglich machen, zu

enact /ɪˈnækt/ vt (*Theat*) aufführen

enamel /ɪˈnæml/ n Email nt; (*on
teeth*) Zahnschmelz m; (*paint*)
Lack m

enchant /ɪnˈtʃɑːnt/ vt bezaubern.
∼**ing** adj bezaubernd. ∼**ment** n
Zauber m

encircle /ɪnˈsɜːkl/ vt einkreisen

enclos|e /ɪnˈkləʊz/ vt einschließen;
(*in letter*) beilegen (**with** dat). ∼**ure**
n (*at zoo*) Gehege nt; (*in letter*) Anlage f

encore /ˈɒŋkɔː(r)/ n Zugabe f ● int
bravo!

encounter /ɪnˈkaʊntə(r)/ n Begegnung f ● vt begegnen (+ dat); (*fig*)
stoßen auf (+ acc)

encourag|e /ɪnˈkʌrɪdʒ/ vt ermuti-
gen; (*promote*) fördern. ∼**ement** n
Ermutigung f. ∼**ing** adj ermutigend

encroach /ɪnˈkrəʊtʃ/ vi ∼ on eindringen in (+ acc) (*land*)

encyclopaed|ia /ɪnsaɪkləˈpiːdɪə/ n
Enzyklopädie f, Lexikon nt. ∼**ic** adj
enzyklopädisch

end /end/ n Ende nt; (*purpose*) Zweck
m; **in the** ∼ schließlich; **at the** ∼ **of
May** Ende Mai; **on** ∼ hochkant; **for
days on** ∼ tagelang; **make** ∼**s
meet** Ⓘ [gerade] auskommen; **no** ∼
of Ⓘ unheimlich viel(e) ● vt beenden
● vi enden; ∼ **up in** (Ⓘ: *arrive at*)
landen in (+ dat)

endanger /ɪnˈdeɪndʒə(r)/ vt gefähr-
den

endeavour /ɪnˈdevə(r)/ n Bemü-
hung f ● vi sich bemühen (**to** zu)

ending /ˈendɪŋ/ n Schluss m, Ende
nt; (*Gram*) Endung f

endless /ˈendlɪs/ adj endlos

endorse /enˈdɔːs/ vt (*Comm*) indos-
sieren; (*confirm*) bestätigen. ∼**ment**
n (*Comm*) Indossament nt; (*fig*) Bestätigung f; (*on driving licence*) Straf-
vermerk m

endow /ɪnˈdaʊ/ vt stiften; **be** ∼**ed
with** (*fig*) haben

endurance /ɪnˈdjʊərəns/ n Durch-
haltevermögen nt; **beyond** ∼ unerträglich

endure /ɪnˈdjʊə(r)/ vt ertragen

enemy /ˈenəmɪ/ n Feind m ● attrib
feindlich

energetic /enəˈdʒetɪk/ adj tatkräf-
tig; **be** ∼ voller Energie sein

energy /ˈenədʒɪ/ n Energie f

enforce /ɪnˈfɔːs/ vt durchsetzen. ∼**d**
adj unfreiwillig

engage /ɪnˈgeɪdʒ/ vt einstellen
(*staff*); (*Theat*) engagieren; (*Auto*)
einlegen (*gear*) ● vi sich beteiligen
(**in** an + dat); (*Techn*) ineinandergrei-
fen. ∼**d** adj besetzt; (*person*) beschäftigt; (*to be married*) verlobt; **get**
∼**d** sich verloben (**to** mit). ∼**ment** n
Verlobung f; (*appointment*) Verabredung f; (*Mil*) Gefecht nt

engaging /ɪnˈgeɪdʒɪŋ/ adj einneh-
mend

engine /ˈendʒɪn/ n Motor m; (*Naut*)
Maschine f; (*Rail*) Lokomotive f; (*of
jet plane*) Triebwerk nt. ∼**-driver** n
Lokomotivführer m

engineer /endʒɪ'nɪə(r)/ n Ingenieur m; (service, installation) Techniker m; (Naut) Maschinist m; (Amer) Lokomotivführer m. ~ing n [mechanical] ~ing Maschinenbau m

England /'ɪŋɡlənd/ n England nt

English /'ɪŋɡlɪʃ/ adj englisch; the ~ Channel der Ärmelkanal ● n (Lang) Englisch nt; in ~ auf Englisch; into ~ ins Englische; the ~ pl die Engländer. ~man n Engländer m. ~woman n Engländerin f

engrav|e /ɪn'ɡreɪv/ vt eingravieren. ~ing n Stich m

enhance /ɪn'hɑːns/ vt verschönern; (fig) steigern

enigma /ɪ'nɪɡmə/ n Rätsel nt. ~tic adj rätselhaft

enjoy /ɪn'dʒɔɪ/ vt genießen; ~ oneself sich amüsieren; ~ cooking gern kochen; I ~ed it es hat mir gut gefallen/ (food:) geschmeckt. ~able adj angenehm, nett. ~ment n Vergnügen nt

enlarge /ɪn'lɑːdʒ/ vt vergrößern. ~ment n Vergrößerung f

enlist /ɪn'lɪst/ vt (Mil) einziehen; ~ s.o.'s help jdn zur Hilfe heranziehen ● vi (Mil) sich melden

enliven /ɪn'laɪvn/ vt beleben

enmity /'enmɪtɪ/ n Feindschaft f

enormity /ɪ'nɔːmətɪ/ n Ungeheuerlichkeit f

enormous /ɪ'nɔːməs/ adj riesig

enough /ɪ'nʌf/ a, adv & n genug; be ~ reichen; **funnily** ~ komischerweise

enquir|e /ɪn'kwaɪə(r)/ vi sich erkundigen (**about** nach). ~y n Erkundigung f; (investigation) Untersuchung f

enrage /ɪn'reɪdʒ/ vt wütend machen

enrich /ɪn'rɪtʃ/ vt bereichern

enrol /ɪn'rəʊl/ v (pt/pp -rolled) ● vt einschreiben ● vi sich einschreiben

ensemble /ɒn'sɒmbl/ n (clothing & Mus) Ensemble nt

enslave /ɪn'sleɪv/ vt versklaven

ensue /ɪn'sjuː/ vi folgen; (result) sich ergeben (**from** aus)

ensure /ɪn'ʃʊə(r)/ vt sicherstellen; ~ that dafür sorgen, dass

entail /ɪn'teɪl/ vt erforderlich machen; **what does it** ~? was ist damit verbunden?

entangle /ɪn'tæŋɡl/ vt get ~d sich verfangen (**in** in + dat)

enter /'entə(r)/ vt eintreten/ (vehicle:) einfahren in (+ acc); einreisen in (+ acc) (country); (register) eintragen; sich anmelden zu (competition) ● vi eintreten; (vehicle:) einfahren; (Theat) auftreten; (register as competitor) sich anmelden; (take part) sich beteiligen (**in** an + dat)

enterpris|e /'entəpraɪz/ n Unternehmen nt; (quality) Unternehmungsgeist m. ~ing adj unternehmend

entertain /entə'teɪn/ vt unterhalten; (invite) einladen; (to meal) bewirten (guest) ● vi unterhalten; (have guests) Gäste haben. ~er n Unterhalter m. ~ment n Unterhaltung f

enthral /ɪn'θrɔːl/ vt (pt/pp enthralled) be ~led gefesselt sein (**by** von)

enthuse /ɪn'θjuːz/ vi ~ over schwärmen von

enthusias|m /ɪn'θjuːzɪæzm/ n Begeisterung f. ~t n Enthusiast m. ~tic adj, -ally adv begeistert

entice /ɪn'taɪs/ vt locken. ~ment n Anreiz m

entire /ɪn'taɪə(r)/ adj ganz. ~ly adv ganz, völlig. ~ty n in its ~ty in seiner Gesamtheit

entitle /ɪn'taɪtl/ vt berechtigen; ~d ... mit dem Titel ...; be ~d to sth das Recht auf etw (acc) haben. ~ment n Berechtigung f; (claim) Anspruch m (**to auf** + acc)

entrance /'entrəns/ n Eintritt m; (Theat) Auftritt m; (way in) Eingang m; (for vehicle) Einfahrt f. ~ fee n Eintrittsgebühr f

entrant /'entrənt/ n Teilnehmer(in) m(f)

entreat /ɪn'triːt/ vt anflehen (**for** um)

entrust /ɪn'trʌst/ vt ~ s.o. with sth, ~ sth to s.o. jdm etw anvertrauen

entry /'entrɪ/ n Eintritt m; (into country) Einreise f; (on list) Eintrag m; **no** ~ Zutritt/ (Auto) Einfahrt verboten

envelop /ɪn'veləp/ vt (pt/pp **enveloped**) einhüllen

envelope /'envələʊp/ n [Brief]umschlag m

enviable /'envɪəbl/ adj beneidenswert

envious /'envɪəs/ adj neidisch (of auf + acc)

environment /ɪn'vaɪərənmənt/ n Umwelt f

environmental /ɪnvaɪərən'mentl/ adj Umwelt-. ~**ist** n Umweltschützer m. ~**ly** adv ~**ly friendly** umweltfreundlich

envisage /ɪn'vɪzɪdʒ/ vt sich (dat) vorstellen

envoy /'envɔɪ/ n Gesandte(r) m

envy /'envɪ/ n Neid m ● vt (pt/pp -ied) ~ **s.o. sth** jdn um etw beneiden

epic /'epɪk/ adj episch ● n Epos nt

epidemic /epɪ'demɪk/ n Epidemie f

epilep|sy /'epɪlepsɪ/ n Epilepsie f. ~**tic** adj epileptisch ● n Epileptiker(in) m(f)

epilogue /'epɪlɒg/ n Epilog m

episode /'epɪsəʊd/ n Episode f; (instalment) Folge f

epitome /ɪ'pɪtəmɪ/ n Inbegriff m

epoch /'iːpɒk/ n Epoche f. ~**-making** adj epochemachend

equal /'iːkwl/ adj gleich (**to** dat); **be** ~ **to a task** einer Aufgabe gewachsen sein ● n Gleichgestellte(r) m/f ● vt (pt/pp **equalled**) gleichen (+ dat); (fig) gleichkommen (+ dat). ~**ity** n Gleichheit f

equalize /'iːkwəlaɪz/ vt/i ausgleichen

equally /'iːkwəlɪ/ adv gleich; (divide) gleichmäßig; (just as) genauso

equat|e /ɪ'kweɪt/ vt gleichsetzen (**with** mit). ~**ion** n (Math) Gleichung f

equator /ɪ'kweɪtə(r)/ n Äquator m

equestrian /ɪ'kwestrɪən/ adj Reit-

equilibrium /iːkwɪ'lɪbrɪəm/ n Gleichgewicht nt

equinox /'iːkwɪnɒks/ n Tagundnachtgleiche f

equip /ɪ'kwɪp/ vt (pt/pp **equipped**) ausrüsten; (furnish) ausstatten. ~**ment** n Ausrüstung f; Ausstattung f

equity /'ekwətɪ/ n Gerechtigkeit f

equivalent /ɪ'kwɪvələnt/ adj gleichwertig; (corresponding) entsprechend ● n Äquivalent nt; (value) Gegenwert m; (counterpart) Gegenstück nt

era /'ɪərə/ n Ära f, Zeitalter nt

eradicate /ɪ'rædɪkeɪt/ vt ausrotten

erase /ɪ'reɪz/ vt ausradieren; (from tape) löschen

erect /ɪ'rekt/ adj aufrecht ● vt errichten. ~**ion** n Errichtung f; (building) Bau m; (Physiology) Erektion f

ero|de /ɪ'rəʊd/ vt (water:) auswaschen; (acid:) angreifen. ~**sion** n Erosion f

erotic /ɪ'rɒtɪk/ adj erotisch

errand /'erənd/ n Botengang m

erratic /ɪ'rætɪk/ adj unregelmäßig; (person) unberechenbar

erroneous /ɪ'rəʊnɪəs/ adj falsch; (belief, assumption) irrig

error /'erə(r)/ n Irrtum m; (mistake) Fehler m; **in** ~ irrtümlicherweise

erupt /ɪ'rʌpt/ vi ausbrechen. ~**ion** n Ausbruch m

escalat|e /'eskəleɪt/ vt/i eskalieren. ~**or** n Rolltreppe f

escape /ɪ'skeɪp/ n Flucht f; (from prison) Ausbruch m; **have a narrow** ~ gerade noch davonkommen ● vi flüchten; (prisoner:) ausbrechen; entkommen (**from** aus; **from s.o.** jdm); (gas:) entweichen ● vt **the name** ~**s me** der Name entfällt mir

escapism /ɪ'skeɪpɪzm/ n Eskapismus m

escort[1] /'eskɔːt/ n (of person) Begleiter m; (Mil) Eskorte f

escort[2] /ɪ'skɔːt/ vt begleiten; (Mil) eskortieren

Eskimo /'eskɪməʊ/ n Eskimo m

esoteric /esə'terɪk/ adj esoterisch

especially /ɪ'speʃəlɪ/ adv besonders

espionage /'espɪənɑːʒ/ n Spionage f

essay /'eseɪ/ n Aufsatz m

essence /'esns/ n Wesen nt; (Chemistry, Culin) Essenz f

essential /ɪ'senʃl/ adj wesentlich; (indispensable) unentbehrlich ● n the ~s das Wesentliche; (items) das Nötigste. ~ly adv im Wesentlichen

establish /ɪ'stæblɪʃ/ vt gründen; (form) bilden; (prove) beweisen

estate /ɪ'steɪt/ n Gut nt; (possessions) Besitz m; (after death) Nachlass m; (housing) [Wohn]siedlung f. ~ agent n Immobilienmakler m. ~ car n Kombi[wagen] m

esteem /ɪ'stiːm/ n Achtung f ● vt hochschätzen

estimate¹ /'estɪmət/ n Schätzung f; (Comm) [Kosten]voranschlag m; at a rough ~ grob geschätzt

estimat|e² /'estɪmeɪt/ vt schätzen. ~ion n Einschätzung f

estuary /'estjʊərɪ/ n Mündung f

etc. /et'setərə/ abbr (et cetera) und so weiter, usw.

eternal /ɪ'tɜːnl/ adj ewig

eternity /ɪ'θɜːnətɪ/ n Ewigkeit f

ethical /'eθɪkl/ adj ethisch; (morally correct) moralisch einwandfrei. ~s n Ethik f

Ethiopia /iːθɪ'əʊpɪə/ n Äthiopien nt

ethnic /'eθnɪk/ adj ethnisch. ~ cleansing n ethnische Säuberung

etiquette /'etɪket/ n Etikette f

EU abbr (European Union) EU f

eulogy /'juːlədʒɪ/ n Lobrede f

euphemis|m /'juːfəmɪzm/ n Euphemismus m. ~tic adj, -ally adv verhüllend

euro /'jʊərəʊ/ n Euro m. E~cheque n Euroscheck m. E~land n Euroland nt

Europe /'jʊərəp/ n Europa nt

European /jʊərə'piːən/ adj europäisch; ~ Union Europäische Union f ● n Europäer(in) m(f)

eurosceptic /'jʊərəʊskeptɪk/ n Euroskeptiker(in) m(f)

evacuat|e /ɪ'vækjʊeɪt/ vt evakuieren; räumen (building, area). ~ion n Evakuierung f; Räumung f

evade /ɪ'veɪd/ vt sich entziehen (+ dat); hinterziehen (taxes)

evaluat|e /ɪvæljʊ'eɪt/ vt einschätzen ~ion n Beurteilung f, Einschätzung f

evange|lical /iːvæn'dʒelɪkl/ adj evangelisch. ~list n Evangelist m

evaporat|e /ɪ'væpəreɪt/ vi verdunsten. ~ion n Verdampfung f

evasion /ɪ'veɪʒn/ n Ausweichen nt; tax ~ Steuerhinterziehung f

evasive /ɪ'veɪsɪv/ adj ausweichend; be ~ ausweichen

even /'iːvn/ adj (level) eben; (same, equal) gleich; (regular) gleichmäßig; (number) gerade; get ~ with ⊞ es jdm heimzahlen ● adv sogar, selbst; ~ so trotzdem; not ~ nicht einmal ● vt ~ the score ausgleichen

evening /'iːvnɪŋ/ n Abend m; this ~ heute Abend; in the ~ abends, am Abend. ~ class n Abendkurs m

evenly /'iːvnlɪ/ adv gleichmäßig

event /ɪ'vent/ n Ereignis nt; (function) Veranstaltung f; (Sport) Wettbewerb m. ~ful adj ereignisreich

eventual /ɪ'ventjʊəl/ adj his ~ success der Erfolg, der ihm schließlich zuteil wurde. ~ly adv schließlich

ever /'evə(r)/ adv je[mals]; not ~ nie; for ~ für immer; hardly ~ fast nie; ~ since seitdem

'evergreen n immergrüner Strauch m/ (tree) Baum m

ever'lasting adj ewig

every /'evrɪ/ adj jede(r,s); ~ one jede(r,s) Einzelne; ~ other day jeden zweiten Tag

every: ~body pron jeder[mann]; alle pl. ~day adj alltäglich. ~ one pron jeder[mann]; alle pl. ~thing pron alles. ~where adv überall

evict /ɪ'vɪkt/ vt [aus der Wohnung] hinausweisen. ~ion n Ausweisung f

eviden|ce /'evɪdəns/ n Beweise pl; (Jur) Beweismaterial nt; (testimony) Aussage f; give ~ce aussagen. ~t adj offensichtlich

evil /'iːvl/ adj böse ● n Böse nt

evoke /ɪ'vəʊk/ vt heraufbeschwören

evolution /iːvə'luːʃn/ n Evolution f

evolve /ɪˈvɒlv/ vt entwickeln ● vi sich entwickeln

ewe /juː/ n Schaf nt

exact /ɪgˈzækt/ adj genau; **not ~ly** nicht gerade. **~ness** n Genauigkeit f

exaggerat|e /ɪgˈzædʒəreɪt/ vt/i übertreiben. **~ion** n Übertreibung f

exam /ɪgˈzæm/ n 🔲 Prüfung f

examination /ɪgzæmɪˈneɪʃn/ n Untersuchung f; (Sch) Prüfung f

examine /ɪgˈzæmɪn/ vt untersuchen; (Sch) prüfen

example /ɪgˈzɑːmpl/ n Beispiel nt (of für); **for ~** zum Beispiel; **make an ~ of** ein Exempel statuieren an (+ dat)

exasperat|e /ɪgˈzæspəreɪt/ vt zur Verzweiflung treiben. **~ion** n Verzweiflung f

excavat|e /ˈekskəveɪt/ vt ausschachten; ausgraben (site). **~ion** n Ausgrabung f

exceed /ɪkˈsiːd/ vt übersteigen. **~ingly** adv äußerst

excel /ɪkˈsel/ v (pt/pp excelled) vi sich auszeichnen ● vt **~ oneself** sich selbst übertreffen

excellen|ce /ˈeksələns/ n Vorzüglichkeit f. **~t** adj ausgezeichnet, vorzüglich

except /ɪkˈsept/ prep außer (+ dat); **~ for** abgesehen von ● vt ausnehmen

exception /ɪkˈsepʃn/ n Ausnahme f. **~al** adj außergewöhnlich

excerpt /ˈeksɜːpt/ n Auszug m

excess /ɪkˈses/ n Übermaß nt (of an + dat); (surplus) Überschuss m; **~es** pl Exzesse pl

excessive /ɪkˈsesɪv/ adj übermäßig

exchange /ɪksˈtʃeɪndʒ/ n Austausch m; (Teleph) Fernsprechamt nt; (Comm) [Geld]wechsel m; **in ~** dafür ● vt austauschen (**for** gegen); tauschen (places). **~ rate** n Wechselkurs m

excitable /ɪkˈsaɪtəbl/ adj [leicht] erregbar

excit|e /ɪkˈsaɪt/ vt aufregen; (cause) erregen. **~ed** adj aufgeregt; **get**

~ed sich aufregen. **~ement** n Aufregung f; Erregung f. **~ing** adj aufregend; (story) spannend

exclaim /ɪkˈskleɪm/ vt/i ausrufen

exclamation /ekskləˈmeɪʃn/ n Ausruf m. **~ mark** n, (Amer) **~ point** n Ausrufezeichen nt

exclu|de /ɪkˈskluːd/ vt ausschließen. **~ding** prep ausschließlich (+ gen). **~sion** n Ausschluss m

exclusive /ɪkˈskluːsɪv/ adj ausschließlich; (select) exklusiv

excrement /ˈekskrɪmənt/ n Kot m

excrete /ɪkˈskriːt/ vt ausscheiden

excruciating /ɪkˈskruːʃɪeɪtɪŋ/ adj grässlich

excursion /ɪkˈskɜːʃn/ n Ausflug m

excusable /ɪkˈskjuːzəbl/ adj entschuldbar

excuse[1] /ɪkˈskjuːs/ n Entschuldigung f; (pretext) Ausrede f

excuse[2] /ɪkˈskjuːz/ vt entschuldigen; **~ me!** Entschuldigung!

ex-di'rectory adj **be ~** nicht im Telefonbuch stehen

execute /ˈeksɪkjuːt/ vt ausführen; (put to death) hinrichten

execution /eksɪˈkjuːʃn/ n Ausführung f; Hinrichtung f

executive /ɪgˈzekjʊtɪv/ adj leitend ● n leitende(r) Angestellte(r) m/f; (Pol) Exekutive f

exemplary /ɪgˈzemplərɪ/ adj beispielhaft

exemplify /ɪgˈzemplɪfaɪ/ vt (pt/pp -ied) veranschaulichen

exempt /ɪgˈzempt/ adj befreit ● vt befreien (**from** von). **~ion** n Befreiung f

exercise /ˈeksəsaɪz/ n Übung f; **physical ~** körperliche Bewegung f ● vt (use) ausüben; bewegen (horse) ● vi sich bewegen. **~ book** n [Schul]heft nt

exert /ɪgˈzɜːt/ vt ausüben; **~ oneself** sich anstrengen. **~ion** n Anstrengung f

exhale /eksˈheɪl/ vt/i ausatmen

exhaust /ɪgˈzɔːst/ n (Auto) Auspuff m; (fumes) Abgase pl ● vt erschöp-

exhibit | expulsion

fen. **~ed** adj erschöpft. **~ing** adj anstrengend. **~ion** n Erschöpfung f. **~ive** adj (fig) erschöpfend

exhibit /ɪɡ'zɪbɪt/ n Ausstellungsstück nt; (Jur) Beweisstück nt ● vt ausstellen

exhibition /eksɪ'bɪʃn/ n Ausstellung f; (Univ) Stipendium nt. **~ist** n Exhibitionist(in) m(f)

exhibitor /ɪɡ'zɪbɪtə(r)/ n Aussteller m

exhilarat|ing /ɪɡ'zɪləreɪtɪŋ/ adj berauschend. **~ion** n Hochgefühl nt

exhume /ɪɡ'zju:m/ vt exhumieren

exile /'eksaɪl/ n Exil nt; (person) im Exil Lebende(r) m/f ● vt ins Exil schicken

exist /ɪɡ'zɪst/ vi bestehen, existieren. **~ence** n Existenz f; be in **~ence** existieren

exit /'eksɪt/ n Ausgang m; (Auto) Ausfahrt f; (Theat) Abgang m

exorbitant /ɪɡ'zɔ:bɪtənt/ adj übermäßig hoch

exotic /ɪɡ'zɒtɪk/ adj exotisch

expand /ɪk'spænd/ vt ausdehnen; (explain better) weiter ausführen ● vi sich ausdehnen; (Comm) expandieren

expans|e /ɪk'spæns/ n Weite f. **~ion** n Ausdehnung f; (Techn, Pol, Comm) Expansion f

expect /ɪk'spekt/ vt erwarten; (suppose) annehmen; **I ~ so** wahrscheinlich

expectan|cy /ɪk'spektənsɪ/ n Erwartung f. **~t** adj erwartungsvoll; **~t mother** werdende Mutter f

expectation /ekspek'teɪʃn/ n Erwartung f

expedient /ɪk'spi:dɪənt/ adj zweckdienlich

expedite /'ekspɪdaɪt/ vt beschleunigen

expedition /ekspɪ'dɪʃn/ n Expedition f

expel /ɪk'spel/ vt (pt/pp expelled) ausweisen (from aus); (from school) von der Schule verweisen

expenditure /ɪk'spendɪtʃə(r)/ n Ausgaben pl

expense /ɪk'spens/ n Kosten pl; **business ~s** pl Spesen pl; **at my ~** auf meine Kosten

expensive /ɪk'spensɪv/ adj teuer

experience /ɪk'spɪərɪəns/ n Erfahrung f; (event) Erlebnis nt ● vt erleben. **~d** adj erfahren

experiment /ɪk'sperɪmənt/ n Versuch m, Experiment nt ● /-ment/ vi experimentieren. **~al** adj experimentell

expert /'ekspɜ:t/ adj fachmännisch ● n Fachmann m, Experte m

expertise /ekspɜ:'ti:z/ n Sachkenntnis f

expire /ɪk'spaɪə(r)/ vi ablaufen

expiry /ɪk'spaɪərɪ/ n Ablauf m

explain /ɪk'spleɪn/ vt erklären

explana|tion /eksplə'neɪʃn/ n Erklärung f. **~tory** adj erklärend

explicit /ɪk'splɪsɪt/ adj deutlich

explode /ɪk'spləʊd/ vi explodieren ● vt zur Explosion bringen

exploit[1] /'eksplɔɪt/ n [Helden]tat f

exploit[2] /ɪk'splɔɪt/ vt ausbeuten. **~ation** n Ausbeutung f

exploration /eksplə'reɪʃn/ n Erforschung f

explore /ɪk'splɔ:(r)/ vt erforschen. **~r** n Forschungsreisende(r) m

explos|ion /ɪk'spləʊʒn/ n Explosion f. **~ive** adj explosiv ● n Sprengstoff m

export[1] /'ekspɔ:t/ n Export m, Ausfuhr f

export[2] /ɪk'spɔ:t/ vt exportieren, ausführen. **~er** n Exporteur m

expos|e /ɪk'spəʊz/ vt freilegen; (to danger) aussetzen (to dat); (reveal) aufdecken; (Phot) belichten. **~ure** n Aussetzung f; (Med) Unterkühlung f; (Phot) Belichtung f; **24 ~ures** 24 Aufnahmen

express /ɪk'spres/ adv (send) per Eilpost ● n (train) Schnellzug m ● vt ausdrücken; **~ oneself** sich ausdrücken. **~ion** n Ausdruck m. **~ive** adj ausdrucksvoll. **~ly** adv ausdrücklich

expulsion /ɪk'spʌlʃn/ n Ausweisung f; (Sch) Verweisung f von der Schule

exquisite /ek'skwɪzɪt/ adj erlesen

extend /ɪk'stend/ vt verlängern; (stretch out) ausstrecken; (enlarge) vergrößern ● vi sich ausdehnen; (table:) sich ausziehen lassen

extension /ɪk'stenʃn/ n Verlängerung f; (to house) Anbau m; (Teleph) Nebenanschluss m

extensive /ɪk'stensɪv/ adj weit; (fig) umfassend. **~ly** adv viel

extent /ɪk'stent/ n Ausdehnung f; (scope) Ausmaß nt, Umfang m; **to a certain ~** in gewissem Maße

exterior /ɪk'stɪərɪə(r)/ adj äußere(r,s) ● n **the ~** das Äußere

exterminat|e /ɪk'stɜ:mɪneɪt/ vt ausrotten. **~ion** n Ausrottung f

external /ɪk'stɜ:nl/ adj äußere(r,s); **for ~ use only** (Med) nur äußerlich. **~ly** adv äußerlich

extinct /ɪk'stɪŋkt/ adj ausgestorben; (volcano) erloschen. **~ion** n Aussterben nt

extinguish /ɪk'stɪŋgwɪʃ/ vt löschen. **~er** n Feuerlöscher m

extort /ɪk'stɔ:t/ vt erpressen. **~ion** n Erpressung f

extortionate /ɪk'stɔ:ʃənət/ adj übermäßig hoch

extra /'ekstrə/ adj zusätzlich ● adv extra; (especially) besonders ● n (Theat) Statist(in) m(f); **~s** pl Nebenkosten pl; (Auto) Extras pl

extract[1] /'ekstrækt/ n Auszug m

extract[2] /ɪk'strækt/ vt herausziehen; ziehen (tooth)

extraordinary /ɪk'strɔ:dɪnərɪ/ adj, **-ily** adv außerordentlich; (strange) seltsam

extravagan|ce /ɪk'strævəgəns/ n Verschwendung f; **an ~ce** ein Luxus m. **~t** adj verschwenderisch

extrem|e /ɪk'stri:m/ adj äußerste(r,s); (fig) extrem ● n Extrem nt; **in the ~e** im höchsten Grade. **~ely** adv äußerst. **~ist** n Extremist m

extricate /'ekstrɪkeɪt/ vt befreien

extrovert /'ekstrəvɜ:t/ n extravertierter Mensch m

exuberant /ɪg'zju:bərənt/ adj überglücklich

exude /ɪg'zju:d/ vt absondern; (fig) ausstrahlen

exult /ɪg'zʌlt/ vi frohlocken

eye /aɪ/ n Auge nt; (of needle) Öhr nt; (for hook) Öse f; **keep an ~ on** aufpassen auf (+ acc) ● vt (pt/pp **eyed**, pres p **ey[e]ing**) ansehen

eye: ~ brow n Augenbraue f. **~lash** n Wimper f. **~lid** n Augenlid nt. **~-shadow** n Lidschatten m. **~sight** n Sehkraft f. **~sore** 🔲 Schandfleck m. **~witness** n Augenzeuge m

•••••••••••••••••••••••••••••••

Ff

•••••••••••••••••••••••••••••••

fable /'feɪbl/ n Fabel f

fabric /'fæbrɪk/ n Stoff m

fabrication /fæbrɪ'keɪʃn/ n Erfindung f

fabulous /'fæbjʊləs/ adj 🔲 phantastisch

façade /fə'sɑ:d/ n Fassade f

face /feɪs/ n Gesicht nt; (surface) Fläche f; (of clock) Zifferblatt nt; **pull ~s** Gesichter schneiden; **in the ~ of** angesichts (+ gen); **on the ~ of it** allem Anschein nach ● vt/i gegenüberstehen (+ dat); **~ north** (house:) nach Norden liegen; **~ the fact that** sich damit abfinden, dass

face: ~-flannel n Waschlappen m. **~less** adj anonym. **~-lift** n Gesichtsstraffung f

facet /'fæsɪt/ n Facette f; (fig) Aspekt m

facetious /fə'si:ʃəs/ adj spöttisch

facial /'feɪʃl/ adj Gesichts-

facile /'fæsaɪl/ adj oberflächlich

facilitate /fə'sɪlɪteɪt/ vt erleichtern

facility /fə'sɪlətɪ/ n Leichtigkeit f; (skill) Gewandtheit f; **~ies** pl Einrichtungen pl

facsimile /fæk'sɪməlɪ/ n Faksimile nt

fact /fækt/ n Tatsache f; **in** ~ tat-

e
f

sächlich; (*actually*) eigentlich

faction /ˈfækʃn/ n Gruppe f

factor /ˈfæktə(r)/ n Faktor m

factory /ˈfæktərɪ/ n Fabrik f

factual /ˈfæktʃʊəl/ adj sachlich

faculty /ˈfækəltɪ/ n Fähigkeit f; (*Univ*) Fakultät f

fad /fæd/ n Fimmel m

fade /feɪd/ vi verblassen; (*material:*) verbleichen; (*sound:*) abklingen; (*flower:*) verwelken.

fag /fæg/ n (*chore*) Plage f; (🔲: *cigarette*) Zigarette f

fail /feɪl/ n **without ~** unbedingt ● vi (*attempt:*) scheitern; (*grow weak*) nachlassen; (*break down*) versagen; (*in exam*) durchfallen; **~ to do sth** etw nicht tun ● vt nicht bestehen (*exam*); durchfallen lassen (*candidate*); (*disappoint*) enttäuschen

failing /ˈfeɪlɪŋ/ n Fehler m

failure /ˈfeɪljə(r)/ n Misserfolg m; (*breakdown*) Versagen nt; (*person*) Versager m

faint /feɪnt/ adj (-er, -est) schwach; **I feel~** mir ist schwach ● n Ohnmacht f ● vi ohnmächtig werden. **~ness** n Schwäche f

fair[1] /feə(r)/ n Jahrmarkt m; (*Comm*) Messe f

fair[2] adj (-er, -est) (*hair*) blond; (*skin*) hell; (*weather*) heiter; (*just*) gerecht, fair; (*quite good*) ziemlich gut; (*Sch*) genügend; **a ~ amount** ziemlich viel ● adv **play ~** fair sein. **~ly** adv gerecht; (*rather*) ziemlich. **~ness** n Blondheit f; Helle f; Gerechtigkeit f; (*Sport*) Fairness f

fairy /ˈfeərɪ/ n Elfe f; **good/wicked ~** gute/böse Fee f. **~ story, ~-tale** n Märchen nt

faith /feɪθ/ n Glaube m; (*trust*) Vertrauen nt (**in** zu)

faithful /ˈfeɪθfl/ adj treu; (*exact*) genau; **Yours ~ly** Hochachtungsvoll. **~ness** n Treue f; Genauigkeit f

fake /feɪk/ adj falsch ● n Fälschung f; (*person*) Schwindler m ● vt fälschen; (*pretend*) vortäuschen

falcon /ˈfɔːlkən/ n Falke m

fall /fɔːl/ n Fall m; (*heavy*) Sturz m; (*in prices*) Fallen nt; (*Amer: autumn*) Herbst m; **have a ~** fallen ● vi (*pt fell, pp fallen*) fallen; (*heavily*) stürzen; (*night:*) anbrechen; **~ in love** sich verlieben; **~ back on** zurückgreifen auf (+ *acc*); **~ for s.o.** 🔲 sich in jdn verlieben; **~ for sth** 🔲 auf etw (*acc*) hereinfallen. **~ about** vi (*with laughter*) sich [vor Lachen] kringeln. **~ down** vi umfallen; (*thing:*) herunterfallen; (*building:*) einstürzen. **~ in** vi hineinfallen; (*collapse*) einfallen; (*Mil*) antreten; **~ in with** sich anschließen (+ *dat*). **~ off** vi herunterfallen; (*diminish*) abnehmen. **~ out** vi herausfallen; (*hair:*) ausfallen; (*quarrel*) sich überwerfen. **~ over** vi hinfallen. **~ through** vi durchfallen; (*plan:*) ins Wasser fallen

fallacy /ˈfæləsɪ/ n Irrtum m

fallible /ˈfæləbl/ adj fehlbar

'fall-out n [radioaktiver] Niederschlag m

false /fɔːls/ adj falsch; (*artificial*) künstlich. **~hood** n Unwahrheit f. **~ly** adv falsch

false 'teeth npl [künstliches] Gebiss nt

falsify /ˈfɔːlsɪfaɪ/ vt (*pt/pp -ied*) fälschen

falter /ˈfɔːltə(r)/ vi zögern

fame /feɪm/ n Ruhm m.

familiar /fəˈmɪlɪə(r)/ adj vertraut; (*known*) bekannt; **too ~** familiär. **~ity** n Vertrautheit f. **~ize** vt vertraut machen (**with** mit)

family /ˈfæməlɪ/ n Familie f

family: ~ 'doctor n Hausarzt m. **~ 'life** n Familienleben nt. **~ 'planning** n Familienplanung f. **~ 'tree** n Stammbaum m

famine /ˈfæmɪn/ n Hungersnot f

famished /ˈfæmɪʃt/ adj sehr hungrig

famous /ˈfeɪməs/ adj berühmt

fan[1] /fæn/ n Fächer m; (*Techn*) Ventilator m

fan[2] n (*admirer*) Fan m

fanatic /fəˈnætɪk/ n Fanatiker m.

339   fanciful | fearful

~al *adj* fanatisch. **~ism** *n* Fanatismus *m*

fanciful /ˈfænsɪfl/ *adj* phantastisch; (*imaginative*) phantasiereich

fancy /ˈfænsɪ/ *n* Phantasie *f*; **I have taken a real ~ to him** er hat es mir angetan ●*adj* ausgefallen ●*vt* (*believe*) meinen; (*imagine*) sich (*dat*) einbilden; (🄙: *want*) Lust haben auf (+ *acc*); **~ that!** stell dir vor! (*really*) tatsächlich! ~ ˈdress *n* Kostüm *nt*

fanfare /ˈfænfeə(r)/ *n* Fanfare *f*

fang /fæŋ/ *n* Fangzahn *m*

ˈfan heater *n* Heizlüfter *m*

fantas|ize /ˈfæntəsaɪz/ *vi* phantasieren. **~tic** *adj* phantastisch. **~y** *n* Phantasie *f*

far /fɑː(r)/ *adv* weit; (*much*) viel; **by ~** bei weitem; **~ away** weit weg; **as ~ as I know** soviel ich weiß; **as ~ as the church** bis zur Kirche ●*adj* at the **~ end** am anderen Ende; **the F~ East** der Ferne Osten

farc|e /fɑːs/ *n* Farce *f*. **~ical** *adj* lächerlich

fare /feə(r)/ *n* Fahrpreis *m*; (*money*) Fahrgeld *nt*; (*food*) Kost *f*; **air ~** Flugpreis *m*

farewell /feəˈwel/ *int* (*literary*) lebe wohl! ● *n* Lebewohl *nt*

far-ˈfetched *adj* weit hergeholt

farm /fɑːm/ *n* Bauernhof *m* ●*vi* Landwirtschaft betreiben ●*vt* bewirtschaften (*land*). **~er** *n* Landwirt *m*

farm: ~house *n* Bauernhaus *nt*. **~ing** *n* Landwirtschaft *f*. **~yard** *n* Hof *m*

far: ~-ˈreaching *adj* weit reichend. **~-ˈsighted** *adj* (*fig*) umsichtig; (*Amer: long-sighted*) weitsichtig

farther /ˈfɑːðə(r)/ *adv* weiter; **~ off** weiter entfernt

fascinat|e /ˈfæsɪneɪt/ *vt* faszinieren. **~ing** *adj* faszinierend. **~ion** *n* Faszination *f*

fascis|m /ˈfæʃɪzm/ *n* Faschismus *m*. **~t** *n* Faschist *m* ●*adj* faschistisch

fashion /ˈfæʃn/ *n* Mode *f*; (*manner*) Art *f*. **~able** *adj*, **-bly** *adv* modisch

fast /fɑːst/ *adj & adv* (**-er, -est**) schnell; (*firm*) fest; (*colour*) waschecht; **be ~** (*clock:*) vorgehen; **be ~ asleep** fest schlafen

fasten /ˈfɑːsn/ *vt* zumachen; (*fix*) befestigen (**to** an + *dat*). **~er** *n*, **~ing** *n* Verschluss *m*

fastidious /fəˈstɪdɪəs/ *adj* wählerisch; (*particular*) penibel

fat /fæt/ *adj* (**fatter, fattest**) dick; (*meat*) fett ● *n* Fett *nt*

fatal /ˈfeɪtl/ *adj* tödlich; (*error*) verhängnisvoll. **~ity** *n* Todesopfer *nt*. **~ly** *adv* tödlich

fate /feɪt/ *n* Schicksal *nt*. **~ful** *adj* verhängnisvoll

ˈfat-head *n* 🄙 Dummkopf *m*

father /ˈfɑːðə(r)/ *n* Vater *m*; **F ~ Christmas** der Weihnachtsmann ●*vt* zeugen

father: ~hood *n* Vaterschaft *f*. **~-in-law** *n* (*pl* **~s-in-law**) Schwiegervater *m*. **~ly** *adj* väterlich

fathom /ˈfæðəm/ *n* (*Naut*) Faden *m* ●*vt* verstehen

fatigue /fəˈtiːg/ *n* Ermüdung *f*

fatten /ˈfætn/ *vt* mästen (*animal*)

fatty /ˈfætɪ/ *adj* fett; (*foods*) fetthaltig

fatuous /ˈfætjʊəs/ *adj* albern

fault /fɔːlt/ *n* Fehler *m*; (*Techn*) Defekt *m*; (*Geology*) Verwerfung *f*; **at ~** im Unrecht; **find ~ with** etwas auszusetzen haben an (+ *dat*); **it's your ~** du bist schuld. **~less** *adj* fehlerfrei

faulty /ˈfɔːltɪ/ *adj* fehlerhaft

favour /ˈfeɪvə(r)/ *n* Gunst *f*; **I am in ~** ich bin dafür; **do s.o. a ~** jdm einen Gefallen tun ●*vt* begünstigen; (*prefer*) bevorzugen. **~able** *adj*, **-bly** *adv* günstig; (*reply*) positiv

favourit|e /ˈfeɪvərɪt/ *adj* Lieblings- ● *n* Liebling *m*; (*Sport*) Favorit(in) *m*(*f*). **~ism** *n* Bevorzugung *f*

fawn /fɔːn/ *adj* rehbraun ●*n* Hirschkalb *nt*

fax /fæks/ *n* Fax *nt* ●*vt* faxen (**s.o.** jdm). **~ machine** *n* Faxgerät *nt*

fear /fɪə(r)/ *n* Furcht *f*, Angst *f* (**of** vor + *dat*) ●*vt/i* fürchten

fear|ful /ˈfɪəfl/ *adj* besorgt; (*awful*)

furchtbar. **~less** adj furchtlos

feas|ibility /fi:zə'bɪlətɪ/ n Durchführbarkeit f. **~ible** adj durchführbar; (possible) möglich

feast /fi:st/ n Festmahl nt; (Relig) Fest nt ● vi ~ [on] schmausen

feat /fi:t/ n Leistung f

feather /'feðə(r)/ n Feder f

feature /'fi:tʃə(r)/ n Gesichtszug m; (quality) Merkmal nt; (article) Feature nt ● vt darstellen

February /'februərɪ/ n Februar m

fed /fed/ see feed ● adj be ~ up ⊞ die Nase voll haben (with von)

federal /'fedərəl/ adj Bundes-

federation /fedə'reɪʃn/ n Föderation f

fee /fi:/ n Gebühr f; (professional) Honorar nt

feeble /'fi:bl/ adj (-r, -st), **-bly** adv schwach

feed /fi:d/ n Futter nt; (for baby) Essen nt ● v (pt/pp fed) ● vt füttern; (support) ernähren; (into machine) eingeben; speisen (computer) ● vi sich ernähren (on von)

'feedback n Feedback nt

feel /fi:l/ v (pt/pp felt) ● vt fühlen; (experience) empfinden; (think) meinen ● vi sich fühlen; ~ soft/hard sich weich/hart anfühlen; I ~ hot/ill mir ist heiß/schlecht; **~ing** n Gefühl nt; **no hard ~ings** nichts für ungut

feet /fi:t/ see foot

feline /'fi:laɪn/ adj Katzen-; (catlike) katzenartig

fell¹ /fel/ vt fällen

fell² see fall

fellow /'feləʊ/ n (⊞: man) Kerl m

fellow: **~-'countryman** n Landsmann m. **~ men** pl Mitmenschen pl

felt¹ /felt/ see feel

felt² n Filz m. **~[-tipped] 'pen** n Filzstift m

female /'fi:meɪl/ adj weiblich ● nt Weibchen nt; (pej: woman) Weib nt

femin|ine /'femɪnɪn/ adj weiblich ● n (Gram) Femininum nt. **~inity** n Weiblichkeit f. **~ist** adj feministisch ● n Feminist(in) m(f)

fenc|e /fens/ n Zaun m; (⊞: person) Hehler m ● vi (Sport) fechten ● vt **~e in** einzäunen. **~er** n Fechter m. **~ing** n Zaun m; (Sport) Fechten nt

fender /'fendə(r)/ n Kaminvorsetzer m; (Naut) Fender m; (Amer: wing) Kotflügel m

ferment /fə'ment/ vi gären ● vt gären lassen

fern /fɜ:n/ n Farn m

feroc|ious /fə'rəʊʃəs/ adj wild. **~ity** n Wildheit f

ferry /'ferɪ/ n Fähre f

fertil|e /'fɜ:taɪl/ adj fruchtbar. **~ity** n Fruchtbarkeit f

fertilize /'fɜ:təlaɪz/ vt befruchten; düngen (land). **~r** n Dünger m

fervent /'fɜ:vənt/ adj leidenschaftlich

fervour /'fɜ:və(r)/ n Leidenschaft f

festival /'festɪvl/ n Fest nt; (Mus, Theat) Festspiele pl

festiv|e /'festɪv/ adj festlich. **~ities** npl Feierlichkeiten pl

festoon /fe'stu:n/ vt behängen (with mit)

fetch /fetʃ/ vt holen; (collect) abholen; (be sold for) einbringen

fetching /'fetʃɪŋ/ adj anziehend

fête /feɪt/ n Fest nt ● vt feiern

feud /fju:d/ n Fehde f

feudal /'fju:dl/ adj Feudal-

fever /'fi:və(r)/ n Fieber nt. **~ish** adj fiebrig; (fig) fieberhaft

few /fju:/ adj (-er, -est) wenige; **every ~ days** alle paar Tage ● n a **~** ein paar; **quite a ~** ziemlich viele

fiancé /fɪ'ɒnseɪ/ n Verlobte(r) m. **fiancée** n Verlobte f

fiasco /fɪ'æskəʊ/ n Fiasko nt

fib /fɪb/ n kleine Lüge

fibre /'faɪbə(r)/ n Faser f

fiction /'fɪkʃn/ n Erfindung f; [works of] ~ Erzählungsliteratur f. **~al** adj erfunden

fictitious /fɪk'tɪʃəs/ adj [frei] erfunden

fiddle /'fɪdl/ n ⊞ Geige f; (cheating) Schwindel m ● vi herumspielen (with mit) ● vt ⊞ frisieren (accounts)

fiddly /'fɪdlɪ/ adj knifflig
fidelity /fɪ'delətɪ/ n Treue f
fidget /'fɪdʒɪt/ vi zappeln. **~y** adj zappelig
field /fiːld/ n Feld nt; (meadow) Wiese f; (subject) Gebiet nt
field: **~ events** npl Sprung- und Wurfdisziplinen pl. **F~ 'Marshal** n Feldmarschall m
fiendish /'fiːndɪʃ/ adj teuflisch
fierce /fɪəs/ adj (-r, -st) wild; (fig) heftig. **~ness** n Wildheit f; (fig) Heftigkeit f
fiery /'faɪərɪ/ adj feurig
fifteen /fɪf'tiːn/ adj fünfzehn ● n Fünfzehn f. **~th** adj fünfzehnte(r,s)
fifth /fɪfθ/ adj fünfte(r,s)
fiftieth /'fɪftɪɪθ/ adj fünfzigste(r,s)
fifty /'fɪftɪ/ adj fünfzig
fig /fɪg/ n Feige f
fight /faɪt/ n Kampf m; (brawl) Schlägerei f; (between children, dogs) Rauferei f ● v (pt/pp fought) ● vt kämpfen gegen; (fig) bekämpfen ● vi kämpfen; (brawl) sich schlagen; (children, dogs:) sich raufen. **~er** n Kämpfer m; (Aviat) Jagdflugzeug nt. **~ing** n Kampf m
figurative /'fɪgjərətɪv/ adj bildlich, übertragen
figure /'fɪgə(r)/ n (digit) Ziffer f; (number) Zahl f; (sum) Summe f; (carving, sculpture, woman's) Figur f; (form) Gestalt f; (illustration) Abbildung f; **good at ~s** gut im Rechnen ● vi (appear) erscheinen ● vt (Amer: think) glauben
filch /fɪltʃ/ vt 🅸 klauen
file¹ /faɪl/ n Akte f; (for documents) [Akten]ordner m ● vt ablegen (documents); (Jur) einreichen
file² n (line) Reihe f; **in single ~** im Gänsemarsch
file³ n (Techn) Feile f ● vt feilen
fill /fɪl/ n **eat one's ~** sich satt essen ● vt füllen; plombieren (tooth) ● vi sich füllen. **~ in** vt auffüllen; ausfüllen (form). **~ out** vt ausfüllen (form). **~ up** vi sich füllen ● vt vollfüllen; (Auto) volltanken; ausfüllen (questionnaire)

fillet /'fɪlɪt/ n Filet nt ● vt (pt/pp filleted) entgräten
filling /'fɪlɪŋ/ n Füllung f; (of tooth) Plombe f. **~ station** n Tankstelle f
filly /'fɪlɪ/ n junge Stute f
film /fɪlm/ n Film m ● vt/i filmen; verfilmen (book). **~ star** n Filmstar m
filter /'fɪltə(r)/ n Filter m ● vt filtern
filth /fɪlθ/ n Dreck m. **~y** adj dreckig
fin /fɪn/ n Flosse f
final /'faɪnl/ adj letzte(r,s); (conclusive) endgültig ● n (Sport) Endspiel nt; **~s** pl (Univ) Abschlussprüfung f
finale /fɪ'nɑːlɪ/ n Finale nt
final|ist /'faɪnəlɪst/ n Finalist(in) m(f)
final|ize /'faɪnəlaɪz/ vt endgültig festlegen. **~ly** adv schließlich
finance /faɪ'næns/ n Finanz f ● vt finanzieren
financial /faɪ'nænʃl/ adj finanziell
find /faɪnd/ n Fund m ● vt (pt/pp found) finden; (establish) feststellen; **go and ~** holen; **try to ~** suchen. **~ out** vt herausfinden; (learn) erfahren ● vi (enquire) sich erkundigen
fine¹ /faɪn/ n Geldstrafe f ● vt zu einer Geldstrafe verurteilen
fine² adj (-r, -st,) **-ly** adv fein; (weather) schön; **he's ~** es geht ihm gut ● adv gut; **cut it ~** 🅸 sich (dat) wenig Zeit lassen
finesse /fɪ'nes/ n Gewandtheit f
finger /'fɪŋgə(r)/ n Finger m ● vt anfassen
finger: **~-nail** n Fingernagel m. **~print** n Fingerabdruck m. **~tip** n Fingerspitze f
finicky /'fɪnɪkɪ/ adj knifflig; (choosy) wählerisch
finish /'fɪnɪʃ/ n Schluss m; (Sport) Finish nt; (line) Ziel nt; (of product) Ausführung f ● vt beenden; (use up) aufbrauchen; **~ one's drink** austrinken; **~ reading** zu Ende lesen ● vi fertig werden; (performance:) zu Ende sein; (runner:) durchs Ziel gehen

Finland /'fɪnlənd/ n Finnland nt

Finn /fɪn/ n Finne m/ Finnin f. **~ish** adj finnisch

fir /fɜ:(r)/ n Tanne f

fire /'faɪə(r)/ n Feuer nt; (forest, house) Brand m; **be on ~** brennen; **catch ~** Feuer fangen; **set ~ to** anzünden; (arsonist:) in Brand stecken; **under ~** unter Beschuss ● vt brennen (pottery); abfeuern (shot); schießen mit (gun); (🔲: dismiss) feuern ● vi schießen (at auf + acc); (engine:) anspringen

fire: ~ alarm n Feuermelder m. **~ brigade** n Feuerwehr f. **~-engine** n Löschfahrzeug nt. **~ extinguisher** n Feuerlöscher m. **~man** n Feuerwehrmann m. **~place** n Kamin m. **~side** n by or at the **~side** am Kamin. **~ station** n Feuerwache f. **~wood** n Brennholz nt. **~work** n Feuerwerkskörper m; **~works** pl (display) Feuerwerk nt

firm¹ /fɜ:m/ n Firma f

firm² adj (-er, -est) fest; (resolute) entschlossen; (strict) streng

first /fɜ:st/ adj & n erste(r,s); **at ~** zuerst; **at ~ sight** auf den ersten Blick; **from the ~** von Anfang an ● adv zuerst; (firstly) erstens

first: ~ 'aid n erste Hilfe. **~-'aid kit** n Verbandkasten m. **~-class** adj erstklassig; (Rail) erster Klasse ● /-'-/ adv (travel) erster Klasse. **~ 'floor** n erster Stock; (Amer: ground floor) Erdgeschoss nt. **~ly** adv erstens. **~name** n Vorname m. **~-rate** adj erstklassig

fish /fɪʃ/ n Fisch m ● vt/i fischen; (with rod) angeln

fish: ~bone n Gräte f. **~erman** n Fischer m. **~ 'finger** n Fischstäbchen nt

fishing /'fɪʃɪŋ/ n Fischerei f. **~ boat** n Fischerboot nt. **~-rod** n Angel[rute] f

fish: ~monger /-'mʌŋgə(r)/ n Fischhändler m. **~y** adj Fisch-; (🔲: suspicious) verdächtig

fission /'fɪʃn/ n (Phys) Spaltung f

fist /fɪst/ n Faust f

fit¹ /fɪt/ n (attack) Anfall m

fit² adj (fitter, fittest) (suitable) geeignet; (healthy) gesund; (Sport) fit; **~ to eat** essbar

fit³ n (of clothes) Sitz m; **be a good ~** gut passen ● v (pt/pp **fitted**) ● vi (be the right size) passen ● vt anbringen (**to** an + dat); (install) einbauen; **~ with** versehen mit. **~ in** vi hineinpassen; (adapt) sich einfügen (**with** in + acc) ● vt (accommodate) unterbringen

fit|ness n Eignung f; **[physical] ~ness** Gesundheit f; (Sport) Fitness f. **~ ted** adj eingebaut; (garment) tailliert

fitted: ~ 'carpet n Teppichboden m. **~ 'kitchen** n Einbauküche f. **~ 'sheet** n Spannlaken nt

fitting /'fɪtɪŋ/ adj passend ● n (of clothes) Anprobe f; (of shoes) Weite f; (Techn) Zubehörteil nt; **~s** pl Zubehör nt

five /faɪv/ adj fünf ● n Fünf f. **~r** n Fünfpfundschein m

fix /fɪks/ n (sl: drugs) Fix m; **be in a ~** 🔲 in der Klemme sitzen ● vt befestigen (**to** an + dat); (arrange) festlegen; (repair) reparieren; (Phot) fixieren; **~ a meal** Essen machen

fixed /fɪkst/ adj fest

fixture /'fɪkstʃə(r)/ n (Sport) Veranstaltung f; **~s and fittings** zu einer Wohnung gehörende Einrichtungen pl

fizz /fɪz/ vi sprudeln

fizzle /'fɪzl/ vi **~ out** verpuffen

fizzy /'fɪzɪ/ adj sprudelnd. **~ drink** n Brause[limonade] f

flabbergasted /'flæbəgɑ:stɪd/ adj **be ~** platt sein 🔲

flabby /'flæbɪ/ adj schlaff

flag /flæg/ n Fahne f; (Naut) Flagge f

'flag-pole n Fahnenstange f

flagrant /'fleɪgrənt/ adj flagrant

'flagstone n [Pflaster]platte f

flair /fleə(r)/ n Begabung f

flake /fleɪk/ n Flocke f ● vi **~[off]** abblättern

flamboyant /flæm'bɔɪənt/ adj extravagant

flame /fleɪm/ n Flamme f

flan /flæn/ n [fruit] ~ Obsttorte f

flank /flæŋk/ n Flanke f

flannel /'flænl/ n Flanell m; (for washing) Waschlappen m

flap /flæp/ n Klappe f; **in a** ~ ⊞ aufgeregt ●v (pt/pp **flapped**) vi flattern; ⊞ sich aufregen ●vt ~ **its wings** mit den Flügeln schlagen

flare /fleə(r)/ n Leuchtsignal nt. ●vi ~ **up** auflodern; (⊞: get angry) aufbrausen

flash /flæʃ/ n Blitz m; **in a** ~ ⊞ im Nu ●vi blitzen; (repeatedly) blinken; ~ **past** vorbeirasen

flash: ~**back** n Rückblende f. ~**er** n (Auto) Blinker m. ~**light** n (Phot) Blitzlicht nt; (Amer: torch) Taschenlampe f. ~**y** a auffällig

flask /fla:sk/ n Flasche f

flat /flæt/ adj (**flatter, flattest**) flach; (surface) eben; (refusal) glatt; (beer) schal; (battery) verbraucht/ (Auto) leer; (tyre) platt; (Mus) **A** ~ As nt; **B** ~ **B** nt ●n Wohnung f; (⊞: puncture) Reifenpanne f

flat: ~**ly** adv (refuse) glatt. ~ **rate** n Einheitspreis m

flatten /'flætn/ vt platt drücken

flatter /'flætə(r)/ vt schmeicheln (+ dat). ~**y** n Schmeichelei f

flat 'tyre n Reifenpanne f

flaunt /flɔ:nt/ vt prunken mit

flautist /'flɔ:tɪst/ n Flötist(in) m(f)

flavour /'fleɪvə(r)/ n Geschmack m ●vt abschmecken. ~**ing** n Aroma nt

flaw /flɔ:/ n Fehler m. ~**less** adj tadellos; (complexion) makellos

flea /fli:/ n Floh m

fleck /flek/ n Tupfen m

fled /fled/ see **flee**

flee /fli:/ v (pt/pp **fled**) ●vi fliehen (**from** vor + dat) ●vt flüchten aus

fleec|e /fli:s/ n Vlies nt ●vt ⊞ schröpfen

fleet /fli:t/ n Flotte f; (of cars) Wagenpark m

fleeting /'fli:tɪŋ/ adj flüchtig

Flemish /'flemɪʃ/ adj flämisch

flesh /fleʃ/ n Fleisch nt

flew /flu:/ see **fly²**

flex¹ /fleks/ vt anspannen (muscle)

flex² n (Electr) Schnur f

flexib|ility /fleksə'bɪlətɪ/ n Biegsamkeit f; (fig) Flexibilität f. ~**le** adj biegsam; (fig) flexibel

flick /flɪk/ vt schnippen

flicker /'flɪkə(r)/ vi flackern

flier /'flaɪə(r)/ n = **flyer**

flight¹ /flaɪt/ n (fleeing) Flucht f

flight² n (flying) Flug m; ~ **of stairs** Treppe f

'flight recorder n Flugschreiber m

flimsy /'flɪmzɪ/ adj dünn; (excuse) fadenscheinig

flinch /flɪntʃ/ vi zurückzucken

fling /flɪŋ/ vt (pt/pp **flung**) schleudern

flint /flɪnt/ n Feuerstein m

flip /flɪp/ vt/i schnippen; ~ **through** durchblättern

flippant /'flɪpənt/ adj leichtfertig

flirt /flɜ:t/ n kokette Frau f ●vi flirten

flirtat|ion /flɜ:'teɪʃn/ n Flirt m. ~**ious** adj kokett

flit /flɪt/ vi (pt/pp **flitted**) flattern

float /fləʊt/ n Schwimmer m; (in procession) Festwagen m; (money) Wechselgeld nt ●vi (thing.) schwimmen; (person:) sich treiben lassen; (in air) schweben

flock /flɒk/ n Herde f; (of birds) Schwarm m ●vi strömen

flog /flɒg/ vt (pt/pp **flogged**) auspeitschen; (⊞: sell) verkloppen

flood /flʌd/ n Überschwemmung f; (fig) Flut f ●vt überschwemmen

'floodlight n Flutlicht nt ●vt (pt/pp **floodlit**) anstrahlen

floor /flɔ:(r)/ n Fußboden m; (storey) Stock m

floor: ~ **board** n Dielenbrett nt. ~**-polish** n Bohnerwachs nt. ~ **show** n Kabarettvorstellung f

flop /flɒp/ n ⊞ (failure) Reinfall m; (Theat) Durchfall m ●vi (pt/pp

floppy | fondle

344

flopped) 🔲 (*fail*) durchfallen

floppy /'flɒpɪ/ *adj* schlapp. ~ **'disc** *n* Diskette *f*

floral /'flɔːrl/ *adj* Blumen-

florid /'flɒrɪd/ *adj* (*complexion*) gerötet; (*style*) blumig

florist /'flɒrɪst/ *n* Blumenhändler(in) *m*(*f*)

flounder /'flaʊndə(r)/ *vi* zappeln

flour /'flaʊə(r)/ *n* Mehl *nt*

flourish /'flʌrɪʃ/ *n* große Geste *f*; (*scroll*) Schnörkel *m* ● *vi* gedeihen; (*fig*) blühen ● *vt* schwenken

flout /flaʊt/ *vt* missachten

flow /fləʊ/ *n* Fluss *m*; (*of traffic, blood*) Strom *m* ● *vi* fließen

flower /'flaʊə(r)/ *n* Blume *f* ● *vi* blühen

flower: ~**-bed** *n* Blumenbeet *nt*. ~**pot** *n* Blumentopf *m*. ~**y** *adj* blumig

flown /fləʊn/ *see* **fly**²

flu /fluː/ *n* 🔲 Grippe *f*

fluctuat|e /'flʌktjʊeɪt/ *vi* schwanken. ~**ion** *n* Schwankung *f*

fluent /'fluːənt/ *adj* fließend

fluff /flʌf/ *n* Fusseln *pl*; (*down*) Flaum *m*. ~**y** *adj* flauschig

fluid /'fluːɪd/ *adj* flüssig, (*fig*) veränderlich ● *n* Flüssigkeit *f*

fluke /fluːk/ *n* [glücklicher] Zufall *m*

flung /flʌŋ/ *see* **fling**

fluorescent /flʊə'resnt/ *adj* fluoreszierend

fluoride /'flʊəraɪd/ *n* Fluor *nt*

flush /flʌʃ/ *n* (*blush*) Erröten *nt* ● *vi* rot werden ● *vt* spülen ● *adj* in einer Ebene (**with** mit); (🔲: *affluent*) gut bei Kasse

flustered /'flʌstəd/ *adj* nervös

flute /fluːt/ *n* Flöte *f*

flutter /'flʌtə(r)/ *n* Flattern *nt* ● *vi* flattern

fly¹ /flaɪ/ *n* (*pl* **flies**) Fliege *f*

fly² *v* (*pt* **flew**, *pp* **flown**) ● *vi* fliegen; (*flag:*) wehen; (*rush*) sausen ● *vt* fliegen; führen (*flag*)

fly³ *n* & **flies** *pl* (*on trousers*) Hosenschlitz *m*

flyer /'flaɪə(r)/ *n* Flieger(in) *m*(*f*); (*leaflet*) Flugblatt *nt*

foal /fəʊl/ *n* Fohlen *nt*

foam /fəʊm/ *n* Schaum *m*; (*synthetic*) Schaumstoff *m* ● *vi* schäumen

fob /fɒb/ *vt* (*pt/pp* **fobbed**) ~ **sth off** etw andrehen (**on s.o.** jdm); ~ **s.o. off** jdn abspeisen (**with** mit)

focal /'fəʊkl/ *n* Brenn-

focus /'fəʊkəs/ *n* Brennpunkt *m*; **in** ~ scharf eingestellt ● *v* (*pt/pp* **focused** *or* **focussed**) ● *vt* einstellen (**on auf** + *acc*) ● *vi* (*fig*) sich konzentrieren (**on auf** + *acc*)

fog /fɒg/ *n* Nebel *m*

foggy /'fɒgɪ/ *adj* (**foggier, foggiest**) neblig

'fog-horn *n* Nebelhorn *nt*

foible /'fɔɪbl/ *n* Eigenart *f*

foil¹ /fɔɪl/ *n* Folie *f*; (*Culin*) Alufolie *f*

foil² *vt* (*thwart*) vereiteln

foil³ *n* (*Fencing*) Florett *nt*

fold *n* Falte *f*; (*in paper*) Kniff *m* ● *vt* falten; ~ **one's arms** die Arme verschränken ● *vi* sich falten lassen; (*fail*) eingehen. ~ **up** *vt* zusammenfalten; zusammenklappen (*chair*) ● *vi* sich zusammenfalten/-klappen lassen; 🔲 (*business:*) eingehen

fold|er /'fəʊldə(r)/ *n* Mappe *f*. ~**ing** *adj* Klapp-

foliage /'fəʊlɪɪdʒ/ *n* Blätter *pl*; (*of tree*) Laub *nt*

folk /fəʊk/ *npl* Leute *pl*

folk: ~**-dance** *n* Volkstanz *m*. ~**-song** *n* Volkslied *nt*

follow /'fɒləʊ/ *vt/i* folgen (+ *dat*); (*pursue*) verfolgen; (*in vehicle*) nachfahren (+ *dat*). ~ **up** *vt* nachgehen (+ *dat*)

follow|er /'fɒləʊə(r)/ *n* Anhänger(in) *m*(*f*). ~**ing** *adj* folgend ● *n* Folgende(s) *nt*; (*supporters*) Anhängerschaft *f* ● *prep* im Anschluss an (+ *acc*)

folly /'fɒlɪ/ *n* Torheit *f*

fond /fɒnd/ *adj* (**-er, -est**) liebevoll; **be** ~ **of** gern haben; gern essen (*food*)

fondle /'fɒndl/ *vt* liebkosen

fondness /ˈfɒndnɪs/ n Liebe f (**for** zu)

food /fuːd/ n Essen nt; (*for animals*) Futter nt; (*groceries*) Lebensmittel pl. **~ poisoning** n Lebensmittelvergiftung f

food poisoning n Lebensmittelvergiftung f

fool¹ /fuːl/ n (*Culin*) Fruchtcreme f

fool² n Narr m; **make a ~ of oneself** sich lächerlich machen ● vt hereinlegen ● vi **~ around** herumalbern

ˈfool|hardy adj tollkühn. **~ish** adj dumm. **~ishness** n Dummheit f. **~proof** adj narrensicher

foot /fʊt/ n (pl **feet**) Fuß m; (*measure*) Fuß m (30,48 cm); (*of bed*) Fußende nt; **on ~** zu Fuß; **on one's feet** auf den Beinen; **put one's ~ in it** ⊺ ins Fettnäpfchen treten

foot: ~-and-ˈmouth [disease] n Maul- und Klauenseuche f. **~ball** n Fußball m. **~baller** n Fußballspieler m. **~ball pools** npl Fußballtoto nt. **~-bridge** n Fußgängerbrücke f. **~hills** npl Vorgebirge nt. **~hold** n Halt m. **~ing** n Halt m. **~lights** npl Rampenlicht nt. **~note** n Fußnote f. **~path** n Fußweg m. **~print** n Fußabdruck m. **~step** n Schritt m; **follow in s.o.'s ~steps** (*fig*) in jds Fußstapfen treten. **~wear** n Schuhwerk nt

---

for /fɔː(r)/, unstressed /fə(r)/
● preposition
····▸ (*on behalf of; in place of; in favour of*) für (+ acc). **I did it for you** ich habe es für dich gemacht. **I work for him/for a bank** ich arbeite für ihn/für die Bank. **be for doing sth** dafür sein, etw zu tun. **cheque/bill for £5** Scheck/Rechnung über 5 Pfund. **for nothing** umsonst. **what have you got for a cold?** was haben Sie gegen Erkältungen?
····▸ (*expressing reason*) wegen (+ gen); (*with emotion*) aus. **famous for these wines** berühmt wegen dieser Weine od für diese Weine.

he was sentenced to death for murder er wurde wegen Mordes zum Tode verurteilt. **were it not for you/your help** ohne dich/deine Hilfe. **for fear/love of** aus Angst vor (+ dat)/aus Liebe zu (+ dat)
····▸ (*expressing purpose*) (*with action, meal*) zu (+ dat); (*with object*) für (+ acc). **it's for washing the car** es ist zum Autowaschen. **we met for a discussion** wir trafen uns zu einer Besprechung. **for pleasure** zum Vergnügen. **meat for lunch** Fleisch zum Mittagessen. **what is that for?** wofür od wozu ist das? **a dish for nuts** eine Schale für Nüsse
····▸ (*expressing direction*) nach (+ dat); (*less precise*) in Richtung. **the train for Oxford** der Zug nach Oxford. **they were heading** od **making for London** sie fuhren in Richtung London
····▸ (*expressing time*) (*completed process*) ... lang; (*continuing process*) seit (+ dat). **I lived here for two years** ich habe zwei Jahre [lang] hier gewohnt. **I have been living here for two years** ich wohne hier seit zwei Jahren. **we are staying for a week** wir werden eine Woche bleiben
····▸ (*expressing difficulty, impossibility, embarrassment etc.*) + dat. **it's impossible/inconvenient for her** es ist ihr unmöglich/ungelegen. **it was embarrassing for our teacher** unserem Lehrer war es peinlich
● conjunction
····▸ denn. **he's not coming for he has no money** er kommt nicht mit, denn er hat kein Geld

---

forbade /fəˈbæd/ see **forbid**

forbid /fəˈbɪd/ vt (pt **forbade**, pp **forbidden**) verbieten (**s.o.** jdm). **~ding** adj bedrohlich; (*stern*) streng

force /fɔːs/ n Kraft f; (*of blow*) Wucht f; (*violence*) Gewalt f; **in ~** gültig; (*in large numbers*) in großer Zahl; **come**

into ~ in Kraft treten; **the ~s** pl die Streitkräfte pl ● vt zwingen; (break open) aufbrechen

forced /fɔːst/ adj gezwungen; ~ **landing** Notlandung f

force: ~-'**feed** vt (pt/pp -fed) zwangsernähren. ~**ful** adj energisch

forceps /'fɔːseps/ n inv Zange f

forcible /'fɔːsəbl/ adj gewaltsam

ford /fɔːd/ n Furt f ● vt durchwaten; (in vehicle) durchfahren

fore /fɔː(r)/ adj vordere(r,s)

fore: ~**arm** n Unterarm m. ~**cast** Voraussage f; (for weather) Vorhersage f ● vt (pt/pp ~**cast**) voraussagen, vorhersagen. ~**finger** n Zeigefinger m. ~**gone** adj **be a** ~**gone conclusion** von vornherein feststehen. ~**ground** n Vordergrund m. ~**head** /'fɒrɪd/ n Stirn f. ~**hand** n Vorhand f

foreign /'fɒrən/ adj ausländisch; (country) fremd; **he is** ~ er ist Ausländer. ~ **currency** n Devisen pl. ~**er** n Ausländer(in) m(f). ~ **language** n Fremdsprache f

Foreign: ~ **Office** n ≈ Außenministerium nt. ~ '**Secretary** n ≈ Außenminister m

fore: ~**leg** n Vorderbein nt. ~**man** n Vorarbeiter m. ~**most** a führend ● adv **first and** ~**most** zuallererst. ~**name** n Vorname m. ~**runner** n Vorläufer m

fore'see vt (pt -saw, pp -seen) voraussehen, vorhersehen. ~**able** adj **in the** ~**able future** in absehbarer Zeit

'**foresight** n Weitblick m

forest /'fɒrɪst/ n Wald m. ~**er** n Förster m

forestry /'fɒrɪstrɪ/ n Forstwirtschaft f

'**foretaste** n Vorgeschmack m

forever /fə'revə(r)/ adv für immer

fore'warn vt vorher warnen

foreword /'fɔːwɜːd/ n Vorwort nt

forfeit /'fɔːfɪt/ n (in game) Pfand nt ● vt verwirken

forgave /fə'geɪv/ see **forgive**

forge /fɔːdʒ/ n Schmiede f ● vt

schmieden; (counterfeit) fälschen. ~**r** n Fälscher m. ~**ry** n Fälschung f

forget /fə'get/ vt/i (pt -got, pp -gotten) vergessen; verlernen (language, skill). ~**ful** adj vergesslich. ~**fulness** n Vergesslichkeit f. ~-**me-not** n Vergissmeinnicht nt

forgive /fə'gɪv/ vt (pt -gave, pp -given) ~ **s.o. for sth** jdm etw vergeben od verzeihen

forgot(ten) /fə'gɒt(n)/ see **forget**

fork /fɔːk/ n Gabel f; (in road) Gabelung f ● vi (road:) sich gabeln; ~ **right** rechts abzweigen

fork-lift '**truck** n Gabelstapler m

forlorn /fə'lɔːn/ adj verlassen; (hope) schwach

form /fɔːm/ n Form f; (document) Formular nt; (bench) Bank f; (Sch) Klasse f ● vt formen (into zu); (create) bilden ● vi sich bilden; (idea:) Gestalt annehmen

formal /'fɔːml/ adj formell, förmlich. ~**ity** n Förmlichkeit f; (requirement) Formalität f

format /'fɔːmæt/ n Format nt ● vt formatieren

formation /fɔː'meɪʃn/ n Formation f

former /'fɔːmə(r)/ adj ehemalig; **the** ~ der/die/das Erstere. ~**ly** adv früher

formidable /'fɒmɪdəbl/ adj gewaltig

formula /'fɔːmjʊlə/ n (pl -ae or -s) Formel f

formulate /'fɔːmjʊleɪt/ vt formulieren

forsake /fə'seɪk/ vt (pt -sook /-sʊk/, pp -saken) verlassen

fort /fɔːt/ n (Mil) Fort nt

forth /fɔːθ/ adv **back and** ~ hin und her; **and so** ~ und so weiter

forth: ~'**coming** adj bevorstehend; (🗓: communicative) mitteilsam. ~**right** adj direkt

fortieth /'fɔːtɪɪθ/ adj vierzigste(r,s)

fortification /fɔːtɪfɪ'keɪʃn/ n Befestigung f

fortify /'fɔːtɪfaɪ/ vt (pt/pp -ied) befestigen; (fig) stärken

fortnight /'fɔːt-/ n vierzehn Tage pl.

~ly *adj* vierzehntäglich ● *adv* alle vierzehn Tage

fortress /'fɔːtrɪs/ *n* Festung *f*

fortunate /'fɔːtʃənət/ *adj* glücklich; **be ~** Glück haben. **~ly** *adv* glüklicherweise

fortune /'fɔːtʃuːn/ *n* Glück *nt*; (*money*) Vermögen *nt*. **~-teller** *n* Wahrsagerin *f*

forty /'fɔːtɪ/ *adj* vierzig

forward /'fɔːwəd/ *adv* vorwärts; (*to the front*) nach vorn ● *adj* Vorwärts-; (*presumptuous*) anmaßend ● *n* (*Sport*) Stürmer *m* ● *vt* nachsenden (*letter*). **~s** *adv* vorwärts

fossil /'fɒsl/ *n* Fossil *nt*

foster /'fɒstə(r)/ *vt* fördern; in Pflege nehmen (*child*). **~-child** *n* Pflegekind *nt*. **~-mother** *n* Pflegemutter *f*

fought /fɔːt/ *see* **fight**

foul /faʊl/ *adj* (**-er, -est**) widerlich; (*language*) unflätig; **~ play** (*Jur*) Mord ● *n* (*Sport*) Foul *nt* ● *vt* verschmutzen; (*obstruct*) blockieren; (*Sport*) foulen

found[1] /faʊnd/ *see* **find**

found[2] *vt* gründen

foundation /faʊn'deɪʃn/ *n* (*basis*) Gundlage *f*; (*charitable*) Stiftung *f*; **~s** *pl* Fundament *nt*

founder /'faʊndə(r)/ *n* Gründer(in) *m(f)*

foundry /'faʊndrɪ/ *n* Gießerei *f*

fountain /'faʊntɪn/ *n* Brunnen *m*

four /fɔː(r)/ *adj* vier ● *n* Vier *f*

four: **~'teen** *adj* vierzehn ● *n* Vierzehn *f*. **~'teenth** *adj* vierzehnte(r,s)

fourth /fɔːθ/ *adj* vierte(r,s)

fowl /faʊl/ *n* Geflügel *nt*

fox /fɒks/ *n* Fuchs *m* ● *vt* (*puzzle*) verblüffen

foyer /'fɔɪeɪ/ *n* Foyer *nt*; (*in hotel*) Empfangshalle *f*

fraction /'frækʃn/ *n* Bruchteil *m*; (*Math*) Bruch *m*

fracture /'fræktʃə(r)/ *n* Bruch *m* ● *vt/i* brechen

fragile /'frædʒaɪl/ *adj* zerbrechlich

fragment /'frægmənt/ *n* Bruchstück *nt*, Fragment *nt*

fragran|ce /'freɪgrəns/ *n* Duft *m*. **~t** *adj* duftend

frail /freɪl/ *adj* (**-er, -est**) gebrechlich

frame /freɪm/ *n* Rahmen *m*; (*of spectacles*) Gestell *nt*; (*Anat*) Körperbau *m* ● *vt* einrahmen; (*fig*) formulieren; ☒ ein Verbrechen anhängen (+ *dat*). **~work** *n* Gerüst *nt*; (*fig*) Gerippe *nt*

franc /fræŋk/ *n* (*French, Belgian*) Franc *m*; (*Swiss*) Franken *m*

France /frɑːns/ *n* Frankreich *nt*

franchise /'fræntʃaɪz/ *n* (*Pol*) Wahlrecht *nt*; (*Comm*) Franchise *nt*

frank /fræŋk/ *adj* offen

frankfurter /'fræŋkfɜːtə(r)/ *n* Frankfurter *f*

frantic /'fræntɪk/ *adj*, **-ally** *adv* verzweifelt; außer sich (*dat*) (**with** vor)

fraternal /frə'tɜːnl/ *adj* brüderlich

fraud /frɔːd/ *n* Betrug *m*; (*person*) Betrüger(in) *m(f)*

fray /freɪ/ *vi* ausfransen

freak /friːk/ *n* Missbildung *f*; (*person*) Missgeburt *f* ● *adj* anormal

freckle /'frekl/ *n* Sommersprosse *f*

free /friː/ *adj* (**freer, freest**) frei; (*ticket, copy, time*) Frei-; (*lavish*) freigebig; **~ [of charge]** kostenlos; **set ~** freilassen; (*rescue*) befreien ● *vt* (*pt/pp* **freed**) freilassen; (*rescue*) befreien; (*disentangle*) freibekommen

free: **~dom** *n* Freiheit *f*. **~hold** *n* [freier] Grundbesitz *m*. **~lance** *adj & adv* freiberuflich. **~ly** *adv* frei; (*voluntarily*) freiwillig; (*generously*) großzügig. **F~mason** *n* Freimaurer *m*. **~-range** *adj* **~-range eggs** Landeier *pl*. **~ 'sample** *n* Gratisprobe *f*. **~style** *n* Freistil *m*. **~way** *n* (*Amer*) Autobahn *f*

freez|e /friːz/ *vt* (*pt* **froze**, *pp* **frozen**) einfrieren; stoppen (*wages*) ● *vi* **it's ~ing** es friert.

freez|er /'friːzə(r)/ *n* Gefriertruhe *f*; (*upright*) Gefrierschrank *m*. **freezing** *adj* eiskalt ● *n* **five degrees below ~ing** fünf Grad unter Null

freight /freɪt/ n Fracht f. ~**er** n Frachter m. ~ **train** n Güterzug m

French /frentʃ/ adj französisch ● n (Lang) Französisch nt; **the** ~ pl die Franzosen

French: ~ **'beans** npl grüne Bohnen pl. ~ **'bread** n Stangenbrot nt. ~' **fries** npl Pommes frites pl. ~**man** n Franzose m. ~ **'window** n Terrassentür f. ~**woman** n Französin f

frenzy /'frenzɪ/ n Raserei f

frequency /'fri:kwənsɪ/ n Häufigkeit f; (Phys) Frequenz f

frequent¹ /'fri:kwənt/ adj häufig

frequent² /frɪ'kwent/ vt regelmäßig besuchen

fresh /freʃ/ adj (-er, -est) frisch; (new) neu; (cheeky) frech

freshness /'freʃnɪs/ n Frische f

'freshwater adj Süßwasser-

fret /fret/ vi (pt/pp fretted) sich grämen. ~**ful** adj weinerlich

'fretsaw n Laubsäge f

friction /'frɪkʃn/ n Reibung f; (fig) Reibereien pl

Friday /'fraɪdeɪ/ n Freitag m

fridge /frɪdʒ/ n Kühlschrank m

fried /fraɪd/ see fry² ● adj gebraten; ~ **egg** Spiegelei nt

friend /frend/ n Freund(in) m(f). ~**liness** n Freundlichkeit f. ~**ly** adj freundlich; ~**ly with** befreundet mit. ~**ship** n Freundschaft f

fright /fraɪt/ n Schreck m

frighten /'fraɪtn/ vt Angst machen (+ dat); (startle) erschrecken; **be** ~**ed** Angst haben (**of** vor + dat). ~**ing** adj Angst erregend

frightful /'fraɪtfl/ adj schrecklich

frigid /'frɪdʒɪd/ adj frostig; (sexually) frigide. ~**ity** n Frostigkeit f; Frigidität f

frill /frɪl/ n Rüsche f; (paper) Manschette f. ~**y** adj rüschenbesetzt

fringe /frɪndʒ/ n Fransen pl; (of hair) Pony m; (fig: edge) Rand m

frisk /frɪsk/ vi herumspringen ● vt (search) durchsuchen

frisky /'frɪskɪ/ adj lebhaft

fritter /'frɪtə(r)/ vt ~ **[away]** verplempern 🔲

frivol|ity /frɪ'vɒlətɪ/ n Frivolität f. ~**ous** adj frivol, leichtfertig

fro /frəʊ/ see to

frock /frɒk/ n Kleid nt

frog /frɒg/ n Frosch m. ~**man** n Froschmann m

frolic /'frɒlɪk/ vi (pt/pp frolicked) herumtollen

from /frɒm/ prep von (+ dat); (out of) aus (+ dat); (according to) nach (+ dat); ~ **Monday** ab Montag; ~ **that day** seit dem Tag

front /frʌnt/ n Vorderseite f; (fig) Fassade f; (of garment) Vorderteil nt; (sea~) Strandpromenade f; (Mil, Pol, Meteorol) Front f; **in** ~ **of** vor; **in** or **at the** ~ vorne; **to the** ~ nach vorne ● adj vordere(r,s); (page, row) erste(r,s); (tooth, wheel) Vorder-

front: ~ **'door** n Haustür f. ~ **'garden** n Vorgarten m

frontier /'frʌntɪə(r)/ n Grenze f

frost /frɒst/ n Frost m; (hoar-~) Raureif m; **ten degrees of** ~ zehn Grad Kälte. ~**bite** n Erfrierung f. ~**bitten** adj erfroren

frost|ed /'frɒstɪd/ adj ~**ed glass** Mattglas nt. ~**ing** n (Amer Culin) Zuckerguss m. ~**y** adj, **-ily** adv frostig

froth /frɒθ/ n Schaum m ● vi schäumen. ~**y** adj schaumig

frown /fraʊn/ n Stirnrunzeln nt ● vi die Stirn runzeln

froze /frəʊz/ see freeze

frozen /'frəʊzn/ see freeze ● adj gefroren; (Culin) tiefgekühlt; **I'm** ~ 🔲 mir ist eiskalt. ~ **food** n Tiefkühlkost f

frugal /'fru:gl/ adj sparsam; (meal) frugal

fruit /fru:t/ n Frucht f; (collectively) Obst nt. ~ **cake** n englischer [Tee]kuchen m

fruitful adj fruchtbar

fruit: ~ **juice** n Obstsaft m. ~**less** adj fruchtlos. ~ **'salad** n Obstsalat m

fruity /'fru:tɪ/ adj fruchtig

frustrat|e /frʌ'streɪt/ vt vereiteln; (*Psychology*) frustrieren. **~ion** n Frustration f

fry /fraɪ/ vt/i (pt/pp **fried**) [in der Pfanne] braten. **~ing-pan** n Bratpfanne f

fuel /'fju:əl/ n Brennstoff m; (for car) Kraftstoff m; (for aircraft) Treibstoff m

fugitive /'fju:dʒɪtɪv/ n Flüchtling m

fulfil /fʊl'fɪl/ vt (pt/pp **-filled**) erfüllen. **~ment** n Erfüllung f

full /fʊl/ adj & adv (**-er, -est**) voll; (detailed) ausführlich; (skirt) weit; **~ of** voll von (+ dat), voller (+ gen); **at ~ speed** in voller Fahrt ● n **in ~** vollständig

full: ~ 'moon n Vollmond m. **~-scale** adj (model) in Originalgröße; (rescue, alert) großangelegt. **~ 'stop** n Punkt m. **~-time** adj ganztägig ● adv ganztags

fully /'fʊlɪ/ adv völlig; (in detail) ausführlich

fumble /'fʌmbl/ vi herumfummeln (**with** an + dat)

fume /fju:m/ vi vor Wut schäumen

fumes /fju:mz/ npl Dämpfe pl; (from car) Abgase pl

fun /fʌn/ n Spaß m; **for ~** aus od zum Spaß; **make ~ of** sich lustig machen über (+ acc); **have ~!** viel Spaß!

function /'fʌŋkʃn/ n Funktion f; (event) Veranstaltung f ● vi funktionieren; (serve) dienen (**as** als). **~al** adj zweckmäßig

fund /fʌnd/ n Fonds m; (fig) Vorrat m; **~s** pl Geldmittel pl ● vt finanzieren

fundamental /fʌndə'mentl/ adj grundlegend; (essential) wesentlich

funeral /'fju:nərl/ n Beerdigung f; (cremation) Feuerbestattung f

funeral: ~ march n Trauermarsch m. **~ service** n Trauergottesdienst m

'funfair n Jahrmarkt m

fungus /'fʌŋgəs/ n (pl **-gi** /-gaɪ/) Pilz m

funnel /'fʌnl/ n Trichter m; (on ship, train) Schornstein m

funnily /'fʌnɪlɪ/ adv komisch; **~ enough** komischerweise

funny /'fʌnɪ/ adj komisch

fur /fɜ:(r)/ n Fell nt; (for clothing) Pelz m; (in kettle) Kesselstein m. **~ 'coat** n Pelzmantel m

furious /'fjʊərɪəs/ adj wütend (**with** auf + acc)

furnace /'fɜ:nɪs/ n (Techn) Ofen m

furnish /'fɜ:nɪʃ/ vt einrichten; (supply) liefern. **~ed** adj **~ed room** möbliertes Zimmer nt. **~ings** npl Einrichtungsgegenstände pl

furniture /'fɜ:nɪtʃə(r)/ n Möbel pl

further /'fɜ:ðə(r)/ adj weitere(r,s); **at the ~ end** am anderen Ende; **until ~ notice** bis auf weiteres ● adv weiter; **~ off** weiter entfernt ● vt fördern

furthermore /fɜ:ðə'mɔ:(r)/ adv außerdem

furthest /'fɜ:ðɪst/ adj am weitesten entfernt ● adv am weitesten

fury /'fjʊərɪ/ n Wut f

fuse¹ /fju:z/ n (of bomb) Zünder m; (cord) Zündschnur f

fuse² n (Electr) Sicherung f ● vt/i verschmelzen; **the lights have ~d** die Sicherung [für das Licht] ist durchgebrannt. **~-box** n Sicherungskasten m

fuselage /'fju:zəlɑ:ʒ/ n (Aviat) Rumpf m

fuss /fʌs/ n Getue nt; **make a ~ of** verwöhnen; (caress) liebkosen ● vi Umstände machen

fussy /'fʌsɪ/ adj wählerisch; (particular) penibel

futil|e /'fju:taɪl/ adj zwecklos. **~ity** n Zwecklosigkeit f

future /'fju:tʃə(r)/ adj zukünftig ● n Zukunft f; (Gram) [erstes] Futur nt

futuristic /fju:tʃə'rɪstɪk/ adj futuristisch

fuzzy /'fʌzɪ/ adj (hair) kraus; (blurred) verschwommen

Gg

gabble /'gæbl/ vi schnell reden

gable /'geɪbl/ n Giebel m

gadget /'gædʒɪt/ n [kleines] Gerät nt

Gaelic /'geɪlɪk/ n Gälisch nt

gag /gæg/ n Knebel m; (joke) Witz m; (Theat) Gag m ● vt (pt/pp **gagged**) knebeln

gaiety /'geɪətɪ/ n Fröhlichkeit f

gaily /'geɪlɪ/ adv fröhlich

gain /geɪn/ n Gewinn m; (increase) Zunahme f ● vt gewinnen; (obtain) erlangen; ~ **weight** zunehmen ● vi (clock:) vorgehen

gait /geɪt/ n Gang m

gala /'gɑːlə/ n Fest nt ● attrib Gala-

galaxy /'gæləksɪ/ n Galaxie f; **the G~** die Milchstraße

gale /geɪl/ n Sturm m

gallant /'gælənt/ adj tapfer; (chivalrous) galant. ~**ry** n Tapferkeit f

'gall-bladder n Gallenblase f

gallery /'gælərɪ/ n Galerie f

galley /'gælɪ/ n (ship's kitchen) Kombüse f; ~ **[proof]** [Druck]fahne f

gallon /'gælən/ n Gallone f (= 4,5 l; Amer = 3,785 l)

gallop /'gæləp/ n Galopp m ● vi galoppieren

gallows /'gæləʊz/ n Galgen m

galore /gə'lɔː(r)/ adv in Hülle und Fülle

gamble /'gæmbl/ n (risk) Risiko nt ● vi [um Geld] spielen; ~ **on** (rely) sich verlassen auf (+ acc). ~**r** n Spieler(in) m(f)

game /geɪm/ n Spiel nt; (animals, birds) Wild nt; ~**s** (Sch) Sport m ● adj (brave) tapfer; (willing) bereit (**for** zu). ~**keeper** n Wildhüter m

gammon /'gæmən/ n [geräucherter] Schinken m

gang /gæŋ/ n Bande f; (of workmen) Kolonne f

gangling /'gæŋglɪŋ/ adj schlaksig

gangmaster /'gæŋmɑːstə(r)/ n Aufseher(in) m(f) von (meist illegalen) Gelegenheitsarbeitern

gangrene /'gæŋgriːn/ n Wundbrand m

gangster /'gæŋstə(r)/ n Gangster m

gangway /'gæŋweɪ/ n Gang m; (Naut, Aviat) Gangway f

gaol /dʒeɪl/ n Gefängnis nt ● vt ins Gefängnis sperren. ~**er** n Gefängniswärter m

gap /gæp/ n Lücke f; (interval) Pause f; (difference) Unterschied m

gap|e /geɪp/ vi gaffen; ~**e at** anstarren. ~**ing** adj klaffend

---

gap year Britische Schulabsolventen legen vor Universitätsbeginn oft eine einjährige Pause ein. In diesem gap year jobben sie, um Arbeitserfahrung zu erwerben oder Geld für ihr Studium zu verdienen. Viele reisen um die Welt, lernen die Kultur anderer Länder kennen, sammeln Auslandserfahrungen, belegen Sprachkurse oder arbeiten ehrenamtlich in Entwickungsländern. *i*

---

garage /'gærɑːʒ/ n Garage f; (for repairs) Werkstatt f; (for petrol) Tankstelle f

garbage /'gɑːbɪdʒ/ n Müll m. ~ **can** n (Amer) Mülleimer m

garbled /'gɑːbld/ adj verworren

garden /'gɑːdn/ n Garten m; **[public] ~s** pl [öffentliche] Anlagen pl ● vi im Garten arbeiten. ~**er** n Gärtner(in) m(f). ~**ing** n Gartenarbeit f

gargle /'gɑːgl/ n (liquid) Gurgelwasser nt ● vi gurgeln

garish /'geərɪʃ/ adj grell

garland /'gɑːlənd/ n Girlande f

garlic /'gɑːlɪk/ n Knoblauch m

garment /'gɑːmənt/ n Kleidungsstück nt

garnet /'gɑːnɪt/ n Granat m

garnish /'gɑːnɪʃ/ n Garnierung f ● vt garnieren

garrison /'gærɪsn/ n Garnison f

garrulous /'gærʊləs/ adj geschwätzig

garter /'gɑːtə(r)/ n Strumpfband nt; (Amer: suspender) Strumpfhalter m

gas /gæs/ n Gas nt; (Amer, fam: petrol) Benzin nt ● v (pt/pp **gassed**) ● vt vergasen ● vi 🔲 schwatzen. ~ **cooker** n Gasherd m. ~ '**fire** n Gasofen m

gash /gæʃ/ n Schnitt m; (wound) klaffende Wunde f

gasket /'gæskɪt/ n (Techn) Dichtung f

gas: ~ **mask** n Gasmaske f. ~-**meter** n Gaszähler m

gasoline /'gæsəliːn/ n (Amer) Benzin nt

gasp /gɑːsp/ vi keuchen; (in surprise) hörbar die Luft einziehen

'**gas station** n (Amer) Tankstelle f

gastric /'gæstrɪk/ adj Magen-

gastronomy /gæ'strɒnəmɪ/ n Gastronomie f

gate /geɪt/ n Tor nt; (to field) Gatter nt; (barrier) Schranke f; (at airport) Flugsteig m

gate: ~**crasher** n ungeladener Gast m. ~**way** n Tor nt

gather /'gæðə(r)/ vt sammeln; (pick) pflücken; (conclude) folgern (**from** aus) ● vi sich versammeln; (storm:) sich zusammenziehen. ~**ing** n family ~**ing** Familientreffen nt

gaudy /'gɔːdɪ/ adj knallig

gauge /geɪdʒ/ n Stärke f; (Rail) Spurweite f; (device) Messinstrument nt

gaunt /gɔːnt/ adj hager

gauze /gɔːz/ n Gaze f

gave /geɪv/ see give

gawky /'gɔːkɪ/ adj schlaksig

gay /geɪ/ adj (-er, -est) fröhlich; (homosexual) homosexuell

gaze /geɪz/ n [langer] Blick m ● vi sehen; ~ **at** ansehen

GB abbr Great Britain

gear /gɪə(r)/ n Ausrüstung f; (Techn) Getriebe nt; (Auto) Gang m; **change** ~ schalten

-**gear:** ~**box** n (Auto) Getriebe nt.

~-**lever** n, (Amer) ~-**shift** n Schalthebel m

geese /giːs/ see goose

gel /dʒel/ n Gel nt

gelatine /'dʒelətɪn/ n Gelatine f

gem /dʒem/ n Juwel nt

gender /'dʒendə(r)/ n (Gram) Geschlecht nt

gene /dʒiːn/ n Gen nt

genealogy /dʒiːnɪ'ælədʒɪ/ n Genealogie f

general /'dʒenrəl/ adj allgemein ● n General m; **in** ~ im Allgemeinen. ~ e'**lection** n allgemeine Wahlen pl

generaliz|ation /dʒenrəlaɪ'zeɪʃn/ n Verallgemeinerung f. ~**e** vi verallgemeinern

generally /'dʒenrəlɪ/ adv im Allgemeinen

general prac'titioner n praktischer Arzt m

generate /'dʒenəreɪt/ vt erzeugen

generation /dʒenə'reɪʃn/ n Generation f

generator /'dʒenəreɪtə(r)/ n Generator m

generosity /dʒenə'rɒsɪtɪ/ n Großzügigkeit f

generous /'dʒenərəs/ adj großzügig

genetic /dʒə'netɪk/ adj, -**ally** adv genetisch. ~**ally modified** gentechnisch verändert; genmanipuliert. ~ **engineering** n Gentechnologie f

Geneva /dʒɪ'niːvə/ n Genf nt

genial /'dʒiːnɪəl/ adj freundlich

genitals /'dʒenɪtlz/ pl [äußere] Geschlechtsteile pl

genitive /'dʒenɪtɪv/ adj & n ~ [**case**] Genitiv m

genius /'dʒiːnɪəs/ n (pl -**uses**) Genie nt; (quality) Genialität f

genome /'dʒiːnəʊm/ n Genom nt

genre /'ʒɑ̃rə/ n Gattung f, Genre nt

gent /dʒent/ n 🔲 Herr m; **the** ~**s** sg die Herrentoilette f

genteel /dʒen'tiːl/ adj vornehm

gentle /'dʒentl/ adj (-r, -st) sanft

gentleman /'dʒentlmən/ n Herr m; (well-mannered) Gentleman m

gent|leness /'dʒentlnɪs/ n Sanftheit f. **~ly** adv sanft

genuine /'dʒenjʊɪn/ adj echt; (sincere) aufrichtig. **~ly** adv (honestly) ehrlich

geograph|ical /dʒɪə'græfɪkl/ adj geographisch. **~y** n Geographie f, Erdkunde f

geological /dʒɪə'lɒdʒɪkl/ adj geologisch

geolog|ist /dʒɪ'ɒlədʒɪst/ n Geologe m/-gin f. **~y** n Geologie f

geometr|ic(al) /dʒɪə'metrɪk(l)/ adj geometrisch. **~y** n Geometrie f

geranium /dʒə'reɪnɪəm/ n Geranie f

geriatric /dʒerɪ'ætrɪk/ adj geriatrisch ● n geriatrischer Patient m

germ /dʒɜːm/ n Keim m; **~s** pl 🗉 Bazillen pl

German /'dʒɜːmən/ adj deutsch ● n (person) Deutsche(r) m/f; (Lang) Deutsch nt; **in ~** auf Deutsch; **into ~** ins Deutsche

Germanic /dʒə'mænɪk/ adj germanisch

Germany /'dʒɜːmənɪ/ n Deutschland nt

germinate /'dʒɜːmɪneɪt/ vi keimen

gesticulate /dʒe'stɪkjʊleɪt/ vi gestikulieren

gesture /'dʒestʃə(r)/ n Geste f

---

get /get/ v

> ❗ pt **got**, pp **got** (Amer also **gotten**), pres p **getting**

● transitive verb

····▸ (obtain, receive) bekommen, 🗉 kriegen; (procure) besorgen; (buy) kaufen; (fetch) holen. **get a job/taxi for s.o.** jdm einen Job verschaffen/ein Taxi besorgen. **I must get some bread** ich muss Brot holen. **get permission** die Erlaubnis erhalten. **I couldn't get her on the phone** ich konnte sie nicht telefonisch erreichen

····▸ (prepare) machen (meal). **he got the breakfast** er machte das Frühstück

····▸ (cause) **get s.o. to do sth** jdn dazu bringen, etw zu tun. **get one's hair cut** sich (dat) die Haare schneiden lassen. **get one's hands dirty** sich (dat) die Hände schmutzig machen

····▸ **get the bus/train.** (travel by) den Bus/Zug nehmen; (be in time for, catch) den Bus/Zug erreichen

····▸ **have got** (🗉: have) haben. **I've got a cold** ich habe eine Erkältung

····▸ **have got to do sth** etw tun müssen. **I've got to hurry** ich muss mich beeilen

····▸ (🗉: understand) kapieren 🗉. **I don't get it** ich kapiere nicht

● intransitive verb

····▸ (become) werden. **get older** älter werden. **the weather got worse** das Wetter wurde schlechter. **get to** kommen zu/nach (town); (reach) erreichen. **get dressed** sich anziehen. **get married** heiraten.

● phrasal verbs

● **get about** vi (move) sich bewegen; (travel) herumkommen; (spread) sich verbreiten. ● **get at** vt (have access) herankommen an (+ acc); (🗉: criticize) anmachen 🗉. (mean) **what are you getting at?** worauf willst du hinaus? ● **get away** vi (leave) wegkommen; (escape) entkommen. ● **get back** vi zurückkommen; vt (recover) zurückbekommen; **get one's own back** sich revanchieren. ● **get by** vi vorbeikommen; (manage) sein Auskommen haben. ● **get down** vi heruntersteigen; vt (depress) deprimieren; **get down to** sich [heran]machen an (+ acc). ● **get in** vi (into bus) einsteigen; vt (fetch) hereinholen. ● **get off** vi (dismount) absteigen; (from bus) aussteigen; (leave) wegkommen; (Jur) freigesprochen werden; vt (remove) abbekommen. ● **get on** vi (mount) aufsteigen; (to bus) einsteigen; (be on good terms) gut auskommen (**with** mit + *dat*); (*make progress*) Fortschritte machen; **how are you getting on?** wie geht's? ● **get out** vi herauskommen; (*of car*) aussteigen; **get out of** (*avoid doing*) sich drücken um; vt (*take out*) herausholen; herausbekommen (*cork, stain*). ● **get over** vi hinübersteigen; vt (*fig*) hinwegkommen über (+ *acc*). ● **get round** vi herumkommen; **I never get round to it** ich komme nie dazu; vt herumkriegen; (*avoid*) umgehen. ● **get through** vi durchkommen. ● **get up** vi aufstehen

get: ~**away** n Flucht f. ~**-up** n Aufmachung f

ghastly /'gɑːstlɪ/ adj grässlich; (*pale*) blass

gherkin /'gɜːkɪn/ n Essiggurke f

ghost /gəʊst/ n Geist m, Gespenst nt. ~**ly** adj geisterhaft

ghoulish /'guːlɪʃ/ adj makaber

giant /'dʒaɪənt/ n Riese m ● adj riesig

gibberish /'dʒɪbərɪʃ/ n Kauderwelsch nt

giblets /'dʒɪblɪts/ npl Geflügelklein nt

giddiness /'gɪdɪnɪs/ n Schwindel m

giddy /'gɪdɪ/ adj schwindlig

gift /gɪft/ n Geschenk nt; (*to charity*) Gabe f; (*talent*) Begabung f. ~**ed** adj begabt

gigantic /dʒaɪ'gæntɪk/ adj riesig, riesengroß

giggle /'gɪgl/ n Kichern nt ● vi kichern

gild /gɪld/ vt vergolden

gilt /gɪlt/ adj vergoldet ● n Vergoldung f. ~**-edged** adj (*Comm*) mündelsicher

gimmick /'gɪmɪk/ n Trick m

gin /dʒɪn/ n Gin m

ginger /'dʒɪndʒə(r)/ adj rotblond; (*cat*) rot ● n Ingwer m. ~**bread** n Pfefferkuchen m

gingerly /'dʒɪndʒəlɪ/ adv vorsichtig

gipsy /'dʒɪpsɪ/ n = **gypsy**

giraffe /dʒɪ'rɑːf/ n Giraffe f

girder /'gɜːdə(r)/ n (*Techn*) Träger m

girl /gɜːl/ n Mädchen nt; (*young woman*) junge Frau f. ~ **band** n Mädchenband f. ~**friend** n Freundin f. ~**ish** adj mädchenhaft

gist /dʒɪst/ n **the** ~ das Wesentliche

give /gɪv/ n Elastizität f ● v (*pt* **gave**, *pp* **given**) ● vt geben/(*as present*) schenken; (**to** dat); (*donate*) spenden; (*lecture*) halten; (*one's name*) angeben ● vi geben; (*yield*) nachgeben. ~ **away** vt verschenken; (*betray*) verraten; (*distribute*) verteilen. ~ **back** vt zurückgeben. ~ **in** vt einreichen ● vi (*yield*) nachgeben. ~ **off** vt abgeben. ~ **up** vt/i aufgeben; ~ **oneself up** sich stellen. ~ **way** vi nachgeben; (*Auto*) die Vorfahrt beachten

glacier /'glæsɪə(r)/ n Gletscher m

glad /glæd/ adj froh (**of** über + *acc*)

gladly /'glædlɪ/ adv gern[e]

glamorous /'glæmərəs/ adj glanzvoll; (*film star*) glamourös

glamour /'glæmə(r)/ n [betörender] Glanz m

glance /glɑːns/ n [flüchtiger] Blick m ● vi ~ **at** einen Blick werfen auf (+ *acc*). ~ **up** vi aufblicken

gland /glænd/ n Drüse f

glare /gleə(r)/ n grelles Licht nt; (*look*) ärgerlicher Blick m ● vi ~ **at** böse ansehen

glaring /'gleərɪŋ/ adj grell; (*mistake*) krass

glass /glɑːs/ n Glas nt; (*mirror*) Spiegel m; ~**es** pl (*spectacles*) Brille f. ~**y** adj glasig

glaze /gleɪz/ n Glasur f

gleam /gliːm/ n Schein m ● vi glänzen

glib /glɪb/ adj (*pej*) gewandt

glid|e /glaɪd/ vi gleiten; (*through the air*) schweben. ~**er** n Segelflugzeug nt. ~**ing** n Segelfliegen nt

glimmer /'glɪmə(r)/ n Glimmen nt ● vi glimmen

glimpse /glɪmps/ vt flüchtig sehen

glint /glɪnt/ n Blitzen nt ● vi blitzen

glisten /'glɪsn/ vi glitzern

glitter /'glɪtə(r)/ vi glitzern

global /'gləʊbl/ adj global

globaliz|e /ˈgləʊbəlaɪz/ vt globalisieren. **~ation** n Globalisierung f

globe /gləʊb/ n Kugel f; (map) Globus m

gloom /gluːm/ n Düsterkeit f; (fig) Pessimismus m

gloomy /ˈgluːmɪ/ adj , **-ily** adv düster; (fig) pessimistisch

glorif|y /ˈglɔːrɪfaɪ/ vt (pt/pp **-ied**) verherrlichen

glorious /ˈglɔːrɪəs/ adj herrlich; (deed, hero) glorreich

glory /ˈglɔːrɪ/ n Ruhm m; (splendour) Pracht f ● vi ~ **in** genießen

gloss /glɒs/ n Glanz m ● adj Glanz- ● vi ~ **over** beschönigen

glossary /ˈglɒsərɪ/ n Glossar nt

glossy /ˈglɒsɪ/ adj glänzend

glove /glʌv/ n Handschuh m

glow /gləʊ/ n Glut f; (of candle) Schein m ● vi glühen; (candle:) scheinen. **~ing** adj glühend; (account) begeistert

glucose /ˈgluːkəʊs/ n Traubenzucker m, Glukose f

glue /gluː/ n Klebstoff m ● vt (pres p **gluing**) kleben (**to** an + acc)

glum /glʌm/ adj (**glummer, glummest**) niedergeschlagen

glut /glʌt/ n Überfluss m (**of** an + dat)

glutton /ˈglʌtən/ n Vielfraß m

GM abbr (**genetically modified**); ~ **crops/food** gentechnisch veränderte Feldfrüchte/Nahrungsmittel

gnash /næʃ/ vt ~ **one's teeth** mit den Zähnen knirschen

gnat /næt/ n Mücke f

gnaw /nɔː/ vt/i nagen (**at** an + dat)

go /gəʊ/

! 3 sg pres tense **goes**; pt **went**; pp **gone**

● intransitive verb

••••▸ gehen; (in vehicle) fahren. **go by air** fliegen. **where are you going?** wo gehst du hin? **I'm going to France** ich fahre nach Frankreich. **go to the doctor's/dentist's** zum Arzt/Zahnarzt gehen. **go to the theatre/cinema** ins Theater/Kino gehen. **I must go to Paris/to the doctor's** ich muss nach Paris/zum Arzt. **go shopping** einkaufen gehen. **go swimming** schwimmen gehen. **go to see s.o.** jdn besuchen [gehen]

••••▸ (leave) weggehen; (on journey) abfahren. **I must go now** ich muss jetzt gehen. **we're going on Friday** wir fahren am Freitag

••••▸ (work, function) (engine, clock) gehen

••••▸ (become) werden. **go deaf** taub werden. **go mad** verrückt werden. **he went red** er wurde rot

••••▸ (pass) (time) vergehen

••••▸ (disappear) weggehen; (coat, hat, stain) verschwinden. **my headache/my coat/the stain has gone** mein Kopfweh/mein Mantel/der Fleck ist weg

••••▸ (turn out, progress) gehen; verlaufen. **everything's going very well** alles geht od verläuft sehr gut. **how did the party go?** wie war die Party? **go smoothly/according to plan** reibungslos/planmäßig verlaufen

••••▸ (match) zusammenpassen. **the two colours don't go [together]** die beiden Farben passen nicht zusammen

••••▸ (cease to function) kaputtgehen; (fuse) durchbrennen. **his memory is going** sein Gedächtnis lässt nach

● auxiliary verb

••••▸ **be going to** werden + inf. **it's going to rain** es wird regnen. **I'm not going to** ich werde es nicht tun

● noun

! pl **goes**

••••▸ (turn) **it's your go** du bist jetzt an der Reihe od dran

····▸ (*attempt*) Versuch. **have a go at doing sth** versuchen, etw zu tun. **have another go!** versuch's noch mal!

····▸ (*energy, drive*) Energie

····▸ (*in phrases*) **on the go** auf Trab. **make a go of sth** das Beste aus etw machen

● *phrasal verbs*

● **go across** *vi* hinübergehen/-fahren; *vt* überqueren. ● **go after** *vt* (*pursue*) jagen. ● **go away** *vi* weggehen/-fahren; (*on holiday or business*) verreisen. ● **go back** *vi* zurückgehen/-fahren. ● **go back on** *vt* nicht [ein]halten (*promise*). ● **go by** *vi* vorbeigehen/-fahren; (*time*) vergehen. ● **go down** *vi* hinuntergehen/-fahren; (*sun, ship*) untergehen; (*prices*) fallen; (*temperature, swelling*) zurückgehen. ● **go for** *vt* holen; (🔲: *attack*) losgehen auf (+ *acc*). ● **go in** *vi* hineingehen/-fahren; ● **go in for** teilnehmen an (+ *dat*) (*competition*); (*take up*) sich verlegen auf (+ *acc*). ● **go off** *vi* weggehen/-fahren; (*alarm clock*) klingeln; (*alarm, gun, bomb*) losgehen; (*light*) ausgehen; (*go bad*) schlecht werden; *vt*: **go off sth** von etw abkommen. ● **go off well** gut verlaufen. ● **go on** *vi* weitergehen/-fahren; (*light*) angehen; (*continue*) weitermachen; (*talking*) fortfahren; (*happen*) vorgehen. ● **go on at** 🔲 herumnörgeln an (+ *dat*). ● **go out** *vi* (*from home*) ausgehen; (*leave*) hinausgehen/-fahren; (*fire, light*) ausgehen; **go out to work/for a meal** arbeiten/essen gehen; **go out with s.o.** (🔲: *date s.o.*) mit jdm gehen. ● **go over** *vi* hinübergehen/-fahren; *vt* (*rehearse*) durchgehen. ● **go round** *vi* herumgehen/-fahren; (*visit*) vorbeigehen; (*turn*) sich drehen; (*be enough*) reichen. ● **go through** *vi* durchgehen/-fahren;

vt (*suffer*) durchmachen; (*rehearse*) durchgehen; (*bags*) durchsuchen. ● **go through with** *vt* zu Ende machen. ● **go under** *vi* untergehen/-fahren; (*fail*) scheitern. ● **go up** *vi* hinaufgehen/-fahren; (*lift*) hochfahren; (*prices*) steigen. ● **go without** *vt*: **go without sth** auf etw (*acc*) verzichten; *vi* darauf verzichten

'go-ahead *adj* fortschrittlich; (*enterprising*) unternehmend ● *n* (*fig*) grünes Licht *nt*

goal /gəʊl/ *n* Ziel *nt*; (*sport*) Tor *nt*. **~keeper** *n* Torwart *m*. **~post** *n* Torpfosten *m*

goat /gəʊt/ *n* Ziege *f*

gobble /'gɒbl/ *vt* hinunterschlingen

God, god /gɒd/ *n* Gott *m*

god: ~child *n* Patenkind *nt*. **~-daughter** *n* Patentochter *f*. **~dess** *n* Göttin *f*. **~father** *n* Pate *m*. **~mother** *n* Patin *f*. **~parents** *npl* Paten *pl*. **~send** *n* Segen *m*. **~son** *n* Patensohn *m*.

goggles /'gɒglz/ *npl* Schutzbrille *f*

going /'gəʊɪŋ/ *adj* (*price, rate*) gängig; (*concern*) gut gehend ● *n* **it is hard ~** es ist schwierig

gold /gəʊld/ *n* Gold *nt* ● *adj* golden

golden /'gəʊldn/ *adj* golden. **~ 'wedding** *n* goldene Hochzeit *f*

gold: ~fish *n inv* Goldfisch *m*. **~-mine** *n* Goldgrube *f*. **~-plated** *adj* vergoldet. **~smith** *n* Goldschmied *m*

golf /gɒlf/ *n* Golf *nt*

golf: ~-club *n* Golfklub *m*; (*implement*) Golfschläger *m*. **~-course** *n* Golfplatz *m*. **~er** *m* Golfspieler(in) *m(f)*

gone /gɒn/ *see* go

good /gʊd/ *adj* (**better, best**) gut; (*well-behaved*) brav, artig; **~ at** gut in (+ *dat*); **a ~ deal** ziemlich viel; **~ morning/evening** guten Morgen/Abend ● *n* **for ~** für immer; **do ~** Gutes tun; **do s.o. ~** jdm gut tun; **it's no ~** es ist nutzlos; (*hopeless*) da ist nichts zu machen

goodbye /gʊdˈbaɪ/ int auf Wiedersehen; (Teleph, Radio) auf Wiederhören

good: G~ 'Friday n Karfreitag m.
~-'looking adj gut aussehend.
~-'natured adj gutmütig

goodness /ˈgʊdnɪs/ n Güte f; **thank
~!** Gott sei Dank!

goods /gʊdz/ npl Waren pl. **~ train**
n Güterzug m

good'will n Wohlwollen nt; (Comm)
Goodwill m

gooey /ˈguːɪ/ adj ☐ klebrig

google /ˈguːgl/ ® vt, vi googeln

goose /guːs/ n (pl **geese**) Gans f

gooseberry /ˈgʊzbərɪ/ n Stachel-
beere f

goose: /guːs/ **~-flesh** n, **~-pimples**
npl Gänsehaut f

gorge /gɔːdʒ/ n (Geog) Schlucht f
● vt **~ oneself** sich vollessen

gorgeous /ˈgɔːdʒəs/ adj prachtvoll;
☐ herrlich

gorilla /gəˈrɪlə/ n Gorilla m

gormless /ˈgɔːmlɪs/ adj ☐ doof

gorse /gɔːs/ n inv Stechginster m

gory /ˈgɔːrɪ/ adj blutig; (story) blut-
rünstig

gosh /gɒʃ/ int ☐ Mensch!

gospel /ˈgɒspl/ n Evangelium nt

gossip /ˈgɒsɪp/ n Klatsch m; (person)
Klatschbase f ● vi klatschen

got /gɒt/ see **get**; **have ~** haben;
have ~ to müssen; **have ~ to do
sth** etw tun müssen

Gothic /ˈgɒθɪk/ adj gotisch

gotten /ˈgɒtn/ see **get**

goulash /ˈguːlæʃ/ n Gulasch nt

gourmet /ˈgʊəmeɪ/ n Feinschme-
cker m

govern /ˈgʌvn/ vt/i regieren; (determine) bestimmen

government /ˈgʌvnmənt/ n Regierung f

governor /ˈgʌvənə(r)/ n Gouverneur
m; (on board) Vorstandsmitglied nt;
(of prison) Direktor m; (☐: boss)
Chef m

gown /gaʊn/ n [elegantes] Kleid nt;
(Univ, Jur) Talar m

GP abbr **general practitioner**

GPS abbr (Global Positioning System) GPS nt

grab /græb/ vt (pt/pp **grabbed**) ergreifen; **~ [hold of]** packen

grace /greɪs/ n Anmut f; (before
meal) Tischgebet nt; **three days' ~**
drei Tage Frist. **~ful** adj anmutig

gracious /ˈgreɪʃəs/ adj gnädig; (elegant) vornehm

grade /greɪd/ n Stufe f; (Comm) Gü-
teklasse f; (Sch) Note f; (Amer, Sch:
class) Klasse f; (Amer) = **gradient** ● vt
einstufen; (Comm) sortieren. **~ crossing** n (Amer) Bahnübergang m

gradient /ˈgreɪdɪənt/ n Steigung f;
(downward) Gefälle nt

gradual /ˈgrædʒʊəl/ adj allmählich

graduate /ˈgrædʒʊət/ n Akademi-
ker(in) m(f)

graffiti /grəˈfiːti/ npl Graffiti pl

graft /grɑːft/ n (Bot) Pfropfreis nt;
(Med) Transplantat nt; (☐: hard
work) Plackerei f

grain /greɪn/ n (sand, salt, rice) Korn
nt; (cereals) Getreide nt; (in wood)
Maserung f

gram /græm/ n Gramm nt

grammar /ˈgræmə(r)/ n Grammatik
f. **~ school** n ≈ Gymnasium nt

grammatical /grəˈmætɪkl/ adj
grammatisch

grand /grænd/ adj (-er, -est) großartig

grandad /ˈgrændæd/ n ☐ Opa m

'grandchild n Enkelkind nt

'granddaughter n Enkelin f

grandeur /ˈgrændʒə(r)/ n Pracht f

'grandfather n Großvater m. **~
clock** n Standuhr f

grandiose /ˈgrændɪəʊs/ adj gran-
dios

grand: ~mother n Großmutter f.
~parents npl Großeltern pl. **~
pi'ano** n Flügel m. **~son** n Enkel m.
~stand n Tribüne f

granite /ˈgrænɪt/ n Granit m

granny /'grænɪ/ n 🔲 Oma f

grant /grɑːnt/ n Subvention f; (Univ) Studienbeihilfe f ● vt gewähren; (admit) zugeben; **take sth for** ∼**ed** etw als selbstverständlich hinnehmen

grape /greɪp/ n [Wein]traube f; **bunch of** ∼**s** [ganze] Weintraube f

grapefruit /'greɪp-/ n invar Grapefruit f

graph /grɑːf/ n grafische Darstellung f

graphic /'græfɪk/ adj, **-ally** adv grafisch; (vivid) anschaulich

'graph paper n Millimeterpapier nt

grapple /'græpl/ vi ringen

grasp /grɑːsp/ n Griff m ● vt ergreifen; (understand) begreifen. ∼**ing** adj habgierig

grass /grɑːs/ n Gras nt; (lawn) Rasen m. ∼**hopper** n Heuschrecke f

grassy /'grɑːsɪ/ adj grasig

grate¹ /greɪt/ n Feuerrost m; (hearth) Kamin m

grate² vt (Culin) reiben

grateful /'greɪtfl/ adj dankbar (**to** dat)

grater /'greɪtə(r)/ n (Culin) Reibe f

gratify /'grætɪfaɪ/ vt (pt/pp **-ied**) befriedigen. ∼**ing** adj erfreulich

gratis /'grɑːtɪs/ adv gratis

gratitude /'grætɪtjuːd/ n Dankbarkeit f

gratuitous /grə'tjuːɪtəs/ adj (uncalled for) überflüssig

grave¹ /greɪv/ adj (-r, -st) ernst; ∼**ly ill** schwer krank

grave² n Grab nt. ∼**-digger** n Totengräber m

gravel /'grævl/ n Kies m

grave: ∼**stone** n Grabstein m. ∼**yard** n Friedhof m

gravity /'grævətɪ/ n Ernst m; (force) Schwerkraft f

gravy /'greɪvɪ/ n [Braten]soße f

gray /greɪ/ adj (Amer) = grey

graze¹ /greɪz/ vi (animal:) weiden

graze² n Schürfwunde f ● vt (car) streifen; (knee) aufschürfen

grease /griːs/ n Fett nt; (lubricant) Schmierfett nt ● vt einfetten; (lubricate) schmieren

greasy /'griːsɪ/ adj fettig

great /greɪt/ adj (-er, -est) groß; (🔲: marvellous) großartig

great: ∼**-'aunt** n Großtante f. **G**∼ '**Britain** n Großbritannien nt. ∼**-'grandchildren** npl Urenkel pl. ∼**-'grandfather** n Urgroßvater m. ∼**-'grandmother** n Urgroßmutter f

great|ly /'greɪtlɪ/ adv sehr. ∼**ness** n Größe f

great-'uncle n Großonkel m

Greece /griːs/ n Griechenland nt

greed /griːd/ n [Hab]gier f

greedy /'griːdɪ/ adj, **-ily** adv gierig

Greek /griːk/ adj griechisch ● n Grieche m/Griechin f; (Lang) Griechisch nt

green /griːn/ adj (-er, -est) grün; (fig) unerfahren ● n Grün nt; (grass) Wiese f; ∼**s** pl Kohl m; **the G**∼**s** pl (Pol) die Grünen pl

> **green card** Ein offizielles 𝒊
> Dokument, das nichtamerikanische Bürger zur Erwerbstätigkeit in den USA berechtigt. Die green card braucht jeder, der beabsichtigt, eine feste Stelle in den USA anzutreten. In Europa ist die grüne Karte ein vom Versicherungsverband ausgestellter grüner Ausweis, mit dem ein Kraftfahrer beim Grenzübertritt nachweist, dass er haftpflichtversichert ist.

greenery /'griːnərɪ/ n Grün nt

green: ∼**fly** n Blattlaus f. ∼**grocer** n Obst- und Gemüsehändler m. ∼**house** n Gewächshaus nt

Greenland /'griːnlənd/ n Grönland nt

greet /griːt/ vt grüßen; (welcome) begrüßen. ∼**ing** n Gruß m; (welcome) Begrüßung f

grew /gruː/ see grow

grey /greɪ/ adj (-er, -est) grau ● n Grau nt ● vi grau werden. ∼**hound** n Windhund m

grid /grɪd/ n Gitter nt

g

grief /griːf/ n Trauer f

grievance /'griːvəns/ n Beschwerde f

grieve /griːv/ vi trauern (**for** um)

grill /grɪl/ n Gitter nt; (Culin) Grill m; **mixed ~** Gemischtes nt vom Grill ● vt/i grillen; (interrogate) [streng] verhören

grille /grɪl/ n Gitter nt

grim /grɪm/ adj (**grimmer, grimmest**) ernst; (determination) verbissen

grimace /grɪ'meɪs/ n Grimasse f ● vi Grimassen schneiden

grime /graɪm/ n Schmutz m

grimy /'graɪmɪ/ adj schmutzig

grin /grɪn/ n Grinsen nt ● vi (pt/pp **grinned**) grinsen

grind /graɪnd/ n (⊞: hard work) Plackerei f ● vt (pt/pp **ground**) mahlen; (smooth, sharpen) schleifen; (Amer: mince) durchdrehen

grip /grɪp/ n Griff m; (bag) Reisetasche f ● vt (pt/pp **gripped**) ergreifen; (hold) festhalten

gripping /'grɪpɪŋ/ adj fesselnd

grisly /'grɪzlɪ/ adj grausig

gristle /'grɪsl/ n Knorpel m

grit /grɪt/ n [grober] Sand m; (for roads) Streugut nt; (courage) Mut m ● vt (pt/pp **gritted**) streuen (road)

groan /grəʊn/ n Stöhnen nt ● vi stöhnen

grocer /'grəʊsə(r)/ n Lebensmittelhändler m; **~'s [shop]** Lebensmittelgeschäft nt. **~ies** npl Lebensmittel pl

groin /grɔɪn/ n (Anat) Leiste f

groom /gruːm/ n Bräutigam m; (for horse) Pferdepfleger(in) m(f) ● vt striegeln (horse)

groove /gruːv/ n Rille f

grope /grəʊp/ vi tasten (**for** nach)

gross /grəʊs/ adj (**-er, -est**) fett; (coarse) derb; (glaring) grob; (Comm) brutto; (salary, weight) Brutto-. **~ly** adv (very) sehr

grotesque /grəʊ'tesk/ adj grotesk

ground[1] /graʊnd/ see **grind**

ground[2] n Boden m; (terrain) Gelände nt; (reason) Grund m; (Amer, Electr) Erde f; **~s** pl (park) Anlagen pl; (of coffee) Satz m

ground: ~ floor n Erdgeschoss nt. **~ing** n Grundlage f. **~less** adj grundlos. **~sheet** n Bodenplane f. **~work** n Vorarbeiten pl

group /gruːp/ n Gruppe f ● vt gruppieren ● vi sich gruppieren

grouse vi ⊞ meckern

grovel /'grɒvl/ vi (pt/pp **grovelled**) kriechen

grow /grəʊ/ v (pt **grew**, pp **grown**) ● vi wachsen; (become) werden; (increase) zunehmen ● vt anbauen. **~ up** vi aufwachsen; (town:) entstehen

growl /graʊl/ n Knurren nt ● vi knurren

grown /grəʊn/ see **grow**. **~-up** adj erwachsen ● n Erwachsene(r) m/f

growth /grəʊθ/ n Wachstum nt; (increase) Zunahme f; (Med) Gewächs nt

grub /grʌb/ n (larva) Made f; (⊞: food) Essen nt

grubby /'grʌbɪ/ adj schmuddelig

grudg|e /grʌdʒ/ n Groll m ● vt **~e s.o. sth** jdm etw missgönnen. **~ing** adj widerwillig

gruelling /'gruːəlɪŋ/ adj strapaziös

gruesome /'gruːsəm/ adj grausig

gruff /grʌf/ adj barsch

grumble /'grʌmbl/ vi schimpfen (**at** mit)

grumpy /'grʌmpɪ/ adj griesgrämig

grunt /grʌnt/ n Grunzen nt ● vi grunzen

guarantee /gærən'tiː/ n Garantie f; (document) Garantieschein m ● vt garantieren; garantieren für (quality, success)

guard /gɑːd/ n Wache f; (security) Wächter m; (on train) ≈ Zugführer m; (Techn) Schutz m; **be on ~** auf der Wache stehen; **on one's ~** auf der Hut ● vt bewachen; (protect) schützen ● vi **~ against** sich hüten vor (+ dat). **~-dog** n Wachhund m

guarded /'gɑːdɪd/ adj vorsichtig

guardian /'gɑːdɪən/ n Vormund m

guess /ges/ n Vermutung f ● vt erraten ● vi raten; (*Amer: believe*) glauben. ~**work** n Vermutung f

guest /gest/ n Gast m. ~**-house** n Pension f

guidance /'gaɪdəns/ n Führung f, Leitung f; (*advice*) Beratung f

guide /gaɪd/ n Führer(in) m(f); (*book*) Führer m; [**Girl**] **G**~ Pfadfinderin f ● vt führen, leiten. ~**book** n Führer m

guided /'gaɪdɪd/ adj ~ **tour** Führung f

guide: ~**-dog** n Blindenhund m. ~**lines** npl Richtlinien pl

guilt /gɪlt/ n Schuld f. ~**ily** adv schuldbewusst

guilty /'gɪltɪ/ adj adj schuldig (**of** *gen*); (*look*) schuldbewusst; (*conscience*) schlecht

guinea-pig /'gɪnɪ-/ n Meerschweinchen nt; (*person*) Versuchskaninchen nt

guitar /gɪ'tɑː(r)/ n Gitarre f. ~**ist** n Gitarrist(in) m(f)

gulf /gʌlf/ n (*Geog*) Golf m; (*fig*) Kluft f

gull /gʌl/ n Möwe f

gullible /'gʌlɪbl/ adj leichtgläubig

gully /'gʌlɪ/ n Schlucht f; (*drain*) Rinne f

gulp /gʌlp/ n Schluck m ● vi schlucken ● vt ~ **down** hinunterschlucken

gum[1] /gʌm/ n (*also pl* **-s**) (*Anat*) Zahnfleisch nt

gum[2] n Gummi[harz] nt; (*glue*) Klebstoff m; (*chewing gum*) Kaugummi m

gummed /gʌmd/ ● adj (*label*) gummiert

gun /gʌn/ n Schusswaffe f; (*pistol*) Pistole f; (*rifle*) Gewehr nt; (*cannon*) Geschütz nt

gun: ~**fire** n Geschützfeuer nt. ~**man** bewaffneter Bandit m

gunner /'gʌnə(r)/ n Artillerist m

gunpowder n Schießpulver nt

gurgle /'gɜːgl/ vi gluckern; (*of baby*) glucksen

gush /gʌʃ/ vi strömen; (*enthuse*) schwärmen (**over** von)

gust /gʌst/ n (*of wind*) Windstoß m; (*Naut*) Bö f

gusto /'gʌstəʊ/ n **with** ~ mit Schwung

gusty /'gʌstɪ/ adj böig

gut /gʌt/ n Darm m; ~**s** pl Eingeweide pl; (☐: *courage*) Schneid m ● vt (*pt/pp* **gutted**) (*Culin*) ausnehmen; ~**ted by fire** ausgebrannt

gutter /'gʌtə(r)/ n Rinnstein m; (*fig*) Gosse f; (*on roof*) Dachrinne f

guy /gaɪ/ n ☐ Kerl m

guzzle /'gʌzl/ vt/i schlingen; (*drink*) schlürfen

gym /dʒɪm/ n ☐ Turnhalle f; (*gymnastics*) Turnen nt

gymnasium /dʒɪm'neɪzɪəm/ n Turnhalle f

gymnast /'dʒɪmnæst/ n Turner(in) m(f). ~**ics** n Turnen nt

gym shoes pl Turnschuhe pl

gynaecolog|ist /gaɪnɪ'kɒlədʒɪst/ n Frauenarzt m /-ärztin f. ~**y** n Gynäkologie f

gypsy /'dʒɪpsɪ/ n Zigeuner(in) m(f)

g

h

Hh

habit /'hæbɪt/ n Gewohnheit f; (*Relig: costume*) Ordenstracht f; **be in the** ~ die Angewohnheit haben (**of** zu)

habitat /'hæbɪtæt/ n Habitat nt

habitation /hæbɪ'teɪʃn/ n **unfit for human** ~ für Wohnzwecke ungeeignet

habitual /hə'bɪtjʊəl/ adj gewohnt; (*inveterate*) gewohnheitsmäßig. ~**ly** adv gewohnheitsmäßig; (*constantly*) ständig

hack[1] /hæk/ n (*writer*) Schreiberling m; (*hired horse*) Mietpferd nt

hack[2] vt hacken; ~ **to pieces** zerhacken

hackneyed /'hæknɪd/ adj abgedroschen

'hacksaw n Metallsäge f
had /hæd/ see **have**
haddock /'hædək/ n inv Schellfisch m
haggard /'hægəd/ adj abgehärmt
haggle /'hægl/ vi feilschen (**over** um)
hail[1] /heɪl/ vt begrüßen; herbeirufen (taxi) ● vi ~ **from** kommen aus
hail[2] n Hagel m ● vi hageln. ~**stone** n Hagelkorn nt
hair /heə(r)/ n Haar nt; **wash one's** ~ sich (dat) die Haare waschen
hair: ~**brush** n Haarbürste f. ~**cut** n Haarschnitt m; **have a** ~**cut** sich (dat) die Haare schneiden lassen. ~**-do** n 🔳 Frisur f. ~**dresser** n Friseur m/Friseuse f. ~**-drier** n Haartrockner m; (hand-held) Föhn m. ~**pin** n Haarnadel f. ~**pin 'bend** n Haarnadelkurve f. ~**-raising** adj haarsträubend. ~**-style** n Frisur f
hairy /'heərɪ/ adj behaart; (excessively) haarig; (🔳 frightening) brenzlig
hake /heɪk/ n inv Seehecht m
half /hɑːf/ n (pl **halves**) Hälfte f; **cut in** ~ halbieren; **one and a** ~ eineinhalb, anderthalb; ~ **a dozen** ein halbes Dutzend; ~ **an hour** eine halbe Stunde ● adj & adv halb; ~ **past two** halb drei; [**at**] ~ **price** zum halben Preis
half: ~**-'hearted** adj lustlos. ~**-'term** n schulfreie Tage nach dem halben Trimester. ~**-'timbered** adj Fachwerk-. ~**-'time** n (Sport) Halbzeit f. ~**-'way** adj the ~**-way mark/ stage** die Hälfte ● adv auf halbem Weg
halibut /'hælɪbət/ n inv Heilbutt m
hall /hɔːl/ n Halle f; (room) Saal m; (Sch) Aula f; (entrance) Flur m; (mansion) Gutshaus nt; ~ **of residence** (Univ) Studentenheim nt
'hallmark n [Feingehalts]stempel m; (fig) Kennzeichen nt (**of** für)
hallo /hə'ləʊ/ int [guten] Tag! 🔳 hallo!
hallucination /həluːsɪ'neɪʃn/ n Halluzination f

halo /'heɪləʊ/ n (pl **-es**) Heiligenschein m; (Astronomy) Hof m
halt /hɔːlt/ n Halt m; **come to a** ~ stehen bleiben; (traffic:) zum Stillstand kommen ● vi Halt machen; ~**! halt!** ~**ing** adj, adv **-ly** zögernd
halve /hɑːv/ vt halbieren; (reduce) um die Hälfte reduzieren
ham /hæm/ n Schinken m
hamburger /'hæmbɜːgə(r)/ n Hamburger m
hammer /'hæmə(r)/ n Hammer m ● vt/i hämmern (**at an** + acc)
hammock /'hæmək/ n Hängematte f
hamper vt behindern
hamster /'hæmstə(r)/ n Hamster m
hand /hænd/ n Hand f; (of clock) Zeiger m; (writing) Handschrift f; (worker) Arbeiter(in) m(f); (Cards) Blatt nt; **on the one/other** ~ einer-/andererseits; **out of** ~ außer Kontrolle; (summarily) kurzerhand; **in** ~ unter Kontrolle; (available) verfügbar; **give s.o. a** ~ jdm behilflich sein ● vt reichen (**to** dat). ~ **in** vt abgeben. ~ **out** vt austeilen. ~ **over** vt überreichen
hand: ~**bag** n Handtasche f. ~**book** n Handbuch nt. ~**brake** n Handbremse f. ~**cuffs** npl Handschellen pl. ~**ful** n Handvoll f; **be [quite] a** ~**ful** 🔳 nicht leicht zu haben sein
handicap /'hændɪkæp/ n Behinderung f; (Sport & fig) Handikap nt. ~**ped** adj **mentally/physically** ~**ped** geistig/körperlich behindert
handkerchief /'hæŋkətʃɪf/ n (pl ~**s** & **-chieves**) Taschentuch nt
handle /'hændl/ n Griff m; (of door) Klinke f; (of cup) Henkel m; (of broom) Stiel m ● vt handhaben; (treat) umgehen mit; (touch) anfassen. ~**bars** npl Lenkstange f
hand: ~**made** adj handgemacht. ~**shake** n Händedruck m
handsome /'hænsəm/ adj gut aussehend; (generous) großzügig; (large) beträchtlich
hand: ~**writing** n Handschrift f. ~**-'written** adj handgeschrieben

handy /ˈhændɪ/ *adj* handlich; (*person*) geschickt; **have/keep** ~ griffbereit haben/halten

hang /hæŋ/ *vt/i* (*pt/pp* hung) hängen; ~ **wallpaper** tapezieren ● *vt* (*pt/pp* hanged) hängen (*criminal*) ● *n* **get the** ~ **of it** 🔲 den Dreh herauskriegen. ~ **about** *vi* sich herumdrücken. ~ **on** *vi* sich festhalten (**to** an + *dat*); (🔲: *wait*) warten. ~ **out** *vi* heraushängen; (🔲: *live*) wohnen ● *vt* draußen aufhängen (*washing*). ~ **up** *vt/i* aufhängen

hangar /ˈhæŋə(r)/ *n* Flugzeughalle *f*

hanger /ˈhæŋə(r)/ *n* [Kleider]bügel *m*

hang: ~**-glider** *n* Drachenflieger *m*. ~**-gliding** *n* Drachenfliegen *nt*. ~**man** *n* Henker *m*. ~**over** *n* 🔲 Kater *m* 🔲. ~**-up** *n* 🔲 Komplex *m*

hanker /ˈhæŋkə(r)/ *vi* ~ **after sth** sich (*dat*) etw wünschen

hanky /ˈhæŋkɪ/ *n* 🔲 Taschentuch *nt*

haphazard /hæpˈhæzəd/ *adj* planlos

happen /ˈhæpn/ *vi* geschehen, passieren; **I** ~**ed to be there** ich war zufällig da; **what has** ~**ed to him?** was ist mit ihm los? (*become of*) was ist aus ihm geworden? ~**ing** *n* Ereignis *nt*

happi|ly /ˈhæpɪlɪ/ *adv* glücklich; (*fortunately*) glücklicherweise. ~**ness** *n* Glück *nt*

happy /ˈhæpɪ/ *adj* glücklich. ~**-go-ˈlucky** *adj* sorglos

harass /ˈhærəs/ *vt* schikanieren. ~**ed** *adj* abgehetzt. ~**ment** *n* Schikane *f*; (*sexual*) Belästigung *f*

harbour /ˈhɑːbə(r)/ *n* Hafen *m*

hard /hɑːd/ *adj* (**-er, -est**) hart; (*difficult*) schwer; ~ **of hearing** schwerhörig ● *adv* hart; (*work*) schwer; (*pull*) kräftig; (*rain, snow*) stark; **be** ~ **up** 🔲 knapp bei Kasse sein

hard: ~**back** *n* gebundene Ausgabe *f*. ~**board** *n* Hartfaserplatte *f*. ~**-boiled** *adj* hart gekocht ~**disk** *n* Festplatte *f*

harden /ˈhɑːdn/ *vi* hart werden

hard-ˈhearted *adj* hartherzig

hard|ly /ˈhɑːdlɪ/ *adv* kaum; ~**ly ever** kaum [jemals]. ~**ness** *n* Härte *f*. ~**ship** *n* Not *f*

hard: ~ ˈ**shoulder** *n* (*Auto*) Randstreifen *m*. ~**ware** *n* Haushaltswaren *pl*; (*Computing*) Hardware *f*. ~**-ˈwearing** *adj* strapazierfähig. ~**-ˈworking** *adj* fleißig

hardy /ˈhɑːdɪ/ *adj* abgehärtet; (*plant*) winterhart

hare /heə(r)/ *n* Hase *m*

harm /hɑːm/ *n* Schaden *m*; **it won't do any** ~ es kann nichts schaden ● *vt* ~ **s.o.** jdm etwas antun. ~**ful** *adj* schädlich. ~**less** *adj* harmlos

harmonious /hɑːˈməʊnɪəs/ *adj* harmonisch

harmon|ize /ˈhɑːmənaɪz/ *vi* (*fig*) harmonieren. ~**y** *n* Harmonie *f*

harness /ˈhɑːnɪs/ *n* Geschirr *nt*; (*of parachute*) Gurtwerk *nt* ● *vt* anschirren (*horse*); (*use*) nutzbar machen

harp /hɑːp/ *n* Harfe *f*. ~**ist** *n* Harfenist(in) *m(f)*

harpsichord /ˈhɑːpsɪkɔːd/ *n* Cembalo *nt*

harrowing /ˈhærəʊɪŋ/ *adj* grauenhaft

harsh /hɑːʃ/ *adj* (**-er, -est**) hart; (*voice*) rau; (*light*) grell. ~**ness** *n* Härte *f*; Rauheit *f*

harvest /ˈhɑːvɪst/ *n* Ernte *f* ● *vt* ernten

has /hæz/ *see* have

hassle /ˈhæsl/ *n* 🔲 Ärger *m* ● *vt* schikanieren

haste /heɪst/ *n* Eile *f*

hasten /ˈheɪsn/ *vi* sich beeilen (**to** zu); (*go quickly*) eilen ● *vt* beschleunigen

hasty /ˈheɪstɪ/ *adj* , **-ily** *adv* hastig; (*decision*) voreilig

hat /hæt/ *n* Hut *m*; (*knitted*) Mütze *f*

hatch¹ /hætʃ/ *n* (*for food*) Durchreiche *f*; (*Naut*) Luke *f*

hatch² *vi* ~**[out]** ausschlüpfen ● *vt* ausbrüten

ˈ**hatchback** *n* (*Auto*) Modell *nt* mit Hecktür

hate /heɪt/ *n* Hass *m* ● *vt* hassen.

h

~**ful** *adj* abscheulich

hatred /'heɪtrɪd/ *n* Hass *m*

haughty /'hɔːtɪ/ *adj* , **-ily** *adv* hochmütig

haul /hɔːl/ *n* (*loot*) Beute *f* ● *vt/i* ziehen (**on** an + *dat*)

haunt /hɔːnt/ *n* Lieblingsaufenthalt *m* ● *vt* umgehen in (+ *dat*); **this house is** ~**ed** in diesem Haus spukt es

have /hæv/, *unbetont* /həv/, /əv/

! 3 sg pres tense **has**; *pt and pp* **had**

● *transitive verb*

····➤ (*possess*) haben. **he has [got] a car** er hat ein Auto. **she has [got] a brother** sie hat einen Bruder. **we have [got] five minutes** wir haben fünf Minuten

····➤ (*eat*) essen; (*drink*) trinken; (*smoke*) rauchen. **have a cup of tea** eine Tasse Tee trinken. **have a pizza** eine Pizza essen. **have a cigarette** eine Zigarette rauchen. **have breakfast/dinner/lunch** frühstücken/zu Abend essen/zu Mittag essen

····➤ (*take esp. in shop, restaurant*) nehmen. **I'll have the soup/the red dress** ich nehme die Suppe/das rote Kleid. **have a cigarette!** nehmen Sie eine Zigarette!

····➤ (*get, receive*) bekommen. **I had a letter from her** ich bekam einen Brief von ihr. **have a baby** ein Baby bekommen

····➤ (*suffer*) haben (*illness, pain, disappointment*); erleiden (*shock*)

····➤ (*organize*) **have a party** eine Party veranstalten. **they had a meeting** sie hielten eine Versammlung ab

····➤ (*take part in*) **have a game of football** Fußball spielen. **have a swim** schwimmen

····➤ (*as guest*) **have s.o. to stay** jdn zu Besuch haben

····➤ **have had it** Ⓘ (*thing*) ausgedient haben; (*person*) geliefert

sein. **you've had it now** jetzt ist es aus

····➤ **have sth done** etw machen lassen. **we had the house painted** wir haben das Haus malen lassen. **have a dress made** sich (*dat*) ein Kleid machen lassen. **have a tooth out** sich (*dat*) einen Zahn ziehen lassen. **have one's hair cut** sich (*dat*) die Haare schneiden lassen

····➤ **have to do sth** etw tun müssen. **I have to go now** ich muss jetzt gehen

● *auxiliary verb*

····➤ (*forming perfect and past perfect tenses*) haben; (*with verbs of motion and some others*) sein. **I have seen him** ich habe ihn gesehen. **he has never been there** er ist nie da gewesen. **I had gone** ich war gegangen. **if I had known ...** wenn ich gewusst hätte ...

····➤ (*in tag questions*) nicht wahr. **you've met her, haven't you?** du kennst sie, nicht wahr?

····➤ (*in short answers*) **Have you seen the film? — Yes, I have** Hast du den Film gesehen? — Ja [, stimmt]

● **have on** *vt* (*be wearing*) anhaben; (*dupe*) anführen

havoc /'hævək/ *n* Verwüstung *f*

hawk /hɔːk/ *n* Falke *m*

hawthorn /'hɔː-/ *n* Hagedorn *m*

hay /heɪ/ *n* Heu *nt*. ~ **fever** *n* Heuschnupfen *m*. ~**stack** *n* Heuschober *m*

hazard /'hæzəd/ *n* Gefahr *f*; (*risk*) Risiko *nt* ● *vt* riskieren. ~**ous** *adj* gefährlich; (*risky*) riskant

haze /heɪz/ *n* Dunst *m*

hazel /'heɪzl/ *n* Haselbusch *m*. ~-**nut** *n* Haselnuss *f*

hazy /'heɪzɪ/ *adj* dunstig; (*fig*) unklar

he /hiː/ *pron* er

head /hed/ *n* Kopf *m*; (*chief*) Oberhaupt *nt*; (*of firm*) Chef(in) *m(f)*; (*of school*) Schulleiter(in) *m(f)*; (*on beer*)

Schaumkrone f; (of bed) Kopfende nt; ~ **first** kopfüber ● vt anführen; (Sport) köpfen (ball) ● vi ~ **for** zusteuern auf (+ acc). **~ache** n Kopfschmerzen pl

head|er /'hedə(r)/ n Kopfball m; (dive) Kopfsprung m. **~ing** n Überschrift f

head: **~lamp, ~light** n (Auto) Scheinwerfer m. **~line** n Schlagzeile f. **~long** adv kopfüber. **~'master** n Schulleiter m. **~'mistress** n Schulleiterin f. **~-on** adj & adv frontal. **~phones** npl Kopfhörer m. **~quarters** npl Hauptquartier nt; (Pol) Zentrale f. **~rest** n Kopfstütze f. **~room** n lichte Höhe f. **~scarf** n Kopftuch nt. **~strong** adj eigenwillig. **~way** n **make ~way** Fortschritte machen. **~word** n Stichwort nt

heady /'hedɪ/ adj berauschend

heal /hiːl/ vt/i heilen

health /helθ/ n Gesundheit f

health: ~ **farm** n Schönheitsfarm f. ~ **foods** npl Reformkost f. **~-food shop** n Reformhaus nt. ~ **insurance** n Krankenversicherung f

healthy /'helθɪ/ adj , **-ily** adv gesund

heap /hiːp/ n Haufen m; **~s** 🔲 jede Menge ● vt ~ **[up]** häufen

hear /hɪə(r)/ vt/i (pt/pp **heard**) hören; **~,~!** hört, hört! **he would not ~ of it** er ließ es nicht zu

hearing /'hɪərɪŋ/ n Gehör nt; (Jur) Verhandlung f. **~-aid** n Hörgerät nt

hearse /hɜːs/ n Leichenwagen m

heart /hɑːt/ n Herz nt; (courage) Mut m; **~s** pl (Cards) Herz nt; **by ~** auswendig

heart: **~ache** n Kummer m. **~attack** n Herzanfall m. **~beat** n Herzschlag m. **~-breaking** adj herzzerreißend. **~-broken** adj untröstlich. **~burn** n Sodbrennen nt. **~en** vt ermutigen. **~felt** adj herzlich[st]

hearth /hɑːθ/ n Herd m; (fireplace) Kamin m

heart|ily /'hɑːtɪlɪ/ adv herzlich; (eat)

viel. **~less** adj herzlos. **~y** adj herzlich; (meal) groß; (person) burschikos

heat /hiːt/ n Hitze f; (Sport) Vorlauf m ● vt heiß machen; heizen (room). **~ed** adj geheizt; (swimming pool) beheizt; (discussion) hitzig. **~er** n Heizgerät nt; (Auto) Heizanlage f

heath /hiːθ/ n Heide f

heathen /'hiːðn/ adj heidnisch ● n Heide m/Heidin f

heather /'heðə(r)/ n Heidekraut nt

heating /'hiːtɪŋ/ n Heizung f

heat wave n Hitzewelle f

heave /hiːv/ vt/i ziehen; (lift) heben; (🔲: throw) schmeißen

heaven /'hevn/ n Himmel m. **~ly** adj himmlisch

heavy /'hevɪ/ adj , **-ily** adv schwer; (traffic, rain) stark. **~weight** n Schwergewicht nt

heckle /'hekl/ vt [durch Zwischenrufe] unterbrechen. **~r** n Zwischenrufer m

hectic /'hektɪk/ adj hektisch

hedge /hedʒ/ n Hecke f. **~hog** n Igel m

heed /hiːd/ vt beachten

heel[1] /hiːl/ n Ferse f; (of shoe) Absatz m; **down at ~** heruntergekommen

heel[2] vi ~ **over** (Naut) sich auf die Seite legen

hefty /'heftɪ/ adj kräftig; (heavy) schwer

height /haɪt/ n Höhe f; (of person) Größe f. **~en** vt (fig) steigern

heir /eə(r)/ n Erbe m. **~ess** n Erbin f. **~loom** n Erbstück nt

held /held/ see **hold**[2]

helicopter /'helɪkɒptə(r)/ n Hubschrauber m

hell /hel/ n Hölle f; **go to ~!** ✖ geh zum Teufel! ● int verdammt!

hello /hə'ləʊ/ int [guten] Tag! 🔲 hallo!

helm /helm/ n [Steuer]ruder nt

helmet /'helmɪt/ n Helm m

help /help/ n Hilfe f; (employees) Hilfskräfte pl; **that's no ~** das nützt

h

nichts ● *vt/i* helfen (**s.o.** jdm); ~
oneself to sth sich (*dat*) etw nehmen; ~ **yourself** (*at table*) greif zu; **I
could not** ~ **laughing** ich musste lachen; **it cannot be** ~**ed** es lässt sich
nicht ändern; **I can't** ~ **it** ich kann
nichts dafür

help|er /'helpə(r)/ *n* Helfer(in) *m(f)*.
~**ful** *adj*, -**ly** *adv* hilfsbereit; (*advice*)
nützlich. ~**ing** *n* Portion *f*. ~**less** *adj*
hilflos

hem /hem/ *n* Saum *m* ● *vt* (*pt/pp*
hemmed) säumen; ~ **in** umzingeln

hemisphere /'hemɪ-/ *n* Hemisphäre *f*

'**hem-line** *n* Rocklänge *f*

hen /hen/ *n* Henne *f*; (*any female
bird*) Weibchen *nt*

hence /hens/ *adv* daher; **five years**
~ in fünf Jahren. ~'**forth** *adv* von
nun an

'**henpecked** *adj* ~ **husband** Pan-
toffelheld *m*

her /hɜ:(r)/ *adj* ihr ● *pron* (*acc*) sie;
(*dat*) ihr

herald /'herəld/ *vt* verkünden. ~**ry**
n Wappenkunde *f*

herb /hɜ:b/ *n* Kraut *nt*

herbaceous /hɜ:'beɪʃəs/ *adj* ~ **border** Staudenrabatte *f*

herd /hɜ:d/ *n* Herde *f*. ~ **together** *vt*
zusammentreiben

here /hɪə(r)/ *adv* hier; (*to this place*)
hierher; **in** ~ hier drinnen; **come/
bring** ~ herkommen/herbringen

hereditary /hə'redɪtərɪ/ *adj* erblich

here|sy /'herəsɪ/ *n* Ketzerei *f*. ~**tic** *n*
Ketzer(in) *m(f)*

here'with *adv* (*Comm*) beiliegend

heritage /'herɪtɪdʒ/ *n* Erbe *nt*. ~
tourism *n* Kulturtourismus *m*

hero /'hɪərəʊ/ *n* (*pl* -**es**) Held *m*

heroic /hɪ'rəʊɪk/ *adj*, -**ally** *adv* hel-
denhaft

heroin /'herəʊɪn/ *n* Heroin *nt*

hero|ine /'herəʊɪn/ *n* Heldin *f*.
~**ism** *n* Heldentum *nt*

heron /'hern/ *n* Reiher *m*

herring /'herɪŋ/ *n* Hering *m*

hers /hɜ:z/ *poss pron* ihre(r), ihrs; **a
friend of** ~ ein Freund von ihr; **that
is** ~ das gehört ihr

her'self *pron* selbst; (*reflexive*) sich;
by ~ allein

hesitant /'hezɪtənt/ *adj* zögernd

hesitat|e /'hezɪteɪt/ *vi* zögern. ~**ion**
n Zögern *nt*; **without** ~**ion** ohne zu
zögern

hexagonal /hek'sægənl/ *adj* sechs-
eckig

heyday /'heɪ-/ *n* Glanzzeit *f*

hi /haɪ/ *int* he! (*hallo*) Tag!

hiatus /haɪ'eɪtəs/ *n* (*pl* -**tuses**)
Lücke *f*

hibernat|e /'haɪbəneɪt/ *vi* Winter-
schlaf halten. ~**ion** *n* Winterschlaf *m*

hiccup /'hɪkʌp/ *n* Hick *m*; (▣: *hitch*)
Panne *f*; **have the** ~**s** den Schluckauf haben ● *vi* hick machen

hid /hɪd/, **hidden** *see* hide[2]

hide *v* (*pt* **hid**, *pp* **hidden**) ● *vt* verstecken; (*keep secret*) verheimlichen
● *vi* sich verstecken

hideous /'hɪdɪəs/ *adj* hässlich; (*horrible*) grässlich

'**hide-out** *n* Versteck *nt*

hiding[1] /'haɪdɪŋ/ *n* ▣ **give s.o. a** ~
jdn verdreschen

hiding[2] *n* **go into** ~ untertauchen

hierarchy /'haɪərɑ:kɪ/ *n* Hierarchie *f*

high /haɪ/ *adj* (-**er**, -**est**) hoch; *attrib*
hohe(r,s); (*meat*) angegangen; (*wind*)
stark; (*on drugs*) high; **it's** ~ **time** es
ist höchste Zeit ● *adv* hoch; ~ **and
low** überall ● *n* Hoch *nt*; (*temperature*) Höchsttemperatur *f*

high: ~**brow** *adj* intellektuell.
~**chair** *n* Kinderhochstuhl *m*.
~'-**handed** *adj* selbstherrlich.
~'-**heeled** *adj* hochhackig. ~ **jump**
n Hochsprung *m*

'**highlight** *n* (*fig*) Höhepunkt *m*; ~**s**
pl (*in hair*) helle Strähnen *pl* ● *vt* (*emphasize*) hervorheben

highly /'haɪlɪ/ *adv* hoch; **speak** ~ **of**
loben; **think** ~ **of** sehr schätzen.
~'-**strung** *adj* nervös

Highness /'haɪnɪs/ n Hoheit f

> **high school** Eine weiterführende Schule in den USA, normalerweise für Schüler von vierzehn bis achtzehn Jahren. Schüler erwerben einen Highschoolabschluss durch Nachweis von *credits* (Punkten) in bestimmten Pflicht- und Wahlkursen. Der Abschluss ist Voraussetzung zum Besuch einer Hochschule. Auch in Großbritannien werden einige weiterführende Schulen als *high schools* bezeichnet.   *i*

high: ~ **season** n Hochsaison f. ~ **street** n Hauptstraße f. ~ **'tide** n Hochwasser nt. **~way** n public **~way** öffentliche Straße f

hijack /'haɪdʒæk/ vt entführen. **~er** n Entführer m

hike /haɪk/ n Wanderung f ● vi wandern. **~r** n Wanderer m

hilarious /hɪ'leərɪəs/ adj sehr komisch

hill /hɪl/ n Berg m; (*mound*) Hügel m; (*slope*) Hang m

hill: **~side** n Hang m. **~y** adj hügelig

him /hɪm/ pron (*acc*) ihn; (*dat*) ihm. **~'self** pron selbst; (*reflexive*) sich; **by ~self** allein

hind /haɪnd/ adj Hinter-

hind|er /'hɪndə(r)/ vt hindern. **~rance** n Hindernis nt

hindsight /'haɪnd-/ n **with ~** rückblickend

Hindu /'hɪnduː/ n Hindu m ● adj Hindu-. **~ism** n Hinduismus m

hinge /hɪndʒ/ n Scharnier nt; (*on door*) Angel f

hint /hɪnt/ n Wink m, Andeutung f; (*advice*) Hinweis m; (*trace*) Spur f ● vi ~ **at** anspielen auf (+ acc)

hip /hɪp/ n Hüfte f

hip 'pocket n Gesäßtasche f

hippopotamus /hɪpə'pɒtəməs/ n (pl **-muses** or **-mi** /-maɪ/) Nilpferd nt

hire /'haɪə(r)/ vt mieten (car); leihen (suit); einstellen (person); **~[out]** vermieten; verleihen

his /hɪz/ adj sein ● poss pron seine(r), seins; **a friend of ~** ein Freund von ihm; **that is ~** das gehört ihm

hiss /hɪs/ n Zischen nt ● vt/i zischen

historian /hɪ'stɔːrɪən/ n Historiker(in) m(f)

historic /hɪ'stɒrɪk/ adj historisch. **~al** adj geschichtlich, historisch

history /'hɪstərɪ/ n Geschichte f

hit /hɪt/ n (blow) Schlag m; (🎵: success) Erfolg m; **direct ~** Volltreffer m ● vt/i (pt/pp **hit**, pres p **hitting**) schlagen; (knock against, collide with, affect) treffen; **~ the target** das Ziel treffen; **~ on** (fig) kommen auf (+ acc); **~ it off** gut auskommen (**with** mit); **~ one's head on sth** sich (dat) den Kopf an etw (dat) stoßen

hitch /hɪtʃ/ n Problem nt; **technical ~** Panne f ● vt festmachen (**to** an + dat); **~ up** hochziehen. **~-hike** vi 🎵 trampen. **~-hiker** n Anhalter(in) m(f)

hive /haɪv/ n Bienenstock m

hoard /hɔːd/ n Hort m ● vt horten, hamstern

hoarding /'hɔːdɪŋ/ n Bauzaun m; (with advertisements) Reklamewand f

hoar-frost /'hɔː-/ n Raureif m

hoarse /hɔːs/ adj (**-r, -st**) heiser. **~ness** n Heiserkeit f

hoax /həʊks/ n übler Scherz m; (false alarm) blinder Alarm m

hobble /'hɒbl/ vi humpeln

hobby /'hɒbɪ/ n Hobby nt. **~-horse** n (fig) Lieblingsthema nt

hockey /'hɒkɪ/ n Hockey nt

hoe /həʊ/ n Hacke f ● vt (pres p **hoeing**) hacken

hog /hɒg/ vt (pt/pp **hogged**) 🎵 mit Beschlag belegen

hoist /hɔɪst/ n Lastenaufzug m ● vt hochziehen; hissen (flag)

hold¹ /həʊld/ n (Naut) Laderaum m

hold² n Halt m; (Sport) Griff m; (fig: influence) Einfluss m; **get ~ of** fassen; (🎵: contact) erreichen ● v (pt/pp **held**) ● vt halten; (container:) fassen; (believe) meinen; (possess) haben; anhalten (*breath*) ● vi (*rope:*) halten; (*weather:*) sich halten. ∼ **back** vt zurückhalten ● vi zögern. ∼ **on** vi (*wait*) warten; (*on telephone*) am Apparat bleiben; ∼ **on to** (*keep*) behalten; (*cling to*) sich festhalten an (+ *dat*). ∼ **out** vt hinhalten ● vi (*resist*) aushalten. ∼ **up** vt hochhalten; (*delay*) aufhalten; (*rob*) überfallen

'**hold|all** n Reisetasche f. ∼**er** n Inhaber(in) m(f); (*container*) Halter m. ∼-**up** n Verzögerung f; (*attack*) Überfall m

hole /həʊl/ n Loch nt

holiday /'hɒlədeɪ/ n Urlaub m; (*Sch*) Ferien pl; (*public*) Feiertag m; (*day off*) freier Tag m; **go on** ∼ in Urlaub fahren

holiness /'həʊlmɪs/ n Heiligkeit f

Holland /'hɒlənd/ n Holland nt

hollow /'hɒləʊ/ adj hohl; (*promise*) leer ● n Vertiefung f; (*in ground*) Mulde f. ∼ **out** vt aushöhlen

holly /'hɒlɪ/ n Stechpalme f

holster /'həʊlstə(r)/ n Pistolentasche f

holy /'həʊlɪ/ adj (-ier, -est) heilig. H∼ **Ghost** or **Spirit** n Heiliger Geist m

homage /'hɒmɪdʒ/ n Huldigung f; **pay** ∼ **to** huldigen (+ *dat*)

home /həʊm/ n Zuhause nt (*house*) Haus nt; (*institution*) Heim nt; (*native land*) Heimat f ● adv at ∼ zu Hause; **come/go** ∼ nach Hause kommen/gehen

home: ∼ **ad'dress** n Heimatanschrift f. ∼ **game** n Heimspiel nt. ∼ **help** n Haushaltshilfe f. ∼**land** n Heimatland nt. ∼**land security** innere Sicherheit f. ∼**less** adj obdachlos

homely /'həʊmlɪ/ adj adj gemütlich; (*Amer: ugly*) unscheinbar

home: ∼-'**made** adj selbst gemacht. H∼ **Office** n Innenministerium nt. ∼ **page** n Homepage f. H∼ '**Secretary** Innenminister m. ∼**sick** adj be ∼**sick** Heimweh haben (**for** nach). ∼**sickness** n Heimweh nt. ∼ '**town**

n Heimatstadt f. ∼**work** n (*Sch*) Hausaufgaben pl

homo'sexual adj homosexuell ● n Homosexuelle(r) m/f

honest /'ɒnɪst/ adj ehrlich. ∼**y** n Ehrlichkeit f

honey /'hʌnɪ/ n Honig m (⚠: *darling*) Schatz m

honey: ∼**comb** n Honigwabe f. ∼**moon** n Flitterwochen pl; (*journey*) Hochzeitsreise f

honorary /'ɒnərərɪ/ adj ehrenamtlich; (*member, doctorate*) Ehren-

honour /'ɒnə(r)/ n Ehre f ● vt ehren; honorieren (*cheque*). ∼**able** adj, **-bly** adv ehrenhaft

hood /hʊd/ n Kapuze f; (*of car, pram*) [Klapp]verdeck nt; (*over cooker*) Abzugshaube f; (*Auto, Amer*) Kühlerhaube f

hoof /huːf/ n (pl ∼s or **hooves**) Huf m

hook /hʊk/ n Haken m ● vt festhaken (**to** an + *acc*)

hook|ed /hʊkt/ adj ∼**ed nose** Hakennase f; ∼**ed on** ⚠ abhängig von; (*keen on*) besessen von. ∼**er** n (*Amer*, 🗙) Nutte f

hookey /'hʊkɪ/ n play ∼ (*Amer*, ⚠) schwänzen

hooligan /'huːlɪgən/ n Rowdy m. ∼**ism** n Rowdytum nt

hooray /hʊ'reɪ/ int & n = **hurrah**

hoot /huːt/ n Ruf m; ∼**s of laughter** schallendes Gelächter nt ● vi (*owl:*) rufen; (*car:*) hupen; (*jeer*) johlen. ∼**er** n (*of factory*) Sirene f; (*Auto*) Hupe f

hoover /'huːvə(r)/ n H∼ ® Staubsauger m ● vt/i [staub]saugen

hop[1] /hɒp/ n, & ∼**s** pl Hopfen m

hop[2] vi (*pt/pp* hopped) hüpfen; ∼ **it!** ⚠ hau ab!

hope /həʊp/ n Hoffnung f; (*prospect*) Aussicht f (**of** auf + *acc*) ● vt/i hoffen (**for** auf + acc); **I** ∼ **so** hoffentlich

hope|ful /'həʊpfl/ adj hoffnungsvoll; **be** ∼**ful that** hoffen, dass. ∼**fully** adv hoffnungsvoll; (*it is hoped*) hoffentlich. ∼**less** adj hoffnungslos;

(*useless*) nutzlos; (*incompetent*) untauglich

horde /hɔːd/ n Horde f

horizon /həˈraɪzn/ n Horizont m

horizontal /hɒrɪˈzɒntl/ adj horizontal. ~ '**bar** n Reck nt

horn /hɔːn/ n Horn nt; (*Auto*) Hupe f

hornet /ˈhɔːnɪt/ n Hornisse f

horoscope /ˈhɒrəskəʊp/ n Horoskop nt

horrible /ˈhɒrɪbl/ adj, **-bly** adv
schrecklich

horrid /ˈhɒrɪd/ adj grässlich

horrific /həˈrɪfɪk/ adj entsetzlich

horrify /ˈhɒrɪfaɪ/ vt (*pt/pp* **-ied**) entsetzen

horror /ˈhɒrə(r)/ n Entsetzen nt

hors-d'œuvre /ɔːˈdɜːvr/ n Vorspeise f

horse /hɔːs/ n Pferd nt

horse: ~**back** n on ~**back** zu
Pferde. ~**man** n Reiter m. ~**power**
n Pferdestärke f. ~**racing** n Pferderennen nt. ~**radish** n Meerrettich m.
~**shoe** n Hufeisen nt

'**horticulture** n Gartenbau m

hose /həʊz/ n (*pipe*) Schlauch m ● vt
~ **down** abspritzen

hosiery /ˈhəʊzɪərɪ/ n Strumpfwa-
ren pl

hospitable /hɒˈspɪtəbl/ adj, **-bly**
adv gastfreundlich

hospital /ˈhɒspɪtl/ n Krankenhaus nt

hospitality /hɒspɪˈtælətɪ/ n Gast-
freundschaft f

host /həʊst/ n Gastgeber m

hostage /ˈhɒstɪdʒ/ n Geisel f

hostel /ˈhɒstl/ n [Wohn]heim nt

hostess /ˈhəʊstɪs/ n Gastgeberin f

hostile /ˈhɒstaɪl/ adj feindlich; (*unfriendly*) feindselig

hostilit|y /hɒˈstɪlətɪ/ n Feindschaft f;
~**ies** pl Feindseligkeiten pl

hot /hɒt/ adj (**hotter, hottest**) heiß;
(*meal*) warm; (*spicy*) scharf; **I am** or
feel ~ mir ist heiß

hotel /həʊˈtel/ n Hotel nt

hot: ~**head** n Hitzkopf m. ~**house** n

Treibhaus nt. ~**ly** adv (*fig*) heiß, heftig. ~**plate** n Tellerwärmer m; (*of
cooker*) Kochplatte f. ~ **tap** n Warm-
wasserhahn m. ~**-tempered** adj jäh-
zornig. ~'**waterbottle** n Wärmfla-
sche f

hound /haʊnd/ n Jagdhund m ● vt
(*fig*) verfolgen

hour /ˈaʊə(r)/ n Stunde f. ~**ly** adj &
adv stündlich

house[1] /haʊs/ n Haus nt; **at my** ~
bei mir

house[2] /haʊz/ vt unterbringen

house: /haʊs/ ~**breaking** n Einbruch m. ~**hold** n Haushalt m.
~**holder** n Hausinhaber(in) m(f).
~**keeper** n Haushälterin f. ~**keeping** n Hauswirtschaft f; (*money*)
Haushaltsgeld nt. ~**plant** n Zim-
merpflanze f. ~**-trained** adj stuben-
rein. ~**-warming** n have a
~**-warming party** Einstand feiern.
~**wife** n Hausfrau f. ~**work** n Hausarbeit f

housing /ˈhaʊzɪŋ/ n Wohnungen pl;
(*Techn*) Gehäuse nt

hovel /ˈhɒvl/ n elende Hütte f

hover /ˈhɒvə(r)/ vi schweben.
~**craft** n Luftkissenfahrzeug nt

how /haʊ/ adv wie; ~ **do you do?**
guten Tag!; **and** ~! und ob!

how'ever adv (*in question*) wie;
(*nevertheless*) jedoch, aber; ~ **small**
wie klein es auch sein mag

howl /haʊl/ n Heulen nt ● vi heulen;
(*baby:*) brüllen

hub /hʌb/ n Nabe f

huddle /ˈhʌdl/ vi ~ **together** sich
zusammendrängen

huff /hʌf/ n **in a** ~ beleidigt

hug /hʌg/ n Umarmung f ● vt (*pt/pp*
hugged) umarmen

huge /hjuːdʒ/ adj riesig

hull /hʌl/ n (*Naut*) Rumpf m

hullo /həˈləʊ/ int = hallo

hum /hʌm/ n Summen nt; Brummen
nt ● vt/i (*pt/pp* **hummed**) summen;
(*motor:*) brummen

human /ˈhjuːmən/ adj menschlich

● *n* Mensch *m*. ~ **'being** *n* Mensch *m*

humane /hjuːˈmeɪn/ *adj* human

humanitarian /hjuːˌmænɪˈteərɪən/ *adj* humanitär

humanity /hjuːˈmænətɪ/ *n* Menschheit *f*

humble /ˈhʌmbl/ *adj* (-r, -st), **-bly** *adv* demütig ● *vt* demütigen

'humdrum *adj* eintönig

humid /ˈhjuːmɪd/ *adj* feucht. ~**ity** *n* Feuchtigkeit *f*

humiliat|e /hjuːˈmɪlɪeɪt/ *vt* demütigen. ~**ion** *n* Demütigung *f*

humility /hjuːˈmɪlətɪ/ *n* Demut *f*

humorous /ˈhjuːmərəs/ *adj* humorvoll; (*story*) humoristisch

humour /ˈhjuːmə(r)/ *n* Humor *m*; (*mood*) Laune *f*; **have a sense of** ~ Humor haben

hump /hʌmp/ *n* Buckel *m*; (*of camel*) Höcker *m* ● *vt* schleppen

hunch /hʌntʃ/ *n* (*idea*) Ahnung *f*

'hunch|back *n* Bucklige(r) *m/f*

hundred /ˈhʌndrəd/ *adj* **one/a** ~ [ein]hundert ● *n* Hundert *nt*; (*written figure*) Hundert *f*. ~**th** *adj* hundertste(r,s) ● *n* Hundertstel *nt*. ~**weight** *n* ≈ Zentner *m*

hung /hʌŋ/ *see* **hang**

Hungarian /hʌŋˈgeərɪən/ *adj* ungarisch ● *n* Ungar(in) *m(f)*

Hungary /ˈhʌŋgərɪ/ *n* Ungarn *nt*

hunger /ˈhʌŋgə(r)/ *n* Hunger *m*. ~**-strike** *n* Hungerstreik *m*

hungry /ˈhʌŋgrɪ/ *adj*, **-ily** *adv* hungrig; **be** ~ Hunger haben

hunt /hʌnt/ *n* Jagd *f*; (*for criminal*) Fahndung *f* ● *vt/i* jagen; fahnden nach (*criminal*); ~ **for** suchen. ~**er** *n* Jäger *m*; (*horse*) Jagdpferd *nt*. ~**ing** *n* Jagd *f*

hurdle /ˈhɜːdl/ *n* (*Sport & fig*) Hürde *f*

hurl /hɜːl/ *vt* schleudern

hurrah /hʊˈraː/, **hurray** /hʊˈreɪ/ *int* hurra! ● *n* Hurra *nt*

hurricane /ˈhʌrɪkən/ *n* Orkan *m*

hurried /ˈhʌrɪd/ *adj* eilig; (*superficial*) flüchtig

hurry /ˈhʌrɪ/ *n* Eile *f*; **be in a** ~ es eilig haben ● *vi* (*pt/pp* **-ied**) sich beeilen; (*go quickly*) eilen. ~ **up** *vi* sich beeilen ● *vt* antreiben

hurt /hɜːt/ *n* Schmerz *m* ● *vt/i* (*pt/pp* **hurt**) weh tun (+ *dat*); (*injure*) verletzen; (*offend*) kränken

hurtle /ˈhɜːtl/ *vi* ~ **along** rasen

husband /ˈhʌzbənd/ *n* [Ehe]mann *m*

hush /hʌʃ/ *n* Stille *f* ● *vt* ~ **up** vertuschen. ~**ed** *adj* gedämpft

husky /ˈhʌskɪ/ *adj* heiser; (*burly*) stämmig

hustle /ˈhʌsl/ *vt* drängen ● *n* Gedränge *nt*

hut /hʌt/ *n* Hütte *f*

hutch /hʌtʃ/ *n* [Kaninchen]stall *m*

hybrid /ˈhaɪbrɪd/ *adj* hybrid ● *n* Hybride *f*

hydraulic /haɪˈdrɔːlɪk/ *adj*, **-ally** *adv* hydraulisch

hydroe'lectric /haɪdrəʊ-/ *adj* hydroelektrisch

hydrogen /ˈhaɪdrədʒən/ *n* Wasserstoff *m*

hygien|e /ˈhaɪdʒiːn/ *n* Hygiene *f*. ~**ic** *adj*, **-ally** *adv* hygienisch

hymn /hɪm/ *n* Kirchenlied *nt*. ~**-book** *n* Gesangbuch *nt*

hyphen /ˈhaɪfn/ *n* Bindestrich *m*. ~**ate** *vt* mit Bindestrich schreiben

hypno|sis /hɪpˈnəʊsɪs/ *n* Hypnose *f*. ~**tic** *adj* hypnotisch

hypno|tism /ˈhɪpnətɪzm/ *n* Hypnotik *f*. ~**tist** *n* Hypnotiseur *m*. ~**tize** *vt* hypnotisieren

hypochondriac /haɪpəˈkɒndrɪæk/ *n* Hypochonder *m*

hypocrisy /hɪˈpɒkrəsɪ/ *n* Heuchelei *f*

hypocrit|e /ˈhɪpəkrɪt/ *n* Heuchler(in) *m(f)*

hypodermic /haɪpəˈdɜːmɪk/ *adj & n* ~ **[syringe]** Injektionsspritze *f*

hypothe|sis /haɪˈpɒθəsɪs/ *n* Hypothese *f*. ~**tical** *adj* hypothetisch

hyster|ia /hɪˈstɪərɪə/ *n* Hysterie *f*. ~**ical** *adj* hysterisch. ~**ics** *npl* hysterischer Anfall *m*

Ii

I /aɪ/ pron ich

ice /aɪs/ n Eis nt ● vt mit Zuckerguss überziehen (cake)

ice: ~**berg** /-bɜːg/ n Eisberg m. ~**box** n (Amer) Kühlschrank m. ~**-'cream** n [Speise]eis nt. ~**-cube** n Eiswürfel m

Iceland /'aɪslənd/ n Island nt

ice: ~**lolly** n Eis nt am Stiel. ~ **rink** n Eisbahn f

icicle /'aɪsɪkl/ n Eiszapfen m

icing /'aɪsɪŋ/ n Zuckerguss m. ~ **sugar** n Puderzucker m

icon /'aɪkɒn/ n Ikone f

icy /'aɪsɪ/ adj , **-ily** adv eisig; (road) vereist

idea /aɪ'dɪə/ n Idee f; (conception) Vorstellung f; **I have no** ~**!** ich habe keine Ahnung!

ideal /aɪ'dɪəl/ adj ideal ● n Ideal nt. ~**ism** n Idealismus m. ~**ist** n Idealist(in) m(f). ~**istic** adj idealistisch. ~**ize** vt idealisieren. ~**ly** adv ideal; (in ideal circumstances) idealerweise

identical /aɪ'dentɪkl/ adj identisch; (twins) eineiig

identi|fication /aɪdentɪfɪ'keɪʃn/ n Identifizierung f; (proof of identity) Ausweispapiere pl. ~**fy** vt (pt/pp -ied) identifizieren

identity /aɪ'dentətɪ/ n Identität f. ~ **card** n [Personal]ausweis m. ~ **theft** Identitätsdiebstahl m

idiom /'ɪdɪəm/ n [feste] Redewendung f. ~**atic** adj, **-ally** adv idiomatisch

idiosyncrasy /ɪdɪə'sɪŋkrəsɪ/ n Eigenart f

idiot /'ɪdɪət/ n Idiot m. ~**ic** adj idiotisch

idle /'aɪdl/ adj (-r, -st) untätig; (lazy) faul; (empty) leer; (machine) nicht in Betrieb ● vi faulenzen; (engine:) leer laufen. ~**ness** n Untätigkeit f; Faulheit f

idol /'aɪdl/ n Idol nt. ~**ize** vt vergöttern

idyllic /ɪ'dɪlɪk/ adj idyllisch

i.e. abbr (id est) d.h.

if /ɪf/ conj wenn; (whether) ob; **as if** als ob

ignition /ɪg'nɪʃn/ n (Auto) Zündung f. ~ **key** n Zündschlüssel m

ignoramus /ɪgnə'reɪməs/ n Ignorant m

ignoran|ce /'ɪgnərəns/ n Unwissenheit f. ~**t** adj unwissend

ignore /ɪg'nɔ:(r)/ vt ignorieren

ill /ɪl/ adj krank; (bad) schlecht; **feel** ~ **at ease** sich unbehaglich fühlen ● adv schlecht

illegal /ɪ'li:gl/ adj illegal

illegible /ɪ'ledʒəbl/ adj, **-bly** adv unleserlich

illegitimate /ɪlɪ'dʒɪtɪmət/ adj unehelich; (claim) unberechtigt

illicit /ɪ'lɪsɪt/ adj illegal

illiterate /ɪ'lɪtərət/ adj be ~ nicht lesen und schreiben können

illness /'ɪlnɪs/ n Krankheit f

illogical /ɪ'lɒdʒɪkl/ adj unlogisch

ill-treat /ɪl'triːt/ vt misshandeln. ~**ment** n Misshandlung f

illuminat|e /ɪ'lu:mɪneɪt/ vt beleuchten. ~**ion** n Beleuchtung f

illusion /ɪ'lu:ʒn/ n Illusion f; **be under the** ~ **that** sich (dat) einbilden, dass

illustrat|e /'ɪləstreɪt/ vt illustrieren. ~**ion** n Illustration f

illustrious /ɪ'lʌstrɪəs/ adj berühmt

image /'ɪmɪdʒ/ n Bild nt; (statue) Standbild nt; (exact likeness) Ebenbild nt; [public] ~ Image nt

imagin|able /ɪ'mædʒɪnəbl/ adj vorstellbar. ~**ary** adj eingebildet

imaginat|ion /ɪmædʒɪ'neɪʃn/ n Phantasie f; (fancy) Einbildung f. ~**ive** adj phantasievoll; (full of ideas) einfallsreich

imagine /ɪ'mædʒɪn/ vt sich (dat) vorstellen; (wrongly) sich (dat) einbilden

im'balance n Unausgeglichenheit f

imbecile /'ɪmbəsiːl/ n Schwachsinnige(r) m/f; (pej) Idiot m

imitat|e /'ɪmɪteɪt/ vt nachahmen, imitieren. ~**ion** n Nachahmung f, Imitation f

immaculate /ɪ'mækjʊlət/ adj tadellos; (Relig) unbefleckt

imma'ture adj unreif

immediate /ɪ'miːdɪət/ adj sofortig; (nearest) nächste(r,s). ~**ly** adv sofort; ~**ly next to** unmittelbar neben ● conj sobald

immemorial /ɪmə'mɔːrɪəl/ adj **from time** ~ seit Urzeiten

immense /ɪ'mens/ adj riesig; ▣ enorm

immerse /ɪ'mɜːs/ vt untertauchen

immigrant /'ɪmɪgrənt/ n Einwanderer m

immigration /ɪmɪ'greɪʃn/ n Einwanderung f

imminent /'ɪmɪnənt/ adj **be** ~ unmittelbar bevorstehen

immobil|e /ɪ'məʊbaɪl/ adj unbeweglich. ~**ize** vt (fig) lähmen; (Med) ruhig stellen. ~**izer** n (Auto) Wegfahrsperre f

immodest /ɪ'mɒdɪst/ adj unbescheiden

immoral /ɪ'mɒrəl/ adj unmoralisch. ~**ity** n Unmoral f

immortal /ɪ'mɔːtl/ adj unsterblich. ~**ity** n Unsterblichkeit f. ~**ize** vt verewigen

immune /ɪ'mjuːn/ adj immun (**to**/**from** gegen)

immunity /ɪ'mjuːnətɪ/ n Immunität f

imp /ɪmp/ n Kobold m

impact /'ɪmpækt/ n Aufprall m; (collision) Zusammenprall m; (of bomb) Einschlag m; (fig) Auswirkung f

impair /ɪm'peə(r)/ vt beeinträchtigen

impart /ɪm'pɑːt/ vt übermitteln (**to** dat); vermitteln (knowledge)

im'parti|al adj unparteiisch. ~'**ality** n Unparteilichkeit f

im'passable adj unpassierbar

impassioned /ɪm'pæʃnd/ adj leidenschaftlich

im'passive adj unbeweglich

im'patien|ce n Ungeduld f. ~**t** adj ungeduldig

impeccable /ɪm'pekəbl/ adj, -**bly** adv tadellos

impede /ɪm'piːd/ vt behindern

impediment /ɪm'pedɪmənt/ n Hindernis nt; (in speech) Sprachfehler m

impel /ɪm'pel/ vt (pt/pp **impelled**) treiben

impending /ɪm'pendɪŋ/ adj bevorstehend

impenetrable /ɪm'penɪtrəbl/ adj undurchdringlich

imperative /ɪm'perətɪv/ adj **be** ~ dringend notwendig sein ● n (Gram) Imperativ m

imper'ceptible adj nicht wahrnehmbar

im'perfect adj unvollkommen; (faulty) fehlerhaft ● n (Gram) Imperfekt nt. ~**ion** n Unvollkommenheit f; (fault) Fehler m

imperial /ɪm'pɪərɪəl/ adj kaiserlich. ~**ism** n Imperialismus m

im'personal adj unpersönlich

impersonat|e /ɪm'pɜːsəneɪt/ vt sich ausgeben als; (Theat) nachahmen, imitieren. ~**or** n Imitator m

impertinen|ce /ɪm'pɜːtɪnəns/ n Frechheit f. ~**t** adj frech

imperturbable /ɪmpə'tɜːbəbl/ adj unerschütterlich

impetuous /ɪm'petjʊəs/ adj ungestüm

impetus /'ɪmpɪtəs/ n Schwung m

implacable /ɪm'plækəbl/ adj unerbittlich

im'plant vt einpflanzen

implement[1] /'ɪmplɪmənt/ n Gerät nt

implement[2] /'ɪmplɪment/ vt ausführen. ~**ation** n Ausführung f, Durchführung f

implication /ɪmplɪ'keɪʃn/ n Verwicklung f; ~**s** pl Auswirkungen pl; **by** ~ implizit

implicit /ɪm'plɪsɪt/ adj unausgesprochen; (absolute) unbedingt

implore /ɪm'plɔː(r)/ vt anflehen

imply /ɪmˈplaɪ/ vt (pt/pp **-ied**) andeuten; **what are you ~ing?** was wollen Sie damit sagen?

impo'lite adj unhöflich

import[1] /ˈɪmpɔːt/ n Import m, Einfuhr f

import[2] /ɪmˈpɔːt/ vt importieren, einführen

importan|ce /ɪmˈpɔːtns/ n Wichtigkeit f. **~t** adj wichtig

importer /ɪmˈpɔːtə(r)/ n Importeur m

impos|e /ɪmˈpəʊz/ vt auferlegen (**on** dat) ● vi sich aufdrängen (**on** dat). **~ing** adj eindrucksvoll

impossi'bility n Unmöglichkeit f

im'possible adj, **-bly** adv unmöglich

impostor /ɪmˈpɒstə(r)/ n Betrüger(in) m(f)

impoten|ce /ˈɪmpətəns/ n Machtlosigkeit f; (Med) Impotenz f. **~t** adj machtlos; (Med) impotent

impoverished /ɪmˈpɒvərɪʃt/ adj verarmt

im'practicable adj undurchführbar

im'practical adj unpraktisch

impre'cise adj ungenau

im'press vt beeindrucken; **~ sth [up]on s.o.** jdm etw einprägen

impression /ɪmˈpreʃn/ n Eindruck m; (imitation) Nachahmung f; (edition) Auflage f. **~ism** n Impressionismus m

impressive /ɪmˈpresɪv/ adj eindrucksvoll

im'prison vt gefangen halten; (put in prison) ins Gefängnis sperren

im'probable adj unwahrscheinlich

impromptu /ɪmˈprɒmptjuː/ adj improvisiert ● adv aus dem Stegreif

im'proper adj inkorrekt; (indecent) unanständig

impro'priety n Unkorrektheit f

improve /ɪmˈpruːv/ vt verbessern; verschönern (appearance) ● vi sich bessern; **~ [up]on** übertreffen. **~ment** n Verbesserung f; (in health) Besserung f

improvise /ˈɪmprəvaɪz/ vt/i improvisieren

im'prudent adj unklug

impuden|ce /ˈɪmpjʊdəns/ n Frechheit f. **~t** adj frech

impuls|e /ˈɪmpʌls/ n Impuls m; **on [an] ~e** impulsiv. **~ive** adj impulsiv

im'pur|e adj unrein. **~ity** n Unreinheit f

in /ɪn/ prep in (+ dat/(into) + acc); **sit in the garden** im Garten sitzen; **go in the garden** in den Garten gehen; **in May** im Mai; **in 1992** [im Jahre] 1992; **in this heat** bei dieser Hitze; **in the evening** am Abend; **in the sky** am Himmel; **in the world** auf der Welt; **in the street** auf der Straße; **deaf in one ear** auf einem Ohr taub; **in the army** beim Militär; **in English/German** auf Englisch/Deutsch; **in ink/pencil** mit Tinte/Bleistift; **in a soft/loud voice** mit leiser/lauter Stimme; **in doing this, he ...** indem er das tut/tat, ... er ● adv (at home) zu Hause; (indoors) drinnen; **he's not in yet** er ist noch nicht da; **all in** alles inbegriffen; (🔲: exhausted) kaputt; **day in, day out** tagaus, tagein; **have it in for s.o.** 🔲 es auf jdn abgesehen haben; **send/go in** hineinschicken/-gehen; **come/bring in** hereinkommen/-bringen ● adj (🔲: in fashion) in ● n **the ins and outs** alle Einzelheiten pl

ina'bility n Unfähigkeit f

inac'cessible adj unzugänglich

in'accura|cy n Ungenauigkeit f. **~te** adj ungenau

in'ac|tive adj untätig. **~'tivity** n Untätigkeit f

in'adequate adj unzulänglich

inad'missable adj unzulässig

inadvertently /ɪnədˈvɜːtntlɪ/ adv versehentlich

inad'visable adj nicht ratsam

inane /ɪˈneɪm/ adj albern

in'animate adj unbelebt

in'applicable adj nicht zutreffend

inap'propriate adj unangebracht

inar'ticulate adj undeutlich; **be ~**

sich nicht gut ausdrücken können

inat'tentive *adj* unaufmerksam

in'audible *adj*, **-bly** *adv* unhörbar

inaugural /ɪˈnɔːgjʊrl/ *adj* Antritts-

inau'spicious *adj* ungünstig

inborn /ˈɪnbɔːn/ *adj* angeboren

inbred /ɪnˈbred/ *adj* angeboren

incalculable /ɪnˈkælkjʊləbl/ *adj* nicht berechenbar; (*fig*) unabsehbar

in'capable *adj* unfähig; **be ~ of doing sth** nicht fähig sein, etw zu tun

incapacitate /ɪnkəˈpæsɪteɪt/ *vt* unfähig machen

incarnation /ɪnkɑːˈneɪʃn/ *n* Inkarnation *f*

incendiary /ɪnˈsendɪərɪ/ *adj* & *n* **~ [bomb]** Brandbombe *f*

incense[1] /ˈɪnsens/ *n* Weihrauch *m*

incense[2] /ɪnˈsens/ *vt* wütend machen

incentive /ɪnˈsentɪv/ *n* Anreiz *m*

incessant /ɪnˈsesnt/ *adj* unaufhörlich

incest /ˈɪnsest/ *n* Inzest *m*, Blutschande *f*

inch /ɪntʃ/ *n* Zoll *m* ● *vi* **~ forward** sich ganz langsam vorwärts schieben

incident /ˈɪnsɪdənt/ *n* Zwischenfall *m*

incidental /ɪnsɪˈdentl/ *adj* nebensächlich; (*remark*) beiläufig; (*expenses*) Neben-. **~ly** *adv* übrigens

incinerat|e /ɪnˈsɪnəreɪt/ *vt* verbrennen

incision /ɪnˈsɪʒn/ *n* Einschnitt *m*

incisive /ɪnˈsaɪsɪv/ *adj* scharfsinnig

incite /ɪnˈsaɪt/ *vt* aufhetzen. **~ment** *n* Aufhetzung *f*

in'clement *adj* rau

inclination /ɪnklɪˈneɪʃn/ *n* Neigung *f*

incline /ɪnˈklaɪn/ *vt* neigen; **be ~d to do sth** dazu neigen, etw zu tun ● *vi* sich neigen

inclu|de /ɪnˈkluːd/ *vt* einschließen; (*contain*) enthalten; (*incorporate*) aufnehmen (**in** in + *acc*). **~ding** *prep*

einschließlich (+ *gen*). **~sion** *n* Aufnahme *f*

inclusive /ɪnˈkluːsɪv/ *adj* Inklusiv-; **~ of** einschließlich (+ *gen*)

incognito /ɪnkɒgˈniːtəʊ/ *adv* inkognito

inco'herent *adj* zusammenhanglos; (*incomprehensible*) unverständlich

income /ˈɪnkəm/ *n* Einkommen *nt*. **~ tax** *n* Einkommensteuer *f*

'incoming *adj* ankommend; (*mail, call*) eingehend

in'comparable *adj* unvergleichlich

incom'patible *adj* unvereinbar; **be ~** (*people:*) nicht zueinander passen

in'competen|ce *n* Unfähigkeit *f*. **~t** *adj* unfähig

incom'plete *adj* unvollständig

incompre'hensible *adj* unverständlich

incon'ceivable *adj* undenkbar

incon'clusive *adj* nicht schlüssig

incongruous /ɪnˈkɒŋgrʊəs/ *adj* unpassend

incon'siderate *adj* rücksichtslos

incon'sistent *adj* widersprüchlich; (*illogical*) inkonsequent; **be ~** nicht übereinstimmen

inconsolable /ɪnkənˈsəʊləbl/ *adj* untröstlich

incon'spicuous *adj* unauffällig

incontinen|ce /ɪnˈkɒntɪnəns/ *n* Inkontinenz *f*. **~t** *adj* inkontinent

incon'venien|ce *n* Unannehmlichkeit *f*; (*drawback*) Nachteil *m*. **~t** *adj* ungünstig; **be ~t for s.o.** jdm nicht passen

incorporate /ɪnˈkɔːpəreɪt/ *vt* aufnehmen; (*contain*) enthalten

incor'rect *adj* inkorrekt

incorrigible /ɪnˈkɒrɪdʒəbl/ *adj* unverbesserlich

incorruptible /ɪnkəˈrʌptəbl/ *adj* unbestechlich

increase[1] /ˈɪnkriːs/ *n* Zunahme *f*; (*rise*) Erhöhung *f*; **be on the ~** zunehmen

increas|e[2] /ɪnˈkriːs/ *vt* vergrößern; (*raise*) erhöhen ● *vi* zunehmen; (*rise*)

i

sich erhöhen. **~ing** adj zunehmend

in'credi|ble adj, **-bly** adv unglaublich

incredulous /ɪn'kredjʊləs/ adj ungläubig

incriminate /ɪn'krɪmɪneɪt/ vt (Jur) belasten

incur /ɪn'kɜː(r)/ vt (pt/pp **incurred**) sich (dat) zuziehen; machen (debts)

in'cura|ble adj, **-bly** adv unheilbar

indebted /ɪn'detɪd/ adj verpflichtet (to dat)

in'decent adj unanständig

inde'cision n Unentschlossenheit f

inde'cisive adj ergebnislos; (person) unentschlossen

indeed /ɪn'diːd/ adv in der Tat, tatsächlich; **very much ~** sehr

indefatigable /ɪndɪ'fætɪɡəbl/ adj unermüdlich

in'definite adj unbestimmt. **~ly** adv unbegrenzt; (postpone) auf unbestimmte Zeit

indent /ɪn'dent/ vt (Printing) einrücken. **~ation** n Einrückung f; (notch) Kerbe f

inde'penden|ce n Unabhängigkeit f; (self-reliance) Selbstständigkeit f. **~t** adj unabhängig; selbstständig

indescriba|ble /ɪndɪ'skraɪbəbl/ adj, **-bly** adv unbeschreiblich

indestructible /ɪndɪ'strʌktəbl/ adj unzerstörbar

indeterminate /ɪndɪ'tɜːmɪnət/ adj unbestimmt

index /'ɪndeks/ n Register nt

index: ~ card n Karteikarte f. **~ finger** n Zeigefinger m. **~-linked** adj (pension) dynamisch

India /'ɪndɪə/ n Indien nt. **~n** adj indisch; (American) indianisch ● n Inder(in) m(f); (American) Indianer(in) m(f)

Indian 'summer n Nachsommer m

indicat|e /'ɪndɪkeɪt/ vt zeigen; (point at) zeigen auf (+ acc); (hint) andeuten; (register) anzeigen ● vi (Auto) blinken. **~ion** n Anzeichen nt

indicative /ɪn'dɪkətɪv/ n (Gram) Indikativ m

indicator /'ɪndɪkeɪtə(r)/ n (Auto) Blinker m

in'differen|ce n Gleichgültigkeit f. **~t** adj gleichgültig; (not good) mittelmäßig

indi'gest|ible adj unverdaulich; (difficult to digest) schwer verdaulich. **~ion** n Magenverstimmung f

indigna|nt /ɪn'dɪɡnənt/ adj entrüstet, empört. **~tion** n Entrüstung f, Empörung f

in'dignity n Demütigung f

indi'rect adj indirekt

indi'screet adj indiskret

indis'cretion n Indiskretion f

indi'spensable adj unentbehrlich

indisposed /ɪndɪ'spəʊzd/ adj indisponiert

indisputable /ɪndɪ'spjuːtəbl/ adj, **-bly** adv unbestreitbar

indi'stinct adj undeutlich

indistinguishable /ɪndɪ'stɪŋɡwɪʃəbl/ adj **be ~** nicht zu unterscheiden sein

individual /ɪndɪ'vɪdjʊəl/ adj individuell; (single) einzeln ● n Individuum nt. **~ity** n Individualität f

indi'visible adj unteilbar

indoctrinate /ɪn'dɒktrɪneɪt/ vt indoktrinieren

indolen|ce /'ɪndələns/ n Faulheit f. **~t** adj faul

indomitable /ɪn'dɒmɪtəbl/ adj unbeugsam

indoor /'ɪndɔː(r)/ adj Innen-; (clothes) Haus-; (plant) Zimmer-; (Sport) Hallen-. **~s** adv im Haus, drinnen; **go ~s** ins Haus gehen

indulge /ɪn'dʌldʒ/ vt frönen (+ dat); verwöhnen (child) ● vi **~ in** frönen (+ dat). **~nce** n Nachgiebigkeit f; (leniency) Nachsicht f. **~nt** adj [zu] nachgiebig; nachsichtig

industrial /ɪn'dʌstrɪəl/ adj Industrie-. **~ist** n Industrielle(r) m

industr|ious /ɪn'dʌstrɪəs/ adj fleißig. **~y** n Industrie f; (zeal) Fleiß m

inebriated /ɪˈniːbrɪeɪtɪd/ adj betrunken

in'edible adj nicht essbar

inef'fective adj unwirksam; (person) untauglich

inef'ficient adj unfähig; (organization) nicht leistungsfähig; (method) nicht rationell

in'eligible adj nicht berechtigt

inept /ɪˈnept/ adj ungeschickt

ine'quality n Ungleichheit f

inertia /ɪˈnɜːʃə/ n Trägheit f

inescapable /ɪnɪˈskeɪpəbl/ adj unvermeidlich

inestimable /ɪnˈestɪməbl/ adj unschätzbar

inevitab|le /ɪnˈevɪtəbl/ adj unvermeidlich. **~ly** adv zwangsläufig

ine'xact adj ungenau

inex'cusable adj unverzeihlich

inexhaustible /ɪnɪgˈzɔːstəbl/ adj unerschöpflich

inex'pensive adj preiswert

inex'perience n Unerfahrenheit f. **~d** adj unerfahren

inexplicable /ɪnɪkˈsplɪkəbl/ adj unerklärlich

in'fallible adj unfehlbar

infamous /ˈɪnfəməs/ adj niederträchtig; (notorious) berüchtigt

infan|cy /ˈɪnfənsɪ/ n frühe Kindheit f; (fig) Anfangsstadium nt. **~t** n Kleinkind nt. **~tile** adj kindisch

infantry /ˈɪnfəntrɪ/ n Infanterie f

infatuated /ɪnˈfætʃʊeɪtɪd/ adj vernarrt (with in + acc)

infect /ɪnˈfekt/ vt anstecken, infizieren; **become ~ed** (wound:) sich infizieren. **~ion** n Infektion f. **~ious** adj ansteckend

inferior /ɪnˈfɪərɪə(r)/ adj minderwertig; (in rank) untergeordnet ● n Untergebene(r) m/f

inferiority /ɪnfɪərɪˈɒrətɪ/ n Minderwertigkeit f. **~ complex** n Minderwertigkeitskomplex m

infern|al /ɪnˈfɜːnl/ adj höllisch. **~o** n flammendes Inferno nt

in'fertile adj unfruchtbar

infest /ɪnˈfest/ vt **be ~ed with** befallen sein von; (place) verseucht sein mit

infi'delity n Untreue f

infighting /ˈɪnfaɪtɪŋ/ n (fig) interne Machtkämpfe pl

infinite /ˈɪnfɪnət/ adj unendlich

infinitive /ɪnˈfɪnətɪv/ n (Gram) Infinitiv m

infinity /ɪnˈfɪnətɪ/ n Unendlichkeit f

inflame /ɪnˈfleɪm/ vt entzünden. **~d** adj entzündet

in'flammable adj feuergefährlich

inflammation /ɪnfləˈmeɪʃn/ n Entzündung f

inflammatory /ɪnˈflæmətrɪ/ adj aufrührerisch

inflat|e /ɪnˈfleɪt/ vt aufblasen; (with pump) aufpumpen. **~ion** n Inflation f. **~ionary** adj inflationär

in'flexible adj starr; (person) unbeugsam

inflict /ɪnˈflɪkt/ vt zufügen (on dat); versetzen (blow) (on dat)

influen|ce /ˈɪnflʊəns/ n Einfluss m ● vt beeinflussen. **~tial** adj einflussreich

influenza /ɪnflʊˈenzə/ n Grippe f

inform /ɪnˈfɔːm/ vt benachrichtigen; (officially) informieren; **~ s.o. of sth** jdm etw mitteilen; **keep s.o. ~ed** jdn auf dem Laufenden halten ● vi **~ against** denunzieren

in'for|mal adj zwanglos; (unofficial) inoffiziell. **~'mality** n Zwanglosigkeit f

informant /ɪnˈfɔːmənt/ n Gewährsmann m

informat|ion /ɪnfəˈmeɪʃn/ n Auskunft f; **a piece of ~ion** eine Auskunft. **~ive** adj aufschlussreich; (instructive) lehrreich

informer /ɪnˈfɔːmə(r)/ n Spitzel m; (Pol) Denunziant m

infra-'red /ɪnfrə-/ adj infrarot

in'frequent adj selten

infringe /ɪnˈfrɪndʒ/ vt/i **~ [on]** verstoßen gegen. **~ment** n Verstoß m

infuriat|e /ɪnˈfjʊərɪeɪt/ vt wütend machen. **~ing** adj ärgerlich

ingenious /ɪn'dʒiːnɪəs/ adj erfinderisch; (thing) raffiniert

ingenuity /ɪndʒɪ'njuːətɪ/ n Geschicklichkeit f

ingrained /ɪn'greɪnd/ adj eingefleischt; **be** ~ (dirt:) tief sitzen

ingratiate /ɪn'greɪʃɪeɪt/ vt ~ oneself sich einschmeicheln (**with** bei)

in'gratitude n Undankbarkeit f

ingredient /ɪn'griːdɪənt/ n (Culin) Zutat f

ingrowing /'ɪngrəʊɪŋ/ adj (nail) eingewachsen

inhabit /ɪn'hæbɪt/ vt bewohnen. ~**ant** n Einwohner(in) m(f)

inhale /ɪn'heɪl/ vt/i einatmen; (Med & when smoking) inhalieren

inherent /ɪn'hɪərənt/ adj natürlich

inherit /ɪn'herɪt/ vt erben. ~**ance** n Erbschaft f, Erbe nt

inhibit|ed /ɪn'hɪbɪtɪd/ adj gehemmt. ~**ion** n Hemmung f

inho'spitable adj ungastlich

in'human adj unmenschlich

inimitable /ɪ'nɪmɪtəbl/ adj unnachahmlich

initial /ɪ'nɪʃl/ adj anfänglich, Anfangs- ● n Anfangsbuchstabe m; **my** ~**s** meine Initialen. ~**ly** adv anfangs, am Anfang

initiat|e /ɪ'nɪʃɪeɪt/ vt einführen. ~**ion** n Einführung f

initiative /ɪ'nɪʃətɪv/ n Initiative f

inject /ɪn'dʒekt/ vt einspritzen, injizieren. ~**ion** n Spritze f, Injektion f

injur|e /'ɪndʒə(r)/ vt verletzen. ~**y** n Verletzung f

in'justice n Ungerechtigkeit f; **do s.o. an** ~ jdm unrecht tun

ink /ɪŋk/ n Tinte f

inlaid /ɪn'leɪd/ adj eingelegt

inland /'ɪnlənd/ adj Binnen- ● adv landeinwärts. **I**~ **Revenue** (UK) ≈ Finanzamt nt

in-laws /'ɪnlɔːz/ npl 🔢 Schwiegereltern pl

inlay /'ɪnleɪ/ n Einlegearbeit f

inlet /'ɪnlet/ n schmale Bucht f; (Techn) Zuleitung f

inmate /'ɪnmeɪt/ n Insasse m

inn /ɪn/ n Gasthaus nt

innate /ɪ'neɪt/ adj angeboren

inner /'ɪnə(r)/ adj innere(r,s). ~**most** adj innerste(r,s)

innocen|ce /'ɪnəsəns/ n Unschuld f. ~**t** adj unschuldig. ~**tly** adv in aller Unschuld

innocuous /ɪ'nɒkjʊəs/ adj harmlos

innovat|ion /ɪnə'veɪʃn/ n Neuerung f. ~**ive** adj innovativ. ~**or** n Neuerer m

innumerable /ɪ'njuːmərəbl/ adj unzählig

inoculat|e /ɪ'nɒkjʊleɪt/ vt impfen. ~**ion** n Impfung f

inof'fensive adj harmlos

in'operable adj nicht operierbar

in'opportune adj unpassend

inor'ganic adj anorganisch

'in-patient n [stationär behandelter] Krankenhauspatient m

input /'ɪnpʊt/ n Input m & nt

inquest /'ɪnkwest/ n gerichtliche Untersuchung f der Todesursache

inquir|e /ɪn'kwaɪə(r)/ vi sich erkundigen (**about** nach); ~**e into** untersuchen ● vt sich erkundigen nach. ~**y** n Erkundigung f; (investigation) Untersuchung f

inquisitive /ɪn'kwɪzətɪv/ adj neugierig

in'sane adj geisteskrank; (fig) wahnsinnig

in'sanitary adj unhygienisch

in'sanity n Geisteskrankheit f

insatiable /ɪn'seɪʃəbl/ adj unersättlich

inscription /ɪn'skrɪpʃn/ n Inschrift f

inscrutable /ɪn'skruːtəbl/ adj unergründlich; (expression) undurchdringlich

insect /'ɪnsekt/ n Insekt nt. ~**icide** n Insektenvertilgungsmittel nt

inse'cur|e adj nicht sicher; (fig) unsicher. ~**ity** n Unsicherheit f

in'sensitive adj gefühllos; ~ **to** unempfindlich gegen

in'separable adj untrennbar;

(*people*) unzertrennlich

insert[1] /'ɪnsɜːt/ n Einsatz m

insert[2] /ɪn'sɜːt/ vt einfügen, einsetzen; einstecken (*key*); einwerfen (*coin*). **~ion** n (*insert*) Einsatz m; (*in text*) Einfügung f

inside /ɪn'saɪd/ n Innenseite f; (*of house*) Innere(s) nt ● *attrib* Innen- ● *adv* innen; (*indoors*) drinnen; **go ~** hineingehen; **come ~** hereinkommen; **~ out** links [herum]; **know sth ~ out** etw in- und auswendig kennen ● *prep* **~ [of]** in (+ *dat*/ (*into*) + *acc*)

insight /'ɪnsaɪt/ n Einblick m (**into** in + *acc*); (*understanding*) Einsicht f

insig'nificant adj unbedeutend

insin'cere adj unaufrichtig

insinuat|e /ɪn'sɪnjʊeɪt/ vt andeuten. **~ion** n Andeutung f

insipid /ɪn'sɪpɪd/ adj fade

insist /ɪn'sɪst/ vi darauf bestehen; **~ on** bestehen auf (+ *dat*) ● vt **~ that** darauf bestehen, dass. **~ence** n Bestehen nt. **~ent** adj beharrlich; **be ~ent** darauf bestehen

'insole n Einlegesohle f

insolen|ce /'ɪnsələns/ n Unverschämtheit f. **~t** adj unverschämt

in'soluble adj unlöslich; (*fig*) unlösbar

in'solvent adj zahlungsunfähig

insomnia /ɪn'sɒmnɪə/ n Schlaflosigkeit f

inspect /ɪn'spekt/ vt inspizieren; (*test*) prüfen; kontrollieren (*ticket*). **~ion** n Inspektion f. **~or** n Inspektor m; (*of tickets*) Kontrolleur m

inspiration /ɪnspə'reɪʃn/ n Inspiration f

inspire /ɪn'spaɪə(r)/ vt inspirieren

insta'bility n Unbeständigkeit f; (*of person*) Labilität f

install /ɪn'stɔːl/ vt installieren. **~ation** n Installation f

instalment /ɪn'stɔːlmənt/ n (*Comm*) Rate f; (*of serial*) Fortsetzung f; (*Radio, TV*) Folge f

instance /'ɪnstəns/ n Fall m; (*example*) Beispiel nt; **in the first ~** zu-

nächst; **for ~** zum Beispiel

instant /'ɪnstənt/ adj sofortig; (*Culin*) Instant- ● n Augenblick m, Moment m. **~aneous** adj unverzüglich, unmittelbar

instant 'coffee n Pulverkaffee m

instantly /'ɪnstəntlɪ/ adv sofort

instead /ɪn'sted/ adv statt dessen; **~ of** statt (+ *gen*), anstelle von; **~ of me** an meiner Stelle; **~ of going** anstatt zu gehen

'instep n Spann m, Rist m

instigat|e /'ɪnstɪgeɪt/ vt anstiften; einleiten (*proceedings*). **~ion** n Anstiftung f; **at his ~ion** auf sein Veranlassung

instil /ɪn'stɪl/ vt (*pt/pp* instilled) einprägen (**into s.o.** jdm)

instinct /'ɪnstɪŋkt/ n Instinkt m. **~ive** adj instinktiv

institut|e /'ɪnstɪtjuːt/ n Institut nt. **~ion** n Institution f; (*home*) Anstalt f

instruct /ɪn'strʌkt/ vt unterrichten; (*order*) anweisen. **~ion** n Unterricht m; Anweisung f; **~ions** pl for use Gebrauchsanweisung f. **~ive** adj lehrreich. **~or** n Lehrer(in) m(f); (*Mil*) Ausbilder m

instrument /'ɪnstrʊmənt/ n Instrument nt. **~al** adj Instrumental-

insu'bordi|nate adj ungehorsam. **~nation** n Ungehorsam m; (*Mil*) Insubordination f

insuf'ficient adj nicht genügend

insulat|e /'ɪnsjʊleɪt/ vt isolieren. **~ing tape** n Isolierband nt. **~ion** n Isolierung f

insult[1] /'ɪnsʌlt/ n Beleidigung f

insult[2] /ɪn'sʌlt/ vt beleidigen

insur|ance /ɪn'ʃʊərəns/ n Versicherung f. **~e** vt versichern

intact /ɪn'tækt/ adj unbeschädigt; (*complete*) vollständig

'intake n Aufnahme f

in'tangible adj nicht greifbar

integral /'ɪntɪgrl/ adj wesentlich

integrat|e /'ɪntɪgreɪt/ vt integrieren ● vi sich integrieren. **~ion** n Integration f

integrity /ɪn'tegrətɪ/ n Integrität f

intellect /'ɪntəlekt/ n Intellekt m.
~**ual** adj intellektuell

intelligen|ce /ɪn'telɪdʒəns/ n Intelligenz f; (Mil) Nachrichtendienst m; (information) Meldungen pl. ~**t** adj intelligent

intelligible /ɪn'telɪdʒəbl/ adj verständlich

intend /ɪn'tend/ vt beabsichtigen; **be** ~**ed for** bestimmt sein für

intense /ɪn'tens/ adj intensiv; (pain) stark. ~**ly** adv äußerst; (study) intensiv

intensify /ɪn'tensɪfaɪ/ v (pt/pp -ied) ● vt intensivieren ● vi zunehmen

intensity /ɪn'tensətɪ/ n Intensität f

intensive /ɪn'tensɪv/ adj intensiv; **be in** ~ **care** auf der Intensivstation sein

intent /ɪn'tent/ adj aufmerksam; ~ **on** (absorbed in) vertieft in (+ acc) ● n Absicht f

intention /ɪn'tenʃn/ n Absicht f. ~**al** adj absichtlich

inter'acti|on n Wechselwirkung f. ~**ve** adj interaktiv

intercede /ɪntə'siːd/ vi Fürsprache einlegen (**on behalf of** für)

intercept /ɪntə'sept/ vt abfangen

'**interchange** n Austausch m; (Auto) Autobahnkreuz nt

intercom /'ɪntəkɒm/ n [Gegen]-sprechanlage f

'**intercourse** n (sexual) Geschlechtsverkehr m

interest /'ɪntrəst/ n Interesse nt; (Comm) Zinsen pl ● vt interessieren; **be** ~**ed** sich interessieren (**in** für). ~**ing** adj interessant. ~ **rate** n Zinssatz m

interface /'ɪntəfeɪs/ n Schnittstelle f

interfere /ɪntə'fɪə(r)/ vi sich einmischen. ~**nce** n Einmischung f; (Radio, TV) Störung f

interim /'ɪntərɪm/ adj Zwischen-; (temporary) vorläufig

interior /ɪn'tɪərɪə(r)/ adj innere(r,s), Innen- ● n Innere(s) nt

interject /ɪntə'dʒekt/ vt einwerfen.

~**ion** n Interjektion f; (remark) Einwurf m

interlude /'ɪntəluːd/ n Pause f; (performance) Zwischenspiel nt

inter'marry vi untereinander heiraten; (different groups:) Mischehen schließen

intermediary /ɪntə'miːdɪərɪ/ n Vermittler(in) m(f)

intermediate /ɪntə'miːdɪət/ adj Zwischen-

interminable /ɪn'tɜːmɪnəbl/ adj endlos [lang]

intermittent /ɪntə'mɪtənt/ adj in Abständen auftretend

internal /ɪn'tɜːnl/ adj innere(r,s); (matter, dispute) intern. **I**~ **Revenue** (USA) ≈ Finanzamt nt. ~**ly** adv innerlich; (deal with) intern

inter'national adj international ● n Länderspiel nt; (player) Nationalspieler(in) m(f)

'**Internet** n Internet nt; **on the** ~ Im Internet

internment /ɪn'tɜːnmənt/ n Internierung f

'**interplay** n Wechselspiel nt

interpolate /ɪn'tɜːpəleɪt/ vt einwerfen

interpret /ɪn'tɜːprɪt/ vt interpretieren; auslegen (text); deuten (dream); (translate) dolmetschen ● vi dolmetschen. ~**ation** n Interpretation f. ~**er** n Dolmetscher(in) m(f)

interrogat|e /ɪn'terəgeɪt/ vt verhören. ~**ion** n Verhör nt

interrogative /ɪntə'rɒgətɪv/ adj & n ~ [**pronoun**] Interrogativpronomen nt

interrupt /ɪntə'rʌpt/ vt/i unterbrechen; **don't** ~! red nicht dazwischen! ~**ion** n Unterbrechung f

intersect /ɪntə'sekt/ vi sich kreuzen; (of lines) sich schneiden. ~**ion** n Kreuzung f

interspersed /ɪntə'spɜːst/ adj ~ **with** durchsetzt mit

inter'twine vi sich ineinanderschlingen

interval /'ɪntəvl/ n Abstand m;

(*Theat*) Pause *f*; (*Mus*) Intervall *nt*; **at hourly ~s** alle Stunde; **bright ~s** *pl* Aufheiterungen *pl*

interven|e /ɪntə'viːn/ *vi* eingreifen; (*occur*) dazwischenkommen. **~tion** *n* Eingreifen *nt*; (*Mil, Pol*) Intervention *f*

interview /'ɪntəvjuː/ *n* (*in media*) Interview *nt*; (*for job*) Vorstellungsgespräch *nt* ● *vt* interviewen; ein Vorstellungsgespräch führen mit. **~er** *n* Interviewer(in) *m*(*f*)

intimacy /'ɪntɪməsɪ/ *n* Vertrautheit *f*; (*sexual*) Intimität *f*

intimate /'ɪntɪmət/ *adj* vertraut; (*friend*) eng; (*sexually*) intim

intimidat|e /ɪn'tɪmɪdeɪt/ *vt* einschüchtern. **~ion** *n* Einschüchterung *f*

into /'ɪntə/, *vor einem Vokal* /'ɪntʊ/ *prep* in (+ *acc*); **be ~** ⓘ sich auskennen mit; **7 ~ 21** 21 [geteilt] durch 7

in'tolerable *adj* unerträglich

in'toleran|ce *n* Intoleranz *f*. **~t** *adj* intolerant

intonation /ɪntə'neɪʃn/ *n* Tonfall *m*

intoxicat|ed /ɪn'tɒksɪkeɪtɪd/ *adj* betrunken; (*fig*) berauscht. **~ion** *n* Rausch *m*

intransigent /ɪn'trænsɪdʒənt/ *adj* unnachgiebig

in'transitive *adj* intransitiv

intrepid /ɪn'trepɪd/ *adj* kühn, unerschrocken

intricate /'ɪntrɪkət/ *adj* kompliziert

intrigu|e /ɪn'triːg/ *n* Intrige *f* ● *vt* faszinieren. **~ing** *adj* faszinierend

intrinsic /ɪn'trɪnsɪk/ *adj* **~ value** Eigenwert *m*

introduce /ɪntrə'djuːs/ *vt* vorstellen; (*bring in, insert*) einführen

introduct|ion /ɪntrə'dʌkʃn/ *n* Einführung *f*; (*to person*) Vorstellung *f*; (*to book*) Einleitung *f*. **~ory** *adj* einleitend

introvert /'ɪntrəvɜːt/ *n* introvertierter Mensch *m*

intru|de /ɪn'truːd/ *vi* stören. **~der** *n* Eindringling *m*. **~sion** *n* Störung *f*

intuit|ion /ɪntjuː'ɪʃn/ *n* Intuition *f*. **~ive** *adj* intuitiv

inundate /'ɪnəndeɪt/ *vt* überschwemmen

invade /ɪn'veɪd/ *vt* einfallen in (+ *acc*). **~r** *n* Angreifer *m*

invalid[1] /'ɪnvəlɪd/ *n* Kranke(r) *m*/*f*

invalid[2] /ɪn'vælɪd/ *adj* ungültig

in'valuable *adj* unschätzbar; (*person*) unersetzlich

in'variab|le *adj* unveränderlich. **~ly** *adv* immer

invasion /ɪn'veɪʒn/ *n* Invasion *f*

invent /ɪn'vent/ *vt* erfinden. **~ion** *n* Erfindung *f*. **~ive** *adj* erfinderisch. **~or** *n* Erfinder *m*

inventory /'ɪnvəntrɪ/ *n* Bestandsliste *f*

invert /ɪn'vɜːt/ *vt* umkehren. **~ed commas** *npl* Anführungszeichen *pl*

invest /ɪn'vest/ *vt* investieren, anlegen; **~ in** (ⓘ: *buy*) sich (*dat*) zulegen

investigat|e /ɪn'vestɪgeɪt/ *vt* untersuchen. **~ion** *n* Untersuchung *f*

invest|ment /ɪn'vestmənt/ *n* Anlage *f*; **be a good ~ment** (*fig*) sich bezahlt machen. **~or** *n* Kapitalanleger *m*

invidious /ɪn'vɪdɪəs/ *adj* unerfreulich; (*unfair*) ungerecht

invincible /ɪn'vɪnsəbl/ *adj* unbesiegbar

inviolable /ɪn'vaɪələbl/ *adj* unantastbar

in'visible *adj* unsichtbar

invitation /ɪnvɪ'teɪʃn/ *n* Einladung *f*

invit|e /ɪn'vaɪt/ *vt* einladen. **~ing** *adj* einladend

invoice /'ɪnvɔɪs/ *n* Rechnung *f* ● *vt* **~ s.o.** jdm eine Rechnung schicken

in'voluntary *adj*, **-ily** *adv* unwillkürlich

involve /ɪn'vɒlv/ *vt* beteiligen; (*affect*) betreffen; (*implicate*) verwickeln; (*entail*) mit sich bringen; (*mean*) bedeuten; **be ~d in** beteiligt sein an (+ *dat*); (*implicated*) verwickelt sein in (+ *acc*); **get ~d with s.o.** sich mit jdm einlassen. **~d** *adj* kompliziert. **~ment** *n* Verbindung *f*

in'vulnerable *adj* unverwundbar;

(*position*) unangreifbar

inward /ˈɪnwəd/ *adj* innere(r,s). ∼**s** *adv* nach innen

iodine /ˈaɪədiːn/ *n* Jod *nt*

IOU *abbr* Schuldschein *m*

Iran /ɪˈrɑːn/ *n* der Iran

Iraq /ɪˈrɑːk/ *n* der Irak

irascible /ɪˈræsəbl/ *adj* aufbrausend

irate /aɪˈreɪt/ *adj* wütend

Ireland /ˈaɪələnd/ *n* Irland *nt*

iris /ˈaɪərɪs/ *n* (*Anat*) Regenbogenhaut *f*, Iris *f*; (*Bot*) Schwertlilie *f*

Irish /ˈaɪərɪʃ/ *adj* irisch ● *n* the ∼ *pl* die Iren. ∼**man** *n* Ire *m*. ∼**woman** *n* Irin *f*

iron /ˈaɪən/ *adj* Eisen-; (*fig*) eisern ● *n* Eisen *nt*; (*appliance*) Bügeleisen *nt* ● *vt/i* bügeln

ironic[al] /aɪˈrɒnɪk[l]/ *adj* ironisch

ironing /ˈaɪənɪŋ/ *n* Bügeln *nt*; (*articles*) Bügelwäsche *f*. ∼**-board** *n* Bügelbrett *nt*

ironmonger /ˈ-mʌŋɡə(r)/ *n* ∼**'s [shop]** Haushaltswarengeschäft *nt*

irony /ˈaɪərənɪ/ *n* Ironie *f*

irrational /ɪˈræʃənl/ *adj* irrational

irreconcilable /ɪˈrekənsaɪləbl/ *adj* unversöhnlich

irrefutable /ɪrɪˈfjuːtəbl/ *adj* unwiderlegbar

irregular /ɪˈreɡjʊlə(r)/ *adj* unregelmäßig; (*against rules*) regelwidrig. ∼**ity** *n* Unregelmäßigkeit *f*; Regelwidrigkeit *f*

irrelevant /ɪˈreləvənt/ *adj* irrelevant

irreparable /ɪˈrepərəbl/ *adj* nicht wieder gutzumachen

irreplaceable /ɪrɪˈpleɪsəbl/ *adj* unersetzlich

irrepressible /ɪrɪˈpresəbl/ *adj* unverwüstlich; **be ∼** (*person:*) nicht unterzukriegen sein

irresistible /ɪrɪˈzɪstəbl/ *adj* unwiderstehlich

irresolute /ɪˈrezəluːt/ *adj* unentschlossen

irrespective /ɪrɪˈspektɪv/ *adj* ∼ of ungeachtet (+ *gen*)

irresponsible /ɪrɪˈspɒnsəbl/ *adj,*

-bly *adv* unverantwortlich; (*person*) verantwortungslos

irreverent /ɪˈrevərənt/ *adj* respektlos

irrevocable /ɪˈrevəkəbl/ *adj,* **-bly** *adv* unwiderruflich

irrigat|e /ˈɪrɪɡeɪt/ *vt* bewässern. ∼**ion** *n* Bewässerung *f*

irritable /ˈɪrɪtəbl/ *adj* reizbar

irritant /ˈɪrɪtənt/ *n* Reizstoff *m*

irritat|e /ˈɪrɪteɪt/ *vt* irritieren; (*Med*) reizen. ∼**ion** *n* Ärger *m*; (*Med*) Reizung *f*

is /ɪz/ *see* be

Islam /ˈɪzlɑːm/ *n* der Islam. ∼**ic** *adj* islamisch

island /ˈaɪlənd/ *n* Insel *f*. ∼**er** *n* Inselbewohner(in) *m(f)*

isolat|e /ˈaɪsəleɪt/ *vt* isolieren. ∼**ed** *adj* (*remote*) abgelegen; (*single*) einzeln. ∼**ion** *n* Isoliertheit *f*; (*Med*) Isolierung *f*

Israel /ˈɪzreɪl/ *n* Israel *nt*. ∼**i** *adj* israelisch ● *n* Israeli *m/f*

issue /ˈɪʃuː/ *n* Frage *f*; (*outcome*) Ergebnis *nt*; (*of magazine, stamps*) Ausgabe *f*; (*offspring*) Nachkommen *pl* ● *vt* ausgeben; ausstellen (*passport*); erteilen (*order*); herausgeben (*book*); **be ∼d with sth** etw erhalten

---

it /ɪt/

● *pronoun*

····▸ (*as subject*) er (*m*), sie (*f*), es (*nt*); (*in impersonal sentence*) es. **where is the spoon? It's on the table** wo ist der Löffel? Er liegt auf dem Tisch. **it was very kind of you** es war sehr nett von Ihnen. **it's five o'clock** es ist fünf Uhr

····▸ (*as direct object*) ihn (*m*), sie (*f*), es (*nt*). **that's my pencil — give it to me** das ist mein Bleistift — gib ihn mir.

····▸ (*as dative object*) ihm (*m*), ihr (*f*), ihm (*nt*). **he found a track and followed it** er fand eine Spur und folgte ihr.

····▶ *(after prepositions)*

> ! Combinations such as *with
> it, from it, to it* are translated
> by the prepositions with the
> prefix **da-** (**damit, davon,
> dazu**). Prepositions beginning
> with a vowel insert an 'r'
> (**daran, darauf, darüber**). **I
> can't do anything with it** ich
> kann nichts damit anfangen.
> **don't lean on it!** lehn dich
> nicht daran!

····▶ *(the person in question)* es. **it's
me** ich bin's. **is it you, Dad?** bist
du es, Vater? **who is it?** wer ist
da?

Italian /ɪˈtæljən/ *adj* italienisch ● *n*
Italiener(in) *m(f)*; *(Lang)* Italienisch *nt*

italics /ɪˈtælɪks/ *npl* Kursivschrift *f*; **in
~s** kursiv

Italy /ˈɪtəlɪ/ *n* Italien *nt*

itch /ɪtʃ/ *n* Juckreiz *m*; **I have an ~**
es juckt mich ● *vi* jucken; **I'm ~ing**
🛈 es juckt mich **(to** zu). **~y** *adj* **be
~y** jucken

item /ˈaɪtəm/ *n* Gegenstand *m*;
(Comm) Artikel *m*; *(on agenda)* Punkt
m; *(on invoice)* Posten *m*; *(act)* Nummer *f*

itinerary /aɪˈtɪnərərɪ/ *n* [Reise]
route *f*

its /ɪts/ *poss pron* sein; *(f)* ihr

it's = it is, it has

itself /ɪtˈself/ *pron* selbst; *(reflexive)*
sich; **by ~** von selbst; *(alone)* allein

ivory /ˈaɪvərɪ/ *n* Elfenbein *nt* ● *attrib*
Elfenbein-

ivy /ˈaɪvɪ/ *n* Efeu *m*

> **Ivy League** Amerikanische
> Universitäten sind in Grupp
> pen von Institutionen aufgeteilt,
> die untereinander sportliche Veran
> staltungen durchführen. Die exklu
> sivste Gruppe ist die *Ivy League* im
> Nordosten der USA. (Efeuliga, nach
> den mit Efeu bewachsenen, alten
> Universitätsgebäuden.) Harvard
> und Yale haben den besten akade
> mischen Ruf der acht Eliteuniversi
> täten. Viele amerikanische Politiker
> haben an einer *Ivy-League* Universi
> tät studiert.

Jj

jab /dʒæb/ *n* Stoß *m*; (🛈: *injection*)
Spritze *f* ● *vt* (*pt/pp* **jabbed**) stoßen

jabber /ˈdʒæbə(r)/ *vi* plappern

jack /dʒæk/ *n* *(Auto)* Wagenheber *m*;
(Cards) Bube *m* ● *vt* **~ up** *(Auto)* aufbocken

jacket /ˈdʒækɪt/ *n* Jacke *f*; *(of book)*
Schutzumschlag *m*

'jackpot *n* **hit the ~** das große Los
ziehen

jade /dʒeɪd/ *n* Jade *m*

jagged /ˈdʒæɡɪd/ *adj* zackig

jail /dʒeɪl/ = gaol

jam¹ /dʒæm/ *n* Marmelade *f*

jam² *n* Gedränge *nt*; *(Auto)* Stau *m*;
(fam. difficulty) Klemme *f* ● *v* (*pt/pp*
jammed) ● *vt* klemmen **(in** in + *acc*);
stören *(broadcast)* ● *vi* klemmen

Jamaica /dʒəˈmeɪkə/ *n* Jamaika *nt*

jangle /ˈdʒæŋɡl/ *vi* klimpern ● *vt*
klimpern mit

January /ˈdʒænjʊərɪ/ *n* Januar *m*

Japan /dʒəˈpæn/ *n* Japan *nt*. **~ese**
adj japanisch ● *n* Japaner(in) *m(f)*;
(Lang) Japanisch *nt*

jar /dʒɑː(r)/ *n* Glas *nt*; *(earthenware)*
Topf *m*

jargon /ˈdʒɑːɡən/ *n* Jargon *m*

jaunt /dʒɔːnt/ *n* Ausflug *m*

jaunt|y /ˈdʒɔːntɪ/ *adj* **-ily** *adv* keck

javelin /ˈdʒævlɪn/ *n* Speer *m*

jaw /dʒɔː/ *n* Kiefer *m*

jazz /dʒæz/ *n* Jazz *m*. **~y** *adj* knallig

jealous /ˈdʒeləs/ *adj* eifersüchtig **(of**
auf + *acc*). **~y** *n* Eifersucht *f*

i

j

jeans /dʒiːnz/ npl Jeans pl

jeer /dʒɪə(r)/ vi johlen; ~ **at** verhöhnen

jelly /'dʒelɪ/ n Gelee nt; (dessert) Götterspeise f. ~**fish** n Qualle f

jeopar|dize /'dʒepədaɪz/ vt gefährden. ~**dy** n **in** ~**dy** gefährdet

jerk /dʒɜːk/ n Ruck m ● vt stoßen; (pull) reißen ● vi rucken; (limb, muscle:) zucken. ~**ily** adv ruckweise. ~**y** adj ruckartig

jersey /'dʒɜːzɪ/ n Pullover m; (Sport) Trikot nt; (fabric) Jersey m

jest /dʒest/ n **in** ~ im Spaß

jet n (of water) [Wasser]strahl m; (nozzle) Düse f; (plane) Düsenflugzeug nt

jet: ~-'**black** adj pechschwarz. ~-**pro'pelled** adj mit Düsenantrieb

jetty /'dʒetɪ/ n Landesteg m; (breakwater) Buhne f

Jew /dʒuː/ n Jude m /Jüdin f

jewel /'dʒuːəl/ n Edelstein m; (fig) Juwel nt. ~**ler** n Juwelier m; ~**ler's [shop]** Juweliergeschäft nt. ~**lery** n Schmuck m

Jew|ess /'dʒuːɪs/ n Jüdin f. ~**ish** adj jüdisch

jib /dʒɪb/ vi (pt/pp jibbed) (fig) sich sträuben (at gegen)

jigsaw /'dʒɪgsɔː/ n ~ **[puzzle]** Puzzlespiel nt

jilt /dʒɪlt/ vt sitzen lassen

jingle /'dʒɪŋgl/ n (rhyme) Verschen nt ● vi klimpern

jinx /dʒɪŋks/ n 🄳 **it's got a** ~ **on it** es ist verhext

jittery /'dʒɪtərɪ/ adj 🄳 nervös

job /dʒɒb/ n Aufgabe f; (post) Stelle f, 🄳 Job m; **be a** ~ nicht leicht sein; **it's a good** ~ **that** es ist [nur] gut, dass. ~**less** adj arbeitslos

jockey /'dʒɒkɪ/ n Jockei m

jocular /'dʒɒkjʊlə(r)/ adj spaßhaft

jog /dʒɒg/ n Stoß m ● v (pt/pp jogged) ● vt anstoßen; ~ **s.o.'s memory** jds Gedächtnis nachhelfen ● vi (Sport) joggen. ~**ging** n Jogging nt

john /dʒɒn/ n (Amer, 🄳) Klo nt

join /dʒɔɪn/ n Nahtstelle f ● vt verbinden (**to** mit); sich anschließen (+ dat) (person); (become member of) beitreten (+ dat); eintreten in (+ acc) (firm) ● vi (roads:) sich treffen. ~ **in** vi mitmachen. ~ **up** vi (Mil) Soldat werden ● vt zusammenfügen

joint /dʒɔɪnt/ adj gemeinsam ● n Gelenk nt; (in wood, brickwork) Fuge f; (Culin) Braten m; (🄳: bar) Lokal nt

jok|e /dʒəʊk/ n Scherz m; (funny story) Witz m; (trick) Streich m ● vi scherzen. ~**er** n Witzbold m; (Cards) Joker m. ~**ing** n ~**ing apart** Spaß beiseite. ~**ingly** adv im Spaß

jolly /'dʒɒlɪ/ adj lustig ● adv 🄳 sehr

jolt /dʒəʊlt/ n Ruck m ● vt einen Ruck versetzen (+ dat) ● vi holpern

Jordan /'dʒɔːdn/ n Jordanien nt

jostle /'dʒɒsl/ vt anrempeln

jot /dʒɒt/ vt (pt/pp jotted) ~ **[down]** sich (dat) notieren

journal /'dʒɜːnl/ n Zeitschrift f; (diary) Tagebuch nt. ~**ese** n Zeitungsjargon m. ~**ism** n Journalismus m. ~**ist** n Journalist(in) m(f)

journey /'dʒɜːnɪ/ n Reise f

jovial /'dʒəʊvɪəl/ adj lustig

joy /dʒɔɪ/ n Freude f. ~**ful** adj freudig, froh. ~**ride** n 🄳 Spritztour f [im gestohlenen Auto]

jubil|ant /'dʒuːbɪlənt/ adj überglücklich. ~**ation** n Jubel m

jubilee /'dʒuːbɪliː/ n Jubiläum nt

judder /'dʒʌdə(r)/ vi rucken

judge /dʒʌdʒ/ n Richter m; (of competition) Preisrichter m ● vt beurteilen; (estimate) [ein]schätzen ● vi urteilen (by nach). ~**ment** n Beurteilung f; (Jur) Urteil nt; (fig) Urteilsvermögen nt

judic|ial /dʒuː'dɪʃl/ adj gerichtlich. ~**ious** adj klug

jug /dʒʌg/ n Kanne f; (small) Kännchen nt; (for water, wine) Krug m

juggle /'dʒʌgl/ vi jonglieren. ~**r** n Jongleur m

juice /dʒuːs/ n Saft m

juicy /'dʒuːsɪ/ adj saftig; 🄳 (story) pikant

juke-box /'dʒuːk-/ n Musikbox f

j

July /dʒʊ'laɪ/ n Juli m

jumble /'dʒʌmbl/ n Durcheinander nt ●vt ~ **[up]** durcheinander bringen. ~ **sale** n [Wohltätigkeits]basar m

jump /dʒʌmp/ n Sprung m; (in prices) Anstieg m; (in horse racing) Hindernis nt ●vi springen; (start) zusammenzucken; **make s.o.** ~ jdn erschrecken; ~ **at** (fig) sofort zugreifen bei (offer); ~ **to conclusions** voreilige Schlüsse ziehen ●vt überspringen. ~ **up** vi aufspringen

jumper /'dʒʌmpə(r)/ n Pullover m, Pulli m

jumpy /'dʒʌmpɪ/ adj nervös

junction /'dʒʌŋkʃn/ n Kreuzung f; (Rail) Knotenpunkt m

June /dʒuːn/ n Juni m

jungle /'dʒʌŋgl/ n Dschungel m

junior /'dʒuːnɪə(r)/ adj jünger; (in rank) untergeordnet; (Sport) Junioren- ●n Junior m

junk /dʒʌŋk/ n Gerümpel nt, Trödel m

junkie /'dʒʌŋkɪ/ n ⊠ Fixer m

'junk-shop n Trödelladen m

jurisdiction /dʒʊərɪs'dɪkʃn/ n Gerichtsbarkeit f

jury /'dʒʊərɪ/ n **the** ~ die Geschworenen pl; (for competition) die Jury

just /dʒʌst/ adj gerecht ●adv gerade; (only) nur; (simply) einfach; (exactly) genau; ~ **as tall** ebenso groß; **I'm** ~ **going** ich gehe schon

justice /'dʒʌstɪs/ n Gerechtigkeit f; **do** ~ **to** gerecht werden (+ dat)

justifiab|le /'dʒʌstɪfaɪəbl/ adj berechtigt. ~**ly** adv berechtigterweise

justi|fication /dʒʌstɪfɪ'keɪʃn/ n Rechtfertigung f. ~**fy** vt (pt/pp -ied) rechtfertigen

justly /'dʒʌstlɪ/ adv zu Recht

jut /dʒʌt/ vi (pt/pp jutted) ~ **out** vorstehen

juvenile /'dʒuːvənaɪl/ adj jugendlich; (childish) kindisch ●n Jugendliche(r) m/f. ~ **delinquency** n Jugendkriminalität f

Kk

kangaroo /kæŋgə'ruː/ n Känguru nt

kebab /kɪ'bæb/ n Spießchen nt

keel /kiːl/ n Kiel m ●vi ~ **over** umkippen; (Naut) kentern

keen /kiːn/ adj (-er, -est) (sharp) scharf; (intense) groß; (eager) eifrig, begeistert; ~ **on** ① erpicht auf (+ acc); ~ **on s.o.** von jdm sehr angetan; **be** ~ **to do sth** etw gerne machen wollen. ~**ly** adv tief. ~**ness** n Eifer m, Begeisterung f

keep /kiːp/ n (maintenance) Unterhalt m; (of castle) Bergfried m; **for** ~**s** für immer ●v (pt/pp **kept**) ●vt behalten; (store) aufbewahren; (not throw away) aufheben; (support) unterhalten; (detain) aufhalten; freihalten (seat); halten (promise, animals); führen, haben (shop); einhalten (law, rules); ~ **s.o. waiting** jdn warten lassen; ~ **sth to oneself** etw nicht weitersagen ●vi (remain) bleiben; (food:) sich halten; ~ **left/right** sich links/rechts halten; ~ **on doing sth** etw weitermachen; (repeatedly) etw dauernd machen; ~ **in with** sich gut stellen mit. ~ **up** vi Schritt halten ●vt (continue) weitermachen

keep|er /'kiːpə(r)/ n Wärter(in) m(f). ~**ing** n **be in** ~**ing with** passen zu

kennel /'kenl/ n Hundehütte f; ~**s** pl (boarding) Hundepension f; (breeding) Zwinger m

Kenya /'kenjə/ n Kenia nt

kept /kept/ see **keep**

kerb /kɜːb/ n Bordstein m

kernel /'kɜːnl/ n Kern m

ketchup /'ketʃʌp/ n Ketschup m

kettle /'ketl/ n [Wasser]kessel m; **put the** ~ **on** Wasser aufsetzen

key /kiː/ n Schlüssel m; (Mus) Tonart f; (of piano, typewriter) Taste f ●vt ~ **in** eintasten

key: ~**board** n Tastatur f; (Mus) Kla-

viatur f. ~**hole** n Schlüsselloch nt.
~**ring** n Schlüsselring m

khaki /ˈkɑːkɪ/ adj khakifarben ● n
Khaki nt

kick /kɪk/ n [Fuß]tritt m; **for** ~**s** 🆃
zum Spaß ● vt treten; ~ **the bucket**
🆃 abkratzen ● vi (animal) ausschlagen

kid /kɪd/ n (🆃: child) Kind nt ● vt (pt/
pp **kidded**) 🆃 ~ **s.o.** jdm etwas vormachen

kidnap /ˈkɪdnæp/ vt (pt/pp -**napped**)
entführen. ~**per** n Entführer m.
~**ping** n Entführung f

kidney /ˈkɪdnɪ/ n Niere f

kill /kɪl/ vt töten; 🆃 totschlagen
(time): ~ **two birds with one stone**
zwei Fliegen mit einer Klappe schlagen. ~**er** n Mörder(in) m(f). ~**ing**
n Tötung f; (murder) Mord m

'killjoy n Spielverderber m

kilo /ˈkiːləʊ/ n Kilo nt

kilo: /ˈkɪlə/: ~**gram** n Kilogramm nt.
~**metre** n Kilometer m. ~**watt** n
Kilowatt nt

kilt /kɪlt/ n Schottenrock m

kind¹ /kaɪnd/ n Art f; (brand, type)
Sorte f; **what** ~ **of car?** was für ein
Auto? ~ **of** 🆃 irgendwie

kind² adj (-**er**, -**est**) nett; ~ **to animals** gut zu Tieren

kind|ly /ˈkaɪndlɪ/ adj nett ● adv net-
terweise; (if you please) gefälligst.
~**ness** n Güte f; (favour) Gefallen m

king /kɪŋ/ n König m; (Draughts)
Dame f. ~**dom** n Königreich nt; (fig
& Relig) Reich nt

king: ~**fisher** n Eisvogel m. ~-**sized**
adj extragroß

kink /kɪŋk/ n Knick m. ~**y** adj 🆃
pervers

kiosk /ˈkiːɒsk/ n Kiosk m

kip /kɪp/ n **have a** ~ 🆃 pennen ● vi
(pt/pp **kipped**) 🆃 pennen

kipper /ˈkɪpə(r)/ n Räucherhering m

kiss /kɪs/ n Kuss m ● vt/i küssen

kit /kɪt/ n Ausrüstung f; (tools) Werkzeug nt; (construction ~) Bausatz m
● vt (pt/pp **kitted**) ~**out** ausrüsten

kitchen /ˈkɪtʃɪn/ n Küche f ● attrib

Küchen-. ~**ette** n Kochnische f

kitchen: ~**'garden** n Gemüsegarten
m. ~**'sink** n Spülbecken nt

kite /kaɪt/ n Drachen m

kitten /ˈkɪtn/ n Kätzchen nt

kitty /ˈkɪtɪ/ n (money) [gemeinsame]
Kasse f

knack /næk/ n Trick m, Dreh m

knead /niːd/ vt kneten

knee /niː/ n Knie nt. ~**cap** n Kniescheibe f

kneel /niːl/ vi (pt/pp **knelt**) knien; ~
[**down**] sich [nieder]knien

knelt /nelt/ see **kneel**

knew /njuː/ see **know**

knickers /ˈnɪkəz/ npl Schlüpfer m

knife /naɪf/ n (pl **knives**) Messer nt
● vt einen Messerstich versetzen (+
dat)

knight /naɪt/ n Ritter m; (Chess)
Springer m ● vt adeln

knit /nɪt/ vt/i (pt/pp **knitted**) stricken; ~ **one's brow** die Stirn runzeln. ~**ting** n Stricken nt; (work)
Strickzeug nt. ~**ting-needle** n
Stricknadel f. ~**wear** n Strickwa-
ren pl

knives /naɪvz/ npl see **knife**

knob /nɒb/ n Knopf m; (on door)
Knauf m; (small lump) Beule f. ~**bly**
adj knorrig; (bony) knochig

knock /nɒk/ n Klopfen nt; (blow)
Schlag m; **there was a** ~ es klopfte
● vt anstoßen; (🆃: criticize) heruntermachen; ~ **a hole in sth** ein Loch in
etw (acc) schlagen; ~ **one's head**
sich (dat) den Kopf stoßen (**on** an +
dat) ● vi klopfen. ~ **about** vt schlagen ● vi 🆃 herumkommen. ~
down vt herunterwerfen; (with fist)
niederschlagen; (in car) anfahren; (demolish) abreißen; (🆃: reduce) herabsetzen. ~ **off** vt herunterwerfen; (🆃:
steal) klauen; (🆃: complete quickly)
hinhauen ● vi (🆃: cease work) Feier-
abend machen. ~ **out** vt ausschlagen; (make unconscious) bewusstlos
schlagen; (Boxing) k.o. schlagen. ~
over vt umwerfen; (in car) anfahren

knock: ~-**down** adj ~-**down prices**

k

Schleuderpreise pl. ~er n Türklopfer m. ~-out n (Boxing) K.o. m

knot /nɒt/ n Knoten m ● vt (pt/pp **knotted**) knoten

know /nəʊ/ vt/i (pt **knew**, pp **known**) wissen; kennen (person); können (language); **get to** ~ kennen lernen ● n **in the** ~ 🛈 im Bild

know: ~-**all** n 🛈 Alleswisser m. ~-**how** n 🛈 [Sach]kenntnis f. ~**ing** adj wissend. ~**ingly** adv wissend; (intentionally) wissentlich

knowledge /'nɒlɪdʒ/ n Kenntnis f (of von/gen); (general) Wissen nt; (specialized) Kenntnisse pl. ~**able** adj **be** ~**able** viel wissen

knuckle /'nʌkl/ n [Finger]knöchel m; (Culin) Hachse f

kosher /'kəʊʃə(r)/ adj koscher

kudos /'kjuːdɒs/ n 🛈 Prestige nt

k

l

L|

lab /læb/ n 🛈 Labor nt

label /'leɪbl/ n Etikett nt ● vt (pt/pp **labelled**) etikettieren

laboratory /lə'bɒrətrɪ/ n Labor nt

laborious /lə'bɔːrɪəs/ adj mühsam

labour /'leɪbə(r)/ n Arbeit f; (workers) Arbeitskräfte pl; (Med) Wehen pl; **L**~ (Pol) die Labourpartei ● attrib Labour- ● vi arbeiten ● vt (fig) sich lange auslassen über (+ acc). ~**er** n Arbeiter m

'labour-saving adj arbeitssparend

lace /leɪs/ n Spitze f; (of shoe) Schnürsenkel m ● vt schnüren

lack /læk/ n Mangel m (**of** an + dat) ● vt **I** ~ **the time** mir fehlt die Zeit ● vi **be** ~**ing** fehlen

laconic /lə'kɒnɪk/ adj, **-ally** adv lakonisch

lacquer /'lækə(r)/ n Lack m; (for hair) [Haar]spray m

lad /læd/ n Junge m

ladder /'lædə(r)/ n Leiter f; (in fabric) Laufmasche f

ladle /'leɪdl/ n [Schöpf]kelle f ● vt schöpfen

lady /'leɪdɪ/ n Dame f; (title) Lady f

lady: ~**bird** n, (Amer) ~**bug** n Marienkäfer m. ~**like** adj damenhaft

lag¹ /læg/ vi (pt/pp **lagged**) ~ **behind** zurückbleiben; (fig) nachhinken

lag² vt (pt/pp **lagged**) umwickeln (pipes)

lager /'lɑːgə(r)/ n Lagerbier nt

laid /leɪd/ see **lay³**

lain /leɪn/ see **lie²**

lake /leɪk/ n See m

lamb /læm/ n Lamm nt

lame /leɪm/ adj (-r, -st) lahm

lament /lə'ment/ n Klage f; (song) Klagelied nt ● vt beklagen ● vi klagen

laminated /'læmɪneɪtɪd/ adj laminiert

lamp /læmp/ n Lampe f; (in street) Laterne f. ~**post** n Laternenpfahl m. ~**shade** n Lampenschirm m

lance /lɑːns/ vt (Med) aufschneiden

land /lænd/ n Land nt; **plot of** ~ Grundstück nt ● vt/i landen; ~ **s.o. with sth** 🛈 jdm etw aufhalsen

landing /'lændɪŋ/ n Landung f; (top of stairs) Treppenflur m. ~-**stage** n Landesteg m

land: ~**lady** n Wirtin f. ~**lord** n Wirt m; (of land) Grundbesitzer m; (of building) Hausbesitzer m. ~**mark** n Erkennungszeichen nt; (fig) Meilenstein m. ~**owner** n Grundbesitzer m. ~**scape** /-skeɪp/ n Landschaft f. ~**slide** n Erdrutsch m

lane /leɪn/ n kleine Landstraße f; (Auto) Spur f; (Sport) Bahn f; **'get in** ~' (Auto) 'bitte einordnen'

language /'læŋgwɪdʒ/ n Sprache f; (speech, style) Ausdrucksweise f

languid /'læŋgwɪd/ adj träge

languish /'læŋgwɪʃ/ vi schmachten

lanky /'læŋkɪ/ adj schlaksig

lantern /'læntən/ n Laterne f

lap¹ /læp/ n Schoß m

lap² n (Sport) Runde f; (of journey)

Etappe f ● vi (pt/pp **lapped**) plätschern (**against** gegen)

lap³ vt (pt/pp **lapped**) ~ **up** aufschlecken

lapel /ləˈpel/ n Revers nt

lapse /læps/ n Fehler m; (moral) Fehltritt m; (of time) Zeitspanne f ● vi (expire) erlöschen; ~ **into** verfallen in (+ acc)

laptop /ˈlæptɒp/ n Laptop m

lard /lɑːd/ n [Schweine]schmalz nt

larder /ˈlɑːdə(r)/ n Speisekammer f

large /lɑːdʒ/ adj (-r, -st) & adv groß; **by and** ~ im Großen und Ganzen; **at** ~ auf freiem Fuß. ~**ly** adv großenteils

lark¹ /lɑːk/ n (bird) Lerche f

lark² n (joke) Jux m ● vi ~ **about** herumalbern

laryngitis /lærɪnˈdʒaɪtɪs/ n Kehlkopfentzündung f

larynx /ˈlærɪŋks/ n Kehlkopf m

laser /ˈleɪzə(r)/ n Laser m

lash /læʃ/ n Peitschenhieb m; (eyelash) Wimper f ● vt peitschen; (tie) festbinden (**to** an + acc). ~ **out** vi um sich schlagen; (spend) viel Geld ausgeben (**on** für)

lass /læs/ n Mädchen nt

lasso /ləˈsuː/ n Lasso nt

last /lɑːst/ adj & n letzte(r,s); ~ **night** heute od gestern Nacht; (evening) gestern Abend; **at** ~ endlich; **for the** ~ **time** zum letzten Mal; **the** ~ **but one** der/die/das vorletzte ● adv zuletzt; (last time) das letzte Mal; **he/she went** ~ er/sie ging als Letzter/Letzte ● vi dauern; (weather:) sich halten; (relationship:) halten. ~**ing** adj dauerhaft. ~**ly** adv schließlich, zum Schluss

latch /lætʃ/ n (einfache) Klinke f

late /leɪt/ adj & adv (-r, -st) spät; (delayed) verspätet; (deceased) verstorben; **the** ~**st news** die neuesten Nachrichten; **stay up** ~ bis spät aufbleiben; **arrive** ~ zu spät ankommen; **I am** ~ ich komme zu spät od habe mich verspätet; **the train is** ~ der Zug hat Verspätung. ~**comer** n

Zuspätkommende(r) m/f. ~**ly** adv in letzter Zeit. ~**ness** n Zuspätkommen nt; (delay) Verspätung f

later /ˈleɪtə(r)/ adj & adv später; ~ **on** nachher

lateral /ˈlætərəl/ adj seitlich

lather /ˈlɑːðə(r)/ n [Seifen]schaum m

Latin /ˈlætɪn/ adj lateinisch ● n Latein nt. ~ **A'merica** n Lateinamerika nt

latitude /ˈlætɪtjuːd/ n (Geog) Breite f; (fig) Freiheit f

latter /ˈlætə(r)/ adj & n **the** ~ der/die/das Letztere

Latvia /ˈlætvɪə/ n Lettland nt

laudable /ˈlɔːdəbl/ adj lobenswert

laugh /lɑːf/ n Lachen nt; **with a** ~ lachend ● vi lachen (**at/about** über + acc); ~ **at s.o.** (mock) jdn auslachen. ~**able** adj lachhaft, lächerlich

laughter /ˈlɑːftə(r)/ n Gelächter nt

launch¹ /lɔːntʃ/ n (boat) Barkasse f

launch² n Stapellauf m; (of rocket) Abschuss m; (of product) Lancierung f ● vt vom Stapel lassen (ship); zu Wasser lassen (lifeboat); abschießen (rocket); starten (attack); (Comm) lancieren (product)

laund(e)rette /lɔːndret/ n Münzwäscherei f

laundry /ˈlɔːndrɪ/ n Wäscherei f; (clothes) Wäsche f

laurel /ˈlɒrl/ n Lorbeer m

lava /ˈlɑːvə/ n Lava f

lavatory /ˈlævətrɪ/ n Toilette f

lavender /ˈlævəndə(r)/ n Lavendel m

lavish /ˈlævɪʃ/ adj großzügig; (wasteful) verschwenderisch ● vt ~ **sth on s.o.** jdn mit etw überschütten

law /lɔː/ n Gesetz nt; (system) Recht nt; **study** ~ Jura studieren; ~ **and order** Recht und Ordnung

law: ~**-abiding** adj gesetzestreu. ~**court** n Gerichtshof m. ~**ful** adj rechtmäßig. ~**less** adj gesetzlos

lawn /lɔːn/ n Rasen m. ~**-mower** n Rasenmäher m

lawyer /ˈlɔːjə(r)/ n Rechtsanwalt m /-anwältin f

lax /læks/ adj lax, locker

laxative | lecture

laxative /'læksətɪv/ n Abführmittel nt

laxity /'læksɪtɪ/ n Laxheit f

lay¹ /loɪ/ see **lie²**

lay² vt (pt/pp **laid**) legen; decken (table); **~ a trap** eine Falle stellen. **~ down** vt hinlegen; festlegen (rules, conditions). **~ off** vt entlassen (workers) ● vi (🔲: stop) aufhören. **~ out** vt hinlegen; aufbahren (corpse); anlegen (garden); (Typography) gestalten

lay-by n Parkbucht f

layer /'leɪə(r)/ n Schicht f

lay: ~man n Laie m. **~out** n Anordnung f; (design) Gestaltung f; (Typography) Layout nt

laze /leɪz/ vi **~[about]** faulenzen

laziness /'leɪzɪnɪs/ n Faulheit f

lazy /'leɪzɪ/ adj faul. **~-bones** n Faulenzer m

lead¹ /led/ n Blei nt; (of pencil) [Bleistift]mine f

lead² /liːd/ n Führung f; (leash) Leine f; (flex) Schnur f; (clue) Hinweis m, Spur f; (Theat) Hauptrolle f; (distance ahead) Vorsprung m; **be in the ~** in Führung liegen ● vt/i (pt/pp **led**) führen; leiten (team); (induce) bringen; (at cards) ausspielen; **~ the way** vorangehen; **~ up to sth** (fig) etw (dat) vorangehen

leader /'liːdə(r)/ n Führer m; (of expedition, group) Leiter(in) m(f); (of orchestra) Konzertmeister m; (in newspaper) Leitartikel m. **~ship** n Führung f; Leitung f

leading /'liːdɪŋ/ adj führend; **~ lady** Hauptdarstellerin f

leaf /liːf/ n (pl **leaves**) Blatt nt ● vi **~ through sth** etw durchblättern. **~let** n Merkblatt nt; (advertising) Reklameblatt nt; (political) Flugblatt nt

league /liːg/ n Liga f

leak /liːk/ n (hole) undichte Stelle f; (Naut) Leck nt; (of gas) Gasausfluss m ● vi undicht sein; (ship:) leck sein, lecken; (liquid:) auslaufen; (gas:) ausströmen ● vt auslaufen lassen; **~ sth to s.o.** (fig) jdm etw zuspielen. **~y** adj undicht; (Naut) leck

lean¹ /liːn/ adj (-er, -est) mager

lean² v (pt/pp **leaned** or **leant** /lent/) ● vt lehnen (against/on an + acc) ● vi (person) sich lehnen (against/on an + acc); (not be straight) sich neigen; **be ~ing against** lehnen an (+ dat). **~ back** vi sich zurücklehnen. **~ forward** vi sich vorbeugen. **~ out** vi sich hinauslehnen. **~ over** vi sich vorbeugen

leaning /'liːnɪŋ/ adj schief ● n Neigung f

leap /liːp/ n Sprung m ● vi (pt/pp **leapt** or **leaped**) springen; **he leapt at it** 🔲 er griff sofort zu. **~ year** n Schaltjahr nt

learn /lɜːn/ vt/i (pt/pp **learnt** or **learned**) lernen; (hear) erfahren; **~ to swim** schwimmen lernen

learn|ed /'lɜːnɪd/ adj gelehrt. **~er** n Anfänger m; **~er [driver]** Fahrschüler(in) m(f). **~ing** n Gelehrsamkeit f; **~ing curve** Lernkurve f

lease /liːs/ n Pacht f; (contract) Mietvertrag m ● vt pachten

leash /liːʃ/ n Leine f

least /liːst/ adj geringste(r,s) ● n **the ~** das wenigste; **at ~** wenigstens, mindestens; **not in the ~** nicht im Geringsten ● adv am wenigsten

leather /'leðə(r)/ n Leder nt

leave /liːv/ n Erlaubnis f; (holiday) Urlaub m; **on ~** auf Urlaub; **take one's ~** sich verabschieden ● v (pt/pp **left**) ● vt lassen; (go out of, abandon) verlassen; (forget) liegen lassen; (bequeath) vermachen (to dat); **~ it to me!** überlassen Sie es mir! **there is nothing left** es ist nichts mehr übrig ● vi [weg]gehen/-fahren; (train, bus:) abfahren. **~ behind** vt zurücklassen; (forget) liegen lassen. **~ out** vt liegen lassen; (leave outside) draußen lassen; (omit) auslassen

leaves /liːvz/ see **leaf**

Lebanon /'lebənən/ n Libanon m

lecherous /'letʃərəs/ adj lüstern

lecture /'lektʃə(r)/ n Vortrag m; (Univ) Vorlesung f; (reproof) Strafpredigt f ● vi einen Vortrag/eine Vorlesung halten (on über + acc) ● vt **~**

s.o. jdm eine Strafpredigt halten. **~r** n Vortragende(r) m/f; (Univ) Dozent(in) m(f)

led /led/ see **lead**[2]

ledge /ledʒ/ n Leiste f; (shelf, of window) Sims m; (in rock) Vorsprung m

ledger /'ledʒə(r)/ n Hauptbuch nt

leech /liːtʃ/ n Blutegel m

leek /liːk/ n Stange f Porree; **~s** pl Porree m

left[1] /left/ see **leave**

left[2] adj linke(r,s) ● adv links; (go) nach links ● n linke Seite f; **on the ~** links; **from/to the ~** von/nach links; **the ~** (Pol) die Linke

left: **~-'handed** adj linkshändig. **~-'luggage [office]** n Gepäckaufbewahrung f. **~overs** npl Reste pl. **~-'wing** adj (Pol) linke(r,s)

leg /leg/ n Bein nt; (Culin) Keule f; (of journey) Etappe f

legacy /'legəsɪ/ n Vermächtnis nt, Erbschaft f

legal /'liːgl/ adj gesetzlich; (matters) rechtlich; (department, position) Rechts-; **be ~** [gesetzlich] erlaubt sein

legality /lɪ'gælətɪ/ n Legalität f

legend /'ledʒənd/ n Legende f. **~ary** adj legendär

legi|ble /'ledʒəbl/ adj, **-bly** adv leserlich

legion /'liːdʒn/ n Legion f

legislat|e /'ledʒɪsleɪt/ vi Gesetze erlassen. **~ion** n Gesetzgebung f; (laws) Gesetze pl

legislative /'ledʒɪslətɪv/ adj gesetzgebend

legitimate /lɪ'dʒɪtɪmət/ adj rechtmäßig; (justifiable) berechtigt

leisure /'leʒə(r)/ n Freizeit f, **at your ~** wenn Sie Zeit haben. **~ly** adj gemächlich

lemon /'lemən/ n Zitrone f. **~ade** n Zitronenlimonade f

lend /lend/ vt (pt/pp lent) leihen (s.o. sth jdm etw)

length /leŋθ/ n Länge f; (piece) Stück nt; (of wallpaper) Bahn f; (of time) Dauer f

length|en /'leŋθən/ vt länger machen ● vi länger werden. **~ways** adv der Länge nach

lengthy /'leŋθɪ/ adj langwierig

lenient /'liːnɪənt/ adj nachsichtig

lens /lenz/ n Linse f; (Phot) Objektiv nt; (of spectacles) Glas nt

lent /lent/ see **lend**

Lent n Fastenzeit f

lentil /'lentl/ n (Bot) Linse f

leopard /'lepəd/ n Leopard m

leotard /'liːətɑːd/ n Trikot nt

lesbian /'lezbɪən/ adj lesbisch ● n Lesbierin f

less /les/ a, adv, n & prep weniger; **~ and ~** immer weniger

lessen /'lesn/ vt verringern ● vi nachlassen; (value:) abnehmen

lesser /'lesə(r)/ adj geringere(r,s)

lesson /'lesn/ n Stunde f; (in textbook) Lektion f; (Relig) Lesung f; **teach s.o. a ~** (fig) jdm eine Lehre erteilen

lest /lest/ conj (literary) damit ... nicht

let /let/ vt (pt/pp let, pres p letting) lassen; (rent) vermieten; **~ alone** (not to mention) geschweige denn; **~ us go** gehen wir; **~ me know** sagen Sie mir Bescheid; **~ oneself in for sth** ⊞ sich (dat) etw einbrocken. **~ down** vt hinunter-/herunterlassen; (lengthen) länger machen; **~ s.o. down** ⊞ jdn im Stich lassen; (disappoint) jdn enttäuschen. **~ in** vt hereinlassen. **~ off** vt abfeuern (gun); hochgehen lassen (firework, bomb); (emit) ausstoßen; (excuse from) befreien von; (not punish) frei ausgehen lassen. **~ out** vt hinaus-/herauslassen; (make larger) auslassen. **~ through** vt durchlassen. **~ up** vi ⊞ nachlassen

'let-down n Enttäuschung f, ⊞ Reinfall m

lethal /'liːθl/ adj tödlich

letharg|ic /lɪ'θɑːdʒɪk/ adj lethargisch. **~y** n Lethargie f

letter /'letə(r)/ n Brief m; (of alphabet) Buchstabe m. **~-box** n Briefkasten m. **~-head** n Briefkopf m.

~ing n Beschriftung f
lettuce /'letɪs/ n [Kopf]salat m
'let-up n 🔲 Nachlassen nt
level /'levl/ adj eben; (horizontal) waagerecht; (in height) auf gleicher Höhe; (spoonful) gestrichen; one's ~ best sein Möglichstes ● n Höhe f; (fig) Ebene f, Niveau nt; (stage) Stufe f; on the ~ 🔲 ehrlich ● vt (pt/pp levelled) einebnen
level 'crossing n Bahnübergang m
lever /'liːvə(r)/ n Hebel m ● vt ~ up mit einem Hebel anheben. ~age n Hebelkraft f
lewd /ljuːd/ adj (-er, -est) anstößig
liabilit|y /laɪə'bɪlətɪ/ n Haftung f; ~ies pl Verbindlichkeiten pl
liable /'laɪəbl/ adj haftbar; be ~ to do sth etw leicht tun können
liaise /lɪ'eɪz/ vi 🔲 Verbindungsperson sein
liaison /lɪ'eɪzɒn/ n Verbindung f; (affair) Verhältnis nt
liar /'laɪə(r)/ n Lügner(in) m(f)
libel /'laɪbl/ n Verleumdung f ● vt (pt/pp libelled) verleumden. ~lous adj verleumderisch
liberal /'lɪbərl/ adj tolerant; (generous) großzügig. L~ adj (Pol) liberal ● n Liberale(r) m/f
liberat|e /'lɪbəreɪt/ vt befreien. ~ed adj (woman) emanzipiert. ~ion n Befreiung f. ~or n Befreier m
liberty /'lɪbətɪ/ n Freiheit f; take liberties sich (dat) Freiheiten erlauben
librarian /laɪ'breərɪən/ n Bibliothekar(in) m(f)
library /'laɪbrərɪ/ n Bibliothek f
Libya /'lɪbɪə/ n Libyen nt
lice /laɪs/ see louse
licence /'laɪsns/ n Genehmigung f; (Comm) Lizenz f; (for TV) ≈ Fernsehgebühr f; (for driving) Führerschein m; (for alcohol) Schankkonzession f
license /'laɪsns/ vt eine Genehmigung/(Comm) Lizenz erteilen (+ dat); be ~d (car:) zugelassen sein; (restaurant:) Schankkonzession haben. ~-plate n (Amer) Nummernschild nt

lick /lɪk/ n Lecken nt; a ~ of paint ein bisschen Farbe ● vt lecken; (🔲: defeat) schlagen
lid /lɪd/ n Deckel m; (of eye) Lid nt
lie¹ /laɪ/ n Lüge f; tell a ~ lügen ● vi (pt/pp lied, pres p lying) lügen; ~ to belügen
lie² vi (pt lay, pp lain, pres p lying) liegen; here ~s ... hier ruht ... ~ down vi sich hinlegen
'lie-in n have a ~ [sich] ausschlafen
lieu /ljuː/ n in ~ of statt (+ gen)
lieutenant /lef'tenənt/ n Oberleutnant m
life /laɪf/ n (pl lives) Leben nt; lose one's ~ ums Leben kommen
life: ~-boat n Rettungsboot nt. ~ coach n Lebensberater(in) m(f). ~-guard n Lebensretter m. ~-jacket n Schwimmweste f. ~less adj leblos. ~like adj naturgetreu. ~long adj lebenslang. ~ preserver n (Amer) Rettungsring m. ~-size(d) adj ... in Lebensgröße. ~time n Leben nt; in s.o.'s ~time zu jds Lebzeiten; the chance of a ~time eine einmalige Gelegenheit
lift /lɪft/ n Aufzug m, Lift m; give s.o. a ~ jdn mitnehmen; get a ~ mitgenommen werden ● vt heben; aufheben (restrictions) ● vi (fog:) sich lichten. ~ up vt hochheben
light¹ /laɪt/ adj (-er, -est) (not dark) hell; ~ blue hellblau ● n Licht nt; (lamp) Lampe f; have you [got] a ~? haben Sie Feuer? ● vt (pt/pp lit or lighted) anzünden (fire, cigarette); (illuminate) beleuchten. ~ up vi (face:) sich erhellen
light² adj (-er, -est) (not heavy) leicht; ~ sentence milde Strafe f ● adv travel ~ mit wenig Gepäck reisen
'light-bulb n Glühbirne f
lighten¹ /'laɪtn/ vt heller machen
lighten² vt leichter machen (load)
lighter /'laɪtə(r)/ n Feuerzeug nt
light: ~-'hearted adj unbekümmert. ~house n Leuchtturm m. ~ing n Beleuchtung f. ~ly adv leicht; get off ~ly glimpflich davonkommen

lightning /'laɪtnɪŋ/ n Blitz m

'lightweight adj leicht ● n (Boxing) Leichtgewicht nt

like¹ /laɪk/ adj ähnlich; (same) gleich ● prep wie; (similar to) ähnlich (+ dat); ~ this so; what's he ~? wie ist er denn? ● conj (🛈: as) wie; (Amer: as if) als ob

like² vt mögen; I should/would ~ ich möchte; I ~ the car das Auto gefällt mir; ~ dancing/singing gern tanzen/singen ● n ~s and dislikes pl Vorlieben und Abneigungen pl

like|able /'laɪkəbl/ adj sympathisch. ~lihood n Wahrscheinlichkeit f. ~ly adj & adv wahrscheinlich; not ~ly! 🛈 auf gar keinen Fall!

'like-minded adj gleich gesinnt

liken /'laɪkən/ vt vergleichen (to mit)

like|ness /'laɪknɪs/ n Ähnlichkeit f. ~wise adv ebenso

liking /'laɪkɪŋ/ n Vorliebe f; is it to your ~? gefällt es Ihnen?

lilac /'laɪlək/ n Flieder m

lily /'lɪlɪ/ n. Lilie f

limb /lɪm/ n Glied nt

lime /laɪm/ n (fruit) Limone f; (tree) Linde f. ~light n be in the ~light im Rampenlicht stehen

limit /'lɪmɪt/ n Grenze f; (limitation) Beschränkung f; that's the ~! 🛈 das ist doch die Höhe! ● vt beschränken (to auf + acc). ~ation n Beschränkung f; ~ed adj beschränkt. ~ed company Gesellschaft f mit beschränkter Haftung

limousine /'lɪməziːn/ n Limousine f

limp¹ /lɪmp/ n Hinken nt ● vi hinken

limp² adj (-er -est) schlaff

limpid /'lɪmpɪd/ adj klar

line¹ /laɪn/ n Linie f, (length of rope, cord) Leine f; (Teleph) Leitung f; (of writing) Zeile f; (row) Reihe f; (wrinkle) Falte f; (of business) f; (Amer: queue) Schlange f; in ~ with gemäß (+ dat) ● vt säumen (street)

line² vt füttern (garment); (Techn) auskleiden

lined¹ /laɪnd/ adj (wrinkled) faltig; (paper) liniert

lined² adj (garment) gefüttert

'line dancing n Linedance-Tanzen nt

linen /'lɪnɪn/ n Leinen nt; (articles) Wäsche f

liner /'laɪnə(r)/ n Passagierschiff nt

'linesman n (-men) (Sport) Linienrichter m

linger /'lɪŋgə(r)/ vi [zurück]bleiben

lingerie /'læ̃ʒərɪ/ n Damenunterwäsche f

linguist /'lɪŋgwɪst/ n Sprachkundige(r) m/f

linguistic /lɪŋ'gwɪstɪk/ adj, -ally adv sprachlich

lining /'laɪnɪŋ/ n (of garment) Futter nt; (Techn) Auskleidung f

link /lɪŋk/ n (of chain) Glied nt (fig) Verbindung f ● vt verbinden; ~ arms sich unterhaken

links /lɪŋks/ n or npl Golfplatz m

lint /lɪnt/ n Verbandstoff m

lion /'laɪən/ n Löwe m; ~'s share (fig) Löwenanteil m. ~ess n Löwin f

lip /lɪp/ n Lippe f; (edge) Rand m; (of jug) Schnabel m

lip: ~-reading n Lippenlesen nt. ~-service n pay ~-service ein Lippenbekenntnis ablegen (to zu). ~stick n Lippenstift m

liqueur /lɪ'kjʊə(r)/ n Likör m

liquid /'lɪkwɪd/ n Flüssigkeit f ● adj flüssig

liquidation /lɪkwɪ'deɪʃn/ n Liquidation f

liquidize /'lɪkwɪdaɪz/ vt [im Mixer] pürieren. ~r n Mixer m

liquor /'lɪkə(r)/ n Alkohol m. ~ store n (Amer) Spirituosengeschäft nt

lisp /lɪsp/ n Lispeln nt ● vt/i lispeln

list¹ /lɪst/ n Liste f ● vt aufführen

list² vi (ship:) Schlagseite haben

listen /'lɪsn/ vi zuhören (to dat); ~ to the radio Radio hören. ~er n Zuhörer(in) m(f); (Radio) Hörer(in) m(f)

listless /'lɪstlɪs/ adj lustlos

lit /lɪt/ see **light¹**

literacy /'lɪtərəsɪ/ n Lese- und Schreibfertigkeit f

literal /'lɪtərl/ adj wörtlich. **~ly** adv buchstäblich

literary /'lɪtərərɪ/ adj literarisch

literate /'lɪtərət/ adj be **~** lesen und schreiben können

literature /'lɪtrətʃə(r)/ n Literatur f; ⊞ Informationsmaterial nt

lithe /laɪð/ adj geschmeidig

Lithuania /lɪθjʊ'eɪnɪə/ n Litauen nt

litre /'li:tə(r)/ n Liter m & nt

litter /'lɪtə(r)/ n Abfall m; (Zool) Wurf m. **~-bin** n Abfalleimer m

little /'lɪtl/ adj klein; (not much) wenig ● adv & n wenig; **a ~** ein bisschen/wenig; **~ by ~** nach und nach

live¹ /laɪv/ adj lebendig; (ammunition) scharf; **~ broadcast** Live-Sendung f; **be ~** (Electr) unter Strom stehen

live² /lɪv/ vi leben; (reside) wohnen. **~ on** vt leben von; (eat) sich ernähren von ● vi weiterleben

liveli|hood /'laɪvlɪhʊd/ n Lebensunterhalt m. **~ness** n Lebendigkeit f

lively /'laɪvlɪ/ adj lebhaft, lebendig

liver /'lɪvə(r)/ n Leber f

lives /laɪvz/ see life

livid /'lɪvɪd/ adj ⊞ wütend

living /'lɪvɪŋ/ adj lebend ● n **earn one's ~** seinen Lebensunterhalt verdienen. **~-room** n Wohnzimmer nt

lizard /'lɪzəd/ n Eidechse f

load /ləʊd/ n Last f; (quantity) Ladung f; (Electr) Belastung f; **~s of** ⊞ jede Menge ● vt laden (goods, gun); beladen (vehicle); **~ a camera** einen Film in eine Kamera einlegen. **~ed** adj beladen; (⊞: rich) steinreich

loaf /ləʊf/ n (pl **loaves**) Brot nt

loan /ləʊn/ n Leihgabe f; (money) Darlehen nt; **on ~** geliehen ● vt leihen (to dat)

loath /ləʊθ/ adj be **~ to do sth** etw ungern tun

loath|e /ləʊð/ vt verabscheuen. **~ing** n Abscheu m

loaves /ləʊvz/ see loaf¹

lobby /'lɒbɪ/ n Foyer nt; (anteroom) Vorraum m; (Pol) Lobby f

lobster /'lɒbstə(r)/ n Hummer m

local /'ləʊkl/ adj hiesig; (time, traffic) Orts-; **~ anaesthetic** örtliche Betäubung; **I'm not ~** ich bin nicht von hier ● n Hiesige(r) m/f; (⊞: public house) Stammkneipe f. **~ call** n (Teleph) Ortsgespräch nt

locality /ləʊ'kælətɪ/ n Gegend f

localization /ləʊkəlaɪ'zeɪʃn/ n Lokalisierung f

locally /'ləʊkəlɪ/ adv am Ort

locat|e /ləʊ'keɪt/ vt ausfindig machen; **be ~ed** sich befinden. **~ion** n Lage f; **filmed on ~ion** als Außenaufnahme gedreht

lock¹ /lɒk/ n (hair) Strähne f

lock² n (on door) Schloss nt; (on canal) Schleuse f ● vt abschließen ● vi sich abschließen lassen. **~ in** vt einschließen. **~ out** vt ausschließen. **~ up** vt abschließen; einsperren (person)

locker /'lɒkə(r)/ n Schließfach nt; (Mil) Spind m

lock: ~-out n Aussperrung f. **~smith** n Schlosser m

locomotive /ləʊkə'məʊtɪv/ n Lokomotive f

locum /'ləʊkəm/ n Vertreter(in) m(f)

locust /'ləʊkəst/ n Heuschrecke f

lodge /lɒdʒ/ n (porter's) Pförtnerhaus nt ● vt (submit) einreichen; (deposit) deponieren ● vi zur Untermiete wohnen (with bei); (become fixed) stecken bleiben. **~r** n Untermieter(in) m(f)

lodging /'lɒdʒɪŋ/ n Unterkunft f; **~s** npl möbliertes Zimmer nt

loft /lɒft/ n Dachboden m

lofty /'lɒftɪ/ adj hoch

log /lɒg/ n Baumstamm m; (for fire) [Holz]scheit nt; **sleep like a ~** ⊞ wie ein Murmeltier schlafen ● vi **~ off** sich abmelden; **~ on** sich anmelden

loggerheads /'lɒgə-/ npl **be at ~** ⊞ sich in den Haaren liegen

logic /'lɒdʒɪk/ n Logik f. ~**al** adj logisch

logo /'ləʊgəʊ/ n Symbol nt, Logo nt

loiter /'lɔɪtə(r)/ vi herumlungern

loll /lɒl/ vi sich lümmeln

loll|ipop /'lɒlɪpɒp/ n Lutscher m. ~**y** n Lutscher m; (🅱: money) Moneten pl

London /'lʌndən/ n London nt ● attrib Londoner. ~**er** n Londoner(in) m(f)

lone /ləʊn/ adj einzeln. ~**liness** n Einsamkeit f

lonely /'ləʊnlɪ/ adj einsam

lone|r /'ləʊnə(r)/ n Einzelgänger m. ~**some** adj einsam

long¹ /lɒŋ/ adj (-er /'lɒŋgə(r)/, -est /'lɒŋgɪst/) lang; (journey) weit; a ~ time lange; a ~ way weit; in the ~ run auf lange Sicht; (in the end) letzten Endes ● adv lange; all day ~ den ganzen Tag; not ~ ago vor kurzem; before ~ bald; no ~er nicht mehr; as or so ~as solange; so ~! 🅱 tschüs!

long² vi ~ for sich sehnen nach

long-'distance adj Fern-; (Sport) Langstrecken-

longing /'lɒŋɪŋ/ adj sehnsüchtig ● n Sehnsucht f

longitude /'lɒŋgɪtjuːd/ n (Geog) Länge f

long: ~ **jump** n Weitsprung m. ~**-lived** /-lɪvd/ adj langlebig. ~**-range** adj (Mil, Aviat) Langstrecken-; (forecast) langfristig. ~**-sighted** adj weitsichtig. ~**-sleeved** adj langärmelig. ~**-suffering** adj langmütig. ~**-term** adj langfristig. ~ **wave** n Langwelle. ~**-winded** /-'wɪndɪd/ adj langatmig

loo /luː/ n 🅱 Klo nt

look /lʊk/ n Blick m; (appearance) Aussehen nt; [good] ~s pl [gutes] Aussehen nt; have a ~ at sich (dat) ansehen; go and have a ~ sieh mal nach ● vi sehen; (search) nachsehen; (seem) aussehen; don't ~ sieh nicht hin; ~ here! hören Sie mal! ~ at ansehen; ~ for suchen; ~ forward to sich freuen auf (+ acc); ~ in on

vorbeischauen bei; ~ into (examine) nachgehen (+ dat); ~ like aussehen wie; ~ on to (room:) gehen auf (+ acc). ~ after vt betreuen. ~ down vi hinuntersehen; ~ down on s.o. (fig) auf jdn herabsehen. ~ out vi hinaus-/heraussehen; (take care) aufpassen; ~ out for Ausschau halten nach; ~ out! Vorsicht! ~ round vi sich umsehen. ~ up vi aufblicken; ~ up to s.o. (fig) zu jdm aufsehen ● vt nachschlagen (word)

'look-out n Wache f; (prospect) Aussicht f; be on the ~ for Ausschau halten nach

loom¹ /luːm/ n Webstuhl m

loom² vi auftauchen

loony /'luːnɪ/ adj 🅱 verrückt

loop /luːp/ n Schlinge f; (in road) Schleife f. ~**hole** n Hintertürchen nt; (in the law) Lücke f

loose /luːs/ adj (-r, -st) lose; (not tight enough) locker; (inexact) frei; be at a ~ end nichts zu tun haben. ~ **'change** n Kleingeld nt

loosen /'luːsn/ vt lockern

loot /luːt/ n Beute f ● vt/i plündern. ~**er** n Plünderer m

lop /lɒp/ vt (pt/pp lopped) stutzen

lop'sided adj schief

lord /lɔːd/ n Herr m; (title) Lord m; **House of L~ s** ≈ Oberhaus nt; **the L~'s Prayer** das Vaterunser

lorry /'lɒrɪ/ n Last[kraft]wagen m

lose /luːz/ v (pt/pp lost) ● vt verlieren; (miss) verpassen ● vi verlieren; (clock:) nachgehen; get lost verloren gehen; (person) sich verlaufen. ~**r** n Verlierer m

loss /lɒs/ n Verlust m; be at a ~ nicht mehr weiter wissen

lost /lɒst/ see lose. ~ **'property office** n Fundbüro nt

lot¹ /lɒt/ n Los nt; (at auction) Posten m; draw ~s losen (for um)

lot² n the ~ alle; (everything) alles; a ~ [of] viel; (many) viele; ~s of 🅱 eine Menge; it has changed a ~ es hat sich sehr verändert

lotion /'ləʊʃn/ n Lotion f

lottery /'lɒtərɪ/ n Lotterie f. ~ **ticket** n Los nt

loud /laʊd/ adj (-er, -est) laut; (colours) grell ● adv [out] ~ laut. ~ **'speaker** n Lautsprecher m

lounge /laʊndʒ/ n Wohnzimmer nt; (in hotel) Aufenthaltsraum m. ● vi sich lümmeln

louse /laʊs/ n (pl lice) Laus f

lousy /'laʊzɪ/ adj 🛈 lausig

lout /laʊt/ n Flegel m, Lümmel m

lovable /'lʌvəbl/ adj liebenswert

love /lʌv/ n Liebe f; (Tennis) null; in ~ verliebt ● vt lieben; ~ doing sth etw sehr gerne machen. ~-**affair** n Liebesverhältnis nt. ~ **letter** n Liebesbrief m

lovely /'lʌvlɪ/ adj schön

lover /'lʌvə(r)/ n Liebhaber m

love: ~**song** n Liebeslied nt. ~ **story** n Liebesgeschichte f

loving /'lʌvɪŋ/ adj liebevoll

low /ləʊ/ adj (-er, -est) niedrig; (cloud, note) tief; (voice) leise; (depressed) niedergeschlagen ● adv niedrig; (fly, sing) tief; (speak) leise ● n (weather) Tief nt; (fig) Tiefstand m

low: ~**brow** adj geistig anspruchslos. ~-**cut** adj (dress) tief ausgeschnitten

lower /'ləʊə(r)/ adj & adv see low ● vt niedriger machen; (let down) herunterlassen; (reduce) senken

low: ~-'**fat** adj fettarm. ~**lands** /-ləndz/ npl Tiefland nt. ~ '**tide** n Ebbe f

loyal /'lɔɪəl/ adj treu. ~**ty** n Treue f. ~**ty card** n Treuekarte f

lozenge /'lɒzɪndʒ/ n Pastille f

Ltd abbr (Limited) GmbH

lubricant /'lu:brɪkənt/ n Schmiermittel nt

lubricat|e /'lu:brɪkeɪt/ vt schmieren. ~**ion** n Schmierung f

lucid /'lu:sɪd/ adj klar. ~**ity** n Klarheit f

luck /lʌk/ n Glück nt; bad ~ Pech nt; good ~! viel Glück! ~**ily** adv glücklicherweise, zum Glück

lucky /'lʌkɪ/ adj glücklich; (day, number) Glücks-; be ~ Glück haben; (thing:) Glück bringen

lucrative /'lu:krətɪv/ adj einträglich

ludicrous /'lu:dɪkrəs/ adj lächerlich

lug /lʌg/ vt (pt/pp lugged) 🛈 schleppen

luggage /'lʌgɪdʒ/ n Gepäck nt

luggage: ~-**rack** in Gepäckablage f. ~-**van** n Gepäckwagen m

lukewarm /'lu:k-/ adj lauwarm

lull /lʌl/ n Pause f ● vt ~ to sleep einschläfern

lullaby /'lʌləbaɪ/ n Wiegenlied nt

lumber /'lʌmbə(r)/ n Gerümpel nt; (Amer: timber) Bauholz nt ● vt ~ s.o. with sth jdm etw aufhalsen. ~ **jack** n (Amer) Holzfäller m

luminous /'lu:mɪnəs/ adj leuchtend

lump /lʌmp/ n Klumpen m; (of sugar) Stück m; (swelling) Beule f; (in breast) Knoten m; (tumour) Geschwulst f; a ~ in one's throat 🛈 ein Kloß im Hals

lump: ~ **sugar** n Würfelzucker m. ~ '**sum** n Pauschalsumme f

lumpy /'lʌmpɪ/ adj klumpig

lunacy /'lu:nəsɪ/ n Wahnsinn m

lunar /'lu:nə(r)/ adj Mond-

lunatic /'lu:nətɪk/ n Wahnsinnige(r) m/f

lunch /lʌntʃ/ n Mittagessen nt ● vi zu Mittag essen

luncheon /'lʌntʃn/ n Mittagessen nt. ~ **voucher** n Essensbon m

lunch: ~-**hour** n Mittagspause f. ~-**time** n Mittagszeit f

lung /lʌŋ/ n Lungenflügel m; ~s pl Lunge f

lunge /lʌndʒ/ vi sich stürzen (at auf + acc)

lurch¹ /lɜ:tʃ/ n leave in the ~ 🛈 im Stich lassen

lurch² vi (person:) torkeln

lure /ljʊə(r)/ vt locken

lurid /'lʊərɪd/ adj grell; (sensational) reißerisch

lurk /lɜ:k/ vi lauern

luscious /'lʌʃəs/ adj lecker, köstlich

lush /lʌʃ/ *adj* üppig

lust /lʌst/ *n* Begierde *f*. **~ful** *adj* lüstern

lustre /'lʌstə(r)/ *n* Glanz *m*

lusty /'lʌstɪ/ *adj* kräftig

luxuriant /lʌg'zʊərɪənt/ *adj* üppig

luxurious /lʌg'zʊərɪəs/ *adj* luxuriös

luxury /'lʌkʃərɪ/ *n* Luxus *m* ● *attrib* Luxus-

lying /'laɪɪŋ/ *see* lie¹, lie²

lynch /lɪntʃ/ *vt* lynchen

lyric /'lɪrɪk/ *adj* lyrisch. **~al** *adj* lyrisch; (*enthusiastic*) schwärmerisch. **~ poetry** *n* Lyrik *f*. **~s** *npl* [Lied]text *m*

Mm

mac /mæk/ *n* 🔲 Regenmantel *m*

macabre /mə'kɑːbr/ *adj* makaber

macaroni /mækə'rəʊnɪ/ *n* Makkaroni *pl*

machinations /mækɪ'neɪʃnz/ *pl* Machenschaften *pl*

machine /mə'ʃiːn/ *n* Maschine *f* ● *vt* (*sew*) mit der Maschine nähen; (*Techn*) maschinell bearbeiten. **~-gun** *n* Maschinengewehr *nt*

machinery /mə'ʃiːnərɪ/ *n* Maschinerie *f*

mackerel /'mækrl/ *n inv* Makrele *f*

mackintosh /'mækɪntɒʃ/ *n* Regenmantel *m*

mad /mæd/ *adj* (**madder, maddest**) verrückt; (*dog*) tollwütig; (🔲: *angry*) böse (**at** auf + *acc*)

madam /'mædəm/ *n* gnädige Frau *f*

mad 'cow disease *n* 🔲 Rinderwahnsinn *m*

madden /'mædn/ *vt* (*make angry*) wütend machen

made /meɪd/ *see* make; **~ to measure** maßgeschneidert

mad|ly /'mædlɪ/ *adv* 🔲 wahnsinnig. **~man** *n* Irre(r) *m*. **~ness** *n* Wahnsinn *m*

madonna /mə'dɒnə/ *n* Madonna *f*

magazine /mægə'ziːn/ *n* Zeitschrift *f*; (*Mil, Phot*) Magazin *nt*

maggot /'mægət/ *n* Made *f*

magic /'mædʒɪk/ *n* Zauber *m*; (*tricks*) Zauberkunst *f* ● *adj* magisch; (*word, wand*) Zauber-. **~al** *adj* zauberhaft

magician /mə'dʒɪʃn/ *n* Zauberer *m*; (*entertainer*) Zauberkünstler *m*

magistrate /'mædʒɪstreɪt/ *n* ≈ Friedensrichter *m*

magnet /'mægnɪt/ *n* Magnet *m*. **~ic** *adj* magnetisch. **~ism** *n* Magnetismus *m*

magnification /mægnɪfɪ'keɪʃn/ *n* Vergrößerung *f*

magnificen|ce /mæg'nɪfɪsəns/ *n* Großartigkeit *f*. **~t** *adj* großartig

magnify /'mægnɪfaɪ/ *vt* (*pt/pp* -**ied**) vergrößern; (*exaggerate*) übertreiben. **~ing glass** *n* Vergrößerungsglas *nt*

magnitude /'mægnɪtjuːd/ *n* Größe *f*; (*importance*) Bedeutung *f*

magpie /'mægpaɪ/ *n* Elster *f*

mahogany /mə'hɒgənɪ/ *n* Mahagoni *nt*

maid /meɪd/ *n* Dienstmädchen *nt*; **old ~** (*pej*) alte Jungfer *f*

maiden /'meɪdn/ *adj* (*speech, voyage*) Jungfern-. **~ name** *n* Mädchenname *m*

mail /meɪl/ *n* Post *f* ● *vt* mit der Post schicken

mail: **~bag** *n* Postsack *m*. **~box** *n* (*Amer*) Briefkasten *m*. **~ing list** *n* Postversandliste *f*. **~man** *n* (*Amer*) Briefträger *m*. **~-order firm** *n* Versandhaus *nt*

maim /meɪm/ *vt* verstümmeln

main /meɪn/ *adj* Haupt- ● *n* (*water, gas, electricity*) Hauptleitung *f*

main: **~land** /-lənd/ *n* Festland *nt*. **~ly** *adv* hauptsächlich. **~stay** *n* (*fig*) Stütze *f*. **~ street** *n* Hauptstraße *f*

maintain /meɪn'teɪn/ *vt* aufrechterhalten; (*keep in repair*) instand halten; (*support*) unterhalten; (*claim*) behaupten

maintenance /'meɪntənəns/ *n* Aufrechterhaltung f; (care) Instandhaltung f; (allowance) Unterhalt m

maize /meɪz/ n Mais m

majestic /mə'dʒestɪk/ adj, -ally adv majestätisch

majesty /'mædʒəstɪ/ n Majestät f

major /'meɪdʒə(r)/ adj größer ● n (Mil) Major m; (Mus) Dur nt ● vi ~ in als Hauptfach studieren

majority /mə'dʒɒrətɪ/ n Mehrheit f; in the ~ in der Mehrzahl

major road n Hauptverkehrsstraße f

make /meɪk/ n (brand) Marke f ● v (pt/pp made) ● vt machen; (force) zwingen; (earn) verdienen; halten (speech); treffen (decision); erreichen (destination) ● vi ~ do vi zurechtkommen (with mit). ~ for vi zusteuern auf (+ acc). ~ off vi sich davonmachen (with mit). ~ out vt (distinguish) ausmachen; (write out) ausstellen; (assert) behaupten. ~ up vt (constitute) bilden; (invent) erfinden; (apply cosmetics to) schminken; ~ up one's mind sich entschließen ● vi sich versöhnen; ~ up for sth etw wieder gutmachen; ~ up for lost time verlorene Zeit aufholen

'make-believe n Phantasie f

maker /'meɪkə(r)/ n Hersteller m

make: ~ **shift** adj behelfsmäßig ● n Notbehelf m. ~-**up** n Make-up nt

maladjusted /mælə'dʒʌstɪd/ adj verhaltensgestört

male /meɪl/ adj männlich ● n Mann m; (animal) Männchen nt. ~ **nurse** n Krankenpfleger m. ~ **voice 'choir** n Männerchor m

malice /'mælɪs/ n Bosheit f

malicious /mə'lɪʃəs/ adj böswillig

malign /mə'laɪn/ vt verleumden

malignant /mə'lɪgnənt/ adj bösartig

mallet /'mælɪt/ n Holzhammer m

malnu'trition /mæl-/ n Unterernährung f

mal'practice n Berufsvergehen nt

malt /mɔːlt/ n Malz nt

mal'treat /mæl-/ vt misshandeln.

~**ment** n Misshandlung f

mammal /'mæml/ n Säugetier nt

mammoth /'mæməθ/ adj riesig

man /mæn/ n (pl men) Mann m; (mankind) der Mensch; (chess) Figur f; (draughts) Stein m ● vt (pt/pp manned) bemannen (ship); bedienen (pump); besetzen (counter)

manage /'mænɪdʒ/ vt leiten; verwalten (estate); (cope with) fertig werden mit; ~ to do sth es schaffen, etw zu tun ● vi zurechtkommen; ~ on auskommen mit. ~**able** adj (tool) handlich; (person) fügsam. ~**ment** n Leitung f; the ~**ment** die Geschäftsleitung f

manager /'mænɪdʒə(r)/ n Geschäftsführer m; (of bank) Direktor m; (of estate) Verwalter m; (Sport) [Chef]trainer m. ~**ess** n Geschäftsführerin f. ~**ial** adj ~**ial staff** Führungskräfte pl

managing /'mænɪdʒɪŋ/ adj ~ **director** Generaldirektor m

mandat|e /'mændeɪt/ n Mandat nt. ~**ory** adj obligatorisch

mane /meɪn/ n Mähne f

manful /'mænfl/ adj mannhaft

man: ~'**handle** vt grob behandeln (person). ~**hole** n Kanalschacht m. ~**hood** n Mannesalter nt; (quality) Männlichkeit f. ~-**hour** n Arbeitsstunde f. ~-**hunt** n Fahndung f

man|ia /'meɪnɪə/ n Manie f. ~**iac** n Wahnsinnige(r) m/f

manicure /'mænɪkjʊə(r)/ n Maniküre f ● vt maniküren

manifest /'mænɪfest/ adj offensichtlich

manifesto /mænɪ'festəʊ/ n Manifest nt

manifold /'mænɪfəʊld/ adj mannigfaltig

manipulat|e /mə'nɪpjʊleɪt/ vt handhaben; (pej) manipulieren. ~**ion** n Manipulation f

man'kind n die Menschheit

manly /'mænlɪ/ adj männlich

'man-made adj künstlich. ~ **fibre** n Kunstfaser f

manner /ˈmænə(r)/ n Weise f; (kind, behaviour) Art f; **[good/bad]** ∼s [gute/schlechte] Manieren pl. ∼ism n Angewohnheit f

manœuvrable /məˈnuːvrəbl/ adj manövrierfähig

manœuvre /məˈnuːvə(r)/ n Manöver nt ● vt/i manövrieren

manor /ˈmænə(r)/ n Gutshof m; (house) Gutshaus nt

'manpower n Arbeitskräfte pl

mansion /ˈmænʃn/ n Villa f

'manslaughter n Totschlag m

mantelpiece /ˈmæntl-/ n Kaminsims m & nt

manual /ˈmænjʊəl/ adj Hand- ● n Handbuch nt

manufacture /mænjʊˈfæktʃə(r)/ vt herstellen ● n Herstellung f. ∼r n Hersteller m

manure /məˈnjʊə(r)/ n Mist m

manuscript /ˈmænjʊskrɪpt/ n Manuskript nt

many /ˈmenɪ/ adj viele ● n **a good/ great** ∼ sehr viele

map /mæp/ n Landkarte f; (of town) Stadtplan m

maple /ˈmeɪpl/ n Ahorn m

mar /mɑː(r)/ vt (pt/pp **marred**) verderben

marathon /ˈmærəθən/ n Marathon m

marble /ˈmɑːbl/ n Marmor m; (for game) Murmel f

March /mɑːtʃ/ n März m

march n Marsch m ● vi marschieren ● vt marschieren lassen; ∼ **s.o. off** jdn abführen

mare /meə(r)/ n Stute f

margarine /mɑːdʒəˈriːn/ n Margarine f

margin /ˈmɑːdʒɪn/ n Rand m; (leeway) Spielraum m; (Comm) Spanne f. ∼al adj geringfügig

marigold /ˈmærɪɡəʊld/ n Ringelblume f

marina /məˈriːnə/ n Jachthafen m

marine /məˈriːn/ adj Meeres- ● n Marine f; (sailor) Marineinfanterist m

marital /ˈmærɪtl/ adj ehelich. ∼ **status** n Familienstand m

maritime /ˈmærɪtaɪm/ adj See-

mark¹ /mɑːk/ n (former German currency) Mark f

mark² n Fleck m; (sign) Zeichen nt; (trace) Spur f; (target) Ziel nt; (Sch) Note f ● vt markieren; (spoil) beschädigen; (characterize) kennzeichnen; (Sch) korrigieren; (Sport) decken; ∼ **time** (Mil) auf der Stelle treten; (fig) abwarten. ∼ **out** vt markieren

marked /mɑːkt/ adj, ∼ly adv deutlich; (pronounced) ausgeprägt

market /ˈmɑːkɪt/ n Markt m ● vt vertreiben; (launch) auf den Markt bringen. ∼ing n Marketing nt. ∼ re-'search n Marktforschung f

marking /ˈmɑːkɪŋ/ n Markierung f; (on animal) Zeichnung f

marksman /ˈmɑːksmən/ n Scharfschütze m

marmalade /ˈmɑːməleɪd/ n Orangenmarmelade f

maroon /məˈruːn/ adj dunkelrot

marooned /məˈruːnd/ adj (fig) von der Außenwelt abgeschnitten

marquee /mɑːˈkiː/ n Festzelt nt

marquetry /ˈmɑːkɪtrɪ/ n Einlegearbeit f

marriage /ˈmærɪdʒ/ n Ehe f; (wedding) Hochzeit f. ∼able adj heiratsfähig

married /ˈmærɪd/ see **marry** ● adj verheiratet. ∼ **life** n Eheleben nt

marrow /ˈmærəʊ/ n (Anat) Mark nt; (vegetable) Kürbis m

marr|y /ˈmærɪ/ vt/i (pt/pp **married**) heiraten; (unite) trauen; **get** ∼**ied** heiraten

marsh /mɑːʃ/ n Sumpf m

marshal /ˈmɑːʃl/ n Marschall m; (steward) Ordner m

marshy /ˈmɑːʃɪ/ adj sumpfig

martial /ˈmɑːʃl/ adj kriegerisch. ∼ 'law n Kriegsrecht nt

martyr /ˈmɑːtə(r)/ n Märtyrer(in) m(f). ∼dom n Martyrium nt

marvel /ˈmɑːvl/ n Wunder nt ● vi (pt/pp **marvelled**) staunen (**at** über

m

+ *acc*). ∼**lous** a, **-ly** adv wunderbar

Marxis|m /'mɑːksɪzm/ n Marxismus m. ∼**t** adj marxistisch ●n Marxist(in) m(f)

marzipan /'mɑːzɪpæn/ n Marzipan nt

mascot /'mæskət/ n Maskottchen nt

masculin|e /'mæskjʊlɪn/ adj männlich ●n (Gram) Maskulinum nt. ∼**ity** n Männlichkeit f

mash /mæʃ/ n 🔲, ∼**ed potatoes** npl Kartoffelpüree nt

mask /mɑːsk/ n Maske f ●vt maskieren

masochis|m /'mæsəkɪzm/ n Masochismus m. ∼**t** n Masochist m

mason /'meɪsn/ n Steinmetz m. ∼**ry** n Mauerwerk nt

mass¹ /mæs/ n (Relig) Messe f

mass² n Masse f ●vi sich sammeln; (Mil) sich massieren

massacre /'mæsəkə(r)/ n Massaker nt ●vt niedermetzeln

massage /'mæsɑːʒ/ n Massage f ●vt massieren

masseu|r /mæ'sɜː(r)/ n Masseur m. ∼**se** n Masseuse f

massive /'mæsɪv/ adj massiv; (huge) riesig

mass: ∼ '**media** npl Massenmedien pl. ∼-**pro'duce** vt in Massenproduktion herstellen. ∼**pro'duction** n Massenproduktion f

mast /mɑːst/ n Mast m

master /'mɑːstə(r)/ n Herr m; (teacher) Lehrer m; (craftsman, artist) Meister m; (of ship) Kapitän m ●vt meistern; beherrschen (language)

master: ∼**ly** adj meisterhaft. ∼-**mind** n führender Kopf m ●vt der führende Kopf sein von. ∼**piece** n Meisterwerk nt. ∼**y** n (of subject) Beherrschung f

mat /mæt/ n Matte f; (on table) Untersatz m

match¹ /mætʃ/ n Wettkampf m; (in ball games) Spiel nt; (Tennis) Match nt; (marriage) Heirat f; **be a good** ∼ (colours:) gut zusammenpassen; **be no** ∼ **for s.o.** jdm nicht gewachsen

sein ●vt (equal) gleichkommen (+ dat); (be like) passen zu; (find sth similar) etwas Passendes finden zu ●vi zusammenpassen

match² n Streichholz nt. ∼**box** n Streichholzschachtel f

mate¹ /meɪt/ n Kumpel m; (assistant) Gehilfe m; (Naut) Maat m; (Zool) Männchen nt; (female) Weibchen nt ●vi sich paaren

mate² n (Chess) Matt nt

material /mə'tɪərɪəl/ n Material nt; (fabric) Stoff m; **raw** ∼**s** Rohstoffe pl ●adj materiell

material|ism /mə'tɪərɪəlɪzm/ n Materialismus m. ∼**istic** adj materialistisch. ∼**ize** vi sich verwirklichen

maternal /mə'tɜːnl/ adj mütterlich

maternity /mə'tɜːnətɪ/ n Mutterschaft f. ∼ **clothes** npl Umstandskleidung f. ∼ **ward** n Entbindungsstation f

mathematic|al /mæθə'mætɪkl/ adj mathematisch. ∼**ian** n Mathematiker(in) m(f)

mathematics /mæθə'mætɪks/ n Mathematik f

maths /mæθs/ n 🔲 Mathe f

matinée /'mætɪneɪ/ n (Theat) Nachmittagsvorstellung f

matrimony /'mætrɪmənɪ/ n Ehe f

matron /'meɪtrən/ n (of hospital) Oberin f; (of school) Hausmutter f

matt /mæt/ adj matt

matted /'mætɪd/ adj verfilzt

matter /'mætə(r)/ n (affair) Sache f; (Phys: substance) Materie f; **money** ∼**s** Geldangelegenheiten pl; **what is the** ∼**?** was ist los? ●vi wichtig sein; ∼ **to s.o.** jdm etwas ausmachen; **it doesn't** ∼ es macht nichts. ∼**-of-fact** adj sachlich

mattress /'mætrɪs/ n Matratze f

matur|e /mə'tjʊə(r)/ adj reif; (Comm) fällig ●vi reifen; (person:) reifer werden; (Comm) fällig werden ●vt reifen lassen. ∼**ity** n Reife f; (Comm) Fälligkeit f

mauve /məʊv/ adj lila

maximum /'mæksɪməm/ adj maximal ● *n* (*pl* **-ima**) Maximum *nt*. ~ **speed** *n* Höchstgeschwindigkeit *f*

may /meɪ/

! *pres* **may**, *pt* **might**

● *modal verb*

····► (*expressing possibility*) können. **she may come** es kann sein, dass sie kommt; es ist möglich, dass sie kommt. **she might come** (*more distant possibility*) sie könnte kommen. **it may/might rain** es könnte regnen. **I may be wrong** vielleicht irre ich mich. **he may have missed his train** vielleicht hat er seinen Zug verpasst

····► (*expressing permission*) dürfen. **may I come in?** darf ich reinkommen? **you may smoke** Sie dürfen rauchen

····► (*expressing wish*) **may the best man win!** auf dass der Beste gewinnt!

····► (*expressing concession*) **he may be slow but he's accurate** mag *od* kann sein, dass er langsam ist, aber dafür ist er auch genau

····► **may/might as well** ebenso gut können. **we may/might as well go** wir könnten eigentlich ebensogut [auch] gehen. **we might as well give up** da können wir gleich aufgeben

May *n* Mai *m*

maybe /ˈmeɪbiː/ *adv* vielleicht

'May Day *n* der Erste Mai

mayonnaise /meɪəˈneɪz/ *n* Mayonnaise *f*

mayor /ˈmeə(r)/ *n* Bürgermeister *m*. ~**ess** *n* Bürgermeisterin *f*; (*wife of mayor*) Frau Bürgermeister *f*

maze /meɪz/ *n* Irrgarten *m*; (*fig*) Labyrinth *nt*

me /miː/ *pron* (*acc*) mich; (*dat*) mir; **it's** ~ 🅸 ich bin es

meadow /ˈmedəʊ/ *n* Wiese *f*

meagre /ˈmiːgə(r)/ *adj* dürftig

meal /miːl/ *n* Mahlzeit *f*; (*food*) Essen

nt; (*grain*) Schrot *m*

mean¹ /miːn/ *adj* (**-er**, **-est**) (*miserly*) geizig; (*unkind*) gemein; (*poor*) schäbig

mean² *adj* mittlere(r,s) ● *n* (*average*) Durchschnitt *m*

mean³ *vt* (*pt/pp* **meant**) heißen; (*signify*) bedeuten; (*intend*) beabsichtigen; **I** ~ **it** das ist mein Ernst; **I** ~ **well** es gut meinen; **be meant for** (*present:*) bestimmt sein für; (*remark:*) gerichtet sein an (+ *acc*)

meaning /ˈmiːnɪŋ/ *n* Bedeutung *f*. ~**ful** *adj* bedeutungsvoll. ~**less** *adj* bedeutungslos

means /miːnz/ *n* Möglichkeit *f*, Mittel *nt*; ~ **of transport** Verkehrsmittel *nt*; **by** ~ **of** durch; **by all** ~! aber natürlich! **by no** ~ keineswegs ● *npl* (*resources*) [Geld]mittel *pl*

meant /ment/ *see* **mean³**

'meantime *n* **in the** ~ in der Zwischenzeit ● *adv* inzwischen

'meanwhile *adv* inzwischen

measles /ˈmiːzlz/ *n* Masern *pl*

measure /ˈmeʒə(r)/ *n* Maß *nt*; (*action*) Maßnahme *f* ● *vt/i* messen; ~ **up to** (*fig*) herankommen an (+ *acc*). ~**d** *adj* gemessen. ~**ment** *n* Maß *nt*

meat /miːt/ *n* Fleisch *nt*

mechan|ic /mɪˈkænɪk/ *n* Mechaniker *m*. ~**ical** *adj* mechanisch. ~**ical engineering** Maschinenbau *m*

mechan|ism /ˈmekənɪzm/ *n* Mechanismus *m*. ~**ize** *vt* mechanisieren

medal /ˈmedl/ *n* Orden *m*; (*Sport*) Medaille *f*

medallist /ˈmedəlɪst/ *n* Medaillengewinner(in) *m(f)*

meddle /ˈmedl/ *vi* sich einmischen (**in** in + *acc*); (*tinker*) herumhantieren (**with** an + *acc*)

media /ˈmiːdɪə/ *see* **medium** ● *n pl* **the** ~ die Medien *pl*

mediat|e /ˈmiːdɪeɪt/ *vi* vermitteln. ~**or** *n* Vermittler(in) *m(f)*

medical /ˈmedɪkl/ *adj* medizinisch; (*treatment*) ärztlich ● *n* ärztliche Untersuchung *f*. ~ **insurance** *n* Kran-

m

kenversicherung f. ～ **student** n Medizinstudent m

medicat|ed /'medɪkeɪtɪd/ adj medizinisch. ～**ion** n (drugs) Medikamente pl

medicinal /mɪ'dɪsɪml/ adj medizinisch; (plant) heilkräftig

medicine /'medsən/ n Medizin f; (preparation) Medikament nt

medieval /medɪ'i:vl/ adj mittelalterlich

mediocr|e /mi:dɪ'əʊkə(r)/ adj mittelmäßig. ～**ity** n Mittelmäßigkeit f

meditat|e /'medɪteɪt/ vi nachdenken (on über + acc). ～**ion** n Meditation f

Mediterranean /medɪtə'reɪnɪən/ n Mittelmeer nt ● adj Mittelmeer-

medium /'mi:dɪəm/ adj mittlere(r,s); (steak) medium; **of** ～ **size** von mittlerer Größe ● n (pl media) Medium nt; (means) Mittel nt

medium: ～-**sized** adj mittelgroß. ～ **wave** n Mittelwelle f

medley /'medlɪ/ n Gemisch nt; (Mus) Potpourri nt

meek /mi:k/ adj (-er, -est) sanftmütig; (unprotesting, compliant) widerspruchslos

meet /mi:t/ v (pt/pp met) ● vt treffen; (by chance) begegnen (+ dat); (at station) abholen; (make the acquaintance of) kennen lernen; stoßen auf (+ acc) (problem); bezahlen (bill); erfüllen (requirements) ● vi sich treffen; (for the first time) sich kennen lernen

meeting /'mi:tɪŋ/ n Treffen nt; (by chance) Begegnung f; (discussion) Besprechung f; (of committee) Sitzung f; (large) Versammlung f

megalomania /megələ'meɪnɪə/ n Größenwahnsinn m

megaphone /'megəfəʊn/ n Megaphon nt

melancholy /'melənkəlɪ/ adj melancholisch ● n Melancholie f

mellow /'meləʊ/ adj(-er, -est) (fruit) ausgereift; (sound, person) sanft ● vi reifer werden

melodious /mɪ'ləʊdɪəs/ adj melodiös

melodramatic /melədrə'mætɪk/ adj, -**ally** adv melodramatisch

melody /'melədɪ/ n Melodie f

melon /'melən/ n Melone f

melt /melt/ vt/i schmelzen

member /'membə(r)/ n Mitglied nt; (of family) Angehörige(r) m/f; **M～ of Parliament** Abgeordnete(r) m/f. ～**ship** n Mitgliedschaft f; (members) Mitgliederzahl f

memento /mɪ'mentəʊ/ n Andenken nt

memo /'meməʊ/ n Mitteilung f

memoirs /'memwɑːz/ n pl Memoiren pl

memorable /'memərəbl/ adj denkwürdig

memorial /mɪ'mɔːrɪəl/ n Denkmal nt. ～ **service** n Gedenkfeier f

memorize /'meməraɪz/ vt sich (dat) einprägen

memory /'memərɪ/ n Gedächtnis nt; (thing remembered) Erinnerung f; (of computer) Speicher m; **from** ～ auswendig; **in** ～ **of** zur Erinnerung an (+ acc)

men /men/ see **man**

menac|e /'menɪs/ n Drohung f; (nuisance) Plage f ● vt bedrohen. ～**ing** adj, ～**ly** adv drohend

mend /mend/ vt reparieren; (patch) flicken; ausbessern (clothes)

'**menfolk** n pl Männer pl

menial /'mi:nɪəl/ adj niedrig

menopause /'menə-/ n Wechseljahre pl

mental /'mentl/ adj geistig; (🄸: mad) verrückt. ～ a'**rithmetic** n Kopfrechnen nt. ～ '**illness** n Geisteskrankheit f

mentality /men'tælətɪ/ n Mentalität f

mention /'menʃn/ n Erwähnung f ● vt erwähnen; **don't** ～ **it** keine Ursache; bitte

menu /'menjuː/ n Speisekarte f

merchandise /'mɜːtʃəndaɪz/ n Ware f

merchant /'mɜːtʃənt/ n Kaufmann

m; (*dealer*) Händler *m*. **~ 'navy** *n* Handelsmarine *f*

merci|ful /'mɜːsɪfl/ *adj* barmherzig. **~fully** *adv* 🎯 glücklicherweise. **~less** *adj* erbarmungslos

mercury /'mɜːkjʊrɪ/ *n* Quecksilber *nt*

mercy /'mɜːsɪ/ *n* Barmherzigkeit *f*, Gnade *f*; **be at s.o.'s ~** jdm ausgeliefert sein

mere /mɪə(r)/ *adj* bloß

merest /'mɪərɪst/ *adj* kleinste(r,s)

merge /mɜːdʒ/ *vi* zusammenlaufen; (*Comm*) fusionieren

merger /'mɜːdʒə(r)/ *n* Fusion *f*

meringue /mə'ræŋ/ *n* Baiser *nt*

merit /'merɪt/ *n* Verdienst *nt*; (*advantage*) Vorzug *m*; (*worth*) Wert *m* ● *vt* verdienen

merry /'merɪ/ *adj* fröhlich

merry-go-round *n* Karussell *nt*

mesh /meʃ/ *n* Masche *f*

mesmerized /'mezməraɪzd/ *adj* (*fig*) [wie] gebannt

mess /mes/ *n* Durcheinander *nt*; (*trouble*) Schwierigkeiten *pl*; (*something spilt*) Bescherung *f* 🎯; (*Mil*) Messe *f*; **make a ~ of** (*botch*) verpfuschen ● *vt* **~ up** in Unordnung bringen; (*botch*) verpfuschen ● *vi* **~ about** herumalbern; (*tinker*) herumspielen (**with** mit)

message /'mesɪdʒ/ *n* Nachricht *f*; **give s.o. a ~** jdm etwas ausrichten

messenger /'mesɪndʒə(r)/ *n* Bote *m*

Messrs /'mesəz/ *n pl see* **Mr**; (*on letter*) **~ Smith** Firma Smith

messy /'mesɪ/ *adj* schmutzig; (*untidy*) unordentlich

met /met/ *see* **meet**

metal /'metl/ *n* Metall *nt* ● *adj* Metall-. **~lic** *adj* metallisch

metaphor /'metəfə(r)/ *n* Metapher *f*. **~ical** *adj* metaphorisch

meteor /'miːtɪə(r)/ *n* Meteor *m*. **~ic** *adj* kometenhaft

meteorological /miːtɪərə'lɒdʒɪkl/ *adj* Wetter-

meteorolog|ist /miːtɪə'rɒlədʒɪst/

n Meteorologe *m*/ -gin *f*. **~y** *n* Meteorologie *f*

meter¹ /'miːtə(r)/ *n* Zähler *m*

meter² *n* (*Amer*) = **metre**

method /'meθəd/ *n* Methode *f*; (*Culin*) Zubereitung *f*

methodical /mɪ'θɒdɪkl/ *adj* systematisch, methodisch

methylated /'meθɪleɪtɪd/ *adj* **~ spirit[s]** Brennspiritus *m*

meticulous /mɪ'tɪkjʊləs/ *adj* sehr genau

metre /'miːtə(r)/ *n* Meter *m* & *n*; (*rhythm*) Versmaß *nt*

metric /'metrɪk/ *adj* metrisch

metropolis /mɪ'trɒpəlɪs/ *n* Metropole *f*

metropolitan /metrə'pɒlɪtən/ *adj* hauptstädtisch; (*international*) weltstädtisch

mew /mjuː/ *n* Miau *nt* ● *vi* miauen

Mexican /'meksɪkən/ *adj* mexikanisch ● *n* Mexikaner(in) *m*(*f*). **'Mexico** *n* Mexiko *nt*

miaow /mɪ'aʊ/ *n* Miau *nt* ● *vi* miauen

mice /maɪs/ *see* **mouse**

micro: **~film** *n* Mikrofilm *m*. **~light** [**aircraft**] *n* Ultraleichtflugzeug *nt*. **~phone** *n* Mikrofon *nt*. **~scope** /-skəʊp/ *n* Mikroskop *nt*. **~scopic** /-'skɒpɪk/ *adj* mikroskopisch. **~wave** [**oven**] *n* Mikrowellenherd *m*

mid /mɪd/ *adj* **~ May** Mitte Mai; **in ~ air** in der Luft

midday /mɪd'deɪ/ *n* Mittag *m*

middle /'mɪdl/ *adj* mittlere(r,s); **the M~ Ages** das Mittelalter; **the ~ class[es]** der Mittelstand; **the M~ East** der Nahe Osten ● *n* Mitte *f*; **in the ~ of the night** mitten in der Nacht

middle: **~-aged** *adj* mittleren Alters. **~-class** *adj* bürgerlich

midge /mɪdʒ/ *n* [kleine] Mücke *f*

midget /'mɪdʒɪt/ *n* Liliputaner(in) *m*(*f*)

Midlands /'mɪdləndz/ *npl* **the ~** Mittelengland *n*

'midnight *n* Mitternacht *f*

midriff /'mɪdrɪf/ n 🔲 Taille f

midst /mɪdst/ n **in the ∼ of** mitten in (+ dat); **in our ∼** unter uns

mid: ∼**summer** n Hochsommer m. ∼**way** adv auf halbem Wege. ∼**wife** n Hebamme f. ∼'**winter** n Mitte f des Winters

might[1] /maɪt/ modal verb **I** ∼ vielleicht; **it ∼ be true** es könnte wahr sein; **he asked if he ∼ go** er fragte, ob er gehen dürfte; **you ∼ have drowned** du hättest ertrinken können

might[2] n Macht f

mighty /'maɪtɪ/ adj mächtig

migraine /'miːgreɪn/ n Migräne f

migrat|e /maɪ'greɪt/ vi abwandern; (birds:) ziehen. ∼**ion** n Wanderung f; (of birds) Zug m

mike /maɪk/ n 🔲 Mikrofon nt

mild /maɪld/ adj (-er, -est) mild

mild|ly /'maɪldlɪ/ adv leicht; **to put it ∼ly** gelinde gesagt. ∼**ness** n Milde f

mile /maɪl/ n Meile f (= 1,6 km); ∼**s too big** 🔲 viel zu groß

mile|age /-ɪdʒ/ n Meilenzahl f; (of car) Meilenstand m

militant /'mɪlɪtənt/ adj militant

military /'mɪlɪtrɪ/ adj militärisch. ∼ **service** n Wehrdienst m

milk /mɪlk/ n Milch f ● vt melken

milk: ∼**man** n Milchmann m. ∼**shake** n Milchmixgetränk nt. ∼**tooth** n Milchzahn m

milky /'mɪlkɪ/ adj milchig. **M∼ Way** n (Astronomy) Milchstraße f

mill /mɪl/ n Mühle f; (factory) Fabrik f

millennium /mɪ'lenɪəm/ n Jahrtausend nt

milli|gram /'mɪlɪ-/ n Milligramm nt. ∼**metre** n Millimeter m & nt

million /'mɪljən/ n Million f; **a ∼ pounds** eine Million Pfund. ∼**aire** n Millionär(in) m(f)

mime /maɪm/ n Pantomime f ● vt pantomimisch darstellen

mimic /'mɪmɪk/ n Imitator m ● vt (pt/pp **mimicked**) nachahmen

mince /mɪns/ n Hackfleisch nt ● vt (Culin) durchdrehen; **not ∼ words** kein Blatt vor den Mund nehmen

mince: ∼**meat** n Masse f aus Korinthen, Zitronat usw; **make ∼ meat of** (fig) vernichtend schlagen. ∼'**pie** n mit 'mincemeat' gefülltes Pastetchen nt

mincer /'mɪnsə(r)/ n Fleischwolf m

mind /maɪnd/ n Geist m; (sanity) Verstand m; **give s.o. a piece of one's ∼** jdm gehörig die Meinung sagen; **make up one's ∼** sich entschließen; **be out of one's ∼** nicht bei Verstand sein; **have sth in ∼** etw im Sinn haben; **bear sth in ∼** an etw (acc) denken; **have a good ∼ to** große Lust haben, zu; **I have changed my ∼** ich habe es mir anders überlegt ● vt aufpassen auf (+ acc); **I don't ∼ the noise** der Lärm stört mich nicht; ∼ **the step!** Achtung Stufe! ● vi (care) sich kümmern (about um); **I don't ∼** mir macht es nichts aus; **never ∼!** macht nichts! **do you ∼ if?** haben Sie etwas dagegen, wenn? ∼ **out** vi aufpassen

'**mindless** adj geistlos

mine[1] /maɪn/ poss pron meine(r), meins; **a friend of ∼** ein Freund von mir; **that is ∼** das gehört mir

mine[2] n Bergwerk nt; (explosive) Mine f ● vt abbauen; (Mil) verminen

miner /'maɪnə(r)/ n Bergarbeiter m

mineral /'mɪnərl/ n Mineral nt. ∼ **water** n Mineralwasser nt

minesweeper /'maɪn-/ n Minenräumboot nt

mingle /'mɪŋgl/ vi ∼ **with** sich mischen unter (+ acc)

miniature /'mɪnɪtʃə(r)/ adj Klein- ● n Miniatur f

mini|bus /'mɪnɪ-/ n Kleinbus m. ∼**cab** n Kleintaxi nt

minim|al /'mɪnɪməl/ adj minimal. ∼**um** n (pl -**ima**) Minimum nt ● adj Mindest-

mining /'maɪnɪŋ/ n Bergbau m

miniskirt /'mɪnɪ-/ n Minirock m

minist|er /'mɪnɪstə(r)/ n Minister m; (Relig) Pastor m. ∼**erial** adj ministeriell

ministry /'mɪnɪstrɪ/ n (Pol) Ministerium nt

mink /mɪŋk/ n Nerz m

minor /'maɪnə(r)/ adj kleiner; (less important) unbedeutend ● n Minderjährige(r) m/f; (Mus) Moll nt

minority /maɪ'nɒrətɪ/ n Minderheit f

minor road n Nebenstraße f

mint[1] /mɪnt/ n Münzstätte f ● adj (stamp) postfrisch; **in ~ condition** wie neu ● vt prägen

mint[2] n (herb) Minze f; (sweet) Pfefferminzbonbon m & nt

minus /'maɪnəs/ prep minus, weniger; (☐: without) ohne

minute[1] /'mɪnɪt/ n Minute f; **in a ~** (shortly) gleich; **~s** pl (of meeting) Protokoll nt

minute[2] /maɪ'njuːt/ adj winzig

miracle /'mɪrəkl/ n Wunder nt. **~ulous** adj wunderbar

mirror /'mɪrə(r)/ n Spiegel m ● vt widerspiegeln

mirth /mɜːθ/ n Heiterkeit f

misadventure /mɪs-/ n Missgeschick nt

misapprehension n Missverständnis nt; **be under a ~** sich irren

misbehav|e vi sich schlecht benehmen. **~iour** n schlechtes Benehmen nt

mis'calcu|late vt falsch berechnen ● vi sich verrechnen. **~'lation** n Fehlkalkulation f

'miscarriage n Fehlgeburt f

miscellaneous /mɪsə'leɪnɪəs/ adj vermischt

mischief /'mɪstʃɪf/ n Unfug m

mischievous /'mɪstʃɪvəs/ adj schelmisch; (malicious) boshaft

miscon'ception n falsche Vorstellung f

mis'conduct n unkorrektes Verhalten nt; (adultery) Ehebruch m

miser /'maɪzə(r)/ n Geizhals m

miserable /'mɪzrəbl/ adj, **-bly** adv unglücklich; (wretched) elend

miserly /'maɪzəlɪ/ adv geizig

misery /'mɪzərɪ/ n Elend nt; (☐: person) Miesepeter m

mis'fire vi fehlzünden; (go wrong) fehschlagen

'misfit n Außenseiter(in) m(f)

mis'fortune n Unglück nt

mis'givings npl Bedenken pl

mis'guided adj töricht

mishap /'mɪshæp/ n Missgeschick nt

misin'form vt falsch unterrichten

misin'terpret vt missdeuten

mis'judge vt falsch beurteilen

mis'lay vt (pt/pp -laid) verlegen

mis'lead vt (pt/pp -led) irreführen. **~ing** adj irreführend

mis'manage vt schlecht verwalten. **~ment** n Misswirtschaft f

misnomer /mɪs'nəʊmə(r)/ n Fehlbezeichnung f

'misprint n Druckfehler m

mis'quote vt falsch zitieren

misrepre'sent vt falsch darstellen

miss /mɪs/ n Fehltreffer m ● vt verpassen; (fail to hit or find) verfehlen; (fail to attend) versäumen; (fail to notice) übersehen; (feel the loss of) vermissen ● vi (fail to hit) nicht treffen. **~ out** vt auslassen

Miss n (pl -es) Fräulein nt

missile /'mɪsaɪl/ n [Wurf]geschoss nt; (Mil) Rakete f

missing /'mɪsɪŋ/ adj fehlend; (lost) verschwunden; (Mil) vermisst; **be ~** fehlen

mission /'mɪʃn/ n Auftrag m; (Mil) Einsatz m; (Relig) Mission f

missionary /'mɪʃənrɪ/ n Missionar(in) m(f)

mis'spell vt (pt/pp -spelt or -spelled) falsch schreiben

mist /mɪst/ n Dunst m; (fog) Nebel m; (on window) Beschlag m ● vi **~ up** beschlagen

mistake /mɪ'steɪk/ n Fehler m; **by ~** aus Versehen ● vt (pt mistook, pp mistaken); **~ for** verwechseln mit

mistaken /mɪ'steɪkən/ adj falsch; **be ~** sich irren. **~ly** adv irrtümlicherweise

m

mistletoe /'mɪsltəʊ/ n Mistel f

mistress /'mɪstrɪs/ n Herrin f; (teacher) Lehrerin f; (lover) Geliebte f

mis'trust n Misstrauen nt ● vt misstrauen (+ dat)

misty /'mɪstɪ/ adj dunstig; (foggy) neblig; (fig) unklar

misunder'stand vt (pt/pp -stood) missverstehen. ~ing n Missverständnis nt

misuse¹ /mɪs'juːz/ vt missbrauchen

misuse² /mɪs'juːs/ n Missbrauch m

mitigating /'mɪtɪgeɪtɪŋ/ adj mildernd

mix /mɪks/ n Mischung f ● vt mischen ● vi sich mischen; ~ with (associate with) verkehren mit. ~ up vt mischen; (muddle) durcheinander bringen; (mistake for) verwechseln (with mit)

mixed /mɪkst/ adj gemischt; **be ~ up** durcheinander sein

mixer /'mɪksə(r)/ n Mischmaschine f; (Culin) Küchenmaschine f

mixture /'mɪkstʃə(r)/ n Mischung f; (medicine) Mixtur f; (Culin) Teig m

'mix-up n Durcheinander nt; (confusion) Verwirrung f; (mistake) Verwechslung f

moan /məʊn/ n Stöhnen nt ● vi stöhnen; (complain) jammern

mob /mɒb/ n Horde f; (rabble) Pöbel m; (🆼: gang) Bande f ● vt (pt/pp mobbed) herfallen über (+ acc); belagern (celebrity)

mobile /'məʊbaɪl/ adj beweglich ● n Mobile nt; (telephone) Handy nt. ~ 'home n Wohnwagen m. ~ 'phone n Handy nt

mobility /mə'bɪlətɪ/ n Beweglichkeit f

mock /mɒk/ adj Schein- ● vt verspotten. ~ery n Spott m

'mock-up n Modell nt

mode /məʊd/ n [Art und] Weise f; (fashion) Mode f

model /'mɒdl/ n Modell nt; (example) Vorbild nt; [fashion] ~ Mannequin nt ● adj Modell-; (exemplary) Muster- ● v (pt/pp modelled) ● vt formen,

modellieren; vorführen (clothes) ● vi Mannequin sein; (for artist) Modell stehen

moderate¹ /'mɒdəreɪt/ vt mäßigen

moderate² /'mɒdərət/ adj mäßig; (opinion) gemäßigt. ~ly adv mäßig; (fairly) einigermaßen

moderation /mɒdə'reɪʃn/ n Mäßigung f; **in ~** mit Maß[en]

modern /'mɒdn/ adj modern. ~ize vt modernisieren. ~ 'languages npl neuere Sprachen pl

modest /'mɒdɪst/ adj bescheiden; (decorous) schamhaft. ~y n Bescheidenheit f

modif|ication /mɒdɪfɪ'keɪʃn/ n Abänderung f. ~y vt (pt/pp -fied) abändern

module /'mɒdjuːl/ n Element nt; (of course) Kurseinheit f

moist /mɔɪst/ adj (-er, -est) feucht

moisten /'mɔɪsn/ vt befeuchten

moistur|e /'mɔɪstʃə(r)/ n Feuchtigkeit f. ~izer n Feuchtigkeitscreme f

molar /'məʊlə(r)/ n Backenzahn m

mole¹ /məʊl/ n Leberfleck m

mole² n (Zool) Maulwurf m

molecule /'mɒlɪkjuːl/ n Molekül nt

molest /mə'lest/ vt belästigen

mollify /'mɒlɪfaɪ/ vt (pt/pp -ied) besänftigen

mollycoddle /'mɒlɪkɒdl/ vt verzärteln

molten /'məʊltən/ adj geschmolzen

mom /mɒm/ n (Amer fam) Mutti f

moment /'məʊmənt/ n Moment m, Augenblick m; **at the ~** im Augenblick, augenblicklich. ~ary adj vorübergehend

momentous /mə'mentəs/ adj bedeutsam

momentum /mə'mentəm/ n Schwung m

monarch /'mɒnək/ n Monarch(in) m(f). ~y n Monarchie f

monastery /'mɒnəstrɪ/ n Kloster nt

Monday /'mʌndeɪ/ n Montag m

money /'mʌnɪ/ n Geld nt

money: ~-box n Sparbüchse f.

∼-lender n Geldverleiher m. **∼ order** n Zahlungsanweisung f

mongrel /'mʌŋgrəl/ n Promenaden-mischung f

monitor /'mɒnɪtə(r)/ n (Techn) Monitor m ● vt überwachen (progress); abhören (broadcast)

monk /mʌŋk/ n Mönch m

monkey /'mʌŋkɪ/ n Affe m

mono /'mɒnəʊ/ n Mono nt

monogram /'mɒnəgræm/ n Monogramm nt

monologue /'mɒnəlɒg/ n Monolog m

monopol|ize /mə'nɒpəlaɪz/ vt monopolisieren. **∼y** n Monopol nt

monosyllable /'mɒnəsɪləbl/ n einsilbiges Wort nt

monotone /'mɒnətəʊn/ n in a ∼ mit monotoner Stimme

monoton|ous /mə'nɒtənəs/ adj eintönig, monoton; (tedious) langweillig. **∼y** n Eintönigkeit f, Monotonie f

monster /'mɒnstə(r)/ n Ungeheuer nt; (cruel person) Unmensch m

monstrosity /mɒn'strɒsətɪ/ n Monstrosität f

monstrous /'mɒnstrəs/ adj ungeheuer; (outrageous) ungeheuerlich

month /mʌnθ/ n Monat m. **∼ly** adj & adv monatlich ● n (periodical) Monatszeitschrift f

monument /'mɒnjʊmənt/ n Denkmal nt. **∼al** adj (fig) monumental

moo /muː/ n Muh nt ● vi (pt/pp mooed) muhen

mood /muːd/ n Laune f; **be in a good/bad ∼** gute/schlechte Laune haben

moody /'muːdɪ/ adj launisch

moon /muːn/ n Mond m; **over the ∼** 🄵 überglücklich

moon: ∼light n Mondschein m. **∼lighting** n 🄵 ≈ Schwarzarbeit f. **∼lit** adj mondhell

moor[1] /mʊə(r)/ n Moor nt

moor[2] vt (Naut) festmachen ● vi anlegen

mop /mɒp/ n Mopp m; **∼ of hair** Wuschelkopf m ● vt (pt/pp mopped) wischen. **∼ up** vt aufwischen

moped /'məʊped/ n Moped nt

moral /'mɒrl/ adj moralisch, sittlich; (virtuous) tugendhaft ● n Moral f; **∼s** pl Moral f

morale /mə'rɑːl/ n Moral f

morality /mə'rælətɪ/ n Sittlichkeit f

morbid /'mɔːbɪd/ adj krankhaft; (gloomy) trübe

more /mɔː(r)/ a, adv & n mehr; (in addition) noch; **a few ∼** noch ein paar; **any ∼** noch etwas; **once ∼** noch einmal; **∼ or less** mehr oder weniger; **some ∼ tea?** noch etwas Tee? **∼ interesting** interessanter; **∼ [and ∼] quickly** [immer] schneller

moreover /mɔː'rəʊvə(r)/ adv außerdem

morgue /mɔːg/ n Leichenschauhaus nt

morning /'mɔːnɪŋ/ n Morgen m; **in the ∼** morgens, am Morgen; (tomorrow) morgen früh

Morocco /mə'rɒkəʊ/ n Marokko nt

moron /'mɔːrɒn/ n 🄵 Idiot m

morose /mə'rəʊs/ adj mürrisch

morsel /'mɔːsl/ n Happen m

mortal /'mɔːtl/ adj sterblich; (fatal) tödlich ● n Sterbliche(r) m/f. **∼ity** n Sterblichkeit f. **∼ly** adv tödlich

mortar /'mɔːtə(r)/ n Mörtel m

mortgage /'mɔːgɪdʒ/ n Hypothek f ● vt hypothekarisch belasten

mortuary /'mɔːtjʊərɪ/ n Leichenhalle f; (public) Leichenschauhaus nt; (Amer: undertaker's) Bestattungsinstitut nt

mosaic /məʊ'zeɪɪk/ n Mosaik nt

Moscow /'mɒskəʊ/ n Moskau nt

mosque /mɒsk/ n Moschee f

mosquito /mɒs'kiːtəʊ/ n (pl -es) [Stech]mücke f, Schnake f; (tropical) Moskito m

moss /mɒs/ n Moos nt. **∼y** adj moosig

most /məʊst/ adj der/die/das meiste; (majority) die meisten; **for the ∼ part** zum größten Teil ● adv am meisten; (very) höchst; **the ∼**

m

interesting day der interessanteste Tag; ~ **unlikely** höchst unwahrscheinlich ● *n* das meiste; ~ **of them** die meisten [von ihnen]; **at [the]** ~ höchstens; ~ **of the time** die meiste Zeit. ~**ly** *adv* meist

MOT *n* ≈ TÜV *m*

motel /məʊ'tel/ *n* Motel *nt*

moth /mɒθ/ *n* Nachtfalter *m*; [**clothes-**] ~ Motte *f*

'**mothball** *n* Mottenkugel *f*

mother /'mʌðə(r)/ *n* Mutter *f*

mother: ~**hood** *n* Mutterschaft *f*. ~**-in-law** *n* (*pl* ~**s-in-law**) Schwiegermutter *f*. ~**land** *n* Mutterland *nt*. ~**ly** *adj* mütterlich. ~**-of-pearl** *n* Perlmutter *f*. ~**-to-be** *n* werdende Mutter *f*

mothproof /'mɒθ-/ *adj* mottenfest

motif /məʊ'tiːf/ *n* Motiv *nt*

motion /'məʊʃn/ *n* Bewegung *f*; (*proposal*) Antrag *m*. ~**less** *adj* bewegungslos

motivat|e /'məʊtɪveɪt/ *vt* motivieren. ~**ion** *n* Motivation *f*

motive /'məʊtɪv/ *n* Motiv *nt*

motor /'məʊtə(r)/ *n* Motor *m*; (*car*) Auto *nt* ● *adj* Motor-; (*Anat*) motorisch ● *vi* [mit dem Auto] fahren

motor: ~ **bike** *n* 🅘 Motorrad *nt*. ~ **boat** *n* Motorboot *nt*. ~ **car** *n* Auto *nt*, Wagen *m*. ~ **cycle** *n* Motorrad *nt*. ~**-cyclist** *n* Motorradfahrer *m*. ~**ing** *n* Autofahren *nt*. ~**ist** *n* Autofahrer(in) *m*(*f*). ~ **vehicle** *n* Kraftfahrzeug *nt*. ~**way** *n* Autobahn *f*

mottled /'mɒtld/ *adj* gesprenkelt

motto /'mɒtəʊ/ *n* (*pl* **-es**) Motto *nt*

mould[1] /məʊld/ *n* (*fungus*) Schimmel *m*

mould[2] *n* Form *f* ● *vt* formen (**into** zu). ~**ing** *n* (*decorative*) Fries *m*

mouldy /'məʊldɪ/ *adj* schimmelig; (🅘: *worthless*) schäbig

mound /maʊnd/ *n* Hügel *m*; (*of stones*) Haufen *m*

mount *n* (*animal*) Reittier *nt*; (*of jewel*) Fassung *f*; (*of photo, picture*) Passepartout *nt* ● *vt* (*get on*) steigen auf (+ *acc*); (*on pedestal*) montieren

auf (+ *acc*); besteigen (*horse*); fassen (*jewel*); aufziehen (*photo, picture*) ● *vi* aufsteigen; (*tension:*) steigen. ~ **up** *vi* sich häufen; (*add up*) sich anhäufen

mountain /'maʊntɪn/ *n* Berg *m*

mountaineer /maʊntɪ'nɪə(r)/ *n* Bergsteiger(in) *m*(*f*). ~**ing** *n* Bergsteigen *nt*

mountainous /'maʊntɪnəs/ *adj* bergig, gebirgig

mourn /mɔːn/ *vt* betrauern ● *vi* trauern (**for** um). ~**er** *n* Trauernde(r) *m/f*. ~**ful** *adj* trauervoll. ~**ing** *n* Trauer *f*

mouse /maʊs/ *n* (*pl* **mice**) Maus *f*. ~**trap** *n* Mausefalle *f*

moustache /mə'stɑːʃ/ *n* Schnurrbart *m*

mouth[1] /maʊð/ *vt* ~ **sth** etw lautlos mit den Lippen sagen

mouth[2] /maʊθ/ *n* Mund *m*; (*of animal*) Maul *nt*; (*of river*) Mündung *f*

mouth: ~**ful** *n* Mundvoll *m*; (*bite*) Bissen *m*. ~**-organ** *n* Mundharmonika *f*. ~**wash** *n* Mundwasser *nt*

movable /'muːvəbl/ *adj* beweglich

move /muːv/ *n* Bewegung *f*; (*fig*) Schritt *m*; (*moving house*) Umzug *m*; (*in board game*) Zug *m*; **on the** ~ unterwegs; **get a** ~ **on** 🅘 sich beeilen ● *vt* bewegen; (*emotionally*) rühren; (*move along*) rücken; (*in board game*) ziehen; (*take away*) wegnehmen; wegfahren (*car*); (*rearrange*) umstellen; (*transfer*) versetzen (*person*); verlegen (*office*); (*propose*) beantragen; ~ **house** umziehen ● *vi* sich bewegen; (*move house*) umziehen; **don't** ~! stillhalten! (*stop*) stillstehen! ~ **along** *vt/i* weiterrücken. ~ **away** *vt/i* wegrücken; (*move house*) wegziehen. ~ **in** *vi* einziehen. ~ **off** *vi* (*vehicle:*) losfahren. ~ **out** *vi* ausziehen. ~ **over** *vt/i* [zur Seite] rücken. ~ **up** *vi* aufrücken

movement /'muːvmənt/ *n* Bewegung *f*; (*Mus*) Satz *m*; (*of clock*) Uhrwerk *nt*

movie /'muːvɪ/ *n* (*Amer*) Film *m*; **go to the** ~**s** ins Kino gehen

moving /'mu:vɪŋ/ adj beweglich; (*touching*) rührend

mow /məʊ/ vt (pt **mowed**, pp **mown** or **mowed**) mähen

mower /'məʊə(r)/ n Rasenmäher m

MP abbr **Member of Parliament**

Mr /'mɪstə(r)/ n (pl **Messrs**) Herr m

Mrs /'mɪsɪz/ n Frau f

Ms /mɪz/ n Frau f

much /mʌtʃ/ a, adv & n viel; **as ～ as** so viel wie; **～ loved** sehr geliebt

muck /mʌk/ n Mist m; (☐: *filth*) Dreck m. **～ about** vi herumalbern; (*tinker*) herumspielen (**with** mit). **～ out** vt ausmisten. **～ up** vt ☐ vermasseln; (*make dirty*) schmutzig machen

mucky /'mʌkɪ/ adj dreckig

mud /mʌd/ n Schlamm m

muddle /'mʌdl/ n Durcheinander nt; (*confusion*) Verwirrung f ● vt ～ **[up]** durcheinander bringen

muddy /'mʌdɪ/ adj schlammig; (*shoes*) schmutzig

'mudguard n Kotflügel m; (*on bicycle*) Schutzblech nt

muffle /'mʌfl/ vt dämpfen

muffler /'mʌflə(r)/ n Schal m; (*Amer, Auto*) Auspufftopf m

mug¹ /mʌg/ n Becher m; (*for beer*) Bierkrug m; (☐: *face*) Visage f; (☐: *simpleton*) Trottel m

mug² vt (pt/pp **mugged**) überfallen. **～ger** n Straßenräuber m. **～ging** n Straßenraub m

muggy /'mʌgɪ/ adj schwül

mule /mju:l/ n Maultier nt

mulled /mʌld/ adj **～ wine** Glühwein m

multi /'mʌltɪ/: **～coloured** adj vielfarbig, bunt. **～lingual** adj mehrsprachig. **～national** adj multinational

multiple /'mʌltɪpl/ adj vielfach; (*with pl*) mehrere ● n Vielfache(s) nt

multiplication /mʌltɪplɪ'keɪʃn/ n Multiplikation f

multiply /'mʌltɪplaɪ/ v (pt/pp -ied) ● vt multiplizieren (**by** mit) ● vi sich vermehren

multistorey adj **～ car park** Parkhaus nt

mum /mʌm/ n ☐ Mutti f

mumble /'mʌmbl/ vt/i murmeln

mummy¹ /'mʌmɪ/ n ☐ Mutti f

mummy² n (*Archaeology*) Mumie f

mumps /mʌmps/ n Mumps m

munch /mʌntʃ/ vt/i mampfen

municipal /mju:'nɪsɪpl/ adj städtisch

munitions /mju:'nɪʃnz/ npl Kriegsmaterial nt

mural /'mjʊərəl/ n Wandgemälde nt

murder /'mɜːdə(r)/ n Mord m ● vt ermorden. **～er** n Mörder m. **～ess** n Mörderin f. **～ous** adj mörderisch

murky /'mɜːkɪ/ adj düster

murmur /'mɜːmə(r)/ n Murmeln nt ● vt/i murmeln

muscle /'mʌsl/ n Muskel m

muscular /'mʌskjʊlə(r)/ adj Muskel-; (*strong*) muskulös

museum /mju:'zɪəm/ n Museum nt

mushroom /'mʌʃrʊm/ n [essbarer] Pilz m, esp Champignon m ● vi (*fig*) wie Pilze aus dem Boden schießen

mushy /'mʌʃɪ/ adj breiig

music /'mju:zɪk/ n Musik f; (*written*) Noten pl; **set to ～** vertonen

musical /'mju:zɪkl/ adj musikalisch ● n Musical nt. **～ box** n Spieldose f. **～ instrument** n Musikinstrument nt

musician /mju:'zɪʃn/ n Musiker(in) m(f)

'music-stand n Notenständer m

Muslim /'mʊzlɪm/ adj muslimisch ● n Muslim(in) m(f)

must /mʌst/ modal verb (nur Präsens) müssen; (*with negative*) dürfen ● n a **～** ☐ ein Muss nt

mustard /'mʌstəd/ n Senf m

musty /'mʌstɪ/ adj muffig

mute /mju:t/ adj stumm

mutilat|e /'mju:tɪleɪt/ vt verstümmeln. **～ion** n Verstümmelung f

mutin|ous /'mju:tɪnəs/ adj meuterisch. **～y** n Meuterei f ● vi (pt/pp -ied) meutern

m

mutter /'mʌtə(r)/ n Murmeln nt
● vt/i murmeln

mutton /'mʌtn/ n Hammelfleisch nt

mutual /'mjuːtjʊəl/ adj gegenseitig;
(🔲: common) gemeinsam. **~ly** adv
gegenseitig

muzzle /'mʌzl/ n (of animal)
Schnauze f; (of firearm) Mündung f;
(for dog) Maulkorb m

my /maɪ/ adj mein

myself /maɪ'self/ pron selbst; (reflexive) mich; **by ~** allein; **I thought to
~** ich habe mir gedacht

mysterious /mɪ'stɪərɪəs/ adj geheimnisvoll; (puzzling) mysteriös, rätselhaft

mystery /'mɪstərɪ/ n Geheimnis nt;
(puzzle) Rätsel nt; **~ [story]** Krimi m

mysti|c[al] /'mɪstɪk[l]/ adj mystisch.
~cism n Mystik f

mystified /'mɪstɪfaɪd/ adj **be ~** vor
einem Rätsel stehen

mystique /mɪ'stiːk/ n geheimnisvoller Zauber m

myth /mɪθ/ n Mythos m; (🔲: untruth) Märchen nt. **~ical** adj mythisch; (fig) erfunden

mythology /mɪ'θɒlədʒɪ/ n Mythologie f

Nn

nab /næb/ vt (pt/pp **nabbed**) 🔲 erwischen

nag¹ /næg/ n (horse) Gaul m

nag² vt/i (pp/pp **nagged**) herumnörgeln **(s.o.** an jdm)

nail /neɪl/ n (Anat, Techn) Nagel m;
on the ~ 🔲 sofort ● vt nageln (**to**
an + acc)

nail: ~-brush n Nagelbürste f.
~-file n Nagelfeile f. **~ scissors** npl
Nagelschere f. **~ varnish** n Nagellack m

naïve /naɪ'iːv/ adj naiv. **~ty** n Naivität f

naked /'neɪkɪd/ adj nackt; (flame)
offen; **with the ~ eye** mit bloßem
Auge. **~ness** n Nacktheit f

name /neɪm/ n Name m; (reputation)
Ruf m; **by ~** dem Namen nach; **by
the ~ of** namens; **call s.o. ~s** 🔲
jdn beschimpfen ● vt nennen; (give a
name to) einen Namen geben (+
dat); (announce publicly) den Namen
bekannt geben von. **~less** adj namenlos. **~ly** adv nämlich

name: ~-plate n Namensschild nt.
~sake n Namensvetter
m/Namensschwester f

nanny /'nænɪ/ n Kindermädchen nt

nap /næp/ n Nickerchen nt

napkin /'næpkɪn/ n Serviette f

nappy /'næpɪ/ n Windel f

narcotic /nɑːˈkɒtɪk/ n (drug) Rauschgift nt

narrat|e /nə'reɪt/ vt erzählen. **~ion**
n Erzählung f

narrative /'nærətɪv/ n Erzählung f

narrator /nə'reɪtə(r)/ n Erzähler(in)
m(f)

narrow /'nærəʊ/ adj (-er, -est)
schmal; (restricted) eng; (margin, majority) knapp; **have a ~ escape** mit
knapper Not davonkommen ● vi sich
verengen. **~-'minded** adj engstirnig

nasal /'neɪzl/ adj nasal; (Med & Anat)
Nasen-

nasty /'nɑːstɪ/ adj übel; (unpleasant)
unangenehm; (unkind) boshaft; (serious) schlimm

nation /'neɪʃn/ n Nation f; (people)
Volk nt

national /'næʃənl/ adj national;
(newspaper) überregional; (campaign)
landesweit ● n Staatsbürger(in) m(f)

national: ~ 'anthem n Nationalhymne f. **N~ 'Health Service** n
staatlicher Gesundheitsdienst m. **N~
In'surance** n Sozialversicherung f

nationalism /'næʃənəlɪzm/ n Nationalismus m

nationality /næʃə'nælətɪ/ n Staatsangehörigkeit f

national|ization
/næʃənəlaɪ'zeɪʃn/ n Verstaatlichung f.

~**ize** vt verstaatlichen

National Trust Eine Stiftung *i*
zur Erhaltung und Pflege von
Stätten von historischem Interesse
oder besonderen Naturschönhei-
ten. Der *National Trust* finanziert
sich aus Stiftungsgeldern und pri-
vaten Spenden und ist der größte
Privateigentümer von Land in
Großbritannien. Er hat riesige
Landflächen, Dörfer und Häuser ge-
kauft oder erhalten, von denen
viele öffentlich zugänglich sind.

native /'neɪtɪv/ adj einheimisch; (*innate*) angeboren ● n Eingeborene(r) m/f; (*local inhabitant*) Einheimische(r) m/f; **a ~ of Vienna** ein gebürtiger Wiener

native: ~ **'land** n Heimatland nt. ~ **'language** n Muttersprache f

natter /'nætə(r)/ vi 🗓 schwatzen

natural /'nætʃrəl/ adj natürlich; ~[-coloured] naturfarben

natural: ~ **'gas** n Erdgas nt. ~ **'history** n Naturkunde f

naturalist /'nætʃrəlɪst/ n Naturforscher m

natural|ization /nætʃrəlaɪ'zeɪʃn/ n Einbürgerung f. ~ize vt einbürgern

nature /'neɪtʃə(r)/ n Natur f; (*kind*) Art f; **by** ~ von Natur aus. ~ **reserve** n Naturschutzgebiet nt

naughty /'nɔːtɪ/ adj , -ily adv unartig; (*slightly indecent*) gewagt

nausea /'nɔːzɪə/ n Übelkeit f

nautical /'nɔːtɪkl/ adj nautisch. ~ **mile** n Seemeile f

naval /'neɪvl/ adj Marine-

nave /neɪv/ n Kirchenschiff nt

navel /'neɪvl/ n Nabel m

navigable /'nævɪgəbl/ adj schiffbar

navigat|e /'nævɪgeɪt/ vi navigieren ● vt befahren (*river*). ~**ion** n Navigation f

navy /'neɪvɪ/ n [Kriegs]marine f ● adj ~ **[blue]** marineblau

near /nɪə(r)/ adj (-er, -est) nah[e]; **the** ~**est bank** die nächste Bank ● adv nahe; **draw** ~ sich nähern

● prep nahe an (+ dat/acc); in der Nähe von

near: ~**by** adj nahe gelegen, nahe liegend. ~**ly** adv fast, beinahe; **not** ~**ly** bei weitem nicht. ~**ness** n Nähe f. ~ **side** n Beifahrerseite f. ~**-sighted** adj (*Amer*) kurzsichtig

neat /niːt/ adj (-er, -est) adrett; (*tidy*) ordentlich; (*clever*) geschickt; (*undiluted*) pur. ~**ness** n Ordentlichkeit f

necessarily /'nesəsərəlɪ/ adv notwendigerweise; **not** ~ nicht unbedingt

necessary /'nesəsərɪ/ adj nötig, notwendig

necessit|ate /nɪ'sesɪteɪt/ vt notwendig machen. ~**y** n Notwendigkeit f; **work from** ~**y** arbeiten, weil man es nötig hat

neck /nek/ n Hals m; ~ **and** ~ Kopf an Kopf

necklace /'neklɪs/ n Halskette f

neckline n Halsausschnitt m

née /neɪ/ adj ~ X geborene X

need /niːd/ n Bedürfnis nt; (*misfortune*) Not f; **be in** ~ **of** brauchen; **in case of** ~ notfalls; **if** ~ **be** wenn nötig; **there is a** ~ **for** es besteht ein Bedarf an (+ dat); **there is no** ~ **for that** das ist nicht nötig ● vt brauchen; **you** ~ **not go** du brauchst nicht zu gehen; ~ **I come?** muss ich kommen? **I** ~ **to know** ich muss es wissen

needle /'niːdl/ n Nadel f

needless /'niːdlɪs/ adj unnötig; ~ **to say** selbstverständlich, natürlich

'needlework n Nadelarbeit f

needy /'niːdɪ/ adj bedürftig

negation /nɪ'geɪʃn/ n Verneinung f

negative /'negətɪv/ adj negativ ● n Verneinung f; (*photo*) Negativ nt

neglect /nɪ'glekt/ n Vernachlässigung f ● vt vernachlässigen; (*omit*) versäumen (**to** zu). ~**ed** adj verwahrlost. ~**ful** adj nachlässig

negligen|ce /'neglɪdʒəns/ n Nachlässigkeit f. ~**t** adj nachlässig

negligible /'neglɪdʒəbl/ *adj* unbedeutend

negotiat|e /nɪ'gəʊʃɪeɪt/ *vt* aushandeln; (*Auto*) nehmen (*bend*) ● *vi* verhandeln. **~ion** *n* Verhandlung *f*. **~or** *n* Unterhändler(in) *m(f)*

Negro /'niːɡrəʊ/ *adj* Neger- ● *n* (*pl* -es) Neger *m*

neigh /neɪ/ *vi* wiehern

neighbour /'neɪbə(r)/ *n* Nachbar(in) *m(f)*. **~hood** *n* Nachbarschaft *f*. **~ing** *adj* Nachbar-. **~ly** *adj* [gut]-nachbarlich

neither /'naɪðə(r)/ *adj & pron* keine(r, s) [von beiden] ● *adv* **~... nor** weder ... noch ● *conj* auch nicht

neon /'niːɒn/ *n* Neon *nt*

nephew /'nevjuː/ *n* Neffe *m*

nepotism /'nepətɪzm/ *n* Vetternwirtschaft *f*

nerve /nɜːv/ *n* Nerv *m*; (🗊: *courage*) Mut *m*; (🗊: *impudence*) Frechheit *f*. **~-racking** *adj* nervenaufreibend

nervous /'nɜːvəs/ *adj* (*afraid*) ängstlich; (*highly strung*) nervös; (*Anat, Med*) Nerven-. **~ 'breakdown** *n* Nervenzusammenbruch *m*. **~ness** Ängstlichkeit *f*

nervy /'nɜːvɪ/ *adj* nervös; (*Amer: impudent*) frech

nest /nest/ *n* Nest *nt* ● *vi* nisten

nestle /'nesl/ *vi* sich schmiegen (**against** an + *acc*)

net[1] /net/ *n* Netz *nt*; (*curtain*) Store *m*

net[2] *adj* netto; (*salary, weight*) Netto-

'netball *n* ≈ Korbball *m*

Netherlands /'neðələndz/ *npl* the **~** die Niederlande *pl*

nettle /'netl/ *n* Nessel *f*

'network *n* Netz *nt*

neurolog|ist /njʊə'rɒlədʒɪst/ *n* Neurologe *m*/ -gin *f*. **~y** *n* Neurologie *f*

neur|osis /njʊə'rəʊsɪs/ *n* (*pl* -oses /-siːz/) Neurose *f*. **~otic** *adj* neurotisch

neuter /'njuːtə(r)/ *adj* (*Gram*) sächlich ● *n* (*Gram*) Neutrum *nt* ● *vt* kastrieren; (*spay*) sterilisieren

neutral /'njuːtrl/ *adj* neutral ● *n* in **~** (*Auto*) im Leerlauf. **~ity** *n* Neutralität *f*

never /'nevə(r)/ *adv* nie, niemals; (🗊: *not*) nicht; **~ mind** macht nichts; **well I ~!** ja so was! **~-ending** *adj* endlos

nevertheless /nevəðə'les/ *adv* dennoch, trotzdem

new /njuː/ *adj* (-er, -est) neu

new: ~comer *n* Neuankömmling *m*. **~fangled** /-'fæŋgld/ *adj* (*pej*) neumodisch. **~-laid** *adj* frisch gelegt

'newly *adv* frisch. **~-weds** *npl* Jungverheiratete *pl*

new: ~ 'moon *n* Neumond *m*. **~ness** *n* Neuheit *f*

news /njuːz/ *n* Nachricht *f*; (*Radio, TV*) Nachrichten *pl*; **piece of ~** Neuigkeit *f*

news: ~agent *n* Zeitungshändler *m*. **~ bulletin** *n* Nachrichtensendung *f*. **~letter** *n* Mitteilungsblatt *nt*. **~paper** *n* Zeitung *f*; (*material*) Zeitungspapier *nt*. **~reader** *n* Nachrichtensprecher(in) *m(f)*

New: ~ Year's 'Day *n* Neujahr *nt*. **~ Year's 'Eve** *n* Silvester *nt*. **~ Zealand** /'ziːlənd/ *n* Neuseeland *nt*

next /nekst/ *adj & n* nächste(r, s); **who's ~?** wer kommt als Nächster dran? **the ~ best** das nächstbeste; **~ door** nebenan; **my ~ of kin** mein nächster Verwandter; **~ to nothing** fast gar nichts; **the week after ~** übernächste Woche ● *adv* als Nächstes; **~ to** neben

nib /nɪb/ *n* Feder *f*

nibble /'nɪbl/ *vt/i* knabbern (**at** an + *dat*)

nice /naɪs/ *adj* (-r, -st) nett; (*day, weather*) schön; (*food*) gut; (*distinction*) fein. **~ly** *adv* nett; (*well*) gut

niche /niːʃ/ *n* Nische *f*; (*fig*) Platz *m*

nick /nɪk/ *n* Kerbe *f*; (🗊: *prison*) Knast *m*; (🗊: *police station*) Revier *nt*; **in good ~** 🗊 in gutem Zustand ● *vt* einkerben; (*steal*) klauen; (🗊: *arrest*) schnappen

nickel /'nɪkl/ *n* Nickel *nt*; (*Amer*) Fünfcentstück *nt* '**nickname** n Spitzname m

nicotine /'nɪkəti:n/ n Nikotin nt

niece /ni:s/ n Nichte f

Nigeria /naɪ'dʒɪərɪə/ n Nigeria nt.
~**n** adj nigerianisch ● n Nigeria-
ner(in) m(f)

night /naɪt/ n Nacht f; (evening)
Abend m; **at** ~ nachts

night: ~-**club** n Nachtklub m.
~-**dress** n Nachthemd nt. ~**fall** n **at**
~**fall** bei Einbruch der Dunkelheit.
~-**gown** n, 🔲 ~**ie** /'naɪti/ n Nachthemd nt

nightingale /'naɪtɪŋgeɪl/ n Nachtigall f

night: ~-**life** n Nachtleben nt. ~**ly**
adj nächtlich ● adv jede Nacht.
~**mare** n Albtraum m. ~-**time** n **at**
~-**time** bei Nacht

nil /nɪl/ n null

nimble /'nɪmbl/ adj (-r, -st), -**bly** adv
flink

nine /naɪn/ adj neun ● n Neun f.
~'**teen** adj neunzehn. ~'**teenth** adj
neunzehnte(r, s)

ninetieth /'naɪntɪɪθ/ adj neunzig-
ste(r, s)

ninety /'naɪntɪ/ adj neunzig

ninth /naɪnθ/ adj neunte(r, s)

nip /nɪp/ vt kneifen; (bite) beißen; ~
in the bud (fig) im Keim ersticken
● vi (🔲: run) laufen

nipple /'nɪpl/ n Brustwarze f; (Amer:
on bottle) Sauger m

nitwit /'nɪtwɪt/ n 🔲 Dummkopf m

no /nəʊ/ adv nein ● n (pl **noes**) Nein
nt ● adj kein(e); (pl) keine; **in no**
time [sehr] schnell; **no parking/**
smoking Parken/Rauchen verboten;
no one = nobody

nobility /nəʊ'bɪlətɪ/ n Adel m

noble /'nəʊbl/ adj (-r, -st) edel; (aris-
tocratic) adlig. ~**man** n Adlige(r) m

nobody /'nəʊbədɪ/ pron niemand,
keiner ● n **a** ~ ein Niemand m

nocturnal /nɒk'tɜ:nl/ adj nächtlich;
(animal, bird) Nacht-

nod /nɒd/ n Nicken nt ● v (pt/pp
nodded) ● vi nicken ● vt ~ **one's**
head mit dem Kopf nicken

noise /nɔɪz/ n Geräusch nt; (loud)
Lärm m. ~**less** adj geräuschlos

noisy /'nɔɪzɪ/ adj , -**ily** adv laut;
(eater) geräuschvoll

nomad /'nəʊmæd/ n Nomade m.
~**ic** adj nomadisch; (life, tribe)
Nomaden-

nominal /'nɒmɪnl/ adj nominell

nominat|e /'nɒmɪneɪt/ vt nominie-
ren, aufstellen; (appoint) ernennen.
~**ion** n Nominierung f; Ernennung f

nominative /'nɒmɪnətɪv/ adj & n
(Gram) ~[**case**] Nominativ m

nonchalant /'nɒnʃələnt/ adj nonchalant; (gesture) lässig

nondescript /'nɒndɪskrɪpt/ adj un-
bestimmbar; (person) unscheinbar

none /nʌn/ pron keine(r)/keins; ~ **of**
it/this nichts davon ● adv ~ **too**
nicht gerade; ~ **too soon** [um]
keine Minute zu früh; ~ **the less**
dennoch

nonentity /nɒ'nentətɪ/ n Null f

non-ex'istent adj nicht vorhanden

non-'fiction n Sachliteratur f

nonplussed /nɒn'plʌst/ adj verblüfft

nonsens|e /'nɒnsəns/ n Unsinn m.
~**ical** adj unsinnig

non-'smoker n Nichtraucher m

non-'stop adv ununterbrochen; (fly)
nonstop

non-'swimmer n Nichtschwimmer m

non-'violent adj gewaltlos

noodles /'nu:dlz/ npl Bandnudeln pl

noon /nu:n/ n Mittag m; **at** ~ um
12 Uhr mittags

noose /nu:s/ n Schlinge f

nor /nɔ:(r)/ adv noch ● conj auch
nicht

Nordic /'nɔ:dɪk/ adj nordisch

norm /nɔ:m/ n Norm f

normal /'nɔ:ml/ adj normal. ~**ity** n
Normalität f. ~**ly** adv normal; (usually) normalerweise

north /nɔ:θ/ n Norden m; **to the** ~
of nördlich von ● adj Nord-, nord-
● adv nach Norden

n

north: N~ America n Nordamerika nt. **~-east** adj Nordost-● n Nordosten m

norther|ly /'nɔːðəlɪ/ adj nördlich. **~n** adj nördlich. **N~n Ireland** n Nordirland nt

north: N~ 'Pole n Nordpol m. **N~ 'Sea** n Nordsee f. **~ward[s]** /-wəd[z]/ adv nach Norden. **~-west** adj Nordwest-● n Nordwesten m

Nor|way /'nɔːweɪ/ n Norwegen nt. **~wegian** adj norwegisch ● n Norweger(in) m(f)

nose /nəʊz/ n Nase

'nosebleed n Nasenbluten nt

nostalg|ia /nɒ'stældʒɪə/ n Nostalgie f. **~ic** adj nostalgisch

nostril /'nɒstrəl/ n Nasenloch nt

nosy /'nəʊzɪ/ adj 🗉 neugierig

---

not /nɒt/
● adverb
····▸ nicht. **I don't know** ich weiß nicht. **isn't she pretty?** ist sie nicht hübsch?
····▸ **not a** kein. **he is not a doctor** er ist kein Arzt. **she didn't wear a hat** sie trug keinen Hut. **there was not a person to be seen** es gab keinen Menschen zu sehen. **not a thing** gar nichts. **not a bit** kein bisschen
····▸ (in elliptical phrases) **I hope not** ich hoffe nicht. **of course not** natürlich nicht. **not at all** überhaupt nicht; (in polite reply to thanks) keine Ursache; gern geschehen. **certainly not!** auf keinen Fall! **not I** ich nicht
····▸ **not ... but ...** nicht ... sondern .... **it was not a small town but a big one** es war keine kleine Stadt, sondern eine große

---

notab|le /'nəʊtəbl/ adj bedeutend; (remarkable) bemerkenswert. **~ly** adv insbesondere

notation /nəʊ'teɪʃn/ n Notation f; (Mus) Notenschrift f

notch /nɒtʃ/ n Kerbe f

note /nəʊt/ n (written comment) Notiz f, Anmerkung f; (short letter) Briefchen nt, Zettel m; (bank ~) Banknote f, Schein m; (Mus) Note f; (sound) Ton m; (on piano) Taste f; **half/whole ~** (Amer) halbe/ganze Note f; **of ~** von Bedeutung; **make a ~ of** notieren ● vt beachten; (notice) bemerken (**that** dass)

'notebook n Notizbuch nt

noted /'nəʊtɪd/ adj bekannt (**for** für)

note: ~paper n Briefpapier nt. **~worthy** adj beachtenswert

nothing /'nʌθɪŋ/ n, pron & adv nichts; **for ~** umsonst; **~ but** nichts als; **~ much** nicht viel; **~ interesting** nichts Interessantes

notice /'nəʊtɪs/ n (on board) Anschlag m, Bekanntmachung f; (announcement) Anzeige f; (review) Kritik f; (termination of lease, employment) Kündigung f; **give [in one's] ~** kündigen; **give s.o. ~** jdm kündigen; **take no ~!** ignoriere es! ● vt bemerken. **~able** /-əbl/, adj, **-bly** adv merklich. **~-board** n Anschlagbrett nt

noti|fication /nəʊtɪfɪ'keɪʃn/ n Benachrichtigung f. **~fy** vt (pt/pp -ied) benachrichtigen

notion /'nəʊʃn/ n Idee f

notorious /nəʊ'tɔːrɪəs/ adj berüchtigt

notwith'standing prep trotz (+ gen) ● adv trotzdem, dennoch

nought /nɔːt/ n Null f

noun /naʊn/ n Substantiv nt

nourish /'nʌrɪʃ/ vt nähren. **~ing** adj nahrhaft. **~ment** n Nahrung f

novel /'nɒvl/ adj neu[artig] ● n Roman m. **~ist** n Romanschriftsteller(in) m(f). **~ty** n Neuheit f

November /nəʊ'vembə(r)/ n November m

novice /'nɒvɪs/ n Neuling m; (Relig) Novize m/Novizin f

now /naʊ/ adv & conj jetzt; **~ [that]** jetzt, wo; **just ~** gerade, eben; **right ~** sofort; **~ and again** hin und wieder; **now, now!** na, na!

'nowadays adv heutzutage

nowhere /'nəʊ-/ adv nirgendwo, nirgends

nozzle /'nɒzl/ n Düse f

nuance /'nju:ɑ̃s/ n Nuance f

nuclear /'nju:klɪə(r)/ adj Kern-. ~ de'terrent n nukleares Abschreckungsmittel nt

nucleus /'nju:klɪəs/ n (pl -lei /-lɪaɪ/) Kern m

nude /nju:d/ adj nackt ● n (Art) Akt m; **in the** ~ nackt

nudge /nʌdʒ/ vt stupsen

nud|ist /'nju:dɪst/ n Nudist m. ~ity n Nacktheit f

nuisance /'nju:sns/ n Ärgernis nt; (pest) Plage f; **be a** ~ ärgerlich sein

null /nʌl/ adj ~ **and void** null und nichtig

numb /nʌm/ adj gefühllos, taub ● vt betäuben

number /'nʌmbə(r)/ n Nummer f; (amount) Anzahl f; (Math) Zahl f ● vt nummerieren; (include) zählen (among zu). ~-**plate** n Nummernschild nt

numeral /'nju:mərl/ n Ziffer f

numerical /nju:'merɪkl/ adj numerisch; **in** ~ **order** zahlenmäßig geordnet

numerous /'nju:mərəs/ adj zahlreich

nun /nʌn/ n Nonne f

nurse /nɜ:s/ n [Kranken]schwester f; (male) Krankenpfleger m; **children's** ~ Kindermädchen nt ● vt pflegen

nursery /'nɜ:sərɪ/ n Kinderzimmer nt; (for plants) Gärtnerei f; [**day**] ~ Kindertagesstätte f. ~ **rhyme** n Kinderreim m. ~ **school** n Kindergarten m

nursing /'nɜ:sɪŋ/ n Krankenpflege f. ~ **home** n Pflegeheim nt

nut /nʌt/ n Nuss f; (Techn) [Schrauben]mutter f; (🄸: head) Birne f 🄸; **be** ~s 🄸 spinnen 🄸. ~**crackers** npl Nussknacker m. ~**meg** n Muskat m

nutrient /'nju:trɪənt/ n Nährstoff m

nutrit|ion /nju:'trɪʃn/ n Ernährung f. ~**ious** adj nahrhaft

'nutshell n Nussschale f; **in a** ~ (fig) kurz gesagt

nylon /'naɪlɒn/ n Nylon nt

Oo

O /əʊ/ n (Teleph) null

oak /əʊk/ n Eiche f

OAP abbr (**old-age pensioner**) Rentner(in) m(f)

oar /ɔ:(r)/ n Ruder nt. ~**sman** n Ruderer m

oasis /əʊ'eɪsɪs/ n (pl **oases** /-si:z/) Oase f

oath /əʊθ/ n Eid m; (swear-word) Fluch m

oatmeal /'əʊt-/ n Hafermehl nt

oats /əʊts/ npl Hafer m; (Culin) [**rolled**] ~ Haferflocken pl

obedien|ce /ə'bi:dɪəns/ n Gehorsam m. ~**t** adj gehorsam

obey /ə'beɪ/ vt/i gehorchen (+ dat); befolgen (instructions, rules)

obituary /ə'bɪtjʊərɪ/ n Nachruf m; (notice) Todesanzeige f

object¹ /'ɒbdʒɪkt/ n Gegenstand m; (aim) Zweck m; (intention) Absicht f; (Gram) Objekt nt; **money is no** ~ Geld spielt keine Rolle

object² /əb'dʒekt/ vi Einspruch erheben (to gegen); (be against) etwas dagegen haben

objection /əb'dʒekʃn/ n Einwand m; **have no** ~ nichts dagegen haben. ~**able** adj anstößig; (person) unangenehm

objectiv|e /əb'dʒektɪv/ adj objektiv ● n Ziel nt. ~**ity** n Objektivität f

objector /əb'dʒektə(r)/ n Gegner m

obligation /ɒblɪ'geɪʃn/ n Pflicht f; **without** ~ unverbindlich

obligatory /ə'blɪgətrɪ/ adj obligatorisch; **be** ~ Vorschrift sein

oblig|e /ə'blaɪdʒ/ vt verpflichten; (compel) zwingen; (do a small service) einen Gefallen tun (+ dat). ~**ing** adj entgegenkommend

oblique /ə'bli:k/ adj schräg; (angle)

schief; (*fig*) indirekt

obliterate /ə'blɪtəreɪt/ *vt* auslöschen

oblivion /ə'blɪvɪən/ *n* Vergessenheit *f*

oblivious /ə'blɪvɪəs/ *adj* be ~ sich (*dat*) nicht bewusst sein (**of** *gen*)

oblong /'ɒblɒŋ/ *adj* rechteckig ● *n* Rechteck *nt*

obnoxious /əb'nɒkʃəs/ *adj* widerlich

oboe /'əʊbəʊ/ *n* Oboe *f*

obscen|e /əb'siːn/ *adj* obszön. ~**ity** *n* Obszönität *f*

obscur|e /əb'skjʊə(r)/ *adj* dunkel; (*unknown*) unbekannt ● *vt* verdecken; (*confuse*) verwischen. ~**ity** *n* Dunkelheit *f*; Unbekanntheit *f*

observa|nce /əb'zɜːvns/ *n* (*of custom*) Einhaltung *f*. ~**nt** *adj* aufmerksam. ~**tion** *n* Beobachtung *f*; (*remark*) Bemerkung *f*

observatory /əb'zɜːvətrɪ/ *n* Sternwarte *f*

observe /əb'zɜːv/ *vt* beobachten; (*say, notice*) bemerken; (*keep, celebrate*) feiern; (*obey*) einhalten. ~**r** *n* Beobachter *m*

obsess /əb'ses/ *vt* be ~**ed by** besessen sein von. ~**ion** *n* Besessenheit *f*; (*persistent idea*) fixe Idee *f*. ~**ive** *adj* zwanghaft

obsolete /'ɒbsəliːt/ *adj* veraltet

obstacle /'ɒbstəkl/ *n* Hindernis *nt*

obstina|cy /'ɒbstɪnəsɪ/ *n* Starrsinn *m*. ~**te** *adj* starrsinnig; (*refusal*) hartnäckig

obstruct /əb'strʌkt/ *vt* blockieren; (*hinder*) behindern. ~**ion** *n* Blockierung *f*; Behinderung *f*; (*obstacle*) Hindernis *nt*. ~**ive** *adj* be ~**ive** Schwierigkeiten bereiten

obtain /əb'teɪn/ *vt* erhalten. ~**able** *adj* erhältlich

obtrusive /əb'truːsɪv/ *adj* aufdringlich; (*thing*) auffällig

obtuse /əb'tjuːs/ *adj* begriffsstutzig

obvious /'ɒbvɪəs/ *adj* offensichtlich, offenbar

occasion /ə'keɪʒn/ *n* Gelegenheit *f*;

(*time*) Mal *nt*; (*event*) Ereignis *nt*; (*cause*) Anlass *m*, Grund *m*; **on the** ~ **of** anlässlich (+ *gen*)

occasional /ə'keɪʒǝnl/ *adj* gelegentlich. ~**ly** *adv* gelegentlich, hin und wieder

occult /ɒ'kʌlt/ *adj* okkult

occupant /'ɒkjʊpənt/ *n* Bewohner(in) *m*(*f*); (*of vehicle*) Insasse *m*

occupation /ɒkjʊ'peɪʃn/ *n* Beschäftigung *f*; (*job*) Beruf *m*; (*Mil*) Besetzung *f*; (*period*) Besatzung *f*. ~**al** *adj* Berufs-. ~**al therapy** *n* Beschäftigungstherapie *f*

occupier /'ɒkjʊpaɪə(r)/ *n* Bewohner(in) *m*(*f*)

occupy /'ɒkjʊpaɪ/ *vt* (*pt/pp* occupied) besetzen (*seat*, (*Mil*) *country*); einnehmen (*space*); in Anspruch nehmen (*time*); (*live in*) bewohnen; (*fig*) bekleiden (*office*); (*keep busy*) beschäftigen

occur /ə'kɜː(r)/ *vi* (*pt/pp* occurred) geschehen; (*exist*) vorkommen, auftreten; **it** ~**red to me that** es fiel mir ein, dass. ~**rence** *n* Auftreten *nt*; (*event*) Ereignis *nt*

ocean /'əʊʃn/ *n* Ozean *m*

o'clock /ə'klɒk/ *adv* [**at**] 7 ~ [um] 7 Uhr

octagonal /ɒk'tægənl/ *adj* achteckig

October /ɒk'təʊbə(r)/ *n* Oktober *m*

octopus /'ɒktəpəs/ *n* (*pl* -puses) Tintenfisch *m*

odd /ɒd/ *adj* (-er, -est) seltsam, merkwürdig; (*number*) ungerade; (*not of set*) einzeln; **forty** ~ über vierzig; ~ **jobs** Gelegenheitsarbeiten *pl*; **the** ~ **one out** die Ausnahme; **at** ~ **moments** zwischendurch

odd|ity /'ɒdɪtɪ/ *n* Kuriosität *f*. ~**ly** *adv* merkwürdig; ~**ly enough** merkwürdigerweise ~**ment** *n* (*of fabric*) Rest *m*

odds /ɒdz/ *npl* (*chances*) Chancen *pl*; **at** ~ uneinig; ~ **and ends** Kleinkram *m*

ode /əʊd/ *n* Ode *f*

odious /'əʊdɪəs/ *adj* widerlich

odour /ˈəʊdə(r)/ n Geruch m. ~less adj geruchlos

---

of /ɒv/, unbetont /əv/

● preposition

····➤ (indicating belonging, origin) von (+ dat); genitive. **the mother of twins** die Mutter von Zwillingen. **the mother of the twins** die Mutter der Zwillinge or von den Zwillingen. **the Queen of England** die Königin von England. **a friend of mine** ein Freund von mir. **a friend of the teacher's** ein Freund des Lehrers. **the brother of her father** der Bruder ihres Vaters. **the works of Shakespeare** Shakespeares Werke. **it was nice of him** es war nett von ihm

····➤ (made of) aus (+ dat). **a dress of cotton** ein Kleid aus Baumwolle

····➤ (following number) **five of us** fünf von uns. **the two of us** wir zwei. **there were four of us waiting** wir waren vier, die warteten

····➤ (followed by number, description) von (+ dat). **a girl of ten** ein Mädchen von zehn Jahren. **a distance of 50 miles** eine Entfernung von 50 Meilen. **a man of character** ein Mann von Charakter. **a woman of exceptional beauty** eine Frau von außerordentlicher Schönheit. **a person of strong views** ein Mensch mit festen Ansichten

---

! **of** is not translated after
■ measures and in some other cases: **a pound of apples** ein Pfund Äpfel; **a cup of tea** eine Tasse Tee; **a glass of wine** ein Glas Wein; **the city of Chicago** die Stadt Chicago; **the fourth of January** der vierte Januar

---

off /ɒf/ prep von (+ dat); ~ **the coast** vor der Küste; **get** ~ **the ladder/bus** von der Leiter/aus dem Bus steigen

● adv weg; (button, lid, handle) ab; (light) aus; (brake) los; (machine) abgeschaltet; (tap) zu; (on appliance) **'off'** 'aus'; **2 kilometres** ~ 2 Kilometer entfernt; **a long way** ~ weit weg; (time) noch lange hin; ~ **and on** hin und wieder; **with his hat/coat** ~ ohne Hut/Mantel; **20%** ~ 20% Nachlass; **be** ~ (leave) [weg]gehen; (Sport) starten; (food:) schlecht sein; **be well** ~ gut dran sein; (financially) wohlhabend sein; **have a day** ~ einen freien Tag haben

offal /ˈɒfl/ n (Culin) Innereien pl

---

off-Broadway Off-Broadway ist eine Bezeichnung für das nichtkommerzielle amerikanische Theater. Diese experimentale Gegenrichtung mit kleineren Truppen und Bühnen gewann nach 1952 an Bedeutung. Viele junge Intendanten sind nicht an kommerziellen Aufführungen interessiert, und ihre Inszenierungen finden in alten Lagerhäusern abseits des Broadway, der großen New Yorker Theaterstraße, statt.

---

offence /əˈfens/ n (illegal act) Vergehen nt; **give/take** ~ Anstoß erregen/nehmen (**at** an + dat)

offend /əˈfend/ vt beleidigen. ~**er** n (Jur) Straftäter m

offensive /əˈfensɪv/ adj anstößig; (Mil, Sport) offensiv ● n Offensive f

offer /ˈɒfə(r)/ n Angebot nt; **on (special)** ~ im Sonderangebot ● vt anbieten (**to** dat); leisten (resistance); ~ **to do sth** sich anbieten, etw zu tun. ~**ing** n Gabe f

off'hand adj brüsk; (casual) lässig

office /ˈɒfɪs/ n Büro nt; (post) Amt nt

officer /ˈɒfɪsə(r)/ n Offizier m; (official) Beamte(r) m/ Beamtin f; (police) Polizeibeamte(r) m/-beamtin f

official /əˈfɪʃl/ adj offiziell, amtlich ● n Beamte(r) m/ Beamtin f; (Sport) Funktionär m. ~**ly** adv offiziell

officious /əˈfɪʃəs/ adj übereifrig

'off-licence n Wein- und Spirituosenhandlung f

off-licence Ein britischer Wein- und Spirituosenladen, der eine Konzession für den Verkauf alkoholischer Getränke hat. *Off-licence*-Läden haben längere Öffnungszeiten als andere Geschäfte und bleiben geöffnet, wenn Bars und Wirtshäuser geschlossen sind. Sie verkaufen auch alkoholfreie Getränke, Süßigkeiten und Tabakwaren und verleihen Gläser für Partys. *i*

off-'load vt ausladen

'off-putting adj 🔟 abstoßend

off'set vt (*pt/pp* -set, *pres p* -setting) ausgleichen

'offshoot n Schössling m; (*fig*) Zweig m

'offshore adj (*oil field*) im Meer; (*breeze*) vom Land kommend ● adv im/ins Ausland

off'side adj (*Sport*) abseits

off'stage adv hinter den Kulissen

off-'white adj fast weiß

often /ˈɒfn/ adv oft; **every so ~** von Zeit zu Zeit

oh /əʊ/ int oh! ach! **oh dear!** o weh!

oil /ɔɪl/ n Öl nt; (*petroleum*) Erdöl nt ● vt ölen

oil: ~field n Ölfeld nt. **~-painting** n Ölgemälde nt. **~ refinery** n [Erd]ölraffinerie f. **~-tanker** n Öltanker m. **~ well** n Ölquelle f

oily /ˈɔɪlɪ/ adj ölig

ointment /ˈɔɪntmənt/ n Salbe f

OK /əʊˈkeɪ/ adj & int 🔟 in Ordnung; okay ● adv (*well*) gut ● vt (*auch* **okay**) (*pt/pp* **okayed**) genehmigen

old /əʊld/ adj (-er, -est) alt; (*former*) ehemalig

old: ~ 'age n Alter nt. **~-age 'pensioner** n Rentner(in) m(f). **~ boy** n ehemaliger Schüler. **~-'fashioned** adj altmodisch. **~ girl** ehemalige Schülerin f

olive /ˈɒlɪv/ n Olive f; (*colour*) Oliv nt ● adj olivgrün. **~ 'oil** n Olivenöl nt

Olympic /əˈlɪmpɪk/ adj olympisch ● n **the ~s** die Olympischen Spiele pl

omelette /ˈɒmlɪt/ n Omelett nt

ominous /ˈɒmɪnəs/ adj bedrohlich

omission /əˈmɪʃn/ n Auslassung f; (*failure to do*) Unterlassung f

omit /əˈmɪt/ vt (*pt/pp* **omitted**) auslassen; **~ to do sth** es unterlassen, etw zu tun

omnipotent /ɒmˈnɪpətənt/ adj allmächtig

on /ɒn/ prep auf (+ dat/(*on to*) + acc); (*on vertical surface*) an (+ dat/(*on to*) + acc); (*about*) über (+ acc); **on Monday** [am] Montag; **on Mondays** montags; **on the first of May** am ersten Mai; **on arriving** als ich ankam; **on one's finger** am Finger; **on the right/left** rechts/links; **on the Rhine** am Rhein; **on the radio/television** im Radio/Fernsehen; **on the bus/train** im Bus/Zug; **go on the bus/train** mit dem Bus/Zug fahren; **on me** (*with me*) bei mir; **it's on me** 🔟 das spendiere ich ● adv (*further on*) weiter; (*switched on*) an; (*brake*) angezogen; (*machine*) angeschaltet; (*on appliance*) 'on' 'ein'; **with/without his hat/coat on** mit/ohne Hut/Mantel; **be on** (*film:*) laufen; (*event:*) stattfinden; **be on at** 🔟 bedrängen (**zu** to); **It's not on** 🔟 das geht nicht; **on and on** immer weiter; **on and off** hin und wieder; **and so on** und so weiter

once /wʌns/ adv einmal; (*formerly*) früher; **at ~** sofort; (*at the same time*) gleichzeitig; **~ and for all** ein für alle Mal ● conj wenn; (*with past tense*) als

'oncoming adj **~ traffic** Gegenverkehr m

one /wʌn/ adj ein(e); (*only*) einzig; **not ~** kein(e); **~ day/evening** eines Tages/Abends ● n Eins f ● pron eine(r)/eins; (*impersonal*) man; **which ~** welche(r,s); **~ another** einander; **~ by ~** einzeln; **~ never knows** man kann nie wissen

one: ~-parent 'family n Einelternfamilie f. **~'self** pron selbst; (*reflexive*) sich; **by ~self** allein. **~-sided** adj einseitig. **~-way** adj (*street*) Einbahn-; (*ticket*) einfach

onion /'ʌnjən/ n Zwiebel f
on-'line adv online
'onlooker n Zuschauer(in) m(f)
only /'əʊnlɪ/ adj einzige(r,s); **an ∼
child** ein Einzelkind nt ● adv & conj
nur; **∼ just** gerade erst; (barely) gerade noch
'onset n Beginn m; (of winter) Einsetzen nt
'on-shore adj (oil field) an Land;
(breeze) vom Meer kommend
onward[s] /'ɒnwəd[z]/ adv vorwärts; **from then ∼** von der Zeit an
ooze /uːz/ vi sickern
opaque /əʊ'peɪk/ adj undurchsichtig
open /'əʊpən/ adj offen; **be ∼** (shop:)
geöffnet sein; **in the ∼ air** im Freien
● n **in the ∼** im Freien ● vt öffnen,
aufmachen; (start, set up) eröffnen
● vi sich öffnen; (flower:) aufgehen;
(shop:) öffnen, aufmachen; (be
started) eröffnet werden. **∼ up** vt
öffnen, aufmachen
'open day n Tag m der offenen Tür
opener /'əʊpənə(r)/ n Öffner m
opening /'əʊpənɪŋ/ n Öffnung f,
(beginning) Eröffnung f; (job) Ein-
stiegsmöglichkeit f. **∼ hours** npl Öffnungszeiten pl
open: ∼-'minded adj aufgeschlossen. **∼ 'sandwich** n belegtes Brot nt

> **Open University - OU** Eine
> britische Fernuniversität, die
> 1969 gegründet wurde und vor
> allem Berufstätigen im Fernstu-
> dium Kurse auf verschiedenem Ni-
> veau bietet. Studenten jeder Alters-
> gruppe, selbst solche ohne die
> erforderlichen Schulabschlüsse,
> können das Studium mit dem
> Bachelor's degree und dem Master's
> degree abschließen. Teilnehmer stu-
> dieren von zu Hause und können
> auch an Direktunterricht teilneh-
> men.

opera /'ɒpərə/ n Oper f. **∼ glasses**
pl Opernglas n **∼-house** n Opern-
haus nt. **∼-singer** n Opernsänger(in)
m(f)
operate /'ɒpəreɪt/ vt bedienen (ma-

chine, lift); betätigen (lever, brake);
(fig: run) betreiben ● vi (Techn) funktionieren; (be in action) in Betrieb
sein; (Mil & fig) operieren; **∼ [on]**
(Med) operieren
operatic /ɒpə'rætɪk/ adj Opern-
operation /ɒpə'reɪʃn/ n (see operate) Bedienung f; Betätigung f; Operation f; **in ∼** (Techn) in Betrieb;
come into ∼ (fig) in Kraft treten;
have an ∼ (Med) operiert werden.
∼al adj einsatzbereit; **be ∼al** in Betrieb sein; (law:) in Kraft sein
operative /'ɒpərətɪv/ adj wirksam
operator /'ɒpərəreɪtə(r)/ n (user)
Bedienungsperson f; (Teleph) Vermitt-
lung f
operetta /ɒpə'retə/ n Operette f
opinion /ə'pɪnjən/ n Meinung f; **in
my ∼** meiner Meinung nach. **∼ated**
adj rechthaberisch
opponent /ə'pəʊnənt/ n Gegner(in)
m(f)
opportun|e /'ɒpətjuːn/ adj günstig.
∼ist n Opportunist m
opportunity /ɒpə'tjuːnɪtɪ/ n Gele
genheit f
oppos|e /ə'pəʊz/ vt Widerstand leis-
ten (+ dat); (argue against) sprechen
gegen; **be ∼ed to sth** gegen etw
sein; **as ∼ed to** im Gegensatz zu.
∼ing adj gegnerisch
opposite /'ɒpəzɪt/ adj entgegengesetzt; (house, side) gegenüberliegend;
∼ number (fig) Gegenstück nt; **the
∼ sex** das andere Geschlecht ● n
Gegenteil nt ● adv gegenüber ● prep
gegenüber (+ dat)
opposition /ɒpə'zɪʃn/ n Widerstand
m; (Pol) Opposition f
oppress /ə'pres/ vt unterdrücken.
∼ion n Unterdrücken f. **∼ive** adj tyrannisch; (heat) drückend
opt /ɒpt/ vi **∼ for** sich entscheiden
für
optical /'ɒptɪkl/ adj optisch
optician /ɒp'tɪʃn/ n Optiker m
optimis|m /'ɒptɪmɪzm/ n Optimis-
mus m. **∼t** n Optimist m. **∼tic** adj,
-ally adv optimistisch

optimum /'ɒptɪməm/ adj optimal

option /'ɒpʃn/ n Wahl f; (Comm) Option f. ~al adj auf Wunsch erhältlich; (subject) wahlfrei

opu|lence /'ɒpjʊləns/ n Prunk m. ~lent adj prunkvoll

or /ɔː(r)/ conj oder; (after negative) noch; **or [else]** sonst; **in a year or two** in ein bis zwei Jahren

oral /'ɔːrl/ adj mündlich; (Med) oral ● n Mündliche(s) nt

orange /'ɒrɪndʒ/ n Apfelsine f, Orange f; (colour) Orange nt ● adj orangefarben

oratorio /ɒrə'tɔːrɪəʊ/ n Oratorium nt

oratory /'ɒrətərɪ/ n Redekunst f

orbit /'ɔːbɪt/ n Umlaufbahn f ● vt umkreisen

orchard /'ɔːtʃəd/ n Obstgarten m

orches|tra /'ɔːkɪstrə/ n Orchester nt. ~tral adj Orchester-. ~trate vt orchestrieren

ordeal /ɔː'diːl/ n (fig) Qual f

order /'ɔːdə(r)/ n Ordnung f; (sequence) Reihenfolge f; (condition) Zustand m; (command) Befehl m; (in restaurant) Bestellung f; (Comm) Auftrag m; (Relig, medal) Orden m; **out of ~** (machine) außer Betrieb; **in ~ that** damit; **in ~ to help** um zu helfen ● vt (put in ~) ordnen; (command) befehlen (+ dat); (Comm, in restaurant) bestellen; (prescribe) verordnen

orderly /'ɔːdəlɪ/ adj ordentlich; (not unruly) friedlich ● n (Mil, Med) Sanitäter m

ordinary /'ɔːdɪnərɪ/ adj gewöhnlich, normal

ore /ɔː(r)/ n Erz nt

organ /'ɔːgən/ n (Biology) Organ nt; (Mus) Orgel f

organic /ɔː'gænɪk/ adj, **-ally** adv organisch; (without chemicals) biodynamisch; (crop) biologisch angebaut; (food) Bio-. **~ farming** n biologischer Anbau m

organism /'ɔːgənɪzm/ n Organismus m

organist /'ɔːgənɪst/ n Organist m

organization /ɔːgənaɪ'zeɪʃn/ n Organisation f

organize /'ɔːgənaɪz/ vt organisieren; veranstalten (event). **~r** n Organisator m; Veranstalter m

orgy /'ɔːdʒɪ/ n Orgie f

Orient /'ɔːrɪənt/ n Orient m. **o~al** adj orientalisch ● n Orientale m/Orientalin f

orientation /ɔːrɪən'teɪʃn/ n Orientierung f

origin /'ɒrɪdʒɪn/ n Ursprung m; (of person, goods) Herkunft f

original /ə'rɪdʒənl/ adj ursprünglich; (not copied) original; (new) originell ● n Original nt. **~ity** n Originalität f. **~ly** adv ursprünglich

originate /ə'rɪdʒɪneɪt/ vi entstehen

ornament /'ɔːnəmənt/ n Ziergegenstand m; (decoration) Verzierung f. **~al** adj dekorativ

ornate /ɔː'neɪt/ adj reich verziert

ornithology /ɔːnɪ'θɒlədʒɪ/ n Vogelkunde f

orphan /'ɔːfn/ n Waisenkind nt, Waise f. **~age** n Waisenhaus nt

orthodox /'ɔːθədɒks/ adj orthodox

ostensible /ɒ'stensəbl/ adj, **-bly** adv angeblich

ostentat|ion /ɒsten'teɪʃn/ n Protzerei f 🔟. **~ious** adj protzig 🔟

osteopath /'ɒstɪəpæθ/ n Osteopath m

ostrich /'ɒstrɪtʃ/ n Strauß m

other /'ʌðə(r)/ adj, pron & n andere(r,s); **the ~ [one]** der/die/das andere; **the ~ two** die zwei anderen; **no ~s** sonst keine; **any ~ questions?** sonst noch Fragen? **every ~ day** jeden zweiten Tag; **the ~ day** neulich; **the ~ evening** neulich abends; **someone/something or ~** irgendjemand/-etwas ● adv anders; **~ than him** außer ihm; **somehow/somewhere or ~** irgendwie/irgendwo

'otherwise adv sonst; (differently) anders

ought /ɔːt/ modal verb I/we ~ to

stay ich sollte/wir sollten eigentlich bleiben; **he ~ not to have done it** er hätte es nicht machen sollen

ounce /aʊns/ n Unze f (28,35 g)

our /'aʊə(r)/ adj unser

ours /'aʊəz/ poss pron unsere(r,s); **a friend of ~** ein Freund von uns; **that is ~** das gehört uns

ourselves /aʊə'selvz/ pron selbst; (reflexive) uns; **by ~** allein

out /aʊt/ adv (not at home) weg; (outside) draußen; (not alight) aus; (unconscious) bewusstlos; **be ~** (sun:) scheinen; (flower) blühen; (workers) streiken; (calculation:) nicht stimmen; (Sport) aus sein; (fig: not feasible) nicht infrage kommen; **~ and about** unterwegs; **have it ~ with s.o.** 🔲 jdn zur Rede stellen; **get ~!** 🔲 raus! **~ with itl** 🔲 heraus damit! ● prep **~ of** aus (+ dat); **go ~ (of) the door** zur Tür hinausgehen; **be ~ of bed/ the room** nicht im Bett/im Zimmer sein; **~ of breath/danger** außer Atem/Gefahr; **~ of work** arbeitslos; **nine ~ of ten** neun von zehn; **be ~ of sugar** keinen Zucker mehr haben

'outboard adj **~ motor** Außenbordmotor m

'outbreak n Ausbruch m

'outbuilding n Nebengebäude nt

'outburst n Ausbruch m

'outcast n Ausgestoßene(r) m/f

'outcome n Ergebnis nt

'outcry n Aufschrei m [der Entrüstung]

out'dated adj überholt

out'do vt (pt -did, pp -done) übertreffen, übertrumpfen

'outdoor adj (life, sports) im Freien; **~ swimming pool** Freibad nt

out'doors adv draußen; **go ~** nach draußen gehen

'outer adj äußere(r,s)

'outfit n Ausstattung f; (clothes) Ensemble nt; (🔲: organization) Laden m

'outgoing adj ausscheidend; (mail) ausgehend; (sociable) kontaktfreudig, **~s** npl Ausgaben pl

out'grow vi (pt -grew, pp -grown) herauswachsen aus

outing /'aʊtɪŋ/ n Ausflug m

'outlaw n Geächtete(r) m/f ● vt ächten

'outlay n Auslagen pl

'outlet n Abzug m; (for water) Abfluss m; (fig) Ventil nt; (Comm) Absatzmöglichkeit f

'outline n Umriss m; (summary) kurze Darstellung f ● vt umreißen

out'live vt überleben

'outlook n Aussicht f; (future prospect) Aussichten pl; (attitude) Einstellung f

out'moded adj überholt

out'number vt zahlenmäßig überlegen sein (+ dat)

'out-patient n ambulanter Patient m

'outpost n Vorposten m

'output n Leistung f; Produktion f

'outrage n Gräueltat f; (fig) Skandal m; (indignation) Empörung f. **~ous** adj empörend

'outright¹ adj völlig, total; (refusal) glatt

out'right² adv ganz; (at once) sofort; (frankly) offen

'outset n Anfang m

'outside¹ adj äußere(r,s); **~ wall** Außenwand f ● n Außenseite f; **from the ~** von außen; **at the ~** höchstens

out'side² adv außen; (out of doors) draußen; **go ~** nach draußen gehen ● prep außerhalb (+ gen); (in front of) vor (+ dat/acc)

out'sider n Außenseiter m

'outsize adj übergroß

'outskirts npl Rand m

out'spoken adj offen; **be ~** kein Blatt vor den Mund nehmen

out'standing adj hervorragend; (conspicuous) bemerkenswert; (Comm) ausstehend

'outstretched adj ausgestreckt

out'vote vt überstimmen

'outward /-wəd/ adj äußerlich; **~**

O

journey Hinreise f ● adv nach außen.
~ly adv nach außen hin, äußerlich.
~s adv nach außen

out'wit vt (pt/pp **-witted**) überlisten

oval /'əʊvl/ adj oval ● n Oval nt

> **Oval Office** Das *Oval Office* i
> ist das Büro des amerikani-
> schen Präsidenten. Es befindet sich
> im westlichen Flügel des Weißen
> Hauses und sein Name bezieht sich
> auf die ovale Form des Raumes.
> George Washington (1. Präsident
> der USA) bestand auf ein ovales
> Büro, damit er bei Besprechungen
> allen Anwesenden in die Augen
> sehen konnte.

ovation /əʊ'veɪʃn/ n Ovation f

oven /'ʌvn/ n Backofen m

over /'əʊvə(r)/ prep über (+ acc/dat);
~ dinner beim Essen; **~ the phone**
am Telefon; **~ the page** auf der
nächsten Seite ● adv (remaining)
übrig; (ended) zu Ende; **~ again**
noch einmal; **~ and ~** immer wieder; **~ here/there** hier/da drüben;
all ~ (everywhere) überall; **it's all ~**
es ist vorbei; **I ache all ~** mir tut
alles weh

overall¹ /'əʊvərɔːl/ n Kittel m; **~s** pl
Overall m

overall² /əʊvər'ɔːl/ adj gesamt; (general) allgemein ● adv insgesamt

over'balance vi das Gleichgewicht
verlieren

over'bearing adj herrisch

'overboard adv (Naut) über Bord

'overcast adj bedeckt

over'charge vt **~ s.o.** jdm zu viel
berechnen ● vi zu viel verlangen

'overcoat n Mantel m

over'come vt (pt **-came**, pp **-come**)
überwinden; **be ~ by** überwältigt
werden von

over'crowded adj überfüllt

over'do vt (pt **-did**, pp **-done**) übertreiben; (cook too long) zu lange kochen; **~ it** (Ⅰ: do too much) sich
übernehmen

'overdose n Überdosis f

'overdraft n [Konto]überziehung f;
have an ~ sein Konto überzogen
haben

over'due adj überfällig

over'estimate vt überschätzen

'overflow¹ n Überschuss m; (outlet)
Überlauf m; **~ car park** zusätzlicher
Parkplatz m

over'flow² vi überlaufen

over'grown adj (garden) über-
wachsen

'overhang¹ n Überhang m

over'hang² vt/i (pt/pp **-hung**) über-
hängen (über + acc)

'overhaul¹ n Überholung f

over'haul² vt (Techn) überholen

over'head¹ adv oben

'overhead² adj Ober-; (ceiling)
Decken-. **~s** npl allgemeine Unkosten pl

over'hear vt (pt/pp **-heard**) mit anhören (conversation)

over'heat vi zu heiß werden

over'joyed adj überglücklich

'overland adj & adv /--'-/ auf dem
Landweg; **~ route** Landroute f

over'lap vi (pt/pp **-lapped**) sich
überschneiden

over'leaf adv umseitig

over'load vt überladen

over'look vt überblicken; (fail to
see, ignore) übersehen

over'night¹ adv über Nacht; **stay**
~ übernachten

'overnight² adj Nacht-; **~ stay**
Übernachtung f

'overpass n Überführung f

over'pay vt (pt/pp **-paid**) überbe-
zahlen

over'populated adj übervölkert

over'power vt überwältigen. **~ing**
adj überwältigend

over'priced adj zu teuer

over'rated adj überbewertet

overre'act vi überreagieren. **~ion** n
Überreaktion f

over'riding adj Haupt-

over'rule vt ablehnen; **we were ~d**
wir wurden überstimmt

over'run vt (pt **-ran**, pp **-run**, pres p **-running**) überrennen; überschreiten (time); **be ~ with** überlaufen sein von

over'seas[1] adv in Übersee; **go ~** nach Übersee gehen

'overseas[2] adj Übersee-

over'see vt (pt **-saw**, pp **-seen**) beaufsichtigen

over'shadow vt überschatten

over'shoot vt (pt/pp **-shot**) hinausschießen über (+ acc)

'oversight n Versehen nt

over'sleep vi (pt/pp **-slept**) [sich] verschlafen

over'step vt (pt/pp **-stepped**) überschreiten

overt /əʊˈvɜːt/ adj offen

over'take vt/i (pt **-took**, pp **-taken**) überholen

over'throw vt (pt **-threw**, pp **-thrown**) (Pol) stürzen

'overtime n Überstunden pl ● adv **work ~** Überstunden machen

over'tired adj übermüdet

overture /ˈəʊvətjʊə(r)/ n (Mus) Ouvertüre f; **~s** pl (fig) Annäherungsversuche pl

over'turn vt umstoßen ● vi umkippen

over'weight adj übergewichtig; **be ~** Übergewicht haben

overwhelm /-ˈwelm/ vt überwältigen. **~ing** adj überwältigend

over'work n Überarbeitung f ● vt überfordern ● vi sich überarbeiten

over'wrought adj überreizt

ow|e /əʊ/ vt schulden/ (fig) verdanken ([to] s.o. jdm); **~e s.o. sth** jdm etw schuldig sein. **'~ing to** prep wegen (+ gen)

owl /aʊl/ n Eule f

own[1] /əʊn/ adj & pron eigen; **it's my ~** es gehört mir; **a car of my ~** mein eigenes Auto; **on one's ~** allein; **get one's ~ back** 🔢 sich revanchieren

own[2] vt besitzen; **I don't ~ it** es gehört mir nicht. **~ up** vi es zugeben

owner /ˈəʊnə(r)/ n Eigentümer(in)

m(f), Besitzer(in) m(f); (of shop) Inhaber(in) m(f). **~ship** n Besitz m

---

Oxbridge Eine Wortbildung aus den Namen Oxford und Cambridge. Diese umgangssprachliche Zusammensetzung wird als Sammelbegriff für die zwei Eliteuniversitäten in England verwendet, um sie von anderen Hochschulen zu unterscheiden. Oxford und Cambridge sind die ältesten britischen Universitäten mit dem besten akademischen Ruf. Oxbridge-Absolventen werden häufig von Arbeitgebern bevorzugt.

---

oxygen /ˈɒksɪdʒən/ n Sauerstoff m

oyster /ˈɔɪstə(r)/ n Auster f

· ·

Pp

· ·

pace /peɪs/ n Schritt m; (speed) Tempo nt; **keep ~ with** Schritt halten mit ● vi **~ up and down** auf und ab gehen. **~-maker** n (Sport & Med) Schrittmacher m

Pacific /pəˈsɪfɪk/ adj & n **the ~ [Ocean]** der Pazifik

pacifist /ˈpæsɪfɪst/ n Pazifist m

pacify /ˈpæsɪfaɪ/ vt (pt/pp **-ied**) beruhigen

pack /pæk/ n Packung f; (Mil) Tornister m; (of cards) [Karten]spiel nt; (gang) Bande f; (of hounds) Meute f; (of wolves) Rudel nt; **a ~ of lies** ein Haufen Lügen ● vt/i packen; einpacken (article); **be ~ed** (crowded) [gedrängt] voll sein. **~ up** vt einpacken ● vi 🔢 (machine:) kaputtgehen

package /ˈpækɪdʒ/ n Paket nt. **~ holiday** n Pauschalreise f

packet /ˈpækɪt/ n Päckchen nt

packing /ˈpækɪŋ/ n Verpackung f

pact /pækt/ n Pakt m

pad /pæd/ n Polster nt; (for writing) [Schreib]block m ● vt (pt/pp **padded**) polstern

padding /'pædɪŋ/ n Polsterung f; (in written work) Füllwerk nt

paddle[1] /'pædl/ n Paddel nt ● vt (row) paddeln

paddle[2] vi waten

paddock /'pædək/ n Koppel f

padlock /'pædlɒk/ n Vorhängeschloss nt ● vt mit einem Vorhängeschloss verschließen

paediatrician /pi:dɪə'trɪʃn/ n Kinderarzt m /-ärztin f

pagan /'peɪɡən/ adj heidnisch ● n Heide m/Heidin f

page[1] /peɪdʒ/ n Seite f

page[2] n (boy) Page m ● vt ausrufen (person)

paid /'peɪd/ see pay ● adj bezahlt; **put ~ to** 🔲 zunichte machen

pail /peɪl/ n Eimer m

pain /peɪn/ n Schmerz m; **be in ~** Schmerzen haben; **take ~s** sich (dat) Mühe geben; **~ in the neck** 🔲 Nervensäge f

pain: **~ful** adj schmerzhaft; (fig) schmerzlich. **~-killer** n schmerzstillendes Mittel nt. **~less** adj schmerzlos

painstaking /'peɪnzteɪkɪŋ/ adj sorgfältig

paint /peɪnt/ n Farbe f ● vt/i streichen; (artist:) malen. **~brush** n Pinsel m. **~er** n Maler m; (decorator) Anstreicher m. **~ing** n Malerei f; (picture) Gemälde nt

pair /peə(r)/ n Paar nt; **~ of trousers** Hose f ● vi **~ off** Paare bilden

pajamas /pə'dʒɑːməz/ n pl (Amer) Schlafanzug m

Pakistan /pɑːkɪ'stɑːn/ n Pakistan nt. **~i** adj pakistanisch ● n Pakistaner(in) m(f)

pal /pæl/ n Freund(in) m(f)

palace /'pælɪs/ n Palast m

palatable /'pælətəbl/ adj schmackhaft

palate /'pælət/ n Gaumen m

palatial /pə'leɪʃl/ adj palastartig

pale adj (-r, -st) blass ● vi blass werden. **~ness** n Blässe f

Palestin|e /'pælɪstaɪn/ n Palästina

nt. **~ian** adj palästinensisch ● n Palästinenser(in) m(f)

palette /'pælɪt/ n Palette f

palm /pɑːm/ n Handfläche f; (tree, symbol) Palme f ● vt **~ sth off on s.o.** jdm etw andrehen. **P~'Sunday** n Palmsonntag m

palpable /'pælpəbl/ adj tastbar; (perceptible) spürbar

palpitations /'pælpɪteɪʃnz/ npl Herzklopfen nt

paltry /'pɔːltrɪ/ adj armselig

pamper /'pæmpə(r)/ vt verwöhnen

pamphlet /'pæmflɪt/ n Broschüre f

pan /pæn/ n Pfanne f; (saucepan) Topf m; (of scales) Schale f

panacea /pænə'siːə/ n Allheilmittel nt

'pancake n Pfannkuchen m

panda /'pændə/ n Panda m

pandemonium /pændɪ'məʊnɪəm/ n Höllenlärm m

pane /peɪn/ n [Glas]scheibe f

panel /'pænl/ n Tafel f, Platte f; **~ of experts** Expertenrunde f; **~ of judges** Jury f. **~ling** n Täfelung f

pang /pæŋ/ n **~s of hunger** Hungergefühl nt; **~s of conscience** Gewissensbisse pl

panic /'pænɪk/ n Panik f ● vi (pt/pp **panicked**) in Panik geraten. **~-stricken** adj von Panik ergriffen

panoram|a /pænə'rɑːmə/ n Panorama nt. **~ic** adj Panorama-

pansy /'pænzɪ/ n Stiefmütterchen nt

pant /pænt/ vi keuchen; (dog:) hecheln

panther /'pænθə(r)/ n Panther m

panties /'pæntɪz/ npl [Damen]slip m

pantomime /'pæntəmaɪm/ n [zu Weihnachten aufgeführte] Märchenvorstellung f

pantry /'pæntrɪ/ n Speisekammer f

pants /pænts/ npl Unterhose f; (woman's) Schlüpfer m; (trousers) Hose f

'pantyhose n (Amer) Strumpfhose f

paper /'peɪpə(r)/ n Papier nt; (newspaper) Zeitung f; (exam~) Testbogen m; (exam) Klausur f; (treatise) Referat

nt; **~s** pl (*documents*) Unterlagen pl;
(*for identification*) [Ausweis]papiere pl
● *vt* tapezieren

paper: ~back n Taschenbuch nt.
~-clip n Büroklammer f. **~weight**
n Briefbeschwerer m. **~work** n
Schreibarbeit f

par /pɑː(r)/ n (*Golf*) Par nt; **on a ~**
gleichwertig (**with** dat)

parable /'pærəbl/ n Gleichnis nt

parachut|e /'pærəʃuːt/ n Fallschirm
m ● *vi* [mit dem Fallschirm] abspring-
en. **~ist** n Fallschirmspringer m

parade /pə'reɪd/ n Parade f; (*procession*) Festzug m ● *vt* (*show off*) zur
Schau stellen

paradise /'pærədaɪs/ n Paradies nt

paradox /'pærədɒks/ n Paradox nt.
~ical paradox

paraffin /'pærəfɪn/ n Paraffin nt

paragraph /'pærəgrɑːf/ n Absatz m

parallel /'pærəlel/ adj & adv parallel
● n (*Geog*) Breitenkreis m; (*fig*) Paral-
lele f

Paralympics /pærə'lɪmpɪks/ npl
the ~ die Paralympics pl

paralyse /'pærəlaɪz/ vt lähmen; (*fig*)
lahmlegen

paralysis /pə'ræləsɪs/ n (pl **-ses**
/-siːz/) Lähmung f

paramedic /pærə'medɪk/ n Ret-
tungssanitäter(in) m(f)

parameter /pə'ræmɪtə(r)/ n Parameter m, Rahmen m

paranoid /'pærənɔɪd/ adj [krank-
haft] misstrauisch

parapet /'pærəpɪt/ n Brüstung f

paraphernalia /pærəfə'neɪlɪə/ n
Kram m

parasite /'pærəsaɪt/ n Parasit m,
Schmarotzer m

paratrooper /'pærətruːpə(r)/ n
Fallschirmjäger m

parcel /'pɑːsl/ n Paket nt

parch /pɑːtʃ/ vt austrocknen; **be
~ed** (*person:*) einen furchtbaren
Durst haben

parchment /'pɑːtʃmənt/ n Pergament nt

pardon /'pɑːdn/ n Verzeihung f; (*Jur*)

Begnadigung f; **~?** Ⓣ bitte? **I beg
your ~** wie bitte? (*sorry*) Verzeihung! ● *vt* verzeihen; (*Jur*) begnadigen

parent /'peərənt/ n Elternteil m; **~s**
pl Eltern pl. **~al** adj elterlich

parenthesis /pə'renθəsɪs/ n (pl
-ses /-siːz/) Klammer f

parish /'pærɪʃ/ n Gemeinde f.
~ioner n Gemeindemitglied nt

park /pɑːk/ n Park m ● *vt/i* parken.
~-and-ride n Park-and-ride-Platz m

parking /'pɑːkɪŋ/ n Parken nt; 'no
~' 'Parken verboten'. **~-lot** n (*Amer*)
Parkplatz m. **~-meter** n Parkuhr f.
~ space n Parkplatz m

parliament /'pɑːləmənt/ n Parlament nt. **~ary** adj parlamentarisch

---

Parliament Das britische   *i*
Parlament ist die oberste gesetzgebende Gewalt in Großbritannien und besteht aus dem Souverän (dem König oder der Königin),
dem *House of Lords* (Oberhaus) und
dem *House of Commons* (Unterhaus). Die Partei mit der Mehrheit
im Unterhaus bildet die Regierung.
▷**DÁIL ÉIREANN**, ▷**SCOTTISH PAR-
LIAMENT**, ▷**WELSH ASSEMBLY**.

---

parochial /pə'rəʊkɪəl/ adj
Gemeinde-; (*fig*) beschränkt

parody /'pærədɪ/ n Parodie f ● *vt*
(*pt/pp* **-ied**) parodieren

parole /pə'rəʊl/ n **on ~** auf Bewährung

parquet /'pɑːkeɪ/ n ~ **floor** Parkett nt

parrot /'pærət/ n Papagei m

parsley /'pɑːslɪ/ n Petersilie f

parsnip /'pɑːsnɪp/ n Pastinake f

parson /'pɑːsn/ n Pfarrer m

part /pɑːt/ n Teil m; (*Techn*) Teil nt;
(*area*) Gegend f; (*Theat*) Rolle f; (*Mus*)
Part m; **spare ~** Ersatzteil nt; **for my
~** meinerseits; **on the ~ of** vonseiten (+ *gen*); **take s.o.'s ~** für jdn
Partei ergreifen; **take ~ in** teilnehmen an (+ *dat*) ● *adv* teils ● *vt* trennen; scheiteln (*hair*) ● *vi* (*people:*)

p

sich trennen; ~ **with** sich trennen von

partial /'pɑːʃl/ adj Teil-; **be ~ to** mögen. **-ly** adv teilweise

particip|ant /pɑː'tɪsɪpənt/ n Teilnehmer(in) m(f). **~ate** vi teilnehmen (**in** an + dat). **~ation** n Teilnahme f

particle /'pɑːtɪkl/ n Körnchen nt; (Phys) Partikel nt; (Gram) Partikel f

particular /pə'tɪkjʊlə(r)/ adj besondere(r,s); (precise) genau; (fastidious) penibel; **in ~** besonders. **~ly** adv besonders. **~s** npl nähere Angaben pl

parting /'pɑːtɪŋ/ n Abschied m; (in hair) Scheitel m

partition /pɑː'tɪʃn/ n Trennwand f; (Pol) Teilung f ● vt teilen

partly /'pɑːtlɪ/ adv teilweise

partner /'pɑːtnə(r)/ n Partner(in) m(f); (Comm) Teilhaber m. **~ship** n Partnerschaft f; (Comm) Teilhaberschaft f

partridge /'pɑːtrɪdʒ/ n Rebhuhn nt

part-'time adj & adv Teilzeit-; **be** or **work ~** Teilzeitarbeit machen

party /'pɑːtɪ/ n Party f, Fest nt; (group) Gruppe f; (Pol, Jur) Partei f

pass /pɑːs/ n Ausweis m; (Geog, Sport) Pass m; (Sch) ≈ ausreichend; **get a ~** bestehen ● vt vorbeigehen/-fahren an (+ dat); (overtake) überholen; (hand) reichen; (Sport) abgeben, abspielen; (approve) annehmen; (exceed) übersteigen; bestehen (exam); machen (remark); fällen (judgement); (Jur) verhängen (sentence); **~ the time** sich (dat) die Zeit vertreiben; **~ one's hand over sth** mit der Hand über etw (acc) fahren ● vi vorbeigehen/-fahren; (get by) vorbeikommen; (overtake) überholen; (time:) vergehen; (in exam) bestehen; **~ away** vi sterben. **~ down** vt herunterreichen; (fig) weitergeben. **~ out** vi ohnmächtig werden. **~ round** vt herumreichen. **~ up** vt heraufreichen; (🔲: miss) vorübergehen lassen

passable /'pɑːsəbl/ adj (road) befahrbar; (satisfactory) passabel

passage /'pæsɪdʒ/ n Durchgang m; (corridor) Gang m; (voyage) Überfahrt f; (in book) Passage f

passenger /'pæsɪndʒə(r)/ n Fahrgast m; (Naut, Aviat) Passagier m; (in car) Mitfahrer m. **~ seat** n Beifahrersitz m

passer-by /pɑːsə'baɪ/ n (pl **-s-by**) Passant(in) m(f)

passion /'pæʃn/ n Leidenschaft f. **~ate** adj leidenschaftlich

passive /'pæsɪv/ adj passiv ● n Passiv nt

pass: ~port n [Reise]pass m. **~word** n Kennwort nt; (Mil) Losung f

past /pɑːst/ adj vergangene(r,s); (former) ehemalig; **that's all ~** das ist jetzt vorbei ● n Vergangenheit f ● prep an (+ dat) ... vorbei; (after) nach; **at ten ~ two** um zehn nach zwei ● adv vorbei; **go ~** vorbeigehen

pasta /'pæstə/ n Nudeln pl

paste /peɪst/ n Brei m; (adhesive) Kleister m; (jewellery) Strass m ● vt kleistern

pastel /'pæstl/ n Pastellfarbe f; (drawing) Pastell nt ● attrib Pastell-

pastime /'pɑːstaɪm/ n Zeitvertreib m

pastr|y /'peɪstrɪ/ n Teig m; **cakes and ~ies** Kuchen und Gebäck

pasture /'pɑːstʃə(r)/ n Weide f

pasty[1] /'pæstɪ/ n Pastete f

pat /pæt/ n Klaps m; (of butter) Stückchen nt ● vt (pt/pp **patted**) tätscheln; **~ s.o. on the back** jdm auf die Schulter klopfen

patch /pætʃ/ n Flicken m; (spot) Fleck m; **not a ~ on** 🔲 gar nicht zu vergleichen mit ● vt flicken. **~ up** vt [zusammen]flicken; beilegen (quarrel)

patchy /'pætʃɪ/ adj ungleichmäßig

patent /'peɪtnt/ n Patent nt ● vt patentieren. **~ leather** n Lackleder nt

paternal /pə'tɜːnl/ adj väterlich

path /pɑːθ/ n (pl **~s** /pɑːðz/) [Fuß]weg m, Pfad m; (orbit, track) Bahn f; (fig) Weg m

pathetic /pə'θetɪk/ adj mitleidrre-

423

patience | peer

gend; (*attempt*) erbärmlich
patience /ˈpeɪʃns/ n Geduld f;
(*game*) Patience f
patient /ˈpeɪʃnt/ adj geduldig ●n
Patient(in) m(f)
patio /ˈpætɪəʊ/ n Terrasse f
patriot /ˈpætrɪət/ n Patriot(in) m(f).
~**ic** adj patriotisch. ~**ism** n Patrio-
tismus m
patrol /pəˈtrəʊl/ n Patrouille f ●vt/i
patrouillieren [in (+ dat)]; (*police:*) auf
Streife gehen/fahren [in (+ dat)]. ~
car n Streifenwagen m
patron /ˈpeɪtrən/ n Gönner m; (*of
charity*) Schirmherr m; (*of the arts*)
Mäzen m; (*customer*) Kunde
m/Kundin f; (*Theat*) Besucher m.
~**age** n Schirmherrschaft f
patroniz|e /ˈpætrənaɪz/ vt (*fig*) her-
ablassend behandeln. ~**ing** adj gön-
nerhaft
patter n (*speech*) Gerede nt
pattern /ˈpætn/ n Muster nt
paunch /pɔːntʃ/ n [Schmer]bauch m
pause /pɔːz/ n Pause f ●vi innehalten
pave /peɪv/ vt pflastern; ~ **the way**
den Weg bereiten (**for** dat). ~**ment**
n Bürgersteig m
paw /pɔː/ n Pfote f; (*of large animal*)
Pranke f, Tatze f
pawn[1] /pɔːn/ n (*Chess*) Bauer m;
(*fig*) Schachfigur f
pawn[2] vt verpfänden. ~ **broker** n
Pfandleiher m
pay /peɪ/ n Lohn m; (*salary*) Gehalt nt;
be in the ~ **of** bezahlt werden von
●v (*pt/pp* **paid**) ●vt bezahlen; zahlen (*money*); ~ **s.o. a visit** jdm einen
Besuch abstatten; ~ **s.o. a compliment** jdm ein Kompliment machen
●vi zahlen; (*be profitable*) sich bezahlt machen; (*fig*) sich lohnen; ~
for sth etw bezahlen. ~ **back** vt zurückzahlen. ~ **in** vt einzahlen. ~ **off**
vt abzahlen (*debt*) ●vi (*fig*) sich auszahlen
payable /ˈpeɪəbl/ adj zahlbar; **make**
~ **to** ausstellen auf (+ acc)
payment /ˈpeɪmənt/ n Bezahlung f;
(*amount*) Zahlung f

pea /piː/ n Erbse f
peace /piːs/ n Frieden m; **for my** ~
of mind zu meiner eigenen Beruhi-
gung
peace|ful adj friedlich. ~**maker** n
Friedensstifter m
peach /piːtʃ/ n Pfirsich m
peacock /ˈpiːkɒk/ n Pfau m
peak /piːk/ n Gipfel m; (*fig*) Höhepunkt m. ~**ed 'cap** n Schirmmütze f.
~ **hours** npl Hauptbelastungszeit f;
(*for traffic*) Hauptverkehrszeit f
peal /piːl/ n (*of bells*) Glockengeläut
nt; ~**s of laughter** schallendes Gelächter nt
'peanut n Erdnuss f
pear /peə(r)/ n Birne f
pearl /pɜːl/ n Perle f
peasant /ˈpeznt/ n Bauer m
peat /piːt/ n Torf m
pebble /ˈpebl/ n Kieselstein m
peck /pek/ n Schnabelhieb m; (*kiss*)
flüchtiger Kuss m ●vt/i picken/(*nip*)
hacken (**at** nach)
peculiar /pɪˈkjuːlɪə(r)/ adj eigenartig, seltsam; ~ **to** eigentümlich (+
dat). ~**ity** n Eigenart f
pedal /ˈpedl/ n Pedal nt ●vt fahren
(*bicycle*) ●vi treten
pedantic /pɪˈdæntɪk/ adj, **-ally** adv
pedantisch
pedestal /ˈpedɪstl/ n Sockel m
pedestrian /pɪˈdestrɪən/ n Fußgän-
ger(in) m(f) ●adj (*fig*) prosaisch. ~
'crossing n Fußgängerüberweg m.
~ **'precinct** n Fußgängerzone f
pedigree /ˈpedɪɡriː/ n Stammbaum
m ●attrib (*animal*) Rasse-
pedlar /ˈpedlə(r)/ n Hausierer m
peek /piːk/ vi 🗓 gucken
peel /piːl/ n Schale f ●vt schälen; ●vi
(*skin:*) sich schälen; (*paint:*) abblättern. ~ **ings** npl Schalen pl
peep /piːp/ n kurzer Blick m ●vi gucken. ~**-hole** n Guckloch nt
peer[1] /pɪə(r)/ vi ~ **at** forschend ansehen
peer[2] n Peer m; **his** ~**s** pl seinesglei-
chen

p

peg /peg/ n (*hook*) Haken m; (*for tent*) Pflock m, Hering m; (*for clothes*) [Wäsche]klammer f; **off the ~** 🔢 von der Stange

pejorative /prˈdʒɒrətɪv/ adj abwertend

pelican /ˈpelɪkən/ n Pelikan m

pellet /ˈpelɪt/ n Kügelchen nt

pelt¹ /pelt/ n (*skin*) Pelz m, Fell nt

pelt² vt bewerfen ● vi ~ **[down]** (*rain:*) [hernieder]prasseln

pelvis /ˈpelvɪs/ n (*Anat*) Becken nt

pen¹ /pen/ n (*for animals*) Hürde f

pen² n Federhalter m; (*ballpoint*) Kugelschreiber m

penal /ˈpiːnl/ adj Straf-. **~ize** vt bestrafen; (*fig*) benachteiligen

penalty /ˈpenltɪ/ n Strafe f; (*fine*) Geldstrafe f; (*Sport*) Strafstoß m; (*Football*) Elfmeter m

penance /ˈpenəns/ n Buße f

pence /pens/ see **penny**

pencil /ˈpensɪl/ n Bleistift m ● vt (pt/pp **pencilled**) mit Bleistift schreiben. **~-sharpener** n Bleistiftspitzer m

pendulum /ˈpendjʊləm/ n Pendel nt

penetrat|e /ˈpenɪtreɪt/ vt durchdringen; ~**e into** eindringen in (+ acc). **~ing** adj durchdringend. **~ion** n Durchdringen nt

'penfriend n Brieffreund(in) m(f)

penguin /ˈpeŋgwɪn/ n Pinguin m

penicillin /penɪˈsɪlɪn/ n Penizillin nt

peninsula /pəˈnɪnsʊlə/ n Halbinsel f

penis /ˈpiːnɪs/ n Penis m

penitentiary /penɪˈtenʃərɪ/ n (*Amer*) Gefängnis nt

pen: ~**knife** n Taschenmesser nt. ~**name** n Pseudonym nt

penniless /ˈpenɪlɪs/ adj mittellos

penny /ˈpenɪ/ n (pl **pence**; *single coins* **pennies**) Penny m; (*Amer*) Centstück nt; **the ~'s dropped** 🔢 der Groschen ist gefallen

pension /ˈpenʃn/ n Rente f; (*of civil servant*) Pension f. **~er** n Rentner(in) m(f); Pensionär(in) m(f)

pensive /ˈpensɪv/ adj nachdenklich

pent-up /ˈpentʌp/ adj angestaut

penultimate /peˈnʌltɪmət/ adj vorletzte(r,s)

people /ˈpiːpl/ npl Leute pl, Menschen pl; (*citizens*) Bevölkerung f; **the ~** das Volk; **English ~** die Engländer; ~ **say** man sagt; **for four ~** für vier Personen ● vt bevölkern

pepper /ˈpepə(r)/ n Pfeffer m; (*vegetable*) Paprika m

pepper: ~**mint** n Pfefferminz nt; (*Bot*) Pfefferminze f. ~**pot** n Pfefferstreuer m

per /pɜː(r)/ prep pro; ~ **cent** Prozent nt

percentage /pəˈsentɪdʒ/ n Prozentsatz m; (*part*) Teil m

perceptible /pəˈseptəbl/ adj wahrnehmbar

percept|ion /pəˈsepʃn/ n Wahrnehmung f. **~ive** adj feinsinnig

perch¹ /pɜːtʃ/ n Stange f ● vi (*bird:*) sich niederlassen

perch² n inv (*fish*) Barsch m

percussion /pəˈkʌʃn/ n Schlagzeug nt. ~ **instrument** n Schlaginstrument nt

perennial /pəˈrenɪəl/ adj (*problem*) immer wiederkehrend ● n (*Bot*) mehrjährige Pflanze f

perfect¹ /ˈpɜːfɪkt/ adj perfekt, vollkommen; (🔢: *utter*) völlig ● n (*Gram*) Perfekt nt

perfect² /pəˈfekt/ vt vervollkommnen. **~ion** n Vollkommenheit f; **to ~ion** perfekt

perfectly /ˈpɜːfɪktlɪ/ adv perfekt; (*completely*) vollkommen, völlig

perforated /ˈpɜːfəreɪtɪd/ adj perforiert

perform /pəˈfɔːm/ vt ausführen; erfüllen (*duty*); (*Theat*) aufführen (*play*); spielen (*role*) ● vi (*Theat*) auftreten; (*Techn*) laufen. **~ance** n Ausführung f; (*at theatre, cinema*) Vorstellung f; (*Techn*) Leistung f. **~er** n Künstler(in) m(f)

perfume /ˈpɜːfjuːm/ n Parfüm nt; (*smell*) Duft m

perhaps /pəˈhæps/ adv vielleicht

perilous /ˈperələs/ adj gefährlich

425

perimeter /pə'rɪmɪtə(r)/ n [äußere]
Grenze f; (Geometry) Umfang m

period /'pɪərɪəd/ n Periode f; (Sch)
Stunde f; (full stop) Punkt m ● attrib
(costume) zeitgenössisch; (furniture)
antik. **~ic** adj, **-ally** adv periodisch.
~ical n Zeitschrift f

peripher|al /pə'rɪfərl/ adj neben-
sächlich. **~y** n Peripherie f

perish /'perɪʃ/ vi (rubber:) verrotten;
(food:) verderben; (to die) ums Leben
kommen. **~able** adj leicht verderb-
lich. **~ing** adj (🆂: cold) eiskalt

perjur|e /'pɜːdʒə(r)/ vt **~e oneself**
einen Meineid leisten. **~y** n Meineid m

perk[1] /pɜːk/ n 🆂 [Sonder]vergünsti-
gung f

perk[2] vi **~ up** munter werden

perm /pɜːm/ n Dauerwelle f ● vt **~
s.o.'s hair** jdm eine Dauerwelle machen

permanent /'pɜːmənənt/ adj ständig; (job, address) fest. **~ly** adv ständig; (work, live) dauernd, permanent;
(employed) fest

permissible /pə'mɪsəbl/ adj erlaubt

permission /pə'mɪʃn/ n Erlaubnis f

permit[1] /pə'mɪt/ vt (pt/pp **-mitted**)
erlauben (**s.o.** jdm)

permit[2] /'pɜːmɪt/ n Genehmigung f

perpendicular /pɜːpən'dɪkjʊlə(r)/
adj senkrecht ● n Senkrechte f

perpetual /pə'petjʊəl/ adj ständig,
dauernd

perpetuate /pə'petjʊeɪt/ vt bewahren; verewigen (error)

perplex /pə'pleks/ vt verblüffen.
~ed adj verblüfft

persecut|e /'pɜːsɪkjuːt/ vt verfolgen.
~ion n Verfolgung f

perseverance /pɜːsɪ'vɪərəns/ n
Ausdauer f

persevere /pɜːsɪ'vɪə(r)/ vi beharrlich
weitermachen

Persia /'pɜːʃə/ n Persien nt

Persian /'pɜːʃn/ adj persisch; (cat,
carpet) Perser-

persist /pə'sɪst/ vi beharrlich weitermachen; (continue) anhalten; (view:)

weiter bestehen; **~ in doing sth**
dabei bleiben, etw zu tun. **~ence** n
Beharrlichkeit f. **~ent** adj beharrlich;
(continuous) anhaltend

person /'pɜːsn/ n Person f; **in ~** persönlich

personal /'pɜːsənl/ adj persönlich.
~ 'hygiene n Körperpflege f

personality /pɜːsə'nælətɪ/ n Persönlichkeit f

personify /pə'sɒnɪfaɪ/ vt (pt/pp
-ied) personifizieren, verkörpern

personnel /pɜːsə'nel/ n Personal nt

perspective /pə'spektɪv/ n Perspek-
tive f

persp|iration /pɜːspɪ'reɪʃn/ n
Schweiß m. **~ire** vi schwitzen

persua|de /pə'sweɪd/ vt überreden;
(convince) überzeugen. **~sion** n
Überredung f; (powers of **~sion**)
Überredungskunst f

persuasive /pə'sweɪsɪv/ adj bered-
sam; (convincing) überzeugend

pertinent /'pɜːtɪnənt/ adj relevant
(**to** für)

perturb /pə'tɜːb/ vt beunruhigen

peruse /pə'ruːz/ vt lesen

pervers|e /pə'vɜːs/ adj eigensinnig.
~ion n Perversion f

pervert[1] /pə'vɜːt/ vt verdrehen; verführen (person)

pervert[2] /'pɜːvɜːt/ n Perverse(r) m

pessimis|m /'pesɪmɪzm/ n Pessimis-
mus m. **~t** n Pessimist m. **~tic** adj,
-ally adv pessimistisch

pest /pest/ n Schädling m; (🆂: person) Nervensäge f

pester /'pestə(r)/ vt belästigen

pesticide /'pestɪsaɪd/ n Schädlings-
bekämpfungsmittel nt

pet /pet/ n Haustier nt; (favourite)
Liebling m ● vt (pt/pp **petted**) liebkosen

petal /'petl/ n Blütenblatt nt

peter /'piːtə(r)/ vi **~ out** allmählich
aufhören

petition /pə'tɪʃn/ n Bittschrift f

pet 'name n Kosename m

petrified /'petrɪfaɪd/ adj vor Angst wie versteinert

petrol /'petrl/ n Benzin nt

petroleum /pɪ'trəʊlɪəm/ n Petroleum nt

petrol: ~-pump n Zapfsäule f. ~ station n Tankstelle f. ~ tank n Benzintank m

petticoat /'petɪkəʊt/ n Unterrock m

petty /'petɪ/ adj kleinlich. ~ 'cash n Portokasse f

petulant /'petjʊlənt/ adj gekränkt

pew /pju:/ n [Kirchen]bank f

pharmaceutical /fɑ:mə'sju:tɪkl/ adj pharmazeutisch

pharmac|ist /'fɑ:məsɪst/ n Apotheker(in) m(f). ~y n Pharmazie f; (shop) Apotheke f

phase /feɪz/ n Phase f ● vt ~ in/out allmählich einführen/abbauen

Ph.D. (abbr **Doctor of Philosophy**) Dr. phil.

pheasant /'feznt/ n Fasan m

phenomen|al /fɪ'nɒmɪnl/ adj phänomenal. ~on n (pl -na) Phänomen nt

philharmonic /fɪlɑ:'mɒnɪk/ n (orchestra) Philharmoniker pl

Philippines /'fɪlɪpi:nz/ npl Philippinen pl

philistine /'fɪlɪstaɪn/ n Banause m

philosoph|er /fɪ'lɒsəfə(r)/ n Philosoph m. ~ical adj philosophisch. ~y n Philosophie f

phlegmatic /fleg'mætɪk/ adj phlegmatisch

phobia /'fəʊbɪə/ n Phobie f

phone /fəʊn/ n Telefon nt; be on the ~ Telefon haben; (be phoning) telefonieren ● vt anrufen ● vi telefonieren. ~ back vt/i zurückrufen. ~ book n Telefonbuch nt. ~ box n Telefonzelle f. ~ card n Telefonkarte f. ~-in n (Radio) Hörersendung f. ~ number n Telefonnummer f

phonetic /fə'netɪk/ adj phonetisch. ~s n Phonetik f

phoney /'fəʊnɪ/ adj falsch; (forged) gefälscht

photo /'fəʊtəʊ/ n Foto nt, Aufnahme f. ~copier n Fotokopiergerät nt. ~copy n Fotokopie f ● vt fotokopieren

photogenic /fəʊtəʊ'dʒenɪk/ adj fotogen

photograph /'fəʊtəgrɑ:f/ n Fotografie f, Aufnahme f ● vt fotografieren

photograph|er /fə'tɒgrəfə(r)/ n Fotograf(in) m(f). ~ic adj, -ally adv fotografisch. ~y n Fotografie f

phrase /freɪz/ n Redensart f ● vt formulieren. ~-book n Sprachführer m

physical /'fɪzɪkl/ adj körperlich

physician /fɪ'zɪʃn/ n Arzt m/ Ärztin f

physic|ist /'fɪzɪsɪst/ n Physiker(in) m(f). ~s n Physik f

physio'therap|ist /fɪzɪəʊ-/ n Physiotherapeut(in) m(f). ~y n Physiotherapie f

physique /fɪ'zi:k/ n Körperbau m

pianist /'pɪənɪst/ n Klavierspieler(in) m(f); (professional) Pianist(in) m(f)

piano /pɪ'ænəʊ/ n Klavier nt

pick¹ /pɪk/ n Spitzhacke f

pick² n Auslese f; take one's ~ sich (dat) aussuchen ● vt/i (pluck) pflücken; (select) wählen, sich (dat) aussuchen; ~ and choose wählerisch sein; ~ a quarrel einen Streit anfangen; ~ holes in ① kritisieren; ~ at one's food im Essen herumstochern. ~ on vt wählen; (①: find fault with) herumhacken auf (+ dat). ~ up vt in die Hand nehmen; (off the ground) aufheben; hochnehmen (baby); (learn) lernen; (acquire) erwerben; (buy) kaufen; (Teleph) abnehmen (receiver); auffangen (signal); (collect) abholen; aufnehmen (passengers); (police:) aufgreifen (criminal); sich holen (illness); ① aufgabeln (girl); ~ oneself up aufstehen ● vi (improve) sich bessern

'pickaxe n Spitzhacke f

picket /'pɪkɪt/ n Streikposten m

pickle /'pɪkl/ n (Amer: gherkin) Essiggurke f; ~s pl [Mixed] Pickles pl ● vt einlegen

pick: ~**pocket** n Taschendieb m.
~**-up** n (truck) Lieferwagen m

picnic /'pɪknɪk/ n Picknick nt ● vi
(pt/pp **-nicked**) picknicken

picture /'pɪktʃə(r)/ n Bild nt; (film)
Film m; **as pretty as a ~** bildhübsch;
put s.o. in the ~ (fig) jdn ins Bild
setzen ● vt (imagine) sich (dat) vorstellen

picturesque /pɪktʃə'resk/ adj malerisch

pie /paɪ/ n Pastete f; (fruit) Kuchen m

piece /pi:s/ n Stück nt; (of set) Teil nt;
(in game) Stein m; (writing) Artikel m;
a ~ of bread/paper ein Stück Brot/
Papier; **a ~ of news/advice** eine
Nachricht/ein Rat; **take to ~s** auseinander nehmen ● vt ~ **together**
zusammensetzen; (fig) zusammen-
stückeln. ~**meal** adv stückweise

pier /pɪə(r)/ n Pier m; (pillar) Pfeiler m

pierc|e /pɪəs/ vt durchstechen. ~**ing**
adj durchdringend

pig /pɪg/ n Schwein nt

pigeon /'pɪdʒɪn/ n Taube f. ~**-hole**
n Fach nt

piggy|back /'pɪgɪbæk/ n **give s.o. a**
~**back** jdn huckepack tragen. ~
bank n Sparschwein nt

pig'headed adj 🗓 starrköpfig

pigment /'pɪgmənt/ n Pigment nt

pig: ~**skin** n Schweinsleder nt. ~**sty**
n Schweinestall m. ~**tail** n 🗓
Zopf m

pilchard /'pɪltʃəd/ n Sardine f

pile[1] /paɪl/ n (of fabric) Flor m

pile[2] n Haufen m ● vt ~ **sth on to**
sth etw auf etw (acc) häufen. ~ **up**
vt häufen ● vi sich häufen

piles /paɪlz/ npl Hämorrhoiden pl

'pile-up n Massenkarambolage f

pilgrim /'pɪlgrɪm/ n Pilger(in) m(f).
~**age** n Pilgerfahrt f, Wallfahrt f

pill /pɪl/ n Pille f

pillar /'pɪlə(r)/ n Säule f. ~**-box** n
Briefkasten m

pillow /'pɪləʊ/ n Kopfkissen nt.
~**case** n Kopfkissenbezug m

pilot /'paɪlət/ n Pilot m; (Naut) Lotse

m ● vt fliegen (plane); lotsen (ship).
~**-light** n Zündflamme f

pimple /'pɪmpl/ n Pickel m

pin /pɪn/ n Stecknadel f; (Techn) Bolzen m, Stift m; (Med) Nagel m; **I**
have ~s and needles in my leg 🗓
mein Bein ist eingeschlafen ● vt (pt/
pp **pinned**) anstecken (**to/on** an +
acc); (sewing) stecken; (hold down)
festhalten

pinafore /'pɪnəfɔː(r)/ n Schürze f. ~
dress n Kleiderrock m

pincers /'pɪnsəz/ npl Kneifzange f;
(Zool) Scheren pl

pinch /pɪntʃ/ n Kniff m; (of salt) Prise
f; **at a ~** 🗓 zur Not ● vt kneifen,
zwicken; (fam; steal) klauen; ~
one's finger sich (dat) den Finger
klemmen ● vi (shoe:) drücken

pine[1] /paɪn/ n (tree) Kiefer f

pine[2] vi ~ **for** sich sehnen nach

pineapple /'paɪn-/ n Ananas f

'ping-pong n Tischtennis nt

pink /pɪŋk/ adj rosa

pinnacle /'pɪnəkl/ n Gipfel m; (on
roof) Turmspitze f

pin: ~**point** vt genau festlegen.
~**stripe** n Nadelstreifen m

pint /paɪnt/ n Pint nt (0,57 l, Amer:
0,47 l)

pioneer /paɪə'nɪə(r)/ n Pionier m
● vt bahnbrechende Arbeit leisten für

pious /'paɪəs/ adj fromm

pip[1] /pɪp/ n (seed) Kern m

pip[2] n (sound) Tonsignal nt

pipe /paɪp/ n Pfeife f; (for water, gas)
Rohr nt ● vt in Rohren leiten; (Culin)
spritzen

pipe: ~**-dream** n Luftschloss nt.
~**line** n Pipeline f; **in the ~line** 🗓
in Vorbereitung

piping /'paɪpɪŋ/ adj ~ **hot** kochend
heiß

pirate /'paɪərət/ n Pirat m

piss /pɪs/ vi 🗷 pissen

pistol /'pɪstl/ n Pistole f

piston /'pɪstən/ n (Techn) Kolben m

pit /pɪt/ n Grube f; (for orchestra) Or-
chestergraben m; (for audience) Par-

p

kett nt; (motor racing) Box f

pitch¹ /pɪtʃ/ n (steepness) Schräge f; (of voice) Stimmlage f; (of sound) [Ton]höhe f; (Sport) Feld nt; (of street-trader) Standplatz m; (fig: degree) Grad m ● vt werfen; aufschlagen (tent) ● vi fallen

pitch² n (tar) Pech nt. ∼-'**black** adj pechschwarz. ∼-'**dark** adj stockdunkel

piteous /'pɪtɪəs/ adj erbärmlich

'**pitfall** n (fig) Falle f

pith /pɪθ/ n (Bot) Mark nt; (of orange) weiße Haut f

pithy /'pɪθɪ/ adj (fig) prägnant

piti|ful /'pɪtɪfl/ adj bedauernswert. ∼**less** adj mitleidslos

'**pit stop** n Boxenstopp m

pittance /'pɪtns/ n Hungerlohn m

pity /'pɪtɪ/ n Mitleid nt, Erbarmen nt; [**what a**] ∼! [wie] schade! **take** ∼ **on** sich erbarmen über (+ acc) ● vt bemitleiden

pivot /'pɪvət/ n Drehzapfen m ● vi sich drehen (**on** um)

pizza /'piːtsə/ n Pizza f

placard /'plækɑːd/ n Plakat nt

placate /plə'keɪt/ vt beschwichtigen

place /pleɪs/ n Platz m; (spot) Stelle f; (town, village) Ort m; (🔢: house) Haus nt; **out of** ∼ fehl am Platze; **take** ∼ stattfinden ● vt setzen; (upright) stellen; (flat) legen; (remember) unterbringen 🔢; ∼ **an order** eine Bestellung aufgeben; **be** ∼**d** (in race) sich platzieren. ∼-**mat** n Set nt

placid /'plæsɪd/ adj gelassen

plague /pleɪg/ n Pest f ● vt plagen

plaice /pleɪs/ n inv Scholle f

plain /pleɪn/ adj (-er, -est) klar; (simple) einfach; (not pretty) nicht hübsch; (not patterned) einfarbig; (chocolate) zartbitter; **in** ∼ **clothes** in Zivil ● adv (simply) einfach ● n Ebene f. ∼**ly** adv klar, deutlich; (simply) einfach; (obviously) offensichtlich

plaintiff /'pleɪntɪf/ n Kläger(in) m(f)

plait /plæt/ n Zopf m ● vt flechten

plan /plæn/ n Plan m ● vt (pt/pp **planned**) planen; (intend) vorhaben

plane¹ /pleɪn/ n (tree) Platane f

plane² /pleɪn/ n Flugzeug nt; (Geometry & fig) Ebene f

plane³ n (Techn) Hobel m ● vt hobeln

planet /'plænɪt/ n Planet m

plank /plæŋk/ n Brett nt; (thick) Planke f

planning /'plænɪŋ/ n Planung f

plant /plɑːnt/ n Pflanze f; (Techn) Anlage f; (factory) Werk nt ● vt pflanzen; (place in position) setzen; ∼ **oneself** sich hinstellen. ∼**ation** n Plantage f

plaque /plɑːk/ n [Gedenk]tafel f; (on teeth) Zahnbelag m

plaster /'plɑːstə(r)/ n Verputz m; (sticking ∼) Pflaster nt; ∼ [**of Paris**] Gips m ● vt verputzen (wall); (cover) bedecken mit

plastic /'plæstɪk/ n Kunststoff m, Plastik nt ● adj Kunststoff-, Plastik-; (malleable) formbar, plastisch

plastic 'surgery n plastische Chirurgie f

plate /pleɪt/ n Teller m; (flat sheet) Platte f; (with name, number) Schild nt; (gold and silverware) vergoldete/ versilberte Ware f; (in book) Tafel f ● vt (with gold) vergolden; (with silver) versilbern

platform /'plætfɔːm/ n Plattform f; (stage) Podium nt; (Rail) Bahnsteig m; ∼ **5** Gleis 5

platinum /'plætɪnəm/ n Platin nt

platitude /'plætɪtjuːd/ n Plattitüde f

plausible /'plɔːzəbl/ adj plausibel

play /pleɪ/ n Spiel nt; [Theater]stück nt; (Radio) Hörspiel nt; (TV) Fernsehspiel nt; ∼ **on words** Wortspiel nt ● vt/i spielen; ausspielen (card); ∼ **safe** sichergehen. ∼ **down** vt herunterspielen. ∼ **up** vi 🔢 Mätzchen machen

play: ∼**er** n Spieler(in) m(f). ∼**ful** adj verspielt. ∼**ground** n Spielplatz m; (Sch) Schulhof m. ∼**group** n Kindergarten m

playing: ∼-**card** n Spielkarte f. ∼-**field** n Sportplatz m

play: ~**mate** n Spielkamerad m.
~**thing** n Spielzeug nt. ~**wright**
/-raɪt/ n Dramatiker m

plc abbr (**public limited company**) ≈
GmbH

plea /pliː/ n Bitte f; **make a** ~ **for**
bitten um

plead /pliːd/ vi flehen (**for** um); ~
guilty sich schuldig bekennen; ~
with s.o. jdn anflehen

pleasant /'plezənt/ adj angenehm;
(person) nett. ~**ly** adv angenehm;
(say, smile) freundlich

pleas|e /pliːz/ adv bitte ● vt gefallen
(+ dat); ~**e s.o.** jdm eine Freude machen; ~**e oneself** tun, was man will.
~**ed** adj erfreut; **be** ~**ed with**/
about sth sich über etw (acc) freuen.
~**ing** adj erfreulich

pleasure /'pleʒə(r)/ n Vergnügen nt;
(joy) Freude f; **with** ~ gern[e]

pleat /pliːt/ n Falte f ● vt fälteln

pledge /pledʒ/ n Versprechen nt ● vt
verpfänden; versprechen

plentiful /'plentɪfl/ adj reichlich

plenty /'plentɪ/ n eine Menge;
(enough) reichlich; ~ **of money**/
people viel Geld/viele Leute

pliable /'plaɪəbl/ adj biegsam

pliers /'plaɪəz/ npl [Flach]zange f

plight /plaɪt/ n [Not]lage f

plinth /plɪnθ/ n Sockel m

plod /plɒd/ vi (pt/pp **plodded**) trot-
ten; (work) sich abmühen

plonk /plɒŋk/ n 🄸 billiger Wein m

plot /plɒt/ n Komplott nt; (of novel)
Handlung f; ~ **of land** Stück nt Land
● vt einzeichnen ● vi ein Komplott
schmieden

plough /plaʊ/ n Pflug m ● vt/i pflügen

ploy /plɔɪ/ n 🄸 Trick m

pluck /plʌk/ n Mut m ● vt zupfen;
rupfen (bird); pflücken (flower); ~
up courage Mut fassen

plucky /'plʌkɪ/ adj tapfer, mutig

plug /plʌɡ/ n Stöpsel m; (wood) Zapfen m; (cotton wool) Bausch m;
(Electr) Stecker m; (Auto) Zündkerze
f; (🄸: advertisement) Schleichwer-

bung f ● vt zustopfen; (🄸: advertise)
Schleichwerbung machen für. ~ **in**
vt (Electr) einstecken

plum /plʌm/ n Pflaume f

plumage /'pluːmɪdʒ/ n Gefieder nt

plumb|er /'plʌmə(r)/ n Klempner m.
~**ing** n Wasserleitungen pl

plume /pluːm/ n Feder f

plump /plʌmp/ adj (-er, -est) mollig,
rundlich ● vt ~ **for** wählen

plunge /plʌndʒ/ n Sprung m; **take**
the ~ 🄸 den Schritt wagen ● vt/i
tauchen

plural /'plʊərl/ adj pluralisch ● n
Mehrzahl f, Plural m

plus /plʌs/ prep plus (+ dat) ● adj
Plus- ● n Pluszeichen nt; (advantage)
Plus nt

plush[y] /'plʌʃ[ɪ]/ adj luxuriös

ply /plaɪ/ vt (pt/pp **plied**) ausüben
(trade); ~ **s.o. with drink** jdm ein
Glas nach dem anderen eingießen.
~**wood** n Sperrholz nt

p.m. adv (abbr **post meridiem**) nach-
mittags

pneumatic /njuː'mætɪk/ adj pneu-
matisch. ~ '**drill** n Pressluftham-
mer m

pneumonia /njuː'məʊnɪə/ n Lun-
genentzündung f

poach /pəʊtʃ/ vt (Culin) pochieren;
(steal) wildern. ~**er** n Wilddieb m

pocket /'pɒkɪt/ n Tasche f; **be out of**
~ [an einem Geschäft] verlieren ● vt
einstecken. ~**-book** n Notizbuch nt;
(wallet) Brieftasche f. ~**-money** n
Taschengeld nt

pod /pɒd/ n Hülse f

poem /'pəʊɪm/ n Gedicht nt

poet /'pəʊɪt/ n Dichter(in) m(f). ~**ic**
adj dichterisch

poetry /'pəʊɪtrɪ/ n Dichtung f

poignant /'pɔɪnjənt/ adj ergreifend

point /pɔɪnt/ n Punkt m; (sharp end)
Spitze f; (meaning) Sinn m; (purpose)
Zweck m; (Electr) Steckdose f; ~**s** pl
(Rail) Weiche f; ~ **of view** Standpunkt m; **good/bad** ~**s** gute/
schlechte Seiten; **what is the** ~?
wozu? **the** ~ **is** es geht darum; **up**

p

to a ~ bis zu einem gewissen Grade; **be on the ~ of doing sth** im Begriff sein, etw zu tun ● *vt* richten (**at** auf + *acc*); ausfugen (*brickwork*) ● *vi* deuten (**at/to** auf + *acc*); (*with finger*) mit dem Finger zeigen. **~ out** *vt* zeigen auf (+ *acc*); **~ sth out to s.o.** jdn auf etw (*acc*) hinweisen

point-'blank *adj* aus nächster Entfernung; (*fig*) rundweg

point|ed /'pɔɪntɪd/ *adj* spitz; (*question*) gezielt. **~less** *adj* zwecklos, sinnlos

poise /pɔɪz/ *n* Haltung *f*

poison /'pɔɪzn/ *n* Gift *nt* ● *vt* vergiften. **~ous** *adj* giftig

poke /pəʊk/ *n* Stoß *m* ● *vt* stoßen; schüren (*fire*); (*put*) stecken

poker[1] /'pəʊkə(r)/ *n* Schüreisen *nt*

poker[2] *n* (*Cards*) Poker *nt*

poky /'pəʊkɪ/ *adj* eng

Poland /'pəʊlənd/ *n* Polen *nt*

polar /'pəʊlə(r)/ *adj* Polar-. **~'bear** *n* Eisbär *m*

Pole /pəʊl/ *n* Pole *m*/Polin *f*

pole[1] *n* Stange *f*

pole[2] *n* (*Geog, Electr*) Pol *m*

'pole-vault *n* Stabhochsprung *m*

police /pə'liːs/ *npl* Polizei *f*

police: ~man *n* Polizist *m*. **~ station** *n* Polizeiwache *f*. **~woman** *n* Polizistin *f*

policy[1] /'pɒlɪsɪ/ *n* Politik *f*

policy[2] *n* (*insurance*) Police *f*

Polish /'pəʊlɪʃ/ *adj* polnisch

polish /'pɒlɪʃ/ *n* (*shine*) Glanz *m*; (*for shoes*) [Schuh]creme *f*; (*for floor*) Bohnerwachs *m*; (*for furniture*) Politur *f*; (*for silver*) Putzmittel *nt*; (*for nails*) Lack *m*; (*fig*) Schliff *m* ● *vt* polieren; bohnern (*floor*). **~ off** *vt* verputzen (*food*); erledigen (*task*)

polite /pə'laɪt/ *adj* höflich. **~ness** *n* Höflichkeit *f*

politic|al /pə'lɪtɪkl/ *adj* politisch. **~ian** *n* Politiker(in) *m(f)*

politics /'pɒlətɪks/ *n* Politik *f*

poll /pəʊl/ *n* Abstimmung *f*; (*election*) Wahl *f*; **[opinion] ~** [Meinungs]umfrage *f*

pollen /'pɒlən/ *n* Blütenstaub *m*, Pollen *m*

polling /'pəʊlɪŋ/: **~-booth** *n* Wahlkabine *f*. **~-station** *n* Wahllokal *nt*

pollut|e /pə'luːt/ *vt* verschmutzen. **~ion** *n* Verschmutzung *f*

polo /'pəʊləʊ/ *n* Polo *nt*. **~-neck** *n* Rollkragen *m*

polystyrene /pɒlɪ'staɪriːn/ *n* Polystyrol *nt*; (*for packing*) Styropor® *nt*

polythene /'pɒlɪθiːn/ *n* Polyäthylen *nt*. **~ bag** *n* Plastiktüte *f*

pomp /pɒmp/ *n* Pomp *m*

pompous /'pɒmpəs/ *adj* großspurig

pond /pɒnd/ *n* Teich *m*

ponder /'pɒndə(r)/ *vi* nachdenken

ponderous /'pɒndərəs/ *adj* schwerfällig

pony /'pəʊnɪ/ *n* Pony *nt*. **~-tail** *n* Pferdeschwanz *m*

poodle /'puːdl/ *n* Pudel *m*

pool /puːl/ *n* [Schwimm]becken *nt*; (*pond*) Teich *m*; (*of blood*) Lache *f*; (*common fund*) [gemeinsame] Kasse *f*; **~s** *pl* [Fußball]toto *nt* ● *vt* zusammenlegen

poor /pʊə(r)/ *adj* (**-er, -est**) arm; (*not good*) schlecht; **in ~ health** nicht gesund. **~ly** *adj* **be ~ly** krank sein ● *adv* ärmlich; (*badly*) schlecht

pop[1] /pɒp/ *n* Knall *m* ● *v* (*pt/pp* **popped**) ● *vt* (🗊: *put*) stecken (**in** in + *acc*) ● *vi* knallen; (*burst*) platzen. **~ in** *vi* 🗊 reinschauen. **~ out** *vi* 🗊 kurz rausgehen

pop[2] *n* 🗊 Popmusik *f*, Pop *m* ● *attrib* Pop-

'popcorn *n* Puffmais *m*

pope /pəʊp/ *n* Papst *m*

poplar /'pɒplə(r)/ *n* Pappel *f*

poppy /'pɒpɪ/ *n* Mohn *m*

popular /'pɒpjʊlə(r)/ *adj* beliebt, populär; (*belief*) volkstümlich. **~ity** *n* Beliebtheit *f*, Popularität *f*

populat|e /'pɒpjʊleɪt/ *vt* bevölkern. **~ion** *n* Bevölkerung *f*

pop-up /'pɒpʌp/ *n* Pop-up-Werbefenster *nt*

porcelain /'pɔːsəlɪn/ *n* Porzellan *nt*

porch /pɔ:tʃ/ n Vorbau m; (Amer) Veranda f

porcupine /'pɔ:kjʊpaɪn/ n Stachelschwein nt

pore /pɔ:(r)/ n Pore f

pork /pɔ:k/ n Schweinefleisch nt

porn /pɔ:n/ n 🛈 Porno m

pornograph|ic /pɔ:nə'græfɪk/ adj pornographisch. **~y** n Pornographie f

porridge /'pɒrɪdʒ/ n Haferbrei m

port¹ /pɔ:t/ n Hafen m; (town) Hafenstadt f

port² n (Naut) Backbord nt

port³ n (wine) Portwein m

portable /'pɔ:təbl/ adj tragbar

porter /'pɔ:tə(r)/ n Portier m; (for luggage) Gepäckträger m

'porthole n Bullauge nt

portion /'pɔ:ʃn/ n Portion f; (part, share) Teil nt

portrait /'pɔ:trɪt/ n Porträt nt

portray /pɔ:'treɪ/ vt darstellen. **~al** n Darstellung f

Portug|al /'pɔ:tjʊgl/ n Portugal nt. **~uese** adj portugiesisch ● n Portugiese m/-giesin f

pose /pəʊz/ n Pose f ● vt aufwerfen (problem); stellen (question) ● vi posieren; (for painter) Modell stehen

posh /pɒʃ/ adj 🛈 feudal

position /pə'zɪʃn/ n Platz m; (posture) Haltung f; (job) Stelle f; (situation) Lage f, Situation f; (status) Stellung f ● vt platzieren; **~ oneself** sich stellen

positive /'pɒzətɪv/ adj positiv; (definite) eindeutig; (real) ausgesprochen ● n Positiv nt

possess /pə'zes/ vt besitzen. **~ion** n Besitz m; **~ions** pl Sachen pl

possess|ive /pə'zesɪv/ adj Possessiv-; **be ~ive about s.o.** zu sehr an jdm hängen

possibility /pɒsə'bɪlətɪ/ n Möglichkeit f

possib|le /'pɒsəbl/ adj möglich. **~ly** adv möglicherweise; **not ~ly** unmöglich

post¹ /pəʊst/ n (pole) Pfosten m

post² n (place of duty) Posten m; (job) Stelle f

post³ n (mail) Post f; **by ~** mit der Post ● vt aufgeben (letter); (send by ~) mit der Post schicken; **keep s.o. ~ed** jdn auf dem Laufenden halten

postage /'pəʊstɪdʒ/ n Porto nt

postal /'pəʊstl/ adj Post-. **~ order** n ≈ Geldanweisung f

post: ~-box n Briefkasten m. **~card** n Postkarte f; (picture) Ansichtskarte f. **~code** n Postleitzahl f. **~-'date** vt vordatieren

poster /'pəʊstə(r)/ n Plakat nt

posterity /pɒ'sterətɪ/ n Nachwelt f

posthumous /'pɒstjʊməs/ adj postum

post: ~man n Briefträger m. **~mark** n Poststempel m

post-mortem /-'mɔ:təm/ n Obduktion f

'post office n Post f

postpone /pəʊst'pəʊn/ vt aufschieben; **~ until** verschieben auf (+ acc). **~ment** n Verschiebung f

postscript /'pəʊstskrɪpt/ n Nachschrift f

posture /'pɒstʃə(r)/ n Haltung f

pot /pɒt/ n Topf m; (for tea, coffee) Kanne f; **~s of money** 🛈 eine Menge Geld

potato /pə'teɪtəʊ/ n (pl -es) Kartoffel f

potent /'pəʊtənt/ adj stark

potential /pə'tenʃl/ adj potenziell ● n Potenzial nt

pot: ~-hole n Höhle f; (in road) Schlagloch nt. **~-shot** n take a **~-shot at** schießen auf (+ acc)

potter /'pɒtə(r)/ n Töpfer(in) m(f). **~y** n Töpferei f; (articles) Töpferwaren pl

potty /'pɒtɪ/ adj 🛈 verrückt ● n Töpfchen nt

pouch /paʊtʃ/ n Beutel m

poultry /'pəʊltrɪ/ n Geflügel nt

pounce /paʊns/ vi zuschlagen; **~ on** sich stürzen auf (+ acc)

p

pound[1] /paʊnd/ n (money & 0,454 kg) Pfund nt

pound[2] vi (heart:) hämmern; (run heavily) stampfen

pour /pɔː(r)/ vt gießen; einschenken (drink) ●vi strömen; (with rain) gießen. **~ out** vi ausströmen ●vt ausschütten; einschenken (drink)

pout /paʊt/ vi einen Schmollmund machen

poverty /'pɒvətɪ/ n Armut f

powder /'paʊdə(r)/ n Pulver nt; (cosmetic) Puder m ●vt pudern

power /'paʊə(r)/ n Macht f; (strength) Kraft f; (Electr) Strom m; (nuclear) Energie f; (Math) Potenz f. **~ cut** n Stromsperre f. **~ed** adj betrieben (**by** mit); **~ed by electricity** mit Elektroantrieb. **~ful** adj mächtig; (strong) stark. **~less** adj machtlos. **~-station** n Kraftwerk nt

practicable /'præktɪkəbl/ adj durchführbar, praktikabel

practical /'præktɪkl/ adj praktisch. **~ 'joke** n Streich m

practice /'præktɪs/ n Praxis f; (custom) Brauch m; (habit) Gewohnheit f; (exercise) Übung f; (Sport) Training nt; **in ~** (in reality) in der Praxis; **out of ~** außer Übung; **put into ~** ausführen

practise /'præktɪs/ vt üben; (carry out) praktizieren; ausüben (profession) ●vi üben; (doctor:) praktizieren. **~d** adj geübt

praise /preɪz/ n Lob nt ●vt loben. **~worthy** adj lobenswert

pram /præm/ n Kinderwagen m

prank /præŋk/ n Streich m

prawn /prɔːn/ n Garnele f, Krabbe f

pray /preɪ/ vi beten. **~er** n Gebet nt

preach /priːtʃ/ vt/i predigen. **~er** n Prediger m

pre-ar'range /priː-/ vt im Voraus arrangieren

precarious /prɪ'keərɪəs/ adj unsicher

precaution /prɪ'kɔːʃn/ n Vorsichtsmaßnahme f

precede /prɪ'siːd/ vt vorangehen (+ dat)

preceden|ce /'presɪdəns/ n Vorrang m. **~t** n Präzedenzfall m

preceding /prɪ'siːdɪŋ/ adj vorhergehend

precinct /'priːsɪŋkt/ n Bereich m; (traffic-free) Fußgängerzone f; (Amer: district) Bezirk m

precious /'preʃəs/ adj kostbar; (style) preziös ●adv 🛈 **~ little** recht wenig

precipice /'presɪpɪs/ n Steilabfall m

precipitation /prɪsɪpɪ'teɪʃn/ n (rain) Niederschlag m

precis|e /prɪ'saɪs/ adj genau. **~ion** n Genauigkeit f

precocious /prɪ'kəʊʃəs/ adj frühreif

pre|con'ceived /priː-/ adj vorgefasst. **~con'ception** n vorgefasste Meinung f

predator /'predətə(r)/ n Raubtier nt

predecessor /'priːdɪsesə(r)/ n Vorgänger(in) m(f)

predicat|e /'predɪkət/ n (Gram) Prädikat nt. **~ive** adj prädikativ

predict /prɪ'dɪkt/ vt voraussagen. **~able** adj voraussehbar; (person) berechenbar. **~ion** n Voraussage f

pre'domin|ant /prɪ-/ adj vorherrschend. **~antly** adv hauptsächlich, überwiegend. **~ate** vi vorherrschen

preen /priːn/ vt putzen

pre|fab /'priːfæb/ n 🛈 [einfaches] Fertighaus nt. **~'fabricated** adj vorgefertigt

preface /'prefɪs/ n Vorwort nt

prefect /'priːfekt/ n Präfekt m

prefer /prɪ'fɜː(r)/ vt (pt/pp **preferred**) vorziehen; **I ~ to walk** ich gehe lieber zu Fuß; **I ~ wine** ich trinke lieber Wein

prefera|ble /'prefərəbl/ adj **be ~ble** vorzuziehen sein (**to** dat). **~bly** adv vorzugsweise

preferen|ce /'prefərəns/ n Vorzug m. **~tial** adj bevorzugt

pregnan|cy /'pregnənsɪ/ n Schwangerschaft f. **~t** adj schwanger; (animal) trächtig

prehi'storic /priː-/ *adj* prähistorisch

prejudice /'predʒʊdɪs/ *n* Vorurteil *nt*; (*bias*) Voreingenommenheit *f* ● *vt* einnehmen (**against** gegen). **~d** *adj* voreingenommen

preliminary /prɪ'lɪmɪnərɪ/ *adj* Vor-

prelude /'prɛljuːd/ *n* Vorspiel *nt*

premature /'prɛmətjʊə(r)/ *adj* vorzeitig; (*birth*) Früh-. **~ly** *adv* zu früh

pre'meditated /priː-/ *adj* vorsätzlich

premier /'prɛmɪə(r)/ *adj* führend ● *n* (*Pol*) Premier[minister] *m*

première /'prɛmɪeə(r)/ *n* Premiere *f*

premise /'prɛmɪs/ *n* Prämisse *f*, Voraussetzung *f*

premises /'prɛmɪsɪz/ *npl* Räumlichkeiten *pl*; **on the ~** im Haus

premium /'priːmɪəm/ *n* Prämie *f*; **be at a ~** hoch im Kurs stehen

premonition /prɛmə'nɪʃn/ *n* Vorahnung *f*

preoccupied /prɪ'ɒkjʊpaɪd/ *adj* [in Gedanken] beschäftigt

preparation /prɛpə'reɪʃn/ *n* Vorbereitung *f*; (*substance*) Präparat *nt*

preparatory /prɪ'pærətrɪ/ *adj* Vor-

prepare /prɪ'peə(r)/ *vt* vorbereiten; anrichten (*meal*) ● *vi* sich vorbereiten (**for** auf + *acc*); **~d to** bereit zu

preposition /prɛpə'zɪʃn/ *n* Präposition *f*

preposterous /prɪ'pɒstərəs/ *adj* absurd

prerequisite /priː'rɛkwɪzɪt/ *n* Voraussetzung *f*

Presbyterian /prɛzbɪ'tɪərɪən/ *adj* presbyterianisch ● *n* Presbyterianer(in) *m*(*f*)

prescribe /prɪ'skraɪb/ *vt* vorschreiben; (*Med*) verschreiben

prescription /prɪ'skrɪpʃn/ *n* (*Med*) Rezept *nt*

presence /'prɛzns/ *n* Anwesenheit *f*, Gegenwart *f*; **~ of mind** Geistesgegenwart *f*

present¹ /'prɛznt/ *adj* gegenwärtig; **be ~** anwesend sein; (*occur*) vorkommen ● *n* Gegenwart *f*; (*Gram*)

Präsens *nt*; **at ~** zurzeit; **for the ~** vorläufig

present² *n* (*gift*) Geschenk *nt*

present³ /prɪ'zɛnt/ *vt* überreichen; (*show*) zeigen; vorlegen (*cheque*); (*introduce*) vorstellen; **~ s.o. with sth** jdm etw überreichen. **~able** *adj* **be ~able** sich zeigen lassen können

presentation /prɛzn'teɪʃn/ *n* Überreichung *f*

presently /'prɛzntlɪ/ *adv* nachher; (*Amer: now*) zurzeit

preservation /prɛzə'veɪʃn/ *n* Erhaltung *f*

preservative /prɪ'zɜːvətɪv/ *n* Konservierungsmittel *nt*

preserve /prɪ'zɜːv/ *vt* erhalten; (*Culin*) konservieren; (*bottle*) einmachen ● *n* (*Hunting & fig*) Revier *nt*; (*jam*) Konfitüre *f*

preside /prɪ'zaɪd/ *vi* den Vorsitz haben (**over** bei)

presidency /'prɛzɪdənsɪ/ *n* Präsidentschaft *f*

president /'prɛzɪdənt/ *n* Präsident *m*; (*Amer: chairman*) Vorsitzende(r) *m/f*. **~ial** *adj* Präsidenten-; (*election*) Präsidentschafts-

press /prɛs/ *n* Presse *f* ● *vt/i* drücken; drücken auf (+ *acc*) (*button*); pressen (*flower*); (*iron*) bügeln; (*urge*) bedrängen; **~ for** drängen auf (+ *acc*); **be ~ed for time** in Zeitdruck sein. **~ on** *vi* weitergehen/-fahren; (*fig*) weitermachen

press: ~ cutting *n* Zeitungsausschnitt *m*. **~ing** *adj* dringend

pressure /'prɛʃə(r)/ *n* Druck *m*. **~-cooker** *n* Schnellkochtopf *m*

pressurize /'prɛʃəraɪz/ *vt* Druck ausüben auf (+ *acc*). **~d** *adj* Druck-

prestig|e /prɛ'stiːʒ/ *n* Prestige *nt*. **~ious** *adj* Prestige-

presumably /prɪ'zjuːməblɪ/ *adv* vermutlich

presume /prɪ'zjuːm/ *vt* vermuten

presumpt|ion /prɪ'zʌmpʃn/ *n* Vermutung *f*; (*boldness*) Anmaßung *f*. **~uous** *adj* anmaßend

pretence /prɪ'tɛns/ *n* Verstellung *f*;

p

(*pretext*) Vorwand *m*

pretend /prɪ'tend/ *vt* (*claim*) vorgeben; ~ **that** so tun, als ob; ~ **to be** sich ausgeben als

pretentious /prɪ'tenʃəs/ *adj* protzig

pretext /'pri:tekst/ *n* Vorwand *m*

prett|y /'prɪtɪ/ *adj* , ~**ily** *adv* hübsch ● *adv* (🔲: *fairly*) ziemlich

prevail /prɪ'veɪl/ *vi* siegen; (*custom:*) vorherrschen; ~ **on s.o. to do sth** jdn dazu bringen, etw zu tun

prevalen|ce /'prevələns/ *n* Häufigkeit *f*. ~**t** *adj* vorherrschend

prevent /prɪ'vent/ *vt* verhindern, verhüten; ~ **s.o. [from] doing sth** jdn daran hindern, etw zu tun. ~**ion** *n* Verhinderung *f*, Verhütung *f*. ~**ive** *adj* vorbeugend

preview /'pri:vju:/ *n* Voraufführung *f*

previous /'pri:vɪəs/ *adj* vorhergehend; ~ **to** vor (+ *dat*). ~**ly** *adv* vorher, früher

prey /preɪ/ *n* Beute *f*; **bird of** ~ Raubvogel *m*

price /praɪs/ *n* Preis *m* ● *vt* (*Comm*) auszeichnen. ~**less** *adj* unschätzbar; (*fig*) unbezahlbar

prick /prɪk/ *n* Stich *m* ● *vt/i* stechen

prickl|e /'prɪkl/ *n* Stachel *m*; (*thorn*) Dorn *m*. ~**y** *adj* stachelig; (*sensation*) stechend

pride /praɪd/ *n* Stolz *m*; (*arrogance*) Hochmut *m* ● *vt* ~ **oneself on** stolz sein auf (+ *acc*)

priest /pri:st/ *n* Priester *m*

prim /prɪm/ *adj* (**primmer**, **primmest**) prüde

primarily /'praɪmərɪlɪ/ *adv* hauptsächlich, in erster Linie

primary /'praɪmərɪ/ *adj* Haupt-. ~ **school** *n* Grundschule *f*

prime¹ /praɪm/ *adj* Haupt-; (*first-rate*) erstklassig

prime² *vt* scharf machen (*bomb*); grundieren (*surface*)

Prime Minister /praɪ'mɪnɪstə(r)/ *n* Premierminister(in) *m*(*f*)

primitive /'prɪmɪtɪv/ *adj* primitiv

primrose /'prɪmrəʊz/ *n* gelbe Schlüsselblume *f*

prince /prɪns/ *n* Prinz *m*

princess /prɪn'ses/ *n* Prinzessin *f*

principal /'prɪnsəpl/ *adj* Haupt- ● *n* (*Sch*) Rektor(in) *m*(*f*)

principally /'prɪnsəplɪ/ *adv* hauptsächlich

principle /'prɪnsəpl/ *n* Prinzip *nt*, Grundsatz *m*; **in/on** ~ im/aus Prinzip

print /prɪnt/ *n* Druck *m*; (*Phot*) Abzug *m*; **in** ~ gedruckt; (*available*) erhältlich; **out of** ~ vergriffen ● *vt* drucken; (*write in capitals*) in Druckschrift schreiben; (*Computing*) ausdrucken; (*Phot*) abziehen. ~**ed matter** *n* Drucksache *f*

print|er /'prɪntə(r)/ *n* Drucker *m*. ~**ing** *n* Druck *m*

'printout *n* (*Computing*) Ausdruck *m*

prior /'praɪə(r)/ *adj* frühere(r,s); ~ **to** vor (+ *dat*)

priority /praɪ'ɒrətɪ/ *n* Priorität *f*, Vorrang *m*

prise /praɪz/ *vt* ~ **open/up** aufstemmen/hochstemmen

prison /'prɪzn/ *n* Gefängnis *nt*. ~**er** *n* Gefangene(r) *m/f*

privacy /'prɪvəsɪ/ *n* Privatsphäre *f*; **have no** ~ nie für sich sein

private /'praɪvət/ *adj* privat; (*confidential*) vertraulich; (*car, secretary, school*) Privat- ● *n* (*Mil*) [einfacher] Soldat *m*; **in** ~ privat; (*confidentially*) vertraulich

privation /praɪ'veɪʃn/ *n* Entbehrung *f*

privilege /'prɪvəlɪdʒ/ *n* Privileg *nt*. ~**d** *adj* privilegiert

prize /praɪz/ *n* Preis *m* ● *vt* schätzen

pro /prəʊ/ *n* 🔲 Profi *m*; **the** ~**s and cons** das Für und Wider

probability /prɒbə'bɪlətɪ/ *n* Wahrscheinlichkeit *f*

proba|ble /'prɒbəbl/ *adj*, **-bly** *adv* wahrscheinlich

probation /prə'beɪʃn/ *n* (*Jur*) Bewährung *f*

probe /prəʊb/ *n* Sonde *f*; (*fig: investigation*) Untersuchung *f*

problem /'prɒbləm/ n Problem nt; (Math) Textaufgabe f. ~**atic** adj problematisch

procedure /prə'siːdʒə(r)/ n Verfahren nt

proceed /prə'siːd/ vi gehen; (in vehicle) fahren; (continue) weitergehen/-fahren; (speaking) fortfahren; (act) verfahren

proceedings /prə'siːdɪŋz/ npl Verfahren nt; (Jur) Prozess m

proceeds /'prəʊsiːdz/ npl Erlös m

process /'prəʊses/ n Prozess m; (procedure) Verfahren nt; **in the** ~ dabei ● vt verarbeiten; (Admin) bearbeiten; (Phot) entwickeln

procession /prə'seʃn/ n Umzug m, Prozession f

processor /'prəʊsesə(r)/ n Prozessor m

proclaim /prə'kleɪm/ vt ausrufen

proclamation /prɒklə'meɪʃn/ n Proklamation f

procure /prə'kjʊə(r)/ vt beschaffen

prod /prɒd/ n Stoß m ● vt stoßen

prodigy /'prɒdɪdʒɪ/ n [**infant**] ~ Wunderkind nt

produce[1] /'prɒdjuːs/ n landwirtschaftliche Erzeugnisse pl

produce[2] /prə'djuːs/ vt erzeugen, produzieren; (manufacture) herstellen; (bring out) hervorholen; (cause) hervorrufen; inszenieren. (play); (Radio, TV) redigieren. ~**r** n Erzeuger m, Produzent m; Hersteller m; (Theat) Regisseur m; (Radio, TV) Redakteur(in) m(f)

product /'prɒdʌkt/ n Erzeugnis nt, Produkt nt. ~**ion** n Produktion f; (Theat) Inszenierung f

productiv|e /prə'dʌktɪv/ adj produktiv; (land, talks) fruchtbar. ~**ity** n Produktivität f

profession /prə'feʃn/ n Beruf m. ~**al** adj beruflich; (not amateur) Berufs-; (expert) fachmännisch; (Sport) professionell ● n Fachmann m; (Sport) Profi m

professor /prə'fesə(r)/ n Professor m

proficien|cy /prə'fɪʃnsɪ/ n Können nt. ~**t** adj **be** ~**t in** beherrschen

profile /'prəʊfaɪl/ n Profil nt; (character study) Porträt nt

profit /'prɒfɪt/ n Gewinn m, Profit m ● vi ~ **from** profitieren von. ~**able** adj, -**bly** adv gewinnbringend; (fig) nutzbringend

profound /prə'faʊnd/ adj tief

program /'prəʊgræm/ n Programm nt; ● vt (pt/pp **programmed**) programmieren

programme /'prəʊgræm/ n Programm nt; (Radio, TV) Sendung f. ~**r** n (Computing) Programmierer(in) m(f)

progress[1] /'prəʊgres/ n Vorankommen nt; (fig) Fortschritt m; **in** ~ im Gange; **make** ~ (fig) Fortschritte machen

progress[2] /prə'gres/ vi vorankommen; (fig) fortschreiten. ~**ion** n Folge f; (development) Entwicklung f

progressive /prə'gresɪv/ adj fortschrittlich. ~**ly** adv zunehmend

prohibit /prə'hɪbɪt/ vt verbieten (s.o. jdm). ~**ive** adj unerschwinglich

project[1] /'prɒdʒekt/ n Projekt nt; (Sch) Arbeit f

project[2] /prə'dʒekt/ vt projizieren (film); (plan) planen ● vi (jut out) vorstehen

projector /prə'dʒektə(r)/ n Projektor m

prolific /prə'lɪfɪk/ adj fruchtbar; (fig) produktiv

prologue /'prəʊlɒg/ n Prolog m

prolong /prə'lɒŋ/ vt verlängern

promenade /prɒmə'nɑːd/ n Promenade f ● vi spazieren gehen

prominent /'prɒmɪnənt/ adj vorstehend; (important) prominent; (conspicuous) auffällig

promiscuous /prə'mɪskjʊəs/ adj **be** ~**ous** häufig den Partner wechseln

promis|e /'prɒmɪs/ n Versprechen nt ● vt/i versprechen (s.o. jdm). ~**ing** adj viel versprechend

promot|e /prə'məʊt/ vt befördern;

p

(*advance*) fördern; (*publicize*) Reklame machen für; **be ~ed** (*Sport*) aufsteigen. **~ion** n Beförderung f; (*Sport*) Aufstieg m; (*Comm*) Reklame f

prompt /prɒmpt/ adj prompt, unverzüglich; (*punctual*) pünktlich ● adv pünktlich ● vt/i veranlassen (**to** zu); (*Theat*) soufflieren (+ dat). **~er** n Souffleur m/Souffleuse f. **~ly** adv prompt

> **Proms** Die Proms, offiziell *BBC Henry Wood Promenade Concerts*, finden jeden Sommer in der Londoner Royal Albert Hall statt. Bei den Promenadenkonzerten steht ein Teil des Publikums vor dem Orchester. In den USA bezeichnet *Prom* einen Ball, den eine ▷**HIGH SCHOOL** veranstaltet, um das Ende des Schuljahrs zu feiern.

prone /prəʊn/ adj **be** or **lie ~** auf dem Bauch liegen; **be ~ to** neigen zu

pronoun /ˈprəʊnaʊn/ n Fürwort nt, Pronomen nt

pronounce /prəˈnaʊns/ vt aussprechen; (*declare*) erklären. **~d** adj ausgeprägt; (*noticeable*) deutlich. **~ment** n Erklärung f

pronunciation /prənʌnsɪˈeɪʃn/ n Aussprache f

proof /pruːf/ n Beweis m; (*Typography*) Korrekturbogen m. **~-reader** n Korrektor m

prop¹ /prɒp/ n Stütze f ● vt (pt/pp **propped**) **~ against** lehnen an (+ acc). **~ up** vt stützen

prop² n (*Theat*, ▯) Requisit nt

propaganda /prɒpəˈgændə/ n Propaganda f

propel /prəˈpel/ vt (pt/pp **propelled**) [an]treiben. **~ler** n Propeller m

proper /ˈprɒpə(r)/ adj richtig; (*decent*) anständig

property /ˈprɒpətɪ/ n Eigentum nt; (*quality*) Eigenschaft f; (*Theat*) Requisit nt; (*land*) [Grund]besitz m; (*house*) Haus nt

prophecy /ˈprɒfəsɪ/ n Prophezeiung f

prophesy /ˈprɒfɪsaɪ/ vt (pt/pp -**ied**) prophezeien

prophet /ˈprɒfɪt/ n Prophet m. **~ic** adj prophetisch

proportion /prəˈpɔːʃn/ n Verhältnis nt; (*share*) Teil m; **~s** pl Proportionen; (*dimensions*) Maße. **~al** adj proportional

proposal /prəˈpəʊzl/ n Vorschlag m; (*of marriage*) [Heirats]antrag m

propose /prəˈpəʊz/ vt vorschlagen; (*intend*) vorhaben; einbringen (*motion*) ● vi einen Heiratsantrag machen

proposition /prɒpəˈzɪʃn/ n Vorschlag m

proprietor /prəˈpraɪətə(r)/ n Inhaber(in) m(f)

propriety /prəˈpraɪətɪ/ n Korrektheit f; (*decorum*) Anstand m

prose /prəʊz/ n Prosa f

prosecut|e /ˈprɒsɪkjuːt/ vt strafrechtlich verfolgen. **~ion** n strafrechtliche Verfolgung f; **the ~ion** die Anklage. **~or** n [**Public**] **P~or** Staatsanwalt m

prospect /ˈprɒspekt/ n Aussicht f

prospect|ive /prəˈspektɪv/ adj (future) zukünftig. **~or** n Prospektor m

prospectus /prəˈspektəs/ n Prospekt m

prosper /ˈprɒspə(r)/ vi gedeihen, florieren; (*person*) Erfolg haben. **~ity** n Wohlstand m

prosperous /ˈprɒspərəs/ adj wohlhabend

prostitut|e /ˈprɒstɪtjuːt/ n Prostituierte f. **~ion** n Prostitution f

prostrate /ˈprɒstreɪt/ adj ausgestreckt

protagonist /prəʊˈtægənɪst/ n Kämpfer m; (fig) Protagonist m

protect /prəˈtekt/ vt schützen (**from** vor + dat); beschützen (*person*). **~ion** n Schutz m. **~ive** adj Schutz-; (fig) beschützend. **~or** n Beschützer m

protein /ˈprəʊtiːn/ n Eiweiß nt

protest¹ /ˈprəʊtest/ n Protest m

protest² /prəˈtest/ vi protestieren

Protestant /ˈprɒtɪstənt/ adj pro-

437 | protester | publish

testantisch ● n Protestant(in) m(f)

protester /prə'testə(r)/ n Protestierende(r) m/f

prototype /'prəʊtə-/ n Prototyp m

protrude /prə'tru:d/ vi [her]vorstehen

proud /praʊd/ adj stolz (**of** auf + acc)

prove /pru:v/ vt beweisen ● vi ~**to be** sich erweisen als

proverb /'prɒvɜ:b/ n Sprichwort nt

provide /prə'vaɪd/ vt zur Verfügung stellen; spenden (shade); ~ **s.o. with sth** jdn mit etw versorgen od versehen ● vi ~ **for** sorgen für

provided /prə'vaɪdɪd/ conj ~ [**that**] vorausgesetzt [dass]

providen|ce /'prɒvɪdəns/ n Vorsehung f. ~**tial** adj **be** ~**tial** ein Glück sein

provinc|e /'prɒvɪns/ n Provinz f; (fig) Bereich m. ~**ial** adj provinziell

provision /prə'vɪʒn/ n Versorgung f (of mit); ~**s** pl Lebensmittel pl. ~**al** adj vorläufig

provocat|ion /prɒvə'keɪʃn/ n Provokation f. ~**ive** adj provozierend; (sexually) aufreizend

provoke /prə'vəʊk/ vt provozieren; (cause) hervorrufen

prow /praʊ/ n Bug m

prowl /praʊl/ vi herumschleichen

proximity /prɒk'sɪmətɪ/ n Nähe f

pruden|ce /'pru:dns/ n Umsicht f. ~**t** adj umsichtig; (wise) klug

prudish /'pru:dɪʃ/ adj prüde

prune¹ /pru:n/ n Backpflaume f

prune² vt beschneiden

pry /praɪ/ vi (pt/pp **pried**) neugierig sein

psalm /sɑ:m/ n Psalm m

psychiatric /saɪkɪ'ætrɪk/ adj psychiatrisch

psychiatr|ist /saɪ'kaɪətrɪst/ n Psychiater(in) m(f). ~**y** n Psychiatrie f

psychic /'saɪkɪk/ adj übersinnlich

psycho|a'nalysis /saɪkəʊ-/ n Psychoanalyse f. ~**'analyst** Psychoanalytiker(in) m(f)

psychological /saɪkə'lɒdʒɪkl/ adj psychologisch; (illness) psychisch

psycholog|ist /saɪ'kɒlədʒɪst/ n Psychologe m/ -login f. ~**y** n Psychologie f

P.T.O. abbr (**please turn over**) b.w.

pub /pʌb/ n ① Kneipe f

> **pub** Ein pub, kurz für public house, ist ein englisches Wirtshaus. Pubs sind bei allen Schichten der britschen Gesellschaft beliebt und Gäste haben oft eine Stammkneipe, wo sie Bier trinken und Darts oder Pool spielen. Öffnungszeiten sind meist von 11-23 Uhr und in vielen pubs kann man auch essen.

puberty /'pju:bətɪ/ n Pubertät f

public /'pʌblɪk/ adj öffentlich; **make** ~ publik machen ● n **the** ~ die Öffentlichkeit

publican /'pʌblɪkən/ n [Gast]wirt m

publication /pʌblɪ'keɪʃn/ n Veröffentlichung f

public: ~ **'holiday** n gesetzlicher Feiertag m. ~ **'house** n [Gast]wirtschaft f

publicity /pʌb'lɪsətɪ/ n Publicity f; (advertising) Reklame f

publicize /'pʌblɪsaɪz/ vt Reklame machen für

public: ~ **'school** n Privatschule f; (Amer) staatliche Schule f. ~**-'spirited** adj **be** ~**-spirited** Gemeinsinn haben

> **public school** Eine Privatschule in England und Wales für Schüler im Alter von dreizehn bis achtzehn Jahren. Die meisten public schools sind Internate, normalerweise entweder für Jungen oder Mädchen. Die Eltern zahlen Schulgeld für die Ausbildung ihrer Kinder. In Schottland und den USA ist eine public school eine staatliche Schule.

publish /'pʌblɪʃ/ vt veröffentlichen.

~**er** n Verleger(in) m(f); (firm) Verlag m. ~**ing** n Verlagswesen nt

pudding /'pʊdɪŋ/ n Pudding m; (course) Nachtisch m

puddle /'pʌdl/ n Pfütze f

puff /pʌf/ n (of wind) Hauch m; (of smoke) Wölkchen nt ● vt blasen, pusten; ~ **out** ausstoßen. ● vi keuchen; ~ **at** paffen an (+ dat) (pipe). ~**ed** adj (out of breath) aus der Puste. ~ **pastry** n Blätterteig m

pull /pʊl/ n Zug m; (jerk) Ruck m; (🔲: influence) Einfluss m ● vt ziehen; ziehen an (+ dat) (rope); ~ **a muscle** sich (dat) einen Muskel zerren; ~ **oneself together** sich zusammennehmen; ~ **one's weight** tüchtig mitarbeiten; ~ **s.o.'s leg** 🔲 jdn auf den Arm nehmen. ~ **down** vt herunterziehen; (demolish) abreißen. ~ **in** vt hereinziehen ● vi (Auto) einscheren. ~ **off** vt abziehen; 🔲 schaffen. ~ **out** vt herausziehen ● vi (Auto) ausscheren. ~ **through** vt durchziehen ● vi (recover) durchkommen. ~ **up** vt heraufziehen; ausziehen (plant) ● vi (Auto) anhalten

pullover /'pʊləʊvə(r)/ n Pullover m

pulp /pʌlp/ n Brei m; (of fruit) [Frucht]fleisch nt

pulpit /'pʊlpɪt/ n Kanzel f

pulse /pʌls/ n Puls m

pulses /'pʌlsɪz/ npl Hülsenfrüchte pl

pummel /'pʌml/ vt (pt/pp **pummelled**) mit den Fäusten bearbeiten

pump /pʌmp/ n Pumpe f ● vt pumpen; 🔲 aushorchen. ~ **up** vt (inflate) aufpumpen

pumpkin /'pʌmpkɪn/ n Kürbis m

pun /pʌn/ n Wortspiel nt

punch[1] /pʌntʃ/ n Faustschlag m; (device) Locher m ● vt boxen; lochen (ticket); stanzen (hole)

punch[2] n (drink) Bowle f

punctual /'pʌŋktjʊəl/ adj pünktlich. ~**ity** n Pünktlichkeit f

punctuat|e /'pʌŋktjʊeɪt/ vt mit Satzzeichen versehen. ~**ion** n Interpunktion f

puncture /'pʌŋktʃə(r)/ n Loch nt; (tyre) Reifenpanne f ● vt durchstechen

punish /'pʌnɪʃ/ vt bestrafen. ~**able** adj strafbar. ~**ment** n Strafe f

punt /pʌnt/ n (boat) Stechkahn m

puny /'pjuːnɪ/ adj mickerig

pup /pʌp/ n = **puppy**

pupil /'pjuːpl/ n Schüler(in) m(f); (of eye) Pupille f

puppet /'pʌpɪt/ n Puppe f; (fig) Marionette f

puppy /'pʌpɪ/ n junger Hund m

purchase /'pɜːtʃəs/ n Kauf m; (leverage) Hebelkraft f ● vt kaufen. ~**r** n Käufer m

pure /pjʊə(r)/ adj (-r, -st,) -**ly** adv rein

purge /pɜːdʒ/ n (Pol) Säuberungsaktion f ● vt reinigen

puri|fication /pjʊərɪfɪ'keɪʃn/ n Reinigung f. ~**fy** vt (pt/pp -**ied**) reinigen

puritanical /pjʊərɪ'tænɪkl/ adj puritanisch

purity /'pjʊərɪtɪ/ n Reinheit f

purple /'pɜːpl/ adj [dunkel]lila

purpose /'pɜːpəs/ n Zweck m; (intention) Absicht f; (determination) Entschlossenheit f; on ~ absichtlich. ~**ful** adj entschlossen. ~**ly** adv absichtlich

purr /pɜː(r)/ vi schnurren

purse /pɜːs/ n Portemonnaie nt; (Amer: handbag) Handtasche f

pursue /pə'sjuː/ vt verfolgen; (fig) nachgehen (+ dat). ~**r** n Verfolger(in) m(f)

pursuit /pə'sjuːt/ n Verfolgung f; Jagd f; (pastime) Beschäftigung f

pus /pʌs/ n Eiter m

push /pʊʃ/ n Stoß m; get the ~ 🔲 hinausfliegen ● vt/i schieben; (press) drücken; (roughly) stoßen. ~ **off** vt hinunterstoßen ● vi (🔲: leave) abhauen. ~ **on** vi (continue) weitergehen/-fahren; (with activity) weitermachen. ~ **up** vt hochschieben; hochtreiben (price)

push: ~**-button** n Druckknopf m. ~**-chair** n [Kinder]sportwagen m

pushy /'pʊʃɪ/ *adj* 🔲 aufdringlich

puss /pʊs/ *n*, **pussy** *n* Mieze *f*

put /pʊt/ *vt* (*pt/pp* put, *pres p* **putting**) tun; (*place*) setzen; (*upright*) stellen; (*flat*) legen; (*express*) ausdrücken; (*say*) sagen; (*estimate*) schätzen (**at** auf + *acc*); ~ **aside** *or* **by** beiseite legen ● *vi* ~ **to sea** auslaufen ● *adj* **stay** ~ dableiben. ~ **away** *vt* wegräumen. ~ **back** *vt* wieder hinsetzen/-stellen/-legen; zurückstellen (*clock*). ~ **down** *vt* hinsetzen/-stellen/-legen; (*suppress*) niederschlagen; (*kill*) töten; (*write*) niederschreiben; (*attribute*) zuschreiben (**to** *dat*). ~ **forward** *vt* vorbringen; vorstellen (*clock*). ~ **in** *vt* hineinsetzen/-stellen/-legen; (*insert*) einstecken; (*submit*) einreichen ● *vi* ~ **in for** beantragen. ~ **off** *vt* ausmachen (*light*); (*postpone*) verschieben; ~ **s.o.** jdn abbestellen; (*disconcert*) jdn aus der Fassung bringen. ~ **on** *vt* anziehen (*clothes*, *brake*); sich (*dat*) aufsetzen (*hat*); (*Culin*) aufsetzen; anmachen (*light*); aufführen (*play*); annehmen (*accent*); ~ **on weight** zunehmen. ~ **out** *vt* hinaussetzen/-stellen/-legen; ausmachen (*fire*, *light*); ausstrecken (*hand*); (*disconcert*) aus der Fassung bringen; ~ **s.o./oneself out** jdm/sich Umstände machen. ~ **through** *vt* durchstecken; (*Teleph*) verbinden (**to** mit). ~ **up** *vt* errichten (*building*); aufschlagen (*tent*); aufspannen (*umbrella*); anschlagen (*notice*); erhöhen (*price*); unterbringen (*guest*) ● *vi* (*at hotel*) absteigen in (+ *dat*); ~ **up with sth** sich (*dat*) etw bieten lassen

putrid /'pjuːtrɪd/ *adj* faulig

putt /pʌt/ *n* Putt *m*

putty /'pʌtɪ/ *n* Kitt *m*

puzzl|e /'pʌzl/ *n* Rätsel *nt*; (*jigsaw*) Puzzlespiel *nt* ● *vt* it ~es me es ist mir rätselhaft. ~**ing** *adj* rätselhaft

pyjamas /pə'dʒɑːməz/ *npl* Schlafanzug *m*

pylon /'paɪlən/ *n* Mast *m*

pyramid /'pɪrəmɪd/ *n* Pyramide *f*

python /'paɪθn/ *n* Pythonschlange *f*

Qq

quack /kwæk/ *n* Quaken *nt*; (*doctor*) Quacksalber *m* ● *vi* quaken

quadrangle /'kwɒdræŋgl/ *n* Viereck *nt*; (*court*) Hof *m*

quadruped /'kwɒdrʊped/ *n* Vierfüßer *m*

quadruple /'kwɒdrʊpl/ *adj* vierfach ● *vt* vervierfachen ● *vi* sich vervierfachen

quaint /kweɪnt/ *adj* (-er, -est) malerisch; (*odd*) putzig

quake /kweɪk/ *n* 🔲 Erdbeben *nt* ● *vi* beben; (*with fear*) zittern

qualif|ication /kwɒlɪfɪ'keɪʃn/ *n* Qualifikation *f*; (*reservation*) Einschränkung *f*. ~**ied** *adj* qualifiziert; (*trained*) ausgebildet; (*limited*) bedingt

qualify /'kwɒlɪfaɪ/ *v* (*pt/pp* -ied) ● *vt* qualifizieren; (*entitle*) berechtigen; (*limit*) einschränken ● *vi* sich qualifizieren

quality /'kwɒlətɪ/ *n* Qualität *f*; (*characteristic*) Eigenschaft *f*

qualm /kwɑːm/ *n* Bedenken *pl*

quantity /'kwɒntətɪ/ *n* Quantität *f*, Menge *f*; **in** ~ in großen Mengen

quarantine /'kwɒrəntiːn/ *n* Quarantäne *f*

quarrel /'kwɒrl/ *n* Streit *m* ● *vi* (*pt/pp* quarrelled) sich streiten. ~**some** *adj* streitsüchtig

quarry[1] /'kwɒrɪ/ *n* (*prey*) Beute *f*

quarry[2] *n* Steinbruch *m*

quart /kwɔːt/ *n* Quart *nt*

quarter /'kwɔːtə(r)/ *n* Viertel *nt*; (*of year*) Vierteljahr *nt*; (*Amer*) 25-Cent-Stück *nt*; ~**s** *pl* Quartier *nt*; **at [a]** ~ **to six** um Viertel vor sechs ● *vt* vierteln; (*Mil*) einquartieren (**on** bei). ~-'**final** *n* Viertelfinale *nt*

quarterly /'kwɔːtəlɪ/ *adj & adv* vierteljährlich

quartet /kwɔː'tet/ *n* Quartett *nt*

p

q

quartz /kwɔːts/ n Quarz m

quay /kiː/ n Kai m

queasy /'kwiːzɪ/ adj **I feel ~** mir ist übel

queen /kwiːn/ n Königin f; (Cards, Chess) Dame f

queer /kwɪə(r)/ adj (-er, -est) eigenartig; (dubious) zweifelhaft; (ill) unwohl

quell /kwel/ vt unterdrücken

quench /kwentʃ/ vt löschen

query /'kwɪərɪ/ n Frage f; (question mark) Fragezeichen nt ● vt (pt/pp -ied) infrage stellen; reklamieren (bill)

quest /kwest/ n Suche f (for nach)

question /'kwestʃn/ n Frage f; (for discussion) Thema nt; **out of the ~** ausgeschlossen; **the person in ~** die fragliche Person ● vt infrage stellen; **~ s.o.** jdn ausfragen; (police:) jdn verhören. **~able** adj zweifelhaft. **~ mark** n Fragezeichen nt

questionnaire /kwestʃə'neə(r)/ n Fragebogen m

queue /kjuː/ n Schlange f ● vi **~ [up]** Schlange stehen, sich anstellen (for nach)

quibble /'kwɪbl/ vi Haarspalterei treiben

quick /kwɪk/ adj (-er, -est) schnell; **be ~!** mach schnell! ● adv schnell. **~en** vt beschleunigen ● vi sich beschleunigen

quick: ~sand n Treibsand m. **~-tempered** adj aufbrausend

quid /kwɪd/ n inv ⬛ Pfund nt

quiet /'kwaɪət/ adj (-er, -est) still; (calm) ruhig; (soft) leise; **keep ~ about** ⬛ nichts sagen von ● n Stille f; Ruhe f

quiet|en /'kwaɪətn/ vt beruhigen ● vi **~en down** ruhig werden. **~ness** n Stille f; Ruhe f

quilt /kwɪlt/ n Steppdecke f. **~ed** adj Stepp-

quintet /kwɪn'tet/ n Quintett nt

quirk /kwɜːk/ n Eigenart f

quit /kwɪt/ v (pt/pp quitted or quit) ● vt verlassen; (give up) aufgeben; **~ doing sth** aufhören, etw zu tun ● vi gehen

quite /kwaɪt/ adv ganz; (really) wirklich; **~ [so]!** genau! **~ a few** ziemlich viele

quits /kwɪts/ adj quitt

quiver /'kwɪvə(r)/ vi zittern

quiz /kwɪz/ n Quiz nt ● vt (pt/pp quizzed) ausfragen. **~zical** adj fragend

quota /'kwəʊtə/ n Anteil m; (Comm) Kontingent nt

quotation /kwəʊ'teɪʃn/ n Zitat nt; (price) Kostenvoranschlag m; (of shares) Notierung f. **~ marks** npl Anführungszeichen pl

quote /kwəʊt/ n ⬛ = quotation; **in ~s** in Anführungszeichen ● vt/i zitieren

Rr

rabbi /'ræbaɪ/ n Rabbiner m; (title) Rabbi m

rabbit /'ræbɪt/ n Kaninchen nt

rabid /'ræbɪd/ adj fanatisch; (animal) tollwütig

rabies /'reɪbiːz/ n Tollwut f

race¹ /reɪs/ n Rasse f

race² n Rennen nt; (fig) Wettlauf m ● vi [am Rennen] teilnehmen; (athlete, horse:) laufen; (⬛: rush) rasen ● vt um die Wette laufen mit; an einem Rennen teilnehmen lassen (horse)

race: ~course n Rennbahn f. **~horse** n Rennpferd nt. **~track** n Rennbahn f

racial /'reɪʃl/ adj rassisch; (discrimination) Rassen-

racing /'reɪsɪŋ/ n Rennsport m; (horse-) Pferderennen nt. **~ car** n Rennwagen m. **~ driver** n Rennfahrer m

racis|m /'reɪsɪzm/ n Rassismus m. **~t** adj rassistisch ● n Rassist m

rack¹ /ræk/ n Ständer m; (for plates)
Gestell nt ● vt ~ one's brains sich
(dat) den Kopf zerbrechen

rack² n go to ~ and ruin verfallen;
(fig) herunterkommen

racket /ˈrækɪt/ n (Sport) Schläger m;
(din) Krach m; (swindle) Schwindelge-
schäft nt

racy /ˈreɪsɪ/ adj schwungvoll; (risqué)
gewagt

radar /ˈreɪdɑː(r)/ n Radar m

radian|ce /ˈreɪdɪəns/ n Strahlen nt.
~t adj strahlend

radiat|e /ˈreɪdɪeɪt/ vt ausstrahlen ● vi
(heat:) ausgestrahlt werden; (roads:)
strahlenförmig ausgehen. ~ion n
Strahlung f

radiator /ˈreɪdɪeɪtə(r)/ n Heizkörper
m; (Auto) Kühler m

radical /ˈrædɪkl/ adj radikal ● n Radi-
kale(r) m/f

radio /ˈreɪdɪəʊ/ n Radio nt; by ~
über Funk ● vt funken (message)

radio|ˈactive adj radioaktiv. ~ac-
ˈtivity n Radioaktivität f

radish /ˈrædɪʃ/ n Radieschen nt

radius /ˈreɪdɪəs/ n (pl -dii /-dɪaɪ/)
Radius m, Halbmesser m

raffle /ˈræfl/ n Tombola f

raft /rɑːft/ n Floß nt

rafter /ˈrɑːftə(r)/ n Dachsparren m

rag /ræg/ n Lumpen m; (pej: newspaper) Käseblatt nt

rage /reɪdʒ/ n Wut f; all the ~ 🄴
der letzte Schrei ● vi rasen

ragged /ˈrægɪd/ adj zerlumpt; (edge)
ausgefranst

raid /reɪd/ n Überfall m; (Mil) Angriff
m; (police) Razzia f ● vt überfallen;
(Mil) angreifen; (police) eine Razzia
durchführen In (+ dat); (break in) eindringen in (+ acc). ~er n Eindring-
ling m; (of bank) Bankräuber m

rail /reɪl/ n Schiene f; (pole) Stange f;
(hand~) Handlauf m; (Naut) Reling f;
by ~ mit der Bahn

railings /ˈreɪlɪŋz/ npl Geländer nt

ˈrailroad n (Amer) = railway

ˈrailway n [Eisen]bahn f. ~ station
n Bahnhof m

rain /reɪn/ n Regen m ● vi regnen

rain: ~bow n Regenbogen m.
~coat n Regenmantel m. ~fall n
Niederschlag m

rainy /ˈreɪnɪ/ adj regnerisch

raise /reɪz/ n (Amer) Lohnerhöhung f
● vt erheben; (upright) aufrichten;
(make higher) erhöhen; (lift) [hoch]-
heben; aufziehen (child, animal); aufwerfen (question); aufbringen
(money)

raisin /ˈreɪzn/ n Rosine f

rake /reɪk/ n Harke f, Rechen m ● vt
harken, rechen

rally /ˈrælɪ/ n Versammlung f; (Auto)
Rallye f; (Tennis) Ballwechsel m ● vt
sammeln

ram /ræm/ n Schafbock m ● vt (pt/pp
rammed) rammen

rambl|e /ˈræmbl/ n Wanderung f
● vi wandern; (in speech) irrereden.
~er n Wanderer m; (rose) Kletter-
rose f. ~ing adj weitschweifig; (club)
Wander-

ramp /ræmp/ n Rampe f; (Aviat)
Gangway f

rampage¹ /ˈræmpeɪdʒ/ n be/go on
the ~ randalieren

rampage² /ræmˈpeɪdʒ/ vi randalieren

ramshackle /ˈræmʃækl/ adj baufällig

ran /ræn/ see run

ranch /rɑːntʃ/ n Ranch f

random /ˈrændəm/ adj willkürlich; a
~ sample eine Stichprobe ● n at ~
aufs Geratewohl; (choose) willkürlich

rang /ræŋ/ see ring²

range /reɪndʒ/ n Serie f, Reihe f;
(Comm) Auswahl f, Angebot nt (of an
+ dat); (of mountains) Kette f; (Mus)
Umfang m; (distance) Reichweite f;
(for shooting) Schießplatz m; (stove)
Kohlenherd m ● vi reichen; ~ from
... to gehen von ... bis. ~r n Aufse-
her m

rank /ræŋk/ n (row) Reihe f; (Mil)
Rang m; (social position) Stand m;
the ~ and file die breite Masse
● vt/i einstufen; ~ among zählen zu

r

ransack /'rænsæk/ vt durchwühlen; (*pillage*) plündern

ransom /'rænsəm/ n Lösegeld nt; **hold s.o. to** ~ Lösegeld für jdn fordern

rape /reɪp/ n Vergewaltigung f ● vt vergewaltigen

rapid /'ræpɪd/ adj schnell. ~**ity** n Schnelligkeit f

rapist /'reɪpɪst/ n Vergewaltiger m

raptur|e /'ræptʃə(r)/ n Entzücken nt. ~**ous** adj begeistert

rare¹ /'reə(r)/ adj (-r, -st) selten

rare² adj (*Culin*) englisch gebraten

rarefied /'reərɪfaɪd/ adj dünn

rarity /'reərətɪ/ n Seltenheit f

rascal /'rɑːskl/ n Schlingel m

rash¹ /ræʃ/ n (*Med*) Ausschlag m

rash² adj (-er, -est) voreilig

rasher /'ræʃə(r)/ n Speckscheibe f

raspberry /'rɑːzbərɪ/ n Himbeere f

rat /ræt/ n Ratte f; (🔲: *person*) Schuft m; **smell a** ~ 🔲 Lunte riechen

rate /reɪt/ n Rate f; (*speed*) Tempo nt; (*of payment*) Satz m; (*of exchange*) Kurs m; ~**s** pl (*taxes*) ≈ Grundsteuer f; **at any** ~ auf jeden Fall; **at this** ~ auf diese Weise ● vt einschätzen; ~ **among** zählen zu ● vi ~ **as** gelten als

rather /'rɑːðə(r)/ adv lieber; (*fairly*) ziemlich; ~**!** und ob!

rating /'reɪtɪŋ/ n Einschätzung f; (*class*) Klasse f; (*sailor*) [einfacher] Matrose m; ~**s** pl (*Radio, TV*) ≈ Einschaltquote f

ratio /'reɪʃɪəʊ/ n Verhältnis nt

ration /'ræʃn/ n Ration f ● vt rationieren

rational /'ræʃənl/ adj rational. ~**ize** vt/i rationalisieren

rattle /'rætl/ n Rasseln nt; (*of windows*) Klappern nt; (*toy*) Klapper f ● vi rasseln; klappern ● vt rasseln mit

raucous /'rɔːkəs/ adj rau

rave /reɪv/ vi toben; ~ **about** schwärmen von

raven /'reɪvn/ n Rabe m

ravenous /'rævənəs/ adj heißhungrig

ravine /rə'viːn/ n Schlucht f

raving /'reɪvɪŋ/ adj ~ **mad** 🔲 total verrückt

ravishing /'rævɪʃɪŋ/ adj hinreißend

raw /rɔː/ adj (-er, -est) roh; (*not processed*) Roh-; (*skin*) wund; (*weather*) nasskalt; (*inexperienced*) unerfahren; **get a** ~ **deal** 🔲 schlecht wegkommen. ~ **ma'terials** npl Rohstoffe pl

ray /reɪ/ n Strahl m

razor /'reɪzə(r)/ n Rasierapparat m. ~ **blade** n Rasierklinge f

re /riː/ prep betreffs (+ gen)

reach /riːtʃ/ n Reichweite f; (*of river*) Strecke f; **within/out of** ~ in/außer Reichweite ● vt erreichen; (*arrive at*) ankommen in (+ dat); (~ *as far as*) reichen bis zu; kommen zu (*decision, conclusion*); (*pass*) reichen ● vi reichen (**to** bis zu); ~ **for** greifen nach

re'act /riː'ækt/ vi reagieren (**to** auf + acc)

re'action /rɪ-/ n Reaktion f. ~**ary** adj reaktionär

reactor /rɪ'æktə(r)/ n Reaktor m

read /riːd/ vt/i (pt/pp read /red/) lesen; (*aloud*) vorlesen (**to** dat); (*Univ*) studieren; ablesen (*meter*). ~ **out** vt vorlesen

readable /'riːdəbl/ adj lesbar

reader /'riːdə(r)/ n Leser(in) m(f); (*book*) Lesebuch nt

readily /'redɪlɪ/ adv bereitwillig; (*easily*) leicht

reading /'riːdɪŋ/ n Lesen nt; (*Pol, Relig*) Lesung f

rea'djust /riː-/ vt neu einstellen ● vi sich umstellen (**to** auf + acc)

ready /'redɪ/ adj fertig; (*willing*) bereit; (*quick*) schnell; **get** ~ sich fertig machen; (*prepare to*) sich bereitmachen

ready: ~**-'made** adj fertig. ~**-to-'wear** adj Konfektions-

real /rɪəl/ adj wirklich; (*genuine*) echt; (*actual*) eigentlich ● adv (*Amer,* 🔲) echt. ~ **estate** n Immobilien pl

realis|m /'rɪəlɪzm/ n Realismus m.

~t n Realist m. ~tic adj, -ally adv
realistisch

reality /rɪˈælətɪ/ n Wirklichkeit f

realization /rɪəlaɪˈzeɪʃn/ n Erkenntnis f

realize /ˈrɪəlaɪz/ vt einsehen; (become aware) gewahr werden; verwirklichen (hopes, plans); einbringen (price)

really /ˈrɪəlɪ/ adv wirklich; (actually) eigentlich

realm /relm/ n Reich nt

realtor /ˈriːəltə(r)/ n (Amer) Immobilienmakler m

reap /riːp/ vt ernten

reap'pear /riː-/ vi wiederkommen

rear[1] /rɪə(r)/ adj Hinter-; (Auto) Heck-
● n the ~ der hintere Teil; from the ~ von hinten

rear[2] vt aufziehen ● vi ~ [up] (horse:) sich aufbäumen

rear'range /riː-/ vt umstellen

reason /ˈriːzn/ n Grund m; (good sense) Vernunft f; (ability to think) Verstand m; **within** ~ in vernünftigen Grenzen ● vi argumentieren; ~ **with** vernünftig reden mit. ~**able** adj vernünftig; (not expensive) preiswert. ~**ably** adv (fairly) ziemlich

reas'sur|ance /riː-/ n Beruhigung f; Versicherung f. ~**e** vt beruhigen; ~**e s.o. of sth** jdm etw (gen) versichern

rebel[1] /ˈrebl/ n Rebell m

rebel[2] /rɪˈbel/ vi (pt/pp rebelled) rebellieren. ~**lion** n Rebellion f. ~**lious** adj rebellisch

re'bound[1] /rɪ-/ vi abprallen

'rebound[2] /riː-/ n Rückprall m

re'build /riː-/ vt (pt/pp -built) wieder aufbauen

rebuke /rɪˈbjuːk/ n Tadel m ● vt tadeln

re'call /rɪ-/ n Erinnerung f ● vt zurückrufen; abberufen (diplomat); (remember) sich erinnern an (+ acc)

recant /rɪˈkænt/ vi widerrufen

recap /ˈriːkæp/ vt/i 🔟 = recapitulate

recapitulate /riːkəˈpɪtjʊleɪt/ vt/i zusammenfassen; rekapitulieren

re'capture /riː-/ vt wieder gefangen

nehmen (person); wieder einfangen (animal)

reced|e /rɪˈsiːd/ vi zurückgehen. ~**ing** adj (forehead, chin) fliehend

receipt /rɪˈsiːt/ n Quittung f; (receiving) Empfang m; ~**s** pl (Comm) Einnahmen pl

receive /rɪˈsiːv/ vt erhalten, bekommen; empfangen (guests). ~**r** n (Teleph) Hörer m; (of stolen goods) Hehler m

recent /ˈriːsənt/ adj kürzlich erfolgte(r,s). ~**ly** adv vor kurzem

receptacle /rɪˈseptəkl/ n Behälter m

reception /rɪˈsepʃn/ n Empfang m; ~ **[desk]** (in hotel) Rezeption f: ~**ist** n Empfangsdame f

receptive /rɪˈseptɪv/ adj aufnahmefähig; ~ **to** empfänglich für

recess /rɪˈses/ n Nische f; (holiday) Ferien pl

recession /rɪˈseʃn/ n Rezession f

re'charge /riː-/ vt [wieder] aufladen

recipe /ˈresəpɪ/ n Rezept nt

recipient /rɪˈsɪpɪənt/ n Empfänger m

recital /rɪˈsaɪtl/ n (of poetry, songs) Vortrag m; (on piano) Konzert nt

recite /rɪˈsaɪt/ vt aufsagen; (before audience) vortragen

reckless /ˈreklɪs/ adj leichtsinnig; (careless) rücksichtslos. ~**ness** n Leichtsinn m; Rücksichtslosigkeit f

reckon /ˈrekən/ vt rechnen; (consider) glauben ● vi ~ **on/with** rechnen mit

re'claim /rɪ-/ vt zurückfordern; zurückgewinnen (land)

reclin|e /rɪˈklaɪn/ vi liegen. ~**ing seat** n Liegesitz m

recluse /rɪˈkluːs/ n Einsiedler(in) m(f)

recognition /rekəgˈnɪʃn/ n Erkennen nt; (acknowledgement) Anerkennung f; **in** ~ als Anerkennung (**of** gen)

recognize /ˈrekəgnaɪz/ vt erkennen; (know again) wieder erkennen; (acknowledge) anerkennen

re'coil /rɪ-/ vi zurückschnellen; (in

fear) zurückschrecken

recollect /rekə'lekt/ *vt* sich erinnern an (+ *acc*). **~ion** *n* Erinnerung *f*

recommend /rekə'mend/ *vt* empfehlen. **~ation** *n* Empfehlung *f*

recon|cile /'rekənsaɪl/ *vt* versöhnen; **~cile oneself to** sich abfinden mit. **~ciliation** *n* Versöhnung *f*

reconnaissance /rɪ'kɒnɪsns/ *n* (*Mil*) Aufklärung *f*

reconnoitre /rekə'nɔɪtə(r)/ *vi* (*pres p* **-tring**) auf Erkundung ausgehen

recon'sider /riː-/ *vt* sich (*dat*) noch einmal überlegen

recon'struct /riː-/ *vt* wieder aufbauen; rekonstruieren (*crime*)

record¹ /rɪ'kɔːd/ *vt* aufzeichnen; (*register*) registrieren; (*on tape*) aufnehmen

record² /'rekɔːd/ *n* Aufzeichnung *f*; (*Jur*) Protokoll *nt*; (*Mus*) [Schall]platte *f*; (*Sport*) Rekord *m*; **~s** *pl* Unterlagen *pl*; **off the ~** inoffiziell; **have a [criminal] ~** vorbestraft sein

recorder /rɪ'kɔːdə(r)/ *n* (*Mus*) Blockflöte *f*

recording /rɪ'kɔːdɪŋ/ *n* Aufnahme *f*

re-'count¹ /riː-/ *vt* nachzählen

're-count² /riː-/ *n* (*Pol*) Nachzählung *f*

recover /rɪ'kʌvə(r)/ *vt* zurückbekommen ● *vi* sich erholen. **~y** *n* Wiedererlangung *f*; (*of health*) Erholung *f*

recreation /rekrɪ'eɪʃn/ *n* Erholung *f*; (*hobby*) Hobby *nt*. **~al** *adj* Freizeit-; **be ~al** erholsam sein

recruit /rɪ'kruːt/ *n* (*Mil*) Rekrut *m*; **new ~** (*member*) neues Mitglied *nt*; (*worker*) neuer Mitarbeiter *m* ● *vt* rekrutieren; anwerben (*staff*). **~ment** *n* Rekrutierung *f*; Anwerbung *f*

rectang|le /'rektæŋgl/ *n* Rechteck *nt*. **~ular** *adj* rechteckig

rectify /'rektɪfaɪ/ *vt* (*pt/pp* **-ied**) berichtigen

rector /'rektə(r)/ *n* Pfarrer *m*; (*Univ*) Rektor *m*. **~y** *n* Pfarrhaus *nt*

recur /rɪ'kɜː(r)/ *vi* (*pt/pp* **recurred**) sich wiederholen; (*illness:*) wiederkehren

recurren|ce /rɪ'kʌrəns/ *n* Wiederkehr *f*. **~t** *adj* wiederkehrend

recycle /riː'saɪkl/ *vt* wieder verwerten

red /red/ *adj* (**redder, reddest**) rot ● *n* Rot *nt*

redd|en /'redn/ *vt* röten ● *vi* rot werden. **~ish** *adj* rötlich

re'decorate /riː-/ *vt* renovieren; (*paint*) neu streichen; (*wallpaper*) neu tapezieren

redeem /rɪ'diːm/ *vt* einlösen; (*Relig*) erlösen

redemption /rɪ'dempʃn/ *n* Erlösung *f*

red: ~-haired *adj* rothaarig. **~-'handed** *adj* **catch s.o. ~-handed** jdn auf frischer Tat ertappen. **~ 'herring** *n* falsche Spur *f*. **~-hot** *adj* glühend heiß. **~ 'light** *n* (*Auto*) rote Ampel *f*. **~ness** *n* Röte *f*

re'do /riː-/ *vt* (*pt* **-did**, *pp* **-done**) noch einmal machen

re'double /riː-/ *vt* verdoppeln

red 'tape *n* ☐ Bürokratie *f*

reduc|e /rɪ'djuːs/ *vt* verringern, vermindern; (*in size*) verkleinern; ermäßigen (*costs*); herabsetzen (*price, goods*); (*Culin*) einkochen lassen. **~tion** *n* Verringerung *f*; (*in price*) Ermäßigung *f*; (*in size*) Verkleinerung *f*

redundan|cy /rɪ'dʌndənsɪ/ *n* Beschäftigungslosigkeit *f*. **~t** *adj* überflüssig; **make ~t** entlassen; **be made ~t** beschäftigungslos werden

reed /riːd/ *n* [Schilf]rohr *nt*; **~s** *pl* Schilf *nt*

reef /riːf/ *n* Riff *nt*

reek /riːk/ *vi* riechen (**of** nach)

reel /riːl/ *n* Rolle *f*, Spule *f* ● *vi* (*stagger*) taumeln ● *vt* **~ off** (*fig*) herunterrasseln

refectory /rɪ'fektərɪ/ *n* Refektorium *nt*; (*Univ*) Mensa *f*

refer /rɪ'fɜː(r)/ *v* (*pt/pp* **referred**) ● *vt* verweisen (**to** an + *acc*); übergeben, weiterleiten (*matter*) (**to** an + *acc*) ● *vi* **~ to** sich beziehen auf (+ *acc*);

(*mention*) erwähnen; (*concern*) betreffen; (*consult*) sich wenden an (+ *acc*); nachschlagen in (+ *dat*) (*book*); **are you ~ring to me?** meinen Sie mich?

referee /refəˈriː/ n Schiedsrichter m; (*Boxing*) Ringrichter m; (*for job*) Referenz f ● vt/i (*pt/pp* **refereed**) Schiedsrichter/Ringrichter sein (bei)

reference /ˈrefərəns/ n Erwähnung f; (*in book*) Verweis m; (*for job*) Referenz f; **with ~ to** in Bezug auf (+ *acc*); **make [a] ~ to** erwähnen. **~ book** n Nachschlagewerk nt

referendum /refəˈrendəm/ n Volksabstimmung f

re'fill¹ /riː-/ vt nachfüllen

'refill² /riː-/ n (*for pen*) Ersatzmine f

refine /rɪˈfaɪn/ vt raffinieren. **~d** adj fein, vornehm. **~ment** n Vornehmheit f; (*Techn*) Verfeinerung f. **~ry** n Raffinerie f

reflect /rɪˈflekt/ vt reflektieren; (*mirror*) [wider]spiegeln; **be ~ed in** sich spiegeln in (+ *dat*) ● vi nachdenken (**on** über + *acc*). **~ion** n Reflexion f; (*image*) Spiegelbild nt; **on ~ion** nach nochmaliger Überlegung. **~or** n Rückstrahler m

reflex /ˈriːfleks/ n Reflex m

reflexive /rɪˈfleksɪv/ adj reflexiv

reform /rɪˈfɔːm/ n Reform f ● vt reformieren ● vi sich bessern

refrain¹ /rɪˈfreɪn/ n Refrain m

refrain² vi ~ **from doing sth** etw nicht tun

refresh /rɪˈfreʃ/ vt erfrischen. **~ing** adj erfrischend. **~ments** npl Erfrischungen pl

refrigerat|e /rɪˈfrɪdʒəreɪt/ vt kühlen. **~or** n Kühlschrank m

re'fuel /riː-/ vt/i (*pt/pp* **-fuelled**) auftanken

refuge /ˈrefjuːdʒ/ n Zuflucht f; **take ~** Zuflucht nehmen

refugee /refjʊˈdʒiː/ n Flüchtling m

'refund¹ /riː-/ **get a ~** sein Geld zurückbekommen

re'fund² /rɪ-/ vt zurückerstatten

refusal /rɪˈfjuːzl/ n (*see* **refuse¹**) Ablehnung f; Weigerung f

refuse¹ /rɪˈfjuːz/ vt ablehnen; (*not grant*) verweigern; ~ **to do sth** sich weigern, etw zu tun ● vi ablehnen; sich weigern

refuse² /ˈrefjuːs/ n Müll m

refute /rɪˈfjuːt/ vt widerlegen

re'gain /rɪ-/ vt wiedergewinnen

regal /ˈriːgl/ adj königlich

regard /rɪˈgɑːd/ n (*heed*) Rücksicht f; (*respect*) Achtung f; ~**s** pl Grüße pl; **with ~ to** in Bezug auf (+ *acc*) ● vt ansehen, betrachten (**as** als). **~ing** prep bezüglich (+ *gen*). **~less** adv ohne Rücksicht (**of** auf + *acc*)

regatta /rɪˈgætə/ n Regatta f

regime /reɪˈʒiːm/ n Regime nt

regiment /ˈredʒɪmənt/ n Regiment nt. **~al** adj Regiments-

region /ˈriːdʒən/ n Region f; **in the ~ of** (*fig*) ungefähr. **~al** adj regional

register /ˈredʒɪstə(r)/ n Register nt; (*Sch*) Anwesenheitsliste f ● vt registrieren; (*report*) anmelden; einschreiben (*letter*); aufgeben (*luggage*) ● vi (*report*) sich anmelden

registrar /redʒɪˈstrɑː(r)/ n Standesbeamte(r) m

registration /redʒɪˈstreɪʃn/ n Registrierung f; Anmeldung f. **~ number** n Autonummer f

registry office /ˈredʒɪstrɪ-/ n Standesamt nt

regret /rɪˈgret/ n Bedauern nt ● vt (*pt/pp* **regretted**) bedauern. **~fully** adv mit Bedauern

regrettab|le /rɪˈgretəbl/ adj bedauerlich. **~ly** adv bedauerlicherweise

regular /ˈregjʊlə(r)/ adj regelmäßig; (*usual*) üblich ● n (*in pub*) Stammgast m; (*in shop*) Stammkunde m. **~ity** n Regelmäßigkeit f

regulat|e /ˈregjʊleɪt/ vt regulieren. **~ion** n (*rule*) Vorschrift f

rehears|al /rɪˈhɜːsl/ n (*Theat*) Probe f. **~e** vt proben

reign /reɪn/ n Herrschaft f ● vi herrschen, regieren

rein /reɪn/ n Zügel m

reindeer /ˈreɪndɪə(r)/ n inv Rentier nt

reinforce /riːɪnˈfɔːs/ vt verstärken. **~ment** n Verstärkung f; **send ~ments** Verstärkung schicken

reiterate /riːˈɪtəreɪt/ vt wiederholen

reject /rɪˈdʒekt/ vt ablehnen. **~ion** n Ablehnung f

rejects /ˈriːdʒekts/ npl (Comm) Ausschussware f

rejoic|e /rɪˈdʒɔɪs/ vi (literary) sich freuen. **~ing** n Freude f

re'join /rɪ-/ vt sich wieder anschließen (+ dat); wieder beitreten (+ dat) (club, party)

rejuvenate /rɪˈdʒuːvəneɪt/ vt verjüngen

relapse /rɪˈlæps/ n Rückfall m ● vi einen Rückfall erleiden

relate /rɪˈleɪt/ vt (tell) erzählen; (connect) verbinden

relation /rɪˈleɪʃn/ n Beziehung f; (person) Verwandte(r) m/f. **~ship** n Beziehung f; (link) Verbindung f; (blood tie) Verwandtschaft f; (affair) Verhältnis nt

relative /ˈrelətɪv/ n Verwandte(r) m/f ● adj relativ; (Gram) Relativ-. **~ly** adv relativ, verhältnismäßig

relax /rɪˈlæks/ vt lockern, entspannen ● vi sich lockern, sich entspannen. **~ation** n Entspannung f. **~ing** adj entspannend

relay[1] /ˈriːleɪ/ vt (pt/pp -layed) weitergeben; (Radio, TV) übertragen

relay[2] /ˈriːleɪ/ n. **~ [race]** n Staffel f

release /rɪˈliːs/ n Freilassung f, Entlassung f; (Techn) Auslöser m ● vt freilassen; (let go of) loslassen; (Techn) auslösen; veröffentlichen (information)

relent /rɪˈlent/ vi nachgeben. **~less** adj erbarmungslos; (unceasing) unaufhörlich

relevan|ce /ˈreləvəns/ n Relevanz f. **~t** adj relevant (to für)

reliab|ility /rɪlaɪəˈbɪlətɪ/ n Zuverlässigkeit f. **~le** adj zuverlässig

relian|ce /rɪˈlaɪəns/ n Abhängigkeit f (on von). **~t** adj angewiesen (on auf + acc)

relic /ˈrelɪk/ n Überbleibsel nt; (Relig) Reliquie f

relief /rɪˈliːf/ n Erleichterung f; (assistance) Hilfe f; (replacement) Ablösung f; (Art) Relief nt

relieve /rɪˈliːv/ vt erleichtern; (take over from) ablösen; **~ of** entlasten von

religion /rɪˈlɪdʒən/ n Religion f

religious /rɪˈlɪdʒəs/ adj religiös

relinquish /rɪˈlɪŋkwɪʃ/ vt loslassen; (give up) aufgeben

relish /ˈrelɪʃ/ n Genuss m; (Culin) Würze f ● vt genießen

reluctan|ce /rɪˈlʌktəns/ n Widerstreben nt. **~t** adj widerstrebend; **be ~t** zögern (to zu). **~tly** adv ungern, widerstrebend

rely /rɪˈlaɪ/ vi (pt/pp -ied) **~ on** sich verlassen auf (+ acc); (be dependent on) angewiesen sein auf (+ acc)

remain /rɪˈmeɪn/ vi bleiben; (be left) übrig bleiben. **~der** n Rest m. **~ing** adj restlich. **~s** npl Reste pl; [mortal] **~s** [sterbliche] Überreste pl

remand /rɪˈmɑːnd/ n **on ~** in Untersuchungshaft ● vt **~ in custody** in Untersuchungshaft schicken

remark /rɪˈmɑːk/ n Bemerkung f ● vt bemerken. **~able** adj, **-bly** adv bemerkenswert

re|marry /riː-/ vi wieder heiraten

remedy /ˈremədɪ/ n [Heil]mittel nt (for gegen); (fig) Abhilfe f ● vt (pt/pp -ied) abhelfen (+ dat); beheben (fault)

rememb|er /rɪˈmembə(r)/ vt sich erinnern an (+ acc); **~er to do sth** daran denken, etw zu tun ● vi sich erinnern

remind /rɪˈmaɪnd/ vt erinnern (of an + acc). **~er** n Andenken nt; (letter, warning) Mahnung f

reminisce /remɪˈnɪs/ vi sich seinen Erinnerungen hingeben. **~nces** npl Erinnerungen pl. **~nt** adj **be ~nt of** erinnern an (+ acc)

remnant /ˈremnənt/ n Rest m

remorse /rɪˈmɔːs/ n Reue f. **~ful** adj reumütig. **~less** adj unerbittlich

remote /rɪ'məʊt/ *adj* fern; (*isolated*) abgelegen; (*slight*) gering. ~ con-'trol *n* Fernsteuerung *f*; (*for TV*) Fernbedienung *f*

remotely /rɪ'məʊtlɪ/ *adv* entfernt; **not** ~ nicht im Entferntesten

re'movable /rɪ-/ *adj* abnehmbar

removal /rɪ'muːvl/ *n* Entfernung *f*; (*from house*) Umzug *m*. ~ **van** *n* Möbelwagen *m*

remove /rɪ'muːv/ *vt* entfernen; (*take off*) abnehmen; (*take out*) herausnehmen

render /'rendə(r)/ *vt* machen; erweisen (*service*); (*translate*) wiedergeben; (*Mus*) vortragen

renegade /'renɪɡeɪd/ *n* Abtrünnige(r) *m/f*

renew /rɪ'njuː/ *vt* erneuern; verlängern (*contract*). ~**al** *n* Erneuerung *f*; Verlängerung *f*

renounce /rɪ'naʊns/ *vt* verzichten auf (+ *acc*)

renovat|e /'renəveɪt/ *vt* renovieren. ~**ion** *n* Renovierung *f*

renown /rɪ'naʊn/ *n* Ruf *m*. ~**ed** *adj* berühmt

rent /rent/ *n* Miete *f* ● *vt* mieten; (*hire*) leihen; ~ [**out**] vermieten; verleihen. ~**al** *n* Mietgebühr *f*; Leihgebühr *f*

renunciation /rɪnʌnsɪ'eɪʃn/ *n* Verzicht *m*

re'open /riː-/ *vt/i* wieder aufmachen

re'organize /riː-/ *vt* reorganisieren

rep /rep/ *n* 🔟 Vertreter *m*

repair /rɪ'peə(r)/ *n* Reparatur *f*; **in good/bad** ~ in gutem/schlechtem Zustand ● *vt* reparieren

repatriat|e /riː'pætrɪeɪt/ *vt* repatriieren

re'pay /riː-/ *vt* (*pt/pp* -**paid**) zurückzahlen; ~ **s.o. for sth** jdm etw zurückzahlen. ~**ment** *n* Rückzahlung *f*

repeal /rɪ'piːl/ *n* Aufhebung *f* ● *vt* aufheben

repeat /rɪ'piːt/ *n* Wiederholung *f* ● *vt/i* wiederholen; ~ **after me** sprechen Sie mir nach. ~**ed** *adj* wiederholt

repel /rɪ'pel/ *vt* (*pt/pp* **repelled**) abwehren; (*fig*) abstoßen. ~**lent** *adj* abstoßend

repent /rɪ'pent/ *vi* Reue zeigen. ~**ance** *n* Reue *f*. ~**ant** *adj* reuig

repercussions /riːpə'kʌʃnz/ *npl* Auswirkungen *pl*

repertoire /'repətwɑː(r)/, **repertory** *n* Repertoire *nt*

repetit|ion /repɪ'tɪʃn/ *n* Wiederholung *f*. ~**ive** *adj* eintönig

re'place /rɪ-/ *vt* zurücktun; (*take the place of*) ersetzen; (*exchange*) austauschen. ~**ment** *n* Ersatz *m*

'**replay** /riː-/ *n* (*Sport*) Wiederholungsspiel *nt*; [**action**] ~ Wiederholung *f*

replenish /rɪ'plenɪʃ/ *vt* auffüllen (*stocks*); (*refill*) nachfüllen

replica /'replɪkə/ *n* Nachbildung *f*

reply /rɪ'plaɪ/ *n* Antwort *f* (**to** auf + *acc*) ● *vt/i* (*pt/pp* **replied**) antworten

report /rɪ'pɔːt/ *n* Bericht *m*, (*Sch*) Zeugnis *nt*; (*rumour*) Gerücht *nt*; (*of gun*) Knall *m* ● *vt* berichten; (*notify*) melden; ~ **s.o. to the police** jdn anzeigen ● *vi* berichten (**on** über + *acc*); (*present oneself*) sich melden (**to** bei). ~**er** *n* Reporter(in) *m(f)*

reprehensible /reprɪ'hensəbl/ *adj* tadelnswert

represent /reprɪ'zent/ *vt* darstellen; (*act for*) vertreten, repräsentieren. ~**ation** *n* Darstellung *f*

representative /reprɪ'zentətɪv/ *adj* repräsentativ (**of** für) ● *n* Bevollmächtigte(r) *m(f)*; (*Comm*) Vertreter(in) *m(f)*; (*Amer, Politics*) Abgeordnete(r) *m/f*

repress /rɪ'pres/ *vt* unterdrücken. ~**ion** *n* Unterdrückung *f*. ~**ive** *adj* repressiv

reprieve /rɪ'priːv/ *n* Begnadigung *f*; (*fig*) Gnadenfrist *f* ● *vt* begnadigen

reprimand /'reprɪmɑːnd/ *n* Tadel *m* ● *vt* tadeln

'**reprint**[1] /riː-/ *n* Nachdruck *m*

re'print[2] /riː-/ *vt* neu auflegen

reprisal /rɪ'praɪzl/ *n* Vergeltungsmaßnahme *f*

r

reproach /rɪˈprəʊtʃ/ n Vorwurf m
● vt Vorwürfe pl machen (+ dat).
~**ful** adj vorwurfsvoll

repro'duc|e /riː-/ vt wiedergeben,
reproduzieren ● vi sich fortpflanzen.
~**tion** n Reproduktion f; (Biology)
Fortpflanzung f

reptile /ˈreptaɪl/ n Reptil nt

republic /rɪˈpʌblɪk/ n Republik f.
~**an** adj republikanisch ● n Republi-
kaner(in) m(f)

repugnan|ce /rɪˈpʌgnəns/ n Wider-
wille m. ~**t** adj widerlich

repuls|ion /rɪˈpʌlʃn/ n Widerwille
m. ~**ive** adj abstoßend, widerlich

reputable /ˈrepjʊtəbl/ adj (firm)
von gutem Ruf; (respectable) anständig

reputation /repjʊˈteɪʃn/ n Ruf m

request /rɪˈkwest/ n Bitte f ● vt bitten

require /rɪˈkwaɪə(r)/ vt (need) brauchen; (demand) erfordern; **be** ~**d to
do sth** etw tun müssen. ~**ment** n
Bedürfnis nt; (condition) Erforder-
nis nt

re'sale /riː-/ n Weiterverkauf m

rescue /ˈreskjuː/ n Rettung f ● vt
retten. ~**r** n Retter m

research /rɪˈsɜːtʃ/ n Forschung f
● vt erforschen; (in media) recherchieren. ~**er** n Forscher m; (for
media) Rechercheur m

resem|blance /rɪˈzembləns/ n Ähn-
lichkeit f. ~**ble** vt ähneln (+ dat)

resent /rɪˈzent/ vt übel nehmen;
einen Groll hegen gegen (person).
~**ful** adj verbittert. ~**ment** n
Groll m

reservation /rezəˈveɪʃn/ n Reser-
vierung f; (doubt) Vorbehalt m; (enclosure) Reservat nt

reserve /rɪˈzɜːv/ n Reserve f; (for
animals) Reservat nt; (Sport) Reserve-
spieler(in) m(f) ● vt reservieren; (client:) reservieren lassen; (keep) aufheben; sich (dat) vorbehalten (right).
~**d** adj reserviert

reservoir /ˈrezəvwɑː(r)/ n Reservoir nt

re'shuffle /riː-/ n (Pol) Umbildung f
● vt (Pol) umbilden

residence /ˈrezɪdəns/ n Wohnsitz
m; (official) Residenz f; (stay) Aufenthalt m

resident /ˈrezɪdənt/ adj ansässig (**in**
in + dat); (housekeeper, nurse) im
Haus wohnend ● n Bewohner(in)
m(f); (of street) Anwohner m. ~**ial**
adj Wohn-

residue /ˈrezɪdjuː/ n Rest m; (Chemistry) Rückstand m

resign /rɪˈzaɪn/ vt ~ **oneself to** sich
abfinden mit ● vi kündigen; (from
public office) zurücktreten. ~**ation** n
Resignation f; (from job) Kündigung
f; Rücktritt m. ~**ed** adj resigniert

resilient /rɪˈzɪliənt/ adj federnd;
(fig) widerstandsfähig

resin /ˈrezɪn/ n Harz nt

resist /rɪˈzɪst/ vt/i sich widersetzen (+
dat), (fig) widerstehen (+ dat).
~**ance** n Widerstand m. ~**ant** adj
widerstandsfähig

resolut|e /ˈrezəluːt/ adj entschlos-
sen. ~**ion** n Entschlossenheit f; (intention) Vorsatz m; (Pol) Resolution f

resolve /rɪˈzɒlv/ n Entschlossenheit
f; (decision) Beschluss m ● vt beschließen; (solve) lösen

resort /rɪˈzɔːt/ n (place) Urlaubsort
m; **as a last** ~ wenn alles andere
fehlschlägt ● vi ~ **to** (fig) greifen zu

resound /rɪˈzaʊnd/ vi widerhallen

resource /rɪˈsɔːs/ n ~**s** pl Ressour-
cen pl. ~**ful** adj findig

respect /rɪˈspekt/ n Respekt m, Achtung f (**for** vor + dat); (aspect) Hinsicht f; **with** ~ **to** in Bezug auf (+
acc) ● vt respektieren, achten

respect|able /rɪˈspektəbl/ adj, **-bly**
adv ehrbar; (decent) anständig; (considerable) ansehnlich. ~**ful** adj res-
pektvoll

respective /rɪˈspektɪv/ adj jeweilig.
~**ly** adv beziehungsweise

respiration /respəˈreɪʃn/ n Atmung f

respite /ˈrespaɪt/ n [Ruhe]pause f;
(delay) Aufschub m

respond /rɪˈspɒnd/ vi antworten; (react) reagieren (**to** auf + acc)

response /rɪˈspɒns/ n Antwort f; Reaktion f

responsibility /rɪspɒnsɪˈbɪlətɪ/ n Verantwortung f; (duty) Verpflichtung f

responsib|le /rɪˈspɒnsəbl/ adj verantwortlich; (trustworthy) verantwortungsvoll. **~ly** adv verantwortungsbewusst

rest¹ /rest/ n Ruhe f; (holiday) Erholung f; (interval & Mus) Pause f; **have a ~** eine Pause machen; (rest) sich ausruhen ● vt ausruhen; (lean) lehnen (**on** an/auf + acc) ● vi ruhen; (have a rest) sich ausruhen

rest² n **the ~** der Rest; (people) die Übrigen pl ● vi **it ~s with you** es ist an Ihnen (**to** zu)

restaurant /ˈrest(ə)rɒnt/ n Restaurant nt, Gaststätte f

restful /ˈrestfl/ adj erholsam

restive /ˈrestɪv/ adj unruhig

restless /ˈrestlɪs/ adj unruhig

restoration /restəˈreɪʃn/ n (of building) Restaurierung f

restore /rɪˈstɔː(r)/ vt wiederherstellen; restaurieren (building)

restrain /rɪˈstreɪn/ vt zurückhalten; **~ oneself** sich beherrschen. **~ed** adj zurückhaltend. **~t** n Zurückhaltung f

restrict /rɪˈstrɪkt/ vt einschränken; **~ to** beschränken auf (+ acc). **~ion** n Einschränkung f; Beschränkung f. **~ive** adj einschränkend

'rest room n (Amer) Toilette f

result /rɪˈzʌlt/ n Ergebnis nt, Resultat nt; (consequence) Folge f; **as a ~** als Folge (**of** gen) ● vi sich ergeben (**from** aus); **~ in** enden in (+ dat); (lead to) führen zu

resume /rɪˈzjuːm/ vt wieder aufnehmen ● vi wieder beginnen

résumé /ˈrezʊmeɪ/ n Zusammenfassung f

resumption /rɪˈzʌmpʃn/ n Wiederaufnahme f

resurrect /rezəˈrekt/ vt (fig) wieder beleben. **~ion** n **the R ~ion** (Relig) die Auferstehung

resuscitat|e /rɪˈsʌsɪteɪt/ vt wieder beleben. **~ion** n Wiederbelebung f

retail /ˈriːteɪl/ n Einzelhandel m ● adj Einzelhandels- ● adv im Einzelhandel ● vt im Einzelhandel verkaufen ● vi **~ at** im Einzelhandel kosten. **~er** n Einzelhändler m

retain /rɪˈteɪn/ vt behalten

retaliat|e /rɪˈtælɪeɪt/ vi zurückschlagen. **~ion** n Vergeltung f; **in ~ion** als Vergeltung

retarded /rɪˈtɑːdɪd/ adj zurückgeblieben

reticen|ce /ˈretɪsns/ n Zurückhaltung f. **~t** adj zurückhaltend

retina /ˈretɪnə/ n Netzhaut f

retinue /ˈretɪnjuː/ n Gefolge nt

retire /rɪˈtaɪə(r)/ vi in den Ruhestand treten; (withdraw) sich zurückziehen. **~d** adj im Ruhestand. **~ment** n Ruhestand m

retiring /rɪˈtaɪərɪŋ/ adj zurückhaltend

retort /rɪˈtɔːt/ n scharfe Erwiderung f; (Chemistry) Retorte f ● vt scharf erwidern

re'trace /riː-/ vt **~ one's steps** denselben Weg zurückgehen

re'train /riː-/ vt umschulen ● vi umgeschult werden

retreat /rɪˈtriːt/ n Rückzug m; (place) Zufluchtsort m ● vi sich zurückziehen

re'trial /riː-/ n Wiederaufnahmeverfahren nt

retrieve /rɪˈtriːv/ vt zurückholen; (from wreckage) bergen; (Computing) wieder auffinden

retrograde /ˈretrəgreɪd/ adj rückschrittlich

retrospect /ˈretrəspekt/ n **in ~** rückblickend. **~ive** adj rückwirkend; (looking back) rückblickend

return /rɪˈtɜːn/ n Rückkehr f; (giving back) Rückgabe f; (Comm) Ertrag m; (ticket) Rückfahrkarte f; (Aviat) Rückflugschein m; **by ~ [of post]** postwendend; **in ~** dafür; **in ~ for** für;

r

many happy ~s! herzlichen Glückwunsch zum Geburtstag! ● *vt* zurückgehen/-fahren; (*come back*) zurückkommen ● *vt* zurückgeben; (*put back*) zurückstellen/-legen; (*send back*) zurückschicken

return ticket *n* Rückfahrkarte *f*; (*Aviat*) Rückflugschein *m*

reunion /riːˈjuːnɪən/ *n* Wiedervereinigung *f*; (*social gathering*) Treffen *nt*

reunite /riːjuːˈnaɪt/ *vt* wieder vereinigen

re'use *vt* wieder verwenden

rev /rev/ *n* (*Auto*, Ⓣ) Umdrehung *f* ● *vt/i* ~ **[up]** den Motor auf Touren bringen

reveal /rɪˈviːl/ *vt* zum Vorschein bringen; (*fig*) enthüllen. **~ing** *adj* (*fig*) aufschlussreich

revel /ˈrevl/ *vi* (*pt/pp* **revelled**) ~ **in** sth etw genießen

revelation /revəˈleɪʃn/ *n* Offenbarung *f*, Enthüllung *f*

revenge /rɪˈvendʒ/ *n* Rache *f*; (*fig & Sport*) Revanche *f* ● *vt* rächen

revenue /ˈrevənjuː/ *n* [Staats]einnahmen *pl*

revere /rɪˈvɪə(r)/ *vt* verehren. **~nce** *n* Ehrfurcht *f*

Reverend /ˈrevərənd/ *adj* the ~ X Pfarrer X; (*Catholic*) Hochwürden X

reverent /ˈrevərənt/ *adj* ehrfürchtig

reversal /rɪˈvɜːsl/ *n* Umkehrung *f*

reverse /rɪˈvɜːs/ *adj* umgekehrt ● *n* Gegenteil *nt*; (*back*) Rückseite *f*; (*Auto*) Rückwärtsgang *m* ● *vt* umkehren; (*Auto*) zurücksetzen ● *vi* zurücksetzen

revert /rɪˈvɜːt/ *vi* ~ **to** zurückfallen an (+ *acc*)

review /rɪˈvjuː/ *n* Rückblick *m* (**of** auf + *acc*); (*re-examination*) Überprüfung *f*; (*Mil*) Truppenschau *f*; (*of book, play*) Kritik *f*, Rezension *f* ● *vt* zurückblicken auf (+ *acc*); überprüfen (*situation*); rezensieren (*book, play*). **~er** *n* Kritiker *m*, Rezensent *m*

revis|e /rɪˈvaɪz/ *vt* revidieren; (*for exam*) wiederholen. **~ion** *n* Revision *f*; Wiederholung *f*

revival /rɪˈvaɪvl/ *n* Wiederbelebung *f*

revive /rɪˈvaɪv/ *vt* wieder beleben; (*fig*) wieder aufleben lassen ● *vi* wieder aufleben

revolt /rɪˈvəʊlt/ *n* Aufstand *m* ● *vi* rebellieren ● *vt* anwidern. **~ing** *adj* widerlich, eklig

revolution /revəˈluːʃn/ *n* Revolution *f*; (*Auto*) Umdrehung *f*. **~ary** *adj* revolutionär. **~ize** *vt* revolutionieren

revolve /rɪˈvɒlv/ *vi* sich drehen; ~ **around** kreisen um

revolv|er /rɪˈvɒlvə(r)/ *n* Revolver *m*. **~ing** *adj* Dreh-

revue /rɪˈvjuː/ *n* Revue *f*; (*satirical*) Kabarett *nt*

revulsion /rɪˈvʌlʃn/ *n* Abscheu *m*

reward /rɪˈwɔːd/ *n* Belohnung *f* ● *vt* belohnen. **~ing** *adj* lohnend

re'write /riː-/ *vt* (*pt* **rewrote**, *pp* **rewritten**) noch einmal [neu] schreiben; (*alter*) umschreiben

rhetoric /ˈretərɪk/ *n* Rhetorik *f*. **~al** *adj* rhetorisch

rheumatism /ˈruːmətɪzm/ *n* Rheumatismus *m*, Rheuma *nt*

Rhine /raɪn/ *n* Rhein *m*

rhinoceros /raɪˈnɒsərəs/ *n* Nashorn *nt*, Rhinozeros *nt*

rhubarb /ˈruːbɑːb/ *n* Rhabarber *m*

rhyme /raɪm/ *n* Reim *m* ● *vt* reimen ● *vi* sich reimen

rhythm /ˈrɪðm/ *n* Rhythmus *m*. **~ic[al]** *adj*, **-ally** *adv* rhythmisch

rib /rɪb/ *n* Rippe *f*

ribbon /ˈrɪbən/ *n* Band *nt*; (*for typewriter*) Farbband *nt*

rice /raɪs/ *n* Reis *m*

rich /rɪtʃ/ *adj* (**-er**, **-est**) reich; (*food*) gehaltvoll; (*heavy*) schwer ● *n* the ~ *pl* die Reichen; **~es** *pl* Reichtum *m*

ricochet /ˈrɪkəʃeɪ/ *vi* abprallen

rid /rɪd/ *vt* (*pt/pp* **rid**, *pres p* **ridding**) befreien (**of** von); **get ~ of** loswerden

riddance /ˈrɪdns/ *n* **good ~!** auf Nimmerwiedersehen!

ridden /ˈrɪdn/ *see* ride

riddle /ˈrɪdl/ *n* Rätsel *nt*

r

riddled /ˈrɪdld/ adj ~ **with** durchlöchert mit

ride /raɪd/ n Ritt m; (in vehicle) Fahrt f; **take s.o. for a** ~ 🔟 jdn reinlegen ● v (pt **rode**, pp **ridden**) ● vt reiten (horse); fahren mit (bicycle) ● vi reiten; (in vehicle) fahren. ~**r** n Reiter(in) m(f); (on bicycle) Fahrer(in) m(f)

ridge /rɪdʒ/ n Erhebung f; (on roof) First m; (of mountain) Grat m, Kamm m

ridicule /ˈrɪdɪkjuːl/ n Spott m ● vt verspotten, spotten über (+ acc)

ridiculous /rɪˈdɪkjʊləs/ adj lächerlich

riding /ˈraɪdɪŋ/ n Reiten nt ● attrib Reit-

riff-raff /ˈrɪfræf/ n Gesindel nt

rifle /ˈraɪfl/ n Gewehr nt ● vt plündern; ~ **through** durchwühlen

rift /rɪft/ n Spalt m; (fig) Riss m

rig /rɪg/ n Ölbohrturm m; (at sea) Bohrinsel f ● vt (pt/pp **rigged**) ~ **out** ausrüsten; ~ **up** aufbauen

right /raɪt/ adj richtig; (not left) rechte(r,s); **be** ~ (person:) Recht haben; (clock:) richtig gehen; **put** ~ wieder in Ordnung bringen; (fig) richtig stellen; **that's** ~! das stimmt! ● adv richtig; (directly) direkt; (completely) ganz; (not left) rechts; (go) nach rechts; ~ **away** sofort ● n Recht nt; (not left) rechte Seite f; **on the** ~ rechts; **from/to the** ~ von/nach rechts; **be in the** ~ Recht haben; **by** ~**s** eigentlich; **the R**~ (Pol) die Rechte. ~ **angle** n rechter Winkel m

rightful /ˈraɪtfl/ adj rechtmäßig

right-'handed adj rechtshändig

rightly /ˈraɪtlɪ/ adv mit Recht

right-'wing adj (Pol) rechte(r,s)

rigid /ˈrɪdʒɪd/ adj starr; (strict) streng. ~**ity** n Starrheit f; Strenge f

rigorous /ˈrɪgərəs/ adj streng

rigour /ˈrɪgə(r)/ n Strenge f

rim /rɪm/ n Rand m; (of wheel) Felge f

rind /raɪnd/ n (on fruit) Schale f; (on cheese) Rinde f; (on bacon) Schwarte f

ring[1] /rɪŋ/ n Ring m; (for circus) Manege f; **stand in a** ~ im Kreis stehen ● vt umringen

ring[2] n Klingeln nt; **give s.o. a** ~ (Teleph) jdn anrufen ● v (pt **rang**, pp **rung**) ● vt läuten; ~ **[up]** (Teleph) anrufen ● vi (bells:) läuten; (telephone:) klingeln. ~ **back** vt/i (Teleph) zurückrufen

ring: ~**leader** n Rädelsführer m. ~ **road** n Umgehungsstraße f

rink /rɪŋk/ n Eisbahn f

rinse /rɪns/ n Spülung f; (hair colour) Tönung f ● vt spülen

riot /ˈraɪət/ n Aufruhr m; ~**s** pl Unruhen pl; **run** ~ randalieren ● vi randalieren. ~**er** n Randalierer m. ~**ous** adj aufrührerisch; (boisterous) wild

rip /rɪp/ n Riss m ● vt/i (pt/pp **ripped**) zerreißen; ~ **open** aufreißen. ~ **off** vt 🔟 neppen

ripe /raɪp/ adj (-r, -st) reif

ripen /ˈraɪpn/ vi reifen ● vt reifen lassen

ripeness /ˈraɪpnɪs/ n Reife f

'rip-off n 🔟 Nepp m

ripple /ˈrɪpl/ n kleine Welle f

rise /raɪz/ n Anstieg m; (fig) Aufstieg m; (increase) Zunahme f; (in wages) Lohnerhöhung f; (in salary) Gehaltserhöhung f; **give** ~ **to** Anlass geben zu ● vi (pt **rose**, pp **risen**) steigen; (ground:) ansteigen; (sun, dough:) aufgehen; (river:) entspringen; (get up) aufstehen; (fig) aufsteigen (**to** zu). ~**r** n **early** ~**r** Frühaufsteher m

rising /ˈraɪzɪŋ/ adj steigend; (sun) aufgehend ● n (revolt) Aufstand m

risk /rɪsk/ n Risiko nt; **at one's own** ~ auf eigene Gefahr ● vt riskieren

risky /ˈrɪskɪ/ adj riskant

rite /raɪt/ n Ritus m

ritual /ˈrɪtjʊəl/ adj rituell ● n Ritual nt

rival /ˈraɪvl/ adj rivalisierend ● n Rivale m/Rivalin f. ~**ry** n Rivalität f; (Comm) Konkurrenzkampf m

river /ˈrɪvə(r)/ n Fluss m

r

rivet /ˈrɪvɪt/ n Niete f ● vt [ver]nieten; ~ed by (fig) gefesselt von

road /rəʊd/ n Straße f; (fig) Weg m

road: ~-map n Straßenkarte f. ~ safety n Verkehrssicherheit f. ~side n Straßenrand m. ~way n Fahrbahn f. ~-works npl Straßenarbeiten pl. ~worthy adj verkehrssicher

roam /rəʊm/ vi wandern

roar /rɔː(r)/ n Gebrüll nt; ~s of laughter schallendes Gelächter nt ● vi brüllen; (with laughter) schallend lachen. ~ing adj (fire) prasselnd; do a ~ing trade 🔲 ein Bombengeschäft machen

roast /rəʊst/ adj gebraten, Brat-; ~ beef/pork Rinder-/Schweinebraten m ● n Braten m ● vt/i braten; rösten (coffee, chestnuts)

rob /rɒb/ vt (pt/pp robbed) berauben (of gen); ausrauben (bank). ~ber n Räuber m. ~bery n Raub m

robe /rəʊb/ n Robe f; (Amer: bathrobe) Bademantel m

robin /ˈrɒbɪn/ n Rotkehlchen nt

robot /ˈrəʊbɒt/ n Roboter m

robust /rəʊˈbʌst/ adj robust

rock¹ /rɒk/ n Fels m; on the ~s (ship) aufgelaufen; (marriage) kaputt; (drink) mit Eis

rock² vt/i schaukeln

rock³ n (Mus) Rock m

rockery /ˈrɒkərɪ/ n Steingarten m

rocket /ˈrɒkɪt/ n Rakete f

rocking: ~-chair n Schaukelstuhl m. ~-horse n Schaukelpferd nt

rocky /ˈrɒkɪ/ adj felsig; (unsteady) wackelig

rod /rɒd/ n Stab m; (stick) Rute f; (for fishing) Angel[rute] f

rode /rəʊd/ see ride

rodent /ˈrəʊdnt/ n Nagetier nt

rogue /rəʊɡ/ n Gauner m

role /rəʊl/ n Rolle f

roll /rəʊl/ n Rolle f; (bread) Brötchen nt; (list) Liste f; (of drum) Wirbel m ● vi rollen; be ~ing in money 🔲 Geld wie Heu haben ● vt rollen; walzen (lawn); ausrollen (pastry). ~ over vi sich auf die andere Seite rollen. ~ up vt aufrollen; hochkrempeln (sleeves) ● vi 🔲 auftauchen

roller /ˈrəʊlə(r)/ n Rolle f; (lawn, road) Walze f; (hair) Lockenwickler m. ~ blind n Rollo nt. R~blades® npl Rollerblades® mpl. ~-coaster n Berg-und-Talbahn f. ~-skate n Rollschuh m

'rolling-pin n Teigrolle f

Roman /ˈrəʊmən/ adj römisch ● n Römer(in) m(f)

romance /rəˈmæns/ n Romantik f; (love-affair) Romanze f; (book) Liebesgeschichte f

Romania /rəʊˈmeɪnɪə/ n Rumänien nt. ~n adj rumänisch ● n Rumäne m/-nin f

romantic /rəʊˈmæntɪk/ adj, -ally adv romantisch. ~ism n Romantik f

Rome /rəʊm/ n Rom nt

romp /rɒmp/ vi [herum]tollen

roof /ruːf/ n Dach nt; (of mouth) Gaumen m ● vt ~ [over] überdachen. ~-top n Dach nt

rook /rʊk/ n Saatkrähe f; (Chess) Turm m

room /ruːm/ n Zimmer nt; (for functions) Saal m; (space) Platz m. ~y adj geräumig

roost /ruːst/ n Hühnerstange f

root¹ /ruːt/ n Wurzel f; take ~ anwachsen ● vi Wurzeln schlagen. ~ out vt (fig) ausrotten

root² vi ~ about wühlen; ~ for s.o. 🔲 für jdn sein

rope /rəʊp/ n Seil nt; know the ~s 🔲 sich auskennen. ~ in vt 🔲 einspannen

rose¹ /rəʊz/ n Rose f; (of wateringcan) Brause f

rose² see rise

rostrum /ˈrɒstrəm/ n Podium nt

rosy /ˈrəʊzɪ/ adj rosig

rot /rɒt/ n Fäulnis f; (🔲: nonsense) Quatsch m ● vi (pt/pp rotted) [ver]faulen

rota /ˈrəʊtə/ n Dienstplan m

rotary /ˈrəʊtərɪ/ adj Dreh-; (Techn) Rotations-

rotat|e /rəʊˈteɪt/ vt drehen ● vi sich

drehen; (*Techn*) rotieren. ~**ion** *n* Drehung *f*; **in** ~**ion** im Wechsel

rote /rəʊt/ *n* **by** ~ auswendig

rotten /'rɒtn/ *adj* faul; 🔲 mies; (*person*) fies

rough /rʌf/ *adj* (**-er, -est**) rau; (*uneven*) uneben; (*coarse, not gentle*) grob; (*brutal*) roh; (*turbulent*) stürmisch; (*approximate*) ungefähr ● *adv* **sleep** ~ im Freien übernachten ● *vt* ~ **it** primitiv leben. ~ **out** *vt* im Groben entwerfen

roughage /'rʌfɪdʒ/ *n* Ballaststoffe *pl*

rough 'draft *n* grober Entwurf *m*

rough|ly /'rʌflɪ/ *adv* (*see* **rough**) rau; grob; roh; ungefähr. ~**ness** *n* Rauheit *f*

'rough paper *n* Konzeptpapier *nt*

round /raʊnd/ *adj* (**-er, -est**) rund ● *n* Runde *f*; (*slice*) Scheibe *f*; **do one's** ~**s** seine Runde machen ● *prep* um (+ *acc*); ~ **the clock** rund um die Uhr ● *adv* **all** ~ ringsherum; **ask s.o.** ~ jdn einladen ● *vt* biegen um (*corner*). ~ **off** *vt* abrunden. ~ **up** *vt* aufrunden; zusammentreiben (*animals*); festnehmen (*criminals*)

roundabout /'raʊndəbaʊt/ *adj* ~ **route** Umweg *m* ● *n* Karussell *nt*; (*for traffic*) Kreisverkehr *m*

round 'trip *n* Rundreise *f*

rous|e /raʊz/ *vt* wecken; (*fig*) erregen. ~**ing** *adj* mitreißend

route /ruːt/ *n* Route *f*; (*of bus*) Linie *f*

routine /ruːˈtiːn/ *adj* routinemäßig ● *n* Routine *f*; (*Theat*) Nummer *f*

row[1] /rəʊ/ *n* (*line*) Reihe *f*

row[2] *vt/i* rudern

row[3] /raʊ/ *n* 🔲 Krach *m* ● *vi* 🔲 sich streiten

rowdy /'raʊdɪ/ *adj* laut

rowing boat /'rəʊɪŋ-/ *n* Ruderboot *nt*

royal /'rɔɪəl/ *adj* königlich

royal|ty /'rɔɪəltɪ/ *n* Königtum *nt*; (*persons*) Mitglieder *pl* der königlichen Familie; **-ies** *pl* (*payments*) Tantiemen *pl*

RSI *abbr* (**repetitive strain injury**) chronisches Überlastungssyndrom *nt*

rub /rʌb/ *vt* (*pt/pp* **rubbed**) reiben; (*polish*) polieren; **don't** ~ **it in** 🔲 reib es mir nicht unter die Nase. ~ **off** *vt* abreiben ● *vi* abgehen. ~ **out** *vt* ausradieren

rubber /'rʌbə(r)/ *n* Gummi *m*; (*eraser*) Radiergummi *m*. ~ **band** *n* Gummiband *nt*

rubbish /'rʌbɪʃ/ *n* Abfall *m*, Müll *m*; (🔲: *nonsense*) Quatsch *m*; (🔲: *junk*) Plunder *m*. ~ **bin** *n* Abfalleimer *m*. ~ **dump** *n* Abfallhaufen *m*; (*official*) Müllhalde *f*

rubble /'rʌbl/ *n* Trümmer *pl*

ruby /'ruːbɪ/ *n* Rubin *m*

rudder /'rʌdə(r)/ *n* [Steuer]ruder *nt*

rude /ruːd/ *adj* (**-r, -st**) unhöflich; (*improper*) unanständig. ~**ness** *n* Unhöflichkeit *f*

rudimentary /ruːdɪˈmentərɪ/ *adj* elementar; (*Biology*) rudimentär

ruffian /'rʌfɪən/ *n* Rüpel *m*

ruffle /'rʌfl/ *vt* zerzausen

rug /rʌg/ *n* Vorleger *m*, [kleiner] Teppich *m*; (*blanket*) Decke *f*

rugged /'rʌgɪd/ *adj* (*coastline*) zerklüftet

ruin /'ruːɪn/ *n* Ruine *f*; (*fig*) Ruin *m* ● *vt* ruinieren

rule /ruːl/ *n* Regel *f*; (*control*) Herrschaft *f*; (*government*) Regierung *f*; (*for measuring*) Lineal *nt*; **as a** ~ in der Regel ● *vt* regieren, herrschen über (+ *acc*); (*fig*) beherrschen; (*decide*) entscheiden; ziehen (*line*) ● *vi* regieren, herrschen. ~ **out** *vt* ausschließen

ruled /ruːld/ *adj* (*paper*) liniert

ruler /'ruːlə(r)/ *n* Herrscher(in) *m*(*f*); (*measure*) Lineal *nt*

ruling /'ruːlɪŋ/ *adj* herrschend; (*factor*) entscheidend; (*Pol*) regierend ● *n* Entscheidung *f*

rum /rʌm/ *n* Rum *m*

rumble /'rʌmbl/ *n* Grollen *nt* ● *vi* grollen; (*stomach*:) knurren

rummage /'rʌmɪdʒ/ *vi* wühlen; ~ **through** durchwühlen

rumour /'ruːmə(r)/ *n* Gerücht *nt*

r

● *vt* **it is ~ed that** es geht das Gerücht, dass

rump /rʌmp/ *n* Hinterteil *nt*. ~ **steak** *n* Rumpsteak *nt*

run /rʌn/ *n* Lauf *m*; (*journey*) Fahrt *f*; (*series*) Serie *f*, Reihe *f*; (*Theat*) Laufzeit *f*; (*Skiing*) Abfahrt *f*; (*enclosure*) Auslauf *m*; (*Amer: ladder*) Laufmasche *f*; ~ **of bad luck** Pechsträhne *f*; **be on the** ~ flüchtig sein; **in the long** ~ auf lange Sicht ● *v* (*pt* **ran**, *pp* **run**, *pres p* **running**) ● *vi* laufen; (*flow*) fließen; (*eyes:*) tränen; (*bus:*) verkehren; (*butter, ink:*) zerfließen; (*colours:*) [ab]färben; (*in election*) kandidieren ● *vt* laufen lassen; einlaufen lassen (*bath*); (*manage*) führen, leiten; (*drive*) fahren; eingehen (*risk*); (*Journalism*) bringen (*story*); ~ **one's hand over sth** mit der Hand über etw (*acc*) fahren. ~ **away** *vi* weglaufen. ~ **down** *vi* hinunter-/herunterlaufen; (*clockwork:*) ablaufen; (*stocks:*) sich verringern ● *vt* (*run over*) überfahren; (*reduce*) verringern; (🔁: *criticize*) heruntermachen. ~ **in** *vi* hinein-/hereinlaufen. ~ **off** *vi* weglaufen ● *vt* abziehen (*copies*). ~ **out** *vi* hinaus-/herauslaufen; (*supplies, money:*) ausgehen; **I've** ~ **out of sugar** ich habe keinen Zucker mehr. ~ **over** *vt* überfahren. ~ **up** *vi* hinauf-/herauflaufen; (*towards*) hinlaufen ● *vt* machen (*debts*); auflaufen lassen (*bill*); (*sew*) schnell nähen

'runaway *n* Ausreißer *m*

run-'down *adj* (*area*) verkommen

rung¹ /rʌŋ/ *n* (*of ladder*) Sprosse *f*

rung² *see* **ring²**

runner /'rʌnə(r)/ *n* Läufer *m*; (*Bot*) Ausläufer *m*; (*on sledge*) Kufe *f*. ~ **bean** *n* Stangenbohne *f*. **~-up** *n* Zweite(r) *m/f*

running /'rʌnɪŋ/ *adj* laufend; (*water*) fließend; **four times** ~ viermal nacheinander ● *n* Laufen *nt*; (*management*) Führung *f*, Leitung *f*; **be/not be in the** ~ eine/keine Chance haben

runny /'rʌnɪ/ *adj* flüssig

run: **~-up** *n* (*Sport*) Anlauf *m*; (*to*

election) Zeit *f* vor der Wahl. **~way** *n* Start- und Landebahn *f*

rupture /'rʌptʃə(r)/ *n* Bruch *m* ● *vt/i* brechen

rural /'rʊərəl/ *adj* ländlich

ruse /ruːz/ *n* List *f*

rush¹ /rʌʃ/ *n* (*Bot*) Binse *f*

rush² *n* Hetze *f*; **in a** ~ in Eile ● *vi* sich hetzen; (*run*) rasen; (*water:*) rauschen ● *vt* hetzen, drängen. **~-hour** *n* Hauptverkehrszeit *f*, Stoßzeit *f*

Russia /'rʌʃə/ *n* Russland *nt*. **~n** *adj* russisch ● *n* Russe *m*/Russin *f*; (*Lang*) Russisch *nt*

rust /rʌst/ *n* Rost *m* ● *vi* rosten

rustle /'rʌsl/ *vi* rascheln ● *vt* rascheln mit; (*Amer*) stehlen (*cattle*). ~ **up** *vt* 🔁 improvisieren

'rustproof *adj* rostfrei

rusty /'rʌstɪ/ *adj* rostig

rut /rʌt/ *n* Furche *f*

ruthless /'ruːθlɪs/ *adj* rücksichtslos. **~ness** *n* Rücksichtslosigkeit *f*

rye /raɪ/ *n* Roggen *m*

························

Ss

························

sabbath /'sæbəθ/ *n* Sabbat *m*

sabot|age /'sæbətɑːʒ/ *n* Sabotage *f* ● *vt* sabotieren

sachet /'sæʃeɪ/ *n* Beutel *m*; (*scented*) Kissen *nt*

sack *n* Sack *m*; **get the** ~ 🔁 rausgeschmissen werden ● *vt* 🔁 rausschmeißen

sacred /'seɪkrɪd/ *adj* heilig

sacrifice /'sækrɪfaɪs/ *n* Opfer *nt* ● *vt* opfern

sacrilege /'sækrɪlɪdʒ/ *n* Sakrileg *nt*

sad /sæd/ *adj* (**sadder, saddest**) traurig: (*loss, death*) schmerzlich. **~den** *vt* traurig machen

saddle /'sædl/ *n* Sattel *m* ● *vt* satteln; ~ **s.o. with sth** 🔁 jdm etw aufhalsen

sadist /'seidist/ n Sadist m. ~**ic** adj, -**ally** adv sadistisch

sad|ly /'sædli/ adv traurig; (unfortunately) leider. ~**ness** n Traurigkeit f

safe /seif/ adj (-r, -st) sicher; (journey) gut; (not dangerous) ungefährlich; ~ **and sound** gesund und wohlbehalten ● n Safe m. ~**guard** n Schutz m ● vt schützen. ~**ly** adv sicher; (arrive) gut

safety /'seifti/ n Sicherheit f. ~**-belt** n Sicherheitsgurt m. ~**-pin** n Sicherheitsnadel f. ~**-valve** n [Sicherheits]-ventil nt

sag /sæg/ vi (pt/pp sagged) durchhängen

saga /'sɑːgə/ n Saga f; (fig) Geschichte f

said /sed/ see **say**

sail /seil/ n Segel nt; (trip) Segelfahrt f ● vi segeln; (on liner) fahren; (leave) abfahren (for nach) ● vt segeln mit

sailing /'seilɪŋ/ n Segelsport m. ~**-boat** n Segelboot nt. ~**-ship** n Segelschiff nt

sailor /'seilə(r)/ n Seemann m; (in navy) Matrose m

saint /seint/ n Heilige(r) m/f. ~**ly** adj heilig

sake /seik/ n for the ~ of ... um ... (gen) willen; for my/your ~ um meinet-/deinetwillen

salad /'sæləd/ n Salat m. ~**-dressing** n Salatsoße f

salary /'sæləri/ n Gehalt nt

sale /seil/ n Verkauf m; (event) Basar m; (at reduced prices) Schlussverkauf m; for ~ zu verkaufen

sales|man n Verkäufer m. ~**woman** n Verkäuferin f

saliva /sə'laivə/ n Speichel m

salmon /'sæmən/ n Lachs m

saloon /sə'luːn/ n Salon m; (Auto) Limousine f; (Amer: bar) Wirtschaft f

salt /sɔːlt/ n Salz nt ● adj salzig; (water, meat) Salz- ● vt salzen; (cure) pökeln; streuen (road). ~**-cellar** n Salzfass nt. ~ '**water** n Salzwasser nt. ~**y** adj salzig

salute /sə'luːt/ n (Mil) Gruß m ● vt/i (Mil) grüßen

salvage /'sælvidʒ/ n (Naut) Bergung f ● vt bergen

salvation /sæl'veiʃn/ n Rettung f; (Relig) Heil nt

same /seim/ adj & pron the ~ der/ die/das gleiche; (pl) die gleichen; (identical) der-/die-/dasselbe; (pl) dieselben ● adv the ~ gleich; all the ~ trotzdem

sample /'sɑːmpl/ n Probe f; (Comm) Muster nt ● vt probieren; kosten (food)

sanatorium /sænə'tɔːriəm/ n Sanatorium nt

sanction /'sæŋkʃn/ n Sanktion f ● vt sanktionieren

sanctuary /'sæŋktjʊəri/ n (Relig) Heiligtum nt; (refuge) Zuflucht f; (for wildlife) Tierschutzgebiet nt

sand /sænd/ n Sand m ● vt ~ [down] [ab]schmirgeln

sandal /'sændl/ n Sandale f

sand: ~**bank** n Sandbank f. ~**paper** n Sandpapier nt. ~**-pit** n Sandkasten m

sandwich /'sænwidʒ/ n; Sandwich m ● vt ~**ed between** eingeklemmt zwischen

sandy /'sændi/ adj sandig; (beach, soil) Sand-; (hair) rotblond

sane /sein/ adj (-r, -st) geistig normal; (sensible) vernünftig

sang /sæŋ/ see **sing**

sanitary /'sænitəri/ adj hygienisch; (system) sanitär. ~ **napkin** n (Amer), ~ **towel** n [Damen]binde f

sanitation /sæni'teiʃn/ n Kanalisation und Abfallbeseitigung pl

sanity /'sæniti/ n [gesunder] Verstand m

sank /sæŋk/ see **sink**

sap /sæp/ n (Bot) Saft m ● vt (pt/pp sapped) schwächen

sarcas|m /'sɑːkæzm/ n Sarkasmus m. ~**tic** adj, -**ally** adv sarkastisch

sardine /sɑː'diːn/ n Sardine f

sash /sæʃ/ n Schärpe f

sat /sæt/ see **sit**

S

satchel /'sætʃl/ n Ranzen m

satellite /'sætəlaɪt/ n Satellit m. **~television** n Satellitenfernsehen nt

satin /'sætɪn/ n Satin m

satire /'sætaɪə(r)/ n Satire f

satirical /sə'tɪrɪkl/ adj satirisch

satirist /'sætərɪst/ n Satiriker(in) m(f)

satisfaction /sætɪs'fækʃn/ n Befriedigung f; to **my ~** zu meiner Zufriedenheit

satisfactory /sætɪs'fæktərɪ/ adj, **-ily** adv zufrieden stellend

satisf|y /'sætɪsfaɪ/ vt (pp/pp **-fied**) befriedigen; zufrieden stellen (customer); (convince) überzeugen; **be ~ied** zufrieden sein. **~ying** adj befriedigend; (meal) sättigend

satphone /'sætfəʊn/ n Satellitentelefon nt

saturate /'sætʃəreɪt/ vt durchtränken; (Chemistry & fig) sättigen

Saturday /'sætədeɪ/ n Samstag m

sauce /sɔːs/ n Soße f; (cheek) Frechheit f. **~pan** n Kochtopf m

saucer /'sɔːsə(r)/ n Untertasse f

saucy /'sɔːʃɪ/ adj frech

Saudi Arabia /saʊdɪə'reɪbɪə/ n Saudi-Arabien n

sauna /'sɔːnə/ n Sauna f

saunter /'sɔːntə(r)/ vi schlendern

sausage /'sɒsɪdʒ/ n Wurst f

savage /'sævɪdʒ/ adj wild; (fierce) scharf; (brutal) brutal ● n Wilde(r) m/f. **~ry** n Brutalität f

save /seɪv/ n (Sport) Abwehr f ● vt retten (**from** vor + dat); (keep) aufheben; (not waste) sparen; (collect) sammeln; (avoid) ersparen; (Sport) verhindern (goal) ● vi **~ [up]** sparen

saver /'seɪvə(r)/ n Sparer m

saving /'seɪvɪŋ/ n (see **save**) Rettung f; Sparen nt; Ersparnis f; **~s** pl (money) Ersparnisse pl

savour /'seɪvə(r)/ n Geschmack m ● vt auskosten. **~y** adj würzig

saw[1] /sɔː/ see **see**[1]

saw[2] n Säge f ● vt/i (pt **sawed**, pp **sawn** or **sawed**) sägen

saxophone /'sæksəfəʊn/ n Saxophon nt

say /seɪ/ n Mitspracherecht nt; **have one's ~** seine Meinung sagen ● vt/i (pt/pp **said**) sagen; sprechen (prayer); **that is to ~** das heißt; **that goes without ~ing** das versteht sich von selbst. **~ing** n Redensart f

scab /skæb/ n Schorf m; (pej) Streikbrecher m

scaffolding /'skæfəldɪŋ/ n Gerüst nt

scald /skɔːld/ vt verbrühen

scale[1] /skeɪl/ n (of fish) Schuppe f

scale[2] n Skala f; (Mus) Tonleiter f; (ratio) Maßstab m ● vt (climb) erklettern. **~ down** vt verkleinern

scales /skeɪlz/ npl (for weighing) Waage f

scalp /skælp/ n Kopfhaut f

scamper /'skæmpə(r)/ vi huschen

scan /skæn/ n (Med) Szintigramm nt ● v (pt/pp **scanned**) ● vt absuchen; (quickly) flüchtig ansehen; (Med) szintigraphisch untersuchen

scandal /'skændl/ n Skandal m; (gossip) Skandalgeschichten pl. **~ize** vt schockieren. **~ous** adj skandalös

Scandinavia /skændɪ'neɪvɪə/ n Skandinavien nt. **~n** adj skandinavisch ● n Skandinavier(in) m(f)

scanner /'skænə(r)/ n Scanner m

scanty /'skæntɪ/ adj, **-ily** adv spärlich; (clothing) knapp

scapegoat /'skeɪp-/ n Sündenbock m

scar /skɑː(r)/ n Narbe f

scarc|e /skeəs/ adj (**-r, -st**) knapp; **make oneself ~e** 🔲 sich aus dem Staub machen. **~ely** adv kaum. **~ity** n Knappheit f

scare /skeə(r)/ n Schreck m; (panic) [allgemeine] Panik f ● vt Angst machen (+ dat); **be ~d** Angst haben (**of** vor + dat)

scarf /skɑːf/ n (pl **scarves**) Schal m; (square) Tuch nt

scarlet /'skɑːlət/ adj scharlachrot

scary /'skeərɪ/ adj unheimlich

scathing /'skeɪðɪŋ/ adj bissig

scatter /'skætə(r)/ vt verstreuen; (disperse) zerstreuen ● vi sich zerstreuen. ~**ed** adj verstreut; (showers) vereinzelt

scatty /'skætɪ/ adj 🄸 verrückt

scene /siːn/ n Szene f; (sight) Anblick m; (place of event) Schauplatz m; **behind the ~s** hinter den Kulissen

scenery /'siːnərɪ/ n Landschaft f; (Theat) Szenerie f

scenic /'siːnɪk/ adj landschaftlich schön

scent /sent/ n Duft m; (trail) Fährte f; (perfume) Parfüm nt. ~**ed** adj parfümiert

sceptic|al /'skeptɪkl/ adj skeptisch. ~**ism** n Skepsis f

schedule /'ʃedjuːl/ n Programm nt; (of work) Zeitplan m; (timetable) Fahrplan m; **behind ~** im Rückstand; **according to ~** planmäßig ● vt planen

scheme /skiːm/ n Programm nt; (plan) Plan m; (plot) Komplott nt ● vi Ränke schmieden

schizophrenic /skɪtsə'frenɪk/ adj schizophren

scholar /'skɒlə(r)/ n Gelehrte(r) m/f. ~**ly** adj gelehrt. ~**ship** n Gelehrtheit f; (grant) Stipendium nt

school /skuːl/ n Schule f; (Univ) Fakultät f ● vt schulen

school: ~**boy** n Schüler m. ~**girl** n Schülerin f. ~**ing** n Schulbildung f. ~**master** n Lehrer m. ~**mistress** n Lehrerin f. ~**-teacher** n Lehrer(in) m(f)

scien|ce /'saɪəns/ n Wissenschaft f. ~**tific** adj wissenschaftlich. ~**tist** n Wissenschaftler(in) m(f)

scissors /'sɪzəz/ npl Schere f; **a pair of ~** eine Schere

scoff[1] /skɒf/ vi ~ **at** spotten über (+ acc)

scoff[2] vt 🄸 verschlingen

scold /skəʊld/ vt ausschimpfen

scoop /skuːp/ n Schaufel f; (Culin) Portionierer m; (story) Exklusivmeldung f ● vt ~ **out** aushöhlen; (remove) auslöffeln

scooter /'skuːtə(r)/ n Roller m

scope /skəʊp/ n Bereich m; (opportunity) Möglichkeiten pl

scorch /skɔːtʃ/ vt versengen. ~**ing** adj glühend heiß

score /skɔː(r)/ n [Spiel]stand m; (individual) Punktzahl f; (Mus) Partitur f; (Cinema) Filmmusik f; **on that ~** was das betrifft ● vt erzielen; schießen (goal); (cut) einritzen ● vi Punkte erzielen; (Sport) ein Tor schießen; (keep score) Punkte zählen. ~**r** n Punktezähler m; (of goals) Torschütze m

scorn /skɔːn/ n Verachtung f ● vt verachten. ~**ful** adj verächtlich

Scot /skɒt/ n Schotte m/Schottin f

Scotch /skɒtʃ/ adj schottisch ● n (whisky) Scotch m

Scot|land /'skɒtlənd/ n Schottland nt. ~**s**, ~**tish** adj schottisch

---

Scottish Parliament Das schottische Parlament, dessen Mitglieder im Holyrood Building in der Hauptstadt Edinburgh zusammentreten. Es wurde 1999 (nach einer Volksabstimmung) eröffnet und verleiht Schottland eine größere Autonomie gegenüber dem britischen Parlament in London. Von den 129 schottischen Abgeordneten werden 73 direkt gewählt und 56 nach dem Verhältniswahlrecht bestimmt.

i

---

scoundrel /'skaʊndrl/ n Schurke m

scour /'skaʊə(r)/ vt (search) absuchen; (clean) scheuern

scout /skaʊt/ n (Mil) Kundschafter m; **[Boy] S~** Pfadfinder m

scowl /skaʊl/ n böser Gesichtsausdruck m ● vi ein böses Gesicht machen

scram /skræm/ vi 🄸 abhauen

scramble /'skræmbl/ n Gerangel nt ● vi klettern; ~ **for** sich drängen nach. ~**d 'egg[s]** n[pl] Rührei nt

scrap[1] /skræp/ n (🄸: fight) Rauferei f ● vi sich raufen

scrap[2] n Stückchen nt; (metal) Schrott m; ~**s** pl Reste; **not a ~** kein bisschen ● vt (pt/pp **scrapped**) aufgeben

S

'**scrapbook** n Sammelalbum nt

scrape /skreɪp/ vt schaben; (clean) abkratzen; (damage) [ver]schrammen. ∼ **through** vi gerade noch durchkommen. ∼ **together** vt zusammenkriegen

scrappy /'skræpɪ/ adj lückenhaft

'**scrapyard** n Schrottplatz m

scratch /skrætʃ/ n Kratzer m; **start from** ∼ von vorne anfangen; **not be up to** ∼ zu wünschen übrig lassen ● vt/i kratzen; (damage) zerkratzen

scrawl /skrɔːl/ n Gekrakel nt ● vt/i krakeln

scream /skriːm/ n Schrei m ● vt/i schreien

screech /skriːtʃ/ n Kreischen nt ● vt/i kreischen

screen /skriːn/ n Schirm m; (Cinema) Leinwand f; (TV) Bildschirm m ● vt schützen; (conceal) verdecken; vorführen (film); (examine) überprüfen; (Med) untersuchen

screw /skruː/ n Schraube f ● vt schrauben. ∼ **up** vt festschrauben; (crumple) zusammenknüllen; zusammenkneifen (eyes); (sl: bungle) vermasseln

'**screwdriver** n Schraubenzieher m

scribble /'skrɪbl/ n Gekritzel nt ● vt/i kritzeln

script /skrɪpt/ n Schrift f; (of speech, play) Text m; (Radio, TV) Skript nt; (of film) Drehbuch nt

scroll /skrəʊl/ n Rolle f ● vt ∼ **up/down** nach oben/unten rollen. ∼ **bar** n Rollbalken m

scrounge /skraʊndʒ/ vt/i schnorren. ∼**r** n Schnorrer m

scrub[1] /skrʌb/ n (land) Buschland nt, Gestrüpp nt

scrub[2] vt/i (pt/pp **scrubbed**) schrubben

scruff /skrʌf/ n **by the** ∼ **of the neck** beim Genick

scruffy /'skrʌfɪ/ adj vergammelt

scrum /skrʌm/ n Gedränge nt

scruple /'skruːpl/ n Skrupel m

scrupulous /'skruːpjʊləs/ adj gewissenhaft

scuffle /'skʌfl/ n Handgemenge nt

sculpt|or /'skʌlptə(r)/ n Bildhauer(in) m(f). ∼**ure** n Bildhauerei f; (piece of work) Skulptur f, Plastik f

scum /skʌm/ n Schmutzschicht f; (people) Abschaum m

scurry /'skʌrɪ/ vi (pt/pp -**ied**) huschen

scuttle[1] /'skʌtl/ vt versenken (ship)

scuttle[2] vi schnell krabbeln

sea /siː/ n Meer nt, See f; **at** ∼ auf See; **by** ∼ mit dem Schiff. ∼**food** n Meeresfrüchte pl. ∼**gull** n Möwe f

seal[1] /siːl/ n (Zool) Seehund m

seal[2] n Siegel nt ● vt versiegeln; (fig) besiegeln. ∼ **off** vt abriegeln

'**sea-level** n Meeresspiegel m

seam /siːm/ n Naht f; (of coal) Flöz nt

'**seaman** n Seemann m; (sailor) Matrose m

seance /'seɪɑːns/ n spiritistische Sitzung f

search /sɜːtʃ/ n Suche f; (official) Durchsuchung f ● vt durchsuchen; absuchen (area) ● vi suchen (**for** nach). ∼ **engine** n Suchmaschine f. ∼**ing** adj prüfend, forschend. ∼**light** n [Such]scheinwerfer m. ∼-**party** n Suchmannschaft f

sea: ∼**sick** adj seekrank. ∼**side** n **at/to the** ∼**side** am/ans Meer

season /'siːzn/ n Jahreszeit f; (social, tourist, sporting) Saison f ● vt (flavour) würzen. ∼**al** adj Saison-. ∼**ing** n Gewürze pl

'**season ticket** n Dauerkarte f

seat /siːt/ n Sitz m; (place) Sitzplatz m; (bottom) Hintern m; **take a** ∼ Platz nehmen ● vt setzen; (have seats for) Sitzplätze bieten (+ dat); **remain** ∼**ed** sitzen bleiben. ∼-**belt** n Sicherheitsgurt m; **fasten one's** ∼-**belt** sich anschnallen

sea: ∼**weed** n [See]tang m. ∼**worthy** adj seetüchtig

seclu|ded /sɪ'kluːdɪd/ adj abgelegen. ∼**sion** n Zurückgezogenheit f

second /'sekənd/ adj zweite(r,s); **on** ∼ **thoughts** nach weiterer Überlegung ● *n* Sekunde *f*; (*Sport*) Sekundant *m*; **~s** *pl* (*goods*) Waren zweiter Wahl ● *adv* (*in race*) an zweiter Stelle ● *vt* unterstützen (*proposal*)

secondary /'sekəndrɪ/ *adj* zweitrangig; (*Phys*) Sekundär-. **~ school** *n* höhere Schule *f*

second: **~-best** *adj* zweitbeste(r,s). **~ 'class** *adv* (*travel, send*) zweiter Klasse. **~-class** *adj* zweitklassig

'second hand *n* (*on clock*) Sekundenzeiger *m*

second-'hand *adj* gebraucht ● *adv* aus zweiter Hand

secondly /'sekəndlɪ/ *adv* zweitens

second-'rate *adj* zweitklassig

secrecy /'si:krəsɪ/ *n* Heimlichkeit *f*

secret /'si:krɪt/ *adj* geheim; (*agent, police*) Geheim-; (*drinker, lover*) heimlich ● *n* Geheimnis *nt*

secretarial /sekrə'teərɪəl/ *adj* Sekretärinnen-; (*work, staff*) Sekretariats-

secretary /'sekrətərɪ/ *n* Sekretär(in) *m(f)*

secretive /'si:krətɪv/ *adj* geheimtuerisch

secretly /'si:krɪtlɪ/ *adv* heimlich

sect /sekt/ *n* Sekte *f*

section /'sekʃn/ *n* Teil *m*; (*of text*) Abschnitt *m*; (*of firm*) Abteilung *f*; (*of organization*) Sektion *f*

sector /'sektə(r)/ *n* Sektor *m*

secular /'sekjʊlə(r)/ *adj* weltlich

secure /sɪ'kjʊə(r)/ *adj* sicher; (*firm*) fest; (*emotionally*) geborgen ● *vt* sichern; (*fasten*) festmachen; (*obtain*) sich (*dat*) sichern

securit|y /sɪ'kjʊərətɪ/ *n* Sicherheit *f*; (*emotional*) Geborgenheit *f*; **~ies** *pl* Wertpapiere *pl*

sedan /sɪ'dæn/ *n* (*Amer*) Limousine *f*

sedate /sɪ'deɪt/ *adj* gesetzt

sedative /'sedətɪv/ *adj* beruhigend ● *n* Beruhigungsmittel *nt*

sediment /'sedɪmənt/ *n* [Boden]-satz *m*

seduce /sɪ'dju:s/ *vt* verführen

seduct|ion /sɪ'dʌkʃn/ *n* Verführung *f*. **~ive** *adj* verführerisch

see /si:/ *v* (*pt* **saw,** *pp* **seen**) ● *vt* sehen; (*understand*) einsehen; (*imagine*) sich (*dat*) vorstellen; (*escort*) begleiten; **go and ~** nachsehen; (*visit*) besuchen; **~ you later!** bis nachher! **~ing that** da ● *vi* sehen; (*check*) nachsehen; **~ about** sich kümmern um. **~ off** *vt* verabschieden; (*chase away*) vertreiben. **~ through** *vt* (*fig*) durchschauen (*person*)

seed /si:d/ *n* Samen *m*; (*of grape*) Kern *m*; (*fig*) Saat *f*; (*Tennis*) gesetzter Spieler *m*; **go to ~** Samen bilden; (*fig*) herunterkommen. **~ed** *adj* (*Tennis*) gesetzt

seedy /'si:dɪ/ *adj* schäbig; (*area*) heruntergekommen

seek /si:k/ *vt* (*pt/pp* **sought**) suchen

seem /si:m/ *vi* scheinen

seen /si:n/ *see* **see¹**

seep /si:p/ *vi* sickern

seethe /si:ð/ *vi* **~ with anger** vor Wut schäumen

'see-through *adj* durchsichtig

segment /'segmənt/ *n* Teil *m*; (*of worm*) Segment *nt*; (*of orange*) Spalte *f*

segregat|e /'segrɪgeɪt/ *vt* trennen. **~ion** *n* Trennung *f*

seize /si:z/ *vt* ergreifen; (*Jur*) beschlagnahmen; **~ s.o. by the arm** jdn am Arm packen. **~ up** *vi* (*Techn*) sich festfressen

seldom /'seldəm/ *adv* selten

select /sɪ'lekt/ *adj* ausgewählt; (*exclusive*) exklusiv ● *vt* auswählen; aufstellen (*team*). **~ion** *n* Auswahl *f*

self /self/ *n* (*pl* **selves**) Ich *nt*

self: **~-as'surance** *n* Selbstsicherheit *f*. **~-as'sured** *adj* selbstsicher. **~-'catering** *n* Selbstversorgung *f*. **~-'centred** *adj* egozentrisch. **~-'confidence** *n* Selbstbewusstsein *nt*, Selbstvertrauen *nt*. **~-'confident** *adj* selbstbewusst. **~-'conscious** *adj* befangen. **~-con'tained** *adj* (*flat*) abgeschlossen. **~-con'trol** *n* Selbstbeherrschung *f*. **~-de'fence** *n* Selbstverteidigung *f*; (*Jur*) Notwehr *f*. **~-em'ployed** selbstständig.

S

∼-e'steem n Selbstachtung f.
∼-'evident adj offensichtlich.
∼-in'dulgent adj maßlos.
∼-'interest n Eigennutz m

self|ish /'selfɪʃ/ adj egoistisch, selbst-
süchtig. ∼less adj selbstlos

self: ∼-'pity n Selbstmitleid nt.
∼-'portrait n Selbstporträt nt.
∼-re'spect n Selbstachtung f.
∼-'righteous adj selbstgerecht.
∼-'sacrifice n Selbstaufopferung f.
∼-'satisfied adj selbstgefällig.
∼-'service n Selbstbedienung f
● attrib Selbstbedienungs-.
∼-suf'ficient adj selbstständig

sell /sel/ v (pt/pp sold) ● vt verkaufen; be sold out ausverkauft sein ● vi
sich verkaufen. ∼ off vt verkaufen

seller /'selə(r)/ n Verkäufer m

Sellotape® /'seləʊ-/, n ≈ Tesa-
film® m

'sell-out n be a ∼ ausverkauft sein;
(🔲: betrayal) Verrat sein

selves /selvz/ see self

semester /sɪ'mestə(r)/ n Semester nt

semi|breve /'semɪbriːv/ n (Mus)
ganze Note f. ∼circle n Halbkreis m.
∼'circular adj halbkreisförmig.
∼'colon n Semikolon nt.
∼-de'tached adj & n ∼-detached
[house] Doppelhaushälfte f. ∼-'final
n Halbfinale nt

seminar /'semɪnɑ:(r)/ n Seminar nt

senat|e /'senət/ n Senat m. ∼or n
Senator m

send /send/ vt/i (pt/pp sent) schicken; ∼ for kommen lassen (person);
sich (dat) schicken lassen (thing).
∼-er n Absender m. ∼-off n Verab-
schiedung f

senil|e /'siːnaɪl/ adj senil

senior /'siːnɪə(r)/ adj älter; (in rank)
höher ● n Ältere(r) m/f; (in rank) Vor-
gesetzte(r) m/f. ∼ 'citizen n Seni-
or(in) m(f)

seniority /siːnɪ'ɒrətɪ/ n höheres
Alter nt; (in rank) höherer Rang m

sensation /sen'seɪʃn/ n Sensation f;
(feeling) Gefühl nt. ∼al adj sensatio-
nell

sense /sens/ n Sinn m; (feeling) Gefühl nt; (common ∼) Verstand m;
make ∼ Sinn ergeben ● vt spüren.
∼less adj sinnlos; (unconscious) bewusstlos

sensible /'sensəbl/ adj, -bly adv vernünftig; (suitable) zweckmäßig

sensitiv|e /'sensətɪv/ adj empfind-
lich; (understanding) einfühlsam.
∼ity n Empfindlichkeit f

sensual /'sensjʊəl/ adj sinnlich. -ity
n Sinnlichkeit f

sensuous /'sensjʊəs/ adj sinnlich

sent /sent/ see send

sentence /'sentəns/ n Satz m; (Jur)
Urteil nt; (punishment) Strafe f ● vt
verurteilen

sentiment /'sentɪmənt/ n Gefühl nt;
(opinion) Meinung f; (sentimentality)
Sentimentalität f ∼al adj sentimental. ∼ality n Sentimentalität f

sentry /'sentrɪ/ n Wache f

separable /'sepərəbl/ adj trennbar

separate¹ /'sepərət/ adj getrennt,
separat

separat|e² /'sepəreɪt/ vt trennen
● vi sich trennen. ∼ion n Trennung f

September /sep'tembə(r)/ n September m

septic /'septɪk/ adj vereitert

sequel /'siːkwl/ n Folge f; (fig) Nach-
spiel nt

sequence /'siːkwəns/ n Reihenfolge f

serenade /serə'neɪd/ n Ständchen
nt ● vt ∼ s.o. jdm ein Ständchen
bringen

seren|e /sɪ'riːn/ adj gelassen. ∼ity n
Gelassenheit f

sergeant /'sɑːdʒənt/ n (Mil) Feldwe-
bel m; (in police) Polizeimeister m

serial /'sɪərɪəl/ n Fortsetzungsge-
schichte f; (Radio, TV) Serie f. ∼ize vt
in Fortsetzungen veröffentlichen/
(Radio, TV) senden

series /'sɪəriːz/ n inv Serie f

serious /'sɪərɪəs/ adj ernst; (illness,
error) schwer. ∼ness n Ernst m

sermon /'sɜːmən/ n Predigt f

servant /'sɜːvənt/ n Diener(in) m(f)

s

serve /sɜːv/ n (*Tennis*) Aufschlag *m*
● *vt* dienen (+ *dat*); bedienen (*customer*, *guest*); servieren (*food*); verbüßen (*sentence*); **it ∼s you right!** das geschieht dir recht! ● *vi* dienen; (*Tennis*) aufschlagen. **∼r** n (*Computing*) Server *m*

service /'sɜːvɪs/ n Dienst *m*; (*Relig*) Gottesdienst *m*; (*in shop, restaurant*) Bedienung *f*; (*transport*) Verbindung *f*; (*maintenance*) Wartung *f*; (*set of crockery*) Service *nt*; (*Tennis*) Aufschlag *m*; **∼s** *pl* Dienstleistungen *pl*; (*on motorway*) Tankstelle und Raststätte *f*; **in the ∼s** beim Militär; **out of/in ∼** (*machine:*) außer/ in Betrieb ● *vt* (*Techn*) warten

service: **∼ area** n Tankstelle und Raststätte *f*. **∼ charge** n Bedienungszuschlag *m*. **∼man** n Soldat *m*. **∼ station** n Tankstelle *f*

serviette /sɜːvɪˈet/ n Serviette *f*

servile /'sɜːvaɪl/ adj unterwürfig

session /'seʃn/ n Sitzung *f*

set /set/ n Satz *m*; (*of crockery*) Service *nt*; (*of cutlery*) Garnitur *f*; (*TV, Radio*) Apparat *m*; (*Math*) Menge *f*; (*Theat*) Bühnenbild *nt*; (*Cinema*) Szenenaufbau *m*; (*of people*) Kreis *m* ● *adj* (*ready*) fertig, bereit; (*rigid*) fest; (*book*) vorgeschrieben; **be ∼ on doing sth** entschlossen sein, etw zu tun ● *v* (*pt/pp* **set**, *pres p* **setting**) ● *vt* setzen; (*adjust*) einstellen; stellen (*task, alarm clock*); festsetzen, festlegen (*date, limit*); aufgeben (*homework*); zusammenstellen (*questions*); [ein]fassen (*gem*); einrichten (*bone*); legen (*hair*); decken (*table*) ● *vi* (*sun:*) untergehen; (*become hard*) fest werden. **∼ back** vt zurücksetzen; (*hold up*) aufhalten; (🄘: *cost*) kosten. **∼ off** vi losgehen; (*in vehicle*) losfahren ● *vt* auslösen (*alarm*); explodieren lassen (*bomb*). **∼ out** vi losgehen; (*in vehicle*) losfahren ● *vt* auslegen; (*state*) darlegen. **∼ up** vt aufbauen; (*fig*) gründen

settee /se'tiː/ n Sofa *nt*, Couch *f*

setting /'setɪŋ/ n Rahmen *m*; (*surroundings*) Umgebung *f*

settle /'setl/ vt (*decide*) entscheiden; (*agree*) regeln; (*fix*) festsetzen; (*calm*) beruhigen; (*pay*) bezahlen ● *vi* sich niederlassen; (*snow, dust:*) liegen bleiben; (*subside*) sich senken; (*sediment:*) sich absetzen. **∼ down** vi sich beruhigen; (*permanently*) sesshaft werden. **∼ up** vi abrechnen

settlement /'setlmənt/ n (*see* **settle**) Entscheidung *f*; Regelung *f*; Bezahlung *f*; (*Jur*) Vergleich *m*; (*colony*) Siedlung *f*

settler /'setlə(r)/ n Siedler *m*

'set-up n System *nt*

seven /'sevn/ adj sieben. **∼'teen** adj siebzehn. **∼'teenth** adj siebzehnte(r,s)

seventh /'sevnθ/ adj siebte(r,s)

seventieth /'sevntɪɪθ/ adj siebzigste(r,s)

seventy /'sevntɪ/ adj siebzig

several /'sevrl/ adj & pron mehrere, einige

sever|e /sɪˈvɪə(r)/ adj (**-r, -st,**) **-ly** adv streng; (*pain*) stark; (*illness*) schwer. **∼ity** n Strenge *f*; Schwere *f*

sew /səʊ/ vt/i (*pt* sewed, *pp* sewn or sewed) nähen

sewage /'suːɪdʒ/ n Abwasser *nt*

sewer /'suːə(r)/ n Abwasserkanal *m*

sewing /'səʊɪŋ/ n Nähen *nt*; (*work*) Näharbeit *f*. **∼ machine** n Nähmaschine *f*

sewn /səʊn/ see sew

sex /seks/ n Geschlecht *nt*; (*sexuality, intercourse*) Sex *m*. **∼ist** adj sexistisch

sexual /'seksjʊəl/ adj sexuell. **∼ 'intercourse** n Geschlechtsverkehr *m*

sexuality /seksjʊˈælətɪ/ n Sexualität *f*

sexy /'seksɪ/ adj sexy

shabby /'ʃæbɪ/ adj , **-ily** adv schäbig

shack /ʃæk/ n Hütte *f*

shade /ʃeɪd/ n Schatten *m*; (*of colour*) [Farb]ton *m*; (*for lamp*) [Lampen]schirm *m*; (*Amer: window-blind*) Jalousie *f* ● *vt* beschatten

shadow /'ʃædəʊ/ n Schatten *m* ● *vt* (*follow*) beschatten

S

shady /'ʃeɪdɪ/ adj schattig; (🛈: disreputable) zwielichtig

shaft /ʃɑːft/ n Schaft m; (Techn) Welle f; (of light) Strahl m; (of lift) Schacht m

shaggy /'ʃægɪ/ adj zottig

shake /ʃeɪk/ n Schütteln nt ● v (pt shook, pp shaken) ● vt schütteln; (shock) erschüttern; ~ hands with s.o. jdm die Hand geben ● vi wackeln; (tremble) zittern. ~ off vt abschütteln

shaky /'ʃeɪkɪ/ adj wackelig; (hand, voice) zittrig

shall /ʃæl/ v aux we ~ see wir werden sehen; what ~ I do? was soll ich machen?

shallow /'ʃæləʊ/ adj (-er, -est) seicht; (dish) flach; (fig) oberflächlich

sham /ʃæm/ adj unecht ● n Heuchelei ● vt (pt/pp shammed) vortäuschen

shambles /'ʃæmblz/ n Durcheinander nt

shame /ʃeɪm/ n Scham f; (disgrace) Schande f; be a ~ schade sein; what a ~! wie schade! **shame|ful** /'ʃeɪmfl/ adj schändlich. ~less adj schamlos

shampoo /ʃæm'puː/ n Shampoo nt ● vt schamponieren

shan't /ʃɑːnt/ = shall not

shape /ʃeɪp/ n Form f; (figure) Gestalt f ● vt formen (into zu). ~less adj formlos; (clothing) unförmig

share /ʃeə(r)/ n [An]teil m; (Comm) Aktie f ● vt/i teilen. ~holder n Aktionär(in) m(f)

shark /ʃɑːk/ n Hai[fisch] m

sharp /ʃɑːp/ adj (-er, -est) scharf; (pointed) spitz; (severe) heftig; (sudden) steil; (alert) clever; (unscrupulous) gerissen ● adv scharf; (Mus) zu hoch; at six o'clock ~ Punkt sechs Uhr ● n (Mus) Kreuz nt. ~en vt schärfen; [an]spitzen (pencil)

shatter /'ʃætə(r)/ vt zertrümmern; (fig) zerstören; ~ed (person:) erschüttert; (🛈: exhausted) kaputt ● vi zersplittern

shave /ʃeɪv/ n Rasur f; **have a** ~ sich rasieren ● vt rasieren ● vi sich rasieren. ~**r** n Rasierapparat m

shawl /ʃɔːl/ n Schultertuch nt

she /ʃiː/ pron sie

shears /ʃɪəz/ npl [große] Schere f

shed¹ /ʃed/ n Schuppen m

shed² vt (pt/pp shed, pres p shedding) verlieren; vergießen (blood, tears); ~ **light on** Licht bringen in (+ acc)

sheep /ʃiːp/ n inv Schaf nt. ~**-dog** n Hütehund m

sheepish /'ʃiːpɪʃ/ adj verlegen

sheer /ʃɪə(r)/ adj rein; (steep) steil; (transparent) hauchdünn

sheet /ʃiːt/ n Laken nt, Betttuch nt; (of paper) Blatt nt; (of glass, metal) Platte f

shelf /ʃelf/ n (pl shelves) Brett nt, Bord nt; (set of shelves) Regal nt

shell /ʃel/ n Schale f; (of snail) Haus nt; (of tortoise) Panzer m; (on beach) Muschel f; (Mil) Granate f ● vt pellen; enthülsen (peas); (Mil) [mit Granaten] beschießen. ~ **out** vi 🛈 blechen

'shellfish n inv Schalentiere pl; (Culin) Meeresfrüchte pl

shelter /'ʃeltə(r)/ n Schutz m; (air-raid ~) Luftschutzraum m ● vt schützen (from vor + dat) ● vi sich unterstellen. ~**ed** adj geschützt; (life) behütet

shelve /ʃelv/ vt auf Eis legen; (abandon) aufgeben

shelving /'ʃelvɪŋ/ n (shelves) Regale pl

shepherd /'ʃepəd/ n Schäfer m ● vt führen

sherry /'ʃerɪ/ n Sherry m

shield /ʃiːld/ n Schild m; (for eyes) Schirm m; (Techn & fig) Schutz m ● vt schützen (from vor + dat)

shift /ʃɪft/ n Verschiebung f; (at work) Schicht f ● vt rücken; (take away) wegnehmen; (rearrange) umstellen; schieben (blame) (on to auf + acc) ● vi sich verschieben; (🛈: rush) rasen

shifty /'ʃɪftɪ/ adj (pej) verschlagen

shimmer /'ʃɪmə(r)/ n Schimmer m ● vi schimmern

shin /ʃɪn/ n Schienbein nt

shine /ʃaɪn/ n Glanz m ● v (pt/pp shone) ● vi leuchten; (reflect light) glänzen; (sun:) scheinen ● vt ~ a light on beleuchten

shingle /'ʃɪŋgl/ n (pebbles) Kiesel pl

shiny /'ʃaɪnɪ/ adj glänzend

ship /ʃɪp/ n Schiff nt ● vt (pt/pp shipped) verschiffen

ship: ~building n Schiffbau m. ~ment n Sendung f. ~per n Spediteur m. ~ping n Versand m; (traffic) Schiffahrt f. ~shape adj & adv in Ordnung. ~wreck n Schiffbruch m. ~wrecked adj schiffbrüchig. ~yard n Werft f

shirt /ʃɜːt/ n [Ober]hemd nt; (for woman) Hemdbluse f

shit /ʃɪt/ n (vulgar) Scheiße f ● vi (pt/pp shit) (vulgar) scheißen

shiver /'ʃɪvə(r)/ n Schauder m ● vi zittern

shoal /ʃəʊl/ n (fish) Schwarm m

shock /ʃɒk/ n Schock m; (Electr) Schlag m; (impact) Erschütterung f ● vt einen Schock versetzen (+ dat); (scandalize) schockieren. ~ing adj schockierend; (🖪: bad) fürchterlich

shoddy /'ʃɒdɪ/ adj minderwertig

shoe /ʃuː/ n Schuh m; (of horse) Hufeisen nt ● vt (pt/pp shod, pres p shoeing) beschlagen (horse)

shoe: ~horn n Schuhanzieher m. ~-lace n Schnürsenkel m. ~-string n on a ~-string 🖪 mit ganz wenig Geld

shone /ʃɒn/ see shine

shoo /ʃuː/ vt scheuchen ● int sch!

shook /ʃʊk/ see shake

shoot /ʃuːt/ n (Bot) Trieb m; (hunt) Jagd f ● v (pt/pp shot) ● vt schießen; (kill) erschießen; drehen (film) ● vi schießen. ~ down vt abschießen. ~ out vi (rush) herausschießen. ~ up vi (grow) in die Höhe schießen/ (prices:) schnellen

shop /ʃɒp/ n Laden m, Geschäft nt; (workshop) Werkstatt f; talk ~ 🖪

fachsimpeln ● vi (pt/pp shopped, pres p shopping) einkaufen; go ~ping einkaufen gehen

shop: ~ assistant n Verkäufer(in) m(f). ~keeper n Ladenbesitzer(in) m(f). ~lifter n Ladendieb m. ~lifting n Ladendiebstahl m

shopping /'ʃɒpɪŋ/ n Einkaufen nt; (articles) Einkäufe pl; do the ~ einkaufen. ~ bag n Einkaufstasche f. ~ centre n Einkaufszentrum nt. ~ trolley n Einkaufswagen m

shop-'window n Schaufenster nt

shore /ʃɔː(r)/ n Strand m; (of lake) Ufer nt

short /ʃɔːt/ (er, -est) kurz; (person) klein; (curt) schroff; a ~ time ago vor kurzem; be ~ of ... zu wenig ... haben; be in ~ supply knapp sein ● adv kurz; (abruptly) plötzlich; (curtly) kurz angebunden; in ~ kurzum; ~ of (except) außer; go ~ Mangel leiden

shortage /'ʃɔːtɪdʒ/ n Mangel m (of an + dat); (scarcity) Knappheit f

short: ~bread n ≈ Mürbekekse pl. ~ 'circuit n Kurzschluss m. ~coming n Fehler m. ~ 'cut n Abkürzung f

shorten /'ʃɔːtn/ vt [ab]kürzen; kürzer machen (garment)

short: ~hand n Kurzschrift f, Stenographie f. ~ list n engere Auswahl f

short|ly /'ʃɔːtlɪ/ adv in Kürze; ~ly before/after kurz vorher/danach. ~ness n Kürze f; (of person) Kleinheit f

shorts /ʃɔːts/ npl Shorts pl

short: ~-'sighted adj kurzsichtig. ~-sleeved adj kurzärmelig. ~ 'story n Kurzgeschichte f. ~-'tempered adj aufbrausend. ~-term adj kurzfristig. ~ wave n Kurzwelle f

shot /ʃɒt/ see shoot ● n Schuss m; (pellets) Schrot m; (person) Schütze m; (Phot) Aufnahme f; (injection) Spritze f; (🖪: attempt) Versuch m; like a ~ 🖪 sofort. ~gun n Schrotflinte f. ~-put n (Sport) Kugelstoßen nt

S

should /ʃʊd/ *modal verb* **you ~ go** du solltest gehen; **I ~ have seen him** ich hätte ihn sehen sollen; **I ~ like** ich möchte; **this ~ be enough** das müsste eigentlich reichen; **if he ~ be there** falls er da sein sollte

shoulder /'ʃəʊldə(r)/ n Schulter f ● vt schultern; (*fig*) auf sich (*acc*) nehmen. **~-blade** n Schulterblatt nt

shout /ʃaʊt/ n Schrei m ● vt/i schreien. **~ down** vt niederschreien

shouting /'ʃaʊtɪŋ/ n Geschrei nt

shove /ʃʌv/ n Stoß m ● vt stoßen; (🅸: *put*) tun ● vi drängeln. **~ off** vi 🅸 abhauen

shovel /'ʃʌvl/ n Schaufel f ● vt (*pt/pp* **shovelled**) schaufeln

show /ʃəʊ/ n (*display*) Pracht f; (*exhibition*) Ausstellung f, Schau f; (*performance*) Vorstellung f; (*Theat, TV*) Show f; **on ~** ausgestellt ● v (*pt* **showed**, *pp* **shown**) ● vt zeigen; (*put on display*) ausstellen; vorführen (*film*) ● vi sichtbar sein; (*film:*) gezeigt werden. **~ in** vt hereinführen. **~ off** vi 🅸 angeben ● vt vorführen; (*flaunt*) angeben mit. **~ up** vi [deutlich] zu sehen sein; (🅸: *arrive*) auftauchen ● vt deutlich zeigen; (🅸: *embarrass*) blamieren

shower /'ʃaʊə(r)/ n Dusche f; (*of rain*) Schauer m; **have a ~** duschen ● vt **~ with** überschütten mit ● vi duschen

'show-jumping n Springreiten nt

shown /ʃəʊn/ *see* **show**

show: ~-off n Angeber(in) m(f). **~room** n Ausstellungsraum m

showy /'ʃəʊɪ/ adj protzig

shrank /ʃræŋk/ *see* **shrink**

shred /ʃred/ n Fetzen m; (*fig*) Spur f ● vt (*pt/pp* **shredded**) zerkleinern; (*Culin*) schnitzeln. **~der** n Reißwolf m; (*Culin*) Schnitzelwerk nt

shrewd /ʃruːd/ adj (**-er, -est**) klug. **~ness** n Klugheit f

shriek /ʃriːk/ n Schrei m ● vt/i schreien

shrill /ʃrɪl/ adj, **-y** adv schrill

shrimp /ʃrɪmp/ n Garnele f, Krabbe f

shrink /ʃrɪŋk/ vi (*pt* **shrank**, *pp* **shrunk**) schrumpfen; (*garment:*) einlaufen; (*draw back*) zurückschrecken (**from** vor + *dat*)

shrivel /'ʃrɪvl/ vi (*pt/pp* **shrivelled**) verschrumpeln

Shrove /ʃrəʊv/ n **~'Tuesday** Fastnachtsdienstag m

shrub /ʃrʌb/ n Strauch m

shrug /ʃrʌg/ n Achselzucken nt ● vt/i (*pt/pp* **shrugged**) **~ [one's shoulders]** die Achseln zucken

shrunk /ʃrʌŋk/ *see* **shrink**

shudder /'ʃʌdə(r)/ n Schauder m ● vi schaudern; (*tremble*) zittern

shuffle /'ʃʌfl/ vi schlurfen ● vt mischen (*cards*)

shun /ʃʌn/ vt (*pt/pp* **shunned**) meiden

shunt /ʃʌnt/ vt rangieren

shut /ʃʌt/ v (*pt/pp* **shut**, *pres p* **shutting**) ● vt zumachen, schließen ● vi sich schließen; (*shop:*) schließen, zumachen. **~ down** vt schließen; stilllegen (*factory*) ● vi schließen. **~ up** vt abschließen; (*lock in*) einsperren ● vi 🅸 den Mund halten

shutter /'ʃʌtə(r)/ n [Fenster]laden m; (*Phot*) Verschluss m

shuttle /'ʃʌtl/ n (*textiles*) Schiffchen nt

shuttle service n Pendelverkehr m

shy /ʃaɪ/ adj (**-er, -est**) schüchtern; (*timid*) scheu. **~ness** n Schüchternheit f

siblings /'sɪblɪŋz/ npl Geschwister pl

Sicily /'sɪsɪlɪ/ n Sizilien nt

sick /sɪk/ adj krank; (*humour*) makaber; **be ~** (*vomit*) sich übergeben; **be ~ of sth** 🅸 etw satt haben; **I feel ~** mir ist schlecht

sick|ly /'sɪklɪ/ adj kränklich. **~ness** n Krankheit f; (*vomiting*) Erbrechen nt

side /saɪd/ n Seite f; **on the ~** (*as sideline*) nebenbei; **~ by ~** nebeneinander; (*fig*) Seite an Seite; **take ~s** Partei ergreifen (**with** für) ● attrib Seiten- ● vi **~ with** Partei ergreifen für

side: ~board n Anrichte f. **~-effect**

n Nebenwirkung *f.* ∼**lights** *npl* Standlicht *nt.* ∼**line** *n* Nebenbeschäftigung *f.* ∼**-show** *n* Nebenattraktion *f.* ∼**-step** *vt* ausweichen (+ *dat*). ∼**walk** *n* (*Amer*) Bürgersteig *m.* ∼**ways** *adv* seitwärts

siding /'saɪdɪŋ/ *n* Abstellgleis *nt*

siege /siːdʒ/ *n* Belagerung *f*; (*by police*) Umstellung *f*

sieve /sɪv/ *n* Sieb *nt* ● *vt* sieben

sift /sɪft/ *vt* sieben; (*fig*) durchsehen

sigh /saɪ/ *n* Seufzer *m* ● *vi* seufzen

sight /saɪt/ *n* Sicht *f*; (*faculty*) Sehvermögen *nt*; (*spectacle*) Anblick *m*; (*on gun*) Visier *nt*; ∼**s** *pl* Sehenswürdigkeiten *pl*; **at first** ∼ auf den ersten Blick; **lose** ∼ **of** aus dem Auge verlieren; **know by** ∼ vom Sehen kennen ● *vt* sichten

'**sightseeing** *n* **go** ∼ die Sehenswürdigkeiten besichtigen

sign /saɪn/ *n* Zeichen *nt*; (*notice*) Schild *nt* ● *vt/i* unterschreiben; (*author, artist:*) signieren. ∼ **on** *vi* (*as unemployed*) sich arbeitslos melden; (*Mil*) sich verpflichten

signal /'sɪgnl/ *n* Signal *nt* ● *vt/i* (*pt/pp* **signalled**) signalisieren; ∼ **to s.o.** jdm ein Signal geben

signature /'sɪgnətʃə(r)/ *n* Unterschrift *f*; (*of artist*) Signatur *f*

significan|ce /sɪg'nɪfɪkəns/ *n* Bedeutung *f.* ∼**t** *adj* (*important*) bedeutend

signify /'sɪgnɪfaɪ/ *vt* (*pt/pp* **-ied**) bedeuten

signpost /'saɪn-/ *n* Wegweiser *m*

silence /'saɪləns/ *n* Stille *f*; (*of person*) Schweigen *nt* ● *vt* zum Schweigen bringen. ∼**r** *n* (*on gun*) Schalldämpfer *m*; (*Auto*) Auspufftopf *m*

silent /'saɪlənt/ *adj* still; (*without speaking*) schweigend; **remain** ∼ schweigen

silhouette /sɪluː'et/ *n* Silhouette *f*; (*picture*) Schattenriss *m* ● *vt* **be** ∼**d** sich als Silhouette abheben

silicon /'sɪlɪkən/ *n* Silizium *nt*

silk /sɪlk/ *n* Seide *f* ● *attrib* Seiden-

silky /'sɪlkɪ/ *adj* seidig

sill /sɪl/ *n* Sims *m & nt*

silly /'sɪlɪ/ *adj* dumm; albern

silver /'sɪlvə(r)/ *adj* silbern; (*coin, paper*) Silber- ● *n* Silber *nt*

silver: ∼**-plated** *adj* versilbert. ∼**ware** *n* Silber *nt*

similar /'sɪmɪlə(r)/ *adj* ähnlich. ∼**ity** *n* Ähnlichkeit *f*

simmer /'sɪmə(r)/ *vi* leise kochen, ziehen ● *vt* ziehen lassen

simple /'sɪmpl/ *adj* (**-r, -st**) einfach; (*person*) einfältig. ∼**-'minded** *adj* einfältig

simplicity /sɪm'plɪsətɪ/ *n* Einfachheit *f*

simpli|fication /sɪmplɪfɪ'keɪʃn/ *n* Vereinfachung *f.* ∼**fy** *vt* (*pt/pp* **-ied**) vereinfachen

simply /'sɪmplɪ/ *adv* einfach

simulat|e /'sɪmjʊleɪt/ *vt* vortäuschen; (*Techn*) simulieren

simultaneous /sɪml'teɪnɪəs/ *adj* gleichzeitig

sin /sɪn/ *n* Sünde *f* ● *vi* (*pt/pp* **sinned**) sündigen

since /sɪns/

● *preposition*

····▶ seit (+ *dat*). **he's been living here since 1991** er wohnt* seit 1991 hier. **I had been waiting since 8 o'clock** ich wartete* [schon] seit 8 Uhr. **since seeing you** seit ich dich gesehen habe. **how long is it since your interview?** wie lange ist es seit deinem Vorstellungsgespräch?

● *adverb*

····▶ seitdem. **I haven't spoken to her since** seitdem habe ich mit ihr nicht gesprochen. **the house has been empty ever since** das Haus steht seitdem leer. **he has since remarried** er hat danach wieder geheiratet. **long since** vor langer Zeit

● *conjunction*

····▶ seit. **since she has been living in Germany** seit sie in Deutschland wohnt*. **since they**

S

had been in London seit sie in London waren*. **how long is it since he left?** wie lange ist es her, dass er weggezogen ist? **it's a year since he left** es ist ein Jahr her, dass er weggezogen ist
····▸ (*because*) da. **since she was ill, I had to do it** da sie krank war, musste ich es tun

❗ *Note the different tenses in German

sincere /sɪnˈsɪə(r)/ adj aufrichtig; (*heartfelt*) herzlich. ~**ly** adv aufrichtig; **Yours** ~**ly** Mit freundlichen Grüßen

sincerity /sɪnˈserətɪ/ n Aufrichtigkeit f

sinful /ˈsɪnfl/ adj sündhaft

sing /sɪŋ/ vt/i (pt **sang**, pp **sung**) singen

singe /sɪndʒ/ vt (pres p **singeing**) versengen

singer /ˈsɪŋə(r)/ n Sänger(in) m(f)

single /ˈsɪŋgl/ adj einzeln; (*one only*) einzig; (*unmarried*) ledig; (*ticket*) einfach; (*room, bed*) Einzel- ● n (*ticket*) einfache Fahrkarte f; (*record*) Single f; ~**s** pl (*Tennis*) Einzel nt ● vt ~**out** auswählen

single: ~**-handed** adj & adv allein. ~ˈ**parent** n Alleinerziehende(r) m/f

singly /ˈsɪŋglɪ/ adv einzeln

singular /ˈsɪŋgjʊlə(r)/ adj eigenartig; (*Gram*) im Singular ● n Singular m

sinister /ˈsɪnɪstə(r)/ adj finster

sink /sɪŋk/ n Spülbecken nt ● v (pt **sank**, pp **sunk**) ● vi sinken ● vt versenken (*ship*); senken (*shaft*). ~ **in** vi einsinken; (🆒: *be understood*) kapiert werden

sinner /ˈsɪnə(r)/ n Sünder(in) m(f)

sip /sɪp/ n Schlückchen nt ● vt (pt/pp **sipped**) in kleinen Schlucken trinken

siphon /ˈsaɪfn/ n (*bottle*) Siphon m. ~ **off** vt mit einem Saugheber ablassen

sir /sɜː(r)/ n mein Herr; **S**~ (*title*) Sir; **Dear S**~**s** Sehr geehrte Herren

siren /ˈsaɪrən/ n Sirene f

sister /ˈsɪstə(r)/ n Schwester f; (*nurse*) Oberschwester f. ~**-in-law** n Schwägerin f

sit /sɪt/ v (pt/pp **sat**, pres p **sitting**) ● vi sitzen; (*sit down*) sich setzen; (*committee:*) tagen ● vt setzen; machen (*exam*). ~ **back** vi sich zurücklehnen. ~ **down** vi sich setzen. ~ **up** vi [aufrecht] sitzen; (*rise*) sich aufsetzen; (*not slouch*) gerade sitzen

site /saɪt/ n Gelände nt; (*for camping*) Platz m; (*Archaeology*) Stätte f

sitting /ˈsɪtɪŋ/ n Sitzung f; (*for meals*) Schub m

situat|e /ˈsɪtjʊeɪt/ vt legen; **be** ~**ed** liegen. ~**ion** n Lage f; (*circumstances*) Situation f; (*job*) Stelle f

six /sɪks/ adj sechs. ~**teen** adj sechzehn. ~**teenth** adj sechzehnte(r,s)

sixth /sɪksθ/ adj sechste(r,s)

sixtieth /ˈsɪkstɪɪθ/ adj sechzigste(r,s)

sixty /ˈsɪkstɪ/ adj sechzig

size /saɪz/ n Größe f

sizzle /ˈsɪzl/ vi brutzeln

skate /skeɪt/ n Schlittschuh m ● vi Schlittschuh laufen. ~**board** n Skateboard nt ● vi Skateboard fahren. ~**boarding** n Skateboardfahren nt. ~**r** n Eisläufer(in) m(f)

skating /ˈskeɪtɪŋ/ n Eislaufen nt. ~**-rink** n Eisbahn f

skeleton /ˈskelɪtn/ n Skelett nt. ~ˈ**key** n Dietrich m

sketch /sketʃ/ n Skizze f; (*Theat*) Sketch m ● vt skizzieren

sketchy /ˈsketʃɪ/ adj , -**ily** adv skizzenhaft

ski /skiː/ n Ski m ● vi (pt/pp **skied**, pres p **skiing**) Ski fahren or laufen

skid /skɪd/ n Schleudern nt ● vi (pt/pp **skidded**) schleudern

skier /ˈskiːə(r)/ n Skiläufer(in) m(f)

skiing /ˈskiːɪŋ/ n Skilaufen nt

skilful /ˈskɪlfl/ adj geschickt

skill /skɪl/ n Geschick nt. ~**ed** adj geschickt; (*trained*) ausgebildet

skim /skɪm/ vt (pt/pp **skimmed**) entrahmen (*milk*)

skimp /skɪmp/ vt sparen an (+ dat)

skimpy /ˈskɪmpɪ/ adj knapp

skin /skɪn/ n Haut f; (on fruit) Schale f ● vt (pt/pp **skinned**) häuten; schälen (fruit)

skin: ∼-**deep** adj oberflächlich. ∼-**diving** n Sporttauchen nt

skinny /'skɪnɪ/ adj dünn

skip¹ /skɪp/ n Container m

skip² n Hüpfer m ● v (pt/pp **skipped**) vi hüpfen; (with rope) seilspringen ● vt überspringen

skipper /'skɪpə(r)/ n Kapitän m

'**skipping-rope** n Sprungseil nt

skirmish /'skɜːmɪʃ/ n Gefecht nt

skirt /skɜːt/ n Rock m ● vt herumgehen um

skittle /'skɪtl/ n Kegel m

skive /skaɪv/ vi 🔲 blaumachen

skull /skʌl/ n Schädel m

sky /skaɪ/ n Himmel m. ∼**light** n Dachluke f. ∼ **marshal** n bewaffneter Flugbegleiter m. ∼**scraper** n Wolkenkratzer m

slab /slæb/ n Platte f; (slice) Scheibe f; (of chocolate) Tafel f

slack /slæk/ adj (-er, -est) schlaff, locker; (person) nachlässig; (Comm) flau ● vi bummeln

slacken /'slækn/ vi sich lockern; (diminish) nachlassen ● vt lockern; (diminish) verringern

slain /sleɪn/ see slay

slam /slæm/ v (pt/pp **slammed**) ● vt zuschlagen; (put) knallen 🔲; (🔲: criticize) verreißen ● vi zuschlagen

slander /'slɑːndə(r)/ n Verleumdung f ● vt verleumden

slang /slæŋ/ n Slang m. ∼**y** adj salopp

slant /slɑːnt/ n Schräge f; on the ∼ schräg ● vt abschrägen; (fig) färben (report) ● vi sich neigen

slap /slæp/ n Schlag m ● vt (pt/pp **slapped**) schlagen; (put) knallen 🔲 ● adv direkt

slapdash adj 🔲 schludrig

slash /slæʃ/ n Schlitz m ● vt aufschlitzen; [drastisch] reduzieren (prices)

slat /slæt/ n Latte f

slate /sleɪt/ n Schiefer m ● vt 🔲 heruntermachen; verreißen (performance)

slaughter /'slɔːtə(r)/ n Schlachten nt; (massacre) Gemetzel nt ● vt schlachten; abschlachten (men)

Slav /slɑːv/ adj slawisch ● n Slawe m/ Slawin f

slave /sleɪv/ n Sklave m/ Sklavin f ● vi ∼ [away] schuften

slavery /'sleɪvərɪ/ n Sklaverei f

slay /sleɪ/ vt (pt slew, pp slain) ermorden

sledge /sledʒ/ n Schlitten m

sleek /sliːk/ adj (-er, -est) seidig; (well-fed) wohlgenährt

sleep /sliːp/ n Schlaf m; go to ∼ einschlafen; put to ∼ einschläfern ● v (pt/pp **slept**) ● vi schlafen ● vt (accommodate) Unterkunft bieten für. ∼**er** n Schläfer(in) m(f); (Rail) Schlafwagen m; (on track) Schwelle f

sleeping: ∼-**bag** n Schlafsack m. ∼-**pill** n Schlaftablette f

sleep: ∼**less** adj schlaflos. ∼-**walking** n Schlafwandeln nt

sleepy /'sliːpɪ/ adj , -**ily** adv schläfrig

sleet /sliːt/ n Schneeregen m

sleeve /sliːv/ n Ärmel m; (for record) Hülle f. ∼**less** adj ärmellos

sleigh /sleɪ/ n [Pferde]schlitten m

slender /'slendə(r)/ adj schlank; (fig) gering

slept /slept/ see sleep

slew see slay

slice /slaɪs/ n Scheibe f ● vt in Scheiben schneiden

slick /slɪk/ adj clever

slid|e /slaɪd/ n Rutschbahn f; (for hair) Spange f; (Phot) Dia nt ● v (pt/pp slid) ● vi rutschen ● vt schieben. ∼**ing** adj gleitend; (door, seat) Schiebe-

slight /slaɪt/ adj (-er, -est) leicht; (importance) gering; (acquaintance) flüchtig; (slender) schlank; not in the ∼**est** nicht im Geringsten; ∼**ly** better ein bisschen besser ● vt kränken, beleidigen ● n Beleidigung f

slim /slɪm/ adj (**slimmer, slimmest**)

schlank; (*volume*) schmal; (*fig*) gering ● *vi* eine Schlankheitskur machen

slim|e /slaɪm/ *n* Schleim *m*. ~**y** *adj* schleimig

sling /slɪŋ/ *n* (*Med*) Schlinge *f* ● *vt* (*pt/pp* **slung**) ⚄ schmeißen

slip /slɪp/ *n* (*mistake*) Fehler *m*, ⚄ Patzer *m*; (*petticoat*) Unterrock *m*; (*paper*) Zettel *m*; **give s.o. the ~** ⚄ jdm entwischen; **~ of the tongue** Versprecher *m* ● *v* (*pt/pp* **slipped**) ● *vi* rutschen; (*fall*) ausrutschen; (*go quickly*) schlüpfen ● *vt* schieben; **~ s.o.'s mind** jdm entfallen. **~ away** *vi* sich fortschleichen. **~ up** *vi* ⚄ einen Schnitzer machen

slipper /'slɪpə(r)/ *n* Hausschuh *m*

slippery /'slɪpərɪ/ *adj* glitschig; (*surface*) glatt

slipshod /'slɪpʃɒd/ *adj* schludrig

'slip-up *n* ⚄ Schnitzer *m*

slit /slɪt/ *n* Schlitz *m* ● *vt* (*pt/pp* **slit**) aufschlitzen

slither /'slɪðə(r)/ *vi* rutschen

slog /slɒg/ *n* [*hard*] ~ Schinderei *f* ● *vi* (*pt/pp* **slogged**) schuften

slogan /'sləʊgən/ *n* Schlagwort *nt*; (*advertising*) Werbespruch *m*

slop|e /sləʊp/ *n* Hang *m*; (*inclination*) Neigung *f* ● *vi* sich neigen. ~**ing** *adj* schräg

sloppy /'slɒpɪ/ *adj* schludrig; (*sentimental*) sentimental

slosh /slɒʃ/ *vi* ⚄ schwappen

slot /slɒt/ *n* Schlitz *m*; (*TV*) Sendezeit *f* ● *v* (*pt/pp* **slotted**) ● *vt* einfügen ● *vi* sich einfügen (**in** in + *acc*)

'slot-machine *n* Münzautomat *m*; (*for gambling*) Spielautomat *m*

slouch /slaʊtʃ/ *vi* sich schlecht halten

slovenly /'slʌvnlɪ/ *adj* schlampig

slow /sləʊ/ *adj* (**-er, -est**) langsam; **be ~** (*clock:*) nachgehen; **in ~ motion** in Zeitlupe ● *adv* langsam ● *vt* verlangsamen ● *vi* ~ **down, ~ up** langsamer werden. ~**ness** *n* Langsamkeit *f*

sludge /slʌdʒ/ *n* Schlamm *m*

slug /slʌg/ *n* Nacktschnecke *f*

sluggish /'slʌgɪʃ/ *adj* träge

sluice /sluːs/ *n* Schleuse *f*

slum /slʌm/ *n* Elendsviertel *nt*

slumber /'slʌmbə(r)/ *n* Schlummer *m* ● *vi* schlummern

slump /slʌmp/ *n* Sturz *m* ● *vi* fallen; (*crumple*) zusammensacken; (*prices:*) stürzen; (*sales:*) zurückgehen

slung /slʌŋ/ *see* **sling**

slur /slɜː(r)/ *vt* (*pt/pp* **slurred**) undeutlich sprechen

slurp /slɜːp/ *vt/i* schlürfen

slush /slʌʃ/ *n* [Schnee]matsch *m*; (*fig*) Kitsch *m*

slut /slʌt/ *n* Schlampe *f* ⚄

sly /slaɪ/ *adj* (**-er, -est**) verschlagen ● *n* **on the ~** heimlich

smack /smæk/ *n* Schlag *m*, Klaps *m* ● *vt* schlagen ● *adv* ⚄ direkt

small /smɔːl/ *adj* (**-er, -est**) klein ● *adv* **chop up ~** klein hacken ● *n* ~ **of the back** Kreuz *nt*

small: ~ **ads** *npl* Kleinanzeigen *pl*. ~ **'change** *n* Kleingeld *nt*. ~**pox** *n* Pocken *pl*. ~ **talk** *n* leichte Konversation *f*

smart /smɑːt/ *adj* (**-er, -est**) schick; (*clever*) schlau, clever; (*brisk*) flott; (*Amer, fam: cheeky*) frech ● *vi* brennen

smarten /'smɑːtn/ *vt* ~ **oneself up** mehr auf sein Äußeres achten

smash /smæʃ/ *n* Krach *m*; (*collision*) Zusammenstoß *m*; (*Tennis*) Schmetterball *m* ● *vt* zerschlagen; (*strike*) schlagen; (*Tennis*) schmettern ● *vi* zerschmettern; (*crash*) krachen (**into** gegen). ~**ing** *adj* ⚄ toll

smear /smɪə(r)/ *n* verschmierter Fleck *m*; (*Med*) Abstrich *m*; (*fig*) Verleumdung *f* ● *vt* schmieren; (*coat*) beschmieren (**with** mit); (*fig*) verleumden ● *vi* schmieren

smell /smel/ *n* Geruch *m*; (*sense*) Geruchssinn *m* ● *v* (*pt/pp* **smelt** or **smelled**) ● *vt* riechen; (*sniff*) riechen an (+ *dat*) ● *vi* riechen (**of** nach)

smelly /'smelɪ/ *adj* übel riechend

smelt /smelt/ *see* **smell**

smile /smaɪl/ *n* Lächeln *nt* ● *vi* lächeln; ~ **at** anlächeln

smirk /smɜːk/ vi feixen

smith /smɪθ/ n Schmied m

smock /smɒk/ n Kittel m

smog /smɒg/ n Smog m

smoke /sməʊk/ n Rauch m ● vt/i rauchen; (Culin) räuchern. ~**less** adj rauchfrei; (fuel) rauchlos

smoker /'sməʊkə(r)/ n Raucher m; (Rail) Raucherabteil nt

smoking /'sməʊkɪŋ/ n Rauchen nt; 'no ~' 'Rauchen verboten'

smoky /'sməʊkɪ/ adj verraucht; (taste) rauchig

smooth /smuːð/ adj (**-er, -est**) glatt ● vt glätten. ~ **out** vt glatt streichen

smother /'smʌðə(r)/ vt ersticken; (cover) bedecken; (suppress) unterdrücken

smoulder /'sməʊldə(r)/ vi schwelen

smudge /smʌdʒ/ n Fleck m ● vt verwischen ● vi schmieren

smug /smʌg/ adj (**smugger, smuggest**) selbstgefällig

smuggl|e /'smʌgl/ vt schmuggeln. ~**er** n Schmuggler m. ~**ing** n Schmuggel m

snack /snæk/ n Imbiss m. ~**-bar** n Imbissstube f

snag /snæg/ n Schwierigkeit f, 🔲 Haken m

snail /sneɪl/ n Schnecke f; **at a** ~**'s pace** im Schneckentempo

snake /sneɪk/ n Schlange f

snap /snæp/ n Knacken nt; (photo) Schnappschuss m ● attrib (decision) plötzlich ● v (pt/pp **snapped**) ● vi [entzwei]brechen; ~ **at** (bite) schnappen nach; (speak sharply) [scharf] anfahren ● vt zerbrechen; (say) fauchen; (Phot) knipsen. ~ **up** vt wegschnappen

snappy /'snæpɪ/ adj (smart) flott; **make it** ~! ein bisschen schnell!

'**snapshot** n Schnappschuss m

snare /sneə(r)/ n Schlinge f

snarl /snɑːl/ vi [mit gefletschten Zähnen] knurren

snatch /snætʃ/ n (fragment) Fetzen pl ● vt schnappen; (steal) klauen; entführen (child); ~ **sth from s.o.** jdm etw entreißen

sneak /sniːk/ n 🔲 Petze f ● vi schleichen; (🔲: tell tales) petzen ● vt (take) mitgehen lassen ● vi ~ **in/out** sich hinein-/hinausschleichen

sneakers /'sniːkəz/ npl (Amer) Turnschuhe pl

sneer /snɪə(r)/ vi höhnisch lächeln; (mock) spotten

sneeze /sniːz/ n Niesen nt ● vi niesen

snide /snaɪd/ adj 🔲 abfällig

sniff /snɪf/ vi schnüffeln ● vt schnüffeln an (+ dat)

snigger /'snɪgə(r)/ vi [boshaft] kichern

snip /snɪp/ n Schnitt m ● vt/i ~ **[at]** schnippeln an (+ dat)

snippet /'snɪpɪt/ n Schnipsel m; (of information) Bruchstück nt

snivel /'snɪvl/ vi (pt/pp **snivelled**) flennen

snob /snɒb/ n Snob m. ~**bery** n Snobismus m. ~**bish** adj snobistisch

snoop /snuːp/ vi 🔲 schnüffeln

snooty /'snuːtɪ/ adj 🔲 hochnäsig

snooze /snuːz/ n Nickerchen nt ● vi dösen

snore /snɔː(r)/ vi schnarchen

snorkel /'snɔːkl/ n Schnorchel m

snort /snɔːt/ vi schnauben

snout /snaʊt/ n Schnauze f

snow /snəʊ/ n Schnee m ● vi schneien; ~**ed under with** (fig) überhäuft mit

snow: ~**ball** n Schneeball m. ~**board** n Snowboard nt. ~**drift** n Schneewehe f. ~**drop** n Schneeglöckchen nt. ~**fall** n Schneefall m. ~**flake** n Schneeflocke f. ~**man** n Schneemann m. ~**plough** n Schneepflug m

snub /snʌb/ n Abfuhr f ● vt (pt/pp **snubbed**) brüskieren

'**snub-nosed** adj stupsnasig

snuffle /'snʌfl/ vi schnüffeln

snug /snʌg/ adj (**snugger, snuggest**) behaglich, gemütlich

S

snuggle /'snʌgl/ vi sich kuscheln (**up to** an + acc)

so /səʊ/ adv so; **so am I** ich auch; **so I see** das sehe ich; **that is so** das stimmt; **so much the better** umso besser; **if so** wenn ja; **so as to** um zu; **so long!** ☒ tschüs! ● pron **I hope so** hoffentlich; **I think so** ich glaube schon; **I'm afraid so** leider ja; **so saying/doing, he/she** ... indem er/sie das sagte/tat, ... ● conj (therefore) also; **so that** damit; **so what!** na und! **so you see** wie du siehst

soak /səʊk/ vt nass machen; (steep) einweichen; (☒: fleece) schröpfen ● vi weichen; (liquid:) sickern. ~ **up** vt aufsaugen

soaking /'səʊkɪŋ/ adj & adv ~ [**wet**] patschnass ☒

soap /səʊp/ n Seife f. ~ **opera** n Seifenoper f. ~ **powder** n Seifenpulver nt

soapy /'səʊpɪ/ adj seifig

soar /sɔː(r)/ vi aufsteigen; (prices:) in die Höhe schnellen

sob /sɒb/ n Schluchzer m ● vi (pt/pp **sobbed**) schluchzen

sober /'səʊbə(r)/ adj nüchtern; (serious) ernst; (colour) gedeckt. ~ **up** vi nüchtern werden

'so-called adj sogenannt

soccer /'sɒkə(r)/ n ☒ Fußball m

sociable /'səʊʃəbl/ adj gesellig

social /'səʊʃl/ adj gesellschaftlich; (Admin, Pol, Zool) sozial

socialis|m /'səʊʃəlɪzm/ n Sozialismus m. ~**t** adj sozialistisch ● n Sozialist m

socialize /'səʊʃəlaɪz/ vi [gesellschaftlich] verkehren

socially /'səʊʃəlɪ/ adv gesellschaftlich; **know** ~ privat kennen

social: ~ **se'curity** n Sozialhilfe f. ~ **worker** n Sozialarbeiter(in) m(f)

society /sə'saɪətɪ/ n Gesellschaft f; (club) Verein m

sociolog|ist /səʊsɪ'ɒlədʒɪst/ n Soziologe m. ~**y** n Soziologie f

sock /sɒk/ n Socke f; (kneelength) Kniestrumpf m

socket /'sɒkɪt/ n (of eye) Augenhöhle f; (of joint) Gelenkpfanne f; (wall plug) Steckdose f

soda /'səʊdə/ n Soda nt; (Amer) Limonade f. ~ **water** n Sodawasser nt

sodden /'sɒdn/ adj durchnässt

sofa /'səʊfə/ n Sofa nt. ~ **bed** n Schlafcouch f

soft /sɒft/ adj (-er, -est) weich; (quiet) leise; (gentle) sanft; (☒: silly) dumm. ~ **drink** n alkoholfreies Getränk nt

soften /'sɒfn/ vt weich machen; (fig) mildern ● vi weich werden

soft: ~ **toy** n Stofftier nt. ~**ware** n Software f

soggy /'sɒgɪ/ adj aufgeweicht

soil[1] /sɔɪl/ n Erde f, Boden m

soil[2] vt verschmutzen

solar /'səʊlə(r)/ adj Sonnen-

sold /səʊld/ see **sell**

soldier /'səʊldʒə(r)/ n Soldat m ● vi ~ **on** [unbeirrbar] weitermachen

sole[1] /səʊl/ n Sohle f

sole[2] n (fish) Seezunge f

sole[3] adj einzig. ~**ly** adv einzig und allein

solemn /'sɒləm/ adj feierlich; (serious) ernst

solicitor /sə'lɪsɪtə(r)/ n Rechtsanwalt m/-anwältin f

solid /'sɒlɪd/ adj fest; (sturdy) stabil; (not hollow, of same substance) massiv; (unanimous) einstimmig; (complete) ganz

solidarity /sɒlɪ'dærətɪ/ n Solidarität f

solidify /sə'lɪdɪfaɪ/ vi (pt/pp -ied) fest werden

solitary /'sɒlɪtərɪ/ adj einsam; (sole) einzig

solitude /'sɒlɪtjuːd/ n Einsamkeit f

solo /'səʊləʊ/ n Solo nt ● adj Solo-; (flight) Allein- ● adv solo. ~**ist** n Solist(in) m(f)

solstice /'sɒlstɪs/ n Sonnenwende f

soluble /'sɒljʊbl/ adj löslich

solution /sə'luːʃn/ n Lösung f

solvable /'sɒlvəbl/ adj lösbar

solve /sɒlv/ vt lösen

solvent /'sɒlvənt/ n Lösungsmittel nt

sombre /'sɒmbə(r)/ adj dunkel; (mood) düster

some /sʌm/ adj & pron etwas; (a little) ein bisschen; (with pl noun) einige; (a few) ein paar; (certain) manche(r,s); (one or the other) [irgend]ein; ~ **day** eines Tages; **I want** ~ ich möchte etwas/ (pl) welche; **will you have** ~ **wine?** möchten Sie Wein? **do** ~ **shopping** einkaufen

some: ~**body** /-bədɪ/ pron & n jemand; (emphatic) irgendjemand. ~**how** adv irgendwie. ~**one** pron & n = **somebody**

somersault /'sʌməsɔːlt/ n Purzelbaum m 🗊; (Sport) Salto m; **turn a** ~ einen Purzelbaum schlagen/einen Salto springen

'something pron & adv etwas; (emphatic) irgendetwas; ~ **different** etwas anderes; ~ **like this** so etwas [wie das]

some: ~**time** adv irgendwann ● adj ehemalig. ~**times** adv manchmal. ~**what** adv ziemlich. ~**where** adv irgendwo; (go) irgendwohin

son /sʌn/ n Sohn m

song /sɒŋ/ n Lied nt. ~**bird** n Singvogel m

'son-in-law n (pl ~s-in-law) Schwiegersohn m

soon /suːn/ adv (-er, -est) bald; (quickly) schnell; **too** ~ zu früh; **as** ~ **as possible** so bald wie möglich; ~**er or later** früher oder später; **no** ~**er had I arrived than ...** kaum war ich angekommen, da ...; **I would** ~**er stay** ich würde lieber bleiben

soot /sʊt/ n Ruß m

sooth|e /suːð/ vt beruhigen; lindern (pain). ~**ing** adj beruhigend; lindernd

sophisticated /sə'fɪstɪkeɪtɪd/ adj weltgewandt; (complex) hoch entwickelt

sopping /'sɒpɪŋ/ adj & adv ~**[wet]** durchnässt

soppy /'sɒpɪ/ adj 🗊 rührselig

soprano /sə'prɑːnəʊ/ n Sopran m;

(woman) Sopranistin f

sordid /'sɔːdɪd/ adj schmutzig

sore /sɔː(r)/ adj (-r, -st) wund; (painful) schmerzhaft; **have a** ~ **throat** Halsschmerzen haben ● n wunde Stelle f. ~**ly** adv sehr

sorrow /'sɒrəʊ/ n Kummer m

sorry /'sɒrɪ/ adj (sad) traurig; (wretched) erbärmlich; **I am** ~ es tut mir Leid; **she is** or **feels** ~ **for him** er tut ihr Leid; **I am** ~ **to say** leider; ~**!** Entschuldigung!

sort /sɔːt/ n Art f; (brand) Sorte f; **he's a good** ~ 🗊 er ist in Ordnung ● vt sortieren. ~ **out** vt sortieren; (fig) klären

sought /sɔːt/ see **seek**

soul /səʊl/ n Seele f

sound¹ /saʊnd/ adj (-er, -est) gesund; (sensible) vernünftig; (secure) solide; (thorough) gehörig ● adv **be** ~ **asleep** fest schlafen

sound² n (strait) Meerenge f

sound³ n Laut m; (noise) Geräusch nt; (Phys) Schall m; (Radio, TV) Ton m; (of bells, music) Klang m; **I don't like the** ~ **of it** 🗊 das hört sich nicht gut an ● vi [er]tönen; (seem) sich anhören ● vt (pronounce) aussprechen; schlagen (alarm); (Med) abhorchen (chest)

soundly /'saʊndlɪ/ adv solide; (sleep) fest; (defeat) vernichtend

'soundproof adj schalldicht

soup /suːp/ n Suppe f

sour /'saʊə(r)/ adj (-er, -est) sauer; (bad-tempered) griesgrämig, verdrießlich

source /sɔːs/ n Quelle f

south /saʊθ/ n Süden m; **to the** ~ **of** südlich von ● adj Süd-, süd- ● adv nach Süden

south: S~ 'Africa n Südafrika nt. S~ A'merica n Südamerika nt. ~-'east n Südosten m

southerly /'sʌðəlɪ/ adj südlich

southern /'sʌðən/ adj südlich

'southward[s] /-wəd[z]/ adv nach Süden

S

souvenir /suːvəˈnɪə(r)/ *n* Andenken *nt*, Souvenir *nt*

Soviet /ˈsəʊvɪət/ *adj* (*History*) sowjetisch; ~ **Union** Sowjetunion *f*

sow¹ /saʊ/ *n* Sau *f*

sow² /səʊ/ *vt* (*pt* **sowed**, *pp* **sown** or **sowed**) säen

soya /ˈsɔɪə/ *n* ~ **bean** Sojabohne *f*

spa /spɑː/ *n* Heilbad *nt*

space /speɪs/ *n* Raum *m*; (*gap*) Platz *m*; (*Astronomy*) Weltraum *m* ● *vt* ~ **[out]** [in Abständen] verteilen

space: ~**craft** *n* Raumfahrzeug *nt*. ~**ship** *n* Raumschiff *nt*

spacious /ˈspeɪʃəs/ *adj* geräumig

spade /speɪd/ *n* Spaten *m*; (*for child*) Schaufel *f*; ~**s** *pl* (*Cards*) Pik *nt*

Spain /speɪn/ *n* Spanien *nt*

span¹ /spæn/ *n* Spanne *f*; (*of arch*) Spannweite *f* ● *vt* (*pt/pp* **spanned**) überspannen; umspannen (*time*)

span² *see* **spick**

Span|iard /ˈspænjəd/ *n* Spanier(in) *m*(*f*). ~**ish** *adj* spanisch ● *n* (*Lang*) Spanisch *nt*; **the** ~**ish** *pl* die Spanier

spank /spæŋk/ *vt* verhauen

spanner /ˈspænə(r)/ *n* Schraubenschlüssel *m*

spare /speə(r)/ *adj* (*surplus*) übrig; (*additional*) zusätzlich; (*seat, time*) frei; (*room*) Gäste-; (*bed, cup*) Extra- ● *n* (*part*) Ersatzteil *nt* ● *vt* ersparen; (*not hurt*) verschonen; (*do without*) entbehren; (*afford to give*) erübrigen. ~ 'wheel *n* Reserverad *nt*

sparing /ˈspeərɪŋ/ *adj* sparsam

spark /spɑːk/ *n* Funke *nt*. ~**[ing]-plug** *n* (*Auto*) Zündkerze *f*

sparkl|e /ˈspɑːkl/ *n* Funkeln *nt* ● *vi* funkeln. ~**ing** *adj* funkelnd; (*wine*) Schaum-

sparrow /ˈspærəʊ/ *n* Spatz *m*

sparse /spɑːs/ *adj* spärlich. ~**ly** *adv* spärlich; (*populated*) dünn

spasm /ˈspæzm/ *n* Anfall *m*; (*cramp*) Krampf *m*. ~**odic** *adj*, **-ally** *adv* sporadisch

spastic /ˈspæstɪk/ *adj* spastisch [gelähmt] ● *n* Spastiker(in) *m*(*f*)

spat /spæt/ *see* **spit**²

spatter /ˈspætə(r)/ *vt* spritzen; ~ **with** bespritzen mit

spawn /spɔːn/ *n* Laich *m* ● *vt* (*fig*) hervorbringen

speak /spiːk/ *v* (*pt* **spoke**, *pp* **spoken**) ● *vi* sprechen (**to** mit) ~**ing!** (*Teleph*) am Apparat! ● *vt* sprechen; sagen (*truth*). ~ **up** *vi* lauter sprechen; ~ **up for oneself** seine Meinung äußern

speaker /ˈspiːkə(r)/ *n* Sprecher(in) *m*(*f*); (*in public*) Redner(in) *m*(*f*); (*loudspeaker*) Lautsprecher *m*

spear /spɪə(r)/ *n* Speer *m* ● *vt* aufspießen

spec /spek/ *n* **on** ~ 🄳 auf gut Glück

special /ˈspeʃl/ *adj* besondere(r,s), speziell. ~**ist** *n* Spezialist *m*; (*Med*) Facharzt *m*/-ärztin *f*. ~**ity** *n* Spezialität *f*

special|ize /ˈspeʃəlaɪz/ *vi* sich spezialisieren (**in** auf + *acc*). ~**ly** *adv* speziell; (*particularly*) besonders

species /ˈspiːʃiːz/ *n* Art *f*

specific /spəˈsɪfɪk/ *adj* bestimmt; (*precise*) genau; (*Phys*) spezifisch. ~**ally** *adv* ausdrücklich

specification /spesɪfɪˈkeɪʃn/ *n* (*also* ~**s**) *pl* genaue Angaben *pl*

specify /ˈspesɪfaɪ/ *vt* (*pt/pp* **-ied**) [genau] angeben

specimen /ˈspesɪmən/ *n* Exemplar *nt*; (*sample*) Probe *f*; (*of urine*) Urinprobe *f*

speck /spek/ *n* Fleck *m*

speckled /ˈspekld/ *adj* gesprenkelt

spectacle /ˈspektəkl/ *n* (*show*) Schauspiel *nt*; (*sight*) Anblick *m*. ~**s** *npl* Brille *f*

spectacular /spekˈtækjʊlə(r)/ *adj* spektakulär

spectator /spekˈteɪtə(r)/ *n* Zuschauer(in) *m*(*f*)

speculat|e /ˈspekjʊleɪt/ *vi* spekulieren. ~**ion** *n* Spekulation *f*. ~**or** *n* Spekulant *m*

sped /sped/ *see* **speed**

speech /spiːtʃ/ *n* Sprache *f*; (*address*) Rede *f*. ~**less** *adj* sprachlos

speed /spiːd/ *n* Geschwindigkeit *f*;

(*rapidity*) Schnelligkeit *f* ● *vi* (*pt/pp* **sped**) schnell fahren ● (*pt/pp* **speeded**) (*go too fast*) zu schnell fahren. **~ up** (*pt/pp* **speeded up**) ● *vt/i* beschleunigen

speed: ~boat *n* Rennboot *nt*. **~ camera** *n* Geschwindigkeitsüberwachungskamera *f*. **~ dating** *n* Speeddating *nt*. **~ing** *n* Geschwindigkeitsüberschreitung *f*. **~ limit** *n* Geschwindigkeitsbeschränkung *f*

speedometer /spiːˈdɒmɪtə(r)/ *n* Tachometer *m*

speedy /ˈspiːdɪ/ *adj*, **-ily** *adv* schnell

spell[1] /spel/ *n* Weile *f*; (*of weather*) Periode *f*

spell[2] *v* (*pt/pp* **spelled** or **spelt**) ● *vt* schreiben; (*aloud*) buchstabieren; (*fig: mean*) bedeuten ● *vi* richtig schreiben; (*aloud*) buchstabieren. **~ out** *vt* buchstabieren; (*fig*) genau erklären

spell[3] *n* Zauber *m*; (*words*) Zauberspruch *m*. **~bound** *adj* wie verzaubert

'spell checker *n* Rechtschreibprogramm *nt*

spelling /ˈspelɪŋ/ *n* (*of a word*) Schreibweise *f*; (*orthography*) Rechtschreibung *f*

spelt /spelt/ *see* **spell**[2]

spend /spend/ *vt/i* (*pt/pp* **spent**) ausgeben; verbringen (*time*)

spent /spent/ *see* **spend**

sperm /spɜːm/ *n* Samen *m*

sphere /sfɪə(r)/ *n* Kugel *f*; (*fig*) Sphäre *f*

spice /spaɪs/ *n* Gewürz *nt*; (*fig*) Würze *f*

spicy /ˈspaɪsɪ/ *adj* würzig, pikant

spider /ˈspaɪdə(r)/ *n* Spinne *f*

spik|e /spaɪk/ *n* Spitze *f*; (*Bot, Zool*) Stachel *m*; (*on shoe*) Spike *m*. **~y** *adj* stachelig

spill /spɪl/ *v* (*pt/pp* **spilt** or **spilled**) ● *vt* verschütten ● *vi* überlaufen

spin /spɪn/ *v* (*pt/pp* **spun**, *pres p* **spinning**) ● *vt* drehen; spinnen (*wool*); schleudern (*washing*) ● *vi* sich drehen

spinach /ˈspɪnɪdʒ/ *n* Spinat *m*

spindl|e /ˈspɪndl/ *n* Spindel *f*. **~y** *adj* spindeldürr

spin-'drier *n* Wäscheschleuder *f*

spine /spaɪn/ *n* Rückgrat *nt*; (*of book*) [Buch]rücken *m*; (*Bot, Zool*) Stachel *m*. **~less** *adj* (*fig*) rückgratlos

'spin-off *n* Nebenprodukt *nt*

spinster /ˈspɪnstə(r)/ *n* ledige Frau *f*

spiral /ˈspaɪrl/ *adj* spiralig ● *n* Spirale *f* ● *vi* (*pt/pp* **spiralled**) sich hochwinden. **~ 'staircase** *n* Wendeltreppe *f*

spire /ˈspaɪə(r)/ *n* Turmspitze *f*

spirit /ˈspɪrɪt/ *n* Geist *m*; (*courage*) Mut *m*; **~s** *pl* (*alcohol*) Spirituosen *pl*; **in low ~s** niedergedrückt. **~ away** *vt* verschwinden lassen

spirited /ˈspɪrɪtɪd/ *adj* lebhaft; (*courageous*) beherzt

spiritual /ˈspɪrɪtjʊəl/ *adj* geistig; (*Relig*) geistlich

spit[1] /spɪt/ *n* (*for roasting*) [Brat]spieß *m*

spit[2] *n* Spucke *f* ● *vt/i* (*pt/pp* **spat**, *pres p* **spitting**) spucken; (*cat:*) fauchen; (*fat:*) spritzen; **it's ~ting with rain** es tröpfelt

spite /spaɪt/ *n* Boshaftigkeit *f*; **in ~ of** trotz (+ *gen*) ● *vt* ärgern. **~ful** *adj* gehässig

splash /splæʃ/ *n* Platschen *nt*; (🔲: *drop*) Schuss *m*; **~ of colour** Farbfleck *m* ● *vt* spritzen; **~ s.o. with sth** jdn mit etw bespritzen ● *vi* spritzen. **~ about** *vi* planschen

splendid /ˈsplendɪd/ *adj* herrlich, großartig

splendour /ˈsplendə(r)/ *n* Pracht *f*

splint /splɪnt/ *n* (*Med*) Schiene *f*

splinter /ˈsplɪntə(r)/ *n* Splitter *m* ● *vi* zersplittern

split /splɪt/ *n* Spaltung *f*; (*Pol*) Bruch *m*; (*tear*) Riss *m* ● *v* (*pt/pp* **split**, *pres p* **splitting**) ● *vt* spalten; (*share*) teilen; (*tear*) zerreißen ● *vi* sich spalten; (*tear*) zerreißen; **~ on s.o.** 🔲 jdn verpfeifen. **~ up** *vt* aufteilen ● *vi* (*couple:*) sich trennen

splutter /ˈsplʌtə(r)/ *vi* prusten

spoil /spɔɪl/ *n* **~s** *pl* Beute *f* ● *v* (*pt/*

pp **spoilt** or **spoiled**) ● *vt* verderben; verwöhnen (*person*) ● *vi* verderben. **~sport** *n* Spielverderber *m*

spoke[1] /spəʊk/ *n* Speiche *f*

spoke[2], **spoken** *see* **speak**

'spokesman *n* Sprecher *m*

sponge /spʌndʒ/ *n* Schwamm *m* ● *vt* abwaschen ● *vi* ~ **on** schmarotzen bei. **~-bag** *n* Waschbeutel *m*. **~-cake** *n* Biskuitkuchen *m*

sponsor /'spɒnsə(r)/ *n* Sponsor *m*; (*godparent*) Pate *m*/Patin *f* ● *vt* sponsern

spontaneous /spɒn'teɪnɪəs/ *adj* spontan

spoof /spu:f/ *n* ⬛ Parodie *f*

spooky /'spu:kɪ/ *adj* ⬛ gespenstisch

spool /spu:l/ *n* Spule *f*

spoon /spu:n/ *n* Löffel *m* ● *vt* löffeln. **~ful** *n* Löffel *m*

sporadic /spə'rædɪk/ *adj*, **-ally** *adv* sporadisch

sport /spɔ:t/ *n* Sport *m* ● *vt* [stolz] tragen. **~ing** *adj* sportlich

sports: **~car** *n* Sportwagen *m*. **~ coat** *n*, **~ jacket** *n* Sakko *m*. **~man** *n* Sportler *m*. **~woman** *n* Sportlerin *f*

sporty /'spɔ:tɪ/ *adj* sportlich

spot /spɒt/ *n* Fleck *m*; (*place*) Stelle *f* (*dot*) Punkt *m*; (*drop*) Tropfen *m*; (*pimple*) Pickel *m*; **~s** *pl* (*rash*) Ausschlag *m*; **on the ~** auf der Stelle ● *vt* (*pt/pp* **spotted**) entdecken

spot: ~ **'check** *n* Stichprobe *f*. **~less** *adj* makellos; (⬛: *very clean*) blitzsauber. **~light** *n* Scheinwerfer *m*; (*fig*) Rampenlicht *nt*

spotted /'spɒtɪd/ *adj* gepunktet

spouse /spaʊz/ *n* Gatte *m*/Gattin *f*

spout /spaʊt/ *n* Schnabel *m*, Tülle *f* ● *vi* schießen (**from** aus)

sprain /spreɪn/ *n* Verstauchung *f* ● *vt* verstauchen

sprang /spræŋ/ *see* **spring**[2]

sprawl /sprɔ:l/ *vi* sich ausstrecken

spray[1] /spreɪ/ *n* (*of flowers*) Strauß *m*

spray[2] *n* Sprühnebel *m*; (*from sea*) Gischt *m*; (*device*) Spritze *f*; (*container*) Sprühdose *f*; (*preparation*)

Spray *nt* ● *vt* spritzen; (*with aerosol*) sprühen

spread /spred/ *n* Verbreitung *f*; (*paste*) Aufstrich *m*; (⬛: *feast*) Festessen *nt* ● *v* (*pt/pp* **spread**) ● *vt* ausbreiten; streichen (*butter, jam*); bestreichen (*bread, surface*); streuen (*sand, manure*); verbreiten (*news, disease*); verteilen (*payments*) ● *vi* sich ausbreiten. ~ **out** *vt* ausbreiten; (*space out*) verteilen ● *vi* sich verteilen

spree /spri:/ *n* ⬛ **go on a shopping** ~ groß einkaufen gehen

sprightly /'spraɪtlɪ/ *adj* rüstig

spring[1] /sprɪŋ/ *n* Frühling *m* ● *attrib* Frühlings-

spring[2] *n* (*jump*) Sprung *m*; (*water*) Quelle *f*; (*device*) Feder *f*; (*elasticity*) Elastizität *f* ● *v* (*pt* **sprang**, *pp* **sprung**) ● *vi* springen; (*arise*) entspringen (**from** *dat*) ● *vt* ~ **sth on s.o.** jdn mit etw überfallen

spring: **~'cleaning** *n* Frühjahrsputz *m*. **~time** *n* Frühling *m*

sprinkle /'sprɪŋkl/ *vt* sprengen; (*scatter*) streuen; bestreuen (*surface*). **~ing** *n* dünne Schicht *f*

sprint /sprɪnt/ *n* Sprint *m* ● *vi* rennen; (*Sport*) sprinten. **~er** *n* Kurzstreckenläufer(in) *m*(*f*)

sprout /spraʊt/ *n* Trieb *m*; [**Brussels**] **~s** *pl* Rosenkohl *m* ● *vi* sprießen

sprung /sprʌŋ/ *see* **spring**[2]

spud /spʌd/ *n* ⬛ Kartoffel *f*

spun /spʌn/ *see* **spin**

spur /spɜ:(r)/ *n* Sporn *m*; (*stimulus*) Ansporn *m*; **on the ~ of the moment** ganz spontan ● *vt* (*pt/pp* **spurred**) ~ [**on**] (*fig*) anspornen

spurn /spɜ:n/ *vt* verschmähen

spurt /spɜ:t/ *n* (*Sport*) Spurt *m*; **put on a ~** spurten ● *vi* spritzen

spy /spaɪ/ *n* Spion(in) *m*(*f*) ● *vi* spionieren; ~ **on s.o.** jdm nachspionieren. ● *vt* (⬛: *see*) sehen

spying /'spaɪɪŋ/ *n* Spionage *f*

squabble /'skwɒbl/ *n* Zank *m* ● *vi* sich zanken

squad /skwɒd/ n Gruppe f; (Sport) Mannschaft f

squadron /'skwɒdrən/ n (Mil) Geschwader nt

squalid /'skwɒlɪd/ adj schmutzig

squall /skwɔ:l/ n Bö f ● vi brüllen

squalor /'skwɒlə(r)/ n Schmutz m

squander /'skwɒndə(r)/ vt vergeuden

square /skweə(r)/ adj quadratisch; (metre, mile) Quadrat-; (meal) anständig; **all ~** 🔟 quitt ● n Quadrat nt; (area) Platz m; (on chessboard) Feld nt ● vt (settle) klären; (Math) quadrieren

squash /skwɒʃ/ n Gedränge nt; (drink) Fruchtsaftgetränk nt; (Sport) Squash nt ● vt zerquetschen; (suppress) niederschlagen. **~y** adj weich

squat /skwɒt/ adj gedrungen ● vi (pt/pp **squatted**) hocken; **~ in a house** ein Haus besetzen. **~ter** n Hausbesetzer m

squawk /skwɔ:k/ vi krächzen

squeak /skwi:k/ n Quieken nt; (of hinge, brakes) Quietschen nt ● vi quieken; quietschen

squeal /skwi:l/ n Kreischen nt ● vi kreischen

squeamish /'skwi:mɪʃ/ adj empfindlich

squeeze /skwi:z/ n Druck m; (crush) Gedränge nt ● vt drücken; (to get juice) ausdrücken; (force) zwängen

squiggle /'skwɪgl/ n Schnörkel m

squint /skwɪnt/ n Schielen nt ● vi schielen

squirm /skwɜ:m/ vi sich winden

squirrel /'skwɪrl/ n Eichhörnchen nt

squirt /skwɜ:t/ n Spritzer m ● vt/i spritzen

St abbr (**Saint**) St.; (**Street**) Str.

stab /stæb/ n Stich m; (🔟: attempt) Versuch m ● vt (pt/pp **stabbed**) stechen; (to death) erstechen

stability /stə'bɪlɪtɪ/ n Stabilität f

stable¹ /'steɪbl/ adj (-r, -st) stabil

stable² n Stall m; (establishment) Reitstall m

stack /stæk/ n Stapel m; (of chimney) Schornstein m ● vt stapeln

stadium /'steɪdɪəm/ n Stadion nt

staff /stɑ:f/ n (stick & Mil) Stab m ● (& pl) (employees) Personal nt; (Sch) Lehrkräfte pl ● vt mit Personal besetzen. **~-room** n (Sch) Lehrerzimmer nt

stag /stæg/ n Hirsch m

stage /steɪdʒ/ n Bühne f; (in journey) Etappe f; (in process) Stadium nt; **by** or **in ~s** in Etappen ● vt aufführen; (arrange) veranstalten

stagger /'stægə(r)/ vi taumeln ● vt staffeln (holidays); versetzt anordnen (seats); **I was ~ed** es hat mir die Sprache verschlagen. **~ing** adj unglaublich

stagnant /'stægnənt/ adj stehend; (fig) stagnierend

stagnate /stæg'neɪt/ vi (fig) stagnieren

stain /steɪn/ n Fleck m; (for wood) Beize f ● vt färben; beizen (wood); **~ed glass** farbiges Glas nt. **~less** adj (steel) rostfrei

stair /steə(r)/ n Stufe f; **~s** pl Treppe f. **~case** n Treppe f

stake /steɪk/ n Pfahl m; (wager) Einsatz m; (Comm) Anteil m; **be at ~** auf dem Spiel stehen ● vt **~ a claim to sth** Anspruch auf etw (acc) erheben

stale /steɪl/ adj (-r, -st) alt; (air) verbraucht. **~mate** n Patt nt

stalk /stɔ:k/ n Stiel m, Stängel m

stall /stɔ:l/ n Stand m; **~s** pl (Theat) Parkett nt ● vi (engine:) stehen bleiben; (fig) ausweichen ● vt abwürgen (engine)

stalwart /'stɔ:lwət/ adj treu ● n treuer Anhänger m

stamina /'stæmɪnə/ n Ausdauer f

stammer /'stæmə(r)/ n Stottern nt ● vt/i stottern

stamp /stæmp/ n Stempel m; (postage ~) [Brief]marke f ● vt stempeln; (impress) prägen; (put postage on) frankieren ● vi stampfen. **~ out** vt [aus]stanzen; (fig) ausmerzen

stampede /stæm'pi:d/ n wilde

Flucht *f* ● *vi* in Panik fliehen

stance /stɑːns/ *n* Haltung *f*

stand /stænd/ *n* Stand *m*; (*rack*) Ständer *m*; (*pedestal*) Sockel *m*; (*Sport*) Tribüne *f*; (*fig*) Einstellung *f* ● *v* (*pt/pp* **stood**) ● *vi* stehen; (*rise*) aufstehen; (*be candidate*) kandidieren; (*stay valid*) gültig bleiben; ~ **still** stillstehen; ~ **firm** (*fig*) festbleiben; ~ **to reason** logisch sein; ~ **in for** vertreten; ~ **for** (*mean*) bedeuten ● *vt* stellen; (*withstand*) standhalten (+ *dat*); (*endure*) ertragen; vertragen (*climate*); (*put up with*) aushalten; haben (*chance*); ~ **s.o. a beer** jdm ein Bier spendieren; **I can't** ~ **her** 🄸 ich kann sie nicht ausstehen. ~ **by** *vi* daneben stehen; (*be ready*) sich bereithalten ● *vt* ~ **by s.o.** (*fig*) zu jdm stehen. ~ **down** *vi* (*retire*) zurücktreten. ~ **out** *vi* hervorstehen; (*fig*) herausragen. ~ **up** *vi* aufstehen; ~ **up for** eintreten für; ~ **up to** sich wehren gegen

standard /'stændəd/ *adj* Normal- ● *n* Maßstab *m*; (*Techn*) Norm *f*; (*level*) Niveau *nt*; (*flag*) Standarte *f*; ~**s** *pl* (*morals*) Prinzipien *pl*. ~**ize** *vt* standardisieren; (*Techn*) normen

'stand-in *n* Ersatz *m*

standing /'stændɪŋ/ *adj* (*erect*) stehend; (*permanent*) ständig ● *n* Rang *m*; (*duration*) Dauer *f*. ~**-room** *n* Stehplätze *pl*

stand: ~**-offish** /stænd'ɒfɪʃ/ *adj* distanziert. ~**point** *n* Standpunkt *m*. ~**still** *n* Stillstand *m*; **come to a** ~**still** zum Stillstand kommen

stank /stæŋk/ *see* **stink**

staple[1] /'steɪpl/ *adj* Grund-

staple[2] *n* Heftklammer *f* ● *vt* heften. ~**r** *n* Heftmaschine *f*

star /stɑː(r)/ *n* Stern *m*; (*asterisk*) Sternchen *nt*; (*Theat, Sport*) Star *m* ● *vi* (*pt/pp* **starred**) die Hauptrolle spielen

starboard /'stɑːbəd/ *n* Steuerbord *nt*

starch /stɑːtʃ/ *n* Stärke *f* ● *vt* stärken. ~**y** *adj* stärkehaltig; (*fig*) steif

stare /steə(r)/ *n* Starren *nt* ● *vt* starren; ~ **at** anstarren

stark /stɑːk/ *adj* (-er, -est) scharf; (*contrast*) krass

starling /'stɑːlɪŋ/ *n* Star *m*

start /stɑːt/ *n* Anfang *m*, Beginn *m*; (*departure*) Aufbruch *m*; (*Sport*) Start *m*; **from the** ~ von Anfang an; **for a** ~ erstens ● *vi* anfangen, beginnen; (*set out*) aufbrechen; (*engine:*) anspringen; (*Auto, Sport*) starten; (*jump*) aufschrecken; **to** ~ **with** zuerst ● *vt* anfangen, beginnen; (*cause*) verursachen; (*found*) gründen; starten (*car, race*); in Umlauf setzen (*rumour*). ~**er** *n* (*Culin*) Vorspeise *f*; (*Auto, Sport*) Starter *m*. ~**ing-point** *n* Ausgangspunkt *m*

startle /'stɑːtl/ *vt* erschrecken

starvation /stɑː'veɪʃn/ *n* Verhungern *nt*

starve /stɑːv/ *vi* hungern; (*to death*) verhungern ● *vt* verhungern lassen

state /steɪt/ *n* Zustand *m*; (*Pol*) Staat *m*; ~ **of play** Spielstand *m*; **be in a** ~ (*person:*) aufgeregt sein ● *attrib* Staats-, staatlich ● *vt* erklären; (*specify*) angeben

stately /'steɪtlɪ/ *adj* stattlich. ~ **'home** *n* Schloss *nt*

statement /'steɪtmənt/ *n* Erklärung *f*; (*Jur*) Aussage *f*; (*Banking*) Auszug *m*

---

state school Eine direkt oder indirekt vom Staat finanzierte Schule in Großbritannien, die keine Schulgebühren verlangt. Der Besuch aller staatlichen Grundschulen und weiterführenden Schulen ist kostenlos. Die meisten Kinder in Großbritannien besuchen solche öffentlichen Schulen. *i*

'statesman *n* Staatsmann *m*

static /'stætɪk/ *adj* statisch; **remain** ~ unverändert bleiben

station /'steɪʃn/ *n* Bahnhof *m*; (*police*) Wache *f*; (*radio*) Sender *m*; (*space, weather*) Station *f*; (*Mil*) Posten *m*; (*status*) Rang *m* ● *vt* stationieren; (*post*) postieren. ~**ary** *adj* stehend; **be** ~**ary** stehen

s

stationery /'steɪʃənrɪ/ n Briefpapier nt; (writing materials) Schreibwaren pl

'**station-wagon** n (Amer) Kombi-[wagen] n

statistic /stə'tɪstɪk/ n statistische Tatsache f. ~**al** adj statistisch. ~**s** n & pl Statistik f

statue /'stætjuː/ n Statue f

stature /'stætʃə(r)/ n Statur f; (fig) Format nt

status /'steɪtəs/ n Status m, Rang m

statut|e /'stætjuːt/ n Statut nt. ~**ory** adj gesetzlich

staunch /stɔːntʃ/ adj (-er, -est) treu

stave /steɪv/ vt ~ **off** abwenden

stay /steɪ/ n Aufenthalt m ● vi bleiben; (reside) wohnen; ~ **the night** übernachten. ~ **behind** vi zurückbleiben. ~ **in** vi zu Hause bleiben; (Sch) nachsitzen. ~ **up** vi (person:) aufbleiben

steadily /'stedɪlɪ/ adv fest; (continually) stetig

steady /'stedɪ/ adj fest; (not wobbly) stabil; (hand) ruhig; (regular) regelmäßig; (dependable) zuverlässig

steak /steɪk/ n Steak nt

steal /stiːl/ vt/i (pt **stole**, pp **stolen**) stehlen (from dat). ~ **in/out** vi sich hinein-/hinausstehlen

stealthy /stelθɪ/ adj heimlich

steam /stiːm/ n Dampf m ● vt (Culin) dämpfen, dünsten ● vi dampfen. ~ **up** vi beschlagen

'**steam engine** n Dampfmaschine f; (Rail) Dampflokomotive f

steamer /'stiːmə(r)/ n Dampfer m

steamy /'stiːmɪ/ adj dampfig

steel /stiːl/ n Stahl m

steep /stiːp/ adj steil; (🛈: exorbitant) gesalzen

steeple /'stiːpl/ n Kirchturm m

steer /stɪə(r)/ vt/i (Auto) lenken; (Naut) steuern; ~ **clear of s.o./sth** jdm/ etw aus dem Weg gehen. ~**ing** n (Auto) Lenkung f. ~**ing-wheel** n Lenkrad nt

stem[1] /stem/ n Stiel m; (of word) Stamm m

stem[2] vt (pt/pp **stemmed**) eindäm-

men; stillen (bleeding)

stench /stentʃ/ n Gestank m

stencil /'stensl/ n Schablone f

step /step/ n Schritt m; (stair) Stufe f; ~**s** pl (ladder) Trittleiter f; **in** ~ im Schritt; ~ **by** ~ Schritt für Schritt; **take** ~**s** (fig) Schritte unternehmen ● vi (pt/pp **stepped**) treten. ~ **in** (fig) eingreifen. ~ **up** vt (increase) erhöhen, steigen; verstärken (efforts)

step: ~**brother** n Stiefbruder m. ~**child** n Stiefkind nt. ~**daughter** n Stieftochter f. ~**father** n Stiefvater m. ~**ladder** n Trittleiter f. ~**mother** n Stiefmutter f. ~**sister** n Stiefschwester f. ~**son** n Stiefsohn m

stereo /'sterɪəʊ/ n Stereo nt; (equipment) Stereoanlage f. ~**phonic** adj stereophon

stereotype /'sterɪətaɪp/ n stereotype Figur f

steril|e /'steraɪl/ adj steril. ~**ize** vt sterilisieren

sterling /'stɜːlɪŋ/ adj Sterling-; (fig) gediegen ● n Sterling m

stern[1] /stɜːn/ adj (-er, -est) streng

stern[2] n (of boat) Heck nt

stew /stjuː/ n Eintopf m; **in a** ~ 🛈 aufgeregt ● vt/i schmoren; ~**ed fruit** Kompott nt

steward /'stjuːəd/ n Ordner m; (on ship, aircraft) Steward m. ~**ess** n Stewardess f

stick[1] /stɪk/ n Stock m; (of chalk) Stück nt; (of rhubarb) Stange f; (Sport) Schläger m

stick[2] v (pt/pp **stuck**) ● vt stecken; (stab) stechen; (glue) kleben; (🛈: put) tun; (🛈: endure) aushalten ● vi stecken; (adhere) kleben, haften (**to** an + dat); (jam) klemmen; ~ **at it** 🛈 dranbleiben; ~ **up for** 🛈 eintreten für; **be stuck** nicht weiterkönnen; (vehicle:) festsitzen, festgefahren sein; (drawer:) klemmen; **be stuck with sth** 🛈 etw am Hals haben. ~ **out** vi abstehen; (project) vorstehen ● vt hinausstrecken; herausstrecken (tongue)

sticker /'stɪkə(r)/ n Aufkleber m

'**sticking plaster** n Heftpflaster nt

sticky /'stɪkɪ/ adj klebrig; (adhesive) Klebe-

stiff /stɪf/ adj (-er, -est) steif; (brush) hart; (dough) fest; (difficult) schwierig; (penalty) schwer; **be bored ~** 🔢 sich zu Tode langweilen. **~en** vt steif machen ● vi steif werden. **~ness** n Steifheit f

stifl|e /'staɪfl/ vt ersticken; (fig) unterdrücken. **~ing** adj **be ~ing** zum Ersticken sein

still /stɪl/ adj still; (drink) ohne Kohlensäure; **keep ~** stillhalten; **stand ~** stillstehen ● adv noch; (emphatic) immer noch; (nevertheless) trotzdem; **~ not** immer noch nicht

'stillborn adj tot geboren

still 'life n Stillleben nt

stilted /'stɪltɪd/ adj gestelzt, geschraubt

stimulant /'stɪmjʊlənt/ n Anregungsmittel nt

stimulat|e /'stɪmjʊleɪt/ vt anregen. **~ion** n Anregung f

stimulus /'stɪmjʊləs/ n (pl -li /-laɪ/) Reiz m

sting /stɪŋ/ n Stich m; (from nettle, jellyfish) Brennen nt; (organ) Stachel m ● v (pt/pp stung) ● vt stechen ● vi brennen; (insect:) stechen

stingy /'stɪndʒɪ/ adj geizig, 🔢 knauserig

stink /stɪŋk/ n Gestank m ● vi (pt stank, pp stunk) stinken (of nach)

stipulat|e /'stɪpjʊleɪt/ vt vorschreiben. **~ion** n Bedingung f

stir /stɜ:(r)/ n (commotion) Aufregung f ● v (pt/pp stirred) vt rühren ● vi sich rühren

stirrup /'stɪrəp/ n Steigbügel m

stitch /stɪtʃ/ n Stich m; (Knitting) Masche f; (pain) Seitenstechen nt; **be in ~es** 🔢 sich kaputtlachen ● vt nähen

stock /stɒk/ n Vorrat m (of an + dat); (in shop) [Waren]bestand m; (livestock) Vieh nt; (lineage) Abstammung f; (Finance) Wertpapiere pl; (Culin) Brühe f; (plant) Levkoje f; **in/out of ~** vorrätig/nicht vorrätig; **take ~** (fig) Bilanz ziehen ● adj Standard-

● vt (shop:) führen; auffüllen (shelves). **~ up** vi sich eindecken (with mit)

stock: ~broker n Börsenmakler m. **S~ Exchange** n Börse f

stocking /'stɒkɪŋ/ n Strumpf m

stock: ~market n Börse f. **~-taking** n (Comm) Inventur f

stocky /'stɒkɪ/ adj untersetzt

stodgy /'stɒdʒɪ/ adj pappig [und schwer verdaulich]

stoke /stəʊk/ vt heizen

stole /stəʊl/, **stolen** see steal

stomach /'stʌmək/ n Magen m. **~-ache** n Magenschmerzen pl

stone /stəʊn/ n Stein m; (weight) 6,35kg ● adj steinern; (wall, Age) Stein- ● vt mit Steinen bewerfen; entsteinen (fruit). **~-cold** adj eiskalt. **~-'deaf** n 🔢 stocktaub

stony /'stəʊnɪ/ adj steinig

stood /stʊd/ see stand

stool /stu:l/ n Hocker m

stoop /stu:p/ n **walk with a ~** gebeugt gehen ● vi sich bücken

stop /stɒp/ n Halt m; (break) Pause f; (for bus) Haltestelle f; (for train) Station f; (Gram) Punkt m; (on organ) Register nt; **come to a ~** stehen bleiben; **put a ~ to sth** etw unterbinden ● v (pt/pp stopped) ● vt anhalten, stoppen; (switch off) abstellen; (plug, block) zustopfen; (prevent) verhindern; **~ s.o. doing sth** jdn daran hindern, etw zu tun; **~ doing sth** aufhören, etw zu tun; **~ that!** hör auf damit! ● vi anhalten; (cease) aufhören; (clock:) stehen bleiben ● int halt!

stop: ~gap n Notlösung f. **~over** n (Aviat) Zwischenlandung f

stoppage /'stɒpɪdʒ/ n Unterbrechung f; (strike) Streik m

stopper /'stɒpə(r)/ n Stöpsel m

stop-watch n Stoppuhr f

storage /'stɔ:rɪdʒ/ n Aufbewahrung f; (in warehouse) Lagerung f; (Computing) Speicherung f

store /stɔ:(r)/ n (stock) Vorrat m; (shop) Laden m; (department ~)

Kaufhaus *nt*; (*depot*) Lager *nt*; **in ~** auf Lager; **be in ~ for s.o.** (*fig*) jdm bevorstehen ● *vt* aufbewahren; (*in warehouse*) lagern; (*Computing*) speichern. **~-room** *n* Lagerraum *m*

storey /'stɔːrɪ/ *n* Stockwerk *nt*

stork /stɔːk/ *n* Storch *m*

storm /stɔːm/ *n* Sturm *m*; (*with thunder*) Gewitter *nt* ● *vt/i* stürmen. **~y** *adj* stürmisch

story /'stɔːrɪ/ *n* Geschichte *f*; (*in newspaper*) Artikel *m*; (🗓: *lie*) Märchen *nt*

stout /staʊt/ *adj* (**-er, -est**) beleibt; (*strong*) fest

stove /stəʊv/ *n* Ofen *m*; (*for cooking*) Herd *m*

stow /stəʊ/ *vt* verstauen. **~away** *n* blinder Passagier *m*

straggl|e /'strægl/ *vi* hinterherhinken. **~er** *n* Nachzügler *m*. **~y** *adj* strähnig

straight /streɪt/ *adj* (**-er, -est**) gerade; (*direct*) direkt; (*clear*) klar; (*hair*) glatt; (*drink*) pur; **be ~** (*tidy*) in Ordnung sein ● *adv* gerade; (*directly*) direkt, geradewegs; (*clearly*) klar; **~ away** sofort; **~ on** *or* **ahead** geradeaus; **~ out** (*fig*) geradeheraus; **sit/ stand up ~** gerade sitzen/stehen

straighten /'streɪtn/ *vt* gerade machen; (*put straight*) gerade richten ● *vi* gerade werden; **~ [up]** (*person:*) sich aufrichten. **~ out** *vt* gerade biegen

straight'forward *adj* offen; (*simple*) einfach

strain /streɪn/ *n* Belastung *f*; **~s** *pl* (*of music*) Klänge *pl* ● *vt* belasten; (*overexert*) überanstrengen; (*injure*) zerren (*muscle*); (*Culin*) durchseihen; abgießen (*vegetables*). **~ed** *adj* (*relations*) gespannt. **~er** *n* Sieb *nt*

strait /streɪt/ *n* Meerenge *f*; **in dire ~s** in großen Nöten

strand[1] /strænd/ *n* (*of thread*) Faden *m*; (*of hair*) Strähne *f*

strand[2] *vt* **be ~ed** festsitzen

strange /streɪndʒ/ *adj* (**-r, -st**) fremd; (*odd*) seltsam, merkwürdig. **~ly** *adv* seltsam, merkwürdig; **~**

enough seltsamerweise. **~r** *n* Fremde(r) *m/f*

strangle /'stræŋgl/ *vt* erwürgen; (*fig*) unterdrücken

strap /stræp/ *n* Riemen *m*; (*for safety*) Gurt *m*; (*to grasp in vehicle*) Halteriemen *m*; (*of watch*) Armband *nt*; (*shoulder~*) Träger *m* ● *vt* (*pt/pp* **strapped**) schnallen

strapping /'stræpɪŋ/ *adj* stramm

strategic /strə'tiːdʒɪk/ *adj*, **-ally** *adv* strategisch

strategy /'strætədʒɪ/ *n* Strategie *f*

straw /strɔː/ *n* Stroh *nt*; (*single piece, drinking*) Strohhalm *m*; **that's the last ~** jetzt reicht's aber

strawberry /'strɔːbərɪ/ *n* Erdbeere *f*

stray /streɪ/ *adj* streunend ● *n* streunendes Tier *nt* ● *vi* sich verirren; (*deviate*) abweichen

streak /striːk/ *n* Streifen *m*; (*in hair*) Strähne *f*; (*fig: trait*) Zug *m*

stream /striːm/ *n* Bach *m*; (*flow*) Strom *m*; (*current*) Strömung *f*; (*Sch*) Parallelzug *m* ● *vi* strömen

'streamline *vt* (*fig*) rationalisieren. **~d** *adj* stromlinienförmig

street /striːt/ *n* Straße *f*. **~car** *n* (*Amer*) Straßenbahn *f*. **~lamp** *n* Straßenlaterne *f*

strength /streŋθ/ *n* Stärke *f*; (*power*) Kraft *f*; **on the ~ of** auf Grund (+ *gen*). **~en** *vt* stärken; (*reinforce*) verstärken

strenuous /'strenjʊəs/ *adj* anstrengend

stress /stres/ *n* (*emphasis*) Betonung *f*; (*strain*) Belastung *f*; (*mental*) Stress *m* ● *vt* betonen; (*put a strain on*) belasten. **~ful** *adj* stressig 🗓

stretch /stretʃ/ *n* (*of road*) Strecke *f*; (*elasticity*) Elastizität *f*; **at a ~** ohne Unterbrechung; **have a ~** sich strecken ● *vt* strecken; (*widen*) dehnen; (*spread*) ausbreiten; fordern (*person*); **~ one's legs** sich (*dat*) die Beine vertreten ● *vt* sich erstrecken; (*become wider*) sich dehnen; (*person:*) sich strecken. **~er** *n* Tragbahre *f*

strict /strɪkt/ *adj* (**-er, -est**) streng; ~**ly speaking** streng genommen

stride /straɪd/ *n* [großer] Schritt *m*, **take sth in one's** ~ mit etw gut fertig werden ● *vi* (*pt* **strode**, *pp* **stridden**) [mit großen Schritten] gehen

strident /ˈstraɪdnt/ *adj* schrill; (*colour*) grell

strife /straɪf/ *n* Streit *m*

strike /straɪk/ *n* Streik *m*; (*Mil*) Angriff *m*; **be on** ~ streiken ● *v* (*pt/pp* **struck**) ● *vt* schlagen; (*knock against, collide with*) treffen; anzünden (*match*); stoßen auf (+ *acc*) (*oil, gold*); abbrechen (*camp*); (*impress*) beeindrucken; (*occur to*) einfallen (+ *dat*); ~ **s.o. a blow** jdm einen Schlag versetzen ● *vi* treffen; (*lightning:*) einschlagen; (*clock:*) schlagen; (*attack*) zuschlagen; (*workers:*) streiken

striker /ˈstraɪkə(r)/ *n* Streikende(r) *m/f*

striking /ˈstraɪkɪŋ/ *adj* auffallend

string /strɪŋ/ *n* Schnur *f*; (*thin*) Bindfaden *m*; (*of musical instrument, racket*) Saite *f*; (*of bow*) Sehne *f*; (*of pearls*) Kette *f*; **the** ~**s** (*Mus*) die Streicher *pl*; **pull** ~**s** 🔢 seine Beziehungen spielen lassen ● *vt* (*pt/pp* **strung**) (*thread*) aufziehen (*beads*)

stringent /ˈstrɪndʒnt/ *adj* streng

strip /strɪp/ *n* Streifen *m* ● *v* (*pt/pp* **stripped**) ● *vt* ablösen; ausziehen (*person, clothes*); abziehen (*bed*); abbeizen (*wood, furniture*); auseinander nehmen (*machine*); (*deprive*) berauben (*of gen*); ~ **sth off sth** etw von etw entfernen ● *vi* (*undress*) sich ausziehen

stripe /straɪp/ *n* Streifen *m*. ~**d** *adj* gestreift

stripper /ˈstrɪpə(r)/ *n* Stripperin *f*; (*male*) Stripper *m*

strive /straɪv/ *vi* (*pt* **strove**, *pp* **striven**) sich bemühen (**to** zu); ~ **for** streben nach

strode /strəʊd/ *see* **stride**

stroke¹ /strəʊk/ *n* Schlag *m*; (*of pen*) Strich *m*; (*Swimming*) Zug *m*; (*style*)

Stil *m*; (*Med*) Schlaganfall *m*; ~ **of luck** Glücksfall *m*

stroke² ● *vt* streicheln

stroll /strəʊl/ *n* Bummel *m* 🔢 ● *vi* bummeln 🔢. ~**er** *n* (*Amer: pushchair*) [Kinder]sportwagen *m*

strong /strɒŋ/ *adj* (**-er** /-gə(r)/, **-est** /-gɪst/) stark; (*powerful, healthy*) kräftig; (*severe*) streng; (*sturdy*) stabil; (*convincing*) gut

strong: ~**hold** *n* Festung *f*; (*fig*) Hochburg *f*. ~**-room** *n* Tresorraum *m*

strove /strəʊv/ *see* **strive**

struck /strʌk/ *see* **strike**

structural /ˈstrʌktʃərl/ *adj* baulich

structure /ˈstrʌktʃə(r)/ *n* Struktur *f*; (*building*) Bau *m*

struggle /ˈstrʌgl/ *n* Kampf *m*; **with a** ~ mit Mühe ● *vt* kämpfen; ~ **to do sth** sich abmühen, etw zutun

strum /strʌm/ *v* (*pt/pp* **strummed**) ● *vt* klimpern auf (+ *dat*) ● *vi* klimpern

strung /strʌŋ/ *see* **string**

strut¹ /strʌt/ *n* Strebe *f*

strut² *vi* (*pt/pp* **strutted**) stolzieren

stub /stʌb/ *n* Stummel *m*; (*counterfoil*) Abschnitt *m*. ~ **out** *vt* (*pt/pp* **stubbed**) ausdrücken (*cigarette*)

stubble /ˈstʌbl/ *n* Stoppeln *pl*

stubborn /ˈstʌbən/ *adj* starrsinnig; (*refusal*) hartnäckig

stubby /ˈstʌbɪ/ *adj*, (**-ier, -iest**) kurz und dick

stuck /stʌk/ *see* **stick**². ~**-'up** *adj* 🔢 hochnäsig

stud /stʌd/ *n* Nagel *m*; (*on clothes*) Niete *f*; (*for collar*) Kragenknopf *m*; (*for ear*) Ohrstecker *m*

student /ˈstjuːdnt/ *n* Student(in) *m(f)*; (*Sch*) Schüler(in) *m(f)*

studio /ˈstjuːdɪəʊ/ *n* Studio *nt*; (*for artist*) Atelier *nt*

studious /ˈstjuːdɪəs/ *adj* lerneifrig; (*earnest*) ernsthaft

stud|y /ˈstʌdɪ/ *n* Studie *f*; (*room*) Arbeitszimmer *nt*; (*investigation*) Untersuchung *f*; ~**ies** *pl* Studium *nt* ● *v* (*pt/pp* **studied**) ● *vt* studieren;

(*examine*) untersuchen ● *vi* lernen; (*at university*) studieren

stuff /stʌf/ *n* Stoff *m*; (**🛈**: *things*) Zeug *nt* ● *vt* vollstopfen; (*with padding, Culin*) füllen; ausstopfen (*animal*); (*cram*) [hinein]stopfen. ~**ing** *n* Füllung *f*

stuffy /ˈstʌfɪ/ *adj* stickig; (*oldfashioned*) spießig

stumbl|e /ˈstʌmbl/ *vi* stolpern; ~**e across** zufällig stoßen auf (+ *acc*). ~**ing-block** *n* Hindernis *nt*

stump /stʌmp/ *n* Stumpf *m* ● ~ **up** *vt/i* **🛈** blechen. ~**ed** *adj* **🛈** überfragt

stun /stʌn/ *vt* (*pt/pp* **stunned**) betäuben

stung /stʌŋ/ *see* **sting**

stunk /stʌŋk/ *see* **stink**

stunning /ˈstʌnɪŋ/ *adj* **🛈** toll

stunt /stʌnt/ *n* **🛈** Kunststück *nt*

stupendous /stjuːˈpendəs/ *adj* enorm

stupid /ˈstjuːpɪd/ *adj* dumm. ~**ity** *n* Dummheit *f*. ~**ly** *adv* dumm; ~**ly [enough]** dummerweise

sturdy /ˈstɜːdɪ/ *adj* stämmig; (*furniture*) stabil; (*shoes*) fest

stutter /ˈstʌtə(r)/ *n* Stottern *nt* ● *vt/i* stottern

sty /staɪ/ *n* (*pl* **sties**) Schweinestall *m*

style /staɪl/ *n* Stil *m*; (*fashion*) Mode *f*; (*sort*) Art *f*; (*hair*~) Frisur *f*; **in** ~ in großem Stil

stylish /ˈstaɪlɪʃ/ *adj*, -**ly** *adv* stilvoll

stylist /ˈstaɪlɪst/ *n* Friseur *m*/ Friseuse *f*. ~**ic** *adj*, -**ally** *adv* stilistisch

suave /swɑːv/ *adj* (*pej*) gewandt

sub'conscious /sʌb-/ *adj* unterbewusst ● *n* Unterbewusstsein *nt*

'subdivi|de *vt* unterteilen. ~**sion** *n* Unterteilung *f*

subdue /səbˈdjuː/ *vt* unterwerfen. ~**d** *adj* gedämpft; (*person*) still

subject[1] /ˈsʌbdʒɪkt/ *adj* **be** ~ **to sth** etw (*dat*) unterworfen sein ● *n* Staatsbürger(in) *m*(*f*); (*of ruler*) Untertan *m*; (*theme*) Thema *nt*; (*of investigation*) Gegenstand *m*; (*Sch*) Fach *nt*; (*Gram*) Subjekt *nt*

subject[2] /səbˈdʒekt/ *vt* unterwerfen

(**to** *dat*); (*expose*) aussetzen (**to** *dat*)

subjective /səbˈdʒektɪv/ *adj* subjektiv

subjunctive /səbˈdʒʌŋktɪv/ *n* Konjunktiv *m*

sublime /səˈblaɪm/ *adj* erhaben

subma'rine *n* Unterseeboot *nt*

submerge /səbˈmɜːdʒ/ *vt* untertauchen; **be** ~**d** unter Wasser stehen ● *vi* tauchen

submission /səbˈmɪʃn/ *n* Unterwerfung *f*

submit /səbˈmɪt/ *v* (*pt/pp* **-mitted**, *pres p* **-mitting**) ● *vt* vorlegen (**to** *dat*); (*hand in*) einreichen ● *vi* sich unterwerfen (**to** *dat*)

subordinate[1] /səˈbɔːdɪnət/ *adj* untergeordnet ● *n* Untergebene(r) *m*/*f*

subordinate[2] /səˈbɔːdɪneɪt/ *vt* unterordnen (**to** *dat*)

subscribe /səbˈskraɪb/ *vi* spenden; ~ **to** (*fig*) abonnieren (*newspaper*). ~**r** *n* Spender *m*; Abonnent *m*

subscription /səbˈskrɪpʃn/ *n* (*to club*) [Mitglieds]beitrag *m*; (*to newspaper*) Abonnement *nt*; **by** ~ mit Spenden; (*buy*) im Abonnement

subsequent /ˈsʌbsɪkwənt/ *adj* folgend; (*later*) später

subside /səbˈsaɪd/ *vi* sinken; (*ground:*) sich senken; (*storm:*) nachlassen

subsidiary /səbˈsɪdɪərɪ/ *adj* untergeordnet ● *n* Tochtergesellschaft *f*

subsid|ize /ˈsʌbsɪdaɪz/ *vt* subventionieren. ~**y** *n* Subvention *f*

substance /ˈsʌbstəns/ *n* Substanz *f*

sub'standard *adj* unzulänglich; (*goods*) minderwertig

substantial /səbˈstænʃl/ *adj* solide; (*meal*) reichhaltig; (*considerable*) beträchtlich. ~**ly** *adv* solide; (*essentially*) im Wesentlichen

substitut|e /ˈsʌbstɪtjuːt/ *n* Ersatz *m*; (*Sport*) Ersatzspieler(in) *m*(*f*) ● *vt* ~**e A for B** B durch A ersetzen ● *vi* ~**e for s.o.** jdn vertreten. ~**ion** *n* Ersetzung *f*

subterranean /sʌbtəˈreɪnɪən/ *adj* unterirdisch

S

'subtitle n Untertitel m

subtle /'sʌtl/ adj (-r, -st), **-tly** adv fein; (fig) subtil

subtract /səb'trækt/ vt abziehen, subtrahieren. **~ion** n Subtraktion f

suburb /'sʌbɜːb/ n Vorort m. **~an** adj Vorort-. **~ia** n die Vororte pl

'subway n Unterführung f; (Amer: railway) U-Bahn f

succeed /sək'siːd/ vi Erfolg haben; (plan:) gelingen; (follow) nachfolgen (+ dat); **I ~ed** es ist mir gelungen; **he ~ed in escaping** es gelang ihm zu entkommen ● vt folgen (+ dat)

success /sək'ses/ n Erfolg m. **~ful** adj,**-ly** adv erfolgreich

succession /sək'seʃn/ n Folge f; (series) Serie f; (to title, office) Nachfolge f; (to throne) Thronfolge f; **in ~** hintereinander

successive /sək'sesɪv/ adj aufeinander folgend

successor /sək'sesə(r)/ n Nachfolger(in) m(f)

succumb /sə'kʌm/ vi erliegen (**to** dat)

such /sʌtʃ/

● adjective

····▸ (of that kind) solch. **such a book** ein solches Buch; so ein Buch 🛈. **such a person** ein solcher Mensch; so ein Mensch 🛈. **such people** solche Leute. **such a thing** so etwas. **no such example** kein solches Beispiel. **there is no such thing** so etwas gibt es nicht; das gibt es gar nicht. **there is no such person** eine solche Person gibt es nicht. **such writers as Goethe and Schiller** Schriftsteller wie Goethe und Schiller

····▸ (so great) solch; derartig. **I've got such a headache!** ich habe solche Kopfschmerzen! **it was such fun!** das machte solchen Spaß! **I got such a fright that ...** ich bekam einen derartigen od 🛈 so einen Schrecken, dass ...

····▸ (with adjective) so. **such a big**

house ein so großes Haus. **he has such lovely blue eyes** er hat so schöne blaue Augen. **such a long time** so lange

● pronoun

····▸ **as such** als solcher/solche/ solches. **the thing as such** die Sache als solche. (strictly speaking) **this is not a promotion as such** dies ist im Grunde genommen keine Beförderung

····▸ **such is**: **such is life** so ist das Leben. **such is not the case** das ist nicht der Fall

····▸ **such as** wie [zum Beispiel]

suchlike /'sʌtʃlaɪk/ pron 🛈 dergleichen

suck /sʌk/ vt/i saugen; lutschen (sweet). **~ up** vt aufsaugen ● vi **~ up to s.o.** 🛈 sich bei jdm einschmeicheln

suction /'sʌkʃn/ n Saugwirkung f

sudden /'sʌdn/ adj plötzlich; (abrupt) jäh ● n **all of a ~** auf einmal

sue /suː/ vt (pres p suing) verklagen (**for** auf + acc) ● vi klagen

suede /sweɪd/ n Wildleder nt

suet /'suːɪt/ n [Nieren]talg m

suffer /'sʌfə(r)/ vi leiden (**from** an + dat) ● vt erleiden; (tolerate) dulden

suffice /sə'faɪs/ vi genügen

sufficient /sə'fɪʃnt/ adj genug, genügend; **be ~** genügen

suffocat|e /'sʌfəkeɪt/ vt/i ersticken. **~ion** n Ersticken nt

sugar /'ʃʊgə(r)/ n Zucker m ● vt zuckern; (fig) versüßen. **~ basin, ~-bowl** n Zuckerschale f. **~y** adj süß; (fig) süßlich

suggest /sə'dʒest/ vt vorschlagen; (indicate, insinuate) andeuten. **~ion** n Vorschlag m; Andeutung f; (trace) Spur f. **~ive** adj anzüglich

suicidal /suːɪ'saɪdl/ adj selbstmörderisch

suicide /'suːɪsaɪd/ n Selbstmord m

suit /suːt/ n Anzug m; (woman's) Kostüm nt; (Cards) Farbe f; (Jur) Prozess *m* ● *vt* (*adapt*) anpassen (**to** *dat*); (*be convenient for*) passen (+ *dat*); (*go with*) passen zu; (*clothing:*) stehen (*s.o. jdm*); **be ~ed for** geeignet sein für; **~ yourself!** wie du willst!

suit|able /'suːtəbl/ *adj* geeignet; (*convenient*) passend; (*appropriate*) angemessen; (*for weather, activity*) zweckmäßig. **~ably** *adv* angemessen; zweckmäßig

'suitcase *n* Koffer *m*

suite /swiːt/ *n* Suite *f*; (*of furniture*) Garnitur *f*

sulk /sʌlk/ *vi* schmollen. **~y** *adj* schmollend

sullen /'sʌlən/ *adj* mürrisch

sultry /'sʌltrɪ/ *adj* (**-ier, -iest**) (*weather*) schwül

sum /sʌm/ *n* Summe *f*; (*Sch*) Rechenaufgabe *f* ● *vt/i* (*pt/pp* **summed**) **~ up** zusammenfassen; (*assess*) einschätzen

summar|ize /'sʌməraɪz/ *vt* zusammenfassen. **~y** *n* Zusammenfassung *f* ● *adj*, **-ily** *adv* summarisch; (*dismissal*) fristlos

summer /'sʌmə(r)/ *n* Sommer *m*. **~time** *n* Sommer *m*

---

summer camp Amerikanische Feriencamps haben eine lange Tradition. Sie bieten ein umfassendes Fitnessprogramm, und Schulkinder haben die Möglichkeit, alle erdenklichen Sportarten und Spiele in den Sommerferien auszuprobieren. Hier erhalten die Teilnehmer Survival-Training und lernen außerdem Unabhängigkeit und Führungseigenschaften. Tausende von Studenten arbeiten während der Sommermonate als Betreuer in den Feriencamps.

---

summery /'sʌmərɪ/ *adj* sommerlich

summit /'sʌmɪt/ *n* Gipfel *m*. **~ conference** *n* Gipfelkonferenz *f*

summon /'sʌmən/ *vt* rufen; holen (*help*); (*Jur*) vorladen

summons /'sʌmənz/ *n* (*Jur*) Vorladung *f* ● *vt* vorladen

sumptuous /'sʌmptjʊəs/ *adj* prunkvoll; (*meal*) üppig

sun /sʌn/ *n* Sonne *f* ● *vt* (*pt/pp* **sunned**) **~ oneself** sich sonnen

sun: ~bathe *vi* sich sonnen. **~bed** *n* Sonnenbank *f*. **~burn** *n* Sonnenbrand *m*

Sunday /'sʌndeɪ/ *n* Sonntag *m*

'sunflower *n* Sonnenblume *f*

sung /sʌŋ/ *see* **sing**

'sunglasses *npl* Sonnenbrille *f*

sunk /sʌŋk/ *see* **sink**

sunny /'sʌnɪ/ *adj* (**-ier, -iest**) sonnig

sun: ~rise *n* Sonnenaufgang *m*. **~-roof** *n* (*Auto*) Schiebedach *nt*. **~set** *n* Sonnenuntergang *m*. **~shade** *n* Sonnenschirm *m*. **~shine** *n* Sonnenschein *m*. **~stroke** *n* Sonnenstich *m*. **~tan** *n* [Sonnen]bräune *f*. **~tanned** *adj* braun [gebrannt]. **~tan oil** *n* Sonnenöl *nt*

super /'suːpə(r)/ *adj* [1] prima, toll

superb /suˈpɜːb/ *adj* erstklassig

superficial /suːpəˈfɪʃl/ *a* oberflächlich

superfluous /suˈpɜːfluəs/ *adj* überflüssig

superintendent /suːpərɪnˈtendənt/ *n* (*of police*) Kommissar *m*

superior /suːˈpɪərɪə(r)/ *a* überlegen; (*in rank*) höher ● *n* Vorgesetzte(r) *m/f*. **~ity** *n* Überlegenheit *f*

superlative /suːˈpɜːlətɪv/ *a* unübertrefflich ● *n* Superlativ *m*

'supermarket *n* Supermarkt *m*

super'natural *adj* übernatürlich

supersede /suːpəˈsiːd/ *vt* ersetzen

superstiti|on /suːpəˈstɪʃn/ *n* Aberglaube *m*. **~ous** *adj* abergläubisch

supervis|e /'suːpəvaɪz/ *vt* beaufsichtigen; überwachen (*work*). **~ion** *n* Aufsicht *f*; Überwachung *f*. **~or** *n* Aufseher(in) *m(f)*

supper /'sʌpə(r)/ *n* Abendessen *nt*

supple /'sʌpl/ *adj* geschmeidig

supplement /'sʌplɪmənt/ *n* Ergänzung *f*; (*addition*) Zusatz *m*; (*to fare*) Zuschlag *m*; (*book*) Ergänzungsband

s

m; (*to newspaper*) Beilage *f* ● *vt* ergänzen. ~**ary** a zusätzlich

supplier /sə'plaɪə(r)/ *n* Lieferant *m*

supply /sə'plaɪ/ *n* Vorrat *m*; **supplies** *pl* (*Mil*) Nachschub *m* ● *vt* (*pt/pp* **-ied**) liefern; ~ **s.o. with sth** jdn mit etw versorgen

support /sə'pɔːt/ *n* Stütze *f*; (*fig*) Unterstützung *f* ● *vt* stützen; (*bear weight of*) tragen; (*keep*) ernähren; (*give money to*) unterstützen; (*speak in favour of*) befürworten; (*Sport*) Fan sein von. ~**er** *n* Anhänger(in) *m(f)*; (*Sport*) Fan *m*

suppose /sə'pəʊz/ *vt* annehmen; (*presume*) vermuten; (*imagine*) sich (*dat*) vorstellen; **be** ~**d to do sth** etw tun sollen; **not be** ~**d to** ⒤ nicht dürfen; **I** ~ **so** vermutlich. ~**dly** *adv* angeblich

supposition /sʌpə'zɪʃn/ *n* Vermutung *f*

suppress /sə'pres/ *vt* unterdrücken. ~**ion** *n* Unterdrückung *f*

supremacy /suː'preməsɪ/ *n* Vorherrschaft *f*

supreme /suː'priːm/ *adj* höchste(r,s); (*court*) oberste(r,s)

sure /ʃʊə(r)/ *adj* (**-r, -st**) sicher; **make** ~ sich vergewissern (**of** *gen*); (*check*) nachprüfen ● *adv* (*Amer*, ⒤) klar; ~ **enough** tatsächlich. ~**ly** *adv* sicher; (*for emphasis*) doch; (*Amer: gladly*) gern

surf /sɜːf/ *n* Brandung *f* ● *vi* surfen

surface /'sɜːfɪs/ *n* Oberfläche *f* ● *vi* (*emerge*) auftauchen

'**surfboard** *n* Surfbrett *nt*

surfing /'sɜːfɪŋ/ *n* Surfen *nt*

surge /sɜːdʒ/ *n* (*of sea*) Branden *nt*; (*fig*) Welle *f* ● *vi* branden; ~ **forward** nach vorn drängen

surgeon /'sɜːdʒən/ *n* Chirurg(in) *m(f)*

surgery /'sɜːdʒərɪ/ *n* Chirurgie *f*; (*place*) Praxis *f*; (*room*) Sprechzimmer *nt*; (*hours*) Sprechstunde *f*; **have** ~ operiert werden

surgical /'sɜːdʒɪkl/ *adj* chirurgisch

surly /'sɜːlɪ/ *adj* mürrisch

surname /'sɜːneɪm/ *n* Nachname *m*

surpass /sə'pɑːs/ *vt* übertreffen

surplus /'sɜːpləs/ *adj* überschüssig ● *n* Überschuss *m* (**of** an + *dat*)

surpris|e /sə'praɪz/ *n* Überraschung *f* ● *vt* überraschen; **be** ~**ed** sich wundern (**at** über + *acc*). ~**ing** *adj* überraschend

surrender /sə'rendə(r)/ *n* Kapitulation *f* ● *vi* sich ergeben; (*Mil*) kapitulieren ● *vt* aufgeben

surround /sə'raʊnd/ *vt* umgeben; (*encircle*) umzingeln; ~**ed by** umgeben von. ~**ing** *adj* umliegend. ~**ings** *npl* Umgebung *f*

surveillance /sə'veɪləns/ *n* Überwachung *f*; **be under** ~ überwacht werden

survey[1] /'sɜːveɪ/ *n* Überblick *m*; (*poll*) Umfrage *f*; (*investigation*) Untersuchung *f*; (*of land*) Vermessung *f*; (*of house*) Gutachten *nt*

survey[2] /sə'veɪ/ *vt* betrachten; vermessen (*land*); begutachten (*building*). ~**or** *n* Landvermesser *m*; Gutachter *m*

survival /sə'vaɪvl/ *n* Überleben *nt*; (*of tradition*) Fortbestand *m*

surviv|e /sə'vaɪv/ *vt* überleben ● *vi* überleben; (*tradition:*) erhalten bleiben. ~**or** *n* Überlebende(r) *m/f*; **be a** ~**or** nicht unterzukriegen sein

susceptible /sə'septəbl/ *adj* empfänglich; (*Med*) anfällig (**to** für)

suspect[1] /sə'spekt/ *vt* verdächtigen; (*assume*) vermuten; **he** ~**s nothing** er ahnt nichts

suspect[2] /'sʌspekt/ *adj* verdächtig ● *n* Verdächtige(r) *m/f*

suspend /sə'spend/ *vt* aufhängen; (*stop*) [vorläufig] einstellen; (*from duty*) vorläufig beurlauben. ~**ders** *npl* (*Amer: braces*) Hosenträger *pl*

suspense /sə'spens/ *n* Spannung *f*

suspension /sə'spenʃn/ *n* (*Auto*) Federung *f*. ~ **bridge** *n* Hängebrücke *f*

suspici|on /sə'spɪʃn/ *n* Verdacht *m*; (*mistrust*) Misstrauen *nt*; (*trace*) Spur

f. ~**ous** adj misstrauisch; (arousing suspicion) verdächtig

sustain /sə'steɪn/ vt tragen; (fig) aufrechterhalten; erhalten (life); erleiden (injury)

sustenance /'sʌstɪnəns/ n Nahrung f

swagger /'swægə(r)/ vi stolzieren

swallow[1] /'swɒləʊ/ vt/i schlucken. ~ **up** vt verschlucken; verschlingen (resources)

swallow[2] n (bird) Schwalbe f

swam /swæm/ see **swim**

swamp /swɒmp/ n Sumpf m ● vt überschwemmen

swan /swɒn/ n Schwan m

swank /swæŋk/ vi 🗉 angeben

swap /swɒp/ n 🗉 Tausch m ● vt/i (pt/pp swapped) 🗉 tauschen (**for** gegen)

swarm /swɔːm/ n Schwarm m ● vi schwärmen; **be** ~**ing with** wimmeln von

swat /swɒt/ vt (pt/pp swatted) totschlagen

sway /sweɪ/ vi schwanken; (gently) sich wiegen ● vt (influence) beeinflussen

swear /sweə(r)/ v (pt swore, pp sworn) ● vt schwören ● vi schwören (**by** auf + acc); (curse) fluchen. ~**-word** n Kraftausdruck m

sweat /swet/ n Schweiß m ● vi schwitzen

sweater /'swetə(r)/ n Pullover m

Swed|e n Schwede m/Schwedin f. ~**en** n Schweden nt. ~**ish** adj schwedisch

sweep /swiːp/ n Schornsteinfeger m; (curve) Bogen m; (movement) ausholende Bewegung f ● v (pt/pp swept) ● vt fegen, kehren ● vi (go swiftly) rauschen; (wind:) fegen

sweeping /'swiːpɪŋ/ adj ausholend; (statement) pauschal; (changes) weit reichend

sweet /swiːt/ a (-er, -est) süß; **have a** ~ **tooth** gern Süßes mögen ● n Bonbon m & nt; (dessert) Nachtisch m

sweeten /'swiːtn/ vt süßen

sweet: ~**heart** n Schatz m. ~**ness** n Süße f. ~ '**pea** n Wicke f. ~**-shop** n Süßwarenladen m

swell /swel/ n Dünung f ● v (pt swelled, pp swollen or swelled) ● vi [an]schwellen; (wood:) aufquellen ● vt anschwellen lassen; (increase) vergrößern. ~**ing** n Schwellung f

swelter /'sweltə(r)/ vi schwitzen

swept /swept/ see **sweep**

swerve /swɜːv/ vi einen Bogen machen

swift /swɪft/ adj (-er, -est) schnell

swig /swɪg/ n 🗉 Schluck m

swim /swɪm/ n **have a** ~ schwimmen ● vi (pt swam, pp swum) schwimmen; **my head is** ~**ming** mir dreht sich der Kopf. ~**mer** n Schwimmer(in) m(f)

swimming /'swɪmɪŋ/ n Schwimmen nt. ~**-baths** npl Schwimmbad nt. ~**-pool** n Schwimmbecken nt; (private) Swimmingpool m

'**swimsuit** n Badeanzug m

swindle /'swɪndl/ n Schwindel m, Betrug m ● vt betrügen. ~**r** n Schwindler m

swine /swaɪn/ n (pej) Schwein nt

swing /swɪŋ/ n Schwung m; (shift) Schwenk m; (seat) Schaukel f; **in full** ~ in vollem Gange ● (pt/pp swung) ● vi schwingen; (on swing) schaukeln; (dangle) baumeln; (turn) schwenken ● vt schwingen; (influence) beeinflussen

swipe /swaɪp/ n 🗉 Schlag m ● vt 🗉 knallen; (steal) klauen

swirl /swɜːl/ n Wirbel m ● vt/i wirbeln

Swiss /swɪs/ adj Schweizer-, schweizerisch ● n Schweizer(in) m(f); **the** ~ pl die Schweizer. ~ '**roll** n Biskuitrolle f

switch /swɪtʃ/ n Schalter m; (change) Wechsel m; (Amer, Rail) Weiche f ● vt wechseln; (exchange) tauschen ● vi wechseln; ~ **to** umstellen auf (+ acc). ~ **off** vt ausschal-

S

ten; abschalten (*engine*). ~ **on** *vt*
einschalten

switchboard *n* [Telefon]zentrale *f*

Switzerland /'swɪtsələnd/ *n* die
Schweiz

swivel /'swɪvl/ *v* (*pt/pp* **swivelled**)
● *vt* drehen ● *vi* sich drehen

swollen /'swəʊlən/ *see* **swell**

swoop /swuːp/ *n* (*by police*) Razzia *f*
● *vi* ~ **down** herabstoßen

sword /sɔːd/ *n* Schwert *nt*

swore /swɔː(r)/ *see* **swear**

sworn /swɔːn/ *see* **swear**

swot /swɒt/ *n* 🔲 Streber *m* ● *vt* (*pt/
pp* **swotted**) 🔲 büffeln

swum /swʌm/ *see* **swim**

swung /swʌŋ/ *see* **swing**

syllable /'sɪləbl/ *n* Silbe *f*

syllabus /'sɪləbəs/ *n* Lehrplan *m*;
(*for exam*) Studienplan *m*

symbol /'sɪmbəl/ *n* Symbol *nt* (*of*
für). ~**ic** *adj*, **-ally** *adv* symbolisch
~**ism** *n* Symbolik *f*. ~**ize** *vt* symboli-
sieren

symmetr|ical /sɪ'metrɪkl/ *adj* sym-
metrisch. ~**y** *n* Symmetrie *f*

sympathetic /sɪmpə'θetɪk/ *adj*,
-ally *adv* mitfühlend; (*likeable*) sympathisch

sympathize /'sɪmpəθaɪz/ *vi* mitfühlen

sympathy /'sɪmpəθɪ/ *n* Mitgefühl
nt; (*condolences*) Beileid *nt*

symphony /'sɪmfənɪ/ *n* Sinfonie *f*

symptom /'sɪmptəm/ *n* Symptom *nt*

synagogue /'sɪnəgɒg/ *n* Synagoge *f*

synchronize /'sɪŋkrənaɪz/ *vt* synchronisieren

synonym /'sɪnənɪm/ *n* Synonym *nt*.
~**ous** *adj* synonym

synthesis /'sɪnθəsɪs/ *n* (*pl* **-ses**
/-siːz/) Synthese *f*

synthetic /sɪn'θetɪk/ *adj* synthetisch

Syria /'sɪrɪə/ *n* Syrien *nt*

syringe /sɪ'rɪndʒ/ *n* Spritze *f*

syrup /'sɪrəp/ *n* Sirup *m*

system /'sɪstəm/ *n* System *nt*. ~**atic**
adj, **-ally** *adv* systematisch

Tt

tab /tæb/ *n* (*projecting*) Zunge *f*; (*with
name*) Namensschild *nt*; (*loop*) Auf-
hänger *m*; **pick up the** ~ 🔲 bezahlen

table /'teɪbl/ *n* Tisch *m*; (*list*) Tabelle
f; **at [the]** ~ bei Tisch. ~**-cloth** *n*
Tischdecke *f*. ~**spoon** *n* Servierlöf-
fel *m*

tablet /'tæblɪt/ *n* Tablette *f*; (*of soap*)
Stück *nt*

'**table tennis** *n* Tischtennis *nt*

tabloid /'tæblɔɪd/ *n* kleinformatige
Zeitung *f*; (*pej*) Boulevardzeitung *f*

taciturn /'tæsɪtɜːn/ *adj* wortkarg

tack /tæk/ *n* (*nail*) Stift *m*; (*stitch*)
Heftstich *m*; (*Naut & fig*) Kurs *m* ● *vt*
festnageln; (*sew*) heften ● *vi* (*Naut*)
kreuzen

tackle /'tækl/ *n* Ausrüstung *f* ● *vt* angehen (*problem*); (*Sport*) angreifen

tact /tækt/ *n* Takt *m*, Taktgefühl *nt*.
~**ful** *adj* taktvoll

tactic|al /'tæktɪkl/ *adj* taktisch. ~**s**
npl Taktik *f*

tactless /'tæktlɪs/ *adj* taktlos.
~**ness** *n* Taktlosigkeit *f*

tag /tæg/ *n* (*label*) Schild *nt* ● *vi* (*pt/
pp* **tagged**) ~ **along** mitkommen

tail /teɪl/ *n* Schwanz *m*; ~**s** *pl* (*tailcoat*) Frack *m*; **heads or** ~**s?** Kopf
oder Zahl? ● *vt* (🔲: *follow*) beschatten ● *vi* ~ **off** zurückgehen

tail: ~**back** *n* Rückstau *m*. ~ **light** *n*
Rücklicht *nt*

tailor /'teɪlə(r)/ *n* Schneider *m*.
~**-made** *adj* maßgeschneidert

taint /teɪnt/ *vt* verderben

take /teɪk/ *v* (*pt* **took**, *pp* **taken**) ● *vt*
nehmen: (*with one*) mitnehmen; (*take
to a place*) bringen; (*steal*) stehlen;
(*win*) gewinnen; (*capture*) einnehmen;
(*require*) brauchen; (*last*) dauern;
(*teach*) geben; machen (*exam, subject, holiday, photograph*); messen
(*pulse, temperature*); ~ **sth to the**

cleaner's etw in die Reinigung bringen; **be ~n ill** krank werden; **~ sth
calmly** etw gelassen aufnehmen ● *vi*
(*plant:*) angehen; **~ after s.o.** jdm
nachschlagen; (*in looks*) jdm ähnlich
sehen; **~ to** (*like*) mögen; (*as a
habit*) sich (*dat*) angewöhnen. **~
away** *vt* wegbringen; (*remove*) wegnehmen; (*subtract*) abziehen; **'to ~
away'** 'zum Mitnehmen'. **~ back** *vt*
zurücknehmen; (*return*) zurückbringen. **~ down** *vt* herunternehmen;
(*remove*) abnehmen; (*write down*)
aufschreiben. **~ in** *vt* hineinbringen;
(*bring indoors*) hereinholen; (*to one's
home*) aufnehmen; (*understand*) begreifen; (*deceive*) hereinlegen; (*make
smaller*) enger machen. **~ off** *vt* abnehmen; ablegen (*coat*); sich (*dat*)
ausziehen (*clothes*); (*deduct*) abziehen; (*mimic*) nachmachen ● *vi* (*Aviat*)
starten. **~ on** *vt* annehmen; (*under-
take*) übernehmen; (*engage*) einstellen; (*as opponent*) antreten gegen. **~
out** *vt* hinausbringen; (*for pleasure*)
ausgehen mit; ausführen (*dog*); (*remove*) herausnehmen; (*withdraw*) abheben (*money*); (*from library*) ausleihen; **~ it out on s.o.** Ⓣ seinen
Ärger an jdm auslassen. **~ over** *vt*
hinüberbringen; übernehmen (*firm,
control*) ● *vi* **~ over from s.o.** jdn
ablösen. **~ up** *vt* hinaufbringen; annehmen (*offer*); ergreifen (*profession*);
sich (*dat*) zulegen (*hobby*); in Anspruch nehmen (*time*); einnehmen
(*space*); aufreißen (*floorboards*); **~
sth up with s.o.** mit jdm über etw
(*acc*) sprechen

take: ~-away *n* Essen *nt* zum Mitnehmen; (*restaurant*) Restaurant *nt*
mit Straßenverkauf. **~-off** *n* (*Aviat*)
Start *m*, Abflug *m*. **~-over** *n* Übernahme *f*

takings /ˈteɪkɪŋz/ *npl* Einnahmen *pl*

talcum /ˈtælkəm/ *n* **~ [powder]**
Körperpuder *m*

tale /teɪl/ *n* Geschichte *f*

talent /ˈtælənt/ *n* Talent *nt*

talk /tɔːk/ *n* Gespräch *nt*; (*lecture*)
Vortrag *m* ● *vi* reden, sprechen (**to/
with** mit) ● *vt* reden; **~ s.o. into sth**

jdn zu etw überreden. **~ over** *vt* besprechen

talkative /ˈtɔːkətɪv/ *adj* gesprächig

tall /tɔːl/ *adj* (**-er, -est**) groß; (*building, tree*) hoch. **~ 'story** *n* übertrie-
bene Geschichte *f*

tally /ˈtælɪ/ *vi* übereinstimmen

tame /teɪm/ *adj* (**-r, -st**) zahm; (*dull*)
lahm Ⓣ ● *vt* zähmen. **~r** *n* Domp-
teur *m*

tamper /ˈtæmpə(r)/ *vi* **~ with** sich
(*dat*) zu schaffen machen an (+ *dat*)

tampon /ˈtæmpɒn/ *n* Tampon *m*

tan /tæn/ *adj* gelbbraun ● *n* Gelbbraun *nt*; (*from sun*) Bräune *f* ● *v*
(*pt/pp* **tanned**) ● *vt* gerben (*hide*)
● *vi* braun werden

tang /tæŋ/ *n* herber Geschmack *m*;
(*smell*) herber Geruch *m*

tangible /ˈtændʒɪbl/ *adj* greifbar

tangle /ˈtæŋgl/ *n* Gewirr *nt*; (*in hair*)
Verfilzung *f* ● *vt* **~ [up]** verheddern
● *vi* sich verheddern

tank /tæŋk/ *n* Tank *m*; (*Mil*) Panzer *m*

tanker /ˈtæŋkə(r)/ *n* Tanker *m*;
(*lorry*) Tank[last]wagen *m*

tantrum /ˈtæntrəm/ *n* Wutanfall *m*

tap /tæp/ *n* Hahn *m*; (*knock*) Klopfen
nt; **on ~** zur Verfügung ● *v* (*pt/pp*
tapped) ● *vt* klopfen an (+ *acc*); anzapfen (*barrel, tree*); erschließen (*resources*); abhören (*telephone*) ● *vi*
klopfen. **~-dance** *n* Stepp[tanz] *m*
● *vi* Stepp tanzen, steppen

tape /teɪp/ *n* Band *nt*; (*adhesive*) Klebstreifen *m*; (*for recording*) Tonband *nt*
● *vt* mit Klebstreifen zukleben; (*record*) auf Band aufnehmen

'tape-measure *n* Bandmaß *nt*

taper /ˈteɪpə(r)/ *vi* sich verjüngen

'tape recorder *n* Tonbandgerät *nt*

tar /tɑː(r)/ *n* Teer *m* ● *vt* (*pt/pp*
tarred) teeren

target /ˈtɑːgɪt/ *n* Ziel *nt*; (*board*)
[Ziel]scheibe *f*

tarnish /ˈtɑːnɪʃ/ *vi* anlaufen

tarpaulin /tɑːˈpɔːlɪn/ *n* Plane *f*

tart¹ /tɑːt/ *adj* (**-er, -est**) sauer

tart² *n* ≈ Obstkuchen *m*; (*individual*)
Törtchen *nt*; (*sl: prostitute*) Nutte *f*

● *vt* ~ **oneself up** 🔲 sich auftakeln

tartan /'tɑːtn/ *n* Schottenmuster *nt*; (*cloth*) Schottenstoff *m*

task /tɑːsk/ *n* Aufgabe *f*; **take s.o. to** ~ jdm Vorhaltungen machen. ~ **force** *n* Sonderkommando *nt*

tassel /'tæsl/ *n* Quaste *f*

taste /teɪst/ *n* Geschmack *m*; (*sample*) Kostprobe *f* ● *vt* kosten, probieren; schmecken (*flavour*) ● *vi* schmecken (**of** nach). ~**ful** *adj* (*fig*) geschmackvoll. ~**less** *adj* geschmacklos

tasty /'teɪstɪ/ *adj* lecker

tat /tæt/ *see* tit²

tatters /'tætəz/ *npl* **in** ~**s** in Fetzen

tattoo /tə'tuː/ *n* Tätowierung *f* ● *vt* tätowieren

tatty /'tætɪ/ *adj* schäbig; (*book*) zerfleddert

taught /tɔːt/ *see* teach

taunt /tɔːnt/ *n* höhnische Bemerkung *f* ● *vt* verhöhnen

taut /tɔːt/ *adj* straff

tawdry /'tɔːdrɪ/ *adj* billig und geschmacklos

tax /tæks/ *n* Steuer *f* ● *vt* besteuern; (*fig*) strapazieren. ~**able** *adj* steuerpflichtig. ~**ation** *n* Besteuerung *f*

taxi /'tæksɪ/ *n* Taxi *nt* ● *vi* (*pt/pp* **taxied**, *pres p* **taxiing**) (*aircraft:*) rollen. ~ **driver** *n* Taxifahrer *m*. ~ **rank** *n* Taxistand *m*

'**taxpayer** *n* Steuerzahler *m*

tea /tiː/ *n* Tee *m*. ~**bag** *n* Teebeutel *m*. ~**break** *n* Teepause *f*

teach /tiːtʃ/ *vt/i* (*pt/pp* **taught**) unterrichten; ~ **s.o. sth** jdm etw beibringen. ~**er** *n* Lehrer(in) *m*(*f*). ~**ing** *n* Unterrichten *nt*

tea: ~**cloth** *n* (*for drying*) Geschirrtuch *nt*. ~**cup** *n* Teetasse *f*

teak /tiːk/ *n* Teakholz *nt*

team /tiːm/ *n* Mannschaft *f*; (*fig*) Team *nt*; (*of animals*) Gespann *nt*

'**teapot** *n* Teekanne *f*

tear¹ /teə(r)/ *n* Riss *m* ● *v* (*pt* **tore**, *pp* **torn**) ● *vt* reißen; (*damage*) zerreißen; ~ **oneself away** sich los-

reißen ● *vi* [zer]reißen; (*run*) rasen. ~ **up** *vt* zerreißen

tear² /tɪə(r)/ *n* Träne *f*. ~**ful** *adj* weinend. ~**fully** *adv* unter Tränen. ~**gas** *n* Tränengas *nt*

tease /tiːz/ *vt* necken

tea: ~**-set** *n* Teeservice *nt*. ~ **shop** *n* Café *nt*. ~**spoon** *n* Teelöffel *m*

teat /tiːt/ *n* Zitze *f*; (*on bottle*) Sauger *m*

'**tea-towel** *n* Geschirrtuch *nt*

technical /'teknɪkl/ *adj* technisch; (*specialized*) fachlich. ~**ity** *n* technisches Detail *nt*; (*Jur*) Formfehler *m*. ~**ly** *adv* technisch; (*strictly*) streng genommen. ~ **term** *n* Fachausdruck *m*

technician /tek'nɪʃn/ *n* Techniker *m*

technique /tek'niːk/ *n* Technik *f*

technological /teknə'lɒdʒɪkl/ *adj* technologisch

technology /tek'nɒlədʒɪ/ *n* Technik *f*

teddy /'tedɪ/ *n* ~ [**bear**] Teddybär *m*

tedious /'tiːdɪəs/ *adj* langweilig

tedium /'tiːdɪəm/ *n* Langeweile *f*

teenage /'tiːneɪdʒ/ *adj* Teenager-; ~ **boy/girl** Junge *m*/Mädchen *nt* im Teenageralter. ~**r** *n* Teenager *m*

teens /tiːnz/ *npl* **the** ~ die Teenagerjahre *pl*

teeter /'tiːtə(r)/ *vi* schwanken

teeth /tiːθ/ *see* tooth

teeth|e /tiːð/ *vi* zahnen. ~**ing troubles** *npl* (*fig*) Anfangsschwierigkeiten *pl*

teetotal /tiː'təʊtl/ *adj* abstinent. ~**ler** *n* Abstinenzler *m*

telebanking /'telɪbæŋkɪŋ/ *n* Telebanking *nt*

telecommunications /telɪkəmjuːnɪ'keɪʃnz/ *npl* Fernmeldewesen *nt*

telegram /'telɪgræm/ *n* Telegramm *nt*

telegraph /'telɪgrɑːf/ ~ **pole** *n* Telegrafenmast *m*

telephone /'telɪfəʊn/ *n* Telefon *nt*; **be on the** ~ Telefon haben; (*be tele-*

phoning) telefonieren ● *vt* anrufen ● *vi* telefonieren

telephone: ∼ **booth** *n*, ∼ **box** *n* Telefonzelle *f*. ∼ **directory** *n* Telefonbuch *nt*. ∼ **number** *n* Telefonnummer *f*

tele'photo /'teli-/ *adj* ∼ **lens** Teleobjektiv *nt*

telescop|e /'teliskəʊp/ *n* Teleskop *nt*, Fernrohr *nt*. ∼**ic** *adj* (*collapsible*) ausziehbar

televise /'telivaiz/ *vt* im Fernsehen übertragen

television /'teliviʒn/ *n* Fernsehen *nt*; **watch** ∼ fernsehen; ∼ **[set]** Fernseher *m* ▣

teleworking /'teliwɜːkiŋ/ *n* Telearbeit *f*

tell /tel/ *vt/i* (*pt/pp* told) sagen (**s.o.** jdm); (*relate*) erzählen; (*know*) wissen; (*distinguish*) erkennen; ∼ **the time** die Uhr lesen; **time will** ∼ das wird man erst sehen; **his age is beginning to** ∼ sein Alter macht sich bemerkbar. ∼ **off** *vt* ausschimpfen

telly /'teli/ *n* ▣ = television

temp /temp/ *n* ▣ Aushilfssekretärin *f*

temper /'tempə(r)/ *n* (*disposition*) Naturell *nt*; (*mood*) Laune *f*; (*anger*) Wut *f*; **lose one's** ∼ wütend werden ● *vt* (*fig*) mäßigen

temperament /'temprəmənt/ *n* Temperament *nt*. ∼**al** *adj* temperamentvoll; (*moody*) launisch

temperate /'tempərət/ *adj* gemäßigt

temperature /'temprətʃə(r)/ *n* Temperatur *f*; **have** *or* **run a** ∼ Fieber haben

temple[1] /'templ/ *n* Tempel *m*

temple[2] *n* (*Anat*) Schläfe *f*

tempo /'tempəʊ/ *n* Tempo *nt*

temporary /'tempərəri/ *adj*, **-ily** *adv* vorübergehend; (*measure, building*) provisorisch

tempt /tempt/ *vt* verleiten; (*Relig*) versuchen; herausfordern (*fate*); (*entice*) [ver]locken; **be** ∼**ed** versucht sein (**to** zu). ∼**ation** *n* Versuchung *f*. ∼**ing** *adj* verlockend

ten /ten/ *adj* zehn

tenaci|ous /tɪ'neɪʃəs/ *adj*, **-ly** *adv* hartnäckig. ∼**ty** *n* Hartnäckigkeit *f*

tenant /'tenənt/ *n* Mieter(in) *m(f)*; (*Comm*) Pächter(in) *m(f)*

tend /tend/ *vi* ∼ **to do sth** dazu neigen, etw zu tun

tendency /'tendənsɪ/ *n* Tendenz *f*; (*inclination*) Neigung *f*

tender /'tendə(r)/ *adj* zart; (*loving*) zärtlich; (*painful*) empfindlich. ∼**ly** *adv* zärtlich. ∼**ness** *n* Zartheit *f*; Zärtlichkeit *f*

tendon /'tendən/ *n* Sehne *f*

tenner /'tenə(r)/ *n* ▣ Zehnpfundschein *m*

tennis /'tenis/ *n* Tennis *nt*. ∼**-court** *n* Tennisplatz *m*

tenor /'tenə(r)/ *n* Tenor *m*

tense /tens/ *adj* (**-r, -st**) gespannt ● *vt* anspannen (*muscle*)

tension /'tenʃn/ *n* Spannung *f*

tent /tent/ *n* Zelt *nt*

tentative /'tentətɪv/ *adj*, **-ly** *adv* vorläufig; (*hesitant*) zaghaft

tenterhooks /'tentəhʊks/ *npl* **be on** ∼ wie auf glühenden Kohlen sitzen

tenth /tenθ/ *adj* zehnte(r,s) ● *n* Zehntel *nt*

tenuous /'tenjʊəs/ *adj* schwach

tepid /'tepɪd/ *adj* lauwarm

term /tɜːm/ *n* Zeitraum *m*; (*Sch*) ≈ Halbjahr *nt*; (*Univ*) ≈ Semester *nt*; (*expression*) Ausdruck *m*; ∼**s** *pl* (*conditions*) Bedingungen *pl*; **in the short/long** ∼ kurz-/langfristig; **be on good/bad** ∼**s** gut/nicht gut miteinander auskommen

terminal /'tɜːmɪnl/ *adj* End-; (*Med*) unheilbar ● *n* (*Aviat*) Terminal *m*; (*of bus*) Endstation *f*; (*on battery*) Pol *m*; (*Computing*) Terminal *nt*

terminat|e /'tɜːmɪneɪt/ *vt* beenden; lösen (*contract*); unterbrechen (*pregnancy*) ● *vi* enden

terminology /tɜːmɪ'nɒlədʒɪ/ *n* Terminologie *f*

terminus /'tɜːmɪnəs/ *n* (*pl* **-ni** /-naɪ/) Endstation *f*

t

terrace /'terəs/ n Terrasse f; (houses) Häuserreihe f. ~**d house** n Reihenhaus nt

terrain /te'reɪn/ n Gelände nt

terrible /'terəbl/ adj, **-bly** adv schrecklich

terrific /tə'rɪfɪk/ adj ① (excellent) sagenhaft; (huge) riesig

terri|fy /'terɪfaɪ/ vt (pt/pp **-ied**) Angst machen (+ dat); **be** ~**fied** Angst haben. ~**fying** adj Furcht erregend

territorial /terɪ'tɔːrɪəl/ adj Territorial-

territory /'terɪtərɪ/ n Gebiet nt

terror /'terə(r)/ n [panische] Angst f; (Pol) Terror m. ~**ism** n Terrorismus m. ~**ist** n Terrorist(in) m(f). ~**ize** vt terrorisieren

terse /tɜːs/ adj kurz, knapp

test /test/ n Test m; (Sch) Klassenarbeit f; **put to the** ~ auf die Probe stellen ● vt prüfen; (examine) untersuchen (**for** auf + acc)

testament /'testəmənt/ n Testament nt

testify /'testɪfaɪ/ v (pt/pp **-ied**) ● vt beweisen; ~ **that** bezeugen, dass ● vi aussagen

testimonial /testɪ'məʊnɪəl/ n Zeugnis nt

testimony /'testɪmənɪ/ n Aussage f

'test-tube n Reagenzglas nt

tether /'teðə(r)/ n **be at the end of one's** ~ am Ende seiner Kraft sein ● vt anbinden

text /tekst/ n Text m ● vt/i texten. ~**book** n Lehrbuch nt

textile /'tekstaɪl/ adj Textil- ● n ~**s** pl Textilien pl

'text message n SMS-Nachricht f

texture /'tekstʃə(r)/ n Beschaffenheit f; (of cloth) Struktur f

Thai /taɪ/ adj thailändisch. ~**land** n Thailand nt

Thames /temz/ n Themse f

than /ðən/, betont /ðæn/ conj als

thank /θæŋk/ vt danken (+ dat); ~ **you [very much]** danke [schön].

~**ful** adj dankbar. ~**less** adj undankbar

thanks /θæŋks/ npl Dank m; ~**!** ① danke! ~ **to** dank (+ dat or gen)

---

that /ðæt/

! pl **those**

● adjective

····▸ der (m), die (f), das (nt), die (pl); (just seen or experienced) dieser (m), diese (f), dieses (nt), diese (pl). **I'll never forget that day** den Tag werde ich nie vergessen. **I liked that house** dieses Haus hat mir gut gefallen

● pronoun

····▸ der (m), die (f), das (nt), die (pl). **that is not true** das ist nicht wahr. **who is that in the garden?** wer ist das [da] im Garten? **I'll take that** ich nehme den/die/das. **I don't like those** die mag ich nicht. **is that you?** bist du es? **that is why** deshalb

····▸ **like that** so. **don't be like that!** sei doch nicht so! **a man like that** ein solcher Mann; so ein Mann ①

····▸ (after prepositions) da .... **after that** danach. **with that** damit. **apart from that** außerdem

····▸ (relative pronoun) der (m), die (f), das (nt), die (pl). **the book that I'm reading** das Buch, das ich lese. **the people that you got it from** die Leute, von denen du es bekommen hast. **everyone that I know** jeder, den ich kenne. **that is all that I have** das ist alles, was ich habe

● adverb

····▸ so. **he's not 'that stupid** so blöd ist er [auch wieder] nicht. **it wasn't 'that bad** so schlecht war es auch nicht. **a nail about 'that long** ein etwa so langer Nagel

····▸ (relative adverb) der (m), die (f), das (nt), die (pl). **the day that I first met her** der Tag, an dem ich sie zum ersten Mal sah.

at the speed that he was going bei der Geschwindigkeit, die er hatte
● *conjunction*
····▸ dass. **I don't think that he'll come** ich denke nicht, dass er kommt. **we know that you're right** wir wissen, dass du Recht hast. **I'm so tired that I can hardly walk** ich bin so müde, dass ich kaum gehen kann
····▸ **so that** (*purpose*) damit; (*result*) sodass. **he came earlier so that they would have more time** er kam früher, damit sie mehr Zeit hatten. **it was late, so that I had to catch the bus** es war spät, sodass ich den Bus nehmen musste

thatch /θætʃ/ *n* Strohdach *nt*. ~**ed** *adj* strohgedeckt

thaw /θɔ:/ *n* Tauwetter *nt* ● *vt/i* auftauen; **it's** ~**ing** es taut

the /ðə/, *vor einem Vokal* /ðɪ:/ *def art* der/die/das; (*pl*) die; **play** ~ **piano**/**violin** Klavier/Geige spielen ● *adv* ~ **more** ~ **better** je mehr, desto besser; **all** ~ **better** umso besser

theatre /'θɪətə(r)/ *n* Theater *nt*; (*Med*) Operationssaal *m*

theatrical /θɪ'ætrɪkl/ *adj* Theater-; (*showy*) theatralisch

theft /θeft/ *n* Diebstahl *m*

their /ðeə(r)/ *adj* ihr

theirs /ðeəz/ *poss pron* ihre(r), ihrs; **a friend of** ~ ein Freund von ihnen; **those are** ~ die gehören ihnen

them /ðem/ *pron* (*acc*) sie; (*dat*) ihnen

theme /θi:m/ *n* Thema *nt*. ~ **park** *n* Themenpark *m*

them'selves *pron* selbst; (*reflexive*) sich; **by** ~ allein

then /ðen/ *adv* dann; (*at that time in past*) damals; **by** ~ seitdem; **since** ~ seitdem; **before** ~ vorher; **from** ~ **on** von da an; **now and** ~ dann und wann; **there and** ~ auf der Stelle ● *adj* damalig

theology /θɪ'ɒlədʒɪ/ *n* Theologie *f*

theoretical /θɪə'retɪkl/ *adj* theoretisch

theory /'θɪərɪ/ *n* Theorie *f*; **in** ~ theoretisch

therap|ist /'θerəpɪst/ *n* Therapeut(in) *m(f)*. ~**y** *n* Therapie *f*

there /ðeə(r)/ *adv* da; (*with movement*) dahin, dorthin; **down**/**up** ~ da unten/oben; ~ **is**/**are** da ist/sind; (*in existence*) es gibt ● *int* ~, ~**!** nun, nun!

there: ~**abouts** *adv* da [in der Nähe]; **or** ~**abouts** (*roughly*) ungefähr. ~**fore** /-fɔ:(r)/ *adv* deshalb, also

thermometer /θə'mɒmɪtə(r)/ *n* Thermometer *nt*

Thermos ® /'θɜ:məs/ *n* ~ **[flask]** Thermosflasche ® *f*

thermostat /'θɜ:məstæt/ *n* Thermostat *m*

these /ði:z/ *see* this

thesis /'θi:sɪs/ *n* (*pl* -**ses** /-si:z/) Dissertation *f*; (*proposition*) These *f*

they /ðeɪ/ *pron* sie; ~ **say** (*generalizing*) man sagt

thick /θɪk/ *adj* (-**er**, -**est**) dick; (*dense*) dicht; (*liquid*) dickflüssig; (🏛: *stupid*) dumm ● *adv* dick ● *n* **in the** ~ **of** mitten in (+ *dat*). ~**en** *vt* dicker machen; eindicken (*sauce*) ● *vi* dicker werden; (*fog:*) dichter werden; (*plot:*) komplizierter werden. ~**ness** *n* Dicke *f*; Dichte *f*; Dickflüssigkeit *f*

thief /θi:f/ *n* (*pl* **thieves**) Dieb(in) *m(f)*

thigh /θaɪ/ *n* Oberschenkel *m*

thimble /'θɪmbl/ *n* Fingerhut *m*

thin /θɪn/ *adj* (**thinner**, **thinnest**) dünn ● *adv* dünn ● *v* (*pt/pp* **thinned**) ● *vt* verdünnen (*liquid*) ● *vi* sich lichten

thing /θɪŋ/ *n* Ding *nt*; (*subject, affair*) Sache *f*; ~**s** *pl* (*belongings*) Sachen *pl*; **for one** ~ erstens; **just the** ~**!** genau das Richtige! **how are** ~**s?** wie geht's? **the latest** ~ 🏛 der letzte Schrei

think /θɪŋk/ *vt/i* (*pt/pp* **thought**) denken (**about**/**of** an + *acc*); (*believe*) meinen; (*consider*) nachdenken; (*re-*

gard as) halten für; **I ~ so** ich glaube schon; **what do you ~ of it?** was halten Sie davon? **~ over** *vt* sich (*dat*) überlegen. **~ up** *vt* sich (*dat*) ausdenken

third /θɜːd/ *adj* dritte(r,s) ● *n* Drittel *nt*. **~ly** *adv* drittens. **~-rate** *adj* drittrangig

thirst /θɜːst/ *n* Durst *m*. **~y** *adj*, **-ily** *adv* durstig; **be ~y** Durst haben

thirteen /θɜːˈtiːn/ *adj* dreizehn. **~th** *adj* dreizehnte(r,s)

thirtieth /ˈθɜːtɪɪθ/ *adj* dreißigste(r,s)

thirty /ˈθɜːtɪ/ *adj* dreißig

this /ðɪs/ *adj* (*pl* **these**) diese(r,s); (*pl*) diese; **~ one** diese(r,s) da; **I'll take ~** ich nehme diesen/diese/ dieses; **~ evening/morning** heute Abend/ Morgen; **these days** heutzutage ● *pron* (*pl* **these**) das, dies[es]; (*pl*) die, diese; **~ and that** dies und das; **~ or that** dieses oder das da; **like ~** so; **~ is Peter** das ist Peter; (*Teleph*) hier [spricht] Peter; **who is ~?** wer ist das? (*Teleph, Amer*) wer ist am Apparat?

thistle /ˈθɪsl/ *n* Distel *f*

thorn /θɔːn/ *n* Dorn *m*

thorough /ˈθʌrə/ *adj* gründlich

thoroughbred *n* reinrassiges Tier *nt*; (*horse*) Rassepferd *nt*

thorough|ly /ˈθʌrəlɪ/ *adv* gründlich; (*completely*) völlig; (*extremely*) äußerst. **~ness** *n* Gründlichkeit *f*

those /ðəʊz/ *see* **that**

though /ðəʊ/ *conj* obgleich, obwohl; **as ~** als ob ● *adv* 🛈 doch

thought /θɔːt/ *see* **think** ● *n* Gedanke *m*; (*thinking*) Denken *nt*. **~ful** *adj* nachdenklich; (*considerate*) rücksichtsvoll. **~less** *adj* gedankenlos

thousand /ˈθaʊznd/ *adj* **one/a ~** [ein]tausend ● *n* Tausend *nt*. **~th** *adj* tausendste(r,s) ● *n* Tausendstel *nt*

thrash /θræʃ/ *vt* verprügeln; (*defeat*) [vernichtend] schlagen

thread /θred/ *n* Faden *m*; (*of screw*) Gewinde *nt* ● *vt* einfädeln; auffädeln (*beads*). **~bare** *adj* fadenscheinig

threat /θret/ *n* Drohung *f*; (*danger*) Bedrohung *f*

threaten /ˈθretn/ *vt* drohen (+ *dat*); (*with weapon*) bedrohen; **~ s.o. with sth** jdm etw androhen ● *vi* drohen. **~ing** *adj* drohend; (*ominous*) bedrohlich

three /θriː/ *adj* drei. **~fold** *adj & adv* dreifach

thresh /θreʃ/ *vt* dreschen

threshold /ˈθreʃəʊld/ *n* Schwelle *f*

threw /θruː/ *see* **throw**

thrift /θrɪft/ *n* Sparsamkeit *f*. **~y** *adj* sparsam

thrill /θrɪl/ *n* Erregung *f*; 🛈 Nervenkitzel *m* ● *vt* (*excite*) erregen; **be ~ed with** sich sehr freuen über (+ *acc*). **~er** *n* Thriller *m*. **~ing** *adj* erregend

thrive /θraɪv/ *vi* (*pt* **thrived** or **throve**, *pp* **thrived** or **thriven** /ˈθrɪvn/) gedeihen (**on** bei); (*business:*) florieren

throat /θrəʊt/ *n* Hals *m*; **cut s.o.'s ~** jdm die Kehle durchschneiden

throb /θrɒb/ *n* Pochen *nt* ● *vi* (*pt/pp* **throbbed**) pochen; (*vibrate*) vibrieren

throes /θrəʊz/ *npl* **in the ~ of** (*fig*) mitten in (+ *dat*)

throne /θrəʊn/ *n* Thron *m*

throttle /ˈθrɒtl/ *vt* erdrosseln

through /θruː/ *prep* durch (+ *acc*); (*during*) während (+ *gen*); (*Amer: up to & including*) bis einschließlich ● *adv* durch; **wet ~** durch und durch nass; **read sth ~** etw durchlesen ● *adj* (*train*) durchgehend; **be ~** (*finished*) fertig sein; (*Teleph*) durch sein

throughout /θruːˈaʊt/ *prep* **~ the country** im ganzen Land; **~ the night** die Nacht durch ● *adv* ganz; (*time*) die ganze Zeit

throve /θrəʊv/ *see* **thrive**

throw /θrəʊ/ *n* Wurf *m* ● *vt* (*pt* **threw**, *pp* **thrown**) werfen; schütten (*liquid*); betätigen (*switch*); abwerfen (*rider*); (🛈: *disconcert*) aus der Fassung bringen; 🛈 geben (*party*); **~ sth to s.o.** jdm etw zuwerfen. **~ away** *vt* wegwerfen. **~ out** *vt* hinauswerfen; (∼ *away*) wegwerfen; verwerfen (*plan*). ∼ **up** *vt* hochwerfen ● *vi* sich übergeben

'**throw-away** *adj* Wegwerf-

thrush /θrʌʃ/ *n* Drossel *f*

thrust /θrʌst/ *n* Stoß *m*; (*Phys*) Schub *m* ● *vt* (*pt/pp* **thrust**) stoßen; (*insert*) stecken

thud /θʌd/ *n* dumpfer Schlag *m*

thug /θʌɡ/ *n* Schläger *m*

thumb /θʌm/ *n* Daumen *m* ● *vt* ∼ **a lift** 🔲 per Anhalter fahren. ∼**tack** *n* (*Amer*) Reißzwecke *f*

thump /θʌmp/ *n* Schlag *m*; (*noise*) dumpfer Schlag *m* ● *vt* schlagen ● *vi* hämmern; (*heart:*) pochen

thunder /'θʌndə(r)/ *n* Donner *m* ● *vi* donnern. ∼**clap** *n* Donnerschlag *m*. ∼**storm** *n* Gewitter *nt*. ∼**y** *adj* gewittrig

Thursday /'θɜ:zdeɪ/ *n* Donnerstag *m*

thus /ðʌs/ *adv* so

thwart /θwɔ:t/ *vt* vereiteln; ∼ **s.o.** jdm einen Strich durch die Rechnung machen

tick¹ /tɪk/ *n* **on** ∼ 🔲 auf Pump

tick² *n* (*sound*) Ticken *nt*; (*mark*) Häkchen *nt*; (🔲: *instant*) Sekunde *f* ● *vi* ticken ● *vt* abhaken. ∼ **off** *vt* abhaken; 🔲 rüffeln

ticket /'tɪkɪt/ *n* Karte *f*; (*for bus, train*) Fahrschein *m*; (*Aviat*) Flugschein *m*; (*for lottery*) Los *nt*; (*for article deposited*) Schein *m*; (*label*) Schild *nt*; (*for library*) Lesekarte *f*; (*fine*) Strafzettel *m*. ∼ **collector** *n* Fahrkartenkontrolleur *m*. ∼ **office** *n* Fahrkartenschalter *m*; (*for entry*) Kasse *f*

tick|le /'tɪkl/ *n* Kitzeln *m* ● *vt/i* kitzeln. ∼**lish** *adj* kitzlig

tidal /'taɪdl/ *adj* ∼ **wave** Flutwelle *f*

tide /taɪd/ *n* Gezeiten *pl*; (*of events*) Strom *m*; **the** ∼ **is in/out** es ist Flut/ Ebbe ● *vt* ∼ **s.o. over** jdm über die Runden helfen

tidiness /'taɪdɪnɪs/ *n* Ordentlichkeit *f*

tidy /'taɪdɪ/ *adj* , **-ily** *adv* ordentlich ● *vt* ∼ **[up]** aufräumen

tie /taɪ/ *n* Krawatte *f*; Schlips *m*; (*cord*) Schnur *f*; (*fig: bond*) Band *nt*;

(*restriction*) Bindung *f*; (*Sport*) Unentschieden *nt*; (*in competition*) Punktgleichheit *f* ● *v* (*pres p* **tying**) ● *vt* binden; machen (*knot*) ● *vi* (*Sport*) unentschieden spielen; (*have equal scores, votes*) punktgleich sein. ∼ **up** *vt* festbinden; verschnüren (*parcel*); fesseln (*person*); **be** ∼**d up** (*busy*) beschäftigt sein

tier /tɪə(r)/ *n* Stufe *f*; (*of cake*) Etage *f*; (*in stadium*) Rang *m*

tiger /'taɪɡə(r)/ *n* Tiger *m*

tight /taɪt/ *adj* (**-er, -est**) fest; (*taut*) straff; (*clothes*) eng; (*control*) streng; (🔲: *drunk*) blau ● *adv* fest

tighten /'taɪtn/ *vt* fester ziehen; straffen (*rope*); anziehen (*screw*); verschärfen (*control*) ● *vi* sich spannen

tightrope *n* Hochseil *nt*

tights /taɪts/ *npl* Strumpfhose *f*

tile /taɪl/ *n* Fliese *f*; (*on wall*) Kachel *f*; (*on roof*) [Dach]ziegel *m* ● *vt* mit Fliesen auslegen; kacheln (*wall*); decken (*roof*)

till¹ /tɪl/ *prep & conj* = **until**

till² *n* Kasse *f*

tilt /tɪlt/ *n* Neigung *f* ● *vt* kippen; [zur Seite] neigen (*head*) ● *vi* sich neigen

timber /'tɪmbə(r)/ *n* [Nutz]holz *nt*

time /taɪm/ *n* Zeit *f*; (*occasion*) Mal *nt*; (*rhythm*) Takt *m*; ∼**s** (*Math*) mal; **at** ∼**s** manchmal; ∼ **and again** immer wieder; **two at a** ∼ zwei auf einmal; **on** ∼ pünktlich; **in** ∼ rechtzeitig; (*eventually*) mit der Zeit; **in no** ∼ im Handumdrehen; **in a year's** ∼ in einem Jahr; **behind** ∼ verspätet; **behind the** ∼**s** rückständig; **for the** ∼ **being** vorläufig; **what is the** ∼? wie spät ist es? wie viel Uhr ist es? **did you have a nice** ∼? hat es dir gut gefallen? ● *vt* stoppen (*race*); **be well** ∼**d** gut abgepaßt sein

time: ∼ **bomb** *n* Zeitbombe *f*. ∼**less** *adj* zeitlos. ∼**ly** *adj* rechtzeitig. ∼**-switch** *n* Zeitschalter *m*. ∼**-table** *n* Fahrplan *m*; (*Sch*) Stundenplan *m*

timid /'tɪmɪd/ *adj* scheu; (*hesitant*) zaghaft

t

timing /'taɪmɪŋ/ n (Sport, Techn) Timing nt

tin /tɪn/ n Zinn nt; (container) Dose f ● vt (pt/pp **tinned**) in Dosen konservieren. ∼ **foil** n Stanniol nt; (Culin) Alufolie f

tinge /tɪndʒ/ n Hauch m

tingle /'tɪŋgl/ vi kribbeln

tinker /'tɪŋkə(r)/ vi herumbasteln (with an + dat)

tinkle /'tɪŋkl/ n Klingeln nt ● vi klingeln

tinned /tɪnd/ adj Dosen-

'tin opener n Dosenöffner m

tinsel /'tɪnsl/ n Lametta nt

tint /tɪnt/ n Farbton m ● vt tönen

tiny /'taɪnɪ/ adj winzig

tip¹ /tɪp/ n Spitze f

tip² n (money) Trinkgeld nt; (advice) Rat m, 🔲 Tipp m; (for rubbish) Müllhalde f ● v (pt/pp **tipped**) ● vt (tilt) kippen; (reward) Trinkgeld geben (s.o. jdm) ● vi kippen. ∼ **out** vt auskippen. ∼ **over** vt/i umkippen

tipped /tɪpt/ adj Filter-

tipsy /'tɪpsɪ/ adj 🔲 beschwipst

tiptoe /'tɪptəʊ/ n on ∼ auf Zehenspitzen

tiptop /tɪp'tɒp/ adj 🔲 erstklassig

tire /'taɪə(r)/ vt/i ermüden. ∼**d** adj müde; **be** ∼**d of sth** etw satt haben; ∼**d out** [völlig] erschöpft. ∼**less** adj unermüdlich. ∼**some** adj lästig

tiring /'taɪrɪŋ/ adj ermüdend

tissue /'tɪʃuː/ n Gewebe nt; (handkerchief) Papiertaschentuch nt

tit /tɪt/ n (bird) Meise f

'titbit n Leckerbissen m

title /'taɪtl/ n Titel m

to /tuː/, unbetont /tə/
● preposition
····➤ (destinations: most cases) zu (+ dat). **go to work/the station** zur Arbeit/zum Bahnhof gehen. **from house to house** von Haus zu Haus. **go/come to s.o.** zu jdm gehen/kommen
····➤ (with name of place or points of compass) nach. **to Paris/Germany** nach Paris/Deutschland. **to Switzerland** in die Schweiz. **from East to West** von Osten nach Westen. **I've never been to Berlin** ich war noch nie in Berlin
····➤ (to cinema, theatre, bed) in (+ acc). **to bed with you!** ins Bett mit dir!
····➤ (to wedding, party, university, the toilet) auf (+ acc).
····➤ (up to) bis zu (+ dat). **to the end** bis zum Schluss. **to this day** bis heute. **5 to 6 pounds** 5 bis 6 Pfund
····➤ (give, say, write) + dat. **give/say sth to s.o.** jdm etw geben/sagen. **she wrote to him/the firm** sie hat ihm/an die Firma geschrieben
····➤ (address, send, fasten) an (+ acc). **she sent it to her brother** sie schickte es an ihren Bruder
····➤ (in telling the time) vor. **five to eight** fünf vor acht. **a quarter to ten** Viertel vor zehn
● before infinitive
····➤ (after modal verb) (not translated). **I want to go** ich will gehen. **he is learning to swim** er lernt schwimmen. **you have to go** du musst [es tun]
····➤ (after adjective) zu. **it is easy to forget** es ist leicht zu vergessen
····➤ (expressing purpose, result) um ... zu. **he did it to annoy me** er tat es, um mich zu ärgern. **she was too tired to go** sie war zu müde um zu gehen
● adverb
····➤ **be to** (door, window) angelehnt sein. **pull a door to** eine Tür anlehnen
····➤ **to and fro** hin und her

toad /təʊd/ n Kröte f

toast /təʊst/ n Toast m ● vt toasten (bread); (drink a ∼ to) trinken auf (+ acc). ∼**er** n Toaster m

tobacco /tə'bækəʊ/ n Tabak m.

~nist's [shop] n Tabakladen m

toboggan /təˈbɒgən/ n Schlitten m ● vi Schlitten fahren

today /təˈdeɪ/ n & adv heute; ~ **week** heute in einer Woche

toddler /ˈtɒdlə(r)/ n Kleinkind nt

toe /təʊ/ n Zeh m; (of footwear) Spitze f ● vt ~ **the line** spuren. ~**nail** n Zehennagel m

toffee /ˈtɒfɪ/ n Karamell m & nt

together /təˈgeðə(r)/ adv zusammen; (at the same time) gleichzeitig

toilet /ˈtɔɪlɪt/ n Toilette f. ~ **bag** n Kulturbeutel m. ~ **paper** n Toilettenpapier m

toiletries /ˈtɔɪlɪtrɪz/ npl Toilettenartikel pl

token /ˈtəʊkən/ n Zeichen nt; (counter) Marke f; (voucher) Gutschein m ● attrib symbolisch

told /təʊld/ see tell ● adj all ~ insgesamt

tolerable /ˈtɒlərəbl/ adj, -**bly** adv erträglich; (not bad) leidlich

toleran|ce /ˈtɒlərəns/ n Toleranz f. ~**t** adj tolerant

tolerate /ˈtɒləreɪt/ vt dulden, tolerieren; (bear) ertragen

toll /təʊl/ n Gebühr f; (for road) Maut f (Aust); **death** ~ Zahl f der Todesopfer

tomato /təˈmɑːtəʊ/ n (pl -**es**) Tomate f

tomb /tuːm/ n Grabmal nt

'**tombstone** n Grabstein m

'**tom-cat** n Kater m

tomorrow /təˈmɒrəʊ/ n & adv morgen; ~ **morning** morgen früh; **the day after** ~ übermorgen; **see you** ~! bis morgen!

ton /tʌn/ n Tonne f; ~**s of** 🔢 jede Menge

tone /təʊn/ n Ton m; (colour) Farbton m ● vt ~ **down** dämpfen; (fig) mäßigen. ~ **up** vt kräftigen; straffen (muscles)

tongs /tɒŋz/ npl Zange f

tongue /tʌŋ/ n Zunge f; ~ **in cheek** 🔢 nicht ernst

tonic /ˈtɒnɪk/ n Tonikum nt; (for hair)

Haarwasser nt; (fig) Wohltat f; ~ [**water**] Tonic nt

tonight /təˈnaɪt/ n & adv heute Nacht; (evening) heute Abend

tonne /tʌn/ n Tonne f

tonsil /ˈtɒnsl/ n (Anat) Mandel f. ~**litis** n Mandelentzündung f

too /tuː/ adv zu; (also) auch; ~ **much/little** zu viel/zu wenig

took /tʊk/ see take

tool /tuːl/ n Werkzeug nt; (for gardening) Gerät nt. ~**bar** n Werkzeugleiste f

tooth /tuːθ/ n (pl teeth) Zahn m

tooth: ~**ache** n Zahnschmerzen pl. ~**brush** n Zahnbürste f. ~**less** adj zahnlos. ~**paste** n Zahnpasta f. ~**pick** n Zahnstocher m

top¹ /tɒp/ n (toy) Kreisel m

top² n oberer Teil m; (apex) Spitze f; (summit) Gipfel m; (Sch) Erste(r) m/f; (top part or half) Oberteil nt; (head) Kopfende nt; (of road) oberes Ende nt; (upper surface) Oberfläche f; (lid) Deckel m; (of bottle) Verschluss m; (garment) Top nt; **at the/on** ~ oben; **on** ~ **of** oben auf (+ dat/acc); **on** ~ **of that** (besides) obendrein; **from** ~ **to bottom** von oben bis unten ● adj oberste(r,s); (highest) höchste(r,s); (best) beste(r,s) ● vt (pt/pp **topped**) an erster Stelle stehen auf (+ dat) (list); (exceed) übersteigen; (remove the ~ of) die Spitze abschneiden von. ~ **up** vt nachfüllen, auffüllen

top: ~ '**hat** n Zylinder[hut] m. ~-**heavy** adj kopflastig

topic /ˈtɒpɪk/ n Thema nt. ~**al** adj aktuell

topple /ˈtɒpl/ vt/i umstürzen

torch /tɔːtʃ/ n Taschenlampe f; (flaming) Fackel f

tore /tɔː(r)/ see tear¹

torment¹ /ˈtɔːment/ n Qual f

torment² /tɔːˈment/ vt quälen

torn /tɔːn/ see tear¹ ● adj zerrissen

torpedo /tɔːˈpiːdəʊ/ n (pl -**es**) Torpedo m ● vt torpedieren

torrent /ˈtɒrənt/ n reißender Strom m. ~**ial** adj (rain) wolkenbruchartig

t

tortoise /'tɔːtəs/ n Schildkröte f.
~**shell** n Schildpatt nt

tortuous /'tɔːtjʊəs/ adj verschlungen; (fig) umständlich

torture /'tɔːtʃə(r)/ n Folter f; (fig)
Qual f ● vt foltern; (fig) quälen

toss /tɒs/ vt werfen; (into the air)
hochwerfen; (shake) schütteln; (unseat) abwerfen; mischen (salad);
wenden (pancake); ~ **a coin** mit
einer Münze losen ● vi ~ **and turn**
(in bed) sich [schlaflos] im Bett wälzen

tot[1] /tɒt/ n kleines Kind nt; (🗌: of liquor) Gläschen nt

tot[2] vt (pt/pp totted) ~ **up** 🗌 zusammenzählen

total /'təʊtl/ adj gesamt; (complete)
völlig, total ● n Gesamtzahl f; (sum)
Gesamtsumme f ● vt (pt/pp totalled); (amount to) sich belaufen auf
(+ acc)

totalitarian /təʊtælɪ'teərɪən/ adj
totalitär

totally /'təʊtəlɪ/ adv völlig, total

totter /'tɒtə(r)/ vi taumeln

touch /tʌtʃ/ n Berührung f; (sense)
Tastsinn m; (Mus) Anschlag m; (contact) Kontakt m; (trace) Spur f; (fig)
Anflug m; **get/be in** ~ sich in Verbindung setzen/in Verbindung stehen
(**with** mit) ● vt berühren; (get hold
of) anfassen; (lightly) tippen auf/an
(+ acc); (brush against) streifen
[gegen]; (fig: move) rühren; anrühren
(food, subject); **don't** ~ **that!** fass
das nicht an! ● vi sich berühren; ~
on (fig) berühren. ~ **down** vi (Aviat)
landen. ~ **up** vt ausbessern

touch|ing /'tʌtʃɪŋ/ adj rührend. ~**y**
adj empfindlich

tough /tʌf/ adj (-er, -est) zäh; (severe, harsh) hart; (difficult) schwierig;
(durable) strapazierfähig

toughen /'tʌfn/ vt härten; ~ **up** abhärten

tour /tʊə(r)/ n Reise f, Tour f; (of
building, town) Besichtigung f; (Theat,
Sport) Tournee f; (of duty) Dienstzeit
f ● vt fahren durch ● vi herumreisen

touris|m /'tʊərɪzm/ n Tourismus m,

Fremdenverkehr m. ~**t** n Tourist(in)
m(f) ● attrib Touristen-. ~**t office** n
Fremdenverkehrsbüro nt

tournament /'tʊənəmənt/ n Turnier nt

'tour operator n Reiseveranstalter m

tousle /'taʊzl/ vt zerzausen

tow /təʊ/ n **give s.o./a car a** ~ jdn/
ein Auto abschleppen ● vt schleppen;
ziehen (trailer)

toward[s] /tə'wɔːdz/ prep zu (+
dat); (with time) gegen (+ acc); (with
respect to) gegenüber (+ dat)

towel /'taʊəl/ n Handtuch nt. ~**ling**
n (cloth) Frottee nt

tower /'taʊə(r)/ n Turm m ● vi ~
above überragen. ~ **block** n Hochhaus nt. ~**ing** adj hoch aufragend

town /taʊn/ n Stadt f. ~ **'hall** n Rathaus nt

tow-rope n Abschleppseil nt

toxic /'tɒksɪk/ adj giftig

toy /tɔɪ/ n Spielzeug nt ● vi ~ **with**
spielen mit; stochern in (+ dat)
(food). ~**shop** n Spielwarengeschäft nt

trac|e /treɪs/ n Spur f ● vt folgen (+
dat); (find) finden; (draw) zeichnen;
(with tracing-paper) durchpausen

track /træk/ n Spur f; (path) [unbefestigter] Weg m; (Sport) Bahn f;
(Rail) Gleis nt; **keep** ~ **of** im Auge
behalten ● vt verfolgen. ~ **down** vt
aufspüren; (find) finden

'tracksuit n Trainingsanzug m

tractor /'træktə(r)/ n Traktor m

trade /treɪd/ n Handel m; (line of
business) Gewerbe nt; (business) Geschäft nt; (craft) Handwerk nt; **by** ~
von Beruf ● vt tauschen; ~ **in** (give
in part exchange) in Zahlung geben
● vi handeln (**in** mit)

'trade mark n Warenzeichen nt

trader /'treɪdə(r)/ n Händler m

trade: ~ **'union** n Gewerkschaft f.
~ **'unionist** n Gewerkschaftler(in)
m(f)

trading /'treɪdɪŋ/ n Handel m

tradition /trə'dɪʃn/ n Tradition f.

~al *adj* traditionell

traffic /'træfɪk/ *n* Verkehr *m*; (*trading*) Handel *m*

traffic: ~ **circle** *n* (*Amer*) Kreisverkehr *m*. ~ **jam** *n* [Verkehrs]stau *m*. ~ **lights** *npl* [Verkehrs]ampel *f*. ~ **warden** *n* ≈ Hilfspolizist *m*; (*woman*) Politesse *f*

tragedy /'trædʒədɪ/ *n* Tragödie *f*

tragic /'trædʒɪk/ *adj*, **-ally** *adv* tragisch

trail /treɪl/ *n* Spur *f*; (*path*) Weg *m*, Pfad *m* ● *vi* schleifen; (*plant:*) sich ranken ● *vt* verfolgen, folgen (+ *dat*); (*drag*) schleifen

trailer /'treɪlə(r)/ *n* (*Auto*) Anhänger *m*; (*Amer: caravan*) Wohnwagen *m*; (*film*) Vorschau *f*

train /treɪn/ *n* Zug *m*; (*of dress*) Schleppe *f* ● *vt* ausbilden; (*Sport*) trainieren; (*aim*) richten auf (+ *acc*); erziehen (*child*); abrichten/(*to do tricks*) dressieren (*animal*); ziehen (*plant*) ● *vi* eine Ausbildung machen; (*Sport*) trainieren. ~**ed** *adj* ausgebildet

trainee /treɪ'niː/ *n* Auszubildende(r) *m/f*, (*Techn*) Praktikant(in) *m(f)*

train|er /'treɪnə(r)/ *n* (*Sport*) Trainer *m*; (*in circus*) Dompteur *m*; ~**ers** *pl* Trainingsschuhe *pl*. ~**ing** *n* Ausbildung *f*; (*Sport*) Training *nt*; (*of animals*) Dressur *f*

trait /treɪt/ *n* Eigenschaft *f*

traitor /'treɪtə(r)/ *n* Verräter *m*

tram /træm/ *n* Straßenbahn *f*

tramp /træmp/ *n* Landstreicher *m* ● *vi* stapfen; (*walk*) marschieren

trample /'træmpl/ *vt/i* trampeln

trance /trɑːns/ *n* Trance *f*

tranquil /'træŋkwɪl/ *adj* ruhig. ~**lity** *n* Ruhe *f*

tranquillizer /'træŋkwɪlaɪzə(r)/ *n* Beruhigungsmittel *nt*

transaction /træn'zækʃn/ *n* Transaktion *f*

transcend /træn'send/ *vt* übersteigen

transfer¹ /'trænsfɜː(r)/ *n* (*see* **transfer²**) Übertragung *f*; Verlegung *f*; Ver-

setzung *f*; Überweisung *f*; (*Sport*) Transfer *m*; (*design*) Abziehbild *nt*

transfer² /træns'fɜː(r)/ *v* (*pt/pp* **transferred**) ● *vt* übertragen; verlegen (*firm, prisoners*); versetzen (*employee*); überweisen (*money*); (*Sport*) transferieren ● *vi* [über]wechseln; (*when travelling*) umsteigen

transform /træns'fɔːm/ *vt* verwandeln. ~**ation** *n* Verwandlung *f*. ~**er** *n* Transformator *m*

transfusion /træns'fjuːʒn/ *n* Transfusion *f*

transistor /træn'zɪstə(r)/ *n* Transistor *m*

transit /'trænsɪt/ *n* Transit *m*; (*of goods*) Transport *m*; **in** ~ (*goods*) auf dem Transport

transition /træn'sɪʒn/ *n* Übergang *m*. ~**al** *adj* Übergangs-

translat|e /træns'leɪt/ *vt* übersetzen. ~**ion** *n* Übersetzung *f*. ~**or** *n* Übersetzer(in) *m(f)*

transmission /trænz'mɪʃn/ *n* Übertragung *f*

transmit /trænz'mɪt/ *vt* (*pt/pp* **transmitted**) übertragen. ~**ter** *n* Sender *m*

transparen|cy /træns'pærənsɪ/ *n* (*Phot*) Dia *nt*. ~**t** *adj* durchsichtig

transplant¹ /'trænsplɑːnt/ *n* Verpflanzung *f*, Transplantation *f*

transplant² /træns'plɑːnt/ *vt* umpflanzen; (*Med*) verpflanzen

transport¹ /'trænspɔːt/ *n* Transport *m*

transport² /træn'spɔːt/ *vt* transportieren. ~**ation** *n* Transport *m*

transpose /træns'pəʊz/ *vt* umstellen

trap /træp/ *n* Falle *f*; (🔲: *mouth*) Klappe *f*; **pony and** ~ Einspänner *m* ● *vt* (*pt/pp* **trapped**) [mit einer Falle] fangen; (*jam*) einklemmen; **be** ~**ped** festsitzen; (*shut in*) eingeschlossen sein. ~'**door** *n* Falltür *f*

trash /træʃ/ *n* Schund *m*; (*rubbish*) Abfall *m*; (*nonsense*) Quatsch *m*. ~**can** *n* (*Amer*) Mülleimer *m*. ~**y** *adj* Schund-

t

trauma /'trɔːmə/ n Trauma nt. **~tic** adj traumatisch

travel /'trævl/ n Reisen nt ● v (pt/pp **travelled**) ● vi reisen; (go in vehicle) fahren; (light, sound:) sich fortpflanzen; (Techn) sich bewegen ● vt bereisen; fahren (distance). **~ agency** n Reisebüro nt. **~ agent** n Reisebürokaufmann m

traveller /'trævələ(r)/ n Reisende(r) m/f; (Comm) Vertreter m; **~s** pl (gypsies) Zigeuner pl. **~'s cheque** n Reisescheck m

trawler /'trɔːlə(r)/ n Fischdampfer m

tray /treɪ/ n Tablett nt; (for baking) [Back]blech nt; (for documents) Ablagekorb m

treacher|ous /'tretʃərəs/ adj treulos; (dangerous, deceptive) tückisch. **~y** n Verrat m

tread /tred/ n Schritt m; (step) Stufe f; (of tyre) Profil nt ● v (pt **trod**, pp **trodden**) ● vi (walk) gehen; **~ on/in** treten auf/ in (+ acc) ● vt treten

treason /'triːzn/ n Verrat m

treasure /'treʒə(r)/ n Schatz m ● vt in Ehren halten. **~r** n Kassenwart m

treasury /'treʒəri/ n Schatzkammer f; **the T~** das Finanzministerium

treat /triːt/ n [besonderes] Vergnügen nt ● vt behandeln; **~ s.o. to sth** jdm etw spendieren

treatment /'triːtmənt/ n Behandlung f

treaty /'triːti/ n Vertrag m

treble /'trebl/ adj dreifach; **~ the amount** dreimal so viel ● n (Mus) Diskant m; (voice) Sopran m ● vt verdreifachen ● vi sich verdreifachen

tree /triː/ n Baum m

trek /trek/ n Marsch m ● vi (pt/pp **trekked**) latschen

trellis /'trelɪs/ n Gitter nt

tremble /'trembl/ vi zittern

tremendous /trɪ'mendəs/ adj gewaltig; (🔲: excellent) großartig

tremor /'tremə(r)/ n Zittern nt; **[earth] ~** Beben nt

trench /trentʃ/ n Graben m; (Mil) Schützengraben m

trend /trend/ n Tendenz f; (fashion) Trend m. **~y** adj 🔲 modisch

trepidation /trepɪ'deɪʃn/ n Beklommenheit f

trespass /'trespəs/ vi **~ on** unerlaubt betreten

trial /'traɪəl/ n (Jur) [Gerichts]verfahren nt, Prozess m; (test) Probe f; (ordeal) Prüfung f; **be on ~** auf Probe sein; (Jur) angeklagt sein (**for** wegen); **by ~ and error** durch Probieren

triang|le /'traɪæŋgl/ n Dreieck nt; (Mus) Triangel m. **~ular** adj dreieckig

tribe /traɪb/ n Stamm m

tribunal /traɪ'bjuːnl/ n Schiedsgericht nt

tributary /'trɪbjʊtəri/ n Nebenfluss m

tribute /'trɪbjuːt/ n Tribut m; **pay ~** Tribut zollen (**to** dat)

trick /trɪk/ n Trick m; (joke) Streich m; (Cards) Stich m; (feat of skill) Kunststück nt ● vt täuschen, 🔲 hereinlegen

trickle /'trɪkl/ vi rinnen

trick|ster /'trɪkstə(r)/ n Schwindler m. **~y** adj adj schwierig

tricycle /'traɪsɪkl/ n Dreirad nt

tried /traɪd/ see **try**

trifl|e /'traɪfl/ n Kleinigkeit f; (Culin) Trifle nt. **~ing** adj unbedeutend

trigger /'trɪgə(r)/ n Abzug m; (fig) Auslöser m ● vt **~ [off]** auslösen

trim /trɪm/ adj (**trimmer, trimmest**) gepflegt ● n (cut) Nachschneiden nt; (decoration) Verzierung f; (condition) Zustand m ● vt schneiden; (decorate) besetzen. **~ming** n Besatz m; **~mings** pl (accessories) Zubehör nt; (decorations) Verzierungen pl

trio /'triːəʊ/ n Trio nt

trip /trɪp/ n Reise f; (excursion) Ausflug m ● v (pt/pp **tripped**) ● vt **~ s.o. up** jdm ein Bein stellen ● vi stolpern (**on/over** über + acc)

tripe /traɪp/ n Kaldaunen pl; (nonsense) Quatsch m

triple /'trɪpl/ adj dreifach ● vt verdreifachen ● *vi* sich verdreifachen

triplets /'trɪplɪts/ *npl* Drillinge *pl*

triplicate /'trɪplɪkət/ *n* **in** ~ in dreifacher Ausfertigung

tripod /'traɪpɒd/ *n* Stativ *nt*

tripper /'trɪpə(r)/ *n* Ausflügler *m*

trite /traɪt/ *adj* banal

triumph /'traɪʌmf/ *n* Triumph *m*
● *vi* triumphieren (**over** über + *acc*).
~**ant** *adj* triumphierend

trivial /'trɪvɪəl/ *adj* belanglos. ~**ity** *n*
Belanglosigkeit *f*

trod, trodden *see* tread

trolley /'trɒlɪ/ *n* (*for food*) Servierwagen *m*; (*for shopping*) Einkaufswagen *m*; (*for luggage*) Kofferkuli *m*;
(*Amer: tram*) Straßenbahn *f*

trombone /trɒm'bəʊn/ *n* Posaune *f*

troop /truːp/ *n* Schar *f*; ~**s** *pl* Truppen *pl*

trophy /'trəʊfɪ/ *n* Trophäe *f*; (*in competition*) ≈ Pokal *m*

tropics /'trɒpɪks/ *npl* Tropen *pl*. ~**al**
adj tropisch; (*fruit*) Süd-

trot /trɒt/ *n* Trab *m* ● *vi* (*pt/pp* **trotted**) traben

trouble /'trʌbl/ *n* Ärger *m*; (*difficulties*) Schwierigkeiten *pl*; (*inconvenience*) Mühe *f*; (*conflict*) Unruhe *f*;
(*Med*) Beschwerden *pl*; (*Techn*) Probleme *pl*; **get into** ~ Ärger bekommen; **take** ~ sich (*dat*) Mühe geben
● *vt* (*disturb*) stören; (*worry*) beunruhigen ● *vi* sich bemühen. ~**-maker**
n Unruhestifter *m*. ~**some** *adj*
schwierig; (*flies, cough*) lästig

trough /trɒf/ *n* Trog *m*

troupe /truːp/ *n* Truppe *f*

trousers /'traʊzəz/ *npl* Hose *f*

trousseau /'truːsəʊ/ *n* Aussteuer *f*

trout /traʊt/ *n inv* Forelle *f*

trowel /'traʊəl/ *n* Kelle *f*

truant /'truːənt/ *n* **play** ~ die Schule
schwänzen

truce /truːs/ *n* Waffenstillstand *m*

truck /trʌk/ *n* Last[kraft]wagen *m*;
(*Rail*) Güterwagen *m*

trudge /trʌdʒ/ *vi* latschen

true /truː/ *adj* (**-r, -st**) wahr; (*loyal*)

treu; (*genuine*) echt; **come** ~ in Erfüllung gehen; **is that** ~**?** stimmt
das?

truly /'truːlɪ/ *adv* wirklich; (*faithfully*)
treu; **Yours** ~ mit freundlichen
Grüßen

trump /trʌmp/ *n* (*Cards*) Trumpf *m*
● *vt* übertrumpfen

trumpet /'trʌmpɪt/ *n* Trompete *f*.
~**er** *n* Trompeter *m*

truncheon /'trʌntʃn/ *n* Schlagstock *m*

trunk /trʌŋk/ *n* [Baum]stamm *m*;
(*body*) Rumpf *m*; (*of elephant*) Rüssel
m; (*for travelling*) [Übersee]koffer *m*;
(*Amer: of car*) Kofferraum *m*; ~**s** *pl*
Badehose *f*

trust /trʌst/ *n* Vertrauen *nt*; (*group
of companies*) Trust *m*; (*organization*)
Treuhandgesellschaft *f*; (*charitable*)
Stiftung *f* ● *vt* trauen (+ *dat*), vertrauen (+ *dat*); (*hope*) hoffen ● *vi* trauen (**in/to** auf + *acc*)

trustee /trʌs'tiː/ *n* Treuhänder *m*

'trust|ful /'trʌstfl/ *adj*, -ly *adv*, ~**ing**
adj vertrauensvoll. ~**worthy** *adj* vertrauenswürdig

truth /truːθ/ *n* (*pl* **-s** /truːðz/) Wahrheit *f*. ~**ful** *adj* ehrlich

try /traɪ/ *n* Versuch *m* ● *v* (*pt/pp*
tried) ● *vt* versuchen; (*sample, taste*)
probieren; (*be a strain on*) anstrengen; (*Jur*) vor Gericht stellen; verhandeln (*case*) ● *vi* versuchen; (*make an
effort*) sich bemühen. ~ **on** *vt* anprobieren; aufprobieren (*hat*). ~ **out** *vt*
ausprobieren

trying /'traɪɪŋ/ *adj* schwierig

T-shirt /'tiː-/ *n* T-Shirt *nt*

tub /tʌb/ *n* Kübel *m*; (*carton*) Becher
m; (*bath*) Wanne *f*

tuba /'tjuːbə/ *n* (*Mus*) Tuba *f*

tubby /'tʌbɪ/ *adj* rundlich

tube /tjuːb/ *n* Röhre *f*; (*pipe*) Rohr *nt*;
(*flexible*) Schlauch *m*; (*of toothpaste*)
Tube *f*; (*Rail*, 🚇) U-Bahn *f*

tuberculosis /tjuːbɜːkjʊ'ləʊsɪs/ *n*
Tuberkulose *f*

tubular /'tjuːbjʊlə(r)/ *adj* röhrenförmig

t

tuck /tʌk/ n Saum m; (decorative) Biese f ● vt (put) stecken. ~ **in** vt hineinstecken; ~ **s.o. in** or **up** jdn zudecken ● vi (🔲: eat) zulangen

Tuesday /'tjuːzdeɪ/ n Dienstag m

tuft /tʌft/ n Büschel nt

tug /tʌg/ n Ruck m; (Naut) Schleppdampfer m ● v (pt/pp **tugged**) ● vt ziehen ● vi zerren (**at** an + dat)

tuition /tjuːˈɪʃn/ n Unterricht m

tulip /'tjuːlɪp/ n Tulpe f

tumble /'tʌmbl/ n Sturz m ● vi fallen. ~**down** adj verfallen. ~**-drier** n Wäschetrockner m

tumbler /'tʌmblə(r)/ n Glas nt

tummy /'tʌmɪ/ n 🔲 Bauch m

tumour /'tjuːmə(r)/ n Tumor m

tumult /'tjuːmʌlt/ n Tumult m

tuna /'tjuːnə/ n Thunfisch m

tune /tjuːn/ n Melodie f; **out of** ~ (instrument) verstimmt ● vt stimmen; (Techn) einstellen. ~ **in** vt einstellen: ● vi ~ **in to a station** einen Sender einstellen. ~ **up** vi (Mus) stimmen

tuneful /'tjuːnfl/ adj melodisch

Tunisia /tjuːˈnɪzɪə/ n Tunesien nt

tunnel /'tʌnl/ n Tunnel m ● vi (pt/pp **tunnelled**) einen Tunnel graben

turban /'tɜːbən/ n Turban m

turbine /'tɜːbaɪn/ n Turbine f

turbulen|ce /'tɜːbjʊləns/ n Turbulenz f. ~**t** adj stürmisch

turf /tɜːf/ n Rasen m; (segment) Rasenstück nt

Turk /tɜːk/ n Türke m/Türkin f

turkey /'tɜːkɪ/ n Truthahn m

Turk|ey n die Türkei. ~**ish** adj türkisch

turmoil /'tɜːmɔɪl/ n Aufruhr m; (confusion) Durcheinander nt

turn /tɜːn/ n (rotation) Drehung f; (bend) Kurve f; (change of direction) Wende f; (Theat) Nummer f; (🔲: attack) Anfall m; **do s.o. a good** ~ jdm einen guten Dienst erweisen; **take** ~**s** sich abwechseln; **in** ~ der Reihe nach; **out of** ~ außer der Reihe; **it's your** ~ du bist an der Reihe ● vt drehen; (~ over) wenden; (reverse) umdrehen; (Techn) drechseln

(wood); ~ **the page** umblättern; ~ **the corner** um die Ecke biegen ● vi sich drehen; (~ round) sich umdrehen; (car:) wenden; (leaves:) sich färben: (weather:) umschlagen; (become) werden; ~ **right/left** nach rechts/ links abbiegen; ~ **to s.o.** sich an jdn wenden. ~ **away** vt abweisen ● vi sich abwenden. ~ **down** vt herunterschlagen (collar); herunterdrehen (heat, gas); leiser stellen (sound); (reject) ablehnen; abweisen (person). ~ **in** vt einschlagen (edges) ● vi (car:) einbiegen; (🔲: go to bed) ins Bett gehen. ~ **off** vt zudrehen (tap); ausschalten (light, radio); abstellen (water, gas, engine, machine) ● vi abbiegen. ~ **on** vt aufdrehen (tap); einschalten (light, radio); anstellen (water, gas, engine, machine). ~ **out** vt (expel) vertreiben; 🔲 hinauswerfen; ausschalten (light); abdrehen (gas); (produce) produzieren; (empty) ausleeren; [gründlich] aufräumen (room, cupboard) ● vi (go out) hinausgehen; (transpire) sich herausstellen. ~ **over** vt umdrehen. ~ **up** vt hochschlagen (collar); aufdrehen (heat, gas); lauter stellen (sound, radio) ● vi auftauchen

turning /'tɜːnɪŋ/ n Abzweigung f. ~**-point** n Wendepunkt m

turnip /'tɜːnɪp/ n weiße Rübe f

turn: ~**-out** n (of people) Beteiligung f. ~**over** n (Comm) Umsatz m; (of staff) Personalwechsel m. ~**pike** n (Amer) gebührenpflichtige Autobahn f. ~**table** n Drehscheibe f; (on record player) Plattenteller m. ~**-up** n [Hosen]aufschlag m

turquoise /'tɜːkwɔɪz/ adj türkis[farben] ● n (gem) Türkis m

turret /'tʌrɪt/ n Türmchen nt

turtle /'tɜːtl/ n Seeschildkröte f

tusk /tʌsk/ n Stoßzahn m

tutor /'tjuːtə(r)/ n [Privat]lehrer m

tuxedo /tʌkˈsiːdəʊ/ n (Amer) Smoking m

TV /tiːˈviː/ abbr television

tweed /twiːd/ n Tweed m

tweezers /'twiːzəz/ npl Pinzette f

501

twelfth | unaware

twelfth /twelfθ/ adj zwölfter(r,s)

twelve /twelv/ adj zwölf

twentieth /'twentɪɪθ/ adj zwanzigste(r,s)

twenty /'twentɪ/ adj zwanzig

twice /twaɪs/ adv zweimal

twig /twɪg/ n Zweig m

twilight /'twaɪ-/ n Dämmerlicht nt

twin /twɪn/ n Zwilling m ● attrib Zwillings-

twine /twaɪn/ n Bindfaden m

twinge /twɪndʒ/ n Stechen nt; ~ of conscience Gewissensbisse pl

twinkle /'twɪŋkl/ n Funkeln nt ● vi funkeln

twin 'town n Partnerstadt f

twirl /twɜːl/ vt/i herumwirbeln

twist /twɪst/ n Drehung f; (curve) Kurve f; (unexpected occurrence) überraschende Wendung f ● vt drehen; (distort) verdrehen; (🆃: swindle) beschummeln; ~ one's ankle sich (dat) den Knöchel verrenken ● vi sich drehen; (road:) sich winden. **~er** n 🆃 Schwindler m

twit /twɪt/ n 🆃 Trottel m

twitch /twɪtʃ/ n Zucken nt ● vi zucken

twitter /'twɪtə(r)/ n Zwitschern nt ● vi zwitschern

two /tuː/ adj zwei

two: **~-faced** adj falsch. **~-piece** adj zweiteilig. **~-way** adj **~-way traffic** Gegenverkehr m

tycoon /taɪ'kuːn/ n Magnat m

tying /'taɪɪŋ/ see **tie**

type /taɪp/ n Art f, Sorte f; (person) Typ m; (printing) Type f ● vt mit der Maschine schreiben, 🆃 tippen ● vi Maschine schreiben, 🆃 tippen. **~writer** n Schreibmaschine f. **~written** adj maschinegeschrieben

typical /'tɪpɪkl/ adj typisch (of für)

typify /'tɪpɪfaɪ/ vt (pt/pp -ied) typisch sein für

typing /'taɪpɪŋ/ n Maschineschreiben nt

typist /'taɪpɪst/ n Schreibkraft f

tyrannical /tɪ'rænɪkl/ adj tyrannisch

tyranny /'tɪrənɪ/ n Tyrannei f

tyrant /'taɪrənt/ n Tyrann m

tyre /'taɪə(r)/ n Reifen m

ugl|iness /'ʌglɪnɪs/ n Hässlichkeit f. **~y** adj hässlich; (nasty) übel

UK abbr **United Kingdom**

ulcer /'ʌlsə(r)/ n Geschwür nt

ultimate /'ʌltɪmət/ adj letzte(r,s); (final) endgültig; (fundamental) grundlegend, eigentlich. **~ly** adv schließlich

ultimatum /ʌltɪ'meɪtəm/ n Ultimatum nt

ultra'violet adj ultraviolett

umbrella /ʌm'brelə/ n [Regen]-schirm m

umpire /'ʌmpaɪə(r)/ n Schiedsrichter m ● vt/i Schiedsrichter sein (bei)

umpteen /ʌmp'tiːn/ adj 🆃 zig. **~th** adj 🆃 zigste(r,s)

un'able /ʌn-/ adj be ~ to do sth etw nicht tun können

una'bridged adj ungekürzt

unac'companied adj ohne Begleitung; (luggage) unbegleitet

unac'countable adj unerklärlich

unac'customed adj ungewohnt; be ~ to sth etw (acc) nicht gewohnt sein

un'aided adj ohne fremde Hilfe

unanimous /juː'nænɪməs/ adj einmütig; (vote, decision) einstimmig

un'armed adj unbewaffnet

unas'suming adj bescheiden

unat'tended adj unbeaufsichtigt

un'authorized adj unbefugt

una'voidable adj unvermeidlich

una'ware adj be ~ of sth sich (dat) etw (gen) nicht bewusst sein. **~s** adv catch s.o. ~s jdn überraschen

t

u

un'bearable *adj*, **-bly** *adv* unerträglich

unbeat|able /ʌn'biːtəbl/ *adj* unschlagbar. **~en** *adj* ungeschlagen; (*record*) ungebrochen

unbe'lievable *adj* unglaublich

un'biased *adj* unvoreingenommen

un'block *vt* frei machen

un'bolt *vt* aufriegeln

un'breakable *adj* unzerbrechlich

un'button *vt* aufknöpfen

uncalled-for /ʌn'kɔːldfɔː(r)/ *adj* unangebracht

un'canny *adj* unheimlich

un'ceasing *adj* unaufhörlich

un'certain *adj* (*doubtful*) ungewiss; (*origins*) unbestimmt; **be ~** nicht sicher sein. **~ty** *n* Ungewissheit *f*

un'changed *adj* unverändert

un'charitable *adj* lieblos

uncle /'ʌŋkl/ *n* Onkel *m*

Uncle Sam Eine Bezeichnung für die USA und ihre Einwohner. Meist dargestellt durch einen mit Frack und Zylinder in den Farben und mit den Sternen der Nationalflagge bekleideten hageren Mann mit weißen Haaren und Backenbart. Die Bezeichnung ist besonders durch das Poster von 1917 zur Rekrutierung von Soldaten *"I want you"* bekannnt geworden.

---

un'comforta|ble *adj*, **-bly** *adv* unbequem; **feel ~** (*fig*) sich nicht wohl fühlen

un'common *adj* ungewöhnlich

un'compromising *adj* kompromisslos

uncon'ditional *adj*, **~ly** *adv* bedingungslos

un'conscious *adj* bewusstlos; (*unintended*) unbewusst; **be ~ of sth** sich (*dat*) etw (*gen*) nicht bewusst sein. **~ly** *adv* unbewusst

uncon'ventional *adj* unkonventionell

unco'operative *adj* nicht hilfsbereit

un'cork *vt* entkorken

uncouth /ʌn'kuːθ/ *adj* ungehobelt

un'cover *vt* aufdecken

unde'cided *adj* unentschlossen; (*not settled*) nicht entschieden

undeniable /ʌndɪ'naɪəbl/ *adj*, **-bly** *adv* unbestreitbar

under /'ʌndə(r)/ *prep* unter (+ *dat/acc*); **~ it** darunter; **~ there** da drunter; **~ repair** in Reparatur; **~ construction** im Bau; **~ age** minderjährig ● *adv* darunter

'undercarriage *n* (*Aviat*) Fahrwerk *nt*, Fahrgestell *nt*

'underclothes *npl* Unterwäsche *f*

under'cover *adj* geheim

'undercurrent *n* Unterströmung *f*; (*fig*) Unterton *m*

'underdog *n* Unterlegene(r) *m*

under'done *adj* nicht gar; (*rare*) nicht durchgebraten

under'estimate *vt* unterschätzen

under'fed *adj* unterernährt

under'foot *adv* am Boden

under'go *vt* (*pt* **-went**, *pp* **-gone**) durchmachen; sich unterziehen (+ *dat*) (*operation, treatment*)

under'graduate *n* Student(in) *m*(*f*)

under'ground[1] *adv* unter der Erde; (*mining*) unter Tage

'underground[2] *adj* unterirdisch; (*secret*) Untergrund- ● *n* (*railway*) U-Bahn *f*. **~ car park** *n* Tiefgarage *f*

'undergrowth *n* Unterholz *nt*

'underhand *adj* hinterhältig

under'lie *vt* (*pt* **-lay**, *pp* **-lain**, *pres p* **-lying**) zugrunde liegen (+ *dat*)

under'line *vt* unterstreichen

under'lying *adj* eigentlich

under'mine *vt* (*fig*) unterminieren, untergraben

underneath /ʌndə'niːθ/ *prep* unter (+ *dat/acc*) ● *adv* darunter

'underpants *npl* Unterhose *f*

'underpass *n* Unterführung *f*

under'privileged *adj* unterprivilegiert

under'rate *vt* unterschätzen

'undershirt n (Amer) Unterhemd nt

under'stand vt/i (pt/pp **-stood**) verstehen; **I ~ that ...** (have heard) ich habe gehört, dass ... **~able** adj verständlich. **~ably** adv verständlicherweise

under'standing adj verständnisvoll ● n Verständnis nt; (agreement) Vereinbarung f; **reach an ~** sich verständigen

'understatement n Untertreibung f

under'take vt (pt **-took**, pp **-taken**) unternehmen; **~ to do sth** sich verpflichten, etw zu tun

'undertaker n Leichenbestatter m; [firm of] **~s** Bestattungsinstitut n

under'taking n Unternehmen nt; (promise) Versprechen nt

'undertone n (fig) Unterton m; **in an ~** mit gedämpfter Stimme

under'value vt unterbewerten

'underwater[1] adj Unterwasser-

under'water[2] adv unter Wasser

'underwear n Unterwäsche f

under'weight adj untergewichtig; **be ~** Untergewicht haben

'underworld n Unterwelt f

unde'sirable adj unerwünscht

un'dignified adj würdelos

un'do vt (pt **-did**, pp **-done**) aufmachen; (fig) ungeschehen machen

un'done adj offen; (not accomplished) unerledigt

un'doubted adj unzweifelhaft. **~ly** adv zweifellos

un'dress vt ausziehen; **get ~ed** sich ausziehen ● vi sich ausziehen

un'due adj übermäßig

und'uly adv übermäßig

un'earth vt ausgraben; (fig) zutage bringen. **~ly** adj unheimlich; **at an ~ly hour** 🄸 in aller Herrgottsfrühe

un'easy adj unbehaglich

uneco'nomic adj, **-ally** adv unwirtschaftlich

unem'ployed adj arbeitslos ● npl **the ~** die Arbeitslosen

unem'ployment n Arbeitslosigkeit f

un'ending adj endlos

un'equal adj unterschiedlich; (struggle) ungleich. **~ly** adv ungleichmäßig

unequivocal /ʌnɪˈkwɪvəkl/ adj eindeutig

un'ethical adj unmoralisch; **be ~** gegen das Berufsethos verstoßen

un'even adj uneben; (unequal) ungleich; (not regular) ungleichmäßig; (number) ungerade

unex'pected adj unerwartet

un'fair adj ungerecht, unfair. **~ness** n Ungerechtigkeit f

un'faithful adj untreu

unfa'miliar adj ungewohnt; (unknown) unbekannt

un'fasten vt aufmachen; (detach) losmachen

un'favourable adj ungünstig

un'feeling adj gefühllos

un'fit adj ungeeignet; (incompetent) unfähig; (Sport) nicht fit; **~ for work** arbeitsunfähig

un'fold vt auseinander falten, entfalten; (spread out) ausbreiten ● vi sich entfalten

unfore'seen adj unvorhergesehen

unforgettable /ʌnfəˈgetəbl/ adj unvergesslich

unforgivable /ʌnfəˈgɪvəbl/ adj unverzeihlich

un'fortunate adj unglücklich; (unfavourable) ungünstig; (regrettable) bedauerlich; **be ~** (person:) Pech haben. **~ly** adv leider

un'founded adj unbegründet

unfurl /ʌnˈfɜːl/ vt entrollen

un'furnished adj unmöbliert

ungainly /ʌnˈgeɪnlɪ/ adj unbeholfen

un'grateful adj undankbar

un'happiness n Kummer m

un'happy adj unglücklich; (not content) unzufrieden

un'harmed adj unverletzt

un'healthy adj ungesund

un'hurt adj unverletzt

u

unification /juːnɪfɪˈkeɪʃn/ n Einigung f

uniform /ˈjuːnɪfɔːm/ adj einheitlich ● n Uniform f

unify /ˈjuːnɪfaɪ/ vt (pt/pp -ied) einigen

uni'lateral /juːnɪ-/ adj einseitig

uni'maginable adj unvorstellbar

unim'portant adj unwichtig

unin'habited adj unbewohnt

unin'tentional adj unabsichtlich

union /ˈjuːnɪən/ n Vereinigung f; (Pol) Union f; (trade ~) Gewerkschaft f

unique /juːˈniːk/ adj einzigartig. ~ly adv einmalig

unison /ˈjuːnɪsn/ n in ~ einstimmig

unit /ˈjuːnɪt/ n Einheit f; (Math) Einer m; (of furniture) Teil nt, Element nt

unite /juːˈnaɪt/ vt vereinigen ● vi sich vereinigen

united /juːˈnaɪtɪd/ adj einig. U~ 'Kingdom n Vereinigtes Königreich nt. U~ 'Nations n Vereinte Nationen pl. U~ States [of America] n Vereinigte Staaten pl [von Amerika]

unity /ˈjuːnətɪ/ n Einheit f; (harmony) Einigkeit f

universal /juːnɪˈvɜːsl/ adj allgemein

universe /ˈjuːnɪvɜːs/ n [Welt]all nt, Universum nt

university /juːnɪˈvɜːsətɪ/ n Universität f ● attrib Universitäts-

un'just adj ungerecht

un'kind adj unfreundlich; (harsh) hässlich

un'known adj unbekannt

un'lawful adj gesetzwidrig

unleaded /ʌnˈledɪd/ adj bleifrei

un'leash vt (fig) entfesseln

unless /ənˈles/ conj wenn ... nicht; ~ I am mistaken wenn ich mich nicht irre

un'like prep im Gegensatz zu (+ dat)

un'likely adj unwahrscheinlich

un'limited adj unbegrenzt

un'load vt entladen; ausladen (luggage)

un'lock vt aufschließen

un'lucky adj unglücklich; (day, number) Unglücks-; be ~ Pech haben; (thing:) Unglück bringen

un'married adj unverheiratet. ~ 'mother n ledige Mutter f

un'mask vt (fig) entlarven

unmistakable /ʌnmɪˈsteɪkəbl/ adj, -bly adv unverkennbar

un'natural adj unnatürlich; (not normal) nicht normal

un'necessary adj, -ily adv unnötig

un'noticed adj unbemerkt

unob'tainable adj nicht erhältlich

unob'trusive adj unaufdringlich; (thing) unauffällig

unof'ficial adj inoffiziell

un'pack vt/i auspacken

un'paid adj unbezahlt

un'pleasant adj unangenehm

un'plug vt (pt/pp -plugged) den Stecker herausziehen von

un'popular adj unbeliebt

un'precedented adj beispiellos

unpre'dictable adj unberechenbar

unpre'pared adj nicht vorbereitet

unpre'tentious adj bescheiden

un'profitable adj unrentabel

un'qualified adj unqualifiziert; (fig: absolute) uneingeschränkt

un'questionable adj unbezweifelbar; (right) unbestreitbar

unravel /ʌnˈrævl/ vt (pt/pp -ravelled) entwirren; (Knitting) aufziehen

un'real adj unwirklich

un'reasonable adj unvernünftig

unre'lated adj unzusammenhängend; be ~ nicht verwandt sein; (events:) nicht miteinander zusammenhängen

unre'liable adj unzuverlässig

un'rest n Unruhen pl

un'rivalled adj unübertroffen

un'roll vt aufrollen ● vi sich aufrollen

unruly /ʌnˈruːlɪ/ adj ungebärdig

un'safe adj nicht sicher

unsatis'factory adj unbefriedigend

un'savoury *adj* unangenehm; (*fig*) unerfreulich

unscathed /ʌnˈskeɪðd/ *adj* unversehrt

un'screw *vt* abschrauben

un'scrupulous *adj* skrupellos

un'seemly *adj* unschicklich

un'selfish *adj* selbstlos

un'settled *adj* ungeklärt; (*weather*) unbeständig; (*bill*) unbezahlt

unshakeable /ʌnˈʃeɪkəbl/ *adj* unerschütterlich

unshaven /ʌnˈʃeɪvn/ *adj* unrasiert

unsightly /ʌnˈsaɪtlɪ/ *adj* unansehnlich

un'skilled *adj* ungelernt; (*work*) unqualifiziert

un'sociable *adj* ungesellig

unso'phisticated *adj* einfach

un'sound *adj* krank, nicht gesund; (*building*) nicht sicher; (*advice*) unzuverlässig; (*reasoning*) nicht stichhaltig

un'stable *adj* nicht stabil; (*mentally*) labil

un'steady *adj*, **-ily** *adv* unsicher; (*wobbly*) wackelig

un'stuck *adj* **come ~** sich lösen; (🔢: *fail*) scheitern

unsuc'cessful *adj* erfolglos; **be ~** keinen Erfolg haben

un'suitable *adj* ungeeignet; (*inappropriate*) unpassend; (*for weather, activity*) unzweckmäßig

unthinkable /ʌnˈθɪŋkəbl/ *adj* unvorstellbar

un'tidiness *n* Unordentlichkeit *f*

un'tidy *adj*, **-ily** *adv* unordentlich

un'tie *vt* aufbinden; losbinden (*person, boat, horse*)

until /ənˈtɪl/ *prep* bis (+ *acc*); **not ~** erst; **~ the evening** bis zum Abend ● *conj* bis; **not ~** erst wenn; (*in past*) erst als

un'told *adj* unermesslich

un'true *adj* unwahr; **that's ~** das ist nicht wahr

unused¹ /ʌnˈjuːzd/ *adj* unbenutzt; (*not utilized*) ungenutzt

unused² /ʌnˈjuːst/ *adj* **be ~ to sth**

etw nicht gewohnt sein

un'usual *adj* ungewöhnlich

un'veil *vt* enthüllen

un'wanted *adj* unerwünscht

un'welcome *adj* unwillkommen

un'well *adj* **be** or **feel ~** sich nicht wohl fühlen

unwieldy /ʌnˈwiːldɪ/ *adj* sperrig

un'willing *adj* widerwillig; **be ~ to do sth** etw nicht tun wollen

un'wind *v* (*pt/pp* **unwound**) ● *vt* abwickeln ● *vi* sich abwickeln; (🔢: *relax*) sich entspannen

un'wise *adj* unklug

un'worthy *adj* unwürdig

un'wrap *vt* (*pt/pp* **-wrapped**) auswickeln; auspacken (*present*)

un'written *adj* ungeschrieben

up /ʌp/ *adv* oben; (*with movement*) nach oben; (*not in bed*) auf; (*road*) aufgerissen; (*price*) gestiegen; **be up for sale** zu verkaufen sein; **up there** da oben; **up to** (*as far as*) bis; **time's up** die Zeit ist um; **what's up?** 🔢 was ist los? **what's he up to?** 🔢 was hat er vor? **I don't feel up to it** ich fühle mich dem nicht gewachsen; **go up** hinaufgehen; **come up** heraufkommen ● *prep* **be up on sth** [oben] auf etw (*dat*) sein; **up the mountain** oben am Berg; (*movement*) den Berg hinauf; **be up the tree** oben im Baum sein; **up the road** die Straße entlang; **up the river** stromaufwärts; **go up the stairs** die Treppe hinaufgehen

'upbringing *n* Erziehung *f*

up'date *vt* auf den neuesten Stand bringen

up'grade *vt* aufstufen

upheaval /ʌpˈhiːvl/ *n* Unruhe *f*; (*Pol*) Umbruch *m*

up'hill *adj* (*fig*) mühsam ● *adv* bergauf

up'hold *vt* (*pt/pp* **upheld**) unterstützen; bestätigen (*verdict*)

upholster /ʌpˈhəʊlstə(r)/ *vt* polstern. **~y** *n* Polsterung *f*

'upkeep *n* Unterhalt *m*

up'market *adj* anspruchsvoll

u

upon /ə'pɒn/ *prep* auf (+ *dat/acc*)

upper /'ʌpə(r)/ *adj* obere(r,s); (*deck, jaw, lip*) Ober-; **have the ~ hand** die Oberhand haben ● *n* (*of shoe*) Obermaterial *nt*

upper class *n* Oberschicht *f*

'upright *adj* aufrecht

'uprising *n* Aufstand *m*

'uproar *n* Aufruhr *m*

up'set¹ *vt* (*pt/pp* upset, *pres p* upsetting) umstoßen; (*spill*) verschütten; durcheinander bringen (*plan*); (*distress*) erschüttern; (*food:*) nicht bekommen (+ *dat*); **get ~ about sth** sich über etw (*acc*) aufregen

'upset² *n* Aufregung *f*; **have a stomach ~** einen verdorbenen Magen haben

'upshot *n* Ergebnis *nt*

upside 'down *adv* verkehrt herum; **turn ~** umdrehen

up'stairs¹ *adv* oben; (*go*) nach oben

'upstairs² *adj* im Obergeschoss

'upstart *n* Emporkömmling *m*

up'stream *adv* stromaufwärts

'uptake *n* **slow on the ~** schwer von Begriff; **be quick on the ~** schnell begreifen

'upturn *n* Aufschwung *m*

upward /'ʌpwəd/ *adj* nach oben; (*movement*) Aufwärts-; **~ slope** Steigung *f* ● *adv* **~[s]** aufwärts, nach oben

uranium /jʊ'reɪnɪəm/ *n* Uran *nt*

urban /'ɜːbən/ *adj* städtisch

urge /ɜːdʒ/ *n* Trieb *m*, Drang *m* ● *vt* drängen; **~ on** antreiben

urgen|cy /'ɜːdʒənsɪ/ *n* Dringlichkeit *f*. **~t** *adj* dringend

urine /'jʊərɪn/ *n* Urin *m*, Harn *m*

us /ʌs/ *pron* uns; **it's us** wir sind es

US[A] *abbr* USA *pl*

usable /'juːzəbl/ *adj* brauchbar

usage /'juːsɪdʒ/ *n* Brauch *m*; (*of word*) [Sprach]gebrauch *m*

use¹ /juːs/ *n* (*see* use²) Benutzung *f*; Verwendung *f*; Gebrauch *m*; **be (of) no ~** nichts nützen; **it is no ~** es

hat keinen Zweck; **what's the ~?** wozu?

use² /juːz/ *vt* benutzen (*implement, room, lift*); verwenden (*ingredient, method, book, money*); gebrauchen (*words, force, brains*); **~ [up]** aufbrauchen

used¹ /juːzd/ *adj* gebraucht; (*towel*) benutzt; (*car*) Gebraucht-

used² /juːst/ *pt* **be ~ to sth** an etw (*acc*) gewöhnt sein; **get ~ to** sich gewöhnen an (+ *acc*); **he ~ to say** er hat immer gesagt; **he ~ to live here** er hat früher hier gewohnt

useful /'juːsfl/ *adj* nützlich. **~ness** *n* Nützlichkeit *f*

useless /'juːslɪs/ *adj* nutzlos; (*not usable*) unbrauchbar; (*pointless*) zwecklos

user /'juːzə(r)/ *n* Benutzer(in) *m(f)*

usher /'ʌʃə(r)/ *n* Platzanweiser *m*; (*in court*) Gerichtsdiener *m*

usherette /ʌʃə'ret/ *n* Platzanweiserin *f*

USSR *abbr* (*History*) UdSSR *f*

usual /'juːʒʊəl/ *adj* üblich. **~ly** *adv* gewöhnlich

utensil /juː'tensl/ *n* Gerät *nt*

utility /juː'tɪlətɪ/ *adj* Gebrauchs-

utilize /'juːtɪlaɪz/ *vt* nutzen

utmost /'ʌtməʊst/ *adj* äußerste(r,s), größte(r,s) ● *n* **do one's ~** sein Möglichstes tun

utter¹ /'ʌtə(r)/ *adj* völlig

utter² *vt* von sich geben (*sigh, sound*); sagen (*word*)

U-turn /'juː-/ *n* (*fig*) Kehrtwendung *f*; **'no ~s'** (*Auto*) 'Wenden verboten'

Vv

vacan|cy /'veɪkənsɪ/ *n* (*job*) freie Stelle *f*; (*room*) freies Zimmer *nt*; **'no ~cies'** 'belegt'. **~t** *adj* frei; (*look*) [gedanken]leer

vacate /və'keɪt/ *vt* räumen

vacation /vəˈkeɪʃn/ n (Univ & Amer) Ferien pl

vaccinat|e /ˈvæksɪmeɪt/ vt impfen. ~**ion** n Impfung f

vaccine /ˈvæksiːn/ n Impfstoff m

vacuum /ˈvækjʊəm/ n Vakuum nt, luftleerer Raum m ● vt saugen. ~ **cleaner** n Staubsauger m

vagina /vəˈdʒaɪnə/ n (Anat) Scheide f

vague /veɪɡ/ adj (-r,-st) vage; (outline) verschwommen

vain /veɪn/ adj (-er,-est) eitel; (hope, attempt) vergeblich; **in** ~ vergeblich. ~**ly** adv vergeblich

valiant /ˈvælɪənt/ adj tapfer

valid /ˈvælɪd/ adj gültig; (claim) berechtigt; (argument) stichhaltig; (reason) triftig. ~**ity** n Gültigkeit f

valley /ˈvælɪ/ n Tal nt

valour /ˈvælə(r)/ n Tapferkeit f

valuable /ˈvæljʊəbl/ adj wertvoll. ~**s** npl Wertsachen pl

valuation /væljʊˈeɪʃn/ n Schätzung f

value /ˈvæljuː/ n Wert m; (usefulness) Nutzen m ● vt schätzen. ~ **'added tax** n Mehrwertsteuer f

valve /vælv/ n Ventil nt; (Anat) Klappe f; (Electr) Röhre f

van /væn/ n Lieferwagen m

vandal /ˈvændl/ n Rowdy m. ~**ism** n mutwillige Zerstörung f. ~**ize** vt demolieren

vanilla /vəˈnɪlə/ n Vanille f

vanish /ˈvænɪʃ/ vi verschwinden

vanity /ˈvænətɪ/ n Eitelkeit f

vapour /ˈveɪpə(r)/ n Dampf m

variable /ˈveərɪəbl/ adj unbeständig; (Math) variabel; (adjustable) regulierbar

variant /ˈveərɪənt/ n Variante f

variation /veərɪˈeɪʃn/ n Variation f; (difference) Unterschied m

varied /ˈveərɪd/ adj vielseitig; (diet:) abwechslungsreich

variety /vəˈraɪətɪ/ n Abwechslung f; (quantity) Vielfalt f; (Comm) Auswahl f; (type) Art f; (Bot) Abart f; (Theat) Varieté nt

various /ˈveərɪəs/ adj verschieden. ~**ly** adv unterschiedlich

varnish /ˈvɑːnɪʃ/ n Lack m ● vt lackieren

vary /ˈveərɪ/ v (pt/pp -ied) ● vi sich ändern; (be different) verschieden sein ● vt [ver]ändern; (add variety to) abwechslungsreicher gestalten

vase /vɑːz/ n Vase f

vast /vɑːst/ adj riesig; (expanse) weit. ~**ly** adv gewaltig

vat /væt/ n Bottich m

VAT /viːeɪˈtiː, væt/ abbr (value added tax) Mehrwertsteuer f, MwSt.

vault¹ /vɔːlt/ n (roof) Gewölbe nt; (in bank) Tresor m; (tomb) Gruft f

vault² n Sprung m ● vt/i ~ **[over]** springen über (+ acc)

VDU abbr (visual display unit) Bildschirmgerät nt

veal /viːl/ n Kalbfleisch nt ● attrib Kalbs-

veer /vɪə(r)/ vi sich drehen; (Auto) ausscheren

vegetable /ˈvedʒtəbl/ n Gemüse nt; ~**s** pl Gemüse nt ● attrib Gemüse-; (oil, fat) Pflanzen-

vegetarian /vedʒɪˈteərɪən/ adj vegetarisch ● n Vegetarier(in) m(f)

vegetation /vedʒɪˈteɪʃn/ n Vegetation f

vehement /ˈviːəmənt/ adj heftig

vehicle /ˈviːɪkl/ n Fahrzeug nt

veil /veɪl/ n Schleier m ● vt verschleiern

vein /veɪn/ n Ader f; (mood) Stimmung f; (manner) Art f

velocity /vɪˈlɒsətɪ/ n Geschwindigkeit f

velvet /ˈvelvɪt/ n Samt m

vending-machine /ˈvendɪŋ-/ n [Verkaufs]automat m

vendor /ˈvendə(r)/ n Verkäufer(in) m(f)

veneer /vəˈnɪə(r)/ n Furnier nt; (fig) Tünche f. ~**ed** adj furniert

venerable /ˈvenərəbl/ adj ehrwürdig

Venetian /vəˈniːʃn/ adj venezia-

v

nisch. **v~ blind** n Jalousie f

vengeance /'vendʒəns/ n Rache f; **with a ~** gewaltig

Venice /'venɪs/ n Venedig nt

venison /'venɪsn/ n (Culin) Reh-[fleisch] nt

venom /'venəm/ n Gift nt; (fig) Hass m. **~ous** adj giftig

vent /vent/ n Öffnung f

ventilat|e /'ventɪleɪt/ vt belüften. **~ion** n Belüftung f; (installation) Lüftung f. **~or** n Lüftungsvorrichtung f; (Med) Beatmungsgerät nt

ventriloquist /ven'trɪləkwɪst/ n Bauchredner m

venture /'ventʃə(r)/ n Unternehmung f ● vt wagen ● vi sich wagen

venue /'venjuː/ n (for event) Veranstaltungsort m

veranda /və'rændə/ n Veranda f

verb /vɜːb/ n Verb nt. **~al** adj mündlich; (Gram) verbal

verbose /vɜː'bəʊs/ adj weitschweifig

verdict /'vɜːdɪkt/ n Urteil nt

verge /vɜːdʒ/ n Rand m ● vi ~ **on** (fig) grenzen an (+ acc)

verify /'verɪfaɪ/ vt (pt/pp -ied) überprüfen; (confirm) bestätigen

vermin /'vɜːmɪn/ n Ungeziefer nt

vermouth /'vɜːməθ/ n Wermut m

versatil|e /'vɜːsətaɪl/ adj vielseitig. **~ity** n Vielseitigkeit f

verse /vɜːs/ n Strophe f; (of Bible) Vers m; (poetry) Lyrik f

version /'vɜːʃn/ n Version f; (translation) Übersetzung f; (model) Modell nt

versus /'vɜːsəs/ prep gegen (+ acc)

vertical /'vɜːtɪkl/ adj senkrecht ● n Senkrechte f

vertigo /'vɜːtɪgəʊ/ n (Med) Schwindel m

verve /vɜːv/ n Schwung m

very /'verɪ/ adv sehr; **~ much** sehr; (quantity) sehr viel; **~ probably** höchstwahrscheinlich; **at the ~ most** allerhöchstens ● adj (mere) bloß; **the ~ first** der/die/das allererste; **the ~ thing** genau das

Richtige; **at the ~ end/beginning** ganz am Ende/Anfang; **only a ~ little** nur ein ganz kleines bisschen

vessel /'vesl/ n Schiff nt; (receptacle & Anat) Gefäß nt

vest /vest/ n [Unter]hemd nt; (Amer: waistcoat) Weste f

vestige /'vestɪdʒ/ n Spur f

vestry /'vestrɪ/ n Sakristei f

vet /vet/ n Tierarzt m /-ärztin f ● vt (pt/pp vetted) überprüfen

veteran /'vetərən/ n Veteran m

veterinary /'vetərɪnərɪ/ adj tierärztlich. **~ surgeon** n Tierarzt m /-ärztin f

veto /'viːtəʊ/ n (pl -es) Veto nt

VHF abbr (very high frequency) UKW

via /'vaɪə/ prep über (+ acc)

viable /'vaɪəbl/ adj lebensfähig; (fig) realisierbar; (firm) rentabel

viaduct /'vaɪədʌkt/ n Viadukt nt

vibrat|e /vaɪ'breɪt/ vi vibrieren. **~ion** n Vibrieren nt

vicar /'vɪkə(r)/ n Pfarrer m. **~age** n Pfarrhaus nt

vice[1] /vaɪs/ n Laster nt

vice[2] n (Techn) Schraubstock m

vice[3] adj Vize-; **~ 'chairman** stellvertretender Vorsitzender m

vice versa /vaɪsɪ'vɜːsə/ adv umgekehrt

vicinity /vɪ'sɪnətɪ/ n Umgebung f; **in the ~ of** in der Nähe von

vicious /'vɪʃəs/ adj boshaft; (animal) bösartig

victim /'vɪktɪm/ n Opfer nt. **~ize** vt schikanieren

victor /'vɪktə(r)/ n Sieger m

victor|ious /vɪk'tɔːrɪəs/ adj siegreich. **~y** n Sieg m

video /'vɪdɪəʊ/ n Video nt; (recorder) Videorecorder m ● attrib

video: ~ cas'sette n Videokassette f. **~ game** n Videospiel nt. **~ recorder** n Videorecorder m

Vienn|a /vɪ'enə/ n Wien nt. **~ese** adj Wiener

view /vjuː/ n Sicht f; (scene) Aussicht

f, Blick m; (picture, opinion) Ansicht f;
in my ∼ meiner Ansicht nach; **in** ∼
of angesichts (+ gen); **be on** ∼ besichtigt werden können ● vt sich
(dat) ansehen; besichtigen (house);
(consider) betrachten ● vi (TV) fernsehen. ∼**er** n (TV) Zuschauer(in) m(f)

view: ∼**finder** n (Phot) Sucher m.
∼**point** n Standpunkt m

vigilan|ce /'vɪdʒɪləns/ n Wachsamkeit f. ∼**t** adj wachsam

vigorous /'vɪɡərəs/ adj kräftig; (fig)
heftig

vigour /'vɪɡə(r)/ n Kraft f; (fig) Heftigkeit f

vile /vaɪl/ adj abscheulich

villa /'vɪlə/ n (for holidays) Ferienhaus nt

village /'vɪlɪdʒ/ n Dorf nt. ∼**r** n
Dorfbewohner(in) m(f)

villain /'vɪlən/ n Schurke m; (in story)
Bösewicht m

vindicat|e /'vɪndɪkeɪt/ vt rechtfertigen. ∼**ion** n Rechtfertigung f

vindictive /vɪn'dɪktɪv/ adj nachtragend

vine /vaɪn/ n Weinrebe f

vinegar /'vɪnɪɡə(r)/ n Essig m

vineyard /'vɪnjɑːd/ n Weinberg m

vintage /'vɪntɪdʒ/ adj erlesen ● n
(year) Jahrgang m. ∼ '**car** n Oldtimer m

viola /vɪ'əʊlə/ n (Mus) Bratsche f

violat|e /'vaɪəleɪt/ vt verletzen;
(break) brechen; (disturb) stören; (defile) schänden. ∼**ion** n Verletzung f;
Schändung f

violen|ce /'vaɪələns/ n Gewalt f;
(fig) Heftigkeit f. ∼**t** adj gewalttätig;
(fig) heftig. ∼**tly** adv brutal; (fig)
heftig

violet /'vaɪələt/ adj violett ● n
(flower) Veilchen nt

violin /vaɪə'lɪn/ n Geige f, Violine f.
∼**ist** n Geiger(in) m(f)

VIP abbr (**very important person**)
Prominente(r) m/f

viper /'vaɪpə(r)/ n Kreuzotter f

virgin /'vɜːdʒɪn/ adj unberührt ● n
Jungfrau f. ∼**ity** n Unschuld f

viril|e /'vɪraɪl/ adj männlich. ∼**ity** n
Männlichkeit f

virtual /'vɜːtjʊəl/ adj a ∼ ... praktisch ein ... ∼**ly** adv praktisch

virtu|e /'vɜːtjuː/ n Tugend f; (advantage) Vorteil m; **by** or **in** ∼**e of** auf
Grund (+ gen)

virtuoso /vɜːtjʊ'əʊzəʊ/ n (pl -**si**
/-ziː/) Virtuose m

virtuous /'vɜːtjʊəs/ adj tugendhaft

virus /'vaɪərəs/ n Virus nt

visa /'viːzə/ n Visum nt

visibility /vɪzə'bɪlətɪ/ n Sichtbarkeit
f; (range) Sichtweite f

visi|ble /'vɪzəbl/ adj, -**bly** adv sichtbar

vision /'vɪʒn/ n Vision f; (sight) Sehkraft f; (foresight) Weitblick m

visit /'vɪzɪt/ n Besuch m ● vt besuchen; besichtigen (town, building).
∼**or** n Besucher(in) m(f); (in hotel)
Gast m; **have** ∼**ors** Besuch haben

visor /'vaɪzə(r)/ n Schirm m; (Auto)
[Sonnen]blende f

vista /'vɪstə/ n Aussicht f

visual /'vɪzjʊəl/ adj visuell. ∼ **dis-
'play unit** n Bildschirmgerät nt

visualize /'vɪzjʊəlaɪz/ vt sich (dat)
vorstellen

vital /'vaɪtl/ adj unbedingt notwendig; (essential to life) lebenswichtig.
∼**ity** n Vitalität f. ∼**ly** adv äußerst

vitamin /'vɪtəmɪn/ n Vitamin nt

vivaci|ous /vɪ'veɪʃəs/ adj lebhaft.
∼**ty** n Lebhaftigkeit f

vivid /'vɪvɪd/ adj lebhaft; (description)
lebendig

vocabulary /və'kæbjʊlərɪ/ n Wortschatz m; (list) Vokabelverzeichnis nt;
learn ∼ Vokabeln lernen

vocal /'vəʊkl/ adj stimmlich; (vociferous) lautstark

vocalist /'vəʊkəlɪst/ n Sänger(in)
m(f)

vocation /və'keɪʃn/ n Berufung f.
∼**al** adj Berufs-

vociferous /və'sɪfərəs/ adj lautstark

vodka /'vɒdkə/ n Wodka m

vogue /vəʊɡ/ n Mode f

V

voice /vɔɪs/ n Stimme f ● vt zum
Ausdruck bringen. ~ **mail** n Voice-
mail f

void /vɔɪd/ adj leer; (not valid) ungültig; ~ **of** ohne ● n Leere f

volatile /'vɒlətaɪl/ adj flüchtig; (person) sprunghaft

volcanic /vɒl'kænɪk/ adj vulkanisch

volcano /vɒl'keɪnəʊ/ n Vulkan m

volley /'vɒlɪ/ n (of gunfire) Salve f;
(Tennis) Volley m

volt /vəʊlt/ n Volt nt. ~**age** n (Electr)
Spannung f

voluble /'vɒljʊbl/ adj, -**bly** adv red-
selig; (protest) wortreich

volume /'vɒljuːm/ n (book) Band m;
(Geometry) Rauminhalt m; (amount)
Ausmaß nt; (Radio, TV) Lautstärke f

voluntary /'vɒləntərɪ/ adj, -**ily** adv
freiwillig

volunteer /vɒlən'tɪə(r)/ n Freiwilli-
ge(r) m/f ● vt anbieten; geben (information) ● vi sich freiwillig melden

vomit /'vɒmɪt/ n Erbrochene(s) nt
● vt erbrechen ● vi sich übergeben

voracious /və'reɪʃəs/ adj gefräßig;
(appetite) unbändig

vot|e /vəʊt/ n Stimme f; (ballot) Ab-
stimmung f; (right) Wahlrecht nt ● vi
abstimmen; (in election) wählen. ~**er**
n Wähler(in) m(f)

vouch /vaʊtʃ/ vi ~ **for** sich verbürgen für. ~**er** n Gutschein m

vowel /'vaʊəl/ n Vokal m

voyage /'vɔɪɪdʒ/ n Seereise f; (in
space) Reise f, Flug m

vulgar /'vʌlgə(r)/ adj vulgär, ordinär.
~**ity** n Vulgarität f

vulnerable /'vʌlnərəbl/ adj ver-
wundbar

vulture /'vʌltʃə(r)/ n Geier m

Ww

wad /wɒd/ n Bausch m; (bundle) Bündel nt. ~**ding** n Wattierung f

waddle /'wɒdl/ vi watscheln

wade /weɪd/ vi waten

wafer /'weɪfə(r)/ n Waffel f

waffle[1] /'wɒfl/ vi 🇬🇧 schwafeln

waffle[2] n (Culin) Waffel f

waft /wɒft/ vt/i wehen

wag /wæg/ v (pt/pp wagged) ● vt
wedeln mit ● vi wedeln

wage /weɪdʒ/ n (also ~s) pl Lohn m

wager /'weɪdʒə(r)/ n Wette f

wagon /'wægən/ n Wagen m; (Rail)
Waggon m

wail /weɪl/ n [klagender] Schrei m
● vi heulen; (lament) klagen

waist /weɪst/ n Taille f. ~**coat** n
Weste f. ~**line** n Taille f

wait /weɪt/ n Wartezeit f; **lie in** ~
for auflauern (+ dat) ● vi warten (**for**
auf + acc); (at table) servieren; ~ **on**
bedienen ● vt ~ **one's turn** warten,
bis man an der Reihe ist

waiter /'weɪtə(r)/ n Kellner m; ~!
Herr Ober!

waiting: ~-**list** n Warteliste f.
~-**room** n Warteraum m; (doctor's)
Wartezimmer nt

waitress /'weɪtrɪs/ n Kellnerin f

waive /weɪv/ vt verzichten auf (+
acc)

wake[1] /weɪk/ n Totenwache f ● v (pt
woke, pp woken) ~ [**up**] ● vt [auf]-
wecken ● vi aufwachen

wake[2] n (Naut) Kielwasser nt; **in the**
~ **of** im Gefolge (+ gen)

Wales /weɪlz/ n Wales nt

walk /wɔːk/ n Spaziergang m; (gait)
Gang m; (path) Weg m; **go for a** ~
spazieren gehen ● vi gehen; (not ride)
laufen, zu Fuß gehen; (ramble) wandern; **learn to** ~ laufen lernen ● vt
ausführen (dog). ~ **out** vi hinausgehen (; workers:) in den Streik treten;

∼ **out on s.o.** jdn verlassen

walker /'wɔːkə(r)/ n Spaziergänger(in) m(f); (rambler) Wanderer m/Wanderin f

walking /'wɔːkɪŋ/ n Gehen nt; (rambling) Wandern nt. ∼**-stick** n Spazierstock m

wall /wɔːl/ n Wand f; (external) Mauer f; **drive s.o. up the** ∼ 🄴 jdn auf die Palme bringen ● vt ∼ **up** zumauern

wallet /'wɒlɪt/ n Brieftasche f

'**wallflower** n Goldlack m

wallop /'wɒləp/ vt (pt/pp walloped) 🄴 schlagen

wallow /'wɒləʊ/ vi sich wälzen; (fig) schwelgen

'**wallpaper** n Tapete f ● vt tapezieren

walnut /'wɔːlnʌt/ n Walnuss f

waltz /wɔːlts/ n Walzer m ● vi Walzer tanzen

wander /'wɒndə(r)/ vi umherwandern, 🄴 bummeln; (fig: digress) abschweifen. ∼ **about** vi umherwandern

wangle /'wæŋgl/ vt 🄴 organisieren

want /wɒnt/ n Mangel m (of an + dat); (hardship) Not f; (desire) Bedürfnis nt ● vt wollen; (need) brauchen; ∼ **[to have]** sth etw haben wollen; ∼ **to do** sth etw tun wollen; **I** ∼ **you to go** ich will, dass du gehst; **it** ∼**s painting** es müsste gestrichen werden ● vi **he doesn't** ∼ **for anything** ihm fehlt es an nichts. ∼**ed** adj (criminal) gesucht

war /wɔː(r)/ n Krieg m; **be at** ∼ sich im Krieg befinden

ward /wɔːd/ n [Kranken]saal m; (unit) Station f; (of town) Wahlbezirk m; (child) Mündel nt ● vt ∼ **off** abwehren

warden /'wɔːdn/ n (of hostel) Heimleiter(in) m(f); (of youth hostel) Herbergsvater m; (supervisor) Aufseher(in) m(f)

warder /'wɔːdə(r)/ n Wärter(in) m(f)

wardrobe /'wɔːdrəʊb/ n Kleiderschrank m; (clothes) Garderobe f

warehouse /'weəhaʊs/ n Lager nt; (building) Lagerhaus nt

wares /weəz/ npl Waren pl

war: ∼**fare** n Krieg m. ∼**like** adj kriegerisch

warm /wɔːm/ adj (-er, -est) warm; (welcome) herzlich; **I am** ∼ mir ist warm ● vt wärmen. ∼ **up** vt aufwärmen ● vi warm werden; (Sport) sich aufwärmen. ∼**-hearted** adj warmherzig

warmth /wɔːmθ/ n Wärme f

warn /wɔːn/ vt warnen (**of** vor + dat). ∼**ing** n Warnung f; (advance notice) Vorwarnung f; (caution) Verwarnung f

warp /wɔːp/ vt verbiegen ● vi sich verziehen

warrant /'wɒrənt/ n (for arrest) Haftbefehl m; (for search) Durchsuchungsbefehl m ● vt (justify) rechtfertigen; (guarantee) garantieren

warranty /'wɒrəntɪ/ n Garantie f

warrior /'wɒrɪə(r)/ n Krieger m

'**warship** n Kriegsschiff nt

wart /wɔːt/ n Warze f

'**wartime** n Kriegszeit f

war|y /'weərɪ/ adj , **-ily** adv vorsichtig; (suspicious) misstrauisch

was /wɒz/ see be

wash /wɒʃ/ n Wäsche f; (Naut) Wellen pl; **have a** ∼ sich waschen ● vt waschen; spülen (dishes); aufwischen (floor); ∼ **one's hands** sich (dat) die Hände waschen ● vi sich waschen. ∼ **out** vt auswaschen; ausspülen (mouth). ∼ **up** vt/i abwaschen, spülen ● vi (Amer) sich waschen

washable /'wɒʃəbl/ adj waschbar

wash-basin n Waschbecken nt

washer /'wɒʃə(r)/ n (Techn) Dichtungsring m; (machine) Waschmaschine f

washing /'wɒʃɪŋ/ n Wäsche f. ∼**-machine** n Waschmaschine f. ∼**-powder** n Waschpulver nt. ∼**-'up** n Abwasch m; **do the** ∼**-up** abwaschen, spülen. ∼**-'up liquid** n Spülmittel nt

wasp /wɒsp/ n Wespe f

waste /weɪst/ n Verschwendung f; (rubbish) Abfall m; ∼s pl Öde f ● adj (product) Abfall- ● vt verschwenden ● vi ∼ away immer mehr abmagern

waste: ∼ful adj verschwenderisch. ∼ land n Ödland nt. ∼ 'paper n Altpapier nt. ∼-'paper basket n Papierkorb m

watch /wɒtʃ/ n Wache f; (timepiece) [Armband]uhr f ● vt beobachten; sich (dat) ansehen (film, match); (keep an eye on) achten auf (+ acc); ∼ television fernsehen ● vi zusehen. ∼ out vi Ausschau halten (for nach); (be careful) aufpassen

watch: ∼-dog n Wachhund m. ∼ful adj wachsam. ∼man n Wachmann m

water /'wɔːtə(r)/ n Wasser nt; ∼s pl Gewässer nt ● vt gießen (garden, plant); (dilute) verdünnen ● vi (eyes:) tränen; **my mouth was** ∼ing mir lief das Wasser im Munde zusammen. ∼ **down** vt verwässern

water: ∼-colour n Wasserfarbe f; (painting) Aquarell nt. ∼cress n Brunnenkresse f. ∼fall n Wasserfall m

'watering-can n Gießkanne f

water: ∼-lily n Seerose f. ∼logged adj be ∼logged (ground:) unter Wasser stehen. ∼ polo n Wasserball m. ∼proof adj wasserdicht. ∼-skiing n Wasserskilaufen nt. ∼tight adj wasserdicht. ∼way n Wasserstraße f

watery /'wɔːtərɪ/ adj wässrig

watt /wɒt/ n Watt nt

wave /weɪv/ n Welle f; (gesture) Handbewegung f; (as greeting) Winken nt ● vt winken mit; (brandish) schwingen; wellen (hair); ∼ one's **hand** winken ● vi winken (to dat); (flag:) wehen. ∼length n Wellenlänge f

waver /'weɪvə(r)/ vi schwanken

wavy /'weɪvɪ/ adj wellig

wax /wæks/ n Wachs nt; (in ear) Schmalz nt ● vt wachsen. ∼works n Wachsfigurenkabinett nt

way /weɪ/ n Weg m; (direction) Richtung f; (respect) Hinsicht f; (manner) Art f; (method) Art und Weise f; ∼s pl Gewohnheiten pl; **on the** ∼ auf dem Weg (**to** nach/zu); (under way) unterwegs; **a little/long** ∼ ein kleines/ganzes Stück; **a long** ∼ **off** weit weg; **this** ∼ hierher; (like this) so; **which** ∼ in welche Richtung; (how) wie; **by the** ∼ übrigens; **in some** ∼s in gewisser Hinsicht; **either** ∼ so oder so; **in this** ∼ auf diese Weise; **in a** ∼ in gewisser Weise; **lead the** ∼ vorausgehen; **make** ∼ Platz machen (**for** dat); **'give** ∼' (Auto) 'Vorfahrt beachten'; **go out of one's** ∼ (fig) sich (dat) besondere Mühe geben (**to** zu); **get one's [own]** ∼ seinen Willen durchsetzen ● adv weit; ∼ **behind** weit zurück. ∼ 'in n Eingang m

way 'out n Ausgang m; (fig) Ausweg m

WC abbr WC nt

we /wiː/ pron wir

weak /wiːk/ adj (-er, -est) schwach; (liquid) dünn. ∼en vt schwächen ● vi schwächer werden. ∼ling n Schwächling m. ∼ness n Schwäche f

wealth /welθ/ n Reichtum m; (fig) Fülle f (**of** an + dat). ∼y adj reich

weapon /'wepən/ n Waffe f; ∼s **of mass destruction** Massenvernichtungswaffen pl

wear /weə(r)/ n (clothing) Kleidung f; ∼ **and tear** Abnutzung f, Verschleiß m ● v (pt **wore**, pp **worn**) ● vt tragen; (damage) abnutzen; **what shall I** ∼? was soll ich anziehen? ● vi sich abnutzen; (last) halten. ∼ **off** vi abgehen; (effect:) nachlassen. ∼ **out** vt abnutzen; (exhaust) erschöpfen ● vi sich abnutzen

weary /'wɪərɪ/ adj , **-ily** adv müde

weather /'weðə(r)/ n Wetter nt; **in this** ∼ bei diesem Wetter; **under the** ∼ 🆒 nicht ganz auf dem Posten ● vt abwettern (storm); (fig) überstehen

weather: ∼-beaten adj verwittert; wettergegerbt (face). ∼ **forecast** n

W

Wettervorhersage *f*

weave[1] /wiːv/ *vi* (*pt/pp* **weaved**)
sich schlängeln (**through** durch)

weave[2] *n* (*of cloth*) Bindung *f* ● *vt*
(*pt* **wove**, *pp* **woven**) weben. **~r** *n*
Weber *m*

web /web/ *n* Netz *nt*; **the W~** das
Web. **~master** *n* Webmaster *m*. **~
page** *n* Webseite *f*. **~site** *n* Website *f*

wed /wed/ *vt/i* (*pt/pp* **wedded**) heiraten. **~ding** *n* Hochzeit *f*

wedding: **~ day** *n* Hochzeitstag *m*.
~ dress *n* Hochzeitskleid *nt*. **~-ring**
n Ehering *m*, Trauring *m*

wedge /wedʒ/ *n* Keil *m* ● *vt* fest-
klemmen

Wednesday /ˈwenzdeɪ/ *n* Mittwoch *m*

wee /wiː/ *adj* 🔲 klein ● *vi* Pipi machen

weed /wiːd/ *n* Unkraut *nt* ● *vt/i*
jäten. **~ out** *vt* (*fig*) aussieben

'**weedkiller** *n* Unkrautvertilgungs-
mittel *nt*

weedy /ˈwiːdɪ/ *adj* 🔲 spillerig

week /wiːk/ *n* Woche *f*. **~day** *n* Wo-
chentag *m*. **~end** *n* Wochenende *nt*

weekly /ˈwiːklɪ/ *adj & adv* wöchentlich ● *n* Wochenzeitschrift *f*

weep /wiːp/ *vi* (*pt/pp* **wept**) weinen

weigh /weɪ/ *vt/i* wiegen. **~ down** *vt*
(*fig*) niederdrücken. **~ up** *vt* (*fig*)
abwägen

weight /weɪt/ *n* Gewicht *nt*; **put
on/lose ~** zunehmen/abnehmen

weight-lifting *n* Gewichtheben *nt*

weighty /ˈweɪtɪ/ *adj* schwer; (*important*) gewichtig

weir /wɪə(r)/ *n* Wehr *nt*.

weird /wɪəd/ *adj* (**-er, -est**) unheimlich; (*bizarre*) bizarr

welcome /ˈwelkəm/ *adj* willkommen; **you're ~!** nichts zu danken!
you're ~ to (have) it das können
Sie gerne haben ● *n* Willkommen *nt*
● *vt* begrüßen

weld /weld/ *vt* schweißen. **~er** *n*
Schweißer *m*

welfare /ˈwelfeə(r)/ *n* Wohl *nt*;

(*Admin*) Fürsorge *f*. **W~ State** *n*
Wohlfahrtsstaat *m*

well[1] /wel/ *n* Brunnen *m*; (*oil* **~**)
Quelle *f*

well[2] *adv* (**better, best**) gut; **as ~**
auch; **as ~ as** (*in addition*) sowohl ...
als auch; **~ done!** gut gemacht!
● *adj* gesund; **he is not ~** es geht
ihm nicht gut; **get ~ soon!** gute
Besserung! ● *int* nun, na

well: **~-behaved** *adj* artig. **~-being**
n Wohl *nt*

wellingtons /ˈwelɪŋtənz/ *npl* Gum-
mistiefel *pl*

well: **~-known** *adj* bekannt. **~-off**
adj wohlhabend; **be ~-off** gut dran-
sein. **~-to-do** *adj* wohlhabend

Welsh /welʃ/ *adj* walisisch ● *n* (*Lang*)
Walisisch *nt*; **the ~** *pl* die Waliser. **~
man** *n* Waliser *m*

> **Welsh Assembly** Das walisi- *i*
> sche Parlament, dessen Mit-
> glieder in der Hauptstadt Cardiff
> zusammentreten. Es wurde 1999
> (nach einer Volksabstimmung) er-
> öffnet und verleiht Wales eine
> größere Autonomie gegenüber
> dem britischen Parlament in Lon-
> don. Das Parlament setzt sich aus
> 60 Mitgliedern zusammen, 40 sind
> direkt gewählt, die restlichen Ab-
> geordneten von Regionallisten und
> nach dem Verhältniswahlrecht.

went /went/ *see* **go**

wept /wept/ *see* **weep**

were /wɜː(r)/ *see* **be**

west /west/ *n* Westen *m*; **to the ~
of** westlich von ● *adj* West-, west-
● *adv* nach Westen. **~erly** *adj* westlich. **~ern** *adj* westlich ● *n* Western *m*

West: **~ 'Germany** *n* Westdeutsch-
land *nt*. **~ 'Indian** *adj* westindisch
● *n* Westinder(in) *m(f)*. **~ 'Indies**
/-ˈɪndɪz/ *npl* Westindische Inseln *pl*

'**westward[s]** /-wəd[z]/ *adv* nach
Westen

wet /wet/ *adj* (**wetter, wettest**) nass;
(*fam: person*) weichlich, lasch; '**~
paint**' 'frisch gestrichen' ● *vt* (*pt/pp*

w

wet or **wetted**) nass machen
whack /wæk/ vt 🔲 schlagen. ∼**ed**
adj 🔲 kaputt
whale /weɪl/ n Wal m
wharf /wɔːf/ n Kai m

what /wɒt/
● pronoun
┄┄➤ (in questions) was. **what is it?**
was ist das? **what do you want?**
was wollen Sie? **what is your
name?** wie heißen Sie? **what?**
(🔲: say that again) wie?; was?
what is the time? wie spät ist
es? (indirect) **I didn't know what
to do** ich wusste nicht, was ich
machen sollte

> ❗ The equivalent of a preposi-
> tion with **what** in English is
> a special word in German be-
> ginning with wo- (wor- before a
> vowel): **for what? what for?** =
> wofür? wozu? **from what?**
> wovon? **on what? what on?**
> worüber? **under what?** worun-
> ter? **with what?** womit? etc.
> **what do you want the money
> for?** wozu willst du das Geld?
> **what is he talking about?**
> wovon redet er?

┄┄➤ (relative pronoun) was. **do
what I tell you** tu, was ich dir
sage. **give me what you can** gib
mir, so viel du kannst. **what little I know** das bisschen, das ich
weiß. **I don't agree with what
you are saying** ich stimme dem
nicht zu, was Sie sagen
┄┄➤ (in phrases) **what about me?**
was ist mit mir? **what about a
cup of coffee?** wie wäre es mit
einer Tasse Kaffee? **what if she
doesn't come?** was ist, wenn sie
nicht kommt? **what of it?** was
ist dabei?
● adjective
┄┄➤ (asking for selection) welcher
(m), welche (f), welches (nt),
welche (pl). **what book do you
want?** welches Buch willst du
haben? **what colour are the**

walls? welche Farbe haben die
Wände? **I asked him what train
to take** ich habe ihn gefragt,
welchen Zug ich nehmen soll
┄┄➤ (asking how much/many) **what
money does he have?** wie viel
Geld hat er? **what time is it?**
wie spät ist es? **what time does
it start?** um wie viel Uhr fängt
es an?
┄┄➤ **what kind of ...?** was für
[ein(e)]? **what kind of man is
he?** was für ein Mensch ist er?
┄┄➤ (in exclamations) was für (+
nom). **what a fool you are!** was
für ein Dummkopf du doch bist!
what cheek/luck! was für eine
Frechheit/ein Glück! **what a
huge house!** was für ein riesiges
Haus! **what a lot of people!** was
für viele Leute!

what'ever adj [egal] welche(r,s)
● pron was ... auch; ∼ **is it?** was ist
das bloß?; ∼ **he does** was er auch
tut; **nothing** ∼ überhaupt nichts
whatso'ever pron & adj ≈ whatever
wheat /wiːt/ n Weizen m
wheel /wiːl/ n Rad nt; (pottery) Töp-
ferscheibe f; (steering ∼) Lenkrad nt;
at the ∼ am Steuer ● vt (push)
schieben ● vi kehrtmachen; (circle)
kreisen
wheel: ∼**barrow** n Schubkarre f.
∼**chair** n Rollstuhl m. ∼-**clamp** n
Parkkralle f
when /wen/ adv wann; **the day** ∼
der Tag, an dem ● conj wenn; (in the
past) als; (although) wo ... doch; ∼
swimming/reading beim
Schwimmen/Lesen
when'ever conj & adv [immer]
wenn; (at whatever time) wann
immer; ∼ **did it happen?** wann ist
das bloß passiert?
where /weə(r)/ adv & conj wo; ∼
[to] wohin; ∼ **[from]** woher
whereabouts¹ /weərə'baʊts/
adv wo
'whereabouts² n Verbleib m; (of

person) Aufenthaltsort *m*

where'as *conj* während; (*in contrast*) wohingegen

whereu'pon *adv* worauf[hin]

wher'ever *conj & adv* wo immer; (*to whatever place*) wohin immer; (*from whatever place*) woher immer; (*everywhere*) überall wo; ~ **possible** wenn irgend möglich

whether /'weðə(r)/ *conj* ob

which /wɪtʃ/
● *adjective*
••••▷ (*in questions*) welcher (*m*), welche (*f*), welches (*nt*), welche (*pl*). **which book do you need?** welches Buch brauchst du? **which one?** welcher/welche/ welches? **which ones?** welche? **which one of you did it?** wer von euch hat es getan? **which way?** (*which direction*) welche Richtung?; (*where*) wohin?; (*how*) wie?
••••▷ (*relative*) **he always comes at one at which time I'm having lunch/by which time I've finished** er kommt immer um ein Uhr; dann esse ich gerade zu Mittag/bis dahin bin ich schon fertig
● *pronoun*
••••▷ (*in questions*) welcher (*m*), welche (*f*), welches (*nt*), welche (*pl*). **which is which?** welcher/ welche/welches ist welcher/ welche/welches? **which of you?** wer von euch?
••••▷ (*relative*) der (*m*), die (*f*), das (*nt*), die (*pl*); (*genitive*) dessen (*m, nt*), deren (*f, pl*); (*dative*) dem (*m, nt*), der (*f*), denen (*pl*); (*referring to a clause*) was. **the book which I gave you** das Buch, das ich dir gab. **the trial, the result of which we are expecting** der Prozess, dessen Ergebnis wir erwarten. **the house of which I was speaking** das Haus, von dem *od* wovon ich redete. **after which** wonach; nach dem. **on which** worauf; auf dem.

the shop opposite which we parked der Laden, gegenüber dem wir parkten. **everything which I tell you** alles, was ich dir sage

which'ever *adj & pron* [egal] welche(r,s); ~ **it is** was es auch ist

while /waɪl/ *n* Weile *f*; **a long ~** lange; **be worth ~** sich lohnen; **it's worth my ~** es lohnt sich für mich ● *conj* während; (*as long as*) solange; (*although*) obgleich ● *vt* ~ **away** sich (*dat*) vertreiben

whilst /waɪlst/ *conj* während

whim /wɪm/ *n* Laune *f*

whimper /'wɪmpə(r)/ *vi* wimmern; (*dog:*) winseln

whine /waɪn/ *vi* winseln

whip /wɪp/ *n* Peitsche *f*; (*Pol*) Einpeitscher *m* ● *vt* (*pt/pp* **whipped**) peitschen; (*Culin*) schlagen. **~ped 'cream** *n* Schlagsahne *f*

whirl /wɜːl/ *vt/i* wirbeln. **~pool** *n* Strudel *m*. **~wind** *n* Wirbelwind *m*

whirr /wɜː(r)/ *vi* surren

whisk /wɪsk/ *n* (*Culin*) Schneebesen *m* ● *vt* (*Culin*) schlagen

whisker /'wɪskə(r)/ *n* Schnurrhaar *nt*

whisky /'wɪskɪ/ *n* Whisky *m*

whisper /'wɪspə(r)/ *n* Flüstern *nt* ● *vt/i* flüstern

whistle /'wɪsl/ *n* Pfiff *m*; (*instrument*) Pfeife *f* ● *vt/i* pfeifen

white /waɪt/ *adj* (**-r, -st**) weiß ● *n* Weiß *nt*; (*of egg*) Eiweiß *nt*; (*person*) Weiße(r) *m/f*

white: ~ **'coffee** *n* Kaffee *m* mit Milch. **~'collar worker** *n* Angestellte(r) *m*. ~ **'lie** *n* Notlüge *f*

whiten /'waɪtn/ *vt* weiß machen ● *vi* weiß werden

whiteness /'waɪtnɪs/ *n* Weiß *nt*

Whitsun /'wɪtsn/ *n* Pfingsten *nt*

whiz[z] /wɪz/ *vi* (*pt/pp* **whizzed**) zischen. **~-kid** *n* 🔟 Senkrechtstarter *m*

who /huː/ *pron* wer; (*acc*) wen; (*dat*) wem ● *rel pron* der/die/das, (*pl*) die

w

who'ever *pron* wer [immer]; ∼ **he
is** wer er auch ist; ∼ **is it?** wer ist
das bloß?

whole /həʊl/ *adj* ganz; (*truth*) voll
● *n* Ganze(s) *nt*; **as a** ∼ als Ganzes;
on the ∼ im Großen und Ganzen;
the ∼ **of Germany** ganz Deutschland

whole: ∼**food** *n* Vollwertkost *f*.
∼-'**hearted** *adj* rückhaltlos. ∼**meal**
adj Vollkorn-

'**wholesale** *adj* Großhandels- ● *adv*
en gros; (*fig*) in Bausch und Bogen.
∼**r** *n* Großhändler *m*

wholly /'həʊlɪ/ *adv* völlig

whom /huːm/ *pron* wen; **to** ∼ wem
● *rel pron* den/die/das, (*pl*) die; (*dat*)
dem/der/dem, (*pl*) denen

whopping /'wɒpɪŋ/ *adj* 🔲 Riesen-

whore /hɔː(r)/ *n* Hure *f*

whose /huːz/ *pron* wessen; ∼ **is
that?** wem gehört das? ● *rel pron*
dessen/deren/dessen, (*pl*) deren

why /waɪ/ *adv* warum; (*for what purpose*) wozu; **that's** ∼ darum

wick /wɪk/ *n* Docht *m*

wicked /'wɪkɪd/ *adj* böse; (*mischievous*) frech, boshaft

wicker /'wɪkə(r)/ *n* Korbgeflecht *nt*
● *attrib* Korb-

wide /waɪd/ *adj* (**-r,-st**) weit; (*broad*)
breit; (*fig*) groß ● *adv* weit; (*off target*) daneben; ∼ **awake** hellwach;
far and ∼ weit und breit. ∼**ly** *adv*
weit; (*known, accepted*) weithin; (*differ*) stark

widen /'waɪdn/ *vt* verbreitern; (*fig*)
erweitern ● *vi* sich verbreitern

'**widespread** *adj* weit verbreitet

widow /'wɪdəʊ/ *n* Witwe *f*. ∼**ed** *adj*
verwitwet. ∼**er** *n* Witwer *m*

width /wɪdθ/ *n* Weite *f*; (*breadth*)
Breite *f*

wield /wiːld/ *vt* schwingen; ausüben
(*power*)

wife /waɪf/ *n* (*pl* **wives**) [Ehe]frau *f*

wig /wɪg/ *n* Perücke *f*

wiggle /'wɪgl/ *vi* wackeln ● *vt* wackeln mit

wild /waɪld/ *adj* (**-er, -est**) wild; (*ani-*

mal) wild lebend; (*flower*) wild wach-
send; (*furious*) wütend ● *adv* wild;
run ∼ frei herumlaufen ● *n* **in the**
∼ wild; **the** ∼**s** *pl* die Wildnis *f*

wilderness /'wɪldənɪs/ *n* Wildnis *f*;
(*desert*) Wüste *f*

wildlife *n* Tierwelt *f*

---

will[1] /wɪl/
● *modal verb*

> ❗ *past* **would**

····▸ (*expressing the future*) werden.
she will arrive tomorrow sie
wird morgen ankommen. **he will
be there by now** er wird jetzt
schon da sein

····▸ (*expressing intention*) (*present
tense*) **will you go?** gehst du? **I
promise I won't do it again** ich
verspreche, ich machs nicht noch
mal

····▸ (*in requests*) **will/would you
please tidy up?** würdest du bitte
aufräumen? **will you be quiet!**
willst du ruhig sein!

····▸ (*in invitations*) **will you have/
would you like some wine?**
wollen Sie/möchten Sie Wein?

····▸ (*negative: refuse to*) nicht wollen. **they won't help me** sie wollen mir nicht helfen. **the car
won't start** das Auto will nicht
anspringen

····▸ (*in tag questions*) nicht wahr.
**you'll be back soon, won't
you?** du kommst bald wieder,
nicht wahr? **you will help her,
won't you?** du hilfst ihr doch,
nicht wahr?

····▸ (*in short answers*) **Will you be
there? — Yes I will** Wirst du da
sein? — Ja

---

will[2] *n* Wille *m*; (*document*) Testament *nt*

willing /'wɪlɪŋ/ *adj* willig; (*eager*) bereitwillig; **be** ∼ bereit sein. ∼**ly** *adv*
bereitwillig; (*gladly*) gern. ∼**ness** *n*
Bereitwilligkeit *f*

willow /ˈwɪləʊ/ n Weide f

'will-power n Willenskraft f

wilt /wɪlt/ vi welk werden, welken

wily /ˈwaɪlɪ/ adj listig

win /wɪn/ n Sieg m ● v (pt/pp **won**; pres p **winning**) ● vt gewinnen; bekommen (scholarship) ● vi gewinnen; (in battle) siegen. ~ **over** vt auf seine Seite bringen

wince /wɪns/ vi zusammenzucken

winch /wɪntʃ/ n Winde f ● vt ~ **up** hochwinden

wind¹ /wɪnd/ n Wind m; (🅘: flatulence) Blähungen pl ● vt ~ **s.o.** jdm den Atem nehmen

wind² /waɪnd/ v (pt/pp **wound**) ● vt (wrap) wickeln; (move by turning) kurbeln; aufziehen (clock) vi (road:) sich winden. ~ **up** vt aufziehen (clock); schließen (proceedings)

wind: ~ **farm** n Windpark m. ~ **instrument** n Blasinstrument nt. ~**mill** n Windmühle f

window /ˈwɪndəʊ/ n Fenster nt; (of shop) Schaufenster nt

window: ~**box** n Blumenkasten m. ~**cleaner** n Fensterputzer m. ~**pane** n Fensterscheibe f. ~**shopping** n Schaufensterbummel m. ~**sill** n Fensterbrett nt

'windpipe n Luftröhre f

'windscreen n, (Amer) **'windshield** n Windschutzscheibe f. ~**wiper** n Scheibenwischer m

wind surfing n Windsurfen nt

windy /ˈwɪndɪ/ adj windig

wine /waɪn/ n Wein m

wine: ~**bar** n Weinstube f. ~**glass** n Weinglas nt. ~**list** n Weinkarte f

winery /ˈwaɪnərɪ/ n (Amer) Weingut nt

'wine-tasting n Weinprobe f

wing /wɪŋ/ n Flügel m; (Auto) Kotflügel m; ~**s** pl (Theat) Kulissen pl

wink /wɪŋk/ n Zwinkern nt; **not sleep a** ~ kein Auge zutun ● vi zwinkern; (light:) blinken

winner /ˈwɪnə(r)/ n Gewinner(in) m(f); (Sport) Sieger(in) m(f)

winning /ˈwɪnɪŋ/ adj siegreich;

(smile) gewinnend. ~**post** n Zielpfosten m. ~**s** npl Gewinn m

wint|er /ˈwɪntə(r)/ n Winter m. ~**ry** adj winterlich

wipe /waɪp/ n **give sth a** ~ etw abwischen ● vt abwischen; aufwischen (floor); (dry) abtrocknen. ~ **out** vt (cancel) löschen; (destroy) ausrotten. ~ **up** vt aufwischen

wire /ˈwaɪə(r)/ n Draht m

wiring /ˈwaɪərɪŋ/ n [elektrische] Leitungen pl

wisdom /ˈwɪzdəm/ n Weisheit f; (prudence) Klugheit f. ~ **tooth** n Weisheitszahn m

wise /waɪz/ adj (-r, -st) weise; (prudent) klug

wish /wɪʃ/ n Wunsch m ● vt wünschen; ~ **s.o. well** jdm alles Gute wünschen; **I** ~ **you could stay** ich wünschte, du könntest hier bleiben ● vi sich (dat) etwas wünschen. ~**ful** adj ~**ful thinking** Wunschdenken nt

wistful /ˈwɪstfl/ adj wehmütig

wit /wɪt/ n Geist m, Witz m; (intelligence) Verstand m; (person) geistreicher Mensch m; **be at one's** ~**s' end** sich (dat) keinen Rat mehr wissen

witch /wɪtʃ/ n Hexe f. ~**craft** n Hexerei f

with /wɪð/ prep mit (+ dat); ~ **fear/cold** vor Angst/Kälte; ~ **it** damit; **I'm going** ~ **you** ich gehe mit; **take it** ~ **you** nimm es mit; **I haven't got it** ~ **me** ich habe es nicht bei mir

with'draw v (pt **-drew**, pp **-drawn**) ● vt zurückziehen; abheben (money) ● vi sich zurückziehen. ~**al** n Zurückziehen nt; (of money) Abhebung f; (from drugs) Entzug m

wither /ˈwɪðə(r)/ vi [ver]welken

with'hold vt (pt/pp **-held**) vorenthalten (**from s.o.** jdm)

with'in prep innerhalb (+ gen) ● adv innen

with'out prep ohne (+ acc); ~ **my noticing it** ohne dass ich es merkte

with'stand vt (pt/pp **-stood**) standhalten (+ dat)

witness /ˈwɪtnɪs/ n Zeuge m/ Zeugin f ● vt Zeuge/Zeugin sein (+ *gen*); bestätigen (*signature*)

witticism /'wɪtɪsɪzm/ n geistreicher Ausspruch m

witty /'wɪtɪ/ adj witzig, geistreich

wives /waɪvz/ see **wife**

wizard /'wɪzəd/ n Zauberer m

wizened /'wɪznd/ adj verhutzelt

wobb‖le /'wɒbl/ vi wackeln. ~**ly** adj wackelig

woke, woken /wəʊk, 'wəʊkn/ see **wake**[1]

wolf /wʊlf/ n (pl **wolves** /wʊlvz/) Wolf m

woman /'wʊmən/ n (pl **women**) Frau f. ~**izer** n Schürzenjäger m

womb /wuːm/ n Gebärmutter f

women /'wɪmɪn/ npl see **woman**

won /wʌn/ see **win**

wonder /'wʌndə(r)/ n Wunder nt; (*surprise*) Staunen nt ● vt/i sich fragen; (*be surprised*) sich wundern; **I** ~ da frage ich mich; **I** ~ **whether she is ill** ob sie wohl krank ist? ~**ful** adj wunderbar

won't /wəʊnt/ = **will not**

wood /wʊd/ n Holz nt; (*forest*) Wald m; **touch** ~! unberufen!

wood: ~**ed** /-ɪd/ adj bewaldet. ~**en** adj Holz-; (*fig*) hölzern. ~**pecker** n Specht m. ~**wind** n Holzbläser pl. ~**work** n (*wooden parts*) Holzteile pl; (*craft*) Tischlerei f. ~**worm** n Holzwurm m

wool /wʊl/ n Wolle f ● attrib Woll-. ~**len** adj wollen

woolly /'wʊlɪ/ adj wollig; (*fig*) unklar

word /wɜːd/ n Wort nt; (*news*) Nachricht f; **by** ~ **of mouth** mündlich; **have a** ~ **with** sprechen mit; **have** ~**s** einen Wortwechsel haben. ~**ing** n Wortlaut m. ~ **processor** n Textverarbeitungssystem nt

wore /wɔː(r)/ see **wear**

work /wɜːk/ n Arbeit f; (*Art, Literature*) Werk nt; ~**s** pl (*factory, mechanism*) Werk nt; **at** ~ bei der Arbeit; **out of** ~ arbeitslos ● vi arbeiten; (*machine, system:*) funktionieren; (*have effect*) wirken; (*study*) lernen; **it**

won't ~ (*fig*) es klappt nicht ● vt arbeiten lassen; bedienen (*machine*); betätigen (*lever*). ~ **off** vt abarbeiten. ~ **out** vt ausrechnen; (*solve*) lösen ● vi gut gehen, Ⓣ klappen. ~ **up** vt aufbauen; sich (*dat*) holen (*appetite*); **get** ~**ed up** sich aufregen

workable /'wɜːkəbl/ adj (*feasible*) durchführbar

worker /'wɜːkə(r)/ n Arbeiter(in) m(f)

working /'wɜːkɪŋ/ adj berufstätig; (*day, clothes*) Arbeits-; **be in** ~ **order** funktionieren. ~ **class** n Arbeiterklasse f

work: ~**man** n Arbeiter m; (*craftsman*) Handwerker m. ~**manship** n Arbeit f. ~**shop** n Werkstatt f

world /wɜːld/ n Welt f; **in the** ~ auf der Welt; **think the** ~ **of s.o.** große Stücke auf jdn halten. ~**ly** adj weltlich; (*person*) weltlich gesinnt. ~**-wide** adj & adv /-'-/ weltweit

worm /wɜːm/ n Wurm m

worn /wɔːn/ see **wear** ● adj abgetragen. ~**-out** adj abgetragen; (*carpet*) abgenutzt; (*person*) erschöpft

worried /'wʌrɪd/ adj besorgt

worry /'wʌrɪ/ n Sorge f ● v (pt/pp **worried**) ● vt beunruhigen; (*bother*) stören ● vi sich beunruhigen, sich (*dat*) Sorgen machen. ~**ing** adj beunruhigend

worse /wɜːs/ adj & adv schlechter; (*more serious*) schlimmer ● n Schlechtere(s) nt; Schlimmere(s) nt

worsen /'wɜːsn/ vt verschlechtern ● vi sich verschlechtern

worship /'wɜːʃɪp/ n Anbetung f; (*service*) Gottesdienst m ● vt (pt/pp **-shipped**) anbeten

worst /wɜːst/ adj schlechteste(r,s); (*most serious*) schlimmste(r,s) ● adv am schlechtesten; am schlimmsten ● n **the** ~ das Schlimmste

worth /wɜːθ/ n Wert m; **£10's** ~ **of petrol** Benzin für £10 ● adj **be** ~ **£5** £5 wert sein; **be** ~ **it** (*fig*) sich lohnen. ~**less** adj wertlos. ~**while** adj lohnend

worthy /'wɜːðɪ/ adj würdig

would /wʊd/ *modal verb* I ～ **do it** ich würde es tun, ich täte es; ～ **you go?** würdest du gehen? **he said he ～n't** er sagte, er würde es nicht tun; **what ～ you like?** was möchten Sie?

wound¹ /wuːnd/ *n* Wunde *f* ● *vt* verwunden

wound² /waʊnd/ *see* **wind²**

wove, woven *see* **weave²**

wrangle /'ræŋgl/ *n* Streit *m*

wrap /ræp/ *n* Umhang *m* ● *vt* (*pt/pp* **wrapped**) ～ [**up**] wickeln; einpacken (*present*) ● *vi* ～ **up warmly** sich warm einpacken. **～per** *n* Hülle *f*. **～ping** *n* Verpackung *f*

wrath /rɒθ/ *n* Zorn *m*

wreath /riːθ/ *n* (*pl* ～**s** /-ðz/) Kranz *m*

wreck /rek/ *n* Wrack *nt* ● *vt* zerstören; zunichte machen (*plans*), zerrütten (*marriage*). **～age** *n* Wrackteile *pl*; (*fig*) Trümmer *pl*

wren /ren/ *n* Zaunkönig *m*

wrench /rentʃ/ *n* Ruck *m*; (*tool*) Schraubenschlüssel *m*; **be a ～** (*fig*) weh tun ● *vt* reißen; ～ **sth from s.o.** jdm etw entreißen

wrestl|e /'resl/ *vi* ringen. **～er** *n* Ringer *m*. **～ing** *n* Ringen *nt*

wretch /retʃ/ *n* Kreatur *f*. **～ed** *adj* elend; (*very bad*) erbärmlich

wriggle /'rɪgl/ *n* Zappeln *nt* ● *vi* zappeln; (*move forward*) sich schlängeln; ～ **out of sth** 🔲 sich vor etw (*dat*) drücken

wring /rɪŋ/ *vt* (*pt/pp* **wrung**) wringen; (～ **out**) auswringen; umdrehen (*neck*); ringen (*hands*)

wrinkle /'rɪŋkl/ *n* Falte *f*; (*on skin*) Runzel *f* ● *vt* kräuseln ● *vi* sich kräuseln, sich falten. **～d** *adj* runzlig

wrist /rɪst/ *n* Handgelenk *nt*. **～-watch** *n* Armbanduhr *f*

write /raɪt/ *vt/i* (*pt* **wrote**, *pp* **written**, *pres p* **writing**) schreiben. ～ **down** *vt* aufschreiben. ～ **off** *vt* abschreiben; zu Schrott fahren (*car*)

'write-off *n* ≈ Totalschaden *m*

writer /'raɪtə(r)/ *n* Schreiber(in) *m(f)*; (*author*) Schriftsteller(in) *m(f)*

writhe /raɪð/ *vi* sich winden

writing /'raɪtɪŋ/ *n* Schreiben *nt*; (*handwriting*) Schrift *f*; **in ～** schriftlich. **～-paper** *n* Schreibpapier *nt*

written /'rɪtn/ *see* **write**

wrong /rɒŋ/ *adj* falsch; (*morally*) unrecht; (*not just*) ungerecht; **be ～** nicht stimmen; (*person:*) Unrecht haben; **what's ～?** was ist los? ● *adv* falsch; **go ～** (*person:*) etwas falsch machen; (*machine:*) kaputtgehen; (*plan:*) schief gehen ● *n* Unrecht *nt* ● *vt* Unrecht tun (+ *dat*). **～ful** *adj* ungerechtfertigt. **～fully** *adv* (*accuse*) zu Unrecht

wrote /rəʊt/ *see* **write**

wrung /rʌŋ/ *see* **wring**

wry /raɪ/ *adj* (**-er, -est**) ironisch; (*humour*) trocken

Xmas /'krɪsməs, 'eksməs/ *n* 🔲 Weihnachten *nt*

X-ray /'eks-/ *n* (*picture*) Röntgenaufnahme *f*; **～s** *pl* Röntgenstrahlen *pl* ● *vt* röntgen; durchleuchten (*luggage*)

yacht /jɒt/ *n* Jacht *f*; (*for racing*) Segeljacht *f*. **～ing** *n* Segeln *nt*

yank /jæŋk/ *vt* 🔲 reißen

Yank *n* 🔲 Ami *m* 🔲

yap /jæp/ *vi* (*pt/pp* **yapped**) (*dog:*) kläffen

yard¹ /jɑːd/ *n* Hof *m*; (*for storage*) Lager *nt*

yard² *n* Yard *nt* (= 0,91 m)

yarn /jɑːn/ *n* Garn *nt*; (🔲: *tale*) Geschichte *f*

 w

 x

 y

yawn /jɔːn/ n Gähnen nt ● vi gähnen

year /jɪə(r)/ n Jahr nt; (of wine) Jahr-gang m; **for ~s** jahrelang. **~ly** adj & adv jährlich

yearn /jɜːn/ vi sich sehnen (**for** nach). **~ing** n Sehnsucht f

yeast /jiːst/ n Hefe f

yell /jel/ n Schrei m ● vi schreien

yellow /'jeləʊ/ adj gelb ● n Gelb nt

yelp /jelp/ vi jaulen

yes /jes/ adv ja; (contradicting) doch ● n Ja nt

yesterday /'jestədeɪ/ n & adv ge-stern; **~'s paper** die gestrige Zei-tung; **the day before ~** vorgestern

yet /jet/ adv noch; (in question) schon; (nevertheless) doch; **as ~** bisher; **not ~** noch nicht; **the best ~** das bisher beste ● conj doch

Yiddish /'jɪdɪʃ/ n Jiddisch nt

yield /jiːld/ n Ertrag m ● vt bringen; abwerfen (profit) ● vi nachgeben; (Amer, Auto) die Vorfahrt beachten

yoga /'jəʊgə/ n Yoga m

yoghurt /'jɒgət/ n Joghurt m

yoke /jəʊk/ n Joch nt; (of garment) Passe f

yolk /jəʊk/ n Dotter m, Eigelb nt

you /juː/ pron du; (acc) dich; (dat) dir; (pl) ihr; (acc, dat) euch; (formal) (nom & acc, sg & pl) Sie; (dat, sg & pl) Ihnen; (one) man; (acc) einen; (dat) einem; **all of ~** ihr/Sie alle; **I know ~** ich kenne dich/euch/Sie; **I'll give ~ the money** ich gebe dir/euch/Ihnen das Geld; **it does ~ good** es tut einem gut; **it's bad for ~** es ist ungesund

young /jʌŋ/ adj (-er /-gə(r)/, -est /-gɪst/) jung ● npl (animals) Junge pl; **the ~** die Jugend f. **~ster** n Jugend-liche(r) m/f; (child) Kleine(r) m/f

your /jɔː(r)/ adj dein; (pl) euer; (for-mal) Ihr

yours /jɔːz/ poss pron deine(r), deins;

(pl) eure(r), euers; (formal, sg & pl) Ihre(r), Ihr[e]s; **a friend of ~** ein Freund von dir/Ihnen/euch; **that is ~** das gehört dir/Ihnen/euch

your'self pron (pl -selves) selbst; (reflexive) dich; (dat) dir; (pl) euch; (formal) sich; **by ~** allein

youth /juːθ/ n (pl youths /-ðːz/) Ju-gend f; (boy) Jugendliche(r) m. **~ful** adj jugendlich. **~ hostel** n Jugend-herberge f

Yugoslavia /juːgə'slɑːvɪə/ n Jugosla-wien nt

Zz

zeal /ziːl/ n Eifer m

zealous /'zeləs/ adj eifrig

zebra /'zebrə/ n Zebra nt. **~ 'cros-sing** n Zebrastreifen m

zero /'zɪərəʊ/ n Null f

zest /zest/ n Begeisterung f

zigzag /'zɪgzæg/ n Zickzack m ● vi (pt/pp -zagged) im Zickzack laufen/ (in vehicle) fahren

zinc /zɪŋk/ n Zink nt

zip /zɪp/ n [fastener] Reißver-schluss m ● vt **~ [up]** den Reißver-schluss zuziehen an (+ dat)

'zip code n (Amer) Postleitzahl f

zipper /'zɪpə(r)/ n Reißverschluss m

zodiac /'zəʊdɪæk/ n Tierkreis m

zone /zəʊn/ n Zone f

zoo /zuː/ n Zoo m

zoological /zuːə'lɒdʒɪkl/ adj zoolo-gisch

zoolog|ist /zuː'ɒlədʒɪst/ n Zoologe m/-gin f. **~y** Zoologie f

zoom /zuːm/ vi sausen. **~ lens** n Zoomobjektiv nt

German irregular verbs

1st, 2nd, and 3rd person present are given after the infinitive, and past subjunctive after the past indicative, where there is a change of vowel or any other irregularity.

Compound verbs are only given if they do not take the same forms as the corresponding simple verb, e.g. *befehlen*, or if there is no corresponding simple verb, e.g. *bewegen*.

An asterisk (*) indicates a verb which is also conjugated regularly.

Infinitive	Past tense	Past participle
abwägen	wog (wöge) ab	abgewogen
ausbedingen	bedang (bedänge) aus	ausbedungen
backen (du bäckst, er bäckt)	backte	gebacken
befehlen (du befiehlst, er befiehlt)	befahl (befähle)	befohlen
beginnen	begann (begänne)	begonnen
beißen (du/er beißt)	biss (bisse)	gebissen
bergen (du birgst, er birgt)	barg (bärge)	geborgen
bewegen[2]	bewog (bewöge)	bewogen
biegen	bog (böge)	gebogen
bieten	bot (böte)	geboten
binden	band (bände)	gebunden
bitten	bat (bäte)	gebeten
blasen (du/er bläst)	blies	geblasen
bleiben	blieb	geblieben
braten (du brätst, er brät)	briet	gebraten
brechen (du brichst, er bricht)	brach (bräche)	gebrochen
brennen	brannte (brennte)	gebrannt
bringen	brachte (brächte)	gebracht
denken	dachte (dächte)	gedacht
dreschen (du drischst, er drischt)	drosch (drösche)	gedroschen
dringen	drang (dränge)	gedrungen
dürfen (ich/er darf, du darfst)	durfte (dürfte)	gedurft
empfehlen (du empfiehlst, er empfiehlt)	empfahl (empföhle)	empfohlen
erlöschen (du erlischst, er erlischt)	erlosch (erlösche)	erloschen
erschrecken* (du erschrickst, er erschrickt)	erschrak (erschäke)	erschrocken
erwägen	erwog (erwöge)	erwogen
essen (du/er isst)	aß (äße)	gegessen
fahren (du fährst, er fährt)	fuhr (führe)	gefahren
fallen (du fällst, er fällt)	fiel	gefallen
fangen (du fängst, er fängt)	fing	gefangen

Infinitive	Past tense	Past participle
fechten (du fichtst, er ficht)	focht (föchte)	gefochten
finden	fand (fände)	gefunden
flechten (du flichtst, er flicht)	flocht (flöchte)	geflochten
fliegen	flog (flöge)	geflogen
fliehen	floh (flöhe)	geflohen
fließen (du/er fließt)	floss (flösse)	geflossen
fressen (du/er frisst)	fraß (fräße)	gefressen
frieren	fror (fröre)	gefroren
gären*	gor (göre)	gegoren
gebären (du gebierst, sie gebiert)	gebar (gebäre)	geboren
geben (du gibst, er gibt)	gab (gäbe)	gegeben
gedeihen	gedieh	gediehen
gehen	ging	gegangen
gelingen	gelang (gelänge)	gelungen
gelten (du giltst, er gilt)	galt (gälte)	gegolten
genesen (du/er genest)	genas (genäse)	genesen
genießen (du/er genießt)	genoss (genösse)	genossen
geschehen (es geschieht)	geschah (geschähe)	geschehen
gewinnen	gewann (gewänne)	gewonnen
gießen (du/er gießt)	goss (gösse)	gegossen
gleichen	glich	geglichen
gleiten	glitt	geglitten
glimmen	glomm (glömme)	geglommen
graben (du gräbst, er gräbt)	grub (grübe)	gegraben
greifen	griff	gegriffen
haben (du hast, er hat)	hatte (hätte)	gehabt
halten (du hältst, er hält)	hielt	gehalten
hängen[2]	hing	gehangen
hauen	haute	gehauen
heben	hob (höbe)	gehoben
heißen (du/er heißt)	hieß	geheißen
helfen (du hilfst, er hilft)	half (hülfe)	geholfen
kennen	kannte (kennte)	gekannt
klingen	klang (klänge)	geklungen
kneifen	kniff	gekniffen
kommen	kam (käme)	gekommen
können (ich/er kann, du kannst)	konnte (könnte)	gekonnt
kriechen	kroch (kröche)	gekrochen
laden (du lädst, er lädt)	lud (lüde)	geladen
lassen (du/er lässt)	ließ	gelassen
laufen (du läufst, er läuft)	lief	gelaufen
leiden	litt	gelitten
leihen	lieh	geliehen
lesen (du/er liest)	las (läse)	gelesen
liegen	lag (läge)	gelegen
lügen	log (löge)	gelogen
mahlen	mahlte	gemahlen
meiden	mied	gemieden

Infinitive	Past tense	Past participle
melken	molk (mölke)	gemolken
messen (du/er misst)	maß (mäße)	gemessen
misslingen	misslang (misslänge)	misslungen
mögen (ich/er mag, du magst)	mochte (möchte)	gemocht
müssen (ich/er muss, du musst)	musste (müsste)	gemusst
nehmen (du nimmst, er nimmt)	nahm (nähme)	genommen
nennen	nannte (nennte)	genannt
pfeifen	pfiff	gepfiffen
preisen (du/er preist)	pries	gepriesen
raten (du rätst, er rät)	riet	geraten
reiben	rieb	gerieben
reißen (du/er reißt)	riss	gerissen
reiten	ritt	geritten
rennen	rannte (rennte)	gerannt
riechen	roch (röche)	gerochen
ringen	rang (ränge)	gerungen
rinnen	rann (ränne)	geronnen
rufen	rief	gerufen
salzen* (du/er salzt)	salzte	gesalzen
saufen (du säufst, er säuft)	soff (söffe)	gesoffen
saugen*	sog (söge)	gesogen
schaffen[1]	schuf (schüfe)	geschaffen
scheiden	schied	geschieden
scheinen	schien	geschienen
scheißen (du/er scheißt)	schiss	geschissen
schelten (du schiltst, er schilt)	schalt (schölte)	gescholten
scheren[1]	schor (schöre)	geschoren
schieben	schob (schöbe)	geschoben
schießen (du/er schießt)	schoss (schösse)	geschossen
schlafen (du schläfst, er schläft)	schlief	geschlafen
schlagen (du schlägst, er schlägt)	schlug (schlüge)	geschlagen
schleichen	schlich	geschlichen
schleifen[2]	schliff	geschliffen
schließen (du/er schießt)	schloss (schlösse)	geschlossen
schlingen	schlang (schlänge)	geschlungen
schmeißen (du/er schmeißt)	schmiss (schmisse)	geschmissen
schmelzen (du/er schmilzt)	schmolz (schmölze)	geschmolzen
schneiden	schnitt	geschnitten
schrecken* (du schrickst, er schrickt)	schrak (schräke)	geschreckt
schreiben	schrieb	geschrieben
schreien	schrie	geschrie[e]n
schreiten	schritt	geschritten
schweigen	schwieg	geschwiegen
schwellen (du schwillst, er schwillt)	schwoll (schwölle)	geschwollen
schwimmen	schwamm (schwömme)	geschwommen
schwinden	schwand (schwände)	geschwunden
schwingen	schwang (schwänge)	geschwungen
schwören	schwor (schwüre)	geschworen

German irregular verbs

Infinitive	Past tense	Past participle
sehen (du siehst, er sieht)	sah (sähe)	gesehen
sein (ich bin, du bist, er ist, wir sind, ihr seid, sie sind)	war (wäre)	gewesen
senden[1]	sandte (sendete)	gesandt
sieden	sott (sötte)	gesotten
singen	sang (sänge)	gesungen
sinken	sank (sänke)	gesunken
sitzen (du/er sitzt)	saß (säße)	gesessen
sollen (ich/er soll, du sollst)	sollte	gesollt
spalten*	spaltete	gespalten
spinnen	spann (spänne)	gesponnen
sprechen (du sprichst, er spricht)	sprach (spräche)	gesprochen
sprießen (du/er sprießt)	spross (sprösse)	gesprossen
springen	sprang (spränge)	gesprungen
stechen (du stichst, er sticht)	stach (stäche)	gestochen
stehen	stand (stünde, stände)	gestanden
stehlen (du stiehlst, er stiehlt)	stahl (stähle)	gestohlen
steigen	stieg	gestiegen
sterben (du stirbst, er stirbt)	starb (stürbe)	gestorben
stinken	stank (stänke)	gestunken
stoßen (du/er stößt)	stieß	gestoßen
streichen	strich	gestrichen
streiten	stritt	gestritten
tragen (du trägst, er trägt)	trug (trüge)	getragen
treffen (du triffst, er trifft)	traf (träfe)	getroffen
treiben	trieb	getrieben
treten (du trittst, er tritt)	trat (träte)	getreten
triefen*	troff (tröffe)	getroffen
trinken	trank (tränke)	getrunken
trügen	trog (tröge)	getrogen
tun (du tust, er tut)	tat (täte)	getan
verderben (du verdirbst, er verdirbt)	verdarb (verdürbe)	verdorben
vergessen (du/er vergisst)	vergaß (vergäße)	vergessen
verlieren	verlor (verlöre)	verloren
verzeihen	verzieh	verziehen
wachsen[1] (du/er wächst)	wuchs (wüchse)	gewachsen
waschen (du wäschst, er wäscht)	wusch (wüsche)	gewaschen
wenden[2]*	wandte (wendete)	gewandt
werben (du wirbst, er wirbt)	warb (würbe)	geworben
werden (du wirst, er wird)	wurde (würde)	geworden
werfen (du wirfst, er wirft)	warf (würfe)	geworfen
wiegen[1]	wog (wöge)	gewogen
winden	wand (wände)	gewunden
wissen (ich/er weiß, du weißt)	wusste (wüsste)	gewusst
wollen (ich/er will, du willst)	wollte	gewollt
wringen	wrang (wränge)	gewrungen
ziehen	zog (zöge)	gezogen
zwingen	zwang (zwänge)	gezwungen

Englische unregelmäßige Verben

Infinitiv	Präteritum	2. Partizip	Infinitiv	Präteritum	2. Partizip
be	was	been	**fly**	flew	flown
bear	bore	borne	**freeze**	froze	frozen
beat	beat	beaten	**get**	got	got, gotten US
become	became	become	**give**	gave	given
begin	began	begun	**go**	went	gone
bend	bent	bent	**grow**	grew	grown
bet	bet, betted	bet, betted	**hang**	hung, hanged	hung, hanged
bid	bade, bid	bidden, bid	**have**	had	had
bind	bound	bound	**hear**	heard	heard
bite	bit	bitten	**hide**	hid	hidden
bleed	bled	bled	**hit**	hit	hit
blow	blew	blown	**hold**	held	held
break	broke	broken	**hurt**	hurt	hurt
breed	bred	bred	**keep**	kept	kept
bring	brought	brought	**kneel**	knelt	knelt
build	built	built	**know**	knew	known
burn	burnt, burned	burnt, burned	**lay**	laid	laid
			lead	led	led
burst	burst	burst	**lean**	leaned, leant	leaned, leant
buy	bought	bought			
catch	caught	caught	**learn**	learnt, learned	learnt, learned
choose	chose	chosen			
cling	clung	clung	**leave**	left	left
come	came	come	**lend**	lent	lent
cost	cost, costed (vt)	cost, costed	**let**	let	let
			lie	lay	lain
cut	cut	cut	**lose**	lost	lost
deal	dealt	dealt	**make**	made	made
dig	dug	dug	**mean**	meant	meant
do	did	done	**meet**	met	met
draw	drew	drawn	**pay**	paid	paid
dream	dreamt, dreamed	dreamt, dreamed	**put**	put	put
			read	read	read
drink	drank	drunk	**ride**	rode	ridden
drive	drove	driven	**ring**	rang	rung
eat	ate	eaten	**rise**	rose	risen
fall	fell	fallen	**run**	ran	run
feed	fed	fed	**say**	said	said
feel	felt	felt	**see**	saw	seen
fight	fought	fought	**seek**	sought	sought
find	found	found	**sell**	sold	sold
flee	fled	fled	**send**	sent	sent

Infinitiv	Präteritum	2. Partizip	Infinitiv	Präteritum	2. Partizip
set	set	set	steal	stole	stolen
sew	sewed	sewn, sewed	stick	stuck	stuck
shake	shook	shaken	sting	stung	stung
shine	shone	shone	stride	strode	stridden
shoe	shod	shod	strike	struck	struck
shoot	shot	shot	swear	swore	sworn
show	showed	shown	sweep	swept	swept
shut	shut	shut	swell	swelled	swollen, swelled
sing	sang	sung			
sink	sank	sunk	swim	swam	swum
sit	sat	sat	swing	swung	swung
sleep	slept	slept	take	took	taken
sling	slung	slung	teach	taught	taught
smell	smelt, smelled	smelt, smelled	tear	tore	torn
			tell	told	told
speak	spoke	spoken	think	thought	thought
spell	spelled, spelt	spelled, spelt	throw	threw	thrown
			thrust	thrust	thrust
spend	spent	spent	tread	trod	trodden
spit	spat	spat	under-stand	under-stood	understood
spoil	spoilt, spoiled	spoilt, spoiled	wake	woke	woken
			wear	wore	worn
spread	spread	spread	win	won	won
spring	sprang	sprung	write	wrote	written
stand	stood	stood			